INSURANCE LAW

CASES AND MATERIALS
Third Edition

By

ROGER C. HENDERSON
Ralph W. Bilby Professor of Law
University of Arizona

ROBERT H. JERRY, II
The Missouri Endowed Floyd R. Gibson Professor of Law
University of Missouri

LEXIS Publishing™

LEXIS°·NEXIS° · MARTINDALE-HUBBELL°
MATTHEW BENDER° · MICHIE™· SHEPARD'S°

Library of Congress Cataloging-in-Publication Data	
Henderson, Roger C.	
Insurance law : cases and materials / Roger C. Henderson; Robert H. Jerry, II—3rd Ed.	
p. cm.	
Includes bibliographical references.	
ISBN 0-8205-4896-0	
1. Insurance law—United States—Cases. I. Jerry, Robert H., 1953– II. Title.	
KF1163 .H46 2000	
346.73'086—dc21	00-065543

Editorial Offices
2 Park Avenue, New York, NY 10016-5675 (212) 448-2000
201 Mission St., San Francisco, CA 94105-1831 (415) 908-3200
701 East Water Street, Charlottesville, VA 22902-7587 (804) 972-7600
www.lexis.com

To Elizabeth, Cecily, Samantha,
Sally, Nancy and Joanie

R.C.H.

To Lisa, John, James and Beth

R.H.J.

PREFACE

Most areas of law quickly reflect social change, and insurance law is no exception. Thus, five years after the second edition was published, we felt it was once again time to collaborate to bring together the best teaching materials while winnowing the old. Although both of us consider insurance to be our primary areas of scholarly interest, the new edition more equally reflects the divergent backgrounds and experiences of each author one who approaches the subject of insurance law from a torts background and the other from an interest in contracts. Having practiced law and consulted in these areas also influences and informs our choices about what should be included in this book, particularly when it is not possible to cover everything one would like to explore in a basic insurance course. We are excited about the new edition and hope the instructors and students enjoy using the materials as much as we did in putting them together.

As with the two prior editions, the materials contained in this book have been selected with three primary goals in mind. First, the cases and notes are designed to impart an understanding of basic insurance law. Second, the materials are designed to raise provocative issues that are fairly debatable, with the object of involving the student in legal analysis and resolution of the problem at hand. Finally, the materials are also chosen for the purpose of informing the student about basic insurance business practices as well as some of the more practical problems faced by attorneys, judges, and insurance regulators in the real world. Special attention has been given to the overall presentation of the materials so that they will accommodate various teaching styles and provide a full opportunity to present and explore various points of view. The overall goal is to impart to the student a sound foundation in law and legal analysis, an understanding of the business of insurance, and an appreciation of the role of insurance in modern society. We believe this approach will serve the student well in resolving those related legal issues and problems which have necessarily been omitted due to the constraints of space.

The book is designed for either a three-or four-unit course in insurance law, but through some judicious editing it may also be used in a two-unit course. Those familiar with the first two editions will observe that this edition has undergone a significant reorganization. A new chapter titled "Fundamental Assumptions" brings together the materials on fortuity, insurable interest, and indemnity. Also, new and reorganized materials on legislative, adminis-trative, and judicial regulation appear early in this edition. Many new cases and notes have been added, and the policy forms in the Appendix have been updated. In some chapters, notes have replaced cases so that more space can be devoted to current topics and areas of controversy. In many ways, the materials raise broader societal concerns and the role and meaning of insurance in those contexts. At the same time, we have retained notes and textual material which point out matters that are so important from an historical or analytical standpoint that they could not conscientiously be omitted. Overall, the emphasis in case selection has been on currency and relevancy to major issues in insurance law.

As far as editing conventions are concerned, those employed in earlier editions have been retained, with one notable exception. As before, omissions in the text of quoted material are indicated by ellipsis. Previously, the omission of case citations was indicated by inserting empty brackets; the present edition does not provide any such indication, and we therefore caution readers against quoting from excerpted materials without checking the original source first. Where footnotes are retained, the original numbers are used. Far more citations are omitted than would ordinarily be preferred, but the gain in substantive material and enhanced readability makes it worthwhile.

We wish to express our gratitude to the American Law Institute, the Insurance Information Institute, the Insurance Services Office, the Defense Research Institute, the American Council of Life Insurance, and the Health Insurance Association of America for their assistance in our research and in providing materials for the book. We also wish to thank Patrick Morgan, Michele Mekel, and Jeff Lasswell for their very helpful research assistance on this third edition. In doing so, we remember with gratitude the research assistance of Christopher Fairchild, Dawn Gabel, Carol Lohmann, Daniel Mickiewicz, Debra Moulton, Terri Pollman, and Julie Witt on prior editions. Finally, Professor Jerry also expresses his appreciation for the support of the trust of the Floyd R. Gibson Missouri Endowed Professorship, the Webb R. Gilmore Research Fund, and the Thomas L. Patten Research Fund during his work on this edition.

Roger C. Henderson
Tucson, Arizona

Robert H. Jerry, II
Columbia, Missouri
December 15, 2000

SUMMARY TABLE OF CONTENTS

———————

TABLE OF CONTENTS

Chapter 1

INTRODUCTION: THE NATURE OF INSURANCE ARRANGEMENTS

AN ACTE concninge matters of Assurances,. . .

And whereas it hathe bene tyme out of mynde an usage amongste Merchantes, both of this Realme and of forraine Nacyons, when they make any greate adventure (speciallie into remote partes) to give some consideracon of Money to other psons (which comonlie are in noe small number) to have from them assurance made of their Goodes Merchandizes Ships and Things adventured, or some parte thereof, at suche rates and in such sorte as the Parties assurers and the Parties assured can agree, whiche course of dealinge is comonly termed a Policie of Assurance; by meanes of whiche Policies of Assurance it comethe to passe, upon the losse or perishinge of any Shippe there followethe not the undoinge of any Man, but the losse lightethe rather easilie upon many, then heavilie upon fewe, and rather upon them that adventure not then those that doe adventure, whereby all Merchantes, spiallie the younger sorte, are allured to venture more winglinglie and more freelie. . . . [Act of 1601, St. 43 Eliz., c. 12.]

§ 1.01 The Essence Of Risk

ROBERT H. JERRY, II, UNDERSTANDING INSURANCE LAW
§ 10[a], at 11 (2d ed. 1996).*

Life is uncertain. We cannot predict with confidence what the future holds. Events are not completely random, but few events are absolutely certain. Every person is certain to die sometime in the future, but the time of death cannot be predicted with certainty. Accidents occur; indeed, if the times at which accidents occur could be predicted with certainty, steps would be taken to prevent many of them. People make promises every day, and the recipients of the promises expect the promises to be kept. Yet, a chance always exists, due either to events outside the promisor's control or to the fact that people sometimes change their minds, that a promise will not be performed.

The inherent uncertainty of events can be described in terms of chance or probability. In insurance, this uncertainty is normally described in terms of

---

1

risk. For every human at a given age, a risk of death exists; the amount of risk is measured on actuarial tables. Every time an automobile is operated, a risk exists that an accident causing injury might occur; the amount of risk is a function of several factors, including the skill of the vehicle's driver, the number of miles driven, the geographic location of the vehicle, and the age and safety features of the vehicle. A risk exists that a building or home will be destroyed by fire or weather; based on the experience of other buildings of similar age, materials, and location, the risk of a particular structure suffering damage can be measured. That some hurricanes will cause great damage in the coastal areas of the eastern United States is certain, but when and where these storms will strike is impossible to know. That earthquakes, including some serious ones, will occur in heavily populated areas in the next fifty to one hundred years is certain; but the precise times of these occurrences are unknown. . . .

People make judgments about risk every day. Before engaging in an activity, an individual makes some sort of calculation, perhaps instinctively, about the activity's probable benefits and costs. After making this calculation, a person might decide not to engage in the activity—although inaction entails risks of its own which must be evaluated. However, if a decision is made to proceed with the activity, the individual might choose to take some steps to manage the risk of a prospective loss.

People cope with risk in various ways. One way to manage risk is *to limit the probability of loss*. Brick buildings are less likely to catch fire than wood buildings; thus, a builder might choose to use masonry rather than wood in a given structure so as to limit the probability of loss. Some people drive defensively in order to reduce the chance that an accident will occur. Many industrial firms utilize complex, dangerous machinery, which place the employees who use them at some risk. The probability, however, that an employee will lose a finger or hand in a cutting machine is reduced if guards or other safety devices are used around the cutting device.

Another way to cope with risk is *to limit the effects of loss*. To return to the foregoing examples, buildings are subject to a risk of fire, regardless of the construction materials used. To limit the effects of a fire should it occur, many building owners install sprinkler systems. A sprinkler system will not prevent a fire, but it will limit the effect of a fire should one occur. Even defensive drivers and their passengers are at risk of injury through accidents. If a vehicle's occupants wear their seat belts, they are less likely to suffer injury should an accident occur, and if an injury is suffered, it is likely to be less severe. Thus, to limit the effects of an accident should it occur, many people choose to "buckle up," thereby limiting the effects of loss. A firm's decision to employ an on-site medic or nurse and have first aid equipment nearby will not prevent accidents, but can mitigate the effects of loss when accidents occur.

Diversification is a particularly important way of limiting the effects of loss. For example, individuals who invest in the stock market expect to make money, but they are also at risk of losing money. To minimize the risk that a sharp decline in the value of one stock will decimate the investor's assets, most investors own a wide variety of the stocks. Through this strategy, losses in one stock are much more likely to be offset by profits in other stocks; if fortunate, the investor will show a net profit from the total portfolio. (Of course, diversification also limits the chance, or "risk," that the investor will benefit from a sharp increase in the value of one stock.) Similarly, the shirt manufacturer who is uncertain whether a new supplier of cloth will provide goods of adequate quality may choose to diversify by placing its order for cloth with several suppliers, thereby minimizing the risk that the entire batch of cloth ordered for a particular job will fail to meet the manufacturer's specifications.

Sometimes people cope with risk through *self-insurance.* For example, a restaurant owner, cognizant of the possibility that a patron may contract food poisoning, is likely to take substantial preventive measures to limit the risk of such an occurrence. After taking such steps, a remote risk nonetheless exists that a customer might be poisoned. The owner may calculate that such an event will rarely occur and may conclude that if it does occur the damages associated with the event could easily be paid from the owner's assets. Alternatively, the owner may choose to set aside a portion of each year's profits into a reserve fund designated to pay the loss should it occur. In either case, the owner chooses to bear the risk. This is the essence of self-insurance.

Sometimes, after weighing the potential benefits and costs of a particular activity, and after taking appropriate steps, if any, to minimize the probability or extent of loss, the individual may choose to engage in the activity without doing anything further with regard to the risk. In other words, some people choose *to ignore* risk. For example, the tightrope walker may purchase special shoes to reduce the risk of falling and may install a safety net to minimize the amount of loss should a fall occur, but if the performer proceeds with the walk, the performer has decided both to assume the risk that remains and to bear the costs of loss should the injury materialize. The performer is not self-insuring, because the performer has no assets to compensate for suffering a loss of life, which is one of the risks. Rather, the performer is choosing to ignore the risk.

In situations where risk cannot be managed sufficiently through preventive measures or through steps that reduce the effects of loss, and where assumption of the risk is not feasible, people usually cope with risk by *transferring* it to someone else. . . .

As the foregoing excerpt indicates, purchasing a policy of insurance is only one of a number of ways that people respond to risk. Consider the risks that you face on a daily basis; how do you respond to them?

Another point of the excerpt is that without risk, there is no need for insurance. If we could foresee the future with certainty, we would not need insurance. For example, if it could be known *ex ante* that tornadoes, fires, windstorms, etc. would never strike a factory, the factory's owners would never purchase insurance against those risks. By the same token, if a person could know *ex ante* that he or she will die from a particular disease before age 50, that person would not purchase insurance that covers nursing home care incurred at age 65 or later. But when one has a risk of suffering a future loss or injury, it may be desirable for a person to pay a certain, periodic premium to another person who is willing to assume the risk of the loss or injury.

It is fair to assert that every contract allocates risk in some way. But an insurance contract involves more than the allocation of risk between contracting parties. In an insurance contract, risk is the item which is exchanged—the equivalent of the commodity in a contract for sale. In other words, the insured bears a risk of some kind of loss; the insured pays money (the premium) to the insurer in exchange for the insurer's promise to assume the risk.

Compare, for example, a contract for sale: the farmer has possession of beans, a commodity which has positive value; the farmer promises to deliver the beans to the buyer if the buyer will pay the agreed-upon price. In contrast, a risk of loss, unlike beans, is something the holder would prefer not to possess, all things being equal. The risk of loss, unlike beans, has negative value, and the insured must pay someone (the insurer) to take the risk from the insured. (For a farmer, a commodity with a negative value might be a pile of garbage; the farmer must pay someone for that other person to take possession of the garbage and dispose of it.)

Like a promise to deliver beans, a promise to assume risk has value. In a wonderful book which covers many topics other than insurance, Professor A. Mitchell Polinsky illustrates in superb fashion how one can calculate the benefit of removing risk. See A. Mitchell Polinsky, An Introduction to Law and Economics 53-55 (2d ed. 1989). The Polinsky hypothetical goes like this: Suppose you are a recent law school graduate. You receive one job offer, which you decide to accept despite its unusual compensation arrangement. You agree to work on one case for your first year, a case that the firm has accepted under a contingency fee arrangement. Your first-year salary will be calculated in this manner: if you win the case, you will be paid $100,000 for the year; but if you lose the case, you will be paid nothing. You (and the firm) are certain, based on the firm's past experience with identical cases, that you have a 50 percent chance of winning the suit, and an equal chance of losing it. Your 50 percent chance of winning the $100,000 salary has an *expected value* of $50,000 (*i.e.*, a 50 percent chance of recovering $100,000). How confident are you of your legal skills? Does the arrangement make you nervous?

Some law graduates will be more nervous than others. One who is *risk preferring* actually welcomes the uncertainty; one who is worried and would prefer to reduce or avoid the risk altogether is *risk averse*, and someone who is ambivalent is *risk neutral*. Where any particular law graduate fits on the continuum between risk aversion and risk preference depends on many factors. One of the most important is the graduate's wealth; for example, a graduate who has independent annual income of $2 million from a family trust may prefer the 50 percent chance to get an extra $100,000 because the risk of getting nothing has no negative consequences, but a graduate with $80,000 of outstanding debt from education loans is likely to be risk averse. Personal preferences are relevant also; some people get pleasure from "living on the edge," and this attitude yields less risk aversion and more risk preference.

With respect to large risks, most people are risk averse, and most law graduates would prefer to find some way around the $^{50}/_{50}$ chance of getting nothing for his or her first year's work. How much would you be willing to accept in certain compensation in lieu of the firm's compensation arrangement? Would you take $40,000 in certain compensation? $30,000? $20,000? At some point on the scale, the certain compensation is so low that one would actually prefer the ⁵⁰⁄₅₀ chance of receiving $100,000 (or $0). There is a point, however, where one is willing to take considerably less (probably) than $50,000 (the expected benefit) in order to avoid the fifty percent chance of getting nothing.

One can flip the Polinsky hypothetical (which involves a *beneficial* or *positive risk*, because whatever the outcome the graduate will suffer no net loss from the proposal) to understand how insurance markets function. Imagine a homeowner who faces a five percent chance of her $500,000 home being destroyed by an earthquake sometime in the next year. This is a *negative risk* because, no matter what happens, the homeowner will not be better off; at best, the homeowner can end up no worse off. (If one of us were facing the five percent chance of a $500,000 loss, we might choose to deal with the risk in some way other than insurance—such as by moving to a different part of the country; the percentage and magnitude of loss in this example are exaggerated for ease of illustration.) The expected loss is $25,000 (*i.e.*, a five percent chance of a $500,000 loss). How much would the insured pay (*i.e.*, lose with certainty) to avoid the five percent chance of losing $500,000? If the insurer offered to assume this risk for a $125,000 annual premium, the insured might not purchase the insurance. Instead, the insured might reason that the odds of the house being destroyed by earthquake in the next 10 years is low; if the insured deposited $125,000 in the bank each year for the next four years, the insured would have a fund large enough to replace the house, and for every year past four years that the earthquake does not strike, the insured will be $125,000 better off. But for some price greater than $25,000, the homeowner (assuming she does not possess great wealth, which would tend to make her less risk averse) will find it desirable to purchase insurance to avoid the five percent chance of losing $500,000. If the insurer is willing to sell and the insured is willing to buy for $30,000 a one-year policy that guarantees replacement of the house if it is destroyed by earthquake, the insurer which enters into the same arrangement with 99 other insureds will collect $3,000,000 in premiums while paying (probably) five claims for $500,000, or $2.5 million, earning the insurer a nice gross profit of $500,000. At the same time, each insured is better off, having purchased the peace of mind that he or she will not lose, whatever happens, $500,000 this year. Because the insured was willing to pay $30,000 to be rid of an expected loss of $25,000, it follows that the insured placed a $5,000 value on "peace of mind," *i.e.*, being free of the expected loss.

By assuming the risk for a price, it does not follow that the insurer is risk preferring. What the insurer has done is to pool the risk with many other identical risks it assumes from many other similarly situated insureds. With the confidence and certainty that come with large numbers, the insurer can make fairly accurate predictions about the number and magnitude of losses and, based on these predictions, set a premium that enables the insurer to pay for the expected losses, cover its expenses, and (if a stock company) earn a profit. At the same time, the insured is freed from the risk, albeit a small one, of a crushing loss, and gains benefit from paying a slight margin over the expected loss to be immunized from the economic effects of the possible large loss. Risk is traded, and then distributed through large pools; the transaction is "efficient" in the economic sense because both insureds and insurers are better off.

If uncertainty were removed from the equation, there would be, of course, no risk. If, for example, it were known that in a group of 100 homeowners (named "No. 1" to "No. 100"), individual person "No. 67" would be the one whose house would be destroyed this year, persons "Nos. 1 to 66" and "Nos. 68 to 100" would not purchase insurance; spending anything for protection from an event they know will not occur would be wasting money. Person "No. 67" knows he or she faces a $500,000 loss, and this person would gladly pay anyone any sum up to $500,000 if that person would take over the certain-to-occur $500,000 loss, but, of course, no rational person would accept an obviously losing proposition of that sort. This necessarily means that there would be no insurer willing to assume the 100 percent risk of loss, and no insurance market would exist where person "No. 67" could make a trade. In other words, insurance depends on uncertainty—the presence of risk. In insurance law, this fundamental economic reality manifests itself in the general requirement of fortuity, which receives more attention in Chapter 2. Much more could be said about the economics of transferring and distributing risk. For further discussion, see Robert H. Jerry, II, Understanding Insurance Law § 10 (2d ed. 1996).

NOTES

1. *The pervasiveness of insurance.* In 1997, there were approximately 5,000 insurance companies based in the United States (a figure which has declined in recent years due to mergers and consolidations), and by 1997 premium receipts for all forms of insurance marketed by these companies exceeded $688 billion. Insurance Information Institute, The Fact Book 2000 (1999), at 1.6, 1.29. This figure accounted for approximately 8.5 percent of gross domestic product and represented an average of more than $2500 annually for every person in the country. At the end of 1998, the insurance industry had responsibility for approximately $3.6 trillion in assets and provided approximately 2.3 million jobs. *Id.* at 1.3. Total premiums in the world for life, non-life, and commercial health insurance totaled $2.14 trillion in 1997. The United States accounted for 32.4 percent of this figure, and the United States and Japan together accounted for 55.0 percent of the total. See The Fact Book 2000, *supra,* at v, 1.29; American Council of Life Insurance, Life Insurance Fact Book 1999, at 156. A full 96 percent of the nation's homeowners, and 29 percent of the renters, carried household insurance in 1998 to protect themselves against potential losses. The Fact Book 2000, at 2.28. In 1997, 70.9 percent of the population under age 65–or 167 million people–had some kind of private health insurance. Health Insurance Association of America, Source Book of Health Insurance Data 1999-2000 (1999), at 14. And, as of 1997, approximately $13.2 trillion of life insurance was in force in the United States. During this period, life insurance was owned by about 85 percent of American

households in the average amount of $178,600. See Life Insurance Fact Book 1999, at 1, 12.

2. *Insurance and the generation of wealth.* From the foregoing figures, it should be obvious that insurance is relatively pervasive and plays an extremely important role in modern, industrialized societies. This is implicitly, if not explicitly, recognized daily in the United States in the manner in which the many insurance and tort cases are addressed in the legal system. The steady expansion of liability in these areas by the courts reflects a symbiotic relationship between an affluent society and the perceived need in that society to transfer and spread risks of loss over large numbers of people.

Realize, too, that affluence creates and enhances the number of situations whereby it is possible for "loss" to be suffered by individuals. Yet affluence also creates and enhances the ability of individuals to avoid the prospect of loss they would otherwise bear. By way of comparison, to take the more extreme case, in a hand–to–mouth society there is relatively less at risk because there is less to lose. Furthermore, to the extent that there is some risk of loss, the necessary marginal or discretionary income which individuals would pool in any risk distribution scheme does not exist. On the other hand, in a relatively affluent society there is much more to lose, and the wherewithal–the discretionary income–exists to transfer and spread the attendant risks. This applies to business and governmental entities, as well as to individuals. Insurance plays a very important role in achieving the requisite levels of stability and predictability that are necessary for effective planning and execution. Could the modern, industrialized nations have progressed to their present position without it?

3. *The "rationality" assumption.* When analyzing the role of insurance in our society and our economy, it is customary to assume rational, informed behavior by those who participate (*i.e.*, insureds, agents, regulators, and insurers) in insurance markets. These assumptions, however, are not always correct. *See, e.g., Ray v. Federated Guaranty Life Insurance Co.*, 381 So. 2d 847 (La. Ct. App. 1980) (insured, insane and under delusion that he possessed supernatural powers, held his head under water in bathtub and drowned). Moreover, there is much data demonstrating that people routinely assess risk incorrectly and therefore respond irrationally to it. *See generally* Stephen Breyer, Breaking the Vicious Circle: Toward Effective Risk Regulation 33-39 (1993). Generally speaking, people tend to overestimate small probabilities and underestimate large ones. Why do you suppose this is so?

4. *Some things are "certain."* A point made earlier is that insurance is designed to deal with the risk of life's uncertain events. Where, then, does death fit in, which is certain to occur for all living things? Of course, the "risk" of death is inherent in the fact that the timing of one's inevitable death is uncertain. Whenever death occurs, it has ramifications beyond the cessation of one's mortal existence. A premature death may create economic difficulty for those who depend on the deceased's earnings for support. Living longer than one reasonably expects (*i.e.*, a "late death") may create economic difficulty for the long-lived person who survives well past his or her economically productive years. An individual may deal with the risk of premature death by purchasing life insurance, and with the risk of "living too long" with annuities, retirement plans, or other investments.

To explore the uncertainty inherent in the risk of death, consider the long-term prospects for the following kind of association. To provide for the cost of burial, 100 individuals form a "burial society." Each individual contributes $100 per year into a common fund; in exchange for the contribution, each person's estate is entitled to withdraw $2000 from the fund upon the person's death in order to pay for burial expenses. To join the association, the individual must be at least 21 years of age. If you were 21 years old, would you join? If you were 70 years old, would you join? If you were a 21-year-old bomb-demolition expert, would you join? See Jerry, *supra*, at 33-34.

5. *Toward a definition of insurance.* The transfer of risk is one ingredient of an insurance contract, but there is more to insurance than that. Consider the materials in the next section.

§ 1.02 What Is (And Is Not) Insurance?

GAF CORP. v. COUNTY SCHOOL BD.
629 F.2d 981 (4th Cir. 1980)

JAMES DICKSON PHILLIPS, CIRCUIT JUDGE:

On this interlocutory appeal defendant GAF Corporation challenges the district court's determination that plaintiff School Board properly invoked the provisions of Virginia's Unauthorized Insurers Process Act, Va. Code § 38.1-63 et seq., in serving process on defendant in this diversity action. We conclude that the Act is not applicable to GAF, reverse and remand to the district court, 478 F. Supp. 44, with instructions to quash the service of process.

I

GAF, a Delaware corporation registered to do business in Virginia, contracted with the School Board to supply roofing materials to contractors constructing two schools. The contracts contained a guarantee in which GAF agreed to repair damage to the roofing membrane and base flashing resulting from leaks caused by natural deterioration of the roofing membrane or base flashing, blisters, bare spots, fish mouths, ridges, splits not caused by structural failure, buckles and wrinkles, thermal shock, gravel stop breaks, plastic pans, workmanship in applying the membrane and base flashing, and slippage of the GAF products. The guarantee excluded leaks caused by natural disasters, structural defects, damage to the building and certain other events unrelated to any defect in GAF's products.

Contending that GAF failed to repair leaks, the School Board brought this diversity action against GAF and effected service of process under the Unauthorized Insurers Process Act on the theory that the guarantee constituted a contract of insurance. GAF contended that the guarantee was a warranty of its products and not a contract of insurance. The district court concluded that the guarantee was a contract of insurance, and GAF was, therefore, an insurer under Virginia's statutory scheme. Because GAF was not an authorized insurer in Virginia, service of process under the Act was held to be valid. The district court certified an interlocutory appeal under 28 U.S.C. § 1292(b).

II

Virginia extensively regulates insurance companies doing business within its borders. Insurers are required to obtain a license from the State Corporation Commission before transacting business in the state. Va. Code § 38.1-85. The Unauthorized Insurers Process Act provides a procedure for service of process on unlicensed insurance companies and requires such an insurer when sued under the Act to post a bond in an amount sufficient to secure any final judgment that might be rendered against it before a responsive pleading may be filed. *Id.* § 38.1-69. The Act allows attorneys' fees to be awarded to a prevailing plaintiff under some circumstances. *Id.* § 38.1-70. The School Board candidly concedes that it sought to effect service under these procedures solely to obtain these collateral benefits.

As noted by the district court, no reported Virginia case has squarely addressed the distinction to be made between a contract of insurance and a warranty accompanying the sale of goods. We therefore address the state law issue unaided by state court interpretation of this "jurisdictional-process" statute which incorporates the problem, or by state court consideration of the question in other contexts. In these circumstances we can only seek the rule of decision by resort to the usual sources to divine what the state's highest court would take as its rule. We conclude that looking to general authorities, considering the practical implications of the rule contended for by the School Board, and applying basic canons of statutory construction, the state court would construe the Act to be inapplicable to the defendant on the facts of this case and accordingly, so hold.

Although "insurance company" is defined as "any company engaged in the business of making contracts of insurance," Va. Code § 38.1-1(8), "insurance contract" is not statutorily defined. In the absence of case law or statutory definition, the district court analyzed the exclusions and inclusions in the policy and applied the principle that a warranty covers defects in the article sold while insurance indemnifies against damage from perils outside the article. Because the guarantee covered leaks caused by faulty workmanship, a peril unrelated to defects in the articles sold, the court held the contract to be one of insurance.

The question whether contracts for sale of goods or for service containing "guarantees" are insurance contracts or warranties arises in a variety of contexts and is a difficult one because these contracts involve the transfer and distribution of risk, which are two elements of insurance. See R. Keeton, Insurance Law § 8.2(c) (1971). Although, as the district court rightly emphasized, the guarantee here possesses some characteristics of insurance, we think that this does not sufficiently address the underlying question and that the guarantee must be viewed as a whole in determining whether it constitutes a contract of insurance or a warranty.

The guarantee does contain an "insurance" component because the risk of damage from leaks caused by faulty workmanship was transferred to GAF.

This element of risk transference, however, was a relatively unimportant element of the transaction and is incidental to the essential character of the guarantee, which is that of a warranty agreement accompanying the sale of goods. *See* R. Keeton, *supra*, at 552. We think that the appropriate rule is that a small element of "insurance" should not be construed to bring a transaction within the reach of the insurance regulatory laws unless the transaction involves "one or more of the evils at which the regulatory statutes were aimed" and the elements of risk transfer and distribution give the transaction its distinctive character. *See id.* We believe that this is the rule that would commend itself to the highest state court and accordingly provides our rule of decision.

GAF guaranteed to repair leaks caused by defects in its products and, incidentally, to repair leaks caused by faulty workmanship. The workmanship guarantee is incidental to the warranty against defects in the products sold. Viewed as a whole under the rule we think proper, the warranty is not a contract of insurance. GAF is, therefore, not an unauthorized insurer and is not amenable to service under the Unauthorized Insurers Process Act.

We remand to the district court with instructions to quash the service of process.

Reversed and remanded.

NOTES

1. *Defining "insurance."* Although the answer to the question of what constitutes "insurance" is rarely determinative—or even at issue—in the run-of-the-mill disputes between claimants and insurers that lawyers seek to resolve, it is still important to identify and examine, at least in a macro sense, this type of jural arrangement at the outset of any attempt to study the subject.

What was the definition of "insurance" employed by the court in the *GAF* case? What evils might the regulatory statutes in the case be designed to address? Does a guarantee, such as that given by GAF, embody any of these evils? Was the court correct in holding that GAF was not amenable to process under the Unauthorized Insurers Process Act?

2. *The "principal object and purpose" test.* One of the leading early cases to consider the meaning of "insurance" was *Jordan v. Group Health Association,* 107 F.2d 239 (D.C. Cir. 1939). The issue in *Jordan* was whether state insurance statutes applied to group health plans, in which medical services are provided as needed in exchange for the payment of a monthly fee. In holding that the Association was not engaged in the business of insurance, the court stated: "That an incidental element of risk distribution or assumption may be present should not outweigh all other factors. If attention is focused only on that feature, the line between insurance or indemnity and other types of legal arrangement and economic function becomes faint, if not extinct. This is especially true when the contract is for the sale of goods or services on contingency. But obviously it was not the purpose of the insurance statutes to regulate all arrangements for assumption or distribution of risk.

That view would cause them to engulf practically all contracts, particularly conditional sales and contingent service agreements. The fallacy is in looking only at the risk element, to the exclusion of all others present or their subordination to it. The question turns, not on whether risk is involved or assumed, but on whether that or something else to which it is related in the particular plan is its principal object and purpose." 107 F.2d at 247-248. This case is usually credited with articulating "the principal object and purpose" test. If the court in *GAF* had applied this test, would the outcome have been different?

3. *Statutory definitions.* If a state has a statutory definition of insurance, this is, of course, the place where one's analysis should begin. Note that Virginia's insurance statutes defined "insurance company" but not "insurance contract." This is typical of many state statutory schemes, but in other states statutes do define "insurance." For example, Cal. Ins. Code § 22 defines insurance as a "contract whereby one undertakes to indemnify another against loss, damage, or liability arising from a contingent or unknown event." Ky. Rev. Stat. § 304.1-030 states that insurance "is a contract whereby one undertakes to pay or indemnify another as to loss from certain specified contingencies or perils called 'risks,' or to pay or grant a specified amount of determinable benefit or annuity in connection with ascertainable risk contingencies, or to act as surety." If either the California or Kentucky statute had been the law in Virginia, would the case have been decided differently? Some state statutory definitions explicitly exempt some kinds of risk-transferring transactions. For example, the Maine statute states that charitable gift annuities, road or tourist service contracts, and home service contracts are not considered insurance. *See* Me. Rev. Stat. Ann. tit. 24-A, § 3.

4. *Implications for state regulation.* The question of what constitutes "insurance" frequently arises in the administrative law context, when a governmental agency attempts to regulate certain types of commercial activity. Every state has an agency or department to which the authority is delegated to regulate those engaging in the "business of insurance" within that state. This regulatory power may include the authority to approve or disapprove policy forms, premiums, rate classification categories, and many other insurer practices and actions. In addition, whether a business is subject to certain income taxes or assessments to support insolvency funds can depend on whether it is classified as being engaged in the business of insurance. If the activity which the state insurance agency seeks to regulate is not "insurance," the agency typically will have no authority over it. It is possible, however, that a legislature might delegate authority to an insurance department to regulate a certain business activity under the reasoning that the activity at least resembles insurance, and there is more logic to authorizing the insurance department to regulate it as opposed to some other government agency. Thus, a group health plan like that at issue in *Jordan, supra*, might not be an insurance contract, but if the legislature specifically delegates to the insurance department the authority to regulate such plans, the question of regulatory authority becomes moot.

5. *Applying the definition.* Compare the following contract provisions used by different automobile tire manufacturers at one time in retail sales to tire customers:

a) Western Auto tires are guaranteed against premature wear and also blowouts, cuts, bruises, rim-cuts, under-inflation, wheels out of alignment, faulty brakes or other road hazards that may render the tire unfit for further service (except fire and theft). In the event that a tire becomes unserviceable from the above conditions, we will (at our option) repair it free of charge, or replace it with a new tire of the same make at any of our stores, ...

b) If the tire fails to give the purchaser satisfactory service under any usual conditions of wear and tear, the liability of Standard Oil Company under this Warranty and Adjustment Agreement is strictly limited either to repairing the tire without charge or to replace it with a new tire of same brand at its option. This Warranty and Adjustment Agreement does not cover punctures, tires ruined in running flat, tires injured or destroyed by fire, wrecks or collisions, tires cut by chains, or by obstruction on vehicle, theft, clincher tires, tubes used in any form, or tires used in taxicab or common carrier bus service.

Which of the two provisions is more likely to be classified as an insurance contract? Why? What might be some of the consequences if one of the provisions was classified as an insurance contract?

6. *Practical reasons for identifying insurance arrangements.* From the public's standpoint, the issue can and does arise in very practical contexts on a regular basis. For example, when you rent a car and are asked whether you would like to purchase the "Collision Damage Waiver" option so that you will not be liable for any property damage to the rented vehicle, are you purchasing "insurance" in a technical or legal sense? *See Truta v. Avis Rent A Car Sys.,* 193 Cal. App. 3d 802, 238 Cal. Rptr. 806 (1987) (holding that the CDW option is not insurance). If you purchase along with your car or appliance a service contract that expands or extends the warranty, have you purchased a contract of insurance? *See Riffe v. Home Finders Associates, Inc.,* 517 S.E.2d 313 (W.Va. 1999) (holding that a home warranty contract constitutes insurance). Might the answer depend on whether you purchased the contract from the manufacturer or retailer of the product, as opposed to purchasing it from a third party? *See Griffin Systems, Inc. v. Washburn,* 153 Ill. App. 3d 113, 505 N.E.2d 1121 (1987) (holding the latter to be an insurance contract, but the former to be either a service contract or a warranty). At least one jurisdiction has addressed the issue regarding the nature of automobile service contracts through amendments to its insurance code. See Cal. Ins. Code § 116(c) (stating that a contract covering only defects in material and workmanship entered into incidental to the business of selling or leasing an automobile is not insurance, provided the maker of the contract is covered by an insurance policy that assumes liability created by the contract). For discussion of whether "non-filing insurance," which is sometimes procured by a lender in lieu of perfecting a security interest, is "insurance," *see Adams v. Plaza Finance Co., Inc.,* 168 F.3d 932 (7th Cir. 1999) (Judge Posner writing the majority opinion, with Judge Easterbrook dissenting). Even the relatively mundane question of subrogation rights can turn on the answer to the question of what constitutes "insurance." For a more extended discussion of the problem and related issues, see Robert H. Jerry, II, Understanding Insurance Law § 12 (2d ed. 1996).

7. *Problem: The case of the religious newsletter.* The "Rescue Mission" is a Christian ministry operating as a nonprofit corporation. It publishes a

newsletter with 35,000 subscribers world-wide. The Mission manages a system for subscribers to share health care costs based on a Biblical passage urging Christians to "bear ye one another's burdens." (Gal. 6:2). Subscribers seeking financial assistance for medical bills submit their bills to the newsletter. If the newsletter staff determines the expenses qualify for assistance, the newsletter publishes the name and address of the claimant, and on the same page assigns enough other subscribers to cover the medical expenses of the claimant. The designated subscribers mail a check ($50 for an individual; $100 for a couple; $150 for a family) directly to the subscriber to whom they have been assigned. Once a year, each subscriber makes a small payment directly to the newsletter to cover administrative costs. A subscriber is eligible for up to $100,000 in medical and health care expenses per person, per incident. Disputed claims are resolved by a rotating panel of members selected at random. Claims are subject to a $200 deductible floor, and the program excludes physical exams and certain routine tests. Each subscriber promises to refrain from using alcohol, tobacco, and illegal drugs. If a subscriber does not mail a check as assigned, he or she is dropped from the subscriber list. The Mission's promotion materials clearly state that no subscriber has a right to receive any benefit under the arrangement, but it also states that all "needs" that were qualified were funded at 100 percent during the past ten years. The Rescue Mission has no license to undertake the business of insurance. Is the Mission in violation of a state law requiring all those who conduct the business of insurance to have a license? *See Barberton Rescue Mission, Inc. v. Insurance Division of Iowa Department of Commerce,* 586 N.W.2d 352 (Iowa 1998).

8. *Does insurance create a "special relationship?"* The answer to what constitutes "insurance" figures prominently in a number of situations, only a few of which have been mentioned here. Some of these situations will be studied in more detail in subsequent sections of this book. However, you should constantly ask yourself as you study these materials whether the same principles and rules would be applied if the relationship were categorized as one other than "insurance." In other words, is the relationship between the insurer and its insured something special, or is it simply one more ordinary kind of contractual relationship? The answer to this question often holds the key that unlocks the logic of court decisions pertaining to insurance law. This receives more attention in the next section.

§ 1.03   The Nature Of The Relationship

RAWLINGS v. APODACA
151 Ariz. 149, 726 P.2d 565 (1986)

Feldman, Justice

David and Elizabeth Rawlings petitioned this court to review an opinion of the court of appeals which reversed the trial court's judgment in their favor. . . . We granted review to clarify the law of this state with regard to the "tort of bad faith." The issues we consider involve analysis of the type of conduct by an insurer that will support a tort action for "bad faith". We also consider what type of conduct will justify the imposition of punitive damages.

FACTS

The case was tried to the court, which made findings of fact and conclusions of law. Taken in the light most favorable to sustaining the judgment, the facts are as follows. On July 25, 1979 a fire near Laveen in Maricopa County caused extensive damage to the dairy farm owned by plaintiffs, David and Elizabeth Rawlings (Rawlings). They believed that the Apodacas, who lived nearby, started the fire by negligently burning trash in violation of Arizona law. Farmers Insurance Co. of Arizona (Farmers) insured Rawlings under a homeowners policy that provided only $10,000 coverage for their haybarn, which was destroyed in the fire along with the hay and seed in it, and nearby farm equipment.

Soon after the fire, Rawlings filed their insurance claim, and Farmers commissioned a private investigating firm to determine the cause of the fire. When the fire investigators came to Rawlings' farm on August 3, Mr. Rawlings told them that he had sizeable uninsured losses and that he was interested in pursuing a claim against the Apodacas. Rawlings specifically asked whether he should have his own investigation done or whether he would have access to the report. They told him that he would receive a copy of their report and need not undertake his own investigation. Rawlings also suggested that Farmers might want to join its subrogation claim with Rawlings' claim against Apodacas. Based on the assurances that they would have access to the investigative report, the Rawlings did not hire their own investigator.

The report was prepared August 17, 1979. The investigators verified that the Apodacas had started the fire. They also learned that the Apodacas had a $100,000 insurance policy covering their liability for the damages sustained by Rawlings. This policy had also been written by Farmers, which found itself in the unhappy position of having insured both a small portion of Rawlings' fire loss and all of Apodacas' liability exposure for that loss.

Both before and after the report was prepared, Mr. Rawlings spoke with Darrell Schultz, the Farmers representative who had retained the fire investigators, and was told that he would receive the report as soon as it was ready. In later conversations, however, Farmers referred Rawlings to the investigative firm, which in turn referred them back to Farmers. Farmers did not tell Rawlings that it already had the report nor that it was Apodacas' liability insurer.

On August 28, 1979 Farmers sent Rawlings a check for $10,000, their policy limit. Having failed to obtain the report, in September Rawlings retained an attorney to pursue the matter. The lawyer contacted Schultz, who said that the report had been received, refused to provide it and said that it contained nothing of interest to Rawlings. The trial judge specifically found that Schultz knew this to be false. Rawlings' attorney then filed a complaint with the Arizona Department of Insurance. Farmers finally agreed to give Rawlings the report, but only if Rawlings paid half its cost. Rawlings refused and instead brought suit against both the Apodacas and Farmers. Rawlings alleged that the Apodacas negligently caused the fire and that Farmers ". . .breached its obligation of good faith and fair dealing with its insureds . . . ." Rawlings also sought punitive damages and attorneys' fees. Having filed a lawsuit against Farmers, Rawlings was finally able to obtain the report through deposition of the custodian of records of the investigative firm.

During trial, James Richardson, an expert witness on insurance practices, testified that when an insurer is faced with a conflict of interest, such as that which faced Farmers, the proper procedure is not to "betray" one insured to protect the company's own purse, but to represent each insured independently. Because the report was prepared for Farmers when it was acting as Rawlings' insurer, the expert testified, Farmers should have cooperated with the Rawlings.

The trial court found that the Apodacas had negligently caused the fire and that Farmers had breached its duty of good faith and fair dealing. The court also found that Rawlings was damaged by Farmers' conduct. The court found the Apodacas liable to Rawlings for compensatory damages and awarded Rawlings $1,000 in compensatory and $50,000 in punitive damages against Farmers. Apodacas and Farmers appealed. The court of appeals affirmed the judgment against the Apodacas, having concluded there was ample evidence to support the finding that they had caused the fire. No review was sought on this issue. However, the court of appeals reversed the trial court judgment on the bad faith claim. It agreed with Farmers that the tort of bad faith was inapplicable to this case. Relying on *Noble v. National American Life Insurance Co.,* 128 Ariz. 188, 624 P.2d 866 (1981), the court held that because Farmers had paid Rawlings' claim in full (the policy limits) and without delay, it could not be liable for the tort of bad faith.

THE ISSUE

This case involves the covenant of good faith and fair dealing which was recognized by Arizona law in *[Noble] v. National American Life Insurance Co., supra.* The facts of this case, in which the first-party insurer is also the tortfeasor's liability insurer, present an issue of first impression in Arizona. The question is whether an insurer violates the covenant of good faith and fair dealing when, for the purpose of protecting its own interests, it acts improperly to impede its insured's recovery of the uninsured portion of the loss. The parties have not cited and our research has not brought to light any reported case that has examined this issue.

Farmers argues that actionable bad faith by an insurer facing a first-party claim is limited to the unfounded refusal or delay in payment of a valid claim. Plaintiffs argue that such a rule grants insurance companies license to abuse their relationship with and power over their insured. They urge that bad faith claims are not limited to situations involving breach of the express promise to pay covered claims.

The issues raised by the foregoing facts cannot be resolved without a brief analysis of the nature of the so-called "tort of bad faith" and the related implied covenant of good faith and fair dealing. Only in this way can we ascertain, first, whether Farmers breached some obligation which it owed to Rawlings and, if so, whether the remedy for the wrong sounds in contract or in tort.

Did Farmers Breach the Covenant of
Good Faith and Fair Dealing?

The Nature of the Covenant

The law implies a covenant of good faith and fair dealing in every contract. *Wagenseller v. Scottsdale Memorial Hospital,* 147 Ariz. 370, 383, 710 P.2d 1025, 1038 (1985); see also Restatement (Second) of Contracts § 205 (1981); 5 Williston on Contracts § 670 at 159 (3rd ed., Jaeger ed. 1961). The duty arises by virtue of a contractual relationship. The essence of that duty is that neither party will act to impair the right of the other to receive the benefits which flow from their agreement or contractual relationship.

Thus, firmly established law indicates that the insurance contract between plaintiffs and Farmers included a covenant of good faith and fair dealing, implied in law, whereby each of the parties was bound to refrain from any action which would impair the benefits which the other had the right to expect from the contract or the contractual relationship. We commented upon this in *Wagenseller*, where we stated that "the relevant inquiry always will focus on the contract itself, to determine what the parties did agree to." In *Wagenseller* we held that the nature of the employment-at-will contract was such that a termination without good cause did not breach the implied covenant of good faith, but that a termination against public policy was a wrong which "violates rights guaranteed to the employee by law and is tortious."

What are the benefits which flow from the insurance contract and the relationship it creates? Obviously, the insured buys the company's express agreement to pay certain types of claims. But the covenant of good faith is an implied covenant. *Wagenseller, supra.* In delineating the benefits which flow from an insurance contract relationship we must recognize that in buying insurance an insured usually does not seek to realize a commercial advantage but, instead, seeks protection and security from economic catastrophe. Thus, the insured's object in buying the company's express covenant to pay claims is security from financial loss which he may sustain from claims against him and protection against economic catastrophe in those situations in which he may be the victim. In both cases, he seeks peace of mind from the fears that accompany such exposure.

Because of the disparity in bargaining power and the nature of the contract, the insurer receives both premium and control. Thus, in third-party situations, the insured surrenders to the insurer the right to control and manage the defense of claims made against him. In first-party situations the insurer sets the conditions for both presentment and payment of claims. In both first-and third-party situations the contract and the nature of the relationship effectively give the insurer an almost adjudicatory responsibility. The insurer evaluates the claim, determines whether it falls within the coverage provided, assesses its monetary value, decides on its validity and passes upon payment. Although the insured is not without remedies if he disagrees with the insurer, the very invocation of those remedies detracts significantly from the protection or security which was the object of the transaction. Thus, the insurance contract and the relationship it creates contain more than the company's bare promise to pay certain claims when forced to do so; implicit in the contract and the relationship is the insurer's obligation to play fairly with its insured.[3]

We hold, therefore, that one of the benefits that flow from the insurance contract is the insured's expectation that his insurance company will not wrongfully deprive him of the very security for which he bargained or expose him to the catastrophe from which he sought protection. Conduct by the insurer which does destroy the security or impair the protection purchased breaches the implied covenant of good faith and fair dealing implied in the contract. This is not to say, of course, that the insurer must pay claims which are not covered, or take any other action inconsistent with the contract. . . .

Similarly, the implied covenant in an insurance contract neither entitles the insured to payment of claims that are excluded by the policy, nor to protection in excess of that which is provided for in the contract, nor to anything inconsistent with the limitations contained in the contract. It does, however, entitle the insured to insist that, to serve its own interests, the insurer not provide the promised protection with one hand while destroying the very objects of the relationship with the other.

Finally, although the insured is entitled to expect that the insurer will be "on his side" at least to the extent of treating him honestly and fairly, we do not go so far as to hold that the insurer is a fiduciary, but do hold that it has some duties of a fiduciary nature. Equal consideration, fairness and honesty are among them.

[The court goes on to consider the elements of the tort of bad faith and related damage issues. These issues are covered in Chapter 8.03[1], where the remainder of the *Rawlings* case is reproduced.]

EDWIN W. PATTERSON, ESSENTIALS OF INSURANCE LAW
62 (2d ed. 1957)*

Most of the peculiar legal aspects of the insurance contract arise from the fact that it is an *aleatory* as distinguished from a *commutative* contract. In making the latter type of contract, the parties contemplate a fairly even exchange of values. In a sale, which is a typical commutative contract, the seller thinks that the price paid is about equal to the value of the goods, and the buyer expects to get goods about equal to his price. On the contrary, in making an insurance contract, the insured knows that he is paying a sum far less than the insurer is to pay him *under certain conditions* that will probably not occur. Insurance is an aleatory contract; the conditions are a part of the bargain. They define the risks that the insurer agrees to bear for a group of persons exposed to similar risks and paying similar contributions to the fund from which losses are to be paid. The law looks back of the contract to the

---

[3] The industry itself seems to recognize these principles. Advertising programs portraying customers as being "in good hands" or dealing with a "good neighbor" emphasize a special type of relationship between the insured and the insurer—one in which trust, confidence and peace of mind have some part.

institution of which it is a part. If the insurer is compelled by law to pay losses for which it never agreed to assume the risk and for which it has collected no corresponding premiums from those who sustain no losses, the insurance enterprise can be maintained, if at all, only as a charitable institution.

Again, the insurance business is different in that the problem of control by a home-office force over the conduct of thousands of agents scattered over the country requires a rigid standardization of policy provisions and of the powers granted to agents. Yet the insured, because of his indifference to an event that will probably never happen, and because of his inability to understand the technical conditions imposed by the insurer, needs guidance and protection to a greater extent than in most of the other business deals in which he engages. The general law of contracts has been considerably distorted by American courts in applying it to insurance controversies, because they have sought to protect the insured.

NOTES

1. *Insurance as chattel?* One authoritative source on contracts points out that perhaps the most significant characteristic of insurance contracts that differentiates them from ordinary, negotiated commercial contracts is the increasing tendency of the public to look upon an insurance policy not as a personal contract between the insurer and insured, but as a special form of chattel:

> The typical [insurance] applicant buys "protection" much as he buys groceries. The protection is intangible, to be sure, but he is reassured by the words of the agent and by the fact that agent and company are regulated by the state and licensed to do business there . . . . [F]or most purposes, insurance must still be considered a contract between insurer and insured, but it is a very special type of contract and one currently involved in a prolonged period of popular gestation from which it may well eventually emerge as a new and special form of chattel, or perhaps, quasi-chattel.

7 Samuel Williston, A Treatise on the Law of Contracts § 900, at 34 (3d ed. Jaeger 1963). What are some of the consequences that might flow from viewing an insurance contract as a chattel? Do any of those consequences help explain the modern judicial treatment of such contracts? Is it more appropriate to view an insurance contract as an exchange involving a very unique kind of "chattel"? Indeed, is it perverse to think of insurance policies as an ordinary product, much like a car or computer?

2. *Insurer as fiduciary?* The court stopped short of declaring the insurer a "fiduciary." What does that make the insurer—a "quasi-fiduciary?" What different consequences would flow from treating the insurer as a fiduciary? Does the characterization turn on what kind of policy is involved?

In insurance cases, the term "fiduciary" appears frequently, but the term's usage is often imprecise in context. In *Tank v. State Farm Fire & Cas. Co.,* 105 Wash. 2d 381, 715 P.2d 1133 (1986), which involved a dispute over the insurer's duties under a liability insurance contract, the court described the insurer's "good faith duty" as having its source in "the fiduciary relationship existing between the insurer and insured. Such a relationship exists not as a result of the contract between insurer and insured, but because of the high stakes involved for both parties to an insurance contract and the elevated level of trust underlying insureds' dependence on their insurers. This fiduciary relationship, as the basis of an insurer's duty of good faith, implies more than the 'honesty and lawfulness of purpose' which comprises a standard definition of good faith. It implies 'a broad obligation of fair dealing,'. . .and a responsibility to give 'equal consideration' to the insured's interests." 715 P.2d at 1136.

Compare *Corrado Brothers, Inc. v. Twin City Fire Ins. Co.,* 562 A.2d 1188 (Del. 1989), which involved a dispute over what premium an insurer could charge an insured for workers compensation coverage, and in which the court stated: "The concept of a fiduciary relationship, which derives from the law of trusts, is more aptly applied in legal relationships where the interests of the fiduciary and the beneficiary incline toward a common goal and in which the fiduciary is required to pursue solely the interests of the beneficiary in the property. . . . The relationship of insurer and insured, however, arises contractually with each party reserving certain rights under the contract, the resolution of which often leads to litigation. . . . This expected clash of interests is clearly not compatible with the concept of a fiduciary." 562 A.2d at 1192.

Is it possible to find a core of common meaning in these two seemingly inconsistent passages? For more discussion (and one point of view), see Douglas R. Richmond, *Trust Me: Insurers are not Fiduciaries to Their Insureds,* 88 Ky. L. J. 1 (1999).

3. *Is the duty of good faith a two-way street?* Is Justice Feldman's thesis only applicable to insurers, or do insureds also owe a duty of good faith and fair dealing to their insurers? If the latter is true in theory, is it ever put into practice by courts? As you study the materials in this book, keep these questions in mind and see if you can identify any situations when courts may have applied the good faith duty to an insured. This issue will be revisited in Section 8.03[1].

4. *Are insurance arrangements special?* As suggested earlier in this chapter, it is plausible to argue that every jural arrangement creates, alters, or confirms patterns of risk. Contractual arrangements and the supporting jurisprudence that has developed to govern such relationships surely fit within this principle. Is there, however, something unique about contracts of insurance and the nature of the risks involved in those relationships that demands the seemingly special treatment that such contracts receive at times by the legal system through administrative, legislative, and judicial regulation?

In many instances, disputes regarding contracts of insurance do not call for the application of unique doctrines. For example, rules regarding contracts of adhesion are not limited to the insurance industry. The last time you purchased an airline ticket, opened a bank account, bought an appliance with a warranty, or purchased a computer or piece of software, was there any realistic opportunity for you to bargain for different terms? Yet does it follow that the subject matter of each of these contracts calls for the same treatment as, for example, a contract of life insurance? Is there a difference to be drawn in terms of how far a court should be willing to go in deciding that the unexpressed but reasonable expectations of the consumer should prevail over the unambiguous terms of the written agreement? Might that depend, for example, on whether the appliance warranty is called into question over bodily injury as compared to pure economic loss? Is it relevant that the subject of insurance contracts primarily deals with indemnification that in some way is related to serious, fortuitous physical losses? And if this is what makes insurance contracts so important, does this also help explain any unique legal treatment that such contracts receive?

It is one thing for courts—or, for that matter, legislatures—to make up the rules of tort law as they go along. (Products liability is often offered as the modern example. The rules of environmental liability is another.) Arguably, it is quite another to rewrite agreements between parties, particularly *ex post facto*. But if insurance contracts are genuinely unique, it may be quite appropriate for courts to engage in judicial regulation of such contracts.

5. *Insurance and social order*. Professor Lon Fuller observed that there are two fundamental forms of social order. *See* Henry M. Hart, Jr. & Albert M. Sacks, The Legal Process: Basic Problems in the Making and Application of Law 402 (William N. Eskridge, Jr. & Phillip P. Frickey ed. 1994). One is a relationship based upon reciprocity or exchange in which people tend to deal more or less at arm's length in such transactions. The other is one of common ends or a shared interest—for example, building a wall to protect against some common problem or threat. Are the perils against which we seek security through insurance contracts more akin to the "common ends," "shared problem" situation described by Professor Fuller? Or is an insurance contract more like a reciprocal, exchange-type relationship? What does this tell us about the nature of the relationship and the goals which it might have? When courts speak of the insurance industry and insurance contracts as being clothed with a public interest, do they have a particular form of social order in mind? Does any of this explain why a contract of insurance might call for a different judicial approach than a contract between a retailer and a consumer for the sale of a cellular phone?

In the excerpt quoted above, the late Professor Edwin W. Patterson, an authority on insurance law, described an insurance contract as an aleatory contract—a contract, the obligation and performance of which depends upon an uncertain event. How does this fit with Professor Fuller's analysis? Is the uncertain event the common problem or threat, and the contract the device for transferring and distributing the risk associated with the event? There is a certain element of "exchange" being effectuated, but does the nature of the subject of the contract lead to more socialization of the relationship — the jural arrangement? Is this what drives the courts, as Patterson put it, to "distort" the law of contracts?

In any event, as you study the materials in this course, the questions and concerns raised at this point should provide a haunting refrain. On a more practical level, these questions and concerns, once addressed, also should provide a frame of reference to guide you in answering the practical questions posed by your clients.

§ 1.04 Risk And The Insurance Contract

As examined more fully in the materials in the first part of this chapter, one of the basic themes of insurance is the following: If life and its assorted events were certain, insurance would be unnecessary. A corollary theme is that if all things were certain, insurance markets as we know them would not exist. Of course, the world is full of uncertainties — hence both the desire and need for insurance as a means of dealing with risk. Insurance companies come to the market and offer a product to individuals and business entities who desire to transfer risk to someone else. But, as noted earlier, insurers are also risk averse; by taking advantage of the certainty that comes with large numbers, insurers can make remarkably accurate predictions about future losses. With this information, insurers can pay expected losses, cover their expenses, and (if a stock company) earn a profit.

The laws of large numbers, however, stop far short of giving insurers absolute certainty. Insurers must make determinations about what degree of risk individual applicants pose (realize that sometimes an applicant is a proxy for a group of individuals, as is the case when an employer purchases a policy of group life insurance for the benefit of its employees), and insurers do not have unlimited resources with which they can do unlimited investigation about those who wish to do business with them. One way insurers deal with imperfect information is through the use of warranties and by conditioning obligations on the accuracy of the applicant's representations. These will receive more attention in Section 3.02[1].

Insurers also deal with risk in insurance contracts themselves. That is, through carefully considered language demarcating the boundary between covered risks and noncovered risks, insurers strive to control the scope of their undertakings. The next case provides an introduction to several aspects of how risk is transferred and managed through the contract between insured and insurer.

DESCHLER v. FIREMAN'S FUND AMERICAN LIFE INSURANCE CO.

663 P.2d 97 (Utah 1983), 39 A.L.R.4th 209 (1985)

DURHAM, JUSTICE:

The respondent filed suit below to recover insurance benefits under an accidental death policy which excludes coverage for death resulting from the use of a "device for aerial navigation." On opposing motions for summary judgment, the lower court granted judgment in favor of the respondent, thereby holding as a matter of law that the insured, who died in an accident involving a water ski kite, was not using a "device for aerial navigation" within the meaning of the policy's exclusionary clause. We reverse.

The facts as produced by the parties in support of their opposing motions for summary judgment show that the insured, Robert W. Deschler, died while operating a water ski kite, constructed of aircraft aluminum and dacron sailcloth, with a 17-foot wingspan. In normal use, the operator of a water ski kite sits in a seat made of seat belt webbing equipped with a safety belt. The seat is attached to a control bar which can be used by the operator by shifting his/her body weight to maneuver the kite to the left or right and to ascend or descend. The kite and operator are lifted into the air by being towed behind a motorboat. They are kept aloft by the airfoil design of the kite which creates lift and retards downward motion as the kite is towed by the boat on a rope 250-300 feet long. While airborne, the kite operator may control the speed of the kite to a limited degree by use of the control bar. The rope tow may be disengaged either by someone in the boat or by the kite operator. On disengagement, the kite descends and is guided by the operator to a selected landing site by use of the control bar and body weight.

The evidence presented showed that water ski kites are unstable, and cannot be safely used if there is any wind because of a danger that the kite and operator may be blown over land and injured in a crash. In this case, the insured's tow rope disengaged and the winds carried his kite over the shoreline at Starvation Reservoir, where he crashed and suffered injuries which resulted in his death. His widow, the respondent, applied for the death benefits payable under her husband's group insurance policy. The appellant denied the respondent's claim based on an exclusionary clause in the policy which reads as follows:

> The policy does not cover any loss, fatal or nonfatal, caused by or resulting from (1) injuries sustained in consequence of riding as a passenger or otherwise in a vehicle or device for aerial navigation.

The sole issue before this Court, which is one of first impression, is whether a water ski kite is a "vehicle or device for aerial navigation" within the meaning of the policy's exclusionary clause. "Interpretation of a written contract is ordinarily a question of law, and this Court need not defer to the trial court's construction, but will make its own independent interpretation of the contract terms."

All of the cases from other jurisdictions which have been cited by the parties deal with parachutes or hang gliders. The majority of these cases hold that the devices in question constitute devices for aerial navigation.[1] The respondent argues, however, that the devices in these cases are distinguishable from a water ski kite in that parachutes and hang gliders are designed for "free flight" whereas a water ski kite is controlled by the speed and direction of a towboat. This distinction is not significant. Although it is true that the operator of a water ski kite cannot maneuver the device to the same extent as a hang glider, he nevertheless has *some* control over speed, direction, and more importantly, the determination of when and where to land.

---

[1] The cases which do not find the devices to be for aerial navigation are all parachute cases.

Although not total, this element of control over direction, speed, and point of landing, together with the design of the kite, renders it a device for aerial navigation. A similar result was reached in the case of *Fireman's Fund American Life Insurance Co. v. Long,* 148 Ga. App. 216, 251 S.E.2d 133 (1978), which, on its facts, is more analogous to the present case than any of the other cases relied on by the parties. That case involved an identical exclusionary clause, and a "hang glider" which was designed to be launched by towing behind a motor vehicle. The court adopted the definition of "navigation" contained in the Webster's Third New International Dictionary at 1509 (1966) (hereinafter "Webster's"), namely, "the science or art of conducting ships or aircraft from one place to another," and found the glider in that case to be an "aircraft." Webster's defines "aircraft" as "a weight-carrying machine or structure for flight in or navigation of the air and designed to be supported by the air either by the buoyancy of the structure or by the dynamic action of the air against its surfaces." The undisputed facts in this case show the water ski kite to be a weight-carrying structure which operates on airfoil principles and depends on the "dynamic action of the air against its surfaces" to stay aloft. Thus, based on two critical factors, we hold as a matter of law that the water ski kite in question here is a "device for aerial navigation" within the meaning of the exclusionary clause: 1) the aerodynamic principles which affect its ability to become and remain airborne and 2) the degree of control which the operator has over direction, speed, and the timing and place of landing.[2]

The judgment of the trial court in favor of respondent is reversed. Judgment should be entered for appellant. No costs awarded.

HALL, C.J., and OAKS, J., concur.

HOWE, JUSTICE (dissenting):

I respectfully dissent.

The majority holds as a matter of law that a water ski kite is a "device for aerial navigation" based on two "critical" factors: (1) the aerodynamic principles which affect its ability to become and remain airborne, and (2) the degree of control which the operator has over its direction, speed, and the timing and place of landing.

I cannot agree that the exclusionary clause should be interpreted so broadly. A snow ski jumper's skis during a jump comply with the "critical" factors outlined by the majority. Yet common sense clearly suggests that they are not devices for aerial navigation even though aerodynamic principles affect their abilities to become and remain airborne and their "operators" exercise a degree of control over direction, speed, and the timing and place of landing.

The majority opinion and other decisions which have interpreted provisions similar to the one in question, have attempted to define "aerial navigation." It has been defined essentially as conducting travel through air. The element of control involved in conducting travel through air has been emphasized by some jurisdictions, as it is by the majority here. I have no quarrel with these

---

[2] We note that this particular combination of factors does not encompass forms of "travel through the air" which, although perhaps affected by some operator control, are accomplished by mechanical means, such as ski lifts, amusement park rides, etc.

definitions. I simply believe that the facts of this case do not require our constructing a general definition.

The question presented by this appeal is restricted to whether a device which is tethered to the earth is a device for aerial navigation. Like many amusement park rides which remain tethered to the ground by cables and other mechanical means, a water ski kite depends for its operation upon its tether to the boat which it trails. Clearly amusement park rides are not devices for aerial navigation. Similarly, water ski kites cannot be so considered. There is no legitimate distinction between them.

I recognize that the court in *Fireman's Fund American Life Ins. Co. v. Long, supra,* held that an insured's death was not covered by the policy because a hang glider which was designed to be launched by towing behind a motor vehicle *was* a vehicle or device for aerial navigation within the policy's aviation exclusion. However, the facts of that case are critically distinctive from the case at bar. There the glider was designed to be launched by towing and the tow rope was to be disengaged by a hand release control at the beginning of the ride. Here the disengaging of the tether is only performed to effect a landing (although that is not how the accident occurred). The glider's ride is untethered in the air while the ride in the kite, like amusement park rides, depends upon the tether for its existence.

Exclusions and words of limitation are to be strictly construed against the insurer.

Accordingly, I would affirm the trial court.

STEWART, J., concurs in the dissenting opinion of HOWE, J.

NOTES

1. *The structure of the insurance contract.* There are, of course, many different kinds of insurance contracts, and the organization and text of the contracts vary enormously. Yet they share, at their most basic level, a common structure: an insurance policy will state what the insurer is willing to cover (commonly called "the insuring agreement"), and this will be followed by a set of exceptions to the grant of coverage (the "exclusions"). A separate set of definitions will pour meaning into both the insuring agreement and the exclusions. This general structure is evident in the various policies in the Appendix to this book; you should review some of them now to get a general sense of how they are assembled.

In *Deschler*, there was no dispute over whether the insured's death was accidental. (What facts would need to be different to make the insured's death nonaccidental in this case?) Thus, the battle in the case is over the meaning of the exclusionary language. The affirmative grant of coverage is not even quoted. What do you surmise was the substance of that grant? For an idea for what the text might have said, look at the accidental death benefit in the whole life policy in Appendix G.

2. *Coverage, exclusions, and burdens of proof.* Limitations on coverage can appear in either the insuring agreement (where the affirmative grant of

coverage might be described narrowly) or in exclusions (which have the effect of negating the affirmative grant of coverage). The distinction is important. Generally, the burden is placed on the insured to establish in the first instance that a loss has occurred within coverage. If this burden is carried, the burden shifts to the insurer to establish the applicability of a particular exclusion. See generally Robert H. Jerry, II, Understanding Insurance Law § 25A[c] (2d ed. 1996). Moreover, it is commonly said that exclusions are to be construed narrowly against the insurer; thus, whether this interpretive principle is relevant depends on the structure of the insurance policy in question.

3. *The insurer's concerns.* When an insurer issues a policy of insurance covering accidental death or injury, the insurer has obvious concerns regarding whether the insured participates in ultrahazardous activities. Did the insurance policy in *Deschler* articulate a principled basis for distinguishing ultrahazardous activity from the kind of activity about which the insurer has no particular concerns? How would you draft a policy to make the distinction?

4. *Aviation exclusions.* It is not uncommon for life and accidental death insurers to employ an "aviation" exclusion clause in their policies. These clauses vary from insurer to insurer, although certain patterns have emerged. Thus, much can depend on the particular wording of the clause. Some policies, as in *Deschler*, speak of a "vehicle or device for aerial navigation," while others simply refer to "aircraft." Would a parachute fall in the former category but not in the latter? *See Edison v. Reliable Life Insurance Co.,* 664 F.2d 1130 (9th Cir. 1981)(a parachute is a device for aerial navigation). *See also Smith v. Mutual Benefit Health & Accident Ass'n,* 175 Kan. 68, 258 P.2d 993 (1953) (parachuting constitutes participation in "aeronautics or air travel" within the meaning of a policy exclusion). A hot air balloon with a passenger gondola would seem to fall within the language of all of the exclusionary clauses mentioned above, would it not? *See Aetna Insurance Co. v. Apollo Sleep Products, Inc.,* 296 S.E.2d 781 (Ga. App. 1982).

5. *Pilots.* Some "aviation" clauses also make distinctions on the basis of whether the insured is a pilot or other member of the crew as compared to being a mere passenger or a fare-paying passenger on a civilian aircraft. Provisions excluding only pilots and crew members from coverage are not uncommon. *See, e.g., Edison v. Reliable Life Insurance Co.,* 664 F.2d 1130 (9th Cir. 1981); *Paul Revere Life Ins. Co. v. First National Bank in Dallas,* 359 F.2d 641 (5th Cir. 1966); *Keyser v. Connecticut General Life Insurance Co.,* 617 F. Supp. 1406 (N.D. Ill. 1985); and *Beckwith v. American Home Assur. Co.,* 565 F. Supp. 458 (W.D.N.C. 1983). There are other variations affecting coverage if the aircraft: (a) is operated for aviation training or experimentation purposes; (b) is a military aircraft; or (c) does not have a valid airworthiness certificate.

To what are most of these exclusions directed—the ordinary civilian using commercial airlines for transportation? Should life and accident insurers be permitted to develop endless permutations of the aviation clause, or should the legislature prescribe a standard clause? If you believe legislative prescription is desirable, would you limit it to accidental death riders in life insurance and to other accidental death policies, or would you extend it to the basic life insurance coverage as well?

6. *Wars and military service.* Military service or "war" exclusion clauses are not uncommon either and have received some interesting interpretations with regard to the United States' military involvement in Vietnam and Korea. *Compare Jackson v. North American Assurance. Soceity of Va.,* 212 Va. 177, 183 S.E.2d 160 (1971) (adopting a legal definition of the term "war" and holding that the Vietnam conflict was not a war because Congress never declared war against North Vietnam under Article I, Section 8 of the U.S. Constitution) *with Bergera v. Ideal National Life Insurance Co.,* 524 P.2d 599 (Utah 1974) (holding that the Vietnam conflict was a "war" within the meaning of the policy). If you represented a life or accidental death insurer that desired to exclude coverage for death suffered in connection with military activity like that which the United States has had in recent decades in Lebanon, Haiti, Panama, Somalia, and the Persian Gulf, how would you draft the exclusion? How would your exclusion apply to an insured member of the military who, while traveling overseas, is killed in a bus explosion caused by a terrorist bomber? See the exclusions to the Accidental Death Benefit in the policy in Appendix G.

7. *Other risks, other language, and other problems.* Of course, there is no end to the exclusions that one might include in a life insurance or accidental death policy, but insurers do have to worry about competition. If you were house counsel to an insurer considering adoption of each of the following types of clauses, what advice would you give?

a) "This policy does not cover any loss caused by or resulting from. . .mental disorder, alcoholism or drug addiction." *Physicians Mutual Insurance Co. v. Savage,* 296 N.E.2d 165 (Ind. App. 1973).

b) "The Insurer shall not be liable for any loss sustained or contracted in consequence of the Insured's being intoxicated or under the influence of any narcotic unless administered on the advice of a physician." *Old Equity Life Insurance Co. v. Combs,* 437 S.W.2d 173 (Ky. 1969).

c) "The insurance under this policy shall not be payable if the insured's death. . .results from. . .homicide or the intentional act of another person." *Hicks v. Durham Life Insurance Co.,* 23 N.C. App. 725, 209 S.E.2d 846 (1974).

8. *Disability insurance for future professional athletes.* Disability insurance for professional athletes is a significant niche market, among many others. Professional athletes in many sports have significant earnings power, but an injury–either on the field or off–can wipe out this asset in an instant. Thus, it is common for such athletes to insure against the risk of disabling injury or illness.

What about the college student-athlete who expects a lucrative professional career? In 1990, the National Collegiate Athletic Association ("NCAA") initiated a disability insurance program for exceptional student-athletes at NCAA institutions in football and men's basketball. By 1998, the program had been extended to baseball, women's basketball, and men's ice hockey. Essentially, the NCAA gave its endorsement to an insurance product sold by a New York insurer and administered by an underwriters group in Massachusetts. Athletes eligible for the NCAA plan are automatically eligible for a loan for the premiums; the loan accrues interest, but is not due and payable until the athlete signs his or her professional contract. The amount of insurance available depends on the athlete's projected draft status. In football, for example, an athlete typically must be projected as a pick in one of the first three rounds of the National Football League draft (a group of fewer than 100 players in any given year). In 2000, a defensive football player under the NCAA-endorsed program could purchase a maximum of $3 million worth of coverage at an annual premium of $29,250. A few other insurers also offer similar products to prospective professional athletes. There are some differences in the policy forms, but these insurers seek to compete with the NCAA-endorsed product on price and policy limits. For example, if one company is willing to sell a policy with higher limits, the athlete may well prefer that policy over one with a lower limit.

A "draft protection" policy form used by Connecticut General Life Insurance Company in 2000 contained the following exclusion: "The Policy does not cover an Accidental Bodily Injury or Sickness or Disease caused by, in whole or in part, or as a result of:. . .8.6 The Insured: (1) being under the influence of any substance in violation of the motor vehicle laws of the state in which this Policy was delivered or issued for delivery." If a prospective insured asked you to explain the meaning of the foregoing exclusion, what advice would you give? What risks is the insurer that uses this form unwilling to assume? A form used by underwriters at Lloyd's of London in 1995 contained the following language: "This Policy does not cover losses wholly or partially, directly or indirectly caused by, contributed to by or aggravated by:. . .e) The insured: 1. being under the influence of alcohol, as defined by the motor vehicle laws of the state in which this Policy was delivered or issued for delivery." Is the Lloyd's policy different? If so, how?

§ 1.05   Types Of Insurers And Insurance

[1]   Insurer Organizations

There are many ways to classify insurers. Private insurers run a gamut of business organizations insofar as forms of legal ownership are concerned. There are capital stock companies, mutual companies, reciprocals or interinsurance exchanges, Lloyds associations, and some unique associations in the health care field. A brief description of each follows.

[a]   Stock and Mutual Companies

A stock company is organized as a profit-making venture, with the stockholders assuming the risks that are transferred by the individual insureds. Of course, the stockholders receive any profits. A mutual company, on the other hand, is owned by its policyholder-members and is organized not for profit as such, but for the purpose of providing insurance for the members. Unlike the capital stock company, the mutual company has no paid-in capital as a guarantee of solvency, but relies on an accumulated surplus. In a mutual company, any money left after paying all costs of operation, including additions to surplus, is returned to the policyholder-members in the form of dividends. There are various types of mutual companies based on whether premiums are payable in advance and whether the policyholder-members are subject to assessments for losses incurred. Fraternal organizations constitute a special form of mutual insurer.

[b] Reciprocal Exchange

A reciprocal exchange (also known as an interinsurance exchange) is in some ways like a mutual company. A reciprocal exchange consists of an unincorporated aggregation of individuals, called subscribers, who exchange insurance risks. A reciprocal, like a mutual, is a cooperative organization and therefore is not operated for profit. Each member (or subscriber) is both an insured and an insurer. As a member of the group, each is insured by each of the other members and *vice versa*. However, in a mutual company the policyholder-members assume their liability collectively, whereas the subscribers to a reciprocal exchange assume liability only severally, *i.e.*, the liability of each subscriber is limited to premiums paid by that member. In fact, the premium of each subscriber is maintained in a separate account and the subscriber's share of each loss is paid from that account. One subscriber cannot be called upon to assume the liability of another subscriber who defaults, unlike the situation in a mutual company. There also are distinguishing differences in the administrative structures of the two types of organizations, which permit a reciprocal exchange to operate at a lower cost to the subscribers. However, reciprocals confine their operations to property and casualty risks and only underwrite a small percentage of that market.

[c] Lloyds Association

A Lloyds association does not issue policies or underwrite insurance as such. It markets the services of a group of individuals, each of whom is an insurer who issues policies and underwrites risks separately or collectively with other members of the group. These organizations bear the name of the legendary Lloyd's of London, the oldest and perhaps the most famous of all insurance organizations in the world. However, "Lloyds" has taken on a generic meaning and other organizations that have the name Lloyds in their title are not to be confused with *the* Lloyd's of London.

Lloyd's of London has been in existence for over three centuries and is one of the major insurance markets of the world. It operates under an Act of Parliament and is governed by a council that establishes standards and rules for it members. From its inception, a distinguishing feature of Lloyd's has been the fact that individuals, each of whom assumes a fraction of the risk, underwrite the insurance. Each underwriter conducts business as an individual proprietor or as a member of one of the many Lloyd's syndicates, and, while liability is several only, each member is personally liable for all the losses he or she underwrites. One interesting legal ramification of this arrangement is that in theory a claimant must sue each of the individuals underwriting the insurance policy in the event of a lawsuit. However, in practice a "lead" underwriter usually serves as the named defendant, a nominee as such, so all underwriters are not actually sued.

Although it is still true that an individual underwriting insurance through Lloyd's is personally liable, in an attempt to gain new infusions of capital Lloyd's now permits corporate members to underwrite risks. In fact, in 1998, for the first time, corporate members made up the majority of the Lloyd's insurance market's capacity to underwrite risk. Consequently, despite the fact that many policies are still underwritten by individuals, the Lloyd's market is starting to look more like that in the United States where, with rare exception, only corporations are allowed to underwrite insurance.

While Lloyd's of London is licensed to do business in only two American states, Illinois and Kentucky, Lloyd's brokers and agents operate throughout the United States and the rest of the world. The Lloyd's policy issued in the United States has a clause whereby the underwriter agrees to submit to the jurisdiction of the courts of Illinois, Kentucky, and any other court of competent jurisdiction in the United States.

In the United States there are a few organizations denominated Lloyds associations. At one time, most of them operated in Texas. These organizations have no connection with Lloyd's of London except the similarity in name and general organizational structure. American Lloyds have not succeeded in emulating their English namesake. In fact, many states prohibit the organization or licensing of such associations.

[d] Hospital and Medical Organizations (and Related Entities)

The explosive growth during the last half of the twentieth century in hospital and medical care costs has led to the creation of a number of risk distribution organizations that are unique to these fields. Indeed, it might be said that health insurance is itself a unique field, given the special status health care access enjoys in the hierarchy of entitlements. With national health care expenditures expected to reach $1.316 trillion in 2000[*] –a full one-seventh of U.S. gross domestic product–the subject of health care financing and access is well deserving of special attention.

Health insurance was relatively slow to develop in the United States.[**] Until 1930, most health care was handled on a fee-for-service basis, with the patient paying the hospital's or physician's bill out of personal resources. When a day in the hospital cost roughly the same as a night in a hotel, few felt a need to purchase health insurance. This changed dramatically, however, during the Great Depression. The middle-class could no longer afford to pay for health care out of personal funds; the decline in use of health care services

---

[*] Statistical data in this section comes from the Health Care Financing Administration, the National Center for Health Statistics, and the U.S. Department of the Census. The data can be found on the foregoing agencies' websites, and much is compiled in National Center for Health Statistics, Health, United States 1999, with Health and Aging Chartbook (1999).

[**] Many good discussions of the history of health care finance exist, but a particularly good summary can be found in Rand E. Rosenblatt, Sylvia A. Law, & Sara Rosenbaum, Law and the American Health Care System 4-24 (1997).

was so severe that many hospitals and doctors were threatened with insolvency. The first insurance plans emerged as a direct response to these economic forces. Initially, these arrangements were created by hospitals or groups of hospitals: in exchange for a monthly premium, a hospital would agree to provide a given number of days of hospital care and a discount on the cost of other services provided during the remainder of the premium period. Similar prepayment plans were organized, somewhat reluctantly, by physicians for their services. These types of plans were typically organized as nonprofit associations, sometimes under special enabling legislation. Their common characteristic was the facilitation of consumers' prepayment of various hospital, medical, and related health care costs; in other words, the *quid pro quo* for the premium was the receipt of a service, not reimbursement for an out-of-pocket loss (*i.e.*, the patient's payment to the hospital or doctor for health care services). Consequently, it was not obvious that these organizations were insurance companies, and in some states they escaped state insurance regulation altogether. Two of the earliest and perhaps the best known of the so-called prepayment plans were the Blue Cross and Blue Shield plans. Blue Cross consisted of members of the American Hospital Association and was originally organized to permit and encourage group prepayment of hospital expenses. Blue Shield plans were organized later by local medical societies for the prepayment of medical care expenses of physicians. The "Blues" were governed by boards of directors or trustees that included representatives from hospitals, the medical profession, and the public. Instead of paying cash benefits to indemnify an insured patient for covered health care expenses, they marketed "service" contracts which could include, for example, a semi-private room in a Blue Cross member hospital or a certain surgical procedure by a Blue Shield member physician. Because many hospitals and physicians participated in these plans, an "insured" had a fair amount of freedom in selecting health care services. Other distinguishing features of most of the "Blues" were open enrollment (anyone could purchase the insurance) and community rating (a single premium for all individuals, and another premium for families, regardless of the insureds' likelihood of needing health care services).

Commercial insurers, impressed by the success and popularity of the prepayment plans, decided to get into the health insurance business. Unlike the typical prepayment plan, these insurers practiced underwriting under traditional insurance principles–good risks were separated from poor risks, and the poor risks were charged a higher premium or denied coverage altogether. Also, the commercial insurers practiced "experience rating," *i.e.*, they varied the premiums based on the loss experience of the individual insured or the group of insureds. These competitive pressures, as well as other changes in health markets in recent decades, have caused the Y2K Blue Cross and Blue Shield plans to undergo change and they now look very different from their 1930s ancestors. For more on this history, see Emily Friedman, *What Price Survival? The Future of Blue Cross and Blue Shield*, 279 J.A.M.A. 1863 (June 17, 1998).

Generally speaking, by 1960 it could be said that two kinds of private health insurance existed. Indemnity plans, primarily sold by commercial insurers, had the patient-insured pay the doctor's or hospital's bill, and then obtain reimbursement from the plan to which premiums had been previously paid. The insured's benefit, then, was money, which indemnified the insured's out-of-pocket expenditure. The other kind could be described as service-benefit plans, with the prime example being the Blue Cross or Blue Shield plans. The plan would persuade doctors and hospitals to accept the plan's payment for services; patients were not limited in their choice of health care provider. Doctors and hospitals would provide care for insureds under the plan, and then be reimbursed directly from the plan. From the insured's perspective, the benefit was not money but was the health care service itself.

In the 1970s, sharply-rising costs led to the rapid growth of a third model of private health insurance–direct service plans. Although health maintenance organizations ("HMOs") had been on the landscape for a few decades, until well into the 1970s they were usually viewed as "wellness" plans. Insureds would pay a monthly premium and would receive health care services from the same organization to which the premium was paid (to be contrasted from the service benefit plan, in which the premium was paid to the plan, which in turn would use the premium to pay the health care provider). In its most basic form, the direct service plan owned the hospital and employed the doctors and other health care professionals on a salaried basis. To the extent the plan kept the insured healthy, the plan would spend less on acute health care and would be able to retain a larger portion of the premium as profit. By the 1970s, these plans became attractive for their cost-saving attributes; by organizing health care providers into larger health care delivery entities, the plans sought to gain efficiencies that enabled the delivery of more care at lower cost. This model was very attractive to employers and employees alike, even though it departed from the indemnity model and to some extent the prior service benefit model by virtue of its restrictions on the insured's choice of physician or hospital. When enrolling in the direct benefit plan, the insured essentially committed to receive his or her care from the plan's hospitals and doctors; if the subscriber chose to go outside the plan, the subscriber would pay for the health care services on the traditional fee-for-service basis.

At 2000, "managed care organizations" (or MCOs), an umbrella term which refers to HMOs and their many permutations, have come to occupy center stage. The line between service benefit plans and direct benefit plans has blurred as players in the health care field have implemented a wide range of organizational structures in an effort to find new efficiencies and a competitive advantage in the health care marketplace. This has generated the proverbial "alphabet soup" of managed care hybrids: IPAs ("Independent Practice Association,"meaning a plan that contracts with individual physicians with independent practices); PPOs ("Preferred Provider Organization," which involves a designated provider network which offers its services to health care purchasers on a discounted, fee-for-service basis; the insured can go outside the network for care, but the insured's out-of-pocket costs will be higher); EPOs ("Exclusive Provider Organization," which is a PPO where the subscriber receives no coverage for care received outside the network); POSs ("Point of Service" plan, which is an HMO that allows subscribers to use non-plan providers if the insured pays a higher share of the cost), and PHOs (a "Physician-Hospital Organization," a hospital-physician group joint venture which markets its services to MCOs and other payers, such as self-insured employers). *See* Elizabeth C. Price, *The Evolution of Health Care Decision-Making: The Political Paradigm and Beyond*, 65 Tenn. L. Rev. 619, 621 (1998). Most come under the jurisdiction of the state insurance regulator in some manner. Moreover, a good number of them are now operated for profit. Many of these are operated by employers as self-insurance programs, which adds further complexities to the landscape. Analysts place the number of persons receiving there health care through some kind of "managed care" system at 85 percent of the insured workforce. Kenneth E. Thorpe, *Managed Care as Victim or Villain?*, 24 J. Health Pol. Pol'y & L. 949 (1999). Because this field is so volatile, new arrangements striving to create efficient and effective risk distribution schemes—and new acronyms—are certain to appear on the landscape. Whatever might be said about them, the public certainly has come to regard such plans as insurance products and usually regards the providers of such plans as insurance companies.

Three other phenomena deserve mention in the health insurance area. First, the years after World War II saw explosive growth in employer-provided group insurance arrangements in the health area. Several factors contributed to this development, not the least of which was favorable tax treatment given health insurance when provided as a fringe benefit in the employment setting. By 1998, 88 percent of all persons with private health insurance received such coverage under group plans. Yet there are still many conventional health insurance companies, both stock and mutual, that underwrite considerable amounts of individual and group cash-indemnity type policies; indeed, in 1996, over 24 million Americans had individual policies of health insurance, even though this number continues to decline in both percentage and absolute terms. Second, in 1965, two major governmental insurance programs were created. Medicare is a federal health insurance program for people age 65 or over, some disabled people under age 65, and people with end-stage renal disease. In 1998, 38.8 million Americans were enrolled in the Medicare program, and total Medicare expenditures reached $216 billion dollars, or almost 20 percent of all U.S. health care expenditures. Medicaid is a joint federal-state program providing health and long-term care insurance for some of the nation's indigent—approximately 29.0 million Americans in 1998 at a cost exceeding $170 billion. This massive government role in financing and providing access to health care services has had extraordinary consequences for the entire health care delivery system. Third, along with the dramatic growth in various kinds of MCOs, there has been a significant increase in self-insured plans by large employers. This has been spurred in large part by the Employee Retirement Income Security Act of 1974 (ERISA), which gives employers more freedom to structure their employee health care programs by relieving them of the obligation to meet certain requirements and pay the taxes that are imposed on insurance companies under state regulatory schemes. But employers in many instances still contract with insurance companies to administer these plans.

With all the different private plans and government programs, it is estimated that more than 44.3 million Americans lacked health insurance coverage—or 16.3 percent of the population—during the entire 1998 calendar year. The number of Americans having no coverage during a significant portion of the year would be considerably larger. Despite Medicaid, nearly one-third of the poor–11.2 million people–had no health insurance of any kind. Although most health insurance continued to be provided through the employment relationship, having a job was no guarantee of coverage: 43.4 percent of the uninsured worked full-time during 1998, and nearly one-half, or 47.5 percent, of poor, full-time workers were uninsured in 1998.

[e] Government Programs

There are various government-sponsored insurance programs. The largest of the public programs are those administered by the federal Social Security Administration—Federal Old Age, Survivors, Disability, and Medicare. Another program, unemployment insurance, is a joint federal-state undertaking, like the previously-discussed Medicaid program. Although some of these are social programs designed to provide only subsistence levels of support, others are more extensive.

There are other public insurance programs that resemble fidelity and guarantee insurance, but are conducted on a scale so large that perhaps only the government could undertake such efforts. The Federal Deposit Insurance Corporation and the Federal Home Administration are the prime examples. Yet some public programs look more like, and in some instances compete directly with, the types of insurance traditionally marketed by private insurance companies. For example, there are government programs for life and crop insurance and for insuring properties against crime, flood, and riots. In some states, workers' compensation insurance is underwritten exclusively by state funds; elsewhere, state funds provide an alternative to and thus compete directly with private insurers. As a result of the so-called medical malpractice insurance crises of the 1970s and 1980s, some states created governmental or quasi-governmental insurance programs for this type of errors and omissions insurance. The foregoing list of government sponsored insurance programs is not exhaustive, but it does provide a basis for comparing public insurance mechanisms with the world of private insurance.

[2] Underwriting Authority

Historically, insurance has been divided into three basic fields or lines: (1) life, (2) fire and marine, and (3) casualty insurance. Underwriters more or less voluntarily limited themselves in the early period of insurance development by specializing in only one of these lines, but there soon followed regulatory laws which formally segregated the underwriters. These laws were passed largely because of the concern that different lines required unique regulatory provisions to ensure financial qualification and stability and to encourage proficiency through specialization. Various conflagrations, such as the New York City fire of 1835 and the Chicago fire of 1871, were instrumental in keeping fire insurers as "monoline" underwriters. The New York fire resulted in the ruin of twenty-three of the twenty-six fire insurers in the state at the time. Needless to say, the Great Depression had an impact on life insurers, and the general concern over solvency has influenced the continued segregation of life underwriters to this day.

Despite the early developments regarding monoline underwriting, the reasons for segregating fire and marine insurers (including the allied forms of property insurance) from casualty insurers became less apparent as both of these areas of underwriting grew to include new types of risks that were not distinctly dissimilar. In addition, insurers circumvented the laws by organizing subsidiaries or developing associations with counterparts to meet the needs of the insuring public. As a result, after World War II many states began to enact legislation permitting "multiple-line" underwriting by companies in the fields of fire and marine and casualty insurance when the capital and surplus requirements of each line were met. However, for historical and other reasons, many insurers today still use separate companies to underwrite different types of insurance in these fields. In addition, although some states have permitted "all-line" underwriting by one company, which permits fire and marine and casualty insurers to write life insurance and *vice versa*, there has been no great movement to break down the barrier between these types of insurers.

Even though multiple-line and all-line legislation did not homogenize the insurance industry in the United States, private insurance is now commonly described as being divided into just two groups: (1) life and health and (2) property and casualty. This break from the earlier trichotomy—life, fire and marine, and casualty insurance—undoubtedly is a result of the multiple-line development, and also of the modern prominence of health care insurance.

Although the original classification into the three categories of life, fire and marine, and casualty insurance still is important for underwriting and regulatory purposes, much of the statistical information regarding the insurance industry is published by organizations representing the more modern classifications. The American Council of Life Insurance has published a "Life Insurance Fact Book" for nearly fifty years and is the principal industry source of statistics about life insurance. The Health Insurance Association of America collects and publishes facts concerning that portion of the industry in the "Source Book of Health Insurance Data," while the Insurance Information Institute publishes the "Property/Casualty Fact Book."

[3] Types of Insurance Policies

[a] Life Insurance

There are essentially four kinds of life insurance policies: whole life, term life, endowment life, and life annuities. The basic feature of a whole life policy is that it provides coverage at a level premium for the entire lifetime of the person whose life is insured. It is described as permanent insurance, which is true as long as the premiums are paid. Thus, one pays premiums until the insured life expires or until the age of (typically) one hundred is achieved (the age at which mortality tables say death should have occurred), at which time the insurer is obligated to pay the face amount of the policy to the designated beneficiary. Whole life is sometimes referred to as "straight life" or "ordinary life" insurance, the basis of the synonyms being readily apparent.

A whole life policy also may be written on a limited payment or on a single-premium basis. The former provides for premium payments for a designated term (thus, the term "20-year pay policy") or until the death of the insured, whichever occurs first. At the end of the specified term, the insurance is "paid up" for the life of the insured. A single-premium policy also provides lifetime coverage and, because it requires that the total premium be paid in a lump sum at the inception of the policy, it is "paid up" at that time. Whole life insurance usually has a savings feature and over time builds up a cash surrender value. Thus, one might think of the whole life premium as purchasing two things: an investment in a savings account (*i.e.*, the cash surrender value) and a policy of term insurance: when the term insurance expires (as explained below), the savings account will remain to make a payment of proceeds to the designated beneficiary or the insured's estate. If the savings account is invested in stocks or other higher-yield instruments, the policy is labeled a "variable life" or "universal life" policy. Not surprisingly, the strength of equity markets during the 1990s has caused consumers to prefer variable or universal life policies over traditional whole life policies.

Term life insurance is temporary insurance in that it is written for a specific period; at the end of this period, it expires. The period usually is defined as a certain number of years or is defined to end at a certain age. The fact that there may be an option to renew merely means that the insured may elect to have the insurance for another succeeding period, usually without proof of insurability, but at a higher premium. It does not mean that the coverage for the original term did not terminate. This may be contrasted to whole life insurance, described above, which is permanent insurance in that it provides coverage for the duration of the insured life. Term insurance is written in a variety of forms, but, whatever the form, it only constitutes protection against death within the contract period. There is no savings element and consequently no cash surrender value. Term insurance may be convertible or nonconvertible. In case of the former, the term policy may be exchanged within a certain period of time for some form of permanent insurance without proof of insurability. Because no portion of the premium is used to fund a surrender value, term life's cost per $1000 of coverage is much less than whole life.

Endowment life insurance has been described as a savings account protected by life insurance. A pure endowment contract is an agreement to pay the face amount only in the event that the "insured" lives for a specified term—the endowment period. If the "insured" dies within the period, nothing is due. The premiums charged must be sufficient, when coupled with the income therefrom, to pay the amount due at the end of the endowment period. This gives the appearance of an enforced savings account. In contrast, endowment life insurance is not a pure endowment contract, but has an insurance feature built into it. The insurance aspect protects the savings or endowment fund prior to maturity, thus leading to the description at the outset of this paragraph. An endowment life insurance policy is more appropriate for funding an income source for use later in life, such as a retirement program, than for protecting against premature death. Protection for the latter is best achieved under a whole or term life policy.

Life annuities are marketed in a variety of forms, but, simply described, they provide for a regular periodic income for the life of the annuitant. This type of contract protects against the risk of living too long—at least in the sense that one might exhaust his or her sources of support prior to death. The other forms of life insurance described above protect against premature death and might be more accurately described as "death insurance"; by that logic, life annuities are true "life insurance." Thus, a young adult may wish to have in his or her insurance portfolio both life insurance (to protect against the risk of dying too soon) and annuities (to protect against the risk of living too long). Ironically, life annuities are not always described as a form of life insurance, perhaps because they resemble investment contracts in some respects.

Life insurance may also be classified on the basis of the manner in which it is marketed. This again calls for at least a four-fold division consisting of ordinary life, industrial life, group life, and credit life insurance. Here the term "ordinary life" is used to distinguish between contracts of life insurance marketed on an individual basis rather than a group basis. The term also is used to distinguish between individual policies in amounts of $2,000 or more and industrial life insurance policies (sometimes called "debit insurance"), which have small face values, typically less than $2,000. The latter also are distinguishable from ordinary life insurance, as defined here, in that industrial life insurance is usually sold in premium units based on what the insured can afford (say fifty cents or one dollar), and the premiums are usually collected weekly by the insurer's representative who calls at the insured's home.

Group insurance involves the marketing of a master contract or policy to a policyholder, such as an employer or a professional association, with an opportunity for individuals within a pre-defined class to subscribe to the benefits. The policyholder contracts with the insurer for the benefit of the individuals in the group. There usually are provisions that the individual subscribers meet certain eligibility requirements such as being full-time, permanent employees; that there be a minimum number of eligible individuals; and that a minimum percentage of the eligible individuals in the group subscribe to the plan. Enrollment periods also are prescribed. All of these requirements are necessary for a successful group plan because one of the usual hallmarks of group coverage is that proof of individual insurability is not required. Group life insurance is a form of term insurance. It has no cash surrender value.

Credit life insurance protects creditors against the risk of nonpayment due to the death of debtors. It also protects the debtor's estate and, in some instances, even facilitates the granting of credit, because it provides security for a personal loan to those whose only means of discharging the debt is through personal earnings. It is sold to short-term borrowers by the lending institutions, and retailers often purchase it to protect charge accounts. In addition to the traditional market where insurers sell to the public, home loan institutions also sell mortgage protection life insurance. Credit life insurance is sold through individual and group policies and, as defined here, takes the form of term insurance.

In 1997, ordinary life insurance and group life insurance together accounted for approximately 98 percent of the total life insurance in force in the United States and about 80 percent of the total number of policies (if each group certificate is counted as a separate policy). Ordinary life insurance accounted for approximately 58 percent of the total amount of insurance (as compared to 40 percent for group policies), and about 37 percent of the total number of policies (as compared to 44 percent for group certificates). Primarily because of the widespread availability of group life insurance through the workplace, industrial life insurance has little importance today. (In fact, some regulators think that the product should be banned because it has so little value. See Allison Bell, *Florida Department Seeks Ban on Sales of Industrial Life*, Nat'l Underwriter (Life-Health), May 8, 2000, at 3.) In 1997, it accounted for just 0.1 percent of the total amount of insurance in force (even though approximately 6.7 percent of all policies in force were industrial life). At one time it comprised a significant portion of the total life insurance in force in America; before World War II, nearly one-fifth of the face value of all life insurance in force was industrial life, and it was not until the early 1970s that the total number of industrial life policies was less than half of the total number of life insurance policies in force. Although credit life accounted for about 12 percent of all policies in force in 1997, the amounts of coverage were, on average, quite small, so that credit life accounted for less than 2 percent of the total amount of life insurance in force.

[b]   Health and Accident Insurance

Perhaps the words "health and accident" should be reversed because "health" insurance, at least as it originated in the mid-1800s, was limited to accidents—usually accidents associated with early forms of transportation. Today, insurance plans providing protection against the expenses associated with hospital and medical care and loss of income, whether caused by accidents or illness, are generally referred to as "health and accident" insurance. This type of insurance comes in many different forms. Some policies combine coverage for accidents and sickness; sometimes the policies are purchased separately. Disability insurance, which provides protection against the loss of income associated with the insured's inability to work due to sickness or accidental injury, is sold separately from health insurance. The coverages are written through individual policies as well as group plans. In their more common forms, coverages include those for: (1) loss of income, such as long term disability insurance; (2) loss of life, sight, or limb, such as accidental death and dismemberment insurance; and (3) health care costs, such as the traditional reimbursement forms of hospital and medical insurance, and the Blue Cross and Blue Shield and health maintenance service contracts. Disability income loss is usually written to pay a specified amount, for example two-thirds of average weekly wages up to a maximum dollar amount, for a specified period of time. Accidental death and dismemberment benefits take the form of specific sums outlined in a schedule of benefits—for example, the policy might pay $15,000 for loss of an arm, and $1,000 for loss of a thumb.

[c]   Property and Casualty Insurance

As explained earlier, what is now referred to in general as property and casualty insurance (due to the influence of multiple-line underwriting) originally consisted of two distinct lines of insurance based on underwriting authority: (1) fire and marine and (2) casualty insurance. Much of the early vestiges of monoline underwriting still remains, particularly with regard to ocean marine insurance, even though many of the coverages described below are sold in multiple peril package policies. The summary of each of the major types of property and casualty insurance which appears below is qualified by the proverbial "fine print" of the standardized forms, which otherwise limits much of what is said below.

Fire insurance contracts are prescribed in a great majority of states by virtue of legislation which adopts the New York Standard Fire Policy (1943 edition). This policy covers all direct loss to the described property by "fire, lightning and removal from premises endangered by the perils insured against." Buildings, machinery, merchandise, household contents, and personal property are common subjects for this coverage. An extended coverage endorsement may be purchased to protect against windstorm, hail, explosion, riot and civil commotion, damage by aircraft or by vehicle, and smoke damage. Selected coverage for less than all of the perils named in the endorsement may be purchased. Other endorsements are available, such as coverage for vandalism or malicious mischief and radioactive contamination. A number of other miscellaneous perils referred to as "allied lines" are written by endorsement or separately by fire insurers because of their close association with the fire business. These include, among others, sprinkler leakage, water damage, tenant's improvement and betterments, builder's risk, flood, and crop insurance.

The New York Standard Fire Policy insures only "direct" losses caused by fire or other covered perils, but indirect losses, such as interruption of income, may be covered by a business-interruption form which can be attached to the fire policy. Standard forms for fire insurance and the other perils mentioned have been developed and are designed to cover particular classes of risks such as dwellings (including apartments), stores, farm buildings, and manufacturing, mercantile, and many other properties.

Marine insurance is divided into ocean and inland marine; the former is sometimes referred to as "wet" and the latter as "dry" marine insurance. To the uninitiated, ocean marine insurance is an arcane world reserved for a few hardy souls who specialize in the subject. Although there are no official uniform or standard forms, happily, at this point at least, the subject can be described as being divided into four types of contracts depending on the type of interest covered: hull, cargo, freight, and liability. Hull and cargo policies cover the property ownership interests in the vessel and goods shipped, respectively. Freight is the tariff or fare for transporting the cargo, another property interest. Liability is used in its common legal sense.

The basic perils covered by the Lloyd's of London ocean marine policy still are described in language adopted in 1779:

> TOUCHING The adventures and Perils which we the assurers are contented to bear and do take upon us in this Voyage, they are, of the Seas, Men-of-War, Fire, Enemies, Pirates, Rovers, Thieves, Jettisons, Letters of Mart and Countermart, Surprisals, Takings at Sea, Arrests, Restraints and Detainments of all Kings, Princes and People, of what Nation, Condition, or Quality soever, Barratry of the Master and

Mariners, and of all the other like Perils, Losses and Misfortunes that have or shall come to the Hurt, Detriment or Damage of the said Goods and Merchandises and Ship, etc., or any Part thereof.

The insuring clause in American policies, although sometimes expressed differently, provides essentially the same coverage as the Lloyd's policy, including stranding, sinking, collision, lightning, and tempestuous action of wind and waves. Of course, there is much more in the way of qualifying and limiting clauses in an ocean marine policy.

The inland marine policy also concerns itself with perils arising from transportation activities. Again, four divisions exist: (1) property in transit; (2) bailee liability; (3) fixed transportation property; and (4) personal and commercial floaters. The first two categories are fairly self-explanatory, but the third includes such unexpected instrumentalities of transportation and communication as bridges, tunnels, piers, wharves, docks, marine railways, dry docks, pipelines, power transmission lines, radio and television towers, and such common traffic control devices as the stop light. A floater policy covers chattels, personal or commercial, that are subject to being moved but that have no particular location or destination. This distinguishes such policies from those in the first category, which in the main cover property destined for a particular location or locations, even though the term "floater" also is used to describe some of these policy forms.

Property and casualty insurance also includes a number of other first-party coverages as well as a host of third-party liability coverages. The former category encompasses physical damage to motor vehicles and aircraft, credit, burglary and theft, boiler and machinery, glass, no-fault automobile, and title insurance and surety and fidelity bonds. Liability policies are available to protect against statutory and contractual liability as well as tort liability for property damage and personal injury. Such policies include private passenger and commercial automobile, aviation, common carrier, employers' liability and workers' compensation, premises and operations, products and completed operations, contractual, errors and omissions, and personal liability coverages.

Many of the types of coverage denominated as property and casualty insurance are marketed today in packages such as the commercial general liability (formerly called comprehensive general liability), homeowners, and personal auto policies. Perhaps with the exception of marine insurance, great progress has been made since World War II through industry and regulatory efforts to standardize the various coverages in all lines of insurance, and the subject is really not as bewildering as it might appear at first blush.

[4] Bibliography of Insurance Texts

For more detailed information regarding the business of insurance, the following standard college textbooks may profitably be consulted. Much of the information in this chapter regarding the types of insurers and insurance is based on these texts:

Bickelhaupt, David L., General Insurance (McGraw-Hill Higher Education, 11th ed. 1983).

Black, Jr., Kenneth & Harold D. Skipper, Jr., Life Insurance (Prentice-Hall, Inc., 12th ed. 1994).

Crawford, Muriel L., Law and Life Insurance Contract (McGraw-Hill, 8th ed. 1998).

Huebner, S.S., Kenneth Black, Jr., & Bernard L. Webb, Property and Liability Insurance (Prentice-Hall, Inc., 4th ed. 1996).

Luthardt, Constance M., Barry D. Smith & Eric A. Wiening, Property and Liability Insurance Principles (Insurance Institute of America, 3d ed. 1999).

Mehr, Robert I., Emerson Cammack, & Terry Rose, Principles of Insurance (Richard D. Irwin, Inc., 8th ed. 1985).

Mowbray, Albert H., Ralph H. Blanchard, & C. Arthur Williams, Jr., Insurance: Its Theory and Practice in the United States (McGraw-Hill Book Co., 6th ed. 1969).

Riegel, Robert, Jerome S. Miller, & C. Arthur Williams, Jr., Insurance Principles and Practices: Property and Liability (Prentice-Hall, Inc., 6th ed. 1976).

Vaughan, Emmett J. & Therese M. Vaughan, Fundamentals of Risk and Insurance (John Wiley & Sons, Inc., 8th ed. 1999).

Williams, C. Arthur, Michael L. Smith & Peter C. Young, Risk Management and Insurance (McGraw-Hill Co., 8th ed. 1997).

Among the legal works on insurance, one may consult:

Abraham, Kenneth S., Distributing Risk: Insurance, Legal Theory, and Public Policy (Yale University Press 1986).

Anderson, Eugene R., Jordan S. Stanzler & Lorelie S. Masters, Insurance Coverage Litigation (John Wiley & Sons, 1997).

Appleman, John A. & Jean Appleman, Insurance Law and Practice (West Publishing Co.).

Dobbyn, John F., Insurance Law in a Nutshell (West Publishing Co., 3rd ed. 1996).

Harnett, Bertram, Responsibilities of Insurance Agents and Brokers (Matthew Bender & Co., 1974 with annual updates)

Jerry, Robert H., II, Understanding Insurance Law (Matthew Bender, Inc., 2d ed. 1996).

Keeton, Robert E. and Alan I. Widiss, Insurance Law, A Guide to Fundamental Principles, Legal Doctrines and Commercial Practices (West Publishing Co., Student Ed. 1988).

Ostrager, Barry R. & Thomas R. Newman, Handbook on Insurance Coverage Disputes (Aspen Law & Business, 10th ed., 2000)

Patterson, Edwin W., Essentials of Insurance Law (McGraw-Hill Book Co., 2d ed. 1957).

Russ, Lee R. & Thomas F. Segalla, Couch on Insurance (Clark Boardman Callaghan, 3d ed.).

Stempel, Jeffrey, Law of Insurance Contract Disputes (Aspen Law & Business, 2d ed., 1999).

Vance, William R., Law of Insurance (West Publishing Co., 3d ed. 1951).

Windt, Allan D., Insurance Claims & Disputes (Shepard's/McGraw-Hill, 3d ed.1995).

Chapter 2

FUNDAMENTAL ASSUMPTIONS

"Perhaps no modern commercial enterprise directly affects so many persons in all walks of life as does the insurance business. Insurance touches the home, the family, and the occupation or the business of almost every person in the United States."—Justice Hugo L. Black, in *United States v. South-Eastern Underwriters Association,* 322 U.S. 533, 540 (1943)

§ 2.01 Fortuity

[1] The General Requirement

COMPAGNIE DES BAUXITES v. INSURANCE CO. OF NORTH AMERICA
724 F.2d 369 (3rd Cir. 1983)

Seitz, Chief Judge.

Compagnie des Bauxites de Guinee (CBG) is appealing an order of the district court granting summary judgment to the Insurance Company of North America (INA) and a number of foreign excess insurers (the excess insurers), in CBG's action to recover on its business interruption insurance policies. . . .

I

This appeal involves one of several suits filed by CBG against its insurers to recover for business interruption losses arising from various casualties at its bauxite mining and processing facility in the Republic of Guinea. . . .

CBG holds all-risk business interruption insurance policies, with a $10 million primary layer carried by INA and a $10 million excess layer carried, in varying percentages, by the excess insurers. At issue is whether CBG may recover from its insurers for the business interruption caused by the structural failure of its tippler building and crusherhouse. This facility raises freight cars loaded with bauxite ore and empties their contents into a feed hopper. Machinery within the structure separates chunks of ore too large to ship and transports them to hammermills where they are crushed to a consistency suitable for shipment. At some time in 1974, not long after the plant became operational, CBG became aware of serious damage to the concrete structural members of the tippler/crusherhouse, as well as to the feeders onto which the ore cars are emptied. CBG alleges that it suffered a protracted and costly business interruption during the time needed to rebuild and reinforce the structure and machinery.

The cause of the damage was the subject of much investigation and discovery. An early report by an adjuster for the insurer of the structure itself concluded that the damage was caused by blocks of bauxite much larger than anticipated being fed into the machinery. CBG claims that only after the damage occurred did it learn that the engineers for the conveyor system had not followed CBG's specifications. The machinery had been designed to accommodate the weight of crushed bauxite, 84 lbs/cubic foot, rather than the weight of bauxite blocks, 159 lbs/cubic foot. It was also discovered that the structural engineers for the building and supports used an incorrect equation to compute the severe stresses to which the structure would be subjected.

INA and the excess insurers separately filed motions for summary judgment based on several grounds. First, they argued that the design defects in the equipment and structure meant that the structural failure and ensuing business interruption was inevitable rather than fortuitous, and that as a matter of law CBG could not recover for losses not caused by a fortuitous event. Second, they alleged that CBG did not file timely notice of loss as required by the terms of the insurance policy, and that they suffered prejudice from this delay. Third, they alleged that CBG did not file suit within 12 months of the date of the loss, also as required by the policy.

The district judge ruled that factual disputes precluded entry of summary judgment based on the latter two grounds, but he granted summary judgment based on the first ground. He held that insurance covers only risks, not certainties, so that a loss must be caused by a fortuitous event in order to be covered. He then held that the design defects made the failure of the tippler/crusherhouse inevitable, and thus that no fortuitous loss had occurred. He further held that regardless of the terms of the insurance contract or the knowledge of the parties at the time it is made, it would be contrary to public policy to cover losses not caused by a fortuitous event.

II

We need not address the public policy rationale if we determine that CBG's loss was fortuitous, and so we proceed directly to that issue. There appears to be no decision by any Pennsylvania court defining a fortuitous event. Thus, the duty of the district judge under the *Erie* doctrine was to predict what definition of a fortuitous event the Pennsylvania Supreme Court would apply if this case were before it. The district judge made his prediction of Pennsylvania law based on cases from other jurisdictions and treatises on insurance law, although he characterized his holding as one of general insurance law rather than a prediction of Pennsylvania law. We must first determine what standard of review we should apply to the district court's holding.

We believe that we should review the district judge's prediction as a determination of law, as to which our review is plenary, rather than as a finding of fact reviewed by the clearly erroneous standard of Fed. R. Civ. P. 52. . . .

Having determined the appropriate standard of review, it remains to decide whether the district court erred as a matter of law in holding that a loss arising from an unknown design defect is not caused by a fortuitous event. We hold that the district court did err, because we believe that the definition of a fortuitous event that Pennsylvania would adopt is that found in the Restatement of Contracts:

> A fortuitous event. . .is an event which *so far as the parties to the contract are aware,* is dependent on chance. It may be beyond the power of any human being to bring the event to pass; it may be within the control of third persons; it may even be a past event, such as the loss of a vessel, *provided that the fact is unknown to the parties.*

Restatement of Contracts § 291 comment a (1932) (emphasis added).

We believe for several reasons that Pennsylvania would adopt this definition of a fortuitous event. The illustrations accompanying this definition make it clear that it applies to insurance policies, and a number of courts have so applied it.

While we know of no Pennsylvania case which has considered the Restatement definition, we have already applied it to an insurance policy in a case controlled by Pennsylvania law. *Panizzi v. State Farm Mutual Auto Insurance Co.,* 386 F.2d 600 (3d Cir. 1967). Furthermore, the parties as well as the district court agree that "accident" is a synonym for 'fortuitous event," and the Restatement definition of a fortuitous event is consistent with Pennsylvania's definition of an accident, which emphasizes its unplanned and unintentional nature. Damage resulting from an unknown design defect is obviously unplanned and unintentional.

We also disagree with the district court's definition of fortuitousness because the court determined what was "certain" based on knowledge gained through hindsight. Since we are reviewing a summary judgment for the insurers, we must credit CBG's statements that it had no knowledge of the design defects. We think it inappropriate to cause the insured to suffer a forfeiture by concluding, with the aid of hindsight, that no fortuitous loss occurred, when at the time the insurance took effect only a risk was involved as far as the parties were aware. *See Millers Mutual Fire Insurance Co. v. Murrell,* 362 S.W.2d 868, 870 (Tex. Civ. App. 1962), *writ ref. n.r.e.:*

> It is true that all the expert witnesses, who, after the damage, examined the underlying structures of the earth, noted the capacity of the soil to absorb water and saw evidences of earth movement, said that damage similar to that which occurred was inevitable. We are not told who, at the time the insurance contract was executed, had certain knowledge that this damage was inevitable. We perceive no error in the court's refusal to hold. . .that the peril was not a risk but a certainty that could not be insured against.

INA and the excess insurers cite numerous cases for the proposition that a loss caused by a design defect is an uninsurable certainty. None of these cases they cite address the Restatement definition of a fortuitous event, much less consider and reject it. Many of the cases cited by insurers' counsel merely mention fortuitousness without any helpful analysis of the meaning of the requirement. In others the finding of non-fortuitousness was based on the insured's own gross negligence or deliberate risk-taking.

The insurers rely heavily on *Greene v. Cheetham,* 293 F.2d 933 (2d Cir. 1961), which involved an insured's attempt to recover for a shipment of frozen catfish which was condemned as unfit for human consumption. The court stated that contaminated fish would inevitably be condemned, so that the insurance policy had to be construed to exclude coverage if contaminated fish were shipped. *Id.* at 937. The court, however, was not stating as a legal principle that coverage could not attach. Instead, the court was construing the policy's "inherent vice" exclusion in order to harmonize it, according to the probable intent of the parties, with the policy's coverage of "any and all risks."

The insurers also rely on language in two pre-Restatement cases. A passage in *Gulf Transportation Co. v. Fireman's Fund Insurance Co.,* 121 Miss. 655, 83 So. 730 (1920), states in dictum that coverage does not apply to a loss caused by a design defect even if it is unknown to the parties at the time of contracting. That case expressly does not decide the issue, however, holding instead that the loss was not caused by a covered "peril of the sea." *Id.* 83 So. at 733. We have also determined that the Pennsylvania courts would not follow *Mellon v. Federal Insurance Co.,* 14 F.2d 997 (S.D.N.Y. 1926). In that case Judge Augustus Hand stated that insurance could only apply to a risk, not a certainty, and held that coverage would not extend to a ship's boiler that cracked from unknown causes. Judge Hand did not consider the issue of fortuitousness in terms of the knowledge of the parties. He also interpreted the coverage of the policy narrowly rather than broadly, and based his holding on this narrow construction of the policy. In contrast, a Pennsylvania court today would interpret the coverage of an all-risks policy broadly.

Because we believe that the Supreme Court of Pennsylvania would hold that a loss arising from an unknown design defect is one caused by a fortuitous event, we will reverse the district court's contrary conclusion. In view of this holding we need not address the district court' ruling that public policy requires that a fortuitous event must occur. We note that our holding does not mean that the event causing CBG's loss is within the coverage of the policy, since a loss can be caused by a fortuitous event and still fall within a contractual exclusion from coverage. In their answer to CBG's complaint the insurers stated defenses based on the policy exclusions for inherent vice, latent defect, wear and tear and gradual degradation. Nothing in the rule of fortuitousness which we adopt today bars the district court from addressing the possible applicability of such exclusions during the proceedings on remand.

[Other issues are omitted.]

Because we have determined that the district court erred when it granted summary judgment to the insurers on the ground that a fortuitous event had not occurred, and that no alternative ground exists for sustaining summary judgment, at least at this stage, we will reverse the judgment of the district court and remand this case for further proceedings consistent with this opinion.

NOTES

1. *Business interruption insurance. Compagnie des Bauxites* involves a kind of insurance that many lawyers would do well to learn more about. After all,

advising business clients about possible ways to protect against various losses is not solely the province of insurance agents. Business interruption or loss of use and occupancy coverages protect the insured against indirect or consequential losses resulting from direct losses by fire, etc., to the insured's property. A similar kind of policy is called contingent business interruption insurance; it protects against losses resulting from direct losses to *another's* property. To illustrate, assume ABC Co.'s manufacturing business depends on receiving a steady supply of a certain electronic component from XYZ Co., the only manufacturer of such a component. If XYZ Co.'s production is interrupted by fire, ABC Co.'s production and profits will suffer. One way to protect against this risk of indirect or consequential loss is for ABC Co. to purchase contingent business interruption insurance. For cases construing the provisions of business interruption policies, see William H. Danne, Jr., Annotation, *Business Interruption Insurance*, 37 A.L.R.5th 41 (1996).

2. *An easy case or a hard case?* Given the risk that the insured sought to cover in *Compagnie des Bauxites*, does it matter what caused the loss? Would it be a harder case if the risk sought to be covered were the damage to the tippler building and crusherhouse? After all, no one could expect the facilities to last forever. As they aged, they would have needed increased maintenance and eventual replacement.

3. *Damage to property, design defects, and fortuity.* Can property damage resulting from a design defect ever be "fortuitous?" In many, and perhaps most, situations, the design defect exists at the time the insurance is purchased. It may well be the case that the damage has been caused already, but not yet discovered. These fact patterns can raise interesting coverage issues depending on the language of the policy, but should such losses be *per se* uninsurable under the fortuity requirement? The loss may in fact be inevitable or even have already occurred, but as long as this information is unknown to the insured and insurer, it would seem that the requirement of fortuity is satisfied. This is the trend in the more recent cases. *See Adams-Arapahoe Joint School District v. Continental Insurance Co.*, 891 F.2d 772 (10th Cir. 1989); Chadwick v. Fire Insurance Exchange, 17 Cal. App. 4th 1112, 21 Cal. Rptr. 2d 871 (Cal. Ct. App. 1993); Jane Massey Draper, Annotation, *Coverage Under All-Risk Insurance*, 30 A.L.R.5th 170, 239–46 (1995).

Should the answer change in the following circumstances? Insured decides to demolish a building instead of renovate it. Federal and state laws require that asbestos-containing materials be removed prior to demolition. The insured knows this at the time the decision to demolish is made. Insured claims that the all-risk property policy provides coverage for the cost of asbestos removal, but the insurer claims the loss is not fortuitous. *See University of Cincinnati v. Arkwright Mutual Insurance Co.*, 51 F.3d 1277 (6th Cir. 1995) (no coverage because removal of ACMs from building prior to demolition was not fortuitous).

4. *Personal insurance and fortuity.* Every sport has its stars, and every musical genre has its highly acclaimed artists. Because time is relentless, the renowned abilities of such persons eventually begin to gradually deteriorate. Should such a person be allowed to insure against this inevitable deterioration, as contrasted with the loss of use of hands and arms due to illness or

accident? Is gradual, inevitable deterioration in ability any different (for purposes of insurability) from death?

5. *All-risk versus specified-risk insurance.* The insurance policy in *Compagnie des Bauxites* is described as an "all-risk" policy. Does the label "all-risk" mean that every risk imaginable is borne by the insurer? In *British & Foreign Marine Insurance Co. v. Gaunt,* 2 A.C. 41 (1921), Lord Sumner wrote: "There are, of course, limits to 'all risks.' They are risks and risks insured against. Accordingly the expression does not cover inherent vice or mere wear and tear or British capture. It covers a risk, not a certainty; it is something, which happens to the subject-matter from without, not the natural behaviour of that subject-matter, being what it is, in the circumstances under which it is carried. Nor is it a loss which the assured brings about by his own act, for then he has not merely exposed the goods to the chance of injury, he has injured them himself. Finally the description 'all risks' does not alter the general law; only risks are covered which it is lawful to cover, and the onus of proof remains where it would have been on a policy against ordinary sea perils." 2 A.C. at 57. Insofar as fortuity is concerned, an all-risk policy covers every risk of fortuitous loss except those specifically excluded.

All-risk coverage is one of two basic types of policy coverage. The other is specified-risk coverage, which is cast in the opposite form. Such a policy might say, for example, that only risks A, B, and C are covered, and even then there may be further exclusions. The fact that there are further exclusions does not work to broaden the coverage to risks other than those specified. *See California Union Insurance Co. v. Spade,* 642 S.W.2d 582 (Ky. 1982).

If all-risk coverage is not really coverage for "all risks," why distinguish between the two forms? The answer involves who bears the burden of proof on causation. Under an all-risk policy, the insured's *prima facie* burden is to show that a loss within coverage occurred; once the insured carries this burden, the insurer has the burden to establish, if it can, that the cause of the loss was an excluded risk. Under a specified-risk policy, the insured's *prima facie* burden is to show not only that a loss occurred but also that the loss was caused by a covered (i.e., specified) peril. If the insured carries this burden, the insurer has the burden to establish that the cause of the loss was actually an excluded peril. When causation is difficult to prove or establish one way or the other, whether the policy is all-risk or specified-risk may determine whether the insured or insurer prevails on the question of coverage. See generally Robert H. Jerry, II, Understanding Insurance Law § 60A (2d ed. 1996).

6. *Intrinsic versus extrinsic causes of diminished value.* In *Chute v. North River Insurance Co.,* 172 Minn. 13, 214 N.W. 473 (1921), the insured purchased a policy that covered "jewelry. . .and/or furs as per schedule attached, against all risks of loss or damage . . . ." Claims for "breakage of glass, overwinding, denting and internal damage" to watches and damage to furs from "wear and tear, or gradual deterioration" were expressly excluded. The insured sought recovery for a fire opal valued at $2,000 because "the opal. . .became cracked." With what the court called "commendable candor" the complaint volunteered that the crack "was due to an inherent vice in said opal and was not the result of outside force." A secondary source on precious

stones quoted by the insured's counsel noted that fire opals are "as 'sensitive' as they are gorgeous." The court affirmed an order sustaining the insurer's general demurrer to the complaint. "It takes explicit language indicating that purpose to extend the effect of insurance beyond damage arising from or contributed to by extraneous causes and make it cover loss from automatic deterioration alone. That rule is applied unequivocally in marine insurance. To apply any other here would make the policy cover natural [disintegration], something clearly not intended. Because the policy must be considered as one against damage from fortuitous and extraneous risks, it is not permissible to resort to an ultraliteral interpretation which will convert it into a contract of warranty against loss resulting wholly from inherent susceptibility to dissolution." 214 N.W. at 474.

Why did the insured not recover? Might the opal have retained its purity indefinitely? Did the insured expect the opal to crack? To crack at the time it did? For a modern version of the "cracking opal" case in which the insured fared no better, *see Harmon v. Safeco Insurance Co. of America*, 954 P.2d 7 (Kan. App. 1998).

If the stakes are higher, the judicial calculus might change. Consider, for example, the owner of a gas station who installs underground storage tanks like those found at all gas stations. After 40 years of use, the tank springs a leak due to normal deterioration and allows gasoline to poison the gas station owner's land as well as the water supply of the station's neighbors. Assume further that it is common knowledge that all underground storage tanks have a lifespan and all such tanks will deteriorate and rupture, leading to the leeching of their contents into surrounding soils and groundwater. How would the court in *Chute* have handled that situation? *See Icarom, PLC v. Howard County, Maryland*, 981 F. Supp. 379 (D. Md. 1997) (damage to insured's and others' property resulting from insured's landfill operations was fortuitous, as required for "all risks" coverage). For more on liability insurance and environmental damage, see § 5.02[3][c], *infra*.

7. *The "overdue market."* Prior to the days of modern communication systems, some underwriters at Lloyd's of London wrote considerable amounts of insurance on ships that were known to be overdue, but not known to be actually lost. G. Hodgson, Lloyd's of London 78 (1984). This was known as the "overdue" market. In fact, one broker succeeded in insuring the *Titanic* against total loss in the overdue market *after* the first news of the disaster was received, but *before* the extent of the loss was learned. *Id.* at 134.

8. *Retroactive liability insurance.* The most notorious example of retroactive liability insurance is probably the $170 million in liability insurance purchased in 1981 with the payment of a $39 million premium by MGM *after* a 1980 fire killed 85 people and injured about 1,000 others at its Las Vegas hotel and casino. The insurers calculated that they could invest the $39 million premium during the lengthy litigation process and ultimately earn a profit. Federal tax law also figured in the deal, since MGM could take a current deduction for the premium but the premium would be counted as income to the insurers much later. Whether anyone ultimately benefitted from the arrangement is an open question; the parties soon found themselves embroiled in bitter litigation over the insurers' obligations when the insurers contended

that MGM was settling victims' claims for excessive amounts. See David Lauter, *MGM Cases Still Smoldering; Settlement Fund Reaches $140M; Hotel Battles Insurers*, Nat'l L. J., May 23, 1983, at 7.

Does retroactive liability insurance violate the principle of fortuity? The insurance for MGM's liability covered losses that were known but which were uncertain in amount and as to the time they would be paid. Retroactive insurance is also sometimes purchased for suspected losses. See generally Michael L. Smith & Robert C. Witt, *An Economic Analysis of Retroactive Liability Insurance*, 52 J. Risk & Ins. 379 (1985).

9. *Fun and games.* If a golfer hits a "hole in one," is that event "fortuitous"? Many golf tournaments (particularly charity events) promise anyone who hits a hole in one on a particular hole a significant prize, such as a new car. It is common for the hosts of such tournaments (i.e., the offerors of the prize) to insure against the possibility that someone will hit a hole in one and thereby win the prize. The premium will typically be a function of the number of golfers participating in the event. Similar policies are typically purchased to protect against the risk that a fan will hit the half-court shot during a half-time promotion at a basketball game, etc.

Not everyone cheered when cyclist Lance Armstrong won the 1999 Tour de France only three years after being diagnosed with testicular cancer and being given a 50 percent chance for survival. One of Armstrong's sponsors agreed to give a cash prize to Armstrong if he led a certain number of stages of the famous race and an additional amount if he actually won it. The sponsor then purchased insurance against the improbable possibility that it would have to make the payment to Armstrong; when Armstrong won, the insurer paid. See David Reich-Hale, *Insurance Company Pays on Cyclist's Victory*, Nat'l Underwriter (Prop.-Cas.), Jan. 31, 2000, at 3.

Have you ever watched the hit U.S. television game show "Who Wants To Be a Millionaire"? The producers of the show and ABC purchased insurance against the risk that a contestant might win one of the show's two top prizes ($500,000 or $1 million). Litigation erupted in early 2000 when the Lloyd's syndicate underwriting the third series of the show claimed that the producers had failed to modify the methods of contestant selection and the degree of difficulty of the game's questions, which the underwriters claim they required after the second series of the show caused a different syndicate significant losses. See Lisa S. Howard, *Insurer Sues to Rescind "Millionaire" Cover*, Nat'l Underwriter (Prop.-Cas.), Feb. 21, 2000, at 2.

[2] The Nonfortuity Defenses

MONTROSE CHEMICAL CORP. v. ADMIRAL INSURANCE CO.

10 Cal. 4th 645, 913 P.2d 878, 42 Cal. Rptr. 2d 324 (1995)

Lucas, Chief Justice.

[Montrose Chemical Corp., the insured, manufactured DDT for use in pesticides from 1947 through 1982. In addition to other insurers that issued comprehensive general liability (CGL) policies to Montrose during this period, Admiral Insurance Co. issued four successive CGL policies covering the period from October 13, 1982 to March 20, 1986. Admiral's policies required it to "pay on behalf of the insured all sums which the insured shall become legally obligated to pay as damages because of. . .bodily injury, or. . .property damage to which this insurance applies, caused by an occurrence . . . ." "Occurrence" was defined as "an accident, including continuous or repeated exposures to conditions, which results in bodily injury or property damage neither expected nor intended from the standpoint of the insured."

Suit was brought by a number of claimants alleging continuous or progressive bodily injury and property damage arising out of Montrose's disposal of hazardous wastes at two locations, referred to as the Stringfellow site and the Levin Metals site. The Stringfellow site, the one regarding which the nonfortuity defenses became an issue, opened in 1956 and closed in 1972. Chemical wastes generated by Montrose were deposited there between 1968 and 1972; Montrose paid a hauling company to transport byproducts of its DDT manufacturing process to the site, which was a state-approved and licensed disposal facility. In 1970, toxic wastes were detected seeping from the site, and the site was declared a public nuisance by a regional water quality control board in 1975. Claimants alleged that the property damage commenced in 1956 and continued through the present, including through the periods that Admiral's CGL policies were in effect.

Montrose sought a declaratory judgment that Admiral and the other insurers had a duty to defend these lawsuits. All the carriers, except Admiral, agreed to defend under a reservation of rights. The trial court granted Admiral's motion for summary judgment, ruling it had no duty to defend or indemnify Montrose. The Court of Appeals reversed and the Supreme Court of California granted Admiral's petition for review.]

In *Prudential-LMI Com. Insurance v. Superior Court* (1990) 51 Cal. 3d 674, 274 Cal. Rptr. 387, 798 P.2d 1230 (*Prudential-LMI*), we examined the issue of allocation of indemnity among insurers in a *first party* property insurance case, where a loss had occurred over several policy periods but was not discovered until several years after it commenced . . . . We expressly reserved the question of what rules should apply in *third party* liability insurance cases involving continuous or progressively deteriorating damage or injury. We recognized there are substantial analytical differences between first party property and third party liability policies, and cautioned that we were intimating no view as to the application of our decision in either the third party liability or commercial liability (including toxic tort) context.

In this case we address the issue reserved in *Prudential-LMI* . . . . [Editor's note: The court's discussion of the trigger of coverage issue appears in § 4.05[4], *infra.*]

As will further be explained, we also conclude, with respect to the "loss-in-progress" rule codified in Insurance Code sections 22 and 250, that in the context of continuous or progressively deteriorating property or bodily injury losses insurable under a third party CGL policy, as long as there remains uncertainty about damage or injury that may occur during the policy period and the imposition of liability upon the insured, and no legal obligation to pay third party claims has been established, there is an insurable risk within the meaning of sections 22 and 250 for which coverage may be sought under such a policy.

. . . .

III

THE LOSS-IN-PROGRESS RULE

Relying on the loss-in-progress rule (sometimes also referred to as the "known loss" rule), Admiral contends there was no potential liability coverage for, and consequently no duty to defend Montrose, in the *Stringfellow* cases. We disagree.

Section 22 defines "insurance" as a "contract whereby one undertakes to indemnify another against loss, damage, or liability arising from a contingent *or* unknown event." (Italics added.) Section 250 provides that "any contingent *or* unknown event, whether past or future, which may damnify a person having an insurable interest, or create a liability against him, may be insured against, subject to the provisions of this code." (Italics added.) Accordingly, when a loss is "known or apparent" before a policy of insurance is issued, there is no coverage.

Critically, the requirement that the "event" be "unknown" *or* "contingent" is stated in the disjunctive in the rules embodied in sections 22 and 250. We long ago recognized that all that is required to establish an insurable risk is that there be *some* contingency. Even where subsequent damage might be deemed inevitable, " 'such "inevitability" does not alter the fact that at the time the contract of insurance was entered into, the event was only a *contingency or risk* that might or might not occur within the term of the policy.' " (*Sabella v. Wisler* (1963) 59 Cal. 2d 21, 34, 27 Cal. Rptr. 689, 377 P.2d 889, italics in original (*Sabella*).)

In *Sabella*, the insurer claimed that damage to the insured's residence was not fortuitous and thus not covered because "the damage occurred as a result of the operation of forces inherent" in the underlying soil conditions (including uncompacted fill and defective workmanship in the installation of a sewer outflow that ultimately broke). Sabella rejected the insurer's contention that the loss was "not fortuitous and hence not a 'risk' properly the subject of insurance." (*Id.* at p. 34, 27 Cal. Rptr. 689, 377 P.2d 889.) Relying on *Snapp, [v. State Farm Fire & Cas. Co.], supra*, 206 Cal. App. 2d 827, 24 Cal. Rptr. 44, *Sabella* held that even if it were inevitable that the damage would have occurred at some time during ownership of the house, the loss was covered because such loss was a contingency or risk at the time the parties entered into the policy. (*Sabella, supra*, 59 Cal. 2d at p. 34, 27 Cal. Rptr. 689, 377 P.2d 889;)

According to Admiral, Montrose's knowledge of the problems at the Stringfellow site defeats coverage. In particular, Admiral points to the fact of Montrose's receipt of the PRP letter from the EPA on August 31, 1982, prior to the inception of the first of Admiral's four successive CGL policies issued to Montrose. * Admiral misses the point. The PRP notice is just what its name suggests C notice that the EPA considered Montrose a "potentially" responsible party. While it may be true that an action to recover cleanup costs was inevitable as of that date, Montrose's *liability* in that action was not a certainty. There was still a contingency, and the fact that Montrose knew it was more probable than not that it would be sued (successfully or otherwise) is not enough to defeat the potential of coverage (and, consequently, the duty to defend).

Moreover, since Admiral's policies did not purport to cover damage or injury that occurred prior to the time those policies went into effect, and only covered those bodily injuries and damages (or continuing bodily injuries and damages resulting from "continuous or repeated exposure to conditions") *that might occur in the future during the policy periods*, the existence and extent of such prospective injuries were clearly unknown and contingent, from Montrose's standpoint, at the time Montrose first purchased its policies from Admiral.

Courts which have addressed the loss-in-progress issue have recognized that "[t]he point at which a threat of loss is so immediate that it may fairly be said that the loss was in progress and the insured knew of it at the time the policy was applied for or issued is generally a question of fact." (*Sentinel Ins. Co. v. First Ins. Co.*, [76 Hawai'i 277, 875 P.2d 894, at] 920 [(1994)]; *Inland Waters Pollution Control, Inc. v. National Union Fire Ins. Co.* (6th Cir. 1993) 997 F.2d 172, 178.) Indeed, several courts have observed that, in the context of third party CGL coverage, a loss-in-progress or known loss contention can seldom be successfully relied on by an insurer *to defeat a duty to defend* because the factual uncertainties needed to be resolved in order to establish the defense generally cannot be resolved on a motion for summary judgment or until the insurer conclusively establishes no possibility of coverage.

In the Court of Appeal, Admiral relied on *Advanced Micro Devices, Inc. v. Great American Surplus Lines Ins. Co.* (1988) 199 Cal. App. 3d 791, 245 Cal. Rptr. 44 in support of its contention that if the insured knows or should have known that there was a problem, the loss is known and there is no insurable risk. *Advanced Micro Devices, Inc.* is inapposite. That case involved interpretation of an express exclusionary clause disavowing coverage of losses arising from " 'any known pre-existing conditions.' " (*Id.* at p. 794, 245 Cal. Rptr. 44.) Although Admiral's policies define "occurrence" as an accident resulting in bodily injury or property damage "neither expected nor intended from the standpoint of the insured," this language is part of the coverage clauses and not an *express exclusionary clause* as was the policy provision at issue in *Advanced Micro Devices, Inc.*. As an integral part of the occurrence-based coverage clause, we must interpret it broadly, in order to protect the objectively reasonable expectations of the insured, and consistent with the rule announced by this court in *Sabella*.

---

* [Editors' note: Anyone who is potentially responsible for CERCLA cleanup costs is called a "potentially responsible party,"or "PRP." When the EPA has reason to believe that someone is a PRP, it sends that person a "PRP letter" or "PRP notice." The substance of these letters vary. It may say that the PRP may be liable for cleanup costs and therefore should voluntarily cleanup the site, or the letter may say that the PRP is liable and that if the PRP does not cleanup the site the EPA will do so and hold the PRP responsible for these expenses. See Kenneth S. Abraham, Environmental Liability Insurance Law 264 (1991).]

Although it is true that the loss-in-progress rule as codified in sections 22 and 250 draws no distinction between, and thus is applicable to, first party property insurance and third party liability insurance policies, the distinctions inherent in the two types of coverage necessarily result in a different analysis when the rule is applied in the liability insurance context. As we have explained, first party property insurance policies provide coverage for damage to the insured's own property. ** In that context, insurance cannot be obtained for damage which has already occurred because the absence of risk precludes coverage. Third party liability insurance policies, in contrast, afford coverage for "sums which the insured shall become legally obligated to pay as damages because of bodily injury or property damage." In the liability insurance context, insurance cannot be obtained for a "known *liability.*"

Where, as here, there is uncertainty about *the imposition of liability* and no "legal obligation to pay" yet established, there is an insurable risk for which coverage may be sought under a third party policy. (*Austero v. National Cas. Co.* (1978) 84 Cal. App. 3d 1, 27–28, 29, 148 Cal. Rptr. 653 ["The fundamental contractual duty of the insurer in the third party case is *to pay such judgments as shall be recovered* against the insured. . . ." "In the usual first party case the promise of the insurer is to pay money, due under the policy, to the insured upon the happening of the event, the risk of which has been insured against." (Original italics deleted, new italics added.)])

The [Second Circuit's] decision in *City of Johnstown, N.Y. v. Bankers Standard Ins.* (2d Cir. 1989), 877 F.2d 1146, is particularly instructive given its analogous facts. In that case, prior to commencement of the liability policy term in issue, the city (the insured) was aware that releases from its dumpsite may have polluted surrounding groundwater, had been notified by the EPA that the "landfill posed a 'potential environmental hazard,' " and had been sued by a family "whose well had reportedly been contaminated by the landfill." The [court] held that because future injury and resulting liability to third parties for damages remained contingent, a loss-in-progress rule would not bar coverage. [25]

We therefore hold that, in the context of continuous or progressively deteriorating property damage or bodily injury insurable under a third party CGL policy, as long as there remains uncertainty about damage or injury that may occur during the policy period and the imposition of *liability* upon the insured, and no legal obligation to pay third party claims has been established, there is a potentially insurable risk within the meaning of sections 22 and 250 for which coverage may be sought. Stated differently, the loss-in-progress rule will not defeat coverage for a claimed loss where it had yet to be established, at the time the insurer entered into the contract of insurance with the policyholder, that the insured had a legal obligation to pay damages to a third party in connection with a loss.

** [Editor's note: The portion of the opinion containing the explanation to which the court refers is contained in the excerpt of the case in § 5.02[2][c], *infra.*]

[25] The Hawaii Supreme Court has likewise concluded that even where an injured third party has filed a lawsuit or claim against the insured, "if the insured's liability is in any degree contingent, there is an insurable risk" within the meaning of the loss-in-progress rule. (*Sentinel Ins. Co. v. First Ins. Co., supra,* 875 P.2d at p. 920, footnote omitted.)

Montrose's receipt of the PRP letter prior to its purchase of Admiral's policies did not establish any legal obligation to pay damages or cleanup costs in connection with the contamination at the Stringfellow site, such as would implicate the loss-in-progress rule and preclude Montrose from seeking to obtain the liability coverage sought. The PRP letter did no more than formally place Montrose on notice of the government's asserted position and initiate proceedings that could result in subsequent findings and orders. Moreover, the PRP letter referred only to the CERCLA cleanup of the Stringfellow site—it did not refer in any way to the injuries, wrongful deaths, or property damage alleged to have occurred off-site by the plaintiffs in *Newman v. Stringfellow* [the toxic tort lawsuit brought by the private parties for property damage and bodily injury].

Accordingly, we conclude that, at least on the facts heretofore alleged in this declaratory relief action, the loss-in-progress rule does not bar potential coverage, or relieve Admiral of its duty to defend, under the policies issued by Admiral to Montrose.

. . . .

The judgment of the Court of Appeal is affirmed, and the matter remanded for further proceedings consistent with the views expressed herein.

Mosk, Kennard, Arabian, George, and Werdegar, JJ., concur.

Baxter, Justice, concurring.

I concur in the judgment, though not in everything the majority say . . . .

1. . . .agree that the statutory "loss-in-progress" rule (Ins.Code, §§ 22, 250) does not conclusively eliminate Admiral's duty to help defend the various contamination-injury suits against Montrose. But the majority appear to offer two separate reasons for this conclusion, and I find only one of them persuasive.

The majority first suggest that because a CGL policy insures against the risk of legal liability to another, insurance of this kind may be purchased for any such legal liability which then remains "contingent" or "unknown." If I understand the majority correctly, a literal application of this theory would allow the purchase of liability insurance for a completed tort up to the moment a final damage judgment is imposed upon the tortfeasor.

But the plain words of the loss-in-progress statutes suggest otherwise. Insurance Code section 22 provides that "[i]nsurance is a contract whereby one undertakes to indemnify another against loss, damage, or *liability* arising from a contingent or unknown *event*." (Italics added.) Insurance Code section 250 provides that, with irrelevant exceptions, "any contingent or unknown *event*, whether past or future, which may damnify a person having an insurable interest, *or create a liability against him*, may be insured against. . . ." (Italics added.) As both statutes make clear, it is the *event or events* which *produce* liability, not merely the liability itself, which must remain "contingent or unknown" at the time the insurance contract is created.

The majority cite no California case on point, and I see no sound reason to depart from the clear statutory language. Consistent with my understanding of insurance, the loss-in-progress statutes imply that the "contingent or unknown" risk insured against is real-world accidents, events, or hazards which produce insurable loss or damage. In the first party context, the relevant risk is direct casualty damage, injury, or loss to the insured person or property. In the third party context, the relevant risk is the insured's act or omission, and the resulting damage, injury, or loss to another, which together form the basis of legal liability against the insured.

Thus, for purposes of liability insurance, once *both* the act or omission *and* the resulting legally compensable damage are no longer "contingent or unknown," no insurable risk remains. As the statutes suggest, it would contravene public policy, and the nature of the insurance contract, to allow a tortfeasor to wait until he has already knowingly caused compensable damage before purchasing protection against his resulting liability.

However, I agree with the majority that the loss-in-progress rule does not preclude liability coverage for *future* or *unknown harm* from a past act or omission, even if the insured does know that some harm may already have arisen from his conduct. The insured cannot be held liable for his act or omission except to the extent it causes compensable harm. Thus, so long as any increment of compensable damage or injury has not yet happened, or is unknown to the insured, it remains a "contingent or unknown event. . .which may. . .create a liability against him." (Ins.Code, § 250.) As such, it is a properly insurable risk.

. . . .

NOTES

1. *First-party versus third-party insurance.* The term "first-party insurance" generally refers to insurance policies that cover the insured's own interest, such as, for example, an insured's own interest in property or a life. If, under a policy of homeowner's insurance, the insured suffers a loss due to fire, the insurance reimburses the insured for the damage caused to the insured's own interest. *Montrose* involve a policy of liability, or third-party, insurance; the insurance protects the insured by indemnifying the insured for liability the insured incurs to other (or "third") parties. Thus, when the insured is determined to be legally responsible to a third party for a claim within the policy's coverage, the insurer pays the proceeds to the third party, thereby discharging the insured's liability. Another important aspect of liability insurance is the insurer's promise to defend the insured against claims for damages within the policy's coverage. Thus, liability insurance is also, in a sense, "litigation insurance." These matters receive more attention throughout this book and particularly in Chapter 8. What difference does the distinction between first-party and third-party insurance make in *Montrose*?

2. *Known losses, known risks, and losses-in-progress.* The core of the nonfortuity defenses is simple enough. If you noticed in the morning that a tree had fallen on your car during the night, could you then purchase insurance protecting your car against such perils? If, while uninsured, you are diagnosed with a terminal illness which will require months of expensive

treatment, could you then purchase a comprehensive health insurance policy? What problems would be created if individuals were allowed to purchase their first policies of health insurance while they were on the way to the hospital? One glimpse into the answers to these questions is provided by *Mason Drug Co., Inc. v. Harris*, 597 F.2d 886 (5th Cir. 1979), where the court held that the "loss in progress" doctrine barred coverage for a store owner, whose store had flooded previously, who purchased flood insurance during a heavy rain and only a few hours before he began caulking the store and moving merchandise out of harm's way.

In situations an insurer concludes that the fortuity principle is implicated, it may assert one (or more) of the "known-loss," "known risk," and "loss-in-progress" defenses. Environmental liability insurance coverage cases are particularly fertile territory for the invocation of this defense. In *Montrose*, the court said that the known-loss and loss-in-progress labels referred to the same rule. The known-loss doctrine has also been equated to the known-risk doctrine. *See Inland Waters Pollution Control, Inc. v. National Union Fire Ins. Co.*, 997 F.2d 172, 177 (6th Cir. 1993). Do the labels themselves suggest different ideas? Plainly, each defense has something to do with "fortuity," but difficulties abound when one attempts to get more specific than that. See generally M. Elizabeth Medaglia, Gregory H. Horowitz, and Gina S. Love, *The Status of Certain Nonfortuity Defenses in Casualty Insurance*, 30 Tort & Ins. L. J. 943 (1995); Richard L. Fruehauf, Note, *The Cost of Knowledge: Making Sense of "Nonfortuity" Defenses in Environmental Liability Insurance Coverage Disputes*, 84 Va. L. Rev. 107 (1998).

3. *Known loss versus known risk.* Is a loss the same thing as a risk? "The known loss rule is based on the fundamental principle [of insurance law] that insurance is intended to cover risks [or contingencies] which are not definitely known to the insured." *Continental Ins. Co. v. Beecham Co.*, 836 F. Supp. 1027, 1046 (D.N.J.1993). Under that formulation, the known-loss defense argues that the insured lacks coverage because the insured knew of the risk that caused the claimed damage at the time the insured purchased the policy. But when you purchase automobile liability insurance, do you know that there is a risk that you might cause and become liable for an accident? It would seem clear enough that under the fortuity doctrine, one cannot insure for damage (i.e., loss) that one already knows has occurred. *See, e.g., Summers v. Harris*, 573 F.2d 869 (5th Cir. 1978).

4. *Known loss versus loss-in-progress.* The loss-in-progress defense argues that the insured lacks coverage because the insured's liability arises out of a loss that was already occurring at the time the insured purchased the policy. Although the court in *Montrose* conflated the analysis of known loss and loss-in-progress in the circumstances of that case, the two doctrines have rather different implications in other circumstances. A risk can be known without the loss being "in progress." On the other hand, a loss can be in progress without either the loss or the risk of loss being known. Why should a loss-in-progress, if not known, be *per se* uninsurable? If, unknown to you, your house burned down while you were en route to the insurer to purchase homeowner's coverage, why should you not be able to purchase a policy of homeowner's coverage effective as of 12:01 a.m. that day? In contrast, if a loss-in-progress

is known, is the harm at least "expected" by the insured and therefore outside the coverage?

5. *Contrarian cases.* Although most courts have followed the same general approach as *Montrose*, there are notable exceptions. For example, in *SCA Services, Inc. v. Transportation Ins. Co.,* 419 Mass. 528, 646 N.E.2d 394 (1995), the court stated:

> By its very nature insurance is based on contingent risks which may or may not occur. Stated differently, the basic purpose of insurance is to protect against fortuitous events and not against known certainties. Parties wager against the occurrence or nonoccurrence of a specified event; the carrier insures against a risk, not a certainty. It follows from this general principle that an insured cannot insure against the consequences of an event which has already begun. Once the risk is eliminated, the contract for insurance no longer exists. Courts have found that the insurable risk is eliminated in the instance where an insured knows, when it purchases a policy, that there is a substantial probability that it will suffer or has already suffered a loss. At that point, the risk ceases to be contingent and becomes a probable or known loss. When the insured has evidence of a probable loss when it purchases the policy, the loss is uninsurable under that policy. This rule has been recognized in Massachusetts and by leading authorities on the subject of insurance. Courts have applied this known loss principle in environmental contamination cases.

See also Outboard Marine Corp. v. Liberty Mut. Ins. Co., 154 Ill. 2d 90, 607 N.E.2d 1204 (1992).

Which side has the better of the argument? Does the logic of the reasoning in *SCA Services* render life insurance invalid? Is it the purpose of liability insurance to enable an insured to cover a risk that the insured will suffer a particular kind of liability? How can the insured know what kind of coverage to purchase if the insured does not know what risks the insured faces? Because liability insurance does not cover harm "expected or intended from the standpoint of the insured," is whether a risk is known relevant to the policy's coverage, as opposed to whether the risk is *per se* uninsurable under the fortuity requirement?

6. *Nonfortuity and the duty to defend.* If one cannot insure a known loss in the first-party setting, it follows, according to the court in *Montrose*, that one cannot insure a known liability in the third-party setting. If a third-party has sued an individual on a claim, would it be possible at that point to secure liability insurance for the purpose of having the insurer provide a defense (i.e., the "litigation insurance" coverage)? What do the majority and dissenting opinions seem to be saying about that? And what, then, are we to make of retroactive liability insurance?

7. *Subsidence, cave-ins, and collapse.* In *Insurance Co. of North America v. U.S. Gypsum Co.,* 870 F.2d 148 (4th Cir. 1989), an all-risk policy was issued by INA to the insured covering over 120 locations. The policy did not exclude subsidence or mine-related perils, but did contain a $250,000 deductible. Several months later the earth subsided beneath part of the insured's gypsum

wallboard plant causing approximately $34 million in damages. The location was in an area that had been mined by various firms since the nineteenth century and numerous cave-ins and natural sinkholes had occurred since that time, although there had only been eight such occurrences in the twenty-five years preceding issuance of the policy and the most serious of these caused only $700 in damages. INA defended on the basis that the loss was not fortuitous. In rejecting the insurer's argument, the court stated: "[T]he fact that it is known that subsidence will occur does not mean that it will occur during the policy period. Moreover, there is a fundamental distinction between the certainty of subsidence and the certainty of resulting loss. An INA expert admitted at trial that there is a certainty of subsidence from the moment that mining operations begin at any location. Thus, if, as INA contends, the certainty of subsidence precludes fortuity, there never could be coverage for subsidence damage. That proposition, however, is contradicted by INA's own underwriting manuals which list subsidence as one of 'the other "all risk" perils which may cause severe loss.'" 870 F.2d at 152.

If one grants the inapplicability of the known-loss defense (is that correct?), why was the catastrophic collapse not a loss-in-progress, given the continual pattern of subsidence at the site?

§ 2.02   Insurable Interests

[1]   Origins of the Doctrine

ROBERT H. JERRY, II, UNDERSTANDING INSURANCE LAW
§ 40, at 233–36 (2d ed. 1996).

The insurable interest doctrine has its origins in the common practice of eighteenth century English marine insurers of not requiring the insured to demonstrate either ownership in or some other legal relationship to the ship or cargo being underwritten. This failure to require the insured to show an "interest" permitted the placing of wagers or bets on whether the insured vessel would successfully complete its voyage. Also, the temptations to frustrate a voyage's success were substantial, and fraud was widespread. . . .

To deter these practices, Parliament enacted a statute requiring, as a prerequisite to the validity of a policy of marine insurance, the insured to possess an interest in the insured property:

> [N]o assurance or assurances shall be made by any person or persons, bodies corporate or politick, on any ship, or ships belonging to his Majesty, or any of his subjects, or on any goods, merchandizes, or effects, laden or to be laden on board of any such ship or ships, interest or no interest, or without further proof of interest than the policy, or by way of gaming or wagering, or without benefit of salvage to the assurer; and that every such assurance shall be null and void to all intents and purposes. [Act of 1746, St. 19 Geo. 2, c. 37 § 1 (Eng.).]

. . . .

In life insurance, similar "gaming" practices developed in the eighteenth century. Popular accounts of the period describe the practice of purchasing insurance on the lives of those being tried for capital crimes. These policies constituted naked wagers on whether the accused would ultimately be convicted and executed for the alleged offense. A related practice was the purchase of insurance on the lives of famous, elderly persons; the premium would be a function of what was known about the person's health, including any recent illnesses. Insuring a life in which one has no interest creates a temptation to bring the insured's life to an early end, but the greater concern in eighteenth-century England was the practice of wagering. Thus, when Parliament enacted an insurable interest statute for life insurance in 1774, the articulated concern in the statute was gaming, not the risk that the insured's life might be destroyed. The 1774 statute prohibited issuing insurance on "the life or lives of any person or persons, or any other event or events whatsoever, wherein the person or persons for whose use, benefit, or on whose account such policy or policies shall be made, shall have no interest, or by way of gaming or wagering." [The Life Assurance Act of 1774, 14 Geo. 3, c. 48 (Eng.).] Like the 1746 Act, the effect of the 1774 Act was to prohibit judicial enforcement of policies issued without satisfying the insurable interest requirement. . . .

In the United States, the insurable interest doctrine was first adopted by courts, although many state legislatures later enacted insurable interest statutes. These statutes are typically written in broad language, leaving considerable room for judicial interpretation. . . .

. . .[T]he purposes of the insurable interest requirement remain those that prompted the doctrine's creation: (1) discouraging the practice of using insurance as a device for gambling or wagering; and (2) removing the incentive for the procurer of the insurance to destroy the subject matter of the insurance, whether it be a life or an item of property. Of these two purposes, the more important is the second: because gambling is not perceived, in and of itself, to be a terrible evil, the reason for disallowing insurance policies to serve as disguised wagers is the incentive such contracts create for destroying the insured property or life. Thus, increased moral hazard is the reason most often given to justify the insurable interest requirement, but it is not uncommon to find courts, when asked to decide whether an insurable interest exists in a particular insurance transaction, inquiring into whether the insurance contract in question functions as a wager.

[2] Property Insurance

The English statutes which created the insurable interest requirement did not define "interest" and did not illuminate what kinds of interests would fulfill the statutes' requirements. Almost immediately, courts were required to decide cases in which the existence of an interest was the issue, and this required courts to articulate principles that explained what sort of interest satisfied the statutes. The first cases arose in the property setting, and controversy over the appropriate test developed almost immediately.

In *Le Cras v. Hughes,* 99 Eng. Rep. 549 (K.B. 1782), Lord Mansfield articulated two tests to explain why an insurer was obligated to pay proceeds for the loss of a ship. British naval forces had captured a Spanish ship during hostilities with Spain; under an act of Parliament, captors of ships taken from the Spanish were entitled to be vested through proclamation by the Crown with rights to seized property. To protect their prize, the captain and crew insured the Spanish ship for the voyage back to England, during which it was lost due to perils of the sea. The insurer refused to pay the claim on the ground that the insureds lacked an insurable interest.

Lord Mansfield reasoned that the legal right to the ship afforded by the act of Parliament and the royal proclamation constituted a "legal interest" that satisfied the statutory insurable interest requirement. As an alternative ground for the conclusion, Lord Mansfield found the existence of a "factual expectancy" as well. He explained that prior case law had not required any particular kind of legal interest, and that in a prior case, expected profits in a voyage, though not a legal or vested interest, was an expectancy of advantage that satisfied the insurable interest requirement. Thus, *Le Cras v. Hughes* indicated that either a legal interest or a factual expectancy could support an insurable interest.

A second case that was influential in the early development of the doctrine was *Lucena v. Craufurd,* 127 Eng. Rep. 630 (H.L. 1805). James Craufurd and others were appointed Royal Commissioners under an act of Parliament, 35 Geo. 3, c. 80, for the purpose of taking into their possession during wartime ships and cargos belonging to subjects of the United Provinces once they were detained in or brought into the ports of Great Britain. Several ships and their cargos belonging to the then-neutral Dutch were seized at sea by English ships of war and were being escorted to England, but were lost by perils of the sea on the voyage. In the meantime, war was declared upon the Dutch; one ship was lost before hostilities were declared, and the others were lost thereafter. The Commissioners had insured these ships and cargos, but the underwriter refused to pay the losses on the basis that the Commissioners had no insurable interest. In an action on the policy, the Commissioners, according to Lord Eldon, alleged that: (1) they "had a right and an interest, as such commissioners;" (2) "the interest of the property insured to be in his majesty, and. . .that the policy was made on his majesty's account;" and (3) "that the property, at the time of the insurance and the loss, belonged to foreigners." *See* 127 Eng. Rep. at 648. The jury found against the plaintiff Commissioners on counts two and three, but in their favor on count one. Judgment was entered for plaintiffs and affirmed on appeal to the Court of Exchequer Chamber. The House of Lords reversed and remanded for a new trial on all counts because of an erroneous jury instruction on count one. At the second trial, a verdict was returned in favor of the plaintiffs on count two, but against the plaintiffs on the first and third counts. Judgment was entered for plaintiffs and affirmed on writ of error to the House of Lords. *See* 1 Taunt. 325, 127 Eng. Rep. 858 (H.L. 1808).

The various opinions in *Lucena v. Crauford* contained two — and perhaps three — different views of the insurable interest doctrine. The opinion of Judge Lawrence approved a broad factual expectancy theory; a full property right is not needed to create an incentive for an insured to preserve property, and that such an incentive exists if the insured's continued advantage (or avoidance of loss) depends on the continued existence of property. See 127 Eng. Rep. at 642–43. In contrast, Lord Eldon disapproved of Judge Mansfield's logic in *Le Cras v. Hughes* and insisted that an insurable interest be predicated on "a right in the property, or a right derivable out of some contract about the property, which in either case may be lost upon some contingency affecting the possession or enjoyment of the party." 127 Eng. Rep. at 650. In a famous portion of this opinion, Lord Eldon reasoned that a technical legal interest would create an insurable interest, even if it were virtually certain that the legal right had no value:

> Suppose A. to be possessed of a ship limited to B. in case A. dies without issue; that A. has 20 children, the eldest of whom is 20 years of age; and B. 90 years of age; it is a moral certainty that B. will never come into possession, yet this is a clear interest. On the other hand, suppose the case of the heir at law of a man who has an estate worth £20,000 a–year, who is 90 years of age; upon his death-bed intestate, and incapable from incurable lunacy of making a will, there is no man who will deny that such an heir at law has a moral certainty of succeeding to the estate; yet the law will not allow that he has any interest, or any thing more than a mere expectation. [127 Eng.Rep. at 652.]

A third opinion in the case attributed to Baron Graham and six others is more difficult to decipher. One reading of the opinion is that it seeks to strike a middle ground between the Lawrence view and the Eldon view. Under this interpretation, the test is essentially cumulative: either a legal interest or factual expectancy will suffice, subject to some caveats. A technical legal right that is certain never to have value (such as Lord Eldon's example) would not suffice to satisfy the statute, and a mere expectancy completely devoid of any grounding in a legal right does not satisfy the requirement either. (For a more detailed discussion of these cases, see Robert H. Jerry, II, Understanding Insurance Law § 42[a] (2d ed. 1996).)

With this rather tumultuous launch of insurable interest doctrine, what can be said about the doctrine at the turn of the twenty-first century? Consider the next cases.

SNETHEN v. OKLAHOMA STATE UNION OF FARMERS EDUCATIONAL & COOPERATIVE UNION OF AMERICA

664 P.2d 377 (Okla. 1983), 38 A.L.R.4th 531 (1985)

OPALA, JUSTICE:

The dispositive issue on certiorari is whether a good-faith purchaser for value of a stolen motor vehicle has an "insurable interest" in the property within the meaning of 36 O.S. 1981 § 3605.[1] We answer in the affirmative.

The insurance company [insurer], defendant below, issued an automobile insurance policy to John O. Snethen [insured], plaintiff below, providing coverage against collision loss for his used 1978 Cadillac automobile. Shortly after the purchase the insured's car was involved in a collision with another vehicle. Before a claim for this damage came to be settled between the insurer and insured, the Oklahoma State Bureau of Investigation [OSBI] discovered that the car was a stolen vehicle. Neither the insured nor the insurer knew this before the accident. The OSBI then seized the car for its return to the rightful owner. The insurer subsequently refused to pay for the loss and the insured pressed his claim under the collision coverage of the policy. The trial court rendered summary judgment for the insurer. The Court of Appeals affirmed based on our opinion in *Ernie Miller Pontiac v. Home Insurance Co.*[2] which holds that a good-faith purchaser for value of a stolen vehicle does not have an insurable interest. We granted certiorari on the petition by the insured to reconsider our holding in *Ernie Miller Pontiac.* We now vacate the Court of Appeals' opinion and reverse the trial court's judgment.

It is well settled that both the validity and enforceability of an insurance contract depend upon the presence of insurable interest in the person who purchased the policy. Considerations underlying the insurable interest concept are generally articulated in terms of policy (1) against allowing wagering contracts under the guise of insurance,[4] (2) against fostering temptation to destroy the insured property in an effort to profit from it and (3) favoring limitation upon the sweep of indemnity contracts.[5]

Most forms of wager agreements were valid at common law. They were deemed enforceable until a series of statutes were passed to outlaw the use of insurance contracts to conduct wagers. Wagering is regarded as detrimental to society. It encourages the wagerer to affect by unnatural means the results of the contingent event and increases the insurer's risk of disproportionate indemnification to an insured who has no relationship to, or pecuniary interest in, the insured subject. The goal of insurance is to indemnify the insured for a loss encountered by the impairment of an interest in the subject. Wagerers

---

[1] The terms of 36 O.S. 1981 § 3605 provide:

"A. No insurance contract on property or of any interest therein or arising therefrom shall be enforceable as to the insurance except for the benefit of persons having an insurable interest in the things insured.

B. 'Insurable interest' as used in this section means any actual, lawful, and substantial economic interest in the safety or preservation of the subject of the insurance free from loss, destruction, or pecuniary damage or impairment.

C. The measure of an insurable interest in property is the extent to which the insured might be damnified by loss, injury, or impairment thereof." [*Emphasis added*].

[2] Okl., 534 P.2d 1 [1975].

[4] *See* Harnett and Thornton, "Insurable Interest in Property: A Socio-Economic Reevaluation of a Legal Concept", 48 Colum. L. Rev. 1162, 1178–1184 [1948]; *Skaff v. United States Fidelity and Guaranty Company,* 215 So. 2d 35, 36 [Fla. App. 1968].

[5] *Harnett and Thornton, supra* note 4 at 1181–1184; *Castle Cars, Inc. v. United States Fire Insurance Company,* 221 Va. 773, 273 S.E.2d 793, 794 [Va. 1981].

suffer no such loss. They actually profit from the occurrence of the contingent event. It is for the purpose of placing a limit on the insurer's indemnification duty that the law undertook to require the insured to have an insurable interest.

Public policy which favors suppression of temptation to destroy one's insured property underlies the law's requirement of an insurable interest. If the insured has no interest in the property, he suffers no loss from its destruction but actually profits from it. The insurable interest concept tends to deter the temptation to destroy the property which is covered against the risk of loss.

While American jurisdictions generally agree with the public policy considerations that underly [sic] the necessity for an insurable interest, they stand divided on what constitutes an insurable interest. Two basic theories were evolved for measuring the nexus which must be present between the property and its insured for an insurable interest to attach. The literature refers to one of these as the "legal interest" and to the other as the "factual expectation" theory.

Jurisdictions holding to the view that no insurable interest attaches to a stolen automobile in the hands of a good-faith purchaser found their conclusion upon the legal interest theory. Those states that adhere to this concept require that insurable interest be rested upon a *legally cognizable interest* in the property.[10] This view has its roots in Lord Eldon's opinion in *Lucena v. Craufurd.*[11] It was there stated that an interest is insurable only if it is a *legal* or *equitable* right enforceable either at law or in chancery.[12] This represents the strict approach to insurable interest.

Those jurisdictions which allow the bonafide owner of a stolen vehicle to recover follow the "factual expectation" theory. Under this theory there is an insurable interest in the property if the insured would gain some economic advantage by its continued existence or would suffer some economic detriment in case of its loss or destruction.[14] This theory — contrary as it is to the one espoused by Lord Eldon — also derives from *Lucena v. Craufurd.* It was expressed there in Lord Lawrence's separate opinion.[15] He believed that a person has an insurable interest if he stands in some relation to, or has concern in, the insured property which may be prejudiced by the happening of the events insured against. It was his view that the insured must be so circumstanced with respect to the insured subject-matter as to make him interested in its preservation.

---

[10] *Granite State Insurance Co. v. Lowe,* 362 So. 2d 240, 241 [Ala. Civ. App. 1978].

[11] 2 Bos. & Pul. (N.R.) 269, 127 Eng. Rep. 630 [1806].

[12] *Lucena v. Craufurd, supra* note 11, 2 Bos. & Pul. (N.R.) at 323, 127 Eng. Rep. at 651. Lord Eldon reasoned further that "[e]xpectation though founded on the highest probability, [is] not interest," and "if moral certainty be a ground of insurable interest, there are hundreds, perhaps thousands, who would be entitled to insure" the same property.

[14] *Granite State Insurance Co. v. Lowe, supra note* 10 at 241. In construing statutory language identical to 36 O S 1981 § 3605, the court in *Granite State Insurance Co. v. Lowe, supra note* 10, held the statute espoused the "factual expectation" theory of insurable interest.

[15] 2 Bos. & Pul. (N.R.) 269, 302, 127 Eng. Rep. 630, 643.

We are inclined to the view articulated by the courts adhering to the "factual expectation" test. An interest held in a stolen vehicle by its good-faith purchaser is by that test regarded as insurable.[17] Once the relationship between the insured and the property is found to be lawful and to create a substantial economic interest, the underlying criteria which make up an insurable interest are met. The insured does hence have a right to enforce the contract regardless of the property's legal status. In the case at bar, the substantial economic interest was created when the insured paid $6,500 for his car and, additionally, parted with his own vehicle as a trade-in. This pecuniary interest, coupled with the insured's undisputed lack of knowledge of the vehicle's stolen status, is adequately substantial. It suffices to negate any notion or intimation of a wager contract. Moreover, the transfer of such a substantial value cannot be viewed as encouraging the insured to destroy the vehicle in order to collect insurance proceeds. Because of the lost investment, indemnification will not amount here to a "profit".

While the insured doubtless does have substantial economic interest, more than that appears to be required. The terms of § 3605(B) explicitly call for an interest that is "lawful".

It is a general rule of law that no one can confer or transfer a better title than that which he has, unless some principle of estoppel should operate to bar an otherwise superior claim. Neither can a person be divested of his property without his consent. While a good-faith purchaser under a defective title cannot hold against the true owner, he does have lawful possession against all the rest of the world. He is said to have a "qualified possessory right" in the property.[21]

In some jurisdictions a qualified possessory right meets the standards of an "actual lawful and substantial economic interest", and is sufficient to create an insurable interest in the vehicle. In *Ernie Miller Pontiac,* we quoted with approval from two Georgia Court of Appeals cases[25] the principle that, while title is not the sole test for determining an insurable interest, there must be a special or limited interest, disconnected from any title, lien or possession, so that the holder of the interest will suffer loss from its destruction. Bond fide possession of stolen property does not, under Georgia case law, meet the

---

[17] *See e.g. Granite State Insurance Co. v. Lowe, supra note 10; Skaff v. United States Fidelity & Guaranty Company, supra* note 4; *Reznick v. Home Insurance Company,* 45 Ill. App. 3d 1058, 4 Ill. Dec. 525, 360 N.E.2d 461 [1977]; *Butler v. Farmers Insurance Company of Arizona,* 126 Ariz. 379, 616 P.2d 54 [Ariz. App. 1980].

[21] Vance, Handbook on the Law of Insurance, § 29 at p. 172; Professor Vance favors the "factual expectation" theory, supra at 172. *See also Duncan v. State Farm Fire & Casualty Co.,* 587 S.W.2d 375 [Tenn. 1979]. The court in Duncan suggested the possibility that the good-faith purchaser has an insurable interest as a potential constructive bailee who might be held liable for the return of the destroyed property if the true owner should be able to locate it and make a demand for it.

[25] *Gordon v. Gulf American Fire and Casualty Co.,* 113 Ga. App. 755, 149 S.E.2d 725 [Ga. App. 1966] and *Giles v. Citizens' Insurance Co. of Missouri,* 32 Ga. App. 207, 122 S.E. 890 [Ga. App.1924].

lawful interest test.[27] We believe that this approach is overly restrictive and does not serve the public interest. We now reject it.

For the purpose of determining an insurable interest under § 3605, it is necessary to make a distinction between "legal" and "lawful" interests. A substantial economic interest is insurable if it is "lawful" in the sense that it was not acquired in violation of law. As used in § 3605(B), the word "lawful" is not synonymous with "legal". A legal interest is enforceable against the whole world. A good-faith purchaser for value acquires an interest that is lawful and enforceable against all the world but the legal owner. Although it is only a qualified possessory interest, it is lawful and enforceable to a very large *extent*. Section 3605 allows *any lawful interest* to be insurable if the economic interest is substantial. We hence hold that a good-faith purchaser for value of a stolen automobile has a substantial economic interest in the property which is lawful and must be treated as insurable under § 3605.

The insured established a lawful and substantial economic interest — innocently acquired — and covered it by insurance. His interest, which clearly meets the § 3605(B) criteria, is hence entitled to judicial protection.

Insofar as *Ernie Miller Pontiac* is in conflict with our pronouncement herein, it is no longer to be regarded as a correct exposition of the current law. Neither fairness nor any principle of public policy dictates that we give a purely prospective application to the change effected by today's decision. The insured should be allowed to reap the benefit of his successful challenge to the insurable interest test we now reject by this opinion. Our pronouncement today shall hence be given effect to this case and, prospectively, to all insurance losses occurring after mandate herein is issued.

Summary judgment is reversed and cause remanded with directions to proceed further in a manner not inconsistent with the views expressed herein.

All Justices concur.

Brewton v. Alabama Farm Bureau Mutual Casualty Insurance Co., 474 So. 2d 1120 (Ala. 1985). Mrs. Browning owned a home, its contents, and one acre of land on which these were located. Mrs. Browning and a Mrs. Brewton went to Farm Bureau's agent to obtain a fire insurance policy. A policy was issued on July 9, 1982, in the name of Mr. & Mrs. Brewton.

Mrs. Browning died intestate in December 1982, and was survived by five sisters who were her heirs. The dwelling and its contents were destroyed by fire on January 27, 1983. Both Mr. and Mrs. Brewton testified that Mrs. Browning left no will and that prior to her death she had not deeded the

---

[27] *Ernie Miller Pontiac, supra* note 2, 534 P.2d at 3.

In *Ernie Miller Pontiac, supra* note 2, the Georgia cases were cited because the statutes are identical. The Oklahoma statute, 36 O.S. 1981 § 3605, although similar to Georgia's, was modeled after A.R.S. § 20-1105 of the Arizona Insurance Code (§ 5 Art. II), enacted in 1954. Current Arizona case law reveals that the courts there adhere to the view that a bona fide purchaser of a stolen automobile has an interest sufficient to qualify as insurable. *Butler v. Farmers Ins. Co. of Arizona*, 126 Ariz. 371, 616 P.2d 46, 48 [Ariz. 1980].

property to them. Mr. Brewton testified that neither he nor his wife had lived in the house after Mrs. Browning's death. The Brewtons apparently had not lived there prior to her death either.

The Brewtons argued that they had an insurable interest in the premises insured because, as Mrs. Brewton explained, Mrs. Browning, the owner, had raised Mr. Brewton and had told them that she would will the property to them, and thus Mr. Brewton had a "reasonable expectation" that he would receive title to the property. The plaintiffs maintained that these facts, together with the alleged fact that the insurer issued the policy knowing that the Brewtons did not hold the legal title at the time of issue, established an insurable interest in the Brewtons. In an opinion by Justice Beatty, the court upheld a summary judgment for Farm Bureau rejecting the Brewtons' claim for the policy's proceeds.

". . . . [I]t is clear that the Brewtons here had no insurable interest in Mrs. Browning's property. They had no title to the property and no actual or constructive possessory interest in it. Neither was related to Mrs. Browning. They knew she had sisters living. They knew that Mrs. Browning owned the house and its contents; thus they did not suffer any economic loss from their destruction. The fact that the Brewtons expected Mrs. Browning to make a testamentary disposition of the property to them because she had raised Mr. Brewton, and thus in gratitude they sought to bear the expense of insuring the property, does not constitute an insurable interest under our authorities. Mere love and affection for the true owner, though laudable, do not constitute the required insurable interest. . . ."

NOTES

1. *The principle of indemnity.* The principle of indemnity—that is, the concept that only actual loss will be reimbursed—is endemic to the subject of insurance. (The indemnity principle receives more attention in § 2.03, *infra*.) Does the requirement of an insurable interest support the principle of indemnity? If so, how?

2. *Distinguishing insurance from wagers.* Insurance and wagering contracts both depend on chance or risk. What is the source of the risk in each of the contracts? Does this make insurance contracts more socially useful than wagering contracts? Consider the following:

> The requirement of an insurable interest to support a contract of insurance is based upon considerations of public policy, which condemn as wagers all agreements for insurance of any subject in which the contracting parties have no such interest. That is to say, proof of circumstances that negative the existence of a wagering intent establishes the existence of an insurable interest. In its broadest aspects, therefore, the question of insurable interest is the question of what facts must be proved in order to satisfy the court that the parties are not engaging in harmful wagering. In the case of property insurance, the satisfaction of this requirement is found in the broad principle of

indemnity, that lies at the very foundation of property insurance law.
The same thing has often been said of life insurance.

William R. Vance, Handbook on the Law of Insurance 156–57 (3d ed. 1951).[*]
What is the relationship between wagering and indemnity? Do you agree that
"proof of circumstances that negative the existence of a wagering intent
establishes the existence of an insurable interest" explains the results in the
cases?

3. *Pernicious practices and other mischief.* In the preambles to the acts of
Parliament mentioned in the quoted excerpt at the beginning of this unit,
Parliament recited the practice of insuring ships in the absence of insurable
interest caused "many pernicious practices, whereby great numbers of ships
with their cargoes, hath either been fraudulently lost or destroyed, or taken
by the enemy in time of war" and that this "introduc[ed] a mischievous kind
of gaming or wagering, under the pretense of assuring the risque on shipping,"
and that this had "perverted" the "institution and laudable design of making
insurance." Act of 1746, St. 19 Geo. 2, c. 37 § 1 (Eng.). Are there modern
analogues to these ancient practices?

4. *Multiple tests.* As *Snethen* indicates, the different explanations of insurable interest articulated in the old English cases survive to the present. The
legal interest test can itself be subdivided into three additional categories.
Under a *property right* theory of legal interest, virtually any kind or quality
of legal or equitable title will suffice to satisfy the insurable interest requirement. Generally speaking, one whose *contract right* depends on the continued
existence of property has an insurable interest in that property. This, for
example, explains why a secured creditor can insure the property which
secures a debt, even though the secured creditor does not own it. If a person
would suffer *legal liability* in the event property were lost or damaged, that
person has an insurable interest in the property. To illustrate, consider *Village
of Constantine v. Home Insurance Co.,* 427 F.2d 1338 (6th Cir. 1970), where
the insured sold some generators to the Village pursuant to title-retaining
conditional sales contracts that required Scott to insure the equipment against
"breakdown." Scott secured the insurance. Scott then sold the contracts to a
Nebraska bank, without making any effort to assign the insurance policy to
the bank, to have the insurance reissued, or to have the bank designated as
an additional insured. When two generators broke down, the insurer refused
to pay on the ground that Scott had no insurable interest in the generators,
given that he had divested his interest in the property. But because Scott was
still liable on his promise to procure insurance, the court concluded that he
possessed an insurable interest: "While Scott had neither ownership interest
in the property insured nor anything to gain from it, he clearly did have
something to lose."

Given these alternative tests, is there any excuse in any kind of transaction
for an attorney's failure to enable his or her client to secure insurance if the
client wishes to do so? What light does your answer shed on the relative merit
of the legal interest and the factual expectancy tests?

5. *Statutory sources of the insurable interest doctrine. Snethen* begins with
a reference to the Oklahoma statute, which underscores the importance of

---

examining statutory text before making assumptions about how the insurable interest doctrine plays out in any particular jurisdiction. What do the statutes provide in your state? Consider the following representative statutes. Do they recognize a definition of insurable interest that requires that there be a legally enforceable right, or do they recognize a more liberal definition?

a. *McKinney's Consolidated New York Insurance Laws Annotated (1999)*

§ 3401. Insurable interest in property

No contract or policy of insurance on property made or issued in this state, or made or issued upon any property in this state, shall be enforceable except for the benefit of some person having an insurable interest in the property insured. In this article, "insurable interest" shall include any lawful and substantial economic interest in the safety or preservation of property from loss, destruction or pecuniary damage.

b. *Arkansas Code (Michie 1999)*

§ 23-79-104. Insurable Interest.

(a) No contract of insurance of property or of any interest in property or arising from property shall be enforceable as to the insurance except for the benefit of persons having an insurable interest in the things insured at the time of the effectuation of the insurance and at the time of the loss.

(b) "Insurable interest" as used in this section means any actual, lawful, and substantial economic interest in the safety or preservation of the subject of the insurance free from loss, destruction, or pecuniary damage or impairment.

c. *West's Annotated California Insurance Code, Art. 4 (2000)*

§ 280. Necessity

If the insured has no insurable interest, the contract is void.

§ 281. Definition

Every interest in property, or any relation thereto, or liability in respect thereof, of such a nature that a contemplated peril might directly damnify the insured, is an insurable interest.

§ 282. Insurable interest in property

An insurable interest in property may consist in:

1. An existing interest;

2. An inchoate interest founded on an existing interest; or,

3. An expectancy, coupled with an existing interest in that out of which the expectancy arises.

§ 283. Contingency or expectancy

A mere contingent or expectant interest in anything, not founded on an actual right to the thing, nor upon any valid contract for it, is not insurable.

§ 284. Measure of interest

Except in the case of a property held by the insured as a carrier or depositary, the measure of an insurable interest in property is the extent to which the insured might be damnified by loss or injury thereof.

§ 287. Stipulations as to interest

Every stipulation in a policy of insurance for the payment of loss whether the person insured has or has not any interest in the property insured, or that the policy shall be received as proof of such interest, is void.

6. *Waiver or estoppel regarding lack of insurable interest.* Given the public policies which underlie the insurable interest requirement, should insurers ever be barred by waiver or estoppel from asserting the insured's lack of an insurable interest? Courts are divided on this issue, with the weight of authority answering the question in the affirmative. See Jonathan M. Purver, Annotation, *Insurer's Waiver of, or Estoppel to Assert, Lack of Insurable Interest in Property Insured Under Fire Policy,* 91 A.L.R.3d 513 (1979). What if the insurer's agent knows about the lack of insurable interest but decides to arrange for the policy's issuance anyway? *See McGehee v. Farmers Insurance Co.,* 734 F.2d 1422 (10th Cir. 1984); *Republic Insurance Co. v. Silverton Elevators, Inc.,* 493 S.W.2d 748 (Tex. 1973).

7. *Timing questions: When must the insurable interest exist?* With property insurance, the choices are (a) at the time the contract is issued, (b) at the time of the loss, or (c) at both times. The general rule in property insurance is that the insurable interest must exist at the time of the loss. Is this answer supported by the public policies which underlie the insurable interest requirement?

In a number of cases, there is language stating that an insurable interest must exist at both the inception of the contract and the time of the loss. On a close reading of most of these cases, it is clear that they did not involve the issue of whether there was an insurable interest at the inception of the policy. The issue was confined to the time of loss. *See, e.g., Bryant v. Transamerica Insurance Co.,* 572 S.W.2d 614 (Ky. App. 1978); *Union Central Life Insurance Co. v. Harp,* 203 La. 806, 14 So. 2d 643 (1943); *Dewitt v. American Family Mutual Insurance Co.,* 667 S.W.2d 700 (Mo. 1984); and *Kingston v. Great Southwest Fire Insurance Co.,* 578 P.2d 1278 (Utah 1978). Professor Patterson described such statements as the "senseless reiteration of a dictum uttered by Lord Chancellor Hardwicke" in *Sadlers' Co. v. Badcock,* 2 Atk. 554, 26 Eng. Rep. 733 (1743). Edwin W. Patterson, Essentials of Insurance Law 130 (2d ed. 1957).

A small minority of cases, however, hold that an insurable interest must exist at the inception as well as at the time of loss. *McCluskey v. Providence Washington Insurance Co.,* 126 Mass. 306 (1878), is illustrative. A policy was mistakenly issued to a former owner of the property sought to be insured. When the mistake was discovered and brought to the attention of the agent, he attempted to correct the error by having the former owner execute an assignment of the policy to the new owner, the intended insured. Even though the agent's assent to the assignment was noted on the policy, the Massachusetts Supreme Judicial Court held that the assignment conveyed no rights since the assignor had no insurable interest, and refused to permit parol evidence to show the mistake. The Court implied, however, that the plaintiff-assignee had pled too narrow of a case, stating: "If there was a mistake in the written contract, it cannot be rectified in this action [which was an action on the contract as written]." *Query:* What other remedy may have been available to the plaintiff? Interestingly, later cases decided by the Massachusetts Supreme Judicial Court, which cite *McCluskey* for the proposition that an inceptive interest is required, do not squarely address the timing issue. *See Mowles v. Boston Insurance Co.*, 226 Mass. 426, 115 N.E. 666 (1917) and *Womble v. Dubuque Fire & Marine Insurance Co.*, 310 Mass. 142, 37 N.E.2d 263 (1941), respectively. Thus, it is fair to wonder whether Massachusetts courts would require an inceptive interest if the issue were raised today.

If an insurable interest is required at the inception, does it have to be the same interest that exists at the time of the loss? *See Bell v. Western Marine & Fire Insurance Co.*, 5 Rob. 423 (La. 1843) (no); *Wriedt v. Beckenhauer*, 183 Neb. 311, 159 N.W.2d 822 (1968) (no). How often do you think a property insurer in California would invoke a defense of no inceptive interest under the following statute?

> An interest in property insured must exist when the insurance takes effect, and when the loss occurs, but need not exist in the meantime; an interest in the life or health of a person insured must exist when the insurance takes effect, but need not exist thereafter or when the loss occurs. *West's Ann. Cal. Ins. Code*, Art. 4, § 286.

Does it surprise you that there are no cases under the annotations to the statute dealing with the issue? Why?

8. *Recurring problems involving motor vehicles.* When parties become lax in the manner in which they sell, buy, and trade cars and trucks, insurable interest problems can easily arise. For example, if a buyer fails to comply with a state titling statute, the buyer might be deemed to lack an insurable interest, even if the buyer has a clear economic stake in the preservation of the vehicle. *See, e.g., Faygal v. Shelter Insurance Co.*, 689 S.W.2d 724 (Mo. App. 1985)(son-in-law to whom truck "belonged" and who treated truck as his own lacked insurable interest, where father-in-law retained title).

Consider the following: Douglas Beatty bought a car for his daughter Kristi on the occasion of her sixteenth birthday. Kristi lived with her mother and guardian Barbara Beatty. Barbara Beatty added the car to her existing insurance policy with USAA Casualty. Several months later, Kristi was involved in an accident, and the car was a total loss (in excess of $13,000). Before paying the claim, USAA discovered that Douglas had retained the certificate of title in his name and that the car was subject to a lien, inasmuch as the car was security for a promissory note executed by Douglas to a credit union (in an amount exceeding $11,000). Neither Barbara nor Kristi knew about the lien; accordingly, the credit union was not named as a loss payee on the USAA policy. Should the insurer pay proceeds to the credit union? Should the insurer pay proceeds to Barbara? Should Kristi have understood that she had no interest in the car if she did not possess a title to it? *See Beatty v. USAA Casualty Insurance Co.*, 954 S.W.2d 250 (Ark. 1997).

9. *Criminal lawyers need to understand insurance law, too.* As part of the nation's anti-drug effort, federal law allows for forfeiture of property used in illegal drug activities. Under 21 U.S.C. § 881(a)(7) the federal government is authorized to seize and seek forfeiture of "[a]ll real property, including any right, title *and interest* . . .which is used, or intended to be used" in illegal

drug activity (emphasis added). A relation-back provision in 21 U.S.C. § 881(h) vests title in the government "upon commission of the act giving rise to forfeiture," which means that the "right, title, and interest" in the property vests in the government as of the date of the illegal drug activity.

Consider the foregoing forfeiture statute in light of the following circumstances: Counihan's house, which she did not occupy but rented to various tenants, was totally destroyed by fire. Thereafter, a final judgment of forfeiture was entered on account of the house's earlier use for illegal drug activities. (The insured's son, a tenant, was arrested for selling cocaine on the premises to a police agent.) Query: Does the relation-back provision of the statute retroactively divest the insured of her insurable interest in the property so as to deprive her of her right to insurance proceeds for a fire loss that occurred after the illegal drug activities but before the final judgment forfeiting the property's title to the government? *See Counihan v. Allstate Insurance Co.,* 827 F. Supp. 132 (E.D.N.Y. 1993) (yes), *reversed by Counihan v. Allstate Insurance Co.,* 25 F.3d 109 (2d Cir. 1994) (no). If the answer is no, does this mean that drug dealers would be well advised to intentionally (and covertly) destroy their insured property after a forfeiture proceeding is commenced but before the final decree of forfeiture? Does this turn the insurable interest doctrine on its head? In a case involving the same insured and the same property, the Second Circuit held that the insured could avoid forfeiture under the federal statute if she lacked knowledge of the illegal activity or, having knowledge, did not consent to it. *See United States v. 890 Noyac Rd.,* 945 F.2d 1252, 1260 (2d Cir. 1991). In subsequent proceedings, the jury apparently found the insured's innocent owner defense lacking, because the forfeiture of the property to the government was upheld. *See United States v. Certain Real Property,* 990 F.2d 1250 (2d Cir. 1993). On remand of the insurance case, the United States intervened, asserting that it was entitled to the insurance proceeds under a theory of constructive trust. Reasoning that Counihan would be unjustly enriched if she kept the insurance proceeds, the court ordered the insurer to pay the proceeds to the United States. *See Counihan v. Allstate Insurance Co.,* 194 F.3d 357 (2d Cir. 1999).

10. *Property and casualty insurance versus personal insurance.* Thus far, insurable interests for property and casualty insurance have been the focus of discussion. But the problem of moral hazard does not disappear in the personal lines, even if the principle of indemnity is weaker in this setting (why is this so?). What, then, are the requirements regarding insurable interests for personal insurance, i.e., life, health, and accident insurance? This topic is considered next.

[3] Personal Insurance

MUTUAL SAVINGS LIFE INSURANCE CO. v. NOAH
291 Ala. 444, 282 So. 2d 271 (1973),
60 A.L.R.3d 81 (1974)

Heflin, Chief Justice.

This is a declaratory judgment action in equity in which the appellee-complainant, Donald R. Noah, alleges in his bill of complaint that he is the named beneficiary in three policies of insurance issued by the appellant-respondent, Mutual Savings Life Insurance Company; that the life of William L. Noah, the brother of the appellee-complainant, was insured under each of these policies; that the insured died by drowning in the City of Galveston, Texas, while the policies were in force; and that the appellant-respondent insurance company refused to pay the amounts due under any of said policies (except that a partial payment [of $434.66] was made on [the burial policy]). The bill seeks a decree construing the policies and declaring the rights of the appellee-complainant and the obligations of the appellant-respondent insurer thereunder, and ultimately that the court declare that the insurer is obligated to pay the death benefits and the balance of the burial benefits prescribed under one of the policies, plus the accidental death benefits provided in all three.

Copies of the three policies were attached as Exhibits A, B and C, respectively, to the bill. . . .

Exhibit A provides for a death benefit of $1,500 and double that sum in case of accidental death, amounting to $3,000. It is provided therein that William L. Noah, who the evidence shows met death by drowning in or near Galveston, Texas, on September 13, 1971, is named therein as the insured and the appellee-complainant is named as the primary beneficiary. The policy bears date of February 15, 1971, which under the evidence is to be taken as the date of issuance.

Exhibit B shows a policy with the same date of issuance and the same terms and beneficiary as that contained in Exhibit A, except that the ordinary death benefit is $1,000 and the accidental death benefit is in double that amount, $2,000. Each of the two policies is characterized as a "Twenty Pay Life Insurance Policy."

Exhibit C is entitled a "Burial Insurance Policy," and provides that the insurer will furnish described funeral services, including, among other things, a casket, if the death of the insured, William L. Noah, should occur within the State of Alabama and within 35 miles of an authorized funeral director. There is the further provision that if the insured's death occurs outside the State of Alabama or more than 35 miles from an authorized funeral director, the company agreed to pay to the beneficiary (Donald) one-half of the retail value of the policy as a cash payment. Since the retail value of the policy is $600, the cash payment to the beneficiary for a death outside the State would be $300. However, there is a further provision that in a case of accidental death the company would pay an additional amount equal to one-third of the retail value, which in this case would be an additional sum of $200, meaning a total cash payment of $500. The date of issuance was February 15, 1971, the same date as the other two policies.

The evidence shows that the beneficiary, Donald R. Noah, by written instrument dated September 16, 1971, declared that he became indebted to Kilgore Funeral Home, Pell City, Alabama, for funeral services and supplies for the burial of William I. Noah in the amount of $434.66, and he thereby assigned unto said funeral firm that amount out of the proceeds of the said burial policy, authorizing Mutual Savings Life Insurance Company to make its check payable to said firm for the assigned amount and directing it to pay the remainder of the proceeds of the policy to the beneficiary, Donald R. Noah. If this burial policy is held to be effective, unquestionably the obligation of the insurer has been partially discharged up to the amount of $434.66, and the insurer owes the beneficiary the unpaid balance of the maximum benefit of $500 due thereunder, viz., $65.34 with interest thereon.

The respondent in its answer and the amendment thereto denies liability under the policies on the ground that the complainant and beneficiary obtained the policies of insurance on his brother's life and that he had no insurable interest which would entitle him to recover, and also on the ground that the policies had lapsed for non-payment of premium.

The trial court rendered a judgment in favor of the appellee-complainant and against the appellant-respondent on all three policies in the total amount of $5,065.34, consisting of $5,000 under the life policies (Exhibits A & B), and $65.34 under the burial policy (Exhibit C), with interest from October 6, 1971, specified as the date the appellant-respondent denies liability.

The most divisive issue with which this court is faced is presented by appellant-respondent's contention that Donald R. Noah has no insurable interest in the life of the insured, and that each of the three policies was invalid by reason thereof. It may be well to note at the outset that this court holds the burial policy not to be subject to the insurable interest requirement. The public policy grounds for requiring an insurable interest, which are discussed below, are not applicable to a burial policy wherein the benefits are substantially restricted to providing burial services. For this reason, it is the named insured in such a policy who is in reality the recipient of the insurance benefits, not the named beneficiary. *Jordan's Mutual Aid Association v. Edwards,* 232 Ala. 80, 166 So. 780. But, even if it could be said that the burial policy is subject to the insurable interest requirement, this court holds, for the reasons stated below, that Donald R. Noah did have an insurable interest in William's life.

Under the evidence the two life policies were procured or "taken out" (an expression used in our cases) by the beneficiary, and thus the long-established rule that the insurance is invalid unless the beneficiary has an "insurable interest" in the life of the insured applies. This rule is to the effect that a person has an unlimited insurable interest in his own life and may designate any person as his beneficiary so long as the insurance was procured or taken out by the insured and the premiums paid by him, but one taking out a policy of insurance for his own benefit, on the life of another person, must have an insurable interest in the continuance of the life of such insured. Tit. 28A, § 316, Code of Alabama, 1940 (Recomp. 1958).[1]

---

[1] Although the Insurance Code, i.e., Title 28A, became effective after all relevant times for purposes of the instant case, this court is of the opinion that the result obtained in the instant case would not be altered by the application of section 316, which provides as follows:

§ 316. Insurable interest; personal insurance.—(1) Insurable interest with reference to personal insurance is an interest based upon a reasonable expectation of pecuniary advantage through the continued life, health or bodily safety of another person and consequent loss by reason of his death or disability, or a substantial interest engendered by love and affection in the case of individuals closely related by blood or by law.

Several reasons have been assigned as the basis for the insurable interest requirement, both of which are grounded upon public policy considerations: a policy taken out by one for his own benefit on the life of another, in whom he has no insurable interest is, in substance, a wagering contract; and such a policy may hold out a temptation to the beneficiary to hasten by improper means the death of the insured.

Certain blood relationships have been held sufficient, in and of themselves to negate the supposition that the beneficiary would take out such a policy for the purpose of wagering on the insured's death, or that such a policy would entice the beneficiary to take the insured's life, and in such cases the relationship alone is said to create an insurable interest. This is true notwithstanding the fact that the beneficiary may have no reasonable expectation of pecuniary advantage through the continued life of the insured or consequent loss by reason of his death, which would otherwise be required in order to find an insurable interest.

The relationship of husband and wife has been held to be sufficiently close to give either an insurable interest in the life of the other. *Jennings v. Jennings,* 250 Ala. 130, 33 So. 2d 251. The parent-child relationship has been accorded the same status as that given to husband and wife in *Jennings.*

On the other hand, the following relationships have been held not to create an insurable interest on the basis of such relationship alone. Cousin and cousin; beneficiary has no interest in the life of the wife of his wife's brother; aunt and niece; aunt-in-law and niece; niece and uncle.

The specific issue presented in the case under review is whether one has an insurable interest in the life of his brother by virtue of the relationship alone. While realizing that this issue is one of first impression in Alabama, and that other jurisdictions are in conflict on this matter, a review of the holdings of other states has convinced this court that the vast majority[2] and best reasoned holdings support the proposition that the brother-brother relationship will, in and of itself, support an insurable interest.

. . . .

The reason most often assigned as the basis of a holding that such relationship will, in and of itself, support an insurable interest is that the natural love and affection prevailing between the two and the expectation that one will render the other aid in time of need is sufficient to overcome any wagering contract argument, as well as any impulse to hasten the death of the insured. . . .

Perhaps the facts of the instant case tend to contradict the closeness and mutual love and affection which the above holdings attribute to the brother-brother relationship, but this court does not write for this case alone. The holding of this court today will govern all future cases, not just the exceptional one where the natural love and affection common to the brother-brother relationship may be missing.

---

[2] This court's research has disclosed that of the nineteen jurisdictions which have written to this issue, fourteen have stated that one has an insurable interest in the life of his brother by virtue of the relationship alone.

In view of the foregoing it is the conclusion of this court that the brother-brother relationship will, standing alone, support an insurable interest.

This court has reviewed the holdings of various other jurisdictions[3] which are contra to the decision announced by this court today, and finds that the rationale underlying these cases is that one would take out an insurance policy on the life of his brother for the purpose of gambling on the time of his death, or would, by virtue of such policy, be induced to take the life of his brother for a price, which is not, in the opinion of this court, substantiated by the common experience of mankind.

. . . .

Accordingly, this court holds that the insurance company is obligated to pay Donald Noah, in addition to the amount due under the life insurance policies, the balance due on the burial policy being the sum of $65.34, with interest from September 16, 1971.

Affirmed.

JONES, JUSTICE (dissenting).

I must disagree with the majority holding that one has an insurable interest in the life of his brother (or sister) on the basis of their relationship alone. The public policy which provides the "insurable interest" requirement has its roots in two related, yet independent, principles. Absent insurable interest such contracts have been discredited for two reasons. One is that they are wagering contracts and the other is that they may be an inducement to homicide. It is not necessary that both reasons exist at the same time or to any given policy. While each might considerably influence the other, these two public policy principles are mutually exclusive and not interdependent.

This brings us to the question whether the relationship of brother and brother (and, incidentally, brother and sister or sister and sister) is such a relationship that it in itself creates an insurable interest. We know that the relationship of husband and wife constitutes such a relationship per se, *Jennings v. Jennings,* 250 Ala. 130, 33 So. 2d 251; and while I do not find that this Court has been specifically called upon to decide whether in every case the relationship of parent and child, or child and parent, in and of itself, with a presumption that is not even rebuttable, gives rise to an insurable interest in either, the overwhelming weight of authority is that this relationship is sufficient to constitute an insurable interest by one in the life of the other (44 C.J.S. Insurance § 204, at 907). But is the relationship of brothers in the same category, or does it depend upon the circumstances of the particular case?

. . . .

---

[3] For cases holding that the relationship of brother-brother does not constitute an insurable interest, *see Lord v. Dall,* 12 Mass. 115, 7 Am. Dec. 38 (1815); *Lewis v. Phoenix Mut. Life Ins. Co.,* 39 Conn. 100 (1872); *Miller v. Travelers' Ins. Co.,* 81 Ind. App. 618, 144 N.E. 554 (1924); *Abernathy v. Springfield Mut. Ass'n,* 284 S.W. 198 (Mo. App. 1926); *Gulf Life Ins. Co. v. Davis,* 52 Ga. App. 464, 183 S.E. 640 (1936); *Dieterle v. Standard Life Ins. Co.,* 119 S.W.2d 440 (Mo. App. 1938); *Williams v. Northeast Mut. Ins. Ass'n,* 72 S.W.2d 166 (Mo. App. 1934); *Masonic Ben. Ass'n of Central Illinois v. Bunch,* 109 Mo. 560, 19 S.W. 25 (1892).

In any case, I think that the relationship alone is not sufficient, that the rule requiring something other than the relation is the sound one and I would so hold. This is based on the rationale that there is but one test for insurable interest — that of a pecuniary interest or some reasonable expectation of monetary benefit from the continuance of the insured's life; and within certain blood or affinity relationships this pecuniary interest or benefit is conclusively presumed. Such relationships are that of husband and wife, parent and child, grandparent and grandchild, and under certain conditions loco parentis relationships. This "conclusive presumption" rule with respect to these relationships does not violate the public policy necessitating insurable interest aimed at preventing homicide and wager contracts. While an extension of this rule to the brother relationship might be permissible as to the homicide aspect, to so extend this rule would facilitate the violation of the second evil which the aforementioned public policy seeks to prevent; vis., wager contracts.

Having adopted the above view, I would hold that the line must be drawn short of the brother relationship, and that insurable interest in such cases should depend upon a pecuniary benefit, or advantage to be gained from the continued life of the insured, which cannot be conclusively presumed, but is subject to proof.

My dissent is limited to the holding of the majority with respect to the insurable interest feature of the life insurance policies, and in all other respects, I concur.

NOTES

1. *Insurable interest requirements for life insurance.* Insurable interest requirements for life insurance can be divided into two general categories based on who takes out the insurance. As indicated in *Noah,* every competent person has an insurable interest in his or her own life and may take out a policy of life insurance thereon, designating whomever the person chooses as beneficiary. There is no requirement that the beneficiary have an insurable interest. How do these rules square with the principle of indemnity?

The second category consists of policies taken out by a person on another's life. Here, as a general rule, the benefits must be payable to: (1) the person whose life is insured or to his or her personal representative, or (2) a person who is related to the insured person by blood, marriage, or adoption, or who has an economic interest in having the insured person's life continue.

2. *Statutory sources of the insurable interest doctrine.* The familial relationship test for insurable interest, which is the subject of dispute in *Noah,* is rather amorphous. Nonetheless, a number of states have statutes similar to the Alabama statute set out in footnote 1 of *Noah* and, of course, these statutes just leave the problem for the courts. Other states have adopted statutes that are more restrictive. Many statutes also specifically reference the economic interest test.

Compare the following statutes. Which approach do you prefer—Alabama's, New York's, or California's?

a. *McKinney's Consolidated New York Insurance Laws Annotated*

§ 3205. Insurable interest in the person; consent required; exceptions

(a) In this section:

(1) The term, "insurable interest" means:

(A) in the case of persons closely related by blood or by law, a substantial interest engendered by love and affection;

(B) in the case of other persons, a lawful and substantial economic interest in the continued life, health or bodily safety of the person insured, as distinguished from an interest which would arise only by, or would be enhanced in value by, the death, disablement or injury of the insured.

(2) The term "contract of insurance upon the person" includes any policy of life insurance and any policy of accident and health insurance.

(3) The term "person insured" means the natural person, or persons, whose life, health or bodily safety is insured.

(b)(1) Any person of lawful age may on his own initiative procure or effect a contract of insurance upon his own person for the benefit of any person, firm, association or corporation. Nothing herein shall be deemed to prohibit the immediate transfer or assignment of a contract so procured or effectuated.

(2) No person shall procure or cause to be procured, directly or by assignment or otherwise any contract of insurance upon the person of another unless the benefits under such contract are payable to the person insured or his personal representatives, or to a person having, at the time when such contract is made, an insurable interest in the person insured.

(3) [Eff. until Aug. 8, 2001.] Notwithstanding the provisions of paragraphs one and two of this subsection, a Type B charitable, educational or religious corporation formed pursuant to paragraph (b) of section two hundred one of the not-for-profit corporation law, or its agent, may procure or cause to be procured, directly or by assignment or otherwise, a contract of life insurance upon the person of another and may designate itself or cause to have itself designated as the beneficiary of such contract.

(4) [Redesignation of former par. (3) as (4) eff. until Aug. 8, 2001.] If the beneficiary, assignee or other payee under any contract made in violation of this subsection receives from the insurer any benefits thereunder accruing upon the death, disablement or injury of the person insured, the person insured or his executor or administrator may maintain an action to recover such benefits from the person receiving them.

(c) No contract of insurance upon the person, except a policy of group life insurance, group or blanket accident and health insurance, or family insurance, as defined in this chapter, shall be made or effectuated unless at or before the making of such contract the person insured, being of lawful age or competent to contract therefor, applies for or consents in writing to the making of the contract, except in the following cases:

(1) A wife or a husband may effectuate insurance upon the person of the other.

(2) Any person having an insurable interest in the life of a minor under the age of fourteen years and six months or any person upon whom such minor is dependent for support and maintenance, may effectuate a contract of insurance upon the life of such minor, in an amount which shall not exceed the limits specified in section three thousand two hundred seven of this article.

Section 3207, referred to in the last paragraph of the New York statute, limits the amount of insurance on the life of a minor according to age. For example, if the child is under two years and six months, the total amount of life insurance may not exceed $1,000; if two years and six months or more of age but under nine years and six months, $2,000; and so on. There are also provisions for exceptions from these limits.

b. *West's Annotated California Insurance Code, Article 1*

§ 10110. Insurable interest

Every person has an insurable interest in the life and health of:

(a) Himself.

(b) Any person on whom he depends wholly or in part for education or support.

(c) Any person under a legal obligation to him for the payment of money or respecting property or services, of which death or illness might delay or prevent the performance.

(d) Any person upon whose life any estate or interest vested in him depends.

3. *Waiver and estoppel reprise.* As with property insurance, courts divide over whether insurers should be barred by waiver or estoppel from asserting a lack of insurable interest, but most courts hold that these doctrines do not bar insurers from asserting lack of insurable interest. *See Beard v. American Agency Life Insurance Co.,* 314 Md. 235, 550 A.2d 677 (1988) (doctrines of waiver and estoppel cannot bar insurers from raising insurable interest defense); *Cundiff v. Cain,* 707 So. 2d 187 (Miss. 1998) (insurer held estopped from avoiding payment to estate, which had standing to raise question of insurable interest); Phoebe Carter, Annotation, *Estoppel of, or Waiver by, Issuer of Life Insurance Policy to Assert Defense of Lack of Insurable Interest,* 86 A.L.R.4th 828 (1991). If a life, health, or accident insurer has actual or constructive knowledge that there is no insurable interest at the inception of the policy and yet is not barred by estoppel or waiver from raising the defense, are there other legal remedies available to the insured or beneficiary (assuming there is an insurable interest at the time of loss)?

4. *Economic interest in the life of another.* When a familial relationship supporting an insurable interest is nonexistent, an economic interest may suffice. Thus, a partner can have an insurable interest in the life of his or her partners, an employer can have an insurable interest in the life of a key employee, and a creditor can have an insurable interest in the life of a debtor. But it is incorrect to say that the mere existence of some kind of economic relationship automatically gives rise to an insurable interest. Moreover, when an economic relationship amounts to an insurable interest, it does not follow

that the insurable interest is unlimited. To explore these and other nuances, consider the next case.

IN THE ESTATE OF BEAN v. HAZEL

972 S.W.2d 290 (Mo. 1998) (en banc)

HOLSTEIN, Judge.

The estate of Jerry N. Bean (Estate) brought a petition for discovery of assets pursuant to sec. 473.340 against Ernest Hazel, III, seeking to determine the title and right to possession of $120,000 in proceeds from Bean's life insurance policy. The trial court concluded that Hazel had no duty to make restitution to the Estate and that Hazel held no part of the proceeds of the policy in trust for the Estate. . . . The judgment is reversed. . . .

On July 5, 1990, Bean and Hazel entered into an agreement under which Bean would borrow $120,000 from Hazel. Their agreement was set forth in a signed promissory note. Among other provisions, it stated:

> [Bean] shall maintain, during the term of this loan, a life insurance policy on his life, in a form acceptable to [Hazel], naming [Hazel] as beneficiary in an amount not less than the unpaid balance of the promissory note and accrued interest at any time. Proof of the maintenance of said policy by the maker hereof shall be given to [Hazel] upon the written request and at least thirty days prior to the premium due date on the policy. Further, [Bean] shall require said insurance company to notify [Hazel] of any termination, cancellation, amendment of beneficiary, or lapse, or transfer of said policy. Any failure to maintain said policy shall, at the option of [Hazel], cause a default of the terms hereof. . . . Proof of coverage will be given to [Hazel] by the maker at the time of execution of this promissory note. [Bean] will also require the company insuring the life of [Bean] that Notice of Premium Due be given not only to [Bean] but also to [Hazel].

The note was to be repaid in monthly installments of $2,609.09.

Thereafter, on July 26, 1990, Bean executed a change of beneficiary form to an existing $200,000 life insurance policy naming Hazel as beneficiary to the extent of $120,000. A subsequent note for $12,000 was executed on February 17, 1992. Bean made all premium payments on the insurance policy. In addition, Bean made periodic payments on the promissory note so that by the time of his death, the amount owing was $79,795.71. However, Bean did not make any changes in the beneficiary status of Hazel.

The trial court entered judgment in favor of Hazel allowing him to keep the entire $120,000. This appeal followed.

The longstanding rule in Missouri is that one must have an insurable interest in a person's life in order to take out a valid policy of insurance on that person's life. *Lakin v. Postal Life & Casualty Ins. Co.,* 316 S.W.2d 542,

549 (Mo.1958). A creditor's insurable interest in the continuing life of the debtor is limited to the amount of the outstanding debt. If a beneficiary insures the life of a person when the beneficiary has no insurable interest, the policy is referred to as a wager life insurance policy. The insurable interest requirement and wager life insurance rules are rooted in public policy.

However, it is also a general rule that a person has an insurable interest in his own life. *Lakin*, 316 S.W.2d at 552. Therefore, a person may purchase an insurance policy on his own life and name as beneficiary a person who has no insurable interest in the person's life "provided it not be done by way of cover for a wagering policy." *Id.* This rule permitting free transfer of the beneficial interest is also rooted in public policy. These two rules come into closest conflict where a creditor contracts with a debtor to assign the proceeds of an insurance policy as a means of securing payment of a debt and the proceeds of the policy are disproportionate to the amount owing on the debt when the insured dies.

While factually different, the legal issues here were addressed by this Court in *Butterworth [v. Mississippi Valley Trust Co.*, 362 Mo. 133, 240 S.W.2d 676 (1951)]. There, the insured and beneficiary of a life insurance policy were close associates, each having a full insurable interest in each other's lives at the time of the assignment of the policy. 240 S.W.2d at 680. The beneficiary then made a gift of the policy to his own family trust for estate planning purposes. *Id.* at 682. These transactions were found to be "wholly free of speculative purpose" and the trust was entitled to the full proceeds of the policy. *Id.* However, the Court in *Butterworth* stopped short of approving contracts for the assignment of a life insurance policy where the contract was merely made to cover up a gambling transaction. "The wager life insurance contract rule. . .applies where a policy has been taken out by, and the premiums paid by, a person who has no insurable interest in the life of the insured, or when [the policy] has been assigned for speculative purposes." *Id.*

In *Strode [v. Meyer Bros. Drug Co.*, 101 Mo.App. 627, 74 S.W. 379 (1903)], like the case at hand, the insured and beneficiary had no relationship other than that of debtor and creditor when the policy was assigned. 74 S.W. at 379. The court determined that the arrangement between the insured and his creditor "was made for the purpose of securing the former's indebtedness to the latter." *Id.* at 380. To the extent of the debt, there was no improper speculative purpose. However, an assignment of proceeds disproportionately large when compared to the debt was deemed an improper speculative purpose. Therefore, the court held that the creditor "acquires the status of beneficiary only as far as is necessary to make him whole, and no further. As to the remainder of the insurance money, he stands as trustee for the estate of the insured." *Id.* at 381 (citations omitted). To hold the assignment of beneficiary valid for the whole proceeds of the policy is to sanction speculative risks on human lives and to "encourage the evils for which wager policies are condemned." *Warnock v. Davis*, 104 U.S. 775, 781, 26 L.Ed. 924 (1881).

In support of his position, Hazel cites several cases from other jurisdictions that have allowed a creditor-beneficiary to recover more than the outstanding debt under an insurance policy on the debtor's life. However, as Hazel himself points out, other jurisdictions have decided that a creditor can only recover the amount of the outstanding debt despite an insurance policy that states otherwise. Equivocal precedent from other jurisdictions is not a compelling reason for overturning precedent of our own courts or for approving the assignment of a policy for a speculative purpose in an amount far in excess of the limited insurable interest of the assignee creditor.

Hazel also attacks the proposition that he holds the excess proceeds in trust for the Estate. Hazel contends that a constructive trust is only proper if he acted fraudulently or breached a confidential or fiduciary relationship. However, "[t]here are numerous situations in which a constructive trust is imposed in the absence of fraud." William F. Fratcher, Scott on Trusts sec. 462 (4th ed.1989). Specifically, "a constructive trust will be imposed where a person wrongfully obtains the proceeds of a life insurance policy as beneficiary of the policy." *[Id.,]* sec. 490. Furthermore, it cannot be said that Hazel was a bystander, wholly uninvolved in procuring the assignment. Bean was required to provide a policy in a "form acceptable" to Hazel. In addition, any failure to maintain the policy, including its beneficiary provisions in a form acceptable to Hazel, would "cause a default" of the promissory note. The contract gave Hazel complete control over both the form of the policy and any subsequent changes in that form. Since Hazel was only entitled to the amount of the debt plus any accrued interest, it was wrongful for him to obtain and claim as his own the remaining proceeds.

Finally, one may speculate that Bean's intent was to make a gift of the excess proceeds of the life insurance policy to Hazel. However, there is no pleading, evidence or argument that Bean intended to make a gift. It is generally said that the person claiming the gift has the burden of proving the gift by clear and convincing evidence. The only evidence here is of a creditor-debtor relationship and that Bean's purpose in assigning the policy was to meet the requirement to "maintain life insurance in a form acceptable to" Hazel.

The judgment is reversed. The cause is remanded for entry of judgment consistent with this opinion.

BENTON, C.J., and PRICE and WHITE, JJ., concur.

LIMBAUGH, JUDGE, dissenting.

Although I agree with the majority's general statement of the law in this case, I cannot agree with the conclusion that the majority reaches when applying the law to the facts. For that reason, I respectfully dissent.

As the majority recognizes, it has long been the rule in Missouri that one must have an insurable interest in a person's life in order to take out a valid policy of insurance on that person's life. If a beneficiary takes out a policy of insurance on the life of a person when the beneficiary has no insurable interest in the life of that person, that policy is referred to as a wager life insurance policy and is against public policy. For this reason, a creditor's ability to insure the life of his debtor is generally limited to the amount of the outstanding debt. However, a person has an insurable interest in his own life and may procure a policy of insurance on his life and name as beneficiary a person who has no insurable interest in his life "provided [that] it not be done by way of cover for a wagering policy." *Lakin*, 316 S.W.2d at 552.

In this case, it is uncontested that the life insurance policy was procured by the insured ("Bean") and not by the beneficiary ("Hazel"). Because Bean had an insurable interest in his own life, the rule against wager life insurance policies normally would not apply, and he was free to name Hazel as a beneficiary regardless of whether Hazel had an insurable interest in Bean's life. Furthermore, the fact that Bean and Hazel were involved in a debtor/creditor relationship generally would not change this result, because the rule against wager life insurance policies only "applies where a policy has been taken out by, and the premiums paid by, a person who has no insurable interest in the life of the insured, or when it has been assigned for speculative purposes." *Butterworth,* 240 S.W.2d at 682.

Apparently, the majority bases its opinion on the assumption that Bean named Hazel as a beneficiary for speculative purposes—as a part of some unstated wager. However, the record simply does not support that conclusion. Bean named Hazel as a beneficiary of $120,000 of the proceeds of a life insurance policy to secure a $120,000 debt that he owed to Hazel. Although Bean chose to name Hazel as the beneficiary of a set amount, Bean was free to have obtained a declining balance policy that would have decreased Hazel's interest as the outstanding debt decreased. In the alternative, Bean could have made subsequent reductions in Hazel's interest as the amount of the outstanding debt decreased. Moreover, nothing in the record indicates that Hazel induced or required Bean to structure the transaction in the manner that he did. In short, while Hazel certainly benefited from Bean's choices regarding the life insurance policy, there is no evidence that Hazel was named as a beneficiary for speculative purposes.

The majority relies heavily on Strode, but the facts in *Strode* were significantly different from those in this case. In *Strode,* the debtor owed the creditor $111, and the debtor took out a life insurance policy in which he named the creditor as a beneficiary of proceeds in the amount of $4,950 as security for the debt. *Strode,* 74 S.W. at 379. The premiums were paid by the creditor, rather than the debtor, and a total of $299.40 had been paid at the time of the debtor's death. *Id.* at 379–80. Thus, the creditor invested $299.40 in an insurance policy that supposedly secured a debt of $111, wagering that the pay-off of $4,950 would substantially exceed the amount of the investment. Given these facts, it is not surprising that the Strode court found evidence of improper speculation in the life of the debtor.

In contrast, the facts in this case indicate that there was no disparity between the amount of the insurance and the amount of the debt at the time Bean named Hazel as a beneficiary under the policy. Furthermore, Bean, the debtor, paid all of the premiums on the policy. Thus, the facts that served as evidence of improper speculation in Strode are simply not present in this case.

The only notable similarity between this case and *Strode* is the existence of a disparity between the amount of the outstanding debt at the time of the debtor's death and the amount actually paid under the insurance policy. Nonetheless, this similarity does not warrant a finding of improper speculation in this case. In *Strode,* the gross disproportion between the amount of insurance and the amount of the debt existed from the very beginning and provided convincing evidence that the transaction served as a means for improper speculation. In this case, the difference between the amount of insurance and the amount of the debt was not present when *Hazel* was named as a beneficiary, but arose solely as a result of the manner in which Bean managed the transaction. Considering that Bean, himself, was responsible for the disparity in this case, it is difficult to see how the disparity could have been the product of improper speculation on the part of Hazel.

In fashioning a remedy, the majority recognizes that "a constructive trust will be imposed where a person wrongfully obtains the proceeds of a life insurance policy as beneficiary of the policy." William F. Fratcher, Scott on Trusts sec. 490 (4th ed.1989); *Strode,* 74 S.W. at 381. However, as indicated by the preceding discussion, Hazel did not "wrongfully" obtain proceeds under Bean's insurance policy. The fact that Hazel received insurance proceeds in excess of the amount of Bean's outstanding debt does not, in itself, prove that Hazel engaged in any wrongful conduct.

The majority makes much of the fact that Bean had to provide insurance in a "form acceptable" to Hazel. Presumably, the majority means to imply that Hazel had some undue influence over Bean's actions, though there is no evidence to support this implication. The facts merely indicate that Bean named Hazel as a beneficiary of a set amount of $120,000 and that Hazel apparently found this arrangement acceptable. Had there been any evidence that Bean attempted to limit or decrease Hazel's interest under the policy, but was unable to do so because of Hazel's control over the form of the policy, then Hazel's control would be relevant. But there is absolutely no indication that Hazel took any such action; thus, the majority's focus on Hazel's possible control over the form of the policy is misplaced. In effect, the majority attempts to build a scenario that never happened.

The law of Missouri is clearly designed to prevent speculation in human life. To this end, a beneficiary is prohibited from insuring the life of another person when the beneficiary has no insurable interest in the life of that person. It follows that a beneficiary may be prohibited from obtaining proceeds under a policy taken out by the insured, when that policy is taken out for improper speculative purposes. In this case, there is no evidence of any conduct that violates the basic policy against speculation in human life. Although Bean was initially required to secure his debt to Hazel by procuring a life insurance policy, he could have reduced Hazel's interest under the policy as the amount of the outstanding debt decreased, and it does not appear that Hazel prevented him from doing so. Indeed, it appears that Hazel received funds in excess of the outstanding debt solely as a result of Bean's voluntary actions. It may very well be that this result was unintentional, that Bean was merely careless in naming Hazel as beneficiary of a set amount and then failing to decrease that amount as the outstanding debt decreased. But the law regarding wager policies is not designed to avoid the unintentional results of an insured's actions; it is designed to avoid speculation in human life. Because I see no evidence of speculation in the facts of this case, I would hold that Hazel is entitled to the full $120,000 he received as beneficiary under the policy taken out by Bean.

ROBERTSON and COVINGTON, JJ., concur in opinion of LIMBAUGH, J.

NOTES

1. *Creditors and debtors.* If the insurable interest doctrine is ultimately grounded in alleviating moral hazard, who has the better of the argument in *Estate of Bean*—the majority or the dissent? How would your assessment of the case change if Hazel and Bean had been long-time personal friends? Suppose the promissory note were given by Bean as an advance, nonrefundable payment for consulting services which Hazel never rendered because of Bean's untimely death. How should this affect the case?

2. *Assignments versus beneficiary designations.* The owner of a life insurance policy need not be the one whose life is insured (sometimes called the "*cestui que vie*," which means "the one who lives," and which is often abbreviated as simply "CQV"). While most individual life insurance policies are purchased on one's own life, it is common for the owner and CQV to be different persons, as is the case where a parent purchases insurance on the life of her child, or where one spouse purchases insurance on the life of the marital partner. The owner of the policy—who is not necessarily the CQV—owns the rights to the policy, which normally include the right to designate the beneficiary, to surrender the policy for any cash value, to borrow against the cash value, or to assign the ownership rights to another. The designated beneficiary has the right to receive the proceeds of the policy upon the CQV's death, but it is the owner of the policy who has the right to change the beneficiary.

If the owner of the policy makes an absolute assignment of the policy to a third person (meaning that the owner assigns all ownership interests to the third person), the assignee is entitled to exercise all rights under the policy and is responsible for maintaining the policy in force. It is common, for example, for someone desiring to make a charitable gift to assign a fully paid-up policy on the donor's life to the charity. Why would the charity be interested in becoming an assignee, instead of a designated beneficiary? At other times, an owner–CQV may assign a policy to the creditor as collateral or security for a loan. This is commonly called a "collateral assignment," and it involves the owner's temporary transfer of some policy rights to a creditor. In the typical collateral assignment, the owner transfers the sole right to receive proceeds to the creditor, but the creditor promises to pay the designated beneficiary any proceeds in excess of the amount of the debt. When the debt is fully repaid, the transferred rights revert to the owner. If you were counsel for Bean and were consulted for purposes of helping draft what would become the July 5, 1990 agreement, what advice would you have given him? Assignments and beneficiary designations receive more attention in § 4.01[4].

3. *Assignments and the insurable interest requirement.* If the owner–CQV assigns the policy to someone else, insurable interest questions do not disappear. If the owner–CQV can designate any beneficiary she chooses, including someone who lacks an insurable interest in the CQV's life, should the owner–CQV be denied the right to assign the policy to someone who lacks an insurable interest in the CQV's life (assuming contractual formalities are satisfied)? *See Grigsby v. Russell,* 222 U.S. 149, 32 S. Ct. 58, 56 L. Ed. 133

(1911); but *See Langford v. National Life & Accident Insurance Co.,* 116 Ark. 527, 173 S.W. 414 (1915) and *Bromley's Adm'r v. Washington Life Insurance Co.,* 122 Ky. 402, 92 S.W. 17 (1906). Should owners who lawfully insure the lives of others be permitted the same freedom? Or should assignment be allowed only to the extent the assignee has an insurable interest in the CQV's life? In *Grigsby,* the CQV lacked money to pay for a needed surgical operation. So, the CQV asked the surgeon to pay for a life insurance policy, which the CQV took out on his own life and then assigned to the surgeon. Is there any cause for concern in this arrangement? (Other aspects of assignments in the context of life insurance receive attention in § 4.01[4]).

4. *May Harvey rest in peace.* Both the majority and dissenting opinions in *Estate of Bean* cited a prior Missouri case—*Lakin v. Postal Life & Casualty Insurance Co.,* 316 S.W.2d 542 (Mo. 1958). In *Lakin,* the insurer issued a $25,000 life insurance policy to Harvey Hankinson, whose wife was named as beneficiary. Harvey, however, refused to accept the policy; instead, he assigned the policy and changed the beneficiary to Lakin, his alleged business partner. These arrangements were made by Lakin (with Harvey's consent), and Lakin paid the premium on the policy. The business partnership did not amount to much; the court said that Lakin's evidence "conclusively establishes that Hankinson made absolutely no financial or capital contribution whatever to the alleged partnership, and that he did not in any way obligate himself to do so; that he had no technical knowledge, skill or ability as a worker or manager to add to the partnership," etc. 316 S.W.2d at 551. Should Lakin be entitled to the $25,000 upon Harvey's death? Harvey died as a result of a shotgun wound suffered during a hunting trip while he was alone with Lakin. Should this be relevant to the outcome of the case? For another hunting accident case where the insurable interest doctrine came into play, *see Rubenstein v. Mutual Life Insurance Co.,* 584 F. Supp. 272 (E.D.La. 1984).

5. *The extent of the economic interest.* Cases like *Lakin* raise the question of how much economic interest is enough—which has its similarities to the question considered in *Noah,* i.e., how much of a familial relationship is enough. In *Estate of Bean,* no one doubted that a creditor has an insurable interest in the life of the debtor. Rather, the parties disagreed over whether this relationship could support Hazel's claim for proceeds exceeding the extent of the interest, which was limited by the amount of Bean's unpaid debt. If the economic interest is slight, does it mean that no insurable interest exists, or that the interest should be valued for what it is worth? Suppose an employer procures a policy of accidental death insurance in the amount of $200,000 on the life of each of its employees without their knowledge, and names itself as beneficiary. One of the clerks in the employer's mail room, who has worked for the employer for three months, dies in a car accident. Why does it matter whether the owner-beneficiary has no insurable interest or only a limited insurable interest? *See Stillwagoner v. Travelers Insurance Co.,* 979 S.W.2d 354 (Tex. Ct. App. 1998).

6. *Implications for insurers.* As will be explored in more detail in Chapter 4(A)(4), life insurers need a dependable set of rules regarding who is entitled to the payment of life insurance proceeds. Indeed, beneficiary designations are as important to insurers as they are to those who purchase insurance.

What are the implications of *Estate of Bean* for life insurers doing business in Missouri?

7. *Funding buy-out agreements.* Assume that Sally and Nancy want to enter a business partnership. In the event of death, the survivor would like to continue the business, but neither particularly wants to be saddled with the heirs of the other as a partner. Their lawyer suggests that they put a clause in the partnership agreement providing an option to the survivor to buy out the heirs of the deceased partner. Since neither Sally nor Nancy may have the money to buy out the other's heirs, the lawyer advises each to take out a policy of life insurance on the life of the other for the purpose of funding the buy-out agreement. (This is also called a "criss-cross" arrangement.) Does the New York or California statute recognize an insurable interest in each partner for this purpose or would you need a statute like the following?

> An individual party to a contract or option for the purchase or sale of an interest in a business partnership or firm, or of shares of stock of a closed corporation or of an interest in the shares, has an insurable interest in the life of each individual party to the contract and for the purposes of the contract only, in addition to any insurable interest which may otherwise exist as to the life of the individual.

Ariz. Rev. Stat. Ann. § 20-1104(C)(3) (West 1990). If the proceeds exceed what is needed to buy out the deceased partner's interest, is the policy an unlawful wager? *See Ridley v. VanderBoegh,* 95 Idaho 456, 511 P.2d 273 (1973) (involving the issue of whether the proceeds in excess of that needed to buy out the deceased partner's interest should be paid to the surviving partner or to the deceased partner's spouse who was bought out).

8. *Timing revisited: When must the insurable interest exist?* Insurable interests may change over time. For example, an employer may have an insurable interest at the inception of an insurance contract in the life of a key employee, but this will not be true at the time of loss if the employment relationship has already terminated. The reverse can be true also; an insurable interest could come into existence sometime after the insurance policy is issued. As discussed in the prior section, the general rule is that an insurable interest in property must exist at the time of loss; in life insurance, the general rule is that the insurable interest must exist at the inception of the contract. Do health and accident policies present any unique problems or are they adequately covered by the general rules? Are these rules supported by sound policy?

One of the reasons given for not requiring an insurable interest in life insurance other than at inception is that some life insurance has a cash surrender value and is partly an investment. Does this mean a policy of term life insurance, which has no cash surrender value, should be treated differently? Where a policy of term life insurance provides that it may be renewed at the expiration of the original term without a medical examination, but subject to the premium for the age then attained by the insured, should the requirement for an insurable interest at inception be applied again at the time of renewal? *See Marquet v. Aetna Life Insurance Co.,* 128 Tenn. 213, 159 S.W. 733 (1913) (holding where policy is extended that insurable interest is to be determined at date of original issue).

9. *Standing to challenge lack of insurable interest.* Whether a party other than the insurer has standing to challenge the lack of insurable interest is not likely to arise in property insurance. Because third parties lack an interest in the proceeds of property insurance, there is nothing to be gained by arguing that the policyholder lacked an insurable interest in insured property. In life insurance, the situation can be different; beneficiaries might wish to claim, for example, that the owner of the policy (*e.g.*, an employer) lacks an insurable interest in the life of the CQV (*e.g.*, an employee) and that the proceeds should therefore be paid to a beneficiary. Of the jurisdictions passing on the question, most have held that only the insurer has standing to challenge the validity of a policy on the basis of lack of insurable interest. *See Ryan v. Tickle,* 210 Neb. 630, 316 N.W.2d 580 (1982); *Secor v. Pioneer Foundary Co.,* 20 Mich.App. 30, 173 N.W.2d 780 (1969). Is the majority rule supported by sound policy considerations?

Some jurisdictions have altered this rule somewhat by permitting an action against a person without an insurable interest who has received the life insurance benefits from the insurer. *See Cundiff v. Cain,* 707 So. 2d 187 (Miss. 1998) (estate of insured, who was owner of life insurance policy procured by beneficiary forging insured's signature on application, had standing to raise question of insurable interest). If you were asked to draft a statute producing this result, whom would you permit to bring the action and to whom would you distribute the benefits?

[4] Duty to Ascertain Insurable Interest

LIBERTY NATIONAL LIFE INSURANCE CO. v. WELDON
267 Ala. 171, 100 So. 2d 696, 61 A.L.R.2d 1346 (1957)

LAWSON, JUSTICE.

This is a suit by Gaston Weldon, who sues as the father of Shirley Dianne Weldon, deceased, his minor daughter, under § 119, Title 7, Code 1940, the so-called homicide statute, against Liberty National Life Insurance Company, a corporation; National Life & Accident Insurance Company, a corporation; and Southern Life & Health Insurance Company, a corporation. . . . [In the trial court there was a verdict and judgment for plaintiff in the amount of $75,000.]

We will sometimes hereafter refer to Gaston Weldon as the plaintiff, to his deceased child as Shirley, and to the defendant insurance companies as Liberty National, National Life and Southern Life.

Shirley died on May 1, 1952, when she was approximately two and one-half years of age. Prior to her death each of the defendant insurance companies had issued a policy wherein Shirley's life was insured. The policy of Liberty National in the amount of $500 was issued on December 1, 1951. National Life's policy in the amount of $1,000 was issued on or about April 23, 1952. The policy of Southern Life in the amount of $5,000 was issued in the latter part of March, 1952. Each of those policies was issued on an application of Mrs. Earle Dennison, who was an aunt-in-law of Shirley, that is, she was the widow of a brother of Shirley's mother. Each of the policies provided that the death benefits be paid to Mrs. Dennison. The Southern Life policy did contain a provision to the effect that Shirley's mother was a contingent beneficiary. . . . [Mrs. Dennison subsequently murdered Shirley.]

The plaintiff has proceeded against these defendants on the theory that Mrs. Dennison did not have an insurable interest in the life of Shirley and hence the policies involved were illegal and void as against public policy; that the defendants were negligent in the issuance of the policies in that they knew there was no such interest or failed to exercise reasonable diligence to ascertain that fact before issuing the policies, although there was a duty upon them to do so; and that the failure to perform that duty was in fact the proximate cause of the child's death.

. . . .

Does a life insurance company have the duty to use reasonable care not to issue a policy of life insurance in favor of a beneficiary who has no interest in the continuation of the life of the insured?

No case has come to our attention where this specific question has been considered by any court. But we are of the opinion that such a duty exists, for there is a duty upon all to exercise reasonable care not to injure another. . . .

The position of the defendants seems to be that if murder results the insurance companies are, of course, sorry that the insured met with such a fate, but they have no liability if there is no insurable interest although they can treat such policies as completely void. If an early death from natural causes makes the policy unprofitable, the defendants can and do refuse to pay the beneficiary for the reason that such policies are void. In other words, the defendants seem to be of the opinion that the insurable interest rule is to protect insurance companies. We do not agree. The rule is designed to protect human life. Policies in violation of the insurable interest rule are not dangerous because they are illegal; they are illegal because they are dangerous.

As we have shown, it has long been recognized by this court and practically all courts in this country that an insured is placed in a position of extreme danger where a policy of insurance is issued on his life in favor of a beneficiary who has no insurable interest. There is no legal justification for the creation of such a risk to an insured and there is no social gain in the writing of a void policy of insurance. Where this court has found that such policies are unreasonably dangerous to the insured because of the risk of murder and for this reason has declared such policies void, it would be an anomaly to hold that insurance companies have no duty to use reasonable care not to create a situation which may prove to be a stimulus for murder.

. . . .

We come now to the contention of the appellants that they were entitled to the affirmative instruction presently under consideration for the reason that the plaintiff failed to meet the burden which was upon him to present some evidence tending to show that the defendants' acts were the proximate cause of Shirley's death. In their brief the defendants say that the evidence shows that "in the instant case, the *separate, independent, superseding, wilful, malicious, crime of murder* became 'the responsible cause' of the death of Shirley Dianne Weldon."

. . . .

We have been cited to a number of cases from other jurisdictions by counsel representing the parties to this litigation which treat the matter of intervening criminal acts of third persons. It is, of course, quite impossible to review all of them in detail within the limits of an ordinary opinion. But our reading of the cases, not only those cited by the plaintiff, but many of those cited by the defendants, show the majority rule to be that stated in the Restatement of the Law of Torts by the American Law Institute, § 448, as follows:

> The act of a third person in committing an intentional tort or crime is a superseding cause of harm to another resulting therefrom, although the actor's negligent conduct created a situation which afforded an opportunity to the third person to commit such a tort or crime, unless the actor at the time of his negligent conduct should have realized the likelihood that such a situation might be created thereby and that a third person might avail himself of the opportunity to commit such a tort or crime.

. . . .

Comment:

a. The rule stated in this Section applies when the actor's conduct creates a situation which is utilized by a third person to intentionally inflict harm upon another or provides a temptation thereto to which the third person yields, the actor having no reason to expect that the third person would so act. Under the rule stated in this Section, the actor is not responsible for the harm thus inflicted merely because the situation which his negligence has created has afforded an opportunity or temptation for its infliction.

b. When special grounds for anticipating criminal action by third person. There are certain situations which are commonly recognized as affording temptations to which a recognizable percentage of humanity is likely to yield. So too, there are situations which create temptations to which no considerable percentage of ordinary mankind is likely to yield but which, if created at a place where persons of peculiarly vicious type are likely to be, should be realized as likely to lead to the commission of fairly definite types of crime. If the situation, which the actor should realize that his negligent conduct might create, is of either of these two sorts, an intentionally criminal or tortious act of the third person is not a superseding cause which relieves the actor from liability.

. . . .

We cannot agree with the defendants in their assertion that we should hold as a matter of law that the murder of the young girl was not reasonably foreseeable. They created a situation of a kind which this court and others have consistently said affords temptation to a recognizable percentage of humanity to commit murder. We quote again from the case of *Helmetag's Adm'r v. Miller,* 76 Ala. 183: "The reason of the law which vitiates wager policies is the pecuniary interest which the holder has in procuring the death of the subject of insurance, *thus opening a wide door by which a constant temptation is created to commit for profit the most atrocious of crimes.*" (Emphasis supplied.)

The question of proximate cause was properly left for the jury's determination.

. . . .

The judgment of the circuit court is affirmed.

Affirmed.

LIVINGSTON, C. J., and SIMPSON, GOODWYN and MERRILL, JJ., concur.

[COLEMAN, J., dissented.]

NOTES

1. *Should there be a duty to investigate?* Given the ambiguities inherent in the definition of insurable interest for life insurance, is it correct to conclude that the insurer has a tort duty to investigate at the inception of the policy? Note that life insurance makes no particular effort to adhere to the principle of indemnity. Thus, even though an insurable interest may exist in a beneficiary, there will be instances when the CQV is worth more to the beneficiary dead than alive. What does this say about the inducement to murder and to the insurer's responsibilities upon the issuance of a policy? Moreover, there is no requirement that an insurable interest at the inception of the policy must continue until the time of the loss. If this is true, how could the court in *Weldon* say that "but for" the insurer's negligence in failing to ascertain whether the aunt-in-law had an insurable interest, the child would have lived? For a criticism of *Weldon,* see Richard W. Duesenberg, *Insurer's Tort Liability for Issuing Policy Without Insurable Interest,* 47 Cal. L. Rev. 64 (1959).

2. *Scope of duty.* Where the beneficiary of a life policy has an insurable interest, would the insurer owe any duty under tort law to the person whose life is insured if the insurer has actual notice of the beneficiary's murderous intent? If so, what should be the scope of the duty? *See Life Insurance Co. of Georgia v. Lopez,* 443 So. 2d 947 (Fla. 1983).

3. *Should there be a duty in property insurance?* Should the rule in *Weldon* be extended to cases involving property insurance? If so, how would it work, given that there is generally no requirement that an insurable interest exist at the inception of the contract?

§ 2.03 Indemnity

In Chapter 1, we examined the nature of insurance arrangements, including the basic point that insureds come to insurance markets to shed undesirable risks and thereby obtain security. Insureds seek protection against losses that would be suffered if particular events, not certain to occur but which might occur, happen. The essence of the insurance contract, then, is to protect against loss, not to profit on account of loss. This fundamental assumption of insurance is often expressed in terms of "indemnity." Under the indemnity principle, an insured is entitled to receive benefits up to or equal to a loss, but not to receive benefits in excess of a loss. Thus, indemnity means that the proceeds paid under insurance contracts should reimburse the insured for loss, not provide the insured with a net gain as a result of the loss. (Note that the principle of indemnity is not violated if the insured recovers less than the loss.) In the preceding section, the close connection between indemnity and the insurable interest doctrine was explored; if the insured has no interest in property or a person, the insured suffers no loss as a result of damage to the property or person, and no proceeds should be paid. In other words, paying proceeds in the absence of an insurable interest would violate the principle of indemnity.

This principle, which is one of the fundamental assumptions of insurance, sets insurance contracts aside from other types of contracts. People contract with one another to generate net gains in all kinds of situations; thus, why not allow insurance contracts to be used to produce net gains? The answer is that insurance does produce "net gain" for the insured, but this gain takes the form of the value the insured places on being relieved of the consequences of an uncertain-to-occur, but possible loss. The indemnity principle means that the insured cannot use insurance contracts to provide compensation that exceeds the insured's economic loss. Otherwise, insureds would have incentives to cause loss in the hope of future gain, an outcome utterly antithetical to basic notions of the public interest.

Like most rules, the indemnity principle is not absolute—nor should it be. There are situations where the costs associated with eliminating minor deviations from the principle are not worth incurring. Moreover, there are situations where other public policies come into play and the indemnity principle is forced to yield somewhat. Finally, to the extent insurance contracts attempt to adhere to the principle of indemnity, it is axiomatic that losses must be measured or valued in order to determine the amount of money that is necessary to make the insured whole under the terms of the contract. As the materials in this section will show, there is a good bit of play in the joints when one undertakes to put a value on property and to calculate the amount of a loss.

Because property and casualty insurance attempt to adhere to the principle of indemnity, most valuation problems arise under these types of insurance. Conversely, life, accident, and disability insurance make less of an attempt, and putting a value on the loss presents relatively few legal problems with those types of insurance. To be sure, there must be a "loss" under the terms of the latter types of insurance, but the benefits due are usually liquidated amounts set out in the policies. For example, a life or accident insurance policy typically provides a fixed amount to be paid once the event insured against comes to pass. The same is true for disability insurance. Health insurance policies which provide cash benefits (as opposed to services) look more like property insurance because only "usual," "customary," and "reasonable" charges for medical care and related services incurred by the insured are reimbursable. In fact, in the health care finance industry, it is common to refer to such policies as "traditional indemnity policies," which has the effect of distinguishing such policies from managed care and direct services arrangements.

Liability insurance is designed to pay a third party for losses caused by an insured. The basis of liability to the third party, whether it be in tort, contract, or civil rights, determines the measure of damages. Generally speaking, the insurer agrees to pay, within the policy limits, all of the damages once the amount is ascertained. Consequently, any disputes usually arise under the law that governs the insured's liability to the third party. There are, however, exceptions. For example, there may be a dispute as to whether punitive damages, as opposed to compensatory damages, are covered. Nevertheless, disputes as to the measure of damages for which the insurer is liable under liability insurance are relatively rare. Disputes over the definitions of loss under first-party property and casualty insurance are more typical.

The materials which follow consider the more common issues and related problems which arise when the indemnity principle is invoked or implicated.

[1]　Valuing Property and Casualty Losses

ELBERON BATHING CO. v. AMBASSADOR INSURANCE CO.
77 N.J. 1, 389 A.2d 439 (1978), 8 A.L.R.4th 519 (1981)

CONFORD, P.J.A.D. (temporarily assigned).

The principal question on this appeal concerns the valuation methods to be used in ascertaining the "actual cash value" of a partial loss under the Standard Form Fire Insurance Policy, *N.J.S.A.* 17:36-5.15 *et seq.* We are also required to determine whether failure to apply the appropriate standard is sufficient cause to set aside an appraisal award. The appeal arises in the context of a judgment in the Law Division in favor of the insured plaintiffs in the amount of $52,000 for excess coverage based on a $77,000 appraisement minus $25,000 primary coverage (on another policy) for a loss due to fire. The Appellate Division affirmed in an unreported opinion.

Defendant, Ambassador Insurance Company, issued a fire insurance policy to plaintiffs, Elberon Bathing Co., Inc. and Elberon Bathing Club, to indemnify them against loss by fire to club facilities and contents situated in Long Branch. The $125,000 policy represented excess coverage over a $25,000 primary policy issued plaintiffs by Great Southwest Fire Insurance Company.

On January 8, 1975, while the policy was in effect, plaintiffs' bathing club was damaged by fire to an amount "greatly in excess of $25,000." Great Southwest promptly paid Elberon the $25,000. However, plaintiffs and defendant were unable to adjust plaintiffs' covered loss under the excess policy. Pursuant to the terms of the policy and an "agreement for submission to appraisers," plaintiffs and defendant each appointed an appraiser. The appraisers were, in turn, to select a disinterested umpire. However, they were unable to reach agreement thereon. Plaintiffs then filed a complaint and an order to show cause requesting the court to appoint an umpire pursuant to the terms of the policy. The court appointed an umpire.

Shortly thereafter the appraisers and umpire went to inspect the insured premises which had already been repaired. According to affidavits of the umpire and defendant's appraiser, the umpire and plaintiffs' appraiser believed that their role was merely to determine the replacement cost of the damaged property. The umpire and plaintiffs' appraiser determined the actual cash value of the entire property to be $180,000 and the amount of fire loss to the property to total $77,000. This consisted of $8,500 for damage to personal property and $68,500 for pure replacement cost of the realty destroyed. Defendant's appraiser refused to sign the award.

Plaintiffs sought entry of judgment on the appraisement. Defendant answered, denying the finality of the award on the basis of its contention that the umpire had not heard all the evidence nor considered all matters submitted to him. It further disclaimed liability because of Elberon's alleged fraud in submitting a claim which it knew was substantially in excess of the actual cost to it to repair the damage. Defendant demanded that the award be vacated, and requested a jury trial on all the issues. In addition, defendant separately sought discovery of various "loss estimates" prepared by plaintiffs' appraiser and gave notice, pursuant to the policy, of defendant's desire to examine plaintiffs' documents and representatives.

The trial judge heard oral argument and reviewed the pleadings and affidavits. He stated that the appraisers could properly determine that replacement cost was the appropriate measure of the actual loss recoverable under the policy. He also found that there was no manifest mistake justifying setting aside the award. After deduction for the primary insurance coverage judgment was entered for plaintiff for $52,000. The Appellate Division, agreeing with the trial judge that under the appropriate narrow standard of review "the facts in the case do not dictate a basis for vacating the award . . .," affirmed. We granted certification. 74 N.J. 284, 377 A.2d 688 (1977).

I

Defendant argues that an award based on replacement cost without deduction for depreciation contravenes the measure of recovery provided for in the policy, that being "actual cash value." We agree.

N.J.S.A. 17:36-5.15 et seq. regulates the subject of fire insurance. As required by N.J.S.A. 17:36-5.19, the policy before us insured Elberon ". . . to the extent of the actual cash value of the property at the time of the loss, but not exceeding the amount which it would cost to repair or replace the property with material of like kind and quality . . . ." This appeal calls for a determination of the meaning of "actual cash value." That phrase is also found in the appraisal provision of the Standard Form Policy which conforms to the statute.

> In case the insured and this Company shall fail to agree as to the actual cash value or the amount of loss, then, on the written demand of either, each shall select a competent and disinterested appraiser and notify the other of the appraiser selected within twenty days of such demand. The appraisers shall first select a competent and disinterested umpire; and failing for fifteen days to agree upon such umpire, then, on request of the insured or this Company, such umpire shall be selected by a judge of a court of record in the State in which the property covered is located. *The appraisers shall then appraise the loss, stating separately actual cash value and loss to each item;* and, failing to agree, shall submit their differences, only, to the umpire. An award in writing, so itemized, of any two when filed with this Company shall *determine the amount of actual cash value and loss.* . . . (emphasis added)

N.J.S.A. 17:36-5.20

The appraisal award here under review purported to follow the stated procedure.

A review of the record indicates that the appraisal was based on replacement cost without consideration of the element of depreciation. Plaintiffs argue that straight replacement cost is a permissible standard. We reject this contention. A standard of replacement without depreciation is inconsistent with the intent and the language of the statute which, as noted above, provides for insurance to the extent of the actual cash value of the property at the time of loss but not to exceed the amount it would cost to repair or replace the property with material of like kind and quality. Repair or replacement costs constitutes an upper limit on, not the absolute measure of, the insurer's liability. *See* Riegel & Miller, Fire Insurance from Insurance Principles and Practices, 360 (3d ed. 1947). To equate "actual cash value" with replacement cost alone would render the limiting phrase meaningless. If actual cash value is less than replacement cost in a particular case the former controls.

Rejection of pure replacement cost is further consonant with the legislative provision permitting insurers to provide for extended coverage to include replacement cost under an extended coverage endorsement. *N.J.S.A.* 17:36-5.22 provides that under such an endorsement the insurer may agree "to reimburse and indemnify the insured for the difference between the actual value of the insured property at the time any loss or damage occurs and the amount actually expended to repair, rebuild or replace with new materials of like size, kind and quality . . . ." Such an endorsement specifically precludes deduction for depreciation. It seems clear that if a specific provision is required to reimburse for pure replacement cost then the basic policy should not be so construed.

Finally, allowing pure replacement cost would violate the principle of indemnity by providing a windfall to the insured:

> To allow the insured to recover the original value of real estate that has depreciated,. . .would be for the insurance company to pay for losses that were not caused by fire. Such prodigality would simply furnish an incentive for the destruction of property, because more could be recovered as insurance than the undamaged property was worth. Even under present conditions it is found that business depressions, which reduce the values of buildings and stocks of goods, are sometimes accompanied by large increases in the fire losses. Such conditions furnish an incentive for a fire.

Riegel & Miller, supra, at 358–359. *See* Bonbright & Katz, "Valuation of Property to Measure Fire Insurance Losses," 29 Colum. L. Rev. 857, 878–879 (1929).

Plaintiffs cite *Farber v. Perkiomen Mutual Ins. Co.,* 370 Pa. 480, 88 A.2d 776 (Sup. Ct. 1952), and *Fedas v. Ins. Co. of the State of Pennsylvania,* 300 Pa. 555, 151 A. 285 (Sup. Ct. 1930), as authority for their position. However, it is not entirely clear that the Pennsylvania cases really so hold. They have been construed not to stand for the proposition that the appraiser may not depreciate a partial loss, but only that "the blanket rate of depreciation taken for purposes of determining actual cash value of the insured structure may not be applied on a blanket basis to [such] loss." *See* Cozen, "Measure and Proof of Loss to Buildings and Structures Under Standard Fire Insurance Policies—the Alternatives and Practical Approaches," 12 Forum 647, 654 (1977). In any event, to the extent that the policy in *Farber* was to the same effect as our statute in respect of coverage, we disagree with the decision if it meant to hold that the insurer is liable for the replacement cost of a loss without deduction for depreciation.

. . . .

We thus conclude that an appraisal based on replacement cost without consideration of depreciation does not measure "actual cash value" under our statute and is therefore improper.

This appeal constitutes an appropriate vehicle for stating the principles which should guide appraisers in determining "actual cash value." The matter of correct standards has been widely litigated elsewhere.[2] Case law reflects three general categories for measuring "actual cash value": (1) market value, (2) replacement cost less depreciation, and (3) the "broad evidence" rule. *See* Note, "Valuation and Measure of Recovery Under Fire Insurance Policies," 49 Colum. L. Rev. 818, 820–823 (1949); Cozen, *op. cit., supra,* 12 Forum at 648–658; Hinkle, "The Meaning of 'Actual Cash Value,'" 1967 Ins. L.J. 711. *See generally* Annot., 61 A.L.R.2d 711 (1958).

Market value is generally defined as the price a willing buyer would pay a willing seller, at a fair and *bona fide* sale by private contract, neither being under any compulsion. But there is a problem in that a building ordinarily has no recognized market value independent of the parcel of property in entirety, land and building together. *See* Note, *op. cit., supra,* 49 Colum. L. Rev. at 820, where it is observed that the majority of courts have rejected

---

[2] Every state has some statutorily prescribed fire insurance policy. Most states, like New Jersey, follow the New York Standard form. *Riegel & Miller, supra,* at 351–352.

market value as the sole criterion or standard of "actual cash value" although they have allowed the fact-finder to consider it as a factor in computing the actual cash value of a building.[3] It is common practice for a valuation expert to develop a residual market value for a structure by deducting from the market value of the whole parcel the appraised market value of the land. In case of a partial loss, the market value approach looks to determination of the difference between the respective market values of the structure before and after the fire. Note, *op. cit., supra,* 49 Colum. L. Rev. at 825–826.

Replacement cost less depreciation has the advantage of relative definiteness. It is also easily ascertained. However, it is inflexible, and this characteristic often results in excessive recovery. Many structures today have a high replacement value because of the inflated cost of building materials even though their true commercial value — represented by rentals, prospective profits, usefulness to the present owner, location and age—is considerably less. *Id.* at 821.

The problem of excessive recovery under the replacement cost less depreciation rule together with the occasional uncertainty of market value prompted development of what is now the most widely accepted rule, generally denominated as the "broad evidence rule." That rule was well explained by the New York Court of Appeals in *McAnarney v. Newark Fire Insurance Co.,* 247 N.Y. 176, 159 N.E. 902 (Ct. App. 1928).

In *McAnarney* the insured built a brewery just before Prohibition. The brewery burned down shortly thereafter (arson was not proven). The insured claimed replacement cost minus depreciation, which because of impending Prohibition was more than the building was worth. The insurer was willing to allow market value, which, for the same reason, was probably less than the building would ordinarily have been worth. The Court of Appeals rejected both of these fixed standards of recovery and held that:

> Where insured buildings have been destroyed, the trier of fact may, and should, call to its aid, in order to effectuate complete indemnity, every fact and circumstance which would logically tend to the formation of a correct estimate of the loss. It may consider original cost and cost of reproduction; the opinions upon value given by qualified witnesses; the declarations against interest which may have been made by the assured; the gainful uses to which the buildings might have been put; as well as any other fact reasonably tending to throw light upon the subject.

159 N.E. at 905.

McAnarney was intended to assure application of the principle of indemnity (*i.e.,* to make the measure of recovery for fire insurance losses correspond to the actual pecuniary loss sustained by the insured). *Id.* at 904–905. *See* Bonbright & Katz, *op. cit., supra,* 29 Colum. L. Rev. at 899. Under-valuation denies the insured the indemnification due him under the policy.

---

[3] California follows the market value rule. *Jefferson Insurance Co. of N. Y. v. Superior Court,* 3 Cal. 3d 398, 90 Cal. Rptr. 608, 475 P.2d 880 (Sup. Ct. 1970), as does Maine. *Forer v. Quincy Mutual Fire Ins. Co.,* 295 A.2d 247 (Maine Sup. Ct. 1972).

Over-valuation tempts the insured to cause the very loss covered, or at least, to provide inadequate safeguards against the loss. *Id.* at 863.

The commentators generally view the broad evidence rule with approval. See *id.* at 898–899 (a flexible test which can be modified in such a way as to accord more nearly with the principle of indemnity); Cozen, *op. cit., supra,* 12 Forum at 657 (sacrificing an easily applied standard for a far more equitable result). It has been adopted in numerous jurisdictions.

. . . .

We find the rationale of the broad evidence rule to be compelling. It requires the fact-finder to consider all evidence an expert would consider relevant to an evaluation, and particularly both fair market value and replacement cost less depreciation. If the appraiser finds it appropriate under the particular circumstances he may, after weighing both factors, settle on either alone. Normally, replacement cost minus depreciation can be significant evidence of value but it is not necessarily conclusive. Thus under the broad evidence rule the two stated criteria do not bind the fact-finder but instead become guidelines, along with other relevant evidence. No evidence is *per se* exclusive of other evidence; any evidence may be used jointly or alternatively according to the circumstances and the property to be evaluated.

The broad evidence rule is consistent with the narrow standard of judicial review generally accorded to appraisal awards. The wider the range of evidence considered by the fact-finder, the more reasonable it is for a court to accept his conclusions. A result reached under the broad evidence rule is more likely to be reliable than one based on either of the other standards alone. If the appraiser gives reasonable consideration to all relevant evidence, his award should ordinarily stand.

We thus hold that the proper standard for evaluating "actual cash value" under the New Jersey Standard Form Policy is the broad evidence rule.[5]

. . . .

The judgment is reversed and the cause is remanded to the Law Division for further proceedings conforming to this opinion.

For reversal and remandment: CHIEF JUSTICE HUGHES, JUSTICES SULLIVAN, PASHMAN, CLIFFORD, SCHREIBER and HANDLER and JUDGE CONFORD—7.

For affirmance: None.

Doelger & Kirsten, Inc. v. National Union Fire Insurance Co., 42 Wis.2d 518, 167 N.W.2d 198 (1969). The insured's wooden patterns for

---

[5] We perceive no reason for distinguishing between the standard of evaluation for a total loss and that for a partial loss. *N.J.S.A.* 17:36-5.19 makes no such distinction; it specifies but one measure of recovery, "actual cash value." Any such distinction may lead to anomalous results. *See* Note, *supra,* 49 Colum. L. Rev. at 826, n. 60 (insured might recover more for a partial loss than a total loss). It is realized, however, that where an appraisal is made after a partial loss there may be difficult proof problems in arriving at the putative market value of the portion of the structure destroyed as distinguished from the entirety.

producing castings for alligator shears were destroyed when a fire destroyed a barn and its contents. The applicable fire insurance policy limited the insurer's liability to "the actual cash value of the property." The trial court entered judgment for the insured in the amount of $4,840, calculating that the replacement cost of the destroyed patterns was $12,100.00 but that a deduction for obsolescence should be made. The insurer appealed. The supreme court affirmed the judgment in an opinion by Justice Hansen.

"What is the proper measuring stick to use in determining the "actual cash value" of wooden patterns of uncertain age, apparently more than 30 years old, last used in 1958 or 1959 and useable only for the producing of castings for alligator shears, an item of heavy industrial equipment for which there no longer seems to be much public demand?

"Plaintiff contends that the proper measuring stick is a replacement cost. Evidence from an expert pattern maker was offered that the cost of reproduction of the destroyed patterns was $12,100.00. Such cost of reproduction, the plaintiff spiritedly contends, is the sole test of value.

"Defendant counters that the measuring stick to be used is that of present market value, actually contending that alligator shears, and consequently patterns used to make them, are obsolete and of no value at all. It is conceded that the patterns had not been used since 1956, and were moved to the barn for storage in 1963. The bottom dropped out of the alligator shears market in the mid-fifties with the development of the guillotine shears, a new and improved type of cutting machine. As background it should be mentioned that we deal here with a piece of expensive equipment. An alligator shears is no scissors to remove warts from crocodiles. One such shears costs $30,000. At the peak of demand, orders came in only two, three or four times a year.

"By the replacement test plaintiff would get $12,100. By the present market value test, plaintiff would get nothing or very near to that. The trial court adopted the measuring stick of replacement cost, minus physical depreciation and minus obsolescence. . . .

"This is in accord with the opinion of experts in valuation of property.

"For example, in the case of used patterns, molds, and designs used as equipment by a manufacturer it has been held that their replacement cost new is not a fair test and that their obsolescence as well as their physical depreciation must be taken into account.[2]

"Applied to the type of equipment here involved and the type of situation here presented, this appears to be a common sense approach to determining present "actual cash value." In the absence of any evidence as to physical depreciation, the trial court made no deduction for the attrition of the aging process, holding that to do so would be "pure speculation." Giving weight both to evidence as to absence of orders and the presence of continuing inquiries as to availability of alligator shears, the trial court found evidence of "substantial obsolescence." . . . .

". . . . Under the fact situation here presented, the court could not be expected to ascertain the "actual cash value" with exact mathematical precision.

---

[2] 1 Bonbright, Valuation of Property, 383.

It was for the trier of fact to set the damages at a reasonable amount, using an acceptable measuring stick. This is what he did.

"Perhaps as a footnote only, we add the warning that sustaining the trial judge here is not laying down an invariable test to be applied in ascertaining "actual cash value" in all fire insurance cases. Actually, this court has consistently followed what has been termed the "broad evidence rule" giving considerable leeway and latitude to the trier of facts. In practice, this broad rule gives to the trial forum the right to consider in a given case all facts reasonably tending to throw light upon the subject. . . .

"Under the "broad evidence rule," we need not find the route travelled by the trier of fact in this case to be the only route that could have been travelled. We need only to find it a proper and acceptable one. This we do. That both parties are outraged by the result reached may be some reassurance that the trial court found and followed a via media between two extremes.

. . . .

"We find no misuse of trial court discretion here, certainly no basis for finding an abuse of discretion."

NOTES

1. *The insurer's duty to indemnify.* The insurer's duty to pay proceeds in the event of a covered loss is, obviously, not unlimited. A "policy limit" will specify the maximum payment the insurer must make; a loss in excess of the policy limit is the insured's responsibility. To get a higher policy limit, the insured must pay a higher premium. Deductibles also limit the insurer's indemnity obligation by requiring the insured to absorb the first dollars of loss up to a stated amount. Essentially, the insurer undertakes no indemnity obligation with respect to small claims, and the insured typically gets a premium reduction if she agrees to a higher deductible. Coinsurance is another kind of loss-sharing between insurer and insured; in essence, the insured must share in the loss based on a percentage or formula, regardless of the size of the loss. These subjects receive more detailed treatment in § 2.03[3] later in this Chapter. Why might it be said that the actual cash value limitation in the policy in *Elberon* is yet another kind of "policy limit"?

2. *Methods of proving loss.* The standards enunciated in *Elberon* for measuring harm to property, real or personal, have been adopted by most courts. Each may be proved in a variety of ways. If you represent a client whose commercial building is completely destroyed by fire, how many different methods for ascertaining the market value of the building can you think of? The number of courts approving the broad evidence rule is increasing. For additional discussion, see Robert H. Jerry, II, Understanding Insurance Law § 93[d][4] (2d ed. 1996).

3. *State statutes.* One should not overlook the possibility that a state statute will affect the choice of valuation standard. For example, Cal. Ins. Code § 10102, as amended in 1993, requires California residential property insurance policies to be accompanied by the following disclosure: "ACTUAL CASH

VALUE COVERAGE PAYS THE FAIR MARKET VALUE OF THE DWELL-
ING AT THE TIME OF LOSS, UP TO POLICY LIMIT. In the event of covered
loss to your home, the insurance company will pay either the depreciated fair
market value of the damaged or destroyed dwelling at the time of the loss
or the cost of replacing or repairing the damaged or destroyed dwelling with
like or equivalent construction up to the policy limit." (Capitals and underline
in original.) Does this statute clarify the valuation standard in California?

This leads to an observation with relevance well beyond the valuation issue
being discussed here. As the court in *Elberon* observed, many jurisdictions
have adopted the New York Standard Fire Insurance Policy, 1943 ed., by
statute. A copy of the policy is contained in Appendix A. Where a state has
adopted this form, or some variation of it, all fire insurance policies issued
to cover property in that state must conform to it. This does not necessarily
mean that the language must be copied word for word. The provisions of the
issued policies, however, must be the same in substance or at least as
favorable to the insured.

4. *Construing the policy.* Replacement or reproduction cost often comes into
play where there is a partial loss. If it would cost $25,000 to repair the damage,
but the "before and after" reduction in market value is only $15,000, would
the insured legally be entitled to elect to have the insurer pay to repair the
property under the policy in *Elberon*?

5. *Who laughs last?* If you were required to explain how the trial judge in
Doelger reached the figure of $4,840, could you offer a rational explanation?
Is there a moral here? The challenges here are illustrated nicely by the split
decision in *General Casualty Co. v. Tracer Industries, Inc.,* 285 Ill. App. 3d
418, 674 N.E.2d 473 (1996). Tracer Industries purchased an old commercial
building on December 23, 1993 for $67,500. At the time of the purchase,
Tracer's appraisers calculated the value of the land to be approximately
$50,000 and the value of the building to be roughly $20,000. One week later,
the building burned. When Tracer and its insurer could not agree on the actual
cash value of the building, each selected an appraiser under the policy's loss
adjustment provisions, and the court appointed an umpire when these two
appraisers disagreed. Tracer's appraiser put the actual cash value at $111,900
based on replacement cost less depreciation for age. The insurer's appraiser
took obsolescence into account, and put actual cash value at $34,065. The
umpire agreed with the insured's appraiser, and the insurer was ordered to
pay the policy limits of $100,000. The majority did not think that failure to
take obsolescence into account was a "gross mistake of law or fact" that would
justify upsetting the award, 674 N.E.2d at 476, but the dissent concluded that
"an appraisal of $111,900 for a building purchased a week earlier for a fair-
market value of $21,000 and having no special value to the insured is
'absurd,'" 674 N.E.2d at 481. What are the implications of all of this for the
principle of indemnity?

6. *Condemnation orders affecting property value.* What if a building, insured
under a policy like that in *Elberon,* has been condemned as a nuisance by the
proper governing authority and ordered to be destroyed? Should this be taken
into account in determining the actual cash value of the building if the
building is completely destroyed by fire after the condemnation order has

become final, but before the building has been razed? What if the condemnation order is not yet final at the time of the fire? In *Bailey v. Gulf Insurance
Co.,* 406 F.2d 47 (10th Cir. 1969), the court, applying Oklahoma law, held that
a city resolution declaring an abandoned fraternity house to be a nuisance
and ordering the owner to raze it had no bearing upon its value in determining
the amount due to the insured under a fire insurance policy. Is this result
defensible on any basis? *See also Myint v. Metropolitan Government of
Nashville, No.* 01A01-9512-CH-0058, 1996 Tenn. App. LEXIS 429, at *1 (Tenn.
Ct. App., July 24, 1996) (insureds had insurable interest in building destroyed
by fire despite demolition order, and order did not limit insureds' recovery
to salvage value).

7. *Replacement cost coverage.* If depreciation is taken into account to reduce
the amount the insurer must pay the insured, the potential hardship to the
insured can be considerable. Orenzo Cheeks' home was damaged in the 1994
Northridge earthquake in California, and the cost of repairs was nearly
$64,000. Cheeks' policy had an $8,800 deductible, and the insurer calculated
that "depreciation and/or betterment" was approximately $10,000. Thus, the
insurer's check to settle Cheeks' claim was less than $45,000. *See Cheeks v.
California Fair Plan Association,* 61 Cal. App. 4th 423, 71 Cal. Rptr. 2d 568
(1998) (reversing trial court's confirmation of arbitration award based on
insurer's settlement and requiring "fair market value" calculation). Would
Cheeks have been better protected under a different kind of policy? See the
next case.

HIGGINS v. INSURANCE CO. OF NORTH AMERICA
256 Or. 151, 469 P.2d 766 (1970), 66 A.L.R.3d 871 (1975)

McAllister, Justice.

This is an action on a fire insurance policy in which the trial court found
for plaintiffs and defendant Insurance Company of North America appeals.
The principal questions on appeal are whether plaintiffs had an insurable
interest in the insured premises, the effect on plaintiffs' claim of other
insurance on the same property, whether the filing of a proof of loss was
waived, and the amount plaintiffs were entitled to recover under the terms
of the policy.

There is little dispute about the facts. John Vickroy owned a house and lot
at 943 Lorane Highway in Eugene which he wanted to sell. On April 21, 1966,
after some negotiation between the parties, an earnest money receipt was
executed by plaintiff Linn D. Higgins and Vickroy by which plaintiffs agreed
to buy the property for $8,000 and to pay the purchase price at the rate of
$85 per month commencing May 15, 1966. The agreement also required four
additional payments of $500 each, payable quarterly commencing August 15,
1966.

Plaintiffs did not purchase the property for a home, but intended to renovate
it for resale. Within a day or two after the earnest money agreement was

signed the plaintiffs took possession of the property and began renovation. Higgins testified that after he took possession he worked evenings and Saturdays on the house doing general cleanup work, painting the exterior, stripping the kitchen and bath and preparing to install new cabinets in the kitchen.

On May 3, 1966, defendant's policy involved in this action was issued to plaintiffs by the Smith and Crakes Agency of Eugene. The policy covered the Lorane Highway property against loss by fire up to $17,000, which Higgins told the agent would be the value of the premises when the house was renovated. The first annual premium was paid. The policy made no mention of Vickroy's interest in the property.

Vickroy had a $10,000 policy of fire insurance covering the premises, also issued by the Smith and Crakes Agency, but in the South Carolina Insurance Company.

On May 15, 1966, the plaintiffs paid Vickroy the $85 payment on the purchase price due on that date. No other payments on the purchase price were made.

On June 4 the house was badly damaged by fire. Smith and Crakes hired an adjuster to adjust the loss on behalf of both the South Carolina Insurance Company and defendant Insurance Company of North America. There was some delay in adjustment while the authorities were investigating the fire, but ultimately the South Carolina Insurance Company paid Vickroy $6,756.55 in settlement under its policy. The defendant did not pay on its policy and plaintiffs brought this action. The trial court found plaintiffs were entitled to recover the policy limit of $17,000, plus $5,000 attorneys' fees, and entered judgment against defendant for $22,000.

[The discussion of whether the plaintiffs had an insurable interest, which was resolved in their favor, is omitted.]

Defendant next contends that the court erred in awarding plaintiffs the policy limit of $17,000 under the provisions dealing with "Replacement Cost" rather than the actual cash value of the property at the time of loss, which, according to the evidence, was $6,500.

The first page or face of the policy insured the insured "to the extent of the actual cash value of the property at the time of loss" against "all direct loss by fire" to the property described in the policy. We shall refer to this as the basic coverage.

Page 4 of the policy is entitled "Provisions Applicable to the Entire Policy" and contains 13 lettered paragraphs, each dealing with a separate subject. Paragraph f is entitled "Replacement Cost" and contains seven numbered subparagraphs. We are concerned primarily with subparagraphs (2), (5) and (7), which read as follows:

> (2) If at the time of loss the limit of liability for the dwelling in Coverage A of this policy is eighty per cent (80%) of the full replacement cost of the dwelling insured, Coverages A and B only of this policy are extended to include the full cost of repair or replacement without deduction for depreciation.

. . . .

(5) This Company's liability for loss under Coverages A and B of this policy, including this replacement cost provision, shall not exceed the smallest of the following amounts: (a) The limit of liability for Coverage A or B, whichever applies; (b) The replacement cost of the building structure or any part thereof identical with such building structure on the same premises and intended for the same occupancy and use; (c) The amount actually and necessarily expended in repairing or replacing said building(s) or any part thereof intended for the same occupancy and use.

. . . .

(7) The insured may elect to disregard this replacement cost provision in making claim under this policy, but such election shall not prejudice the Insured's right to make further claim within a reasonable time after loss for any additional liability brought about by this replacement cost provision.

It is conceded that, if the policy did not contain subparagraph (5) plaintiffs would be entitled to recover $17,000 under the provisions of subparagraph (2). The policy insures a dwelling under Coverage A and the 80% requirement of subparagraph (2) is met.

Defendant contends that subparagraph (5) limits its liability to the smallest of three amounts, and that the smallest of the three, clause (c), is "The amount actually and necessarily expended in repairing or replacing said building(s) or any part thereof intended for the same occupancy and use." There is no evidence that plaintiffs expended anything after the fire for replacement or repair of the insured building. Defendant contends that since plaintiffs have expended nothing in repairing or replacing the insured building they are entitled to nothing under the replacement clause provisions of the policy, but are entitled only to the actual cash value of the insured property under the basic coverage.

Since the amount of recovery turns on whether the basic coverage or the replacement cost extension is applicable we need to consider the relationship of the alternative coverages. The purpose of Replacement Cost insurance is explained in Fire, Casualty & Surety Bulletins published by The National Underwriter as follows:

Though the concept underlying the use of actual cash value as a Property insurance standard is sound, beyond challenge, the business has for many decades recognized that its strictest application can and does leave uninsured a very real source of potential loss. A property owner may indeed realize a betterment through the reconstruction of a damaged building, but that betterment may be one for which he cannot at the time of loss afford to pay. In other words, one's building may be, say 25% depreciated at the time of loss, but he needs sufficient funds with which to replace the building and the depreciation may represent nothing more to him at that time than an accounting entry. To be prepared for this contingency, he must have some sort of reserve. Otherwise, whatever the theory — depreciation, betterment, use, indemnity—this man is faced with an eminently *practical problem* which may quite realistically be viewed as an *insurable risk of loss.*

The recognition of this element of risk led to what the business now speaks of as *Replacement Cost insurance.* Fundamentally, this is any type of coverage under which the insurance company agrees, in effect, to pay *the difference* between actual cash value and full replacement cost. What is insured, therefore, is *depreciation* and, in fact, some of the earliest approaches to this protection involved *specific additional amounts* of coverage of this part of the exposure, hence, the early (and still not entirely extinct) title "Depreciation insurance."[1]

The following explanation of replacement cost insurance is taken from Magee and Bickelhaupt, General Insurance (7th ed. 1964) at 309:

> *Depreciation insurance,* sometimes called *replacement cost* insurance, pays for full replacement cost new of the insured property, without deduction for depreciation. It provides indemnity for the expenditures the insured is obliged to make over and above the amount of the loss covered by full insurance under the standard fire policy in order to restore the property to its full usefulness as before the loss or damage. Depreciation insurance substitutes a figure representing the cost of replacement new for the term "actual cash value."

It appears that replacement cost insurance has been written only under very definite limitations. The basic limitation is that "the insured collects on this 'new for old' basis only if the property is repaired or replaced."[2] The "Replacement Requirement" is described in F.C. & S. Bulletins, Dwellings, Rc-2, June, 1966, as follows:

> There is to be no recovery of the part of the loss which exceeds the actual cash value of the damaged part *unless and until actual repair or replacement is completed.* In other words, repair or replacement is *prerequisite* to recovery under the extension. The insured can submit a claim for *actual cash value* when he chooses and collect any *additional amount* he may have coming under the Replacement Cost extension subject to a requirement that the additional claim be made *within 180 days* after the loss. (The number of days is 120 in some states.) [The policy involved in this case specifies "a reasonable time after loss."]
>
> . . . .

The purpose of repair or replacement as a condition precedent to recovery under Replacement Cost insurance is protection against the moral hazard. This thought is expressed in Magee and Bickelhaupt, *op. cit. supra* at 309, as follows:

> Not all insurers are willing to write insurance in an amount sufficient to insure the full replacement cost of the insured property. They point out that there is an element of moral hazard in providing insurance that will replace in its entirety an old and partly obsolete building in

---

[1] F.C. & S. Bulletins, Fire & Marine Section, Misc. Fire, Acb-1, Third Printing, Sept. 1966.

[2] F. C. & S. Bulletins, Fire & Marine Section, Misc. Fire, Acd-1, Second Printing, Sept. 1966.

a new condition. There are others who contend that in most instances the element of moral hazard is negligible and that an insured has every right to buy insurance that will place him back in business after a fire without contributing to the replacement cost of his building an amount measured by depreciation.

. . . .

The limitations on recovery under the replacement cost provision of the policy involved in this case closely parallel the usual limitations as described in F. C. & S. Bulletins as follows:

> Replacement Cost insurance does *not* provide *valued coverage*. A loss under this type of form is adjusted in the same manner as one under a conventional form, the difference being that *depreciation*—routinely deducted whenever feasible is an actual cash value loss — is not considered.
>
> *The Replacement Cost endorsement specifies that the insurer is to pay not more than the <u>smallest</u> of three amounts:*
>
> 1. The amount of the policy applicable to the damaged or destroyed property.
>
> 2. The replacement cost of the property (or part thereof) *identical* with the insured property, *on the same premises* and *intended for the same occupancy and use.*
>
> 3. The *actual* and necessary *expenditure* in repairing or replacing the insured property. Note that this limit no longer refers to replacement *on the same premises.. . .*[3]

The reasons for limiting recovery to the amount actually expended for repair or replacement seem reasonable, and such a limitation should be enforced if it is clearly stated in the insurance contract. We think that the language employed in the policy under consideration is sufficiently clear, and that the intent to limit the company's liability to amounts actually expended is apparent from a careful reading of the replacement cost provision. We conclude that since plaintiffs have not expended anything in repairing or replacing the insured building they are not eligible to recover under the "Replacement Cost" extension of the policy. For a similar conclusion *see Bourazak v. North River Insurance Company,* 379 F.2d 530 (7th Cir. 1967).

Plaintiff's recovery, then, is under the basic coverage of the policy. There is evidence in the record from which the trial court can make findings as to the appropriate amount. The judgment should be modified according to these findings, and should represent what the trial court finds to be the actual cash value of the property at the time of the loss as defined in the policy.

. . . .

Reversed and remanded for modification of judgment in accordance with this opinion.

---

[3] F. C. & S. Bulletins, Fire & Marine Section, Misc. Fire, Acd-4 and 5, Third Printing, August, 1967.

NOTES

1. *A violation of the indemnity principle?* Note the court's reference to "moral hazard" in its use of a quotation from a prominent insurance textbook. Moral hazard refers to the inherent tendency of insurance to increase the probability of loss by reducing the insured's incentives to take precautions to prevent loss or increasing the insured's incentives to cause loss (with the hope he does not get caught doing so). Why does replacement cost coverage arguably increase moral hazard, and how does the requirement that the insured actually repair or replace damaged property to obtain replacement cost proceeds tend to mitigate this?

Recall that ordinary wear and tear and the effects of ordinary aging are not "fortuitous" losses. (See § 2.01 *supra.*) Assume that in 1980 homeowner replaces the roof on her home for $6000, and homeowner uses shingles that are expected to last for 30 years. In 2000, a hailstorm damages the roof to the extent that it must be replaced. In 2000, replacing the roof with shingles of like kind and quality costs $9000. What is necessary to make the homeowner "whole" in the sense of being put in the position she would have occupied if no hailstorm had occurred? How much of this should be insurable? Do the answers change if the property covered is an automobile and the peril is collision?

For more information about the structure of replacement cost coverage, see Johnny Parker, *Replacement Cost Coverage: A Legal Primer,* 34 Wake Forest L. Rev. 295 (1999).

2. *Protecting against inflation.* In addition to the feature in *Higgins* that protects against the risk that replacement cost will exceed the amount of the adjusted loss because of depreciation, insurers also offer a similar feature that protects against inflation. This endorsement is available for residential as well as commercial property and is designed to automatically increase the amount of coverage so that the policy limit keeps pace with increases in property value due to inflation. Otherwise, in times of rapid inflation the property may not be adequately insured without frequent revaluation and adjustment in the amount of insurance.

3. *Code upgrades.* One of the things that insurers typically try to exclude from the replacement cost coverage is the cost of building code upgrades. For example, between the time a building is constructed and the loss, a particular governing body may require that buildings meet certain architectural, structural, mechanical, or electrical requirements. Existing buildings are usually exempted, but if any major construction work is subsequently performed, the building must meet the new requirements. However, many replacement cost coverage provisions exclude the cost of bringing a building "up to code" even though the insured-owner may be required to do so in repairing or rebuilding after an insured loss. Even if the policy does not explicitly exclude such costs, an insurer may argue that code upgrades are not included because the coverage only extends to "like construction" and "the cost, at the time of the loss, to repair or replace the damaged property with new materials of like kind

and quality." With code upgrades costing many thousands of dollars in some instances, this has been a fertile ground for litigation. *See Bering Strait School District v. RLI Insurance Co.,* 873 P.2d 1292 (Alaska 1994) (holding, under fire policy, insured entitled to recover expenditures attributable to building code changes under doctrine of reasonable expectations); *Dombrosky v. Farmers Insurance Co. of Washington,* 84 Wash. App. 245, 928 P.2d 1127 (1996) (homeowners policy limited insured to recovery of actual cash value, and insured could not recover additional costs of compliance with new building codes). For a discussion of the issue in the context of the devastation caused by Hurricane Andrew, see Hugh L. Wood, Jr., Comment, *The Insurance Fallout Following Hurricane Andrew: Whether Insurance Companies Are Legally Obligated to Pay for Building Code Upgrades Despite the "Ordinance or Law" Exclusion Contained in Most Homeowners Policies,* 48 U. Miami L. Rev. 949 (1994).

4. *Overhead and sales tax.* If the plaintiffs in *Higgins* had rebuilt, the insurer's replacement cost payout would have included enough to cover the cost of materials, the general contractor's charges (including overhead), and applicable sales taxes on materials used in the reconstruction. But Higgins was a renovator. If Higgins had rebuilt the property himself, should the insurer have paid him a sum for overhead? Higgins, of course, did not rebuild, but he was still entitled to an actual cash value reimbursement. If actual cash value is defined as "replacement cost less depreciation," is the insurer also allowed to deduct the overhead and sales tax expense from replacement cost under the reasoning that these costs are not incurred and therefore cannot be a part of the replacement cost? *Compare Salesin v. State Farm Fire & Casualty Co.,* 229 Mich. App. 346, 581 N.W.2d 781 (1998) (no), with *Snellen v. State Farm Fire & Casualty Co.,* 675 F. Supp. 1064 (W.D. Ky. 1987) (yes). How does your answer square with the principle of indemnity?

5. *Valuation problems regarding personal property.* In *Crisp v. Security National Insurance Co.,* 369 S.W.2d 326 (Tex. 1963), the court recognized a distinction between marketable chattels possessed for purposes of resale and other types of chattels that have no readily ascertainable market value and had the following to say about losses regarding the latter:

> It is a matter of common knowledge and of usual acceptation by the courts that used household goods, clothing and personal effects have no market value in the ordinary meaning of that term. They may be sold but only at considerable sacrifice which by no means represents the value of the articles to the owner. We find no recognized authority which would hold the insured to a recovery based solely on the proceeds obtainable on a secondhand market. Likewise, replacement costs do not afford a fair test. In some instances on account of obsolescence, change in style and fashion, this measure might represent an economic gain to the insured quite aside from the difficulty of application and proof. The measure of damage that should be applied in case of destruction of this kind of property is the actual worth or value of the articles to the owner for use in the condition in which they were at the time of the fire excluding any fanciful or sentimental considerations.

Id. at 328. In applying the *McAnarney* rule, the court noted that the trier of fact may consider original cost, replacement cost, the opinions upon value by qualified witnesses (including that of the owner), and the gainful uses to which the property has been put, as well as any other facts reasonably tending to shed light upon the value of the property. *Id.* at 329. Does this place a premium on the ingenuity of counsel in representing parties to disputes over the amount of the loss regarding this type of property?

6. *Sentimental value.* In *Crisp* (discussed in the prior note), the Texas Supreme Court held that an insured may not recover based on fanciful or sentimental considerations. What if part of the property destroyed consisted of a number of irreplaceable reels of movies or videotapes of family weddings, honeymoons, vacations, religious rites, and other family activities, including pictures of members at various stages of their lives? Does *Crisp* mean that the insured's recovery should be limited to the cost of replacing the film? In *Mieske v. Bartell Drug Co.*, 92 Wash. 2d 40, 593 P.2d 1308 (1979), 6 A.L.R.4th 923 (1981), the court upheld a jury award of $7,500 in a tort action against defendants for loss of thirty-two reels of family home movies on the basis that plaintiffs, although not entitled to recover for fanciful or sentimental value, were entitled to recover the "actual or intrinsic" value to them. Would the same result obtain if the claimants were seeking recovery under their homeowners policy which, in conformance with the New York Standard Fire Policy, covered "all direct loss by fire"?

[2] Valued Policies

HEADY v. FARMERS MUTUAL INSURANCE CO.
217 Neb. 172, 349 N.W.2d 366 (1984)

CAPORALE, JUSTICE.

Gary L. Heady, plaintiff below, appeals from the trial court's judgment which, pursuant to the jury's verdict in favor of defendant-appellee, Farmers Mutual Insurance Company, denied him recovery on a fire insurance binder. Farmers Mutual has filed a cross-appeal. We reverse and remand for a new trial.

In June of 1981 Gary Heady contacted Patricia Hohman of Insurance Agents, Inc., an independent insurance agency located in Omaha, Nebraska, in order to obtain a fire insurance policy on a house located in Omaha. After Hohman asked Heady questions pertinent to the property, she issued, without prior inspection, a 1-month binder commencing on July 2, 1981, for Farmers Mutual, extending $60,000 of fire and extended coverage insurance on the property. The $60,000 figure represented the reproduction cost of the house, which was in a rundown condition and for which Heady paid a total of $5,000.

Heady was engaged in the business of buying older homes and refurbishing them for resale or rental. He began to remodel the house in question 2 days prior to completing the purchase on July 2, 1981. The work was primarily confined to scraping the exterior paint and doing other work on the outside of the house until July 8, 1981. On that day Heady directed his workmen to remove damaged plaster from the inside walls and ceiling. In the early morning hours of July 9, 1981, the house was destroyed beyond repair by fire.

. . . .

Farmers Mutual refused to honor Heady's claim, and Heady instituted this suit to recover the $60,000 face value of the insurance binder. Farmers Mutual did not contest the issuance of the binder, but defended on the grounds that the binder was void due to misrepresentations made by Heady to Insurance Agents, and also that Heady had deliberately caused or procured another to cause the fire.

[The court reversed for a new trial on the ground that some of the evidence of arson was inadmissible.]

Since the judgment must be reversed and a new trial granted, we address the additional issues raised by both the appeal and cross-appeal in order to answer questions of law which will likely be present again in such new trial. Those issues are: (1) Is Neb. Rev. Stat. § 44-380 (Reissue 1978), the valued policy statute, a viable statute with respect to fire insurance? (2) Does the valued policy statute preclude evidence of the actual value of the premises to establish that the coverage was procured fraudulently? (3) If so, does it preclude evidence of the actual value of the premises to establish a motive for arson? . . .

Turning to the first of these issues, § 44-380 provides:

> Whenever any policy of insurance shall be written to insure any real property in this state against loss by fire, tornado, windstorm, lightning, or explosion and the property insured shall be wholly destroyed, without criminal fault on the part of the insured or his assignee, the amount of the insurance written in such policy shall be taken conclusively to be the true value of the property insured and the true amount of loss and measure of damages.

[The court considered whether § 44-380 was repealed by implication by a subsequent Nebraska statute, § 44-501.] The clear intent of § 44-501(10) is that the written value provisions of § 44-380 apply to fire insurance policies. We are bound by that intent.

The remaining issues are all concerned with the effect of the valued policy statute on certain fraud defenses asserted by Farmers Mutual.

By its answer to Heady's petition Farmers Mutual claims that Heady should not be allowed to recover on the insurance binder and the binder should be declared void because Heady fraudulently obtained the coverage by misrepresenting the value of the subject dwelling. Farmers Mutual presented evidence that, if believed, would establish that the actual value of the property was $5,000, while the insured value was $60,000. Farmers Mutual claims the trial court erred in failing to instruct the jury on this defense, while Heady claims that the valued policy statute precludes the introduction of such evidence.

In *Aetna Ins. Co. v. Simmons,* 49 Neb. 811, 69 N.W. 125 (1896), the elements of the fraudulent overinsurance defense are illuminated by language quoted with approval from *Franklin Fire Ins. Co. v. Vaughan,* 92 U.S. 516, 23 L. Ed. 740 (1875):

"The law exacts the utmost good faith in contracts of insurance, both on the part of the insured and the insurer, and a knowing and willful overvaluation of property by the insured, with a view and purpose of obtaining insurance thereon for a greater sum than could otherwise be obtained, is a fraud upon the insurance company that avoids the policy. It is a question of good faith and honest intention on the part of the insured, and though he may have put a value on his property greatly in excess of its cash value in the market, yet if he did so in the honest belief that the property was worth the valuation put upon it, and the excessive valuation was made in good faith, and not intended to mislead or defraud the insurance company, then such overvaluation is not a fraudulent overvaluation that will defeat a recovery."

49 Neb. at 838–39, 69 N.W. at 134.

Farmers Mutual asserts that *Aetna* supports its position that the valued policy statute does not preclude a fraudulent overvaluation defense. We cannot read the case in that manner. While it is true that a form of the valued policy statute was in effect at that time, the *Aetna* court did not resolve the exact issue we confront here, because the matter was resolved on the basis that the insurer failed to plead or prove that the insured intentionally overvalued the property, that the representations were material to the risk, and that the insurer had relied upon them. *Aetna* therefore does no more than say that if there were such a defense, it was neither pled nor proved.

On the other hand, in *United States Fire Ins. Co. v. Sullivan*, 25 F.2d 40 (8th Cir. 1928), *cert. denied*, 278 U.S. 608, 49 S. Ct. 12, 73 L. Ed. 534, the insured sought recovery against his insurance company for $5,000 after a dwelling valued at $2,500 was destroyed by fire. The insurance company defended on the grounds the policy was void, first, because the insured breached an affirmative duty to disclose the actual value was no more than $2,500 and, second, because the insured stated in the application that the dwelling was worth $5,000. The eighth circuit held that, under Nebraska law, these fraud defenses were unavailable to the insurance company to defeat its insured's recovery. It based its decision on Nebraska's then valued policy statute, which was identical to our present statute except that it did not cover insurance policies covering windstorm or explosion. Comp. Stat. § 7809 (1922). We find the reasoning and analysis of the eighth circuit persuasive, and adopt it as our own.

It is a well-known fact that it has been the practice of some fire insurance companies to insure property at any value the insured cared to put thereon without any investigation as to such value. The natural impulse of the insured was toward amply sufficient or even over valuation. The higher the valuation, the greater the premium. If there were no loss, the insurance company profited through the high valuation. If loss occurred, the insurer would contest the value or amount of recovery and the insured might recover less than the value stipulated in the policy, although he had honestly estimated the value at the time the insurance was taken and had paid premiums on the basis of such estimated value. This situation produced dissatisfaction and litigation. It was to correct this condition, that this section was enacted. *Lancashire Ins. Co.*

v. Bush, 60 Neb. 116, 120, 82 N.W. 313; *Calnon v. Ins. Co.,* 114 Neb. 194, 199, 206 N.W. 765. Also, overvaluation was a temptation to commit arson, which might endanger lives or other property. The statute is not merely for the protection of the insured but "rests on considerations of public policy, and it is probable that the insured could not, even by express contract, relinquish the benefit of its provisions." *Lancashire Ins. Co. v. Bush,* 60 Neb. 116, 122, 82 N.W. 313, 314; also *see Reilly v. Franklin Ins. Co.,* 43 Wis. 449, 28 Am. Rep. 552; *Emery v. Piscataqua Ins. Co.,* 52 Me. 322; *Queen Ins. Co. v. Leslie,* 47 Ohio St. 409, 24 N.E. 1072, 9 L.R.A. 45; 14 R.C.L. p. 1306.

The method of the section is to have the value liquidated in the policy by the parties to the contract and removed from dispute and determination "by evidence, agreement or arbitration." *Lancashire Ins. Co. v. Bush,* 60 Neb. 116, 121, 82 N.W. 313. The statute is confined to real property because values thereof are relatively fixed and certain. *Calnon v. Ins. Co.,* 114 Neb. 194, 198, 206 N.W. 765. The result of this method of making the policy valuation binding was to place on the insurer the duty to make its own investigation and binding determination of value before such is agreed upon and placed in the contract. *Insurance Co. v. Barron,* 91 Miss. 722, 727, 45 So. 875; *Queen Ins. Co. v. Leslie,* 47 Ohio St. 409, 24 N.E. 1072, 9 L.R.A. 45. Neither party can evade the statute by avoiding this duty. If the insurer performs its full duty, in this respect, it is bound by its estimate of value based thereon unless conditions (reducing value), not ascertainable by a reasonably careful inspection and known to the insured, are withheld by the insured. But the insurer cannot close its eyes, make no reasonable investigation, take the bare word of the insured as to value and thereafter challenge such value. To permit this would be to nullify the good effect intended by the statute. It would reinstate the very situation and condition which the statute sought to destroy and prevent. It would encourage conscious overvaluation and, possibly, resulting arson.

25 F.2d at 41–42.

We recognize that at least one jurisdiction has reached the opposite conclusion. *Zuraff v. Empire Fire & Marine Ins. Co.,* 252 N.W.2d 302 (N.D. 1977). We do not find that case persuasive except for its dissenting opinion. We hold, therefore, as the eighth circuit in this instance correctly foreshadowed in 1928, that the valued policy statute precludes Farmers Mutual from asserting as a defense to liability on its fire insurance contract the fact that its insured either affirmatively misrepresented or failed to disclose the actual value of the subject property.

The next issue is raised by Heady's assertion that the valued policy statute forecloses evidence of the actual value of the destroyed premises in order to show that the insured had a motive to commit arson. . . . .

In *Weiner v. Aetna Ins. Co.,* 127 Neb. 572, 587, 256 N.W. 71, 77 (1934), we stated with respect to arson cases:

> [I]t is firmly established that in cases of this kind circumstantial evidence is not only admissible, but is usually the only evidence obtainable, since it is very evident that in almost no instance can direct testimony of eyewitnesses be obtained. Persons desiring to burn their property for the purpose of collecting the insurance, or for any other

illegal purpose, do not discuss their intentions with others, nor do they carry out such intentions in the light of day.

In light of the facts of this case it was proper for the district court to allow evidence of the actual value of the property to supply a motive to Heady, if the jury wished to so believe, for the commission of the unquestioned act of arson. Failure to allow such evidence would deprive the insurer of one of its vehicles to connect the arson to Heady and not to some other person. We think the proper rule to be that when the loss complained of is shown to be the result of an intentional act of destruction, § 44-380 does not preclude admission of the actual value of the property into evidence for the jury to consider in assessing whether the insured had a motive for committing arson.

. . . .

For the reasons hereinabove stated the judgment is reversed and the cause remanded for a new trial conducted in accordance with this opinion.

Reversed and remanded for a new trial.

NOTES

1. *Statutes with a purpose?* Many states have enacted valued policy statutes that apply to total losses under fire insurance contracts covering real property. These statutes vary as to other details, such as whether: (a) losses caused by hazards other than fire are subject to the statute; (b) personal property is covered; (c) partial losses are governed by the statute; (d) depreciation is deductible from the agreed value; and (e) mobile homes are covered. *See generally* 12 Lee R. Russ & Thomas F. Segalla, Couch on Insurance § 175:66, 96, 103–17 (3d ed. 1998).

Even in the absence of a statute, it is possible for the parties to agree to a valued policy. Such agreements are common in marine insurance, and they can also be found in personal property floater policies or endorsements. *See, e.g., Nichols v. Hartford Fire Insurance Co.,* 61 App. Div. 2d 555, 403 N.Y.S.2d 335 (1978) (involving a painting purchased for $5 and insured for $35,000). This type of policy is an example of an inland marine policy. Marine insurance receives more attention in Chapter 2.03[6], *infra.*

Some have argued that the valued policy statutes should be repealed. Is there more justification for permitting valued policies in marine insurance, including personal property floater policies, than in fire insurance on real property? See Robert H. Jerry II, Understanding Insurance Law § 93[c] (2d ed. 1996).

2. *Indemnity, fortuity, and valued policies.* As is explicit in the structure of this chapter, the fortuity principle is distinct from the indemnity principle. Can you explain the distinction? But the two principles connect to each other in some situations, as *Heady* illustrates. If insureds are allowed to collect insurance proceeds exceeding their losses, are nonfortuitous losses more likely to occur? Was the fortuity principle more important to the court in *Heady* than the indemnity principle?

3. *Limiting the reach of valued policy statutes.* If judges are unsympathetic to the policies underlying valued policy statutes, one might expect that courts would embrace opportunities to narrow the reach of the statutes in some situations. Does that prediction explain the following holdings?

a. The Missouri Supreme Court held that the valued policy statutes of that state do not apply to insurance coverage procured through the Missouri FAIR Plan. *Wells v. Missouri Property Insurance Placement Facility,* 653 S.W.2d 207 (Mo. 1983). FAIR is an acronym for "Fair Access to Insurance Requirements," which is a federal reinsurance program designed to encourage private insurers to write fire and extended coverage and theft insurance for homeowners and businesses in urban areas. This program was established after urban riots in the mid-1960s precipitated a mass withdrawal of coverage by private insurers.

b. In *St. Paul Fire & Marine Insurance Co. v. Griffin Construction Co.,* 338 Ark. 289, 993 S.W.2d 485 (1999), a contractor renovating an historic building was issued a "builder's risk policy" to cover its financial interest as a contractor in the renovation of several buildings. The contractor estimated its interest in one of those buildings as $1.5 million, and this building was totally destroyed by fire four months into the renovation. Reversing the trial court which held for the contractor, the Supreme Court held that the policy was an "open policy," not a "valued policy," and the Arkansas valued policy statute was therefore irrelevant.

c. In *Hallcom v. Allstate Insurance Co., USAA,* 654 So. 2d 245 (Fla. Ct. App. 1995), the court interpreted the Florida valued policy law to allow multiple insurers to prorate their payment of proceeds when multiple policies applied to the same loss. Would this result be possible under Missouri law? Mo. Stat. § 379.145 reads in relevant part: "When fire insurance policies shall be hereafter issued or renewed by more than one company upon the same property, and suit shall be brought upon any of said policies, the defendant shall not be permitted to deny that the property insured was worth the aggregate of the several amounts for which it was insured at the time the policy was issued or renewed thereon, unless willful fraud or misrepresentation is shown on part of the insured in obtaining such additional insurance . . . ." If you were a legislator and the Missouri statute were proposed for your state, would you vote for it?

4. *Do valued policy statutes preclude an insurer's fraud defense?* In *Zuraff v. Empire Fire & Marine Insurance Co.,* 252 N.W.2d 302, 306 (N.D. 1977), cited in *Heady,* the court held that fraud in the procurement of insurance is a defense under North Dakota's valued policy statute: "We are satisfied that the North Dakota Legislature did not enact § 26-18-08, NDCC to encourage, shelter, or reward fraud which would be the result if we were to give this statute the narrow construction contended by Zuraff." The North Dakota statute provided:

> Whenever any policy of insurance shall be written to insure any real property in this state against loss by fire and the insured property shall be destroyed by fire without fraud on the part of the insured or his assigns, the stated amount of the insurance written in such policy shall be taken conclusively to be the true value of the property insured.

Do you agree with the Nebraska or North Dakota court? Is the North Dakota statute distinguishable from the Nebraska statute? Is there a compromise position that is more supportable? *See also Filiatreau v. Allstate Insurance Co.,* 358 S.E.2d 829 (W. Va. 1987); *DeWitt v. American Family Mutual Insurance Co.,* 667 S.W.2d 700, 708 (Mo. 1984).

[3] Indemnity in Other Contexts

AETNA CASUALTY & SURETY CO. v. INSURANCE DEPARTMENT OF IOWA
299 N.W.2d 484 (Iowa 1980)

HARRIS, JUSTICE.

. . . .

Petitioner insurance company wished to initiate a new method of settling third party claims under the liability portion of its automobile insurance policies. The new method was challenged by the Iowa insurance department because it was inconsistent with Iowa law. Aetna thereafter discontinued the practice but, pursuant to section 17A.19, The Code 1977, and insurance department rule 510-2.2(502.505), Iowa Administrative Code, petitioned for a declaratory ruling by the commissioner. The insurance commissioner, thereafter affirmed by the district court upon judicial review (section 17A.19, The Code 1977), ruled adversely to Aetna.

For more than 50 years our cases on the subject have generally cited *Langham v. Chicago, R.I. & P.R. Co.,* 201 Iowa 897, 901, 208 N.W. 356, 358 (1926), to describe the measure of damages for destroyed or damaged automobiles:

> 1. When the automobile is totally destroyed, the measure of damages is its reasonable market value immediately before its destruction.
>
> 2. Where the injury to the car can be repaired, so that, when repaired, it will be in as good condition as it was before the injury, then the measure of damages is the reasonable cost of repair plus the reasonable value of the use of the car while being repaired, with ordinary diligence, not exceeding the value of the car before the injury.
>
> 3. When the car cannot, by repair, be placed in as good condition as it was in before the injury, then the measure of damages is the difference between its reasonable market value immediately before and immediately after the accident.

See State v. Urbanek, 177 N.W.2d 14, 16–17 (Iowa 1970).

The petitioner's challenge is to the second of the *Langham* situations. Petitioner starts with "the reasonable cost of repair plus the reasonable value of use of the car while being repaired, with ordinary diligence, not exceeding the value of the car before the injury." To this petitioner would add a further limitation and in this proceeding asks us to adopt it as a part of the measure of damages. The change would add, as another limitation in the second

Langham situation, the diminution in value of the car caused by the accident unless and until a repair is actually undertaken. The effect would be to compel the car owner to invest from personal funds any amount by which the repairs exceeded the proposed diminution limitation. After repairs were done the company would reimburse the owner.

The petitioner argues that there is an increased tendency on the part of automobile owners to pocket the proceeds from insurance claims and to leave damage unrepaired. The petitioner also complains that independent body shop owners have interjected themselves into negotiating the price of repairs. In the petitioner's view these two developments have increased the costs incurred by the companies, costs which it says "are necessarily being passed on to the consumer in the form of higher insurance premiums."

We are not inclined to disturb the rules set down in *Langham*. We are not persuaded that the rule change proposed by the petitioner would be an improvement. Some savings might result to petitioner. But unnecessary inconvenience and loss would likely result to owners of the damaged vehicles. Some investment of their private funds, as noticed, would be necessary at least temporarily.

A more serious criticism of the proposed change is that it complicates and blurs the clear and well understood rule we have applied for over half a century. The market value after the vehicle was damaged would be another estimate, subject to all the uncertainties and disputes inherent in any estimate. These uncertainties and disputes would become added factors in the settlement of claims. We doubt the proposed change would lead to more just or prompt settlements. We are sure the change would not be worth the cost.

We continue to subscribe to the measure of damages set down in *Langham*. So doing we affirm the district court.

Affirmed.

NOTES

1. *Third-party compared to first-party coverage.* Ignore insurance for a moment, and explain how these two situations are different: (a) you fall asleep while driving your car, and you crash it into a tree; (b) someone else falls asleep while driving, and that person crashes his car into yours. Who is legally responsible for these losses? What legal rules determine the amount of the losses? If both you and the other driver have insurance for your own losses and for damage you cause others, how would you describe the relationship between the insurance contracts and the losses you described?

Note that the *Aetna* case deals with the tort measure of damages and the obligation of the liability insurer to pay a third party. Even so, does the insurance industry still have a legitimate concern? Would you support the insurer's proposal if it were confined to first-party property damage coverage, such as collision or comprehensive coverage, as opposed to third-party liability coverage for property damage?

2. *A review of first-party valuation rules.* Examine the provisions in the policy in Appendix E regarding the first-party physical damage coverage ("Part D—Coverage for Damage to Your Auto"). What is owed under this policy in the three situations described in *Aetna? See Johnson v. State Farm Mutual Automobile Insurance Co.,* 754 P.2d 330 (Ariz. Ct. App. 1988); *Delledonne v. State Farm Mutual Automobile Insurance Co.,* 621 A.2d 350 (Del. Super. Ct. 1992).

3. *Loss of use.* Should loss of use damages only be permitted in the second situation set out in the *Aetna* case, i.e., where the car can be repaired? In a subsequent decision, the Supreme Court of Iowa followed the growing trend that permits loss of use damages in all three situations described. *Long v. McAllister,* 319 N.W.2d 256 (Iowa 1982).

4. *Stock in trade.* When stock in trade is destroyed, such as the inventory of a shoe store, a number of courts have held that retail value is an inappropriate measure of fair market value. It is reasoned that the merchant should not be compensated for the retail value because it includes a mark-up for overhead and profit. Instead, the merchant is entitled to recover at such rate as she would have to pay in the nearest market where a like quantity could be bought to replace the property lost plus interest from the date of damage and other costs of replacement such as shipping charges. See Dan B. Dobbs, Law of Remedies § 5.13(3) (2d ed. 1993). Does this mean that retail value would never be appropriate? What if the merchant lost the only remaining stock of a very popular but expensive line of shoes that no longer were being manufactured?

5. *Other property valuation problems.* For a discussion of the special valuation problems confronted where there is no suitable market for personal property or the property is unique, see Dan B. Dobbs, Law of Remedies § 5.16 (2d ed.1993).

6. *Indemnity and the life insurance contract (and other kinds of personal insurance).* When insurance companies first marketed life insurance, the product met with considerable hostility, largely because the relationship between insuring a life and the principle of indemnity seemed attenuated. Early critics thought that the product was more like a wager on how long the CQV (the person whose life was the basis for the insurance) would live, as opposed to a product that protected beneficiaries against the economic consequences associated with an untimely demise of the CQV. To the extent that the product was used to build up cash values, it seemed to more closely resemble an investment product, as opposed to a risk-transferring arrangement. In time, these concerns faded, as the economic value of life insurance became better understood. In fact, life insurance does have a loose relationship to indemnity in the sense that the life insurer compensates for the economic losses associated with loss of life. Because it is difficult to value these losses, the relationship between the coverage and the indemnity principle is more attenuated than, for example, in property insurance. Although no one questions the viability of life insurance as a product, it is fair to say that strict adherence to the principle of indemnity is not always required in life insurance.

Similar observations are appropriate for other kinds of personal insurance. In accidental dismemberment insurance, the schedule of benefits is, arguably, intended to compensate the insured for the economic loss associated with the particular body part or bodily function. But, again, because it is difficult to value these losses, strict adherence to the indemnity principle is not required. Accidental death insurance's relationship to indemnity is more difficult to explain (if one is worried about the economic loss associated with death, why purchase insurance that only covers loss of life in an accident?), but if a policy covers the loss of a body part in an accident, it would be odd if one could not insure the destruction of the entire body in an accident. The relationship of disability insurance to indemnity is more apparent; if illness or accident disables one from pursuing gainful employment, the insurance steps in to compensate that economic loss. As explained in the introductory note which began this section, health insurance policies where the insurer reimburses the insured for the out-of-pocket expense incurred in paying a doctor's or hospital's bill look very much like classic indemnity arrangements, such as those found in property insurance. But health insurance policies typically have a schedule of benefits payable for particular kinds of services, and to that extent these policies more closely resemble life insurance or AD&D policies that pay a stipulated sum for certain kinds of losses. Not surprisingly, courts have been inconsistent when forced to decide whether the principle of indemnity must be honored in health insurance.

[4] Coordination of Benefits I: Subrogation

CUNNINGHAM v. METROPOLITAN LIFE INSURANCE CO.
121 Wis. 2d 437, 360 N.W.2d 33 (1985)

WILLIAM A. BABLITCH, JUSTICE.

Michael Cunningham seeks review of a court of appeals' decision that Metropolitan Life Insurance Company (Metropolitan) was equitably subrogated to Cunningham's interest in the settlement proceeds of Cunningham's wrongful death action against third-party tortfeasors.

. . . .

Background

The parties stipulated to the facts. On September 11, 1978, Helene Cunningham, the plaintiff's minor daughter, was involved in an automobile accident. She sustained serious injuries, for which she was hospitalized, and which ultimately resulted in her death four months later.

At the time of the accident, Michael Cunningham was employed by the American Can Company. As an employee, he and his dependents were covered under Metropolitan's group insurance policy which contained two riders: 1) "Group Hospitalization and Physicians' Services Benefits Insurance Rider" and 2) "Group Medical Expense Insurance-Extended Coverage". [Editor's note: These riders are quoted later in the opinion.] Metropolitan paid Cunningham $80,069 in benefits, representing medical expenses incurred by Cunningham, as a result of his daughter's injuries. . . . The parties stipulated that the policy contained no express subrogation clause.

Cunningham made and settled claims for the wrongful death of his minor daughter against third-party tortfeasors, including the liability insurer of the automobile in which Helene was riding. The parties agreed that $20,000 of the settlement proceeds from the liability insurer would be held in a trust account pending a judicial determination of Metropolitan's subrogation rights. If subrogation rights were found to exist, the parties agreed that the $20,000 plus interest, less certain disbursements, would fully satisfy Metropolitan's claim. The policy was appended in its entirety to the agreed statement of facts.

On the basis of these stipulated facts, Cunningham moved for summary judgment. The court denied this motion on December 2, 1981, finding that the group policy was one of indemnity. The parties subsequently stipulated to a supplementary statement of facts in light of the trial court's determination that the policy was an indemnity contract and that Metropolitan had subrogation rights. It was agreed that Cunningham had been made whole by Metropolitan's payments, the settlement proceeds of the wrongful death claim, and further settlement proceeds from another contributing tortfeasor. An additional $5,248.75, representing 40 percent of another settlement from a contributing tortfeasor, was placed in the trust account. The trial court then ordered judgment for Metropolitan.

On Cunningham's appeal, the court of appeals affirmed the trial court's judgment. Relying on this court's decision in *Rixmann v. Somerset Public Schools,* 83 Wis. 2d 571, 266 N.W.2d 326 (1978), the court determined that the applicable provisions of the policy provided coverage "for the actual medical expenses incurred", rather than for a "fixed sum upon the occurrence of a specified event." *Cunningham v. Metropolitan Life Ins. Co.,* 116 Wis. 2d 331, 336, 342 N.W.2d 60 (Ct. App. 1983). Therefore, the court said, the policy was an indemnity contract, not an investment contract, and Metropolitan was equitably subrogated to the proceeds of Cunningham's tort recovery. *Id.* at 339, 342 N.W.2d 60.

Cunningham subsequently filed a petition for review, which was granted. The sole issue for review is:

Under the specific language in the group medical and the group hospitalization riders under which Metropolitan reimbursed Cunningham for his daughter's medical expenses, is Metropolitan subrogated to Cunningham's recovery of expenses from third party tortfeasors in the absence of an express subrogation clause? We hold that the medical expense rider of the policy was one of indemnity and that Metropolitan was equitably subrogated to the medical expense portion of Cunningham's recovery. We find, however, that the hospitalization rider of the policy was one of investment, and that Metropolitan has no subrogation rights as to this portion of Cunningham's recovery. The record before this court is devoid of any accounting which reveals how much Metropolitan paid under each of the insurance riders, and how much of the settlement proceeds were paid under each of the insurance categories. Therefore, we remand to the trial court for further proceedings consistent with this opinion.

Subrogation is an equitable remedy which operates when a victim of loss is entitled to recover from two sources, one of whom bears a primary legal responsibility. If the secondary source pays the obligation, it succeeds to the rights of the party it has paid, against the third party, who was the primarily responsible party. *See* 1 G.E. Palmer, Law of Restitution § 1.5(b) (1978).

The doctrine of subrogation, when applied in the insurance context, deals with the right of the insurer to be put in the position of the insured in order to pursue recovery from third parties, legally responsible to the insured, for a loss paid by the insurer to the insured. 16 G. Couch, Couch on Insurance 2d (Rev. ed.) section 61:1 (1983). If the insured has been compensated in full by the insurer for the loss sustained, and subsequently receives recovery from a third party, the insurer's right becomes a right to the proceeds if subrogation is found to apply. 16 G. Couch, section 61:29.

The purpose of subrogation is to place the loss ultimately on the wrongdoers. 3 J.A. Appleman, Insurance Law and Practice, § 1675 (1967, Supp. 1984);. It also prevents the insured from recouping a windfall double recovery. 3 J.A. Appleman, section 1675. This court has acknowledged this purpose and has stated:

> ". . . in the absence of this doctrine the insured might often recover more than a full indemnity, and to prevent such result the courts have adopted the rule that the insured shall be entitled to only one full indemnity for the injury sustained, and from this the doctrine of subrogation has arisen. As a general rule, therefore, applicable to insurance and indemnity contracts of all kinds, the insurer, on paying to the insured the amount of the loss on the property insured, is subrogated in a corresponding amount to the insured's right of action against any other person responsible for the loss. Likewise, where the tortious conduct of a third person is the cause of a loss covered by an insurance policy, the insurer, upon payment of the loss, becomes subrogated pro tanto by operation of law to whatever right the insured may have against the wrongdoer. The theory is that to permit the insured to receive payment from both the wrongdoer and the insured would be to give him double compensation for his loss, and that it would be unjust to compel the insurer to suffer the consequences of the wrongful act of another by permitting such wrongdoer to shield himself by the theory that the loss was covered by insurance."

D'Angelo v. Cornell Paperboard Products Co., 19 Wis. 2d 390, 401–02, 120 N.W.2d 70 (1963) (quoting 8 G. Couch, Couch on Insurance. Section 1977, at 6590 (1st edition)).

An additional purpose which underlies the doctrine of subrogation is that it prevents the policy holder from receiving more than he or she bargained for from the contract of insurance. Commentators in the field have suggested that if the insurer has only contracted to indemnify the insured for losses incurred, denying the insurer subrogation rights in effect rewrites the policy and allows the insured to retain benefits not contracted for. Kimball & Davis, *The Extension of Insurance Subrogation,* 60 Mich. L. Rev. 841, 841–42 (1962). Other proponents of the subrogation doctrine assert that it returns the excess, duplicative proceeds to the insurer who can then recycle them in the form of lower insurance premiums. Fleming, *The Collateral Source Rule and Loss Allocation in Tort Law,* 54 Calif. L. Rev. 1478, 1481–84 (1966).

Subrogation may exist by operation of law, i.e. equitable subrogation, or may arise by contract of the parties, i.e. conventional subrogation. G. Couch, *supra* at sections 61:1, 61:2. The party who is seeking to prove subrogation has the burden of introducing evidence to that effect.

This court has given effect to express subrogation clauses contained in insurance contracts, including medical and hospital expense insurance contracts. Where there is no express subrogation clause, however, the policy itself must be analyzed to determine whether it is a policy of investment or a policy of indemnity.

If the contract is found to be one of indemnity, this court will allow the insurer to receive subrogation, even in the absence of an express subrogation clause. If the contract is found to be one of investment, this court will not permit the insurer to receive subrogation in the absence of an express subrogation clause. *Gatzweiler v. Milwaukee E.R. & L. Co.,* 136 Wis. 34, 38, 116 N.W. 633 (1908).

As we stated in *Gatzweiler:*

> . . . if such a company desires protection against loss caused by the wrongs of third persons who would ordinarily be liable they must do so by the contracts they make; that in the absence of a feature expressly making the policy of insurance an indemnity contract, it should not be regarded as such, but held to be an investment contract in which the only parties concerned are the insurer and the assured or the beneficiary.

Id. at 39, 116 N.W. 633. . . .

The investment-indemnity contract distinction has historically turned upon more than merely the measurement of liability, whether it be measured by fixed sum or by the extent of the insured's loss. The availability of subrogation has generally depended on the type of coverage involved; courts have implied rights of subrogation under policies covering property damages, i.e. fire insurance and property insurance. *Frost v. Porter Leasing Corp.,* 386 Mass. 425, 436 N.E.2d 387, (1982). *See generally* 3 J.A. Appleman, *supra* section 1675 at 495. The insurer's obligation under a property insurance policy is only viewed as a duty to indemnify the insured for actual loss. *Frost,* 436 N.E.2d at 389; 16 G. Couch, *supra* section 61:8. The insured's loss for property damage can generally be liquidated, and tort recovery is comparable, if not the same as the insurance coverage. *Frost,* 436 N.E.2d at 389.

Courts have not recognized implied rights of subrogation in the area of personal insurance, a category that has included life insurance benefits, medical expense and hospitalization benefits, and accident benefits.

The case law. . .is summarized in 3 J.A. Appleman, *supra,* section 1675 at 495 as follows:

> In personal insurance contracts, however the loss is never capable of ascertainment. Life and death, health, physical well being, and such

matters, are incapable of exact financial estimation. There are, accordingly, not the same reasons militating against a double recovery. The general rule is, therefore, that the insurer is not subrogated to the beneficiary's rights under contracts of personal insurance, at least in the absence of a policy provision so providing.

See also 73 A.L.R.3d 1140, pp. 1142–43. This unwillingness to recognize legal subrogation in the area of personal injury may be based on the court's recognition that the insured's receipt of both tort damages and insurance benefits may not produce a duplicative result given that the insured is likely to have suffered intangible losses that are not indemnified by either the insurer or the third-party tortfeasor.

Our case law has not explicitly embraced the property versus personal insurance distinctions, but it has nonetheless proven to be entirely consistent with the general trends in each of these areas. . . .

. . . .

We begin by noting that the construction of an insurance policy is generally a question of law to be determined independently on appeal. We further note that this state follows a policy of strict construction of insurance policies, resolving ambiguities against the insurer and in favor of the insured. Therefore, subrogation clauses and indemnity clauses must be strictly construed against the insurer in the event of any ambiguity or obscurity.

We conclude that the "Group Medical Expense Insurance-Extended Coverage" rider, issued in 1973, is one of indemnity. Therefore, Metropolitan is equitably subrogated to the extent of the payments it made under this rider to Cunningham's claims against third party proceeds paid under this policy. We base our conclusion on the express language of this rider which provides unambiguous language regarding the indemnity nature of this contract. The relevant language provides:

> If benefits have been paid hereunder on account of services received by the Employee or by a Dependent and thereafter it is established that the charges for such services were not paid by the Employee or the Dependent, or said Employee or Dependent was otherwise reimbursed therefor, the Insurance Company shall be entitled to a refund of the amount of the benefits paid which is in excess of the benefits that would have been payable based on the actual charges incurred and paid by the Employee or the Dependent.

It is clear that the purpose of this rider was to indemnify the insured from whatever loss *he or a dependent* sustained by reason of a specified hazard. Metropolitan expressly contracted to receive a refund for reimbursements the insured received for medical expenses paid by Metropolitan under this rider for the insured's dependent's care.

If the above language were the only language in the group policy to be construed, our conclusion would be in agreement with the court of appeals. However, our review of the "Group Hospitalization and Physicians' Services Benefits Rider" leads us to conclude that this rider is one of investment.

Metropolitan, in its briefs before this court and the court of appeals, argues that "Metropolitan did unambiguously define the nature of its obligation in

the policy." In support of its position with respect to the "Group Hospitalization and Physicians' Services Benefits Insurance Rider", Metropolitan's briefs
in both courts quoted language from that rider as follows: "[Section 1(A)(7)
of the 'Group Hospitalization and Physicians Services Benefits' (Appendix,
Exhibit A, p. 56)] provides that benefits payable pursuant to it 'shall be reduced by benefits paid or payable. . .from any fund, other insurance, or other
arrangement.' "

However, a reading of the language referred to in the rider itself indicates
that a comma, rather than a period, follows the word "arrangement". The
language in the policy actually reads:

> The hospitalization benefits otherwise provided for any hospital
> confinement of the *Employee* shall be reduced by any benefits paid or
> payable on account of hospital confinement for the same period or any
> part thereof from any fund, other insurance, or other arrangement,
> *provided or established in conformity with any state or other govern-
> mental disability or cash sickness or hospital benefits law.* (Emphasis
> added.)

The omitted language in the briefs ("provided or established in conformity
with any state or other governmental disability or cash sickness or hospital
benefits law.") contradicts the position of Metropolitan that "the policy itself
makes clear that its purpose is to indemnify the insured only for those out-of-
pocket losses which are not otherwise compensated." Quite to the contrary,
the omitted language makes it clear that this rider is one of investment. We
make this finding because Metropolitan has failed to put any evidence into
the record which would demonstrate that the settlement proceeds came from
a fund referred to in the omitted language. . . .

Viewing the language of the hospitalization rider as a whole further
substantiates our conclusion. The hospitalization benefits are only reduced
if the initial proceeds are paid to provide payment for the hospital confinement
of the *employee*. Nothing in this limitation paragraph permits Metropolitan
to reduce benefits paid or payable on account of benefits paid for the hospital
confinement of an insured employee's *dependent*. The definitions in the group
policy specifically define employee and dependent separately. Thus, the
limitation found in 1.A(7) is inapplicable as it applies to payments made for
Helene Cunningham's hospital confinement. Additionally we note that the
rider in 1973 for the Group Medical Expenses coverage specifically provided
for reimbursement to the insurer for duplicative benefits paid for the insured's
dependent. Having failed to do so in the hospitalization rider but not in the
medical expense rider, the omission of the word "dependent" does not appear
to be unintentional. We conclude that the hospitalization and physicians' service rider is one of investment.

We are unable to determine, based on the record presently before us, how
much of Metropolitan's insurance proceeds were paid under the Group Medical
Expense rider for which Metropolitan is entitled to equitable subrogation, and
how much of the proceeds were paid under the Group Hospitalization and
Physicians' Services rider for which Metropolitan is not entitled to equitable
subrogation. Nor are we able to determine how much of the trust proceeds

were paid to compensate Cunningham for medical expenses which Metropolitan had previously paid under its Group Medical Expense rider of the policy. We therefore remand to the trial court.

First, we direct the trial court to make a determination as to how much of the insurance benefits were paid for medical expenses, for which there is equitable subrogation, and how much of the insurance benefits were paid for the hospitalization and physicians' services, for which there is no equitable subrogation. . . .

We also direct the trial court to make a determination as to how much of the settlement proceeds were paid to compensate Cunningham for medical expenses, which were previously paid by Metropolitan under the Group Medical Expense rider. This determination is essential because legal subrogation gives indemnity only; the insurer is only entitled to that part of the tort recovery which the insurer is able to establish was paid in compensation for the same loss. G.E. Palmer, *supra* at section 23.16 at 444. An insurer who possesses a cause of action for subrogation cannot recover beyond the amount actually dispersed by it. *D'Angelo,* 19 Wis. 2d at 402, 120 N.W.2d 70. Nor can it recover from any source unless the settlement from that source actually compensates the insured for the same specific loss the insurer previously compensated it for. G.E. Palmer section 23.15 at 440. "If there is any doubt as to the facts, the doubt should be resolved in favor of the tort victim." *Id.*

In reaching the result we have, we note that controversies such as this one would not arise had the parties included an express subrogation clause in the insurance contract. We have held that an express subrogation clause in a medical insurance contract effectively serves to assign an insured's claim to his insurer.

Nevertheless, we decline to dispose of our long standing doctrine of equitable subrogation. Where it can be clearly and unequivocally determined that an insurance contract requires only that the insurer make whole the insured, then the insurer is subrogated *pro tanto* to the insured's claims against third parties. To rule otherwise would vitiate the agreement between the insurer and the insured. The right to equitable subrogation rests on the fact that the insured bargained only for indemnification of his out-of-pocket losses. Thus, the doctrine of equitable subrogation serves to promote the expectations of the parties.

Moreover, the doctrine helps to facilitate sound distribution of compensation resources. Nowhere is the need for cost control more pressing than in the field of hospitalization and medical insurance. Where a hospitalization or medical insurance policy clearly promises to indemnify the insured only for out-of-pocket losses, then the equitable subrogation doctrine serves to make the health care payment system more efficient.

The opinion of the court of appeals is affirmed in part, and reversed in part, and the cause remanded to the circuit court for further proceedings consistent with this opinion.

ABRAHAMSON, JUSTICE (concurring in part and dissenting in part).

The parties have stipulated that the policy in question contains no express subrogation provision. Were such a provision contained in the policy, it probably would have been given effect.

The insurance policy before the court is a single group policy of insurance incorporating multiple coverages — life, accident and health, hospitalization and physicians service benefits insurance and medical expense insurance extended coverage. It is a participating contract under which the employer may receive dividends. This court has not previously analyzed such a policy in terms of the doctrine of equitable (a/k/a legal) subrogation which evolved in an earlier era of insurance.

A primary function of the doctrine of equitable subrogation is to prevent an insurer from paying and an insured from receiving more than the parties bargained for in the contract of insurance. The determinative question in each case is whether the policy should be interpreted to mean that the insurer will reimburse the insured for losses not otherwise compensated or will reimburse the insured upon the occurrence of an event, notwithstanding that the loss associated with that event may be reimbursed from some other source. The indemnity/investment analysis of the policy used by the majority is a means of deciding this question.

The distinction between indemnity and investment contracts for purposes of determining legal subrogation is a tenuous one, and courts have been viewed as inept in applying it. Kimball and Davis, *The Extension of Insurance Subrogation,* 60 Mich. L. Rev. 841 (1962). This case demonstrates the futility of attempting to fit today's multitude of policies into indemnity/investment boxes.[1] Courts should not be reviewing each coverage in the myriad of multiple coverage health insurance policies to determine the insurance company's right to subrogation.

On the facts presently before the court, I would hold that in the absence of an express subrogation clause, the insurance company has no subrogation rights. If the insurance company desires subrogation in this kind of policy, it should disclose its intent to assert subrogation rights through express policy language. When subrogation rights are expressly set forth in the policy, the premiums can then be calculated properly, and the opportunity for either the insured or the insurer to receive a windfall is minimized.

If the court were to adopt the result I reach, it should come as no surprise to the insurance industry. From our prior cases, insurance companies know: first, that certain express subrogation clauses used by insurance companies writing medical and expense payment coverage and medical payment coverage have been held valid; second, that a company's failure to include an express subrogation clause puts the company at the risk of a court's affixing the label "investment" to the policy, thereby deciding that the company has no subrogation rights; and third, that "this state follows a policy of strict construction

---

[1] As the insurer implies (Brief, p. 17), and as the majority apparently holds, different provisions of the policy may dictate different resolutions of the indemnity/investment question necessary to a determination of equitable subrogation. The majority's language that only portions of the policy are examined, and not the policy as a whole, to determine the nature of the diverse coverages and the intent of the parties, if read literally, contravenes the generally accepted doctrine of contract interpretation. This language should not, I believe, be read literally. I believe it is the intent of the majority to state that it need not label the policy in toto as either an indemnity or an investment contract. Rather, it can consider each type of coverage in the policy independently, examining the policy provisions applicable to that coverage as well as the policy provisions applicable to all coverages.

of insurance policies, resolving ambiguities against the insurer and in favor of the insured."

For the reasons set forth, I concur in part and dissent in part.

STEINMETZ, JUSTICE (dissenting).

I disagree with the result and reasoning of the majority in this case. I believe it is significant that the policies were before the trial court and the court of appeals and that at no level of judicial review have the parties referred to specifically or relied on the select provisions of the policy that are relied on by the majority. I believe the policies must be looked at as a total contract. This was the view of the court of appeals also.

I would adopt as the decision in this case the one written by the court of appeals and found at *Cunningham v. Metropolitan Life Ins. Co.,* 116 Wis. 2d 331, 342 N.W.2d 60 (Ct. App. 1983).

NOTES

1. *The origins of subrogation and the "primary-secondary" distinction.* The Latin root of the word "subrogation" is *subrogare*, which means "to substitute." In Anglo-American law, subrogation is used "to describe a process by which one party is substituted for another so that he may enforce that other's rights against a third party for his own benefit." Charles Mitchell, The Law of Subrogation 3 (1994). The "primary-secondary" distinction mentioned in *Cunningham* reflects the origins of equitable, or what is often referred to as "legal," subrogation. See Edwin W. Patterson, Essentials of Insurance Law § 33, at 147–52 (2d ed. 1957). If a guarantor or surety discharged the obligation of her debtor, the guarantor or surety, who was secondarily responsible, succeeded or became subrogated to the claim of the creditor against the debtor, who was primarily responsible. This right was originally recognized in equity and was available even though there was no express provision for it in the guaranty or suretyship contract. *See* Dan B. Dobbs, Law of Remedies § 4.3(4) (2d ed. 1993). In fact, it has been suggested that subrogation is a kind of judicially created "equitable assignment" or "constructive assignment" for situations where the creditor does not expressly give this right to the party making the payment. See Ronald C. Horn, Subrogation in Insurance Theory and Practice 15 (1964). As a protection for the party making the payment, subrogation also has a very close connection to the law of restitution. The assertion of a subrogation right prevents the unjust enrichment of the debtor, who otherwise receives a windfall by virtue of the payment of her debt by a third party, which would occur at the expense of another person (i.e., the party making the payment). Is preventing unjust enrichment and promoting the principle of indemnity the same thing?

Although subrogation is not confined to insurance matters, the doctrine is often identified with insurance law because most subrogation litigation involves insurers. Does an insurer occupy the same position as a guarantor or surety in their respective relationships with the insured and the debtor? Is the primary-secondary distinction helpful in deciding which insurers have a common law right of subrogation when benefits are paid under a policy of insurance?

2. *The indemnity-investment distinction.* The court in *Cunningham* also referred to another test for recognizing a right of subrogation. This test involved an inquiry into the nature of the contract, and distinguishes indemnity contracts from investment contracts. In its most straightforward application, a property insurance policy will be viewed differently from a personal insurance policy. Is this a more efficacious test than the primary-secondary test? Does this type of analysis give the best answer to the question of whether a court should enforce an express subrogation provision in an insurance contract? If an express subrogation clause were found in a policy of term life insurance or accident insurance, should it be enforced?

3. *Subrogation rights of insurers of joint tortfeasors.* Subrogation rights have not been limited to situations involving first-party insurers pursuing their insureds' claims against third-party tortfeasors, such as a physical damage insurer under an auto collision coverage pursuing its insured's claim against a third-party who negligently damages the insured vehicle. There is precedent for the proposition that an insurer of a joint tortfeasor who settles with the tort victim may pursue a right of contribution or indemnity possessed by the insured against another joint tortfeasor. *See Zeglen v. Minkiewicz,* 12 N.Y.2d 497, 191 N.E.2d 450, 240 N.Y.S.2d 965 (1963) (contribution) and *American Home Assurance Co. v. City of Opa Locka,* 368 So. 2d 416 (Fla. Dist. Ct. App. 1979) (indemnity). Would it be possible to resolve all of these cases under the law of restitution?

4. *Statutory subrogation rights.* Subrogation rights can also be created by statute. For example, workers' compensation statutes commonly provide for subrogation rights on behalf of the state fund or carrier to any third-party tort claims of an injured employee. *See, e.g.,* Ariz. Rev. Stat. § 23-1023. In a similar vein, the Federal Medical Care Recovery Act (FMCRA) was passed in 1962 to provide the United States government with a right to reimbursement as subrogee to any third-party tort claims of certain individuals, such as military personnel and their dependents, who receive free medical or dental care from the federal government as a result of injuries caused by third parties. 42 U.S.C. § 2651. In automobile insurance, it is common for statutes to create, limit, or prohibit subrogation with respect to uninsured, underinsured, first-party medical payments, and no-fault coverages. Statutory subrogation provisions trump inconsistent terms in the insurance contract under the reasoning that the insurer consents to the requirements of state law when in does business in the state. Furthermore, policies are deemed to contain statutorily-required provisions, whatever the text of the policy might say.

5. *Subrogation and personal injury claims.* The general rule is that assigning a cause of action for personal injury is against public policy. See generally Andrea G. Nadel, Annotation, Assignability of Proceeds of Claim for Personal Injury or Death, 33 A.L.R.4th 82 (1984). So, what happens when the insurer makes a payment to its insured for medical expenses (or, in the case of an HMO, provides medical care) required on account of a third-party's negligence, and the insurer seeks subrogation against the tortfeasor? If the essence of subrogation is giving the insurer the right to bring the insured's claim against

the tortfeasor, is this tantamount to an impermissible assignment of the insured's personal injury cause of action to the insurer? Consider the next case.

MAHLER v. SZUCS

135 Wash. 2d 398, 957 P.2d 632 (1998) (en banc)

TALMADGE, Justice.

In this case we analyze an insurer's right to recover payments made to an insured pursuant to a Personal Injury Protection (PIP) provision * in a liability insurance policy when an insured recovers against a tortfeasor. Specifically, we are asked to determine the extent to which the insurer, State Farm Mutual Automobile Insurance Company (State Farm), must pay the insured a share of the expenses the insured incurred to recover from the tortfeasor. . . .

. . . .

[Two separate actions were consolidated for review by the court. The underlying facts of each case involved State Farm's insured being injured in an auto accident due to the negligence of a third party. State Farm paid PIP benefits to each of its insureds. Thereafter, each insured, represented by respective counsel, secured a settlement from the tortfeasor, each of which was insured by other insurance companies. In each case, an amount equal to the PIP benefits paid was placed in escrow pending determination of the amount of State Farm's interest in the recovery. In neither case did State Farm assist the attorney in procuring the settlement. The attorneys in each action demanded that State Farm accept in its status as subrogee less than the full amount of PIP benefits paid under the reasoning that State Farm should share in the cost of securing the settlement. State Farm refused both requests.

In the "Mahler action," State Farm filed a claim against the tortfeasor's insurer for the amount of the PIP benefits. A private arbitration panel, convened under the auspices of the insurance companies' inter-company arbitration agreement, decided in State Farm's favor under the reasoning that the tortfeasor's insurer had failed to protect State Farm's interests. In the meantime, an arbitrator awarded Mahler an attorney fee credit of $1,391 against the PIP funds in the trust account. State Farm challenged the award in the trial court, but the trial court entered a judgment for $1,612 in favor of Mahler (the additional amount representing an award of attorney fees for her being forced to litigate her rights under the policy), but without any

---

* [Editors' note: PIP benefits are first-party benefits provided by many automobile insurance policies. Exactly what is denominated a PIP benefit varies from state to state, but medical expenses and wage losses suffered as a result of an accident, funeral expenses, and rehabilitation expenses are common coverages. They are paid without regard to whether the insured is at fault in an accident. If a third-party is (solely) at fault, that third-party — or his liability insurer—will be responsible for all damages, including the medical expenses incurred by the insured. If the PIP insurer pays these benefits to an insured-victim, the PIP insurer will desire to recover the amount of these payments from the tortfeasor or the tortfeasor's insurer.]

findings and conclusions in support of the award. Both parties sought direct review of the award in the Washington Supreme Court.

In the "Fisher action," State Farm sought reimbursement of its PIP payments from the tortfeasor's insurer, but the insurer refused on the ground that it had already paid Fisher's settlement amount and would not pay twice for the same loss. State Farm did not invoke inter-company arbitration in this instance. In Fisher's interpleader action to determine the fate of the funds placed in the court's registry, the trial court agreed with State Farm and ordered the entire sum to be disbursed to State Farm, without any payment to Fisher. The Court of Appeals reversed. *Fisher v. Aldi Tire, Inc.*, 78 Wash.App. 902, 902 P.2d 166 (1995), review denied, 128 Wash.2d 1025, 913 P.2d 816 (1996). On remand, the trial court held that state Farm's PIP payments were recoverable through intercompany arbitration "but for the interference by the insured's attorney." Fisher sought direct review, and the case was consolidated with the Mahler action.]

We are confronted in these cases with a series of practical and theoretical concerns in interpreting State Farm's policy provisions regarding reimbursement for PIP benefits advanced to insureds and whether State Farm must share with its insureds the expenses necessary to secure recoveries from tortfeasors. However, the issues in this case so starkly divide the plaintiffs' personal injury bar on the one hand, and the insurance industry and the insurance defense bar on the other, both sides are often emotional and not well-focused on the real issues at stake in this case. For this reason, it is useful to resort to basic principles to resolve the issues here.

. . . .

All of the parties have argued subrogation principles resolve the issues in these cases. Subrogation is an equitable doctrine the essential purpose of which is to provide for a proper allocation of payment responsibility. It seeks to impose ultimate responsibility for a wrong or loss on the party who, in equity and good conscience, ought to bear it. Ronald C. Horn, Subrogation in Insurance Theory and Practice 3 (1964). Two law review commentators have referred to this allocation rationale as stemming from "the moralistic basis of tort law as it has developed in our system." Spencer L. Kimball & Don A. Davis, *The Extension of Insurance Subrogation*, 60 Mich. L. Rev. 841, 841(1962).[4] "The general purpose of subrogation is to facilitate placement of the financial consequences of loss on the party primarily responsible in law for such loss." Horn, *supra*, at 24.

---

[4] We are not persuaded that one rationale for subrogation in the insurance context is "to prevent unjust enrichment of the insured," as the Court of Appeals said below. *Fisher*, 78 Wash.App. at 906, 902 P.2d 166. The notion is the insured would be unjustly enriched if he or she received PIP payments from an insurer and subsequently recovered special damages from the tortfeasor duplicating the PIP payments. First, the asserted rationale does not appear in classical discussions of the purposes of subrogation. *See, e.g., Aetna Life Ins. Co. v. Town of Middleport*, 124 U.S. 534, 8 S.Ct. 625, 31 L.Ed. 537 (1888). Second, Washington public policy is altogether to the contrary. "It is a well settled rule in tort actions that a party has a cause of action notwithstanding the payment of his loss by an insurance company." *Consolidated Freightways v. Moore*, 38 Wash.2d 427, 430, 229 P.2d 882 (1951); *Ciminski v. SCI Corp.*, 90 Wash.2d 802, 585 P.2d 1182 (1978). The Legislature has abolished the collateral source rule in the specific case of injuries occurring as a result of health care, but not in other contexts. RCW 7.70.080. We reject the notion that subrogation principles trump the collateral source rule.

Subrogation has existed in civil law longer than in common law. Henry N. Sheldon, Subrogation 3 (2d ed. 1893); James Morfit Mullen, *The Equitable Doctrine of Subrogation*, 3 Md. L. Rev. 201, 201 (1939). It applies in cases involving multiple claims upon the same property, suretyship, joint debtors, parties to bills and notes, the administration of estates, and contracts of insurance. Subrogation is favored in Washington law. "Subrogation is always liberally allowed in the interests of justice and equity." *J.D. O'Malley & Co. v. Lewis,* 176 Wash. 194, 201, 28 P.2d 283 (1934).

There are, in effect, two features to subrogation. The first is the right to reimbursement. The second is the mechanism for the enforcement of the right. The right to reimbursement may arise by operation of law, termed legal or equitable subrogation, or by contract, called conventional subrogation. *Ross v. Jones,* 174 Wash. 205, 216, 24 P.2d 622 (1933).

The more troublesome question is the precise enforcement mechanism for the subrogee's right of reimbursement. Considerable imprecision on this question is present in case law on subrogation. By virtue of payments made to a subrogor stemming from the actions of a third party, a subrogee has a right of reimbursement under general subrogation principles. That reimbursement may be enforced as a type of lien against any recovery the subrogor secures from the third party. Alternatively, the subrogee, standing in the shoes of its subrogor, may pursue an action in the subrogor's name against the third party to enforce the reimbursement right.

In the insurance context, the "doctrine of subrogation enables an insurer that has paid an insured's loss pursuant to a policy. . .to recoup the payment from the party responsible for the loss." Elaine M. Rinaldi, *Apportionment of Recovery Between Insured and Insurer in a Subrogation Case*, 29 Tort & Ins. L. J. 803, 803 (1994). Traditionally, subrogation in the context of insurance concerned cases of marine and fire losses. In a typical case of a fire loss, upon payment of the loss to the insured, the property insurer would be subrogated to the extent of its payment to the remedies of the insured against the party that caused the loss. This traditional application of subrogation principles is in accord with the policy of allocating to the causer of the loss the cost of reimbursing the person (the insurer) who paid for the loss. Property loss subrogation caused few disputes between the insurer and the insured, because once the insured had recovered from the insurer the economic value of the loss, the insured had little or no interest in competing with the insurer for the right to sue the tortfeasor; economic damages could make the insured whole.

It has been only in the last 30 to 40 years that subrogation disputes regarding personal injury cases have arisen. "During this period, subrogation clauses have been inserted in first party medical payments coverage in automobile policies, uninsured and underinsured motorist coverage, and medical and hospitalization coverages." Roger M. Baron, *Subrogation on Medical Expense Claims: The "Double Recovery" Myth and the Feasibility of Anti-Subrogation Laws*, 96 Dick. L. Rev. 581, 583 (1992).[6] In the personal injury

---

[6] For instance, "until 1958 the subrogation clauses that were included in the standard forms for automobile insurance specifically were not applicable to medical payments coverages." Robert E. Keeton & Alan I. Widiss, Insurance Law 228 (1988). "Automobile medical payments coverage

context, where insureds may wish to pursue claims for noneconomic damages, i.e., pain and suffering, disputes regarding the right to subrogation have proliferated.

The complexities are readily apparent. By contrast with a property loss case, where the damages are all economic and usually readily determinable, so that the insured can be made whole by the payment of money, in a personal injury case, the claimed noneconomic damages typically amount to many multiples of the economic damages and are almost always disputed because they are not objectively ascertainable. Thus, rather than stepping aside and allowing the insurer to pursue the tortfeasor by means of subrogation for the money it paid its insured, the injured insured will often sue the tortfeasor to recover noneconomic damages, and include in the claim the medical expenses and other special damages he or she has incurred as a result of the injury. In effect, the injured insured does not abandon its shoes, and its insurer thus has no shoes to step into to pursue subrogation.

The potential for conflict of interest abounds in such circumstances. Both insurer and insured, having entered into an insurance contract, are bound by the common law duty of good faith and fair dealing, as well as the statutory duty "to practice honesty and equity in all insurance matters." RCW 48.01.030. We have said the statute creates a fiduciary duty for insurers running to their insureds. *Industrial Indem. Co. of the Northwest, Inc. v. Kallevig,* 114 Wash.2d 907, 916–17, 792 P.2d 520 (1990). Yet the injured insured seeks recovery from the tortfeasor, the same source to which the insurer may look to recover its payments to its insured.[7]

As a result of these new conflicts, some courts initially refused to allow subrogation in the personal injury context, basing their denials on the common law rules against splitting causes of action and assigning personal injury claims. Baron, *supra,* at 583 (citing cases). Most jurisdictions, however, now allow subrogation. J.A. Bock, Annotation, *Subrogation Rights of Insurer Under Medical Payments Provision of Automobile Insurance Policy,* 19 A.L.R.3d 1054.

We have dealt with some of these difficulties as they have arisen since the advent of subrogation in insurance contracts involving personal injury claims. In general, the right of reimbursement in the insurance setting may arise by contract or equitable means. The right may be enforced contractually by an insurer's right to recover from the insured the amount of payments made from any recovery the insured secures from a third party tortfeasor or by a legal action in the name of the insured against the tortfeasor. We have articulated

---

is of comparatively recent origin. It was conceived and reared without benefit of subrogation, and only during the past few years have *some* automobile insurers undertaken to wrap it in a mantle of subrogation." *Travelers Indem. Co. v. Chumbley,* 394 S.W.2d 418, 425, 19 A.L.R.3d 1043 (Mo.App.1965).

[7] We are dubious that two actions arising from the same tort against a tortfeasor may proceed either simultaneously or consecutively, one by the injured insured seeking noneconomic damages, and another by the injured insured's PIP carrier seeking recovery of its PIP payments. Elementary considerations of the undesirability of claim splitting and of fairness to the defendant tortfeasor militate against such an outcome. "The doctrine of claim preclusion prohibits claim splitting as a matter of policy, primarily in order to conserve judicial resources and to ensure repose for parties who have already responded adequately to the plaintiff's claims." *Babcock v. State,* 112 Wash.2d 83, 93, 768 P.2d 481 (1989).

basic principles of subrogation in the insurance setting in three decisions: *Metropolitan Life Ins. Co. v. Ritz*, 70 Wash.2d 317, 422 P.2d 780 (1967); *Thiringer v. American Motors Ins. Co.*, 91 Wash.2d 215, 588 P.2d 191 (1978); and *Leader Nat'l Ins. Co. v. Torres*, 113 Wash.2d 366, 779 P.2d 722 (1989).

In *Metropolitan Life*, the insurer paid medical benefits to the insured, pursuant to a group policy which contained a subrogation provision. Nevertheless, the insured entered into a complete release of all claims against a third party tortfeasor without specifically referencing the insurer's interest. We stated the general release "deprived" the insurer of subrogation rights, noting the insurer "was entitled either to reimbursement from [the insured] or to be subrogated to [the insured's] claim for medical expenses against the tortfeasor." *Metropolitan Life*, 70 Wash.2d at 321, 422 P.2d 780. The Court held the insurer could secure reimbursement from the insured's recovery from the tortfeasor, subject to the insurer's obligation to share proportionately in the insured's expenses incurred to obtain the settlement.

In *Thiringer*, an insurer refused to pay PIP benefits to an insured, and the insured settled with a tortfeasor. The insured then demanded PIP benefits because his damages exceeded the amount of the settlement. The trial court held the settlement reasonable and the insurer's subrogation rights were not prejudiced by it. The trial court held further that the settlement amount was to be first applied to the insured's general damages and then, if any excess remained, toward the payment of the special damages to which the insurer's PIP coverage applied. We held the insured's release did not prejudice the insurer's subrogation right so as to invalidate the insured's right to PIP benefits, noting *Thiringer*, 91 Wash.2d at 219, 588 P.2d 191:

> the policy quite reasonably contemplates that the insured may pursue his remedy against a third party, and the only restriction is that he must not do any act to prejudice the rights of the insurer. Since the losses covered by the PIP provision may represent only a minor portion of an insured's total damage, it would be patently unfair to require him to surrender his right of action against a third party in order to receive this payment. Also, it is unrealistic to expect that a third party will accept only a partial release when he settles a claim, under circumstances such as those presented here.

Moreover, with respect to the allocation of benefits, we articulated a rule of full compensation, that is, no right of reimbursement existed for the insurer until the insured was fully compensated for a loss:

> The general rule is that, while an insurer is entitled to be reimbursed to the extent that its insured recovers payment for the same loss from a tortfeasor responsible for the damage, it can recover only the excess which the insured has received from the wrongdoer, remaining after the insured is fully compensated for his loss.
>
> > This rule embodies a policy deemed socially desirable in this state, in that it fosters the adequate indemnification of innocent automobile accident victims.

Thiringer, 91 Wash.2d at 219–20, 588 P.2d 191 (citations omitted). *Thiringer* is in accord with the great majority of jurisdictions in following this "full compensation for the insured" rule. Rinaldi, *supra*, at 807.

Finally, in *Leader Nat'l*, the insured received $10,000 in medical payments under a PIP policy provision. The insured then sought $5,211.10 in unreimbursed special damages and general damages from a tortfeasor, ultimately settling with the tortfeasor for a total of $10,000. Both the insured and the tortfeasor were aware of the insured's subrogation right, the insurer did not consent to the settlement, and the tortfeasor had additional assets. Under these circumstances, we held the settlement between the insured and the tortfeasor did not extinguish the insurer's subrogation right *against the third party tortfeasor*. We held the risk of loss in such a context must be borne, not by the insured, but by the tortfeasor or the insurer. *Leader Nat'l,* 113 Wash.2d at 372, 779 P.2d 722.

These cases are consistent with the general view that subrogation creates in the insurer, by contract or equity, a right to be reimbursed. The enforcement of the interest, whether by a type of lien against the subrogor/insured's recovery from a tortfeasor or by an action by the subrogee/insurer in the name of the insured against the tortfeasor, is governed by the general public policy of full compensation of the insured, tempered by the principle that the insured and/or a tortfeasor may not knowingly prejudice the right of the insurer to be reimbursed.

With these principles at hand, we proceed to discuss the issues in the present cases.

. . . .

The State Farm policy language with respect to recovery of its PIP payments and the sharing of expenses is essentially identical in both the Mahler and Fisher policies. In the "Conditions" section of the policy, under the heading, "Our Right to Recover Our Payments," the following language appears:

a. Medical payments, death, dismemberment and loss of sight and total disability coverage payments are not recoverable by us.

b. Under personal injury protection and underinsured motor vehicle coverages, we are subrogated to the extent of our payments to the proceeds of any settlement the injured person recovers from any party liable for the bodily injury or property damage.

If the person to or for whom we have made payment has not recovered our payment from the party at fault, he or she shall:

(1) keep these rights in trust for us and do nothing to impair them;

(2) execute any legal papers we need; and

(3) when we ask, take legal action through our representative to recover our payments.

We are to be repaid our payments, costs and fees of collection out of any recovery.

c. Under all other coverages the right of recovery of any party we pay passes to us. Such party shall:

(1) not hurt our rights to recover; and

(2) help us get our money back.

d. If the insured recovers from the party at fault and we share in the recovery, we will pay our share of the legal expenses. Our share is that percent of the legal expenses that the amount we recover bears to the total recovery. This does not apply to any amounts recovered or recoverable by us from any other insurer under any inter-insurer arbitration agreement.

Our right to recover our payments applies only after the insured has been fully compensated for the bodily injury, property damage or loss.

Paragraph b of the State Farm policy establishes State Farm's right to reimbursement, but it articulates two distinct mechanisms for enforcement of the right.

In the first paragraph of Paragraph b, the phrase "[w]e are subrogated to the extent of our payments to the proceeds of any settlement the injured person recovers from any party liable for the bodily injury or property damage" is significant. First, this phrase refers only to the proceeds of settlements, and not to the proceeds of any judgments the insured might obtain. Second, the phrase speaks of the "proceeds of any settlement," thereby suggesting State Farm's contractual right to recover payments from its insureds under PIP or UIM coverage arises only *after* settlement. There are obviously no proceeds of a settlement until the settlement occurs.

The policy language says State Farm is "subrogated" to those proceeds. The meaning here is indistinct. "No right of subrogation can arise in favor of an insurer against its own insured since, by definition, subrogation exists only with respect to rights of the insurer against third persons to whom the insurer owes no duty." *Stetina v. State Farm Mut. Auto. Ins. Co.,* 196 Neb. 441, 243 N.W.2d 341, 346 (1976). This language plainly does not contemplate State Farm will step into the shoes of its insureds and pursue their claims against the tortfeasors. Instead, State Farm has simply contracted for a right to reimbursement of its PIP payments *from its insureds* from the proceeds of a settlement.

The Supreme Court of Oregon considered nearly identical policy language in *State Farm Mut. Auto. Ins. Co. v. Pohl,* 255 Or. 46, 464 P.2d 321 (1970). The State Farm policy provided:

Upon payment. . .the company shall be subrogated to the extent of such payment to the proceeds of any settlement or judgment that may result from the exercise of any rights of recovery which the injured person or anyone receiving such payment may have against any person or organization and such person shall execute and deliver instruments and papers and do whatever else is necessary to secure such rights. Such person shall do nothing after loss to prejudice such rights.

Id. 464 P.2d at 322 (alteration in original). The specific issue before the Oregon court was whether this language created a right of subrogation in State Farm. The court held it did not: "The literal language of the clause only purports to transfer an interest in moneys after they become the property of the insured. The clause creates a right in the proceeds, not against the tortfeasor." *Id.* at 324. We agree.

By contrast, in the second paragraph of Paragraph b and in Paragraph c, State Farm contracted with its insureds for a traditional subrogation right to recover payments made to its insureds. In the second paragraph of Paragraph b, State Farm indicated it would "take legal action through our representative to recover our [PIP or UIM] payments" when "the person to or for whom we have made payment has not recovered our payment from the party at fault." Thus, State Farm has reserved a traditional subrogation right to sue in the shoes of the insured *only* when it makes PIP payments to the insured and the insured does not pursue a tortfeasor. Similarly, Paragraph c quoted above succinctly creates a subrogation right: "Under all other coverages the right of recovery of any party we pay passes to us." This assignment of rights is a proper, classical subrogation clause.

Thus, by its terms Paragraph b creates a contractual right of reimbursement, not a right to subrogation, when an insured pursues an action or seeks recovery from a tortfeasor.[10] With this understanding of State Farm's insurance contract, we proceed to the central issue in this case: whether, and to what extent, State Farm must share with its insureds any expenses necessary to obtain a settlement from a tortfeasor.

[In the remainder of the opinion, the court held that State Farm's policy required it to pay its insureds a portion of their expenses necessary to obtain a recovery from the tortfeasors. State Farm was not obligated to pay prejudgment interest on Mahler's expenses, but it was obligated to pay Mahler's attorney fees to enforce the sharing of expenses. The case was remanded to the trial court for the entry of findings and conclusions with respect to the reasonable amount of the fees.]

DOLLIVER, SMITH, GUY and JOHNSON, JJ., concur.

[The separate concurring opinion of Justice Madsen is omitted, as is the dissenting opinion of Justice Alexander.].

NOTES

1. *A public policy prohibiting subrogation?* The court in *Mahler* endorsed the rule that the PIP insurer has a right of reimbursement out of any recovery the insureds obtained from the tortfeasor. Not all courts, however, agree with this result, as the court in *Mahler* acknowledged. A minority of jurisdictions holds that a subrogation clause regarding medical payments coverage in an auto policy which gives the insurer a right to bring the insured's action against a tortfeasor is an attempt to assign a cause of action for personal injuries and, consequently, is void because such assignments violate public policy. *Allstate Insurance Co. v. Reitler*, 628 P.2d 667 (Mont. 1981) (listing cases in the minority and majority). The minority rule has been extended, in some

---

[10] State Farm does not argue equitable subrogation applies in these cases. If equitable subrogation did apply, we would be compelled to consider under equitable principles the sharing of legal fees incurred in obtaining recoveries from the tortfeasors.

jurisdictions, to the "right to proceeds" type of clause (like that found in paragraph (b) of the State Farm policy in *Mahler*) and also to a clause which states that the insured is to "repay [the insurer] out of the proceeds," which is similar to the subparagraph (3) portion of paragraph (b) in the *Mahler* policy. *See Allstate Insurance Co. v. Druke,* 118 Ariz. 301, 576 P.2d 489 (1978). What public policies arguably support the minority rule? What public policies support the majority approach?

If a jurisdiction refuses to enforce a subrogation clause under medical payments coverage in an auto policy on the basis that it is an attempted assignment of a cause of action for personal injuries, should the same rule apply to all insurance contracts for medical expenses in that jurisdiction? Is there any problem in recognizing the subrogation rights of the insurer under first-party coverages for property damage, as compared to coverages for medical care, in a jurisdiction that follows the minority rule?

2. *Comparing subrogation to assignments.* Is a subrogation clause the same thing as, or tantamount to, an assignment? What are the evils or problems in permitting assignments of causes of action for personal injuries? Do those same evils or problems exist with subrogation clauses in insurance policies that provide indemnity? *Compare Westchester Fire Insurance Co. v. Allstate Insurance Co.,* 672 A.2d 939, 945 (1996) ("equitable subrogation is not the equivalent of the assignment of a personal injury action"), with *Wine v. Globe American Casualty Co.,* 917 S.W.2d 558, 564 (Ky. 1996) ("Although in abstract terms an assignment differs from subrogation, in the field of insurance subrogation the distinction is academic and not a substantive matter.").

When insurers attempt to avoid the effect of the rule against assignments of causes of action for personal injuries by casting the subrogation clause in terms of creating a right against the proceeds as opposed to a right against the tortfeasor, other difficulties can appear. In *State Farm Mutual Automobile Insurance Co. v. Pohl,* 255 Or. 46, 464 P.2d 321 (1970), which the court in *Mahler* cited with approval, State Farm's insured was injured while riding in a car when it was struck by a truck being negligently operated by Pohl. State Farm paid its insured's medical expenses, notified the Pohls of its subrogation rights, and requested reimbursement. The Pohls subsequently settled with State Farm's insured for an amount that included medical expenses, and State Farm brought a subrogation action against the Pohls. The prior iteration of the State Farm policy provided, in relevant part, that "[u]pon payment. . .the company shall be subrogated to the extent of such payment to the proceeds of any settlement or judgment that may result from the exercise of any rights of recovery" the insured might have against third parties. The court observed that the "to the proceeds" phrase was designed to circumvent some courts' holdings that a subrogation clause not similarly restricted was invalid as an attempt to assign a personal injury claim. See 464 P.2d at 323. The Pohls argued, however, that this clause gave State Farm a right only to proceeds, not to a claim against the tortfeasor, and the court agreed. *Id.* at 324. How does the text of the policy in the *Mahler* case avoid the problem faced by State Farm in *Pohl*?

3. *Express versus implied right of subrogation.* Should it make any difference that there is a written or express subrogation provision in an auto medical

payments coverage or in a group hospital or medical policy, as compared to a similar policy that is silent on the subject of subrogation? If a court would enforce the written or express provision, should it also recognize an implied or equitable right of subrogation where the contract is silent? *See Frost v. Porter Leasing Corp.*, 386 Mass. 425, 436 N.E.2d 387 (1982).

4. *Subrogation by HMOs.* HMOs and other managed care entities provide health care services directly, instead of reimbursing the insured for payments the insured has made to doctors and hospitals (or simply making the payment directly to the health care provider in satisfaction of the insured's debt for services received). Should a health maintenance organization have an enforceable right of subrogation, either at common law or by virtue of a written contract provision, where it renders medical services to a tortiously injured subscriber? *See Medica, Inc. v. Atlantic Mutual Insurance Co.*, 566 N.W.2d 74 (Minn. 1997) (yes); *Shumpert v. Time Insurance Co.*, 496 S.E.2d 653 (S.C. 1998) (no equitable right of subrogation where policy does not have subrogation provision). For more discussion of the issue in the context of employer-provided health care plans, see David M. Kono, Comment, *Unraveling the Lining of ERISA Health Insurer Pockets—A Vote for National Federal Common Law Adoption of the Make Whole Doctrine*, 2000 B.Y.U. L. Rev. 427.

5. *Subrogation to contract rights?* Assume that Ralph has medical payments coverage under his auto policy (see Personal Auto Policy—Part B, in Appendix E) and is also covered for health care expenses under his wife's group health plan provided through her employer. If Ralph's auto insurer pays for his medical expenses resulting from a one car auto accident, should the auto carrier be allowed a right of subrogation to the extent Ralph's expenses are also covered through his wife's group insurance plan? If the group insurer pays first, should it have a right of subrogation against the auto insurer? *See Medica, Inc. v. Atlantic Mutual Insurance Co.*, 566 N.W.2d 74 (Minn. 1997)(contractual language providing for subrogation against "any party, individual or other entity who may be legally responsible for your injuries" entitles HMO, after paying its insureds' medical costs, to recovery under medical expense coverage of third party's general liability policy). *See also Morin v. Massachusetts Blue Cross, Inc.*, 365 Mass. 379, 311 N.E.2d 914 (1974) (issue identified but not resolved).

6. *Defenses and limitations.* Subrogation merely permits the insurer to bring the original claim of the insured; any defenses available against the insured are applicable in a subrogation proceeding, and can be used to defeat or limit the subrogee's claim. A common way to phrase the principle is as follows: The rights of a subrogated insurer against a third party can rise no higher than the rights of its insured. *See State Automobile & Casualty Underwriters v. Farmers Insurance Exchange*, 204 Neb. 414, 282 N.W.2d 601 (1979). The court in *Mahler* acknowledged this rule in its discussion of a trilogy of prior Washington subrogation cases.

Consider how this rule plays out if an insured gives a release to a tortfeasor. The tortfeasor acquires a complete defense to the insured's claim (assuming the release is valid), and this defense will defeat the insurer's subrogation claim. If the release is given without the insurer's involvement, the insured probably has also violated policy provisions that forbid the insured from interfering with the insurer's subrogation rights. This can have the further effect of defeating the insured's coverage. *See, e.g., Brantley v. State Farm Mutual Automobile Insurance Co.,* 586 So. 2d 184 (Ala. 1991); *Kentucky National Insurance Co. v. Gardner,* 6 S.W.3d 493 (Tenn. Ct. App. 1999). Should this result follow if the insurer has not been prejudiced by the settlement between insured and tortfeasor?

But if the tortfeasor has notice of the insurer's subrogation interest at the time the tortfeasor settles the claim with the insured and secures a release, the landscape changes, as the court in *Mahler* noted. Why should prior notice to the tortfeasor matter? By definition, if the insurer's subrogation right is not affected, the insured has not interfered with the right, and the insured's coverage is not at risk.

Another limitation on subrogation is that, as a general rule, there is no right of subrogation in favor of the insurer against its own insured. This is true both as to the named insured and as to any person to whom coverage is otherwise extended under the terms of the policy. *See Truck Insurance Exchange v. Transport Indemnity Co.,* 180 Mont. 419, 591 P.2d 188 (1979).

7. *Pre-loss exculpatory clauses.* As discussed in the prior note, the insured runs risks when she releases the tortfeasor without the insurer's consent. What about exculpatory clauses in contracts? In construction contracts, leases, and many other kinds of commercial deals, clauses where one party releases the other from liability for future wrongs are common. Can the insurer pursue subrogation against a party that has been contractually exculpated? Assuming the clause is valid, the answer is no, as this is a defense against the subrogor that limits the rights of the subrogee. Do such clauses interfere with the insurer's subrogation rights and thereby defeat coverage? Courts have answered this question in the negative. *See Insurance Co. of North America v. Universal Mortgage Corp. of Wisconsin,* 82 Wis.2d 170, 262 N.W.2d 92 (1978); *Great Northern Oil Co. v. St. Paul Fire and Marine Insurance Co.,* 291 Minn. 97, 189 N.W.2d 404 (1971). Why should this be? Exculpatory clauses clearly hurt the insurer, but is this a situation where insurers are providing the coverage that insureds want?

8. *The "made whole" rule.* The *Mahler* court referred to its prior decision in *Thiringer,* where it endorsed the general rule that an insurer is entitled to subrogation only after the insured has been fully compensated. While most courts favor this approach, it is not the only possible answer. *See, e.g., Franklin v. Healthsource of Arkansas,* 942 S.W.2d 837 (Ark. 1997) (insured not entitled to subrogation because insured not made whole by liability insurance payments); *Continental Western Insurance Co. v. Swartzendruber,* 570 N.W.2d 708 (Neb. 1997) (insured must be made whole first). The opposite result—that the subrogor-insurer has the right to be reimbursed fully first before the insured receives anything—is sometimes dictated by statutory language. *See United States v. Lorenzetti,* 467 U.S. 167 (1984) (federal workers compensation statute); *Grayam v. Department of Health & Human Resources,* 201 W.Va. 444, 298 S.E.2d 12 (W.Va. 1997)(state statute gives priority to DHHR to reimbursement for payment of medical bills); but *see Blankenship v. Estate of Bain,* 5 S.W.3d 647 (Tenn. 1999) (Medicaid statute interpreted to deny subrogation to state until recipient is made whole). Some courts have

held that the "made whole" rule, while appropriate in the genre of equitable subrogation, can be trumped by policy language to the contrary, *see Fields v. Farmers Insurance Co.,* 18 F.3d 831 (10th Cir. 1994) (applying Oklahoma law). This answer is not, however, universally favored. *See Hare v. State,* 733 So. 2d 277, 284 (Miss. 1999) (" 'made whole' rule. . .is not to be overridden by contract language, because the intent of subrogation is to prevent a double recovery by the insured").

Beyond the "made whole" rule, three other possible solutions on how the proceeds from the third-party claim might be distributed have some support in precedents: (1) the insurer is entitled to all the proceeds; (2) the insured is entitled to all the proceeds; and (3) the proceeds are prorated between the insured and the insurer on the basis that the amount of money paid by the insurer to the insured bears to the original loss sustained by the insured. There is little support for the first alternative. The second alternative amounts to a "no right of subrogation" rule. The third has some precedential support, but it is probably more commonly followed as a result of settlement negotiations between the insured and insurer. See generally John Dwight Ingram, *Priority Between Insurer and Insured in Subrogation Recoveries,* 3 Conn. Ins. L. J. 105 (1996); Robert E. Keeton & Alan I. Widiss, Insurance Law 236 (Student Ed. 1988).

9. *Transaction costs—is subrogation worth the candle?* Subrogation has been examined in this section as a technique of preventing multiple recoveries for the same loss by insureds and, thus, adhering to the principle of indemnity. This technique, however, is not without its costs because resources have to be expended to enforce such a right, i.e., there are transaction costs. This raises a policy question regarding the social utility of permitting such claims, especially if there is a more efficient alternative that would achieve the same goal of adhering to the principle of indemnity.

If the recoveries by insurers under subrogation are used to reduce premiums, one could make a strong argument that first-party insureds should be given the option of purchasing less expensive policies in exchange for insurer's having a robust subrogation right—including, perhaps, the right to the first reimbursement out of any recovery obtained by third parties. See Jeffrey A. Greenblatt, Comment, *Insurance and Subrogation: When the Pie Isn't Big Enough, Who Eats Last?,* 64 U. Chi. L. Rev. 1337 (1997). But many are skeptical that subrogation recoveries have much to do with premium rates. As one court stated, "Admittedly, subrogation has been a two-edge sword. Unfortunately, it has frequently become a source of windfall to insurers in that the anticipated recoveries under subrogation rights are generally not reflected in the computation of premium rates. . . . . This, however, is a legislative or administrative problem rather than one that bears on the inherent validity of such a clause." *De Cespedes v. Prudence Mutual Casualty Co.,* 193 So. 2d 224, 227–228 (Fla. Dist. Ct. App. 1966), *aff'd,* 202 So. 2d 561 (Fla. 1967). This skepticism, however, is a partial explanation for some other courts denying insurers a right of subrogation. *See, e.g., Allstate Insurance Co. v. Druke,* 118 Ariz. 301, 576 P.2d 489 (1978) and *Maxwell v. Allstate Insurance Co.,* 728 P.2d 812 (Nev. 1986).

In a portion of the *Mahler* decision not included in these materials, the court considered (and ultimately rejected, over a dissent) State Farm's contention that paragraph (d) of the policy provided for an exception to its promise to contribute to the expenses of procuring recoveries from third parties when the recovery is secured through inter-company arbitration. See 957 P.2d at 645–646. Under this agreement, signatory companies are bound to arbitrate disputes among themselves arising out of the pursuit of subrogation, reimbursement, and other recovery action claims. The court noted: "Insurance companies recognized many years ago the disadvantages in costs, delay, and public relations stemming from litigation of subrogation actions among insurers. The use of arbitration to resolve such disputes occurred first in New York in 1929. A Nationwide Inter-Company Arbitration Agreement was drafted and became effective on February 1, 1952. Approximately 2,000 insurance companies are signatories to the current version of the agreement." *Id.* at 645, n. 12. Is inter-company arbitration the answer, or is it simply proof of the problem?

10. *ERISA wars, episode I.* The minority position prevailing in some states that refuses to recognize a right of subrogation has been preempted by federal law in some situations. In 1974 Congress passed the Employee Retirement Income Security Act (ERISA), 88 Stat. 829, as amended, 29 U.S.C. § 1001 *et seq.*, to protect the interests of participants in employee benefit plans. Since most group insurance plans provided by employers to their employees fall within the ambit of ERISA, many group life, health, accident, and disability insurance policies and self-insurance plans are now governed by federal law. In order to achieve uniform treatment, ERISA specifically preempts "any and all state laws insofar as they may now or hereafter relate to any employee benefit plan," except for those laws that "regulate insurance." 29 U.S.C §§ 1144(a) and 1144(b)(2)(A). Consequently, a state statute or common law rule that prohibits an ERISA self-insurer or insurer from asserting a subrogation right under the plan may be unenforceable. *See Holliday v. FMC Corp.,* 498 U.S. 52 (1990); *Baxter v. Lynn,* 886 F.2d 182 (8th Cir. 1989) (*en banc*); *Blue Cross & Blue Shield of Alabama v. Sanders,* 974 F. Supp. 1416 (N.D. Ala. 1997).

11. *Other issues.* Much more could be said about subrogation. For a discussion of other issues with regard to enforcement of subrogation rights, including proper parties, splitting causes of action, conflicts of interest, and breaches and other interferences, see Robert E. Keeton & Alan I. Widiss, Insurance Law § 3.10(c) (Student Ed. 1988); Robert H. Jerry, II, Understanding Insurance Law § 96 (2d ed. 1996).

[5]   Coordination of Benefits II: "Other Insurance" Clauses

CARRIERS INSURANCE CO. v. AMERICAN POLICYHOLDERS' INSURANCE CO.
404 A.2d 216 (Me. 1979)

DELAHANTY, JUSTICE.

This action was brought in the Superior Court, Kennebec County, by the plaintiff, Carriers Insurance Company (Carriers), seeking contribution from the defendant, American Policyholders' Insurance Co. (American). The parties joined issue upon whether and to what extent American was required to contribute to a settlement made by the plaintiff. Upon an agreed statement of facts, the presiding Justice found for Carriers, and American has appealed. We deny the appeal.

During April of 1963, Cummings Bros. (Cummings) entered into a contractual agreement with Merrill's Rental Service, Inc. (Merrill's) whereby it leased certain motor vehicles from Merrill's. Pursuant to the lease and for Cummings' benefit, Merrill's agreed to provide insurance coverage — both personal injury and property damage—for its vehicles while they were being operated by Cummings' employees. In 1971, this personal injury liability coverage which Merrill's obtained through Carriers stood at approximately $3,000,000 with $500,000 of property damage coverage. In the meantime, Cummings independently procured $250,000 of liability insurance through the defendant, American.

In March of 1972, one of Cummings' employees, while negligently driving a vehicle leased from Merrill's, collided with a Lincoln Continental killing the driver and extensively damaging his automobile. Carriers, acting in good faith and in the best interests of its insured, settled a wrongful death claim for $200,000 and a property damage claim for approximately $8,000. . . . . Thereafter, Carriers instituted the present action and received a judgment against the defendant for approximately $104,000. Both Carriers and American had "other insurance" clauses in their insurance policies. Carriers' contract stated:

OTHER INSURANCE

If there is other insurance against an occurrence covered by this policy, the insurance afforded by this policy shall be deemed *excess insurance* over and above the applicable limits of all such other insurance. (emphasis supplied.)

American's policy contained an endorsement specifically covering "hired automobiles" which provided:

OTHER INSURANCE

This insurance shall be *excess insurance* over any other valid and collectible insurance for Bodily Injury Liability, for Property Damage Liability and for Automobile Medical Payments. (emphasis supplied.)

Faced with these competing clauses, the presiding Justice disregarded them as "mutually repugnant." American assigns this as error and insists that its clause should be given preference over Carriers'.

I

We begin our discussion by acknowledging the utter confusion that pervades the entire realm of "other insurance" clauses. Originating in the property insurance field, these clauses were designed to prevent fraudulent claims induced by overinsuring. With automobiles, however, the fear of death or injury was in itself sufficient to deter specious accidents. The original purpose of other insurance clauses has little relevance, therefore, to automobile liability insurance other than to limit, reduce, or avoid an insurer's loss in those cases where there is multiple coverage. *See* Comment, *"Other Insurance"*

Clauses: The Lamb-Weston Doctrine, 47 Or. L. Rev. 430 (1968); Note, *Concurrent Coverage in Automobile Liability Insurance,* 65 Colum. L. Rev. 319 (1965). However, these clauses violate no public policy and in the absence of a statute to the contrary they will be given effect, even if the insured is unaware of the existence of the other insurance. 8 D. Blashfield, Automobile Law and Practice § 345.10 (3rd ed. 1966).

There are three basic types of other insurance clauses which regulate how liability is to be divided when multiple coverage exists. The first, a "pro-rata" clause, limits the liability of an insurer to a proportion of the total loss. The second, an "escape" clause, seeks to avoid all liability. The third, an "excess" clause, the provision used in the present case, provides that the insurance will only be excess. *See* 8 J. Appleman, Insurance Law and Practice § 4911 (Cum. Supp. 1973); 7 Am. Jur. 2d *Automobile Insurance* §§ 200–202 (2d ed. 1963).

No problems arise as long as only one policy contains an other insurance clause since the particular provision can be given effect as written. Complications and conflicts occur where more than one applicable policy contains an other insurance clause. In that situation, the court is faced with a battle of the clauses.[2]

In the case at bar, each policy, in virtually identical language, states that it will be excess over any other valid and collectible insurance. Any attempt at a literal reconciliation of the clauses involves hopeless circular reasoning. One clause cannot be given effect as "excess" unless the other is considered "primary." Since both claim to be excess, neither could operate as primary and hence neither could take effect as excess. Taken to its *reductio ad absurdum* conclusion, even though each insurer concedes that its policy would have covered the loss in the absence of the other, where there is double coverage both would escape liability, a result which neither party advocates. As well stated in *State Farm Mutual Insurance Co. v. Travelers Insurance Co.,* 184 So. 2d 750, 753–54 (La. App. 1966) (Tate, J., concurring),

> [i]ndeed, there is actually no way by logic or word-sense to reconcile two such clauses, where each policy by itself can apply as a primary insurer, but where the clause in each policy nevertheless attempts to make its own liability secondary to that of any other policy issued by a similar primary insurer: For then the primary and (attempted) secondary liability of each policy chase the other through infinity, something like trying to answer the question: Which came first, the chicken or the egg?

Faced with this logical logjam, a number of different and conflicting methods have at various times been used to determine which policy is primary and hence which should bear the brunt of the loss. Thus, it has been stated that the primary policy is the one: covering the tortfeasor; issued prior in time;

---

[2] Some of the more common interchanges have been commented upon: excess clause v. pro-rata clause, *see* Annot., 76 A.L.R.2d 502 (1961); escape clause v. pro-rata clause, *see* Annot., 46 A.L.R.2d 1163, 1167 (1956); excess clause v. excess clause, *see* Annot., 69 A.L.R.2d 1122 (1960); excess clause v. escape clause, *see* 46 A.L.R.2d, *supra* at 1165. *See Union Ins. Co. (Mut.) v. Iowa Hardware Mut. Ins. Co.,* 175 N.W.2d 413, 415 (Iowa 1970).

insuring the vehicle's owner; whose policy covered the particular loss more specifically; or whose other insurance clause is written in more general terms.

Seizing on one of these approaches, American argues that Carriers' policy should be construed as primary based upon minute differences in the language of the excess insurance clauses. We prefer not to engage in such semantic microscopy. "It [merely] encourages the continuing draftsmanship battle by which insurers seek still more specific policy terms, and the end is not in sight." Note, *Concurrent Coverage in Automobile Liability Insurance, supra* at 322. Fairly read, each insurer, through its excess clause, seeks to place the initial loss on any other applicable insurance, saving for itself a role as secondary insurer.

As an alternative argument, American asserts that the intent of the underlying parties should be given effect. Merrill's, for valuable consideration, contractually agreed to insure Cummings.[3] Merrill's' insurance should therefore be considered primary.

We disagree.

American's argument would be well taken were this suit simply one for breach of contract between Cummings and Merrill's. We fail, however, to see the relevance in this case of the lease agreement to which the insurers were neither parties nor beneficiaries. The only appropriate considerations are the two insurance policies through which the respective insurers and insureds manifested their contractual intent. An examination of the policies issued is the single criteria for analyzing an insurer's obligations which can neither be enlarged nor diminished beyond the terms employed A determination of the primary insurer must turn, therefore, upon a construction of the insurance contracts and not upon a collateral agreement between an insured and a third party.

We perceive no methodology which is neither arbitrary nor utterly mechanical by which we could rationally resolve the enigma of which policy should be given effect over the other. Both clauses attempt to occupy the same legal status. Any construction this Court renders should attempt to maintain this

---

[3] In pertinent part, the lease provided:

F. INSURANCE COVERAGE AND LIABILITY

Subject to the following conditions, MERRILL shall provide, at its expense, insurance coverage for its benefit and the benefit of CUMMINGS and the drivers and/or operators of CUMMINGS.

1. All rental units described in Schedule A including any emergency spares or other vehicles or trailers of MERRILL's used by CUMMINGS under the terms hereof will be covered, for the benefit of CUMMINGS and its operating and driving personnel:

(a). Personal injury, [$2,990,000.00].

(b). Property damage, $500,000.00.

2. CUMMINGS shall not be liable to MERRILL for any damages or injuries sustained to the rental units described in Schedule A while being used by CUMMINGS under the terms hereof if occasioned by:

(a). The negligent operation of CUMMINGS' drivers or operators while operating or driving said rental units in the scope of their employment with CUMMINGS.

status quo. This goal can be achieved only by abandoning the search for the mythical "primary" insurer and insisting instead that both insurers share in the loss. Such an approach best carries out the intent of the insurers which was to reduce or limit their liability.

There are additional benefits to adopting this rule. It would introduce certainty and uniformity into the insurance industry, discourage litigation between insurers, and enable underwriters to predict the losses of the insurers more accurately. Note, *Conflicts Between "Other Insurance" Clauses in Automobile Liability Insurance Policies,* 20 Hastings L.J. 1292, 1304 (1969). We hold that where there are conflicting excess insurance clause provisions they are to be disregarded as mutually repugnant thus rendering applicable the general coverage of each policy. This, we note, is the clear majority rule.

II

Having found that both policies are to be considered "primary," we are brought to the question of how should the liability be prorated where the total loss does not exceed the limits of either policy. American argues that the loss should be prorated according to the policy limits. Because Carriers provided $2,990,000 of coverage compared to only $250,000 for American, appellant contends that Carriers should bear close to ninety percent of the settlement cost. Carriers, on the other hand, argues that the loss should be shared equally between the insurers, the approach adopted by the presiding Justice.

There are three basic methods of proration. The majority rule, the one urged upon by appellant, prorates liability according to the limits contained in each policy. The next, which is seldom followed, prorates on the basis of the premiums paid to each insurer. Finally, there is a minority but growing number of courts which prorate the loss equally up to the limits of the lower policy,[7] the approach adopted by the court below.

Each method is grounded on the premises, often unarticulated, that on equitable principles the loss should be shared among the insurers either on the basis of the risk that they have undertaken or the benefit they have received. In its clearest expression, the majority rule has been justified on the theory that

> the burden imposed on each insurer is generally proportional to the benefit which he received, since the size of the premium is most always directly related to the size of the policy.

Lamb-Weston, Inc. v. Oregon Automobile Insurance Company, [219 Or. 129, 137, 346 P.2d 643, 647 (1959)]. On precisely these grounds, the majority rule has been criticized since "[i]t is commonly known that the cost of liability insurance does not increase proportionately with the policy limits." Once minimum coverage has been obtained, significant supplemental coverage can be provided at only a modest increase in cost.

On the other hand, if the majority rule is less equitable than that minority approach which apportions on the basis of premiums received, it has the advantage of facile application. Unless the multiple policies cover the identical

---

[7] *See, e.g., Ruan Transport Corp. v. Truck Rentals, Inc.,* 278 F. Supp. 692 (D. Colo. 1968);.

risks, there would be too many variables affecting the premiums to permit them to serve as a benchmark for an equitable adjustment.

The minority rule adopted by the presiding Justice utilizes the best aspects of both approaches without the limitations. Like the majority rule, it is easy to administer. It would simply require each company to contribute equally until the limits of the smaller policy were exhausted, with any remaining portion of the loss then being paid from the larger policy up to its limits.

Unlike the majority rule, this Solomon-like approach comports with a most basic sense of justice. *See* Exodus, ch. 21, par. 35 ("When one man's ox hurts another's ox so badly that it dies, they shall sell the live ox and divide this money as well as the dead animal they shall divide equally between them.") Moreover, the majority rule unfairly discriminates against the larger policy by apportioning the loss in proportion to the respective policy limits, utterly forgetting that both insurers, by their contracts, have in fact agreed to cover a loss up to the limits of the lesser policy. Until that point is reached, the majority rule amounts to no more than an unacceptable subsidy from the high-coverage to the low-coverage carrier. We are in complete accord with the presiding Justice when he adopted the persuasive opinion of Judge Doyle in *Ruan Transport Corp. v. Truck Rentals, Inc., supra note 7 at 696.*

The majority method of prorating operates inequitably in its differentiating treatment of the high-loss and low-loss insurer. In return for a greater premium the insurer providing higher coverage has undertaken to protect the insured against accidents involving high losses. Yet because of this undertaking to protect against high loss the larger insurer is in an unfavorable position vis-à-vis the other insurer even in cases of low loss, since under the majority method of prorating the insurer affording the greater maximum coverage pays the greater segment of any loss incurred, regardless of the amount of the loss. This seems inequitable since both insurers have equally undertaken to insure against the low-loss accident.

The majority rule would hardly encourage an insurer from increasing its coverage where it is aware that there is a lesser policy. It would increase the insurer's potential liability not only in the high-risk situation which the additional premiums are presumably meant to recompense, but it would have the untoward effect of increasing liability in the more likely to occur low-risk situation. Carried to its extreme, it would further increase the cost of additional insurance thereby reducing the likelihood that an insured would choose such coverage. The Court would be reluctant to adopt a rule which would seemingly have little social utility.

For all of the aforesaid reasons, the presiding Justice correctly prorated the loss between Carriers and American.

Accordingly, the entry shall be:

Appeal denied.

Judgment affirmed.

WERNICK, J., did not sit.

NOTES

1. *Types of clauses.* The court in *Carriers* identified the three principle categories of "other insurance" clauses. Some courts and commentators recognize a fourth—the "excess-escape" clause, which, as the name suggests, combines the features of an excess and escape clause. Under this provision, the insurer is liable only in excess of other available insurance, but has no liability if the other insurance is equal to or in excess of its own limits. There are also many "tailor-made" variations on these categories, which appear when insurers have specific coordination objectives in mind with respect to particular risks. For example, some property insurance policies have a variation on the "escape" clause, which states that if there is other insurance on the property described in the policy, and if the insurer does not consent to such other insurance, the policy is void. Generally speaking, in order to constitute "other insurance" so as to avoid a property insurance policy by operation of such an "escape" clause, the "other insurance" must cover the same risks, the same property, and the same interests as those covered by the policy containing the "escape" provision. See David B. Harrison, Annotation, *What Constitutes "Other Insurance" Within Meaning of Insurance Policy Provisions Prohibiting Insured From Obtaining Other Insurance on Same Property,* 7 A.L.R.4th 494 (1981). Health insurance policies also contain the equivalent of "other insurance" clauses, but they are typically labeled "coordination of benefit" (or "COB") clauses. For an exhaustive survey of other insurance clauses and how they operate, see Douglas R. Richmond, *Issues and Problems in "Other Insurance," Multiple Insurance, and Self-Insurance,* 22 Pepp. L. Rev. 1373 (1995).

2. *Property loss versus liability to third parties.* In property insurance, "other insurance" clauses have an obvious connection to the principle of indemnity, in that they prevent the insured from recovering multiple times for the same loss. The issue in *Carriers* concerned overlapping liability coverages. In this context, "other insurance" clauses are not designed to prevent net gain because the policies themselves merely agree to pay for losses caused by the insured to a third party. Since the third party is not entitled to collect more than her loss from the insured, there is no danger that the liability insurer or insurers will have to pay an amount that would result in a net gain by the third party. On the other hand, "other insurance" clauses in liability policies can have the effect of reducing the insurers' obligations to something less than full recovery by the third party. This is especially true where effect is given to an "escape" clause. This can also happen in property insurance if the policy limits of all of the policies are less than the value of the property and one or more of these policies has an "escape" clause. "Other insurance" clauses in liability insurance policies receive further attention in § 5.03[2].

Property insurance presents fewer problems today regarding conflicts between "other insurance" clauses because most states have adopted the New York Standard Fire Insurance Policy, 1943 edition, as the prescribed form. This policy contains two relevant provisions:

> Other Insurance. Other insurance may be prohibited or the amount of insurance may be limited by endorsement attached hereto. . . .
>
> Pro rata Liability. This Company shall not be liable for a greater proportion of any loss than the amount hereby insured shall bear to the whole insurance covering the property against the peril involved, whether collectible or not.

See Appendix A, lines 25–27 and 86–89, respectively. Since the same pro rata clause appears in so many fire insurance policies, there is less opportunity for conflict, but other issues may arise. *See, e.g., Concord General Mutual Insurance Co. v. Patrons-Oxford Mutual Insurance Co.,* 411 A.2d 1017 (Me. 1980) (holding that the requirement under the standard fire policy regarding prohibiting or limiting other insurance is not satisfied by a clause in the *body* of the policy prohibiting other insurance, but must be by separate "attachment" to the policy).

3. *The matter of "layering."* The prototype "other insurance" case involves two insurers providing overlapping coverage at the same level (or in the same "layer"). It is important to distinguish this from the situation where the coverage from multiple insurers is designed to apply in layers. For example, the insured might purchase a policy from Insurer A for "layer one" covering all losses up to $500,000. Then, a second policy might be purchased from Insurer B for "layer two" in the amount of $2 million. In the trade, Insurer A would be referred to as the "primary" carrier and B would be called the "first level excess" carrier. If a loss is under $500,000, it is entirely the responsibility of Insurer A. If the loss exceeds $500,000, Insurer B pays for any loss exceeding $500,000 and up to the policy limits of $2 million. Thus, for example, if the loss were $1.5 million, Insurer A would pay $500,000 of the loss and Insurer B would pay $1 million of the loss. Large corporations (*e.g.,* of the Fortune 500 variety) are likely to structure their coverages in multiple layers, with a first excess, second excess, third excess, and perhaps other carriers. To complicate things further, the insured might have several insurers participating concurrently in one (or more) of the excess levels. It is also likely that such a company will have a large self-insured retention, which functions as a large deductible.

The "umbrella policy," purchased by many individuals, is mostly designed to provide excess coverage over the primary coverage provided by the homeowner's and the automobile policies. The umbrella policy is sometimes called a "true excess" policy to underscore its intent to operate in a different layer than the primary coverages. *See, e.g., Bosco v. Bauermeister,* 456 Mich. 279, 571 N.W.2d 509 (1997) (employer's auto policy, which contained excess clause, was not excess over umbrella policies, which were "true excess" policies).

In both commercial and personal insurance, difficulties can arise in determining whether an "excess" policy was meant to operate at a primary or a secondary layer. With the layering concept in mind, how would you explain the effect of the "other insurance" clause in the liability section "Section II—Liability Coverages" of the standard homeowner's form (see "Section II—Conditions" in Appendix C)? Why is it drafted differently from the "other insurance" clause in the property coverages ("Section I—Conditions") of that form?

4. *Judicial frustration.* If you detect a sense of frustration by the courts in attempting to reconcile the variety of "other insurance" clauses in liability policies, you are perceptive. The "other insurance" morass has led to some very colorful language in reported cases. One court recently offered this assessment:

> When judges first set about the task of interpreting insurance policies, we looked confidently to tried and true principles of contract law. After all, lawyers are taught in their earliest classes that the common law rules of contract are the bedrock of all Anglo-American jurisprudence, thus judges clearly had at hand the perfect tools for crafting fair and lucid interpretations of insurance agreements. We failed utterly to anticipate the linguistic excesses to which the insurance industry would resort in order to avoid paying claims when "other insurance" may be available. This is an area in which hair splitting and nit picking has been elevated to an art form. "Other insurance" clauses have been variously described as: "the catacombs of insurance policy English, a dimly lit underworld where many have lost their way," a circular riddle, and "polic[ies] which cross one's eyes and boggle one's mind. [footnotes and citations omitted.]

South Carolina Insurance Co. v. Fidelity and Guaranty Insurance Underwriters, Inc., 327 S.C. 207, 489 S.E.2d 200 (1997). In 1966, one court recalled an old Vaudeville comedy routine as a metaphor for the "other insurance" morass, a metaphor which has been borrowed by opinion writers in at least ten subsequent cases: "This court believes it is good public policy not to put an injured plaintiff, or a defendant who is fortunate to enough to have duplicate coverage, in a position where there is any possibility one insurer can say, 'After you, my dear Alphonse!' while the other says, 'Oh, no, after you, my dear Gaston.' They must walk arm in arm through the door of responsibility."[*] *Firemen's Insurance Co. v. St. Paul Fire & Marine Insurance Co.,* 243 Or. 10, 411 P.2d 271 (1965) (en banc). Given the intensity of judicial frustration, is the failure of the insurance industry to arrive at a comprehensive solution to "other insurance" conflicts defensible? See Susan Randall, *Coordinating Liability Insurance,* 1995 Wis. L. Rev. 1339, 1360–1365.

5. *Resolving conflicts among clauses.* Most courts try to reconcile "other insurance" conflicts by resort to rules of contract interpretation. When, for example, a pro rata clause faces an excess clause, most courts have concluded that the clauses are not inconsistent, and the policy with the pro rata clause is primary and the policy with the excess clause is secondary. See Richmond, *supra* (in note 1), at 1392 n. 73 (listing cases). Some courts have become quick to declare that conflicting clauses are mutually repugnant and that the coverages are to be prorated, usually on the basis of the policy limits. An early leading case, and perhaps the landmark case, on the subject is that of *Lamb-Weston, Inc. v. Oregon Auto. Insurance Co.,* 219 Or. 110, 341 P.2d 110,

---

[*] [Editors' Note: "Alphonse and Gaston," two comically deferential Frenchmen, were the creation of American cartoonist Frederick Burr Opper (1857-1937). The popularity of their long-running comic strip (1902-1920s) eventually brought them into Vaudeville acts, the latter being a theatrical medium for "cultural icons" of that period. Ruth Muldrew, Vaudeville Q&A (last modified Jan. 3, 1999) personal.nbnet.nb.ca./muldrew/vaudeville2.htm.]

modified and reh'g denied, 219 Or. 129, 346 P.2d 643 (1959), 76 A.L.R.2d 485 and 498 (1961), which involved "excess" and "pro rata" clauses. Holding both insurers liable in proportion to their policy limits, the Oregon Supreme Court reasoned that "whether one policy uses one clause or another, when any come in conflict with the 'other insurance' clause of another insurer, regardless of the nature of the clause, they are in fact repugnant and each should be rejected in toto." *Id.* 219 Or. at 129, 341 P.2d at 119.

Escape clauses have, in general, been met with judicial hostility, although much depends on the nature of the risk and other circumstances. *See, e.g., CSE Insurance Group v. Northbrook Property and Casualty Co.,* 23 Cal. App. 4th 1839, 29 Cal. Rptr. 2d 120, 124 (1994); *Connecticut Indemnity Co. v. Cordasco,* 369 Pa. Super. 439, 535 A.2d 631, 633 (1987). Are there reasons to treat escape clauses differently from excess clauses in conflict situations? Does the nature of the insured risk matter? What if, for example, two policies have escape clauses, but one insures a building against fire damage and the other insures crops against hail damage?

6. *The Minnesota rule for conflicts.* In a series of cases, the Minnesota Supreme Court has developed a "closest to the risk" analysis to resolve "other insurance" conflicts. The essence of the test involves analyzing the insurance as a whole and looking for the risk which gives rise to the loss in light of the "total insuring intent." *See Interstate Fire & Casualty Co. v. Auto-Owners Insurance Co.,* 433 N.W.2d 82 (Minn. 1988). At the core of the test are three questions: "(1) Which policy specifically described the accident-causing instrumentality? (2) Which premium is reflective of the greater contemplated exposure? (3) Does one policy contemplate the risk and use of the accident-causing instrumentality with greater specificity than the other policy — that is, is the coverage of the risk primary in one policy and incidental in the other?" *Auto Owners Insurance Co. v. Northstar Mutual Insurance Co.,* 281 N.W.2d 700, 704 (1979). Has Minnesota found a path out of the forest? Or do you see problems with the Minnesota approach? *See Illinois National Insurance Co. v. Farm Bureau Mutual Insurance Co.,* 578 N.W.2d 670 (Iowa 1998)(rejecting "closest to the risk" test).

7. *Methods of proration.* Do you agree with the choice and the reasoning of the court in *Carriers* as to the method of prorating the loss between the two insurance policies? The total loss in *Carriers,* as represented by the settlement, did not exceed the limits of either policy. If the loss had exceeded the limits of the smaller policy, would the choice of method of proration matter? For example, assume that there was no property damage but that the settlement in the wrongful death action amounted to $750,000. Also, assume that the Carriers' policy limit was $3,000,000 and American's was $250,000. What would each insurer have to pay under the holding in *Carriers*? What would each insurer have to pay if the settlement were prorated on the basis of the policy limits, the position advocated by American? Which method is the fairest? *See Western Casualty and Surety Co. v. Universal Underwriters Insurance Co.,* 232 Kan. 606, 657 P.2d 576 (1983) (favoring "equal shares" approach and criticizing *pro rata* approach).

8. *Workers' compensation offset.* The medical payments provision in standard automobile liability insurance forms provides that there is no coverage

for medical expenses for bodily injury to the extent workers' compensation benefits "are required or available" for the injury. See Appendix E ("Part B—Medical Payments Coverage," Exclusion 4). Similar provisions exist in individual and group health insurance policies to avoid duplicating benefits under workers' compensation.

9. *Valued policy statutes reprise.* Assume that there is in force on the same property two policies of fire insurance. One policy is a standard policy which will pay for loss caused by fire up to the policy limits. The other policy is a valued policy. Both contain pro rata "other insurance" clauses. Does the fact one is a valued policy foreclose proration of any loss? See *Commercial Union Insurance Co. v. Sneed,* 541 S.W.2d 943 (Tenn. 1976). If you were inclined to support a valued policy statute for your state, how would you handle the overlapping coverage problem in this context?

10. *Life insurance.* Life insurers rarely, if ever, resort to "other insurance" clauses as attested to by the dearth of cases on the subject. See West's American Digest System Key No. "217K2444 Other Insurance." Of the relatively few cases on the subject, many of them are older ones involving burial insurance or industrial life insurance. Life insurers tend to address the matter by making inquiries in the application process and limiting the amount sold accordingly. What does this say about the principle of indemnity?

[6] Marine Losses

LENFEST v. COLDWELL
525 F.2d 717 (2d Cir. 1975)

GURFEIN, CIRCUIT JUDGE:

This is an appeal from a decision by Judge Carter in the United States District Court for the Southern District of New York, denying plaintiffs any recovery on their "Anticipated Profits" marine insurance policy. Plaintiff Ferro-Bet Corporation was the time charterer of the vessel S.S. PANOCEAN from October, 1963 until sometime in the summer of 1964.[1] Plaintiffs Lenfest[2] and Yarrington were financiers of Ferro-Bet. All plaintiffs were insured under an "Anticipated Profits" policy issued by a group of London marine insurers who have designated Harold Coldwell as their nominee in this action. The question presented on appeal is whether the district court erred in finding that plaintiffs failed to prove the vessel either an actual total loss, a constructive total loss, or a compromised total loss, as the policy required, and were hence not entitled to recover.

---

[1] Under the time charter, the owner remained responsible for providing the crew, and running, maintaining and repairing the ship, while the charterer was responsible for the vessel's itinerary and her cargo, to be arranged through the grant of subcharters. See G. Gilmore and C. Black, The Law of Admiralty § 4–14, at 230–31 (2d ed. 1975).

[2] Harold C. Lenfest died after consolidation of the actions. The executors of his estate, Inez Lenfest and Marine Midland Grace Trust Co., were substituted as plaintiffs.

I

A. *The Policies and Other Preliminaries*

When the charter was arranged, the owners of PANOCEAN (not parties to this suit) had insurance policies on the hull and machinery of the vessel for $240,000. Under such policies, not directly in issue, the owners were insured against the partial or total destruction or loss of the vessel's structure and machinery (*e.g.*, engines, auxiliaries and boilers).[3]

The "Anticipated Profits" "honor"[4] insurance policy issued to the plaintiffs was to run for a twelve-month period beginning on October 29, 1963. The policy provides for payment to the plaintiffs "On—Anticipated Profits—Amount $150,000."[5] The insurers were

> to pay the above sum in the event the vessel becomes a total and/or constructive and/or arranged and/or compromised *total* loss as a result of Marine or War perils (emphasis added).

The "Institute T.L.O." or "Inchmaree" clause, to which these insurance contracts were also subject, further provides that

> 1. This insurance covers only: — Total Loss (Actual or Constructive) of the Vessel (including total loss directly caused by: —
>
> . . . Bursting of boilers, breakage of shafts, or latent defect in the machinery or hull
>
> . . . Negligence of Master, Officers, Crew or Pilots)
>
> provided such loss or damage has not resulted from want of due diligence by the Assured, Owners or Managers.

The policy provides further that

> [i]n ascertaining whether the Vessel is a constructive total loss. . .nothing in respect of the damaged or break-up value of the Vessel. . .shall be taken into account. No claim for constructive total loss based upon the cost of recovery and/or repair of the Vessel shall

---

[3] The owners also had a policy on "increased value" on the hull and machinery for $60,000 recoverable only in the event that the vessel became a *total* and/or constructive *total* and/or arranged *total* and/or compromised *total* loss.

[4] An "honor" policy is one in which the underwriters agree (in this case, through a "Policy Proof of Interest," "FULL INTEREST ADMITTED" clause) not to contest whether the insureds have an "insurable interest." In the United States "honor" policies are not necessarily binding, and the insurer may affirmatively show the absence of an insurable interest. Gilmore & Black, *supra*, § 2–5, at 61 n. 45; *Frank B. Hall & Co. v. Jefferson Ins. Co.*, 279 F. 892 (S.D.N.Y. 1921). However, the insurers have made no challenge on the grounds of "interest" here.

[5] Other forms of anticipated profits insurance provide an insured amount which varies from month to month, as the insureds declare their expected profits, which generally depend on the state of the subcharter market. *See, e.g., Continental Grain Co., Inc. v. Twitchell,* [1945] 78 Lloyd's List L.R. 251 (C.A.). Still others provide for a pro-rated return of expected profit which will provide a different recovery depending on when, during the period of risk, the insured-against risk occurs. L. J. Buglass, Marine Insurance and General Average in the United States 288 (1973). Here, the parties chose to insure the total profit expected in one year and made no provisions for apportionment of actual loss.

be recoverable hereunder unless such cost would exceed the insured value in the policies on hull and machinery.[6]

By the terms of the policy, plaintiffs could recover on "anticipated profits" in the event that the vessel became a) an actual total loss; b) an arranged or compromised total loss; or c) a constructive total loss, as a result of marine or war perils, or crew negligence (unless due to lack of due diligence by owners or insureds). For the ship to become a constructive total loss, the costs of recovery and/or repairs to the ship would have had to exceed $240,000 (the insured value on hull and machinery).

B. *The Calamitous Voyage*

The PANOCEAN's charter began comfortably enough. In late November 1963 the vessel proceeded in ballast from Curacao to New Orleans where a cargo under a Cook Grains, Inc., subcharterparty was loaded and carried to Marseilles.[7] She went on to Seville where baryte ore destined for New Orleans was loaded. At Leixos, Portugal, she took on other cargo. She then proceeded to London to discharge cargo and incurred some minor damage while in her berth. After loading at Immingham steel coils destined for Baltimore, PANOCEAN proceeded to Flushing, Netherlands, for bunkers.

In the subsequent passage between Flushing and Baltimore it was stipulated that the vessel encountered heavy weather, and that the voyage lasted from February 24 to April 3, 1964. The stipulation continued:

> Damages and/or equipment losses occurred on the forecastle deck, the main deck, the upper bridge deck, the boat deck, the "02" deck, and the poop deck; and in the engineering spaces of the vessel. The vessel's Scotch Boiler was subjected to heavy accumulation of salt, scale and soot from use of raw sea water; and both the starboard and the port Lamont boilers were subjected to use of raw sea water, and heavy accumulation of salt, scale and soot. It was necessary for the vessel to put into Azores and Bermuda as "ports of refuge" before Baltimore could be reached.

Stipulation # 8.

Under the charterparty, the PANOCEAN was "off hire" while the owner had her repaired in Baltimore, for about two months, until June 5, 1964, when she was tendered back to the time charterer as ready. She sailed out of Baltimore on June 12, 1964, but within two hours suffered a steering engine telemotor control system failure (apparently due to negligently made repairs), and was forced to anchor for repairs.[8]

After further repairs were made, the voyage resumed on June 16, but the ship again ran into trouble, and was forced to drop anchor off Port Everglades,

---

[6] It is therefore irrelevant under the policy that the estimated domestic scrap value of the vessel in September 1964 was $28,875, or that she was shortly thereafter sold by the owners for just over $29,000.

[7] It is not clear how many (if any) subcharters plaintiffs had arranged at the time of delivery on November 19, 1963.

[8] The marine adjuster's handwritten notes read: "Detention in Chesapeake Bay effecting telemotor repairs consequent on Repairer's Negligence—$635.00; Crew wages and provisions during detention—2 days—$332.78."

Florida, to make repairs on account of boiler carryover problems unconnected with earlier damage. On June 22, the vessel stranded while at anchor off Port Everglades, suffering numerous bottom "setups" and indentations from the sand and coral bottom. She was refloated with the assistance of a tug on June 26 and docked the next day at Port Everglades for repairs.

She did not arrive in New Orleans until July 18, 1964, almost a month later. There she was drydocked for engine repairs which were effected by July 31. Various permanent hull repairs costing some $40,000 should have been made at this time, but were deferred by the owner. After she arrived at New Orleans and before she departed, a dispute arose between the charterer and the owner, and the status of the charterparty went to arbitration. The vessel left New Orleans again, off charter, and sustained additional serious injuries in the Gulf of Mexico in September 1964. The owners sold the vessel as scrap in late 1964.

On June 26, 1964, while the vessel was in drydock for repairs at Port Everglades, Tradax Export cancelled a subcharter with plaintiff Ferro-Bet, pursuant to its option to cancel if the PANOCEAN was not ready to load soybeans in New Orleans by June 20. Plaintiffs claim that they also lost the Cook Grains subcharter when Ferro-Bet's chief financiers, Marine Midland Bank, refused to permit substitution of a vessel, forcing an abandonment of the enterprise.

C. *The Course of Adjustment*

On May 20, 1964, while the vessel was under repair in Baltimore and after serious expressions of anxiety by its subcharterers and lenders, Ferro-Bet made its first demand for payment under the Anticipated Profits policy.[9] On February 25, 1965, the owners of PANOCEAN authorized their average adjuster,[10] Great Eastern Associates, Inc., to settle all PANOCEAN claims (exclusive of salvage costs) arising during 1964 for $235,000. Two days later, however, the owners reduced the figure to $225,000. On March 4, 1965, Great Eastern Associates cabled the insurance brokers in London with a breakdown of disbursements and unrepaired damages making up the owner's gross claim against the insurers of $444,246. The insurers had already advanced some $126,794 for repairs in Baltimore. After deducting $15,000 for estimated general average contributions[11] from cargo interests, Great Eastern's cable

---

[9] Lenfest and Yarrington made a similar demand about a year later, on March 24, 1965.

[10] An average adjuster is an experienced professional in the field of marine insurance, who itemizes and classifies expenditures, damages and necessary repairs according to whether they are "general" or "particular" average items for purposes of determining insurer's liability and the liabilities of various interests one to the other. Buglass, *supra,* at 73. In the United States, the average adjuster is employed by the shipowner and paid by the underwriter, and his findings are "seldom questioned." *Id.*

[11] Not all items allowable in general average are allowable in the determination of constructive total loss. A "general average act" is a sacrifice or expenditure voluntarily made to save ship or cargo from imminent total loss, whose costs are shared proportionally by those benefited. Gilmore & Black, *supra,* ch. 5. The key question in determining whether an item is includible in a calculation of a constructive total loss figure is whether or not the act related to the ship's repair. By way of contrast, a general average act need not be related to an effort to repair the vessel. Some costs generally are common to both, such as *salvage* expenses when unobligated third parties refloat or otherwise assist a vessel to shore for repairs. Buglass, *supra,* at 209. *See also* note 18, *infra.*

indicated a "balance due" from the insurers of $302,452 (on an aggregate claim of $429,246). An exchange of telegrams resulted in Great Eastern and the owners accepting an immediate settlement of $225,000; an additional $45,220.07 was later paid over for general average costs at Port Everglades.[12]

D. *The Decision Below*

The District Court correctly held that the Baltimore repairs and damages had resulted from insured-against marine perils. Relying on the report of the underwriter's survey, done on behalf of the London Salvage Association, the court found that $155,006 in necessary repairs had been accomplished at Baltimore, and that estimated repairs of $49,340 on the Port Lamont boiler had been deferred. Appellees concede that these two sums may properly be added in determining the existence of a constructive total loss.

The district court also found that the Azores and Bermuda were ports of refuge, as was stipulated, and that the claimed costs at those ports were properly to be included in determining the costs of repair and recovery. The court relied on *Compania Maritima Astra, S. A. v. Archdale (The ARMAR)*, 134 N.Y.S.2d 20 (S. Ct. 1954), which held the costs of "salvage, pilotage, towage and super-intendence" includible in computing constructive total loss costs. The costs accepted were, at the Azores, $538.15 for "disbursements" and $2,380.29 for "vessel allowances," and, at Bermuda, $1,028.60 for "disbursements" and $3,166.67 for "vessel allowances." Since all these expenses in the aggregate did not total over $240,000 (but amounted to only $211,459.71), the court found that there was no constructive total loss at Baltimore.

The court did not take into account, however, certain items of cost incurred at Baltimore, namely, "disbursements, vessel allowances and survey fees," though these appeared to be like the items of disbursements and allowances at Azores and Bermuda which were allowed. The court gave no explanation for the different treatment of costs incurred at Baltimore. Though Baltimore was a scheduled port of call, it was also the first port at which heavy repairs could be made in drydock. Appellants contend that the court should have included as admissible costs at Baltimore the following:[13]

Disbursements	$11,097.76
Survey fees	$13,151.10
Allowances	$10,095.42
TOTAL	$34,344.28

Appellees contend that the evidence is insufficient to establish the claimed costs at Baltimore, or, indeed, the allowed costs at the Azores and Bermuda, the stipulated ports of refuge.

The district court held the $40,000 in deferred hull repairs at New Orleans to be irrelevant on the ground that the plaintiffs had not proved that the damage from the Port Everglades stranding had resulted from marine perils

---

[12] The PANOCEAN's hull underwriters' proportion of the Port Everglades general average liability was $40,139.91, with special charges on the underwriters amounting to $5,090.16.

[13] These charges may be inferred from a telegram sent by John Wood, the average adjuster with Great Eastern Associates, to the London underwriters on March 4, 1965, and are supported by his more detailed handwritten notes in plaintiffs' exhibit 27.

covered by the insurance. The court limited the allowable costs to those incurred before the vessel left Baltimore.

There is no contention by the underwriters that if the cost of repairs exceeded $240,000, the plaintiffs are not entitled to recovery. This court need not consider, therefore, whether, if that amount is reached, the constructive total loss was the proximate cause of the plaintiffs' loss of profits, for the underwriters have not tendered such an issue.

II

To determine whether the plaintiffs were entitled to recover, we must explore the meaning of the terms "total loss," "constructive total loss," and "arranged and/or compromised total loss."[14] Although these phrases have evolved out of long-standing custom and practice in marine insurance, they nonetheless leave unclear some of the key issues in this case.

We readily find that there was no "total loss."

A total loss of a vessel occurs when the vessel no longer exists in specie or when she is absolutely and irretrievably sunk or otherwise beyond the possible control of the insured. Since the PANOCEAN was afloat and was capable of being repaired, there was no *actual* total loss.

The doctrine of "constructive total loss" was designed to alleviate the harshness of the requirement of an "actual total loss," where a shipowner is the insured, and where the costs of repairs would exceed the repaired value of the ship. It enables the shipowner to "abandon" the vessel as if she were a total loss, while preserving to the insurer the right to recoup what it might from the sale or other disposition of the vessel abandoned to it. In time, common law admiralty rules concerning the measure of value to be applied in determining whether there was a constructive total loss were, to some extent, superseded by the British Marine Insurance Act of 1906,[15] and through policies which abrogated common law presumptions by their express terms. Thus, where the policy provides that the insured value shall be taken as the repaired value, the insured value controls absolutely even if the insured value exceeds the actual value of the vessel at the time of the insurance or of the accident.

---

[14] The "loss" referred to in the policies is that of a vessel. Plaintiffs' argument that they are entitled to recover for loss of profits alone is frivolous. *Continental Grain Co. v. Christie,* 22 N.Y.S.2d 57, 60 (S. Ct. 1940).

[15] *See, e.g.,* Marine Insurance Act of 1906 §§ 55–63. English and American law of marine insurance have developed on rather similar lines. It is the general rule in this country, as the parties have agreed, that American courts will look to British law for meaning and definition in this field. *Queen Ins. Co. v. Globe & Rutgers Fire Ins. Co.,* 263 U.S. 487, 493, 44 S. Ct. 175, 68 L. Ed. 402 (1924); *Calmar Steamship Corp. v. Scott,* 345 U.S. 427, 442–43, 73 S. Ct. 739, 97 L. Ed. 1125 (1953). Although the Marine Insurance Act generally requires notice of abandonment for recovery on a constructive total loss, such notice is not an absolute prerequisite to recovery on anticipated profits for a constructive total loss where the insured is a charterer. *Robertson v. Nomikos,* [1933] A.C. 371; *Roura & Fourgas v. Townsend,* [1919] 1 K.B. 189. *See also Canada Sugar Refining Co. v. Insurance Co. of North America,* 175 U.S. 609, 619–20, 20 S. Ct. 239, 44 L. Ed. 292 (1900); Buglass, *supra,* at 274.

A. *Constructive Total Loss at Baltimore*

Several factors are of importance in approaching the question of whether there was a constructive total loss at Baltimore. Plaintiffs-insureds are time charterers, and not the owners of the vessel. As a consequence, the *res* which they insured was their anticipated profit, and not the vessel itself. The condition precedent to their right to recover was the occurrence of a total loss as defined in the owner's policy on the vessel; yet without physical control of the vessel, the interests of the time charterer could be more easily defeated than those of the owner. A constructive total loss of the vessel is only a *condition precedent* to the charterer's right to recover, while for the owner, the constructive total loss of the ship is not only the condition of recovery but the insured *res* itself. The relatively helpless position of the charterer in the face of loss of freight and anticipated profit, a condition known in advance to the insurer, suggests that we interpret with some liberality the costs allowable in the determination of whether there was a constructive total loss.

There is no dispute that the damage repaired at Baltimore resulted from insured-against perils—heavy weather and crew negligence. There was ample evidence in the record to support this finding. The primary questions on this appeal are the correctness of the district court's calculation of allowable costs at Baltimore and its exclusion of any costs subsequent to the Baltimore repairs.

The few cases which have considered what costs are allowable in computing whether there has been a constructive total loss have involved vessels which had actually been abandoned, and in which the claimed figures for costs of repair and recovery were largely estimates. The teaching of cases such as *THE MEDINA PRINCESS,* [1965] 1 Lloyd's List L.R. 361; *Calmar Steamship Corp. v. Scott,* 209 F.2d 852 (2 Cir. 1954), and *Compania Maritima Astra, S. A. v. Archdale (The ARMAR), supra,* is that the trier of fact must scrutinize with care anticipated expenses, making an independent determination of what the expenses really would have been.[17] It is within the discretion of the trial court wholly to disallow certain items of anticipated expenses as unrealistic.

Here the claimed expenses were in large part actually incurred by the owners and the determination of which of these expenses, if reasonable, should be allowed is a question of law. To determine the legal questions, however, we need more detailed findings on what these costs were for, and particularly, how they relate to the repair of the vessel. A remand for more detailed findings is required, especially since the figure arrived at by the court was less than $30,000 short of the crucial sum of $240,000. The district court should make clear on remand whether particular claimed expenses fall into the category of "salvage, pilotage, towage and superintendence."

Of particular difficulty is the absence of a finding which describes in detail what the claimed figure of $10,095.42 for "vessel allowances" at Baltimore (without which the Baltimore costs could in any event not exceed $240,000) consists of. There is some evidence that the "vessel allowances" were for "crew

---

[17] The difficulties in reaching accurate estimates of what repair costs would have been is to some extent compensated by the practice of adding a "contingency allowance" to the amounts calculated in determining constructive total loss. *THE MEDINA PRINCESS,* [1965] 1 Lloyd's List L.R. 361, 408; *Irvin v. Hine,* [1949] 83 Lloyd's List L.R. 162, 172–73.

wages and overtime." If the allowances in the Azores and Bermuda were actually for "crew wages and overtime," they were properly included as maintenance of necessary crew in a port of refuge pending substantial repairs. At Baltimore, where it could have been anticipated that substantial repairs would cause the ship to be laid up for close to two months, the rule may be otherwise.

Generally, wages and crew maintenance are not allowable as items unless the crew assisted in or was "necessary in connection with the repair of the vessel." On the other hand, where the crew makes repairs or would have assisted in repairs, or where the crew is necessary to guard the vessel or to superintend the repair work, the expenses may properly be considered in determining whether there was a constructive total loss.[18]

We must, therefore, as part of our remand, ask for particular findings on what the "allowances" item of $10,095.42 was for, and, if for the crew, which of the crew remained on board and for what purposes. On remand the district court will also make findings on the other expenses at Baltimore, and on the Azores and Bermuda expenses.

Though we may ultimately conclude that plaintiffs failed to meet their burden of proof by a preponderance of the evidence, we think, in view of the dearth of authority on the construction of this type of marine insurance policy and the absence of detailed findings, justice suggests that on remand the district court may, if necessary to its findings, take further evidence on the limited issues remanded.

In reconsidering its findings with respect to the Baltimore expenses, the district court should also be more specific in explaining why certain expenses were not included, or if they were, under what heading. For instance, the surveyor's report relied on by the district court failed to include the cost of replacing lifeboat equipment lost in the storm. This is a legitimate expense to be counted in determining whether there was a constructive total loss. Also, a summary by the average adjuster indicated that a pump filter had to be replaced at additional cost beyond the $155,006 estimate relied on by the court; more detailed findings are necessary here to clarify whether expenses which were disallowed were disbelieved, or whether they were disallowed as a matter of law. Additionally, we note that expenses properly incurred to repair damage from negligently made repairs may be included in computing constructive total loss costs; this requires more detailed findings concerning the costs of the repairs just outside Baltimore and whether the repairs were made necessary by earlier negligent repairs, including failure to repair the port boiler. These costs may include wages and victualling of crew during the two-day layover to make repairs.

---

[18] There is some confusion in this area, since the standards for determining whether crew wages may be included are different for general average costs than for determining constructive total loss; in this country, as in England, wages of crew while a vessel is being repaired have come to be considered general average costs. *See* York/Antwerp Rules # 11; Buglass, *supra,* at 159. Under the rule's expanded definition of "port of refuge" all the Baltimore crew expenses might well have been allowable as general average items.

B. *Constructive Total Loss After Baltimore—The Question of Cumulation*

Appellant contends that, even if the ship was not a constructive total loss at Baltimore, repair costs arising after the ship left Baltimore may be cumulated with the repairs made and deferred at Baltimore.[19] In opposing this view, appellee argues that once the ship has been repaired and sails again, subsequent repair costs incurred from successive casualties may not be cumulated for constructive total loss purposes.

Although this question was left open in *THE MEDINA PRINCESS, supra,* we agree that independent successive casualties incurred after the ship has been repaired may not be cumulated. It is true that the anticipated profits policy is silent on whether the "costs of recovery and/or repair" must arise out of a single incident or exist at a single time.[20] To permit cumulation of repairs after the ship has been repaired, however, would obliterate the difference between insurance policies on partial loss (under which the insurer may be required to pay out, over the term of the policy, amounts which in toto exceed the insured valuation limit applicable to any one partial loss)[21] and total loss policies. Had the plaintiffs desired protection against the loss of profits caused by successive partial losses, they were free to negotiate with the insurers to pay the higher premiums such additional insurance would doubtless have required. Moreover, conceptually, once the ship has been adequately restored to service, she is a seaworthy ship, and it could hardly have been intended that the cost of repairs from a new, independent cause should be added to repairs already done to the restored ship.[22]

That is not to say that the ship, once restored, may not later, on the basis of a new serious catastrophe, become a constructive total loss. If the costs incurred from repairing the new damage exceed the insured value of the owner's policy, the charterer is, indeed, in a position to contend that a constructive total loss has occurred. We think also there is a carryforward of costs from damage incurred in the earlier incidents but not repaired at Baltimore. In this case, the carryforward would be $49,340 in deferred boiler expense at Baltimore. The district court did not address the issue of determining

---

[19] In Baltimore the deferred repairs were only $49,000; at New Orleans they were at the maximum $130,000; and at the end of September, the amount claimed as deferred was only $188,000. Thus, plaintiffs' cumulation theory requires aggregation of both deferred and accomplished repairs. Appellees have not challenged the correctness of cumulating actual and deferred expenses necessary at any single point in time.

[20] Although the rules of construction might tend to favor an interpretation in favor of the plaintiffs-insureds since the policy was prepared by the insurer, later amendment of the standard form insurance policies in 1970 specifically provides that the costs of recovery and repair must, indeed, arise out of a *single* incident to make a constructive total loss. It may be that, before the amendment, the industry thought that to be the rule in any event, before Mr. Justice Roskill raised the question in *THE MEDINA PRINCESS, supra.*

[21] Marine Insurance Act of 1906, § 77(1).

[22] Although the baryte ore was loaded in Seville and apparently destined for New Orleans, on the record before us it would be difficult to describe the voyage as a "single voyage," though it may well have been intended to be continuous. We therefore do not consider the question whether, if we treated the PANOCEAN as having been on a single voyage all the way to the port of ultimate destination, New Orleans, we would allow cumulation of the costs after departure from Baltimore for New Orleans with the costs incurred at Baltimore.

possibly allowable subsequent repair costs, for the simple reason that it found that the damages caused by the stranding at Port Everglades had not resulted from "perils of the sea" insured under the policy. While we hold that this finding was error on this record,[23] our ruling will not affect the plaintiffs' right to recovery. Even if the stranding was due to a "peril of the sea" or to negligence of the crew under the *Inchmaree* clause, the claimed damages[24] *thereafter could not aggregate $240,000 even including the deferred expense at Baltimore of $49,340.*

C. *Arranged or Compromised Total Loss*

In the absence of findings below, we cannot determine whether the settlement between the shipowner and its underwriters was for a "total constructive loss" or for a series of "partial losses" as appellees contend.

The case is remanded to the district court to make findings of fact and conclusions of law under F.R. Civ. P. 52(a) in conformity with this opinion with respect to (a) whether allowable costs exceed $240,000 and (b) whether the amounts paid by the insurers to the owners were in settlement of a constructive total loss claim.

Lenfest v. Coldwell, 557 F.2d 993, 994–995 (2d Cir. 1977). "This is an appeal from a judgment of the United States District Court for the Southern District of New York, HON. ROBERT L. CARTER, entered after this court, upon appeal from a prior judgment in this case, remanded for further proceedings. . . . Following the remand, Judge Carter held a further evidentiary hearing on April 6, 1976. In an opinion dated June 1, 1976, he concluded that the amounts received by the owners were not paid in settlement of a constructive total loss claim. However, his revised calculations of allowable expenses yielded alternate sums of $240,664.04 and $246,433.19 resulting in a constructive total loss. On that basis, judgment for the plaintiffs was entered on July 26, 1976.

"We agree with the district court that no arranged or compromised total loss was proven. In fact, the evidence established that no claim for constructive total loss was ever submitted.

"On the issue of whether the total allowable expenses equal a constructive total loss, it becomes essential to determine if an allowance of $9,631.91 for crew wages at Baltimore was proper since allowable expenses exceeded the $240,000 amount by at most $6,443.19. Our prior opinion in this case fully sets forth the applicable legal principles governing the treatment of this expense, 525 F.2d at 725–26 (footnote omitted):

---

[23] Stranding is generally considered a peril of the sea under a marine insurance policy, *Lanasa Fruit Steamship Co. v. Universal Insurance Co.,* 302 U.S. 556, 561, 58 S. Ct. 371, 82 L. Ed. 422 (1938); Gilmore & Black, *supra,* § 2–9, unless due to scuttling. *See Northwestern Mutual Life Ins. Co. v. Linard,* 498 F.2d 556 (2 Cir. 1974).

[24] These claims include the following: 1) between $40,000 and $51,000 in deferred hull repairs at New Orleans, 2) $45,230 salvage costs at Port Everglades, 3) $5,877 for repairs at Port Everglades, 4) engine repairs at New Orleans of $3,385, and 5) hull repairs of $5,771, totalling at most $111,263.

Generally, wages and crew maintenance are not allowable as items unless the crew assisted in or was "necessary in connection with the repair of the vessel." On the other hand, where the crew makes repairs or would have assisted in repairs, or where the crew is necessary to guard the vessel or to superintend the repair work, the expenses may properly be considered in determining whether there was a constructive total loss.

"With these considerations in mind, we remanded for 'more detailed findings on what these costs were for, and particularly, *how they relate to the repair of the vessel.' Id.* at 725 (emphasis added).

"No such relation was found below. The court simply noted that the crew members of the Panocean were foreign residents, and that it would have been expensive to have discharged them upon arrival in Baltimore and then assemble another crew after repairs were completed. While that fact is not controverted, it does not justify shifting that expense to the underwriters absent some nexus with the repairs that the vessel underwent.

"Since plaintiffs claim that some part of crew wages was incurred in relation to the safekeeping and repair of the vessel, we remand solely for a further hearing on this issue.

"Affirmed in part, reversed in part and remanded."

NOTES

1. *The origins of insurance.* Although many ancient societies, religious groups, and social groups had primitive insurance arrangements, a significant commercial practice of insurance did not emerge until the requirements of the maritime industry made it economically desirable to disperse the risks of marine travel. As early as the twelfth century, a relatively robust insurance business could be found in the maritime states of Italy. In fact, it was the "Lombards," a group of northern Italian merchants, who introduced insurance to England in the mid-thirteenth century. For about four more centuries, the insurance business in England was predominately a marine insurance business; it was not until the late seventeenth century that other lines of insurance began to emerge and grow. A common theme in the development of commercial insurance begins with marine insurance: it is the need for risk dispersion which precedes the product. For example, it was about fifteen years after the London fire of 1666 that an informal organization for insuring against fire risk was established in the rear of the Royal Exchange, which was then a marine insurance enterprise. See generally Robert H. Jerry, II, Understanding Insurance Law § 11, at 17–18 (2d ed. 1996).

Modern marine insurance descends directly from the early practices in England, particularly those at Lloyd's Coffee House in London, the ancient precursor of Lloyd's of London. As marketed today, marine insurance is a form of all-risk coverage (meaning, it extends to all forms of loss not specifically excluded) for ships and their cargoes against "perils of the sea."

No attempt is made in these materials to examine marine insurance in great depth. The law of admiralty, a highly specialized and unique area of jurisprudence, is not offered in many law schools for a variety of reasons. As a consequence, it is not possible to give ocean marine insurance, the underpinnings of which are steeped in maritime law, the attention in a basic insurance law course necessary to make one familiar with the subject, must less master it. On the other hand, because marine insurance is one of the oldest forms of insurance, it has influenced and affected other forms of insurance, which makes it both appropriate and useful to introduce some marine insurance concepts in these materials for their broader relevance and for comparative purposes. Indeed, there are few jurisdictions that do not border upon or contain within them a navigable body of water; thus, the odds that a lawyer will encounter admiralty and marine insurance issues sometime in her career are higher than one might think.

Additional materials on the nature of the risk covered in marine insurance policies appear in § 4.06.

2. *Types of total losses.* Losses in maritime law, as elsewhere, may be total or partial. These losses may occur to the traditional maritime interests in the vessel or to cargo. However, total and partial losses are not defined in maritime law in the traditional way. Total losses, as explained in *Lenfest,* may be actual or constructive. The general rule under American maritime law is that an owner of a vessel may claim a constructive total loss of the insured vessel if the cost of repairs and other expenses required to get the ship to its destination would exceed one half the value of the vessel after the repairs are made. *Marcardier v. Chesapeake Insurance Co.,* 8 Cranch 39, 12 U.S. 39, 3 L. Ed. 48 (1814). The English maritime rule, on the other hand, requires that the costs exceed the full value of the vessel after repairs. The respective rules also apply to cargo. However, this difference in maritime law has been obviated to some extent through special clauses in hull policies requiring, as in *Lenfest,* that the expense of recovering and repairing the vessel must exceed the insured value. See Grant Gilmore & Charles L. Black, Jr., The Law of Admiralty 83–84 (2d ed. 1975). Apparently, the difference in the law of the two nations regarding the definition of constructive total losses has not led marine insurers to put similar clauses in their policies regarding property other than vessels.

If the owners of the vessel in *Lenfest* had not been insured for partial losses, but only for total losses, could they have recovered under their insurance?

3. *Types of partial losses.* There are three other types of marine losses that merit brief discussion. Two of these deal with partial loss claims and are referred to as general average and particular average losses, respectively. The word "average" denominates a partial loss as compared to an actual or constructive total loss. General average losses involve sacrifices to save lives and property interests in the maritime venture:

> General average contribution is defined to be a contribution by all the parties in a sea adventure to make good the loss sustained by one of their number on account of sacrifices voluntarily made of part of the ship or cargo to save the residue and the lives of those on board from an impending peril, or for extraordinary expenses necessarily

incurred by one or more of the parties for the general benefit of all the interests embarked in the enterprise. Losses which give a claim to general average are usually divided into two great classes: (1.) Those which arise from sacrifices of part of the ship or part of the cargo, purposely made in order to save the whole adventure from perishing. (2.) Those which arise out of extraordinary expenses incurred for the joint benefit of ship and cargo.

Star of Hope, 76 U.S. (9 Wall.) 203, 228, 19 L. Ed. 638, 645 (1869). Rules of general average can be traced at least as far back as the maritime law of Rhodes (circa 900 B.C.) and probably existed in still earlier times. Essentially, it made no sense in a storm for merchants to argue over whose cargo should be jettisoned to save the vessel, their lives, and at least some of the cargo. Thus, discretion was vested in the pilot of the vessel to make the decision about what cargo should be jettisoned. However, at the end of the voyage, the various merchants whose goods were saved were required to make a *pro rata* contribution to the merchants whose goods were tossed overboard so that all would share the loss.

Particular average is a partial loss which falls alone on the owner of the property (vessel or cargo) damaged, usually due to accidents or inherent susceptibility to loss. For example, partial damage to a vessel or its cargo by collision or fire would be classified as a particular average loss, as would some spoilage or normal deterioration of perishable goods. Grant Gilmore & Charles L. Black, Jr., The Law of Admiralty 80 (2d ed. 1975).

4. *Total loss of a part.* Finally, the fourth type of marine loss is referred to as a total loss of a part of a shipment:

A particular average should be distinguished from the total loss of a part, which may occur when a shipment consists of various units, as when, out of a shipment of 50 bars of copper, 1 is lost during transshipment or, out of a lot of 50 bales of cotton, 1 is totally destroyed by fire. This is not a particular average loss, but a total loss of an integral part of the entire shipment. Particular average is damage or loss suffered by a particular interest or by part of it which destroys less than the total value of the particular interest or the part of the particular interest involved. A particular average may attain such a percentage of the total value involved that the assured may, by exercising the right of abandonment, convert such particular average into a constructive total loss.

William D. Winter, Marine Insurance 370 (3d ed. 1952). The significance of this distinction arises where particular average losses are excluded, in whole or part, under marine policies. A total loss of a part would be covered, whereas other partial losses to a particular interest may not be covered.

5. *Valued policies in marine insurance.* Marine insurance policies were the first kinds of "valued policies," a topic which received more attention in § 2.03[2], *supra.* In *Lenfest,* the parties apparently agreed upon and insured the total profits expected during the time charter. The insurer was obligated to pay $150,000 once one of the three types of total loss was proved or agreed upon. In the absence of fraud, concealment, or an intent to wager, the

stipulation as to the value is binding, regardless of what the actual profits may have been. Grant Gilmore & Charles L. Black, Jr., The Law of Admiralty 86–87 (2d ed. 1975). Why do you think the parties were moved to enter this type of arrangement in marine insurance? Is there greater justification for valued policies where the insurer and insured agree in advance on the total value of the insured subject matter in maritime ventures than under the statutes discussed in § 2.03[2]?

[7] The Relationship Between Policy Limits and Indemnity

Most persons understand that an insurer's obligation to pay for a loss is not unlimited. An insurer will only pay for claims covered by the policy; thus, if the policy covers the insured's business property, the insured should not even ask the insurer to consider paying for a personal property claim. The policy will also exclude coverage for certain kinds of losses; thus, if the insured, for example, intentionally destroys her property, the insurer will not be liable to pay for the loss, even if the property was what the insurance policy covered. These provisions, which will receive further attention through the remainder of the book (along with many other kinds of clauses), are all in the nature of "limits" on the insurer's obligation.

In the vocabulary of the business of insurance, the phrase "policy limits" refers to the maximum dollar amount which the insurer is obligated to pay for a covered loss. The "policy limits" are part of the insurance contract, and they operate independently of the indemnity principle. Except for compulsory insurance situations (e.g., the requirement in almost all states that car owners purchase liability insurance for their vehicles), a person with a risk is not obligated to purchase coverage. Thus, there is no requirement, for example, that a property owner purchase full coverage for her property. Although the indemnity principle will place an outer limit on the insured's recovery, policy limits may create a lower limit, which has the effect of preventing—pursuant to the contract between insurer and insured—the insured from being fully indemnified for a loss.

Limits are important to insurers, because they indicate the maximum amount the insurer will have to pay for a covered loss. Insurers must be certain to collect enough premium to pay for expected losses; policy limits are key to the insurer's overall exposure for covered losses. Thus, the policy limit will be directly related to what the insured pays for coverage. The most familiar limits in insurance policies are the limits on maximum or aggregate payments, and these receive our attention first. The more complicated limitations on initial and sequential payments will be discussed last.

[a] Limits on Maximum or Aggregate Payments

Property insurance. A "policy limit" in first-party property insurance is usually thought of as the maximum amount the insurer has to pay. These limits can vary with the type of property insurance. For example, there may be a separate limit within a homeowners policy regarding personal property in addition to the maximum dollar limit which applies to loss to the residence.

In addition, there are usually specific dollar limitations on certain types of personal property such as jewelry, firearms, and other valuables.

Life and health insurance. In life insurance, the face amount of the policy is the limit unless the policy contains a "double indemnity" feature. In the latter situation, the beneficiary receives twice the face amount of the policy if the insured dies in an accident. Indemnity-type health insurance policies commonly contain several types of monetary limits. There may be limits on the amount of benefits payable for certain kinds of procedures or services (*e.g.*, separate limits for surgery, for hospital stays, for prescription drug coverages). There may be an overall lifetime limit (*e.g.*, $1 million during a lifetime is not uncommon). Managed care plans tend to have fewer limits, but the insured's ability to get services without the approval of the plan is more limited than in other arrangements.

Disability insurance. Disability insurance usually employs two kinds of limits. The first is an "overall" limit on benefits, sometimes expressed in units of time (such as $X per week for Y number of weeks). The second is a percentage limitation, i.e., disability benefits are usually limited to some percentage (60 to 70 percent depending on the type of policy) of the insured's average weekly wage, if that figure is less than the maximum weekly benefit. The percentage limitation is designed to approximate the after-tax take-home pay of the insured, but the overall limit may cause the proceeds to fall short of the percentage figure when the disabled person is a high-income individual. Is there any justification for insurers imposing a maximum per week benefit where the insured's take-home pay substantially exceeds that benefit? Finally, there is usually a waiting period before disability benefits begin, 180 days being the usual period for long-term disability policies.

Liability insurance. As observed earlier in this Chapter, indemnity is not irrelevant to liability insurance, but its role is much more limited. Thus, liability insurance has its own array of policy limits (*e.g.*, aggregate limits, per-occurrence limits, per-person limits, per-claim limits, etc.) depending on the type of policy. These receive more attention in the sections of this book devoted to liability insurance.

[b] Limits on Initial and Sequential Payments

There are a number of other techniques to limit the liability of an insurer with respect to the amount of money that is to be paid under the policy. These vary with the type of insurance, and only the basic techniques will be discussed here. Co-insurance and the use of deductibles are two of the most common; although not normally thought of as "policy limits," they do function as such. They limit initial and sequential payments rather than aggregate or maximum payments. Each mainly serves a different function, but there is some overlap.

[i] Deductibles

Deductibles are used by insurers to exclude small, frequent losses which by their nature are relatively expensive to handle. For example, insurers do not pay claims without taking some steps to become satisfied that the claim is one for which the insurer is contractually obligated. Small claims are simply too expensive to investigate; if the insurer is unwilling to simply pay all claims, it may be better to give the insured a premium reduction in exchange for self-insurance of small claims.

To illustrate, consider the collision and comprehensive coverages of an automobile policy, a familiar form of deductible. If you choose a $200 deductible and you suffer a physical damage loss of $500, the insurer pays only $300. The administrative costs of processing small claims in many instances exceed the value of the claim, and the premium for such coverages would be disproportionate to such losses. If the insurer had to charge a premium of $1.25 for every $1.00 of coverage, you would not purchase the insurance because it would be a poor value from your perspective; in economic terms, it is inefficient to use the insurance mechanism to distribute losses that can be easily absorbed by the insured. Insurance works best when it is designed to reimburse the type of loss that cannot readily be absorbed by the insured. In short, by using deductibles, insurers operate more efficiently and insureds achieve significant savings in premiums.

Also, the principle of moral hazard tells us that insureds are less likely to take precautions to prevent loss if their losses are covered by insurance. How do deductibles help insurers deal with the problem of moral hazard?

In addition to the physical damage coverages under auto policies, deductibles are commonly used in many other first-party insurance policies providing similar coverages, such as homeowners and commercial property policies, as well as other types of insurance, such as health care policies. Deductibles are also common in many forms of liability insurance, particularly malpractice and product liability coverages.

There are many kinds of deductibles; a few of the more common ones are:

(a) *straight deductible*: The deductible under the auto physical damage coverages and the homeowners policy is a straight deductible. This type of deductible means that the insured must bear the deductible amount in every loss. If the insured has the misfortune to have a car damaged four times in a year, the deductible will be subtracted from the repair cost each time.

(b) *aggregate deductible*: A straight deductible should be contrasted with an aggregate deductible that is commonly used in health insurance policies. For example, the health policy may utilize a $150 annual deductible per person with an overall deductible of $300 for the entire family. The claims of each family member are charged against an individual deductible until the $150 figure is reached for that person. At that point, the individual deductible has been met for the year for that person and no longer applies to the claims of that person. However, as soon as the claims of all of the individuals in the family reach an aggregate of $300 in the policy year, regardless of whether each individual deductible has been met, the family deductible is satisfied and there no longer is any deductible that applies to any claim of any family member.

(c) *franchise deductible*: Still another type of deductible is found in ocean marine insurance where deductibles originated. Under the franchise deductible, no loss is payable unless the amount of the loss equals or exceeds a percentage of value (the percentage is called the "franchise"). Once the franchise is met, the entire loss is paid. This was designed to relieve the underwriter from liability for partial losses on certain items that were to some extent inherently perishable or susceptible to damage during shipment. Franchise deductibles that use a dollar amount rather than a percentage of value are also used in some forms of nonmarine property insurance.

(d) *variable deductible*: As suggested above, a straight deductible eliminates the small claim, and in so doing has the beneficial effect of decreasing moral hazard. Simply put, if the insured has to pay part of each loss, this will encourage loss prevention. This is not the case, however, with all types of deductibles, particularly the aggregate and franchise deductibles. Here there may actually be an incentive to incur medical bills to meet an annual aggregate deductible or to exaggerate a partial loss claim in marine insurance so as to collect the entire loss.

In an attempt to combat the moral hazard problem created by the franchise-type deductible in marine and property insurance, insurers developed a deductible that combines the features of the straight and franchise deductibles. This deductible is referred to as a variable, diminishing, disappearing or modified deductible and works as follows. For losses less than a minimum amount (*e.g.*, $100), no payment is due. For losses above a maximum amount (*e.g.*, $500), the deductible does not apply. For losses between the two amounts (i.e., between $100 and $500), the insured receives a percentage of the amount by which the loss exceeds the minimum amount. In marine insurance, the percentage or franchise is stipulated in the policy. Assume the percentage is 125 percent. If two insureds, A and B, sustain losses of $300 and $480, respectively, A would recover $250 and B would recover $475. This is calculated by multiplying the amount of the loss that exceeds $100 by 125% (or 1.25). A little further arithmetic reveals that a $100 loss produces no payment because $100 − $100 = $0 and 1.25 × $0 = $0, and a $500 loss produces full recovery because $500—$100 = $400 and 1.25 × $400 = $500. You are probably glad to know that this has not been a popular form of deductible, due in part to its complexity.

[ii] Co-insurance: Its Purpose

In contrast to the deductible, co-insurance requires the insured to share in the loss along with the insurer, regardless of the amount of the loss. Like the deductible, co-insurance requires the insured to share a portion of the risk. Thus, both clauses help mitigate moral hazard, but co-insurance clauses have the potential to be stronger in this respect, given that the insured is required to share in a percentage of the entire covered loss, regardless of its size. To illustrate, once the deductible in an indemnity-type health insurance policy is satisfied (meaning, once the insured has incurred medical expenses equal to the amount of the deductible), neither the insured nor the provider has as much (if any) incentive to control utilization of medical services. Thus, a co-insurance factor requiring the insured to pay 20 percent of all claims out-of-pocket where the deductible has been met should help deter unnecessary utilization. The point is actually quite simple: If you have a sore shoulder from playing too much tennis, the chances are high that you can find a doctor somewhere who will diagnose a rotator cuff problem and will recommend surgery. If the surgery costs $4000 to perform, will more surgeries be performed if each patient's out-of-pocket cost is $100 (a per-person deductible) as opposed to $800 (a 20 percent co-pay)? Obviously, many people will prefer to "tough it out" and see if the shoulder gets better on its own if they can save $800 by doing so, but the number of "tough it out" choosers will go down as the costs get lower.

It is fair to ask whether it is necessary to the purpose of combating moral hazard that the co-insurance factor apply to all claims regardless of amount. After all, 20 percent of a $250,000 medical bill for a catastrophic illness would result in the insured being responsible for $50,000, an amount that would mean financial ruin for many persons. Similarly, $250,000 in claims can hardly be "run up" without a real and serious medical problem. Thus, a well designed health plan should eliminate the co-insurance factor at some level; a few thousand dollars is common. This kind of adjustment does not exist, however, with all forms of insurance; marine insurance is the classic example, as explained below.

Co-insurance has other facets to it too that have less to do with moral hazards and more to do with how losses are adjusted or premiums are calculated in some forms of insurance. The net result—the insured shares in the loss—is the same, however. Some of these situations are discussed below.

[iii] Co-insurance in Ocean Marine Insurance

Ocean marine insurance on cargos, unless in an amount as great as the market value of the property (or the value stipulated if it is a valued policy), is customarily pure co-insurance. This results from the way losses are calculated under marine policies. For example, if the value, either market or stipulated, of insured cargo is $100,000 and the amount of insurance is $80,000, the insurer would be liable for only 80 percent of any loss, unless there is a total loss of a part. In that latter case, the total loss of a part is paid in full up to the policy limit. Thus, if a partial loss (general or particular average) is determined to be $40,000, the insurer bears $32,000 and the insured bears $8,000 of the loss. If the entire cargo is lost, the insurer owes $80,000, the policy limit. Only where the actual or stipulated value is fully insured would there be no co-insurance.

As to marine hull insurance, there would be co-insurance under the British rule where the insured amount does not equal the value of the vessel, but there is some question as to whether there is co-insurance under the American rule on hull losses. There is some authority for the proposition that it should be treated as nonmarine property insurance (which is explained below). See Robert E. Keeton & Alan I. Widiss, Insurance Law § 3.7(c) (Student Ed. 1988).

[iv] Co-insurance in Nonmarine Property Insurance

Nonmarine property insurance is not co-insurance unless the policy so provides. Thus, the insurer is liable for the full amount of the loss, whether partial or total, up to the policy limits. For example, using the figures from the marine cargo situation above, if property valued at $100,000 is insured for only $80,000 and a partial loss of $40,000 is suffered, the insurer would owe $40,000 unless the nonmarine policy contained a specific co-insurance clause. As it turns out, most standard forms do have a co-insurance clause.

Due to the way some types of nonmarine property insurance is rated, an inequity results unless insurers take steps to eliminate it. Rates for fire, windstorm, and certain other types of nonmarine property insurance are based on the ratio of losses to the total values insured, but the insurer charges the same percentage or rate for the last dollar of coverage as it does for the first dollar. For example, a person who buys $30,000 of insurance on a building worth $100,000 pays the same amount per $1,000 of insurance, say $5.00, as the owner of an identical building who insures it for the full $100,000. Statistics collected by fire rating organizations conclusively demonstrate that there are, and will be, many more partial losses than total losses. Thus, from the standpoint of the two hypothetical insureds, the $30,000 insured is getting a better deal and the $100,000 insured is getting a worse deal than either deserves.

From an underwriting standpoint, nonmarine property insurers may also have rate adequacy problems if their book of business tends toward those only partially insuring. One way to correct both the rating inequity and the rate adequacy problem is to charge a sliding scale premium, meaning to charge a higher rate for the first $1,000 of coverage than for the last $1,000. Sliding scale premium structures are used for some forms of insurance, such as crime insurance. After all, there is a point of diminishing return even with burglars, i.e., they can carry only so much when they steal from you. Another way to eliminate the inequity would be for the insurer to charge a lower rate to those who insure a higher percentage of the value of the property.

Fire insurers, instead of adopting either of the approaches described above, developed a clause which has the effect of reducing the amount of the insurer's contribution to a loss based on the ratio of the amount of insurance to the value of the property insured. A clause which accomplishes this reduction evolved and is generally known as "the New York standard co-insurance clause." It reads in relevant part as follows:

> This Company shall not be liable for a greater proportion of any loss or damage to the property described herein than the sum hereby insured bears to the percentage specified on the first page of this policy of the actual cash value of said property at the time such loss shall happen, nor for more than the proportion which this policy bears to the total insurance thereon.

To accomplish the purposes of the clause, the specified percentage would normally be 70 to 90 percent, with 80 percent being the most common coinsurance percentage.

This clause is most common in insurance policies on commercial property, but it is not uncommon for some insurers to use it in homeowners policies. The Sample Homeowners Policy in Appendix C ("Section I-Conditions," par. 3(b)) contains the substance of the New York clause in more modern–but almost equally challenging–language:

(2) If, at the time of loss, the amount of insurance in this policy on the damaged building is less than 80% of the full replacement cost of the building immediately before the loss, we will pay the greater of the following amounts, but not more than the limit of liability under this policy that applies to the building:

> (a) The actual cash value of that part of the building damaged; or
>
> (b) That proportion of the cost to repair or replace, after application of the deductible and without deduction for depreciation, which the total amount of insurance in this policy on the damaged building bears to 80% of the replacement cost of the building.

How do these clauses work? One way to understand the clause is to reduce its elements to an algebraic formula, and then memorize the formula. See Robert H. Jerry, II, Understanding Insurance Law § 93[b] (2d ed. 1996) (showing how one derives a formula from the New York standard coinsurance clause). If one does this work, one arrives at the following for the New York standard coinsurance clause: Where X equals the proceeds to be paid by the insurer, U equals the policy limits (or underwritten amount), L equals the amount of loss, ACV equals the actual cash value of the property (measured at the time of the loss), and the coinsurance percentage is 80 percent,

$$X = (U/.80ACV)L$$

In the provision from the homeowners policy, one would simply use replacement cost ("RC") instead of ACV, so that:

$$X = (U/.80RC)L$$

To take an example, assume that the insured has property with an actual cash value (or replacement cost, in the case of the homeowners policy) at the time of the loss of $125,000, and the insured insures the house for $75,000 under a policy that uses an 80 percent coinsurance percentage. In a windstorm, the house suffers damage of $20,000. The insured has purchased coverage for only 60 percent of its value. If one does the math, one finds that the insurer pays $15,000, or 75 percent of the loss, in these circumstances. The point? By failing to insure the property for at least 80 percent of its actual cash value (or replacement cost in the homeowners policy), the insured is prevented from receiving 100 percent reimbursement for a partial loss. If, however, the insured had insured the property for $100,000, one would discover, after doing the math, that the insured would recover $20,000 for the partial loss. Of course, by failing to insure the property for its full value ($125,000), the insured would not receive full reimbursement in the event of a total, or nearly total, loss.

What risk does the insured run with the co-insurance clause in times of rapid inflation? Does this militate against the use of the clause in noncommercial property insurance policies such as a homeowners policy? This problem can surface in other areas as well. For example, where a warehouseman or bailee buys one policy which insures her property as well as the bailor's or customer's property, coverage for the latter is usually accomplished through an "in trust or on commission" clause in conjunction with a standard fire insurance policy. (See note 5 regarding bailments following the Berman & Bourne essay in Chapter 4(E)(3)(c)). Where the fire policy also contains a New York standard co-insurance clause, the question may arise as to what is meant by the language "the property described herein" in the co-insurance clause. If that language includes the bailor's property in custody of the bailee, this could work to reduce the percentage of the value of the property insured so that the bailee no longer would be covered for the total amount of a partial loss to his or her property. In addition to inflation on her own property, the bailee would also have to worry about the value, including inflation, of property bailed. There is little authority addressing the issue of whether the language "the property described herein" includes the bailee's property as well as that of the bailor. See Robert E. Keeton & Alan I. Widiss, Insurance Law § 4.5(b) (Student Ed. 1988).

What does all of this accomplish from the insurer's perspective? The insurer anticipates that many people will realize that small losses are the most common, and therefore given a choice will self-insure (i.e., roll the dice) on the large, catastrophic loss. After all, total losses are relatively rare; thus, the saavy insured would purchase only partial coverage if that provided full reimbursement of partial losses, and would self-insure for the remainder. But by using the coinsurance clause, the insurer will encourage people to insure the full value of their properties—by taking away full coverage for partial losses in the absence of insuring the property for an amount at least equal to the coinsurance percentage. For a good example of the coinsurance clause in action, *see Templeton v. Insurance Co. of North America,* 201 S.W.2d 784 (Mo. Ct. App. 1947).

Chapter 3

REGULATING THE INSURANCE RELATIONSHIP

"Insurance is a small world that reflects the purposes of the larger world outside it." —Professor Spencer Kimball, in *The Purpose of Insurance Regulation: A Preliminary Inquiry in the Theory of Insurance Law*, 45 Minn. L. Rev. 471, 524 (1961)

§ 3.01 An Overview of State Legislative and Administrative Regulation *

In § 1.02's materials on the question of "what is (and is not) insurance," we encountered the fact that the business of insurance is a regulated industry. For most of the twentieth century, the proposition that the insurance industry should be regulated was not questioned; rather, the only question was *who* should regulate it, i.e., whether regulation should occur at the federal or at the state level of government. At 2000, some of the assumptions about the proper mix of regulation and free competition in the business of insurance are being questioned, particularly with respect to commercial lines.

a. *Rationales for regulation.* Why should any industry be regulated? The classic rationales for regulation which are possibly relevant to the insurance industry include restraining excessive competition, compensating for inadequate information, remedying unequal bargaining power, and implementing paternalism (i.e., regulation is required to trump irrational decisions of market participants). Which of these are plausible justifications for regulating the business of insurance? Sometimes regulation is justified on the ground of producing desirable social outcomes that the market will not, if left to its own devices, achieve. Does this help explain why health insurance, to take a prominent example, not only is regulated but also has a significant government presence as an insurance provider and financier? How successfully would an unregulated market provide health insurance, and consequently health care access, to the nation's elderly?

b. *The dominance of state regulation.* One of the most striking characteristics of the insurance business is the extent to which it has escaped significant federal regulation. Indeed, the business of insurance is easily the largest U.S. industry to elude such oversight. To understand how this happened, one must take a quick look at the history of the industry.

---

* The material in this section is an adaptation of Robert H. Jerry, II, Understanding Insurance Law §§ 11, 20-23 (2d ed. 1996).

In the early years of the colonies, insurance on domestic risk was normally placed with British underwriters; in short, there was not much of an insurance business to regulate. Slowly but surely, however, the American insurance industry emerged and began to grow. During the last years of the colonial period, insurance offices opened in Philadelphia, New York, and other port cities. The first fire insurance company was established in Philadelphia in 1752, and the first American insurance corporation was chartered in 1792. Seventeen more companies were chartered by 1803.

During this early period, regulation, such as it was, occurred primarily through restrictions in specific corporate charters granted by state legislatures. From the beginning, colonial and state governments did not ignore the fledgling industry; at the least, they understood the industry's revenue potential, so there was a desire to tax insurers and their agents. As one would expect, the practice of granting specific charters for insurance companies fell into disuse when general incorporation statutes were enacted early in the nineteenth century. When states enacted general incorporation legislation, many states also passed legislation governing the establishment of insurance companies. These statutes imposed requirements similar to those contained in a typical insurer's corporate charter. Insurers were required to make periodic reports to a state official, avoid certain kinds of investments, and maintain certain minimum levels of capitalization and reserves. States often imposed more onerous burdens on out-of-state insurers.

Insurance companies were inclined to view the developing patchwork system of state regulation as burdensome, and by the 1860s insurers were urging Congress to adopt national standards that would make insurers federal institutions analogous to banks. As part of an effort to encourage the federal government to take over the function of insurance regulation, a number of New York insurance companies set up a case they hoped would invalidate the system of state regulation. Paul, a Virginia resident, was appointed by these companies as their agent. He applied for a Virginia license, but refused to deposit bonds with the state treasurer as required by state law. Paul was not granted a license, but he proceeded to sell a policy of insurance to a Virginia resident anyway, and he was convicted for violating the Virginia licensing statute. The Virginia Supreme Court affirmed his conviction. Paul challenged his conviction in the United States Supreme Court on the grounds that Virginia's stricter requirements for foreign insurers violated the Privileges and Immunities Clause of the United States Constitution, that the federal commerce power allowed regulation of insurers, and that this power resided exclusively with the federal government.

In 1869, the Supreme Court rejected Paul's arguments, thereby dashing the hopes of the insurers who were interested in promoting federal regulation. The Court held in *Paul v. Virginia,* 75 U.S. (8 Wall.) 168 (1869), that a corporation is not a citizen within the meaning of the Privileges and Immunities Clause. More importantly, the Court held that "issuing a policy of insurance is not a transaction of commerce," which was tantamount to placing the business of insurance outside the constitutional authority of Congress. Under this ruling, to which the Court adhered for seventy-five years, individual states retained the authority to regulate insurance companies.

The insurance industry grew with the rest of the country; as the business became bigger and more complex, the public urged more rigorous state regulation. By 1900, most states had some kind of licensing procedure for companies and agents, but abuses in the life insurance industry attracted the public's attention. These practices included the payment of excessively large commissions to agents, the making of false representations about future dividends, the waste of company assets on lobbying activities and the inability of many companies to account for related expenditures, nepotism in the hiring of insurance company employees, and other practices where company officials abused their positions for personal gain. It was not coincidental that populist fervor at the turn of the century was hostile to combinations of capital and restraints of trade, and insurance companies bore their fair share of public disdain.

These pressures culminated in an investigation by a New York legislative committee led by Senator William W. Armstrong. In 1906, the Armstrong Committee issued a lengthy report on insurer abuses, which led to the enactment of remedial legislation in New York. Among other changes, the New York law required detailed year-end reporting by insurers, ordered the allocation of policy dividends to insureds, limited the amount of new business insurers could write each year, and imposed strict regulations on agent commissions. New York's initiatives were influential in other states, and by 1919, thirty-six states had separate insurance departments vested with the exclusive task of administering regulatory statutes. By 1930, insurance departments in most states were not only given greater authority to collect information from insurers but were also charged with the responsibility of preserving insurer solvency. The departments were likewise authorized to review insurers' business decisions on reserve levels, valuation of assets, and investments. In addition, regulators were given some authority over policy forms and unfair trade practices, such as rebating, misrepresentation, twisting, and discrimination. By 1944, state insurance regulation was relatively comprehensive in all areas but ratemaking, even if it was not always particularly aggressive.

In the early 1940s, the Attorney General of Missouri, frustrated with the ineffectiveness of state ratemaking regulation and hoping to encourage federal involvement, sought a determination in federal court that the business of insurance constituted interstate commerce subject to the antitrust laws. He obtained an indictment against the South-Eastern Underwriters Association, an association of 198 stock fire insurance companies in six states, its officers, and its member companies. The indictment charged the defendants with violating the Sherman Act by agreeing to fix rates and boycotting nonmembers. The district court dismissed the indictment on the authority of *Paul v. Virginia*, ruling that insurance was not interstate commerce. In 1944, however, the U.S. Supreme Court reversed the dismissal in a four-to-three decision. In *United States v. South-Eastern Underwriters Association*, 322 U.S. 533 (1944), the Court overruled the longstanding precedent of *Paul v. Virginia* and held that insurance transactions were subject to federal regulation under the Commerce Clause. In short, the *SEUA* decision removed the constitutional impediment to federal regulation of the insurance industry.

Ironically, by 1944, the insurance industry preferred the generally lax regulation of the authorities in many states. Moreover, the industry was concerned that federal antitrust laws might be applied in a way that prohibited the pooling of actuarial data, a practice central to the ratemaking process. For other reasons, too, the industry feared both the potential havoc that federal antitrust regulation might create and the uncertainties inherent in substituting federal for state regulation. The industry knew that the Court's holding in *SEUA* regarding the scope of the Commerce Clause could not be overturned. Therefore, the industry rallied behind legislation proposed by the National Association of Insurance Commissioners (an entity, also known as the NAIC, which is discussed below) to limit the impact of *SEUA*. Congress enacted this proposal, which became known as the McCarran-Ferguson Act, 15 U.S.C. §§ 1011 et seq.

c. *Congressional "preemption" of federal regulation in McCarran-Ferguson.* In section 1 of the McCarran-Ferguson Act, Congress stated the underlying policy of the statute as one favoring state regulation of the insurance business:

> Congress declares that the continued regulation and taxation by the several States of the business of insurance is in the public interest, and that silence on the part of the Congress shall not be construed to impose any barrier to the regulation or taxation of such business by the several States.

If one takes the foregoing preamble at face value, Congress presumably favored state regulation because of both the states' closer proximity to the kinds of problems needing regulation and its concern over the effect of supplanting existing structures of state regulation with untested, yet-to-be devised federal structures.

The operative language of the Act appeared in section 2:

> (a) The business of insurance, and every person engaged therein, shall be subject to the laws of the several States which relate to the regulation or taxation of such business.

> (b) No Act of Congress shall be construed to invalidate, impair, or supersede any law enacted by any State for the purpose of regulating the business of insurance, or which imposes a fee or tax upon such business, unless such Act specifically relates to the business of insurance: *Provided,* That after June 30, 1948, [the Sherman Act of 1890, the Clayton Act of 1914, and the Federal Trade Commission Act of 1914] shall be applicable to the business of insurance to the extent that such business is not regulated by State law.

Section 3(b) of the Act stated that the Sherman Act would apply to some insurer activities regardless of whatever regulation the states might enact: "Nothing contained in this chapter shall render the said Sherman Act inapplicable to any agreement to boycott, coerce, or intimidate, or act of boycott, coercion, or intimidation." Section 4 similarly ensured the supremacy of three labor statutes: "Nothing contained in this chapter shall be construed to affect in any manner the application to the business of insurance of the. . .National Labor Relations Act, or. . .the Fair Labor Standards Act of

1938, or. . .the Merchant Marine Act, 1920." Whatever motives underlay behind the statute, its significance was unmistakable. As the Supreme Court soon explained, "[o]bviously Congress' purpose was broadly to give support to the existing and future state systems for regulating and taxing the business of insurance. . . .; [I]ts purpose was evidently to throw the whole weight of its power behind the state systems." *Prudential Insurance Co. v. Benjamin,* 328 U.S. 408, 429–430 (1946).

d. *States' acceptance of the McCarran-Ferguson invitation.* In essence, the McCarran-Ferguson Act gave supremacy to state regulation of the business of insurance to the extent the states chose to occupy the regulatory field. Accordingly, shortly after the Act was passed, state insurance commissioners and representatives of the industry collaborated in an effort to draft and propose state legislation to occupy the areas exempted from federal regulation. The NAIC, with the input of industry representatives, drafted model rate regulation and unfair trade practices statutes. The model ratemaking legislation reflected the beliefs that concerted ratemaking was essential to insurer solvency and that such joint activity should proceed under state supervision. By 1950, some form of rate regulation had been adopted in every state.

The states were somewhat slower to enact unfair trade practices legislation. In the mid-1950s, the Federal Trade Commission initiated inquiries into unsavory practices in the advertising of accident and health insurance. Concern about possible federal intervention encouraged the states to act, and, by 1963, unfair trade practices statutes were adopted in all the states. This legislation, as enacted in most states, empowered the state insurance commissioner to issue cease and desist orders for misrepresentations and false advertising, for defamation, boycotts, coercion, and intimidation, for issuing false financial statements, providing stock options and advisory board contracts, and unfairly discriminating in life insurance, annuities, accident, and health insurance, and for rebating.

The process repeated itself in the 1960s and early 1970s when public concern over automobile insurance rates led to a Department of Transportation inquiry. With the prospect of federal intervention looming, a majority of the states enacted some kind of no-fault automobile insurance statute; in about half of these states, the statutory changes reformed the tort system with respect to compensation of victims of auto accidents.

e. *State regulation at 2000.* Throughout the 1980s and 1990s, efforts to shift more regulatory responsibility to the federal government arose from time to time, typically prompted by consumer advocates and, more recently, by some insurers frustrated with the difficulties of dealing with up to fifty different regulatory authorities. But none of these initiatives progressed very far, and it was fair to assert that at 2000 the state regulatory system was well entrenched.

But it would not be correct to assert that the state regulatory system was static, as changes in the financial services marketplace were placing a great deal of pressure on the NAIC and the state regulatory system at 2000. In the late 1990s, both the Federal Reserve Board and the Comptroller of the Currency had supported banks' efforts to sell insurance either directly or through subsidiaries or affiliates. Insurers, of course, did not welcome the competition, but as banks moved into insurers' territories, some insurers responded by opening thrifts and acquiring savings banks—i.e., by entering into the banking business. (For a summary of these developments, see Alex Maurice, *Insurance Players Rush Into Banking Game*, Nat'l Underwriter (Prop.-Cas.), April 19, 1999, at 9.) Because the federal government has long had a significant role in regulating the banking industry, the presence of banks in the insurance business and insurers in the banking business naturally raised the question of whether state regulation continued to be appropriate in this rapidly changing environment. The banking industry had long sought an overhaul of federal regulation, but until 1999, Congress was unable to agree upon the parameters of this reform in the face of disagreements among the banking, insurance, securities, and thrift industries, consumer groups, and federal and state regulators. A major breakthrough (and compromise) was the enactment of the Gramm-Leach-Bliley Act of 1999, Pub. L. No. 106-102, 1999 U.S.C.C.A.N. (113 Stat.) 1338 (the "GLB Act"). The statute's primary thrust was to modernize banking regulation, but it also lowered the barriers between the banking and insurance industries.

The extent to which the GLB Act will affect state regulation of the insurance business remains to be seen. The Act affirms the McCarran-Ferguson Act and the primary role of the states in regulating the business of insurance. It also affirms the role of the states in licensing entities and individuals which provide or market insurance. But because "financial holding companies" will be allowed to own both banks and insurance companies, cooperation between federal and state regulators is expected. The GLB Act does preempt some state laws governing the sale of insurance by depository institutions and their affiliates (the general principle is that states cannot interfere with the ability of depository institutions to sell insurance), but states are specifically authorized to apply consumer protection statutes against depository institutions selling insurance on a nondiscriminatory basis. For more on the relevance of the GLB Act to the insurance industry, see James M. Cain & John J. Fahey, Survey, *Banks and Insurance Companies—Together in the New Millennium*, 55 Bus. Law. 1409 (2000); Paul J. Polking & Scott A. Cammam, *Overview of the Gramm-Leach-Bliley Act*, 4 N.C. Banking Inst. 1 (2000); Mitchell S. Eitel, William D. Torchiana, & Donald J. Tourney, *Gramm-Leach-Bliley Act Provisions of Particular Interest to Insurers and Banks*, 1184 PLI/Corp 495 (Mar. 2000).

A particularly interesting aspect of the GLB Act encourages states to establish a uniform system of insurance agent and broker licensing. If within a three-year period after the enactment of the GLB Act the NAIC determines that a majority of states have not established such a system, the NAIC is given two years to establish a "National Association of Registered Agents and Brokers." If the NAIC fails to establish "NARAB," the President is authorized to create and supervise NARAB, with certain appointment and supervision powers to be carried out with the advice and consent of the U.S. Senate. Thus, the possibility exists that a significant shift of regulatory authority from the states to the federal government could occur if the states (or the NAIC) fail to exercise regulatory authority themselves. This, of course, was how the state regulatory system emerged in the wake of the McCarran-Ferguson Act in the late 1940s.

At mid-2000, the NAIC has had some difficulty drafting a model licensing statute. *See* Mark E. Ruquet, *Licensing Model Hits "One-Word" Impasse*, Nat'l Underwriter (Life-Health), July 17, 2000, at 1. But the NAIC has been active in trying to reform and update its regulatory efforts, in part due to pressure from congressional leaders who see federal regulation as a superior alternative to the current state regulatory regime. *See* Alex Maurice, *NAIC Seeks Transformation to Stay Viable*, Nat'l Underwriter (Life-Health), Mar. 27, 2000, at 6; Steven Brostoff, *Federal Regulation Possible: GOP Leaders*, Nat'l Underwriter (Life-Health), July 31, 2000, at 5 (two leading Republicans asserting that Congress will consider federal regulation of insurance if the state system is not reformed). It is difficult to predict how all of this will evolve. As one commentator observed, "[o]n its face, GLB appears unequivocally to protect the prerogatives of the states to regulate insurance and indeed that scenario may well come to pass. Due to its intentional ambiguity, however, the potential exists for courts and regulators to implement the federal regulation of a significant portion of the insurance industry." Douglas P. Faucette, *Could GLB Be a 'Wolf in Sheep's Clothing'?*, Nat'l Underwriter (Life-Health), June 19, 2000, at 33.

f. *The "limits" of state regulation.* Generally speaking, the McCarran-Ferguson Act gives state insurance statutes supremacy over federal laws, but this statement is subject to significant qualification. The Act does not give the states supremacy over *all* activities of insurance companies; activities of insurers not within the "business of insurance" are subject to the full reach of Congress's authority under the Commerce Clause. Thus, many activities of insurers are subject to "paramount federal regulation" where the "business of insurance" is not involved. *See Securities and Exchange Commission v. National Securities, Inc.*, 393 U.S. 453, 459–460 (1969). Insurance companies must comply with federal tax laws, many of the filing and disclosure requirements of the securities laws, and federal labor laws. Moreover, Congress's decision in the McCarran-Ferguson Act to give state statutes primacy over Congress's exercise of its commerce power does not limit the applicability of the Equal Protection Clause. *See Metropolitan Life Insurance Co. v. Ward*, 470 U.S. 869 (1985).

g. *The structure of state regulation.* Because each state separately regulates the business of insurance, the statutory law of each state is the starting point for sketching the legislative regulatory framework. The sheer volume of this statutory law precludes a detailed discussion of it in this book. A number of generalizations, however, are possible.

All states have some sort of office that is charged with the duty of administering the state's regulatory insurance laws. In most states, the office is called the "Department of Insurance," and the official who heads the Department is usually called the "Insurance Commissioner." In about two-thirds of the states, the department is a separate regulatory entity; in the remaining states, the insurance agency is a part of some other state department, such as a "Department of Insurance and Banking" or a "Corporation Commission." In a majority of the states, the commissioner is appointed by and serves at the pleasure of the governor. In about half the remaining states, the commissioner is appointed by some other governmental entity, and in the other half the commissioner is elected by the voting public.

The department of insurance (or whatever it might be named) exercises authority delegated to it by the legislature. The primary responsibility of the insurance commissioner (or other head of the department) is to protect the public, and to that end the authority of the commissioner is usually stated broadly. As an implementer of law, the commissioner makes "law"; administering and applying a statute inevitably requires interpreting its substance and designing procedural rules for implementation of the substantive standards. As any administrative lawyer knows, the substantive and procedural rules generated in the administrative process have a tangible effect on the conduct of regulated parties.

Given that the insurance business is regulated by fifty different state agencies, it would not be unreasonable to predict utter disarray and chaos in this industry. Such a prediction, surprisingly enough, misses the mark, except perhaps in one respect: when compared to state commercial legislation, state insurance legislation is extremely disorganized. There is nothing in state insurance law that even comes close to the unifying influence of the Uniform Commercial Code. In fact, few states have insurance "codes" in the ordinary sense of the term. Most state insurance "codes" are a hodge-podge of many independently drafted and enacted provisions. In fact, Professor Kimball once described state insurance statutes as a "rubbish heap without parallel in the law-making of modern man." Spencer L. Kimball, *Unfinished Business in Insurance Regulation*, 1969 Wis. L. Rev. 1019.

But when one gets past the disarray in many state "insurance codes," one finds in discrete areas of statutory regulation a surprising degree of uniformity from state to state. This is due primarily to two factors. First, many states have enacted model acts promulgated by the NAIC, which has resulted in substantial uniformity in many state statutes. The NAIC is an association of the chief insurance regulatory officials of the fifty states, the District of Columbia, and the territories. It was organized in 1871, shortly after the Supreme Court's decision in *Paul v. Virginia* made it clear that the states had the exclusive authority to regulate the insurance business. The NAIC, through its staff and various committees currently headquartered in Kansas City, Missouri, proposes model laws and regulations for possible adoption by the states, studies problems of insurance regulation, gathers and distributes information on regulatory matters, and maintains financial data for the purpose of detecting insurer insolvency at an early stage. The proceedings of the NAIC's regular biannual meetings are published; these volumes serve as an important source of research information. The NAIC's model laws, regulations, and guidelines are now published in a multivolume looseleaf and annotated format, making it easier to assess the national status of various NAIC initiatives. The NAIC has no legal authority, but it does provide a significant coordinating influence on the regulation of the insurance industry by the several states.

Second, and perhaps more important, the purposes of the statutory schemes are virtually identical. As a result, many state insurance statutes are similar in both content and wording. The objectives of state legislative regulation, as articulated somewhere in most states' insurance codes, are essentially fourfold: (1) ensuring that consumers are charged fair and reasonable prices for insurance products; (2) protecting the solvency of insurers; (3) preventing unfair practices and overreaching by insurers; and (4) guaranteeing the availability of coverage to the public. To a large extent, these objectives overlap. For example, in regulating rates, the first and second objectives overlap: it is important not only that a fair price be charged for the risk assumed but also that a sufficiently high price be charged to maintain insurers' solvency. Similarly, the first and third objectives overlap: unfair prices may be related to an unfair practice of discriminating against particular groups. And to some extent, these objectives are contradictory. For example, the second and fourth objectives are sometimes difficult to achieve simultaneously: charging a premium sufficiently high to maintain adequate reserves may result in coverage being unaffordable to certain segments of the population. To some extent, the first and third objectives are inconsistent: eliminating discrimination in insurance rating is potentially at odds with setting a fair or reasonable rate, given that insurance rates should be a function of risk; however, owing to the expense of risk evaluation, an unbounded effort to categorize and subdivide risks in search of the fair rate would eventually lead to prohibitively expensive rates.

h. *Rate regulation.* The current methods of rate regulation in the states are quite diverse, and therefore defy easy generalization. Not every line of insurance is subject to the same kind of regulation, and different states approach the task in different ways. Prescription of rates by the state regulator is uncommon. It is more typical for insurers to file proposed rates with the insurance department, which must approve them before they can be used. The "prior approval" approach usually has a mechanism under which a filed rate becomes effective unless the department disapproves the rate within a specified period of time. The "file and use" approach allows the insurer to use the filed rate, unless the insurance department takes steps to disapprove the rate within a specified period of time. It is possible to combine these two methods pursuant to what is commonly called "flex rating." Insurers can file and use their rates provided they are within a specified range; but any rate changes outside the range must receive the department's prior approval. The "open competition" method relies upon market forces to set rates, although the insurance department can take steps to intercede in appropriate circumstances. Rate regulation has some connection to solvency regulation, to be sure, but other state statutes also seek to secure insurer insolvency.

i. *Solvency regulation.* The modern era of solvency regulation dates to the 1960s, when a wave of insurer insolvencies developed primarily among companies writing substandard auto insurance. In the wake of these insolvencies, the NAIC proposed model statutes to create guaranty associations. These statutes create an association of insurers to satisfy the obligations of insolvent insurers through assessments on insurers doing business in the state. In effect, these statutes create a safety net for insureds who happen to do business with a financially unstable insurer. The NAIC also created a centralized database and early warning system to help identify troubled insurance companies in the early 1970s, and in 1989 the NAIC created a working group to help identify potentially troubled companies of national significance.

Another important aspect of solvency regulation are those statutes that provide for periodic examinations of insurers and audits of their annual reports. By investigating detailed accounting information submitted by insurers, state regulators, working with the NAIC, seek to determine whether insurers doing business in the state have the financial ability to meet their commitments. The examination-audit statutes dovetail with the licensing statutes: state regulators will only license an insurer to do business in the state if it appears that the insurer is a financially stable institution. The financial requirements for insurers to obtain a license vary greatly in the different states.

Several other kinds of statutes have as a predominant purpose the protection and furtherance of insurer solvency. For example, all states have statutes prescribing the kinds of investments insurers are allowed to make. Similar statutes regulate the methods by which insurer assets are valued, so that a true picture of the insurer's financial health is available. All states have statutes that require insurers to create as a liability on their balance sheets a "reserve" thought adequate to provide a fund to meet policy obligations as they are incurred. Most states have adopted statutes or regulations that regulate insurer holding company systems; this regulation is intended to ensure that those who control or seek to acquire control of insurers will not manage the insurer contrary to the interests of policyholders.

j. *Regulation of trade practices.* The special relationship between insurer and insured was explored in § 1.03, *supra.* As one would expect, much early statutory law (and judicial case law) was designed to equalize the relationship between insurer and insured. Initially, specific problems were often met with specific solutions. In the nineteenth century, some states enacted statutes providing that no condition in an application for insurance would be valid unless specifically stated in the policy itself. These statutes were designed to prevent insurers from relying on obscure conditions outside the text of the policy that purported to relieve the insurer of liability in certain circumstances. Throughout most of the nineteenth century, it was assumed that an insured who discontinued his premium payments under a whole-life insurance policy forfeited any equity he had previously accumulated. But statutes enacted in many states in the late nineteenth and early twentieth centuries required the insurer to provide some sort of minimum cash surrender value in the event of default after a specified period of time. The rule of contract law that allowed a party to void a contract upon the other party's breach of a warranty provision, regardless of the provision's materiality, worked great hardship on many policyholders. Thus, statutes enacted in many states around the turn of the century declared that no policy would be voided for breach of warranty unless the fact warranted was material or was intentionally misrepresented. (The successors to these statutes are examined in subsection 3.02[1], *infra.*)

Under the impetus of the McCarran-Ferguson Act, state legislatures took steps to regulate the bargaining relationship between the insurer and the applicant in the late 1940s and early 1950s, thereby preempting federal entry into this regulatory field. Each state enacted statutes to prohibit such practices as false or misleading advertising, misrepresentation of a competitor's product, and failing to pay valid claims. Most of these statutes authorize the state insurance commissioner to commence an investigation into alleged unfair trade practices and to issue cease and desist orders where such practices are occurring.

More recently, legislative efforts to combat overreaching and unfairness in the marketplace take the form of increasing the availability of, and access to, information. For example, much attention has been given to making more information available about the price of insurance at the point of sale. One important source of information for consumers in the insurance business is advertising. Advertising, by making consumers aware of available products and the alternatives, both promotes distribution of coverage and enhances product competition. Inaccurate advertising, however, has an equal potential for frustrating the public interest by encouraging unnecessary and incorrect purchases. Thus, much modern regulation can fairly be described as "truth-in-advertising" regulation. Under the reasoning that a consumer who understands his or her rights and obligations under a contract is less likely to be the victim of sharp practices and is more likely to purchase a useful product, statutes in some states mandate minimum standards for language used in policies, often using "reading ease tests" to determine whether the policy's language is sufficiently "plain." Insurance commissioners usually have the express authority to disapprove forms that are obscure, misleading, or unclear.

Most statutes on insurer overreaching are aimed at the marketing practices of insurers and their agents. Claims processing is regulated legislatively by statutes that assess penalties for delays in paying claims. Also, a number of states have statutes that impose penalties against an insurance company that refuses to pay a claim, forces the insured to sue the insurer to recover, and subsequently loses the insured's suit. All states have some procedure by which the insurance department can receive consumer complaints. Some legitimate complaints will fall within an area where the department has the authority to investigate and give relief. However, even if the department lacks authority to resolve a complaint or it is otherwise inappropriate for the department to take specific action, which will often be the case, the procedure for merely receiving the complaint may provide considerable benefit to the consumer. Such procedures are an important method of transmitting information to consumers about insurance statutes and regulations, consumer rights, and available remedies.

k. *Coverage regulation.* States regulate the coverage of insurance policies in a number of ways. The most pervasive kind of coverage regulation seeks to increase the amount of coverage that insureds possess, perhaps even by mandating the purchase of coverage. For example, all states have financial responsibility statutes for owners of automobiles, and these statutes effectively require owners of automobiles to have liability insurance or the financial wherewithal to pay for losses they cause. In 47 states, liability insurance is compulsory. The public policy underlying these statutes is to ensure that adequate funds will exist to reimburse individuals who suffer physical injury or economic loss in most automobile accidents.

Legislatures commonly specify the content of insurance policies, and this has obvious effects on coverage. For example, some statutes mandate that health policies cover the insured's dependents from the moment of birth. Statutes in some states prohibit insurers from offsetting increased social security benefits in group disability income policies. In a majority of states, statutes now limit insurers' use of genetic information to make risk or premium classifications in health insurance and sometimes in life and disability insurance as well.

States also regulate coverage by prescribing rules for access to insurance. For example, all states have some kind of so-called "residual market plan" through which automobile insurance is sold to people unable to obtain insurance in the voluntary market. The most common mechanism in the states is the "assigned risk" plan, under which insurers doing business in a state are required to insure some portion of otherwise uninsurable risks.

1. *Meshing insurance, the market, and social goals.* ** A market that allocates resources in a perfectly efficient manner may be utterly unresponsive to social goals. If the public prefers for reasons of fairness or justice a different allocation than what an unregulated market produces, the state may intervene to produce a particular outcome that trumps the result reached in the market. As Arthur Okun has explained, society's elevation of certain values over what the market would allow can be explained in terms of "rights." Because certain rights cannot be purchased or sold, they are inefficient; they lack the benefit of the price mechanism that would induce trading in rights to maximize the utility to buyer and seller (*e.g.*, a ban on baby selling prevents adults who would value children more from acquiring them from a parent who values them less). Okun explains that these rights are justified on grounds of liberty (the primacy of the value of protecting the individual against encroachments of the state), pluralism (material gain is only one of the values that motivate humans, and the other motivating values sometimes need protection from market forces), and humanism (the inherent, fundamental rights of human beings that must be declared invulnerable to trading). To the extent the market's perspective on these rights is one of neutrality, the market must be subordinated to the values reflected in these rights. See Arthur Okun, Equality and Efficiency: The Big Tradeoff 6–15 (1975).

In health insurance and some other areas of personal insurance, the inconsistencies between the values of a neutral market and the norms of social welfare are particularly striking. Under traditional insurance principles, those who are predisposed to illness through either family history or genetics, the elderly (who tend to use more health care), the unemployed and the indigent (who tend to have more adverse health events), and other groups should pay more for health insurance than others. Under the neutral actuarial principle that low-risk insureds should get premium advantages, only the healthiest, who by definition need health care access the least, should pay relatively low amounts for health insurance. Given a normative judgment that health care deserves the status of a right or entitlement, the neutral market will undervalue the importance of providing insurance, and concomitantly health care access, to the sick, the elderly, and the poor. If insurance is deemed a public good, the market will not allocate it fairly; regulation, through subsidy and allocation, improves upon the market's choices by furthering higher-order social goals.

** This subsection "1" is derived from an unpublished manuscript. Robert H. Jerry, II, *Justifying Regulation in a Market-Oriented Insurance Industry* (unpub. man. Sept. 17, 1998.) Copyright © 1998 by the author. Reprinted with permission.

The observation that the neutral market undervalues some social goals is a variant of the point that market efficiency and fairness are not always congruent. As Professor Abraham explains, "[t]he concept of efficiency ignores questions about the appropriate distribution of wealth and protection against risk, because the preferability of a given allocation of resources is measured by consumer willingness to pay for those resources . . . . A natural consideration, therefore, is whether the distribution of risk produced by insurance and regulated or altered by insurance law is fair, regardless of whether the allocation involved is efficient." Kenneth S. Abraham, Distributing Risk: Insurance, Legal Theory, and Public Policy 18 (1986). Insurers must, of course, discriminate; without discrimination, an insurer cannot, as it must, separate high-risks from low-risks. As an insurer's pool attracts an increasing proportion of high risks (which is inevitable due to the phenomenon of adverse selection), the insurer that fails to discriminate must increase premiums until lower-risk insureds are priced out of the market or decide to self-insure. In the meantime, a competing insurer that does discriminate among risks is likely to enter the market and lure the lower-risk insureds to its product with the promise of a lower premium. In short, insurers must discriminate among insureds in order to compete.

This does not mean, however, that the risk classifications insurers will develop when responding to market forces will necessarily be "fair." For example, even if it is cost-effective for insurers to use factors such as race, ethnicity, or religion to distinguish among risks, it does not follow that the use of such factors is justifiable. If there is a social consensus that the use of a particular rating is morally repugnant, regulation can deny the use of the unacceptable factor. Indeed, it is possible in an unregulated market that insurance will be used for what society perceives to be immoral, antisocial, or unlawful purposes. By prohibiting insurance contracts on specified kinds of losses, regulation reduces the tendency that insurance has to increase behavior leading to such losses. For example, history shows that some persons purchase insurance on property or lives with the intention of causing a loss so that proceeds can be collected. The criminal law has much to say about such behavior, but insurance law does as well. A number of insurance law doctrines—the insurable interest requirement; the fortuity rules; rules defining "accident" for the purpose of excluding coverage for intentionally-caused loss; and rules governing disqualification of life insurance beneficiaries—operate to eliminate coverage where the person entitled to proceeds or protection contributes to, or is in a position to contribute to, the loss. At the margin, this has the effect of deterring some antisocial or unlawful conduct that would otherwise occur. In short, these principles favor social values that an unregulated market would not necessarily achieve and deter conduct to which an unregulated market would not necessarily object.

In other words, there is no guarantee that insurers will develop fair, socially acceptable classification schemes in an unregulated market. Thus, regulation can achieve the fairness that the unregulated market is unable to attain. In short, when "justice" is defined in terms other than efficiency, the unregulated market does not necessarily further it; in such circumstances, what constitutes "justice" must be determined in the political process, where the interactions of individual actors and interest groups decide which values among many are predominant.

NOTES

1. *State or federal regulation?* Which is better—state or federal regulation? What are the advantages and disadvantages of each approach? See generally Robert H. Jerry, II, Understanding Insurance Law § 23[c] (2d ed. 1996). For more information on insurance regulation, see Susan Randall, *Insurance Regulation in the United States: Regulatory Federalism and the National Association of Insurance Commissioners*, 26 Fla. St. U. L. Rev. 625 (1999); John Dembeck, *Regulation of Insurance*, 602 PLI/Lit 119 (April 1999); Jonathan Macey & Geoffrey Miller, Costly Policies: State Regulation and Antitrust Exemption in Insurance Markets (1993); Francine Semaya & Vincent Vitkowskey, eds., The State of Insurance Regulation (1991).

2. *Gender discrimination in insurance.* As of 1997, the average life expectancy at birth in the United States was 73.6 years for a male and 79.2 years for a female. By 2010, the figures are expected to increase to 74.1 and 80.6 for men and women, respectively. U.S. Dep't of the Census, Statistical Abstract of the United States 1999, at 93 (Table No. 127). Suppose an insurer offers a life insurance product which charges older applicants more than younger (based on a table that sets a higher premium for each additional year of an applicant's age), but makes no distinction based on the applicant's sex. Would you expect more men or more women to purchase the product? How would the insurer's risk pool be affected if a competing insurer decided to offer the same product except that women would pay slightly less (at each age) than men to account for the average advantage women enjoy in longevity?

Under the logic of two U.S. Supreme Court cases, it is a violation of Title VII of the Civil Rights Act of 1964, 42 U.S.C. § 2000e-2(a)(1), for an employer to provide its employees any kind of insurance benefit, including life insurance or a retirement plan, unless identical benefits are provided to both men and women and unless contributions, if any, are the same for both sexes. *See Los Angeles Department of Water & Power v. Manhart,* 435 U.S. 702 (1978); *Arizona Governing Committee v. Norris,* 463 U.S. 1073 (1983). How do Title VII's requirements affect your assessment of the issues raised in the preceding paragraph?

Unless the practice is prohibited by state law or unless insurance coverage is provided as a fringe benefit in the employment setting, insurers may permissibly charge men and women different prices for the same coverage. Is this unfairly discriminatory? The evidence shows that young male drivers have many more injury-producing and damage-causing accidents than young female drivers. Should young men pay more for auto insurance than young women, or should young men and young women pay the same? Why not use the frequency of injury-producing and damage-causing accidents to set auto insurance premiums instead of sex and age? For more discussion, see Jerry, *supra* note 1, § 24[a].

3. *Race and other classifications.* Prior to the mid-1960s, many life insurers made distinctions between whites and non-whites in the coverage provided and premiums charged for life insurance. Why do you suppose race-distinct actuarial tables seemed to disappear from the marketplace in the mid-1960s? Current data show that whites, on average, enjoy longevity advantages over most minority groups. Should insurers be allowed to distinguish among individuals in the pricing of insurance based on the individual's race? If the evidence showed that Baptists have shorter average life spans than non-Baptists (and we are aware of no evidence one way or the other on this question), would it be appropriate for insurers to charge Baptists more for life insurance (and less for annuities)? Are your answers to these questions consistent with your answers to the questions posed with respect to insurance distinctions based on the individual's sex?

Although race-based insurance life insurance pricing "seemed to disappear" in the 1960s, it apparently did not vanish. According to one report, "[i]nvestigations in Florida, New York and other state insurance departments have turned up evidence of race-based pricing. Discrimination was maintained in a variety of ways, ranging from use of different premium and agent compensation rates to the use of separate sets of risk classification systems." Jim Connolly, *NAIC Acts on Race-Based Premium Rates*, Nat'l Underwriter (Life-Health), June 19, 2000, at 3. Florida regulators recently reached a settlement with one insurer that it claimed used race-based pricing practices. *See* Jim Connolly, *States Huddle on Race-Based Policies*, Nat'l Underwriter (Life-Health), July 10, 2000, at 3. Insurance regulators in Florida and Georgia recently sent "cease and desist" letters to 28 insurers, ordering them to eliminate racial discrimination in the pricing of industrial life policies. *See* Allison Bell, *Florida, Georgia Warn 28 Insurers Against Race-Based Premiums*, Nat'l Underwriter (Life-Health), July 24, 2000, at 3.

"Redlining" refers to the practice of drawing "red lines" around certain geographic areas on a map and then declining to sell products or services in that location. For example, a bank might decide that residents of a particular area are poor risks for repayment of loans, and therefore it might decide not to make loans to anyone in that area. If an insurer is concerned that properties in a particular geographic area present particularly high risks, the insurer might "redline" that area. If redlining has the effect of denying insurance coverage to disproportionate numbers of members of racial and ethnic minority groups, should the practice be allowed? If the practice is disallowed, can insurers be effectively prevented from achieving the same result by declining to designate agents to service particular areas, by charging higher prices for properties in certain areas, or by making discriminatory use of property inspections? Exactly what is wrong with insurers charging higher prices to higher-risk insureds? *See* William E. Murray, Note, *Homeowners Insurance Redlining: The Inadequacy of Federal Remedies and the Future of the Property Insurance War*, 4 Conn. Ins. L. J. 735 (1998).

4. *Genetic classifications.* Suppose A applies for a policy of life insurance. A review of A's ancestry shows that A's parents and grandparents had a history of premature death due to heart disease. Suppose further that the evidence shows that A is more likely than other persons whose ancestors had

no history of heart disease to die prematurely. B also applies for life insurance. B is identically situated to A, except that B has no indications or family history of heart disease. Should an insurer be allowed to charge A more for life insurance than Applicant B? Does your answer change if the product is health insurance?

The Human Genome Initiative is a massive research project, coordinated by the National Institute for Health, which is soon to complete the construction of a map of the human genome, the chromosomal material (i.e., DNA) where human genes reside and which define many individual physical characteristics. The project has already identified many genes that correlate with diseases such as Huntington's disease, sickle cell anemia, and cystic fibrosis, and at 2000 new discoveries are being announced on almost a daily basis. If a genetic marker should be discovered for certain kinds of heart disease and an inexpensive test is devised to identify the gene, should insurers be allowed to use the test for the purpose of charging those who have the gene higher premiums for life, disability, and health insurance? Scholarly commentaries on this subject are voluminous. For a survey of the arguments for and against allowing insurers to use genetic information, see Mark A. Hall, *Insurers' Use of Genetic Information*, 37 Jurimetrics J. 13 (1996).

5. *Insurance and AIDS*. AIDS is one of the most serious health afflictions in human history. The Centers for Disease Control estimates that as many as two million Americans are afflicted with the Human Immunodeficiency Virus ("HIV"), representing at least one in every 135 Americans, and the World Health Organization estimates that over thirty million people worldwide are afflicted. Barring a breakthrough in the treatment of the virus, it appears that 100 percent of HIV-positive persons will progress to clinical AIDS, which is fatal in all cases.

AIDS is a heterosexual phenomenon in many parts of the world; in the United States the most significant increase in HIV-infection is occurring as a result of heterosexual sexual activity. But because about 60 percent of all AIDS cases in the U.S. involve men who have had a sexual experience with other men, many insurers in the 1980s considered AIDS to be a "gay disease" and sought to use sexual orientation as a basis for denying life, health, or disability insurance. These practices were widely condemned (see NAIC, *Medical/Lifestyle Questions and Underwriting Guidelines*, in 1 NAIC, Model Laws, Regulations and Guidelines 60-1 (1995)), and seem not to be, at least overtly, a part of insurers' underwriting practices today. It is common, however, for insurers to ask questions on applications about an applicant's HIV status and in some instances to require an HIV test as a prerequisite to approval of an application for life or disability insurance and individual policies of health insurance (i.e., to be distinguished from group policies sold to employers for the benefit of employees).

Persons who are HIV-positive or who have AIDS have shorter life expectancies and are certain to incur large medical bills in the latter stages of their illnesses. Should such persons pay the same for health and life insurance as persons who are not HIV-positive or who do not have AIDS? Should an insurer be allowed to refuse an application for health insurance because the applicant is HIV-positive? See generally Jerry, *supra* note 1, §§ 23[b].

6. *What does "fairness" mean in insurance?* No two persons are identical in all respects, and no two persons or situations present identical degrees of risk of loss. One view of fairness implies that people with different risks should pay different premiums for the same insurance coverage. This view, however, often collides with a different view of fairness, one that values treating human beings equally, notwithstanding provable differences among them or demonstrated differences in loss experience (which may or may not be caused by the factors with which the losses correlate).

"Maximizing access to insurance. . .is a goal that cannot be perfectly reconciled with the economic forces that underlie the operation of insurance markets. This paradox will require our society to grapple in future years with two fundamentally opposed notions of what insurance really is. Should, on the one hand, insurance be viewed as a product to be purchased and sold in predominately unregulated markets, where access to insurance is a function of a person's risk and ability to pay? In this paradigm, insurance will be unavailable to many people, sometimes people with high risks and great needs . . .. Or, on the other hand, should insurance be viewed as a public good, where access is an entitlement and the costs are spread across the widest groups possible, perhaps even the entire population in some instances? . . . To some extent, this dichotomy is already apparent in the debate over health care reform and the issue of whether health insurance should become a national program. These issues are certain to be with us for many years to come." Jerry, *supra,* at 122.

§ 3.02 Judicial and Legislative Regulation of Policy Provisions and Insurer Defenses

[1] Breach of Warranty, Misrepresentation, and Concealment

[a] Breach of Warranty: Basic Principles

The starting point was developed in Chapter 1: Insurance companies come to the market and offer a product to individuals and business entities who desire to transfer risk to someone else. If insurers possessed perfect information about the risk they are invited to assume, insurers could make perfect decisions about which risks to accept and how much premium to charge. Insurers, of course, begin with little or no information about the risks they are asked to assume; by expending resources to learn about risks (insurers acquire expertise over time about risk, and this knowledge is an important asset) and to investigate individual applicants for insurance, insurers acquire information they need to make good decisions. With unlimited resources, insurers could do unlimited investigation, acquire unlimited information, and make absolutely perfect decisions. But resources are not unlimited, and investigation is a cost that insurers must account for, one way or another, on the insurers' balance sheet. Thus, insurers, although they strive to get the best information possible at reasonable cost, cannot acquire perfect information about risks through their own efforts.

Moreover, some information is simply inaccessible to insurers. Consider, for example, an insurer who is asked to insure a building against loss by fire, windstorm, hurricanes, tornados, etc. With respect to the weather-related risk, the insurer can learn about the frequency of damaging winds, tornados, and hurricanes by investigating weather patterns; as a result, the insured in Florida will pay more for protection against the risks posed by hurricanes than the insured in Michigan. With respect to the fire risk, however, the behavior of the insured is a material factor affecting the likelihood of damage to the building due to fire. For example, whether the insured installs and adequately maintains a sprinkler system is highly relevant to the amount of damage that would occur if a fire should break out. Thus, the insured who installs and maintains a sprinkler system will pay less for the insurance. The insurer can check on whether the system has been installed easily enough. But how is the insurer to know whether the insured leaves the system on all the time? Obviously, the insurer cannot cost-effectively post one of its agents at the insured's building to make sure that the sprinkler system is always properly maintained and functional.

To deal with this kind of imperfect information, the insurer may ask the insured to "warrant" that a sprinkler system will be properly maintained and fully functional at all times. Alternatively, the insurer may seek to "condition" the coverage on the presence of a functional sprinkler system. If the insurer does not wish to inspect the inside of the building (after all, the inspection is a cost to the insurer; for homeowners insurance, would you expect the insurer's agent to tour the house on which coverage is sought to check for the presence of fire alarms and a security system?), the insurer may ask the insured to "represent" that the building has a sprinkler system. To that end, the application for insurance may ask "Do the premises for which insurance is sought have a sprinkler system?"; if the applicant answers the question incorrectly, this misrepresentation may have consequences for coverage should the property be damaged by fire in the future. (For a case involving warranty law and a sprinkler system, *see American Home Assur. Co. v. Harvey's Wagon Wheel, Inc.,* 398 F. Supp. 379 (D. Nev. 1975), *aff'd without opinion,* 554 F.2d 1067 (9th Cir. 1977).) In sum, insurers respond to the problem of imperfect information by asking for warranties and representations and by limiting coverage. Much insurance law addresses the question of the extent the insurer has the power in particular cases to limit its obligations in these ways.

Consequently, the history of the law of warranties is a story about the extent to which courts and legislatures have allowed insurers to rely on an insured's breach of warranty as a basis for refusing to provide coverage to the insured. The seminal article on the history of warranties in the early common law was written by Professor William R. Vance, and all subsequent treatments of the subject, including this one, depend mightily on Professor Vance's insights. *See* William R. Vance, *The History of the Development of the Warranty in Insurance Law,* 20 Yale L. J. 523 (1911).

Prior to the late eighteenth century, warranties in insurance law, such as it was, were indistinguishable in legal effect from warranties in any other type of contract. A warranty was merely an agreed-upon condition, set forth in the contract itself, that had to be strictly performed; if not strictly performed, the policy was voidable by the underwriter. In this early time, warranties and representations were similar in all important respects. Both required a material relation to the risk transferred in order for noncompliance or nonsatisfaction to have an effect on the insurance contract. Thus, both the nonsatisfaction of an immaterial warranty and an immaterial noncompliance with an otherwise material warranty were inconsequential.

All of this changed by the late eighteenth century, and Lord Mansfield deserves most of the credit (or blame, depending on your perspective) for these changes. First, in a line of cases beginning in 1763 with *Woolmer v. Muilman,* 1 W. Bl. 427, Burr, 1419, and culminating in 1786 with *De Hahn v. Hartley,* 1 T.R. 343, Lord Mansfield eliminated the materiality requirement for warranties. Professor Vance describes the effect of the latter case:

> But it is not until 1786 that we find the fully developed warranty really in action. In *De Hahn v. Hartley,* a vessel was insured for a voyage from Africa to the West Indies. The vessel was described as "warranted copper sheathed, and sailed from Liverpool with fourteen six-pounders,. . .fifty hands or upwards." The vessel having been captured during the period covered by the policy, the underwriter paid the loss. Subsequently, learning that the vessel had sailed from Liverpool with only forty-six hands, although it had, six hours later, taken on six additional men at Anglesea, thus sailing from that island with fifty-two men, the broker brought his action to recover the money paid on the ground that the insurance was void for breach of warranty. It is very clear that the risk assumed for the voyage from Africa to the West Indies was in no wise enhanced by the fact that the vessel had only forty-six hands during the short voyage on inland waters from Liverpool to Anglesea, yet it was held that the policy was avoided by the breach of the warranty. In his opinion, Lord Mansfield stated the law in this characteristic fashion: "There is a material distinction between a warranty and a representation. A representation may be equitably and substantially answered; but a warranty must be strictly complied with. Supposing a warranty to sail on the first of August, and the ship did not sail till the second, the warranty would not be complied with. A warranty in a policy of insurance is a condition or a contingency, and unless that be performed, there is no contract. It is perfectly immaterial for what purpose a warranty is introduced; but being inserted, the contract does not exist unless it be literally complied with. Now, in the present case, the condition was the sailing of the ship with a certain number of men; which not being complied with, the policy is void."

20 Yale L.J. at 529–30. *

Professor Vance also describes how the change wrought by *De Hahn* and its progeny necessitated a further distinction:

Since the court had decided that the distinction between warranties and representations was accompanied by such striking and surprising legal consequences, it naturally was a matter of great interest to the underwriters to know when a statement descriptive of a risk was a warranty and when a representation. Lord Mansfield very quickly decided that a statement written in the policy was a warranty, while one written anywhere else, or not written at all, was only a representation. Then the question arose, How must it be written in the policy? It was determined that a statement should bear the magical potency of the warranty if it was written anywhere on the face of the policy as on the margin, straight or obliquely; but if the written statement was inscribed on a different paper folded within the policy, or even fastened by a wafer to the policy, it was no more than a representation, which could not destroy the rights of the insured or enable the underwriter to escape his liability, unless it had really prejudiced the underwriter. It will be observed that the mere fact that a stipulation or a descriptive term was written in the policy was of itself sufficient to determine its character as a warranty. No other evidence of the intention of the parties to make it a warranty was deemed necessary.

Id. at 530.

Although the strict compliance rule left the insured with a high risk that coverage might be forfeited, the strict compliance rule had a significant commercial purpose in marine insurance in eighteenth century England. Recurrent wars of that period made it highly desirable that ships sail in a convoy; therefore, an insured might be asked to warrant that the ship would not sail alone. Sailing at certain times of the year was more dangerous; so, an insured might be asked to warrant that the ship would sail at a particular time. See Edwin W. Patterson, Essentials of Insurance Law 274 (2d ed. 1957). Insurers were not, of course, in a position to monitor the ship's compliance with the warranty after it had left port, particularly given the primitive methods of communication in that era. Thus, warranties were important to marine insurers as a method of dealing with imperfect information. At least initially, underwriters sought to limit their exposure to certain risks, and the warranties they inserted in policies did, by their nature, pertain to matters that materially affected the risk. However, as Professor Patterson described it, things soon got out of hand:

These decisions [about warranties] were deemed necessary by Lord Mansfield and other English judges in order to protect the "infant industry," marine insurance, which was a valuable aid to British overseas commerce. Hence the adoption of the rule, after a long period of development, that the materiality of a breach of warranty will not be inquired into, because the expert underwriter took the risk on the assumption that certain facts (warranted to be so) existed or would exist, and no judge or jury should be allowed to substitute his or its judgment for the underwriter's. . . .

The earlier warranties were few in number, and were drawn for each individual contract between persons of equal bargaining power. If anything, the shrewd shipowner or trader, often insuring a ship "lost or not lost" long after she had sailed and after she had last been heard from, was in a better position to know the risk than the underwriter at Lloyds. In the nineteenth century this English doctrine of warranty was transferred to the popular forms of insurance in the United States, especially life insurance and above all fire insurance, with warranties drawn by insurance-company lawyers to guard against every potential hazard, multiplied by the printing press into an array of formal and stilted clauses which the insured could not understand even if he tried to read them. Thus, as a New York court said in a notable opinion [*Van Schroick v. Niagara Fire Ins. Co.,* 68 N.Y. 434 (1877)], a fact well known to both the insured and the insurer's agent might create a defense for the insurer "by force of some condition, crouched unseen in the jungle of printed matter with which a modern policy is overgrown." . . .

Patterson, *supra,* at 274–275. *

This kind of forfeiture suffered by insureds led courts and eventually legislatures to find ways to mitigate the potentially harsh effects of warranties. For an example of judicial mitigation of warranties in modern times, consider the following case.

VLASTOS v. SUMITOMO MARINE & FIRE INSURANCE CO. (EUROPE), LTD.

707 F.2d 775 (3d Cir. 1983)

ADAMS, Circuit Judge.

Evelyn Vlastos appeals from a judgment denying her recovery on an insurance policy for a fire that occurred in a commercial building that she owned. Applying Pennsylvania law, the district court declared that Vlastos had unambiguously warranted that the third floor of her building was occupied exclusively as a janitor's residence. Based on this ruling by the court, the jury found that Vlastos had breached the warranty, and the court declined to set aside the jury verdict. Inasmuch as we hold that it was error to determine that the warranty clause in question is unambiguous, the order of the district court will be vacated and the case remanded for further proceedings.

I.

Vlastos owned a 20′ × 80′ four-story building at 823 Pennsylvania Avenue, Pittsburgh, Pennsylvania. Prior to a fire on April 23, 1980, Vlastos and her son operated a luncheonette and a bar on the first floor of the building. The second and third floors were leased to Spartacus, Inc., which conducted a massage parlor on the second floor. Evidence was introduced at trial tending to show that the massage parlor also utilized at least a portion of the third

---

floor. At the rear of the third floor there was a section variously described as a padlocked room or a section partitioned off from the remainder of the floor. It was in this area that Philip "Red" Pinkney, Vlastos' handyman and janitor, is alleged to have lived. Vlastos kept supplies on the fourth floor, and maintained a small office there as well. She occasionally remained overnight on the fourth floor rather than return to her residence. Vlastos was not staying there the night of the fire, but two friends of hers were residing there temporarily and were killed. A third person was also killed in the fire.

All of Vlastos' insurance matters were handled by her broker, John Mitchell. Mitchell obtained insurance for Vlastos from a group of European insurance companies through two sub-brokers. The policy in question, dated November 22, 1979, provided $345,000 of fire insurance with a $1,000 deductible provision. It contained a section, Endorsement No. 4, expressly incorporated into the policy, which stated in part: "Warranted that the 3rd floor is occupied as Janitor's residence."

After the building and its contents were destroyed by the fire, the insurers refused to pay the claim, citing an alleged breach of the warranty. Vlastos filed a complaint based on diversity jurisdiction. The jury trial was bifurcated as to liability and damages; the parties agreed that Pennsylvania law is applicable. During the trial on liability, the district court ruled that the insurers were not required to produce evidence that the warranty was material to the risk insured against, holding that materiality was irrelevant. At the conclusion of the evidence, the court denied Vlastos' motion for a directed verdict, and proceeded to charge the jury that the warranty regarding the third floor was breached if a massage parlor occupied any significant portion of the floor, regardless of whether the janitor had a residence there as well. The jury was also instructed that if the third floor was totally unoccupied this too would constitute a breach of the warranty. The sole question put to the jury was: "Have the defendants proved by a preponderance of the evidence that the plaintiff breached the warranty?" The jury answered affirmatively. Vlastos' motions for judgment notwithstanding the verdict or a new trial were denied in a memorandum opinion and order. Vlastos has appealed, raising numerous points, including the contention that the jury was incorrectly instructed that the warranty was unambiguous.

II.

Vlastos objects that "no proof was offered that the provision in Endorsement No. 4 actually was a warranty." Reply Br. 1. Although her brief does not specify an alternate characterization of the provision, presumably she means to assert that it was a representation. If, as Vlastos implies, it was a representation, then the insurers would be under an obligation to show that the provision was material to the risk insured against in order for the insurers to avoid their obligations under the contract.

A representation, unlike a warranty, is not part of the insurance contract but is collateral to it. If a representation is not material to the risk, its falsity does not avoid the contract. On the other hand, the materiality of a warranty to the risk insured against is irrelevant; if the fact is not as warranted, the insurer may deny recovery. In case of doubt, courts normally construe a statement in an insurance contract as a representation rather than a warranty. But no reason has been advanced for doubting that the provision in question here—which by its terms "warrant[s]" a fact and is part of the insurance contract — is a warranty. Accordingly, we cannot hold that it was improper for the trial judge to read this provision as a warranty. The district court therefore did not err in ruling that evidence of materiality would not have been relevant to the question whether Vlastos can recover on the policy.

The parties agree that the provision in question concerned a state of affairs existing at the time the contract was signed, and was not a promise that a janitor *would* occupy the third floor in the future. In other words, the provision is satisfied if a janitor occupied the floor on Nov. 22, 1979, the date the policy was issued, even if the situation had changed by the time of the fire several months later.[2] The district court erroneously instructed the jury on this issue at two points. It stated that Vlastos agreed that the floor "*would be* occupied as a janitor's residence" (App. 389, emphasis added) and that the warranty was breached if "*at the time of the fire*" a massage parlor occupied any significant portion of the floor (App. 390, emphasis added). If the district court on remand decides that the case must be retried (see *infra*, Part III), then it should instruct the jury that the relevant time for purposes of the warranty is the time at which the parties entered into the contract.

III.

Having established that Vlastos did warrant that at the time she entered into the contract "the 3rd floor [was] occupied as Janitor's residence," it must be determined what the language of the warranty should be construed to mean. For the reasons set forth below, the provision must be read in Vlastos' favor, as warranting merely that a janitor occupied some portion of the third floor.

Under Pennsylvania law, the question "whether a written contract is ambiguous is one for the court to decide as a matter of law. . . . Our review therefore is plenary." *Northbrook Insurance Co. v. Kuljian Corp.,* 690 F.2d 368, 371 (3d Cir. 1982). "[T]he language of the policy may not be tortured to create ambiguities where none exist." *Houghton v. American Life Insurance Co.,* 692 F.2d 289, 291 (3d Cir. 1982);. If any ambiguity exists, however, it is well-settled that the ambiguity "*must* be construed against the insurer, and in a manner which is more favorable to coverage." *Houghton,* 692 F.2d at 291 (quoting *Buntin v. Continental Insurance Co.,* 583 F.2d 1201, 1207 (3d Cir. 1978)) (emphasis in original).

"A provision of an insurance policy is ambiguous if reasonably intelligent [persons] on considering it in the context of the entire policy would honestly differ as to its meaning." *Northbrook,* 690 F.2d at 372(quoting *Celley v. Mutual Benefit Health & Accident Association,* 229 Pa. Super. 475, 481–82, 324 A.2d 430, 434 (1974)). In determining whether there is any ambiguity, the court need not confine its attention to the "four corners" of the contract but may consider external evidence. *Celley,* 229 Pa. Super. at 482, 324 A.2d at 434, states that the court may consider "whether alternative or more precise language, if used, would have put the matter beyond reasonable question."

---

[2] Thus there is no contention that this provision was a so-called "promissory warranty."

Applying Pennsylvania law to the facts of this case, we conclude that the warranty here was ambiguous. Although the view of the insurance companies—that Vlastos stated that the floor was to be the janitor's exclusive province—is a possible construction, a reasonable person could have understood Vlastos to have warranted merely that her janitor lived on the third floor.

Even if one takes the warranty clause in isolation, it is questionable that the reading proffered by the insurance companies is the only plausible one. If Pinkney resided on the third floor, then it is not simply and unambiguously false to say that he occupied that floor, even assuming the existence of a significant competing or concurrent use. In response to the query "does a janitor occupy the third floor?" a categorical "no" surely would be misleading at best, and even a qualified "no" ("no, he occupies only part of it" or "no, a massage parlor occupies it as well") is strained. It seems that the most appropriate reply, making the relevant factual assumptions, would be a qualified affirmative ("yes, although he occupies it along with a massage parlor").[6]

When the relevant language is examined in the context of the remainder of the policy, and in light of the alleged purposes for the insertion of the warranty, it becomes even more difficult to say that Vlastos unambiguously warranted that her janitor alone occupied the third floor.

It is significant that the warranty was not made in the course of a description of the various uses to which the building was being put. The policy did not make any warranties as to any other floors of the building. Thus, it would be reasonable to infer that the warranty evinced a concern that there be a resident janitor rather than an intent that the various floors of the building, such as the third floor, be put to relatively safe uses.

Although the actual reasons for the insertion of the warranty are not clear from the record, the insurers represented at trial that one reason was that a resident janitor decreases the risk of losses due to fire. See App. at 358, 372. This purpose of the provision would be fulfilled if Pinkney lived on the third floor, regardless of the proportion of this floor that was reserved for his sole use. Occupancy of the premises by a janitor might increase the likelihood that fire hazards would be taken care of promptly. It also might mean that there is a good chance that if a fire were to begin a responsible person would be on the scene to put it out or call the fire department, thus minimizing the damage from fires that do occur. A full-time resident janitor might also deter prowlers and vandals from entering the building. For reasons such as these, Vlastos could have assumed that the insurance companies looked kindly upon her having a resident janitor, without understanding that the insurance companies had any interest in whether the janitor occupied all or only part of the floor.

It is true that a second reason has been proposed for the insertion of the warranty. If a janitor occupied all of the third floor, then no occupant more dangerous—as a massage parlor perhaps is—would be there. Viewed in light

---

[6] *Cf.* 45 C.J.S. Insurance § 556 at 304 (1946) ("The mere fact that only one room in the house is actually used by the occupant does not render the building vacant or unoccupied.")

of this possible motive, the warranty would have been intended to contemplate the occupancy of the entire third floor. Although this suggestion as to the purpose of the warranty is plausible, it is less obvious than the first suggested reason, especially when it is recalled that the insurers did not request any assurance that extremely dangerous usages were absent from the other three floors of the building.

The conclusion that the warranty is ambiguous is buttressed by the consideration that the insurers easily could have precluded doubt by the addition of one word. Had the provision read: "Warranted that the 3rd Floor is occupied solely as Janitor's residence," then the question whether there would be a breach if a massage parlor operated in some of the space would have been unlikely to arise.

Because the provision is ambiguous, under Pennsylvania law it must be construed in a manner favorable to insurance coverage. We therefore hold that Vlastos warranted only that a janitor resided on the third floor, not that there was no other occupancy of the floor.

If any jury issue existed at all, it was simply whether or not a janitor resided on the third floor at the time of the contract. The district court at several points indicated that the insurers had presented no evidence that Pinkney did not live on the third floor, and that it would not let the insurers go to the jury on this question.[7] On the other hand, the district court did instruct the jury that it could find "that nothing occupied the space at all . . . ." App. 391. There also is some uncertainty whether the district court, in considering the sufficiency of the evidence that Pinkney did not occupy the third floor, focused on the time of the fire as distinguished from the time that the parties entered into the contract. *See supra*, Part II. Accordingly, on remand the district court should clarify whether, in its view, there was a jury question whether Pinkney lived on the third floor at the time the contract was made. If it determines that there was sufficient evidence to go to the jury on this issue, then a new trial on the liability issue should be held. If there is no jury question, then under the facts of this case a new trial would be unwarranted, and the district court should enter judgment for Vlastos on liability.

IV.

For the reasons set forth above, the judgment of the district court will be vacated, and the matter remanded for further proceedings consistent with this opinion.

NOTES

1. *The insurer's purpose.* Why did the insurer care about who occupied the third floor? If the janitor changed his location to the second floor to

---

[7] See App. 357 ("You [the insurers] haven't produced any evidence that he [Pinkney] was not there or that he was not a janitor in the ordinary sense of the word. . .[the insurers'] only substantial contention. . .is that there was a massage parlor there"); App. 360 ("The only evidence I think that you've introduced, at least the evidence that I'm letting you go to the Jury on, is that there may have been a massage parlor there.") See also App. 358, 359. The insurers have not questioned that they bear the burden of proof.

accommodate a change in use of the building, should coverage be invalidated on account of breach of warranty?

Presumably the insurance policy at issue in *Vlastos* was a standardized form, and the warranty provision was, obviously, not standard policy language. What implications does this have? Would the court have decided the case differently if the policy had said "We do not cover: . . .(7) losses that occur while a janitor is not occupying the third floor"? Why do you suppose the insurer drafted in terms of warranty?

2. *Affirmative versus promissory warranties.* One method of mitigating the harsh consequences of literal noncompliance with a warranty involved a distinction between *affirmative* and *promissory* warranties. In essence, affirmative warranties involve a stipulation or recital of an existing fact made in the application process. Promissory (or "executory") warranties involve a stipulation that certain action or nonaction will take place after the policy has been entered into or that certain facts shall or will continue to exist.

To illustrate the distinction, assume a shipowner and underwriter agree that insurance on the hull (i.e., the ship) would be effective only if the ship had sailed by or will sail on a date certain, say August 1. This would constitute a condition of the contract, *i.e.*, a warranty. The condition that the ship *had* sailed on August 1 is an example of an affirmative warranty—a stipulation or recital of an existing fact. The condition that the ship *will* sail on August 1 is an example of what is an executory or promissory warranty—a stipulation for the future performance of an act or that a certain fact will come into existence in the future. Affirmative warranties only need to be true on the date of the policy's effectiveness; but promissory warranties have no such temporal limitation, and are promises of the continued existence of a given state of things.

The paradigmatic promissory warranty is the provision found in many kinds of business policies under which the insured promises to keep inventories, books, and records of the business (which will be used to establish the amount of any ensuing loss) and to provide a safe place for their keeping. Obviously, such a warranty is useless if the insured need only keep records and provide a safe location for them on the date the policy is issued. But unless a warranty is clearly shown to be promissory, courts usually presume that the warranty is affirmative. *See, e.g., Reid v. Hardware Mutual Insurance Co.,* 252 S.C. 339, 166 S.E.2d 317 (1969); *Smith v. Mechanics' & Traders' Fire Insurance Co.,* 32 N.Y. 399 (1865).

In eighteenth century England, would the distinction between affirmative and promissory warranties with respect to the date of a ship's sailing matter? Does the distinction matter in *Vlastos*?

3. *Occupancy of personal dwellings.* Why should an insurer of residential property care who lives there? In *Reid, supra* note 2, the insureds purchased a homeowner's policy that described the insured premises as "one story frame constructed, approved roof, owner occupied, one family dwelling." 166 S.E.2d at 319. The court concluded that the phrase "owner occupied" was an affirmative warranty that the Reids occupied the home at the time the policy was issued, not that the Reids promised to continue to live there. Thus, the policy

was not invalidated by the fact that the Reids sold the home to a buyer who resided in the premises when the house burned. *Id.* at 320. If you are an insurer to whom owner occupancy matters, how would you redraft the policy? *See Heniser v. Frankenmuth Mutual Insurance,* 449 Mich. 155, 534 N.W.2d 502 (1995) (policy's definition of "residence premises" was unambiguous statement of coverage requiring insured to "reside" at premises at the time of the loss).

4. *Interpretation.* When parties give different meanings to the same words, it is sometimes necessary for a court to employ techniques of interpretation to determine what the words mean. Interpretation can also serve a "policing" function, however. If one interpretation of language produces a harsh result for one party, this harsh result can be avoided by interpreting the words to mean something else. What role did interpretation play in *Vlastos*? Some courts have avoided the harsh consequences of warranties by construing the relevant language as a representation, instead of a warranty. Would this have been too much of a stretch in *Vlastos*?

[b] Misrepresentation and Concealment: Basic Principles

The law with regard to misrepresentation is fairly easy to state insofar as the basic elements are concerned. There must be a representation that (1) is substantially false or misleading, (2) is material, (3) induces reasonable reliance, and (4) causes harm or detriment. If one adds the element of intent to the mix, one has the common law doctrine of fraud or, as it is sometimes called, deceit. The relying party that suffers harm or detriment may sue for damages or for rescission of the contract. Although relief for misrepresentation and fraud in the insurance context is equally available to insured and insurer, it is the insurer that most frequently raises it, usually as a defense, to avoid the insurance contract for something the insured has allegedly done in the formation of the contract or in claiming benefits under it.

Today there is little in the way of procedural or other jurisdictional formalities to hinder an insurer in asserting a defense based on misrepresentation or in seeking to rescind an insurance policy, but that has not always been the case. It was not that long ago that a clear distinction existed in most states between the common law action for damages, which went by the name of fraud and deceit and required a showing that the representation was knowingly false, and the equitable remedy of rescission, which did not have such a requirement. *See New York Life Insurance Co. v. Miller,* 73 F.2d 350 (8th Cir. 1934), 97 A.L.R. 562 (1935). In this earlier time, courts of law and courts of equity had separate jurisdictional requirements, and neither could dispense relief that was within the power of the other. One of the jurisdictional requirements for equitable relief was that the petitioner have no adequate remedy at law. Thus, if the ability of an insurer to raise fraud as a defense in an action on the policy was viewed as an adequate remedy at law, as it was in most jurisdictions, the insurer could not seek rescission in a court of equity. This was true even though the insurer would have to show that the insured was guilty of an intentional falsehood to succeed in the law court, whereas in the equity court a completely innocent misrepresentation would be grounds for avoiding the policy. *Id.*

Several things have happened to change the situation described in the preceding paragraph. First, many matters which were cognizable only in equity came to be recognized by courts of law. Second, modern rules of civil procedure have worked a merger of law and equity so that there is no longer any problem of the insurer asserting a right to rescind in response to an insured's claim on the policy. *See* Fleming James, Jr., Geoffrey C. Hazard, Jr., & John Leubsdorf, Civil Procedure § 8.9 (4th ed. 1992). Finally, the fact that the insurer can resort to a declaratory judgment proceeding in most jurisdictions today has blurred, if not eliminated, the old distinction between proceedings in law and equity, thereby obviating the question of the adequacy of the remedy at law. In many cases, the declaratory judgment action provides an adequate remedy to resolve the issue of the validity of the policy as well as issues regarding policy interpretation. There still may be a difference, however, as to whether there is a right to a jury trial, particularly in declaratory judgment proceedings. *Id.* at § 8.11.

Eventually, partly as a result of the merger of law and equity, a majority of courts came to recognize that a material misrepresentation is grounds for avoiding a policy, irrespective of whether the representation was made with knowledge of its falsity. In other words, a completely innocent, material misrepresentation was enough to avoid the policy. This had long been the rule in marine insurance, *see McDowell v. Fraser,* 1 Doug. 260 (1779), but now it is also applied to other areas of insurance law. Edwin W. Patterson, Essentials of Insurance Law 382-383 (2d ed. 1957). *See* 1 Eric Mills Holmes & Mark S. Rhodes, Holmes's Appleman on Insurance § 4.34 (2d ed. 1996). Nevertheless, there are still some cases that follow a minority rule and require knowledge of falsity or reckless indifference as to truth or falsity. *See, e.g., Union Bankers Insurance Co. v. Shelton,* 889 S.W.2d 278 (Tex. 1994). Some of these cases may be reconcilable, but it is clear that some courts are diverging from the above-described majority view. *See also* 7 George J. Couch, Cyclopedia of Insurance Law §§ 35:119–124 (2nd ed. 1985).

The foregoing describes common law developments regarding fraud and misrepresentation. Courts have attempted—not always with perfect clarity—to draw a distinction between these situations and concealment. Generally speaking, misrepresentation involves an inaccurate disclosure (fraud involves an intentionally inaccurate disclosure), whereas concealment involves a failure to make disclosure. Under these definitions, if an insurer asks an applicant "have you received any traffic tickets during the last three years?" and the applicant falsely answers "no," the applicant has made a misrepresentation because the response is inaccurate. Concealment involves failing to make a material disclosure without being asked, but many judicial discussions blur the boundaries between misrepresentation and concealment.

Be that as it may, the law with regard to concealment took a little different tack. In marine insurance, either an intentional or a good faith failure to disclose a material fact is a good defense for the insurer:

> Mr. Duer (Lect. 13, pt. 1, sect. 13; 2 Ins. 398) states as a part of the rule the following proposition: —

> "Sect. 13. The assured will not be allowed to protect himself against the charge of an undue concealment by evidence that he had disclosed

to the underwriters, in *general* terms, the information that he possessed. Where his own information is specific, it must be communicated in the terms in which it was received. General terms may include the truth, but may fail to convey it with its proper force and in all its extent. Nor will the assured be permitted to urge, as an excuse for his omission to communicate material facts, that they were actually known to the underwriters, unless it appears that their knowledge was as particular and full as his own information. It is the duty of the assured to place the underwriter in the same situation as himself; to give to him the same means and opportunity of judging of the value of the risks; and when any circumstance is withheld, however slight and immaterial it may have seemed to himself, that, if disclosed, would probably have influenced the terms of the insurance, the concealment vitiates the policy."

Sun Mutual Insurance Co. v. Ocean Insurance Co., 107 U.S. 485, 510–11 (1882). This rule, which originated in England, has now been incorporated into the British Marine Insurance Act of 1906. *See* 2 Sir Michael J. Mustill & Jonathan C.B. Gilman, Arnould's Law of Marine Insurance and Average 475–77 (16th ed. 1981). It is summed up by the Latin phrase *uberrimae fidei*, which means that the parties to the contract have a duty of "utmost good faith" and the insured is obligated to reveal any fact that affects the risk that the underwriter is asked to assume. It also is observed in the United States. *See, e.g., Certain Underwriters at Lloyd's v. Montford*, 52 F.3d 219 (9th Cir. 1995). The foregoing, however, is not the rule in non-marine insurance. Under the non-marine rule, an intentional concealment of a material fact by an applicant for insurance is generally a good defense for an insurer unaware of that fact, but an applicant's *good faith* failure to disclose a material fact is ordinarily not a good defense. For more details about the defense of concealment, see Robert H. Jerry, II, Understanding Insurance Law § 103 (2d ed. 1996).

As one might expect, insurers typically ask the important questions when taking an application for insurance. Thus, applicants rarely get the opportunity to conceal material information from insurers, and usually find themselves in the position of misrepresenting—more often innocently rather than deliberately—facts in response to insurers' questions. Although most litigation, then, involves misrepresentation rather than concealment, there are occasional situations where material information resides in gaps between the insurer's questions, and the law of concealment comes into play.

The above summary is what one would generally expect to find regarding the common law of misrepresentation, fraud, and concealment in the field of insurance. However, a number of states have passed statutes that impact the common law rules. Often the statutes are aimed at changing the common law rules with regard to warranties in insurance contracts, but in some instances these statutes also change the rules with regard to misrepresentations. Some of the statutes apply only to specific types of insurance, such as life, health and disability insurance, while others apply more generally. These provisions will receive more attention later in this section. The next two cases illuminate basic principles regarding elements of misrepresentation and concealment that arise both under common law rules and the statutes.

BERGER v. MINNESOTA MUTUAL LIFE INSURANCE CO.

723 P.2d 388 (Utah 1986)

PER CURIAM:

Plaintiff Anna Marie Berger appeals from the judgment entered on a jury verdict that denied her recovery of the proceeds of her husband's credit life insurance policy issued by defendant Minnesota Mutual Life Insurance Co. ("Minnesota Mutual"). Minnesota Mutual declined coverage under the policy, claiming that plaintiff's deceased husband materially misrepresented his medical condition when he submitted his insurance application form.

In a 1974 preemployment physical examination at Kennecott Copper Corporation, David Berger was diagnosed as afflicted with mild diabetes mellitus. The physician discussed with Berger the diabetes tests given him and any past family history of the disease. Medication was prescribed for Berger, and the doctor noted that the diabetes could be controlled as long as Berger continued with prescribed medication and dietary restrictions. When Kennecott was advised that Berger's diabetes could be controlled if treated, Berger was hired by the company.

On subsequent occasions between 1975 and 1979, Berger had several contacts with medical clinics and doctors who examined and discussed his diabetic condition and medication. In connection with another employment physical in June 1976, Berger listed his diabetes on his medical history form. There was also evidence that he often ignored the medication and dietary restrictions imposed to control his diabetes, which required more extensive medical treatment for his condition.

In April 1979, Berger applied for and received group credit life insurance from Minnesota Mutual to satisfy his home mortgage in the event of his death. On the insurance application concerning his medical history, he wrote that in the past three years he had only consulted with a physician regarding an earache and sore throat and that he had never been treated for or advised that he had diabetes. The jury found these representations to be false but not fraudulently made.

In February 1981, Berger was admitted to the hospital to bring his diabetes under control. A few weeks after his release, on March 8, 1981, he died of an acute codeine overdose. When a claim was made on the life policy, Minnesota Mutual undertook an independent investigation of the death. Discovering the preexisting diabetic condition, the insurer refused payment under its policy, claiming that the misrepresentation on the policy application was material to Berger's insurability and that Minnesota Mutual would not have issued the policy had the truth been disclosed at the time the application for insurance was made.

Under our statute enacted in 1963, a misrepresentation, omission, or concealment of facts shall not prevent recovery under an insurance policy unless:

    (a) fraudulent; or

(b) material either to the acceptance of the risk, or to the hazard assumed by the insurer; or

(c) the insurer in good faith either would not have issued the policy,. . .or would not have issued. . .a policy or contract in as large an amount, or would not have provided coverage with respect to the hazard resulting in the loss, if the true facts had been made known to the insurer as required either by the application for the policy or contract or otherwise.

U.C.A., 1953, § 31-19-8(1) (1974 ed.).[1] The statutory alternatives are stated in the disjunctive, not the conjunctive. In order to invalidate a policy because of a misrepresentation by the insured, an insurer need prove applicable only one of the above provisions.[2]

The court submitted the matter to the jury under instructions setting forth the alternative provisions of section 31-19-8(1). Responding to special interrogatories, the jury found, inter alia, that:

a. David Berger failed to disclose to Minnesota Mutual that he had been treated for and/or advised that he had diabetes;

b. David Berger's diabetic condition was material either to the acceptance of the risk or the hazard assumed by Minnesota Mutual under the policy;

c. Had David Berger disclosed his diabetic treatment, Minnesota Mutual, in good faith, either would not have issued the policy, or would not have issued the policy at the same rate or in as large an amount, or would not have provided coverage with respect to the hazard resulting in the loss.

d. David Berger's diabetes did not cause or contribute to his death.

e. The plaintiff was not entitled to recover on the policy.

Consistent with these findings, the trial court entered judgment for defendants, voiding the policy.

On appeal, we view the record in a light most favorable to the jury's findings and special verdict, which are entitled to a presumption of validity and will not be disturbed if supported by substantial evidence. We find a reasonable basis in the evidence to support the jury's verdict.

Regardless of section 31-19-8, plaintiff claims that our prior decisions require that in order to defeat coverage, a misrepresentation by an insured must be made with a knowing and willful intent to deceive. However, our prior cases, cited by plaintiff to support this requirement, were decided under the

---

[1] This section has now been replaced with the recodification of the Utah Insurance Code, effective July 1, 1986, Utah Laws ch. 242, § 26; U.C.A., 1953, § 31A-21-105 (Supp. 1985).

[2] Our statute is essentially identical to Okla. Stat. tit. 36, § 3609 (1981), and Idaho Code § 41-1811 (1977 ed.), see *Industrial Indemnity Co. v. United States Fidelity & Guar. Co.*, 93 Idaho 59, 454 P.2d 956, 959 (1969). Similar provisions regarding the materiality of a misrepresentation are also found in other states' statutes, *e.g.*, Ill. Rev. Stat. ch. 73, § 766 (1965), Or. Rev. Stat. §743.042(1) (1984); Colo. Rev. Stat. § 10-8-111(2) (1973). But compare Ariz. Rev. Stat. Ann. § 20-1109 (1975 ed.), where the identical provisions are held to be in the conjunctive and an insurer must show all three conditions. *Keplinger v. Mid-Century Ins. Co.*, 115 Ariz. 387, 565 P.2d 893 (App. 1977).

statute which existed prior to 1963 and which allowed avoidance of a policy only if the misrepresentations materially affected the acceptance of the risk assumed *and* were made with an intent to deceive. *See* U.C.A., 1953, § 31-19-8 (repealed 1963 Utah Laws ch. 45, § 3).

When a statutory defense is asserted, a defendant is entitled to rely upon the language of the existing statute for the requisite elements of that defense. The jury was properly instructed regarding the statutory elements required to determine whether the misrepresentation was sufficient to avoid the policy.

The evidence supports the conclusion that, although not fraudulent, Berger's concealment of his diabetic condition was knowing and intentional. The misrepresentation was not merely considered as an expression or representation of his general health condition, but was a falsehood and a concealment of a significant medical illness. *See* 43 Am. Jur. 2d *Insurance* § 1055, at 1059-61 (1982).

We also reject plaintiff's second argument, that in order for the misrepresentation to be material, the insurer must prove that the fact misrepresented resulted in the insured's death. Again, plaintiff relies upon decisions under our prior statute. Under our present statute, a misrepresentation may prevent recovery under an insurance contract when it is material to the risk of death assumed by the insurer. There is substantial evidence to support the jury's verdict that Berger's diabetic condition was material to his insurability and to the acceptance by Minnesota Mutual of the risk of death. The materiality of a fact misrepresented or withheld is determined by the probable and reasonable effect that a truthful disclosure would have had upon the insurer in determining the advantages of the proposed contract.

Because the materiality of a misrepresentation by the insured is determined by the extent to which it initially influenced the insurer to assume the risk of coverage, materiality is measured at the time that the risk is assumed and not at the subsequent death. Therefore, the misrepresentation in an insurance application may be material if it diminishes the insurer's opportunity to determine or estimate its risk. By withholding facts relevant to his insurability, the decedent prevented Minnesota Mutual from appraising its risk on the basis of the facts as they truly existed at the time the contract was made.

According to the medical testimony, diabetes is associated with an acceleration of arthrosclerosis and heart and circulatory complications, resulting in a lower average life expectancy. There is also a greater risk of dangerous side effects from the controlling medication, particularly when used with alcohol and codeine. A finding that Berger did not die from diabetes does not necessarily determine the immateriality of the misrepresentation. Because the materiality of a misrepresentation is related to the insurer's willingness to initially accept the risk, the ultimate cause of death may be a factor considered by the jury, but is not of itself necessarily determinative. Other jurisdictions have also held that the concealment or misrepresentation by the insured of a diabetic condition is material to the risk assumed by the insurer, even though the insured's death or injury results from other causes.

The materiality of the misrepresentation in this case was for the jury to determine on the basis of what a reasonable and prudent insurer would do

in the industry. The evidence was unrebutted that a truthful representation
. by Berger of his diabetic condition would have caused rejection of this type
of credit life policy. The jury was entitled to conclude that Minnesota Mutual's
practice to deny group life insurance to applicants with diabetes was reasonable and prudent. Therefore, we decline to disturb the jury's determination
that the misrepresentation by the insured was material to the risk of death
assumed by Minnesota Mutual and that it would not have issued the policy
to Berger under truthful circumstances. . . .

The verdict and judgment below in favor of defendants are affirmed.

Mutual Benefit Life Insurance Co. v. JMR Electrics Corp. 848 F.2d
30 (2d Cir. 1988). The defendant insurer issued a nonsmoker, discounted
premium "key man" life insurance policy based on the representation by the
cestui que vie that he had never smoked cigarettes when in fact he had been
smoking one-half a pack per day for a continuous period of not less than 10
years. The *cestui que vie* died and the insurer sued to rescind on the basis
of misrepresentation. The corporate beneficiary counterclaimed for the policy
proceeds. The trial court denied the latter claim and entered an order
rescinding the policy, ruling that the misrepresentation was material as a
matter of law. On appeal the corporate beneficiary argued that the misrepresentation was not material as a matter of law because a jury could reasonably
have found that even had the insurer been aware of the smoking history, a
policy at the smoker's premium rate would have been issued and that the
appropriate remedy was to permit recovery under the policy in the amount
that the premium actually paid would have purchased for a smoker. Applying
New York law, the Court of Appeals in a *per curiam* opinion affirmed the trial
court and held for the insurer.

". . . .We agree with Judge Sweet that the novel theory is without basis
in New York law. The plain language of the statutory definition of "materiality," found in section 3105(b), permits avoidance of liability under the policy
where "knowledge of. . .the facts misrepresented would have led to a refusal
by the insurer to make *such contract.*" (Emphasis added). Moreover, numerous
courts have observed that the materiality inquiry under New York law is made
with respect to the particular policy issued in reliance upon the
misrepresentation. . . .

"There is no doubt that Mutual was induced to issue the non-smoker,
discounted-premium policy to JMR precisely as a result of the misrepresentations made by Gaon concerning his smoking history. That Mutual might not
have refused the risk on *any* terms had it known the undisclosed facts is
irrelevant. Most risks are insurable at some price. The purpose of the
materiality inquiry is not to permit the jury to rewrite the terms of the insurance agreement to conform to the newly disclosed facts but to make certain
that the risk insured was the risk covered by the policy agreed upon. If a fact
is material to the risk, the insurer may avoid liability under a policy if that
fact was misrepresented in an application for that policy whether or not the

parties might have agreed to some other contractual arrangement had the critical fact been disclosed. . . ."

Waxse v. Reserve Life Ins. Co. 809 P.2d 533 (Kan. 1991). The Supreme Court vacated the trial court's entry of summary judgment for the insurer, which had denied coverage based on Behnke's alleged fraudulent misrepresentation of his HIV status. (Waxse was the administrator of Behnke's estate.) Behnke, because of his prior hepatitis and multiple sexual partners, believed that he might be carrying the HIV virus. He therefore underwent a blood test at a private laboratory, and he was notified in July 1987 that he had tested positive for the presence of HIV antibodies. He was informed that testing positive for HIV did not mean that he currently had AIDS or AIDS-Related Complex (ARC). In September 1987, Behnke completed an application for a major medical and life insurance policy with defendant insurer. The court described the application and Behnke's answers as follows:

"No question on the application specifically asked whether the applicant had undergone HIV antibody testing for AIDS or any other questions concerning AIDS.

"Question 5(c) of the application asked whether the applicant had been treated for or had any indication of specific disorders, including any blood disorders. Behnke answered negatively.

"Question 7 asked, 'Do you know of any other impairment now existing in the health or physical condition of any proposed insured?' Behnke responded "No," on the theory his health was not impaired even though he had received a positive HIV test. At the time of filing the application Behnke felt well.

"Question 8 asked, 'Has any proposed insured been examined or treated by a doctor during the past three years for anything other than the conditions listed above?' Behnke responded "Yes" and explained in Paragraph 9 he had suffered minor sore throats, colds, etc.

"Behnke did not indicate he had tested HIV positive because he found none of the questions were applicable. However, Behnke realized Question 8 was propounded to determine if the applicant had any pre-existing condition. Behnke also determined that Question 8 did not require revelation of the HIV test because it inquired about examinations conducted by doctors and the blood test he had undergone was not administered by a doctor.

"[The estate argued that Behnke did not make an untrue statement on the application.] We find the estate's argument valid. Behnke answered the questionnaire honestly. No inquiry was made as to AIDS or HIV. Admittedly, Behnke could have gone farther in his disclosure, but to do so he would have had to act as a volunteer about a matter which he did not consider an impairment of his health. It was the insurance company's responsibility to ask the questions to which it wanted answers. This it did not do."

NOTES

1. *Test for materiality.* The test for materiality has been stated in many different forms, but most courts would probably agree that the information sought is material if it would significantly affect the decision of the under-writer in issuing the policy at all, or in estimating the degree or character of the risk, or in fixing the amount of premium to be charged for the coverage. It is when one tries to refine the test that things become more difficult. Should the test be based on what would have affected the particular insurer in question (a subjective test)? An ordinary prudent insurer writing the type of insurance sought to be sold by the particular insurer (an objective test)? Or a reasonable insurer in the particular insurer's position (a hybrid test)? Which test is more favorable to the insured? Which test did the court apply in *Berger*? Should the same test be applied regardless of the type of insurance, i.e., life, health and accident; property and casualty; or fire and marine? *See New York Life Insurance Co. v. Kuhlenschmidt,* 218 Ind. 404, 33 N.E.2d 340, 135 A.L.R. 397 (1941).

2. *Nature of insurer's inquiries: fact versus opinion.* If an insurer is to prevail on a theory that the insured misrepresented certain information sought in an application, the insurer must prove that the information was not true, i.e., that it was substantially false. Whether the information is false can depend on what the insurer intended to elicit. Did the insurer intend to elicit a factual response, such as: "Have you consulted or been examined or treated by any physician or practitioner in the past 5 years?" A negative response to this question when the insured knows she has seen a physician for medical care on a number of occasions in the past five years would clearly be false. Some courts call this an "objective" inquiry. *See Ledley v. William Penn Life Insurance Co.,* 138 N.J. 627, 651 A.2d 92 (1995).

What if the insured answers the question in the above paragraph in the negative, but claims that she actually forgot about the visits? Some courts have described this as "legal fraud" and permit the insurer to avoid the policy. *Illinois Bankers' Life Ass'n v. Theodore,* 44 Ariz. 160, 34 P.2d 423 (1934). Perhaps a better explanation of legal fraud is that the courts are saying that such situations amount to constructive knowledge.

A different situation arises, however, where the question on the application does not elicit a factual response but instead asks for an opinion. Suppose, for example, the question asks "Are you now in good health?" and the insured answers in the affirmative even though he knows he has had certain medical problems in the past and that he may even still be suffering from some of these problems. If the insured in good faith believes he is in good health, is the answer false? Most courts say "no" because the insured was asked for an opinion, which if truly held cannot be false. In short, there has been no misrepresentation and therefore the situation does not afford relief to the insurer. Again, some courts call this a "subjective" inquiry. *See Ledley, supra.* Does this help explain why courts in some cases have opined that intent is an element of the defense of misrepresentation?

3. *Reliance*. It would seem that rational insurers would rely on material information and ignore immaterial information. Thus, it is fair to wonder whether the reliance element has independent significance. The materiality element and the reliance element do conflate to some extent. Material information is important to insurers; it is upon material information that insurers will rely. Thus, the same evidence that proves reliance will usually also prove materiality, although the advocate must be careful to make sure that all elements are documented. *See American States Insurance Co. v. Ehrlich,* 237 Kan. 449, 701 P.2d 676 (1985) (insurer denied rescission on account of misrepresentation where insurer offered evidence on materiality but none on reliance). But there are situations where reliance has critical importance independent of the materiality requirement. Without reliance one need not reach the materiality question, and vice versa.

The essence of reliance is inducement. The insurer is induced to issue a policy because it believed certain information provided by the insurance applicant is true. If the insurer does not believe the applicant, then it should be obvious that the insurer did not rely, and the information, if incorrect, should not be a basis for rescinding the policy. The cases that come to court, however, are hardly ever this clear, and typically involve the question of whether the insurer was *reasonable* in relying on the information, such as it is, provided by the applicant. *See New York Life Insurance Co. v. Strudel,* 243 F.2d 90 (5th Cir. 1957).

Insurers use applications so that they do not have to investigate every fact potentially relevant to the applicant's risk. Investigation is a cost of doing business; by not investigating and instead relying upon answers given in applications, insurers can keep premiums lower, which benefits insureds. At what point does an insurer acquire an obligation to conduct some investigation independent of the answers given by an applicant? Should this depend on whether the applicant is attempting to intentionally deceive the insurer, as opposed to merely being careless or negligent in giving answers to the insurer's questions? *See Ledley v. William Penn Life Insurance Co.,* 138 N.J. 627, 651 A.2d 92 (1995)(holding insurer is entitled to rely on applicant's statements and has no duty to investigate further in absence of something that casts doubt on the validity of the statements).

4. *Misstatements of age and keeping the contract in force.* Although age can be a material fact in whether a life insurance company either issues a policy at all or as to the amount it is willing to sell to a particular applicant, most states have statutes that alter the common law rule with regard to misrepresentations of age. It is probable that these statutes had their origins in the absence of official records of births in many areas of this country until well into the twentieth century, not to mention problems that immigrants faced in recounting their correct ages. The typical statute provides that if the age of the insured has been misstated, the benefit payable is limited to that which the premium would have purchased at the correct age. Of course, if some other material matter has been misrepresented in addition to a misstatement of age, the insurer may have a complete defense. Does the manner in which age misrepresentations are handled suggest another answer the Second Circuit might have given in the *Mutual Benefit Life* case?

If one assumes, as seems fair, that the applicant's misrepresentation in *Mutual Benefit Life* was deliberate, did the court have any real choice other than the result it reached? If the only consequence of a deliberate misrepresentation is to reduce the amount paid under the policy if the insured is caught in the lie, what incentives would this state of affairs create from applicants' viewpoints? If you are an honest person (particularly in your dealings with insurance companies), how do you react to these incentives? *See New York Life Insurance Co. v. Johnson,* 923 F.2d 279 (3d Cir. 1991) (following rule in Pennsylvania that life insurance policy obtained by fraudulent misrepresentation in the application is void *ab initio*).

5. *Misrepresentation by applicant or by agent?* Simply because an application is attached to the policy, it hardly follows that the insurer will prevail when the application contains misinformation. It is very common for agents or brokers to fill out the application based on the applicant's oral answers to questions posed by the agent or broker. Thus, in many instances, the insured will assert that the insurer's agent was correctly informed but mistakenly recorded or even intentionally omitted information supplied by the applicant. Despite the insured's opportunity to read the application and point out any misinformation, courts have held that the insurer is deemed to have knowledge of facts known to its agent and therefore estopped from asserting the defense of misrepresentation, except where there is collusion between the agent and the insured. *See, e.g., Bunn v. Monarch Life Insurance Co.,* 257 Or. 409, 478 P.2d 363 (1970); *Ward v. Durham Life Insurance Co.,* 90 N.C. App. 286, 368 S.E.2d 391 (1988). One court has held this to be the result even though the insured signed an application containing a clause in which the insured purported to verify the information contained in it and, in addition to which, the clause stated that the agent had no authority "to accept risks, to pass on the acceptability for insurance, or to make, change, or end any insurance contract." *See Marchiori v. American Republic Insurance Co.,* 662 A.2d 932 (Me. 1995). But compare *Marionjoy Rehab. Hospital v. Lo,* 180 Ill. App. 3d 49, 535 N.E.2d 1061 (App. Ct. 1989) (insured's subsequent review and reaffirmation of answers in application was an affirmative act of bad faith relieving insurer of liability under policy).

6. *Obligation of applicant to volunteer information.* With regard to the *Waxse* case, did the insurer have a legitimate interest in keeping Behnke out of its risk pool? What does the court's decision do to the integrity of the pool? The court concluded that Behnke omitted the information about the HIV test "in good faith" and that there was "no evidence of fraud." *Id.* at 537. Is the court saying that Behnke did not intend to mislead the insurer? If so, do you agree with that conclusion? In circumstances where the insurer's question about HIV or AIDS is clearly stated, is the insured's failure to disclose a positive test result a material misrepresentation? *See Kieser v. Old Line Life Insurance Co.,* 712 So. 2d 1261 (Fla. Dist. Ct. App 1998); *Northern Life Insurance Co. v. Ippolito Real Estate Partnership,* 234 Ill. App. 3d 792, 601 N.E.2d 773 (1992). Should the insurer even be allowed to ask such questions? Are there public policy considerations that justify prohibiting insurers from seeking out such information?

There is no doubt that an applicant has an obligation to answer all of the insurer's questions as honestly and truthfully as is reasonably possible. But does the applicant have a duty to volunteer material information about which no inquiry is made? If the application is for marine insurance, the answer is yes; however, for other types of insurance a good faith failure to volunteer information may not rise to the level of a misrepresentation or wrongful concealment. Do you agree that the facts of *Waxse* did not rise to that level? Compare *Jackson v. Travelers Insurance Co.,* 113 F.3d 367 (2d Cir. 1997) (under New York law, questions in application for disability insurance policy that asked whether applicant had received treatment for "disease or disorder" and whether he had had any other "illness or disorder" during last five years held unambiguous, and negative answers by applicant who had been diagnosed with and treated for back, neck, and wrist injuries by various physicians held to constitute misrepresentations); *Russell v. Royal Maccabees Life Insurance Co.,* 193 Ariz. 464, 974 P.2d 443 (1998) ("no" response to question whether applicant had ever been convicted of a felony was misrepresentation even though insured's conviction had been expunged).

7. *Applicant's continuing obligation to supply information.* Does an applicant for insurance have any obligation to inform the insurer of material information coming to light after the application is submitted, but before the insurer has accepted it? If the time of completion of the application is the critical date for determining insurability, changes in the applicant's condition after this date are irrelevant. But what about situations where the insurer allows itself the option to make an insurability determination at any time up to and until the application is accepted? Needless to say, the scope of the applicant's duty, if any, has been the subject of considerable dispute in a number of cases. In *American General Life Insurance Co. v. Gilbert,* 595 S.W.2d 83 (Tenn. App. 1979), the court made the following statement:

> The general rule pertaining to the applicant's duty to disclose changes in his health occurring between the date of his application and the delivery of policy is set forth in 9 Couch on Insurance 2d, § 38.22, pp. 347–348:

> The mutual good faith which is required in a contract of life insurance will not permit a recovery where the insured withholds or conceals material changes in the condition of his health between the date of his examination by the insurer's physician and the delivery of the policy and which is of such a nature as to affect his insurability, make him a hazardous risk and thus amount to a fraud on the insurer. For example, where one, after applying for life insurance, learns that he is afflicted with a fatal disease, his failure to disclose that information constitutes an intentional concealment of a material fact which will avoid a policy subsequently delivered in ignorance of the insured's diseased condition.

> Where between the date of the application and the issuance of the policy the insured consulted a physician who reported a serious ailment, the insured must disclose this even though there has been no change in the physical condition of the applicant after the application was made.

Tennessee decisions are in accord with the general rule.

Id. at 86–87.

What if the applicant truthfully answers the questions on the application to the effect she is in good health, but unknown either to the applicant or the insurer the applicant is suffering from a fatal disease, and this is not discovered until after the policy is issued? Can the insurer still rescind on the grounds of mutual mistake of fact? If the disease is discovered before the policy is issued, there may be a duty to reveal the information. But where the policy has already been issued, at least one court has held that the insurer may not avoid the policy. *Metropolitan Life Insurance Co. v. Devore,* 66 Cal. 2d 129, 424 P.2d 321, 56 Cal. Rptr. 881 (1967), 30 A.L.R.3d 376 (1970). For a more complete discussion of these issues, see Robert H. Jerry, II, Understanding Insurance Law § 102[i] (2d ed. 1996).

8. *"Concealment or fraud" clause in New York Standard Fire Policy.* Fraud and misrepresentation is not limited to the application process, but can occur in many different contexts. If it does, is the policy voidable by the insurer? The New York Standard Fire Policy (1943 ed.) provides a very sweeping answer to this question:

> This entire policy shall be void if, whether before or after a loss, the insured has wilfully concealed or misrepresented any material fact or circumstance concerning this insurance or the subject thereof, or the interest of the insured therein, or in case of any fraud or false swearing by the insured related thereto.

See Appendix A. This language and its more modern versions have afforded insurers with a broad defense. For example, in *McCullough v. State Farm Fire & Casualty Co.,* 80 F.3d 269 (8th Cir. 1996), the insured misrepresented that a fire loss was accidental when in fact it was caused by his son's arson. Consequently, there was no coverage for a burglary that occurred a few days after the fire. Exaggerating claims or filing claims for nonexistent personal property, even though there was a covered fire loss to the premises, has also allowed the insurer to avoid all claims under the policy. *See, e.g., Home Insurance Co. v. Hardin,* 528 S.W.2d 723 (Ky. 1975).

[c]   Regulation of the Defenses

As discussed earlier in this section, the first warranties in insurance contracts were strictly construed and enforced with a vengeance. Interestingly enough, a number of states still do not have statutes modifying the common law rule that an immaterial breach of warranty avoids the contract. Where there is no statutory relief, either in general or for particular types of insurance, courts have developed techniques of mitigating the harsh effects of warranties, as *Vlastos v. Sumitomo Marine & Fire Insurance Co. (Europe), Ltd.* illustrated.

In addition to the distinction between affirmative and promissory warranty which figured prominently in *Vlastos*, the court observed that "[a] representation, unlike a warranty, is not part of the insurance contract but is collateral to it. . . . In case of doubt, courts normally construe a statement in an insurance contract as a representation rather than a warranty." 707 F.2d at 777. This softens the potentially harsh consequences of the warranty. As another court explained it: "A warranty in insurance enters into and is part of the contract, and must be literally true to permit a recovery on the policy while a representation is not part of the contract but an inducement thereto. A representation must relate to a material matter, and is only required to be substantially true." *Whitehead v. Fleet Towing Co.,* 442 N.E.2d 1362, 1365 (Ill. Ct. App. 1982).

Another technique involves arguing that the warranty has been breached only "temporarily," which invokes the rule followed by many courts that coverage is only suspended during the breach and that the breach does not void the policy for the entire term. Another limiting technique interprets the warranty as extending only to a particular risk or a severable part of the policy. Under this approach, a breach of warranty with respect to one facet of the coverage does not invalidate other parts of the coverage. For more discussion of judicial mitigating techniques, see Robert H. Jerry, II, Understanding Insurance Law § 101[e][2] (2d ed. 1996).

In many situations, courts' regulatory efforts devolve from statutory prescriptions. It is to this kind of regulation that we now turn. Four representative statutes follow; if the state in which you reside is not among these five, which of these statutes is your state's law most like?

McKINNEY'S CONSOLIDATED NEW YORK INSURANCE LAWS ANNOTATED
§§ 3105, 3106, 3204 (1999)

§ 3105 Representations by the insured

(a) A representation is a statement as to past or present fact, made to the insurer by, or by the authority of, the applicant for insurance or the prospective insured, at or before the making of the insurance contract as an inducement to the making thereof. A misrepresentation is a false representation, and the facts misrepresented are those facts which make the representation false.

(b) No misrepresentation shall avoid any contract of insurance or defeat recovery thereunder unless such misrepresentation was material. No misrepresentation shall be deemed material unless knowledge by the insurer of the facts misrepresented would have led to a refusal by the insurer to make such contract.

(c) In determining the question of materiality, evidence of the practice of the insurer which made such contract with respect to the acceptance or rejection of similar risks shall be admissible.

(d) A misrepresentation that an applicant for life or accident and health insurance has not had previous medical treatment, consultation or observation, or has not had previous treatment or care in a hospital or other like institution, shall be deemed, for the purpose of determining its materiality, a misrepresentation that the applicant has not had the disease, ailment or other medical impairment for which such treatment or care was given or which was discovered by any licensed medical practitioner as a result of such consultation or observation. If in any action to rescind any such contract or to recover thereon, any such misrepresentation is proved by the insurer, and the insured or any other person having or claiming a right under such contract shall prevent full disclosure and proof of the nature of such medical impairment, such misrepresentation shall be presumed to have been material.

§ 3106 Warranty defined; effect of breach

(a) In this section "warranty" means any provision of an insurance contract which has the effect of requiring, as a condition precedent of the taking effect of such contract or as a condition precedent of the insurer's liability thereunder, the existence of a fact which tends to diminish, or the non-existence of a fact which tends to increase, the risk of the occurrence of any loss, damage, or injury within the coverage of the contract. The term "occurrence of loss, damage, or injury" includes the occurrence of death, disability, injury, or any other contingency insured against, and the term "risk" includes both physical and moral hazards.

(b) A breach of warranty shall not avoid an insurance contract or defeat recovery thereunder unless such breach materially increases the risk of loss, damage or injury within the coverage of the contract. If the insurance contract specified two or more distinct kinds of loss, damage or injury which are within its coverage, a breach of warranty shall not avoid such contract or defeat recovery thereunder with respect to any kind or kinds of loss, damage or injury other than the kind or kinds to which such warranty relates and the risk of which is materially increased by the breach of such warranty.

(c) This section shall not affect the express or implied warranties under a contract of marine insurance in respect to, appertaining to or in connection with any and all risks or perils of navigation, transit, or transportation, including war risks, on, over or under any seas or inland waters, nor shall it affect any provision in an insurance contract requiring notice, proof or other conduct of the insured after the occurrence of loss, damage or injury.

§ 3204 Policy to contain entire contract; statements of applicant to be representations and not warranties; alterations

(a)(1) Every policy of life, accident or health insurance, or contract of annuity, delivered or issued for delivery in this state, shall contain the entire contract between the parties, and nothing shall be incorporated therein by reference to any writing, unless a copy thereof is endorsed upon or attached to the policy or contract when issued.

(2) No application for the issuance of any such policy or contract shall be admissible in evidence unless a true copy was attached to such policy or contract when issued.

(3) Such policy or contract cannot be modified, nor can any rights or requirements be waived, except in a writing signed by a person specified by the insurer in such policy or contract.

(b) Subsection (a) hereof shall not apply to a table or schedule of rates, premiums or other payments which is on file with the superintendent for use in connection with such policy or contract.

(c) All statements made by, or by the authority of, the applicant for the issuance, reinstatement or renewal of any such policy or contract shall be deemed representations and not warranties.

(d) No insertion in or other alteration of any written application for any such policy or contract shall be made by any person other than the applicant without his written consent, except that insertions may be made by the insurer for administrative purposes only in such manner as to indicate clearly that the insertions are not to be ascribed to the applicant.

. . . .

(f) Any waiver of the provisions of this section shall be void.

MASSACHUSETTS GENERAL LAWS ANNOTATED (West 2000)

Chapter 175, § 186. Misrepresentations by insured; effect.

No oral or written misrepresentation or warranty made in the negotiation of a policy of insurance by the insured or in his behalf shall be deemed material or defeat or avoid the policy or prevent its attaching unless such misrepresentation or warranty is made with actual intent to deceive, or unless the matter misrepresented or made a warranty increased the risk of loss.

UTAH 2000 SESSION LAWS

Chapter 114, Senate Bill 190, Section 5.

Section 31A-21-105 is amended to read:

31A-21-105. Representations, warranties, and conditions.

. . . .

(2) . . . [N]o misrepresentation or breach of an affirmative warranty affects the insurer's obligations under the policy unless:

(a) the insurer relies on it and it is either material or is made with intent to deceive; or

(b) the fact misrepresented or falsely warranted contributes to the loss.

(3) No failure of a condition prior to the loss and no breach of a promissory warranty affects the insurer's obligations under the policy unless it exists at the time of the loss and either increases the risk at the time of the loss or

contributes to the loss. This Subsection (3) does not apply to failure to tender payment of premium.

(4) Nondisclosure of information not requested by the insurer is not a defense to an action against the insurer. Failure to correct within a reasonable time any representation that becomes incorrect because of changes in circumstances is misrepresentation, not nondisclosure.

. . . .

(7) No trivial or transitory breach of or noncompliance with any provision of this chapter is a basis for avoiding an insurance contract.

NEBRASKA REVISED STATUTES
§ 44-358 (1998)

§ 44-358. Policies; misrepresentations; warranties; conditions; effect.

No oral or written misrepresentation or warranty made in the negotiation for a contract or policy of insurance by the insured, or in his behalf, shall be deemed material or defeat or avoid the policy, or prevent its attaching, unless such misrepresentation or warranty deceived the company to its injury. The breach of a warranty or condition in any contract or policy of insurance shall not avoid the policy nor avail the insurer to avoid liability, unless such breach shall exist at the time of the loss and contribute to the loss, anything in the policy or contract of insurance to the contrary notwithstanding.

NOTES

1. *The New York influence.* New York has exerted considerable influence on insurance law and regulation throughout the United States, and some of this influence is apparent in the area of warranties. The New York statutes involve two somewhat different attempts to regulate warranties by legislation. The original version of section 3204 was enacted in 1906 and has been modified only slightly since then. Subsection (a)(1) limits its application to policies of life, accident, and health insurance and annuity contracts. By virtue of subsection (c), it simply treats all statements by the applicant in effecting these types of coverage as representations. Thus, it is limited to statements or affirmations in the application process. It does not appear to cover provisions inside the policy which would be classified as warranties unless statements of the applicant are somehow embodied in the provision. This type of statute has been adopted by many states, although its application may have been expanded to cover other types of insurance.

Section 3106 was enacted in 1939, apparently in response to the burgeoning practice of insurers to insert warranties into the text of all types of policies. *See Glickman v. New York Life Insurance Co.,* 291 N.Y. 45, 50 N.E.2d 538

(1943). Note, however, that the statute does not apply, according to subsection (c), to marine insurance or to policy provisions that may be implicated in claims processing. Section 3106 is the work of Professor Edwin W. Patterson, a leading authority on insurance law in his time, and is the most carefully drafted statute of its kind. It is one of the few statutes that attempts in any way to define the term "warranty." In section 3106(a) Patterson defined "warranty" in such a way as to include within its scope all clauses, however denominated, that prescribe, as a condition of the insurer's liability, the existence of a fact affecting the risk. He re-introduced the requirement that any breach must be material in order to afford relief to the insurer. This, in effect, puts warranties on a par with the law regarding misrepresentations. Thus, a material breach of warranty will still allow the insurer to avoid the policy but an immaterial breach will not. This statute has not been copied by other jurisdictions.

Section 3105 was also enacted in 1939 and in essence codifies the common law requirement that a misrepresentation has to be material before it will avoid the policy or defeat recovery. It also defines materiality in terms of whether the insurer would have issued *the* policy applied for had it known the truth.

2. *Scope limitations in the statutes.* Even though some states have passed statutes in an attempt to modify the harsh consequences of the common law rule, the statutes in some instances only apply to certain types of insurance. The prior note observed that section 3106 of the New York statute leaves the common law rule in effect as to ocean marine insurance. This means that Lord Mansfield's pronouncement that even an immaterial breach of warranty will avoid the policy may prevail. *See, e.g., Certain Underwriters at Lloyd's v. Montford,* 52 F.3d 219 (9th Cir. 1995) (applying California law). It also should be noted that the British Marine Insurance Act of 1906 expressly preserves the rule as laid down by Lord Mansfield.

Moreover, some of the statutes are limited to affirmative warranties, which leaves the regulation of promissory warranties to the common law. Is that a fair reading of the Massachusetts and Nebraska statutes? In *Coppi v. West American Insurance Co.,* 524 N.W.2d 804 (Neb. 1994), the insured operated a beauty salon and was insured for theft under a policy requiring, as a condition of coverage, that certain business records be maintained so that any loss could be determined. The records were not maintained and, despite the fact the insured submitted other evidence of the loss, the insurer refused to pay for a burglary of cash kept in the insured's safe for day to day operation of the salon. The insured argued that Neb. Stat. § 44-358 prevented the insurer from demanding strict compliance with the policy condition. The court agreed that the condition constituted a warranty, but construed it to be a promissory warranty and held that the statute only "deals with warranties which are conditions precedent to the very existence of an insurance contract, not with promissory warranties the fulfillment of which are conditions precedent to recovery under an insurance contract which has come into being." *Id.* at 812. Do you agree that the text of the Nebraska statute requires that result? Did the Nebraska legislature intend to require a contribute-to-the-loss test for post-loss lapses by the insured?

3. *Other approaches to warranty regulation.* The basic approach in section 3204(c) of the New York statute embodies the most prevalent attempt to change the common law regarding warranties in insurance contracts. Do you agree that the Utah statute applied in *Berger* essentially adheres to the New York approach, albeit with different terminology? The structure and text of the Utah statute applied in *Berger* more closely resembles statutes in other states than does the New York statute, whatever their similarities. The Nebraska statute, on the other hand, is what is known as a "contribute to the loss" statute and further limits the rights of the insurer. Imagine a warranty in a policy of insurance on an aircraft under which the insured "warrants that only pilots with a valid medical certificate will operate said aircraft." The plane crashes when its landing gear fails, and it turns out that the medical certificate of the pilot flying the aircraft at the time of the crash had expired two days earlier. Do the New York and Nebraska statutes give different answers?

The Massachusetts statute is an example of an intermediate type of statute that declares that a breach of warranty shall not prevent recovery by the insured unless it increased the risk of loss. What are the textual differences among the Massachusetts, Nebraska, and New York statutes, and what significance would these differences have when the statutes are applied?

Of the different statutory approaches outlined above, which one is the fairest to those concerned — insureds, insurers, and the public?

4. *Regulating the misrepresentation defense.* In footnote 1 of *Berger v. Minnesota Mutual Life Insurance Co.*, set out in subsection 3.01[1][b] of this section, the court mentioned that the 1963 Utah statute had been replaced with U.C.A. § 31A-21-105 pursuant to a 1986 recodification of the Utah insurance code. (This statute also received minor modifications during the 2000 Utah legislative session.) Both the Massachusetts statute and the 1963 Utah statute differ from the other statutes excerpted in these materials in that they articulate with a fair amount of precision what the insurer must show to make out a misrepresentation defense.

Notice further that the 1963 Utah statute not only covers misrepresentations but also includes "omission" and "concealment" of facts. Does this alter the common law regarding good faith failures to reveal information in non-marine insurance? Do you see any real difference between subsections (b) and (c) in the 1963 Utah statute, or are those subsections redundant?

The 1963 Utah statute says that a "fraudulent" misrepresentation, omission, or concealment is sufficient for the insurer to avoid the policy. Similarly, the Massachusetts and 2000 Utah statutes both indicate that a misrepresentation made with "intent to deceive" is sufficient for the insurer to avoid the policy. Does this mean that the insured's mere intent to deceive provides the insurer with a defense, without regard to whether it is about a material matter or the insurer relies? How often will insurers rely on immaterial misrepresentations anyway?

5. *Entire-contract statutes.* New York Ins. Law § 3204(a)(1) is what is called an "entire-contract" statute; these statutes have been enacted in many states. They originally applied only to contracts of life insurance, but some of them

have been extended to health and accident insurance. Essentially, these statutes state that the policy and any attachments constitute the only agreement between the parties. In a sense, the laws create the equivalent of a "statutory merger clause." A principal purpose of the statutes is to force insurers to furnish the insured a copy of all statements made by him that might thereafter be relied upon as grounds for avoiding the policy. (The statutes, at least originally, had the additional purpose of protecting the insured against a particular form of abuse—the incorporation into the policy of terms, such as the bylaws of a mutual insurance company, merely referred to and hence actually inaccessible to the insured.) See Edwin W. Patterson, Essentials of Insurance Law § 86, at 436–42 (2d ed. 1957). Some insurance policies and applications contain "entire-contract" clauses even where there is no statutory requirement that they do so. What advantages do these clauses have for insurers?

Entire-contract statutes are relevant to an insurer's ability to rely on the defense of fraud and misrepresentation. Courts have construed these statutes to exclude proof by the insurer of any misrepresentation made by the insured in an application not attached to the policy. *See id.* at 439. Moreover, to the extent insurers are motivated to attach the applications to policies they issue to preserve possible defenses, insureds have the opportunity to correct any misinformation once having perused the application on receipt, which (at least in theory) reduces the instances in which a misrepresentation occurs.

6. *ERISA preemption and state statutes regulating misrepresentation defense.* ERISA, which first appeared in note 10 after the *Mahler* case in § 2.03 [4], periodically rears its head in the insurance world, and thus necessarily surfaces from time to time throughout these materials. Recall that ERISA preempts any state law that "relates to" certain insurance policies, unless the state law is designed to "regulate insurance." In the 1990s, a number of federal courts held that ERISA preempted state statutes regulating the warranty and misrepresentation defenses. *See, e.g., Security Life Insurance Co. v. Meyling,* 146 F.3d 1184 (9th Cir. 1998) (ERISA preempts California insurance statute allowing insurer to rescind insurance contract for concealment or misrepresentation of material facts); *Tingle v. Pacific Mutual Insurance Co.,* 996 F.2d 105 (5th Cir. 1993) (Louisiana statute defining circumstances under which policy may be rescinded based on insured's misrepresentation in an application is preempted under ERISA). If the federal common law to be applied in cases of alleged breach of warranty and misrepresentation is the same as the displaced state statutory law, nothing will change in terms of results, although this is not meant to diminish the important question of the proper situs of the federal-state regulatory boundary. *See Jones v. United States Life Insurance Co.,* 12 F. Supp. 2d 383 (D.N.J. 1998) (ERISA preemption issue not decided because court determines that New Jersey law of misrepresentation and federal common law are the same).

7. *Coverage and related clauses.* The Massachusetts, Utah and Nebraska statutes, unlike the New York statute, do not expressly cover clauses that prescribe, as a condition of the insurer's liability, the existence of a fact affecting the risk. Thus, clauses which are couched in terms of coverage have been held to escape such statutes even though they have the same effect as

a warranty at common law. It is somewhat ironic, though, that some courts have refused to enforce such clauses even though the policy provision has not been satisfied or fulfilled, *i.e.*, where the failure to satisfy or fulfill the policy provision had no causal relationship to the loss. In doing so, it would seem that the courts have adopted a "contribute to the loss" approach similar to the Nebraska statutory approach. If the court has the power to construe a coverage provision in contravention of its text, could it also construe warranties or conditions precedent similarly? This receives more attention in the next subsection.

[d]　The Limits of Regulation

OMAHA SKY DIVERS PARACHUTE CLUB, INC. v. RANGER INSURANCE CO.
189 Neb. 610, 204 N.W.2d 162 (1973)

McCOWN, JUSTICE.

This is an action on an aircraft insurance policy to recover for damage to the insured aircraft. The district court sustained a motion for summary judgment for the defendant and dismissed plaintiff's petition.

The plaintiff, Omaha Sky Divers Parachute Club, Incorporated, was the owner of a 1959 Cessna aircraft. On September 2, 1970, the defendant, Ranger Insurance Company, issued an insurance policy insuring the aircraft for a term of 1 year. The coverage included loss of or damage to the aircraft while in motion. On January 12, 1971, a brake on the plane failed upon landing and the aircraft was damaged in the resulting wreck. The plane was piloted by John F. Peters. He held a valid and effective F.A.A. pilot certificate, but his previously valid F.A.A. medical certificate had expired on August 9, 1970. On January 14, 1971, 2 days after the accident an F.A.A. medical certificate with no limitations was issued to John F. Peters. On the date of the accident, Peters had no medical infirmity that would have prevented his having a valid medical certificate and his failure to have such a certificate in no way contributed to the accident.

Item 7 of the declarations page, Part Two of the policy, provided: "PILOT CLAUSE: Only the following pilot or pilots holding valid and effective pilot and medical certificates with ratings as required by the Federal Aviation Administration for the flight involved will operate the aircraft in flight: STAN SEARLES; OTHERWISE, PRIVATE OR COMMERCIAL PILOTS HAVING A MINIMUM OF 300 TOTAL LOGGED HOURS, INCLUDING 20 HOURS IN INSURED MAKE AND MODEL."

Under the heading of "EXCLUSIONS," on page 2 of the policy, is the following language: "This Policy does not apply:

. . . .

"2. to any occurrence or to any loss or damage occurring while the aircraft is operated in flight by other than the pilot or pilots set forth under Item 7 of the Declarations;".

The district court found that the applicable F.A.A. regulations require that a pilot have in his possession a valid medical certificate issued within the preceding 24 months; that the insurance policy provisions quoted above are clear and unambiguous; and that the policy provided no coverage for an aircraft operated in flight by a pilot not having a valid and effective medical certificate. The district court then overruled a motion for summary judgment by the plaintiff, granted the defendant's motion for summary judgment, and dismissed the plaintiff's action.

The sole issue here is whether the insurance policy excluded coverage for damage which occurred while the aircraft was being operated in flight by a pilot whose medical certificate had expired.

The plaintiff contends that the provisions of the insurance policy previously quoted constitute only a warranty or condition and that a breach of such warranty or condition will not permit the insurer to avoid liability unless the breach contributed to the loss. Plaintiff relies on section 44-358, R.R.S. 1943, which provides in part: "The breach of a warranty or condition in any contract or policy of insurance shall not avoid the policy nor avail the insurer to avoid liability, unless such breach shall exist at the time of the loss and contribute to the loss, anything in the policy or contract of insurance to the contrary notwithstanding."

Item 7 of the declarations standing alone might well be interpreted as a warranty or a condition, but any such interpretation cannot be extended to the separate exclusion clause. The exclusion clause here provides that the policy does not apply to any "damage occurring while the aircraft is operated in flight by other than the pilot or pilots set forth under Item 7 of the Declarations." Coverage is excluded while the plane is operated in flight by anyone except the pilot or pilots described separately in the declarations. Both the exclusion clause and the declaration are clear and unambiguous. The exclusion does not constitute either a warranty or a condition within the meaning of section 44-358, R.R.S. 1943.

It is well established that an aircraft insurance policy may exclude coverage when the airplane is flown by certain types of persons or pilots. See 11 Couch on Insurance 2d, § 42:634, at 315. The insurer under an aircraft insurance policy may lawfully exclude certain risks from the coverage of its policy and where damage occurs during the operation of the insured aircraft under circumstances as to which the policy excludes coverage, there is no coverage.

The policy provisions here require that a pilot hold "valid and effective pilot and medical certificates with ratings as required by the Federal Aviation Administration . . ." That language is unambiguous. The evidence establishes that the medical certificate of the pilot in command of the aircraft at the time of the accident had lapsed even before the insurance policy here had been issued. Under language in an aircraft policy excluding coverage "while such aircraft is in flight unless the pilot in command of the aircraft is properly certificated . . .," it has been held that the lapse of a pilot's medical certificate excluded coverage whether or not there was any causal connection between the breach of an exclusionary clause and the accident.

Here the terms of the policy specifically exclude coverage while the aircraft is operated in flight by any pilot not "holding valid and effective pilot and medical certificates." A medical certificate which had lapsed 5 months before the accident occurred, and before the issuance of the policy was not a "valid and effective" medical certificate. A renewal shortly thereafter did not validate it retroactively. Federal aviation regulations prohibited Peters from acting as a pilot unless he had in his personal possession an appropriate current medical certificate. He could not lawfully act as a pilot in command at the time of the crash. The subsequent renewal did not wipe out the violation nor alter the fact that the violation had occurred. Under an aircraft insurance policy that excludes coverage while the aircraft is operated in flight by other than a pilot or pilots holding valid and effective pilot and medical certificates, there is no coverage where a pilot's medical certificate lapsed 5 months before an accident occurred.

The judgment of the trial court was correct and is affirmed.

Affirmed.

NOTES

1. *An end-run?* Insurers can and do avoid using the word "warranty" and attempt to achieve the same common law result by using other language. Is that what was going on in *Omaha Sky Divers*? This practice poses a problem with regard to identifying warranties so that one knows whether the statutes or court decisions apply. If they do not apply, underwriters may be able to achieve the same result as under Lord Mansfield's rule—a breach of a condition works a forfeiture of the policy or at least suspends coverage during the period the condition is not met, regardless of whether the breach was material to the risk that was the subject of the condition. But is there anything wrong with this "end-run"? Should insurers be allowed to determine what they will cover and what they will not?

Recall the *Deschler* case in § 1.04. Should the insurer have insisted that the insured warrant that he would not operate water ski kites?

2. *Unfair surprise?* Many insureds read their policies for the first time after they suffer a loss, and sometimes what they find in the text of the policies surprises them. As a general matter, which is more likely to surprise an insured—an insurer's defense that the insured has breached a warranty, or an insurer's defense that the loss which occurred was not within the policy's coverage? Is *Omaha Sky Divers* essentially a case where the insured was unfairly surprised by a technical coverage exclusion that was immaterial to the risk that produced the loss?

3. *An alternative perspective.* In *Bayers v. Omni Aviation Managers, Inc.,* 510 F. Supp. 1204 (D. Mont. 1981), the court held that a pilot's failure to hold a valid effective medical certificate at the time of the plane's crash did not preclude coverage under a aircraft liability insurance policy due to the lack of a causal connection between the failure to hold the medical certificate and the crash. Would this approach make sense if the pilot's deficiency were that he or she had not logged a minimum number of hours in the make and model of aircraft and had not received the requisite training, all as specified in the

insurance policy? *See Ranger Insurance Co. v. Kovach,* 63 F. Supp. 2d 174 (D. Conn. 1999) (crash of aircraft flown under instrument flight rules by pilot certified to fly only under visual flight rules); *Macalco, Inc. v. Gulf Insurance Co.,* 550 S.W.2d 883 (Mo. App. 1977) (crash of aircraft when pilot, who possessed student license, lacked proper FAA certificate and rating). Likewise, the insurer may wish to issue a policy only if the insured aircraft is flown while it has a valid FAA airworthiness certificate and if the insured has taken steps to comply with all applicable FAA rules and regulations. If it turns out that at the time of the aircraft's crash at least one FAA rule was being violated, is it unfair surprise when the insurer denies coverage? *See Avemco Insurance Co. v. White,* 841 P.2d 588 (Okla. 1992) (crash of aircraft lacking airworthiness certificate; held, no coverage and causation not required); *O'Connor v. Proprietors Insurance Co.,* 696 P.2d 282 (Colo. 1985)(similar facts; held, no coverage because insured failed to show that the violation of the regulation was not a cause of the accident).

4. *Warranties and coverage provisions in aviation policies.* How the questions in the preceding note are resolved will depend mightily on whether the clause in question is a warranty or a coverage provision. If, for example, a pilot qualification provision is deemed a warranty, then, under the affirmative warranty rule referenced in *Vlastos,* the pilot need only be qualified (i.e., competent and properly trained) at the time the policy is issued. To avoid the obvious problems from such a construction, it is common for current aviation policies to state that the policy provides coverage only when pilots with the designated credentials and training are flying the aircraft. But drafting in terms of coverage can also result in situations where the pilot's failure to be suitably qualified to operate the aircraft has no relationship to the accident. Some courts and commentators have taken the position that noncompliance with a coverage provision should result in loss of coverage only if the noncompliance has a causal relationship to the loss. See Derrick J. Hahn, *General Aviation Aircraft Insurance: Provisions Denying Coverage for Breaches That Do Not Contribute to the Loss,* 64 J. Air L. & Com. 675 (1999); Dawn R. Gabel, Note, *Warranties and Representations in Aviation Insurance: A Contribute-to-the-Loss Solution to the Confusion Created by the Common Law and the Statutory Response,* 30 Ariz. L. Rev. 515 (1988). How this approach plays out in particular cases can depend on whether the insured has the burden to establish that noncompliance did not cause the loss, or whether the insurer has the burden to establish that noncompliance did cause the loss. *See O'Connor v. Proprietors Insurance Co., supra (in note 3).* How would you expect insurers to react to a requirement that an insurer can assert an exclusion to coverage only if it can establish that the exclusion was causally related to the loss? If you were a policyholder, particularly one who took great pains to make sure that your fleet of aircraft are only operated by pilots with the requisite skills and training, would you favor the requirement?

5. *Statutory regulation reprise.* If the *Omaha Sky Divers* case were governed by New York law, would section 3106 of the New York statute apply to the pertinent clauses in that insurance policy? What would be the effect if it did?

Why, according to the Supreme Court of Nebraska, did not the Nebraska statute regulating warranties apply? Is this result required by the text of the

Nebraska statute? If the Nebraska statute did apply to the policy in *Omaha Sky Divers*, what would be the result?

If the case were governed by Massachusetts law, what result would the Massachusetts statute require?

CHARLES, HENRY & CROWLEY, CO. v. HOME INSURANCE CO.

349 Mass. 723, 212 N.E.2d 240 (1965)

KIRK, JUSTICE.

This case is here on the defendant's exceptions to the judge's denial of nine of its eleven requests for rulings. The first request sought a ruling that, "[o]n all the evidence and the law, a finding for the defendant is warranted." The judge denied the request "in view of the facts found and the application of" G.L. c. 175, § 186.[1] The second request, also denied, was for a ruling that the evidence and the law required a finding for the defendant. Our consideration of the disposition of these requests is decisive of the case.

The statement of agreed facts, which was submitted to the judge, recited that the plaintiff, a Boston jewelry firm, on October 6, 1960, made a written proposal to the defendant for a "Jewelers' Block Policy" insuring against theft from the plaintiff's display windows. Question 14B of the proposal form asked the plaintiff to indicate the maximum value of jewelry to be displayed in the windows. The plaintiff answered that, during business hours, the value of jewelry displayed in ". . . windows. . .outside show cases. . .[or] any one window" would not exceed $14,500 where the window or case was protected by swinging shatterproof glass, and $500 where the window or case was not so protected.

The policy issued by the defendant on November 16, 1960, stated that the proposal form was made part of the policy. The policy also carried a "Jewelers' Block Combination Endorsement." Section 1A of the combination endorsement provided that the insurer's maximum liability for theft of displayed jewels during business hours was $14,500 where the jewels were protected by the swinging shatterproof glass, and $500 where unprotected. Section 1B stated: "It is a condition of this insurance precedent to any recovery hereunder that the values of property displayed will not exceed the amount represented in answer to Question 14B of the Proposal form attached to this policy."

On the morning of March 24, 1961, while the plaintiff was open for business, a rock was thrown through one of the store's display windows and jewelry worth $13,620 was stolen. At the time of the theft the jewelry on display in

---

[1] "No oral or written misrepresentation or warranty made in the negotiation of a policy of insurance by the insured or in his behalf shall be deemed material or defeat or avoid the policy or prevent its attaching unless such misrepresentation or warranty is made with actual intent to deceive, or unless the matter misrepresented or made a warranty increased the risk of loss."

the protected area of the window was worth $18,512, and in the unprotected area was worth $1,118.40.

The single question presented is whether the provision in § 1B of the policy, referring to the plaintiff's representation in answer to question 14B that the displayed jewelry would not exceed certain amounts in value was, on the one hand, a condition precedent which, if not complied with, would bar recovery, or was, on the other hand, a representation or warranty which, if not fulfilled, would bar recovery only if the proof required by G.L. c. 175, § 186, was forthcoming. The judge treated the provision as a representation or warranty. He found that the insurer's risk had not been materially increased by the display of the more valuable jewelry and, since the parties had stipulated that there was no intent to deceive the insurer, made a finding for the plaintiff in the sum of $13,620.

We think that the judge was in error. General Laws c. 175, § 186, applies only to representations and warranties and does not apply to conditions precedent included expressly within the terms of a policy. The statement made by the plaintiff in the proposal was, at first, a representation. The statement, however, was expressly made a condition precedent to recovery in the combination endorsement.

Whether a warranty or representation made in an application for a policy may be converted into a condition of a policy was briefly discussed but not decided in *Everson v. General Acc. Fire & Life Assur. Corp. Ltd.*, 202 Mass. 169, 172, 88 N.E. 658, where representations respecting income were in a rider pasted to a page of an insurance contract under the heading, "Schedule of warranties." The court there held that since there was no clear expression in the policy whereby these negotiatory warranties were to be made conditions precedent, the mere attachment of them to the policy did not change their legal significance, and accordingly they were to be regarded as subject to the predecessor of G.L. c. 175, § 186. The question, however, was decided in *Kravit v. United States Cas. Co.*, 278 Mass. 178, 179 N.E. 399, and *Faris v. Travelers' Indem. Co.*, 278 Mass. 204, 179 N.E. 605, where statements by the prospective insured, essential to an intelligent decision by the insurer to incur liability, were expressly made conditions precedent to recovery under the policy, and so were not subject to G.L. c. 175, § 186. Although the statements in the *Kravit* and *Faris* cases referred to existing facts, representations concerning future events have also been held conditions precedent where the policies have so provided as in *Elder v. Federal Ins. Co.*, 213 Mass. 389, 100 N.E. 655 (where the insured's statement that his insured vehicle would not be used for hire was made a condition precedent to recovery), and *Krause v. Equitable Life Ins. Co.*, 333 Mass. 200, 203, 204, 129 N.E.2d 617 (where the insured agreed that his life insurance policy would not be effective if he consulted or was treated by a physician in the interval between the time of his examination by the company's doctor and the time of his receipt of the policy and payment of the premium). The result of the foregoing is that a statement made in an application for a policy of insurance may become a condition of the policy rather than remain a warranty or representation if: (1) the statement made by the insured relates essentially to the insurer's intelligent decision to issue the policy; and (2) the statement is made a condition precedent to recovery under the policy, either by using the precise words "condition precedent" or their equivalent. Both tests are met in the instant case. First, it is clear that the value of the jewelry to be displayed was a fundamental fact which the insurer considered in deciding to issue the policy. Second, the representations made in question 14B were expressly made conditions precedent to recovery in § 1B of the combination endorsement. Since the words of a contract for insurance are as "binding upon both parties as that of any other contract,", the language of the endorsement must be read as constituting an agreement to treat the representations as a condition precedent to recovery. General Laws c. 175, § 186, therefore was not applicable to the policy. The defendant's first two requests should have been granted. The plaintiff relies heavily on *Goldstein v. Royal Indem. Co.,* 297 Mass. 55, 7 N.E.2d 420. We have considered that case and do not think it applicable here.

A finding for the defendant was required. It is not necessary to discuss the remaining exceptions.

Exceptions sustained. Judgment for the defendant.

* * *

NOTES

1. *"You say to-may-toe, and I say to-mah-toe."* The use of the words "condition precedent" escaped the reach of the Massachusetts statute according to the court in the principal case. But the position that a condition precedent is different from a warranty is subject to question. As one treatise observes, "[t]he terms 'warranty' and 'condition precedent' are often used interchangeably or as synonymous, a confusion of terms which has been to a large degree engendered by the fact that in a broad sense the nonbreach of the warranties of a policy is a condition precedent to recovery thereon." 6 Couch on Insurance § 81:24 (3d ed. 1999). Given the Massachusetts interpretation, does it also follow that the words "condition precedent" are immune from the judicial techniques for regulating forfeitures discussed in *Vlastos* and in the notes following that case? Does the fact that a statute has been enacted on the subject, for example, like the one in Massachusetts, prevent the court from regulating forfeitures through judicial interpretation?

The looseness with which courts use the concept of "condition" breeds no small amount of confusion in the cases. In what sense is the court using the term "condition" in the following passage? "[Neb. Stat.] § 44-358 deals with warranties which are conditions precedent to the very existence of an insurance contract, not with promissory warranties the fulfillment of which are conditions precedent to recovery under an insurance contract which has come into being." *Coppi v. West American Insurance Co.,* 247 Neb. 1, 524 N.W.2d 804, 812 (1994).

2. *Are all conditions warranties?* If a condition precedent is synonymous with a warranty because it works a forfeiture, what types of conditions in a policy might be classified as a warranty? Claims processing issues will receive attention in Chapter 8. Policy provisions which are in play in those cases include, for example, notice of loss provisions, proof of loss clauses, cooperation clauses, and many more.

[2] Interpretation

Are insurance contracts only one more kind of contract? Judge Cuthbert Pound apparently thought not: "The tendency on the part of the courts to treat insurance contracts as standing in a class by themselves and to protect against forfeitures invoked in defense of honest claims has led to much subtlety. As Professor Woodruff says. . .'What do they know of the law of the insurance contract who only the law of contract know?'" *Satz v. Massachusetts Bonding & Insurance Co.*, 243 N.Y. 385, 393, 153 N.E. 844, 846 (1926). Indeed, subtlety abounds in that statement. From one perspective, the entire subject of contract law is nothing more than an attempt to regulate such jural arrangements; if one knows contract law, one can intuit most answers to questions involving the meaning of the insurance policy. Although it is impossible to seriously dispute the proposition that contract law is highly relevant when insurance policies must be interpreted, insurance law principles often add significant nuances to the contract law principles with which law students and lawyers are well familiar.

The basic rules have a familiar ring to any lawyer. One court recently summarized the "principles of insurance policy interpretation" as follows:

> Under statutory rules of contract interpretation,[*] the mutual intention of the parties at the time the contract is formed governs interpretation. Such intent is to be inferred, if possible, solely from the written provisions of the contract. The "clear and explicit" meaning of these provisions, in their "ordinary and popular sense," unless "used by the parties in a technical sense or a special meaning is given to them by usage", controls judicial interpretation. Thus, if the meaning a layperson would ascribe to contract language is not ambiguous, we apply that meaning.
>
> If there is ambiguity, however, it is resolved by interpreting the ambiguous provision in the sense the promisor (i.e., the insurer) believed the promisee understood them at the time of formation. If application of this rule does not eliminate the ambiguity, ambiguous language is construed against the party who caused the uncertainty to exist. In the insurance context, we generally resolve ambiguities in favor of coverage. Similarly, we generally interpret the coverage clauses of insurance policies broadly, protecting the objectively reasonable expectations of the insured. These rules stem from the fact that the insurer typically drafts policy language, leaving the insured little or no meaningful opportunity or ability to bargain for modifications. Because the insurer writes the policy, it is held "responsible" for ambiguous policy language, which is therefore construed in favor of coverage.
>
> It follows, however, that where the policyholder does not suffer from lack of legal sophistication or a relative lack of bargaining power, and where it is clear that an insurance policy was actually negotiated and jointly drafted, we need not go so far in protecting the insured from

---

[*] [Editors' note: California has some statutory rules which essentially codify the common law principles.]

ambiguous or highly technical drafting. . . .. In the absence of evidence that the parties, at the time they entered into the policies, intended the provisions at issue. . .to carry technical meanings and implemented this intention by specially crafting policy language, however, we see little reason to depart from ordinary principles of interpretation.

AIU Insurance Co. v. Superior Court, 51 Cal. 3d 807, 799 P.2d 1253, 1265, 274 Cal. Rptr. 820 (1990). In application, however, the easy-to-state principles frequently fail to point to obvious results. Indeed, at times it seems that the distinctions being drawn by contestants in litigation require the legal equivalent of an electron microscope to observe and understand. Yet there is much at stake in many of these cases, which explains the extraordinary scrutiny which insurance policy text receives in the cases. Consider, for example, the following:

McHUGH v. UNITED SERVICE AUTOMOBILE ASSOCIATION
164 F.3d 451 (9th Cir. 1999)

LAY, Circuit Judge:

Frank and Mary McHugh filed a complaint for a declaratory judgment against the United Service Automobile Association insurance company ("USAA") and the Director of the Federal Emergency Management Agency ("FEMA") alleging that (1) their beach house which was insured by USAA under a Standard Flood Insurance Policy ("SFIP") was damaged by a mudslide, (2) they made a claim to USAA under the SFIP, and (3) USAA improperly denied their claim. The district court granted summary judgment for USAA, holding that the damage to the McHughs' home was caused by a landslide which is not covered by the policy. We reverse the decision of the district court.

Background

Under the National Flood Insurance Act of 1968 ("Act"), codified at 42 U.S.C. §§ 4001 et seq. (1994), the FEMA is authorized to provide federally subsidized flood insurance to individual homeowners. The language of the SFIP is prescribed by the Act and FEMA regulations, although the policy itself is issued through a private insurer. Frank and Mary McHugh purchased a SFIP from USAA to provide coverage for their beach house located on the Hood Canal in Seabeck, Washington.

The McHughs' Flood Policy defines "Direct Physical Loss By or From Flood" as "any loss in the nature of actual loss of or physical damage, evidenced by physical changes, to the insured property. . .which is directly and proximately caused by a 'flood' (as defined in this policy)." The policy also defines "Flood" as:

A. A general and temporary condition of partial or complete inundation of normally dry land area from:

1. The overflow of inland or tidal waters.

2. The unusual and rapid accumulation or runoff of surface waters from any source.

3. Mudslides (i.e., mudflows) which are proximately caused by flooding as defined in subparagraph A-2 above and are akin to a river of liquid and flowing mud on the surfaces of normally dry land areas, including your premises, as when earth is carried by a current of water and deposited along the path of the current.

B. The collapse or subsidence of land along the shore of a lake or other body of water as a result of erosion or undermining caused by waves or currents of water exceeding the cyclical levels which result in flooding as defined in subparagraph A-1 above.

The Flood Policy also contains the following exclusion:

We only provide coverage for direct physical loss by or from flood which means we do not cover:

. . . .

B. Losses from other casualties, including loss caused by:

1. Theft, fire, windstorm, wind, explosion, earthquake, land sinkage, landslide, destabilization or movement of land resulting from the accumulation of water in subsurface land areas, gradual erosion, or any other earth movement except such mudslides (i.e., mudflows) or erosion as is covered under the peril of flood.

The federal courts have stated that flood insurance polices normally are subject to limitations on coverage imposed by applicable federal regulations. However, this makes little difference in the instant case because the definitions of the terms "flood" and "flooding" in the policy are the same in all material respects as the definitions found in the regulations. . . .

On December 28, 1994, the McHughs reported to USAA that their beach house had been damaged by a flood-related mudslide that occurred after heavy rains and an overflow of a drainage ditch situated at the top of the slope on which the house was located. The house, located at the base of a steep sloping hill, was knocked off its foundation and partially destroyed after being hit by a saturated mixture of soil, gravel, vegetation, and rock. After receiving the McHughs' claim under the SFIP, USAA hired an independent adjustor, who took several photographs, and then hired Martin Page from the geo-technical engineering firm of Shannon & Wilson to determine the exact cause of the damage to the McHughs' house. In a written report, Page concluded that the slide was caused by a combination of factors including saturation of the surface soils by heavy rainfall and a build-up of groundwater in the underlying sand and gravel. Page's report concludes, however, that "it is our opinion that the soil instability that occurred at the subject site is classified as a landslide, not a mudslide."

The McHughs hired their own geo-technical engineer, Robert Pride, to assess the cause of the damage. Contrary to Page's report, Pride found that the damage to the beach house was caused by a mudslide, not a landslide, precipitated by soil saturation and surface-water runoff from a natural drainage channel above the slide area.

In December 1995, the McHughs filed a complaint against USAA and the director of FEMA[1] seeking coverage for damage to the beach house. USAA moved for summary judgment in November 1996 to dismiss all claims with prejudice. The McHughs filed a cross-motion for summary judgment a month later asking the district court to hold that their claim was covered by the policy as a matter of law.

On December 6, 1996, the district court granted USAA's motion for summary judgment, holding the damage to the McHughs' home was caused by a landslide, not a mudslide, and therefore was excluded from coverage under the SFIP. This appeal followed.

Discussion

The law is clear that, as contracts, SFIPs issued under the National Flood Insurance Program ("NFIP") are governed by federal law applying standard insurance law principles. Furthermore, the interpretation of the insurance policy is a question of law for the court and is reviewed de novo.

There were two diverging expert testimonies in this case. Although experts may disagree in their conclusions, their testimony cannot be used to provide legal meaning or interpret the policies as written. Therefore, we view the experts' testimony in this case as only relevant for the historical facts that they observed and not for their legal conclusions as to what conditions were covered or excluded under the terms of the policy.

The historical facts of this case are not in dispute. Robert Pride, the McHughs' expert, characterized the event as a "saturated soil mass that flowed down towards the [McHughs'] house." He stated that this signified to him the fluid movement of saturated soils, whatever their makeup. The insurance company's expert did not differ from this observation. In fact, Martin Page, the defendant's geo-technical engineer, also characterized the event as "a saturated mass of soil and trees" that slid down the slope. Page stated in his report:

> The slide debris generally consists of gravel and sand mixed with surface vegetation, several large tree stumps, and previously cut tree tops. In our opinion, the presence of cut trees and decayed tree stumps on the surface of the slope may also have contributed to the instability. . . . The soils that have accumulated against the side of the beach house appear to have slid down the slope as a saturated mass of soil and trees.

Pride also observed that the "slide was not a 'landslide'" because the "slide did not involve a deep-seated earth movement or other geo-technical conditions associated with landslides." Furthermore, in his report, Pride stated "[l]andslides are typically in excess of five to fifteen feet deep, usually involve large quantities of earth or rock, and may move downslope with much of the slide mass relatively intact."

It is a fundamental principle that unless the contract terms are specifically different than the common usage of the terms, that the common usage of the

---

[1] The director of FEMA was dismissed as a party on March 11, 1996.

terms will be adopted. For example, under the SFIP, a "landslide" as opposed to a mudflow is excluded from coverage. Yet the term landslide is not otherwise defined in the policy. Webster's dictionary defines a landslide as "the rapid downward movement under the influence of gravity of a mass of rock, earth, or artificial fill on a slope." Webster's Third New International Dictionary 1269 (1981).

However, the fundamental question involved here is not so much the interpretation of the exclusionary clause but whether a mudflow occurred and was the proximate cause of the damage to the house. The definition of "mudflow" as set forth in the policy and regulation is reinforced by the common usage of that term. According to Webster's Ninth New Collegiate Dictionary 778 (1984), "mudflow" is defined as "a moving mass of soil made fluid by rain or melting snow." We find nothing in the policy itself or in the regulations which defines "mudflow" any differently than the common usage of the term. Under the common usage, the "saturated soil mass" that destroyed the McHughs' house was a mudslide.

The dissent faults our interpretation of the record on the basis that there is no evidence offered by the McHughs to show that there was a "liquid river of mud." However, we think that common sense and common meaning must prevail. Under the terms of the policy, "liquid and flowing mud" surely means nothing more than a saturated soil mass moving by liquidity down a slope. The torrential rain and the overflow of the natural drainage channel formed a liquidity which flowed down the slope and brought with it a saturated soil mass composed of soil, sand, gravel, and underbrush. As a result, the McHughs' house was hit by this saturated mixture of soil, gravel, vegetation and rock, and was knocked off its foundation. The policy itself describes a mudflow "as when earth is carried by a current of water and deposited along the path of the current." This statement is no different than the definition of the mudflow quoted from Webster's that it is "a moving mass of soil made fluid by rain or melting snow."

The district court found that "soil saturation was the predominant cause" of the event which occurred. In denying coverage, however, the district court relied upon *Wagner v. Director, Federal Emergency Management Agency,* 847 F.2d 515, 521 (9th Cir.1988). The Wagner case is clearly distinguishable from the facts adduced in this case. First and foremost, as the Wagner court points out, in that case the plaintiffs admitted that floodwaters did not damage their property directly and all of their losses were caused by the shifting of the saturated earth beneath their home. Unlike the facts in Wagner, the McHughs' home was hit by the liquid flow of soil mass which in turn knocked the home off its foundation. There is no evidence that the saturation of the land underneath the McHughs' home gave way or was caused to move by reason of that saturation. The pictures submitted to the court by exhibit clearly demonstrate to the contrary. Neither expert testified that saturation of the land underneath the house caused the movement of the house.

In the *Wagner* case, the court stated that "the courts have all but universally held, federal flood insurance policies do not cover losses stemming from water-caused earth movements." *Wagner,* 847 F.2d at 522. It is clear from the facts involved and the cases cited to support this statement, that the court did not mean to exclude water-caused mudflows. In other words, *Wagner*'s statement was not intended to change the policy terms which define mudflow "as when earth is carried by a current of water. . . ."

. . . .

Under the reading of the policy urged by USSA, a policyholder whose home was inundated with flood waters mixed with fine, granular soil would receive coverage, while a homeowner unfortunate enough to be located below a slope with sand and gravel where flood waters are mixed with fine, granular soil would be denied coverage. While FEMA should be free to draw a mudslide/ landslide distinction when allocating its flood coverage, as a matter of fairness such a distinction should not lead to such a seemingly arbitrary result.

. . . .

Conclusion

As we earlier observed, whether coverage exists under an insurance policy is a question of law. The historical facts in the present case are not materially disputed by the experts' reports and depositions. What is disputed is their legal conclusions as to whether the facts fall within the terms of "mudflow" or the exclusion of a "landslide" within the policy. This is a question of law for the court to be decided from the definitions within the policy as reinforced by the common usage of the terms. The following facts are undisputed:

> (1) At the time of the damage to McHughs' home, there was a heavy rainfall and overflow of waters from a drainage ditch located above the house and slope.

> (2) The waters came down the slope, inundated the slope, and carried a mass of saturated soil, gravel, vegetation and rock.

> (3) The saturated soil mass flowed down the slope, hit the McHughs' home, and knocked it off its foundation.

> (4) The damage to the foundation did not occur because of settlement of saturated soil underneath the house.

We conclude that the policy is not ambiguous in its terms. We also conclude that the occurrence was "akin to a river of liquid, flowing mud" and constituted "earth carried by a current of water and deposited along the path of the current." These definitions simply mean that coverage will be extended to the common usage of the term "mudflow" as when damage is proximately caused "by a moving mass of soil made fluid by rain."

We, therefore, conclude that under the undisputed historical facts the coverage of the SFIP policy clearly extends to the flooding (i.e., mudflow) that proximately caused the damage to the McHughs' home. We vacate the judgment of the district court and remand the case for entry of judgment in favor of the plaintiffs.

GRABER, Circuit Judge, dissenting:

I respectfully dissent. The majority's opinion is inconsistent with the record, conflicts with precedent on important matters of federal law, modifies a valid federal regulation, and reaches an unjust result.

The Insurance Policy and the Governing Regulations

This appeal involves the interpretation of a Standard Flood Insurance Policy (SFIP), the wording of which is prescribed by the National Flood Insurance Act of 1968(Act) and by Federal Emergency Management Agency (FEMA) regulations, found at 44 C.F.R. Pt. 61, App. A(1). The Act grants to the Director of FEMA the authority to promulgate regulations pertaining to SFIPs. 42 U.S.C. § 4121(a)(1). The SFIP is a single-risk insurance policy that "only provide[s] coverage for direct physical loss by or from flood." 44 C.F.R. Pt. 61, App. A(1) (emphasis in original). The emphasized phrase is defined as "any loss in the nature of actual loss of or physical damage, evidenced by physical changes, to the insured property (building or personal property) which is directly and proximately caused by a flood." *Id.* (emphasis added; emphasis omitted).

FEMA regulations define the terms "flood" and "flooding" to include:

> (a) A general and temporary condition of partial or complete inunda-tion of normally dry land areas from:
>
> . . . .
>
> (3) Mudslides (i.e., mudflows) which are proximately caused by flood-ing as defined in paragraph (a)(2) of this definition and are akin to a river of liquid and flowing mud on the surfaces of normally dry land areas, as when earth is carried by a current of water and deposited along the path of the current.

44 C.F.R. § 59.1 (emphasis added). "Inundation" is not defined in the regula-tions, but commonly means, as pertinent, "a rising and spreading of water over land not usu[ally] submerged." Webster's Third New Int'l Dictionary 1188 (unabridged ed.1993).

The regulations further define "mudslide (i.e., mudflow)" as

> a condition where there is a river, flow or inundation of liquid mud down a hillside usually as a result of a dual condition of loss of brush cover, and the subsequent accumulation of water on the ground preceded by a period of unusually heavy or sustained rain. A mudslide (i.e., mudflow) may occur as a distinct phenomenon while a landslide is in progress, and will be recognized as such by the Administrator only if the mudflow, and not the landslide, is the proximate cause of damage that occurs.

44 C.F.R. § 59.1 (emphasis added). That regulatory definition of "mudslide (i.e., mudflow)" as "a river, flow or inundation of liquid mud" is very similar to the SFIP's definition of that term as "akin to a river of liquid and flowing mud." Under either definition, a "mudslide (i.e., mudflow)" must consist of liquid mud.

The Issue for Decision and the Facts in the Record

We must decide whether, based on the evidence in this record, a "mudslide" directly caused the damage to plaintiffs' property. If so, defendant must provide insurance coverage. If not, defendant need not provide coverage.

. . . .

Defendant's geotechnical engineer unequivocally concluded that plaintiffs' property damage was the result of a landslide, not a mudslide. His report stated in part:

> The slide debris generally consists of gravel and sand mixed with surface vegetation, several large tree stumps, and previously cut tree tops. In our opinion, the presence of cut trees and decayed tree stumps on the surface of the slope may also have contributed to the instability.
>
> . . . .
>
> Based on our visual evaluation of the property, it is our opinion that the soil instability that occurred at the subject site is classified as a landslide, not a mudslide. The soils that have accumulated against the side of the beach house appear to have slid down the slope as a saturated mass of soil and trees. There was no evidence of soils having flowed around the sides of or into the house, as would have occurred if there had been significant flowing of wet or saturated soils. (Emphasis added.)

Plaintiffs' expert, in his report, presented "arguments for classifying this slope failure as a 'mudslide' in accordance with [defendant's] flood policy terminology." (Emphasis added.) Notwithstanding the availability of those "arguments," however, plaintiffs' expert, too, ultimately concluded that the directly damage-causing event was not a mudslide:

> If the saturated soils on the slope consisted of silts and clays, or even sands and silts, the failure most certainly would have been labeled a "mudflow." Saturated fine-grained soils would behave more like a slurry because of its particle size, strength and viscosity characteristics. In contrast, these soils on your slope are basically coarse-grained granular materials with higher strength and greater resistance to failure—thereby resulting in steeper natural slopes. The causes of failure are the same (i.e.: rainfall, surface runoff and groundwater seepage), but the appearance is different. Saturated sands and gravels are not carried as far by water flow, nor do they create mud or slurry-like consistencies. Although excess surface water runoff is more readily absorbed by the native granular soils, the net effect of saturated soils on your steep slope is a "sand-gravel flow" instead of a "mudflow." (Emphasis added.)

Plaintiffs' expert did not refer to the mass of material that directly damaged the house as "liquid mud" or even "mud." Rather, the words that he used in his report to describe the material include "sand," "gravel," "rock," "vegetation," "coarse-grained granular materials," and "debris."

Nowhere in the record is there any indication that the directly damage-causing material was liquid mud or that it flowed or resembled a river at any time, as required by the definition of "mudslide" in the SFIP and the FEMA regulations. In colloquial terms, it rained a lot. The rain caused the hill behind plaintiffs' house to fail, and the hill—soil, rock, gravel, sand, trees, plants, and debris—fell on the house. That kind of earth movement is not a "mudslide," because it lacks the essential characteristic of a "mudslide" as defined in the SFIP and the regulations—liquidity.

The majority writes that "[t]he torrential rain and the overflow of the natural drainage channel formed a liquidity which flowed down the slope and brought with it a saturated soil mass composed of soil, sand, gravel, and underbrush." This passage still means that rain caused the ground to get wet and give way, and that the wet ground then damaged plaintiffs' house. Using the word "liquidity" in the sentence does not change the nature of the directly damage-causing event from a slope failure to a mudflow.

Federal Judicial Interpretation of the SFIP

As the courts have all but universally held, federal flood insurance policies do not cover losses stemming from water-caused earth movements." *Wagner v. Director, Fed. Emergency Management Agency,* 847 F.2d 515, 522 (9th Cir.1988). That is so because of the SFIP's requirement that property damage be caused "directly and proximately" by a flood. Because of that requirement, it is not enough for heavy rainfall to cause an earth movement and for the earth movement in turn to cause property damage. Rather, the flood must be the immediate and actual cause of the damage. . . .

. . . .

Contractual and Regulatory Definition of Terms

When an insurance policy defines a term, the court is bound by that definition. *Enterprise Tools, Inc. v. Export-Import Bank,* 799 F.2d 437, 439 (8th Cir.1986). The SFIP defines "flood" and "mudslide (i.e., mudflow)." As noted earlier, the policy covers "[m]udslides (i.e., mudflows) which are. . .akin to a river of liquid and flowing mud on the surfaces of normally dry land areas, as when earth is carried by a current of water and deposited along the path of the current."

Although the majority recognizes that a court must employ the contractual definition of a term when that definition differs from common usage, the majority conducts its analysis using the common meaning of "mudflow," after asserting that the contractual and common definitions match. That reasoning is flawed, because the contractual definition and the common meaning of "mudflow" differ materially. The SFIP's narrow definition of "mudslide (i.e., mudflow)" requires liquidity. The majority, instead, adopts a broader meaning for "mudflow" as " 'a moving mass of soil made fluid by rain or melting snow.' " The majority thereby ignores the contractual requirement that a mudslide "be akin to a river of liquid and flowing mud," and contradicts the precedential requirement that a contractual definition govern, when it says that "common sense and common meaning must prevail."

There is a second flaw in the majority's analysis of terms: By adopting the "common meaning" of terms for interpreting SFIPs, the majority unjustifiably modifies a valid FEMA regulation. The SFIP's definition of "mudflow" derives from and is mandated by a FEMA regulation, 44 C.F.R. § 59.1. Regulations issued by an agency pursuant to statutory authority have the force and effect of law. A court has no power to set aside valid administrative regulations simply because it would interpret differently the statute under which they were promulgated.

. . . .

Unfair Result

As noted, the majority uses the common, rather than the contractual and regulatory, definition of the term "mudflow" to avoid a "seemingly arbitrary result." Although what befell plaintiffs was unquestionably a disaster, disallowing recovery under an insurance policy that plainly does not cover their loss is entirely reasonable and just.

Simply put, it is not unjust to deny coverage when the insured has not bought coverage for the particular kind of disaster that occurred. The majority thinks it unfair that "a policyholder whose home was inundated with flood waters mixed with fine, granular soil would receive coverage, while a homeowner unfortunate enough to be located below a slope with sand and gravel where flood waters are mixed with fine, granular soil would be denied coverage." *Id.* Although that result surely is unfortunate for the second homeowner, it is not unfair. The first homeowner bought insurance that covered the damage, while the second did not.

Indeed, the opposite result is what would be unfair. Others who have purchased flood insurance must pay for the claim in the form of increased premiums. Purchasers of flood insurance agree to share only the risk of flood, not any of the many other risks for which other forms of insurance are designed.

. . . .

IN THE MATTER OF MOSTOW v. STATE FARM INSURANCE COS.
88 N.Y.2d 321, 668 N.E.2d 392 (1996). Petitioners Sandell and Alan Mostow were involved in an auto accident in 1992. The insurer for the other vehicle paid its $10,000 policy limits to the Mostows. Thereafter, the Mostows served State Farm with a demand for arbitration under the underinsured coverage of the Mostows' policy. (Generally speaking, underinsured coverage is first-party coverage for bodily injury; if the tortfeasor's liability insurance is not adequate to cover the victim-insured's damages, the victim-insured's own insurer pays for the loss exceeding the amount paid by the tortfeasor's insurer, up to the victim-insured's policy limits.) The court's opinion was written by Judge Titone.

"The question presented is whether the terms of a policy of insurance providing that the $100,000 per person policy limit "is the amount of coverage for all damages due to bodily injury to one person" and that the $300,000 limits of liability for " 'Each Accident' is the total amount of coverage for all damages due to bodily injury to two or more persons in the same accident" are ambiguous. Because the policy may be reasonably construed as both limiting recovery to $100,000 per person or alternatively as permitting the full $300,000 policy limits to be apportioned among persons without reference to the per person limit where two or more persons are injured, we conclude that the policy is ambiguous and that its provisions should be construed in favor of the insured.

". . . . The [Mostow's] policy provided in a declarations page that where the insured seeks damages for bodily injury caused by an underinsured motorist, the limits of liability are "$100,000 each person, $300,000 each accident." Policy provisions pertaining to the amount of coverage shown on the declarations page explain that:

> "[u]nder 'Each Person' is the amount of coverage for all damages due to bodily injury to one person. Under 'Each Accident' is the total amount of coverage for all damages due to bodily injury to two or more persons in the same accident".

After arbitration, petitioner Sandell Mostow was awarded $190,000, and Alan Mostow was awarded $100,000. The arbitrators concluded that the policy "affords coverage for an underinsured vehicle in the amount of $300,000 in an accident involving bodily injuries to 'two' people or more and therefore where two or more suffer bodily injury, the limit of $100,000 per person no longer applies." [The Mostows brought an action to confirm the award, and State Farm cross-petitioned to reduce Sandell's recovery to $100,000. The trial court modified the award, holding that "the insurer's liability to any one person is limited to $100,000 regardless of how many persons were injured in one accident." The Appellate Division reversed and reinstated the arbitrators' decision, and the Court of Appeal affirmed.]

"Insurance Law § 3420 states that all automobile policies insuring against personal injury or property damage must, at the insured's option, provide for Supplementary Uninsured Motorist (SUM) insurance coverage in terms that are "equally or more favorable to the insured" (subd [a]) than the statutory language, which provides:

> "Any such policy shall, at the option of the insured, * * * provide supplementary uninsured motorists insurance for bodily injury * * * subject to a maximum of one hundred thousand dollars because of bodily injury to or death of one person in any one accident and, *subject to such limit for one person*, up to three hundred thousand dollars because of bodily injury to or death of two or more persons in any one accident" (Insurance Law § 3420 [f][2][A] [emphasis added]).

By rendering the $300,000 per accident maximum "subject to" the per-person limit of $100,000, the Insurance Law makes clear that no injured person may recover greater than $100,000 under the provision.

"The policy at issue here does not contain any language deeming the $300,000 per accident limit "subject to" the per-person limit. The absence of such language, coupled with the policy provision stating that the $300,000 limit for " 'Each Accident' is the total amount of coverage for all damages due to bodily injury to two or more persons in the same accident" renders the policy language susceptible of two reasonable interpretations. First, the policy may be reasonably construed by an insured to limit any injured person to a recovery of $100,000, regardless of the number of injured claimants. Alternatively, the policy may be construed to provide that $100,000 is available where bodily injury damages are owed only to "one person," but that when two or more persons are injured in an automobile accident, the full $300,000 per accident policy limit is available.

"The Insurance Law does not bar the latter construction which would permit, as here, an injured claimant to recover over $100,000 where more than one person makes a claim under this endorsement because it would merely provide coverage that is "more favorable to the insured" than the statutory provisions (*see*, Insurance Law § 3420 [f][2][A]). Thus, both constructions of the policy are reasonable and not contrary to law. Because the policy may be reasonably interpreted in two conflicting manners, its terms are ambiguous.

"We are not alone in concluding that this policy language is ambiguous. The courts of at least four other jurisdictions have reached the same conclusion in construing essentially similar policy language that lacked any terms indicating that the available per accident coverage was subject to the stated per-person limits.

"Given that our precedent establishes that ambiguities in an insurance policy should be construed in favor of the insured and against the insurer, the drafter of the policy language, the construction favoring petitioner in this case, afforded by a fair interpretation of the policy, prevails. Thus, the Appellate Division properly declined to reduce the award of $190,000 to petitioner Sandell Mostow to $100,000 as respondent requested.

"Although the common understanding of the insurance industry and the legal profession may well be that the total per accident coverage is subject to the per-person limits-i.e.-classic "split limit" coverage-the test to determine whether an insurance contract is ambiguous focuses on the reasonable expectations of the average insured upon reading the policy and employing common speech.

"Additionally, while the Superintendent of Insurance has recently promulgated a regulation mandating that all policies issued or renewed after October 1, 1993[2] include a SUM endorsement that employs language identical to that contained in policy provisions at issue here, that regulation does not purport to provide guidance on the construction of this policy or otherwise demonstrate that the policy at issue is free from ambiguity. Indeed, this dilemma could have been avoided had the insurer simply drafted the policy to include the "subject to" language employed in Insurance Law § 3420 (f) (2) (A).

"Accordingly, the order of the Appellate Division should be affirmed, with costs."

NOTES

1. *Land use in coastal areas.* The extraordinary pace of development during the late twentieth century of beachfront property throughout the United States is a source of great concern for insurers. Since 1972, the population along the U.S. coastline has increased by about 62 persons per square mile of coastal land. Between 1974 and 1999, an average of 2,000 new homes were built along U.S. coastline every day. Charles A. Bookman et al., Trends in U.S. Coastal Regions, 1970-1998 (August 1999) state-of-the-coast.noaa.gove/ natdialog/coastal_trends /summaries.html. In addition, the coastline of the U.S. supports 40 percent of new commercial development and 46 percent of

---

[2] The mandatory SUM endorsement is not applicable to this accident because the policy was not issued or renewed after October 1993.

new residential development, according to the Office of Ocean and Coastal Resource Management. Outreach and Communications: Fast Facts (revised May 9, 2000) www.ocrm.nos.noaa.gove/pcd/outreach.html. Hurricanes are an obvious worry, but *McHugh* shows that this is not the only problem on some coasts. Landslides (or "mudslides"; do you agree there is a difference?) are also a concern in some western states, where it is fashionable to perch upscale homes on the edge, or sometimes over the edge, of a cliff. The McHughs urged an expansive interpretation of coverage in the principal case; who can blame them? But why should those who do not own beachfront homes or choose not to build homes in precarious locations subsidize in insurance markets those who suffer loss due to earth movement?

The McHughs' policy was purchased through the National Flood Insurance Program, which, as the court mentioned, was created by Congress in 1968 and is administered by the director of the Federal Emergency Management Agency. The essence of the program is to provide federal subsidies so that an insurance product will be available to people who would not otherwise be able to purchase it in private markets. The program has not escaped criticism in recent years. Does it make sense to subsidize the construction of homes in midwestern flood plains? Or on the beach? For more on the program and some of the special issues surrounding flood insurance, see Craig M. Collins, *Flood Insurance Is Not All Created Equal*, 74 N.D. L. Rev. 35 (1998); Charles T. Griffith, Note, *The National Flood Insurance Program: Unattained Purposes, Liability in Contract, and Takings*, 35 Wm. & Mary L. Rev. 727 (1994); Gary Knapp, Annotation, *National Flood Insurance Risks and Coverage*, 81 A.L.R. Fed. 416 (1987).

The McHughs bought a "Flood Policy." Why does the owner of beachfront property purchase flood insurance? What expectations, then, is it probable that the McHughs had at the time of contracting? Should this affect how their policy is interpreted with respect to the kind of loss they suffered? Would the court's analysis have been different if the agent who sold the policy advised them that they needed a different kind of policy to cover losses resulting from earth movement, unless the earth movement occurred in connection with flooding?

2. *General principles revisited.* If the words in the insurance policy are clear and unambiguous, they are to be given their plain and ordinary meaning. Is this what happened in *McHugh*? If both the majority and dissent think the term is unambiguous, does this not demonstrate that the term "mudslide" is ambiguous? Would you agree with the proposition that there is an ambiguity whenever two or more courts have come to different interpretations of the same provision? *See Cimarron Insurance Co. v. Travelers Insurance Co.*, 224 Or. 57, 65–66, 355 P.2d 742, 746 (1960).

If ambiguity is present, the insured gets the benefit of any reasonable doubt regarding the meaning because the policy is to be strictly construed against the drafter. But when is a term ambiguous? Stating the test for determining whether there is an ambiguity is easy: "The language of a contract of insurance is ambiguous if it is reasonably susceptible of different interpretations." *Brackett v. Middlesex Insurance Co.*, 486 A.2d 1188 (Me. 1985), 46 A.L.R.4th 765 (1986). Under this test, a disagreement between contracting parties over the meaning of a term or phrase is not, by itself, enough to establish ambiguity; indeed, if one party is asserting an unreasonable interpretation, it may be that the disputed text is clear. Stating the test is easy, but applying it is often not, as *McHugh* illustrates. Was the term "mudslide" reasonably susceptible of different interpretations? Or did that case involve a dispute about interpreting facts to which a term with one meaning would be applied? What about the fact that some policies have reached a point of such technical and complex language that many people cannot understand them, even with a very careful reading or studied effort? Does that qualify as an ambiguity? If so, does the policy in *McHugh* fall into that category?

The rule of strict construction against the drafter is known as *contra proferentum*. It is applied primarily where the parties to the contract occupy unequal bargaining positions and, since most insurance policies are contracts of adhesion, it almost always favors the insured, as *Mostow* illustrates. If it is true, as the court suggests, that few people with special knowledge of insurance would have foreseen the interpretation which the Mostows' attorney gave the provision on policy limits (do you disagree with the assumption that the Mostows' attorney came up with this interpretation, not the Mostows themselves?), why should the Mostows get the financial benefit of this bizarre—at least from the perspective of insurers and attorneys familiar with the form—interpretation? What light does this shed on the purpose of *contra proferentum*?

How should *contra proferentum* apply if the purchaser of an insurance policy on commercial operations is a large corporation, instead of individual purchasing personal insurance for home or auto? Should different interpretive rules apply? There is authority for the proposition that the rule of strict construction against the insurer has no application when the policy language is supplied by the insured, an agent of the insured, or a broker representing the insured. *Travelers Indemnity Co. v. United States,* 543 F.2d 71 (9th Cir. 1976). If the policyholder is "sophisticated," does that mean the policyholder cannot take advantage of *contra proferentum? See Eagle Leasing Corp. v. Hartford Fire Insurance Co.,* 540 F.2d 1257 (5th Cir. 1976), *cert. denied,* 431 U.S. 967 (1977)(applying Missouri law). Can you think of arguments why the insured should still get the benefit of the doubt in these situations? For more discussion, see Jeffrey W. Stempel, Law of Insurance Contract Disputes § 4.11 (2d ed. 1999).

There are other indications in some cases of limits to the doctrine of *contra proferentum*. First and foremost, to the extent a court is inclined to conclude that the disputed text has "plain meaning," it necessarily follows that *contra proferentum* can have no field of operation. *See, e.g., Money Store/ Massachusetts, Inc. v. Hingham Mutual Fire Insurance Co.,* 430 Mass. 298, 718 N.E.2d 840, 841–43 (1999) (unambiguous standard mortgage clause is enforced in accordance with plain meaning); *Nedrow v. Unigard Security Insurance Co.,* 132 Idaho 421, 974 P.2d 67, 69 (1998) (" 'Farm employee' is not reasonably subject to conflicting interpretation . . . ."); *Andersen v. Highland House Co.,* No. 75769, 2000 Ohio App. LEXIS 2020, at *18 (Ohio Ct. App., May 11, 2000)("pollution exclusion. . .clearly and unambiguosly precluded coverage"; "trial court erred in straining to find an ambiguity where none existed"). Indeed, a growing number of courts have refused to engage in a rote application of *contra proferentum*. As the court in *State Farm Mutual Automobile Insurance Co. v. Wilson,* 162 Ariz. 251, 257, 782 P.2d 727, 733 (1989), remarked:

> We marvel, as Corbin did nearly forty years ago, that judges insist upon applying such rules [construing ambiguities] "innumerable times, sometimes to apply them though justice weeps at her own blindness, sometimes to avoid them by making fine and specious distinctions, sometimes merely to state them with respect while disregarding them, and sometimes to voice criticism and disapproval." 3 A. Corbin, CONTRACTS § 536 (2d ed. 1960). We prefer to adopt a rule of common sense and have attempted to do so on numerous occasions.
>
> . . . .[W]e construe a clause subject to different interpretations by examining the language of the clause, public policy considerations, and the purpose of the transaction as a whole.
>
> . . . .However, when a question of interpretation arises, we are not compelled in every case of apparent ambiguity to blindly follow the interpretation least favorable to the insurer.

A more specific articulation of a limitation on *contra proferentum* can be found in the California cases. Recall the excerpt from *AIU Insurance* in the introductory note on interpretation preceding *McHugh*: if the insurer and insured claim different understandings of the same phrase, one asks whether the insurer knew or had reason to know of a different meaning attached to the phrase by the insured. If so, the insured's understanding controls. Should this be the case regardless of what the text of the policy says? In *Bank of the West v. Superior Court,* 2 Cal. 4th 1254, 833 P.2d 545, 10 Cal. Rptr. 2d 538 (1992), the court explained that *contra proferentum* could not be invoked until after an inquiry had been made into what the insurer should have expected the insured understood in the circumstances:

> The [insured] has invoked this rule of construction [*contra proferentum*] too early in the interpretive process. While insurance contracts have special features, they are still contracts to which the ordinary rules of contractual interpretation apply. The fundamental goal of contractual interpretation is to give effect to the mutual intention of the parties. If contractual language is clear and explicit, it governs. On the other hand, "[i]f the terms of a promise are in any respect ambiguous or uncertain, it must be interpreted in the sense in which the promisor believed, at the time of making it, that the promisee understood it." This rule, as applied to a promise of coverage in an insurance policy, protects not the subjective beliefs of the insurer but, rather, "the objectively reasonable expectations of the insured." Only if this rule does not resolve the ambiguity do we then resolve it against the insurer.

Id. at 1265–66, 833 P.2d at 551–52, 10 Cal. Rptr. 2d at 544–45. Should this interpretive approach be a two-way street? That is, if the insured understands what the insurer means by a particular provision, should the insured be bound to that meaning? If so, does that mean that insureds would be well-advised not to read their policies? For more on *contra proferentum* and other interpretation issues, see Ken Abraham, *A Theory of Insurance Policy Interpretation*, 95 Mich. L. Rev. 531 (1996).

3. *Interpreting policy text mandated by statute.* Some policies or particular provisions are mandated by statute. For example, the New York Standard Fire Policy (1943 ed.) is legislatively prescribed in most states. See Appendix A. Does this mean that rules of statutory construction should be applied instead of the usual contract rules (*see Olson Enterprises, Inc. v. Citizens Insurance Co.*, 255 Iowa 141, 121 N.W.2d 510 (1963)), or that such policy language should not be liberally construed in favor of the insured? *Compare Bilodeau v. Lumbermens Mutual Casualty Co.*, 392 Mass. 537, 467 N.E.2d 137 (1984), 46 A.L.R.4th 725 (1986) (refusing to construe ambiguities against insurer where policy language prescribed by statute) *with Hoekstra v. Farm Bureau Mutual Insurance Co.*, 382 N.W.2d 100 (Iowa 1986) (construing legislatively prescribed policy liberally in favor of insured, treating policy like any other insurance contract). Should the insured get the benefit of the doubt when the policy text is prescribed by statute?

Interestingly, in *Mostow*, the court observed that the Department of Insurance had approved the specific language contained in the policy at issue for use in the future. Apparently the interpretation that the Mostows' attorney would give the language never occurred to the state regulator, presumably an expert in such matters. Why, then, should the insureds get the benefit of an interpretation which apparently no one involved in the drafting of the form foresaw as even remotely possible?

4. *The insurer's next steps.* If you were the insurer in *McHugh* or *Mostow*, would you change future iterations of the insurance form? Would you be more likely to change the form in one case rather than the other? In *Leone v. Ameco Insurance Co.*, 249 A.D.2d 516, 672 N.Y.S.2d 116 (App. Div. 1998), the court reversed a summary judgment entered for plaintiffs in an underlying action against an insured, pursuant to which the trial court had declared that $500,000 in policy limits was available to each plaintiff, and ordered the entry of judgment for the insurer: "The subject insurance policy issued to the deceased insured is not ambiguous, and clearly limits coverage to $50,000 liability for 'each person' per bodily injury claim (including death). . . . The case of [*Mostow*] relied upon by the Supreme Court is distinguishable and has no application here." 672 N.Y.S.2d at 117.

McHugh presents a more difficult situation for the insurer. Naturally, the role of the federal government in subsidizing the underwriting of the risk and its consequent interest in regulating the coverage provisions is a huge complicating factor. But even if this were not so, is it obvious that the insurer would want to change the form? It is certainly true that many changes in standardized forms have been prompted by adverse results insurers encountered in litigation with insureds. But losing a case is not necessarily a reason to change the form. If the policy in *McHugh* were a standardized form shared by other insurers throughout the nation and the insurers collaborate by sharing information with each other about losses incurred and premiums charged, what problems might the insurer anticipate if it reacts to its loss in *McHugh* by drafting a new form? Indeed, if you were the insurer in

McHugh, would you assume that courts in other jurisdictions would adopt the reasoning of the majority's opinion? Suppose that you, the insurer, believe that a new, better form is possible, and you have an idea for what it might look like. Are there reasons why you would not want to do the research and make the investment in designing a new form?

5. *Question of law or fact?* It is well settled that the construction of an insurance policy, including the question of whether there is an ambiguity, is a matter for the court. *Cody v. Connecticut General Life Insurance Co.,* 387 Mass. 142, 439 N.E.2d 234 (1982). But there are occasions when jury issues are raised. If the legal interpretation of the contract depends on the resolution of controverted facts, such as where extrinsic evidence is admissible to determine the intent of the parties, a jury trial may be warranted. *M-Z Enters. v. Hawkeye-Security Insurance Co.,* 318 N.W.2d 408 (Iowa 1982). Whether a certain set of facts exists so as to bring a loss within the policy (*e.g.*, whether an activity took place within one's "business," or whether a car was furnished for the "regular use" of a person), may also be an issue to be determined by the trier of fact. *See Jones v. Utica Mutual Insurance Co.,* 463 So. 2d 1153 (Fla. 1985) (activity and "business"); *Foster v. Johnstone,* 107 Idaho 61, 685 P.2d 802 (1984) (car and "regular use"). Once the facts are established, however, the question of contract coverage generally is a legal matter for the court to resolve.

6. *The role of drafting history.* Is evidence of the drafter's intention when preparing a policy relevant to interpreting its meaning? The Insurance Services Office ("ISO") is a private trade association of property and casualty insurers that drafts for the benefit of member insurers standardized property and casualty forms. Some examples are reprinted with the ISO's permission in the Appendix of this book. The drafting process is not open to the public, but drafting documents, memoranda, etc. have been discovered in some cases where the meaning of an ISO form has been at issue. See Jeffrey W. Stempel, Law of Insurance Contract Disputes § 4.05, at 4–24 to 4–27 (2d ed. 1999). Sometimes industry officials involved in the drafting of particular forms have written articles or made published presentations on drafting history. Whether such evidence is admissible in disputes over meaning is controversial. For more discussion, see Robert H. Jerry, II, Understanding Insurance Law § 25A[d] (2d ed. 1996).

7. *"Easy read" policies.* In recent years, the insurance industry has taken steps to reduce the complexities of insurance policies. In particular, the ISO has drafted what are referred to as "easy read" policies which a number of companies have adopted. See the policies in Appendices C and D. Some legislatures and insurance commissioners have even required certain policies to be written in the "easy read" style. Whether these efforts have led to better communication and, consequently, to fewer legal disputes is difficult, if not impossible, to test empirically. No one suggests that it is undesirable to strive for clearer contracts. But it is naive to suggest that clearer contracts will make all misunderstandings go away. For example, prior to March 1980, Public Employees Mutual Insurance Company used a homeowners form which said that "This policy does not insure against loss: . . . . 2. caused by, resulting from, contributed to or aggravated by any earth movement, including but not

limited to. . .volcanic eruption . . . ." To simplify the policy and supposedly make it clearer, PEMCO's new form stated "We do not cover loss resulting directly or indirectly from:. . .2. Earth Movement. Direct loss by fire, explosion, theft, or breakage of glass or safety glazing materials resulting from earth movement is covered." In May 1980, Mt. St. Helens erupted with catastrophic consequences for many of PEMCO's insureds and for insureds of other companies that also used the new form. Do you think in the aftermath of the eruption that PEMCO wished it still used the old form? *See Graham v. Public Employees Mutual Insurance Co.,* 98 Wash. 2d 533, 656 P.2d 1077 (1983).

8. *More on regulation of policy text: "fairness in labeling."* In the homeowners form in Appendix C, look at "Section I—Perils Insured Against," and notice that several of the subsections have text which negates the grant of coverage under some of the enumerated perils. Why do you suppose these "exclusions" do not appear in the following section titled "Section I—Exclusions"? Does the presence of the coverage-limiting provisions in the "Perils Insured Against" section make the policy hard to understand? Were you misled by the section's title? An Oregon statute provides that "[a]ny provision restricting or abridging the rights of the insured under the policy must be preceded by a sufficiently explanatory title printed or written in type not smaller than eight-point capital letters." Or. Rev. Stat. § 742.246(2) (1999). In *Fleming v. United Services Automobile Ass'n,* 329 Or. 449, 988 P.2d 378 (1999), *modified on reconsideration in other respects,* 330 Or. 62, 996 P.2d 501 (2000), the insured owner of residential rental property sued the insurer after it relied on a pollution exclusion in the "Perils Insured Against" section of the homeowners policy to deny coverage for lead and mercury contamination caused by a tenant's clandestine operation of an illegal methamphetamine laboratory. The court held that the appearance of a pollution exclusion in a section titled "Perils Insured Against" violated the statute because the title did not explain that the section contained provisions which excluded the right to coverage under the policy. What would this holding do to other provisions in the standard homeowner's form in a jurisdiction with a statute like the referenced Oregon law? Do you agree that insurance policies should be regulated to this extent?

9. *Reformation of policy text.* Reformation is not the same thing as interpretation; it is, however, a potentially potent remedy that counsel for insureds should not overlook. "Reformation is an ancient remedy used to reframe written contracts to reflect accurately the real agreement between contracting parties when, either through mutual mistake or unilateral mistake coupled with actual or equitable fraud by the other party, the writing does not embody the contract as actually made. . . . [R]eformation is an extraordinary remedy, and courts exercise it with great caution. Even in situations where obvious mistakes have been made, courts will not rewrite the contract between the parties, but will only enforce the legal obligations of the parties according to their original agreement." *Mutual of Omaha Insurance Co. v. Russell,* 402 F.2d 339, 344–45 (10th Cir. 1968), *cert. denied,* 394 U.S. 973 (1969). Reformation usually is not an end in itself; it is sought so that the moving party can then seek the real remedy desired. An action usually is brought first to reform the contract and then to enforce the contract as reformed or to seek damages for

its breach. All of this may be accomplished in one lawsuit. *See* Dan B. Dobbs, Law of Remedies § 4.3(7) (2d ed. 1993).

Reformation is available only if both the insured and the insurer are mistaken (mutual mistake) or if one of them knows that the other is mistaken (unilateral mistake). If the basis for reformation is unilateral mistake, the instrument may be reformed only if the knowledgeable party is guilty of fraud or inequitable conduct. The term "constructive fraud" sometimes is used to describe inequitable conduct not amounting to actual fraud. For example, if the insurer has made a mistake as to the amount of the policy, the insured knows this, and the insured conceals the mistake from or fails to inform the insurer, the insured's conduct may be characterized as constructive fraud and reformation may be an appropriate remedy. *See Flax v. Prudential Life Insurance Co.,* 148 F. Supp. 720 (S.D. Cal. 1957). Although reformation can correct many kinds of errors in a policy, it is commonly invoked to correct mistakes in designating the persons who are covered or who are entitled to benefits. *See, e.g., Justarr Corp. v. Buckeye Union Insurance Co.,* 102 Ohio App. 3d 222, 656 N.E.2d 1345 (1995) (policy reformed to add corporation operating health care facility as named insured); *Emmert v. Prade,* 711 A.2d 1217 (Del. Ch.1997) (reformation to change beneficiary designation to mirror disposition of assets in decedent's will denied); *Koskey v. Pacific Indemnity Co.,* 704 N.Y.S.2d 656 (App. Div. 2000)(fire insurance policy reformed to add trust, to which property had been conveyed, as owner and loss payee).

There is a fundamental difference between reformation and rescission. An action for reformation seeks to modify or change a written instrument to make it reflect the parties' true intentions, *i.e.,* the real deal, not the one embodied in the writing. An action to rescind lies to obviate or cancel the written agreement, *i.e.,* to call the deal off. The fact that an agreement is induced, for example, by a fraudulent misrepresentation does not mean that there is no agreement. Unless the agreement is terminable or unenforceable for some reason other than that it was fraudulently induced, there is an enforceable deal until the aggrieved party takes steps to avoid it. Avoidance may be accomplished through the equitable remedy of rescission or the common law defense of fraud.

Although fraud may be a basis for either reformation or rescission, the object of the fraud is different in each remedy. Fraud in inducing the formation of an agreement warrants rescission (or damages), but not reformation. There is no agreement other than the written one entered into by the parties and, therefore, nothing else to which it can be conformed. In contrast, fraud in expressing or writing down an agreement warrants reformation, but not rescission of the agreement. In the latter case, there is an agreement, albeit not expressed in the writing, that should be enforceable once reformation reveals it. See Dan B. Dobbs, Law of Remedies § 9.5 (2d ed. 1993).

[3]　Waiver, Estoppel, and Election

REPUBLIC INSURANCE CO. v. SILVERTON ELEVATORS, INC.

493 S.W.2d 748 (Tex. 1973), 91 A.L.R.3d 500 (1979)

DANIEL, JUSTICE.

This suit was brought by Respondents, Silverton Elevators, Inc. and Carl L. Tidwell, against Petitioner, Republic Insurance Company, to recover under a Texas Standard Fire Policy issued to Silverton Elevators by Republic covering a residential dwelling and household goods contained therein. In a non-jury trial, Silverton was awarded $3,000 "for the use and benefit" of Carl L. Tidwell for the loss of the household goods. The Court of Civil Appeals affirmed. We affirm.

Carl L. Tidwell was at all times material to this controversy, an officer, director and the general manager of Silverton Elevators, Inc. Silverton owned and furnished to Tidwell a house near its elevators, together with the insurance on the house and on Tidwell's household goods, as part of his compensation as general manager. Since 1964, Republic's local agent had issued and renewed insurance policies in the name of Silverton covering the dwelling and its household goods. It is undisputed that the local agent, who had authority to issue the policies and receive the premiums, knew that the household goods belonged to Tidwell and that Silverton was carrying the insurance for the benefit of Tidwell. On April 17, 1970, a tornado destroyed the house and the household goods.

On the date of the tornado there was in effect a Texas Standard Fire Policy with Extended Coverage on DWELLING & HOUSEHOLD GOODS in the sum of $10,000 issued by Republic to Silverton for the period of April 20, 1969 to April 20, 1972, insuring against loss from windstorm the specifically described "occupied dwelling" for $7,000 and "household goods. . .while in the described building" for $3,000.00. It is undisputed that Silverton paid the $227.00 premium, and the local agent admitted that at the time he issued the policy he knew the facts heretofore mentioned with respect to actual ownership of the insured property. He testified that he wrote the policy to cover Tidwell's household goods located in the dwelling which Tidwell and his family occupied; that he knew Silverton was carrying the policy on the household goods for the benefit of Tidwell; that when he issued the policy he did not think it made any difference that it was in the name of Silverton because "they were paying the premium"; and that he told Tidwell that the policy covered his household goods both before and after the tornado.

Republic acknowledged coverage on the house and paid Silverton $7,000 for its damage, but it denied any liability to Silverton or Tidwell on the household goods. Thereupon, Silverton and Tidwell brought this suit against Republic claiming coverage to the limit of the policy ($3,000) on the household goods owned by Tidwell. Republic defended on the grounds that Silverton had no ownership and therefore no insurable interest in the household goods and that the policy as written was limited by its terms to household goods owned by Silverton Elevators, Inc., the named insured.

Silverton and Tidwell's pleadings asserted that they both had insurable interests; that the insurance was purchased by Silverton and extended to Tidwell as part of his compensation as manager and as "a legal representative of Silverton Elevators, Inc.," and that when Republic issued its policy and accepted premiums with full knowledge of the true ownership and relations between Silverton and Tidwell, it waived the right to complain about any lack of ownership or insurable interest of the named insured and was estopped from denying coverage on behalf of Tidwell. As heretofore indicated, the trial court awarded Silverton Elevators $3,000 "for the use and benefit of Carl L. Tidwell."

Since the policy refers to and clearly purports to cover the household goods located in the specifically described dwelling, we agree with the Court of Civil Appeals that the knowledge of Tidwell's ownership of the household goods by Republic's local agent and his actions with respect thereto were imputed to and binding upon Republic. Issuance of the policy and collection of the premiums with such knowledge operates as a waiver of any requirement that the named insured own or possess a beneficial interest in the insured property. *National Fire Ins. Co. of Hartford v. Carter,* 257 S.W. 531 (Tex. Comm'n App. 1924, jdgmt adopted); *Continental Ins. Co. v. Cummings,* 98 Tex. 115, 81 S.W. 705 (1904); *Wagner v. Westchester Fire Ins. Co.,* 92 Tex. 549, 50 S.W. 569 (1899); *Liverpool and London and Globe Insurance Company v. Ende,* 65 Tex. 118 (1885); *Old Colony Insurance Company v. S.D. Messer,* 328 S.W.2d 335 (Tex. Civ. App. 1959, writ ref., n.r.e.); *Germania Mutual Aid Association v. Trotti,* 318 S.W.2d 918 (Tex. Civ. App. 1958, no writ).

In the above cases, the named insureds were not the owners or sole owners of the insured properties. In each case, the true owner was known to the insurance agent and was allowed direct recovery, or recovery for his benefit, on the grounds that the insurance company had waived warranties of sole ownership or lack of insurable interest. There is no conflict between the above cases and those which hold that waiver and estoppel cannot operate to bring within the terms of a policy liabilities or benefits which were expressly excepted therefrom, such as liability from injuries due to gunshot wounds; loss for injuries while in military service in time of war; or payment of benefits beyond a specified termination date at age 65. The latter cases recognize that waiver and estoppel may operate to avoid forfeiture of coverage and benefits stated in the policy, but not to add specifically excluded risks or to enlarge the benefits or risks therein set forth. In the present case, plaintiffs seek to recover only on the risk assumed by Republic under the terms of the written policy. Republic's policy insured against the destruction of precisely the same household goods identified in its policy and for which it collected its premiums. There is no evidence that its risk was enlarged because the household goods were owned by Tidwell rather than Silverton.

. . . .

It has been suggested, but not by Republic, that the building item provision contained in the "Mortgage or Trustee" clause at the bottom of the face of the policy, and particularly the last sentence thereof, limits liability for compensation to the "interest of the insured," and that this applies to personal property.[3] Even though the provision does not speak of "named insured," and for all practical purposes Tidwell was the "insured" because the policy as to household goods was written for his benefit, there are other more compelling reasons why this provision is inapplicable to the personal property involved in this case. Clearly, the entire clause refers to loss on "building items," their value at the time of loss less depreciation, repair, replacement and reconstruction, etc. None of the language refers to personal property. Furthermore, the last sentence begins with the words, "Subject to Article 6.13 of the Texas Insurance Code," and this Article contains the specific provision that: "The provisions of this article shall not apply to personal property."

The above clause has been a part of the Texas Standard Fire Policy form prescribed by the Insurance Commission since 1943. Since then we have found no case involving a claim of an actual owner for whose benefit a policy was taken out with full knowledge by the insurance company of the true ownership, in which this clause has been applied to deny recovery by or on behalf of the true owner. In the later case the clause was specifically raised as a defense and overruled on the grounds (1) that the company was estopped by its knowledge that the named insured was not the true owner and (2) that one for whose benefit a policy is issued under such circumstances is entitled to recover thereon. The latter reason was based on a well-established rule of contract law which is applicable to insurance contracts.

Whether applicable to personal property or not, we hold that the portion of the clause relating to limitation of liability to "the interest of the insured" falls within the category of ownership provisions which may be waived; the insurer may be estopped from denying liability to the true owner on policies issued in the names of third parties covering the risks on identified property with full knowledge by the company that the property is actually owned by the one for whose benefit the policy was written or maintained.

Republic insists that reformation of the policy is the only proper remedy, if any, for recovery by Silverton on behalf of Tidwell, because of failure of the written policy to identify the household goods as belonging to Tidwell. We disagree. As heretofore indicated, under the undisputed facts, the household goods described in the policy belonged to Tidwell and were insured by Silverton for his benefit in a policy drawn by Republic's agent for such purpose, with assurances from the agent that it would cover Tidwell's furniture. If this was a mistake, it was made by Republic's agent, and it was mutual, because Tidwell and Silverton took the agent's word that it expressed the true

---

[3] The clause reads:

Loss on building items shall be payable to ASSURED ONLY

Address as Mortgagee or Trustee, as their interest may appear at time of loss, subject to Mortgage Clause (without contribution) printed elsewhere in this policy. Subject to Article 6.13 of the Texas Insurance Code, 1951, liability hereunder shall not exceed the actual cash value of the property at the time of loss, ascertained with proper deduction for depreciation; nor shall it exceed the amount it would cost to repair or replace the property with material of like kind and quality within a reasonable time after the loss, without allowance for any increased cost of repair or reconstruction by reason of any ordinance or law regulating construction or repair, and without compensation for loss resulting from interruption of business or manufacture; nor shall it exceed the interest of the insured, or the specific amounts shown under "Amount of Insurance."

agreement. With this evidence being fully developed in the present record, there is no reason to require another trial for reformation of the written policy. It has been held that even without a plea for reformation, when the facts show the true agreement intended and a mutual mistake, or mistake of the agent, in preparing the written policy, the agreement intended will be enforced without going through the formal proceedings of reformation.

Silverton and Tidwell made every proof in this case that would entitle recovery on the policy as written. Under the above cited authorities, the trial court and Court of Civil Appeals have properly held that Silverton is entitled to recover for the benefit of Tidwell on the written policy without seeking a reformation thereof.

Accordingly, the judgments of the lower courts are affirmed.

Dissenting Opinion by WALKER, J., joined by GREENHILL, C.J., and POPE and REAVLEY, JJ.

WALKER, JUSTICE (dissenting).

I respectfully dissent. . . . . .

The provision limiting liability to the interest of the insured obviously applies to both real and personal property. Since the Court does not hold otherwise, no purpose will be served by a discussion of the point. According to the majority opinion, the provision limiting liability "falls within the category of ownership provisions which may be waived; the insurer may be estopped from denying liability to the true owner on policies issued in the names of third parties *covering the risks on identified property* with full knowledge by the company that the property is actually owned by one for whose benefit the policy was written and maintained." (Emphasis supplied) It will be noted that the Court there assumes that the policy covered Tidwell's property, and that is the question presented for decision. There is no contention and has been no suggestion that the limitation of liability would, in itself and under the facts of this case, deprive respondents of a recovery to which they might otherwise be entitled under the provisions of the policy. It is, however, one of the provisions that should be considered in determining the coverage afforded by the policy as written. It must be eliminated in some way before the policy can be said to cover all household goods, regardless of by whom owned, located in the described dwelling. This the Court attempts to do by holding that the limitation of liability provision has been waived. I do not agree.

The net effect of the majority holding is to extend the policy coverage and create an entirely different contract by waiver or estoppel. That is contrary, of course, to the established rule in Texas and most other jurisdictions.

As pointed out by the Supreme Court of Michigan in *Ruddock v. Detroit Life Ins. Co.,* 209 Mich. 638, 177 N.W. 242, "to apply the doctrine of estoppel and waiver here would make this contract of insurance cover a loss it never covered by its terms, to create a liability not created by the contract and never assumed by the defendant under the terms of the policy." Neither doctrine can properly be made to serve that purpose. In *Great American Reserve Ins. Co. v. Mitchell, Tex. Civ. App.,* 335 S.W.2d 707 (wr. ref.), the court reviewed the authorities and correctly stated the Texas rule as follows:

. . . Waiver and estoppel may operate to avoid a forfeiture of a policy, but they have consistently been denied operative force to change, re-write and enlarge the risks covered by a policy. In other words, waiver and estoppel can not create a new and different contract with respect to risks covered by the policy. This has been the settled law in Texas since the decision in *Washington Nat. Ins. Co. v. Craddock,* 130 Tex. 251, 109 S.W.2d 165, 113 A.L.R. 854 . . . .

None of the cases cited in support of the waiver holding is pertinent here. Most of them involved the so-called sole and unconditional ownership clause, which provided that the entire policy would be void if the interest of the insured was other than sole and unconditional ownership. Others involved a stipulation that the policy would be void in case of a change of ownership unless otherwise provided by agreement endorsed on the policy. The policy in *Old Colony Insurance Co. v. Messer, Tex. Civ. App.,* 328 S.W.2d 335 (wr. ref. n.r.e.) covered the dwelling that was damaged by fire, but it contained a provision limiting liability to the interest of the insured and another making the policy void if the insured had concealed any material fact. These provisions as well as lack of insurable interest were pled by the insurance company in bar. Although the jury made findings tending to support an estoppel theory, the Court of Civil Appeals affirmed the trial court's judgment in favor of the true owner on the basis of its holding that the provisions in question had been waived by issuance of the policy and acceptance of the premiums with knowledge of the ownership of the property. Be that as it may, there was no question of coverage in the case, and the decision does not stand for the proposition that the limitation of liability may be waived out of the policy for the purpose of determining coverage.

There is no sole and unconditional ownership or similar provision involved in the present case. Petitioner does not urge lack of insurable interest and, contrary to the suggestion in the majority opinion, we are not concerned with a "requirement that the named insured own or possess a beneficial interest in the insured property." The provision limiting liability to the interest of the insured is not a requirement, warranty or representation. It is not a condition of forfeiture, but it is of considerable importance here in determining the property covered by the policy. So far as I am able to determine, the present case is the first in which our Court has held, albeit somewhat circuitously, that an insurance company may "waive" itself into liability for a loss not covered by the policy.

It is my opinion that respondents are not entitled to recover on the policy as written, and that is all they have attempted to do thus far. Tidwell may show his right to recover by offering evidence and obtaining findings that establish mutual mistake and the terms of the true agreement. The trial court would then be in position to enter a judgment based on the coverage actually agreed upon and intended by the parties. It would also be in position to insure that petitioner receives the appropriate premium for the risk actually as-sumed. I would reverse the judgments of the courts below and remand the cause in the interest of justice.

GREENHILL, C.J., and POPE and REAVLEY, J.J., join in this dissent.

NOTES

1. *Role of waiver and estoppel in insurance.* The doctrines of waiver and estoppel have come to play a formidable role in insurance litigation. Next to claims that the policy contains an ambiguity, these doctrines probably are advanced more often by claimants than any other legal theory. Much of this has to do with the way insurance contracts are marketed. With hundreds and sometimes thousands of agents negotiating on behalf of insurers, the field is fertile for claims by insureds that they obtained something more than what the insurer intended to sell. Professor Clarence Morris theorized nearly fifty years ago that "waiver and estoppel are two of several guises that cloak the courts' part in changing insurance from a service safely bought only by sophisticated businessmen to a commodity bought with confidence by untrained consumers" and that "[j]udges, at the urging of policyholders' advocates, have used waiver and estoppel to convert insurance from a custom-made document designed in part by knowing buyers to a brandname staple sold over the counter by mine-run salesmen to the trusting public." Clarence Morris, *Waiver and Estoppel in Insurance Policy Litigation,* 105 U. Pa. L. Rev. 925 (1957). No doubt there are many cases where the facts justify a finding of waiver or estoppel, but one can hardly avoid the impression that the technical requirements of the doctrines are not always strictly enforced.

2. *Elements of waiver.* Waiver is the voluntary and intentional relinquishment of a known right. First, did the agent in *Silverton Elevators* have the authority, actual or apparent, to waive policy provisions? Second, did the agent understand that he was relinquishing the right of the insurance company to enforce the policy as written? Assuming the answers to these questions are "yes," if the agent had thought through what he was doing, is it not more plausible that he would have written the insurance in a way to make it clear that Mr. Tidwell's interest was covered? The parties probably never really focused on the point; if that is true, how could the agent have intended to waive anything?

3. *Elements of estoppel.* Estoppel differs from waiver. Estoppel is available where one with knowledge of the facts has acted in a particular manner so that she ought not to be allowed to assert a position inconsistent with the former acts to the prejudice of others who have relied thereon. One key difference between estoppel and waiver is that detrimental reliance is required in the former, but not in the latter. Another difference is that waiver involves consent on the part of the waiving party whereas in most instances the party sought to be estopped did not actually agree or consent to give up anything by taking the earlier position. There is a very practical consequence to this difference aside from the different burden of proof that is placed upon the person asserting either waiver or estoppel. As Judge Keeton and Professor Widiss point out:

> When a claimant bases a claim for rights at variance with policy provisions on the conduct of persons alleged to have acted on behalf of an insurer, the difference between estoppel and waiver can be

particularly significant if agency concepts are also invoked. Estoppel often is more compatible than waiver with applying a relatively "broad" agency concept that precludes an insurer from objecting to the actions of the insurer's representative, and this is especially the case when the individual has exceeded the scope of authority prescribed by express provisions in the contractual relationship between the insurer and agent.

Robert E. Keeton & Alan I. Widiss, Insurance Law 618 (Student Ed. 1988). In other words, under estoppel it may be argued that the insurer-principal should be liable on a *respondeat superior* basis, as occurs in tort law when the agent acts within the course and scope of the employment. See Restatement (Second) of Agency § 8B, cmt. *a* (1958). In contrast, the theory of waiver seems to lend itself more to an analysis based on contract law, *i.e.*, a determination as to whether the agent had the authority to relinquish the right. Because agents seldom have the authority to waive policy provisions, or at least the ones that insureds typically assert were waived, the difference between waiver and estoppel can be crucial to many insureds' cases.

Based on these observations, what would you argue as plaintiff's counsel in the *Silverton Elevators* case regarding estoppel? Do you have a better case based on estoppel as compared to waiver?

4. *What remedy was most appropriate in* Silverton*?* After considering the above observations concerning waiver and estoppel, do you agree with the dissent in *Silverton Elevators* that reformation was the appropriate remedy? If you had the opportunity to plead the case anew, how would you proceed?

5. *Creating coverage by waiver or estoppel.* Most courts continue to adhere to the position, mentioned by the court in *Silverton Elevators,* that neither waiver nor estoppel may be employed to expand coverage not otherwise provided in an insurance contract. *See, e.g., Laidlaw Environmental Services (TOC), Inc. v. Aetna Casualty & Surety Co.,* 338 S.C. 43, 524 S.E.2d 847, 852 (S.C. Ct. App. 1999) (waiver cannot create coverage that does not otherwise exist); *Martin v. United States Fidelity and Guaranty Co.,* 996 S.W.2d 506, 511 (Mo. 1999)(estoppel cannot be used to create coverage); *Shepard v. Keystone Insurance Co.,* 743 F. Supp. 429, 433 (D. Md. 1990) (under Maryland law, "waiver and estoppel cannot be used to create liability where none previously existed, or to extend coverage beyond what was originally intended"); *Fli-Back Co., Inc. v. Philadelphia Manufacturers Mutual Insurance Co.,* 502 F.2d 214, 216 (4th Cir. 1974) (same under North Carolina law). The leading case for the minority view is *Harr v. Allstate Insurance Co.,* 54 N.J. 287, 255 A.2d 208 (1969):

> Although we have not previously passed upon the question here involved, we have no hesitation in deciding, in line with the rationale just outlined, that, speaking broadly, equitable estoppel is available to bar a defense in an action on a policy even where the estopping conduct arose before or at the inception of the contract, and that the parol evidence rule does not apply in such situations.

> . . . .

> However, many jurisdictions which have long followed this view nevertheless hold that equitable estoppel is not available to broaden

the coverage of a policy so as to protect the insured against risks not included therein or expressly excluded therefrom, as distinct from alleviation of other limitations or conditions of the contract. . . . While there is a clear split of authority, with the decisions holding estoppel not available to broaden coverage presently representing the majority view, many of the cases so stating are confusing and not clear cut. Estoppel and waiver are often interchangeably and improperly used, and in many cases where estoppel is held unavailable the necessary elements have not been made out anyway, or the insured by reason of his own conduct is clearly not entitled to relief. The reasons generally advanced in support of the majority view are that a court cannot create a new contract for the parties, that an insurer should not be required by estoppel to pay a loss for which it charged no premium, and perhaps that a risk or peril should not be imposed upon an insurer which it might have declined.

We are more impressed with the decisions in those jurisdictions which hold that equitable estoppel is utilizable to bar a defense of non-coverage of the loss claimed, *i.e.,* the minority rule.

These decisions all proceed on the thesis that where an insurer or its agent misrepresents, even though innocently, the coverage of an insurance contract, or the exclusions therefrom, to an insured before or at the inception of the contract, and the insured reasonably relies thereupon to his ultimate detriment, the insurer is estopped to deny coverage after a loss on a risk or from a peril actually not covered by the terms of the policy. The proposition is one of elementary and simple justice. By justifiably relying on the insurer's superior knowledge, the insured has been prevented from procuring the desired coverage elsewhere. To reject this approach because a new contract is thereby made for the parties would be an unfortunate triumph of form over substance. The fact that the insurer has received no premium for the risk or peril as to which the loss ensued is no obstacle. Any additional premium due can be deducted from the amount of the loss. If the insurer is saddled with coverage it may not have intended or desired, it is of its own making, because of its responsibility for the acts and representations of its employees and agents. It alone has the capacity to guard against such a result by the proper selection, training and supervision of its representatives. Of course, the burden of proof of equitable estoppel rests on the insured and, since evidence of representations is almost always oral, a trial court must be convinced that the requisite elements have been established by reliable proof and that the insured has met his burden by a fair preponderance of the evidence.

We agree with the Appellate Division that New Jersey should adopt the view that equitable estoppel is available, under appropriate circumstances, to bring within insurance coverage risks or perils which are not provided for in the policy or which are expressly excluded.

Id. at 304–07, 255 A.2d at 218–19. Although *Silverton* may still represent the majority rule on this point, the position is eroding as a number of states have followed the line of reasoning represented in *Harr. See, e.g., Bill Brown Construction Co. v. Glens Falls Insurance Co.,* 818 S.W.2d 1 (Tenn. 1991); *Crown Life Insurance Co. v. McBride,* 517 So. 2d 660 (Fla. 1988); *Darner Motor Sales, Inc. v. Universal Underwriters Insurance Co.,* 140 Ariz. 383, 682 P.2d 388 (1984); *Martini v. Lafayette Studios Corp.,* 676 N.Y.S.2d 808 (App. Div. 1998). In *Potesta v. United States Fidelity & Guaranty Co.,* 202 W. Va. 308, 504 S.E.2d 135 (1998), the Supreme Court of West Virginia affirmed the rule that waiver and estoppel may not be used to extend coverage, but then allowed that the rule is subject to exceptions-such as when the insurer's or agent's misrepresentation at the policy's inception prevented the insured from getting the coverage she desired, the insurer defends the insured without a reservation of rights, and the insurer acts in bad faith. 504 S.E.2d at 147–150. With which position do you agree?

Is it all relevant that the doctrine of promissory estoppel, as compared to estoppel in pais, had not been fully recognized at the time most of the early cases espousing the majority view were decided? Indeed, is it possible to follow the majority view with respect to equitable estoppel but allow coverage to be created under the doctrine of promissory estoppel? In *Verschoor v. Mountain West Farm Bureau Mutual Insurance Co.,* 907 P.2d 1293 (Wyo. 1995), the court stated: "Estoppel and waiver will not operate to create additional coverage in an existing contract of insurance . . . . However, no retreat from [that rule] is required to make room for the possibility that [the insurer's agent's] promises to Chad [an employee under a policy of group health insurance] resulted in the formation of an entirely new contract of insurance, not under a theory of equitable estoppel but by virtue of promissory estoppel." *Id.* at 1298.

6. *Election.* There also is another doctrine that somewhat resembles waiver and estoppel and which is commonly grouped with these other doctrines for purposes of discussion. Contracts scholar E. Allan Farnsworth explains the doctrine of election as follows:

> The word *election* signifies a choice, one that is often binding on the party that makes it. Holmes called election 'a choice, shown by an overt act, between two inconsistent rights, either of which may be asserted at the will of the chooser alone.' [*Wm. W. Bierce, Ltd. v. Hutchins,* 205 U.S. 340, 346 (1907) (Holmes, J.).] When the time for occurrence of a condition has expired, the party whose duty is conditional has such a choice. That party can take advantage of the nonoccurrence of the condition and treat the duty as discharged or can disregard the nonoccurrence of the condition and treat the duty as unconditional. Courts often hold that a party that chooses to disregard the nonoccurrence of a condition is bound by an election to treat the duty as unconditional; that party cannot reinstate the condition even if the other party has not relied on this choice.

E. Allan Farnsworth, Contracts § 8.5, at 543 (3d ed. 1999). Professor Farnsworth goes on to point out that "[t]he parties that have most often been bound by election waivers are insurers." *Id.* For example, in circumstances where the insured's notice of loss is arguably late, thereby giving rise (perhaps) to a defense (a subject discussed in § 8.01[1], *infra*) the insurer that proceeds to adjust the claim will subsequently be foreclosed from asserting late notice as a defense. There are various ways to explain this result—that the insurer has not been prejudiced by the lack of notice and therefore has no defense is one; that the insurer is now estopped to assert late notice is another. Another is to say that the insurer that adjusts the claim despite the late notice is foreclosed by its *election* from defending against the claim on the ground of late notice. Note that an insured which raises estoppel will need to show reliance; but this is not a part of the election analysis. This can be advantageous to insureds in situations where the evidence does not seem to make out the insurer's known, voluntary relinquishment of a right, and the insured's reliance on the insurer's course of conduct is unclear.

As it turns out, the benefits of the doctrine of election can be attained by dispensing with some of the requirements of estoppel. One court put it this way: "We have stated that the party invoking equitable estoppel must show that 'he or she has detrimentally relied on the representation or conduct of the person sought to be estopped, and that such reliance was reasonable.' Such requirement, however, may be dispensed with in order to prevent manifest injustice." *AIG Hawai'i Insurance Co. v. Smith,* 78 Hawai'i 174, 891 P.2d 261, 266 (1995). Does this mean that if the insured cannot prove reliance and is being hurt badly, the court can simply dispense with the reliance requirement? In *Smith,* the insurer undertook to defend the insured without a reservation of rights to contest coverage at a later time, and the court held that because the coverage defense should have been known to the insurer at the time it undertook the defense, the insurer was estopped to deny coverage. Could this result have been explained by use of the doctrine of election? *See also Home Insurance Co. v. Rice,* 585 So. 2d 859 (Ala. 1991) (insurer waived ability to deny duty to defend when it assumed defense without reservation thirteen months earlier; insured need not show actual prejudice).

To review your understanding of the doctrine of election, consider the following problem: Assume that ABC Insurance Company routinely notifies its insureds when a policy is about to expire. The written notice ABC uses states that "any late payment for renewal will not continue the current policy in force." In other words, the old policy will expire and the late payment will result—assuming the insurer accepts it—in a new policy which takes effect as of the date of receipt of the late premium. It turns out, however, that ABC's actual practice is to treat late payments for renewal as continuing the old policy in force. Insured, who has a policy with ABC, receives an expiration letter, and she fails to tender her first renewal premium on time. She is unaware of ABC's actual practice. Two days after the old policy expires Insured is involved in an accident. Insured, aware that the renewal due date has passed, sends in the premium anyway and it is received by ABC four days after the accident. Should ABC be permitted to deny coverage on the basis that Insured's premium, at best, would be used only to begin a new policy and that there was no policy in effect at the time of the accident? Was there a voluntary relinquishment of a known right by ABC insofar as Insured is concerned? Was there any detrimental reliance by Insured? Would election be an appropriate theory for Insured to pursue? *See* Robert E. Keeton & Alan I. Widiss, Insurance Law § 6.1(b)(4), 6.8(c)(3) (Student Ed. 1988) (urging that the doctrine of election should apply in such a situation).

[4] Honoring Reasonable Expectations

The idea that the reasonable expectations of a contracting party should be protected is deeply embedded in contract law. For example, the fundamental premise of the law of contract remedies is that the aggrieved party is entitled to be put in the position she expected to occupy if the contract had been performed. Cases where the issue is whether or how to interpret contract text are replete with statements that the reasonable expectations of the parties should be protected. Many other examples could be offered. See Robert H. Jerry, II, *Insurance, Contract, and the Doctrine of Reasonable Expectations*, 5 Conn. Ins. L. J. 21, 23–35 (1998) (giving these and other examples). Thus, it should come as no particular surprise that courts have long honored the reasonable expectations of insureds where a policy provision is ambiguous.

It is also true, however, that courts on occasion have taken a more liberal view of what constitutes an ambiguity. This, too, is not a foreign concept in the law of contract. *See, e.g.,Henningsen v. Bloomfield Motors, Inc.,* 161 A.2d 69 (N.J. 1960) (refusal to enforce limitation on personal injury liability in automobile warranty provision); *Campbell Soup Co. v. Wentz,* 172 F.2d 80, 84 (3d Cir. 1948) ("sum total" of contract provisions "drives too hard a bargain for a court of conscience to assist"). But an observer of insurance law cases over a period of many years would have a very thick file of examples, dating back to the early cases regulating warranties in insurance policies. In addition, the observer would also note that in insurance cases courts seemed more willing to apply doctrines like waiver, estoppel, or election than one would expect from a representative sample of cases in other fields. It was this situation that attracted the attention of Professor Robert E. Keeton (later to become a United States District Judge) and caused him to conclude that something new was actually going on in the way of doctrinal development— something that could not be explained by such existing orthodoxy as construing ambiguities, waiver, estoppel, election, reformation, and rescission. Recognition of two broad principles, he submitted, would explain most of what otherwise appeared to be an undue number of aberrational decisions in insurance cases. He stated the principles as follows: (1) an insurer will be denied any unconscionable advantage in an insurance transaction, and (2) the reasonable expectations of insurance applicants and intended beneficiaries will be honored. *See* Robert E. Keeton, *Insurance Law Rights at Variance with Policy Provisions* (pts. 1 & 2), 83 Harv. L. Rev. 961, 1281 (1970).

The second of these two principles has come to be known as the doctrine of reasonable expectations and, in one formulation or another, has been embraced by a growing number of jurisdictions. *See* Roger C. Henderson, *The Doctrine of Reasonable Expectations in Insurance Law After Two Decades,* 51 Ohio St. L.J. 823 (1990). It has also prompted an enormous amount of discussion in the secondary literature. See, *e.g.*, Peter Swisher, *A Realistic Consensus Approach to the Insurance Law Doctrine of Reasonable Expectations*, 35 Tort & Ins. L. J. 729 (2000); Symposium, *The Doctrine of Reasonable Expectations,* 5 Conn. Ins. L. J. 1-473 (1998) (a set of articles reviewing the state of the doctrine at three decades); Kenneth S. Abraham, *Judge-Made Law and Judge-Made Insurance: Honoring the Reasonable Expectations of the Insured,* 67 Va. L. Rev. 1151 (1981). Exactly what constitutes the doctrine of reasonable expectations (or "DRE," as it is sometimes called) remains a source of considerable controversy. If anything is clear at the year 2000, it is that courts have conceptualized the doctrine differently, as the following cases show.

CLARK-PETERSON COMPANY, INC. v. INDEPENDENT INSURANCE ASSOCIATES, LTD.

492 N.W.2d 675 (Iowa 1992) (en banc)

HARRIS, JUSTICE.

Plaintiff Clark-Peterson Company, Inc., became liable in an underlying suit for intentional discrimination. Neil Brown, plaintiff in the underlying case, obtained a substantial judgment on a theory of improper employment termination, that is, discrimination due to alcoholism. *See Consolidated Freightways, Inc. v. Cedar Rapids Civil Rights Comm'n*, 366 N.W.2d 522, 526–28 (Iowa 1985)(holding damages are recoverable for disparate treatment because of disability in the form of alcoholism). *See also* Iowa Code § 601A.6(1)(a) (1991). The appropriateness of that recovery was not appealed and is not challenged in the present suit.

Clark-Peterson brought this declaratory judgment action against defendant Cincinnati Insurance Co. (the insurer), which had issued plaintiffs a "contractor's umbrella liability policy." The district court ruled, and we agree, that the policy[3] did not cover the employment claim because the discrimination

---

[3] The relevant provisions of the liability insurance policy at issue are as follows:

PART I—DEFINED WORDS AND PHRASES

A. "You", "your" and "yours" mean a person or organization shown as the Named Insured in the declarations;

. . . .

G. "Occurrence" means an accident, or a happening or event, or a continuous or repeated exposure to conditions which occurs during the policy period which unexpectedly or unintentionally results in Personal Injury. . .;

H. Personal Injury means:

(3) Discrimination or humiliation;

. . . .

PART II—THE COVERAGE

A. WE WILL PAY

We will pay on behalf of the Insured the ultimate net loss for occurrences during the policy period in excess of the underlying insurance or for occurrences covered by this policy which are either excluded or not covered by underlying insurance because of Personal Injury

. . . .

B. THIS POLICY DOES NOT APPLY—EXCLUSIONS

This policy does not apply:

. . . .

(h) To any liability for Personal Injury arising out of discrimination including fines or penalties imposed by law, if (1) insurance coverage therefor is prohibited by law or statute, or (2) committed by or at your direction; . . .

was intentional.[4] The court nevertheless ruled that coverage should be afforded under the doctrine of reasonable expectations, a holding with which we also agree.

I

The first issue presented is the insurer's contention that, because the act complained of was intentional, the policy did not cover Brown's discrimination claim. The district court specifically found that the discrimination against Brown was an intended act by the Clarks and thus, under the precise terms of the policy, there was no coverage. The court was prompted to this view by two policy clauses: (1) the intentional acts clause accompanying the definition of "occurrence" found in part I section G; and (2) the exclusion of discrimination "committed by or at your direction" found in part II section B(h)(2). Our reading of the two clauses leads us to the same conclusion. Brown's claim is not covered under the precise wording of the policy.

The district court's view that the discharge was not an "occurrence" is consistent with our subsequent holding in *Smithway Motor Xpress, Inc. v. Liberty Mutual Insurance Co.,* 484 N.W.2d 192, 194–95 (Iowa 1992)(holding a wrongful discharge is not an "occurrence").

II

A closer question is presented on Clark-Peterson's claim of coverage on the basis of the reasonable expectations doctrine. Originating with *Rodman v. State Farm Mutual Automobile Insurance Co.,* 208 N.W.2d 903, 906 (Iowa 1973), the doctrine has become a vital part of our law interpreting insurance policies. But the doctrine does not contemplate the expansion of insurance coverage on a general equitable basis. The doctrine is carefully circumscribed; it can only be invoked where an exclusion "(1) is bizarre or oppressive, (2) eviscerates terms explicitly agreed to, or (3) eliminates the dominant purpose of the transaction." *Aid (Mut.) Ins. v. Steffen,* 423 N.W.2d 189, 192 (Iowa 1988); *Farm Bureau Mut. Ins. Co. v. Sandbulte,* 302 N.W.2d 104, 112 (Iowa 1981).

Before the doctrine can be considered, a preliminary criterion must be satisfied. Either the policy must be such that an ordinary layperson would misunderstand its coverage, or there must be circumstances attributable to the insurer which would foster coverage expectations. *Steffen,* 423 N.W.2d at 192; *Sandbulte,* 302 N.W.2d at 112–13. Once the doctrine has been shown to

---

. . . .

D. WHO IS AN INSURED—PERSONS OR ORGANIZATIONS WE WILL COVER

. . . .

Each of the following is an Insured under this policy to the extent set forth below:

. . . .

    (f) Any executive officer, director, or employee or stockholders of yours while acting within the scope of his duties as such;

. . . .

[4] The discrimination would also qualify as an occurrence under part I section G of the policy if it was unexpected. The district court made no determination with respect to whether or not the discrimination was unexpected. The omission can however be ignored because the termination was "at [the] direction" of Clark-Peterson, and thus coverage was excluded under part II section B(h)(2) of the policy.

be applicable, "the objectively reasonable expectations of applicants and intended beneficiaries regarding insurance [policies] will be honored even though painstaking study of the policy provisions would have negated those expectations." *Steffen,* 423 N.W.2d at 192 (quoting *Rodman,* 208 N.W.2d at 906). When they are honored, "[r]easonable expectations may be established by proof of the underlying negotiations or inferred from the circumstances." *Steffen,* 423 N.W.2d at 192 (citing *Sandbulte,* 302 N.W.2d at 112).

In applying the doctrine, the district court reasoned this way. The policy purports to provide protection for discrimination in part I section H(3). The intentional acts clause in part I section G excludes from coverage acts of intentional discrimination (disparate treatment). The "at your direction" clause in part II section B(h)(2) excludes disparate impact claims from coverage. The district court determined that, contrary to part I section H(3), the policy under no circumstances provides coverage for liability based on discriminatory acts. Thus the court said, "The policy exclusions act to eviscerate all coverage for discrimination, a term explicitly agreed to in part I section H(3)." This was particularly unfair in view of another finding: that Clark-Peterson, in deciding to purchase the policy, was prompted in part by its provision of discrimination coverage. As a result, according to the district court, "the policy must be viewed to be oppressive to the [insured]." Thus the district court found application of the doctrine appropriate on all three grounds.

We review applications of the reasonable expectations doctrine with a view to the liability for which insurance coverage was sought. The coverage sought in this case was for liability arising from firing an employee, firing which the underlying suit established to constitute intentional discrimination because it was due to the employee's alcoholism. The issue becomes whether an ordinary layperson could reasonably expect coverage under this policy under these circumstances. The district court answered in the affirmative. Its finding that an ordinary layperson could reasonably expect coverage was certainly validated during the appellate process following that finding.

We also think the answer is clearly yes, that an ordinary layperson could expect coverage. The policy purports to provide some discrimination coverage; the insured here seeks coverage for an unusual and controversial liability, liability which no doubt came as a shock to it.[6]

Coverage does not necessarily follow from the finding that an ordinary layperson could expect coverage. It cannot be awarded unless we agree with

---

[6] As mentioned, liability in the underlying case was on a theory contemplated in Consolidated Freightways, 366 N.W.2d at 526–28, a case we considered on judicial review of agency action. Our majority acknowledged, pursuant to a municipal civil rights ordinance, that an alcoholic person could be a disabled person, entitled to civil rights protection.

We were not blind to the fact that finding disability on such a basis was unique and differed substantially from discrimination based on the more traditional bases of race, color, religion, sex or national origin. The uniqueness of our Consolidated Freightways holding has some bearing on Clark-Peterson's understanding of the coverage under the policy here. This case is a far cry from the more traditional ones mentioned. It does no offense to the public policy protecting disabled persons to acknowledge that an employer in the position of Clark-Peterson, having employed an alcoholic person, faces a dilemma. If the alcoholic person is retained, the very survival of the business might be jeopardized. But if the alcoholic person is for that reason discharged, liability for extensive damages might be sought.

the district court on at least one of its three findings that denial of coverage: (1) is bizarre or oppressive; (2) eviscerates terms explicitly agreed to; or (3) eliminates the dominant purpose of the transaction. *Steffen,* 423 N.W.2d at 192. Under the special circumstances here, we agree with respect to the second ground; the exclusion effectively guts the discrimination coverage previously agreed to. The insurer contends that evisceration is not complete and therefore not achieved because a form of discrimination (disparate impact)[7] can be imagined which, it is said, would be covered under the policy. So doing, the insurer calls upon us to hold for liability in a situation not supported by the facts here; this is not a disparate impact case.

We decline to speculate on the policy's coverage for liability arising from disparate impact because we believe evisceration can occur on something less than total obliteration of all possibilities of coverage. "Eviscerate," according to its dictionary meaning, is to disembowel—or to gut. Webster's New International Dictionary (3d ed. 1964). To qualify under the definition, it is enough if an exclusion deprives coverage in a vital and substantial way. Disemboweling is the taking of a vital organ, not the taking of all of them.[8]

To deny discrimination coverage in the present case would be to withdraw with the policy's left hand what is given with its right. In a fundamental sense, of course, this is the proper function of any exclusion clause in an insurance policy. The reasonable expectations doctrine does no violence to this proper function by its limited intrusion into it. The doctrine means only that when, within its metes and bounds definition, an exclusion acts in technical ways to withdraw a promised coverage, it must do so forthrightly, with words that are, if not flashing, at least sufficient to assure that a reasonable policy purchaser will not be caught unawares.

The reasonable expectations doctrine is a recognition that insurance policies are sold on the basis of the coverage they promise. When later exclusions work to eat up all, or even substantially all, of a vital coverage, they cannot rest on technical wording, obscure to the average insurance purchaser. At some point fairness demands that the coverage clause itself be self-limiting. Clark-Peterson's claim could not have arisen if the coverage promised in the coverage clause had been clearly worded so as to extend coverage only as far as the insurer contends it does extend. The difficulty arises because a much broader

---

[7] The distinction between "disparate treatment" and "disparate impact" was explained in *Hy-Vee Food Stores v. Civil Rights Commission,* 453 N.W.2d 512, 516–19 (Iowa 1990). Disparate treatment cases involve discrimination which is addressed to persons on the basis of race, color, religion, etc.; disparate impact cases involve discrimination which, though not addressed on such a basis, results in it. The present case does not turn on this distinction. Here the termination was intended to be, and was directed toward, Brown personally on the basis of his alcoholism.

[8] The policy's "by or at your direction" clause is worded to exclude coverage for intentional discrimination. Although we are not called upon to decide the question, it seems likely that the sweep of that clause extends beyond intentional discrimination, certainly far beyond the present unique case. If the clause were to deny coverage, not only for disparate treatment cases, but also for disparate impact cases, its effect would extend to deny coverage in all, or substantially all, discrimination cases. Stated otherwise, the clause would eviscerate all, or substantially all, of a purported coverage. This would clearly be contrary to the reasonable expectations doctrine. We revisited the reasonable expectations doctrine in a similar circumstance and applied it in *Wohlenhaus v. Pottawattamie Mutual Insurance,* 407 N.W.2d 572, 576 (Iowa 1987) (holding exclusion does not apply if it eliminates dominant purpose of the transaction).

coverage is promised, but an attempt is made to withdraw it in violation of the doctrine of reasonable expectations.

We agree with the district court that the special facts here qualify for application of reasonable expectations on the second ground for the doctrine. The exclusions upon which the insurer relies would eviscerate the discrimination coverage explicitly agreed to.

DECISION OF COURT OF APPEALS AND JUDGMENT OF DISTRICT COURT AFFIRMED.

All Justices concur except LARSON and LAVORATO, JJ., who take no part.

NOTES

1. *General principles.* The court concluded that the policy in *Clark-Peterson* was not ambiguous. Thus, at least in Iowa, the doctrine of reasonable expectations may apply regardless of whether there is an ambiguity in the policy. Accordingly, the doctrine of reasonable expectations is substantive in nature and is not just a rule of construction used to resolve competing interpretations of policy language.

Does it matter where the insured in *Clark-Peterson* obtained its "reasonable expectation"? Is it possible that the insured reasonably understood it was purchasing coverage only for disparate treatment claims? Is any expectation the insured has, regardless of its source, enforced as long as it is "reasonable"? The court in *Clark-Peterson* refers to "special circumstances" present in that case. What were they? If the clause had been brought to the insured's attention before the policy was purchased, would the court's decision have been different?

2. *Application of doctrine of reasonable expectations.* A number of the initial cases that recognized that an insured has rights based on reasonable expectations despite unambiguous policy language dealt with conditional receipts in marketing life insurance. There the courts held that a temporary contract of insurance came into existence if the applicant paid the first premium at the time the conditional receipt was issued unless it was made clear to the applicant that there would not be any temporary insurance. Of course, the wording of the receipt rarely made it clear and that was the problem. Some of these cases are cited in the dissenting opinions and the notes following *Grandpre v. Northwestern National Life Insurance Co. in § 7.02[1][b].*

The doctrine also has been applied with regard to provisions in other types of insurance. *See, e.g., National Indemnity Co. v. Flesher,* 469 P.2d 360 (Alaska 1970) (duty to defend under auto liability policy); *Gordinier v. Aetna Casualty & Surety Co.,* 154 Ariz. 266, 742 P.2d 277 (1987) (resident of same household clause in uninsured motorist coverage); *Ponder v. Blue Cross,* 145 Cal. App. 3d 709, 193 Cal. Rptr. 632 (1983) (whether treatment for temporomandibular joint syndrome was covered under health insurance policy); *Sparks v. St. Paul Insurance Co.,* 100 N.J. 325, 495 A.2d 406 (1985) ("claims made" professional liability insurance policy). If a court recognizes the doctrine, apparently it does not matter what kind of insurance or policy provision is involved.

3. *Visible marks.* One of the early reasonable expectation cases in Iowa was *C & J Fertilizer v. Allied Mutual Insurance Co.*, 227 N.W.2d 169 (Iowa 1975). That case involved a burglary policy which contained a "visible marks" exclusion, meaning that the insured could not recover for a burglary if the thief did not leave "visible marks" as evidence of a forceful entry into the premises. The purpose of the clause is to exclude coverage for "inside jobs," under the reasoning that the employee who embezzles or steals from the employer will have access to the premises and will therefore not leave visible marks. The clause also has some connection to encouraging the insured to take steps to secure their property so that thieves do not have easy access to it. The court in *C & J Fertilizer* held that the insured reasonably expected coverage for a burglary in circumstances where a talented burglar managed to steal from the insured without leaving visible marks. If the clause had been brought to the insured's attention before the policy was purchased, should the insured have been allowed to recover? Would it matter if the insured had received a premium reduction in exchange for accepting the visible marks exclusion? If you purchased insurance from Allied Mutual and you were very conscientious about securing your premises, would you be pleased with the result in *C & J Fertilizer*?

4. *Unconscionability.* Was the exclusion in *Clark-Peterson* unconscionable? Should the case have been decided for the insured on this ground instead of the reasonable expectations doctrine? Does the concept of unconscionability add anything to the reasonable expectations doctrine? If so, when should it apply? If the particular insured in *Clark Peterson* fully understood what the insurer intended by the exclusion, would the insured nevertheless have an argument under the facts of the case that the limitation was unconscionable? See Robert E. Keeton & Alan I. Widiss, Insurance Law § 6.2 (Student Ed. 1988).

Arthur Corbin used insurance to make one of his points about unconscionability: "Standardized contracts such as insurance policies, drafted by powerful commercial units and put before individuals on the 'accept this or get nothing' basis, are carefully scrutinized by the courts for the purpose of avoiding enforcement of 'unconscionable' clauses." 6A Corbin on Contracts, § 1376, at 21 (1962). Indeed, before then-Professor Keeton wrote his seminal 1970 article (see introductory note on reasonable expectation doctrine) which is credited for articulating the doctrine of reasonable expectations, the idea that the reasonable expectations of a party forced to adhere to unfair terms in a standardized form should be protected was already in circulation, and prominent scholars used insurance policies to illustrate their point. See Robert H. Jerry, II, *Insurance, Contract, and the Doctrine of Reasonable Expectations*, 5 Conn. Ins. L. J. 21, 23–35 (1998) (discussing early writings of Karl Llewellyn, Friedreich Kessler, and Spencer Kimball). Unconscionability figured prominently in the *C & J Fertilizer* case, discussed above.

5. *Implied warranties under insurance contracts?* The *C & J Fertilizer* opinion offered "implied warranty" as an independent basis for the insured's recovery: "Plaintiff should also prevail because defendant breached an implied warranty that the policy later delivered would be reasonably fit for its intended purpose: to set out in writing the obligations of the parties (1) without

altering or impairing the fair meaning of the protection bargained for when read alone, and (2) in terms that are neither in the particular nor in the net manifestly unreasonably and unfair." *C & J Fertilizer, supra*, 227 N.W.2d at 177–78. But only a minority of the court subscribed to the implied warranty theory. In a subsequent decision cited in *Clark-Peterson*, a majority of the Supreme Court of Iowa embraced it in an insurance case, but went on to hold that it was inapplicable under the facts. *Farm Bureau Mutual Insurance Co. v. Sandbulte,* 302 N.W.2d 104 (1981). Does the implied warranty theory really add anything to the reasonable expectations doctrine? Should it be applied to what are essentially service contracts as compared to contracts involving sales of goods? Whatever might be said for applying the doctrine of implied warranty in insurance cases, this idea has not garnered support elsewhere. See Robert H. Jerry, II, Understanding Insurance Law § 25F (2d ed. 1996).

6. *"Strong form" versus "weak form" DRE.* The court in *Clark-Peterson* endorsed a "strong form" of the reasonable expectations doctrine. Other courts also endorsed the doctrine, but upon a closer look, it became clear that at least some of these courts were making a different point. Consider the next case.

MAX TRUE PLASTERING CO. v. UNITED STATES FIDELITY AND GUARANTY CO.

912 P.2d 861 (Okla. 1996)

Kauger, Vice Chief Judge.

Two issues are presented by the questions certified: 1) whether the doctrine of reasonable expectations applies to the construction of insurance contracts in Oklahoma; and 2) what circumstances give rise to the doctrine's operation. Under the reasonable expectations doctrine, the objectively reasonable expectations of applicants, insureds and intended beneficiaries concerning the terms of insurance contracts are honored even though painstaking study of the policy provisions might have negated those expectations. We find that the reasonable expectations doctrine may apply to the construction of ambiguous insurance contracts or to contracts containing exclusions which are masked by technical or obscure language or which are hidden in policy provisions.

FACTS

The third-party defendant, Jeff R. Johnson (Johnson/agent), sold a fidelity bond to the plaintiff, Max True Plastering Company (True/insured), insuring True for some losses arising from employee dishonesty.[3] "The bond was purchased from the defendant, United States Fidelity and Guaranty Company (USF & G/insurer).

---

[3] The policy provides in pertinent part:

"A. COVERAGE

1. Covered Property: 'Money', 'securities', and 'property other than money and securities'. . . ."

In the summer of 1991, True discovered that employees in his Dallas office had formed a corporation, LCR, Inc. (LCR), and that they were diverting True business to it. True filed suit against LCR and the employees in October of 1991. The following June, True wrote the agent notifying him of losses from employee dishonesty; and he claimed coverage under the USF & G policy. USF & G denied coverage on August 16, 1993, asserting that True had not complied with the policy's notice and proof of loss requirements and that losses of intellectual property, such as the diversion of job opportunities and lost profits, were not covered by the policy.

True filed suit against USF & G to recover under the policy on August 30, 1993. True contended that coverage existed either under the express terms of the policy or that he was insured because of his reasonable expectations that the losses were covered. On July 28, 1994, USF & G filed a third-party petition against Johnson and his agency claiming indemnity if True prevailed. USF & G and Johnson both filed motions for summary judgment on December 2, 1994. True filed an objection to USF & G'S motion on December 9th claiming coverage either under the plain reading of the policy or pursuant to his reasonable expectations. Finding no Oklahoma precedent to resolve the questions of law, the trial court certified two questions to this Court . . . .

I.

UNDER OKLAHOMA LAW, THE REASONABLE EXPECTATIONS DOCTRINE MAY BE
APPLICABLE TO CONSTRUE INSURANCE CONTRACTS.

True argues that although this Court has not expressly adopted the reasonable expectations doctrine, many of the principles applied in Oklahoma to the construction of insurance contracts conform to the spirit of the doctrine. It urges us to join the majority* of jurisdictions which have considered the doctrine by recognizing it as part of Oklahoma law. USF & G and Johnson insist that insureds are adequately protected by existing principles applied to the construction of insurance contracts and they contend that those courts which have rejected the doctrine offer the better reasoned opinions.

An adhesion contract is a standardized contract prepared entirely by one party to the transaction for the acceptance of the other. These contracts, because of the disparity in bargaining power between the draftsman and the second party, must be accepted or rejected on a "take it or leave it" basis without opportunity for bargaining—the services contracted for cannot be obtained except by acquiescing to the form agreement. Insurance contracts are contracts of adhesion because of the uneven bargaining positions of the parties. The doctrine of reasonable expectations has evolved as an interpretative tool to aid courts in discerning the intention of the parties bound by adhesion contracts. It developed in part because established equitable doctrines were inadequate, and it takes into account the realities of present day commercial practice.

Under the doctrine, if the insurer or its agent creates a reasonable expectation of coverage in the insured which is not supported by policy language, the

---

* [Editors' note: The court's opinion is replete with lengthy footnotes citing to relevant case authority. These have been omitted in this edited version of the case.]

expectation will prevail over the language of the policy. The doctrine does not negate the importance of policy language. Rather, it is justified by the underlying principle that generally the language of the policy will provide the best indication of the parties' reasonable expectations. The standard under the doctrine is a "reasonable expectation"; and courts must examine the policy language objectively to determine whether an insured could reasonably have expected coverage. Courts adopting the reasonable expectations doctrine have found its rationale for interpretation of the usual insurance contract to be sensible. They also recognize that insurance law is the basis of the doctrine. These courts acknowledge that different rules of construction have traditionally been applied to insurance contracts because of their adhesive nature. Tribunals embracing the doctrine recognize that it is consistent with numerous other interpretive rules pertaining to adhesion contracts. Many of these rules are a part of Oklahoma law. For instance: 1) ambiguities are construed most strongly against the insurer; 2) in cases of doubt, words of inclusion are liberally applied in favor of the insured and words of exclusion are strictly construed against the insurer; 3) an interpretation which makes a contract fair and reasonable is selected over that which yields a harsh or unreasonable result; 4) insurance contracts are construed to give effect to the parties' intentions; 5) the scope of an agreement is not determined in a vacuum, but instead with reference to extrinsic circumstances; and 6) words are given effect according to their ordinary or popular meaning. Nevertheless, these rules of construction are often inadequate because they may fail to recognize the realities of the insurance business and the methods used in modern insurance practice.

Of the thirty-six jurisdictions which have addressed the reasonable expectations doctrine, our research reveals only four courts which have rejected the rule. Although the Utah court recognized its duty to invalidate insurance provisions contrary to public policy, it refused to adopt the doctrine on the basis that its operation is not well-defined, and its deference to the occupation of the insurance field by the legislative and the executive branches.[27] The three other courts rejected the doctrine in favor of traditional construction guidelines relating to insurance contracts.

Although the reasonable expectations doctrine has not been adopted per se in Oklahoma, several cases indicate that the reasonable expectations of an insured will be considered in the construction of insurance contracts. In *Homestead Fire Ins. Co. v. De Witt*, 206 Okla. 570, 245 P.2d 92, 94 (1952), this Court quoted from *Bird v. St. Paul Fire & Marine Ins. Co.*, 224 N.Y. 47, 120 N.E. 86–87, 13 A.L.R. 875 (1918) referring to the construction of an insurance policy:

> "Our guide is the reasonable expectation and purpose of the ordinary business man making an ordinary business contract. It is his intention, expressed or fairly to be inferred, that counts." (Emphasis supplied.)

In *Conner v. Transamerica Ins. Co.*, 496 P.2d 770, 774 (Okla.1972), we held that the insurer was obligated to defend its insureds in actions involving

---

[27] *Allen v. Prudential Property & Casualty Ins. Co.*, [839 P.2d 798] at 804 [(Utah 1992)].

dishonest, fraudulent, criminal and malicious conduct or omissions. The Court's holding in *Conner* was buttressed by a quotation from *Gray v. Zurich Ins. Co.,* 65 Cal.2d 263, 54 Cal.Rptr. 104, 419 P.2d 168 (1966) providing in pertinent part:

> ". . . This language, in its broad sweep, would lead the insured **reasonably to expect** defense of any suit regardless of merit or cause. . . . The basic promise would support the insured's **reasonable expectation** that he had bought the rendition of legal services to defend against a suit for bodily injury which alleged he had caused it, negligently, nonintentionally, intentionally or in any other manner . . ." (Emphasis supplied.)
>
> . . . .

Some courts rely upon a form of the reasonable expectations doctrine espoused in § 211 of the Restatement (Second) of Contracts[30] to protect the expectations of the contracting parties. Under the Restatement, reformation of an insurance contract is allowed if the insurer has reason to believe that the insured would not have signed the contract if the inclusion of certain limitations had been known.

---

[30] Restatement (Second) of Contracts § 211 (1979) formulates the doctrine in a manner which allows a fact finder to look at the totality of the circumstances in determining the intent of the parties, rather than being strictly confined to the four corners of a standardized agreement. Section 211 provides:

> "(1) Except as stated in Subsection (3), where a party to an agreement signs or otherwise manifests assent to a writing and has reason to believe that like writings are regularly used to embody terms of agreements of the same type, he adopts the writing as an integrated agreement with respect to the terms included in the writing.
>
> (2) Such a writing is interpreted whenever reasonable as treating alike all those similarly situated, without regard to their knowledge or understanding of the standard terms of the writing.
>
> (3) Where the other party has reason to believe that the party manifesting such assent would not do so if he knew that the writing contained a particular term, the term is not part of the agreement."

Comment (b) to § 211 points out that parties regularly using standardized agreements ordinarily do not expect customers to understand or even to read the standard terms. Customers trust to the good faith of the party using the form and to the tacit representation that like terms are being accepted regularly by others similarly situated. Subsection (3) of § 211 is the Restatement's characterization of the reasonable expectations doctrine. Comment (f) to the subsection outlines a sensible rationale for interpretation of the usual insurance agreement. It provides in pertinent part:

> "Although customers typically adhere to standardized agreements and are bound by them without even appearing to know the standard terms in detail, they are not bound to unknown terms which are beyond the range of reasonable expectation. . . . [An insured] who adheres to the [insurer's] standard terms does not assent to a term if the [insurer] has reason to believe that the [insured] would not have accepted the agreement if he had known that the agreement contained the particular term. Such a belief or assumption may be shown by the prior negotiations or inferred from the circumstances. Reason to believe may be inferred from the fact that the term is bizarre or oppressive, from the fact that it eviscerates the non-standard terms explicitly agreed to, or from the fact that it eliminates the dominant purpose of the transaction. The inference is reinforced if the adhering party never had an opportunity to read the term, or if it is illegible or otherwise hidden from view. This rule is closely related to the policy against unconscionable terms and the rule of interpretations against the draftsman."

In *Gay v. Hartford Underwriters Ins. Co.,* 904 P.2d 83 (Okla.1995) (*Gay* II), we held that the insurer was bound by the settled law of case of *Gay I*.[31] In *Gay I*, the Court of Appeals found that despite contract language providing for uninsured motorist coverage of $10,000/$20,000, the insurance company had acted in a manner indicating a mutual mistake warranting contract reformation to allow coverage of $100,000/$300,000. The insured in the *Gay* cases had on at least two occasions requested that his coverage be upgraded to $100,000/$300,000, and the insurance agent had indicated that the policy change would be made. Nevertheless, at the time Gay was injured, the policy language provided only for $10,000/$20,000 in coverage. We held in *Gay II* that the insurer was bound by the settled law of *Gay I* finding a mutual mistake. Although in doing so, we did not cite § 211 of the Restatement or refer to the reasonable expectations doctrine, the reasoning of the case coincides with the doctrine as outlined in § 211—the insurer was required to provide the higher coverage because of the expectations it had induced in the insured to believe that he had purchased coverage of $100,000/$300,000 as uninsured motorist insurance.

Generally, absent an ambiguity, insurance contracts are subject to the same rules of construction as other contracts. However, because of their adhesive nature, these contracts are liberally construed to give reasonable effect to all their provisions. Our case law and the interpretive rules applied to insurance contracts demonstrate that Oklahoma law is consistent with the spirit and the policy of the reasonable expectations doctrine. The same case law coincides with the reasoning of the majority of jurisdictions adopting the doctrine.

II.
THE REASONABLE EXPECTATIONS DOCTRINE MAY APPLY TO THE CONSTRUCTION OF AMBIGUOUS INSURANCE CONTRACTS OR TO CONTRACTS CONTAINING EXCLUSIONS MASKED BY TECHNICAL OR OBSCURE LANGUAGE OR HIDDEN POLICY PROVISIONS.

True urges us to adopt a version of the reasonable expectations doctrine which does not require a finding of ambiguity in policy language before the doctrine is applied. Although they urge us not to adopt the doctrine, USF & G and Johnson argue that if the doctrine is to apply in Oklahoma, it should be limited to situations in which the policy contains an ambiguity or to contracts containing unexpected exclusions arising from technical or obscure language or which are hidden in policy provisions. We agree with this limitation.

If the doctrine is not put in the proper perspective, insureds could develop a "reasonable expectation" that every loss will be covered by their policy and courts would find themselves engaging in wholesale rewriting of insurance policies. Therefore, the jurisdictions which have adopted the doctrine apply it to cases where an ambiguity is found in the policy language or where the exclusions are obscure or technical or are hidden in complex policy language. In these cases, the doctrine is utilized to resolve ambiguities in insurance

---

[31] *Gay v. Hartford Underwriters Ins. Co.,* No. 76,577 (Okla.Ct.App.1992).

policies and considers the language of the policies in a manner which conforms the policies with the parties' "reasonable expectations."

A policy term is ambiguous under the reasonable expectations doctrine if it is reasonably susceptible to more than one meaning. When defining a term found in an insurance contract, the language is given the meaning understood by a person of ordinary intelligence. The doctrine does not mandate either a pro-insurer or pro-insured result because only **reasonable** expectations of coverage are warranted.

In Oklahoma, unambiguous insurance contracts are construed, as are other contracts, according to their terms. The interpretation of an insurance contract and whether it is ambiguous is determined by the court as a matter of law. Insurance contracts are ambiguous only if they are susceptible to two constructions. In interpreting an insurance contract, this Court will not make a better contract by altering a term for a party's benefit. We do not indulge in forced or constrained interpretations to create and then to construe ambiguities in insurance contracts.

However, in *Conner v. Transamerica Ins. Co.,* 496 P.2d 770, 773 (Okla.1972), this Court found coverage for the defense of an action based on groundless, false or fraudulent conduct by the insured. The *Conner* policy provided coverage for "any suit. . .even if any of the allegations of the suit are groundless, false or fraudulent." A subsequent provision of the same policy eliminated coverage for "any dishonest, fraudulent, criminal or malicious act of omission of any insured, partner or employee." This Court refused to allow a later provision of the policy to eviscerate coverage clearly delineated in a prior provision—the hidden exclusion was not given effect.

The stacking cases—*Scott v. Cimarron Ins. Co., Inc.,* 774 P.2d 456, 458 (Okla.1989), *Withrow v. Pickard,* 905 P.2d 800, 804–06 (Okla.1995), and *Kramer v. Allstate Ins., No.* 83,822 (Okla.Ct.App.1995) all provide that an insured will benefit from the coverage paid for regardless of whether a policy allows stacking of uninsured motorist coverage. *Conner,* disallowing a hidden exclusion and these cases relating the payment of premiums to the coverage which may be expected despite policy language demonstrate that crafty drafting of coverage language will not defeat the reasonable expectations of policy holders in Oklahoma.

The reasonable expectations doctrine comports with our case law and with the rules of construction applied to insurance contracts. Oklahoma law mandates that we join the majority of jurisdictions which have considered application of the doctrine and apply it to cases in which policy language is ambiguous and to situations where, although clear, the policy contains exclusions masked by technical or obscure language or hidden exclusions.

CONCLUSION

The reasonable expectations doctrine recognizes the true origin of standardized contract provisions, frees the courts from having to write a contract for the parties, and removes the temptation to create ambiguity or invent intent to reach a result. The underlying principle of the reasonable expectations doctrine—that reasonable expectations of insurance coverage should be honored— has been recognized by the majority of jurisdictions which have considered the issue and by a steady progression of Oklahoma law beginning in 1952 with *Homestead Fire Ins. Co. v. De Witt,* 206 Okla. 570, 245 P.2d 92, 94 (1952), and continuing through 1995 in *Withrow v. Pickard,* 905 P.2d 800, 804–06 (Okla. 1995), in *Gay v. hartford Underwriters Ins. Co.,* 904 P.2d 83 (Okla. 1995) (*Gay II*), and in *Kramer v. Allstate Ins., No.* 83,822 (Okla.Ct.App. 1995). By adopting the reasonable expectations doctrine, we recognize that it is important that ambiguous clauses or carefully drafted exclusions should not be permitted to serve as traps for policy holders. Nevertheless, it is equally imperative that the provisions of insurance policies which are clearly and definitely set forth in appropriate language, and upon which the calculations of the company are based, should be maintained unimpaired by loose and ill-considered judicial interpretation. Today, we hold that the doctrine of reasonable expectations may be applicable to the interpretation of insurance contracts in Oklahoma, and that the doctrine may apply to ambiguous contract language or to exclusions which are masked by technical or obscure language or which are hidden in a policy's provisions.

QUESTIONS ANSWERED

We find that under Oklahoma law, the reasonable expectations doctrine may be applied in the construction of insurance contracts and that the doctrine may apply to ambiguous contract language or to exclusions which are masked by technical or obscure language or which are hidden in a policy's provisions.

ALMA WILSON, C.J., KAUGER, V.C.J., and LAVENDER, SIMMS, HARGRAVE, SUMMERS and WATT, JJ., concur.

OPALA, J., concurs in part and dissents in part.

HODGES, J., dissents.

NOTES

1. *The "ambiguity requirement."* If Part II of the *Max True Plastering* did not have the tag "or to contracts containing exclusions masked by technical or obscure language or hidden policy provisions," would Part I of the opinion have changed anything from garden-variety contract law principles? What exactly does the quoted rule add to the traditional rules of contract interpretation? Was the exclusion in *Clark-Peterson* "masked by technical or obscure language or hidden policy provisions"?

The Missouri Supreme Court described the "objective reasonable expectations doctrine" as a "rule provid[ing] the objective reasonable expectations of adherents and beneficiaries to insurance contracts will be honored even though a thorough study of the policy provisions would have negated these expectations." *Robin v. Blue Cross Hospital Service, Inc.,* 637 S.W.2d 695, 697 (Mo. 1982). In *Robin,* the court declined to either approve or disapprove the doctrine because it said that its application depended on the existence of a contract of adhesion, which the court reasoned was not present in that case. 637 S.W.2d at 697–98. Subsequently, the court held with respect to a claim for underinsured motorist benefits that "[e]ven were we to assume for the sake of argument that the contract in question here is a contract of adhesion, the [insureds'] argument for the application of the objective reasonable expectation doctrine depends on the presence of an ambiguity in the contract language. . . . [W]here insurance policies are unambiguous, they will be enforced as written absent a statute or public policy requiring coverage." *Rodriguez v. General Accident Insurance Co.*, 808 S.W.2d 379, 382 (Mo. 1991). Has Missouri stopped one step beneath Oklahoma's ascent to a more robust doctrine of reasonable expectations?

2. *Restatement (Second) of Contracts § 211.* The court's reference in *Max True Plastering* to section 211 of the *Restatement (Second) of Contracts* merits a closer look. This section has received attention in a few other insurance cases where reasonable expectations has been put in play. *See, e.g., Mitchell v. Broadnzx,* 2000 W. Va. Lexis 7 (Feb. 18, 2000) (Starcher, J., concurring); *Sutton v. Banner Life Insurance Co.,* 686 A.2d 1045 (D.C. 1996); *Darner Motor Sales, Inc. v. Universal Underwriters Ins. Co.,* 140 Ariz. 383, 682 P.2d 388 (1984); *C & J Fertilizer, Inc. v. Allied Mutual Insurance Co.,* 227 N.W.2d 169 (Iowa 1975). The thrust of the rule under section 211 is that standard form contracts will be enforced as written, without regard to knowledge or understanding of the standard terms, if a party has reason to believe that like writings are regularly used to embody terms of the same type. The rule, however, is qualified. Where the other party—the insurer in our case—has reason to believe that the party manifesting assent—the insured—would not do so if he knew that the writing contained a particular term, the term is not part of the agreement. Comment *f* of the *Restatement*, also quoted by the court, attempts to clarify when it is that the drafter—for example, an insurer—would have "reason to believe" that some one like an insured would not have assented to what is later found objectionable. How is the doctrine of reasonable expectations as articulated by Professor Keeton different from the formulation in section 211? Do the differences matter? Did they matter to the court in *Max True Plastering*? Is there any other formulation that would result in an efficacious test and not contain a bias in favor of one party or the other, and that would provide a test distinct from one that would be used to determine that a term or provision is "unconscionable"? See Roger C. Henderson, *The Formulation of the Doctrine of Reasonable Expectations and the Influence of Forces Outside Insurance Law,* 5 Conn. Ins. L. J. 70, 73–80 (1998); John E. Murray, Jr., *The Parole Evidence Process and Standardized Agreements Under the Restatement (Second) of Contracts,* 123 U. Pa. L. Rev. 1342, 1372-89 (1975).

3. *"Strong form," "weak form,"* or *"no form"?* By this point, it should be clear that "reasonable expectations" means different things to different courts. Once they find the meaning of the doctrine, not all courts like what they see, as the next case illustrates.

DENI ASSOCIATES OF FLORIDA, INC. v. STATE FARM FIRE & CASUALTY INSURANCE CO.
711 So. 2d 1135 (Fla. 1998)

GRIMES, SENIOR JUSTICE.

We review *State Farm Fire & Casualty Insurance Co. v. Deni Associates of Florida, Inc.,* 678 So.2d 397, 404 (Fla. 4th DCA 1996), in which the court certified the following as a question of great public importance:

Where an ambiguity is shown to exist in a CGL policy, is the court limited to resolving the ambiguity in favor of coverage, or may the court apply the doctrine of reasonable expectations of the insured to resolve ambiguities in CGL policies?

. . . . In addressing this question, the court below decided two unrelated cases which involved the same issue.

Deni Associates of Florida, Inc. (Deni), an architectural engineering firm, was one of several tenants in a two-story commercial building. In the course of moving equipment in the building, ammonia was accidentally spilled from a blueprint machine. Responding to a 911 call, the fire department evacuated the building, set up ventilators, and broke windows in order to expedite ventilation. The building was turned back over to the building manager six hours later. Thereafter, claims were made against Deni for personal injuries sustained from inhalation of the ammonia fumes. Claims were also made by several cotenants seeking reimbursement for loss of income due to evacuation of the building. Deni carried a comprehensive general liability (CGL) policy with State Farm Fire and Casualty Insurance Company.

E.C. Fogg and others, doing business as the partnership of Land-O-Sun Groves (Land-O-Sun), contracted with Colony Services, Inc. (Colony) to aerially spray chemical insecticide furnished by Land-O-Sun on its citrus groves. In the course of spraying, the helicopter splashed insecticide on two men who were standing on adjacent property. The two men subsequently sued Land-O-Sun and Colony for injuries allegedly suffered as a result of being exposed to the insecticide. Land-O-Sun carried a CGL policy with Florida Farm Bureau Mutual Insurance Company.

In both instances, the insurance companies disputed coverage based upon a pollution exclusion provision in their respective policies. In the ensuing declaratory judgment actions, the trial courts in both cases entered summary judgments against the insurance companies. Sitting en banc, the Fourth District Court of Appeal unanimously reversed the judgment in favor of Land-O-Sun and by a split decision reversed the judgment in favor of Deni.

Both pollution exclusion clauses are substantially the same. They exclude from liability coverage any personal injury or property damage "arising out of the actual, alleged or threatened discharge, dispersal, release or escape of pollutants."[1] Further, each policy contained the following language:

Pollutants means any solid, liquid, gaseous or thermal irritant or contaminant, including smoke, vapor, soot, fumes, acids, alkalines, chemicals and waste.

In its opinion, the court rejected a rule of construction employed in many jurisdictions known as the doctrine of reasonable expectations. The court pointed out that this doctrine had not been adopted in Florida and that in any event because there was no ambiguity in the exclusions, there was no reason to

---

[1] The State Farm policy contained the additional words "seepage," "ingestion," and "spill."

analyze the expectations of the insureds. However, the court chose to pose the certified question with respect to the doctrine of reasonable expectations.

At the outset, we note that the certified question presupposes an ambiguity, whereas the court held that no such ambiguity existed. Notwithstanding, we believe that the legal efficacy of the pollution exclusion is an important issue which should be decided by this Court.

Apparently, the language of this pollution exclusion, sometimes called the absolute pollution exclusion, is in widespread use throughout the country because many courts have addressed the same arguments contained in the briefs filed in the instant cases. A substantial majority of these courts have concluded that the pollution exclusion is clear and unambiguous so as to preclude coverage for all pollution related liability.

We, too, agree that the pollution exclusion clause is clear and unambiguous. In *State Farm Mutual Automobile Insurance Co. v. Pridgen*, 498 So.2d 1245 (Fla.1986), this Court announced the rule to be followed in the interpretation of exclusionary clauses in insurance policies:

> [E]xclusionary provisions which are ambiguous or otherwise suscepti- ble to more than one meaning must be construed in favor of the in- sured, since it is the insurer who usually drafts the policy. However, "[o]nly when a genuine inconsistency, uncertainty, or ambiguity in meaning remains after resort to the ordinary rules of construction is the rule apposite. It does not allow courts to rewrite contracts, add meaning that is not present, or otherwise reach results contrary to the intentions of the parties."

Id. at 1248.

. . . .

Finally, we address the substance of the certified question which asks whether the doctrine of reasonable expectations should be applied to interpret CGL policies. Under this doctrine, the insured's expectations as to the scope of coverage is upheld provided that such expectations are objectively reason- able. *Max True Plastering Co. v. United States Fidelity & Guar. Co.*, 912 P.2d 861 (Okla.1996). Among those courts which have adopted the doctrine, most only apply it when it can be said that the policy language is ambiguous. *Id.* Notably, a number of courts which have adopted the doctrine of reasonable expectations have refused to apply it to this very pollution exclusion because they have deemed the language of the exclusion to be unambiguous. Yet, a few courts have invoked the doctrine even in cases where the language of the pollution exclusion was clear and unambiguous.

We decline to adopt the doctrine of reasonable expectations.[4] There is no need for it if the policy provisions are ambiguous because in Florida ambigui- ties are construed against the insurer. To apply the doctrine to an

---

[4] While supporting the insureds' claim for coverage in these cases, the Florida Department of Insurance categorically opposes the adoption of the doctrine of reasonable expectations. According to its answer brief: "Adopting the reasonable expectations doctrine will negate the traditional construction guidelines and create greater uncertainty. This Court should not resort to the reasonable expectations doctrine because it will only spawn more litigation to determine the parties' expectations."

unambiguous provision would be to rewrite the contract and the basis upon which the premiums are charged. *See Sterling Merchandise Co. v. Hartford Ins. Co.,* 30 Ohio App.3d 131, 506 N.E.2d 1192, 1197 (1986) ("[T]he reasonable expectation doctrine requires a court to rewrite an insurance contract which does not meet popular expectations. Such rewriting is done regardless of the bargain entered into by the parties to the contract.").

Construing insurance policies upon a determination as to whether the insured's subjective expectations are reasonable can only lead to uncertainty and unnecessary litigation. As noted in *Allen v. Prudential Property & Casualty Insurance Co.,* 839 P.2d 798, 803 (Utah 1992):

> Today, after more than twenty years of attention to the doctrine in various forms by different courts, there is still great uncertainty as to the theoretical underpinnings of the doctrine, its scope, and the details of its application.

We see no reason to address what might be the holding under certain hypothetical situations if we interpret the pollution exclusion clause as it is written because none of those facts are before us. Suffice it to say that insurance policies will not be construed to reach an absurd result. Applying the unambiguous language of the pollution exclusion clause to the facts of these two cases, it is clear that the incidents at issue were excluded from coverage under the respective insurance policies.

All the claims against Deni came about when chemical fumes were released as a result of the ammonia spill. Ammonia is a colorless, gaseous alkaline compound which is extremely pungent in smell. Webster's Third New International Dictionary 70–71 (1976). The Federal Clean Air Act categorizes ammonia as an extremely hazardous substance, the release of which is known to have serious adverse effects to human health. 42 U.S.C. § 7412(r)(3) (1994). There is no doubt that the incident involved in the *Deni* case was excluded from coverage under the CGL policy. Other jurisdictions have also held that the pollution exclusion is applicable to ammonia leaks and spills which cause respiratory injuries to persons exposed to the ammonia fumes.

In the *Fogg* case, the injuries resulted from the spraying of Ethion 4 Miscible used to control mites and other pests. Ethion is recognized as a "pollutant" in regulations promulgated under Florida's "Pollutant Discharge Prevention and Control Act"[5] and is regulated under the "Florida Pesticide Law."[6] We reject Land-O-Sun's premise that when used properly Ethion causes no harm and is not a pollutant. It can obviously cause harm when it is not used properly. Thus, the pollution exclusion of the Florida Farm Bureau policy clearly precludes coverage for the incident in the *Land-O-Sun* case. We also note that other jurisdictions have reached the same conclusions involving pesticide sprays similar to Ethion.

We approve the decision of the court below in both cases.

It is so ordered.

---

[5] Ch. 376, Fla. Stat. (1995); Fla. Admin. Code., R. 38I-30.003.

[6] Ch. 487, Part I, Fla. Stat. (1995).

KOGAN, C.J., and SHAW, HARDING and ANSTEAD, JJ., concur.

WELLS, J., concurs and dissents with an opinion, in which OVERTON, J., concurs.

WELLS, Justice, concurring and dissenting.

I concur as to the spraying case involving Florida Farm Bureau. I dissent as to the case involving the printing machine. I adopt the well-reasoned dissent of Judge Klein in the district court's opinion. I believe to do otherwise allows the exclusion to swallow the coverage, rendering the policy to no longer be a comprehensive general liability policy as it was sold to be by State Farm.

OVERTON, J., concurs.

NOTES

1. *Counting the cases.* One must be wary of statements that a given number of courts have approved the doctrine of reasonable expectations; the statement means little unless one knows to which "doctrine" one is referring. For cases sitting somewhere between *Clark-Peterson* and *Deni Associates*, some interpretation of a court's opinion is needed before one concludes that the opinion endorses, or does not endorse, the reasonable expectations principle. As of 1990, it was fair to say that the number of courts embracing the doctrine was growing notwithstanding observable signs of ambivalence in some jurisdictions, and that somewhere between ten and sixteen state courts of last resort had approved the doctrine in its strong form (i.e., as originally formulated by then-Professor Keeton). See Roger C. Henderson, *The Doctrine of Reasonable Expectations in Insurance Law After Two Decades,* 51 Ohio St. L.J. 823, 827–38 (1990). In the cases decided since 1990 (including those in these materials), a clear trend is not obvious. *See, e.g., Lewis v. West American Insurance Co.,* 927 S.W.2d 829 (Ky. 1996)(unambiguous family exclusions in liability insurance policies are inconsistent with reasonable expectations of insureds); *State Farm Mutual Automobile Insurance Co. v. Nissen,* 851 P.2d 165 (Colo. 1993) (clear exclusion in uninsured motorist provisions violates reasonable expectations of insured); *Allen v. Prudential Property and Casualty Insurance Co.,* 839 P.2d 798 (Utah. 1992) (rejecting doctrine of reasonable expectations). "The cases of the 1990s suggest that the reasonable expectations 'plebiscite' among the states is remaining relatively stable, with few states changing their respective roles on the doctrine." Jeffrey W. Stempel, *Unmet Expectations: Undue Restriction of the Reasonable Expectations Approach and the Misleading Mythology of Judicial Role,* 5 Conn. Ins. L. J. 181, 185 (1998).

If the facts of *Clark-Peterson* had been presented to the Florida Supreme Court, how do you suppose that court would have decided it?

2. *Which view is the best?* Contract law has long reflected the tension between "formal" rules on the one hand (*e.g.*, plain meaning rule of interpretation, strict enforcement of merger clauses) and "functional"rules on the other (*e.g.*, searching for what the parties intended in context, rather than plain meaning; merger clauses are important, but not dispositive). The acuteness

of this tension was apparent decades ago with the advent of standardization, and it remains very troublesome in modern times. Is the debate of the doctrine of reasonable expectations in insurance law simply another facet of this longstanding contract law controversy? Which side has the better of the debate?

[5] Parol Evidence (and Related Matters)

TAYLOR v. STATE FARM MUTUAL AUTOMOBILE INSURANCE CO.

175 Ariz. 148, 854 P.2d 1134 (1993)

FELDMAN, CHIEF JUSTICE.

[The insured, Bobby Sid Taylor, was involved in an auto accident for which he was sued by others. His insurer, State Farm, undertook his defense, but a verdict was returned against him for an amount far exceeding his liability limits. Taylor then sued State Farm for bad faith, alleging that the latter had improperly failed to settle the auto accident claim that resulted in the excess verdict. In the meantime, Taylor had filed a claim for uninsured motorist benefits under his State Farm policy and in settlement thereof signed a release. State Farm took the position that the release also applied to Taylor's bad faith claim and moved for summary judgment on that ground. Taylor also moved for partial summary judgment, seeking a ruling that as a matter of law the release did not preclude his bad faith claim. The judge denied both motions, finding that the release was ambiguous and, therefore, that parol evidence was admissible at trial to aid in interpreting the release. A second judge, who presided at trial, also denied State Farm's motion for directed verdict based on the release. After being instructed on the interpretation of the release, the jury returned a verdict in favor of Taylor on the bad faith claim.

The court of appeals reversed, holding that the release agreement was not ambiguous and therefore the judge erred by admitting parol evidence to vary its terms. Based on the agreement's "four corners," the court found that "it clearly release[d] all policy contract rights, claims, and causes of action that Taylor has or may have against State Farm." According to the court, because the release should have been strictly enforced, there was no basis for Taylor's bad faith claim. Taylor's petition for review to the Arizona Supreme Court was granted.]

DISCUSSION

Much of the dispute in this case centers on the events that surround the drafting of the release and the inferences that can be drawn from those events. As noted, the trial court found that the release was ambiguous and admitted extrinsic evidence to aid in its interpretation. The court of appeals found no ambiguity. In resolving this issue, we must address the scope and application of the parol evidence rule in Arizona and decide whether, under these facts, the trial court properly admitted extrinsic evidence to interpret the release.

A. Legal principles

The application of the parol evidence rule has been the subject of much controversy and scholarly debate. *See generally Darner Motor Sales, Inc. v. Universal Underwriters Ins. Co.,* 140 Ariz. 383, 392–93, 682 P.2d 388, 397–98 (1984); John D. Calamari & Joseph M. Perillo, THE LAW OF CONTRACTS §§ 3-2 to 3-16, at 135-77 (3d ed. 1987); *Robert L. Gottsfield, Darner Motor Sales v. Universal Underwriters: Corbin, Williston and the Continued Viability of the Parol Evidence Rule in Arizona, 25 ARIZ. ST. L.J. 377 (1993). "When two parties have made a contract and have expressed it in a writing to which they have both assented as the complete and accurate integration of that contract, evidence, whether parol or otherwise, of antecedent understandings and negotiations will not be admitted for the purpose of varying or contradicting the writing." 3 Arthur L. Corbin, CORBIN ON CONTRACTS § 573, at 357 (1960) ("CORBIN");. Antecedent understandings and negotiations may be admissible, however, for purposes other than varying or contradicting a final agreement. 3 CORBIN § 576, at 384. Interpretation is one such purpose. 3 CORBIN § 579, at 412–13; Restatement (Second) of Contracts § 214(c) & cmt. b (1979) ("Restatement").*

Interpretation is the process by which we determine the meaning of words in a contract. *See* Restatement § 200. Generally, and in Arizona, a court will attempt to enforce a contract according to the parties' intent. "The primary and ultimate purpose of interpretation" is to discover that intent and to make it effective. 3 CORBIN § 572B, at 421 (1992 Supp.). The court must decide what evidence, other than the writing, is admissible in the interpretation process, bearing in mind that the parol evidence rule prohibits extrinsic evidence to vary or contradict, but not to interpret, the agreement. These substantive principles are clear, but their application has been troublesome.

1. *Restrictive view*

Under the restrictive "plain meaning" view of the parol evidence rule, evidence of prior negotiations may be used for interpretation only upon a finding that some language in the contract is unclear, ambiguous, or vague. E. Allan Farnsworth, FARNSWORTH ON CONTRACTS § 7.12, at 270 (1990) ("FARNSWORTH"). Under this approach, "if a writing, or the term in question, appears to be plain and unambiguous on its face, its meaning must be determined from the four corners of the instrument without resort to extrinsic evidence of any nature." Calamari & Perillo, *supra* § 3-10, at 166–67;. Thus, if the judge finds from the face of a document that it conveys only one meaning, parol evidence is neither considered nor admitted for any purpose. The danger here, of course, is that what appears plain and clear to one judge may not be so plain to another (as in this case), and the judge's decision, uninformed by context, may not reflect the intent of the parties.

2. *Corbin view*

Under the view embraced by Professor Corbin and the Second Restatement, there is no need to make a preliminary finding of ambiguity before the *judge considers* extrinsic evidence. Instead, the court considers all of the proffered evidence to determine its relevance to the parties' intent and then applies the parol evidence rule to exclude from the fact finder's consideration only the evidence that contradicts or varies the meaning of the agreement. According to Corbin, the court cannot apply the parol evidence rule without first understanding the meaning the parties intended to give the agreement. To understand the agreement, the judge cannot be restricted to the four corners of the document. Again, even under the Corbin view, the court can admit evidence for *interpretation* but must stop short of *contradiction*.

3. Arizona view

Writing for a unanimous court in *Smith v. Melson, Inc.*, 135 Ariz. 119, 121–22, 659 P.2d 1264, 1266–67 (1983), Chief Justice Holohan expressly committed Arizona to the Corbin view of contract interpretation. We have not, however, fully explored *Melson*'s application. We have held that a court may consider surrounding circumstances, including negotiation, prior understandings, and subsequent conduct, but have not elaborated much further.

According to Corbin, the proper analysis has two steps. First, the court *considers* the evidence that is alleged to determine the extent of integration, illuminate the meaning of the contract language, or demonstrate the parties' intent. The court's function at this stage is to eliminate the evidence that has no probative value in determining the parties' intent. The second step involves "finalizing" the court's understanding of the contract. Here, the parol evidence rule applies and *precludes admission* of the extrinsic evidence that would vary or contradict the meaning of the written words.

Even during the first step, the judge may properly decide not to consider certain offered evidence because it does not aid in interpretation but, instead, varies or contradicts the written words. This might occur when the court decides that the asserted meaning of the contract language is so unreasonable or extraordinary that it is improbable that the parties actually subscribed to the interpretation asserted by the proponent of the extrinsic evidence. "The more bizarre and unusual an asserted interpretation is, the more convincing must be the testimony that supports it." 3 CORBIN § 579, at 420. At what point a judge stops "listening to testimony that white is black and that a dollar is fifty cents is a matter for sound judicial discretion and common sense." *Id.*

When interpreting a contract, nevertheless, it is fundamental that a court attempt to "ascertain and give effect to the intention of the parties at the time the contract was made if at all possible." If, for example, parties use language that is mutually intended to have a special meaning, and that meaning is proved by credible evidence, a court is obligated to enforce the agreement according to the parties' intent, even if the language ordinarily might mean something different. See Restatement § 212 cmt. b, illus. 3 & 4. The judge, therefore, must avoid the often irresistible temptation to automatically interpret contract language as he or she would understand the words. This natural tendency is sometimes disguised in the judge's ruling that contract language is "unambiguous." *See* 3 CORBIN § 543A, at 159 (1992 Supp.). Words, however, are seldom so clear that they "apply themselves to the subject matter." Restatement § 214 cmt. b. On occasion, exposition of the evidence regarding the intention of the parties will illuminate plausible interpretations other than the one that is facially obvious to the judge. *See id.* Thus, ambiguity determined by the judge's view of "clear meaning" is a troublesome concept that often obstructs the court's proper and primary function in this area—to enforce the meaning intended by the contracting parties.

Recognizing these problems, we are hesitant to endorse, without explanation, the often repeated and usually over-simplified construct that ambiguity must exist before parol evidence is admissible. We have previously criticized the ambiguity prerequisite in the context of non-negotiated agreements. Moreover, a contract may be susceptible to multiple interpretations and therefore truly ambiguous yet, given the context in which it was negotiated, not susceptible to a clearly contradicting and wholly unpersuasive interpretation asserted by the proponent of extrinsic evidence. In such a case, it seems clear that a court should exclude that evidence as violating the parol evidence rule despite the presence of some contract ambiguity. Finally, and most important, the ambiguity determination distracts the court from its primary objective — to enforce the contract as intended by the parties. Consequently, although relevant, contract ambiguity is not the only linchpin of a court's decision to admit parol evidence.

The better rule is that the judge first considers the offered evidence and, if he or she finds that the contract language is "reasonably susceptible" to the interpretation asserted by its proponent, the evidence is admissible to determine the meaning intended by the parties. *See* Restatement § 215 cmt. b; *see also Pacific Gas & Elec. Co. v. G.W. Thomas Dray. & Rigging Co.,* 69 Cal. 2d 33, 69 Cal. Rptr. 561, 564, 566, 567–68, 442 P.2d 641, 644, 645–46 (1968);[2] *cf. Melson,* 135 Ariz. at 121, 659 P.2d at 1266("A contract should be read in light of the parties' intentions as reflected by their language and in view of all the circumstances."). The meaning that appears plain and unambiguous on the first reading of a document may not appear nearly so plain once the judge considers the evidence. In such a case, the parol evidence rule is not violated because the evidence is not being offered to contradict or vary the meaning of the agreement. To the contrary, it is being offered to explain what the parties truly may have intended. We believe that this rule embodies the concepts endorsed by Corbin and adopted by this court ten years ago in *Melson.* Other courts more recently have expressed approval of the position taken by Corbin and the Restatement (Second) of Contracts.

A judge may not always be in a position to rule on a parol evidence objection at first blush, having not yet heard enough relevant evidence on the issue. If this occurs, the judge might, for example, admit the extrinsic evidence

---

[2] We recognize that Pacific Gas has its critics. [¶] We nevertheless believe that the rule correctly embodies the Corbin view adopted in Melson. See 3 CORBIN §§ 542, at 102 (1992 Supp.) (citing Pacific Gas as an "excellent example of correct analytical thinking"). We believe that these cases read much more in Pacific Gas than is there. We too would recoil if Pacific Gas meant that mere complexity required a finding of ambiguity or that courts must listen to wholly unpersuasive extrinsic evidence to create ambiguity where words are clear beyond dispute. What this means, at least in Arizona, is that the parol evidence rule does not apply to exclude evidence unless the evidence varies or contradicts the agreement. But the court must first decide what the agreement says and, as a preliminary matter, must decide if it reasonably could be interpreted in different ways, given the language and the factual context surrounding the making of the agreement. Admittedly, the process is not without risk, but we believe the game is worth the candle. After all, the purpose is to produce the contract result the parties intended, not that which the judge intends. Some words are clear beyond dispute. Some may mean one thing to the judge but could have meant something else to the parties. It is the latter meaning that is important.

conditionally, reserve ruling on the issue until enough relevant evidence is presented, or, if the case is being tried to a jury, consider the evidence outside the jury's presence. Because the judge is in the best position to decide how to proceed, we leave this decision to his or her sound discretion. As noted also, the judge need not waste much time if the asserted interpretation is unreasonable or the offered evidence is not persuasive. A proffered interpretation that is highly improbable would necessarily require very convincing evidence. In such a case, the judge might quickly decide that the contract language is not reasonably susceptible to the asserted meaning, stop listening to evidence supporting it, and rule that its admission would violate the parol evidence rule.

We now apply these principles to the facts of this case. [The court went on to consider the release and concluded that it was not so clear that the trial court erred in admitting parol evidence to determine its meaning and, once having admitted the evidence, the trial court did not err in holding that it could not be determined as a matter of law whether it was meant to release the bad faith claim. Therefore, the issue was properly submitted to the jury.]

CONCLUSION

The trial court properly considered and then admitted extrinsic evidence to interpret the release and determine whether it included Taylor's bad faith claim. That question, in this case, was appropriately left to the trier of fact. There remain other issues not resolved by the court of appeals. . . . . The decision of the court of appeals pertaining to the release is vacated and the matter is remanded to the court of appeals for resolution of the remaining issues.

MOELLER, V.C.J., ZLAKET, J., and JAMES D. HATHAWAY, JUDGE, concur.

JUSTICE FREDERICK J. MARTONE did not participate in this matter; pursuant to Ariz. Const. art. VI, § 3, JUDGE JAMES D. HATHAWAY of the Court of Appeals, Division Two, was designated to sit in his stead.

CORCORAN, JUSTICE, specially concurring:

I concur with the opinion—but without enthusiasm. It is certainly true that wavering and overlapping lines of interpretation, rather than bright straight borders prevail in this area of contract interpretation. I don't know whether our opinion helps.

The canon of interpretation which we propound today is amorphous. The problem with an amorphous rule is that in the end, only this court can make a final determination in construing any contract. Our interpretation will be based upon which parol evidence impresses us the most. That ultimately means that this court must decide every contract dispute subject to this analysis. As the history of this case shows, the trial court may go one way and the court of appeals another and this court yet another.

I fear that this opinion makes this court the supreme court of arguments "that white is black and that a dollar is fifty cents"—to use the colorful words of Professor Corbin.

. . . .

NOTES

1. *A parol evidence rule review.* Contracting parties often reduce their agreements (or parts of their agreements) to writing, intending to create trustworthy, reliable evidence of their understandings and perhaps to supersede prior expressions, negotiations, or understandings. If one party tries to introduce evidence of prior (or perhaps even contemporaneous) statements, evidence, or understandings, the other party may assert the parol evidence rule for the purpose of barring the introduction of such statements, etc. to contradict or perhaps even to supplement the writing. It does not matter whether the evidence offered is oral or written; the parol evidence rule applies to both. If the court determines that the parties intended their writing as a final expression of their agreement, the parol evidence rule will bar any prior or contemporaneous statements, etc. that would contradict the writing; and if the court determines that the parties also intended their writing to be a complete expression of their agreement, the statements, etc. are barred even if they are consistent with the writing (i.e., the statements cannot be used even to supplement the writing). An important exception to the parol evidence rule involves interpretation; the rule does not prevent evidence from being offered for the purpose of interpreting the writing. In this sense, then, the parol evidence rules speaks only to what the terms of the contract are, not what they mean. Also, there are exceptions for fraud, duress, mistake, and other causes that might be shown to invalidate a contract. For example, where reformation is sought, the parol evidence rule does not apply. Of course, whether the entire agreement was intended to be finally or completely expressed in the writing may be the subject of dispute; parol evidence may be admitted to resolve that issue. It should also be remembered that the parol evidence rule does not bar evidence that arises subsequent to the formation of a contract—for example, evidence of modification.

2. *Williston versus Corbin.* The so-called "restrictive" and "liberal" views of the parol evidence rule often are identified with the two of the most highly regarded contract law scholars of their time—Samuel H. Williston and Arthur L. Corbin. Exactly how do their positions differ? Were there any doctrinal developments taking place during their lives that would lead to a difference in attitude about the parol evidence rule? As a general proposition, with which position do you agree? If you were an insurer, would you favor the Williston view or the Corbin view? Does Justice Corcoran have a point?

Of course, the writing in *Taylor* did not involve an insurance contract; it dealt with a release. Is there any reason why the so-called Corbin rule may not work quite the same with contracts of insurance as with other types of contracts?

3. *Parol evidence rule and the doctrine of reasonable expectations.* By the time the American Law Institute undertook to revise the first Restatement of Contracts, it was clear that there were many situations where parties to a contract no longer actually negotiated its terms. The age of the form contract had arrived and it had to be dealt with in the Restatement. The result was

section 211 of the second Restatement (discussed in the prior subsection in this Chapter); it was designed to state how standard form contracts should be interpreted. How does section 211 relate to the parol evidence rule? Note that in the organization of the second Restatement, section 211 is sited in the midst of the various parol evidence rule sections. If the contract consists of a standard form and the disputed language was not the subject of negotiation but was offered on a "take it or leave it" basis by the insurer, for what purpose might parol evidence be admissible? *See Darner Motor Sales, Inc. v. Universal Underwriters Ins. Co.,* 140 Ariz. 383, 393–394, 682 P.2d 388, 397–398 (1984).

4. *"Entire-contract" provisions.* As discussed earlier (see note 5 in § 3.02[1][c], many states have enacted "entire-contract" statutes. Essentially, these statutes and clauses state that the policy and any attachments constitute the only agreement between the parties and are designed in part to require the insurer to furnish the insured a copy of all statements made by him that might thereafter be relied upon as grounds for avoiding the policy. Could it be plausibly argued that the effect of these statutes and clauses is to adopt the so-called "restrictive" parol evidence rule? Would an "entire-contract" statute or clause prevent a court from adopting the approach taken in *Taylor?*

5. *Statute of Frauds.* Oral contracts of insurance, as such, rarely run afoul of the Statute of Frauds. The traditional "five-category statute" as well as the statute of frauds pertaining to sales of goods for a monetary value in excess of a certain amount have no application. The so-called "guaranty provision" of the five-category statute does not, under the prevailing view, cover guarantee and fidelity bonds because the latter are construed as contracts to indemnify the creditor against loss or damage from the debtor's nonperformance rather than contracts to perform the debtor's original obligation. The fact that almost any insurance contract can be performed within one year from the making thereof because of the possibility of a loss during that time also removes such contracts from this peculiar provision. There are cases, however, which hold that the Statute of Frauds may apply to oral contracts or agreements to procure or to renew contracts of insurance. See Robert E. Keeton & Alan I. Widiss, Insurance Law § 2.2(c)(1) (Student Ed. 1988), at 47–49.

Also, some states have specific statutes that require (or have been interpreted to require) certain types of insurance, or certain kinds of insurance transactions, to be in writing to be enforceable. *Id.* at § 2.2(e). *See, e.g.,* New York Gen. Oblig. Law § 5-701 (contract to assign, or an assignment, of a life, health, or accident policy, or a promise to designate a beneficiary, must be in writing, unless the insurance is industrial life); Mass. Gen. Laws Ann. ch. 175, §§177C (no contract with an "insurance adviser" is enforceable by the adviser unless it is in writing).

Chapter 4

COMMON FIRST-PARTY COVERAGES AND RECURRING ISSUES

[Henry Clay Frick, 1849-1919, was a prominent industrialist. He was chairman of Carnegie Steel from 1889-1900 and played an important role in the formation of U.S. Steel in 1901.] "Frick spent his summers at Pride's Crossing in Massachusetts, and every year he had his priceless collection of paintings loaded in a steel railroad car, specially built to transport them, and brought them from New York to his Pride's Crossing estate. When [journalist] Oswald Garrison Villard asked Frick if he was not afraid of the paintings being stolen or damaged in transit, he replied, 'Oh, no. They are insured.'" —Page Smith, The Rise of Industrial America 773 (1984)

Henry Clay Frick's insurance on his art treasures was a first-party coverage on property. The materials in this Chapter discuss the coverage provided by the most common first-party insurance policies: life insurance; accidental death and dismemberment insurance; disability insurance; health insurance; property insurance; and marine insurance. The types of questions confronted in this Chapter concern the risks which the insurer assumes when it issues an insurance policy, limitations on the risks assumed (i.e., limitations on the coverage), and other related, commonly recurring issues.

It is worth noting at this early juncture that although the distinction between first-party and third-party coverage is a clear one, it is not uncommon to combine first-party and third-party coverage in the same policy. For example, the standard homeowners policy contains both first-party coverage on the property and third-party coverage for the insured's liability exposures. In contrast, commercial property and liability coverages are typically sold in separate policies. Automobile insurance, however, is another example of a "combination" policy. The usual automobile policy includes liability coverage and first-party property coverage, as well as other kinds of coverage (first-party medical benefits; perhaps first-party disability; perhaps a first-party death benefit; uninsured and underinsured motorist protection; etc.). No-fault auto insurance, for example, is a first-party coverage; uninsured and underinsured motorist insurance also has features of first-party insurance. Liability— that is, third-party coverage — is addressed, in general, in Chapter 5. Both first-and third-party coverages in auto insurance are discussed in Chapter 6.

No-fault auto insurance bears elaboration for an additional reason. The essence of no-fault involves (a) abolishing a portion of the tort liability system, i.e., taking away a portion of an individual's right to sue a third party in tort for damage tortiously caused by the third party, and (b) compelling that individual to purchase first-party coverage in order to provide protection from the consequences of the torts of third parties. Workers' compensation insurance, which is ordinarily studied in a law school course that focuses exclusively on the workers' compensation system, is a first-party coverage purchased by employers for the benefit of employees. To be more specific, "[t]he stated theory of workmen's compensation in the United States is that it 'is a mechanism for providing cash-wage benefits and medical care to victims of work-connected injuries, and for placing the cost of these injuries ultimately on the consumer, through the medium of insurance, whose premiums are passed on in the cost of the product.'" Roger C. Henderson, *Should Workmen's Compensation Be Extended to Nonoccupational Injuries?* 48 Tex. L. Rev. 117, 119 (1969) (quoting 1 A. Larson, Workmen's Compensation § 1, at 1 (1964)). The insurance that backs up the remedial scheme, then, provides the compensation for employee injuries that but for the preemptive effects of the workers' compensation system would have been remedied in a tort action against the negligent employer and, in most cases, paid by a liability insurer. One of the important public policy issues of the day is whether more third-party liabilities should be replaced by first-party insurance compensation mechanisms. See generally *id*; Robert H. Jerry, II, Understanding Insurance Law § 132, at 849–859 (2d ed. 1996) (discussing various proposals). In short, one should not be confused simply because third-party liability concepts are discussed in proximity to first-party insurance coverage. Chances are that the discussion involves one of the kinds of first-party coverage that has a strong nexus to third-party liabilities.

§ 4.01   Life Insurance

[1]   Determining Death

CROBONS v. WISCONSIN NATIONAL LIFE INSURANCE CO.
790 F.2d 475 (6th Cir. 1986)

KEITH, CIRCUIT JUDGE.

This is a cross appeal from a district court order, 594 F. Supp. 379, denying the defendant's motions for summary judgment and granting partial summary judgment to plaintiff. For the following reasons, we affirm.

The plaintiff, Anne Marie Crobons, brought this action to recover insurance policy proceeds from a policy on the life of Gene Crobons, her deceased husband. The defendant, Wisconsin National Life Insurance Company (Wisconsin National) issued the policy and paid the controverted proceeds to defendant Marvin Wyant, former business partner of Gene Crobons. Defendant Brian Wyant, Marvin Wyant's son, and an insurance agent, serviced the Wisconsin National policy on Gene Crobons' life.

Gene Crobons and Marvin Wyant allegedly entered an oral agreement to take out life insurance policies on each other's lives. In December 1981, Marvin Wyant purchased from Wisconsin National a $100,000 term life insurance policy on the life of Gene Crobons. Defendant Brian Wyant, Marvin Wyant's son and a Wisconsin National insurance agent, serviced the policy. In February 1982, Marvin Wyant and Gene Crobons designated plaintiff Marie Crobons as the primary beneficiary of the policy insuring Gene Crobons' life. The policy provided for change of beneficiary while Mr. Crobons was still living.

On September 3, 1982, Gene Crobons entered Foote Hospital in Jackson, Michigan. Hospital personnel diagnosed massive subarachnoid hemorrhage and placed Mr. Crobons on a life support system. The district court determined that Mr. Crobons' treating physician, Dr. Rawal, submitted unchallenged testimony that readings of Mr. Crobons' brain waves on September 13, 1982 confirmed the doctor's earlier conclusion that Mr. Crobons had suffered irreversible brain death. Dr. Rawal so informed Mrs. Crobons. A day earlier Dr. Rawal had written in his progress notes dated September 12th, that Mr. Crobons' neuro examination was "consistent with brain death". The doctor had no doubt his clinical examination meant Mr. Crobons' spontaneous brain functions had irreversibly ceased. However, because Dr. Rawal encountered reluctance by the family to accept Mr. Crobons' death, he awaited results of an EEG requested by Mrs. Crobons and the family's decision to disconnect life support before certifying Mr. Crobons as deceased. On September 15, 1982, Dr. Rawal certified Mr. Crobons' time of death as September 14, 1982 at 2:55 p.m.

During the interim between Dr. Rawal's September 12th notation of brain death and the certification of Mr. Crobons' death on September 15th, Marvin Wyant was fully aware of the deceased's comatose state and a report by Pat Vincent that Crobons had suffered brain death on September 11th. On September 13th, 1982, Marvin Wyant executed and Brian witnessed a change of beneficiary form which substituted Marvin Wyant as the principal beneficiary of the life insurance policy and left plaintiff as beneficiary in the then moot possibility of Mr. Crobons' accidental death.

The district court determined that Wisconsin National agent John Basinger knew about Crobons' comatose state before September 13th and was aware the Wyants were trying to change the policy beneficiary quickly. After conducting an investigation, Wisconsin National nonetheless determined the change of beneficiary form had been properly executed and paid Marvin Wyant the $100,000 in policy proceeds in November, 1982.

Plaintiff first learned of the policy and her former status as beneficiary in the summer of 1983. In November of 1983, plaintiff filed a constructive fraud and breach of contract action in Michigan Circuit Court, Jackson County. Plaintiff alleged in Count I of the complaint that Wisconsin National had breached its contractual duty to pay the proceeds of the policy to her, the designated beneficiary. The defendants removed the suit to federal district court based on diversity of citizenship and Wisconsin National and Brian Wyant moved for summary judgment.

The district court determined that even accepting defendants' contention that Marvin Wyant executed the change of beneficiary form the afternoon of September 12, 1982, the change was not completed prior to Gene Crobons' brain death. The court concluded that under the Michigan Death Act, Mich. Comp. Laws Ann. § 333.1021 (1980), Gene Crobons died when his doctor observed and noted the "irreversible cessation of spontaneous brain functions." The court then determined that on September 12, 1982, Dr. Rawal first announced his opinion of "brain death" in his progress notes and informed Mrs. Crobons of the opinion one day later. The court concluded that since Mr. Crobons died at some point before execution of the change of beneficiary form, the date on the death certificate denoted only when life support was removed and therefore presented no genuine issue of material fact. Under such circumstances, the court concluded, Wisconsin National unreasonably relied upon the death certificate. The court denied defendants' motions for summary judgment and on its own motion granted summary judgment against Wisconsin National on Count I of the complaint.

. . . .

Our review on appeal is limited to determining whether any issue of material fact precluded summary judgment. The key issue before the district court was whether Mr. Crobons died before or after the Wyants executed the change of beneficiary form. The court entered summary judgment on Count 1 in favor of plaintiff because the record showed Mr. Crobons suffered brain death prior to execution of the form. In the district court's view, this fact negated the presumptive validity of the later time of death noted on the death certificate, and left no issue of material fact precluding summary judgment against Wisconsin National on the charge that it had breached the policy contract and wrongfully paid Marvin Wyant the policy proceeds.

On appeal, Wisconsin National first contends that the provisions of the Michigan Death Act[1] defining brain death should not be used for determining the time of death for purposes of disbursing insurance policy proceeds. Specifically, defendant contends the legislature intended the Death Act be used only to protect transplant surgeons from liability in determining the death of a potential donor. We do not agree. The plain language of the statute requires that the method of determining death prescribed under the Act

---

[1] The Michigan Death Act, Mich. Comp. Laws Ann. §§ 333.1021-1023 (1985), provides:

333.1021 Death; spontaneous respiratory and circulatory functions, cessation; artificial support, spontaneous brain functions, cessation; time

Sec. 1. A person will be considered dead if in the announced opinion of a physician, based on ordinary standards of medical practice in the community, there is the irreversible cessation of spontaneous respiratory and circulatory functions. If artificial means of support preclude a determination that these functions have ceased, a person will be considered dead if in the announced opinion of a physician, based on ordinary standards of medical practice in the community, there is the irreversible cessation of spontaneous brain functions. Death will have occurred at the time when the relevant functions ceased.

P.A. 1979, No. 124, § 1, Imd. Eff. Oct. 19.

333.1022 Pronouncement before artificial support terminated

Sec. 2. Death is to be pronounced before artificial means of supporting respiratory and circulatory functions are terminated.

P.A. 1979, No. 124, § 2, Imd. Eff. Oct. 19.

333.1023 Means of determining death, use

Sec. 3. The means of determining death in section 1 shall be used for all purposes in this state, including the trials of civil and criminal cases.

P.A. 1979, No. 124, § 3, Imd. Eff. Oct. 19.

". . .shall be used *for all purposes* in this state, including the trials of civil and criminal cases." The clarity of the statutory language precludes further judicial interpretation.

Defendant next contends that the time of death for purposes of identifying the beneficiary of life insurance is the time certified on the official death certificate. We agree that the certified time of death is presumptively correct. However, the death certificate provides only prima facie evidence of identity, occurrence, time and place of death. Where, as here, evidence of death as defined under the Death Act contravenes the time of death stated in the death certificate, the presumptive correctness of the latter is rebutted. We find no error in the district court's conclusion that in cases involving life support systems the Death Act excludes reference to the death certificate and unambiguously designates the moment of death as the time when there is irreversible cessation of spontaneous brain functions.

Wisconsin National further contends that, assuming general applicability of the Death Act to this case, it was entitled to rely on the time of death stated on the death certificate because it was the only "announced opinion" of death and because the record fails to show Dr. Rawal "announced" his opinion of brain death within the meaning of the Act. Additionally, Wisconsin National argues it reasonably relied on the certified time of death because no other available information indicated Crobons was brain dead before the time of death noted on the certificate. The district court, however, concluded that Dr. Rawal's statement to Mrs. Crobons and his September 12th notation of brain death constituted "announced opinions" under the Death Act. The court further concluded that an announcement is not a necessary predicate to a determination of death under the Act. Moreover, the court determined that in any event Wisconsin National was not entitled to rely on the certificate because it had failed to heed sufficient warning of a potential dispute over Mr. Crobons' time of death.

We agree with the district court that the Michigan Death Act does not impose a prescribed or formal method of communicating an opinion of brain death. The statute provides that "a person will be considered dead if in the announced opinion of a physician, based on ordinary standards of medical practice in the community, there is irreversible cessation of spontaneous brain functions. Death will have occurred at the time when the relevant functions ceased." Section 2 of the Death Act, however, requires that death be *"pronounced"* before life support systems are disconnected. In order to give the statute full effect, we must accord the terms "announcement" and "pronouncement" distinct meanings. Under ordinary definitions of these terms, we conclude that unlike a pronouncement, an announcement does not entail a formal, authoritative declaration of opinion and requires the doctor to communicate written or oral opinion of brain death such that a third person can determine when irreversible cessation of spontaneous brain functions occurred.

The district court's factual determination that Dr. Rawal announced his opinion of brain death to the family and in his progress notes between September 10th and 12th is not clearly erroneous. Time of death, therefore, occurred prior to the time noted on the death certificate and prior to execution of the change of beneficiary form. Nor can we find clear error in the court's finding that Wisconsin National had constructive notice Mr. Crobons may have suffered brain death prior to the time of death noted on the death certificate or at minimum that a potential conflict over the policy was brewing. Wisconsin National agent John Basinger testified he knew of Crobons' comatose state prior to September 13th and that the Wyants desired a quick change of beneficiary. The record also reveals that the hospital discharge summary, received by Wisconsin National, states that "[o]n 9/13/82 the EEG was performed which was consistent with electrocerebal silence" or brain death. This entry presented sufficient indication that brain death may have occurred prior to September 14th, 1982, the certified time of death. Moreover, the record shows Wisconsin National could have obtained access to Dr. Rawal's notes or at minimum a determination of when Mr. Crobons' brain functions irreversibly ceased, an inquiry required by the Death Act in cases involving artificial life support systems.

In our view, the district court correctly determined that the Michigan Death Act applies to this case. Further, the court did not err in determining that no dispute exists over the evidence that Dr. Rawal announced Mr. Crobons' brain death in his progress notes prior to the change in beneficiary. We do not see where in the record Wisconsin National proffered proof challenging the doctor's conclusion of irreversible brain death prior to September 13, 1982. As no material dispute on this key issue exists, we affirm the district court judgment on Count 1.

Plaintiff cross appeals contending the district court erred in refusing to order Wisconsin National to pay interest on the insurance policy proceeds from the date of death until the filing of the complaint. We affirm the district court judgment. Under Michigan law, absent policy provisions providing for interest payment from date of death, plaintiff is not entitled to interest prior to the filing of her complaint.

Accordingly, the judgment of the Honorable Charles W. Joiner is hereby affirmed.

UNIFORM DETERMINATION OF DEATH ACT (1980 ACT)
12A U.L.A. 589 (1996)

This Act provides comprehensive bases for determining death in all situations. It is based on a ten-year evolution of statutory language on this subject. The first statute passed in Kansas in 1970. In 1972, Professor Alexander Capron and Dr. Leon Kass refined the concept further in "A Statutory Definition of the Standards for Determining Human Death: An Appraisal and a Proposal," 121 Pa. L. Rev. 87. In 1975, the Law and Medicine Committee of the American Bar Association (ABA) drafted a Model Definition of Death Act. In 1978, the National Conference of Commissioners on Uniform State Laws (NCCUSL) completed the Uniform Brain Death Act. It was based on the prior work of the ABA. In 1979, the American Medical Association (AMA) created its own Model Determination of Death statute. In the meantime, some twenty-five state legislatures adopted statutes based on one or another of the existing models.

The interest in these statutes arises from modern advances in lifesaving technology. A person may be artificially supported for respiration and circulation after all brain functions cease irreversibly. The medical profession, also, has developed techniques for determining loss of brain functions while cardiorespiratory support is administered. At the same time, the common law definition of death cannot assure recognition of these techniques. The common law standard for determining death is the cessation of all vital functions, traditionally demonstrated by "an absence of spontaneous respiratory and cardiac functions." There is, then, a potential disparity between current and accepted biomedical practice and the common law.

The proliferation of model acts and uniform acts, while indicating a legislative need, also may be confusing. All existing acts have the same principal goal—extension of the common law to include the new techniques for determination of death. With no essential disagreement on policy, the associations which have drafted statutes met to find common language. This Act contains that common language, and is the result of agreement between the ABA, AMA, and NCCUSL.

Part (1) codifies the existing common law basis for determining death—total failure of the cardiorespiratory system. Part (2) extends the common law to include the new procedures for determination of death based upon irreversible loss of all brain functions. The overwhelming majority of cases will continue to be determined according to part (1). When artificial means of support preclude a determination under part (1), the Act recognizes that death can be determined by the alternative procedures.

Under part (2), the entire brain must cease to function, irreversibly. The "entire brain" includes the brain stem, as well as the neocortex. The concept of "entire brain" distinguishes determination of death under this Act from "neocortical death" or "persistent vegetative state." These are not deemed valid medical or legal bases for determining death.

This Act also does not concern itself with living wills, death with dignity, euthanasia, rules on death certificates, maintaining life support beyond brain death in cases of pregnant women or of organ donors, and protection for the dead body. These subjects are left to other law.

This Act is silent on acceptable diagnostic tests and medical procedures. It sets the general legal standard for determining death, but not the medical criteria for doing so. The medical profession remains free to formulate acceptable medical practices and to utilize new biomedical knowledge, diagnostic tests, and equipment.

It is unnecessary for the Act to address specifically the liability of persons who make determinations. No person authorized by law to determine death, who makes such a determination in accordance with the Act, should, or will be, liable for damages in any civil action or subject to prosecution in any criminal proceeding for his acts or the acts of others based on that determination. No person who acts in good faith, in reliance on a determination of death, should, or will be, liable for damages in any civil action or subject to prosecution in any criminal proceeding for his acts. There is no need to deal with these issues in the text of this Act.

Time of death, also, is not specifically addressed. In those instances in which time of death affects legal rights, this Act states the bases for determining death. Time of death is a fact to be determined with all others in each individual case, and may be resolved, when in doubt, upon expert testimony before the appropriate court.

Finally, since this Act should apply to all situations, it should not be joined with the Uniform Anatomical Gift Act so that its application is limited to cases of organ donation.

§ 1. [Determination of Death]

An individual who has sustained either (1) irreversible cessation of circulatory and respiratory functions, or (2) irreversible cessation of all functions of the entire brain, including the brain stem, is dead. A determination of death must be made in accordance with accepted medical standards.

. . . .

NOTES

1. *Is death "certain"?* In most situations, death is among the most unambiguous of all events. Modern technology, however, complicates what is otherwise a straightforward concept, and the factual dimensions of the question "when does death occur" will not become simpler. Many legal consequences flow from the factual determination of when death occurs, and these consequences are not confined to insurance. *See, e.g.,* James M. DuBois, *Non-Heart-Beating Organ Donation: A Defense of the Required Determination of Death,* 27 J. of Law, Med., & Ethics 126 (1999).

During the last two decades, much effort has been given to achieving more certain and easier-to-apply legal rules in this area. One important effort is the Uniform Determination of Death Act, now adopted in over 40 states. Although aimed mainly at addressing the problem of the health care provider's exposure to legal sanctions for terminating life support, the Uniform Act has obvious relevance to life insurance. The Uniform Act was not the law that the court dealt with in *Crobons.* Would the Act be an improvement over the Michigan statute as far as life insurance is concerned?

2. *"Proving" death.* When death occurs, a beneficiary usually "proves" the fact of death with a death certificate. In the typical situation, this is not problematic. But Mr. Crobons' death was not typical. Should a death certificate be contestable, and, if so, on what grounds?

Beyond problems with determining the time of death, a situation in which death itself might be said to be "ambiguous" involves the insured's unexplained disappearance and the absence of a body. Issues that can arise in connection with proof of death are considered in more detail in a note in § 8.01[2].

3. *Causation.* Life insurance, using that term in a generic sense, generally protects against premature death without regard to cause, unless the policy specifically excludes a certain cause or certain causes. Of course, there may be judicially or legislatively created exceptions to this statement, such as when a beneficiary intentionally kills the insured to collect the insurance proceeds. Even in that instance, however, the insurer seldom is relieved from paying someone. (This issue is taken up in § 4.01[5].) Some insurance protecting against premature death is limited to certain activities, such as death or injury from aviation or other means of transportation. This type of insurance is normally thought of as accident insurance, although it may be written by a life insurance company.

4. *Fortuity revisited.* Although death is certain to occur, the time at which death will occur is uncertain. This is enough to satisfy the fortuity requirement, at last insofar as life insurance is concerned. The analysis changes, however, if the *cestui que vie* deliberately acts to cause her own death. Almost all life insurance policies contain an exclusion for suicide that occurs within two years of the issuance of the policy. Why a two-year period? Why not exclude suicide altogether? If the insured who commits suicide is "insane," should this fact matter? For more on these and other questions, consider the materials in the next subsection.

[2] Intentional Self-destruction

NIELSEN v. PROVIDENT LIFE & ACCIDENT INSURANCE CO.
100 Idaho 223, 596 P.2d 95 (1979)

SHEPARD, CHIEF JUSTICE.

This is an appeal from a summary judgment in favor of defendant-respondent Provident Life and Accident Insurance Company in an action brought by plaintiff-appellant Mary Nielsen seeking to recover death benefits under an insurance policy on the life of her husband William Nielsen, who died as a result of a self-inflicted gunshot wound. We are required for the first time in Idaho to construe an insurance policy excluding benefits where death results from "suicide, while sane or insane." We affirm the judgment of the trial court.

William Nielsen, on January 14, 1976, purchased a Provident 20-year decreasing term life insurance policy with death benefits of $150,000.00. The primary beneficiary was Mary Nielsen. William Nielsen died on December 25, 1976, as a result of a self-inflicted gunshot wound to the head. The policy was at that time in full force and effect. It contained the following provision:

> "SUICIDE. If the insured should commit suicide, while sane or insane, within two years from the date of issue of this policy, the amount payable by the company, in place of all other benefits, will be the premiums paid without interest. This amount will be paid in one sum to the beneficiary."

Following the death of William Nielsen, Provident denied the policy death benefits and, rather, tendered the total premiums paid on the policy. Mary Nielsen brought this action for the recovery of the death benefits under the policy and Provident filed alternative motions to dismiss under I.R.C.P. 12(b)(6) and/or for summary judgment under I.R.C.P. 56. The trial court granted Provident's motion for summary judgment.

There appear to be no issues of fact presented to the trial court. Provident filed the affidavit of the Chief Deputy Corner for Ada County, which stated that "the death of William Nielsen was not an accident but was suicide and that the cause of death was due to a deliberate and self-inflicted gunshot wound to the head." Nielsen admits decedent died as a result of a self-inflicted gunshot wound, but she filed an affidavit in opposition to summary judgment, stating:

"   . . . .

2. That William S. Nielsen, affiant's deceased husband, was involved in an automobile accident on or about the 7th day of November, 1975.

3. That, as a result of the aforementioned automobile accident, William S. Nielsen suffered serious mental and physical injuries.

4. That, as a result of said injuries William S. Nielsen was, until the date of his death, under constant care of several doctors.

5. That said injuries caused William S. Nielsen, until the date of his death, to behave in an irrational manner. That said irrationality was markedly distinct from his behavior before said automobile accident."

Nielsen argues on appeal that the proximate cause of the death was the automobile accident and that the fatal self-inflicted gunshot wound was the result of an irresistible impulse of the decedent which was proximately caused by certain mental injuries received in the automobile accident 13 months prior to his death. There is no contention that the insured accidently shot himself.

When a motion to dismiss under I.R.C.P. 12(b)(6) is supported by affidavits and other materials, the motion may then properly be considered as one for summary judgment. Upon motion for summary judgment, it is axiomatic that all facts and inferences arising are construed most favorably towards the party against whom summary judgment is sought. If any genuine issue of material fact remains unresolved, summary judgment is improper.

Provisions in insurance policies excluding or limiting the insurer's liability where injury or death results from suicide have usually been held valid. Annot., 9 A.L.R.3d 1015 (1966); Appleman, Insurance Law and Practice § 363 (1965). Such provisions are statutorily authorized in Idaho. I.C. § 41-1925(1)(b)(v).

Early cases interpreting suicide exclusions in insurance policies held that self-destruction while insane was not suicide because there could be no suicide unless the insured could form a conscious intention to kill himself and carry out the act, realizing its moral and physical conditions and consequences. Thereafter, and as a result of those cases, the suicide exclusion clauses were expanded so as to include the words "suicide, sane or insane," or words having substantially the same meaning. Annot., 9 A.L.R.3d 1015 (1966); 9 Couch on Insurance 2d § 40:39, 40:40 (R. Anderson ed. 1962). The effect of that change in policy language is demonstrated by the case of *Bigelow v. Berkshire L. Ins. Co.,* 98 U.S. 284, 23 L.Ed. 918 (1876), in contrast with the earlier case of *Mutual Life Ins. Co. v. Terry,* 15 Wall. 580, 21 L. Ed. 236 (1873). In *Bigelow* the court concluded that the proviso "suicide, sane or insane" effectively removed the necessity of grappling with the "shadowy and difficult to define" line between sanity and insanity, stating:

> "Nothing can be clearer than that the words, 'sane or insane,' were introduced for the purpose of excepting from the operation of the policy any intended self-destruction, whether the insured was of sound mind or in a state of insanity. These words have a precise, definite, well-understood meaning. No one could be misled by them; nor could an expansion of this language more clearly express the intention of the parties. In the popular, as well as in the legal, sense, suicide means, as we have seen, the death of a party by his own voluntary act; and this condition, based, as it is, on the construction of this language, informed the holder of the policy, that, if he purposely destroyed his own life, the company would be relieved from liability."

93 U.S. at 287.

The numerical weight of authority states that in order for an insurer to avoid liability on the basis of a suicide clause with the words "sane or insane," it is not necessary for the insured to realize the physical nature or consequence of his act or to form a conscious purpose to take his life. If the act of self-destruction would be regarded as suicide in the case of a sane person, it would be so treated as to an insane insured, regardless of whether the insured realized or was capable of realizing that such an act would cause his death or whether he could form an intent to kill himself.

In a minority of jurisdictions, it is held that a policy exclusion for "suicide, sane or insane" is not operative absent an intent by the insured to kill himself and such intent could not be formed by the insured if he were so far insane as to be without appreciation of the physical consequences of his action or without power to resist the disordered impulse that caused him to take his own life.

The divergent lines of authority stem from varying concepts of the term "suicide." The majority view adopts a plain meaning and popular definition of the term as covering any act of self-destruction. The minority views the term in essentially a criminal law or technical concept holding that understanding and intent are deemed essential elements of a suicide. *See* Annot., 9 A.L.R.3d 1015 (1966). In *Aetna Life Ins. Co. v. McLaughlin, supra* at 106, it was stated:

> "In our opinion, the minority rule would lead to confusion and attempts by courts to define varying degrees or aspects of insanity. . . . The broader exclusion afforded to the exclusionary clause by the majority rule is in no way obnoxious to public policy. . . . [F]urther, and of most importance, we think the majority construction gives to the clause, in light of its history, the plain common sense meaning of the words employed."

See Atkinson v. Life Ins. Co. of Virginia, supra 228 S.E.2d at 120.

Nielsen argues that the exclusion of liability for suicide, sane or insane, does not exclude liability for a self-destructive act resulting from an irresistible impulse. We disagree.

In Idaho an insurance contract is to be construed most favorably to the insured and in such a manner as to provide full coverage for the indicated risks, and a construction of the insurer's contract will not be sanctioned which will defeat the very purpose or object of the insurance. However, where a word or phrase used in an insurance contract has a settled legal meaning or interpretation, that meaning or interpretation will be given effect although other interpretations are possible. A new liability not assumed by the insurer will not be created, nor will a new contract be made for the parties.

We find the reasoning of what appears to be the majority view persuasive. The self-destructive act of the decedent here constituted either a "sane or insane" suicide and was expressly excluded under the terms of the insurance contract. The fact that decedent may have suffered from a mental aberration caused by an automobile accident does not remove the act of self-destruction from the plain language of the policy excluding liability. The cause of the mental aberration is irrelevant to the applicability of the exclusionary language. The decedent's self-destructive act would clearly have constituted an act of suicide in the case of a sane person and thus remains a "suicide" under the language of the policy in the case of an insane person or one suffering a mental aberration. On the facts presented here, there is no question of "accidental" self-destruction and it is admitted that death resulted from a self-inflicted gunshot wound. Therefore, even construing all the facts and inferences in favor of the plaintiff Nielsen, as we are required to do on a motion for summary judgment, we hold there is no liability on the part of Provident under the terms of the insurance policy.

The judgment of the district court is affirmed.

DONALDSON, BAKES and BISTLINE, JJ., and SCOGGIN, J. pro tem., concur.

NOTES

1. *Legislative regulation of suicide clauses.* Most states have enacted statutes which permit life insurers to include suicide clauses in their policies like the one in *Nielsen.* These statutes either expressly or by implication prohibit any other suicide clauses that would be more disfavorable to the insured. Most modern policies contain such a provision; the typical provision is two years. See Appendix G. Should an insurer be permitted to exclude suicide from coverage altogether? Why do insurers not do so?

2. *"While sane or insane."* As the court points out in *Nielsen,* there was a time when the suicide clauses did not include the phrase "while sane or insane." This invited an argument that self-inflicted death was not suicide under some situations. Needless to say, insurers were not pleased with many of the court decisions attempting to resolve this issue and eventually they inserted the "sane or insane" language. Most courts have held that this text puts

outside the coverage "all nonaccidental acts of self-destruction, regardless of the insured's mental condition or understanding of the moral character of the act." See Gary Schuman, *Suicide and the Life Insurance Contract: Was the Insured Sane or Insane? That is the Question—Or Is It?*, 28 Tort & Ins. L. J. 745, 759 (1993). This change in policy language, however, has not solved all of the problems. What if the insured is so insane that she has no comprehension whatever of what she is doing? Does this degree of insanity negate "suicidal intent"? *See Searle v. Allstate Life Insurance Co.*, 38 Cal.3d 425, 212 Cal.Rptr. 466, 696 P.2d 1308 (1985) (exclusion does not apply if insured does not understand the physical nature and consequences of the act).

3. *Calculating the duration of the suicide period.* Normally, the policy will specify the date from which the suicide period will be calculated. How does the sample policy in Appendix G handle the matter? In fact, the policy might have one date for calculating the suicide period and another date for determining when premiums are due and other matters. *See Metropolitan Life Insurance Co. v. Daniels*, 745 So. 2d 1062 (Fla. Dist. Ct. App. 1999) (two-year suicide period began to run on "Date of Issue" as defined in policy, not on date temporary binding receipt was issued). On a related point, it is generally held that when a policy of life insurance is canceled or surrendered and replaced by a new agreement, which is identical or at least substantially similar to the old policy, the new policy does not create a new date of issue so as to commence again the suicide clause time period. *See Swanson v. First Fidelity Life Insurance Co.*, 214 Neb. 654, 335 N.W.2d 538 (1983); *Founders Life Assurance Co. v. Poe*, 242 Ga. 748, 251 S.E.2d 247 (1978); *cf. Sutton v. Banner Life Insurance Co.*, 686 A.2d 1045 (D.C. 1996) (vacating summary judgment for insurer which denied coverage based on two-year suicide exclusion in replacement policy on ground that material dispute existed as to whether insurer knew or should have known that insured had not agreed to new two-year suicide exclusion).

4. *Foolish, highly risky activities.* If the insured engages in an act that is likely, but not certain, to produce death, is the insured's death within the suicide exclusion? Normally this issue will arise in the context of whether beneficiaries are entitled to an accidental death benefit, but it is possible for this issue to arise under the basic life insurance coverage. If the insured, despondent over the breakup of his marriage, places one round in a revolver and plays Russian Roulette with fatal consequences, is the insured's death within the exclusion? *See C.M. Life Insurance Co. v. Ortega*, 562 So. 2d 702 (Fla. Dist. Ct. App. 1990). Does it make a difference if the insured thought the "safety" was on, but was mistaken? *See Butler v. Group Life and Health Insurance Co.*, 962 S.W.2d 296 (Tex. Ct. App. 1998) (under life and accidental death policies, insured's death from self-inflicted gunshot wound suffered when he fired what he incorrectly thought was an unloaded gun at his head was not suicide).

5. *Second thoughts.* If the insured commences the act of suicide, has a change of heart, and then tries to abort the suicide attempt without success, is the insured's death outside coverage by virtue of the suicide exclusion? *See Estate of Tedrow v. Standard Life Insurance Co.*, 558 N.W.2d 195 (Iowa 1997) (insured changes mind about suicide attempt and attempts without success to escape carbon monoxide fumes).

6. *Suicide and terminal illnesses.* Is it "suicide" for a patient in a hospital suffering from a terminal illness to knowingly and voluntarily refuse food and water? Is your answer the same if the circumstances involve a patient who faces an inevitable, painful death within a matter of days, but death will be hastened (and suffering reduced) by refusing nourishment? See Phyllis Coleman & Ronald A. Shellow, *Suicide: Unpredictable and Unavoidable-Proposed Guidelines Provide Rational Test for Physician's Liability*, 71 Neb. L. Rev. 643 (1992); George P. Smith, II, *All's Well that Ends Well: Toward a Policy of Assisted Rational Suicide or Merely Enlightened Self-Determination*, 22 U.C. Davis L. Rev. 275 (1989). Is there any argument for *not* applying the suicide exclusion as it reads in circumstances when the terminal illness was discovered after the insured purchased the policy? What issues are raised by the controversy over physician-assisted suicide, an issue made prominent by the activities of the infamous Dr. Kevorkian? *See Charney v. Illinois Mutual Life Casualty Co.,* 764 F.2d 1441 (11th Cir. 1985) (policy contains provisions stating "SUICIDE. If the Insured, whether sane or insane, shall die by his own hand or act within 2 years after the Date of the Policy . . .").

7. *Other statutorily prescribed clauses.* The suicide clause is but one example of an insurance provision that is statutorily prescribed. There are others, such as, for example, statutory provisions regarding grace periods extending premium payment due dates and misstatement of age. *See, e.g.,* N.Y. Ins. Law § 3203(a). A perusal of the statutes in your state may produce other interesting provisions. One of the most important of the statutorily prescribed clauses is the incontestability clause, which is explored in the next subsection.

[3] Incontestability

CRAWFORD v. EQUITABLE LIFE ASSURANCE SOCIETY OF U.S.
56 Ill. 2d 41, 305 N.E.2d 144 (1973)

WARD, JUSTICE.

This appeal presents the question whether an incontestability clause contained in a group life insurance policy bars the insurer from defending against a claim on the ground that the insured was not an employee eligible for insurance under the terms of the policy. The question is one of first impression in this court.

The plaintiff, Harvey A. Crawford, brought an action in the circuit court of Rock Island County against the defendant, The Equitable Life Assurance Society of the United States, to recover the sum of $10,000 as the beneficiary of his wife under a group insurance policy issued by the defendant. The case was heard upon the complaint, the defendant's answer, the motion of the plaintiff for summary judgment, and affidavits and stipulations filed by the parties. The circuit court granted the motion for summary judgment, and the appellate court affirmed. We granted the defendant's petition for leave to appeal. Leave was also granted to three other life insurance companies to file a joint brief *amici curiae.*

The undisputed facts are that effective January 1, 1965, the defendant issued a group life insurance policy to the Warm Air Heating and Air Conditioning Group Insurance Trust. The trust was established by the Warm Air Heating and Air Conditioning Association, for the purpose of providing insurance on the lives of employees of companies which were members of the association, as authorized by section 230(2)(e) of the Insurance Code Ill. Rev. Stat. 1971, ch. 73, par. 842(2)(e).

One of the members of the association was the Crawford Heating and Cooling Company, Inc., whose president was the plaintiff. In December, 1964, shortly prior to the issuance of the policy, the plaintiff executed and delivered to the association an enrollment form which requested insurance for three persons, each of whom he represented to be employees of his company. Among the three were the plaintiff himself and his wife, Rose A. Crawford. A certificate of insurance was thereafter issued to Mrs. Crawford in the face amount of $10,000. The certificate also provided for certain hospital and medical expense benefits. The plaintiff was named as the beneficiary. The premiums were paid by the Crawford Heating and Cooling Company. Mrs. Crawford died in February, 1969.

The master policy contained a provision that only a "full time employee" would be eligible for insurance, subject to a proviso that any employee "whose work week calls for a schedule of less than 32 hours shall not be eligible for insurance hereunder."

The insurance certificate issued to the decedent, while stating that the insurance provided under the policy was effective "only if the Employee is eligible for insurance," did not contain the specific full-time employment requirement found in the master policy. The enrollment form executed by the plaintiff, however, did state that an employee must work at least 32 hours a week, and the plaintiff marked the form in such fashion as to indicate that each of the three persons listed did meet that requirement. The same representation was made in regularly monthly statements submitted by the plaintiff to the trustee with his premium payments from February, 1965, until February, 1969.

An individual application for insurance executed by the decedent also included a representation by her that she worked 32 hours a week or more. She stated further in her application that her position with the company was that of Secretary-Treasurer, and that she earned $7500 or more a year. Information as to position and salary was significant under the policy because these factors affected the amount of death benefits payable.

In point of fact the representations made by the plaintiff and by the decedent were false. Neither at the time when the policy issued nor at any time thereafter did the decedent ever complete a week in which she worked 32 or more hours. According to the complaint the extent of her duties was to spend several hours a month in assisting the plaintiff in drawing up proposals for contracts, and in taking night telephone calls when he was on a job or out of town. She received no compensation for these functions.

It is admitted that the defendant made no inquiry into the circumstances of the decedent's employment until after her death. The facts came to light when the plaintiff submitted his claim to the trustee accompanied by a death certificate, which listed the decedent's occupation as that of housewife. The trustee notified the defendant, and requested it to verify the decedent's eligibility. An employee of the defendant then made a single call to the bookkeeper of the plaintiff's company, from whom the decedent's employment status was ascertained. The defendant thereafter wrote to the plaintiff denying the latter's claim.

The master policy contains an incontestability clause which reads as follows:

"The validity of this policy shall not be contested, except for the non-payment of premiums, after it has been in force for two years from the date of issue; and no statement made by any employee insured under this policy relating to his insurability shall be used in contesting the validity of the insurance with respect to which such statement was made, after such insurance has been in force prior to the contest for a period of two years during such employee's lifetime nor unless it is contained in a written application signed by such employee and a copy of such application is or has been furnished to such employee or his beneficiary."

The provision quoted above incorporates portions of section 231 of the Illinois Insurance Code (Ill. Rev. Stat. 1971, ch. 73, par. 843), which specifies certain provisions which must be contained in any policy of group life insurance issued or delivered in this State. Subsection (a) of section 231 requires inclusion of "A provision that the policy shall be incontestable after two years from its date of issue during the lifetime of the insured, except for nonpayment of premiums and except for violation of the conditions of the policy relating to military or naval services in time of war." Subsection (b) requires inclusion of "A provision . . . that all statements made by the employer or trustee or by the individual employees shall, in the absence of fraud, be deemed representations and not warranties, and that no such statement shall be used in defense to a claim under the policy, unless it is contained in a written application."

As presented by the parties, the basic issue in this case is whether the eligibility of an employee relates to the "coverage" of the policy and may, therefore, be challenged notwithstanding the incontestability clause. Each party apparently considers that only the first portion of the incontestability clause in the policy, reading "The validity of this policy shall not be contested, except for non-payment of premiums, after it has been in force for two years from the date of issue," is relevant in determining this issue. This view is presumably based on the assumption that the succeeding portion of the clause is intended only to deal with cases where proof of individual insurability is required. See Gregg, Group Life Insurance (2d ed.) 92.

The parties are in agreement that this case is governed by Illinois law. As we have previously noted, there appears to be no direct precedent in the decisions of this court applicable to the specific question presented.

An incontestability clause was considered in *Baker v. Prudential Insurance Company of America,* 279 Ill. App. 5, where recovery was sought under a group life insurance policy for the death of a former employee who had been discharged shortly prior to his death. The master policy specified that insurance should cease upon the termination of employment. Despite the incontestability clause, the appellate court held that the insurer was not liable, stating (279 Ill. App. 5, 10):

> "The incontestable provision did not prevent the defendant insurance company from showing the policy was no longer in effect because Baker had been discharged a month before death. That provision of the policy would prevent the defendant in the instant case from contending that the policy was obtained by fraud or misrepresentation or upon any other ground, going to the original validity of the policy."

Historically the uncontestability [sic] clause arose in the context of individual life insurance policies, and typically involved situations where the insured, in connection with his application for insurance, made statements respecting his health. In the absence of an incontestability clause, the insurer, upon the death of the insured, would be entitled to resist payment of the claim upon a showing that there had been a material misrepresentation of fact made by the insured or on his behalf, and that the contract of insurance was therefore voidable. The nature of the showing required is now defined by section 154 of the Insurance Code (Ill. Rev. Stat. 1971, ch. 73, par. 766), and for present purposes we need not review the "refined distinctions" which had been applied prior to the enactment of section 154 in 1937. The insurer, if he had no knowledge of the misrepresentation, was not ordinarily barred by the passage of time from making this defense, but might preserve it for use at such time as the insured died and the claim was presented for payment. The resulting situation was described by this court in *Powell v. Mutual Life Insurance Company of New York,* 313 Ill. 161, 164–165, 144 N.E. 825, 826, in the following language:

> "In the earlier development of insurance contracts it not infrequently occurred that, after the insured had paid premiums for a large number of years, the beneficiaries under the policy found, after the maturity thereof by the death of the insured, that they were facing a lawsuit in order to recover the insurance; that in certain answers in the application it was said by the insurer, the insured had made statements which were not true, and the beneficiaries were not entitled to recover on the policy. It is needless to call attention to the fact that this situation gave rise to a widespread suspicion in the minds of the public that an insurance contract was designed largely for the benefit of the company. Recognizing this fact and seeing the effect of it on the insurance business, numerous insurance companies inserted in their policies what is now known as an incontestable clause."

Whatever the manner of its origin, in most States, as in Illinois, the matter of incontestability is now covered by statute. (See Keeton, Basic Text on Insurance, sec. 6.5(d) (1971).) It is evident that one effect of an incontestability clause is to permit recovery in cases of false or even fraudulent representations, simply because these had not been discovered prior to the expiration of the contestable period. Balanced against this undesirable result, however, was the social desirability of assuring a beneficiary that his claim could not be put to a challenge at some remote future time when the insured was dead and when others who might have testified in the beneficiary's behalf might also be unable to do so.

The conventional incontestability clause contains certain exceptions, most commonly one for the nonpayment of premiums. It is clear, however, that there are other, unenumerated grounds on which an insurer may refuse to pay a claim after the period of contestability has run. The clause obviously does not preclude a refusal based on the fact that the particular event insured against has not taken place, and the insurer is thus not barred from "contesting" the claim or the interpretation of the coverage provisions advanced by the claimant. This point of distinction was described by Justice Cardozo, then the Chief Judge of the New York Court of Appeals, in the often cited case of *Metropolitan Life Insurance Co. v. Conway* (1930), 252 N.Y. 449, 169 N.E. 642. It was urged in that case that a rider in a policy excluding from protection death resulting from travel in an aircraft (except as a fare-paying passenger) conflicted with the incontestability provision contained in the New York insurance laws. The Court of Appeals held to the contrary, stating: "The provision that a policy shall be incontestable after it has been in force during the lifetime of the insured for a period of two years is not a mandate as to coverage, a definition of the hazard to be borne by the insurer. It means only this, that within the limits of the coverage the policy shall stand, unaffected by any defense that it was invalid in its inception, or thereafter became invalid by reason of a condition broken."

While the broad distinction drawn in *Conway* between a policy's limits of coverage and its validity has been quite generally recognized, differences of opinion have arisen as to its application, particularly with respect to group life insurance. (*See, e.g.*, Keeton, Basic Text on Insurance, sec. 6.5(d); Young, *"Incontestable—As to What?"*, 1964 U. Ill. L. F.) With individual life insurance the policy identifies a specific individual by name, and it is relatively easy to distinguish between a question of coverage (the death of the insured or his death from some specific cause) and a question of validity created by antecedent misrepresentations on the part of the insured. In the case of group life insurance, however, the master policy undertakes to provide insurance for a collection of unnamed persons defined only in terms of membership in a class, such as the employees of a certain company. To ascertain whether a person is insured necessitates a determination of whether he is in fact a member of the class. To the extent that that determination is based upon information furnished by the employer or by an employee or alleged employee, the question whether coverage exists tends to become intertwined with the question whether the coverage was obtained by false representations.

The courts of other States have considered a number of factual situations relating to eligibility, such as whether the insured is an employee at all, whether he was actively employed, whether he exceeded a specific maximum age, whether he was disqualified for some other reason, and whether he was incorrectly classified as to position. The decisions, which are collected in an annotation appearing in 26 A.L.R.3d 632, are not uniform in result.

The proposition that an insurer may challenge the eligibility of the insured has been advanced, either by direct holding or otherwise, with regard to the States of Arkansas, Idaho, Louisiana, Michigan, New Hampshire, Pennsylvania, Texas and Wisconsin, the decisions in some instances having been rendered by a Federal court called upon to ascertain and apply the law of the State in question.

The contrary view has been taken with respect to California, Oklahoma, Utah, and West Virginia.

The rule originally announced in Georgia was that eligibility could not be challenged, but a subsequent Federal decision applying Georgia law looks the other way. Conversely, the New York view, as first expressed in a Federal decision, was that the insurer might raise the defense of ineligibility, but a subsequent decision in 1969 by the New York Court of Appeals holds to the contrary (*Simpson v. Phoenix Mutual Life Insurance Co.* (1969), 24 N.Y.2d 262, 299 N.Y.S.2d 835, 247 N.E.2d 655). It is the *Simpson* decision on which the appellate court principally relied in the case now before us.

We, however, consider that the question of eligibility is one which relates to the risk assumed and that a defense based on lack of eligibility is therefore not foreclosed by an incontestability clause.

It is, of course, true that eligibility may relate to circumstances existing at the inception of the contract (although it may also arise subsequently because of a change in employment status). It is also true that it may have been determined initially upon the basis of statements made by the insured or by his employer. And it may be assumed that whether a person is an employee or is a full-time employee is a matter affecting the willingness of the insurer to assume the defined risk at the defined premium charge, since employment or active or full-time employment may protect the insurer against adverse selection. See Gregg, Group Life Insurance (2d ed.) 34–36.

A challenge to eligibility does not, however, involve an attack by the insurer on the validity of the master policy. The defendant is not seeking to set aside the policy because of the misrepresentations made and the only aspect of the insurance plan which is affected is the payment sought by a single beneficiary. Moreover, even as to that beneficiary, while the defendant may have relied on his representations as well as those of the decedent, the defendant's success in this litigation does not require that the defendant establish the falsity of those representations as such. Had the plaintiff alleged that the decedent had been a full-time employee, instead of admitting that she was not, the defendant would of course have been put to his proof of ineligibility. But it would be the fact of eligibility or ineligibility which would be decisive, not what prior representations had been made on the subject.

As we read *Simpson,* it represents a basic departure from the distinction announced in *Conway* between matters concerning validity, to which the incontestable clause applies, and the risk assumed, to which it does not. The court in *Simpson* takes the position that some matters which relate only to the risk assumed are nevertheless covered by the incontestable clause, namely those risks which could have been discovered at the time the contract was entered into. We consider that conclusion both inapplicable to the policy we consider here as well as unsuitable to the group insurance situation with its constantly changing body of insured employees.

The incontestability clause of the policy, to begin with, provides only that the validity of the policy may not be contested, and, as we have seen, its validity is not disputed.

A further factor which we deem significant was expressed in *Rasmussen v. Equitable Life Assurance Society of the United States,* 293 Mich. 482, 487, 292 N.W. 377, 380, in connection with a group policy excluding employees over a certain age: "[A] greater social good is served by enabling employed groups to obtain the most advantageous protection that their status warrants by restricting the invitation to particular age groups. Those who deliberately misstate their age and thus tend to lower the experience record of the group should not be placed by construction within the aegis of the incontestability provision."

Similarly, in the present case we can envisage the possibility of an adverse effect upon other employers if, by virtue of the incontestability clause, claims must be paid out upon the death of persons not meeting the standards of eligibility contained in the policy, in that actuarial calculations upon which the premium rate had been determined could be distorted, with the consequence of increased rates being imposed as the result of experience rating. See Gregg, Group Life Insurance (2d ed.) 220–229.

We do not mean to intimate that the occasions in which an employer would intentionally make a misrepresentation as to the eligibility of an employee would be of frequent occurrence. In the ordinary case the employer, who is paying all or a portion of the premiums, would not appear to have any incentive to create a supply of fictitious employees. The risk does exist, however, as indicated by the facts of this case and the somewhat similar facts in such cases as *Fisher v. Prudential Insurance Co.* (1966), 107 N.H. 101, 218 A.2d 62.

A third consideration underlying the decision we reach lies in the possibility that an employee who is eligible at the time when the policy is issued might, at some point more than two years after the issuance date, cease to be a full-time employee, or, indeed, even terminate his employment. Were the incontestability clause to be applied in such a situation, there would appear to be no manner in which payment of a claim could be resisted if the employer or employer group had failed to notify the insurer of the change in the status of the employee. We think that the termination of employment is clearly a matter which the insurer may raise. On the same reasoning we believe that raising the question whether a person ever became an employee or became an employee of the type eligible for insurance is also not barred by an incontestability clause.

The principle of discoverability which governed the *Simpson* decision would put the insurer to an election between the risk of making payment on unwarranted claims or conducting an investigation, in some manner not dependent upon information provided by the employer or employee, into the employment status of every person purportedly insured. The contention is made here that the latter course of action would cause substantial expense and the unnecessary duplication of records. It would undermine group life insurance which is customarily conducted on a "self administrative" fashion with the employer or employer group maintaining the record of individual employees, thus reducing the cost of premiums. The record made in this case does not supply us with evidence as to what overall method of administration was followed under the insurance plan involved or as to what the costs of some alternative method might be, and we therefore do not consider this contention in reaching our decision.

In addition to his contentions regarding the question of incontestability the plaintiff argued before the appellate court that certain actions by the defendant constituted a waiver or an estoppel. These further issues were not considered by the appellate court nor were they argued here. We therefore reverse the decision of the court for the reasons given in this opinion, and remand the cause for disposition of any other contentions of the plaintiff which are properly before the appellate court.

Reversed and remanded, with directions.

GOLDENHERSH, JUSTICE (dissenting).

I dissent. As stated by the majority, the parties are in agreement that this case is governed by Illinois law, and under Illinois law the fact that Mrs. Crawford was not a full-time employee working 32 or more hours per week cannot be raised as a defense. The majority appears to conclude that under the incontestability clause it is only the validity of the policy which may not be contested. This is clearly erroneous. The incontestability clause provides:

> "[A]nd no statement made by any employee insured under this policy relating to his insurability shall be used in contesting the validity of the insurance with respect to which such statement was made, after such insurance has been in force prior to the contest for a period of two years during such employee's lifetime nor unless it is contained in a written application signed by such employee and a copy of such application is or has been furnished to such employee or his beneficiary."

As used in this policy the term "insurability" does not refer solely to the condition of the employee's health; it means "capable of being insured" or the "quality or condition of being insurable," and the only contention made by defendant of her ineligibility or lack of insurability is her failure to be regularly employed. Defendant accepted premiums covering Mrs. Crawford for 52 months, and admittedly, if she had been afflicted with some incurable malady at the time the policy was issued, her "insurability" could not, after two years, have been contested. Neither logic nor the authorities cited support the drawing of a distinction between noninsurability based on illness and noninsurability based on failure to be employed for a minimum number of hours during each week. Indeed, if any distinction were to be drawn it should serve to more rigidly apply the incontestability clause to the latter situation for the reason that it is so easily discoverable.

The reason for the inclusion of the incontestability clause in policies of this type is obvious, and the fixing of the two-year period is clearly for the purpose of providing ample time for the insurer to investigate the veracity of the representations made. It is naive to believe that group insurers are trusting souls who accept, without question, the representations of the groups whom they insure, and the fact is that the policies provide for, and the insurers make, periodic inspections and audits. I cannot share the majority's apprehension with regard to the hypothetical case of the terminated employee. If the insurer failed to learn of the termination, and accepted premiums for a period of two years after its occurrence, that too should be governed by the incontestability clause. Under the terms of this policy the defendant was entitled to inspect and audit payroll records, and its failure to discover within the two-year period that Mrs. Crawford was not employed should not permit it to invoke a defense in clear violation of the express provisions of its policy. The rationale of *Simpson v. Phoenix Mutual Life Insurance Co.*, 24 N.Y.2d 262, 299 N.Y.S.2d 835, 247 N.E.2d 655, which the appellate court followed, is preferable to the grounds upon which the majority rests its decision, and I would affirm the judgment.

NOTES

1. *Statutory mandates.* Most states require life insurance contracts to contain an incontestability clause. This requirement may apply to group contracts as well as individual contracts. Some states also require that prescribed incontestability clauses appear in accident, disability, and health insurance contracts. It is not uncommon, however, to find statutes permitting insurers to except disability and accidental death benefits in life insurance contracts from the operation of such a clause. See generally Dale Joseph Gilsinger, Annotation, *Construction of Incontestable Clause Applicable to Disability Insurance*, 67 A.L.R.5th 513 (1999).

2. *Standard text.* The standard incontestability clause reads as follows: "This policy shall be incontestable after it has been in force during the lifetime of the insured, for a period of two years from the issue date, except for nonpayment of premiums." Note that if the *cestui que vie* dies within the two-year period, this particular clause permits the insurer to contest the validity of the policy beyond the two-year period.

Earlier versions of the clause did not contain this feature and it was held that the insurer lost the right to contest the policy after two years regardless of when the death occurred. *See, e.g., Monahan v. Metropolitan Life Ins. Co.*, 283 Ill. 136, 119 N.E. 68 (1918). This was true even though the death occurred so close to the end of the two-year period that it was not possible for the insurer to learn of it or bring an action to rescind before the two years expired. Under this rule, if there was any doubt about the validity of the policy, an astute claimant could wait until the two years expired, assuming this would not breach some other time limitation, and thereby preclude the insurer's defenses.

Some insurers continued to use the earlier version as a result of some courts holding that the new version made the equitable remedy of rescission unavailable to the insurer. The logic of these decisions was that because the insurer could defend at any time against claims on the policy, the insurer had an adequate remedy at law and the rescission remedy was therefore unavailable. By omitting the phrase "during the lifetime of the insured," the insurer preserved the right to the equitable remedy. *Massachusetts Mutual Life Insurance Co. v. Goodelman*, 160 F. Supp. 510 (E.D.N.Y. 1958). Under modern rules of civil procedure and with the merger of law and equity, there is little reason today for insurers to continue to use the earlier version.

3. *Calculating the duration of the incontestability period.* The language "after it has been in force" can give rise to disputes regarding the date from which the two years is to be measured. Does this mean the date of issue stated in the policy or could it be some other date? For example, if the policy has a "delivered while in good health" clause, could it be argued that the incontestability period does not begin to run until the policy is delivered, regardless of the date of issue? Or, if the insurer uses a conditional receipt in a jurisdiction that treats this as creating temporary coverage, does the temporary coverage period count as part of the incontestability period?

4. *To which defenses does the clause apply?* The incontestability clause was designed to preclude an insurer from raising certain defenses after the stated time period has elapsed. But which ones? It is commonly said that the clause "is designed to require the insurer to investigate and act with reasonable promptness if it wishes to deny liability on the ground of false representation or warranty by the insured." 18 Couch on Ins. § 72:2, at 283 (2d rev. ed. 1983). Misrepresentation is the defense to which the incontestability clause is most often applied. As for breach of warranty, should a distinction be drawn between affirmative warranties and promissory warranties? *See Vetter v. Massachusetts Nat. Life Ass'n,* 29 A.D. 72, 51 N.Y.S. 393 (App. Div. 1898).

What about the defense of fraud? If an applicant for insurance deliberately misrepresents his health status and the insurer fails to catch the falsehood within two years, should the insurer be foreclosed from contesting the policy? If your answer is "yes," what kinds of incentives does this create for dishonest individuals who learn that they suffer from a terminal or disabling illness? In many cases, courts have held the insurer's defense of fraud to be subject to the incontestability clause. *See, e.g., Bankers Security Life Insurance Society v. Kane,* 885 F.2d 820 (11th Cir. 1989) (applying Florida law); *Perry v. Bankers Life and Casualty Co.,* 362 S.W.2d 213 (Tex. Ct. Civ. App. 1962); *See also Paul Revere Life Insurance Co. v. Fima,* 105 F.3d 490 (9th Cir. 1997) (applying California law to disability policy).

What if the statute mandating the incontestability clause does not specifically mention fraud, and the insurer has a policy provision excepting fraud from the scope of the clause? Courts have not answered this question consistently. In *Protective Life Insurance Co. v. Sullivan,* 682 N.E.2d 624 (Mass. 1997), the court held that the insurer could not rescind the policy for fraud after passage of a two-year incontestability period, in circumstances in which the insured knew but failed to disclose he was HIV positive at the time of the application. That the insurance policy, the form of which was approved by the state insurance department, provided it was contestable for fraud at any time did not matter. The Massachusetts incontestability statute was held to prohibit an insurer from enforcing a fraud exception in the policy. *Id.* at 627–628. In *New England Mutual Life Insurance Co. v. Doe,* 93 N.Y.2d 122, 710 N.E.2d 1060, 688 N.Y.S.2d 459 (1999), the court held that once the incontestability period had passed, a disability insurer could not deny coverage by claiming that the applicant, who was being treated for HIV, falsely stated at the time of the application that he was not receiving any medical treatment. But the insurer had not reserved a right to contest the policy for fraud at any time, and the court stated "[a] carrier may, compatibly with the incontestability clause, protect itself by including a provision in its incontestability clause creating an exception for 'fraudulent misstatements.'" 710 N.E.2d at 1063. Should insurers be allowed to include a fraud exception to the incontestability clause? Should they be allowed to do so if the premium charged for the coverage is reduced? On what basis might one argue that fraud differs from breach of warranty or negligent misrepresentation?

5. *Coverage versus validity.* Most jurisdictions have held that incontestability clauses do not affect the scope of coverage, but only go to defenses relating to the policy's validity. But this principle is easier to state than to apply. The problem is basically one of trying to distinguish coverage provisions, to which the clause does not apply, from other provisions which give rise to defenses or grounds for avoidance and which should be preempted by the clause. For example, suppose an employee under an employer-provided group life insurance plan is eligible to purchase $100,000 of life insurance, but due to his employer's clerical error he is mistakenly enrolled for $200,000 of coverage (for which he is not eligible). But he pays monthly premiums for the full amount of coverage for five years until his death, whereupon the mistake is caught and the insurer refuses to pay more than $100,000 in proceeds plus a refund of the excess premiums. Is there no coverage for the extra $100,000 because he was never eligible for it, or is the issue one of the contract's validity which the insurer cannot now contest? *See Baseheart v. Life Insurance Co. of North America,* 960 F. Supp. 1210 (W.D. Ky. 1997) (favoring answer of incontestability, but holding that insurer can contest under prior Sixth Circuit precedent which court deemed binding authority).

This issue has arisen most prominently in cases involving eligibility requirements for group life insurance. For a list of cases categorized by holdings, *see Bonitz v. Travelers Insurance Co.,* 374 Mass. 327, 372 N.E.2d 254 (1978). As can be seen in *Crawford,* the eligibility requirement could be viewed as a condition which affects the validity of the contract between the insured and the insurer, in which case the clause would preclude any contest. On the other hand, the eligibility requirement could be viewed as a coverage provision because the insurer intends to insure only full-time employees. How could Mrs. Simpson *ever* become covered under the policy if she was never eligible for coverage? *See Turner v. Safeco Life Insurance Co.,* 17 F.3d 141 (6th Cir. 1994) (approving *Crawford*). The *Simpson* case, discussed in *Crawford,* used a test of whether the condition or situation which would give rise to a defense or grounds for avoidance was discoverable. The emphasis is put on the insurer's obligation to investigate on pain of being denied a defense on the basis that the insured did not meet the eligibility requirements. One of the advantages of group insurance is cost efficiency. Does the *Simpson* rationale promote cost efficiency? The *Crawford* case rejected *Simpson,* but did it provide a rationale of its own that will be useful in deciding other cases?

The cases addressing the issue raised in *Crawford* are still almost evenly divided in their results. *See McDaniel v. Medical Life Insurance Co.,* 195 F.3d 999 (8th Cir. 1999) (using Ohio law to inform on federal common law under ERISA, approving *Crawford*); *Groll v. Safeco Life Insurance Co.,* 388 Pa. Super. 556, 566 A.2d 269 (1989) (approving *Simpson* rule); *Halstead Consultants, Inc. v. Continental Cas. Co.,* 181 Ariz. 459, 891 P.2d 926 (Ariz. Ct. App.

1995) (citing cases). For more discussion of the scope of incontestability clauses, see Robert H. Jerry, II, Understanding Insurance Law § 104B (2d ed. 1996).

6. *Other exceptions to incontestability.* There are some other areas where courts have held that the policy's validity remains contestable notwithstanding the incontestability clause. For example, it has been held that the incontestability clause does not bar a defense or grounds for avoidance when there is no insurable interest, *Carter v. Continental Life Insurance Co.,* 115 F.2d 947 (D.C. Cir. 1940), and where the policy was procured with intent to murder the *cestui que vie, Henderson v. Life Insurance Co. of Va.,* 176 S.C. 100, 179 S.E. 680 (1935). If policies are contestable on these grounds, then why not on the basis of the applicant's fraud? Is there a difference between a defense or grounds for avoidance that is based on a theory that the policy was void *ab initio* as compared to a theory that the policy is merely voidable?

What if someone fraudulently impersonates the proposed insured at the time of the application, and this scheme is not discovered until the incontestability period has passed? *See Wood v. New York Life Insurance Co.,* 783 F.2d 990 (11th Cir. 1986) (policy remains contestable). Does the so-called "imposter defense" apply when the insured personally applies for the coverage, but sends an imposter to take the mandatory medical examination? *See Amex Life Insurance Co. v. Superior Court,* 14 Cal. 4th 1231, 930 P.2d 1264, 60 Cal. Rptr. 2d 898 (1997) (policy is incontestable). What if the beneficiary of a policy forges the insured's name on a reinstatement authorization without the insured's authorization? *See North American Co. for Life and Health Insurance v. Rypins,* 29 F. Supp. 2d 619 (N.D. Cal. 1998) (policy is incontestable).

7. *Risks covered versus interests protected.* To this point in this section, the subjects covered—determining death; intentional self-destruction; and incontestability—have focused on what *risks* are covered under the life insurance policy. A different dimension of insurance coverage involves the *interests protected* by a policy. Different kinds of legal issues arise when one asks "who" is protected under the policy, and the remainder of the section will address the most significant ones in life insurance.

[4]   Owners, Beneficiaries, and Assignees

LEMKE v. SCHWARZ
286 N.W.2d 693 (Minn. 1979)

KELLY, JUSTICE.

This is an appeal from a judgment entered in the District Court of St. Louis County. The district court, after a full hearing, ruled that by reason of her status as named beneficiary, defendant, Bernadine Schwarz, was entitled to the entire proceeds of two insurance policies in the name of her deceased husband. Judgment was entered accordingly, and plaintiffs appealed. We reverse.

At the time of his death, decedent was the named insured under the terms of two life insurance policies which listed defendant as the beneficiary. Both policies provided that the insured could from time to time designate a change of beneficiary by filing a written request with the company.

Shortly before his death on September 8, 1975, the insured wrote a letter, entirely in his own handwriting, to his daughter, Debora, one of the plaintiffs herein. The letter was dated September 7, 1975, and postmarked the following day. The letter read in part as follows:

". . . [T]here are a few things that I want you to know & I want you to keep because of legal matters that might arise in the near future. I should have kept a copy of this letter, but I haven't & so it's up to you. Hang on to this because sometimes it takes a long time for things to develop & then you may need some evidence & this letter should be a part of a record."

Decedent then set forth the following provision between quotation marks:

"I hereby decree & make it known to all persons that whatever are my possessions-material things such as shall be known by my wife Bernie Schwarz to be things as housewares, painting and misc. items that I contributed to our household, let it be known that my daughters Debora Schwarz & Denise Lemke (Schwarz) have the right to share and share alike in these items and that my wife Bernie Schwarz, has not one right to withhold these items.

"Also let it be known that I also bequeath to my two daughters, Debora & Denise, all other assets that I have at the time of my death. These assets namely would be to the best of my knowledge at this writing a life insurance policy with Goodwill Industries in the amount of $5,000-a Retirement Benefit with the National Health and Welfare Association-all my retirement benefits plus a death benefit of two years of my salary. Also at the time of this writing & date I have been informed by my brother-in-law Omer Larson, that I am the benefactor of at least $5,000 from the estate of my late, father, Walter Schwarz. This also should be considered a part of my estate & divided equally between my two daughters."

At the conclusion of these provisions, it stated:

"All parts enclosed under the sign of 'marks are to be known as my last will & testament.' Let no one contest my last wishes."

Thereafter, insured concluded this letter as follows:

"Share nothing with Bernie [defendant] because she has not been willing to share her life with me.

"I love you,

Daddy"

This letter did not reach Debora until after she had returned from her father's funeral. After receipt of that letter, plaintiffs retained legal counsel and notified the respective insurance companies, indicating their belief that the insured had intended them to be the beneficiaries on the insurance policies and demanding that no payment be made to anyone until an appropriate resolution had been reached. Both insurance companies subsequently paid the proceeds of the insurance policies to the plaintiffs' attorney to be held in trust pending the resolution of this matter. The insurance companies are not parties to this action.

The district court made no findings respecting the legal effect of the letter which insured sent to his daughter, Debora, nor did it make a finding as to insured's intent in drafting the letter. The court merely ruled that, as the named beneficiary, defendant was entitled to the entire proceeds of both insurance policies.

On this appeal, plaintiffs do not argue that decedent's letter to his daughter constituted a valid will. They do contend, however, that the letter was effective to change the beneficiary on the two policies in question from decedent's wife, Bernadine, the named beneficiary, to decedent's daughters, the plaintiffs herein. We agree.

This court has, in our prior decisions, made it clear that a change of beneficiary may properly be effected in spite of the failure of the insured to comply with each and every policy requirement. *Pabst v. Hesse*, 286 Minn. 33, 173 N.W.2d 925 (1970); *Brown v. Agin*, 260 Minn. 104, 109 N.W.2d 147 (1961). In *Brown v. Agin, supra*, speaking to this issue, we reasoned as follows (260 Minn. 109, 109 N.W.2d 150):

> ". . .Such provisions are for the protection of the insurer, and where, as here, the insurance company has deposited the proceeds of the policy to be paid in accordance with the order of the court, it has waived any defense it might have to the claim of either party."

We therefore determined that in cases such as these equitable principles should control. We additionally adopted a two-pronged test as a guideline for future determinations:

> ". . .(1) whether the insured intended to change the beneficiary and (2) whether he took affirmative action or otherwise did substantially all that he could do to demonstrate that intention without regard to whether he complied with the change-of-beneficiary provisions in the policy." 260 Minn. 109, 109 N.W.2d 151.

In order to utilize the above test, a close examination of the facts before us becomes necessary. Here, the insured had been married three times. At the time of his death, he had been married to defendant for a little more than a year. There was testimony that during the last 6 months of their marriage the relationship between defendant and the insured became progressively worse, to the extent that at one point defendant left her husband and remained separated from him for a period of a week. On the evening prior to his death, defendant informed the insured of her intent to leave him. It was sometime subsequent to this that the insured wrote the letter in question.

Defendant claims that the insured's act of sending the letter to his daughter neither evidences an intent to change beneficiaries nor constitutes a substantial effort to demonstrate that intent. We disagree. The language of the letter expresses the insured's clear and unambiguous intent that his daughters rather than his wife receive the entire proceeds of the policies. It is also apparent that the insured expected and fully intended the letter to have legal signifi-cance.[1]

Defendant maintains that even assuming that the insured had the requisite intent, his subsequent acts were not sufficient to effect the change claimed by the plaintiffs. Defendant suggests that had the insured simultaneously written to his employer or to the insurer or even sent them copies of the original letter, the policy provisions may have been satisfied. It is undisputed that the insured could have changed his mind several times regarding the choice of beneficiary on the life insurance policies. There seems to be, however, little, if any, distinction between writing a letter to the insurer of the change and making an unequivocal statement of such intent in a letter to another, so long as the insurer, for whose benefit the notice requirements exist, is not thereby prejudiced.

Many courts that have required relatively strict compliance with the policy formalities have reasoned that this best effectuates the original intent of the parties and insures that the insured ". . .unequivocally desired to make that change, and that he did not at some time thereafter abandon his purpose by failing to take affirmative steps to carry out his intent." *Allen v. Abrahamson,* 12 Wash. App. 103, 107, 529 P.2d 469, 471 (1974). We do not find this reasoning persuasive. We hold that where an insured has clearly and unam-biguously demonstrated an intent to change the beneficiary on a life insurance policy, this intent should be given effect unless prejudice to the insurer would result. If there exists any confusion as to the insured's intent or conflicting expressions of intent, then the named beneficiary should be entitled to the proceeds. This will avoid the practical difficulties which have troubled some courts.

In the instant case, the trial court made no findings of fact regarding the insured's mental state. However, because the letter written by the insured constitutes the primary evidence on this issue, this court is as able as the trial court to make the ultimate determination.

As we have already stated, we believe that the insured intended to substi-tute his daughters as beneficiaries on his insurance policies in place of his wife. In addition, we find that the insured made affirmative efforts to effect this change and under the circumstances substantially complied with the relevant policy provisions. For the foregoing reasons, we reverse the judgment of the trial court and hold that the plaintiffs are entitled to the proceeds of both policies. *Reversed.*

OTIS, J., took no part in the consideration or decision of this case.

NOTES

1. *Types of interests in life insurance.* There are a number of interests or rights in contracts of life insurance that may be held by different persons or entities. The three main persons or entities, aside from the insurer, are the

---

[1] "Hang on to this because sometimes it takes a long time for things to develop & then you may need some evidence & this letter should be a part of a record."

owner of the policy, the *beneficiary*, and the person whose life is insured, or *cestui que vie* (or simply "CQV"). The earliest forms of life insurance were contracts taken out by the beneficiary on the life of the *cestui que vie*; consequently, the beneficiary held all the ownership rights. Today, the *cestui que vie* most often applies for, and therefore owns, the policy on her own life. Where a person takes out a policy on her own life and makes another the beneficiary, the ownership rights are held by the *cestui que vie* unless otherwise alienated. The beneficiary may be entitled to the proceeds on the death of the *cestui que vie*, but the owner, in the meantime, may change the beneficiary; surrender the policy for any cash value; borrow against the cash surrender value or on the security of the policy; assign the policy in whole or in part; and exercise any other rights under the contract. Thus, the owner has the power to alienate or convey any number of distinct rights or interests to various persons or entities.

2. *Modern policy forms and the right to change beneficiary.* Modern policy forms reserve the right to change beneficiaries. But where that right is waived or otherwise foreclosed under the contract the beneficiary has a vested right to the proceeds upon death, subject to the policy being maintained in force. *See Morton v. United States,* 457 F.2d 750 (4th Cir. 1972).

3. *Attempts to change beneficiary.* Would the attempt to change the beneficiary in *Lemke* be effective under the change of beneficiary provision in the policy in Appendix G? Should courts require that attempts to change beneficiaries meet the exact conditions set out in the policy? Should the subject be approached with the same sanctity as that of wills? The substantial compliance rule with the two-pronged test set out in *Lemke* is the approach favored by a majority of jurisdictions today. *See, e.g., Engelman v. Connecticut General Life Insurance Co.,* 240 Conn. 287, 690 A.2d 882 (1997); *IDS Life Insurance Co. v. Estate of Groshong,* 112 Idaho 847, 736 P.2d 1301 (1987).

Attempts to change a life insurance beneficiary by will have been held void where the policy, as most policies do today, sets out specific procedures for making beneficiary changes and which do not authorize change by that method. *See, e.g., McCarthy v. Aetna Life Insurance Co.,* 92 N.Y.2d 436, 704 N.E.2d 557, 681 N.Y.S.2d 790 (1998); *Stone v. Stephens,* 155 Ohio St. 595, 99 N.E.2d 766 (1951), 25 A.L.R.2d 992 (1952). Is the rationale of these decisions undermined if the jurisdiction adheres to the "substantial compliance" rule outlined in *Lemke? See Rindlaub v. Travelers Insurance Co.,* 119 Ohio App. 77, 196 N.E.2d 602 (Ct. App. 1962). Note that a will, like a life insurance contract, is not operative until the *cestui que vie* dies. Consequently, at the moment of death the original beneficiary is entitled to the proceeds so that the will cannot operate simultaneously to change the beneficiary. This may be a more formidable reason for voiding testamentary attempts to change a beneficiary; some courts have adhered to this reasoning in holding that such an attempt is inherently ineffective. *See Cook v. Cook,* 17 Cal. 2d 639, 111 P.2d 322 (1941).

Lemke involved a writing. Should oral statements ever be deemed sufficient by themselves (i.e., without a writing) to change a beneficiary under the substantial compliance rule? *Compare DeCeglia v. Estate of Colletti,* 265 N.J. Super. 128, 625 A.2d 590 (N.J. Super. Ct. 1993) (insured's oral statements did not accomplish a beneficiary change), with *Bell v. Parker,* 563 So.2d 594 (Miss. 1990) (insured's oral request for change of beneficiary constituted substantial compliance with policy terms requiring request for change to be in writing).

4. *Effect of divorce.* The general rule is that a divorce decree or settlement agreement does not, in and of itself, automatically terminate a spouse's rights as a named beneficiary of a life insurance policy. Instead, courts look for—and drafters of such decrees and agreements must be careful to insert—language which clearly manifests an intent to terminate a beneficiary's interest. As one court explained it, the "manifestation can take the form of either an express renunciation of the expectancy as beneficiary or other language which unmistakenly evidences an intent to waive the expectancy." *Christensen v. Sabad,* 773 P.2d 538, 540 (Colo. 1989) (holding that marital property separation agreement lacked sufficiently clear language to extinguish respondent's expectancy). *See also Ohran v. Sierra Health and Life Insurance Co.,* 111 Nev. 688, 895 P.2d 1321 (1995) (divorce decree did not contain explicit language needed to divest former husband of rights as designated life insurance beneficiary). Thus, with sufficiently clear language, a beneficiary's interest may be effectively terminated by an agreement or court order, and this is true even where there is no reservation in the policy of the right to change the beneficiary or, if there is a right to do so, the beneficiary is never actually changed or is not changed in accordance with the policy provisions after the divorce. *See, e.g., Napper v. Schmeh,* 773 P.2d 531 (Colo. 1989) (en banc); *Beneficial Life Insurance Co. v. Stoddard,* 95 Idaho 628, 516 P.2d 187 (1973), 70 A.L.R.3d 344 (1976); *Larsen v. Northwestern National Life Insurance Co.,* 463 N.W.2d 777 (Minn. Ct. App. 1990). Likewise, the policy owner's right to change a beneficiary may be limited by a divorce decree, property settlement, or other contractual agreement. *See Holt v. Holt,* 995 S.W.2d 68 (Tenn. 1999).

Careful thought needs to be given to how the obligation under any one of these devices may be enforced if there is a breach. In that event, is the contempt power of the court available, or may the court impose a constructive trust or order any unauthorized beneficiary change set aside? Or, is the remedy one for damages only? See Annotation, *Divorce: Provision in Decree that One Party Obtain or Maintain Life Insurance for Benefit of Other Party or Child,* 59 A.L.R.3d 9 (1974) (particularly §§ 18-20, which discuss remedies for enforcement).

5. *Statutory changes in common law rule regarding effect of divorce.* Until recently, only a few states had adopted statutes that affect the rights of the owner of a life insurance policy and the beneficiary upon divorce. These statutes, in effect, treat the beneficiary-spouse as having predeceased the owner-spouse, unless steps are taken at the time of divorce or otherwise to counteract the statutes. *See, e.g.,* Mich. Comp. Laws Ann. § 552.101 (West 1988); Ohio Rev. Code Ann. § 1339.63 (Anderson 1993); Okla. Stat. Ann. tit. 15, § 178 (West 1993 & Supp. 2000); Tex. Fam. Code §§ 7.005 (West 1998). This paucity in legislation has begun to change, however, because the Uniform Probate Code was amended in 1990 to contain a provision that automatically revokes a life insurance spousal beneficiary designation upon divorce unless the insurance policy, a court order, or an agreement of the parties precludes

such a change. The effect of the revocation is to treat the situation as if the former beneficiary-spouse disclaimed the policy benefits. See Uniform Probate Code § 2-804(b) and (d), 8 U.L.A. 23–24 (Supp. 2000). This means that a contingent beneficiary or, in the absence of such, the estate of the owner-spouse would be entitled to the benefits. The life insurance industry was not in favor of including this provision in the UPC. Can you think of any good reasons for their opposition?

6. *ERISA and divorce.* Federal law now governs most employer sponsored insurance benefit programs because ERISA preempts all state law insofar as it may "relate to any employee benefit plan," except for those laws that "regulate insurance." (See note 10 following *Mahler* in § 2.03[4].) Accordingly, a number of federal circuit courts of appeals have held that state law dealing with designation of beneficiaries under ERISA benefit plans has been preempted, including state law dealing with the effect of divorce upon beneficiary designation. The preemption applies to state common law rules discussed in note 4 as well as state statutes discussed in note 5 (both notes above) unless ERISA provides for an exception (discussed below). If state law is preempted, what law governs? Federal circuit courts that have faced this issue have split as to whether ERISA itself supplies the rule of law or whether judges must look to federal common law for the controlling principles. *See Manning v. Hayes,* 212 F.3d 866 (5th Cir. 2000) (describing split of authority; holding that federal common law provides governing rule, which is that "a named ERISA beneficiary may waive his or her entitlement to the proceeds of an ERISA plan providing life insurance benefits, provided that the waiver is explicit, voluntary, and made in good faith").

If a state court enters a judgment, decree, or order (including approval of a property settlement agreement) in a domestic relations proceeding, which would include a divorce, overriding the beneficiary designation or otherwise altering the rights to receive benefits as prescribed in an ERISA plan, such as in an employer provided group life insurance policy, the court action may survive the ERISA preemption. ERISA specifically provides that the preemption-of-state-law clause does not apply to a "qualified domestic relations order," *see* 29 U.S.C. § 1144(7), as defined in 29 U.S.C. §§ 1056(d)(3)(C)(i), (ii), (iv). Consequently, if the court order meets the requirements of a "QDRO," it would not be invalidated by the preemption clause. *See Metropolitan Life Insurance Co. v. Wheaton,* 42 F.3d 1080 (7th Cir. 1994); *Carland v. Metropolitan Life Insurance Co.,* 935 F.2d 1114 (10th Cir.), *cert. denied,* 502 U.S. 1020 (1991). The operative language in the statute refers to the "right to. . .receive. . .benefits payable with respect to a participant under a plan"; it has been held that a decree which merely waives a beneficiary's interest in an ERISA plan is not a QDRO because "it does not require that anyone be maintained as a beneficiary." *See Metropolitan Life Insurance Co. v. Barlow,* 884 F. Supp. 1118, 1122 (E.D. Mich. 1995).

7. *Persons protected under health insurance.* Policies of health insurance and health service contracts can be written for an individual insured (or, more commonly, the employee in a group insurance plan) or for the insured and family members. The latter includes the spouse of the insured (often referred to in policies as the "legal spouse") and dependent children of the spouses.

"Family" also is usually defined to include step-children and foster children who reside in the same household as and are supported by the insured. Children who have reached the age of 19 may be continued under many plans until age 24 if they are full-time students and dependent on the insured for support. Not surprisingly, young adults comprise a significant percentage of the nation's uninsured population.

8. *Domestic partners.* The "legal spouse" requirement has received much attention in recent years. By the literal terminology of the typical policy, non-married partners, such as lovers who reside together or roommates, are not entitled to coverage as dependents, even if the relationship is a longstanding one with considerable economic dependency. But according to the Human Rights Campaign (a Washington, D.C-based gay and lesbian rights organiza-tion), 93 of the five hundred largest U.S. companies and about 3,400 employers nationwide (including nonprofit organizations, universities, and local and state governments) have extended health benefits to domestic partners. See Norihiko Shirouzu, *Gay Couples to Get Benefits at Auto Makers,* Wall St. J., June 9, 2000, at A3. A 1994 study found that fewer than 150 employers nationwide offered domestic partner benefits; it is indisputable that the number has grown significantly in recent years. See Roberto Ceniceros, *Seattle, L.A. pass mandates on partner benefits,* Bus. Ins., Dec. 6, 1999, at 1. On August 1, 2000, the nation's three largest automakers (DaimlerChrylser; Ford; and General Motors) made domestic partner benefits available to their 465,000 U.S. employees. The automakers' programs provided that recipients "must reside in a state where marriage between persons of the same sex is not recognized as a valid marriage, or, if residing in a state which recognizes same-sex unions, enter into such union as recognized by the state." See *Top Auto Firms to Offer Benefits to Gay Partners Workplace,* L.A. Times, June 9, 2000, at A1.

Do such plans have any adverse selection implications? One report indicated that roughly half of all employers who provide coverage to domestic partners limit the coverage to same-sex couples. *Partner Benefits May Not Apply to Heterosexuals,* Minneapolis-St. Paul Star Tribune, June 7, 1996, at 1A. The automakers' programs described above do not apply to unmarried heterosex-ual partners. See *Top Auto Firms, supra.* Is this lawful? Appropriate? Imagine two siblings, each of whom has never married, and both of whom have continued to live in the family residence long after their parents' deaths. Should sibling A be entitled to health insurance coverage as a dependent on the plan provided sibling B where sibling B works? What if sibling B supports both of them by working outside the home, and sibling A works at home by taking care of the family residence?

9. *Eligibility for group coverage.* Contracts for group insurance contain provisions defining who is eligible to take out the coverage. A common provision in contracts covering employees of a particular business excludes coverage for "part-time or temporary" employees. *See Hargraves v. Continental Assurance Co.,* 247 Ark. 965, 448 S.W.2d 942 (1970), 41 A.L.R.3d 1411 (1972). Why would a group insurer want to exclude such employees from coverage? For more details regarding eligibility requirements based on employment status, see Robert H. Jerry, II, Understanding Insurance Law § 122[b] (2d ed. 1996).

DAVIS v. MODERN INDUSTRIAL BANK

279 N.Y. 405, 18 N.E.2d 639 (1939), 135 A.L.R. 1035 (1941)

HUBBS, JUDGE.

Clarence M. Davis, on June 1, 1932, procured from the Prudential Life Insurance Company a $5,000 straight life policy of insurance on his own life, dated that day. His wife, Eleanor H. Davis, was the named beneficiary. The policy contained clauses reserving to the insured the right to change the beneficiary and to assign the policy. The insured, Clarence M. Davis, died October 26, 1936.

The plaintiffs commenced an action against the insurance company to recover the proceeds of the policy. There being other claimants, the insurance company impleaded the several claimants and paid the proceeds of the policy into court to the credit of the action. The respondent Griffiths by answer alleged that the insured, Clarence M. Davis, by an instrument in writing, assigned the policy to him "as his interest may appear" to protect him on account of his indorsement of the assured's note, paid by respondent, upon which there remained due and unpaid to respondent $3,357.25, and which sum respondent contends he became entitled to receive from the proceeds of the policy. There is no claim that the beneficiary paid the premiums on the policy or that she was named as beneficiary pursuant to the terms of a contract.

The plaintiffs moved for summary judgment, which was granted at Special Term, and defendant Griffiths' counterclaim was dismissed. The Appellate Division reversed and granted summary judgment in favor of defendant Griffiths for the amount of his counterclaim. The facts are not in dispute. Only a very interesting question of law is involved. That question is whether the rights of the beneficiary named in the policy are superior to the rights of the assignee of the policy, the assignment having been taken from the insured in good faith for a valuable consideration but without the knowledge or consent of the beneficiary named in the policy.

The right to change the beneficiary named in the policy was reserved by the insured; also the right to assign the policy. The policy provided:

> "If the right to change the Beneficiary has been reserved, the Insured may at any time while this Policy is in force, by written notice to the Company at its Home Office, change the Beneficiary or Beneficiaries under this Policy, such change to be subject to the rights of any previous assignee and to become effective only when a provision to that effect is endorsed on or attached to the Policy by the Company, whereupon all rights of the former Beneficiary or Beneficiaries shall cease."

> "Any assignment of this Policy must be in writing, and the Company shall not be deemed to have such knowledge of such assignment unless

the original or a duplicate thereof is filed at the Home Office of the Company. The Company will not assume any responsibility for the validity of an assignment."

It is not questioned that the assignment in question was in writing and duly filed with the company at its home office as required by the terms of the policy. The fact that the beneficiary named in the policy was the wife of the insured does not affect the question here involved. It is urged by the appellants that the only interest taken by respondent Griffiths under the assignment was that which the assignor, the insured, possessed, i.e., to have his estate take under the policy in case of the death of the beneficiary before the death of the insured; also the right to appoint a new beneficiary in case the insured survived the beneficiary, or to change the beneficiary in the exact method provided in the policy. The position of the respondent is that the written assignment conveyed to him an interest in the proceeds of the policy sufficient to require payment to him of the amount due him from the insured.

Concededly an assignment of a policy by the insured will not convey any interest as against the beneficiary named in the policy unless the right to change the beneficiary is reserved therein. It makes no difference what the interest of the beneficiary is denominated, as a vested interest or by some other name. In any event it is such an interest that the beneficiary cannot be deprived of it without consent unless such right is reserved in the policy. That is the law in every jurisdiction in this country except Wisconsin. *Boehmer v. Kalk,* 155 Wis. 156, 144 N.W. 182, 49 L.R.A., N.S., 487; Richards on Insurance (4th ed.) p. 557. That rule is known as the vested interest rule. It was because the law had become settled to the effect that an insured could not change the beneficiary or assign a policy that the insurance companies, in answer to an extensive demand therefor, provided in some policies that the insured reserved the right to change the beneficiary and to assign the policy. (31 Yale Law Journal, p. 358.) The very purpose of reserving the right to change the beneficiary and to assign the policy was to overcome the old rule that the beneficiary had a valuable interest which could not be incumbered or changed by the insured without the consent of the beneficiary. When those privileges are reserved in an attempt by an insured to retain control of the policy for which he has paid, the courts have determined that the interests of the parties are affected in either of two ways.

The first view is that the insured takes no rights in the policy during the life of the beneficiary; that he has merely the power to divest the named beneficiary of his rights and to vest those rights in a new beneficiary; that he has power only to revoke the appointment already made and make a new appointment, such power to be exercised only in the manner provided in the policy. That rule is sometimes spoken of as the New Jersey rule. *Sullivan v. Maroney,* 77 N.J.Eq. 565, 78 A. 150. The second view is that the insured, by reserving the right to change the beneficiary and to assign the policy, retains the beneficial ownership of the policy during life, and that the naming of a beneficiary constitutes only an instruction to the company to pay at his death to the person named unless such instruction is changed by the insured. Under this view of the law the beneficiary has a mere expectancy or vested interest subject to be divested or an inchoate right depending entirely upon the will of the insured. The beneficiary has no interest in the form provided in the policy for assigning it, that being a provision inserted for the benefit of the company which it can refuse to assert, sometimes improperly called a waiver. See Richards on Insurance (4th ed.) p. 565.

There is no controlling decision in this jurisdiction on the question here involved. In various opinions there may be found statements which indicate conflicting views. We are at liberty, therefore, to adopt the view which seems to us to be supported by the best reasons . . . .

The leading textbook writers and writers of law review articles favor the view last expressed.

It is a matter of common knowledge that since the depression of 1929 the use of life insurance policies as collateral upon which to raise much needed funds has become more common. *Cf.* "Power of Pledgee of Life Insurance Policy to Exercise Surrender Options," 48 Yale L.J. 315.

"It is desirable that the insured should have the opportunity of making free commercial use of his life insurance as available property for it may often be convenient to secure money by loan or otherwise upon it." Richards on Insurance (4th ed.) p. 678.

. . . .

It seems to us that upon principle as well as weight of authority the Appellate Division has reached the correct conclusion and that the insured, having reserved the right to change the beneficiary and assign the policy, did all that the law required him to do to constitute a valid transfer of the proceeds of the policy to the assignee, to the extent of the indebtedness thereby secured, in the absence of objection on the part of the company. . . .

From an every day, practical standpoint it is desirable to hold that an assignee of a policy containing a clause permitting a change of beneficiary and an assignment of the policy secures a right in the proceeds of the policy superior to the rights of the named beneficiary. If an assignee, in the absence of the consent of the beneficiary, does not obtain such right it will be practically impossible for an insured to borrow on a policy in time of need of financial aid in those cases where compliance with the form prescribed in the policy cannot be followed. No bank or individual would be likely to lend on the security of a policy where the right to enforce the reduction of the security to cash would only mature in case the insured outlived the beneficiary, and where the continued life of the policy depends upon the payment of the annual premium. As stated in the case of Matter of Whiting, D.C., 3 F.2d 440, 441: "To hold that the beneficiary of such policy has a vested interest would be tantamount to destroying the 'changed beneficiary' provisions of the policy itself." *Cf.* Vance on Insurance (2d ed.), 646; 48 Yale L.J. 315.

That the question is a practical one is illustrated by the large number of decisions involving the issue.

The judgment should be affirmed, with costs.

CRANE, CHIEF JUDGE (dissenting).

The policy as stated in the opinion provided: ". . . such change to be subject to the rights of any previous assignee and to become effective only when a provision to that effect is endorsed on or attached to the Policy by the Company, whereupon all rights of the former Beneficiary or Beneficiaries shall cease." The opinion fails to state that the assignee failed to procure the indorsement required to make the assignment effective. Judge HUBBS states that the indorsement is for the benefit of the company and may be waived. If this be so then it rests arbitrarily with the insurance company whether the beneficiary or assignee be paid. The better law, in my judgment, is to take agreements as they are written and made by the parties. Anybody reading the clear language, that no assignment is to be effective until the assignment is indorsed on or attached to the policy by the company, would naturally think that it meant what it said.

LEHMAN, O'BRIEN, LOUGHRAN, and FINCH, JJ., concur with HUBBS, J.

CRANE, C.J., dissents in opinion in which RIPPEY, J., concurs.

Judgment affirmed.

NOTES

1. *Types of assignments.* Where the policy owner intends an absolute assignment of the policy, i.e., all ownership interests, the assignee is entitled to exercise all rights thereunder and is responsible for maintaining the policy in force. It is not always the case, however, that an absolute assignment is intended. As the court mentions in *Davis,* it is not uncommon for the owner to assign a policy as collateral or as security for a loan. In cases of collateral assignment, should the assignee receive the entire policy proceeds upon the death of the *cestui que vie* or just the amount outstanding on the debt which is secured by the assignment? What if there is nothing on the face of the assignment to indicate it is merely to secure a debt? In *Boyle v. Crimm,* 363 Mo. 731, 740, 253 S.W.2d 149, 155 (1952), the court was faced with this question and the argument that parol evidence could not be introduced to vary the terms of the written assignment. The court held that the assignee was entitled only to the amount of the debt, quoting with approval from various sources:

> "The majority of courts at the present time, however, are prone to look with reluctance upon absolute assignments and hold that if the assignment, though absolute in form, was intended only as collateral security, it will have only such effect. Thus, one having an equitable claim may show by parol that an apparently absolute assignment was intended as security, and such showing, whether demonstrated by written agreement or parol evidence, will be conclusive. And such evidence is admissible though contrary to the clear and unambiguous language of the assignment." 2 Appleman, Insurance Law & Practice, Sec. 1312, pp. 759–761. "And it has also been held that the purpose of the written assignment may be shown by parol, although the assignment is absolute in terms." 2 Cooley's Briefs on Insurance, 2d Ed., p. 1839. "It is generally considered that parol evidence is admissible where it is offered, not for the purpose of varying the terms of a written contract or instrument, but for the purpose of explaining and showing

the true nature and character of the transaction evidenced thereby
. . . ." 32 C.J.S., Evidence, § 1015, p. 1037, citing *Service Purchasing
Co. v. Brennan,* 226 Mo. App. 110, 42 S.W.2d 39.

Where the assignment states on its face that it is an absolute assignment,
should parol evidence be admissible to show a contrary intent? Is this different
from any other written instrument governed by the parol evidence rule?

Recall that assignments can also raise insurable interest questions. These
were considered in § 2.02[3], *supra.*

2. *Modern policy provisions.* Examine the provisions with regard to transfer
of ownership and assignments in the policy in Appendix G. Will these efforts
help eliminate problems over the nature or extent of assignments?

3. *Insurer's risk of paying wrong person.* Even though modern policy forms
attempt to protect the insurer that in good faith pays a beneficiary when there
is a superior, but unknown, right outstanding in an assignee, the insurer still
may end up paying twice under certain circumstances. In *American West Life
Insurance Co. v. Hooker,* 622 P.2d 775 (Utah 1980), the *cestui que vie* assigned
the policy in question to his then–wife in accordance with the contract terms.
She was already the beneficiary of the policy. Later the insurer advised the
cestui que vie that he could change the beneficiary to his second wife, which
he did relying on the insurer's representation. Upon the *cestui que vie*'s death,
the insurer paid the policy proceeds to the second wife, but subsequently was
held liable to the first wife for the same amount because of the assignment
to her. The insurer was denied any right of reimbursement from the second
wife on the basis that the insurer was estopped to deny that the change in
beneficiary was effective. If the insurer had paid the first wife initially, would
it also have to pay the second wife?

4. *Terminal illnesses, "viatical settlements," and accelerated benefits.* During
the early 1980s, largely as a result of the onset of the AIDS epidemic, some
individuals started businesses that offer to provide immediate cash payments
to terminally ill owners of life insurance policies in an amount less than the
expected death benefit in exchange for an assignment of the right to the policy
proceeds. Depending on the insured's life expectancy, the cash payment might
range anywhere from fifty to eighty percent of the expected death benefit. The
market ebbed somewhat in the mid-1980s; observers attributed this to
unanticipated medical developments which extended the life expectancies of
terminally ill AIDS patients, which reduced the profits of assignees of the
policies. In the early 1990s, the market again saw significant growth, particularly with respect to non-terminally ill insureds who, no longer having a need
for life insurance to protect against economic loss, were solicited to assign their
policies to an investor rather than to allow the policy to lapse. See Barry A.
Wilkinson, *New Market Ripe for Fraud,* Best's Review-Life/Health Insurance
Edition, Oct 1, 1999, at 86. If you were the insurance commissioner in your
state, would you be concerned about viatical settlements and, if so, why? Do
you see any risks to insureds from these sort of arrangements? Is there
anything wrong with an insured wanting to get present value from a death
benefit she does not need and will not be able to enjoy?

In 1993, the National Association of Insurance Commissioners promulgated
the Viatical Settlements Model Act which regulates any viatical settlement

business in an enacting state by requiring that the business be licensed and settlement contracts approved by the insurance regulator. The Act requires certain disclosures regarding benefit calculations and ordinarily regulates the amount of proceeds payable to the *cestui que vie* through a formula that references a stated percentage of the person's income at the time of disability or by resort to a schedule of benefits based on the nature of the disability. In addition, the regulator has the power to examine the financial aspects of the business. As of 1999, 24 states had substantially adopted the model. See IV NAIC, VIATICAL SETTLEMENTS MODEL ACT, Model Laws, Regulations & Guidelines 697-1 (1999).

More recently, a number of insurance companies have added a rider to their policies that allow, under certain conditions, a terminally ill insured to receive a percentage of the policy's benefits prior to death. Eligibility for accelerated benefits is typically triggered by a medical condition that limits the insured's life expectancy to two or less years, a condition requiring extraordinary medical intervention (*e.g.*, through an organ transplant or continuous life support), a condition requiring lifetime institutionalization of the insured, and specified illnesses or conditions that have one or more of these characteristics (*e.g.*, AIDS, end-stage renal failure, severe brain injury, etc.). For more discussion of viatical arrangements and state regulation of them, see Miriam R. Albert, *Selling Death Short: The Regulatory and Policy Implications of Viatical Settlements*, 61 Alb. L. Rev. 1013 (1998).

5. *Creditors' rights to life insurance.* It also should be noted that many states have statutes, either as part of the insurance laws or as part of the exemption laws, which protect various interests in life insurance, and sometimes related types of insurance such as disability insurance, from the reach of creditors. However, the content of these statutes varies widely. Compare Ariz. Rev. Stat. Ann. § 33-1126(A)(1) (2000); Tex. Ins. Code Ann. art. 21.22 (West 1981); Vt. Stat. Ann. tit. 12, § 2740 (1993 & Supp. 1999); and Wash. Rev. Code Ann. §§ 48.18.400-.430 (West 1999). Exemptions for life insurance also exist under the bankruptcy laws. See Robert H. Jerry, II, Understanding Insurance Law § 52A[d](1)-(3) (2d ed. 1996).

[5]   Disqualification of Beneficiaries

PRUDENTIAL INSURANCE COMPANY OF AMERICA v. ATHMER

178 F.3d 473 (7th Cir.), cert. denied, 120 S. Ct. 342 (1999)

POSNER, Chief Judge.

A pair of insurance companies brought this interpleader action to determine who should receive the proceeds of two life insurance policies owned by a man who was murdered by his wife. The contenders are the victim's natural daughter, and the murderess's natural son and sister. Upon stipulated facts, the district judge rendered judgment for the latter two, and the daughter appeals.

Kevin Spann, a soldier in the U.S. Army, was the insured. Prudential had issued him a life insurance policy pursuant to the Servicemen's Group Life Insurance Act of 1965 (SGLI), 38 U.S.C. §§ 1965 et seq., for $200,000 in 1992 when he was stationed in Germany. The policy named Spann's wife, Gina Spann, as primary beneficiary and Gina's natural son, Steven Hill, as contingent or secondary beneficiary. Steven was 13 and had been living with Kevin and Gina throughout the eleven years of their marriage. The other policy, which was for $100,000, had been issued in 1994, also in Germany, by Boston Mutual. This policy also named Gina as primary beneficiary, but it named her sister, Betty Jo Pierce, rather than Steven, as the contingent beneficiary, and it was not issued under SGLI. Neither policy mentioned Chrystal Athmer, Kevin Spann's natural daughter. He had never lived with her or even acknowledged the relationship, which was established by DNA testing after his death. In his will Spann devised his estate to Steven, describing him as "my son."

At the time of his death in 1997, Spann was a permanent resident of Illinois but was stationed in Georgia. His wife had him murdered there by her 18-year-old lover and three of his 16-year old pals. She pleaded guilty to the murder and was sentenced to life in prison without parole plus five additional years (as the district judge judiciously put it, "the State of Georgia even tacked an additional five years onto that already lengthy sentence"). She no longer has custody of her son. In fact, as Steven's lawyer explained without contradiction, "the whole family is estranged from her. The sister [Betty Jo Pierce] didn't have anything to do with her. They've been trying to get Kevin away from her for years. Gina is somewhere else." The sister is Steven's legal guardian, and has instituted a proceeding to adopt him; neither was complicit in Kevin Spann's murder. Gina is conceded to be disqualified from taking anything under the life insurance policies. The question is whether Steven and his aunt are also disqualified. The district judge held not.

There is an initial issue, not adequately dealt with by the parties or the district judge, concerning choice of law. The insurance policies were issued in Germany to a citizen of Illinois. We assume that Kevin Spann was a citizen of Illinois at the time because he was when he died and because the policies list an Illinois address as his permanent mailing address; on the special rules governing the domicile of members of the armed forces, see Restatement (Second) of Conflicts § 17, comment d and illustration 1 (1971). The beneficiaries named in the life insurance policies, Steven and his aunt, are (and, we assume, were) also citizens of Illinois. But the controversy over entitlement to the proceeds was precipitated by a murder in Georgia.

The choice of law issue must be analyzed separately for each policy. The cases say or imply that when a question relating to the interpretation and administration of an insurance policy issued under the authority of the servicemen's insurance statute arises that is not answered by the statute itself, then as with other government contracts, the answer is to be supplied by federal common law. Since the concept of "federal common law" is nebulous when a statute is in the picture, it might be better to jettison the concept in that context and say simply that in filling gaps left by Congress in a federal program the courts seek to effectuate federal policies. SGLI is a federal program; in fact, technically the government rather than the serviceman is the policyholder. 38 U.S.C. § 1966. The government's concern with beneficiary issues is shown by SGLI's detailed provisions concerning who the beneficiary is if the policy doesn't say, 38 U.S.C. § 1970(a), although the contingency of a beneficiary's murdering the insured is not addressed. As we have both a government contract and a federal statute (we might have the government contract yet only a procedural issue not governed by a statute, or at least by the statute authorizing the contract), the case for using federal law to answer the question of who is to receive the proceeds of the insurance policy is compelling.

Often a court asked to fill a gap in a federal statute will do so by borrowing a state's common law, because in most areas of the law state common law is more highly developed than federal. But borrowing state law would be a mistake in the case of soldiers' life insurance policies. Frequently as in this case the policy is issued wherever the soldier happens to be stationed when thoughts of mortality assail him. Although soldiers generally designate a U.S. state as their domicile, their connection with that state is often tenuous until retirement. It would be arbitrary to subject issues arising under the policy to the law of a particular state. Better that these policies should be governed by a uniform set of rules untethered to any particular jurisdiction. Congress's desire for uniformity is reflected in the statute's detailed provision mentioned earlier regarding who shall receive the proceeds if a beneficiary is not named.

The principle that no person shall be permitted to benefit from the consequences of his or her wrongdoing has long been applied to disqualify murderers from inheriting from their victims, whether the route of inheritance is a will, an intestacy statute, or a life insurance policy. *E.g., Mutual Life Ins. Co. v. Armstrong,* 117 U.S. 591, 600, 6 S.Ct. 877, 29 L.Ed. 997 (1886); *Riggs v. Palmer,* 115 N.Y. 506, 22 N.E. 188 (N.Y.1889); *Swietlik v. United States,* 779 F.2d 1306 (7th Cir.1985); see annotations at 25 A.L.R.4th 787 (1981 & 1998 Supp.), 27 A.L.R.3d 794 (1970 & 1997 Supp.). It is undoubtedly an implicit provision of the Servicemen's Group Life Insurance Act of 1965, and it disqualifies Gina Spann from receiving any of the proceeds of Kevin's SGLI policy, even though she is the primary beneficiary named in it.

The usual consequence when a primary beneficiary disclaims or is forced to disclaim an interest under an insurance policy, will, pension plan, or other such instrument is that the contingent beneficiary takes in the place of the primary one. And this is the approach that a majority of courts take when the beneficiary is disqualified by reason of having murdered his benefactor. *E.g., Lee v. Aylward,* 790 S.W.2d 462 (Mo.1990); *Spencer v. Floyd,* 30 Ark.App. 230, 785 S.W.2d 60 (Ark.App.1990); *Seidlitz v. Eames,* 753 P.2d 775 (Colo.App.1987); *National Home Life Assurance Co. v. Patterson,* 746 P.2d 696 (Okl.App.1987). (There is a slew of minority rules, see Annot., 26 A.L.R.2d 987 (1952 & 1998 Supp.); Lee R. Russ & Thomas F. Segalla, Couch on Insurance, § 62:19 (3d ed.1997)—which is a good reason for having a uniform federal rule for SGLI policies.) We take it, although the case law is sparse, that if the contingent beneficiary is himself a wrongdoer and his wrongdoing contributed to the death of his benefactor, as where the contingent beneficiary is the accomplice of the primary beneficiary in the benefactor's murder, the same rule that disqualifies the primary beneficiary disqualifies the contingent beneficiary. *In re Estate of Vallerius,* 259 Ill.App.3d 350, 196 Ill.Dec. 341, 629 N.E.2d 1185, 1188 (Ill.App.1996). We are surprised that *Reynolds v. American-Amicable Life Ins. Co.,* 591 F.2d 343 (5th Cir.1979) (per curiam), allowed an accessory after the fact to inherit.

But this leaves the case in which the primary beneficiary may derive an indirect benefit if the contingent beneficiary (assumed to be completely innocent) is allowed to obtain the benefits. *Estate of Vallerius* is the plainest illustration: the grandchildren murdered their grandmother, who had left her estate to their (innocent) mother, who died, having devised her estate, now including the grandmother's money, to her children—the murderers. They were, of course, barred from taking under their mother's will. Subtler cases of indirect benefit can be imagined. Suppose that Steven Hill (the murderess's son and victim's stepson) were an adult and he promised that he would use the life insurance proceeds to pay for his mother's lawyer or to buy her books or other goods that the prison would allow her to receive. Or suppose that Steven needed an expensive operation that Kevin could not or would not pay for and Gina killed Kevin so that the proceeds of his life insurance could be used to pay for the operation; or that Gina had been given a short prison sentence and Kevin had promised to support her in style out of the life insurance proceeds when she was released. The lawyer for Steven and Betty Jo argued to us that the fulfillment of such a promise would be barred by the "murdering heir" rule itself, but that is not correct. The rule forbids the murderer to take under the will or other instrument; it does not impress on the benefits a kind of reverse constructive trust placing them forever beyond the murderer's reach.

These cases can be multiplied indefinitely. Some states have decided that the best way to deal with them and make utterly certain that the murderer does not profit from his crime is to disqualify all the murderer's relatives, except his or her children if they are also the victim's children. *E.g.,* Ga. Stat. 53-4-64(c); *Crawford v. Coleman,* 726 S.W.2d 9 (Tex.1987). Under that rule, Steven and Betty Jo would be disqualified. We need not decide whether that is or should be the federal common law rule governing murders by beneficiaries of Servicemen's Group Life Insurance policies, because Chrystal, the daughter, the party who would benefit from such a rule, does not advocate a uniform federal rule. She argues for the rule of the insured's domicile, here Illinois. Steven and Betty Jo argue for a uniform federal rule, not a borrowed state rule—a uniform rule that does not cut out the murderer's bloodline, that instead requires proof that the murderer will in fact benefit if the contingent beneficiary is allowed to take in the murderer's place. We could turn the tables on Steven and Betty Jo and say, yes, we agree with you that a uniform federal rule is desirable, but we don't like your rule; we like the rule that would entitle the natural daughter to a victory in this suit. But we do not reverse judgments in civil cases on the basis of grounds not argued by the appellant at any stage of the litigation— grounds, therefore, that the appellee had no opportunity to meet. *See,* for the general principle, *Cosgrove v. Bartolotta,* 150 F.3d 729, 735 (7th Cir.1998), and for its application to murdering-heir cases, *Reynolds v. American Amicable Life Ins. Co., supra,* 591 F.2d at 344.

The life insurance policy issued by Boston Mutual was not issued under the aegis of the Servicemen's Group Life Insurance Act, and so federal common law is not in the picture. The choice of law rule of the forum state, that is, Illinois, must therefore be used to determine which jurisdiction shall supply the rule of decision. In the case of life insurance, that rule picks the law of the state where the insured was domiciled when the policy was applied for, hence in this case Illinois, unless some other state has a more significant relationship. That at any rate is the rule of the Second Restatement, see section 192 (and note that comment b to that section confirms Kevin Spann's status as an Illinois domiciliary), which Illinois follows. But one could argue, consistent with the principle—which is a principle of Illinois law—that the law of the place of the tort is the presumptive or default rule of choice of law in tort cases, that the law of Georgia should govern this case instead. For it was a tort, namely the wrongful death that Gina Spann inflicted on her husband, that is the basis for refusing to enforce the contract as written. Georgia has the paramount interest in deciding whether to refuse to enforce a contract as a means of increasing the punishment for a murder committed in Georgia. But just to show how complicated choice of law analysis can be, we point out that arguably what is at stake in "murdering heir" cases is donative intent rather than deterrence. Deterrence of murdering heirs is a legitimate concern, given the number of murders by spouses and children (more than 1,000 in 1997, see FBI, Uniform Crime Reports for the United States 1997 21 (1998) (tab.2.12)), but could be achieved by imposing on the murderer a fine equal to the amount he inherited from his victim. Even so, the victim would not have made the murderer his heir (or the beneficiary of his life insurance policy) had he known what the future held. And if this is the important thing it would point us back toward Illinois.

Neither side argues for the application of German law. Although that is where the contracts were made, the parties to the contracts had only the most adventitious connection to Germany and it is highly doubtful that they contemplated the application of German law to any dispute under the policy that might arise. The choice is thus between Illinois and Georgia.

Both states have "slayer statutes," but they are not the same. The Illinois statute forbids the murderer to "receive any property, benefit or other interest by reason of the death [of the murderer's victim], whether as heir, legatee, beneficiary. . .or in any other capacity," and provides that if the murderer is disqualified, the property, etc. shall "pass as if the person causing the death died before the decedent." 755 ILCS 5/2-6. Judicial interpretation has established that the statute is applicable to life insurance. Georgia has a statute that deals expressly with murder by the beneficiary of a life insurance policy, and provides that in such a case the property goes to the secondary beneficiary if one is named in the policy. Ga.Code Ann. § 33-25-13. So the Illinois statute defines "benefit" broadly enough to encompass cases of indirect benefit such as we posited earlier, while the Georgia statute, read literally, allows no room for such consideration. This creates a tension with Georgia's will statute, which, as noted earlier, absolutely excludes the murderer's family, provided there is no blood relationship between them and the victim.

Kevin Spann's daughter pitches her appeal with regard to both policies on cases interpreting the Illinois statute, and since those cases do not carry the day for her, we have no need to delve into Georgia case law, and anyway we cannot find any relevant cases. The daughter relies primarily on a case in which an Illinois court refused to allow the children of a convicted murderess to take under the victim's will. *In re Estate of Mueller*, 275 Ill.App.3d 128, 211 Ill.Dec. 657, 655 N.E.2d 1040 (Ill.App.1995). As in this case, the victim was the murderess's husband and the children were hers, not his. But Chrystal has missed the real significance of *Estate of Mueller*. What it shows is that Illinois does not cut off the murderess's bloodline regardless of circumstances. The court thought it important that the murderess had already been released from prison and had custody of one of her children (the other was an adult) and that the marriage had been a sham and the children had not lived with her husband. *Id.* at 1043, 1046. It was quite likely in these circumstances that the murderess would benefit if her husband's bequest went to the children; indeed, it was almost certain so far as the bequest to the younger child was concerned, since she was living with her murderous mom.

Estate of Mueller suggests that Illinois "murdering heir" case law requires the trial court to make a factual determination whether allowing a relative of the murderer to take in the place of the murderer is likely to confer a significant benefit on him. *Estate of Vallerius*, discussed earlier, is consistent with that approach, and we cannot find any contrary precedent in Illinois. Which is not to say that it is necessarily the best approach. Rejected by many states, *see, e.g.*, *Lee v. Aylward, supra*, 790 S.W.2d at 463; *Neff v. Massachusetts Mutual Life Ins. Co.*, 158 Ohio St. 45, 107 N.E.2d 100 (Ohio 1952); *In re Estate of Benson*, 548 So.2d 775, 777 (Fla.App.1989), it requires an inherently speculative judgment about the future and an investigation of family relations quite likely to be of Faulknerian opacity, but it is Illinois's approach and we are bound by it. It is the approach followed by the district judge, and, as should be apparent from the stipulated facts sketched at the outset of this opinion, the conclusion he reached cannot be adjudged clearly erroneous. It is exceedingly unlikely that Gina Spann will ever benefit significantly from the proceeds of her husband's life insurance policies in the hands of her son and her sister.

But we do not think the judge was right to place any weight on the tenuousness of Chrystal's claim to any place in her father's affections. The question of indirect benefit to the murderer is the focus of inquiry under Illinois law as we understand it and it is unaffected by the victim's affection for the person who will take under the will or the insurance policy if the named beneficiary is disqualified. The "person" could be the state under an escheat statute, so far as anything to do with the policy behind Illinois's murdering-heir rule is concerned. But we do not think the judge's decision would have been different had he ignored the affective dimensions of Chrystal's relationship with her father; his emphasis was quite properly on the remoteness of Gina's prospects of ever deriving any benefit from the life insurance policies.

Affirmed.

CARTER v. CARTER

88 So. 2d 153 (Fla. 1956)

THORNAL, JUSTICE.

[Hunter J. Carter, Jr. was shot and killed by his wife, Ruby J. Carter. Hunter's life was insured by the Equitable Life Assurance Society of the United States under a group policy, and Ruby was named as beneficiary. Ruby was tried on a charge of second degree murder, and was acquitted. She earlier had pled guilty to the charge of manslaughter, but was allowed to withdraw the plea to go to trial on the murder charge, which turned out to be good judgment on her part. The Equitable filed an interpleader action against Ruby, Hunter's father, and Hunter's estate to determine who was entitled to the proceeds. Ruby claimed entitlement to the proceeds under the reasoning that her acquittal established that "the killing was clearly not felonious." The father claimed that Ruby was disqualified and that he as a "surviving parent" was designated by the policy as the successive beneficiary. The administratrix of the estate claimed that Ruby was a surviving, albeit disqualified beneficiary who held the proceeds in trust for the benefit of the estate. Ruby moved for summary judgment, and the trial judge denied her motion, decreeing that the "issues will be made up to determine by a *preponderance of the evidence* whether the claimant wife feloniously killed her husband." Ruby sought review of this order by petition for certiorari.

On review, the court rejected Ruby's position that the acquittal established her right to proceeds:] . . . . we conclude the initial aspect of our problem by adhering to the rule that since a wrongdoer will not be permitted to profit by his own wrong, the beneficiary of a life insurance policy will not be permitted to receive the proceeds of a policy on the life of one whom he unlawfully and intentionally killed.

By the order under review, the trial judge decreed that the issues in this cause would be decided by a "preponderance of the evidence". The petitioner insists that the verdict of acquittal in her trial on the charge of second degree murder is admissible in this civil action to preclude any consideration of her guilt in the homicide of her husband. This court is committed to the rule that the verdict and judgment in a criminal proceeding are not admissible in a civil proceeding as evidence of the guilt or innocence of a party to the civil cause. The rule is not without some exceptions, for example, under Section 731.31, Florida Statutes, F.S.A., where the ultimate fact of conviction of murder is a condition precedent to denying inheritance to one entitled to inherit. The instant case, however, is not within any of the exceptions and we agree with the trial judge that the verdict and judgment acquitting the petitioner in the criminal action is not admissible in evidence in this case.

The respondents on the other hand contend that the felonious nature of the killing was established by the petitioner's plea of guilty to manslaughter which was withdrawn in the criminal case. Consistent with the rule that the judgment of acquittal is not admissible, we do not feel that the plea of guilty to manslaughter, which was withdrawn, is admissible as evidence against the petitioner in this civil action. It could hardly be fairly contended that a defendant in a criminal proceeding should be charged with the pleadings on some obviously tactical maneuver on the criminal side of the court and at the same time be denied the benefit of the judgment and verdict in her favor. The issues in this civil case, as the trial judge ruled, should be decided on the basis of the preponderance of the evidence produced in this case entirely exclusive of the record in the criminal proceeding. This likewise has been the rule in similar cases in other courts.

The record before us reveals nothing at all with reference to the facts that produced the homicide. However, if at the trial a preponderance of the evidence should establish the fact that the homicide was intentional and unlawful in nature and therefore was without the purifying effect of excuse or justification, the petitioner insofar as this cause is concerned would be confronted by the rule heretofore announced that a person will not be permitted to profit by his own wrong. If, however, the evidence preponderates in favor of justification or excuse, an example of which would be self-defense, accident or insanity, then there would be no area for the application of the rule that would prevent her recovery. The burden of proof in the first instance will rest on the party who alleges that the killing was intentional and unlawful. The order of the Chancellor provided that a preponderance of the evidence would govern whether the claimant-wife "feloniously killed" her husband. By the expression "feloniously killed" in this particular type of situation, we understand the Chancellor to have reference to an "unlawful and intentional" killing. As so construed, we find no objection to the use of the word "feloniously". It is altogether appropriate to permit the establishment of these facts by a preponderance of the evidence which is the degree of proof required in civil cases, for the perfectly obvious reason that in a criminal proceeding, which imposes upon the State the burden of proving guilt beyond a reasonable doubt, a jury, being conscious that it is the custodian of the life and liberty of an accused is often apt to emphasize in its thinking extraneous facts and circumstances that are allowed to mitigate the severe penalties of the criminal law. These misplaced emphases cannot be permitted to influence the decision in a civil proceeding where the rights of the parties are evaluated in an entirely different atmosphere undisturbed by those invisible and intangible cross-currents that we all know oftentimes subconsciously influence the judgment of the criminal court jury.

Finally, we are confronted with a decision as to the ultimate recipient of the proceeds of the insurance money here involved in the event that it should be determined that the petitioner is not entitled thereto. The trial judge decided that the father of the deceased should receive the proceeds, there being no surviving children, and the father being next in order of designated priority. The respondent, Clara Brown, as administratrix of the estate of the deceased, claims the proceeds and the petitioner says that even though she is precluded from receiving the insurance as a designated beneficiary, nevertheless, if the money goes to the estate then she is entitled to receive it as a beneficiary of her husband's estate.

Although the problem is not without difficulty, we are of the view that the trial judge again ruled correctly. . . . .

. . . . There is sound reason for this position [i.e., that "the beneficiary next in priority to the excluded beneficiary should receive the proceeds of the policy in preference to the estate of the deceased"]. Although obviously not a will, the beneficiary clause of a life insurance policy is in some measure analogous in principle to the disposition of one's estate by will. It is usually ambulatory. It is almost always donative, and in a sense it is testamentary in character in that payment is customarily contingent upon the death of the insured. In view of the nature of the beneficiary clause, it would appear to be appropriate in construing it to endeavor to give effect to the intent of the insured if it is possible to do so without doing violence to the expressed language of the policy.

Some of the writers have undertaken to resolve the problem by declaring that the primary beneficiary becomes the trustee of a constructive trust and holds the proceeds for the use and benefit of the beneficiary next in priority. We think it unnecessary to complicate the problem with involved trust principles. It is perfectly clear that it was the intent of this decedent that if his widow could not receive the insurance, then it would go to his parents in the event that he had no children. While in this case we cannot conclude that the petitioner would be relegated to a status of one civilly dead, we can with safety conclude that when the policy provided for the distribution of the proceeds to various contingent beneficiaries if there was no designated beneficiary "surviving at the death" of the insured, the language was intended to mean a beneficiary entitled to receive the proceeds. Undoubtedly, the deceased never contemplated that he would be killed by his wife, if he was. Certainly, if he had so contemplated, he would not have encouraged the act by establishing a reward in the form of a policy of insurance on his life.

We must assume that the word "beneficiary" as used in a life insurance policy comprehends beneficiary in its broadest legal aspect and in that sense it necessarily must be considered as having reference to the survival of a beneficiary eligible to take. Admittedly, there are those who apply a rule of strict construction to such provisions and by so doing arrive at the conclusion that the words "beneficiary surviving at the death" of the insured mean just exactly that, without the implication of the additional inference of an eligible beneficiary and that if the designated beneficiary survives but becomes ineligible by operation of law then the members of the various successive classes are prevented from taking because of the "survival" of the designated beneficiary. Under this rule the proceeds of the policy would go to the estate of the deceased. . . .

We prefer to adhere to what we consider to be the better rule which is the one that appears to give effect to the intent of the insured by paying the proceeds to the beneficiary first in priority who is eligible under the law to receive the money. In this case it would be the respondent, Hunter J. Carter, Sr., in the event the petitioner is found to be disqualified. This would be so because in the absence of an express provision of the insurance policy, the insurance company itself is not to be relieved of the obligation to pay the amount which it contracted to pay merely because of the alleged wrongdoing of a particular beneficiary.

. . . .

For the reasons hereinabove stated, the prayer of the petition for certiorari is hereby —

Denied.

DREW, C.J., HOBSON, J., and PRUNTY, Associate Justice, concur.

NOTES

1. *General principles.* That a beneficiary who slays the *cestui que vie* should not be allowed to benefit from the wrongful act is well settled. "It would be a reproach to the jurisprudence of the country, if one could recover insurance money payable on the death of a party whose life he had feloniously taken." *Mutual Life Insurance Co. v. Armstrong,* 117 U.S. 591, 600 (1886). On the questions of who receives the proceeds when the beneficiary is disqualified, the court in *Athmer* made clear that it was not at liberty to choose whatever rule it thought best. Thus, the court did not decide what rule should be applied in the future for SGLI beneficiary disqualification cases. It is undisputed that the slayer should be disqualified. But should this also disqualify all in the slayer's bloodline as well? This is the rule in some states, but not in Illinois. Judge Posner does not like the Illinois rule, but is there a better one?

One of the questions in *Carter* was whether the slaying beneficiary could *directly* benefit from the proceeds by inheriting through the estate. That she thought there was some chance of winning this argument had something to do with the then-applicable Florida statute relative to disqualification of heirs: "Any person convicted of murder of a decedent shall not be permitted to inherit from the decedent or to take any portion of his estate as a legatee or devisee." Fla. Stat. Ann. § 731.31. The Florida statute did not pertain to life insurance beneficiaries, although statutes in some states do cover legatees, devisees, insurance beneficiaries, and trust beneficiaries in the same text. What weakness do you see in the Florida statute, and how would you propose to fix it?

2. *The intent of the CQV.* If the *cestui que vie* designates primary and contingent beneficiaries, and if the primary beneficiary slays the *cestui que vie* in circumstances where the contingent beneficiary is innocent, should the contingent benficiary receive the proceeds? Or should the slaying beneficiary hold the proceeds in constructive trust for the *cestui que vie's* estate, which means that the proceeds will be distributed in accordance with the *cestui que vie's* will or the laws of intestate succession? Does your answer change if the slayer was also the owner of the policy and the one who designated the beneficiaries? Should the dominant consideration be making sure the slayer does not benefit or trying to determine what the deceased *cestui que vie* would have wanted?

If the primary beneficiary predeceases the insured, contingent beneficiaries recover. Should the slayer be treated as predeceasing the insured? If the slayer is disqualified but is not treated as predeceasing the insured, then the slayer presumably holds the proceeds in constructive trust for someone, and some courts have held that this person is the estate of the insured. *See, e.g., Webb v. Voirol,* 773 F.2d 208, 212 (8th Cir. 1985) (applying Missouri law); *Crawford v. Coleman,* 726 S.W.2d 9 (Tex. 1987).

To make matters more difficult, what if the slayer commits suicide after murdering the insured? What if the slayer lays a fatal wound upon the insured before committing suicide, but the insured does not finally succumb until after the slayer's death? To get a glimpse of the complexities that arise in the murder-suicide situation, *see Diep v. Rivas,* 357 Md. 668, 745 A.2d 1098 (2000) (policy entitled siblings of victim's husband, the slayer who then committed suicide, to benefits, and slayer's rule did not bar siblings from recovery). It is worth noting that *Diep* involved an accidental death policy, and that the disqualification rules do not change for that very similar product. (Why is the murder of the insured an "accidental" death?)

3. *The intent of the slayer.* If the slayer purchases insurance on the *cestui que vie* with a simultaneous, and necessarily undisclosed, intent to slay the *cestui que vie,* and if the slayer successfully implements the plan, the accepted rule is that the policy is void *ab initio. See New England Mutual Life Insurance Co. v. Null,* 605 F.2d 421 (8th Cir. 1979) (applying Missouri law); *Chute v. Old American Insurance Co.,* 6 Kan. App. 2d 412, 629 P.2d 734 (1981). Why should this be so? Why not have the slayer hold the proceeds in constructive trust for the benefit of the deceased insured's estate? What does this rule have to do with concealment?

4. *The role of interpleader.* Why is interpleader important to insurers in these kinds of cases? Note that interpleader is not costless. Courts can award the insurer the costs of the interpleader action out of the "stake," *i.e.,* the proceeds of the policy deposited in court, and the successful defendant's litigation expenses will offset some of the proceeds.

When the insurer is discharged pursuant to a judgment in the interpleader, the insurer's contractual obligations under the insurance contract are fulfilled. Does this mean that the contract is "discharged" for all purposes? If the policy has provisions relevant to beneficiary's rights, why do these continue to be relevant if the contract itself has been discharged? Why not decide who is entitled to the proceeds based on equitable principles (assuming no statute provides the answer)?

5. *Criminal versus civil proceedings.* If the slayer in *Carter* had been convicted of murdering her husband, would she have been at liberty to argue in the interpleader action that the criminal conviction was incorrect? Should a guilty plea be treated the same as a conviction after a full trial? *See State Farm Fire and Casualty Co. v. Fullerton,* 118 F.3d 374 (5th Cir. 1997) (in context of intentional act exclusion in liability policy).

6. *A duty to investigate?* If the insured perishes in circumstances where the primary beneficiary is a suspect, is the insurer obligated to conduct an independent investigation of the circumstances of the insured's death in order to determine who is entitled to the proceeds? If the insurer is notified that the primary beneficiary is being investigated for possible involvement in the insured's death, can the insurer discharge its obligations by making payment to the primary beneficiary? *See Harper v. Prudential Insurance Co.,* 233 Kan.

358, 662 P.2d 1264 (1983). Can the insurer withhold paying proceeds if the insured has simply died in "suspicious circumstances"? It is commonly said that the insurer has the duty to act reasonably in paying the policy proceeds. *See Lunsford v. Western States Life Insurance,* 908 P.2d 79, 86 (Colo. 1995) (en banc). Can being "too quick" to file an interpleader constitute a breach of this duty?

7. *Choice of law rules.* In insurance law, like all other substantive fields of law, choice of law can be pivotal to the outcome of cases. There are some special rules for insurance contracts, as *Athmer* indicates. For more discussion of this subject, see Robert H. Jerry, II, Understanding Insurance Law § 36 (2d ed. 1996).

UNIFORM PROBATE CODE § 2-803

8 U.L.A. 20 (Supp. 2000)

2-803   Effect of Homicide on Intestate Succession, Wills, Trusts, Joint Assets, Life Insurance, and Beneficiary Designations.

(a) [Definitions.] In this section·

"Disposition or appointment of property" includes a transfer of an item of property or any other benefit to a beneficiary designated in a governing instrument.

"Governing instrument" means a governing instrument executed by the decedent.

"Revocable," with respect to a disposition, appointment, provision, or nomination, means one under which the decedent, at the time of or immediately before death, was alone empowered, by law or under the governing instrument, to cancel the designation in favor of the killer, whether or not the decedent was then empowered to designate himself [or herself] in place of his [or her] killer and or the decedent then had capacity to exercise the power.

(b) [Forfeiture of Statutory Benefits.] . . . .

(c) [Revocation of Benefits Under Governing Instrument.] The felonious and intentional killing of the decedent:

revokes any revocable (i) disposition or appointment of property made by the decedent to the killer in a governing instrument, ...

. . . .

(d) [Effect of Severance.] . . . .

(e) [Effect of Revocation.] Provisions of a governing instrument are given effect as if the killer disclaimed all provisions revoked by this section . . . .

(f) [Wrongful Acquisition of Property.] A wrongful acquisition of property or interest by a killer not covered by this section must be treated in accordance with the principle that a killer cannot profit from his [or her] wrong.

(g) [Felonious and Intentional Killing; How Determined.] After all right to appeal has been exhausted, a judgment of conviction establishing criminal accountability for the felonious and intentional killing of the decedent conclusively establishes the convicted individual as the decedent's killer for purposes of this section. In the absence of a conviction, the court, upon the petition of an interested person, must determine whether, under the preponderance of evidence standard, the individual would be found criminally accountable for the felonious and intentional killing of the decedent. If the court determines that, under that standard, the individual would be found criminally accountable for the felonious and intentional killing of the decedent, the determination conclusively establishes that individual as the decedent's killer for purposes of this section.

(h) [Protection of Payors and Other Third Parties.] . . . .

(i) [Protection of Bona Fide Purchasers; Personal Liability of Recipient.] . . . .

NOTES

1. *Comparing common law to UPC.* The term "governing instrument" is defined in Section 1-201(19) of the Uniform Probate Code to include an insurance policy and Section 2-803 is designed, among other things, to answer the questions being confronted in *Athmer* and *Carter*. Does it resolve the questions satisfactorily?

2. *Protection for insurers who pay without notice.* The Uniform Probate Code was substantially revised in 1990, and this section had further technical amendments in 1993 and 1997. Unlike the pre-1990 versions of the Uniform Probate Code, the version set out above contains a provision protecting payors who pay before receiving notice of a claimed forfeiture or revocation, and imposing personal liability on the recipient or killer. This is located in subsection (h), which was omitted from the above quote.

3. *ERISA preemption.* Also omitted from the above excerpt from Section 2-803 was subsection (i)(2), which attempts to deal with the problem of ERISA preemption. It reads as follows:

> If this section or any part of this section is preempted by federal law with respect to a payment, an item of property, or any other benefit covered by this section, a person who, not for value, receives the payment, item of property, or any other benefit to which the person is not entitled under this section is obligated to return the payment, item of property, or benefit, or is personally liable for the amount of the payment or the value of the item of property or benefit, to the person who would have been entitled to it were this section or part of this section not preempted.

If ERISA preempts the applicability of Section 2-803 to any employer-provided life insurance plan, would it not also preempt subsection (i)(2)? So what good is this provision? If all of Section 2-803 is preempted, what law would a federal court apply in passing on the issue of disqualification of a beneficiary for having killed the *cestui que vie*? See note 6 following *Lemke v. Schwarz, supra*, § 4.01[4]. Would you expect the court to follow federal common law? If so, would you expect that law to different from what is provided under Section 2-803?

---

[6]   Community Property Interests

AETNA LIFE INSURANCE CO. v. WADSWORTH
102 Wash. 2d 652, 689 P.2d 46 (1984)

DORE, JUSTICE.

This interpleader action involves a dispute between decedent Lawrence Wadsworth's first wife and his wife at the time of his death over the proceeds of a group term life insurance policy. The dissolution decree between the decedent and his first wife purported to transfer all of her interests in all life insurance policies on the decedent's life to him. The first wife, however, remained the named beneficiary of the term insurance at the time of his death.

This action raises two issues. First, what is the proper characterization under our community property law of the group term life insurance policy? We hold that the character should be determined by the identity of funds used to pay for the most recent term.

Second, does a dissolution decree purporting to divest a spouse of her interests in all life insurance policies also divest her of all interest as a named beneficiary? We hold that it does not.

Facts

Joan and Lawrence Wadsworth were married in 1949. In 1952, Lawrence commenced work for the Boeing Company. In 1963, Aetna Life Insurance Company issued a group term life insurance policy covering Boeing employees, including Lawrence. The policy has no cash surrender value and each premium is paid in full on a monthly basis as a benefit of employment by the Boeing Company. Lawrence designated Joan as beneficiary.

Joan and Lawrence were divorced on August 3, 1978. The dissolution decree incorporated a separation contract in which Joan conveyed to Lawrence "as his sole and separate property, free and clear of any right, title, or interest on her part. . .[a]ll life insurance policies" insuring his life. Lawrence Wadsworth married Sharon Wadsworth on the same day. Lawrence never changed the designation of Joan as beneficiary of the group policy.

Lawrence Wadsworth died intestate on January 10, 1981. Sharon, as surviving spouse and administratrix of his estate, claimed the proceeds of the group policy. Pursuant to the terms of the policy, Aetna commenced an interpleader action to determine whether Sharon or Joan should receive the policy proceeds. Joan moved for partial summary judgment, arguing that she was entitled to one-half of the policy proceeds as named beneficiary. Sharon brought a cross motion, claiming all of the proceeds.

The trial court denied Joan's motion and granted Sharon's motion for summary judgment, and awarded her the policy proceeds.

Joan appealed. The Court of Appeals found that the dissolution decree divested Joan of any interest she had in the group policy, including her right to be named as beneficiary. It further held that the dissolution of Joan and Lawrence's marriage converted the group policy into Lawrence's separate property. Thereafter, ownership of the policy or its proceeds was both separate and community property in proportion to the percentage of the total premiums paid. Thus, the Court of Appeals held that Sharon obtained a community property interest in only that portion of the proceeds attributable to the premiums paid with community funds after her marriage to Lawrence. It reversed and remanded to the trial court for resolution of two factual issues: (1) did Lawrence intend Joan to be the beneficiary of the policy, and (2) if so, what portion of the policy proceeds are attributable to premiums paid by funds of the marital community of Lawrence and Sharon.

Judicial History

Application of community property principles to life insurance policies in Washington has its roots in *Occidental Life Ins. Co. v. Powers,* 192 Wash. 475, 74 P.2d 27, 114 A.L.R. 531 (1937). In *Powers,* the husband changed the beneficiary of a life insurance policy purchased with community funds from his wife to his mother and secretary. This change was made without the wife's knowledge or consent. After the husband's death, the wife and the named beneficiaries made conflicting claims to the proceeds. This court held that a nonconsenting spouse could void her husband's designation of a beneficiary of a policy purchased with community funds. The court reasoned:

> In this state, insurance or the proceeds of insurance are not mere expectancies or choses in action, but are property; and if the premiums are paid by the assets of the community, they constitute community property.

Powers, at 484, 74 P.2d 27. Since substantial gifts of community property may not be made without the consent of both spouses, the change of beneficiaries was held void ab initio.

Powers has been consistently questioned over the years on several grounds. *E.g.,* Cross, *The Community Property Law in Washington,* 49 Wash. L. Rev. 729, 790–93 (1974); Comment, *Life Insurance Process* [sic] *as Community Property,* 13 Wash. L. Rev. 321 (1939).

One criticism of *Powers* revolves around its characterization of the designation of a life insurance beneficiary as a present property interest rather than an expectancy. Where the policy owner has the right to change the beneficiary, the named beneficiary has no vested right in the nomination. Even if the insured cannot change the beneficiary, the beneficiary's interest is not indefeasibly vested so long as there remain premiums to be paid. *Francis v.*

Francis, 89 Wash. 2d 511, 573 P.2d 369 (1978). Thus, the characterization of the right to proceeds as a present property interest rather than an expectancy is wrong.

The effect of *Powers* was somewhat diminished by *In re Estate of Towey,* 22 Wash. 2d 212, 155 P.2d 273 (1945) which upheld an insured husband's change of beneficiary from his wife to his executor. Under *Towey,* the wife's half interest in the proceeds was preserved but the husband could dispose of his half of the policy proceeds by will.

Finally, in *Francis v. Francis, supra,* this court overruled *Powers,* at least insofar as the *Francis* court held that the insured spouse may designate a person other than his or her spouse as beneficiary of up to one-half of the proceeds of a community-owned policy. *Francis* recognized that designation of a beneficiary is quasi-testamentary rather than a means of making a gift of community property. Since the insured spouse has the right to dispose of one-half of the community property upon his or her death, designation of a beneficiary other than his or her spouse as to one-half of the proceeds is permissible.

Risk Payment Approach

Powers was also the progenitor of the apportionment rule under which ownership of an insurance policy or its proceeds is separate or community property in proportion to the premiums paid by separate or community property. *See Wilson v. Wilson,* 35 Wash. 2d 364, 212 P.2d 1022 (1949); *Small v. Bartyzel,* 27 Wash. 2d 176, 177 P.2d 391 (1947). Critics of this apportionment rule argue that it fails to take into account the nature of life insurance, especially term life insurance.

Although numerous variations of life insurance exist, life insurance policies generally may be divided into two broad classes: term insurance and cash value insurance. Premiums purchasing cash value insurance pay for both cash value and protection from risk of death. The cash value, somewhat akin to a savings account, is a permanent cumulative asset against which the owner may borrow, and which the owner may receive upon cancellation of the policy. On the other hand, term insurance has no cash surrender value; premiums purchase only protection from risk of death for a fixed period of time. At the end of that period, there is no asset remaining. The length of time the insured has had the policy and the number of premiums paid are irrelevant.

Based upon these differences in life insurance policies, critics of the apportionment theory argue for adoption of a risk payment theory. The risk payment theory is a functional approach which takes into account the manner in which values accrue under various types of policies. Under this theory, the proceeds of a life insurance policy are characterized by determining the source of funds which paid for the risk portion of the policy. In the case of term insurance, only the character of funds used to purchase the most recent premium is significant because term insurance premiums purchase solely protection from risk of death. Hence, the character of a term policy should depend upon whether payment for the most recent premium was made with community or separate funds.

Courts in several community property jurisdictions have adopted, at least implicitly, a risk payment approach to characterization of term life insurance policies. For example, in *Lock v. Lock,* 8 Ariz. App. 138, 145, 444 P.2d 163 (1968), the Arizona Court of Appeals stated:

> [S]eparate funds paid for *all* of the coverage that resulted at the time of Mr. Lock's death. The fact that the community that had existed between [the decedent insured,] Charles Henry Lock and [his first wife,] Hazel Margaret Lock had paid a premium for a risk long since expired without loss would not give this community estate any vested interest in the proceeds of the policy.

The California courts have rejected the risk payment approach. These courts reason that insurability; *i.e.,* the right of the insured to keep the policy in force past the time when he or she could obtain an identical policy from the same company, is a valuable right. According to these courts, this valuable right is derived at the inception of the contract and is, therefore, subject to apportionment.

While we recognize that insurability may have value in certain policies, we reject the approach of the California courts. This approach is based in part upon the questionable assumption that uninsurability occurs at the inception of the contract. Generally, however, uninsurability occurs as one grows older, and any value attached to insurability is, therefore, more likely to be attributable to later premium payments than to initial payments. Further, valuation of insurability can be complex. While the complexity of determining values alone may not be a sufficient reason to reject apportionment, we seek to adopt a rule that will add simplicity to the determination of life insurance beneficiaries. Finally, the California courts' approach does not take into account the fact that many term life insurance policies, especially group policies, do not require evidence of insurability for participation.

We could adopt a rule requiring inquiry into the various aspects of each insurance policy to determine what, if any, features have present value. We prefer, however, to take a broader approach requiring inquiry only into whether the insurance policy is a term or cash value policy. The rule we adopt will, we hope, have the advantage of ease of application and thus avoid the time and expense of extensive litigation.

In the past, we have expressly reserved the question whether the risk payment theory should be applied as a method of characterizing life insurance policies. We now resolve that question with respect to term life insurance policies.[2] We hold that the character of funds used to pay for the most recent term should determine the character of a term life insurance policy. Accordingly, insofar as *Small v. Bartyzel, supra, Estate of Madsen v. Commissioner,* 97 Wash. 2d 792, 650 P.2d 196 (1982) and *Stephen v. Gallion,* 5 Wash. App. 747, 491 P.2d 238 (1971) indicate the characterization of a term life insurance policy should be determined by apportionment, they are overruled.

We now apply the risk payment doctrine to the Wadsworth policy.

Because the community funds of Sharon and Lawrence Wadsworth were used to purchase coverage for the most recent term, the policy was the

---

[2] We need not decide whether the risk payment doctrine should be applied, in whole or in part, to cash value policies.

community property of Sharon and Lawrence. Any coverage paid for by the marital community of Joan and Lawrence Wadsworth had expired without loss long before Lawrence's death. The adequacy of identification of the policy in their separation agreement is no longer material.

Upon Lawrence's death, Sharon became entitled to one-half of the proceeds from this community property source. The decedent had the power to direct the disposition of the other half of the proceeds. The disposition of the decedent's share depends upon whether his designation of Joan Wadsworth as beneficiary is valid. We turn next to this issue.

New Rule for Determination of Beneficiary

In a separation agreement, incorporated into their dissolution decree, Joan Wadsworth transferred to Lawrence Wadsworth "as his sole and separate property, free and clear of any right, title, or interest on her part. . .all life insurance policies insuring his life." [The court went on to find that the language of the decree was neither sufficiently clear nor sufficiently specific to indicate an intent to divest Joan Wadsworth of her expectancy and held that a former spouse named beneficiary in a life insurance policy is entitled to the proceeds unless (1) a dissolution decree specifically states that the former spouse is divested of his or her expectancy as named beneficiary *and* (2) the policy owner formally executes this previously stated intention to change the beneficiary within a reasonable time (but no longer than 1 year) after dissolution. After this reasonable time period, assuming no community property rights are invaded, the beneficiary named in the insurance policy is entitled to the proceeds despite a statement in the dissolution decree indicating a contrary intent.]

Conclusion

In this case, Joan Wadsworth, the named beneficiary, is entitled to the life insurance proceeds to the extent that no community property rights are invaded. The policy was purchased with the community funds of Sharon and Lawrence Wadsworth. Therefore, Sharon is entitled to one-half of the proceeds. Lawrence had dispositive power over the other half of the proceeds. Consequently, his named beneficiary is entitled to his half of the proceeds.

Our resolution of this issue makes it unnecessary to decide whether Lawrence intended to make a gift to Joan by naming her beneficiary.

The case is reversed and remanded to the trial court for entry of judgment, vesting one-half of the subject life insurance proceeds in Joan Wadsworth and the remaining half in Sharon Wadsworth. We award no attorney fees to either party. Joan Wadsworth should be awarded her costs.

WILLIAM H. WILLIAMS, C.J., ROSELLINI, UTTER&esc:, BRACHTENBACH, DOLLIVER, DIMMICK, and PEARSON, JJ., and CUNNINGHAM, J. Pro Tem., concur.

NOTES

1. *General rules.* Ten jurisdictions presently have the community property system of marital property law—Arizona, California, Idaho, Louisiana,

Nevada, New Mexico, Texas, Washington, Wisconsin, and the Commonwealth of Puerto Rico. In general the community property system dictates that property acquired prior to marriage is the separate property of each spouse, but that all property acquired after marriage other than by gift, devise, or descent is the community property of both spouses. Each spouse owns a one-half undivided interest in community property. Originally, the husband was the sole manager of the community property, but that has been changed in modern times in most states to give the wife more powers to control and manage community property. See generally W.S. McClanahan, Community Property Law in the United States (1982).

2. *Unique problems of life insurance.* Life insurance presents some unique problems in community property jurisdictions. The cash surrender value in a policy purchased with community funds constitutes community property, but how should the proceeds be characterized upon the death of the *cestui que vie*? Are the entire death proceeds to be treated as a gift, subject only to the restrictions upon a spouse's ability to dispose of community property without the consent of the other spouse? If the surviving spouse is the beneficiary, there is usually no competing ownership claim, but issues can arise under inheritance and estate tax laws and creditor's rights that turn on whether the surviving spouse acquired the proceeds totally as beneficiary or partly as an owner. *See* McClanahan, *supra*, § 6.20.

If the surviving spouse is not the beneficiary of a community-owned life insurance policy, the issue may turn on the dispositive powers of the *cestui que vie* spouse. If it is within the power of the *cestui que vie* spouse to dispose of the entire policy proceeds without the consent of the other spouse, the latter may be entitled to a return of one-half of the premiums paid with community funds. On the other hand, the power may be limited to disposition of the *cestui que vie*'s community one-half. The latter is the rule set out in *Francis v. Francis,* 89 Wash. 2d 511, 573 P.2d 369 (1978), which is discussed in *Wadsworth.* This rule has support in other jurisdictions as well. *Pacific Mut. Life Insurance Co. v. Cleverdon,* 16 Cal. 2d 788, 108 P.2d 405 (1940); *Travelers Insurance Co. v. Johnson,* 97 Idaho 336, 544 P.2d 294 (1975); *Murphy v. Metropolitan Life Insurance Co.,* 498 S.W.2d 278 (Tex. Civ. App. 1973).

3. *Term versus whole life insurance.* The *Wadsworth* court was called upon to decide how the proceeds of a term life insurance policy should be characterized under the community property law of that state and opted for the so-called "risk payment" approach. The policy in question was a group term policy made available through Lawrence Wadsworth's employer, the Boeing Company. Presumably the premium was paid solely by Wadsworth through a payroll deduction plan. What if Boeing provided $25,000 of term insurance without any charge to each employee who had been continuously employed by the company for a certain period of time? Would it make a difference in characterizing the proceeds under the risk payment rule whether the insurance was (1) only in force during the employment or (2) continued in force even if the employee quit or retired?

As the *Wadsworth* court pointed out, term life insurance has no cash surrender value, but whole or ordinary life insurance typically does employ such a feature. Should the fact that the insurance has a cash value make a difference in how to characterize the proceeds in a community property state? In a subsequent case involving four life insurance policies that had a cash surrender value, the Supreme Court of Washington, without any real discussion of the issue, held that the "apportionment" rule applied and that ownership of the proceeds will be separate property or community property in proportion to the percentage of total premiums which have been paid with separate or community funds. *Porter v. Porter*, 726 P.2d 459 (Wash. 1986). Is this result reconcilable with the *Wadsworth* decision?

4. *Statutory changes.* Some jurisdictions have attempted to deal with some of the issues regarding community property interests in life insurance through legislation. *See, e.g.,* Ariz. Rev. Stat. § 20-1128 (1990). As to the effect of divorce on a life insurance beneficiary designation, the common law and statutory changes were explored in the notes following *Lemke v. Schwarz,* in § 4.01[4], *supra*. In fact, the State of Washington revised its probate code in 1993 and, in the process, nullified the holding in *Wadsworth* on the failure to change beneficiary issue. The Washington statute, RCW 11.07.010, which is similar to what a number of other states have done, revokes entitlement of a former spouse to life insurance benefits upon dissolution of marriage unless the parties take appropriate steps to preserve that entitlement.

§ 4.02   Accidental Death and Dismemberment Insurance

[1]   The Meaning of "Accident"

INA LIFE INSURANCE CO. v. BRUNDIN
533 P.2d 236 (Alaska 1975), 91 A.L.R.3d 1027 (1979)

RABINOWITZ, CHIEF JUSTICE.

This appeal arises from a superior court jury verdict rendered in favor of appellee LuVerne J. Brundin in a suit to recover benefits under several identical accidental death and dismemberment policies. Milton Brundin, appellee's husband, died following surgery for hemorrhoids in July 1972. During the surgery, Brundin's heart stopped without warning. The physicians in attendance managed to restore his heartbeat, but Brundin had lapsed into a coma from which he never recovered.

Shortly after the death, LuVerne Brundin filed claims as beneficiary under the policies at issue here. Appellants rejected the claims on the grounds that the death was not covered by the terms of the policies. Appellee then filed suit. After a trial and verdict in favor of appellee, appellants filed this appeal and appellee cross-appealed on the issue of the amount awarded to her as costs for expert witness fees.

At trial, appellee offered several expert witnesses to testify as to the facts surrounding Brundin's death and possible causes of his death. There was agreement that the immediate cause of death was a cardiac arrest. However, the expert witnesses could not arrive at a conclusion as to the exact cause of the cardiac arrest. Among the possible etiologies mentioned were acute myocardial infarction or arrhythmia; hypotension; anoxia secondary to position;[1] idiosyncratic reaction to the anesthesia; pulmonary embolism; dissecting aneurysm, and a sudden tearing of the aorta. Other unknown factors could also have been contributing causes.[2]

Further, it was established at trial that at the time of the operation Brundin was 58 years old, was 75 pounds overweight, had high blood pressure, may have been diabetic, drank several martinis a night and smoked a pack and a half of cigarettes a day. Testimony indicated that these factors could predispose a person to cardiovascular problems.

Appellants attempted to demonstrate that none of the experts testifying was able to connect the cardiac arrest and subsequent death with any particular causative incident within the surgical process. Appellee was content to elicit testimony that the cardiac arrest was somehow related to the surgery, although the exact mechanism of the cardiac arrest could not be determined with any certainty. It is from these conflicting approaches to the cause of Brundin's death that the major issues in this appeal arise.

Each of the policies at issue here insures against death through bodily injury and defines "injury" as:

> bodily injury caused by an accident resulting directly and independently of all other causes in loss . . . .

The primary issue in this appeal focuses on the superior court's interpretation of the coverage provided by this provision. In the instructions to the jury, the court defined "accident" as "an unexpected, unforeseen and abnormal occurrence". Appellants contend that this instruction could have led the jury to conclude that the cardiac arrest was the "accident" causing death. In appellants' view, the proper definition of "accident" would require a showing that a mistake or misstep occurred in the course of the operation, and that that misstep was the direct cause of the cardiac arrest. Thus, we must first determine the legal meaning of the policy language.

There are two main lines of authority interpreting insurance provisions like that quoted above. The cases relied upon by appellants construe such provisions strictly and emphasize the distinction between accidental results and accidental means.[4] These precedents would have required LuVerne Brundin to prove that the cause of the death was itself an accident, that is, that some actual mistake or misstep occurred during the surgery which caused the death. It would not be enough under this line of authority to prove that the result itself was accidental in the sense of being unexpected and unforeseen. As stated in 10 Couch on Insurance 2d section 41:112, at 142 (2d ed. R. Anderson 1962):

---

[1] Due to the nature of the surgery, the patient was placed on his stomach, a position made more uncomfortable by his obesity.

[2] The possibility of a stroke was mentioned as well, although a partial autopsy of the brain revealed no evidence of damage which could be attributed to a stroke. A full autopsy of the body was never performed.

[4] Phrases such as "resulting from", "caused by", "sustained by", and "effected by" have generally been interpreted similarly because they have identical meanings for laymen. .

> [I]f an operation is not necessitated by an injury resulting from an accident, death occurring during or following the operation can be considered 'accidental' only when it is the result of mishap or misadventure in operative procedure.

Under the court decisions relied on by appellants, the fact that the death was unexpected does not alone make it accidental. For example, in *Caldwell v. Travelers' Ins. Co.,* 305 Mo. 619, 267 S.W. 907 (1924), the court found no "accidental means" in a death following surgery for hernia repair. It noted that where the insured voluntarily undertook the surgery, it must be proven that something unforeseen or unusual occurred during the operation, and that the unforeseen or unusual occurrence caused the death.[7] Some cases hold that even if the result is not clearly foreseeable, death as the result of a voluntary undertaking is still not covered. In the case at bar, appellants point out that there was no evidence presented here of any misstep or mistake in operative procedures relating to hemorrhoidectomy,[9] and that the insured undertook the surgery voluntarily, knowing that unexpected death can occur during surgery without any misstep in surgical procedures.

Appellee points to a growing number of jurisdictions which have adopted a broader reading of policy language like that at issue here. This other main line of authority strives to apply the controlling policy language in a manner in which the average man would understand it. An early expression of the rationale behind this approach was expressed by Justice Cardozo in his dissent in *Landress v. Phoenix Mutual Life Insurance Co.,* 291 U.S. 491, 54 S. Ct. 461, 78 L. Ed. 934 (1934). There Justice Cardozo said:

> The attempted distinction between accidental results and accidental means will plunge this branch of the law into a Serbonian Bog. 'Probably it is true to say that in the strictest sense and dealing with the region of physical nature there is no such thing as an accident.' . . .On the other hand, the average man is convinced that there is, and so certainly is the man who takes out a policy of accident insurance. It is his reading of the policy that is to be accepted as our guide, with the help of the established rule that ambiguities and uncertainties are to be resolved against the company.
>
>   . . . .
>
> When a man has died in such a way that his death is spoken of as an accident, he has died because of an accident, and hence by accidental means. . . .
>
>   . . . .
>
> If there was no accident in the means, there was none in the results, for the two are unseparable. . . . There was an accident throughout, or there was no accident at all.

---

[7] Thus, there are holdings to the effect that if a course of action is undertaken voluntarily, with the expectation that a certain result is probable, that result is neither an accident nor occurs by accidental means; the result is presumed to be intended.

[9] The operation was apparently performed as planned. The cardiac arrest occurred without warning just as the surgery was being completed.

The cases comprising this second line of authority generally look to the reasonable understanding or expectations of the average person: if in common parlance an "accidental result" is an "accident", the accidental results should be covered. *See, e.g., Gaskins v. New York Life Insurance Co.,* 235 La. 461, 104 So. 2d 171 (1958).

An example of the reasoning behind this line of cases is found in *Knight v. Metropolitan Life Insurance Co.,* 103 Ariz. 100, 104, 437 P.2d 416, 420 (1968):

> One paying the premium for a policy which insures against 'death by accidental means' intends to provide benefits to his family or named beneficiary in the event he should suffer death *caused by accident* as opposed to death caused by other means, such as suicide, murder, disease or natural death. . . .
>
> The term 'accidental means' as used in this policy should not be construed in a technical sense but should be given its ordinary and popular meaning according to common speech and usage and the understanding of the average man . . . . Insurance policies upon which the public relies for security in case of accident should be free from fine distinctions which few can understand until pointed out by lawyers and judges . . . . (citations omitted)

Similarly, the New York Court of Appeals approved of a jury instruction which defined "accidental means" as "those which produce effects which are not their natural and probable consequences".[14] The court said:

> Legal scholars have spent much effort in attempts to evolve a sound theory of causation and to explain the nature of an "accident". Philosophers and lexicographers have attempted definition with results which have been productive of immediate criticism. No doubt the average man would find himself at a loss if asked to formulate a written definition of the word. Certainly he would say that the term applied only to an unusual and extraordinary happening; that it must be the result of chance; that the cause must be unanticipated or, if known, the result must be unexpected. . . .
>
>   . . . .
>
> In this State there is no longer any distinction made between accidental death and death by accidental means, nor between accidental means and accidental results. As was said by Chief Judge Crane . . .: "Accidental death means death by accident, and excludes suicide; death occurring through 'accidental means' in this case and under these circumstances is the same as death occurring 'by means of an accident.' " . . . [A]ccidental means are those which produce effects which are not their natural and probable consequences. . . . [I]nsurance policies upon which the public relies for security in case of accident should be plainly written in understandable English "free from fine distinctions which few can understand until pointed out by lawyers and judges." A distinction between "accidental means" and

---

[14] *Burr v. Commercial Travelers Mut. Acc. Ass'n,* 295 N.Y. 294, 301, 67 N.E.2d 248, 251 (1946).

"accidental results" is certainly not understood by the average man and he is the one for whom the policy is written. . . . (citations omitted)

Events similar to the instant case occurred in *Whatcott v. Continental Casualty Co.,* 85 Utah 406, 39 P.2d 733 (1935), where a patient suffered a cardiac arrest and died during a routine appendectomy. The operation had been performed in the normal manner, without mishap. The court found that policy language requiring "an external, violent and purely accidental event" was met where the "accident" amounted to an unusual or unexpected result of an intentional act, though occurring without mischance, slip, or mishap. According to this theory of interpretation, LuVerne Brundin needed only to demonstrate that the cardiac arrest was somehow related to the surgery, that is, that it would not have occurred on that day anyway in the normal course of events. Appellee would not be required to prove that any actual misstep or mischance occurred during the operation.

In order to decide which line of authority to follow and therefore the extent of coverage in the instant case, we think it necessary to examine the principles which we have applied in past contract litigation, and particularly to insurance policy disputes. In our recent opinion in *Day v. A & G Construction Co.,* [528 P.2d 440 (Alaska 1974)] we discussed the possible standards of interpretation which could be applied to a bilateral commercial contract. There we held that the proper standard was the reasonable expectations of the parties as to the remaining of the contract terms. We also noted in *Day* that the interpretation of insurance contracts is controlled by somewhat different standards, due in part to the inequality in bargaining power and to the greater necessity for certainty required for ascertaining rates to be paid for policies. Further, in other cases we have concluded that ambiguities in the meaning of insurance contracts are to be resolved against the drafters of the language, the insurers. And we have said [that] an insurance policy may be considered a contract of adhesion and as such should be construed so as to provide the coverage which a layman would reasonably have expected, given his lay interpretation of the policy language.

A lay person's expectations of insurance coverage are of course formed by many factors besides the language of the policies themselves. Typically, a salesman explains the technical terminology to the prospective purchaser of insurance. Often, as in this case, purchase of insurance is induced by printed advertising flyers which describe the coverage. It cannot realistically be said that the expectations of a purchaser of insurance are not generated in part by such representations. Moreover, it has frequently been held that an insurer is under a duty not to misrepresent the existence of coverage, either deliberately or negligently. For this reason and in order to give effect to our rule of interpretation that a policyholder's reasonable expectations of coverage are to control, all representations of the insurer to the prospective purchaser must be taken into account. An insurer will in fact be bound by its representations to the extent that they form, with the policy itself, the expectations of a reasonable policyholder.

Applying these principles of Alaska contract law to the issue before us, we find that our law is generally compatible with the broader definition of "accident" urged by appellee. Thus, we conclude that the policy coverage at issue here is sufficiently broad to encompass accidents in the sense of accidental results, that is, instances when unintended injury or death results despite lack of any identifiable accidental causative agent. In our view, the language of the policies in question is inherently ambiguous, for "caused by an accident" is sufficiently close to "caused by accident" that we cannot say the average layman would necessarily understand accidental results to be excluded from coverage under the language in question.[23]

Moreover, in the case at bar the prospective purchaser's expectations almost certainly were influenced by certain advertising flyers, which he obtained prior to purchasing the insurance, toward a broad interpretation of coverage. These flyers contained boldface and large-type statements such as the following: "EXTENT OF COVERAGE: Covers all accidents . . . ."; "Your coverage is all-risk. . . ."; "You are covered wherever and whenever an accident happens . . . ."; "[the policy] covers ANY ACCIDENTAL LOSS OF LIFE . . . ." In view of these representations which the deceased Milton Brundin was aware of and which were made without accompanying limiting language, we think a close construction of the language of the policies inappropriate. The language simply is not sufficiently unambiguous or prominent in restricting coverage that a layman would be disabused of the impression of broad coverage generated by the policy and the advertising flyers taken together. We hold that the policies' language here extends coverage to results and conditions which are unexpected and unforeseen and hence "accidental" in common usage.[24] We believe the result to be in harmony with this court's decisions involving construction of insurance contracts, as well as the rationale of the judicial precedents relied upon by appellee.[25] Moreover, we are

---

[23] Webster's Third New International Dictionary, 1971, defines "accident" as "an event or condition occurring by chance or arising from unknown or remote causes. . .lack of intention or necessity. . .an unexpected medical development. . .an unexpected happening causing loss or injury . . . ."

"An 'accident,' within the meaning of policies of accident insurance may be anything that begins to be, that happens, or that is a result which is not anticipated and is unforeseen and unexpected . . . ." 10 Couch on Insurance § 41:6 (2d ed. 1962).

[24] Of course, we do not consider the policy language here broad enough to cover deaths which are unexpected but natural. This is an accident policy, not a life policy, and appellee never argued that she should recover under the policy if her husband would have suffered the cardiac arrest on the day it occurred no matter where he was and what he was doing. To recover she must prove that the cardiac arrest was related to the surgery.

It should also be apparent that when one undertakes an activity, such as certain types of surgery, in which there is a substantial chance that death or disability may occur, such a result, if it occurs, cannot properly be called accidental. If the activity is undertaken with full knowledge of a substantial risk, the resulting death or injury is not accidental, unless a positive mistake or misstep in fact occurred. In the instant case, the death occurred during a routine hemorrhoidectomy, in which the risk is ordinarily not substantial, so the insured cannot be said to have foreseen the result.

[25] In reaching this conclusion, we are influenced by the considerable semantic difficulties which courts have encountered in distinguishing between accidental "means" and accidental "results." As was noted in 166 A.L.R. 469, at 477:

This whole branch of insurance law has become shrouded in a semantic and polemical maze, and the result has been 'almost a wilderness of cases in which varying facts and situations have been applied in varying principles'. The situation is fast approaching

not convinced that insurers are incapable of writing policy provisions whose limitations are clear to the layman, and then advertising them in a manner which does not mislead the purchasers.[26]

. . . .

Appellants also complain that the court's instructions were erroneous in several respects.

At one point in his instructions to the jury, the trial court addressed the language in the policies requiring the injury to be caused by an "accident" and "resulting directly and independently of all other causes." More particularly, the instructions stated:

> [T]he court has determined as a matter of law that this terminology is descriptive of the requirement of proximate cause.
>
> The term 'proximate cause' means a cause which, in natural or probable sequence, produced the death complained of.
>
> If you find from the evidence that there were concurring causes of death, the cause to which the death is to be attributed is the dominant one, the one that sets the other causes in operation, and causes which are incidental are not the ones to which the death is to be attributed, even though they may be nearer in time and place to the death. That is, you must determine from the evidence which fatal injury or injuries occurred first in time. Any other injury or injuries, later in time, set in motion by the first injury, are not the dominant cause, even though they might have also caused the death.

Appellants contend that this instruction misstated the standard and applied a tort test of proximate cause rather than the stricter test contained in the language of the policies.

We disagree. Proximate cause is a familiar phrase to attorneys. But here it is addressed to laymen, who undoubtedly did not have fixed prior conceptions as to the meaning of proximate cause. They were not likely to apply the phrase except as it was defined by the court. Thus, if the court's definition of proximate cause ("a cause which in natural or probable sequence, produced the death complained of") and the limiting material which follows adequately

---

a point where the slight flame of legal theory involved is being smothered. Some of the courts have felt it necessary to resort to tortuous and tortured legal jiu-jitsu to distinguish and differentiate between 'accidental means' and 'accident,' 'accidental injury,' etc. Accordingly, the courts of last resort in several jurisdictions have accepted and approved Mr. Justice Cardozo's views as expressed above as a common-sense approach to the legal theory involved.

We are also persuaded by the logic of Professor Keeton in his article, *Insurance Law Rights At Variance With Policy Provisions*, 83 Harv. L. Rev. 960 (1970), which advocates rejection of technical analysis of policy terms in favor of emphasizing the reasonable expectations of the policyholders.

[26] For instance, the policies at issue here could have provided that deaths resulting from surgery shall not be covered unless it is established that there was a mistake or misstep occurring in the course of the operation which was the direct cause of death.

instructed on what appellee had to show, there was no error in the use of the phrase.[32]

Secondly, the court's instruction on proximate cause would be clarified by more closely tying it to the policy language. For example, the first paragraph quoted above could begin, "As pertaining to the assertion that the death result 'directly and independently of all other causes,' the court has determined, etc."

As to the definition and accompanying language, we cannot say it was erroneous. The final paragraph above does limit the jury to finding the original causative factor and disregarding subsequent and incidental ones. Moreover, as a matter of law the policy language should not be taken as requiring a strict exclusion of all other possible contributing causes. And at least one court has even used the phrase "proximate cause" to refer to nonexclusive causes:

> [T]he loss must be produced by 'external', by 'violent', and by 'accidental' means. Such means must be the proximate cause of the resulting death, but a total absence of latent contributing causes is not required for coverage to be afforded.

Gaskins v. New York Life Ins. Co., [235 La. 461,] 104 So. 2d 171 (1958). A similar instruction utilizing the term "proximate cause" was approved in *Burr v. Commercial Travelers Accident Insurance Co.,* 295 N.Y. 294, 67 N.E.2d 248 (1946).

Appellants also complain that the instructions erroneously submitted to the jury the question of what reasonable expectations of coverage under the policy were. The superior court in effect told the jury to interpret the policy language themselves. We find it unnecessary to address the question in view of the disposition we reach here. On retrial, the superior court should instruct the jury in accord with the interpretation of the policy language which we have placed upon it as a matter of law. More particularly, the superior court should instruct that the insured's death falls within the coverage of the policies if it was caused by the surgery and was unexpected or unforeseen.

In light of the foregoing, the case is reversed and remanded for a new trial.

NOTES

1. *The nature and purpose of the coverage.* It is common for life insurance policies to have an accidental death "rider" or "endorsement" pursuant to which the insurer will pay twice the face amount of the policy if the insured's death is caused by "accident." The doubling of the policy's face value has led to the label "double indemnity" for this kind of insurance. Accident insurance is also sold as a separate policy. The dismemberment feature of this kind of insurance pays an insured, according to a schedule, for loss of a limb, loss of sight, and other injuries. For what reasons would a person want to purchase accident insurance? Would it make more sense to purchase an accidental

---

[32] Two aspects of the jury instructions, while not manifest error, are somewhat confusing and in our opinion should be modified upon retrial. The last two sentences in the instruction quoted above are proper in cases involving multiple injuries. Such is not the case here.

death and dismemberment policy as a rider on an automobile insurance policy than on a life insurance policy? Why is there no equivalent "double indemnity" policy in property insurance?

2. *Perceptions and perspectives on the term "accident."* In common parlance, the word "accident" connotes a loss that occurs suddenly, usually with an accompanying force or act of violence. Is the common parlance understanding of "accident" sufficient for insurance purposes? Is the fact that a harm or loss is unexpected enough to make the harm or loss "accidental"? In *Brundin*, what was the insurer's perception of the meaning of "accident"? What was the insured's perception? What was the court's perception? With whose perception do you agree?

Brundin involved an intrasurgical death. Does it make sense to treat all such deaths as a special category, and deem them all nonaccidental? In *Senkier v. Hartford Life & Accident Insurance Co.*, 948 F.2d 1050 (7th Cir. 1991), the court offered this perspective:

> Any time one undergoes a medical procedure there is a risk that the procedure will inflict an injury, illustrating the adage that "the cure is worse than the disease." The surgeon might nick an artery; might in fusing two vertebrae to correct a disk problem cause paraplegia; might in removing a tumor from the patient's neck sever a nerve, so that the patient could never hold his head upright again. A simple injection will, in a tiny fraction of cases, induce paralysis. An injection of penicillin could kill a person allergic to the drug. A blood transfusion can infect a patient with hepatitis or AIDS. All these injuries are accidental in the sense of unintended and infrequent. But they are not "accidents" as the term is used in insurance policies for accidental injuries. The term is used to carve out physical injuries not caused by illness from those that are so caused, and while injuries caused not by the illness itself but by the treatment of the illness could be put in either bin, the normal understnading is that they belong with illness, not with accident.

948 F.2d at 1051–52. For a recent decision approving the *Senkier* analysis, *see Austin v. CUNA Mutual Life Insurance Co.*, 603 N.W.2d 577 (Iowa 1999) (14-year-old's death during surgery to repair a defective aorta held not accidental, even though the surgery's mortality rate was only five percent).

If the insured is murdered, is the insured's death "accidental?" Whether a certain result is accidental is usually determined by looking at the casualty from the insured's perspective. That is, whether the loss was unexpected, unusual, and unforeseen is determined from the insured's point of view. See 1A John A. Appleman and Jean Appleman, Insurance Law and Practice § 360, at 452–53 (rev.ed. 1981).

3. *"Accidental means" versus "accidental results."* Insurance policies that explicitly limited the coverage to death caused by "accidental means" were much more common three or four decades (or longer) ago. Even though the literal words "accidental means" are not found as often in modern policies, the issues raised by the means-results distinction still find their way into cases. The rejection of any distinction between "accidental means" and

"accidental results" is clearly the majority rule insofar as modern case law is concerned. *See, e.g., Harrell v. Minnesota Mutual Life Insurance Co.,* 937 S.W.2d 809 (Tenn. 1996); *Carroll v. CUNA Mutual Insurance Society,* 894 P.2d 746 (Colo. 1995); *Wall v. Pennsylvania Life Insurance Co.,* 274 N.W.2d 208 (N.D. 1979); *Vallejos v. Colonial Life & Accident Insurance Co.,* 91 N.M. 137, 571 P.2d 404 (1977). There are, however, jurisdictions which continue to adhere to the distinction. *See, e.g., Weil v. Federal Kemper Life Assurance Co.,* 7 Cal. 4th 125, 866 P.2d 774, 27 Cal. Rptr. 2d 316 (1994) (en banc) (voluntary ingestion of cocaine, which resulted in death, does not provide basis for coverage within terms of policy covering death "effected solely through external, violent, and accidental means"); *Gottfried v. Prudential Insurance Co. of Am.,* 173 N.J. Super. 370, 414 A.2d 545 (1977), *aff'd,* 173 N.J. Super. 381, 414 A.2d 551 (1979), *rev'd,* 82 N.J. 478, 414 A.2d 544 (1980); *Linder v. Prudential Insurance Co. of Am.,* 39 N.C. App. 486, 250 S.E.2d 662, *cert. denied,* 297 N.C. 300, 254 S.E.2d 918 (1979). Is there any argument that was not mentioned in *Brundin* for abolishing the distinction?

4. *Risky or foolish behavior, or both.* The court in *Brundin* quoted with approval from *Knight v. Metropolitan Life Insurance Co.,* 437 P.2d 416 (Ariz. 1968). In *Knight,* the insured was a 22-year-old high-diver of considerable skill and experience. His last dive was from the top of the Coolidge Dam, a place from which he had previously executed a successful, and no doubt spectacular, dive. Unfortunately, his final dive did not go nearly as well. The policy provided for coverage if the insured died "solely through violent, external and accidental means." Should Jackie Knight's beneficiaries collect accidental death benefits? In *Wickman v. Northwestern National Insurance Co.,* 908 F.2d 1077 (1st Cir.), *cert. denied,* 498 U.S. 1013 (1990), the insured died from injuries sustained when he climbed over a bridge guardrail, hung onto the guardrail with one hand, and fell 50 feet to railroad tracks below the bridge. In holding the death was not accidental under the terms of an ERISA accidental death policy, the court noted that the insured "possessed no extraordinary gymnastic, acrobatic, or other athletic skills" that would enable him to hold onto the guardrail. 908 F.2d at 1088. Should it have mattered if he did?

The kinds of risky and/or foolish activities in which humans engage are virtually unlimited. If the insured intentionally injects heroin into his or her bloodstream and dies as a result, is the insured's death accidental? *See Patch v. Metropolitan Life Insurance Co.,* 733 F.2d 302 (4th Cir. 1984). Is the answer different if the drug is cocaine? *See Weil v. Federal Kemper Life Assurance Co.,* 7 Cal. 4th 125, 866 P.2d 774, 27 Cal. Rptr. 2d 316 (1994) (en banc); *O'Toole v. New York Life Insurance Co.,* 671 F.2d 913 (5th Cir. 1982). A surprising number of cases involve the practice of auto-erotic hanging with fatal consequences; are those deaths accidental? See Alan Stephens, Annotation, *Accident or Life Insurance: Death by Autoerotic Asphyxiation as Accidental,* 62 A.L.R. 4th 823 (1988). If death results while the insured is pointing a loaded gun at his or her head, can the death be accidental? *See Linder v. Prudential Insurance Co. of America,* 250 S.E.2d 662 (N.C. Ct. App. 1979).

Intoxication plays a role in many deaths. If an insured perishes from alcohol poisoning after drinking to excess at a fraternity or sorority party, is the death accidental? *See Collins v. Nationwide Life Insurance Co.,* 294 N.W.2d 194 (Mich. 1980). If an insured voluntarily becomes intoxicated and then proceeds to operate a vehicle with fatal consequences, is the death accidental for purposes of an accidental death policy? Courts have divided on this issue. See *Harrell v. Minnesota Mutual Life Insurance Co.,* 937 S.W.2d 809 (Tenn. 1996) (death was accidental despite voluntary intoxication); *Cats v. Metropolitan Life Insurance Co.,* 14 F. Supp. 2d 1024 (E.D. Tenn. 1996) (driving with blood alcohol content of .18% rendered the infliction of serious injury or death reasonably foreseeable and, hence, not accidental; applying federal common law under ERISA, instead of Tennessee law to contrary); *Frypan v. Pilot Life Insurance Co.,* 704 S.W.2d 205 (Ky. 1986) (insured's death while operating his motorcycle at an excessive rate of speed and with a blood alcohol content of .20 deemed "accidental"). In *Hearn v. Southern Life and Health Insurance Co.,* 454 So. 2d 932 (Ala. 1984), the insured, whose blood alcohol content would later be determined to be .11, became involved in a high-speed chase with police officers at speeds of between 70 and 80 miles per hour. The insured's pickup truck left the roadway and crashed into a gully; the insured, while trying to escape via a jammed door, died of smoke inhalation in a fire that engulfed the wrecked vehicle. Is the insured's death "accidental" for purposes of a policy providing accidental death benefits?

The common issue in these cases is this: if the insured places herself in a situation where death is a natural, foreseeable, and perhaps even probable consequence, but the insured does not necessarily intend to die, is the death accidental for purposes of the accidental death benefit? If the policy has a specific exclusion for the exact kind of conduct in which the insured engaged, coverage should be denied. Should the failure of insurers to draft more explicit language covering situations like those described above cause courts to find coverage in these situations?

5. *Death while intentionally involved in criminal conduct.* The general rule is that basic life insurance benefits should not be denied the insured's beneficiaries simply because the insured dies while committing a crime. Why should this be so? See Robert H. Jerry, II, Understanding Insurance Law § 63B[b] (2d ed. 1996). Should the same result be reached under accidental death benefit coverage in the absence of an explicit exclusion barring coverage in such circumstances? *See Howard v. Southern Life & Health Insurance Co.,* 474 So. 2d 1109 (Ala. 1985); *Roque v. Nationwide Mutual Insurance Co.,* 467 A.2d 1128 (Pa. 1983). If the insured is shot and killed by a police officer while fleeing the scene of robbery, is the insured's death accidental? Does it make a difference if the insured was pointing a gun at the police officer when the police officer shot and killed the insured? Does your answer change if the insured was insane or otherwise mentally incapacitated at the time of the crime and his or her death? *See Hoffman v. Life Insurance Co. of N. Am.,* 669 P.2d 410 (Utah 1983); *Herbst v. J.C. Penney Insurance Co.,* 679 S.W.2d 381 (Mo. Ct. App. 1984).

Suppose the insured is tried, convicted, and executed for committing a crime. Is the insured's death "accidental" for purposes of the accidental death benefit? What if the crime the insured committed was murdering a police officer, and the crime occurred while the insured was involved in a face-to-face gun battle with the officer?

6. *The insurers' response.* As the foregoing discussion illustrates, life insurers have gone to great pains to refine the meaning of "accident" in order to distinguish the basic coverage under the policy from that offered for accidental death. The foregoing also illustrates that this is a complicated and difficult effort. If you were asked to advise a life insurer on how to avoid the reasoning of the court in *Brundin,* what approach would you take? Before trying to answer the question, you may wish to consider the next case.

KASPER v. PROVIDENT LIFE INSURANCE CO.

285 N.W.2d 548 (N.D. 1979), 1 A.L.R.4th 1305 (1980)

PAULSON, JUSTICE.

Monica R. Kasper ["Monica"] is the widow of Robert W. Kasper ["Kasper"], and is the beneficiary on several life insurance policies insuring against the accidental injury and death of Kasper. Shortly after Kasper's death, Monica made a claim for the accidental death benefits ("double indemnity") provided under the policies. The companies refused to pay and Monica brought suit in the Morton County District Court. The actions against the companies were consolidated and, after trial, judgment was entered in favor of the companies. Monica appeals from that judgment. We affirm.

. . . .

On the day of Robert W. Kasper's death, he was bird hunting south of Fort Rice in Morton County with a group of family members and friends. A prairie fire was started accidentally when a fiery wad fell into the tall grass nearby, caused by the discharge of a companion's shotgun. Kasper, a rather heavy man weighing 200 pounds and only 5'6" in height, ran over to assist his companions. Kasper vigorously fought the blaze, stamping it with his feet and swinging his jacket, in an attempt to extinguish the fire. After a few minutes of such activity, Kasper was observed to suddenly collapse and fall forward into the fire, and his death was apparently instantaneous.

Kasper's companions attempted to revive him by artificial respiration, but to no avail. He was taken to Mandan Hospital where he was pronounced dead on arrival by Dr. P.M. Ocampo, Jr., acting coroner for Morton County. Dr. Ocampo signed the death certificate on September 19, 1972, and noted thereon that the cause of death was acute myocardial infarction (heart failure). No autopsy was ever performed on the body of Robert Kasper.

. . . .

There is no dispute that all of the premiums were paid and that all of the policies were in effect at the time of Kasper's death. The companies have paid the regular life insurance benefits but have withheld payment of the extra "accidental death" benefits.

. . . .

Monica also contends that there was error in Finding of Fact No. 9, which reads as follows:

9. The cause of death was an acute myocardial infarction, causing instant death. Mr. Kasper was an extremely obese person. The myocardial infarction resulted directly or indirectly from, or was contributed to, by bodily disease or infirmity of Robert Kasper. Sudden and strenuous exertion combined with the bodily infirmity caused the myocardial infarction and sudden death of Robert Kasper. The exertion entered into by Mr. Kasper was entirely voluntary (although seemingly demanded by the exigency of the fire), the excitement he no doubt experienced was involuntary but cannot be held to be accidental. Only the fire was an accident, and Mr. Kasper's viewing it (and fighting it) cannot be reasons to be accidental.

Her contention is basically that it was erroneous to conclude that the exertion required to fight the fire was voluntary and not accidental. Monica contends that this was a conclusion of law and not a finding of fact and is therefore subject to stricter scrutiny on review. Even if we were to disagree, the error would not be prejudicial because the trial court also found that the death was caused or contributed to by bodily disease or infirmity which would alone be dispositive of the case in accordance with the terms of each policy.

. . . .

All three of the policies involved on appeal contained an "accidental means" clause as well as an "exclusionary clause". An accidental means clause requires that death must result "directly and independently of all other causes" from bodily "injury effected solely through external, violent and accidental means". In some policies the accidental means clause appears alone, but in the three policies involved on appeal there was an additional "exclusionary clause". The exclusionary clause is as follows: "This benefit does not cover death caused or contributed to directly or indirectly, wholly or partly, by: disease or bodily or mental infirmity . . .". It then goes on to list several other contributing causes excluded from coverage which are not relevant to this appeal.

The following excerpt from 10 Couch on Insurance 2d § 41:380 (1962) explains the distinction between the two clauses:

§ 41:380. Distinction between express exclusion clause and "caused solely by accident" clause.

There is a distinction between an accident policy covering loss "resulting directly, independently and exclusively" from other causes and a similar policy containing the additional phrase excluding disability "wholly or in part, directly or indirectly, from disease or other bodily infirmities," or phrases of like nature. The phrase "resulting directly, independently and exclusively" refers to the efficient, substantial, and proximate cause of the disability at the time it occurs. On the other hand, *a policy containing the additional phrase set out above refers to another contributory cause, whether proximate or remote.* Where, under a policy containing only the first phrase, the accidental injury acts upon a pre-existing disease causing total disability which except for such disease would not have occurred, the injury is deemed to be the proximate cause of the disability entitling recovery. But it is otherwise where the policy contains the additional phrase indicated above. Of course, the result would be otherwise in this latter situation where the disease resulted from the accidental injury or if the accidental injury caused the disablement independently of the disease. Otherwise stated, where the policy covers accidental death resulting directly and independently of all other causes through external, violent, and accidental means, liability arises if the accident is the moving, sole, and proximate cause of death, even though a pre-existing disease or physical infirmity is a necessary condition to the result. However, where the insurer's liability is further restricted by a clause avoiding liability where death results directly or indirectly from disease or from bodily or mental infirmity, it is not sufficient to create liability to establish a direct causal relation between the accident and the death or disability, but the plaintiff must show that the resulting condition was caused solely by external and accidental means, if the evidence points to a pre-existing infirmity or abnormality which may have been a contributing factor, the burden is upon him to produce further evidence to exclude this possibility.[Emphasis added.]

In the instant case, there seems to be no question but that the exclusionary clause stating "death caused or contributed to . . . by: disease or bodily . . . infirmity" would work to deny coverage. The trial court accepted the medical testimony that death was at least partially contributed to by preexisting bodily disease or infirmity. This is an application of the facts to the clear wording of the exclusionary clause.

Although there is a divergence of opinion, the cases which deny coverage because of a preexisting bodily infirmity are legion where the policy includes an exclusionary clause. In *Berger v. Travelers Insurance Company,* 379 Mich. 51, 149 N.W.2d 441, 442 (1967), the Michigan Supreme Court said that "such 'exclusionary' clauses necessarily *do preclude* recovery when death results from a preexisting disease or from a combination of accident and preexisting disease" [emphasis in original]. In *Berger,* the insured died soon after an automobile accident but the court held that an arteriosclerotic heart disease contributed to his death and, therefore, denied coverage. The Florida Court of Appeals took a similar position in *Nationwide Mutual Insurance Company v. Anglin,* 306 So. 2d 147, 149 (Fla. App. 1975), when it said:

> . . . [W]hen an accident and a pre-existing physical condition combine to bring about death, there will ordinarily be a question of fact if the policy provides for coverage whenever the death occurs directly and independently of all other causes. If the policy also contains a provision excluding coverage where the death arises in part from disease or other bodily infirmity, the insurance company will be entitled to judgment as a matter of law whenever the undisputed facts show that disease materially contributed to the death.

Accord Neeman v. John Hancock Mutual Life Insurance Co., 182 Neb. 144, 153 N.W.2d 448 (1967).

An exclusionary clause will not operate to deny coverage where the accident is the sole cause of death, independent of a preexisting bodily infirmity. If the trial court had found that Kasper was in good physical condition and his exertion in fighting the fire was the sole cause of his death, then Monica would be entitled to the double indemnity benefits. *See Rankin v. United Commercial Travelers of America,* 193 Kan. 248, 392 P.2d 894, 901–02 (1964), wherein the court said:

> We are forced to conclude that . . . where an able bodied man, *without apparent physical or health impairment,* dies of a heart attack *caused exclusively* from emotional strain, heat and physical exertion while engaged in fighting a pasture fire, the death is the result of bodily injury effected solely through external, violent and accidental means. [Emphasis added.]

Even though the *Rankin* court was interpreting the accidental means clause, under the facts we think the result would have been the same even with the addition of an exclusionary clause. See cases discussed and cited at 84 A.L.R.2d 270–81, for the proposition that accident must be the sole cause of death where there is a preexisting heart condition.

In summary, where a policy contains only an accidental means clause, the finder of fact can determine that death resulted from the accident even though a preexisting condition contributed to the death. Where it is difficult to determine whether the accident or a preexisting disease or condition was the motivating or precipitating cause of death, it necessarily becomes a question of fact. But where the policy also contains an "exclusionary" clause and it is found that a preexisting bodily infirmity contributed to the death of the insured, the court should enter judgment in favor of the company. *See Grabau v. Hartford Accident & Indemnity Company,* 149 N.W.2d 361 (N.D. 1967), wherein we held that there could be no recovery under the policy because a preexisting bodily condition contributed to the death of the insured. Where the policy contains both an "accidental means clause" and an "exclusionary clause", and the accident alone causes death or the condition which brings about death without any contribution from a preexisting bodily condition, the beneficiary is entitled to recover the accidental death benefit. Courts should not, by strained construction, extend the coverage contracted for in a provision of an insurance policy for double indemnity where there is no ambiguity in the words used in the policy.

The trial court found that the death of Kasper was contributed to by a preexisting heart condition. This finding was not clearly erroneous, and under a plain reading of the "exclusionary clause" in the policy, Monica Kasper is not entitled to recover the double indemnity benefits.

Judgment affirmed.

ERICKSTAD, C.J., and PEDERSON, VANDE WALLE and SAND, JJ., concur.

NOTES

1. *Causation revisited.* Does an accident ever occur that is not connected in some way to a preexisting physical condition? As one court explained, "[n]o individual is completely free from the normal degeneration that might cause weakness or susceptibility to an accident. Requiring an individual to be highly fit in order to recover under an accidental insurance policy would effectively nullify the value of these policies for an ordinary purchaser." *Carroll v. CUNA Mutual Insurance Society,* 894 P.2d 746, 754 (Colo. 1995). *See also Henry v. Home Insurance Co.,* 907 F. Supp. 1392 (C.D. Cal. 1995) (literal interpretation of phrase "direct result, independent of all other causes" violated reasonable expectations doctrine); *Kievit v. Loyal Protective Life Insurance Co.,* 34 N.J. 475, 170 A.2d 22 (1961) (pre-existing dormant condition, activated by accident into incapacitating condition, did not preclude coverage under accident policy covering loss "resulting directly and independently of all other causes from accidental bodily injuries"). Should courts therefore conclude that the exclusion applies only when the preexisting condition is the dominant cause of the death?

Suppose the insured receives a pacemaker implant to control a heart condition. The pacemaker works properly for ten months, but then it suddenly malfunctions due to a mechanical defect in the device, and this malfunction causes the insured's death. An autopsy reveals that the insured's heart was no better or worse at the time of death than it was at the time of the pacemaker implant. In these circumstances, is the insured's death "accidental" under a policy like that in *Brundin?* Like that in *Kasper? See Pirkheim v. First Unum Life Insurance Co.,* 50 F. Supp. 2d 1018 (D. Colo. 1999). If you are a prospective purchaser of accidental death insurance, what kind of answer would you prefer that a court give?

2. *The insurers' response revisited.* Although there have been some efforts by the life, health, and accident insurance industries to standardize their policy forms, one tends to encounter far more variety in policy language in these areas than in property and casualty insurance. Nowhere is this better illustrated than in the variations found in policy provisions dealing with accidental death and bodily injuries.

Consider, for example, *Reid v. Aetna Life Insurance Co.,* 440 F. Supp. 1182 (S.D. Ill. 1977), *aff'd,* 588 F.2d 835 (7th Cir. 1978), where the policy covered accidental bodily injury "caused by violent, external and accidental means," but excluded such injuries if "caused or contributed to by, or as a consequence of,. . .medical or surgical treatment." The insured, while recuperating from surgery performed for nonaccidental ailments, was erroneously administered intravenously a drug known as succinylcholine, instead of a normal saline solution, as a carrier for an intended antibiotic known as keflin. After two injections of correct fluids, at 10:42 A.M. and 4:00 P.M., respectively, the error in ingredients was made by the nurse on the 9:40 P.M. dosage. Shortly after this, the insured went into respiratory arrest from which he never fully recovered. He died five days later. It was agreed that this erroneous injection of succinylcholine, a muscle relaxant, was the proximate cause of death. On cross motions for summary judgment, the trial court denied plaintiff's motion and entered judgment for defendant-insurer and held: "[O]bjective consideration seems to this court to find inescapable the conclusion that. . .[the insured] died as a direct consequence of medical treatment, even though the proximate or precipitating cause of death must also be recognized as having been the accidental injection of a lethal drug." *Id.* at 1184.

In *Aetna Life Ins. Co. v. Kegley,* 389 F.2d 348 (5th Cir. 1967), *cert. denied,* 390 U.S. 946 (1968), 28 A.L.R.3d 400 (1969), the policy covered bodily injury caused by accident, provided that "the injury is evidenced by one or more visible contusions or wounds on the exterior of the body, except in the case of drowning." The insured, age forty and apparently in good health, collapsed and died of coronary thrombosis. Witnesses testified that after the insured collapsed, his lips turned a bluish color, indicating cyanosis, which is normally associated with a severe blood vessel occlusion. Plaintiff contended that the coronary thrombosis was the result of an accidental bodily injury, namely a ruptured blood vessel brought on by several days of overexertion and lack of sleep. In the trial court, verdict and judgment were entered for plaintiff. However, the appellate court held: "As a matter of law, cyanosis is not a visible contusion or wound on the exterior of the body, as those terms are normally understood and as intended in the policy. Therefore, there being no evidence of a contusion or wound upon the exterior of the body, the death did not come within the terms of the policy, and appellee cannot recover." *Id.* at 356. See generally, Jean F. Rydstrom, Annotation, *Construction and Effect of "Visible Sign of Injury" and Similar Clauses in Accident Provision of Insurance Policy,* 28 A.L.R.3d 413 (1969).

3. *Intoxication revisited.* Many accidental death policies have recently added an exclusion which narrows coverage if the insured's intoxication is somehow involved in the death. For example, in *Ober v. CUNA Mutual Society,* 645 So. 2d 231 (La. Ct. App. 1994), the insured suffered fatal injuries in a one-car auto accident; his blood-alcohol level was at least .11 percent; a person with a .10 percent blood alcohol level is legally intoxicated in Louisiana. The policy in question excluded coverage when "the loss to the insured person [is] caused by or resulting from. . .operating a motor vehicle while intoxicated." The court rejected the beneficiaries' argument that "intoxicated," which was not defined in the policy, was ambiguous. Concluding that "intoxicated" includes being legally intoxicated or "decidedly drunk," the court held that the exclusion barred coverage.

Statutory regulation can, of course, be important in this area. In *Olson v. American Bankers Insurance Co.,* 30 Cal. App. 4th 816, 35 Cal. Rptr. 897 (1994), the policy provided that "[t]his insurance does not cover any loss caused in whole or in part, directly or indirectly, from . . . 5. the influence of any intoxicant." The insured drowned in a hot tub during a July 4th barbecue party hosted at the insured's home; her blood alcohol level was .14 percent and included a therapeutic amount of Valium. An autopsy revealed some evidence that she had fallen into the tub; the coroner ruled her death accidental. The insurer denied coverage based on the exclusion, but the court held the exclusion invalid because it was less favorable than the intoxication clause allowed by Cal. Ins. Code § 10369.12, which provided: "The insurer shall not be liable for any loss sustained or contracted in consequence of the insured's being intoxicated or under the influence of any controlled substance unless administered on the advice of a physician."

Should an insurer be allowed to exclude coverage if death is caused while the insured is intoxicated, without regard to whether the intoxication causes the loss? This is what is called a "status exclusion," to distinguish the exclusion from one where the intoxication must have some kind of causal connection to the death. In an unpublished Wisconsin decision, the accidental death policy contained the following exclusion: "No benefit shall be paid for [l]oss that. . .occurs while the [c]overed person's blood alcohol is .10 percent weight per volume or higher; a causal connection between the injury and the loss is not required." Jensen died in an auto accident while he was driving home after some heavy drinking in a tavern; at the time of his accident, his blood alcohol level was .234 percent. The insurer denied coverage because of the intoxication exclusion, and this denial was upheld against the beneficiary's claim that the exclusion violated public policy. *Jensen v. J.C. Penney Life Insurance Co.,* 549 N.W.2d 287 (Wis. Ct. App. 1996). But in *Holloway v. J.C. Penney Life Insurance Co.,* 190 F.3d 838 (7th Cir. 1999), the court reversed a summary judgment for an insurer, holding that the same status exclusion contravened an Illinois statute mandating model language for accidental death policies and that the state insurance department did not have authority to approve, as it did with respect to the J.C. Penney policy, policies that are less favorable to insureds.

4. *The choking-to-death cases.* What if the insured chokes to death on regurgitated food (i.e., his vomit)? Does it matter what causes the vomiting? *See Ike v. Jefferson National Life Insurance Co.,* 267 Mont. 396, 884 P.2d 471 (1994) (insured's death by pulmonary aspiration when choked to death on his own vomit deemed accidental; evidence deemed insufficient to connect choking to cardiac arrest or insured's beer consumption the night before). What if a person, after eating food that has spoiled, regurgitates and chokes to death? Is contaminated meat containing botulinus (a bacterium which causes acute food poisoning) any less lethal, if the poisoning is left untreated, than a bullet? With respect to the policy language in *Reid, supra,* in particular, are both botulinus and bullets "external" and "violent"? What if a person merely chokes on improperly chewed, but nevertheless wholesome, food? *See Spaid v. Cal-Western States Life Insurance Co.,* 130 Cal. App. 3d 803, 182 Cal. Rptr. 3, 29 A.L.R.4th 1224 (1982). What if the insured chokes to death on her vomit, which occurred as a result of her voluntarily drinking alcoholic beverages to excess?

5. *How much risk?* Do you think there is a significant statistical risk of death by any of the causes attempted to be excluded in the cases discussed above that would result in an appreciable difference in premium? If not, should insurers be permitted to employ such exclusions?

6. *Burdens of pleading and proof.* Does the insurer or the insured have the burden of pleading and of proof on the issue raised by such exclusionary language in the notes above? *See Page Flooring & Construction Co. v. Nationwide Life Insurance Co.,* 840 F.2d 159 (7th Cir. 1988) (applying Rhode

Island law); *Employees Retirement System of Texas v. Cash,* 906 S.W.2d 204 (Tex. Ct. App. 1995).

[2]   Temporal Limitations

KIRK v. FINANCIAL SECURITY LIFE INSURANCE CO.
75 Ill. 2d 367, 389 N.E.2d 144 (1978)

RYAN, JUSTICE:

Christine Kirk brought this action as beneficiary under the double indemnity accident provision of her husband's life insurance policy. The defendant insurer, Financial Security Life Insurance Company, moved to dismiss the complaint because the insured died 92 days after the accident. The double indemnity provision takes effect only if the assured dies within 90 days of the accident. The Sangamon County circuit court dismissed the complaint and the appellate court reversed, holding that the 90-day provision violates public policy. One justice dissented. 54 Ill. App. 3d 192, 11 Ill. Dec. 886, 369 N.E.2d 340.

The facts are not disputed. On January 26, 1974, John Kirk was seriously injured in an automobile accident in Jackson, Mississippi. From that day until his death, Kirk was given little chance of survival. He died at the University Hospital in Jackson on April 28, 1974, 92 days after the accident.

The defendant insurance company paid the face amount of Kirk's life insurance policy, but refused to pay under the double indemnity provision because the assured died more than 90 days after the accident. The policy provided double indemnity benefits if the following provision was complied with:

> ACCIDENTAL DEATH BENEFIT. The Company, while this policy is in full force and effect, other than under the nonforfeiture provisions, WILL PAY an Accidental Death Benefit to the Beneficiary upon receipt at its Home Office of due proof of the accidental death of the Insured which directly shows the accidental death occurred; (1) death resulted directly and solely from an accidental bodily injury, and (2) death occurred within ninety (90) days after the bodily injury, and (3) both the injury and death occurred while this policy was in full force and effect.

Thus, the benefit provision specifically limits double indemnity recovery to death occurring within 90 days of the fatal accident. The primary question posed by this appeal is whether this 90-day limitation on double indemnity recovery for accidental death is void as against public policy. We hold that this limitation is not against the public policy of Illinois and, as a consequence, we reverse.

As a preliminary matter, it is important to note that where the provisions of an insurance policy are clear and unambiguous, courts do not hesitate to enforce those provisions fully. If there is an ambiguity in the policy then that ambiguity is resolved against the maker of the policy, the insurance company.

Here, the 90-day provision is clear and unambiguous. In order to collect double the face amount of the policy, the assured must meet three requirements. The death must result directly and solely from an accident, the date of death must be within 90 days of the accident, and both the injury and death must occur while the policy is in full force. There is no ambiguity in these three requirements.

The primary question posed is whether this unambiguous 90-day requirement violates Illinois public policy. Similar limitation periods appear in many life insurance policies and until very recently every jurisdiction faced with a challenge to these provisions had upheld them. 1A J. Appleman, Insurance sec. 612 (1965); Annot., 39 A.L.R.3d 1311 (1971).) Recently, at least two courts have held these provisions invalid on public policy grounds. *Burne v. Franklin Life Insurance Co.* (1973), 451 Pa. 218, 301 A.2d 799; *Karl v. New York Life Insurance Co.* (1977), 154 N.J. Super. 182, 381 A.2d 62.

Though this precise issue has not previously been addressed by this court, several Illinois appellate courts have approved this type of time limitation. In *Clarke v. Illinois Commercial Men's Association* (1913), 180 Ill. App. 300, the decedent had been injured on June 14, 1909, and died November 17, 1909. The insurer refused to pay under the double indemnity provision noting that the assured had died beyond the association's 90-day limitation period. The appellate court affirmed the dismissal of the suit, noting:

> The proximate cause of death, especially when it follows at a time somewhat remote from the accident to which it may be attributed, is often the subject of controversy and litigation. Provisions of different kinds, designed to remove or limit a controversy on that subject, are found sometimes in the policies and sometimes in by-laws. Doubtless, the by-law in question had some such end in view.
>
> Its reasonableness would seem to rest upon a theory that if death does not usually result from the injuries received from an accident within ninety days therefrom, it may be reasonably ascribed to other causes prior or intervening. We cannot say that such a time limit is unreasonable.

(180 Ill. App. 300, 302.) A similar time limitation was upheld in *Hickey v. Washington National Insurance Co.* (1939), 302 Ill. App. 388, 23 N.E.2d 933, where the assured died 60 days after an accident and the accident policy provided benefits only if the assured died within 30 days. Finally, in *Shelton v. Equitable Life Assurance Society of the United States* (1961), 28 Ill. App. 2d 461, 171 N.E.2d 787, the assured lost his leg nearly 3 years after the precipitating accident. Benefits under his policy were denied when the court held that a 90-day provision in the policy violated no known public policy.

Until 1973 the Illinois cases reflected a unanimous rule. In that year the primary case relied on by the plaintiff, *Burne v. Franklin Life Insurance Co.,* held that a 90-day time limitation for double indemnity accidental death benefits violated public policy. In *Burne,* the assured was kept alive 4½ years by sophisticated medical techniques. The insurer conceded that the sole cause of death was the accident, but argued that under the 90-day requirement the assured's death was outside the policy. The Pennsylvania Supreme Court held that requirement invalid. First, the court noted that the leading cases were well before modern advances in medical science. Such advances had, in that court's view, made the 90-day limit obsolete. Second, the court felt that extraneous matters, such as the eventual receipt of insurance proceeds should not be a factor in the deliberations on whether and how to prolong life. Third, the court considered it fundamentally unjust to allow full recovery to a beneficiary who has endured little or no prolonged expense and anxiety, and yet allow no recovery for those who suffer the longest and endure the greatest expense.

In a similar case, a trial level court in New Jersey followed *Burne* and held both a 90-day and 120-day limitation invalid. (139 N.J. Super. 318, 353 A.2d 564.) A New Jersey appellate court upheld that decision on the premise that the life policy's underlying purposes would not be frustrated where it was conceded that the assured died as a result of the accident, albeit beyond the 90-day limit. 154 N.J. Super. 182, 381 A.2d 62.

In contrast, the Ohio Supreme Court and Louisiana appellate court have recently rejected the policy arguments of Pennsylvania and New Jersey and upheld 90-day limitations. *Rhoades v. Equitable Life Assurance Society of the United States* (1978), 54 Ohio St. 2d 45, 374 N.E.2d 643, 645 n.3; *Fontenot v. New York Life Insurance Co.* (La. App. 1978), 357 So. 2d 1185.

The long line of authority supporting these time-limitations requirements in insurance policies, the recent departure from these holdings by the Pennsylvania Supreme Court in *Burne* and the New Jersey appellate court in *Karl,* and the subsequent rejection of *Burne* by the Ohio Supreme Court and Louisiana appellate court indicate that the issue is not one where there are clearly defined and objective rules and standards of public policy. This is not a matter where public policy is so clear that objective criteria compel us to hold the 90-day limitation invalid. Furthermore, public policy of a State or the nation is found imbedded in its constitution and its statutes, and, when these are silent on a subject, in the decisions of the courts. The legislature has not been silent on the matter of public policy as it relates to the contents of insurance policies. The Director of the Department of Insurance is required by statute to review policies of insurance in certain categories and approve or disapprove them, based on criteria including the established public policy of this State. The statute, section 143 of the Illinois Insurance Code, provides:

> No company transacting the kind or kinds of business enumerated in Classes 1(a), 1(b) and 2(a) of section 4 shall issue or deliver in this State a policy or certificate of insurance, attach an endorsement or rider thereto, incorporate by reference by-laws or other matter therein or use an application blank, in this State until the form and content of such policy, certificate, endorsement, rider, by-law or other matter incorporated by reference or application blank has been filed with and approved by the Director. It shall be the *duty of the* Director to withhold approval of any such policy, certificate, endorsement, rider, by-law or other matter incorporated by reference or application blank filed with him if it contains provisions which encourage misrepresentation or are unjust, unfair, inequitable, ambiguous, misleading, inconsistent, deceptive, *contrary to law or to the public policy* of this

State, or contains exceptions and conditions that unreasonably or deceptively affect the risk purported to be assumed in the general coverage of the policy. In all other cases the Director shall give his approval. Failure of the Director to act within sixty days after submission shall constitute approval unless the Director extends by not more than an additional 30 days the period within which he may approve or disapprove any such form by giving notice to the insurer of such extension before expiration of the initial 60 days period. The action of the Director in disapproving such form shall be subject to judicial review as set forth in Section 407. (Emphasis added.)

Ill. Rev. Stat. 1977, ch. 73, par. 755.

Additional statutory authority to proscribe certain policy provisions, by rule, is found in section 401 of the Illinois Insurance Code (Ill. Rev. Stat. 1977, ch. 73, par. 1013). Specifically, "The Director is charged with the rights, powers and duties appertaining to the enforcement and execution of all the insurance laws of this State. He shall have the power (a) to make reasonable rules and regulations as may be necessary for making effective such laws." (Ill. Rev. Stat. 1977, ch. 73, par. 1013.) Through these two sections the Director of Insurance is clearly given the duty to make judgments as to the validity of the 90-day requirement.

Here, we may assume that the Financial Security Life insurance policy was approved pursuant to section 143 by the Department of Insurance. In addition, the Department of Insurance has specifically authorized the use of the 90-day limitation in its rules and regulations. Rule 20.07 approved August 1, 1978, sets out the "Minimum Standards of Individual Accident and Health Insurance." That rule authorizes the following:

> Accidental death and dismemberment benefits shall be payable if the loss occurs within 90 days from the date of the accident, irrespective of total disability.

Department of Insurance Rule 20.07, sec. 7(A)(10), 2 Ill. Reg. No. 30, at 57 (July 28, 1978).

The approval of the use of 90-day limitation period in policies of insurance by the Department, although not conclusive upon the courts, is, however, entitled to great weight as against the contention that such a provision is against public policy. In *Stofer v. Motor Vehicle Casualty Co.* (1977), 68 Ill. 2d 361, 12 Ill. Dec. 168, 369 N.E.2d 875, this court upheld the constitutionality of legislation which allowed the Department of Insurance to prohibit conditions in fire insurance policies which "unreasonably or deceptively affect the risks." In that case it was acknowledged that the Department was acting to carry forward the mandate of the legislature and the court stated:

> We hold that the legislature may delegate to the Director the power to prescribe a uniform insurance contract containing a clause limiting the time during which actions may be brought by the insured against his insurer.

(68 Ill. 2d 361, 369, 12 Ill. Dec. 168, 171, 369 N.E.2d 875, 878.) In our case, pursuant to the command of the legislature, we must assume that the Director

has reviewed the provisions of the insurance policy in question to ascertain whether its provisions were "unjust, unfair," etc., or "contrary to law or to the public policy of this State" (Ill. Rev. Stat. 1977, ch. 73, par. 755). The long-established approval of the usage of time limitations in insurance policies similar to that contained in the policy in question, in the absence of any action by the legislature countermanding the approval by the Director of such provisions, is strong evidence that the General Assembly does not consider the use of such limitation periods violative of public policy.

That this 90-day provision is a matter best left to the legislature and Department of Insurance is clear from an analysis of the issues involved. While there may be valid reasons which support the validity of the decisions in *Burne* and *Karl* (*see* Note, *Death Be Not Proud — The Demise of Double Indemnity Time Limitations,* 23 DePaul L. Rev. 854 (1974)), there are numerous policy arguments favoring the 90-day limitation.

It has been held in several cases that these provisions minimize uncertainty as to the cause of the assured's death. Without the finality of a time limitation, the accompanying uncertainty as to the cause of death as the time between that event and the injury increases will spawn a substantial amount of litigation as beneficiaries attempt to establish some injury-connected cause of their insured decedent's death.

Also, several cases have acknowledged that these provisions reflect risk decisions. An insurance company sets policy rates based on the risks of recovery. As a consequence, the 90-day limitation, which clearly affects the risk, is reflected in the rate charged an assured. Thus, these cases hold, as a matter of contract law, that the assured is receiving what he has paid for. The limitation is thus reasonable as a reflection of the insurer's risk.

We find unpersuasive the argument that the limitations on the time within which death must occur should be abandoned in light of the advancements made by the medical profession in the ability to prolong life or to defer death. Regardless of the state of the art of healing or preserving life, there has always been and there always will be those who will die on the 89th day following the injury and those who will die on the 91st day following an injury. In the cases cited above, we note that this problem has been in litigation since prior to the advent of this century.

The suggestion that the injection of financial matters may detrimentally affect decisions by double indemnity life insurance beneficiaries is not sub-stantiated by the case at bar. Indeed, the beneficiary appears to have done precisely the opposite of what she argues. She maintained her husband, despite the policy, for more than 90 days. The 90-day requirement did not act as a disincentive in the provision of medical services.

As a general matter, the suggestion that persons will be encouraged to "pull the plug" is already dealt with by the concept of "insurable interest." A person may not purchase insurance on another unless he has a positive incentive to keep that person alive. The law already has a requirement that will protect the assured.

If the 90-day provision is invalid as injecting financial motives into life-saving decisions, then a whole host of other provisions and laws must be invalidated. What of term insurance? What of the termination of some insurance benefits at age 60? What of life insurance itself? Justice Holmes, speaking of insurable interest, noted aptly:

> The law has no universal cynic fear of the temptation opened by a pecuniary benefit accruing upon a death. It shows no prejudice against remainders after life estates, even by the rule in *Shelley's Case.*

Grigsby v. Russell (1911), 222 U.S. 149, 155–56, 32 S. Ct. 58, 59, 56 L. Ed. 133, 137.

The implications of a decision invalidating 90-day limitations are quite broad. See, *e.g., INA Life Insurance Co. v. Pennsylvania Insurance Department* (1977), 31 Pa. Cmwlth. 416, 376 A.2d 670 (invalidation of *all* time limits in accidental death provisions).

It is clear on review of the many arguments that favor and oppose the 90-day restriction that continued approval is best left to the Department of Insurance and the legislature. The regulation of insurance has long been the prerogative of the legislature, and we should not usurp that authority.

Because of the use of a 90-day limitation in a double indemnity accident clause of a life insurance policy is not clearly against public policy, the judgment of the appellate court is reversed and the judgment of the circuit court of Sangamon County is affirmed.

Appellate court reversed; circuit court affirmed.

CLARK, JUSTICE, dissenting:

I would affirm the appellate court for the reasons stated there. 54 Ill. App. 3d 192, 194–97, 11 Ill. Dec. 886, 369 N.E.2d 340.

The majority opinion has amassed an impressive array of cases and arguments supporting the 90-day limitation on double or additional indemnity payments in life insurance policies and evidencing that the limitation is not against public policy. Moreover, the majority's view that deference, not absolute, should be given to decisions, made by the Director of the Department of Insurance pursuant to legislative command, is correct. However, I am not persuaded by the majority's implication that the Director's approval of the 90-day limitation was the only reasonable exercise of his discretion. I believe that consideration of public policy dictates disapproval of the 90-day limitation: "[W]henever any contract conflicts with the morals of the time, and contravenes any established interest of society, it is void as being against public policy."

In *Burne v. Franklin Life Ins. Co.* (1973), 451 Pa. 218, 221–24, 301 A.2d 799, 801–02, the Supreme Court of Pennsylvania said:

> There are strong public policy reasons which militate against the enforceability of the ninety day limitation. The provision has its origins at a much earlier stage of medicine. Accordingly, the leading case construing the provision predates three decades of progress in the field of curative medicine. *Advancements made during that period have enabled the medical profession to become startlingly adept at delaying death for indeterminate periods.* Physicians and surgeons now stand

at the very citadel of death, possessing the awesome responsibility of sometimes deciding whether and what measure should be used to prolong, even though momentarily, an individual's life. The legal and ethical issues attending such deliberations are gravely complex.

The result reached by the trial court presents a gruesome paradox indeed—it would permit double indemnity recovery for the death of an accident victim who dies instantly or within ninety days of an accident, but would deny such recovery for the death of an accident victim who endures the agony of prolonged illness, suffers longer, and necessitates greater expense by his family in hopes of sustaining life even momentarily beyond the ninety day period. To predicate liability under a life insurance policy upon death occurring only on or prior to a specific date, while denying policy recovery if death occurs after that fixed date, offends the basic concepts and fundamental objectives of life insurance and its [sic] contrary to public policy. Hence, the ninety day limitation is unenforceable.

. . . [T]he decisions as to what medical treatment should be accorded an accident victim should be unhampered by considerations which might have a tendency to encourage something less than the maximum medical care on penalty of financial loss if such care succeeds in extending life beyond the 90th day. All such factors should, wherever possible, be removed from the antiseptic halls of the hospital. Rejection of the arbitrary ninety day provision does exactly that.

. . . [V]irtually every. . .case [which has] construed a ninety day limitation provision, is based on considerations which have no pragmatic applicability to the factual situation here. The earlier judicial interpretation of the ninety day provision was that its underlying purpose was to govern situations where there existed some possible uncertainty over whether injuries sustained in an accident would actually result in death. The ninety day provision attempted to delineate a line governing cases where the injuries may or may not cause death. Ninety days was the arbitrary period advanced by the carrier within which to ascertain whether death will in fact result from the accident.(Emphasis added.)

I agree with those statements.

I further believe that an insured is placed at a distinct disadvantage, as is frequently the case where insurance contracts and policies are concerned, of not having been able to negotiate any of the provisions. The 90-day limitation "within the provision is not reached by process of negotiation between the parties but is a standard time which the individual must accept if he desires the accidental death protection." The insurance applicant is relegated to the role of either adhering to or rejecting, but not changing or amending, a standardized contract drafted by a party with greater bargaining strength.

The majority has missed an opportunity to establish a more humane practice of permitting additional indemnity recovery where causation is not at issue. Modern medical technology and medical ethics have dictated a public policy which requires terminating adherence to an arbitrary time limit devised decades ago.

WARD, C. J., joins in the dissent.

NOTES

1. *Putting* Kirk *in context.* If you purchase a policy of automobile insurance for a term beginning on January 1, 2000 and ending on December 31, 2000, and you suffer a loss in an accident which occurs on January 1, 2001, would you expect a court to take seriously your argument that because the loss occurred just one day after the policy's term, the December 31, 2000 termination date is arbitrary and should be extended by one more day? If your answer is "no," why should the beneficiary's argument in *Kirk* be treated with any more respect? Is the situation in *Kirk* distinguishable?

In *Reliance Mutual Life Insurance v. Booher,* 166 So. 2d 222 (Fla. Dist. App. 1964), a case which appears in § 6.04, *infra*, the insured incurred medical expenses as a result of injuries she suffered in an automobile accident. The policy covered such expenses "provided that such expense shall be incurred within 52 weeks from the date of such injury." On advice of her physician, some reconstructive surgery was postponed for medical reasons until after the 52 week period expired. When the insured sought to recover for these expenses, the insurer denied coverage, and the court agreed with the insurer. Would a result in favor of coverage in *Kirk* require a different answer in *Booher?* Or are the cases distinguishable?

The minority position adopted by the two courts — Pennsylvania and New Jersey—cited in *Kirk* has also been rejected by the Supreme Court of Kansas. *Hawes v. Kansas Farm Bureau,* 238 Kan. 404, 710 P.2d 1312 (1985). *Kirk* still represents the majority view.

2. *Is there a better way?* Given the nature of the problem that the insurer is attempting to avoid — litigation over the causation issue—is there any better way of designing the coverage in *Kirk* to eliminate what some would consider to be a patently unfair result?

3. *Fortuity revisited.* Is the issue in *Kirk* one that implicates fundamental concerns about the need for a fortuitous loss? Does Justice Clark's analysis suggest a problem of "moral hazard," i.e., a possibility that an insured or beneficiary may cause a loss to obtain coverage? What should "public policy" have to say about that?

§ 4.03   Disability Insurance

SHAPIRO v. BERKSHIRE LIFE INSURANCE CO.

212 F.3d 121 (2d Cir. 2000)

JACOBS, CIRCUIT JUDGE:

Paul Shapiro, a licensed dentist, brought this diversity action against Berkshire Life Insurance Co. ("Berkshire") contesting Berkshire's denial of his claim for total disability benefits. Berkshire appeals from the judgment of the United States District Court for the Southern District of New York (Schwartz, J.) awarding summary judgment in Shapiro's favor on his claim for total disability benefits against Berkshire. Shapiro cross-appeals the court's grant of summary judgment in favor of Berkshire on his claim under § 349 of the New York General Business Law. We affirm.

BACKGROUND

A. *The Insurance Contracts*

On November 1, 1990, Berkshire issued a Disability Income Insurance Policy, which provided a monthly $3,100 benefit in the event of Shapiro's total disability (the "1990 policy"). On November 1, 1995, Berkshire issued a second, identical policy, which provided Shapiro an additional $1,000 monthly benefit (the "1995 policy"). [1]

The policies define "total disability" as "the inability to perform the material and substantial duties of your occupation," and "your occupation" is limited to "the occupation you are engaged in immediately preceding the onset of disability." In another clause, the policies also provide benefits for residual disability, and define it: "Residual disability means that due to injury or sickness you are unable: (1) to do one or more of the substantial and material duties of your business or profession; or (2) to perform your duties for the length of time that they usually require." The insured is ineligible for residual disability benefits unless he has suffered a 20 percent drop in income as a result of the disability.

B. *Shapiro's Responsibilities*

Shapiro has been a licensed dentist since 1981. In 1988, he opened his own practice called Park South Dental. In that office, patients were treated by Shapiro as well as by another full-time dentist, a periodontist and an orthodontist employed by Shapiro. Shapiro also owns North Hill Dental, a one-dentist office at which Shapiro treated patients only rarely. Shapiro is also the 44 percent owner and President of Sharraty Properties, Inc. ("Sharraty"), a for-profit corporation he founded with his brother-in-law, Dr. Monte Ezratty,

---

[1] The 1990 policy and the 1995 policy will be referenced collectively as the "policies" or the "insurance contracts."

to provide dental assistants, receptionists and clerical personnel for their offices.

Shapiro testified that before the onset of his disability he worked four or five days a week for a total of 40 to 45 hours. In 1995, the year before he became disabled, Shapiro saw nine to eleven patients a day, and performed an average of 275 procedures per month.

In addition to this dentistry work, Shapiro also spent between one and a half and four hours per week attending to various administrative and managerial duties related to Park South Dental, North Hill Dental and Sharraty.[2] Shapiro's non-dentistry responsibilities included, inter alia, personnel decisions, staff evaluations, staff meetings, consultations with his office manager on major equipment purchases and difficult billing disputes, troubleshooting the computer, and insurance and health plan proposal reviews.

C. Shapiro's Disability & Berkshire's Denial of His Claim

In December 1995, Shapiro concluded that progressive skeletal illnesses (osteoarthritis and spondylosis of the elbow, neck and other joints) had left him medically unable to perform "chair dentistry," which is the sum of procedures involved in treating dental patients in the dentist's chair. Shapiro stopped treating patients on January 30, 1996. The parties agree that this event marked the "onset of [Shapiro's] disability" within the meaning of the insurance contracts.

On March 26, 1996, Shapiro filed his claim for total disability benefits. Berkshire investigated the claim, agreed that Shapiro was unable to perform chair dentistry, and undertook to pay total disability benefits for a limited time only, while Shapiro recovered from arm surgery, after which time, benefits could be paid only under the "residual disability" provisions of the policies. Berkshire's coverage position was that Shapiro's occupation immediately preceding the onset of his disability was as an administrator and manager of his various dental practices as well as a practitioner of chair dentistry; because the disability did not prevent Shapiro from doing his administrative or managerial work, Berkshire reasoned, Shapiro did not satisfy the policies' definition of total disability: "the inability to perform the material and substantial duties of your occupation."

D. Procedural History

Shapiro brought this diversity action against Berkshire, alleging, inter alia, breach of contract and deceptive business conduct in violation of § 349 of the General Business Law of New York. The parties cross-moved for summary judgment. The district court granted summary judgment in favor of Shapiro on his breach of contract claim. As to the § 349 claim, the court concluded there was no violation and granted summary judgment in favor of Berkshire. Berkshire appeals and Shapiro cross-appeals.

DISCUSSION

The substantive law of New York controls this diversity case. We review a district court's grant of summary judgment de novo, construing the evidence

---

[2] Shapiro testified that his "nondental duties" at Sharraty and Park South Dental were "commingled."

in the light most favorable to and drawing all reasonable inferences in favor of the non-moving party.

A. *The Contract Claim*

Under New York law, Shapiro bears the burden of proving that he is totally disabled within the meaning of the policies. The definition of total disability in Berkshire's policies tracks the standard articulated by the New York courts: "[A] claimant is 'totally disabled' when he or she is no longer able to perform the 'material' and 'substantial' responsibilities of his or her job." *Klein v. National Life of Vt.*, 7 F.Supp.2d 223, 227 (E.D.N.Y.1998) (Trager, J.) (citing, inter alia, *McGrail v. Equitable Life Assurance Soc'y*, 292 N.Y. 419, 425–26, 55 N.E.2d 483 (1944)). The coverage question entails a "fact-oriented, functional approach that look[s] to the professional activities in which the insured was regularly engaged at the time of the onset of the insured's disability." *Id.*

After reviewing the record, we conclude that the district court properly granted summary judgment in Shapiro's favor on the breach of contract claim because in the relevant period Shapiro's occupation was that of a dentist. It is uncontested that he spent the vast majority of his time performing chair dentistry. Viewing the evidence in the light most favorable to Berkshire, Shapiro's administrative duties consumed no more than four of his forty working hours per week: 90 percent of his time was spent fixing the teeth of patients and 10 percent on non-dentistry duties. He saw several patients every day, four or five days a week. His office manager described his schedule as being "booked every day" with patients. Shapiro was thus regularly engaged in chair dentistry at the time of the onset of his disability. His administrative work was incidental to his material and substantial duties as a full-time dentist. *See Brumer v. National Life of Vt.*, 874 F.Supp. 60, 64 (E.D.N.Y.1995) (Trager, J.) ("[W]ere one able to find that the plaintiff's managerial activities were peripheral or incidental when considered in light of the medical or surgical tasks he performed, the court would have to find that he did not have a separate occupation as a medical administrator."), *aff'd sub nom. Brumer v. Paul Revere Life Ins. Co.*, 133 F.3d 906 (2d Cir.1998) (unpublished summary order).

Berkshire relies primarily on *Klein* and *Brumer*, and argues that Shapiro, like the two podiatrist partners in those cases, is not entitled to total disability benefits because of his continued ability to perform administrative duties. On the whole, however, *Klein* and *Brumer* support Shapiro's argument, because the plaintiff in neither case could make a credible claim of being a full-time podiatrist. Klein spent (at most) 24 percent of his time performing (or assisting with) a total of 251 surgeries in the thirteen months preceding his disability. *See Klein*, 7 F.Supp.2d at 229–30. The bulk of his time was spent operating and managing his six podiatric clinics. Brumer performed no podiatric surgery in the year preceding the onset of his disability, because (for all but the final eight weeks of that year) his podiatry license was suspended. *See Brumer*, 874 F.Supp. at 61–62. Thus Klein and Brumer were predominantly administrators and managers. *See, e.g., Klein*, 7 F.Supp.2d at 227 ("[T]he record is clear that [immediately preceding onset of disability] plaintiff was predominantly engaged in operating and managing his podiatric clinics while practicing, at most, a minimal amount of podiatric surgery.").

In the period relevant to this claim, Shapiro devoted 90 percent of his full-time working hours to treating patients, and performed 275 procedures per month. Berkshire emphasizes, however, that the onset of Shapiro's disability caused no change in the gross revenues of his three businesses.[3] We reject this argument for three reasons:

(i) It is well-settled in New York that "occupational disability policies are designed to indemnify against loss of capacity to work, not against loss of income." *Blasbalg v. Massachusetts Cas. Ins. Co.,* 962 F.Supp. 362, 368 (E.D.N.Y.1997). "[R]ecovery will not, therefore, be precluded even if plaintiff were to earn a larger income from his new occupation." *Id.*

(ii) Although earnings may have some bearing on the question of a policy-holder's capacity to work, the appropriate inquiry in this case concerns net income of the individual, rather than his gross revenue (much less the gross revenue of his business). An individual whose sole occupation had been the practice of chair dentistry could suffer total disability without losing a cent of gross revenue simply by hiring a substitute dentist to treat his patients. Here, the record evidence shows that Shapiro's net income decreased following the onset of his disability. This fact thus tends to support Shapiro's argument that he was, in fact, a dentist.

(iii) The stability of gross revenues cited by Berkshire does not tend to refute the idea that Shapiro was a full-time dentist because Shapiro in fact hired a dentist to replace himself.

* * * * * *

At some point, a medical entrepreneur's administrative and managerial responsibilities may well become the material and substantial duties of the insured's occupation. But we need not decide where to fix that point in order to resolve this appeal. Immediately preceding the onset of his disability, Paul Shapiro was a dentist. Because his disability prevents him from performing the material and substantial duties of that occupation, he is entitled to total disability benefits under the insurance contracts.

. . . .

[In an omitted part of the opinion, the court upheld the summary judgment for the insurer on the insured's claim that Berkshire engaged in deceptive conduct in violation of Section 349 of the General Business Law.]

CONCLUSION

For the foregoing reasons, the judgment is affirmed.

---

[3] In mid-1997 (well after the onset of Shapiro's disability), Shapiro sold North Hill Dental and subsequently purchased the Elgar Dental practice. Shapiro never treated any patients at Elgar Dental.

———

Prudence Life Insurance Co. v. Wooley, 254 Miss. 500, 182 So. 2d 393 (1966), 21 A.L.R.3d 1149 (1968). On June 12, 1959, Prudence issued a policy of insurance containing disability coverage to the insured. On June 2, 1960, the insured suffered a heart attack and was paid disability benefits from that time through June 10, 1962. Prudence denied that the insured was disabled within the meaning of the policy on June 10, 1962, and claimed that in May 1963 the insured had ceased to be active in his business even though he was not totally disabled, thereby justifying Prudence's refusal to renew the policy. The insured sued for payments not made since June 10, 1962, and recovered a judgment in the trial court, which the Supreme Court of Mississippi reversed and remanded because of an error in a jury instruction.

"The policy contained the following definition of total disability, 'Complete loss of business time due to the inability of the insured to engage in his regular occupation or in any gainful occupation for which he is reasonably fitted by education, training or experience.' Appellee was fifty-four years of age and was and had been engaged in the occupation of farming and raising chickens. He is a high school graduate. Other than his experience as a farmer and broiler producer, he had worked as a carpenter, truck driver and equipment operator on construction jobs.

"Evidence by the appellee, his wife and doctors was sufficient, though conflicting, to justify the jury's finding that he was totally disabled, and unable to perform acts required of him in his farming and chicken producing business, but there was evidence, if believed by the jury, to show he was not disabled from engaging 'in any gainful occupation for which he is reasonably fitted by education, training or experience.' The appellee requested and received an instruction which said if the jury believed from the evidence that plaintiff was prevented by his disease from performing the substantial acts required of him in his business, he was totally disabled within the meaning of the policy. The plaintiff's instruction said nothing about his ability or inability to engage in any other occupation as described in the policy's definition of disability. The appellant requested an instruction to the effect that 'total disability' meant not only complete loss of time due to the inability of the insured to engage in his regular occupation, but also in any gainful occupation for which he is reasonably fitted by education, training or experience. This instruction was refused.

"The question is therefore presented to us as to the construction of this particular disability provision of the policy involved. . . .

"None of these cases [relied upon by the parties] include the provision contained in this policy. All of them have what is known as a 'general disability' clause, but not one mentions the occupation of the insured. In construing the disability definitions there, this Court several times refers to the fact that no mention of present occupation is made. . . . .

"In 29A Am. Jur. Insurance § 1518 at 622-3-4 (1960), it is said:

The question whether there is a total disability when the insured, notwithstanding his injury, is able to work in other occupations, depends largely on the terms of the contract defining the disability. In the case of an "occupational disability" policy, inability to perform all the substantial and material acts necessary to the prosecution of the insured's business or occupation is sufficient to constitute total disability of the insured.

In the case of a "general disability" policy, the courts are in conflict as to the type of work which the insured must be unable to perform in order to be totally disabled within the meaning of the policy. Some courts refuse to distinguish between policies which relate specifically to disability in respect to a particular occupation and those which undertake to insure against disability from performing any sort of remunerative labor, holding that total disability occurs in either case if the insured becomes unable to perform the duties of, or labor pertaining to, his particular occupation. According to this rule, recovery will not be prevented by the fact that the insured is able to perform all the substantial and material acts of some other business or occupation. At the other extreme, there is authority for the view that an insured person may not be regarded as totally disabled within a "general disability" clause until he is unable to follow any occupation whatsoever. Under this theory the liability of the insurer does not extend to cases where the insured is still capable of engaging in some occupation for profit. A majority of the courts, however, take the middle ground that it is not sufficient, in order to recover under the "general disability" clause, that the insured is disabled only from engaging in his usual business or occupation, but that he must also be unable to engage in any comparable occupation or employment for which he is fitted by education, experience, and physical condition. These cases proceed upon the theory that the term "total disability" as used in general disability clauses is a relative one depending in a large measure upon the character of the occupation or employment and the capabilities of the insured, and upon the circumstances of the particular case. While under this rule it is not sufficient, in order to recover under the disability clause, that the insured is disabled from engaging in his usual business or occupation, he need not be disabled from following any occupation whatsoever regardless of its character. The majority rule is particularly applicable where the plaintiff is insured as belonging to a particular group, such as railroad employees, and a general policy form is used. Under the majority rule, expressions such as "any occupation" and "any work," in the coverage clause, are converted into words of concrete significance and must be construed to mean the ordinary employment of the particular person insured, or such other employment, if any, approximating the same livelihood as the insured might fairly be expected to follow, in view of his station, circumstances, and physical and mental capabilities.

"This policy is worded so as to bring it squarely within the rule of the majority of courts which took the middle ground as hereinbefore shown. . . .

"This provision is what may be termed a 'double-barrel provision,' which requires that disability be shown as inability to follow his regular occupation, or any other occupation for which insured is reasonably fitted by education, training or experience. This provision is entirely different from any stated in the cases cited and brings it squarely within the majority rule announced in 29A Am. Jur., *supra*.

"The instruction given for appellee, who was required to prove his case, should have required a finding in addition to that stated that he was disabled and incapable of performing any gainful occupation for which he was fitted by education, training or experience—or the substantial acts required thereby.

. . . ."

NOTES

1. *The nature and purpose of the coverage.* If a worker or business owner is suddenly disabled, what kinds of economic dislocations would you expect that person to suffer? The answers to that question provide insight into the purposes—and limitations—of disability insurance. Disability insurance is designed to protect against loss of income due to illness or injury. Some policies limit coverage to disability from accidental injuries, but the more common forms, and the customary coverage with group programs, cover disability from both illness and accidents. The coverage may be short-term (a typical "short term period" is six months) or long-term, meaning that the policy provides benefits for what is essentially permanent impairment. The payment of benefits under a long-term policy typically must be preceded by the expiration of a waiting period (called an "elimination period" or "qualification period") that may range from 30 days to two years, although a six-month period is common. If a range of possible waiting periods is offered, the cost of the policy will go down as the length of the period increases. Life insurance policies often include a provision that waives the insured's obligation to make future premium payments if he becomes disabled; in fact, this is how disability insurance first originated. Not surprisingly, most disability policies also have waiver of premium provisions.

2. *Policy language matters.* As the excerpt from *Wooley* discusses, there are two basic kinds of disability coverages, occupational and general, although occupational coverage is more commonly encountered. Note that each defines disability by reference to a person's capacity to do work, not by reference to the person's loss of income. Should it be otherwise? Within these general categories, subtle variations in policy language are common, and they matter mightily in specific cases. In *Mossa v. Provident Life and Casualty Insurance Co.,* 36 F. Supp. 2d 524 (E.D.N.Y. 1999), the insured's policy defined "total disability" as "that due to Injuries or Sickness: 1) you are not able to engage in any gainful occupation in which you might reasonably be expected to engage because of education, training, or experience; and 2) you are receiving care by a Physician which is appropriate for the condition causing the disability." If this policy language had applied in *Shapiro*, would the case have been decided the same way?

What is an "occupation" anyway? If Shapiro had been a part of a dental clinic with ten dentists who divided the administrative work among themselves, and if after his disability he had undertaken, with no loss of income, 100 percent of the administrative work while his colleagues were engaged 100 percent in chair dentistry, would this court have still found Shapiro to be totally disabled? What would be the answer under the *Mossa* policy? *See Dym v. Provident Life and Accident Insurance Co.,* 19 F.Supp. 2d 1147 (S.D. Cal. 1998) (insured does not suffer from "total disability" if he can perform one of the significant duties of his occupation). If a law professor loses her voice, is she disabled from her "occupation"? What if she is able to move into a full-time research position? Or into full-time work, with no loss of income, in the admissions office? Is a concert pianist disabled if she can earn a reasonable income as a piano teacher, but nowhere near the income commanded prior to a disabling accident? What if the insured cannot instruct, but can earn a modest living as a salesperson in a music store or as a piano tuner? Is it the amount of money or the nature of the work, or both, which is to be compared to the former situation?

3. *More on determining the existence of a disability.* The three rules described in *Wooley* for determining when a person is totally disabled under a general disability policy are easy to state, but not as easily applied. In particular, because of the highly individual characteristics of the insureds, the majority rule has produced much litigation as to when a person is incapable of performing "any gainful occupation for which he is reasonably fitted by education, training or experience." The difficulties here are much like those presented in the prior note with respect to occupational policies.

Some disability policies state that the insured is not totally disabled if she is receiving any income from any business activity. In what circumstances might this present a special problem for an insured? Some policies create "presumptions" of total disability if certain kinds of disabilities are incurred, such as loss of sight in both eyes, loss of use of both hands or both feet (or one hand and one foot), or loss of hearing in both ears. If the insured fits within one of these presumptions, benefits are payable even if the insured is able to continue work and does not need continuing medical treatment. What is the point of having such presumptions?

4. *Partial versus total disability.* Disability insurance may cover partial disability, as well as total disability. The following clause is one example of the former:

> B. Partial Disability. When, as the result of injury and commencing while this policy is in force or immediately following a period of total disability for which indemnity is payable under Paragraph A of this Part, the Insured is continuously disabled and prevented from performing one or more of the important duties of his occupation, the Company will pay forty per cent of the Monthly Indemnity stated in the Schedule for the period of such disability, not to exceed three consecutive months as the result of any one accident.

Dittmar v. Continental Casualty Co., 29 N.J. 532, 150 A.2d 666 (1959). What phrases in this clause are magnets for possible litigation?

One way to deal with the problems presented in determining whether the insured is partially disabled has the insurer tier the coverage: the insured who is partially disabled is treated as totally disabled for a specific period of time (*e.g.*, two years), but thereafter the insurer provides coverage only for total disability. *See, e.g., Ryan v. ITT Life Insurance Corp.*, 450 N.W.2d 126 (Minn. 1990) (occupational coverage for five years, followed by general disability coverage).

Most disability policies do not cover anything less than a total disability (either occupational or general). This sets most disability insurance apart from the disability benefits available under state workers compensation systems, where much energy is expended attempting to calculate the degree of disability in individual cases. *See, e.g.*, Alaska Code § 23.30.190, 23.30.200 (Michie Supp. 1997); Ariz. Rev. Stat. Ann. § 23-1044 (1995); Ala. Code § 25-5-57 (1992). On the other hand, the typical disability policy puts the partially disabled person in an "either-or" predicament that is not without some risk— either the insured is totally disabled or is "not-at-all disabled."

5. *Other facets of the typical disability policy.* The amount of the insured's monthly benefit is typically the lesser of a percentage of the insured's income (typically 60 to 80 percent), or a specified dollar amount. Disability payments are not subject to federal income tax if the individual insured pays the premium, but if the employer pays for the coverage as a fringe benefit, the benefit is taxable income to the employee. It is common for policies to have "other insurance" provisions so that the coverages of multiple policies cannot be stacked. It is also common for policies to link the definition of disability to the insured's continued receipt of medical care for the disabling condition.

Disability policies typically have "pre-existing condition" clauses. The language of these clauses varies, but the general effect is to deny coverage for any disability that occurs as a result of a condition that existed at the time the application was filed (or policy issued), or perhaps during a period of time prior to the issuance of the policy. (These provisions receive more attention in the materials on health insurance, which is the next section of this Chapter; the issues that arise are similar with respect to both kinds of policies.) A less common provision excludes coverage for any disability that arises during a period of time (*e.g.*, up to two years) after the application for the policy. For more details on the structure of disability policies, see Frank J. Rief, III, *Disability Insurance: Its Uses and Tax Implications*, in ALI-ABA, Uses of Insurance in Estate and Tax Planning, SE14 ALI-ABA 667, 669 (Oct. 28, 1999).

6. *Factual versus social or legal disability.* Being disabled by illness or accident is called a "factual" disability to distinguish it from other kinds of disability. For example, in *Gates v. Prudential Insurance Co.*, 240 A.D. 444, 270 N.Y.S. 282 (App. Div. 1934), the insured was declared a "typhoid carrier," meaning that he was not ill with typhoid or physically impaired from working in any respect, but carried the typhoid bacilli and was for that reason banned by state statute from his occupation of milking cows and handling milk. Indeed, he would not have known he was a carrier but for laboratory tests that showed the condition. The court concluded that "[w]hen public good with regard to the safety of others steps in and puts a limitation upon his activities,

the disability resulting is social in its nature rather than physical," and that the insured was not disabled within the meaning of the policy. 270 N.Y.S.2d at 286–287. This reasoning was followed more recently in *Dang v. Northwestern Mutual Life Insurance Co.*, 960 F. Supp. 215 (D. Neb. 1997), in which a surgeon, who was discovered to be a hepatitis B virus carrier, was banned from certain surgical procedures without a patient's informed consent. The court held that he was not totally or partially disabled under the terms of the policy, given that he remained physically able to perform these duties. 960 F. Supp. at 218. Why should the insureds in these cases be treated differently than an insured whose virus is manifested in a present disabling illness?

If the policy requires that the insured be disabled by accident or illness, it should be obvious that an insured who is "disabled" from working due to revocation of a professional license or being imprisoned for a crime is not entitled to monthly benefits. When this kind of "legal" disability commingles with an accident or illness, however, the question is more difficult. *See, e.g., Massachusetts Mutual Life Insurance Co. v. Millstein*, 129 F.3d 688 (2d Cir. 1997) (attorney claimed he was disabled by attention deficit disorder, conduct disorder, and chemical dependency; held, insured's loss of income was caused not by disability but by loss of license to practice on account of illegal use of client funds); *BLH v. Northwestern Mutual Life Insurance Co.*, 92 F. Supp. 2d 910 (D. Minn. 2000) (fact questions as to whether doctor's sexual disorder rendered him disabled precluded summary judgment); *Goomar v. Centennial Life Insurance Co.*, 855 F. Supp. 319 (S.D. Cal. 1994), aff'd, 76 F.3d 1059 (9th Cir. 1996) (even if insured doctor was seeing astral beings because of psychological disorder when license was revoked due to molestation of patients allegedly caused by disorder, doctor was not totally disabled); *Holzer v. MBL Life Assurance Corp.*, 97 Civ. 5834 (TPG), 1999 U.S. Dist. LEXIS 13094, at *1 (S.D.N.Y. Aug. 25, 1999) (material question of fact presented by anesthesiologist who surrendered license due to opioid dependence). Suppose, for example, the insured is disabled by accident, starts receiving monthly disability benefits, and is then convicted of a crime and incarcerated. Does the imprisonment act as a superseding legal disability that cuts off the insured's right to benefits, under the reasoning that the policy protects against lost income and the insured cannot earn income while in prison? *See Weissman v. First Unum Life Insurance Co.*, 44 F. Supp. 2d 512 (S.D.N.Y. 1999). What if the order is reversed—the insured is incarcerated and then suffers what would have been a disabling illness? *See Allmerica Financial Life Insurance and Annuity Co. v. Llewellyn*, 139 F.3d 664 (9th Cir. 1997) (chiropractor's license is revoked and he subsequently becomes mentally ill). Why does it not violate public policy for convicted felons to receive disability payments while in prison? If you were the insurance commissioner, would you approve a form that contained an provision eliminating coverage in the event of the insured's incarceration for a felony? *See Ohio National Life Assurance Corp. v. Crampton, No.* 93-1850, 1995 U.S. App. LEXIS 16744, at *1 (4th Cir. 1995) (unpub. dec.).

7. *Accidental dismemberment policies compared.* Part of the logic, presumably, of a dismemberment policy, which covers the loss of a limb or a bodily function (*e.g.*, sight) due to accident or (sometimes) illness, is that the insured who suffers the physical loss suffers a loss of future earnings; the payment, at least in theory, compensates for this loss. Of course, the match between

the present value of lost future income and the proceeds is likely to be crude, if it exists at all. Disability coverage is more general in the sense that no specific body member has to be impaired in order for the insured to recover; rather, the coverage has a closer nexus to the loss the proceeds are designed to replace. On the other hand, a dismemberment policy usually has easier tests to apply than a disability policy, i.e., either you have lost a leg or you have not. There are situations, though, where the answers to the coverage questions are not obvious. *See, e.g., Buchanan v. Reliance Standard Life Insurance Co.,* 5 F. Supp. 2d 1172 (D. Kan. 1998) (determining that "entire and irrevocable loss of sight" had not occurred where insured's sight could be corrected to 20/100, with loss of near vision and depth perception); *Rice v. Military Sales & Service Co.,* 621 F.2d 83 (4th Cir. 1980) ("entire" or "total" loss of the use or sight of one eye does not mean total blindness, but means that the sight left is of no practical use); *Galindo v. Guarantee Trust Life Insurance Co.,* 91 Ill. App. 3d 61, 414 N.E.2d 265 (1980) ("loss" of arms or legs does not require actual severance or dismemberment unless policy specifically states this requirement).

Suppose the policy provides a payment in the event an insured loses the use of a kidney due to accident or illness. The insured's sibling suffers an illness that causes the loss of both kidneys, and the insured donates one kidney for an organ transplant to the sibling. Is the insured entitled to proceeds under the policy?

8. *A duty to mitigate?* The insured is disabled by an accidental injury. The insurer's doctors, who have examined the insured, conclude that the insured's disability can be completely remedied if the insured submits to a surgical procedure. Must the insured submit to the procedure as a condition to continued coverage under the disability policy? See *Heller v. The Equitable Life Assurance Society of the U.S.,* 833 F.2d 1253 (7th Cir. 1987). Would you enforce a policy provision requiring an insured to submit to surgery if that would minimize the insurer's payments under the policy? Would you make a distinction between "major" and "minor" surgery? Is such a requirement distinguishable from a requirement that a disabled insured make periodic visits to a physician for the purpose of determining whether the disability continues?

9. *Is America underinsured for the risk of disability?* "Disability insurance is the least prevalent form of private loss insurance. About 60 million people (roughly 55% of the workforce) are covered by private short-term disability insurance, defined as coverage against disability lasting for less than two years; but only about 24 million people (roughly 22% of the workforce) are covered by long-term disability insurance. Private disability insurance pays only about $6 billion in benefits annually." Kenneth S. Abraham & Lance Liebman, *Private Insurance, Social Insurance, and Tort Reform: Toward a New Vision of Compensation for Illness and Injury,* 93 Colum. L. Rev. 75, 81–82 (1993) (citing 1986 data from Health Insurance Association of America). One commentator described the potential ramifications this way: "Most American workers (particularly professionals) are better prepared to die than they are to become disabled for an extended period of time. This is disturbing because there is a greater likelihood that an individual will become disabled

for a substantial period of time (more than 90 days) during his working years (particularly the younger years) than there is that he will die during those years." Rief, *supra* at note 4, at 669. Citing data supplied by state insurance departments, Rief observed that the average male worker aged 30 has a 23.5% chance of dying before age 65, but a 33.1% chance of being disabled for more than 30 days. *Id.* Moreover, he indicated that the *average* duration of a disability lasting more than 90 days and starting at age 30 is 4.7 years, and the average duration *increases* for older workers. *Id.* (citing J. of Am. Soc'y of Chartered Life Underwriters, Vol. 8, no. 1).

Part of the reason the market for private disability insurance is not robust has to do with the prevalence of workers compensation, which replaces some lost income of disabled workers, and two federal programs, Social Security Disability (SSD) and Supplemental Security Income (SSI), both of which provide benefits to persons who are disabled. SSD is available as a supplement to workers compensation benefits for most disabled workers, but it "replaces only a small percentage of wages for all but the lowest-income workers," meaning that without private disability insurance a person who suffers a disability not covered under the workers compensation system will suffer a significant loss of income. Abraham & Liebman, *supra*, at 84. SSI is available for persons who could not work and therefore qualify for SSD or who have so little income and assets as to make them eligible for supplementation through the program. *Id.* at 85. SSD and SSI together paid annual benefits of approximately $45 billion in 1997 to over six million disabled workers and their dependents (U.S. Dep't of the Census, Statistical Abstract of the United States 1999, at 392 (Table No. 617). When workers compensation disability benefits are added in, the figure jumped to almost $90 billion. *Id.* at 397 (Table No. 629) (reporting $42.4 billion in workers compensation benefits paid in 1996). Although this number greatly exceeds proceeds paid by private disability insurance (in 1994, total private expenditures for long-term disability benefits were $2.9 billion, and the same figure for all private short-term sickness and disability benefits were $15.9 billion; see Social Security Bulletin, Annual Statistical Supplement 1999, Table 3.A4, at 140), the fact remains that government disability programs fall far short of substantially reimbursing the lost income of a person who becomes disabled by accident or illness.

Another reason that the market for disability insurance is not robust is that disability insurance sold by commercial insurers is more expensive than life insurance (i.e., when a worker compares the cost per $1000 of coverage, the cost of disability protection is much higher). Why is this so? See Abraham & Liebman, *supra*, at 101–06. Realizing that many policies will reimburse only up to 60 percent of an insured's income, does all of this mean that most American workers are underinsured for the risk of disability?

§ 4.04   Health Insurance

[1]   The Nexus Between Health Insurance and Health Care

If one sought to compile a short list of the five most significant public policy issues to have confounded the United States in the last half of the twentieth century, health care would be on that list. If one were to make a prediction of the five most important issues facing the country during the first half of the twenty-first century, health care would still surely be upon it, particularly given the profound changes facing our society as a result of its rapid aging.

The United States health care delivery system is a complicated mix of many complicated components. Insurance is one of the most important parts of the system, and the relationship between insurance and health care is itself an enormously complicated matter. Moreover, the subject is so vast that any effort to deal with the subject comprehensively, particularly in a basic insurance law course, is doomed to failure. The materials in this section attempt to provide an overview of some of the important issues in health insurance and to provide a flavor of the public policies that are implicated by some of the legal questions that arise when health insurance coverage is contested. But it is difficult, if not impossible, to appreciate the full ramifications of health insurance cases and statutes without some sense of the nexus between health insurance and health care access.

The next two readings and the notes which follow them explore that nexus. This subsection begins with a foray into the portrayal of health insurance in popular culture. John Grisham is one of the most popular writers of recent years; his series of novels involving a variety of legal story-lines have all been best-sellers, and most have been made into very successful movies. In his 1995 book titled *The Rainmaker*, which was also made into a movie directed and produced by Francis Ford Coppola, Rudy Baylor, the main character, is a recent law school graduate (from the University of Memphis, one is led to think) who sues on his client's behalf an insurance company that refused to pay for a bone marrow transplant that would have saved the life of its insured, who is stricken with leukemia. While most of the book concerns Rudy's preparation and trial of the bad-faith claim, other aspects of the book provide insights into the nexus between health insurance and the nation's health care delivery system. In one scene in the book, Rudy visits Donny Ray Black when his death is imminent; when Rudy leaves, he says to himself, "so this is how the uninsured die." Many of these themes are also important in the movie. For an analysis of *The Rainmaker* from an insurance perspective, see Alan I. Widiss, *"Bad Faith" in Fact and Fiction: Ruminations on John Grisham's Tale About Insurance Coverages, Punitive Damages, and the Great Benefit Life Insurance Company*, 26 U. Memphis L. Rev. 1377 (1996); Robert H. Jerry, II, *Health Insurance Coverage for High-Cost Health Care: Reflections on The Rainmaker*, 26 U. Memphis L. Rev. 1347 (1996). After the excerpt from the second of the two cited articles, we consider Professor Stone's thoughtful reflections on fundamental questions regarding the nature of health insurance should play in twenty-first century America.

As you reflect on the materials which follow, try to articulate the reasons why health insurance differs from all other kinds of insurance examined in this book.

Robert H. Jerry, II, *Health Insurance Coverage for High-cost Health Care: Reflections on the Rainmaker,* **26 U. Memphis L. Rev. 1347, 1349–62 (1996)** *

The story of Donny Ray's demise is actually quite simple. When he is diagnosed as having acute leukemia, he is given about a year to live. Desperately needing a bone marrow transplant (BMT), Donny Ray is ideally suited for such a procedure; he has an identical twin brother who is willing to donate his bone marrow to save his sibling. The insurer, however, refuses to pay for the procedure, which costs approximately $150,000. Lacking another way to pay for the treatment, the hospital discharges Donny Ray. Repeated requests to the insurer by his mother for coverage are denied. Months pass, and Donny Ray deteriorates, getting little medical care because he cannot afford it. Eventually, enough months pass to eliminate the BMT procedure as a viable option, even if the insurer were to reverse its denial of coverage and thereby enable Donny Ray to receive it. In late September, some thirteen months after Donny Ray learned he was ill, Rudy Baylor visits Donny Ray, now on his deathbed, and observes, "So this is how the uninsured die." A brief amount of time passes, and on a Sunday morning, Donny Ray's mother calls Rudy to give him the news that Donny Ray is dead. The insurer's denial of coverage is a major contributing factor in, if not the outright cause of, Donny Ray's death because if the BMT had been performed soon after the discovery of his illness, the chances of Donny Ray surviving his illness were fairly estimated at eighty to ninety percent. Without the transplant, Donny Ray had no chance of surviving his illness.

The essence of the story is simpler still. Donny Ray needed access to a high-cost treatment. Because he could not obtain that access, he died. In that simple equation lie the twin imperatives of our nation's health care system—providing access to adequate health care at an affordable cost. Although the problems of access and affordability are profoundly interrelated, their ramifications are perhaps best understood by reflecting on each in turn.

II. THE PROBLEMS OF ACCESS AND AFFORDABILITY

The access issue is complicated, to put it mildly. The dimensions of the problem are usually described by reference to the number of people in the nation who lack health insurance. This makes sense: because health care is expensive, lack of insurance can equate to lack of access to care. An estimated 39.7 million Americans are thought to lack health insurance of any kind at any particular time, but a closer look shows this group to be both diverse and fluid. Not surprisingly, the poor are disproportionately represented among the uninsureds, as are minorities. Because most health insurance is provided by employers as a fringe benefit in employee compensation packages, those who are chronically unemployed as well as those who are between jobs make up a significant portion of the uninsured population. In addition, many uninsured people are employed, but in low-wage positions where the employer does not offer health insurance. Likewise, many young adults who have recently departed their parents' households, where they were covered as dependents on one or both parents' policies, are also uninsured. In short, the uninsured population is much more diverse than most people realize.

Lack of insurance is, however, only one facet of the access issue. Many people who obtain insurance learn later that their coverage has significant exclusions or limitations. For example, most health insurance policies have preexisting condition clauses, which provide that insureds have no coverage, usually for a specific period of time after a policy is issued, for illnesses or conditions that predated the policy's effective date. Thus, a person who changes jobs and obtains new insurance through a new employer may find that his or her (or his or her dependent's) existing condition is not covered by the new policy.** Most policies have deductibles or coinsurance clauses. The presence of these loss-sharing clauses helps reduce the premium charged for insurance. To the extent this makes insurance more affordable, more people may be able to purchase it, but the deductibles and coinsurance requirements themselves may make it difficult for insureds to obtain health care if the insured cannot afford the out-of-pocket payment. Some policies have lifetime limits which place a cap on the insurer's total payments under the policy; this leaves some insureds without coverage for catastrophic illnesses or injuries once the policy limits are exhausted.

The access issue is, however, even more involved than this. Just because an individual lacks insurance or just because his or her affliction falls within a gap in coverage, it does not necessarily follow that the person receives no medical care. An uninsured person may be more likely to forego preventive care, but when that person suffers a very serious medical condition, he or she is likely to go to a health care provider—most probably the emergency room of the nearest hospital—where that person will receive treatment. If a person is too poor to have insurance, then he or she will be too poor to pay the hospital's bill, and, even if the person is not indigent, the expenses of even a short hospital stay are likely to exceed his or her ability to pay. Hospitals and physicians write off some of these bills as uncompensated professional services, but the cost of many of these unpaid bills must be shifted to other paying patients, a redistribution that increases the cost of care and hence the cost of insurance for the insured population. As these costs rise, some insureds lose their ability to afford coverage, and these people become part of the uninsured population whose health care expenses will, in turn, be shouldered by the remaining insureds (or by taxpayers if the person is or becomes eligible for Medicaid or a similar state program, such as TennCare).

Furthermore, the uninsured person who receives care at an emergency room only after a condition has become acute receives one of the most expensive forms of medical care possible. The care is also inefficient in the economic sense in at least two respects. First, it would have been better to treat the person's condition earlier when it would have been less expensive to do so, rather than delay to a point when more expensive treatments are needed. Second, it is inefficient to use trauma centers to treat ear or sinus infections, even painful ones. To add to the problem, an uninsured who is a rational economic actor is unwilling to invest his or her first discretionary dollars in health insurance when he or she knows that free care is available at the emergency room or from other health care providers. This is particularly true of young adults who tend to be healthy and, therefore, do not perceive a need for health insurance; for many such persons, making a monthly car payment

---

** [Editors' note: After this article was published, Congress passed and President Clinton signed the Health Insurance Portability and Accountability Act, otherwise known as "HIPAA." The provisions of HIPAA, most of which became effective on July 1, 1997, significantly limit exclusions for preexisting conditions in health insurance policies. HIPAA is discussed in the notes after these excerpts.]

may seem to have more utility than paying a health insurance premium. To the extent young, healthy people do not purchase insurance, the insured population tends to be older and, therefore, more prone to use health care services. This makes health insurance relatively more expensive, which makes it even less likely that a young, healthy adult will perceive health insurance to be a sensible investment.

The issue of health care's affordability is no less intransigent. The statistics quickly become dated, but the trends are unmistakable and widely documented: as a percentage of gross domestic product, total spending on health care has increased significantly;[38] health care costs are growing at about twice the general rate of inflation; per-family spending for health care as a percentage of total family income has increased significantly; and spending on health care is consuming an ever-increasing percentage of the federal budget. Of course, increased spending on health care is not necessarily cause for alarm if the increased expenditures simply reflect the desire of a more affluent society to spend more on health care than on other goods and services. In other words, spending a lot on something is not necessarily bad if this reflects a conscious, voluntary allocation of resources, in the same sense that if people like to play golf often, people will spend a disproportionate amount of their wealth on golf.

Receiving medical care is not, of course, the same thing as playing golf. People do not aspire to receive more health care in the same way they aspire to play more golf, own a new car, purchase a cellular phone, etc. But when health care is needed, people usually want the very best care possible. Depending on the circumstances, this may mean receiving large quantities of care, the attention of the highest quality (and most expensive) specialists, elaborate tests, etc.[43] In other words, health care is a peculiar kind of consumable; when a parent's child is ill, a parent is likely to insist on the very best care available, regardless of cost. When faced with a life-or-death illness or injury, few people make medical care decisions motivated primarily—or even significantly — by cost. Indeed, many, and perhaps most, people prefer extensive medical care when faced with life-threatening illnesses, even if much of the care only extends life briefly with no chance of altering an inevitable outcome. All of these motivations are understandable, but it means that the

---

[38] [Editors' note: The data set forth in this footnote, as well as other footnotes which appeared in the vicinity of this one, are updated in the notes following the principal readings.]

[43] This description does not, of course, fit everyone. Some people simply do not like to go to doctors, regardless of their illness or other circumstances. Some people are satisfied with a minimum amount of high quality care, assuming this degree of intervention resolves the ailment. All things being equal, I would prefer that my physician spare no expense to cure a persistent earache, but I tend to avoid visiting the doctor for such afflictions at all, even though the out-of-pocket cost to me for such services is de minimis. This is because large quantities of time are lost anytime I visit my physician. This is, of course, an access problem: to keep my premiums low, my health maintenance organization (HMO) has an extremely large patient membership, which frequently leads to long waits in the physicians' offices, which is a cost—lost time — that deters me from seeking care (that is, I consider lost time a greater cost than the annoyance of the earache). If the earache goes away on its own, as most of them do, the HMO saves money (thereby permitting lower premiums) by deterring my visit. This outcome is efficient, however, only if these savings exceed the additional costs incurred by patients who delay the receipt of health care for minor afflictions until the conditions become more serious and, hence, much more expensive to treat.

incentives to consume medical care differ from the reasons one has to purchase cars, movie tickets, and other consumer goods and services.

Yet, even if some portion of increased expenditures for health care reflects an increase that is "desired" by most people, much of the increased expenditure occurs because health care costs more. In other words, cost containment is a problem in health care, and it translates directly into reduced affordability of health care services.

The affordability problem has many dimensions. Few would question that large segments of the current system have excessively high administrative costs.[45] We praise the effectiveness of new technologies, but their use increases the cost of medical care. Although the magnitude of the effect is vigorously debated, many people believe that the legal system encourages enough unnecessary medical care to affect the cost of health care paid by everyone. Unnecessary duplication of expensive medical technologies also increases costs. To illustrate, it is doubtful that each of two adjacent hospitals in most urban centers needs an open-heart surgery capability. It is doubtful that every county in rural areas of the Central Plains needs a hospital, but the controversy over this issue is easy to imagine. The resident of a county with an under-utilized hospital that should be closed does not want the ambulance to have to travel an extra fifty miles to reach the neighboring county's hospital after his or her heart attack. But if an under-utilized hospital is kept open and consolidation is spurned, then the cost of each service must go up in order to pay for the excess overhead. The extent to which the health care industry is sufficiently competitive is much discussed; some believe that certain parts of the industry, such as drug companies, earn excess profits, while others view high drug prices as necessary to cover the high costs of bringing new drugs to the market. Each of these cost factors is complex, and the extent to which each contributes to the problem of affordability is much debated.

Perhaps the most important factor increasing the cost of medical care is the one most deeply entrenched. The federal tax code allows employers to deduct health insurance provided as a fringe benefit to employees, and the benefit is excluded from the employee's income. This has greatly increased the amount of health insurance in force, which has greatly increased the demand for health care: to the extent an insured's decision to consume health care is motivated by cost considerations, an insured who has eighty percent of his or her health care bill covered by insurance will continue to consume health care until an additional one dollar of health care services is worth less

---

[45] The problem is, of course, more complicated than the text allows. For example, the advent of "managed care" and "managed care organizations," such as HMOs and PPOs, is a direct consequence of the cost problem. To the extent many health services rendered are thought to be unnecessary or inappropriate, thereby driving up overall system-wide costs, managed care, through review or intervention, seeks to deter health care providers from prescribing unnecessary or inappropriate treatments. Managed care may also involve a managed care organization negotiating, on behalf of a large group of consumers, with health care providers to receive discounted prices for services. Thus, managed care often requires new or additional administrative mechanisms, which have the effect of increasing administrative costs. If these additional administrative costs result in net savings to the health care system, then the increased administrative costs are desirable.

than twenty cents to the insured. This translates into an enormous increase in demand for health care services: total health care expenditures increase, and to the extent demand rises faster than supply, prices must increase. When to this increased demand for services is added the increased demand generated by government-funded health care programs (i.e., Medicare and Medicaid, or Medicaid substitutes in some states), a simple supply-demand curve predicts significant increases in price, which means health care's affordability is reduced.

Moreover, even if every bit of health care services currently consumed were voluntarily and willingly purchased in a perfectly functioning market, the percentage of federal and state governmental budgets devoted to health care would be a serious concern. Neither the federal nor state government can continue to increase spending for health care without either increasing taxes (a politically unpopular and often impossible option), increasing the size of budget deficits (which creates another diverse set of problems), or cutting expenditures for other government programs (an extraordinarily difficult and perhaps impossible strategy). Thus, even if the health care system currently operated with perfect efficiency, governments would still be searching for ways to reduce the cost of, and hence expenditures for, health care.

The problems of access and affordability are, of course, interrelated: when the price of health care increases, more people find health care unaffordable, which further reduces access. When access is provided for those for whom cost is otherwise an insurmountable barrier, system-wide expenditures for health care inevitably increase. These additional expenses must be paid by someone, but there are few alternatives. Physicians and hospitals might provide the care without charge; indeed, the amount of uncompensated care provided by health care professionals is large. But it is unrealistic to expect health care providers to provide the uninsured population with all their health care needs for free.

Two alternatives remain. First, higher prices can be charged to those who already pay for health care, in effect making the group of people who receive care in today's system subsidize the care of those who lack access. To the extent the higher prices are paid through an insurance mechanism, the additional insurance payouts must be funded through higher premiums charged the insured population, which further constricts the affordability of insurance.

Second, the government could provide the subsidy rather than impose the burden only on those who receive health care. In other words, those who lack access might be assisted through either publicly provided or publicly compensated health care. This would spread the cost of the subsidy across the tax base, with whatever distributive consequences result from federal or state tax policies. This approach, however, adds to tax burdens at a time when the prevailing mood in our country is that the governmental role (and the concomitant tax burden) should be decreased, not expanded.

Sadly, no alternative resonates much excitement, or even hope. Once the generosity of health care providers is exhausted, the cost of providing health care services to the uninsured can be paid either with higher prices charged to insureds or with government funds provided through the tax base, or some combination of the two. Moreover, whatever mechanism is used to increase access to health care services, the increased demand for health care leads to higher prices, which has the ironic effect of compounding the access problem. [49]

III. CAUGHT IN THE CROSS-CURRENTS: HOW INSURERS COPE

Insurance companies like Great Benefit Life are in the middle of all of this. Insurers must collect sufficient premiums to cover payments and administrative costs and (if not a not-for-profit company) to earn a reasonable profit. Employers purchase most health insurance under group arrangements for the benefit of their employees; with health insurance making up an increasing percentage of employers' total expenses, employers exert pressure on insurers to keep premiums low. Individual consumers often act likewise. To compete, insurers must try to accommodate this desire, but it necessarily follows, in a market where costs of services are increasing, that stable premiums are likely to be accompanied by either reductions in coverage or at least constraints on expansion of coverage.

In *The Rainmaker*, Great Benefit Life responds to these pressures in the most extreme manner imaginable by adhering to a corporate policy of initially denying coverage in virtually all cases and citing highly dubious and sometimes overtly frivolous grounds . . . . Yet as the reader reacts with anger to the consequences of Great Benefit Life's miserably callous conduct, he or she should not lose sight of the act that the grounds asserted by Great Benefit Life-the definition of "insured," the preexisting condition clause, the misrepresentation defense, and the experimental treatment exclusion-are important, even essential tools in many other settings where insurers have legitimate reasons for limiting their obligations to their insureds . . . .

Deborah A. Stone, *The Struggle for the Soul of Health Insurance,* **18 J. of Health Politics, Policy & Law 287, 287–90, 308, 314 (1993).** [*]

In the late 1980s, the trade associations of the health and life insurance industry sponsored an advertising campaign to persuade the reading public that "paying for some else's risks" is a bad idea. In one of these ads, a photo of a workman in hard hat and tool belt straddling the girders of a steel tower was captioned: "If you don't take risks, why should you pay for someone else's?" Another ad showed a young man and woman playing basketball one-on-one and asked: "Why should men and women pay different rates for their health and life insurance?" The choral refrain at the bottom of each ad in the series went: "The lower your risk, the lower your premium," and the small print explained the relevant facts. For example:

---

[49] In this discussion, it is assumed that access for the uninsured will not be increased by reducing benefits for the insured population—a solution which merely transfers some of one group's access to another group, i.e., the group lacking access. Such a solution would not increase demand, but would merely shift the access problem, not solve it. . . .

Women under 55 normally incur more health care expenses than men of the same age, so they pay more for individual health insurance than men. After age 55, women generally have lower claims costs, so they normally pay less for individual health insurance than men of the same age.

That's why insurers have to group people with similar risks when they calculate premiums. If they didn't, people with low risks would end up subsidizing people with high risks. And that wouldn't be fair.

In late 1991, The Prudential Insurance Company ran a very different sort of ad campaign. In the *New York Times, Wall Street Journal*, and many newsweeklies, readers saw a photo of a chest X ray with a large white mass in the lower right quadrant. Though most readers couldn't interpret the X ray, the caption explained its significance: "Because he works for a small company, the prognosis isn't good for his fellow workers either." The small-print text went on to explain how one employee's serious illness might cause a small company to be charged "excessively high premiums" come renewal time and how the company might even be forced to drop its health insurance coverage. The Prudential, readers were assured, didn't consider this situation fair and was backing legislation to "regulate the guidelines and rating practices of insurers." Offering a rather different interpretation of fairness from the one in the trade association series a few years back, The Prudential opined, "After all, a small company shouldn't be forced to drop its health plan because an employee was sick enough to need it."

These advertisements have many layers of meaning. On the surface, the issue is how commercial insurers ought to price their health insurance policies. Just below the surface lurks the struggle over health insurance reform proposals in the states and Congress. But the underlying question is whether medical care will be distributed as a right of citizenship or as a market commodity. If, as "the-lower-your-risk-the-lower-your-premium" series commends, we charge people as closely as possible for the medical care they need and consume, then we are treating medical care like other consumer goods distributed through the market. If, like The Prudential, we are unwilling to throw sick people and their fellow employees out of the insurance lifeboat, if we think perhaps the healthy should help pay for the care of others, then medical care becomes more like things we distribute as a right of citizenship, such as education. These advertisements symbolize two very different logics of insurance: the actuarial fairness principle and the solidarity principle.

At a deeper level still, these advertisements offer competing visions of community. They suggest how Americans should think about what ties them together and to whom they have ties. Consider hard hats and other workers in dangerous trades who get injuries and diseases doing constructive work for society: no one else, the ads say, should feel an obligation to pay for their risks. Take women of childbearing age, who are daily exhorted to assure the health of their babies, even those not yet conceived: no one else should finance their extra medical care for that purpose, least of all the men with whom they create the next generation (and recreate on the basketball courts). Alternatively, says the Prudential ad, we should not abandon those who are sick or attached in some way to people who are sick; sick and healthy, we are all one community.

. . . .

While in most societies sickness is widely accepted as a condition that should trigger mutual aid, the American polity has had a weak and wavering commitment to that principle. The politics of health insurance can only be understood as a struggle over the meaning of sickness and whether it should be a condition that automatically generates mutual assistance. However, this is more than a cultural conflict or a fight over meanings. The private insurance industry, the first line of defense in the U.S. system of mutual aid for sickness, is organized around a principle profoundly antithetical to the idea of mutual aid, and indeed, the growth and survival of the industry depends on its ability to finance health care by charging the sick and to convince the public that "each person should pay for his own risk."

. . . Actuarial fairness-each person paying for his own risk-is more than an idea about distributive justice. It is a method of organizing mutual aid by fragmenting communities into ever-smaller, more homogenous groups and a method that leads ultimately to the destruction of mutual aid. This fragmentation must be accomplished by fostering in people a sense of their differences, rather than their commonalities, and their responsibility for themselves only, rather than their interdependence. Moreover, insurance necessarily operates on the logic of actuarial fairness when it, in turn, is organized as a competitive market.

. . . .

The logic and methods of actuarial fairness mean denying insurance to those who most need medical care. The principle actually distributes medical care in *inverse* relation to need, and to the large extent that commercial insurers operate on this principle, the American reliance on the private sector as its main provider of health insurance establishes a system that is perfectly and perversely designed to keep sick people away from doctors. Many insurance regulators accept this view of insurance as well. A state insurance commissioner defends commercial insurers' use of HIV tests in medical underwriting by saying:

> We encourage insurers to test where appropriate because *we don't want insurance companies to issue policies to people who are sick, likely to be sick, or likely to die.*

The commercial industry needs advertisements like "the-lower-your-risk-the-lower-your-premium" series because it is not easy to persuade the public or its elected officials that the task of health insurers and their regulators is to keep sick people away from medical care. These ads were designed to persuade people that actuarial fairness, not solidarity or subsidy, is what insurance is all about.

. . . .

If risk classification is central to the economic organization of commercial insurance, it is perhaps even more central to the social and political organization of American life. The underwriting criteria that insurers have found so necessary to preserve the fiscal soundness and actuarial fairness of their business dovetail precisely with those identities that have formed our major social cleavages: race, ethnicity, class, and more recently sexual orientation

and disability. Underwriting makes and perpetuates a series of internal social divisions, so that, in a far broader sense than insurers usually mean, "likes share their risks with likes." Just as social insurance is a mechanism for implementing mutual aid and a means of defining a diverse and integrated community, the principle of actuarial fairness in all its institutional forms is a marvellously invisible way of creating and perpetuating a segregated society. It explains misfortune as the result of unalterable natural characteristics of individuals, for which the only possible solution is a division of society into the Purgatory of the unfortunate and the Paradise of the blessed.

NOTES

1. *The goals of the system.* Although Professor Jerry's commentary focuses on access and affordability, there are arguably three key variables in the health care mix: access; affordability; and *quality*. Why is it impossible to maximize all three simultaneously?

Is the primary goal of the health care system to provide health care for the sick? How is achieving this goal hindered by the desire of health care providers, pharmaceutical manufacturers, and those who insure the risk of illness to be compensated for their services and contributions? Is providing employment now a primary goal of the health care system? According to the Bureau of Labor Statistics, approximately 13.2 million people were employed in some capacity in the U.S. health care system in 1994, and the BLS predicts that this number will grow to 20.8 million by 2005. Health Insurance Association of America, Source Book of Health Insurance Data 1999-2000, Table 6.23, at 151.

2. *A snapshot of the system I: four routes to insurance and the gaps.* In theory, all Americans should acquire health insurance through one of four routes: (a) Medicare for the elderly and disabled; (b) Medicaid for the indigent and some disabled citizens; (c) employer-provided coverage; (d) individually purchased policies if a person is ineligible for all of the three other categories. Medicaid, however, reaches less than one-half of the poor, and many people under the age of 65 not only lack employer-provided coverage, but are unable to afford their own. Emily Friedman, *The Uninsured: From Dilemma to Crisis*, 265 J.A.M.A. 2491, 2492 (1991). And the trends in these numbers are not promising:

> The most prominent feature of American health insurance coverage is its slow erosion, even as the government seeks to plug the gaps in coverage through such new programs as Medicare+Choice, the Health Insurance Portability and Accountability Act (HIPAA), expansions of state Medicaid programs, and the $24 billion Children's Health Insurance Program of 1997. Despite these efforts, the proportion of Americans without insurance increased from 14.2 percent in 1995 to 15.3 percent in 1996 to 16.1 percent in 1997, when 43.4 million people were uninsured. Not as well appreciated is the fact that the number of people who are underinsured, and thus must either pay out of pocket or forgo medical care, is growing even faster.

Robert Kuttner, *The American Health Care System—Health Insurance Coverage (Health Policy Report)*, 340 N. Eng. J. Med. 163 (1999). In 1998, the proportion of uninsured Americans stood at 16.3 percent, meaning that an estimated 44.3 million people were without health insurance during the 1998 calendar year. Jennifer A. Campbell, *Health Insurance Coverage 1998*, (U.S. Census Bureau) Current Population Reports (Oct. 1999). Because almost 100 percent of the 65 and over population are in Medicare, the 44.3 million uninsureds constituted 18.8 percent of the nonelderly population in 1998. Moreover, the uninsured population is surprisingly fluid; it is believed that approximately 25 percent of all persons under age 65 go without health insurance for a period of at least one month during any given year. Katherine Swartz, *Dynamics of People Without Health Insurance: Don't Let the Numbers Fool You*, 271 J.A.M.A. 64, 64–66 (1994). Kuttner points to several factors that have caused insurance coverage to steadily erode: rising health insurance premiums; the trend toward temporary and part-time work; reductions in the scope of benefits (especially for pharmaceutical benefits) and increases in deductibles and copayments; increased denials of cares (especially by managed care organizations); declining Medicaid eligibility due to welfare reform; the increased cost of Medigap plans (which supplement Medicare coverage); and a trend away from community rating toward individual rating. Kuttner, *supra*, at 163.

3. *A snapshot of the system II: health care expenditures.* The health care delivery system presents a rapidly changing target.[*] In 1998, national health care expenditures exceeded $1.1 trillion, a 5.6 percent increase from the prior year. Despite the size of these numbers, the growth rates of the five years prior to 1998 were the lowest in about 35 years, and roughly matched overall economic growth rates of the same period. Thus, the share of GDP spent on health care remained stable during this period, and stood at 13.5 percent in 1998. But analysts at the Health Care Financing Administration predict that total health care spending will soon begin to grow faster than the overall rate of growth in the economy, and will rise by 2008 to $2.2 trillion, an estimated 16.2 percent of GDP.

Of the $1.1 trillion spent on health care in 1998, about 89 percent of this— about $1 trillion—was spent on personal health care services. Not surprisingly, hospital care and physician services accounted for over half of this figure. After extraordinary growth in the early 1990s, spending on home health care is decelerating, double-digit increases in spending on prescriptions, fueled by rapidly inflating prices and increased insurance coverage, is the big growth area, accounting for 8 percent of total spending in 1998 and for 20 percent of the increase in health spending in 1998. Of the $626.4 billion spent in the private sector for health care in 1998, about 60 percent — or $375.0 billion—was spent by employers and employees on private health insurance premiums. Health insurance benefits paid in 1998 were $337 billion, which represented a growth rate approximately equal to the premium

---

[*] Unless otherwise noted, data cited in these notes comes from the Health Care Financing Administration; the most recent data can be obtained at HCFA's web site, which can be accessed at www.hcfa.gov/stats/nhe-oact. For a useful summary of the data, see Katharine Levit, et al., *Health Spending in 1998: Signals of Change*, Health Affairs, Jan./Feb. 2000, available at http://www.projhope.org/HA/janfeb00/190109.htm

growth rate. Medicare and Medicaid were easily the largest components of public sector spending, accounting for a total of $386.6 billion in expenditures in 1998.

4. *A snapshot of the system III: assessing quality.* Does the U.S. get enough "quality" for these expenditures? The U.S. health care system is widely touted as the best in the world. Yet U.S. infant mortality is among the worst in the developed world (in 1995, 7.59 deaths of infants under one year per 1,000 live births, as compared, for example, to 4.26 deaths in Japan and 5.30 deaths in Germany), and life expectancy at birth lags behind that of many other nations (in 1995 in the U.S., 72.5 years for males and 78.9 years for females, as compared to 76.4 and 82.9 respectively in Japan, and 73.4 and 79.8 respectively in Germany). This occurs even though the U.S. spends more per capita on health care than any other nation in the world (in 1997, $3,925 in the U.S., versus $2,339 in Germany and $1,741 in Japan). Does the quality of "health" depend on different things than the quality of "health care"?

5. *The significant governmental role.* One thing that distinguishes health insurance from all of the other major categories of insurance is the significant governmental presence as financier and provider. The federal government provides health care directly for veterans and for members of the Armed Forces, the Bureau of Indian Affairs operates some facilities that provide care directly, and public health clinics are important in some locales. But the government role in the Medicare and Medicaid programs is overwhelming relative to these other examples.

For many years, government expenditures—primarily Medicare and Medicaid—have accounted for between 40 and 50 percent of total health care expenditures, and a steady upward trend in public funding has only recently showed signs of abating. The growth in public sector spending declined in 1998, increasing by only 4.1 percent; this was largely the result of successful cost-cutting measures in the Medicare program. Private sector health care spending increased from 4.8 percent in 1997 to 6.9 percent in 1998, due largely to steep increases in private health insurance premiums. These premiums increased 8.2 percent in 1998, more than twice the increase of each of the preceding three years. Analysts attribute this to insurers' efforts to reverse deteriorating profit margins and consumers' desire for increased choice in health care plans and increased coverage. In fact, because the trend in recent years had been steady increases in the proportion of health care spending funded by the government (in 1990, the public share was 40 percent and the private share was 60 percent), 1998 marked the first time in a decade that the overall share of private sector spending on health care increased—to 54.5 percent of total spending.

Medicare is the largest federal health program of any kind; it financed 19 percent of all health care spending in 1998 — $216.6 billion in spending for its 38.8 million aged and disabled enrollees. It provides benefits for people over age 65, the disabled, and those with end-stage kidney disease. The program has four sources of funding: mandatory contributions by employers and employees, general tax revenues, beneficiaries' premiums, and deductibles and copayments paid by patients (or supplemental health insurance, which is commonly referred to as "Medigap" coverage). Medicare Part A pays for hospital care, subject to deductibles, length of stay limits, etc. Part A's "Hospital Insurance Trust Fund" is essentially a social insurance program akin to Social Security. Workers make mandatory payments into the fund during their working years, with the expectation of receiving payments from the fund upon retirement. Medicare Part B finances care provided by physicians and other outpatient, some home health, and some other services; it is commonly referred to as the Supplementary Medical Insurance Program. The funding for Part B comes mostly from general tax revenues, although Medicare beneficiaries who enroll in Part B are required (unlike Part A) to pay monthly premiums (in 2000, the monthly premium was $45.50). Enrollment in Part B, unlike Part A, is voluntary. Unlike Medicaid, everyone pays the same premiums, regardless of income. Do you agree with this premise of the system? For a more detailed explanation of Medicare (including Part C, enacted in 1997, which allows Medicare recipients to opt for some kinds of managed care arrangements), see Health Care Financing Administration, A Profile of Medicare Chart Book (1998); Barry R. Furrow, et al., Health Law, ch. 11 (2d ed. 2000).

Medicaid financed 15 percent of all health care spending in 1998. In 1998, Medicaid paid for acute care and long-term care services for 29.0 million aged, blind, and disabled persons with low incomes, as well as poor mothers and children, at a cost of $170.6 billion. The number of Medicaid recipients actually declined in 1998 due to the combined effect of federal welfare reform and strong job growth in the nation's economy. Both the federal and state governments finance the Medicaid program; the federal share ranges from 50 to 83 percent of the state's program costs, depending on the per capita income of the state. Overall, Medicaid accounts for about 40 percent of all federal grants to the states, and accounts for about 60 percent of total costs of all state Medicaid programs. Medicaid defies easy generalization because each state is allowed to set its own guidelines within parameters set by Congress. In fact, several states have HCFA-authorized "Medicaid waivers" that permit local experimentation with delivery of health care services to the poor. (The TennCare program in Tennessee, mentioned in the first excerpt, is one such program.) Compared to Medicare, the coverage provided by Medicaid is generally much more robust; why is this so? For more on Medicaid (and other aspects of health care finance as well), see Furrow, *supra*, ch. 12.

6. *A closer look at the private component.* In 1997, approximately 79.5 percent of all persons under age 65 who had health insurance obtained it through group plans. See U.S. Dep't of the Census, Statistical Abstract of the United States 1999, at 127 (Table No. 185). These are usually employer-provided plans. This phenomenon is in large measure a result of incentives created by federal tax law. Some employers self-insure; in that event, an outside entity— often an insurance company—is retained to manage the health insurance program, but the costs of the program are funded directly by the employer. A large proportion of private health insurance is provided under Blue Cross/Blue Shield plans, which grew out of health insurance plans offered directly by health care providers (i.e., physicians and hospitals) beginning in the 1930s. (The "Blues" are explained in more detail in § 1.05[1], *supra.*) The remainder of private health insurance consists of cash-indemnity plans sold by commercial insurers, of which there are about 350 currently

selling health insurance in the United States. This landscape is rapidly changing, however, as the material in § 1.05[1] explains in more detail.

An individual insurance policy usually has two components: one covers physicians' services, and the other provides hospitalization coverage. The typical policy has a bundle of provisions (*e.g.*, exclusions, deductibles, co-payment, etc.) pertinent to each. The term "major medical" coverage refers to a policy which either is subject to a very large deductible or is excess over other health insurance; this kind of coverage is intended to provide protection against catastrophic medical expenses, but these policies will have their own exclusions and limitations.

7. *Is health insurance "insurance"?* Should health insurance be sold much like any other insurance product? In other words, should high-risk insureds pay higher premiums or be denied coverage altogether? Has this model already been abandoned? The creation of expansive government programs (Medicare, Medicaid) to provide health insurance to groups who will struggle in private markets (the elderly because they are high-risk and the poor because they lack the resources to acquire coverage) suggests a society-wide consensus that the private market model has intolerable limitations. The effort to expand access to health care through governmental subsidy implies that health care is an entitlement or right. If our society arrives at a consensus that some basic quantity of access to health care is to be provided to all citizens (a "social welfare model"), health insurance is likely to become the device through which this universal access will be provided. A system of universal, compulsory health insurance may still involve private entities, but such a system will no doubt have many features which resemble the Social Security system, including its wealth-redistributing features.

Professor Stone argues that the insurance world's actuarial model is irreconcilable with the social welfare model. When private insurers segment health insurance risk pools, are they forcing on the general public a product that the public does not want? Assume that you are in excellent health, you have a policy of health insurance from a private insurer, and you receive a letter indicating that the insurer intends to increase the number of insureds in your pool by 25 percent by adding individuals with terminal illnesses. You are also told that your monthly premium will increase by 25 percent so that these persons can be covered. What is your reaction to this proposal? Would you consider switching to another insurer's plan? Is acquiescing to the insurer's plan your "moral obligation"? Would your reaction be different if you were told that the plan were going to cover a previously excluded illness that could strike anyone in the plan, and that all were going to have to pay more for the coverage?

Is Professor Stone's argument equally applicable to life insurance? When life insurers refuse to issue insurance to the terminally ill, to those whose family histories suggest the probability of early death, or to those who have adverse health conditions relevant to mortality which they cannot control, are insurers "creating and perpetuating a segregated society"? Should regulatory steps be taken to make life insurance more widely available to those who currently cannot afford it or acquire it? What about disability insurance?

8. *Health care reform in the 1990s.* In 1993 President Bill Clinton proposed a far-reaching reform of the health care system. Among the many features of the proposed "Health Security Act" were minimum benefits for all citizens; placing all citizens ineligible for Medicare in regional Health Alliances that would use their bargaining power to purchase coverage at competitive rates from "Health Plans," i.e., health insurers or networks of hospitals, HMOs, and physicians; employer-financing of health insurance premiums for employees, and federal government financing of premiums for the unemployed through surcharges placed on the premiums paid by everyone else; and the option for individuals to purchase benefits above the minimum package. After an extended national debate, President Clinton withdrew the plan when it became clear that it could not get the support of a majority in the Congress.

As a result of the failure of the Clinton initiative, it appears that reforms will be incremental for the indefinite future. What future president will be willing to take the political risks associated with comprehensive reform? Indeed, it is fair to say that the American approach to health care reform has always been one of "incrementalism." Although Medicare is a massive program, its essence when enacted and at present is to address one piece of a very large puzzle — how to provide health care access to the elderly, an inexorably high-risk group. Medicaid is also incremental in the sense that it targets another at-risk group—the poor. Shoring up the funding of these programs remains a very hot issue at Y2K. What political problems will be confronted in increasing funding for Medicaid? What are the political problems with finding a Medicare funding plan, and how are they different? Professor Mark Hall reported on one senior citizen's response to President Clinton's failed health care reform proposal: "I don't want the government coming between me and my Medicare." Does this help prove Professor Stone's point? What does this say about the political climate for health care reform?

A few other incremental reforms are discussed in the notes which follow. Future reforms are likely to be incremental as well. During the next several years, much attention will be given to solving the problem of the high cost of prescription drugs and to the high cost of coverage for early retirees. The problems of providing long-term care for the increasing number of elderly — and the high cost of long-term care insurance — will also figure prominently in public discussions.

9. *Incremental reform: COBRA.* The access issue has, obviously, much to do with who is entitled to the benefits of particular policies. For example, because group policies in the employment setting are so common, many people have health insurance by virtue of their dependency relationship (spouse or child) to the employee. If this relationship ends (either through divorce or because a child ceases to be a dependent), the coverage may cease. Moreover, an employee may be fired or laid off, or the employee may die, thereby terminating the coverage of the dependents. Further, an employer may terminate or modify a plan, leaving the employee without coverage. Some of these problems are addressed, at least partially, by a 1985 federal statute which is commonly referred to as "COBRA," an acronym for "The Consolidated Omnibus Budget Reconciliation Act of 1985" (COBRA), P.L. 99-272, 99th Cong., 2nd Sess., 100 Stat. 82 (1986).

Under COBRA, most employers who maintain group health plans are required to offer participating employees and their covered dependents the option to continue health coverage for a specified period. The law is intended to make health care coverage available for a limited time at group rates to people who would otherwise lose their employer-sponsored coverage and could not afford or obtain the same coverage at individual rates. The principal limitations in the statute are: (a) it does not create new classes of covered employees; (b) it does not regulate what benefits, if any, the employer must provide; (c) it does not apply to employers who have less than 20 employees or to employees that are terminated for "gross misconduct." Some state statutes provide "continuation benefits" for other categories of employees; for example, Mo. Stat. § 376.397 (West 1991) extends some COBRA protections to any employer having two or more employees.

COBRA applies to a "group health plan," which is defined as an employee welfare benefit plan providing medical care to participants or beneficiaries directly or through insurance, reimbursement, or otherwise. The option to elect continuation coverage is triggered by a "qualifying event," after which a "qualified beneficiary" has 60 days to exercise the option. Generally, any specified person who experiences one of the following "qualifying events" is a "qualified beneficiary" entitled to the option to purchase continuation coverage: (a) *voluntary termination* (i.e., employees who lose coverage because they quit their jobs); (b) *involuntary termination* (i.e., employees who lose coverage because they are fired, unless terminated for "gross misconduct"); (c) *reduction in hours* (i.e., employees who experience a reduction in hours that drops them below a minimum hours' requirement under the plan); (d) *events affecting spouses and other dependents of covered employees* (i.e., spouses and other dependents if they were previously covered by the plan but lose their coverage because of death of the covered employee, divorce or legal separation from the covered employee, or the covered employee becomes eligible for Medicare); (e) *discontinuance of coverage for ineligible dependents* (i.e., children of employees who cease to be covered dependents under the plan's definition, as in the situation where the plan provides that dependent children of employees are no longer covered upon marriage or reaching age 21).

The maximum period of continuation coverage, once elected, depends on the type of "qualifying event." If there is a voluntary or involuntary termination of employment or a reduction in hours worked, coverage must be available for up to 18 months commencing on the date health coverage otherwise would expire. On the other hand, coverage arising due to (1) the death of a covered employee or divorce or legal separation from the covered employee; (2) the covered employee becoming eligible for Medicare; or (3) a child becoming ineligible as a covered dependent under the plan, must be available for up to 36 months commencing on the date health coverage otherwise would expire. There also are special provisions for those who are disabled.

The act goes on to detail (1) notice procedures requiring that employees and qualified beneficiaries be provided both an initial notice of their rights to continuation coverage when they become eligible to participate in the plan and a more extensive notice upon the occurrence of a qualifying event, (2) election procedures, (3) what type of coverage is required to be offered (generally, the eligible person must be offered the same coverage that the person had before the qualifying event took place), (4) what happens when an individual is afforded coverage under another group health plan during the COBRA continuation period, (5) the maximum premium that can be charged for the continuation coverage (generally, it is 102% of the total premium under the plan, including both the employer's and employee's contribution), and (6) penalties for employer noncompliance.

Although COBRA is a very important milestone in the development of health care coverage, it is no panacea. For example, it does nothing for those who lose their health care coverage because the employer cancels or modifies the group contract. In addition, the premium—although capped at 102%—is still formidable for most people and can even be prohibitive for some. Would it be advisable to allow employers to provide alternative plans with less extensive coverage at lower rates? Would it be advisable to expand the time periods for continuation coverage for certain employees—for example, those who have been in the group for a certain number of years, but who want to retire more than 18 months before they are eligible for Medicare? Or should the Medicare eligibility age be dropped for early retirees? For more information about COBRA, see Roberta Casper Watson, *COBRA Health Continuation Benefits Under the New and Old Regulations*, SE04 ALI-ABA 109 (Sept. 16, 1999). When "incrementalism" is the style of health care reform, one looks at existing programs and asks how they might be expanded or what gaps in them might be plugged.

10. *Incremental reform: HIPAA.* In 1996, Congress passed and President Clinton signed into law the Health Insurance Portability and Accountability Act of 1996 (" HIPAA"), Pub. L. No. 104-191, 110 Stat. 1936 (1996). HIPAA, which as amended is codified in scattered sections of titles 18, 26, 29, and 42 of the U.S. Code, has three main components: 1) the "portability rules" make it easier for those who remain continuously covered under employer-sponsored health plans to change jobs without having to meet new eligibility requirements; 2) the "anti-discrimination provisions" prohibit discrimination against employees and dependents based on health status, which has the effect of eliminating barriers to access for some persons; 3) the "guaranteed access" provisions guarantee renewability and availability of coverage to certain employees and individuals. The portability rules regulate health insurers' use of preexisting condition clauses, and this receives more attention in § 4.04[4] below. The anti-discrimination provisions are complicated, but it is questionable whether they will have much impact in any event. HIPAA does not regulate the cost of coverage; thus, even if people have the right to purchase coverage without health status limitations, whether they can afford it is another matter altogether. The same problem exists with guaranteed renewability and availability rules; if the insurance is unaffordable, the fact that it is technically "available" is of little worth. For more information about HIPAA (and other recent statutes), see Phyllis C. Borzi, *Recent Health Care Legislation*, Q285 ALI-ABA 1 (Mar. 16, 1999).

11. *Other incremental reforms.* In recent years, Congress has become enamored of "mandated benefit" statutes. COBRA, for example, is a "mandate," but it mandates employers to offer coverage. COBRA, by its terms, does

not state what specific benefits must be provided by an employer (although an employer may not offer less as a continuation benefit than what it provides to full-time employees). The first mandated benefit was probably the Pregnancy Discrimination Act of 1978, 92 Stat. 2076, 42 U.S.C. § 2000e(k) (1994). Before this statute was enacted, the U.S. Supreme Court had ruled that a workplace policy or rule which discriminates against unmarried, pregnant women does not constitute discrimination based on sex in violation of Title VII of the Civil Rights Act, 42 U.S.C. § 2000e (1994). The reasoning was that the distinction drawn was not between men and women, but rather was between pregnant and nonpregnant persons; because some women are in the category of nonpregnant persons, the Court ruled that such a policy does not unlawfully discriminate against women. In the Pregnancy Discrimination Act, Congress rejected this reasoning and made clear that discrimination based on a woman's pregnancy is discrimination because of her sex. Although the essence of the statute was establishing nondiscrimination rules for women in the workplace, this was relevant to health insurance in that employer-provided health plans (of employers with 15 or more workers) were required, if they covered prenatal and maternity services at all, to provide coverage for prenatal and maternity services comparable to coverage for other conditions.

For many years, a number of states had required insurers issuing group or blanket health and accident policies providing benefits for hospital or medical expenses to include coverage for treatment of mental illness and nervous disorders. *See, e.g.,* Cal. Ins. Code § 10125 (West 1993); D.C. Code Ann. § 35-2302 (1997). Others merely require the insurers to offer such coverage as an option. *See, e.g.,* La. Rev. Stat. § 22:669 (West 1995 & Supp. 2000). Congress entered this territory when it enacted the Mental Health Parity Act of 1996 (the "MHPA"), 29 U.S.C. § 1185a, and 42 U.S.C. §§ 300gg-5 (Supp. III 1996). Originally included in the bill that would become HIPAA, the mental health provisions (which initially called for full parity) were stripped out of the HIPAA bill during intense, partisan debate in conference committee. A more limited bill was tacked onto an Veterans Affairs appropriations bill, and this bill became law. The essence of the MHPA is to require parity in the application of annual dollar limits and aggregate lifetime dollar limits for medical/surgical benefits relative to mental health benefits. Small employers (those with fewer than 50 employees) are exempt, and there is an exemption for health plans that can demonstrate that compliance will result in a cost increase of one percent or more. The statute does not require any plan to provide mental health benefits, and does not prevent a plan from dropping mental health benefits. It also does not affect any other terms and conditions of coverage, including medical necessity requirements, deductibles, or limits on numbers of visits or days of coverage. Moreover, the MHPA has a sunset provision that runs in 2001. Having mandated the benefit for health plans, what are the odds that Congress will allow the mandate to expire and that employers will take the coverage away? Why do you suppose Congress was worried about providing "full parity" for mental health benefits? For more discussion of the MHPA, see Brian D. Shannon, *Paving the Path to Parity in Health Insurance Coverage for Mental Illness: New Law or Merely Good Intentions?*, 68 U. Colo. L. Rev. 63 (1997).

In 1996, Congress also passed the Newborns' and Mothers' Health Protection Act of 1996 (the "NMHPA"), 29 U.S.C. § 1185, 42 U.S.C. §§ 300gg-4, -51 (Supp. II 1996). The essence of this statute is to forbid group plans from restricting benefits for any hospital length of stay in connection with childbirth for the mother or newborn following a normal vaginal delivery to less than 48 hours (or 96 hours in the case of a cesarean birth). Is there any coincidence in the fact that this statute (as well as HIPAA and MHPA) was enacted during an election year? This statute was a reaction to a number of highly publicized stories of insurers forcing mothers and newborns to leave hospitals earlier than their doctors advised or they wished, sometimes with tragic consequences. The statute enjoys widespread popular support; for a dissenting view, see David A. Hyman, *Drive-Through Deliveries: Is "Consumer Protection" Just What the Doctor Ordered?*, 78 N.C. L. Rev. 5 (1999). Two years later, Congress passed the Women's Health and Cancer Rights Act of 1998 (the "WHCRA"), 29 U.S.C.A. § 1185b, and 42 U.S.C.A. §§ 300gg-6, -52 (West 1999), which requires health care plans offering mastectomy coverage to also provide coverage for reconstructive surgery in a manner determined in consultation with the attending physician and the patient.

Numerous other mandates have been proposed in Congress, involving such diverse matters as infertility treatments, prescription drug coverage, hair prostheses for scalp diseases, asthma treatments for children, contraceptive drugs and services, obstetric and gynecological care, colorectal cancer screening, and minimum hospital stays for lymph node dissections. Are these the kinds of details in which Congress should become involved?

12. *State mandates.* In recent years, many state legislatures have enacted "mandated benefits" statutes requiring that health insurance policies sold in the state contain certain minimum coverages. Benefits which have been the subject of legislation in one or more states include, for example, coverage for inpatient and outpatient kidney disease treatment, in-patient treatment for alcoholism and drug abuse, infertility treatments (including in vitro fertilization), and payment for blood products. Scholars debate to what extent these mandates have increased the cost of health insurance. See Gail A. Jensen & Michael A. Morrisey, *Employer-Sponsored Health Insurance and Mandated Benefit Laws*, 77 Milbank Quar. 425 (1999). Why do you suppose these mandates have been so popular in state legislatures? It is noteworthy that because ERISA preempts state efforts to regulate self-insured plans, the state mandates do not apply to such plans. The same is not true, however, of the federal mandates discussed in the prior notes (COBRA, HIPAA, MHPA, WHCRA, NMHPA). Those mandates apply to employer-provided plans, including self-insured plans.

13. *Prospects for the future.* It seems that no one—doctors; patients; insurers; politicians — is satisfied with the current health care and health insurance system. So what is to be done about it? As one observer stated, "Millions of our citizens do not now have a full measure of opportunity to achieve and enjoy good health. Millions do not now have protection or security against the economic effects of sickness. The time has arrived for action to help them attain that opportunity and that protection. . . . We should resolve now that the health of this Nation is a national concern; that financial barriers

in the way of attaining health shall be removed; that the health of all its citizens deserves the help of all the Nation." Those words were spoken by President Harry Truman in an address to the Congress on November 19, 1945. *Special Message to the Congress Recommending a Comprehensive Health Program*, in Public Papers of the Presidents of the United States: Harry S. Truman, 1945, at 475, 476–477. Why have these problems been so enduring?

[2]   The Nature of "Risk" in Health Insurance

CONNECTICUT GENERAL LIFE INSURANCE CO. v. SHELTON

611 S.W.2d 928 (Tex. Civ. App. 1981)

Massey, Chief Justice.

[Mr. & Mrs. Shelton, insureds, obtained a judgment against the defendant insurer in a bench trial for hospital and medical expenses in connection with "elective" surgery performed on Mrs. Shelton. The insurer, Connecticut General Life Insurance Company, appealed.]

We reverse and render a take nothing judgment.

Years ago Mrs. Shelton was married to a man by whom children were born in a state of health such that her physician advised that there would be extreme hazard to the health of any subsequent child born of the marriage. This was because of incompatibility of the Rh factor in the blood of the parents. There was no evidence of any danger to the mother; only to any child she might bear. The advice received was that any such child would probably perish. Because of this the woman, who later became Mrs. Shelton, decided that she should have tubal ligation, i.e. the operation commonly referred to as "having one's tubes tied". She did have such an operation and it was successful in that future pregnancy was thereby prevented.

Thereafter she married Shelton. She became "covered" by the policy of insurance upon which the instant suit was predicated. She and her husband desired to have a child of such marriage if that should be possible. By recourse to medical examinations and advice they learned that the state of the art of medical and surgical practice had advanced so that restoration of Mrs. Shelton's fallopian tubes to a condition that she might become pregnant was more likely to be successful than unsuccessful. Also determined was that the Rh factors in the blood of Mr. and Mrs. Shelton were compatible; that in the event of the birth of a child there should be no expectation of complication or difficulty to either such child or to the mother.

Based upon this advice Mrs. Shelton elected to have the restorative surgery. An operation was performed and it was successful. In due course she and her husband have a reasonable expectation that a healthy child might be born of their marriage.

The policy of insurance was in force and effect at the time of the restorative surgery. If and in the event it should be properly construed to cover and provide for the payment of the expenses attendant thereto the Sheltons would be entitled to collect the benefits provided. The amount of these benefits are stipulated for purposes of the appeal; if the Sheltons have entitlement to any benefits it is for those awarded them by judgment.

The sole point of error of the company is that there was "no evidence that the Plaintiffs' claims for expenses were incurred for the necessary care and treatment of an injury or sickness as defined in the group insurance contract."

We will express our opinion at the outset, to be later elaborated, that absent any language of the policy of an intent to cover operations of the character here involved—either expressed or by necessary implication,—the general principles of the law relative to insurance forbid the holding that there was liability of the company therefor as a covered risk for which insurance was afforded. We do not find any such language in the policy and therefore have no doubt but that the decision is controlled by these general principles.

We copy from provisions found in the Shelton policy. The insuring provisions, in pertinent part, under the title "Major Medical Benefits", provide as follows:

> If. . .a dependent, while insured for Major Medical Benefits, incurs Covered Expenses as a result of an injury or a sickness, the Insurance Company will pay an amount determined as follows: [here the measure to be applied, not copied because immaterial under the only point of error presented]
>
> . . . .
>
> COVERED EXPENSES: The term Covered Expenses means the expenses actually incurred by or on behalf of. . .dependent for charges listed below,. . .only to the extent that the services or supplies provided are recommended by a physician as essential for the necessary care and treatment of an injury or sickness.

The group insurance contract defines the term "injury" as follows:

> The term injury will include all injuries received by an individual in any one accident.

The group insurance contract defines the term "sickness" as follows:

> . . . physical sickness, mental illness, functional nervous disorder and covered pregnancy. . . .

From the presentation of both parties we think it not to be doubted that the test to be made of coverage by the policy of insurance is upon the premise that the operation resulted because there was election to submit thereto by reason of either "injury" or "sickness" as defined by the policy, or — if not contradictory thereto—by legal definitions to be attributed to these terms. In any event, as already stated, we do not find any policy language which would alter general principles of the law of insurance so as to express an intent of the parties to the contract that an operation of the character involved should be a covered risk.

By the history of insurance in the United States the beginning theory was that risks or the chance of loss, to be insurable, must be pure risks and should not be based on a moral hazard. In addition to be insurable the risk must be measurable in quantitative terms for which purpose the law of large numbers and the theories of probability and chance are employed. The law of large numbers is based on the observation that the larger the number of instances taken, the closer the result approaches the theoretical probability, and, as applied to insurance, that means the probability of loss. Carried to the ultimate this means to have converted the probability of loss into "expectation of loss" or value of the risk. Thereby is determinable the consideration to be charged (ultimately or in advance, with — as applied to mutual companies—reasonably assured profits to be shared without likelihood of a necessity to make a greater payment, to insure an individual or group of individuals. Noticed is that in the case of a stock company the individual insured is generally not entitled to share in the company's profits; but at the same time he is not expected to pay more in the event there should be a loss and not a profit for the term insured.).

In addition to the requirement that risks, to be insurable, must be of the pure variety as described above, and must also lend themselves to measurement in quantitative terms, certain other conditions must be met before the institution of insurance may function. (1) The risk must be genuine, must exist for large groups of people, and its existence must be recognized by a sufficient number of people to warrant the establishment of organization(s) to insure it. (2) Persons exposed to the risk must feel a responsibility for the possible loss and its consequences. (3) Those concerned (in the instance of mutual insurance) must possess the resources with which to pay their prorata share of the costs or premiums. (4) The magnitude of the potential loss must be sufficient to cause a real hardship for the individuals upon whom actual losses may fall. (5) *The events concerned must be accidental or fortuitous* in character; they must occur according to the laws of chance and not be subject to control by those seeking to insure. (6) And, finally, a catastrophe hazard must not exist.

As we view it the matters set out in the foregoing paragraph provide a method for considering applicable limitations upon the well recognized rule that in the construction of insurance contracts the terms and provisions are to be considered to afford insurance whenever no violence is done by giving them meaning and effect in accomplishing to the fullest extent the intention of the parties as expressed by the policy.

Generally it is contemplated to be that in attaining the objective of insurance and insurability the moral hazard should not be permitted to exist. The simplest example of such a moral hazard is that applicable to fire insurance on property; as applied thereto the moral hazard is the risk or probability that the individual insured will destroy or permit to be destroyed the insured property for purpose of collecting insurance benefits. There has been qualification of this principle in insurance policies, perhaps in those related to health insurance more than in any others. In many of such policies are found provisions for payment of insurance benefits indemnifying the insured for costs incidental to pregnancy and childbirth. However, these benefits of insurance are payable because of their inclusion by contractual provision. They are not payable otherwise — assuming normalcy of the term of pregnancy and absence of complications attendant thereto or to ensuing childbirth.

In its brief the company has included a good many citations of cases exemplifying application of basic insurance principles; where in each the result has been the holding that there was no liability under various policies of insurance. We list these:

McGregor v. General Acc. Fire and Life Assur. Corporation, 214 N.C. 201, 198 S.E. 641 (N.C. 1938) (holding that impacted wisdom teeth which caused no trouble, pain or illness prior to their removal did not constitute a disease).

Myers v. Metropolitan Life Insurance Company, 152 Pa. Super. 507, 33 A.2d 253 (1943) (holding that a congenital eye defect was not a disease, i.e., not an illness, malady or disorder).

Beaudoin v. La Societe St. Jean Baptiste De Bienfaisance De Biddeford, et al., 116 Me. 428, 102 A. 234 (1917) (holding that a broken leg was not a sickness; there was no accidental bodily injury coverage).

Fazekas v. Perth Amboy Holy Mary Roman Catholic Sick Ben. Soc., 13 N.J. Misc. 822, 181 A. 631 (1935) (holding that a broken elbow was not a sickness; there was no accidental bodily injury coverage).

Callison v. Continental Casualty Company, 221 Cal. App. 2d 363, 34 Cal. Rptr. 444 (Cal. App., 1963) (holding that burns were not a sickness and disallowing additional benefits in the policy for sickness where the coverage limits for injury had been exhausted).

Diez v. Accident Indemnity Insurance Company, 162 So. 2d 206 (La. App., 1964) (holding absence of liability of the company for expenses attendant to claims for benefits under "sickness" provisions of the insurance policy to pay for children's tonsillectomies—because the surgical procedures were purely preventative, or in other words elective, and not done in treatment of a sickness).

Reserve Life Insurance Company v. Whitten, 38 Ala. App. 455, 88 So. 2d 573 (Ala. App., 1956) (holding that where a tubal ligation had been performed on the insured to prevent future pregnancy shown to be dangerous to the insured in the event it should occur there was not coverage under a sickness policy for medical expenses, the operation not having been performed to relieve any existing condition).

Fullerton v. General Motors Corporation, etc., 46 A.D.2d 251, 362 N.Y. Supp. 2d 581 (1974) (holding, in an instance where there was a claim for disability under the New York Workmen's Compensation Law for time lost due to an elective bilateral tubal ligation, there was no liability of the company for the insurance benefits of the policy because it was conceded by the claimant that the surgery was performed solely at her request because she desired sterilization. The applicable statute defined disability as "inability of an employee to perform the regular duties of his employment as the result of injury or sickness").

We view the objectives of the surgical procedures in this case, as applied to the insurance afforded by the policy, to be the same as would have been existent had Mrs. Shelton been well able to become pregnant and bear a child, but desired for reasons other than the security of existent health in her own person to "have her tubes tied". In either case the procedure would be elective surgery unrelated to sickness or accident. (We assume absence of any complication following surgical procedures.)

The event, the surgical procedure, though undoubtedly necessitating hospital and medical expense and a period of physical disability for a period to follow, was neither accidental or fortuitous in character, nor was it necessitated to cure or alleviate any condition of sickness of Mrs. Shelton. While we recognize that she would have greatly preferred to be in physical condition so that she might become pregnant without necessity of the operation, yet, from the standpoint of the company the moral hazard which should not be permitted to exist under basic insurance principles would have application to any claim for benefits predicated upon the expense attendant to and incident to the accomplishment of the elective surgery.

We reject the resourceful argument of the [Sheltons'] attorney that the evidence raised the issue of "sickness" in Mrs. Shelton by reason of the earlier operation, so that the corrective surgery was made necessary. We deem that in this case it would be a distortion of the terms "unsound", "impaired", "morbid condition of the body which hinders and prevents the organs from normally discharging their functions", etc., to force the company to afford insurance by its policy.

We reverse the judgment of the trial court and render judgment that Gray W. Shelton, et ux., take nothing by the suit against Connecticut General Life Insurance Company.

SPURLOCK, JUSTICE, dissenting.

The group health insurance contract in question defines "sickness" as "physical sickness, mental illness, functional nervous disorder and Covered Pregnancy." I will limit my dissent to the discussion of the term "physical sickness" in an attempt to demonstrate why Mae Janell Shelton's condition falls within this category.

A small percentage of the women in our population are born with an Rh negative factor in their blood. That by itself presents no problem. However, as the bulk of the population is Rh positive a woman with a Rh negative factor runs the risk of marrying and conceiving children with a man whose blood type is Rh positive and thus incompatible with hers. Again, the husband's blood, should it be Rh positive is incompatible in the situational sense only, that situation being the conceiving and the giving of birth to children. Even at this point the first child is usually "a freebie". During the first pregnancy, assuming it to be normal, the newborn's blood does not mix with the mother's until birth. If the child's blood is Rh positive, as mathematics dictate it usually will be, at the point of mixing the child's incompatible blood with the mother's, the mother's body responds as if it were being invaded by an "antigen", a substance perceived by her body as deleterious to it. This triggers the mother's body to produce antibodies specifically tailored to destroy the invading antigen; in this case, the baby's blood. As her body is not so alerted until the birth of the first child the complications that arise affect only subsequent pregnancies. During the course of any future pregnancies the mother's system, now alerted to the antigens (the Rh positive blood of the fetus) "attacks" the fetus' blood supply with antibodies. Normally her system does what is intended; the fetus dies and the mother miscarries.

To avoid the continuous and recurring possibility of this gruesome scene our plaintiff, a woman born (and borne) with an Rh negative factor "chose" to become sterilized. It is this capacity to choose that has singled her out to be denied coverage. People normally don't choose to become physically ill. In line with the majority opinion it is this inability to choose that allows for insurable risks. There exists that element of chance, a chance that the group as a pool seeks to insure against.

Mrs. Shelton is perceived as having denied chance by having chosen to receive elective surgery. What the insurance company and the majority fail to realize is that the ailment for which Mrs. Shelton seeks redress is not the undoing of the tubal ligation but the condition that made it necessary in the first place. For Mrs. Shelton, despite the limits of the English language, did not "choose" to become physically sick. The term choice as it is normally applied to elective surgery has no significance here. It would be far more accurate to depict Mrs. Shelton's situation, when she "chose" to have a tubal ligation sixteen years ago as one in which she was *forced* to *trade* one illness for another. She may have had some input as to what effect her condition would impose on her body (inability to conceive as opposed to the inability to bear children.) But Mae Shelton did not choose to be sick; she merely chose from limited possibilities what form that sickness would take. It was chance that made her sick, chance that created her Rh negative and chance that exposed her to the perilous environment of conceiving children with a male that was Rh positive. In this regard Mae Shelton was no better and no worse than anybody else born with a susceptibility to a particular disease.

To argue that surgery to avoid the complications arising from her Rh negative factor was elective is preposterous. To argue further that the inability to produce healthy, live born children does not somehow demonstrate a serious impairment in a female body borders on the far reaches of common sense. A primary ability of a healthy, normally functioning female is the ability to successfully bear children. The fact that Mae Shelton, as previously married and without a tubal ligation, would have birthed still-born children or miscarried indicates a deficiency in an otherwise normal female.

The majority would have us believe that such a deficiency manifests itself only on the fetus; that the mother's health is in no way affected. Are we to presume that the ability to give birth to healthy, alive children is not the function of a healthy female? Somehow, because there temporarily and frailly exists a child to accept, unwillingly, the onus of this failure, we are expected to conclude that such a condition affects only the health of the child. As these frail souls depart into the next world we are expected to sit here content in the knowledge that the mother is a healthy and unimpaired woman. In fact it is her body that is possessed by the disease. The miscarried child exists as sad testament to this disease. Only by curing the mother can the tragedy to the child be avoided. Mae Shelton did not choose to become sterile, not in the true sense of the word. It was a decision forced upon her as she sought the lesser of two evils. Such a Hobson's choice is a choice in name only. And now she seeks to have removed a deficiency the yoke of which she had no choice but to struggle under.

Connecticut General, in its brief, cited and relied upon the following definition from *Couch on Insurance* 2d § 41:803:

"Disease" has been defined as an alteration in the state of the human body or some of its organs or parts interrupting or disturbing the performance of the vital functions or as a deviation from the healthy or normal condition of any of the body, and as a morbid condition of any of the functions or tissues of the body.

The words "sickness" and "disease" are technically synonymous, but given their popular meaning as required in construing a contract of insurance, "sickness" is a condition interfering with one's usual activities, whereas disease may exist without such result; in other words, one is not ordinarily considered sick who performs his usual occupation, though some organ of the body may be affected, but is regarded as sick when that diseased condition has advanced far enough to incapacitate him.

The definition speaks for itself. The Rh negative factor incapacitated Mae Shelton's ability to have a normal pregnancy and childbirth. The tubal ligation in no way altered that symptom; it only allowed her a little greater freedom in her sex life. Her present operation stems from a desire to cure the illness and restore Mae Shelton to a normal state. I would affirm the lower court.

I respectfully dissent.

NOTES

1. *What is a "sickness"?* Suppose the battle in *Shelton* were over the expense of the original tubal ligation. Should that procedure be covered under the policy? Compare *Poche v. Travelers Insurance Co.,* 491 So. 2d 185 (La. App. 1986). How would the majority and dissent each answer that question?

Is infertility a "sickness"? *See Ralston v. Connecticut General Life Insurance Co.,* 617 So. 2d 1379 (La. Ct. App.), *vacated,* 625 So. 2d 156 (La. 1993). If Mrs. Shelton's tubal ligation had nothing to do with the problem of the incompatible Rh factor and was motivated solely by her desire never to be pregnant again, should the insurer be required to pay for the restorative surgery? See *Reuss v. Time Insurance Co.,* 177 Ga. App. 672, 340 S.E.2d 625 (1986) (involving insured who sought restoration through vasovasotomy of sterilization resulting from prior voluntary vasectomy). Should the answer to the question of whether infertility is a sickness depend on the fortuity involved in the cause of the infertility? For more discussion, see D'Andra Millsap, *Sex, Lies and Health Insurance: Employer-Provided Health Insurance Coverage of Abortion and Infertility Services and the ADA,* 22 Am. J. L. & Med. 51 (1996).

What are the implications of insisting upon a "fortuitous cause" as a prerequisite to coverage? The insured whose elbow trouble is caused by arthritis would be covered, presumably, for the expenses incurred in treating the elbow. If the insured's elbow trouble is caused by voluntarily playing too much tennis with a poor backhand, should the health care expenses be covered? What about coverage of the expenses associated with childbirth?

If "sickness or injury" is the threshold for health insurance coverage, what about preventive care, such as immunizations, EKGs, mammograms, and other physical examinations?

2. *The importance of policy language.* In these cases, much can turn on the precise language of the insurance contract. Most policies do provide coverage for the most common and useful kinds of preventive care; indeed, it would be incredibly cost-ineffective for an insurance policy not to pay for immunizations, to take one example. Moreover, a policy might exclude coverage for some treatments under the reasoning that they are too costly and the benefits are too few. In vitro fertilization as a treatment for infertility is frequently excluded from coverage, arguably for the reasons just mentioned.

3. *Dental care.* Dental care, both preventive and restorative, is viewed as important to a person's well-being and health. Why is dental care typically excluded from health insurance plans, except when the expense is incurred as the result of an accident? The standard health insurance policy usually contains a provision excluding certain conditions from coverage, such as the following:

> "Mouth Conditions—Charges for doctors' services or X-ray examinations for mouth conditions due to periodontal or periapical disease or any treatment of the teeth, surrounding tissue or structure, the alveolar process on the gingival tissue, except for treatment or removal of malignant tumors."

Moorman v. Prudential Insurance Co. of Am., 4 Ohio St. 3d 20, 445 N.E.2d 1122 (1983). Separate policies of dental insurance can be purchased. Yet the words "sickness" or "disease," as used in the typical health insurance policy, could be construed to cover many services provided by dentists, particularly oral surgeons.

The type of clause quoted above has been troublesome with regard to expenses for treatment of temporomandibular joint syndrome ("TMJ"), a misalignment of the temporomandibular joint which causes pain in the ear, jaw, head, neck, or shoulder areas. In addition to the use of splints and even surgery to realign the jaw joint, crown and bridge work is often prescribed. Insurers have resisted paying for the latter under exclusions similar to that above on the basis that it constitutes "any treatment of the teeth" or under clauses that exclude charges for "dentistry." So far the insurers have lost most of the time. *See, e.g., Bocalbos v. Kapiloani Medical Center for Women and Children,* 997 P.2d 42 (Haw. Ct. App. 2000); *Cotton v. Wal-Mart Stores, Inc.,* 552 So. 2d 14 (La. App. 1989); *Celtic Life Insurance Co. v. Fox,* 544 So. 2d 245 (Fla. Dist. Ct. App. 1989); *Moorman v. Prudential Insurance Co. of Am.,* 4 Ohio St. 3d 20, 445 N.E.2d 1122 (1983). But *see Humphrey v. Aetna Life and Casualty Insurance Co.,* 572 So. 2d 105 (La. App. 1990) (treatment for TMJ was not covered by major medical provisions of group plan because it did not arise due to an "injury"). In one case, the insurer specifically excluded coverage for "treatment for or prevention of temporomandibular joint syndrome" and still lost because the exclusion was not conspicuous, plain, and clear. *Ponder v. Blue Cross of S. Cal.,* 145 Cal. App. 3d 709, 193 Cal. Rptr. 632 (1983). In the 1980s, TMJ was diagnosed and treated with an unprecedented frequency. Did the frequency of TMJ increase across the country, or did dentists need more work? One commentator provided this answer: "Dentists, having controlled tooth decay, have stumbled upon an epidemic of alleged whiplash-induced temporomandibular joint (TMJ) syndromes, many of which either do not exist or arose from an uninsured natural cause. Practice-building seminars teach dentists how to find this new source of business and how to link the condition to an accident to ensure reimbursement." Ronald E. Gots, *Applying the Brakes to Medical Casualty Costs*, 90 Best's Review—Prop.-Cas. Ins. Ed. 50 (Feb. 1990).

4. *The "medical necessity" connection.* Whether an health care expense is a treatment for a sickness or injury and is therefore covered blends into the closely-related issue of "medical necessity." It is common for health insurance plans to limit coverage to "medically necessary" services; if there is no sickness or injury, the argument follows that health care expenses incurred were not "medically necessary." But one can, of course, have a sickness or injury and still confront an insurer's contention that the care received was not "medically necessary." Consider the following materials.

[3]   Medical Appropriateness

FULLER v. CBT CORP.

905 F.2d 1055 (7th Cir. 1990)

Posner, Circuit Judge.

This is an appeal from the dismissal, on motion for summary judgment, of a suit that charges two separate violations of an employee health plan. (The basis of federal jurisdiction is ERISA, the federal pension and welfare plan statute. Employee Retirement Income Security Act, 29 U.S.C. §§ 1001 et seq.) The plaintiff, James Fuller, was employed as an auditor by the Board of Trade, and the first violation charged arises out of an operation that he had in March of 1986 to remove a sperm granuloma (a type of growth) that had developed at the site of a vasectomy. In the same operation he had the vasectomy reversed so that he and his wife could have additional children. The bill exceeded $7,500 but the plan was unwilling to reimburse him more than $300, the plan's estimate of the cost allocable to the removal of the granuloma. Fuller contends that this allocation is too low, and in addition that he is entitled to the cost of his overnight stay at the hospital, which was necessitated by his reaction to the anesthesia. But in this court he has abandoned his argument that the plan covers vasectomy reversals; and while arguing that employees of the plan told him that it did cover that procedure he does not argue that their statements bind the plan, for example on a theory of estoppel.

The plan confines coverage of medical expenses to "conditions," defined as "illness" or "pregnancy," the former being "an injury or sickness." "Injury" means "accidental bodily injury," and "sickness" "any physical or mental disease or any emotional or nervous disorder, [including] alcoholism, drug addiction, and pregnancy." The reversal of a vasectomy is not the treatment of a disease or disorder in any obvious sense, but that is not critical. We are not devotees of literal interpretation. Sterility is a condition for which medical treatment is commonly sought, and, as in *Egert v. Connecticut General Life Ins. Co.*, 900 F.2d 1032 (7th Cir. 1990), we find it difficult to believe that the plan excludes all fertility treatment. Now a vasectomy produces sterility; but it is self-induced sterility, and that makes all the difference. The plan, no doubt reflecting concern with the "moral hazard" (the temptation to alter one's behavior because one is insured) that is created when a person buys insurance against the consequences of his deliberate behavior, *Connecticut General Life Ins. Co. v. Shelton*, 611 S.W.2d 928, 930–32 (Tex. Civ. App. 1981), excludes from coverage treatment of "any condition resulting from an intentional self-inflicted injury." If sterility could fairly be called an "injury," the reversal of a vasectomy would be treatment of a condition resulting from an intentional self-inflicted injury. While we grant that the consequence of a vasectomy is better described as a condition than as an injury, the exclusionary intention of the provision we have quoted seems both clear and clearly applicable to vasectomy reversals.

The plan muddies these waters a bit, though, by grounding its denial of liability not on the definition of sickness but on a provision in the plan that "medical services or supplies not certified as necessary by a physician" are not covered. The purpose of this exclusion is not to confine coverage to conditions that a physician might think "necessary" to treat, but to avoid coverage of extravagant procedures. Few conditions are necessary to treat in the sense that if they are left untreated the patient will die, be crippled, or suffer excruciating pain. A patient might have a disfiguring scar; in what sense would its removal be "necessary"? A physician might think it unnecessary to treat a fertility problem, because people can live in perfect physical health and adequate mental health without being fertile; we do not think that on this account no fertility treatments are covered by the plan. The plan covers cosmetic surgery, provided that it is required to correct a disfigurement due to a nonoccupational accident; the line drawn is (approximately) between the frivolous and the sober resort to discretionary medical treatment, and the treatment of fertility is surely on the sober side of the line.

The significance of the "certified as necessary" provision in this case lies not in determining whether vasectomy reversals are covered, but in making clear that, since they are not, the presence of the granuloma (a covered condition) does not bring Fuller's vasectomy reversal within the scope of coverage. One does not require a vasectomy reversal in order to remove a granuloma that has developed at the site of the vasectomy.

Fuller is left to argue over the cost allocable to the removal of the granuloma, an admittedly covered expense. He failed to submit evidence on what the removal of a granuloma should cost. As for the overnight stay in the hospital, it plainly was not caused by the simple out-patient procedure of removing a granuloma; it was caused by the operation to reverse the vasectomy. Now even if vasectomy reversal is not a covered procedure, an illness incident to the procedure — infection, complications, a iatrogenic injury, whatever — would be covered. Playing tennis is not a covered procedure either, but if you are injured playing tennis your medical expenses are covered. The record contains a letter from Fuller's physician suggesting (in the fractured prose that is the hallmark of physicians' epistolary endeavors) that the overnight stay was necessary because of complications resulting from the operation to reverse the vasectomy and remove the granuloma, as distinct from being a necessary incident of a normal vasectomy reversal. But Fuller does not argue the point in this court, and it is therefore forfeited.

To defeat the plan's motion for summary judgment on this point, all Fuller had to do was to submit an affidavit from a reputable surgeon concerning the cost of removing a sperm granuloma. But that much he had to do; he could not rest on his pleadings when the plan had submitted evidence on the cost allocable to the removal of the granuloma. Fed. R. Civ. P. 56(e). . . . We therefore need not consider the subtle issue of cost allocation that would be presented if the cost of removing the granuloma were low by virtue of the fact that the procedure was done in conjunction with reversing the vasectomy. The issue would then be whether Fuller or the plan was entitled to the benefits of this economy of scope. The issue is not before us, because Fuller failed to present intelligible evidence of the relevant costs.

. . . .

The grant of summary judgment on the question whether the trustees violated the uniformity provision of the plan by refusing to extend Fuller's (dependent) benefits for six months was premature, and is reversed; in all other respects the judgment of the district court is affirmed. No costs in this court.

Affirmed in part, reversed in part.

NOTES

1. *Where is the line?* What makes a treatment unnecessary under the standard adopted by Judge Posner? Why did Mr. Fuller not have coverage? Should the insurer redraft the "medical necessity" clause? If so, how?

Does "medical necessity" have different meanings in different contexts? Professor Jost observes that asserting that a treatment is "not necessary" could mean that the procedure or test is inappropriate for the patient's particular condition, that the second-best treatment is comparatively more appropriate in terms of costs and benefits, or that the benefit to the patient is unknown. See Timothy S. Jost, *The American Difference in Health Care Costs: Is There a Problem? Is Medical Necessity the Solution?*, 43 St. Louis U. L. J. 1, 13 (1999).

Medical necessity is also important in the public insurance programs. The Medicare statute excludes from coverage services which "are not reasonable and necessary for the diagnosis or treatment of illness or injury or to improve the functioning of a malformed body member." 42 U.S.C. § 1395y(a) (1994). The Medicaid statute does not have a similar provision, but the Supreme Court held in an early case that Medicaid covers "necessary medical treatment." *See Beal v. Doe*, 432 U.S. 438, 444 (1977).

2. *Who draws the line?* Under the provision at issue in *Fuller* and the court's construction of it, is it possible for a health care expense to be "medically unnecessary" if a physician certifies necessity? If the clause "muddies the waters," does this mean the clause is ambiguous? And if it is, does this mean the physician's certification should always be determinative? In *Mount Sinai Hospital v. Zorek*, 271 N.Y.S.2d 1012 (N.Y. Civ. Ct. 1966), a case typical of its era and the utilization review practices of those times, the court rejected

the insurer's challenge to a doctor's decision to hospitalize the insured during a "rigid starvation" weight loss regimen, stating "we may of course review [the doctor's] judgment as to whether or not hospital confinement was necessary for the particular treatment prescribed. . . [, but] [o]nce the treating doctor has decided on a course of treatment for which hospitalization is necessary, his judgment cannot be retrospectively challenged." 271 N.Y.S.2d at 1016. If you are worried about giving health care providers the key to the safe, do you have any concern about letting the insurer make the determination of medical necessity? By the end of the 1970s, most health insurance policies specified that medical necessity would be determined in the insurer's judgment, not the physician's.

3. *Sickness, injury, and necessity. Fuller* illustrates how the illness or injury determination is closely connected to the determination of medical necessity. Much, of course, can turn on the precise language of the insurance contract. Predictably, the kinds of disputes that can arise are almost endless. Should the following be considered a "necessary" medical expense resulting from sickness or injury? (a) laetrile (amygdalin) and related nutritional therapy prescribed for a metabolic disorder (*Shumake v. Travelers Insurance Co.,* 147 Mich. App. 600, 383 N.W.2d 259 (1986)); (b) reconstructive breast surgery due only in part to birth defects (*Aetna Life Ins. Co. v. Martin,* 386 So. 2d 468 (Ala. Civ. App. 1980)); (c) soft palate operation to correct congenital defect of two-year-old child (*Beggs v. Pacific Mutual Life Insurance Co.,* 171 Ga. App. 204, 318 S.E.2d 836 (1984)); (d) Gerson therapy, involving a dietary regimen consisting of large numbers of organically grown fruits and vegetables and their juices, together with certain medications, digestive aids and vitamins, to treat cancer (*Zuckerberg v. Blue Cross and Blue Shield,* 108 A.D.2d 56, 487 N.Y.S.2d 595 (1985), *aff'd on other grounds,* 67 N.Y.2d 688, 490 N.E.2d 839, 499 N.Y.S.2d 920 (1986)); (e) physician-prescribed massage therapy for back strain resulting from insured lifting her children (*Wait v. Metropolitan Life Insurance,* 168 A.D.2d 867, 564 N.Y.S.2d 535 (1990); (f) a "cranial hair vacuum prosthesis" used to protect the insured, who suffered from alopecia universalis, from weather extremes and sunburns (*Hendley v. South Carolina State Budget and Control Bd. ex rel. Division of Insurance Services,* 333 S.C. 455, 510 S.E.2d 421 (1999); (g) prescribed intravenous antibiotic treatment of Lyme disease for "seriously ill" 40-year-old woman suffering from, *inter alia,* epileptic seizures and migraines (*Risenhoover v. Bayer Corp. Group Health Plan,* 83 F. Supp. 2d 408 (S.D.N.Y. 2000).

4. *The connection between "medical necessity" and experimental or investigational treatments.* Judge Posner viewed the medical necessity provision as a brake on coverage for the elaborate and extravagant treatment, such as an in-patient hospital stay for the removal of stitches that closed a wound. A different question than the one addressed in *Fuller* is this: Is a treatment that does not comport with accepted medical care protocols "medically necessary"? Even if the treatment is the last card to be played in an effort to avoid death? Consider the next case.

BECHTOLD v. PHYSICIANS HEALTH PLAN OF NORTHERN INDIANA, INC.

19 F.3d 322 (7th Cir. 1994)

COFFEY, CIRCUIT JUDGE.

Penny Jo Bechtold, a female diagnosed and treated for breast cancer, brought this action under the Employee Retirement Income Security Act ("ERISA"), 29 U.S.C. § 1132(a)(1)(B), to recover benefits under an ERISA-governed employee welfare benefit plan. In her suit against Physicians Health Plan of Northern Indiana ("PHP"), Bechtold is seeking coverage for high-dose chemotherapy with autologous bone marrow transplantation ("HDC/ABMT"). The case was assigned to a U.S. Magistrate Judge by consent pursuant to 28 U.S.C. § 636(c). On March 18, 1993, the magistrate judge denied the plaintiff's motion for summary judgment but granted the defendant's motion for summary judgment. We affirm.

BACKGROUND

The parties have stipulated to the relevant facts in this case and legal issues only need be determined. Penny Jo Bechtold is a forty year-old pre-menopausal adult female. She is employed by Magnavox Electronic Systems which maintains a health plan administered by the defendant Physicians Health Plan of Northern Indiana. The plan is an "employee welfare benefit plan" as defined in 29 U.S.C. § 1002(1).

In October, 1991, the plaintiff was diagnosed as having breast cancer and underwent a modified radical mastectomy. The surgery disclosed heavy lymph node involvement with the breast cancer cells. After the removal of the tumor she was treated with standard chemotherapy and radiation. Her oncologist recommended that she receive heavy dose chemotherapy with an autologous bone marrow transplant (HDC/ABMT) and referred her to the Cleveland Clinic for this treatment.

HDC/ABMT is a two-step procedure. Physicians first extract ("harvest") the bone marrow cells from the patient's body and place them temporarily in frozen storage. Next, the patient undergoes a cycle of high-dose chemotherapy in hopes of killing the cancer cells. Because the high-dose chemotherapy also attacks the bone marrow cells, it is necessary to withdraw some of the bone marrow prior to undergoing the high-dose chemotherapy. Without initially removing a portion of the bone marrow cells, the high-dose chemotherapy would be lethal because of its myeloblative effect (it destroys bone marrow cells which produce blood cells (red and white) as well as platelets) rendering the patient highly susceptible to infection. After completing the administration of the high-dose chemotherapy, the patient's own ("autologous") stored marrow is reinfused intravenously into the bloodstream to relieve the patient from the toxic effects of the chemotherapy. HDC/ABMT has proven effective in treating certain cancerous blood diseases such as leukemia and Hodgkin's disease but to date it has not been universally accepted treatment for solid-type tumors including breast cancer.

Before Bechtold proceeded with the treatment, PHP advised her that the HDC/ABMT treatment was not a covered service under the plan. Under the policy, a claimant is entitled to a hearing following the denial of a claim, and the plaintiff did in fact appeal the denial of benefits and received a hearing before a committee selected by PHP.[1] The committee recommended that even though the insurer had met its obligations to the plaintiff under the contract, that the insurer should change its policy and authorize payment for the procedure because the treatment was reasonable for a patient of Bechtold's age. PHP did not agree with the committee's recommendation, and refused to pay for the treatment stating that it had "lived up to its Contract obligations" under the "clear and unambiguous language in the Contract." PHP advised the plaintiff it was denying her appeal in a letter dated October 2, 1992. With her administrative remedies exhausted, the plaintiff initiated this suit in the U.S. District Court for the Northern District of Indiana.

ISSUES

On appeal, the plaintiff raises two issues: (1) whether PHP erroneously denied coverage for HDC/ABMT under the plan, and (2) whether she was denied a "full and fair review" of her claim for benefits when PHP declined to accept the recommendation of the complaints committee.

DISCUSSION

We are aware that Mrs. Bechtold and her immediate family have undoubtedly endured a great deal of heartache, frustration and depression during her battle with cancer.[2] There is no doubt that the policy questions posed in cases like this are of grave concern to all of us, yet we, as a court of law, are called upon to make legal determinations.[3] The issue in this case is very

---

[1] The "Complaint Procedures" section of the policy, contains the following requirements regarding the hearing:

Section 5.2 Complaint Hearing. If the Covered Person requests a hearing, a committee shall be appointed by the Chief Executive Officer of PLAN, consisting of at least one PLAN Participating Physician, at least one consumer Enrollee of PLAN, and a representative of PLAN management. The complaint committee shall be empowered to resolve or recommend the resolution of the complaint.

[2] Fortunately for Mrs. Bechtold she has secondary insurance that paid for the treatment and thus this action will merely determine which of two insurers will pay for the treatment.

[3] In *Harris v. Mutual of Omaha Cos.*, 1992 WL 421489, 1992 U.S.Dist. LEXIS 21393 (S.D.Ind. Aug. 26, 1992), aff'd, 992 F.2d 706 (7th Cir.1993), a similar case of a claimant seeking coverage for HDC/ABMT, U.S. District Judge Tinder succinctly summarized the problem facing courts in these difficult claims for medical coverage:

Despite rumors to the contrary, those who wear judicial robes are human beings, and as persons, are inspired and motivated by compassion as anyone would be. Consequently, we often must remind ourselves that in our official capacities, we have authority only to issue rulings within the narrow parameters of the law and the facts before us. The temptation to go about, doing good where we see fit, and to make things less difficult for those who come before us, regardless of the law, is strong. But the law, without which judges are nothing, abjures such unlicensed formulation of unauthorized social policy by the judiciary.

Plaintiff Judy Harris well deserves, and in a perfect world would be entitled to, all known medical treatments to control the horrid disease from which she suffers. In ruling as this court must, no personal satisfaction is taken, but that the law was followed. The court will have to

straightforward: Does the PHP benefit plan authorize coverage of HDC/ABMT? This is a matter of contract interpretation that does not implicate the broader policy issues involved in whether insurers should cover medical procedures that are presently of unknown medical value and extremely costly.

A claim for benefits under an ERISA-governed plan "is a matter of contract interpretation. When there are no triable issues of fact, we have held that '[c]ontract interpretation is a subject particularly suited to disposition by summary judgment.'" The interpretation of an unambiguous contract is a question of law for the court. "A term is [only] ambiguous if it is subject to reasonable alternative interpretations."

The parties have devoted considerable time arguing what the proper standard of review is in this case. . . . We need not decide what level of deference to give to the defendant's interpretation of the contract term because under the facts in this case, even applying de novo review, the clear and unambiguous language of the policy dictates that the defendant, Physicians Health Plan of Northern Indiana, properly denied coverage for the HDC/ABMT treatment.

Denial of Coverage

In part, the Plan provides:

"Experimental or Unproven Procedures" means any procedures, devices, drugs or medicines or the use thereof which falls within any of the following categories:

1. Which is considered by any government agency or subdivision, including but not limited to the Food and Drug Administration, the Office of Health Technology Assessment, or *HCFA Medicare Coverage Issues Manual* to be:

    a. experimental or investigational;

    b. *not considered reasonable and necessary*; or

    c. any similar finding;

2. Which is not covered under Medicare reimbursement laws, regulations or interpretations; or

3. Which is not commonly and customarily recognized by the medical profession in the state of Indiana as appropriate for the condition being treated.

PLAN reserves the right to change, from time to time, the procedures considered to be Experimental or Unproven. Contact PLAN to determine if a particular procedure, treatment, or device is considered to be Experimental or Unproven."

(Emphasis added).

---

live with the haunting thought that Ms. Harris, and perhaps others insured by the Mutual of Omaha Companies under similar plans, may not ultimately receive the treatment they need and deserve. Perhaps the question most importantly raised about this case, and similar cases, is who should pay for the hopeful treatments that are being developed in this rapidly developing area of medical science?

The HCFA Medicare Coverage Issues Manual (which is referenced in the PHP Plan) provides in section 35-31:

> "C. *Autologous Bone Marrow Transplantation (Effective for Services Performed on or After 04/28/89).*—Autologous bone marrow transplantation is a technique for restoring bone marrow stem cells using the patient's own previously stored marrow.

* * *

> 2. *Noncovered Conditions.*—Insufficient data exist to establish definite conclusions regarding the efficacy of autologous bone marrow transplantation for the following conditions:
>
> • Acute leukemia in relapse (ICD-9-CM codes 204.0, 205.0, 206.0, and 208.0);
>
> • *Chronic granulocytic leukemia (ICD-9-CM code 205.1);* or.
>
> • *Solid tumors* (other than neuroblastoma) (ICD-9-CM codes 140-199).
>
> *In these cases, autologous bone marrow transplantation is not considered reasonable and necessary within the meaning of § 1862(a)(1)(A) of the Act and is not covered under Medicare.*" (Emphasis added). [5]

The plaintiff does not challenge the language of the HCFA Medicare Coverage Issues Manual but argues that the phrase in the Plan that PHP "reserves the right to change, from time to time, the procedures considered to be Experimental or Unproven" creates an obligation on the part of PHP to cover the contested treatment in light of recent medical research endorsing the procedure for solid tumors like breast cancer. She argues that the "right to change" implies that PHP will update the list of experimental treatments as medical research and science allows. Bechtold claims that an unsuspecting lay person would conclude that the phrase "right to change" implies that PHP's intent was to stay current with advances in the medical sciences rather than to hide behind outdated or inapplicable guidelines and therefore if the treatment is no longer experimental-as the plaintiff argues-she is entitled to coverage. Bechtold further argues that because the phrase "right to change" is not defined anywhere in the contract, it is ambiguous.

We are of the opinion that Bechtold is attempting to create an ambiguity in the contract language where no ambiguity exists. The "right to change" clause is merely a reservation of rights and is not "subject to reasonable alternative interpretations." The "right to change" the classification of procedures certainly does not obligate PHP to reclassify hourly, weekly, monthly or annually whether a treatment should be covered on the basis of competing views of medical experts (oncologists). Rather, PHP chose to link the experimental nature of a treatment to the neutral (third party) determination of the medical experts responsible for drafting the HCFA Medicare Coverage

---

[5] Breast cancer falls under the solid tumor exclusion.

Issues Manual. Clearly, PHP's intent was to avoid a case-by-case battle of the experts in which PHP would be required to re-evaluate covered treatments each time a self-proclaimed "expert" publishes a new article. As recited above, PHP chose to rely on the neutral HCFA Medicare Coverage Issues Manual to determine whether a procedure is "experimental."[6] The section of the policy that defines experimental procedures states "[e]xperimental or [u]nproven [p]rocedures means any procedure . . . [w]hich is considered by. . .[the] HCFA Medicare Coverage Issues Manual to be. . .not considered reasonable and necessary. . . ." The HCFA manual clearly states that for solid tumors, including breast cancer, "autologous bone marrow transplantation is not considered reasonable and necessary. . . ." This language is clear and unambiguous. *See Awbrey v. Pennzoil Co.*, 961 F.2d 928, 930–31 (10th Cir.1992) ("[a] court is without authority to alter or amend contract terms and provisions absent an ambiguity in the contract *** [w]e will not read into the [contract] a requirement that, by its clear and unambiguous language, is absent"); *Senn v. United Dominion Indust., Inc.*, 951 F.2d 806, 818 (7th Cir.) ("we are not permitted to allow our sympathies and desires to vitiate clear principles of contract and labor law, and in particular, we refuse to amend the clear terms of the health and welfare benefits contained in the [agreement]"), *reh'g en banc denied*, 962 F.2d 655 (7th Cir.1992), *cert. denied*, 509 U.S. 903, 113 S.Ct. 2992, 125 L.Ed.2d 687 (1993); *Heller v. Equitable Life Assur. Soc.*, 833 F.2d 1253, 1257 (7th Cir.1987) ("In the absence of a clear, unequivocal and specific contractual requirement [placing a duty on a party,] we refuse to order the same.[7] To hold otherwise and to impose such a requirement would, in effect, enlarge the terms of the policy beyond those clearly defined in the policy agreed to by the parties.").

---

[6] The HCFA Medicare Coverage Issues Manual is updated when new medical data becomes available and the updates are published quarterly in the Federal Register. *See* Joint Exhibit No. 7. The provision relating to autologous bone marrow transplants for solid tumors (breast cancer) was published in the Federal Register on June 11, 1992, *see* 57 Fed.Reg. 24797, 24804 (June 11, 1992), and was in effect at all times relevant to this proceeding (Bechtold was denied coverage in October 1992).

[7] In *Heller*, the insurance company was attempting to require the insured (a physician) to undergo surgery to correct carpal tunnel syndrome, however, there was no such requirement in the disability insurance contract. We noted that the plaintiff "entered into a mutually binding private insurance contract for professional disability insurance with [the defendant] and obligated himself to pay a substantial bi-annual premium. In the absence of an express provision obligating the insured to undergo surgery, we refuse to place such a requirement upon the insured." 833 F.2d at 1258. We also added that

"The insurance company seeking to condition coverage on its insureds' acquiescence to undergo surgery to minimize the extent of their disabilities, as well as the financial loss to the insurer, need only incorporate a specific requirement to that effect in the policy, and we would not hesitate to enforce the same. On the other hand, insurers who fail to include this express surgical contractual requirement, and who refuse to cover an insured after entering into a binding and enforceable agreement after accepting substantial premiums, in circumstances such as those before us, cause problems not only for the insured, but for the insurance industry as well. Insurance companies, members of a service industry, must recognize that, like their insureds, they have corresponding duties and obligations under the policy and must conduct themselves accordingly instead of attempting to rely on the courts to correct their own deficiencies in underwriting and/or careless policy drafting."

Id. at 1259–60 (footnote omitted).

In effect, the plaintiff is arguing that PHP should cover the treatment. Clearly there is no authority for such a proposition under ERISA which does not dictate what a plan such as the PHP plan before us should cover. Therefore, we hold that the language of the PHP Plan excludes coverage for HDC/ABMT as a treatment for breast cancer.

Full and Fair Review

Bechtold's second argument is that she was denied full and fair review under 29 U.S.C. § 1133 because PHP refused to accept the recommendation of its own complaints committee and instead denied the benefits based on the Plan Chief Operating Officer's disagreement with the committee's recommendation. We cannot agree with Bechtold's argument on this account because a review of the letter from PHP denying the benefits (the October 2, 1992 letter) makes clear that the committee recognized that the HDC/ABMT treatment was not covered under the plan. The committee, however, recommended a change of policy by the insurer to allow coverage of the procedure because:

1) the procedure was not experimental and PHP has an express intent of providing reasonable care for patients of this type;

2) Medicare supporting claims for this type of non-covered condition, is not that of a patient of Ms. Bechtold's age;

3) supportive data suggests the proposed treatment as very appropriate.

The committee was called upon to make a recommendation within the parameters of the contract entered into between the insured and the insurance carrier. The committee found that according to the language in the policy that the parties agreed upon, Bechtold was not entitled to coverage. This should have signaled the end of their report but they chose to go beyond their authority and responsibility and recommend a material policy reformation. See 29 U.S.C. § 1133 and Art. 5 of PHP Plan (referring to resolution of the claim not reformation of the plan to cover previously noncovered services). The only authority vested in the committee was to recommend whether a specific claim for benefits had been properly denied based upon the language of the policy; it was not free to cast aside the agreed upon terms of the insurance contract. Based on the clear and unambiguous terms of the policy, we agree with the defendant that the Plan did not authorize reimbursement for the procedure (HDC/ABMT for breast cancer) and that the complaints committee lacked authorization to recommend a significant reformation of the Plan (i.e., the Plan should cover the treatment). Accordingly we hold that the plaintiff received a full and fair review as required under 29 U.S.C. § 1133.

CONCLUSION

As stated above, cases of this nature pose troubling social as well as ethical questions that go well beyond the legal issues. As a court of law we are empowered to decide legal issues presented by specific cases or controversies. The greater social questions must be decided by the political branches of government which can engage in "legislative fact-finding" and "benefit from public hearings and constituent expression of opinion." Chesterfield Smith, the former president of the American Bar Association once stated in a Law Day address: "courts are being asked today to solve problems for which they are not institutionally equipped. . . . The American public perceives the courts as a jack-of-all trades available to furnish the answer to whatever may trouble them." The question of what procedures insurance companies should cover is just the type of problem to which Mr. Smith was referring.

In order to resolve the question of whether health insurance providers should cover treatments like HDC/ABMT, the prudent course of action might be to establish some sort of regional cooperative committees comprised of oncologists, internists, surgeons, experts in medical ethics, medical school administrators, economists, representatives of the insurance industry, patient advocates and politicians. Through such a collective task force perhaps some consensus might be reached concerning the definition of experimental procedures, as well as agreement on the procedures, which are so cost prohibitive that requiring insurers to cover them might result in the collapse of the healthcare industry. While such a committee would in no way be a panacea for our skyrocketing health care costs, it may help to reduce the incidence of suits in which one "expert" testifies that a procedure is experimental and another equally qualified "expert" testifies to the opposite effect. This so called battle of the experts occurs all too frequently in federal court.

Under the present state of the law, we are bound to interpret the language of the specific contract before us and cannot amend or expand the coverage contained therein. In this case, that contract is unambiguous and clearly states that HDC/ABMT is not a reasonable or necessary treatment for solid tumors such as breast cancer. Accordingly, the judgment of the magistrate is

AFFIRMED.

NOTES

1. *Where is the line?* Every treatment in medical science was, at one point, experimental. When does a treatment cease to be experimental? If a treatment consistently achieves a 90 percent cure rate for some kinds of cancer in some kinds of patients over an extended period of time, and these results are validated in clinical trials, presumably one would conclude that the treatment is no longer experimental in that application. As for *Bechtold*, does it make sense to use a Medicare standard for senior citizens to decide whether a 40-year-old woman's illness is covered by insurance?

Experts are likely to disagree about the efficacy of some treatments. Is a treatment no longer experimental when "most" experts say so? When "at least half" of all experts say so? When "some" experts say so? And then there is the question of what makes someone an "expert." Is conducting a clinical study enough? Is being a licensed physician enough?

If you were Mrs. Bechtold's personal physician, would you have certified the treatment as "medically necessary?" Assuming you felt strongly about your decision (you know that Mrs. Bechtold and her family does), how would you feel about having it reviewed by an insurer? See Mark A. Hall & Gerald F. Anderson, *Health Insurers' Assessment of Medical Necessity*, 140 U. Pa. L. Rev.

1637 (1992); Sharona Hoffman, *A Proposal for Federal Legislation to Address Health Insurance Coverage for Experimental and Investigational Treatments*, 78 Or. L. Rev. 203 (1999).

2. *Equal treatment?* How would it affect your assessment of Mrs. Bechtold's claim if the data showed that ABMT is routinely covered by insurers for some rare forms of cancer, such as testicular cancer, where there is even less evidence of ABMT's utility than with breast cancer? Would it affect your assessment if the data showed that patients with lawyers were more likely to get approval of coverage than patients without lawyers?

3. *Breast cancer and HDCT-ABMT.* There is a great deal riding on the question of how to treat breast cancer for millions of women. The illness strikes more than one out of every ten women at some time in their lives. More than 180,000 new cases are diagnosed annually, and each year more than 45,000 women succumb to the disease. Nancy A. Wynstra, *Breast Cancer: Selected Legal Issues*, 74 Cancer Supp. 491 (July 1, 1994). There is also a great deal riding on this question for the health care system, given that the expense of providing HDCT-ABMT for all breast cancer patients who might be good candidates for it is in the vicinity of $2.25 billion. Marilyn Chase, *Medical Quandary: Breast-Cancer Patients Seeking New Therapy Face Tough Obstacles,* Wall St. J., Feb. 17, 1993, at A1, A9.

For many years, expert opinion on whether bone-marrow transplants accompanied by high-dose chemotherapy is superior to conventional treatment was sharply divided. See *Breast Cancer: Bone-Marrow Transplants*, Harvard Health Letter, July 1, 1995, at 1. Predictably, this uncertainty was reflected in disparate outcomes when similarly situated women sought coverage. In April 2000, the *New England Journal of Medicine* published the results of a study which concluded that "[a]s compared with maintenance chemotherapy in conventional doses, high-dose chemotherapy plus autologous stem-cell transplantation soon after the induction of a complete or partial remission with conventional-dose chemotherapy does not improve survival in women with metastatic breast cancer." Edward A. Stadtmauer, et al., *Conventional-Dose Chemotherapy Compared with High-Dose Chemotherapy plus Autologous Hematopoietic Stem-Cell Transplantation for Metastatic Breast Cancer*, 342 N. Eng. J. Med. 1069 (2000). What, if anything, does this portend for future cases where insureds seek coverage for experimental treatments?

4. *Procedure.* If a person in Mrs. Bechtold's position lacks sufficient personal resources to pay for the treatment and cannot find a physician or hospital willing to perform the treatment when reimbursement is uncertain, the speed with which the insurance coverage issue can be resolved can be literally a life-or-death matter. For the insured, the cause may be lost for all practical purposes if the insured cannot meet the standards for obtaining a preliminary injunction against the insurer's denial of coverage.

5. *Counting the cases.* When insureds sued insurers for refusal to provide coverage for HDCT-ABMT to treat certain kinds of cancers, some insureds prevailed. *See, e.g., Kekis v. Blue Cross & Blue Shield of Utica-Watertown, Inc.,* 815 F. Supp. 571 (N.D.N.Y. 1993); *White v. Caterpillar, Inc.,* 765 F. Supp. 1418 (W.D. Mo.), *aff'd,* 985 F.2d 564 (8th Cir. 1991). But other insureds lost, particularly in the more recent cases. *See, e.g., Martin v. Blue Cross & Blue*

Shield of Virginia, Inc., 115 F.3d 1201 (4th Cir. 1997); *Wolf v. Prudential Insurance Co. of Am.,* 50 F.3d 793 (10th Cir. 1995); *Fuja v. Benefit Trust Life Insurance Co.,* 18 F.3d 1405 (7th Cir. 1993); *Nusseim v. Mail Handlers Benefit Plan,* 995 F.2d 804 (8th Cir. 1993); *Glausner-Nagy v. Medical Mutual of Ohio,* 987 F. Supp. 1002 (N.D. Ohio 1997). Does it make sense that coverage in a life-or-death matter turn on the jurisdiction in which a person lives?

If you were in-house counsel for an insurer on the losing end of these cases, would you recommend that the insurer draft an exclusion that specifically refers to ABMT for breast cancer? Insurers have generally prevailed when they have done so. *See, e.g., Pitman v. Blue Cross and Blue Shield of Oklahoma,* 217 F.3d 1291 (10th Cir. 2000) (ABMT was expressly excluded as a covered service under the plan and was therefore not covered; but HDCT was not excluded, and insurer acted arbitrarily and capriciously in denying coverage for HDCT); *Bailey v. Blue Cross & Blue Shield of Virginia,* 67 F.3d 53 (4th Cir. 1995) (to same effect). In some cases, however, insureds have argued with some success that explicit exclusions of coverage for HDCT-BMT for most cancers violates the Americans with Disabilities Act, 42 U.S.C. §§ 12101-12213 (1990). *See Henderson v. Bodine Aluminum, Inc.,* 70 F.3d 958 (8th Cir. 1995). As in-house counsel for the insurer, what would be your next response?

[4] Preexisting Condition Exclusions

BULLWINKEL v. NEW ENGLAND MUTUAL LIFE INSURANCE CO.

18 F.3d 429 (7th Cir. 1994)

MANION, CIRCUIT JUDGE.

In September 1991, Madelaine Bullwinkel had a lump removed from her left breast. The lump was later discovered to be cancerous. She filed a claim with her insurance company seeking coverage for the lump removal and subsequent cancer treatments. The insurance company denied coverage under the pre-existing condition limitation in the insurance policy. The company concluded that the lump, which Madelaine first discovered in July, and which was treated by a physician on July 20, predated the July 31 effective date of the insurance policy. Madelaine and her husband filed suit under the Employee Retirement Income Security Act of 1974 (ERISA). 29 U.S.C. §§ 1001-1461. The district court granted summary judgment for the insurance company. Madelaine and her husband appeal. We affirm.

I.

This case highlights the perils of changing health insurance companies during the course of medical treatment. Madelaine's husband, George Bullwinkel, operates Bullwinkel Partners Limited, a law firm. For reasons not relevant to this case, George decided to offer his law firm's employees and their dependents health insurance benefits. He negotiated a deal with New England Mutual Life Insurance Company, which agreed to begin providing health insurance on July 31, 1991. George and Madelaine enlisted under this plan.

In July 1991, Madelaine noticed a lump in her left breast. She had detected a similar lump the previous February, but a mammogram did not reveal any abnormality. On July 20, 1991 Madelaine visited her physician, who performed an ultrasound examination. This time, he detected what he diagnosed as a cyst. He made no definite conclusion whether the cyst was cancerous or benign. He assured Madelaine, however, that more than likely the cyst was benign. But he was concerned about the possibility of cancer. He referred Madelaine to a surgeon for removal and biopsy of the cyst, telling her "Let's be safe and take it out."

On August 15-two weeks after the New England Mutual insurance policy became effective-Madelaine visited the surgeon, who examined her breast. The surgeon removed the lump on September 6. Tests on the removed tissue revealed that the lump was cancerous. Since that discovery, Madelaine has had additional cancer treatment, including surgery, radiation treatment, and chemotherapy.

Madelaine sought coverage from New England Mutual for her initial surgery and subsequent cancer treatments. New England Mutual denied coverage, claiming that the cancer was a pre-existing condition, for which the insurance policy explicitly precluded coverage. The insurance policy contained the following "Pre-Existing Condition Limitation":

> No benefits are payable for a condition, sickness, or injury for which you or your dependent were seen, treated, diagnosed, or incurred medical expense in the six-month period just before insurance starts until the earlier of:. . .for you or your dependent, the end of a period of twelve consecutive months after insurance starts.

The insurance policy defined the term "sickness" as a "bodily disorder, disease, or mental infirmity or complication of pregnancy."

The Bullwinkels sued New England Mutual under ERISA, seeking coverage for the surgery and cancer treatments. . . . The district court determined that, under the undisputed facts, the cancer was a pre-existing condition. The court therefore granted summary judgment in favor of New England Mutual. Significantly, in its order granting summary judgment, the court noted: "There is no suggestion that the lump became malignant after the coverage commenced or that it was removed for cosmetic reasons without any thought or concern that it might be cancerous. Rather, it is clear that the purpose of the surgery was to excise and biopsy the lump because of the risk, small though it may have been, that it was cancerous."

The Bullwinkels have appealed. We must determine whether the July treatment triggered the pre-existing condition limitation in the insurance policy. If so, then New England Mutual prevails, and the post-policy treatments at issue are not covered. If not, the Bullwinkels prevail, and they are entitled to coverage.

II. Analysis

Generally, this case concerns an insurance policy, which is a contract. Like all contracts, the writing represents an agreement between the parties. In consideration for premiums paid, New England Mutual promised to pay health benefits to the Bullwinkels under certain terms and conditions. New England Mutual specifically refused to cover any "condition, sickness, or injury" which pre-existed the policy.[1] The Bullwinkels agreed to this provision, but they and the company disagree on its meaning.

This case is governed by ERISA, a law which requires us to apply federal common law rules of contract interpretation when interpreting the terms of an employee health insurance policy. . . . The Bullwinkels commit a large portion of their brief to making public policy arguments favoring their position. But we are restricted by federal common law rules of contract interpretation to view the language of the insurance policy to determine where the parties' minds met. . . . Therefore, we must give effect to the words which denote the bargain, not in light of public policy considerations, but in light of their plain meaning.

The first portion of the pre-existing condition limitation succinctly states the exclusion: "No benefits are payable for a condition, sickness, or injury for which you or your dependent were seen, treated, diagnosed, or incurred medical expense in the six-month period just before insurance starts. . . ." Both sides agree that the breast lump was a condition which was diagnosed and treated in July, before the effective date of the policy. Therefore, both sides essentially concede that the post-policy treatment of the lump—the August 15 visit to the surgeon and the September 6 lump removal—is not covered under the policy. This appeal, then, focuses on the cancer treatments which took place after the lump was removed. The Bullwinkels argue that cancer was never diagnosed in July, and therefore that Madelaine was never "seen, treated, diagnosed," nor did she incur medical expenses for cancer in July. In short, they argue that while the lump may have been a pre-existing condition under the policy, the cancer was not since it was not actually diagnosed. New England Mutual does not make the same distinction between the lump and the cancer. According to New England Mutual, the September biopsy conclusively established that the lump was cancerous. Therefore, any treatment for the lump in July was actually treatment for cancer, and cancer was a pre-existing condition for which coverage was excluded.

The Bullwinkels cite a number of cases to support the distinction they draw between the lump and the cancer. . . . Unfortunately, the cases the Bullwinkels cite are not very helpful. Most did not involve interpretation of a pre-existing condition limitation in an insurance policy. . . .

Only *Kirk [v. Provident Life & Acc. Ins. Co.]*, 942 F.2d 504 [8th Cir. 1991], approaches similarity with the case at hand. But that case, which the Bullwinkels introduce "[b]y way of contrast," actually supports New England Mutual's position. In that case, Kirk was treated for a number of symptoms-pain in his right side, night sweats, an ache in his leg, a lesion on his knee, and swelling-which led his doctor to suspect congenital heart disease. But a blood culture which might have detected such a disease proved negative.

---

[1] Under the terms of the policy, the pre-existing condition provision limited coverage only for one year after the insurance became effective. The treatments at issue in this case all took place in that year. The parties have not asked us to determine whether Madelaine would be entitled to coverage for treatments occurring after the one year period.

Subsequently, Kirk obtained an insurance policy which contained a pre-existing condition exclusion. Kirk began once again to display symptoms of congenital heart disease. This time, a heart specialist diagnosed the disease as bacterial endocarditis, a heart illness. The heart specialist, as well as a specialist in infectious diseases, both concluded that the disease had been present before insurance coverage commenced.

The court was asked to interpret a pre-existing condition exclusion which provided that "[n]o benefits [are] payable for expenses due to any Injury or Illness beginning before the effective date of coverage." That case, like this one, was governed by ERISA. The court determined that Kirk was not covered for the heart condition, because it pre-dated the policy. The court was unpersuaded by the fact that the condition was not accurately diagnosed until after the policy became effective. The court also separated its decision from the type of case where "'the insured has some supposedly trivial infirmity or abnormality when the policy took effect. Later on, however, the condition changed for the worse and for the first time either actually became, or became diagnosable as, a sickness or disease falling within the coverage of the policy.'" *Kirk,* 942 F.2d at 506, quoting *Lincoln Income Life Ins. Co. v. Milton,* 242 Ark. 124, 412 S.W.2d 291 (1967). The court reasoned that Kirk did not exhibit only trivial symptoms; he exhibited symptoms which led to the inescapable conclusion that he had a heart condition before his insurance commenced.

If we were to base our decision on *Kirk,* we would affirm the district court's denial of coverage in this case. As in *Kirk,* the condition in this case was not fully diagnosed until after the insurance became effective. And as in *Kirk,* the symptoms which Madelaine exhibited were not trivial and inconclusive—like a cough or a rash which might imply any of a variety of maladies, or none at all. The breast lump was anything but trivial; in September it was determined to be cancer.

Though instructive, *Kirk* is not the last word in this case. The insurance policy language which the court interpreted in *Kirk* differs significantly from the language in the policy before us. Therefore, our analysis returns to the policy language which this case presents. Is a malignant breast lump—discovered before the effective date of an insurance policy but not definitely diagnosed as cancer until after coverage commenced—a "condition, sickness, or injury" for which Madelaine was "seen, treated, diagnosed, or incurred medical expenses" in July? Certainly, a malignant breast tumor is a "condition" and a "sickness." True, Madelaine was never "seen, treated, diagnosed" specifically for breast cancer in July, nor did she incur medical expenses specifically for breast cancer in July. But she was "seen, treated, diagnosed" and she did incur medical expenses for a breast lump in July. The lump was discovered in September to be cancerous. We may infer from this fact that the lump was also cancerous in July. So, even though Madelaine did not know the lump was cancerous in July, her visit with the doctor in that month concerning the lump actually concerned cancer. It follows that Madelaine was "seen" and "treated" and incurred medical expenses for her cancer in July. Therefore, any post-policy treatment concerning the same condition is not covered.

Ultimately, the Bullwinkels rest their entire appeal on one argument. They claim that a court cannot conclude on summary judgment that a lump discovered to be cancerous in September was also cancerous in July. They argue that this conclusion can only be made by a fact-finder. They request a remand to give the fact-finder an opportunity to consider the competing inferences. At oral argument, the Bullwinkels' attorney conceded that if the lump was cancerous in July, then the pre-existing condition limitation would preclude coverage. He made this concession during questioning by the court:

COURT: But what fact can be revealed [on remand]?

ATTORNEY: Did she have breast cancer for which she was treated [in July]?

COURT: Suppose every doctor that knows anything about cancer says that this was there for a year?

ATTORNEY: But no doctor said that.

COURT: But suppose they do. Do you lose?

ATTORNEY: We lose.

The problem with granting a remand is that the record does not present competing inferences. The only reasonable inference which the record in this case allows is that the lump discovered to be cancerous in September was also cancerous in July. . . . If the Bullwinkels desired to negate this inference, or at least to create a question of fact, they should have submitted some kind of medical affidavit stating that a breast lump can be benign in one month, but cancerous two months later. . . . They do not do this. Really, they do not even attempt to argue that the lump was benign in July. They just argue that the district court was not permitted to determine that the lump was cancerous in July. Therefore, the Bullwinkels have not shown a genuine issue of material fact. It follows that the district court was correct to grant summary judgment in favor of the insurance company.

Obviously, this case is not an authorization for summary judgment in all future cases dealing with pre-existing condition limitations. Several attributes make this case unique. First, the lump discovered in July was not a trivial and inconclusive symptom. *See Kirk,* 942 F.2d at 506. Consider the hypothetical where a person purchased cough medicine in one month, then obtained insurance, only to learn in the next month that he had lung cancer, which possible caused his hacking. A district court would not be able to conclusively determine whether treatment for the cough was actually treatment for cancer, without the benefit of an evidentiary hearing. Here, there is no need for an evidentiary hearing, because we may reasonably infer that the breast lump was cancerous in July, and the record presents no competing inferences. This case is also unique because the Bullwinkels never really attempt to argue that the breast lump was benign in July. In the previous hypothetical, the insured would likely argue that the cough could have been caused by any number of maladies other than cancer. That type of argument-which was not made here-would at least get the case to the fact-finder. . . .

III. Conclusion

For the foregoing reasons we

AFFIRM.

NOTES

1. *Fortuity revisited.* Suppose you own a car which you have not insured for loss due to collision. If you run your car into a tree and then seek to purchase insurance for the accident you just had, how would you expect the insurer to react? The answer is obvious. So why should health insurance be any different? Insurers believe that in the absence of preexisting condition clauses, insureds would wait to purchase health insurance (or opt into group plans, if possible) until their first illness, thereby avoiding the payment of premiums for the time period during which they were healthy and obtaining coverage as soon as they first need it. By excluding coverage for preexisting conditions, insurers are able to reduce health insurance premiums. Do you agree with the insurers' perspective on this issue? Do you have health insurance?

In one of the readings in § 4.01[1], Professor Stone spoke of the values of community in health insurance. Does it promote these values to prohibit preexisting condition clauses? Or would you favor some other approach? For example, would it make more sense for insurers to simply exclude health conditions that are operative on the first day the coverage is effective?

2. *First versus subsequent acquisitions of insurance.* Is there a basis for distinguishing preexisting condition clauses as they are applied to the first purchase of insurance, and preexisting condition clauses as they are applied to subsequent acquisitions of insurance?

3. *The structure of the clause.* Note that the preexisting condition clause has two key elements. The first is the "look-back period," i.e., one "looks back" to see if the insured has been seen, treated, diagnosed, or incurred expenses for conditions, sicknesses, or injuries during the designated period. The "exclusion period" states how long there is no coverage for conditions that are captured by the look-back period.

Many cases, of course, turn on the precise wording of the clause at issue. For example, if the clause defines conditions in terms of symptoms for which the insured has received "treatment" in the past, an insured whose condition has been diagnosed but not treated has been held to be outside the exclusion. *See Franceschi v. American Motorists, Inc.,* 852 F.2d 1217 (9th Cir. 1988); *Thompson v. Simon United States Holdings, Inc.,* 956 F. Supp. 1344 (N.D. Ohio 1997); *Indiana Comprehensive Health Insurance Ass'n v. Dye,* 531 N.E.2d 505 (Ind. Ct. App. 1988).

4. *The "existence" of a condition.* A health condition or illness might be said to have an "inception," a time when the condition first becomes "manifest" or apparent to the person, and a time when the condition is first diagnosed. Is it fair to say that a disease "exists" at all three times?

Is what the insured "knows" about the condition or illness relevant? The insured in *Bullwinkel* did not know that she had cancer on July 31. If she did not know, why should she not have coverage? How is the principle of fortuity violated if an insured secures coverage in ignorance of an underlying health condition which the insurer now seeks to put outside coverage? *See State v. Carper,* 545 So. 2d 1 (Miss. 1989); *Holub v. Holy Family Society,* 518 N.E.2d 419 (Ill. Ct. App. 1987). Why are insurers interested in an objective test, as opposed to a subjective test?

In *Bullwinkel,* the mass which turned out to be cancerous was discovered before the policy's effective date. What if the insured were being treated before the policy's effective date for a condition unrelated to cancer (*e.g.,* fibrocystic disease), and in the course of this treatment tissue was removed which was discovered after the policy's effective date to be cancerous? *See Pitcher v. Principal Mutual Life Insurance Co.,* 93 F.3d 407 (7th Cir. 1996) (coverage; routine physical and mammogram prior to effective date of policy was not treatment for breast cancer, when mammogram revealed fibrous material that turned out to be cancerous); *Hardester v. Lincoln National Life Insurance Co.,* 33 F.3d 330 (4th Cir. 1994) (no coverage), *vacated after rehearing en banc,* 52 F.3d 70 (4th Cir. 1995) (coverage), *cert. denied,* 516 U.S. 864 (1995).

Under the text of the exclusion in *Bullwinkel,* if the insured has a condition that he or she can live with for awhile (*e.g.,* a hernia, hemorrhoids, or tennis elbow), and the insured waits to seek care until 12 months after the insurance plan becomes effective, the insured is then eligible for coverage for the condition. (Does this make good policy sense?) Why then exclude coverage when the insured is unaware that he or she has a medical condition just because it is diagnosable?

5. *HIPAA's portability rules.* In 1996, Congress passed the Health Insurance Portability and Accountability Act of 1996 (" HIPAA"), Pub. L. No. 104-191, 110 Stat. 1936 (1996). Of HIPAA's three main components (see note 10 in § 4.04[1], *supra*), the portability rules are most often associated with HIPAA, no doubt because many people change employment at one time or another and thus encounter this aspect of the law. HIPAA is applicable to all employer-sponsored plans, both fully insured and self-insured, having two or more participants who are current employees. Indeed, the principal purpose of the portability rules is to make it easier for those who remain continuously covered under employer-sponsored health plans to change jobs without having to meet new eligibility requirements.

The portability rules essentially state that preexisting conditions are permissible subject to certain conditions. A preexisting condition exclusion (or "PCE") must relate to a condition for which medical advice, diagnosis, care or treatment was recommended or received during the six-month period prior to an individual's enrollment in a plan. Then, the maximum exclusion period is 12 months (or 18 months for late enrollees), except that a health plan must reduce the maximum exclusion period based on the number of days of "creditable coverage." Most health insurance coverage is "creditable coverage," with the noteworthy exception that creditable coverage which precedes a break in coverage of 63 days or more need not be counted against the maximum exclusion period. Thus, if an individual has had coverage for four months when she changes jobs, the individual would face a maximum eight-month PCE in his or her new employment, provided the individual did not allow the coverage to lapse for 63 days (*e.g.,* did not take a more than 63 day break between employment or insurance plans). What personal planning imperatives do these requirements create? Further, some persons can never face a PCE: women who are pregnant when coverage begins; and newborns and adopted children under age 18, provided the child does not incur a subsequent 63 day or longer "break in coverage." Also, genetic information is declared not to constitute a preexisting condition in the absence of a diagnosis.

Because HIPAA's basic purpose is to eliminate the coverage gaps and "job lock" pressures caused by PCEs, the Act is not concerned with some other issues that affect access to and affordability of health insurance and health care. For example, HIPAA does not affect the rates that insurers can charge, and therefore is not expected to materially improve the circumstances of most Americans who lack health insurance altogether. Also, HIPAA's anti-discrimination provisions prevent an insurer from canceling an individual's coverage simply because the individual gets sick, but HIPAA does not require employers to offer health insurance to their employees in the first place.

Some people think that HIPAA prohibits PCEs, but this is incorrect. Even after HIPAA is fully implemented, PCEs will continue to be relevant to the first purchase of insurance and in some other situations (such as where the insured lets her coverage lapse for 63 days or more and then starts work for a new employer whose group plan has a preexisting condition clause).

6. *Ongoing illness and termination of health coverage.* A related, but different problem arises when coverage terminates. Assume, for example, that Mary is covered for hospital and medical care for the 1999 calendar year. Mary undergoes treatment for an illness that becomes manifest on July 1, 1999. Periodically, Mary receives treatment for this illness, which is within the coverage of the policy, but she permits the policy to lapse at the end of 1999. If Mary receives treatment in 2000 for the condition which originated in 1999 and thereafter receives a bill for such services, is the 2000 expense covered? Most modern health insurance policies require that the expense of treatment occur within the policy period. In the absence of an ambiguity or some other exception, courts will usually enforce a provision that limits the insurer's liability for expenses incurred after the policy period has ended for accidents, illness, or other medical conditions which occurred during the policy period. *See, e.g., Forbau v. Aetna Life Insurance Co.,* 876 S.W.2d 132 (Tex. 1994); *Guardian Life Insurance Co. of Am. v. Zerance,* 505 Pa. 345, 479 A.2d 949 (1984).

[5] Utilization Review

SARCHETT v. BLUE SHIELD OF CALIFORNIA
43 Cal. 3d 1, 729 P.2d 267, 233 Cal. Rptr. 76 (1987)

BROUSSARD, JUSTICE.

This dispute arose when defendant Blue Shield of California (Blue Shield) denied plaintiff John Sarchett's claim for hospitalization benefits in the amount of $1,203.05. Sarchett sued Blue Shield for the hospital expenses and also for a breach of the implied covenant of good faith and fair dealing. The trial court directed a verdict for Sarchett on breach of the covenant of good faith and fair dealing, and the jury awarded his hospital costs, $20,000 in compensatory damages and $80,000 in punitive damages. Blue Shield appeals from this verdict.

FACTS AND PROCEDURAL BACKGROUND

In 1966, John Sarchett, a Los Angeles County employee, elected to be insured under a group policy provided by Blue Shield. In January 1976, Sarchett was hospitalized for three days by his family physician, Dr. Bruce Van Vranken, who is a member physician of Blue Shield. Dr. Van Vranken testified that Sarchett, usually a healthy and robust person, reported symptoms during January of fatigue, tremor, disorientation, painful swelling and distension of the stomach and back, changing bowel habits and peculiar stools. His blood test showed low hemoglobin and low white blood cell counts. Sarchett's condition appeared to be deteriorating rapidly during January, and Dr. Van Vranken feared Sarchett might be suffering from a life-threatening bleeding duodenal ulcer or leukemia.

Blue Shield paid Sarchett's medical and diagnostic testing bills, but denied his claim for the hospital stay, amounting to $1,203.05. Its denial was based on two separate provisions of Sarchett's policy: (1) an exclusion for "[s]ervices when hospitalized primarily for *diagnostic purposes* or medical observation, rest or convalescent care . . ." (italics added) and (2) exclusion for services not "medically necessary."[2] The latter exclusion reads as follows: "Medical Necessity: Benefits will be provided under this contract only for such services, whether provided on an Inpatient or Outpatient basis, as are reasonably intended, in the exercise of good medical practice, for the treatment of illness or injury." Blue Shield contended that Dr. Van Vranken's orders for Sarchett's care in the hospital were inconsistent with a belief that Sarchett was seriously ill and hospitalized for medical treatment.[3]

Plaintiff, Dr. Van Vranken, and the hospital utilization review committee protested the denial of coverage. The matter was submitted to arbitration, but the arbitrator's award in favor of plaintiff was vacated by the superior court. The matter was then set for trial de novo in the superior court.

. . . .

I.

The trial court found that the Blue Shield policy was ambiguous because it did not indicate who would determine when the diagnostic services or medical necessity exclusion barred coverage. Construing that ambiguity in favor of the member, it concluded that he should be able to rely on the

---

[2] Similar exclusions appear in the subscriber's brochure under "Services Not Covered."

[3] For instance, Dr. Van Vranken's admitting orders allowed Sarchett to ambulate and to eat the regular house diet, and he did not order serial blood counts, regular monitoring of vital signs, multiple position blood pressure readings, placement of an intravenous line, blood typing and cross-matching in case a blood transfusion became necessary, nasogastric tube insertion to monitor internal bleeding, serial stool checks, or a barium enema—all of which steps Blue Shield claims should have been taken if the admitting physician actually suspected a bleeding duodenal ulcer or leukemia. Blue Shield asserts that Sarchett was suffering only from chronic anemia and a reaction to some "gall bladder pills" ingested in preparation for a gall bladder series, though Sarchett and Dr. Van Vranken claim the symptoms antedate the gall bladder tests.

judgment of his treating physician as to the purpose and necessity of hospitalization, and that Blue Shield could not question that judgment. Blue Shield contends that the trial court erred in interpreting the policy, and that its right to review claims is inherent in the insurance contract. Sarchett, on the other hand, maintains that only the addition of an explicit statement asserting the insurer's right of retrospective review would cure the ambiguity and, going beyond the ruling of the trial judge, argues that regardless of policy language retrospective review should be banned as contrary to public policy.

We begin with the specific language of the policy. The diagnostic exclusion denies coverage for "[s]ervices when hospitalized primarily for diagnostic purposes or medical observation, rest or convalescent care." The "medical necessity" provision provides coverage "only for such services. . .as are reasonably intended, in the exercise of good medical practice, for the treatment of illness or injury." When the two provisions are read together, certain ambiguities appear. In some cases, for example, some diagnostic procedures may be so difficult or hazardous that hospitalization is medically necessary. In others a patient's medical condition may be so serious as to require hospitalization even though the physician is unable to treat that condition without diagnostic tests which ordinarily could be performed on an outpatient basis. Policy coverage for both cases is unclear.

At oral argument, however, counsel for Blue Shield explained that the diagnostic exclusion is intended as a subset of the implied exclusion for unnecessary medical treatment, and that the insurer would cover "medically necessary" hospitalization even if done for diagnostic purposes.[5] Consequently, coverage for plaintiff's hospitalization does not turn on whether he was hospitalized for diagnosis, but simply on whether hospitalization was "medically necessary." Furthermore, strict necessity is not required. The policy language requires only that the services be "reasonably intended. . .for the treatment of illness or injury." The intent in question is apparently that of the treating physician, and "treatment," Blue Shield acknowledges, includes hospitalization required by the subscriber's medical condition even if further diagnosis is essential for further treatment.

Plaintiff's insurance coverage would therefore appear to depend upon three questions of fact: (1) whether Dr. Van Vranken ordered hospitalization with the intention of treating plaintiff's illness or injury, (2) whether the physician's intention was reasonable, and (3) whether that intention conforms to good medical practice. Blue Shield concedes the question of good medical practice, but disputes the other issues, claiming that Dr. Van Vranken did not reasonably believe plaintiff's medical condition called for hospital treatment.

Plaintiff, however, seeks to eliminate even these factual questions, arguing that the policy is ambiguous as to who decides whether hospitalization is

---

[5] Contrary to the assertion of the dissent, we do not maintain that counsel's concession eliminated ambiguity as to who decides whether a treatment was medically necessary. As we explain later in this opinion, we think the policy unambiguously provides that this decision will ultimately be made by a disinterested third party—a review committee, an arbitrator, or a court. We believe, instead, that counsel's concession resolved an ambiguity concerning the policy's substantive coverage in favor of the insured, thus making it unnecessary for us to employ established rules of construction to reach that same result.

medically necessary. As we have noted, the trial court agreed, and directed the jury that Blue Shield violated its duty of good faith and fair dealing by challenging the treating physician's determination of medical necessity.

Upon review of the entire policy, however, we find no ambiguity in this respect. It is true that neither the diagnostic exclusion nor the medical necessity provision provides expressly how coverage disputes will be resolved, but neither does any other exclusionary clause.[6] Instead, Blue Shield has provided a separate provision, entitled "Settlement of Disputes," which applies to all disputes under the policy. That section first provides that "[a] dispute concerning the therapeutic justification for any services rendered to the member shall be resolved by the decision of the appropriate review committee of that medical society. . .for the geographical area in which such services were provided. . . ." It then states that "all other disputes, including disputes with respect to the decisions of the medical society. . .shall be resolved. . .in accordance with the Rules of the American Arbitration Association."

We find no ambiguity in this language relevant to the present case. The dispute between Sarchett and Blue Shield is "a dispute concerning the therapeutic justification" for plaintiff's hospitalization, and even if it were not, it would then be among the "other disputes" governed by the arbitration provision. The point is not that this dispute must be remanded to a medical review committee or an arbitrator—such remedies have been waived or exhausted, and the case was properly in the superior court. It is, instead, that since the policy itself provides unambiguously how disputes are to be resolved, including disputes concerning the "medical necessity" of hospitalization,[8] there is no room for the argument that the policy contains an ambiguity which, construed in plaintiff's favor, would vest the final determination of medical necessity in the treating physician.[9]

Sarchett relies on the decision of the Illinois Court of Appeal in *Van Vactor v. Blue Cross Association* (1977) 50 Ill. App. 3d 709, 8 Ill. Dec. 400, 365 N.E.2d 638. *Van Vactor* was a class action by members who had been denied coverage for hospitalization for oral surgery. The policy provided for payment of hospital bills incident to removal of impacted teeth where hospitalization was "medically necessary." The court held that since "nowhere does either the master contract or the brochure provide that a judgment on medical necessity for such inpatient hospitalization is required to be made by anyone other than the duly licensed treating physician as a condition to payment of benefits, there is no

---

[6] Besides the exclusions at issue in this case, the policy also generally excluded coverage for, *e.g.*, mental disorders, routine eye refractions, routine physical examinations, hospitalization for tuberculosis, physical therapy, dental services, organ transplants, and treatment for alcoholism and narcoticism.

[8] The wording of the "medical necessity" provision itself supports this analysis. The clause refers to services reasonably intended for treatment, yet plaintiff's interpretation would leave the treating physician the sole judge of his own reasonableness. The clause also requires the "exercise of good medical practice," language which suggests an objective standard, not one under which the physician himself decides whether his intentions conform to good medical practice.

[9] Plaintiff accused Blue Shield of claiming that it has the final right to determine the "medical necessity" of treatment. But as we understand defendant's position, it is only claiming the right to contest plaintiff's claim, with the ultimate decision confided to an impartial review committee, arbitrator, or court.

justification for the denial of benefits *solely* on the ground that the insurer disagrees with the honest judgment of the treating physician." (365 N.E.2d at p. 642, italics in original.) The court then interpreted the policy to provide that the "determination of whether and to what extent hospital services are medically necessary is 'vested solely and exclusively in the judgment and discretion of the treating physician.'" (p. 647.)

The *Van Vactor* decision, however, stands alone. It has not been followed by any other court. Numerous decisions from other jurisdictions take the position that "medical necessity" or similar policy language is an objective standard to be applied by the trier of fact, not a delegation of power to the treating physician.

We note in particular the last cited case, *Lockshin v. Blue Cross of Northeast Ohio, supra*, 434 N.E.2d 754. In that case Blue Cross denied a subscriber's claim for two days of private nursing care following a Cesarean section on the ground that care was ordered to "allay. . .misapprehension" (p. 757) and was not "necessary" within the purview of the insurance policy. "The trial court held that the term 'necessary' was ambiguous, vis-à-vis who must ultimately decide what is 'necessary.' Consequently, the trial court strictly construed the policy against the drafter and found for the claimant (plaintiff)." (p. 755.) The Court of Appeal, however, rejected this view, stating: "[A] function, basic to the insurer, is the right '. . . to determine whether. . .[a] claim should be allowed or rejected.' [Citation.] The function of reviewing claims is obviously reserved by the insurer and implied by the mandatory process of submitting a proof of claim. [Citations.] Without such a right, an orderly establishment, administration and dispensation of insurance benefits would be virtually impossible." (p. 756.) "While the decision of a physician is both relevant and probative on the issue of necessity, it is not dispositive of the question. . . ." (Ibid.)

In short, we find the policy unambiguous on the question of who decides "medical necessity": in the event of a dispute the decision is made by an impartial review committee, subject to further review through arbitration. Since this is clearly set out in the settlement of disputes section of the policy, it is not necessary for the insurer, to avoid ambiguity, to repeat that language in the diagnostic exclusion or medical necessity clauses. We do not seek to discourage inserting such language into appropriate exclusions; a little judicious repetition may illuminate the meaning of the policy and avert controversy.[12] We hold, however, that the absence of such language does not preclude the insurer from challenging the medical necessity of hospitalization recommended by the treating physician. Thus we conclude that the trial court erred in directing a verdict that Blue Shield violated its duty of good faith and fair dealing by disagreeing with the judgment of the treating physician on retrospective review.

Plaintiff argues, however, even if the policy is not ambiguous upon close reading, it should still be construed in light of the "reasonable expectation

---

[12] Some insurers include such language in the policy. For instance, in *Franks v. Louisiana Health Services & Indemnity Co. (La. App.* 1980) 382 So. 2d 1064, 1066, the policy contained the following provision: "The fact that a physician may prescribe, order, recommend, or approve a service or supply does not, of itself, make it medically necessary or make the charge an allowable expense, even though it is not specifically listed as an exclusion." . . . .

of the insured." (*Gray v. Zurich Insurance Co.* (1966) 65 Cal. 2d 263, 271, 54 Cal. Rptr. 104, 419 P.2d 168.) The subscriber under a Blue Shield policy, he contends, would reasonably expect to be covered for hospitalization recommended by the treating physician. We do not question this description of the subscriber's expectations, but we doubt that it arises from any belief that Blue Shield will cover all treatment recommended by a physician, however unreasonable the recommendation. Instead, the subscriber expects coverage because he trusts that his physician has recommended a reasonable treatment consistent with good medical practice. Consequently we believe the subscriber's expectations can be best fulfilled not by giving his physician an unreviewable power to determine coverage, but by construing the policy language liberally, so that uncertainties about the reasonableness of treatment will be resolved in favor of coverage.

Finally, plaintiff argues that, entirely apart from the policy language, the courts as a matter of public policy should bar insurers from refusing coverage for hospitalization ordered by the treating physician. He points to the dilemma faced by the subscriber when his doctor tells him that hospitalization is necessary. Unless a physician himself, the subscriber lacks competence to question his doctor's recommendation. If he follows the recommendation, he takes the risk that the insurer may later deny coverage, leaving the subscriber liable for a hospital bill he cannot afford. Yet if he does not follow the recommendation, he may be foregoing needed treatment. Faced with this dilemma, most subscribers would follow their doctor's recommendation and risk the denial of insurance coverage. Subscribers purchase insurance not only for financial advantage, but to obtain the peace of mind and sense of security that follows from assured payment (*cf. Crisci v. Security Ins. Co.* (1967) 66 Cal. 2d 425, 434, 58 Cal. Rptr. 13, 426 P.2d 173), and retrospective review frustrates those objectives.

There are, however, countervailing policy considerations. Sarchett had a choice between the Blue Shield plan, which offered him unlimited selection of physicians but provided for retrospective review, and alternative plans which would require him to choose from among a limited list of physicians but guaranteed payment. A holding that retrospective review is against public policy would narrow the range of choices available to the prospective subscriber, since it is unlikely that any insurer could permit the subscriber free selection of a physician if it were required to accept without question the physician's view of reasonable treatment and good medical practice. If the treating physician makes the final decision whether the treatment he prescribes is covered by the policy, inevitably a few will abuse that power by overutilization of medical procedures, imposing excessive costs on the insurer.

This view finds support in the decision of the Kentucky Supreme Court. In *Blue Cross and Blue Shield of Kentucky, Inc. v. Smither, supra,* 573 S.W.2d 363, the policy covered "medically necessary" hospital services, and warned expressly that the fact that a physician may recommend a service does not of itself make that service medically necessary. Unable to argue ambiguity in the policy, the subscriber nevertheless contended that the decision of the treating physician should always control the question of medical necessity, and that contrary views of nontreating physicians were insufficient to raise a triable issue of fact. The court commented: "Smither's argument is, in essence, that the only medical advice the patient has concerning his hospital stay is that provided by the treating physician, and therefore his opinion should be treated as correct and not be subject to contradiction. We do not believe a treating physician should be placed in this unassailable position. One need only look to the Medicare and Medicaid System for alleged evidence of fraud w,hich may occur on the part of doctors and other persons in the medical care professions, if their decisions are always assumed correct." (p. 365.)

Both the federal Medicare program (42 U.S.C. § 1395y(a)) and the state MediCal program (Welf. & Inst. Code, § 14110, subd. (e)), which permit the patient free choice of physician, also contemplate retrospective review. We cannot declare contrary to public policy a feature found necessary whenever the public, through its representatives, itself sets out the terms of a health insurance program.

In summary, we appreciate the plight of the subscriber, forced to decide whether to follow his doctor's recommendation without assurance that his policy will cover the expense. We do not, however, believe it would be alleviated by requiring the insurer to insert redundant language into the policy to make doubly clear to the subscriber that he really is in a dilemma and cannot count on coverage. And although a judicial ruling that retrospective review violates public policy would protect against retrospective denial of coverage, subscribers would pay the price in reduced insurance alternatives and increased premiums.

The problem of retrospective denial of coverage can be reduced through the growing practice of preadmission screening of nonemergency hospital admissions. When such screening is not feasible, as in the present case, we think the best the courts can do is give the policy every reasonable interpretation in favor of coverage. We trust that, with doubts respecting coverage resolved in favor of the subscriber, there will be few cases in which the physician's judgment is so plainly unreasonable, or contrary to good medical practice, that coverage will be refused.

. . . .

The judgment is reversed, and the matter remanded for further proceedings in accordance with the views expressed in this opinion. The parties shall bear their own costs on appeal.

GRODIN AND PANELLI, JJ., concur. [The opinion of Justice Lucas, concurring in part and dissenting in part, is omitted.]

MOSK, JUSTICE.

I dissent to the conclusion reached in Part I of the majority's opinion. In my view, the policy is ambiguous because, as the trial court found, it does not state that Blue Shield had the right, on the basis of a retrospective review, to disagree with the judgment of the treating physician to hospitalize Sarchett.

The majority admit that the diagnostic exclusion is ambiguous when read in the light of the medical necessity exclusion. However, because of an explanation offered by Blue Shield at oral argument, the majority fail to apply the usual rule of interpreting ambiguous language in favor of the insured. But the question of ambiguity cannot be determined from the 11th-hour concession of an insurer before this court as to the meaning of the policy. It must be decided from the terms of the policy itself—terms which the majority concede are ambiguous.

The interpretation now advanced by Blue Shield, i.e., that the diagnostic exclusion is a subset of the implied exclusion for unnecessary medical treatment, and that it would cover medically necessary hospitalization even if done for diagnostic purposes, is not evident from the policy or the subscriber's brochure, which lists 16 categories of "Services Not Covered." The first is the diagnostic exclusion, and the last the "medical necessity" exclusion. There is no indication in the policy that one has any relation to the other. In my view, therefore, the ambiguities in the policy recognized by the majority should be resolved against Blue Shield, in accordance with the usual rule.

Nor do I agree with the majority's second reason for finding that the "medical necessity" exclusion is unambiguous. They conclude because the policy contains a provision that disputes relating to the "therapeutic justification" for services are to be resolved by a review committee, a subscriber is unambiguously notified that Blue Shield may second-guess the subscriber's physician on the issue of medical necessity.

An exclusionary clause in a policy must be "conspicuous, plain and clear." The burden is on the insurer to "phrase exceptions and exclusions in clear and unmistakable language" and to "draft its policy to avoid any misinterpretation by the average layman" These rules must be applied with special care in the present case, since the exclusion which Blue Shield seeks to invoke amounts to a "vast, additional exclusionary condition to coverage."

The provision relating to resolution of disputes does not meet the foregoing standard. It does not state that Blue Shield reserves the right to second-guess the judgment of the subscriber's doctor as to medical necessity. At most, it allows the subscriber, if he ponders the subject at length, to draw an inference that because there exists a right to review of disputes concerning "therapeutic justification" for services, Blue Shield may challenge the judgment of his doctor. On the other hand, the provision relied on by the majority does not even appear on the same page in the subscriber's brochure as the "medical necessity" exclusion. Thus I do not see how it can be said that the power which Blue Shield seeks to exercise is set forth in language clear and unmistakable to the average layman.

. . . .

Finally, I am unable to concur in the determination of the majority that Sarchett did not have a reasonable expectation of coverage. The opinion states a subscriber could not reasonably expect that Blue Shield would cover all treatment recommended by his physician "however unreasonable the recommendation." A subscriber, unless he is knowledgeable in medical science, is unable to assess the reasonableness of his physician's recommendation for hospitalization. Since in this sense he is controlled by the opinion of his doctor, it is not unreasonable for him to expect that his insurer would likewise be bound by his doctor's judgment regarding the necessity for hospitalization, absent clear notification to the contrary.

The failure of Blue Shield to make clear its claimed right to decide after-the-fact that hospitalization was not a medical necessity deprives a subscriber of his opportunity to make a meaningful selection between various available types of health plans. If the policy and the brochure had made it known to Sarchett that Blue Shield claimed this right, he could have made a meaningful choice between the plan offered by Blue Shield and one with a limited choice of physicians but guaranteed payment. In my view, Sarchett should not be personally burdened with medical expenses which he could have avoided if Blue Shield had fulfilled its duty to make clear the important qualification of coverage which it belatedly advances in this case.

I would affirm the judgment.

BIRD, C.J., and REYNOSO, J., concur.

NOTES

1. *HMOs versus traditional delivery systems.* Sarchett had a choice of two types of health care plans, one in which he selected his own doctor and one in which he did not. The plan in which he selected his own doctor required retrospective review of the doctor's decisions. Why? Under what circumstances would the doctor be likely to say that treatment he ordered was not medically necessary? Why does the HMO not have retrospective review?

2. *Reasonable expectations?* Do you think Sarchett understood the full implications of his decision when he selected his health care plan? Do most insureds? Was Sarchett acting reasonably in relying on his doctor's advice? How could Sarchett have avoided the predicament in which he found himself? What does this decision suggest about the importance of the cost-containment issue in health care today?

3. *Reviewing utilization review.* The growth of managed care has put the topic of "patients' rights" near the top of the health care agenda. The genesis for this set of concerns is, ultimately, utilization review; denials of care in prospective review systems has led to calls for—and debate over—granting patients the right to sue their HMOs for refusing care, allowing managed care enrollees to see specialists without prior approval from their "gatekeeper" physicians, mandating coverage for emergency room visits if the insured believes she needs immediate medical care, and creating external appeals processes for denials of care. This is all part of a broader transformation in health insurance generally. One observer describes these changes as follows:

> Before the emergence of managed care, it was largely physicians, act-ing individually on behalf of their patients, who decided how most health care dollars were spent. They billed for their services, and third-party insurers usually reimbursed them without asking any questions, because the ultimate payers-employers-demanded no greater accounting. Now, many employers have changed from passive payers to aggressive purchasers and are exerting more influence on payment rates, on where patients are cared for, and on the content of care. Through selective contracting with physicians, stringent

review of the use of services, practice protocols, and payment on a fixed, per capita basis, plans have pressured doctors to furnish fewer services and to improve the coordination and management of care, thereby altering the way in which many physicians treat patients. In striving to balance the conflicts that arise in caring for patients within these constraints, physicians have become "double agents." The ideological tie that long linked many physicians and private executives-a belief in capitalism and free enterprise-has been weakened by the aggressive intervention of business into the practice of medicine through managed care . . . .

John K. Iglehart, *The American Health Care System-Expenditures (Health Policy Report)*, 340 N. Eng. J. Med. 70, 76 (1999). Is it fair to say that market forces have produced some of the conditions that opponents of the failed Clinton national health care plan claimed would arise if it were enacted? For more developments in the area of utilization review, see David A. Hyman, *Regulating Managed Care: What's Wrong with a Patient Bill of Rights*, 73 S.Cal. L. Rev. 221 (2000); Michael E. Ginsberg, *HMO Grievance Processes*, 37 Harv. J. on Legis. 237 (2000); Marc A. Rodwin, *Backlash As Prelude to Managing Managed Care*, 24 J. Health Pol. Pol'y & L. 1115 (1999); Tracey E. Miller, *Center Stage on the Patient Protection Agenda: Grievance and Appeal Rights*, 26 J. L. Med. & Ethics 89 (1998).

4. *Reprise: Other methods of cost containment.* The medical necessity requirement is one of the most important ways that insurers limit their exposure to what would otherwise be nearly unlimited liability, but it is hardly the only device. As in property and liability insurance, health insurers have "other insurance" provisions which coordinate coverage when policies overlap, or when one insured is covered under multiple policies (for example, when the person is insured at his or her own place of employment and is an additional insured under the spouse's coverage). These "coordination of coverage" clauses have important cost-containment objectives. *See Blue Cross and Blue Shield of Kansas, Inc. v. Riverside Hospital,* 703 P.2d 1384 (Kan. 1985). Subrogation rules, discussed in § 2.03[4], are also important to cost containment.

§ 4.05 Property Insurance

[1] The Risks Covered

ENGEL v. REDWOOD COUNTY FARMERS MUTUAL INSURANCE CO.

281 N.W.2d 331 (Minn. 1979)

KELLY, JUSTICE.

This is an appeal from a judgment entered in the District Court of Redwood County. The plaintiff brought this action alleging that defendant-insurer was liable under a fire insurance policy for a loss occasioned by the death of a number of plaintiff's sows.

The trial court, after trying the case on a stipulated set of facts, found that the loss was covered under the terms of plaintiff's policy and accordingly entered judgment for the plaintiff. We affirm.

The issue presented on appeal is whether a loss caused by excessive heat from a fire intentionally kindled and wholly confined to the furnace wherein it was intended to burn is covered under an insurance policy providing coverage for all losses or damage by fire.

The facts are not in dispute. The plaintiff was insured under a "Minnesota Standard Township Mutual Fire Insurance Policy" issued by defendant. In 1973, the plaintiff constructed a hog barn on his farm for use in farrowing hogs. The barn was heated by an L.B. White furnace which was located just outside the building and which blew hot air into the barn by means of a fan. The furnace was controlled by a thermostat which could be adjusted to shut off the fan and furnace at a pre-set temperature.

On January 1, 1976, the plaintiff discovered that 15 of the 16 sows then in the hog barn were dead. Subsequent investigation revealed that the sows died from an inadequate supply of oxygen in the hog barn, caused by increased temperature. The high temperatures resulted from a "short" which rendered the thermostat inoperable allowing the furnace to blow hot air into the barn until the high limit control, set at 120°, shut down the furnace. The thermostat was set at 75° and this was normally as high as temperatures inside the building would rise. At all times the fire inside the furnace burned and produced heat at its usual rate and was confined within the furnace causing no damage to the hog barn or to the furnace nor producing any soot or other foreign material.

Defendant refused to compensate plaintiff, claiming that the loss was not recoverable under his policy as it was the result of a so-called "friendly" rather than "hostile" fire.

The hostile fire doctrine is said to have originated in the early English case of *Austin v. Drew,* 4 Campb. 360 (1815).[1] In that case, sugar being refined in plaintiff's factory was damaged by excessive heat and smoke. The sugar was contained in various rooms of an 8-story building through which ran a flue supplying the heat necessary for the refining process. At the top of the flue was a register which was normally kept open when the fire was high. An employee started the fire without opening the register. As a result, the fire overheated, smoking up the rooms containing the sugar and causing the damage complained of. The court, in denying recovery, stated:

> I am of the opinion that this action is not maintainable. There was no more fire than always exists when the manufacture is going on. Nothing was consumed by fire. The plaintiff's loss arose from the negligent management of their machinery. The sugars were chiefly damaged by the heat; and what produced that heat? Not any fire

---

[1] Although this case is often cited as first originating the hostile fire doctrine, the terms hostile and friendly fire first appeared in the case of *Way v. Abington Mutual Fire Ins. Co.,* 166 Mass. 67, 43 N.E. 1032 (1896).

against which the company insures, but the fire for heating the pans, which continued all the time to burn without any excess. The servant forgot to open the register by which the smoke ought to have escaped and the heat to have been tempered.

4 Campb. 361.

From this opinion has emerged a rule of law known as the hostile fire doctrine. It is recognized in a majority of jurisdictions where the issue has been raised, 44 Am. Jur. 2d, *Insurance*, § 1348; 5 Appleman, Insurance Law and Practice, § 3082, although it has been criticized by many commentators. *See* Vance, *Friendly Fires,* 1 Conn. Bar J. 284; Reis, *The Friendly Versus Hostile Fire Dichotomy,* 12 Vill. L. Rev. 109; Morrison, *Concerning Friendly Fires,* 3 Boston C. Indus. & Com. L. Rev. 15. In brief, the rule generally states that a fire which is intentionally kindled and which remains at all times confined to the place where it was intended to be will be characterized as friendly and will not subject the insurer to any liability for the resulting loss. By adopting this doctrine, courts have in effect established a presumption, seemingly irrebuttable, that the parties to the transaction, particularly the prospective insured, were aware of this doctrine and contemplated its inclusion in the policy. Common sense tells us that this is more than likely not the case. When an insured buys a fire insurance policy which "covers all losses or damage by fire" his expectation is that it will cover all unintentional losses from fire, except listed exclusions, regardless of the nature or character of the fire. The doctrine thus seems to protect the insurer at the expense of the unwitting insured.

In Minnesota, this problem is avoided because of the judicially created limitations on friendly fires. In *L.L. Freeberg Pie Co. v. St. Paul Mutual Insurance Co.,* 257 Minn. 244, 100 N.W.2d 753 (1960), we joined a minority of courts which require that a friendly fire, in addition to the elements listed above, be non-excessive. In the *Freeberg* case, the thermostat on a bake oven failed and, as a result, the flame inside the oven continued to build up to such a degree as to seriously warp and damage the oven. The lower court determined that, because the fire in the oven was intentionally kindled and only burned in its intended place, it was a friendly fire and recovery was precluded.

On appeal, we reexamined the *Austin* decision and aligned ourselves with the minority, reasoning as follows:

As has been stated, the rule originated with *Austin v. Drew,* 4 Campb. 360. However, a reading of that case will disclose that Lord Chief Justice Gibbs did not base the distinction between what is now called a "friendly" fire and a "hostile" fire only on the locus or the place where the fire was burning. He stated in the opinion (4 Campb. 361):

. . . There was no more fire than always exists. . .which [the fire] continued all the time to burn without any excess. . . .

. . . .

. . . Had the fire been brought out of the flue, and any thing had been burnt, the Company would have been liable. But can this be said, where the fire never was at all excessive, and was always confined within its proper limits?

The rule as stated in the texts above cited and in the decided cases ignores entirely these references to the nature of the fire in question, that it continued "to burn without any excess" and "never was at all excessive." The excessiveness of the fire, however great and destructive it might be if confined to the place where it was intended to be, has been considered immaterial in determining whether a fire was "friendly" or "hostile." Although the result we are reaching is contrary to the great majority of decided cases, there is a respectable minority supporting it.

257 Minn. at 248, 100 N.W.2d at 755. Under the *Freeberg* case, a fire may be found to be hostile although it was intentionally kindled and never escaped its confines if it was excessive or uncontrolled. 257 Minn. 251, 100 N.W.2d 757.

In the case before us defendant argues that even under the minority rule it should not be held liable because the fire was in no way excessive. In support of this contention, defendant points to the stipulated facts which state:

The fire inside the furnace burned and produced heat at its usual rate.

Defendant reasons that if the furnace burned only at its usual rate it could not possibly be excessive. We disagree. A fire which causes damage by burning for a greater length of time than intended is no less uncontrolled merely because it continues to burn at its usual rate. See, generally, Morrison, *Concerning Friendly Fires,* 3 Boston C. Indus. & Com. L. Rev. 15.

Returning to the facts before us, the malfunctioning thermostat caused the furnace to burn continuously until the temperature reached 120°—well beyond the pre-set temperature of 75°. We do not believe that under these circumstances this fire can be described as controlled. It burned for an excessive period of time resulting in temperatures much greater than those intended, causing the loss complained of. By characterizing this fire as hostile we are in no way departing from our prior decisions. We merely hold that a fire may be hostile although burning at its usual rate if it burns substantially longer or in some fashion other than expected. For the above reasons, we affirm the decision of the trial court.

Affirmed.

Youse v. Employers' Fire Insurance Co., 172 Kan. 111, 238 P.2d 472 (1951). The wife of the insured carried a star sapphire ring wrapped in a handkerchief in her purse. When she arrived home, she put the handkerchief together with some Kleenex on the dresser in her bedroom. Subsequently, her maid inadvertently picked up the handkerchief along with the tissues and threw them in a wastebasket. Another servant put the wastebasket's contents, along with other trash, into a trash burner on the premises (which was intended to be used to burn trash), lit a fire, and burned the trash. The ring was found about a week later in the burner; it had suffered $900 in damage. The insured sued to recover for the damage to the ring caused by fire. The lower court overruled a demurrer to the evidence and entered judgment for the insured; the Supreme Court reversed, and ordered that judgment be entered for the insurer.

"The policy, a standard form, insured household goods and personal property, usual or incidental to the occupancy of the premises as a dwelling, belonging to insured or a member of his family while contained on the premises, '. . . against all direct loss or damage by fire, except as hereinafter provided, . . .' in an amount not exceeding $2,000. . . .

"The insured also carried a 'floater policy' in another company (not a party to this action) by the terms of which the ring was insured to the extent of $250. The company issuing the 'floater policy' offered to pay that amount to insured, but as of the time of trial of this action such offer had not been accepted.

"
. . . .

"The company contends here, as it did in the court below, that the quoted insuring clause of the policy, 'against all direct loss or damage by fire' covers only loss or damage resulting from a 'hostile' fire as distinguished from a 'friendly' fire; that here, the fire being intentionally lighted in and confined to a place or receptacle where it was intended to be, was not a hostile fire within the usual and well-established meaning of the term and therefore no recovery can be had.

"The insured argues that he purchased and paid for *fire insurance*—not just for fire insurance to cover loss resulting only from so-called 'hostile' fires; that the direct loss and damage to the ring by fire is undisputed; that the company would have the court write into the policy an unauthorized and unreasonable restriction; . . . .

"
. . . .

"We think it cannot be denied that in common parlance and everyday usage one has not 'had a fire' so long as it has burned only in the place where it was intended to burn, and where fire ordinarily is maintained. By way of illustration, when a person maintains a fire in his furnace, cookstove or fireplace, or when he burns trash in his incinerator, he has not 'had a fire' in the ordinary, common acceptation of the term. On the other hand, if a fire on the roof results from sparks from fire in the furnace, cookstove or fireplace, if sparks from the latter should burn a rug or furniture or if the fire in the trash burner escapes therefrom and sets fire to the garage or fence, such person has 'had a fire' for which recovery can be had, notwithstanding the fire was originally friendly.

"We think it is quite true to say that when one purchases standard fire insurance he does so with the idea in mind of protecting himself from loss or damage resulting from what the law defines as a 'hostile' fire, and that the word 'fire,' as used in fire insurance policies, has, in common parlance, such well-understood meaning. In [*Mode, Ltd. v. Fireman's Fund Ins. Co.*, 62 Idaho 270, 110 P.2d 840, 843 (1941),] it was stated: 'The meaning of the term 'loss by fire' as being a 'hostile' and not a 'friendly fire' has been so extensively and long recognized that reasonably we must consider, even under liberal interpretation that both insured and insurer contracted with such definition in mind, determinative of what losses were covered.'

"
. . . .

"In our opinion there can be no question but that the fire which damaged or destroyed the sapphire ring was what in law is known as a 'friendly' fire. It was intentionally lighted, was for the usual and ordinary purpose of burning trash, and was at all times confined to the place where it was intended, and did not escape.

"We are not concerned here with the provisions of a 'floater policy,' and neither are we concerned with the question of the negligence or inadvertence of insured's servant in throwing the ring into the trash burner, which latter fact, according to insured's argument, made the fire a 'hostile' fire so far as insured is concerned. Negligence or inadvertence of an insured or of one of his employees of course ordinarily would not bar recovery—*provided* the fire causing the loss or damage is what is known in law as a *hostile* fire. True, here the loss was occasioned by fire—but, it was a *friendly* fire, and under such circumstances no recovery may be had."

NOTES

1. *The nature and purpose of the coverage.* Property insurance does not cover property as much as it covers the insured's *interest* in property. When property is destroyed, the contract of insurance compensates the damage to the insured's interest. Legal issues, and there are many, that relate to the *interest protected* are considered in the subsections following this one. *Engel* and *Youse* explore what *risks* are covered by property insurance.

What are the two most valuable pieces of property commonly owned by individuals? "[T]he two items. . .are real estate improvements and vehicles. These assets can be insured by a homeowners policy and a personal auto policy, respectively. Prior to the late 1950s, a homeowner needed to purchase several different kinds of policies, such as fire insurance, theft insurance, and other coverages to get complete coverage. In the late 1950s, insurers developed the homeowners' policy — known in the trade as the HO policy—which incorporated into one policy several kinds of property coverages, additional living expenses in the event of the dwelling's damage or destruction, comprehensive personal liability coverage, and replacement-cost coverage on the dwelling and sometimes the contents." Robert H. Jerry, II, Understanding Insurance Law § 60B, at 341 (2d ed. 1996). Many automobiles are acquired by a long-term lease as opposed to purchase; the personal auto policy treats the leased vehicle the same as an owned vehicle. When someone leases a house or apartment, the landlord typically insures the premises, but this is something that the landlord and tenant can negotiate in the rental agreement. If a tenant, for example, leases realty in a "rent-to-own" arrangement, the tenant may assume responsibility for insuring the premises. Owners of commercial property can obtain coverage via similar kinds of forms, but with provisions that differ to account for the different nature of the property.

With the benefit of the foregoing background, can you explain why the insurer on the "floater policy" mentioned in *Youse* was so willing to pay the $250 under its policy?

2. *Fortuity revisited.* Do you agree that the losses in both cases were fortuitous? If so, why does the insured not recover in *Youse?* That is, what is the rationale for the pro-insurer outcome in *Youse?*

If the law of Minnesota were applied to the facts in *Youse,* would the result in *Youse* have been different? Is there any other rationale that would permit the insured to recover in *Youse* and, at the same time, preserve the "friendly fire" rule for those cases where it might be justified? Does the rationale turn on whether there was a fire (which there surely was), whether there was a loss (which there surely was), or whether the loss by the fire was fortuitous (a more debatable proposition)?

3. *Friendship versus hostility.* The friendly fire/hostile fire distinction is easy to state, but is often less clear in practical application. The test has a "you know it when you see it" quality to it, having something to do with the difference, for example, between a romantic campfire and a grease fire roaring across a kitchen counter or a blaze in the middle of the living room sofa. In other situations, the test is often applied with less confidence, as *Engel* and *Youse* suggest. Some of this uncertainty can be traced to *Austin v. Drew,* which as the seminal case in the area has had much influence on the development of the friendly fire/hostile fire distinction. One of the difficulties, however, is that reasonable people can read *Austin* and have important differences of opinion about the nature of the fire in that case—and hence the scope of the rule employed to decide it. For more discussion of *Austin,* see Robert H. Jerry, II, Understanding Insurance Law § 66, at 477–79 (2d ed. 1996).

4. *Commercial liability insurance and the hostile-friendly distinction.* The Commercial General Liability ("CGL") policy receives attention in § 5.02, *infra.* Since 1973, the CGL has had a pollution exclusion, the text of which has changed through the years. (The exclusion receives special attention in § 5.02[3][c], *infra*). A much broader exclusion (i.e., one placing greater limits on the coverage) appeared in 1986, but the exclusion has an exception for some kinds of bodily injury or property damage "arising out of heat, smoke or fumes from a 'hostile fire.'" See "Section I-Coverages," par. f of "Exclusions," in Appendix B. An earlier iteration of the 1986 exclusion (see the exclusion in CG 00 01 01 96) also stated: "As used in this exclusion, a hostile fire means one which becomes uncontrollable or breaks out from where it was intended to be." (The latest CGL places this text in "Section V-Definitions." See the forms in Appendix B. Why do you suppose the definition was moved from the exclusion to the definition section? Does this make the exclusion clearer?) Does the earlier iteration limit the meaning of "hostile fire" relative to how that term is interpreted in case law? If a fire spontaneously erupts in a factory but remains under control due to expert work of on-site firefighters, and the fire nevertheless produces fumes that cause some pollution damage, is this damage covered by the CGL? See *Associated Wholesale Grocers, Inc. v. Americold Corp.,* 261 Kan. 806, 934 P.2d 65 (1997); *Mid-Continent Casualty Co. v. Safe Tire Disposal Corp.,* 16 S.W.3d 418 (Tex. Ct. App. 2000).

5. *The limits of the friendly fire doctrine.* What if the insured in *Engel* had negligently set the thermostat at too high a heat, thereby causing the loss? Should the policy provide coverage in that event? Suppose the baker burns a batch of pies because the thermostat malfunctions. Should the baker recover

for the lost pies under her fire insurance policy? Would your answer be different if the malfunctioning thermostat caused the destruction of a $100,000 oven? What if the baker's losses (pies in one instance and the oven in the other) were caused by her negligence in setting the thermostat too high for too long a period? Is it time to jettison the distinction altogether in favor of another approach? Would you favor using the doctrine of reasonable expectations to resolve the close cases? *See Sadlowski v. Liberty Mutual Insurance Co.,* 487 A.2d 1146 (Del. Super. Ct. 1984).

[2] Partial Interests

[a] Vendors and Vendees

BROWNELL v. BOARD OF EDUCATION
239 N.Y. 369, 146 N.E. 630, 37 A.L.R. 1319 (1925)

POUND, J. [Defendant Board of Education owned property (the "Lake Avenue property") on which was situated a high school building and two other small structures. The Board was constructing a new high school on other land it owned, and therefore on September 10, 1923 entered into a contract to sell the Lake Avenue property to plaintiff. The contract price was $30,000, of which $3,000 was paid at the time the contract was executed. The balance was to be paid when the new high school was completed (estimated to be about one year later), at which time a deed to the Lake Avenue property was to be given to plaintiff and plaintiff would be allowed to take possession.] . . . . The contract provided that the premises were to be delivered "in as good condition as they now are, natural wear excepted;" that defendant was to pay taxes and assessments during the period of its occupancy and until the delivery of the deed; and that in case either party failed to perform, the party so failing should pay to the other the sum of $3,000, which was agreed upon as liquidated damages for such failure. The contract was silent as to insurance. However, at the time of the contract, and for a considerable period prior thereto, defendant carried insurance on the premises and the contents thereof in substantial amounts, including $28,000 upon the high school building. This insurance was payable to defendant in the event of loss. No change in the form of the insurance was made at any time. It was continued after the contract was executed. Plaintiff did not secure other insurance. On October 26, 1923, while the premises were still in defendant's exclusive possession, a fire occurred without fault of either party which totally destroyed the roofs and interior of the high school building, and practically destroyed its outer walls. Defendant by reason thereof was compelled to vacate the building, and no repairs have been made upon it. The building was considered by defendant and the insurance companies as a total loss, and defendant has received from the insurers and still retains the full sum of $28,000 insurance carried thereon. This is exclusive of other amounts of insurance received by it for loss on the building's contents.

On this state of facts plaintiff asks that the contract of September 10, 1923, be specifically performed by defendant, by a conveyance of the title to the real estate, and by application of the insurance money upon the purchase price. Defendant declines to do this, but offers to return to plaintiff the $3,000, with interest paid by him upon the execution of the contract.

The courts below have held that defendant continued to hold the insurance money in place of the destroyed building in trust for plaintiff. With this conclusion we are not in accord. The benefit of the vendor's policy belonged to the vendor, and the vendee had no claim on the insurance money. Such is the weight of English and American authority resting on *Rayner v. Preston, [*1881] 18 Ch. Div. 1.[1]

The English rule has been changed by act of Parliament, [1922] (12 & 13 Geo. V, c. 16, § 105), so as to provide that the vendee may claim the insurance money received by the vendor, subject, however, to any stipulation to the contrary. The question is unsettled in this court. When the risk of loss falls on an uninsured vendee (*Sewell v. Underhill,* 197 N.Y. 168, 90 N.E. 430, 27 L.R.A. [N.S.] 233, 134 Am. St. Rep. 863, 18 Ann. Cas. 795), the rule in *Rayner v. Preston* has given some dissatisfaction. In some jurisdictions the courts have sought to follow the general and manifestly unsound reasoning of Lord Justice James in his dissenting opinion, to the effect that the policy is for the benefit of all persons interested in the property. Professor Vance, in the note in the Yale Law Journal (see footnote), suggests that in the business world the insurance runs with the land, and that the courts should give effect to that understanding. Other jurisdictions have sought so to extend the rule that the vendee becomes the beneficial owner of the land for certain purposes (*Sewell v. Underhill, supra*) as to include the insurance money. In *Millville Aerie No. 1836, Fraternal Order of Eagles v. Weatherby* (1913) 82 N.J. Eq. 455, 88 A. 847, the court says:

> "As purchaser under a valid contract of purchase vendee became the equitable owner of the property, in equity the property is regarded as belonging to him; the vendor retaining the legal title simply as trustee and as security for the unpaid purchase money. By reason of this equitable relation of the parties to a contract of sale of land, it has been determined by the great weight of American authority that money accruing on a policy of insurance, where the loss has occurred subsequent to the execution of the contract, will, in equity, inure to the benefit of the vendee; the vendor still retaining his character as trustee, and the insurance money in his hands representing the property that has been destroyed."

These reasons may savor of layman's ideas of equity, but they are not law. The majority of the court in *Rayner v. Preston* were sound in principle. Insurance is a mere personal contract to pay a sum of money by way of indemnity to protect the interest of the insured. In common parlance the buildings are insured; but every one who stops to consider the nature of the insurance contract understands that they are not. Both in the forum and the

---

[1] *See* Woodruff's Cases on Insurance (2d Ed. p. 223); "Risk of Loss in Equity between the Date of Contract to Sell Real Estate and Transfer of Title," by Prof. Vannemore, 8 Minn. Law Review, 127; also, note on the decision below, 34 Yale Law Journal, 87.

market place it is known that the insurance runs to the individual insured, and not with the land. The vendor has a beneficial interest to protect, i.e., his own. The vendee has an insurable interest and may protect himself. The trustee as such has no insurable interest, and can only act for the cestui qui trust. Plaintiff may not have the insurance money collected by defendant. It is not a part of the res bargained for, and no trust relation exists in regard to it.

Plaintiff asks that, if the relief he seeks cannot be granted, the rights of the parties be stated. In this regard the parties have by the terms of their contract taken themselves out of the old rule of *Paine v. Meller,* 6 Ves. Jr. 349, adopted in *Sewell v. Underhill, supra,* which places the loss on the vendee when the buildings are destroyed before the transfer is made. The vendor contracted to deliver the premises "in as good condition as they now are," and the parties agreed that in case of failure to perform the defaulting party should pay the sum of $3,000 as liquidated damages. The loss must therefore be borne by the defendant, except as it has protected itself from such loss by insurance. By reason of the accidental destruction of a substantial part of the premises, it can neither perform nor compel performance. The purchaser may seek to rescind the contract or take the position that it is at an end for impossibility of performance and recover back the $3,000 he has paid on the purchase price, or he may stand on the contract under the terms of which he paid the $3,000 and claim the stipulated damages. He is not in a position to do both. The measure of defendant's liability in either case is the sum of $3,000.

The judgments below should be reversed and a declaratory judgment granted in accordance with opinion, with costs in all courts.

HISCOCK, C. J., and CARDOZO, CRANE, ANDREWS, and LEHMAN, JJ., concur. MCLAUGHLIN, J., absent.

Judgments reversed, etc.

NOTES

1. *First things about real estate sales.* In most real estate sales, a contract for sale is executed, and this contract typically calls for a transfer of title (i.e., the deed) at a "closing" which is to be held at some date in the future. The parties are free to contract for a particular closing date, and the date is frequently the subject of negotiation. With respect to sales of residential real estate, it is common for the date to be in the vicinity of thirty to sixty days in the future. Normally, there are a variety of conditions in the contract (*e.g.,* the vendee being able to get financing; the premises passing various inspections; etc.) which must occur before the vendee's obligation to proceed to the closing becomes due and owing. Obviously, there is a risk that the premises could be destroyed or damaged between the date of the sales contract and the date of the closing. In *Brownell,* who agreed to bear this risk? Most standard form real estate contracts allocate the risk of loss during this interim period. If the vendor assumes this risk and insures it, as is common, the vendee will have difficulty making out a claim that she is entitled to the benefit of the vendor's policy.

2. *Risk of loss in the absence of contract.* If the sales contract in *Brownell* had not covered the situation, under New York law at that time who would have had the risk of loss at the time of the fire? Where a contract for the sale of land is subject to specific performance, a majority of jurisdictions treat the purchaser as the owner of the land pending completion of the contract. This is known as the doctrine of equitable conversion. The vendor is viewed as retaining only legal title, which in effect gives the vendor a security interest, whereas the equitable or beneficial title is placed in the purchaser. Under this doctrine the purchaser bears the risk of loss. Those jurisdictions that also have a common law rule but that have rejected the doctrine of equitable conversion usually follow one of two minority rules during the executory period: (1) the risk is on the purchaser only if the purchaser has taken possession or (2) the risk is always on the vendor.

Other states following a minority position have done so by adopting the Uniform Vendor and Purchaser Risk Act, 14 U.L.A. 469 (1990). Generally speaking, this Act, along with the more recent Uniform Land Transactions Act, 13 U.L.A. 469 (1986), both promulgated by the National Conference of Commissioners on Uniform State Laws, leaves the risk of loss on the vendor until possession or legal title is transferred to the purchaser. They deny the vendor the remedy of specific performance and compel the vendor to return any earnest money deposit if a material loss occurs during the executory period. Of course, as *Brownell* indicates, the common law and statutory rules can be overridden by an express provision in the contract allocating the risk of loss. *See Holscher v. James*, 124 Idaho 443, 860 P.2d 646 (1993) (purchase agreement placing risk of loss on vendors renders doctrine of equitable conversion inapplicable).

3. *The New York rule today.* In 1963, the New York legislature enacted a modified version of the Uniform Vendor and Purchaser Act. See N.Y. Gen. Oblig. Law § 5-1311 (McKinney 2000). The New York statute, like the Uniform Act, leaves the risk of loss on the vendor until title or possession passes, but only prohibits specific performance if there is a "material" casualty loss. If an "immaterial" part of the property is destroyed without the fault of the purchaser, either the vendor or purchaser may enforce the contract of sale, but the purchaser is entitled to a reduction in the purchase price to reflect the reduction in value due to the damage. *See National Factors, Inc. V. Winslow,* 52 Misc. 2d 194, 274 N.Y.S.2d 400 (N.Y. Sup. Ct. 1966). For more on the doctrine of equitable conversion in real estate transactions, see Roger A. Cunningham, William B. Stoebuck & Dale Whitman, The Law of Property § 10.13 (2nd ed. 1993).

4. *Matching coverage with risk.* As the foregoing suggests, the entangled nature of these rules creates the possibility that the party who bears the risk of loss may not have insured it. This is perhaps most likely in situations where the parties do not use a standardized form which allocates risk, the parties are not aware of a default rule allocating risk to the vendee, the vendor leaves his insurance in force during the pre-closing period, and it never occurs to the vendee to acquire insurance prior to the closing. There are, of course, other possible gaps and mismatches. To explore how courts handle these situations, consider the following cases.

WOLF v. HOME INSURANCE CO.

100 N.J. Super. 27, 241 A.2d 28 (Law Div. 1968)

STAMLER, (JOSEPH H.) J.S.C.

Plaintiffs sue to recover on a fire insurance policy issued by defendant. The case is before the court on cross-motions for summary judgment . . . .

There is no dispute as to the relevant facts. On October 8, 1964, a fire occurred damaging or destroying plaintiffs' three-story frame apartment dwelling located at 80–82 Orchard Street in the City of Orange. Defendant had insured the premises for three years beginning on September 9, 1963 against fire with a limit of coverage under the policy of $25,000 (subject to an 80% co-insurance clause not here pertinent). The policy term had not yet expired on the date of the fire.

Prior thereto, on May 11, 1964 the plaintiffs had entered into an agreement with the State of New Jersey to sell the property in question together with another piece of property owned by plaintiffs which was located at 76 Orchard Street in the City of Orange. The successful negotiations, which were with the State Highway Department, were in lieu of condemnation proceedings. The sale price was $27,000 for the properties, without any allocation of this sum among the separate parcels of land or buildings. As of the date of purchase, the insured premises had already been vacated, and the State took possession of the property on July 29, 1964. The State's possession was evidenced by signs posted at the premises.

Following the fire of October 8, 1964 there was no downward revision in the original purchase price of $27,000. Plaintiffs were paid the agreed sum on March 4, 1965 and the State took title. It is alleged that the fire was reported to the defendant one day after its occurrence. Defendant having refused to pay for damages resulting from the fire, plaintiffs bring this action seeking to recover $25,000, the maximum coverage under the policy.

. . . .

Defendant's principal contention is that plaintiffs did not sustain any loss which is covered under the policy of insurance. Plaintiffs insist with equal vigor that they have suffered a loss under this set of facts. The insuring provisions in the case at bar conform precisely with the language found in the first sentence of N.J.S.A. 17:36-5.19:

> "Every such fire insurance policy shall insure, limited to the amounts of insurance specified therein, the named insured and legal represen-tatives, to the extent of the *actual cash value of the property at the time of loss,* but not exceeding the amount which it would cost to repair or replace the property with material of like kind and quality within a reasonable time after such loss, without allowance for any increased cost of repair or reconstruction by reason of any ordinance or law

regulating construction or repair and without compensation for loss resulting from interruption of business or manufacture, *nor in any event for more than the interest of the insured, against all direct loss by fire,* lightning, and by removal from premises endangered by the perils insured against in such policy, except as thereinafter provided, *to the property described therein* while located or contained as described in such policy, or pro rata for 5 days at each proper place to which any of the property shall necessarily be removed for preservation from the perils insured against in such policy, but not elsewhere." (Emphasis added).

There can be no dispute that an insured must sustain a loss before he can recover on a standard form fire insurance policy. The question before this court is: precisely when does one measure or ascertain whether a fire loss has occurred? What is the "time of loss" referred to in N.J.S.A. 17:36-5.19? Does the "loss" become fixed as of the date of the fire so that, as long as the insured has an insurable interest at that time, the insurer becomes obligated to pay under its policy; or can subsequent collateral events, such as the fact that the sale between insureds and the State of New Jersey was ultimately consummated nearly five months after the fire, with insureds receiving the full previously agreed upon contract price, be taken into account in determining the existence of an insurable "loss"?

This is a controversy which "has been raging in Anglo-American law since 1801." Cribbet, "Insurance and the Executory Contract for the Sale of Real Estate," 51 Ill. Bar J. 124 (1962). As noted in *First National Bank of Highland Park v. Boston Ins. Co.,* 17 Ill. 2d 147, 150, 160 N.E.2d 802, 804 (Sup. Ct. 1959):

> "The problem that the case presents is not an easy one. When insured property is in a single ownership, it is not hard to hold to the orthodox concept of an insurance contract as a personal contract of indemnity. But there are inherent difficulties when there are multiple interests in the property. Those inherent difficulties are augmented because the effect given to an executory contract to sell realty, and to the doctrine of equitable conversion, differs significantly from one jurisdiction to another. The result is that neither courts nor commentators are agreed upon proper solutions for the many variations on the vendor-vendee-insurer theme."

In an excellent note by William F. Young entitled "Some 'Windfall Coverages' in Property and Liability Insurance," 60 Colum.L.Rev. 1063, 1071 (1960), the author feels that the Illinois court "understates the case" to say that neither the courts nor the commentators are agreed upon the proper solutions in this area.

It would appear that there are two broad lines of authority upon this question. What may be referred to as the "New York Rule" is derived from *Foley v. Manufacturers' & Builders' Fire Ins. Co.,* 152 N.Y. 131, 46 N.E. 318, 43 L.R.A. 664 (Ct. of App. 1897) and a subsequent series of New York cases, especially *Alexandra Restaurant, Inc. v. New Hampshire Ins. Co.,* 272 App. Div. 346, 71 N.Y.S.2d 515 (App. Div. 1947), *affirmed* 297 N.Y.S.2d 515 (App. Div. 1947), *affirmed* 297 N.Y. 858, 79 N.E.2d 268 (Ct. of App. 1948). This rule is to the effect that in the absence of any contractual agreement to the contrary, a fire insurance policy is a contract of indemnification, the premiums for which are computed according to the value of the property and the risk involved without the knowledge of collateral remedies, so that recovery on the policy will not be denied as long as the insured has a valuable insurable interest at the time of the casualty, even though there is an executory contract for the sale of the real property outstanding which is later consummated. A large majority of the courts in this country that have dealt with the question adhere to the New York Rule. The contrary view, known as the "Wisconsin Rule" is an outgrowth of *Ramsdell v. Insurance Co. of North America,* 197 Wis. 136, 221 N.W. 654 (Sup. Ct. 1928). This rule also regards a contract of fire insurance as a contract of indemnity but it denies recovery to the vendor-insured where the existence of a collateral executory contract for the sale of the real property eventually results in shielding the vendor from sustaining any actual pecuniary loss from the casualty.

. . . .

The topic has received judicial attention in one reported New Jersey case. *Tauriello v. Aetna Insurance Co.,* 14 N.J. Super. 530, 82 A.2d 226 (Law Div. 1951) dealt squarely with the same factual situation now before this court. There is no relevant distinction. In holding for the defendant insurer on the theory that the plaintiffs had not been able to show any loss, the court in *Tauriello* in effect followed that line of cases referred to as the Wisconsin Rule, when it said:

> "The general rule is that a contract for insurance against fire is ordinarily one of indemnity under which the insured is entitled to receive indemnity or to be reimbursed for any loss that he may have sustained and cannot recover if he has sustained no loss. *See* 45 C.J.S. Insurance § 915, page 1009, section 915. In *Draper v. Delaware State Grange Mutual Fire Insurance Co.,* 5 Boyce 143, 28 Del. 143, 91 A. 206 [Super. Ct. 1914], it was pointed out that a fire insurance policy is a contract not to insure the property against fire but to insure the owner against loss by fire, and that the insurance company can be called upon when, and only when, the insured has sustained a loss which under the terms of the policy calls for indemnification. The same rule finds support in *Patterson v. Durand Farmers Mutual Insurance Co.,* 303 Ill. App. 128, 24 N.E.2d 740 (1940)." (14 N.J. Super. at p. 532, 82 A.2d at pp. 227, 228)

The court goes on to state that the rationale of *United Bond & Mortgage Co. of Hackensack v. Concordia Fire Ins. Co.,* 113 N.J.L. 28, 172 A. 373 (E. & A. 1934) and *Power Building & Loan Association v. Ajax Fire Ins. Co.,* 110 N.J.L. 256, 164 A. 410 (E. & A. 1933), lends support to its decision.

Plaintiffs submit that in light of the persuasive appellate authority from other states before and after *Tauriello,* that holding is erroneous. Our system of jurisprudence envisions that while the opinions of courts of coordinate jurisdiction be taken into consideration, they are nevertheless not binding on a court of equivalent rank.

An examination of the cases relied upon by the court in *Tauriello* leads this court to the conclusion that the question before it is deserving of fresh study. . . .

The difficulty with the opinion in *Tauriello* may lie in its stress on the term "indemnity". In talking about labels, Chief Justice Weintraub observed in *Spina v. Consolidated Police, etc., Pension Fund Com.,* 41 N.J. 391, 197 A.2d 169 (1964) that:

> "There is no profit in dealing in labels such as 'gratuity,' 'compensation,' 'contract,' and 'vested rights.' None fits precisely, and it would be a mistake to choose one and be driven by that choice to some inevitable consequence." (at p. 401, 197 A.2d at p. 174)

This is exactly what the court did in *Tauriello*. Instead of analyzing and determining just what interest of the insured was protected by the policy in force, it applied the label "indemnity" and was thus bound by what it considered to be the "general rule" for contracts of indemnity.

. . . .

The cases of *United Bond & Mortgage Co. of Hackensack v. Concordia Fire Ins. Co.,* 113 N.J.L. 28, 172 A. 373 (E. & A. 1934) and *Power Building & Loan Association v. Ajax Fire Ins. Co.,* 110 N.J.L. 256, 164 A. 410 (E. & A. 1933), cited by the court in *Tauriello v. Aetna Insurance Co.,* 14 N.J. Super. 530 at p. 532, 82 A.2d 226 (Law Div. 1951), deal with a situation where the insured is a mortgagee who had insured his interest in the mortgaged premises. The test utilized by the two cases in determining whether the insured had suffered any loss is whether the debt represented by the mortgage was subsequently fully satisfied or not. Any analysis of this topic must also consider the opinion of our Supreme Court in *Flint Frozen Foods, Inc. v. Firemen's Ins. Co. of Newark, N.J.,* 8 N.J. 606, 86 A.2d 673 (1952). In that case Einhorn's Inc., a creditor of the plaintiff, held warehouse receipts as collateral security upon a debt and obtained fire insurance which insured the creditor to the extent of its interest in groceries stored in a subsidiary of the plaintiff. A fire occurred which destroyed the goods covered by the warehouse receipts. Within a month after the fire the plaintiff-debtor had paid the debt in full. The insurance policy was assigned to plaintiff, which sued thereon notwithstanding that the assignor-creditor had never filed any claim under the policy. Plaintiff recovered below and the judgment was reversed on appeal. In holding that the plaintiff, as loss-claim assignee, could not recover because its assignor had suffered no loss, the Supreme Court made the following observations:

> "A policy of fire insurance is a contract the terms of which are prescribed by statute, N.J.S.A. 17:36-5.7 [presently found in N.J.S.A. 17:36-5.20]. Like any contract, when its terms are clear the court must enforce the contract as it finds it, *James v. Federal Insurance Co.,* 5 N.J. 21, 24, 73 A.2d 720 (1950). Its meaning 'is to be governed by its own terms without recourse to other documents unless its own language so requires,' *Herbert L. Farkas Co., v. New York Fire Ins. Co.,* 5 N.J. 604, 609, 76 A.2d 895, 897 (1950). By the policy here in litigation the insurance company insured Einhorn's to the extent of its interest against loss by fire with respect to groceries which Einhorn's held as collateral security for a debt owed it by the plaintiff. The debt having been paid in full by the plaintiff, it necessarily follows that Einhorn's suffered no loss. Therefore, neither Einhorn's nor the plaintiff as its

assignee can recover on the policy which expressly provides that there shall be no recovery 'in any event for more than the interest of the insured.' This conclusion, reached under the clear terms of the policy, is consonant with the fundamental principle of all insurance on property that the policy is a contract of indemnity. If the insured has suffered no loss with respect to the property covered by the policy, there is, of course, no liability on the policy, for there is nothing for the insurer to indemnify." (at p. 610, 86 A.2d at p. 674.)

Defendant argues that the above-mentioned authorities place New Jersey under what has been referred to as the Wisconsin Rule and that, pursuant to this rule, this court must look to related transactions to determine whether the insured plaintiffs have sustained a loss. The contention is that even if the plaintiffs had an insurable interest at the time of fire, the subsequent culmination of the sale of the insured property to the New Jersey Highway Department nearly five months after the fire for the same amount the plaintiffs had agreed to accept prior to the fire "wiped out" any loss; and in this State if there is no loss, there is nothing to indemnify. Plaintiffs maintain, on the other hand, that the New Jersey cases are distinguishable from the present set of facts because there it was the debt due the property owner that was insured while here, pursuant to the terms of the contract and N.J.S.A. 17:36-5.19, the property itself is insured. Furthermore, they insist that any collateral arrangements or outside agreements a vendor may have are of no concern to the insurance company and that to make the payment of claims which are ostensibly due dependent on extraneous matters does violence to the express terms of the insurance policy.

This court is, of course, bound by all pronouncements of the present or former high tribunal of New Jersey. A fair and proper reading of *Flint Frozen Foods, Inc. v. Firemen's Ins. Co. of Newark, N.J., supra,* and the earlier opinions of the Court of Errors and Appeals, cited previously, can only mean that when the insured in a contract of fire insurance is a creditor, mortgagee, lienholder or the like who is insuring the obligation due to him, related transactions occurring subsequent to the fire can be taken into account in determining whether the insured has sustained a loss. The question before this court is whether the same rule obtains in non-creditor situations when the insured is simply an individual insuring himself against damage loss to property that he owns.

This court is aware of the seemingly broad import given the words "loss" and "indemnity" in *Flint Frozen Foods, supra.* But the court would also like to focus on p. 612, 86 A.2d on p. 675 of the same opinion. There the Supreme Court, after stating that it is now entirely appropriate for a person having merely a security interest to take out a fire insurance policy in his own name covering property in which he has an interest, finds that recovery by the plaintiff (the debtor and assignee of the former assured)

> "is precluded by the fact that the policy did not purport to insure its interest as owners of the property destroyed *and* because as assignee its claim could rise no higher than that of its assignor, Einhorn's, which suffered no loss." (Emphasis added).

The intimation is that had the policy therein purported to insure a full ownership interest in the property, as does the one now before this court, the result might well have been different.

. . . .

When the underlying nature of the respective interests being insured by a creditor and by an owner are examined, it becomes completely logical and consistent that a different rule should prevail in each instance. A creditor is interested only in having the debt or obligation owing to him assured. He seeks to have his *status* as creditor protected. An owner, on the other hand, already holds what our law considers to be the most complete type of interest and he wishes to insure his *physical property* rather than his status. In short, if a piece of property held as security burns down, the "loss" is not yet a proven fact because the creditor may still be able to pursue successfully his underlying obligation; but if the same property held in outright ownership burns, the "loss" is then complete because the "owner" has nothing left to his [ownership] status except the ashes and rubble unless he can collect insurance that will enable him to rebuild or purchase some new property to evidence his ownership.

. . . .

The views expressed herein with respect to the nature of the insured owner's interest and the determination of when he has sustained a loss by fire are thoroughly buttressed by an examination of the fire policy issued to the plaintiffs. The rights of the parties are controlled by this insurance contract. And its meaning is to be governed by its own terms without recourse to other documents unless its language so requires.

In accordance with the mandate of N.J.S.A. 17:36-5.19, the present policy insures, but not "for more than the *interest of the insured,* against all direct loss by fire,. . .*to the property* described therein." (Emphasis added). Here, unlike in *Flint Frozen Foods, Inc., supra,* the policy does purport to insure an ownership interest in the property. It is undisputed that plaintiffs held full legal title to the insured premises on the date of the fire. Did they also sustain a "loss" as of that date? The statute and policy allow for a recovery up to the maximum coverage specified "to the extent of the actual cash value of the property at the time of loss." The "time of loss" can only intend the time of fire damage or destruction. If any other meaning were inferred, then the time for valuing the loss would be uncertain in every case. Defendant insurer offers this court no fixed standard for determining when a casualty loss is to be measured and argues only that *here,* after taking cognizance of collateral events not involving the insurer which came to be realized nearly five months after the fire, there was no loss. Nothing in New Jersey law commits this court to such a view for a non-creditor fire insurance situation.

. . . .

To give any meaning other than "time of fire" to the words "time of loss", moreover, results in totally contradictory interpretations to the word "loss" in the several sections of this fire insurance policy. The insurance contract provides that:

"The insured shall give immediate written notice to this Company of any *loss,*. . .and within sixty days after the *loss,* unless such time is extended in writing by this Company, the insured shall render to this Company a proof of loss, . . ." (Emphasis added).

On the facts *sub judice,* the insurance company maintains that if we look at the closing date between insureds and their vendee, nearly five months after the date of the fire, it becomes apparent that the plaintiffs have ultimately sustained no "loss" within the intendment of the policy. If this is the time of determining "loss", then, consistently, the "immediate" written notice to the Company of any loss and the sixty day requirement for filing a proof of loss only come into play as of the closing date. The defendant cannot have it both ways. A contract of insurance must be construed as a whole. While a party may plead inconsistent claims or defenses and may argue inconsistent principles of law, he cannot be heard to contend for two diametrically opposed sets of facts.

Certainly the only conceivable day meant by the terms of the policy after which notice of any loss must be given and proof of loss filed is the day on which the casualty occurred. Consistency dictates that the "time of loss" for purposes of arriving at the "actual cash value of the property" also be taken as the date of fire.

One of the arguments presented by the courts adhering to the minority Wisconsin Rule is that an insurance contract is one of indemnity and to permit the assured to recover without taking into account collateral events would convert insurance into a wagering or profit-making device. It is this court's belief that if the facts of a particular case so warrant, our courts can always deal adequately with a case involving fraud. In holding that the plaintiff was entitled to the insurance proceeds and that the defendant insurer could not be subrogated to the plaintiff's rights in the matter, the Supreme Court of Minnesota dealt squarely with this contention of profit-making:

"In considering the asserted right of the insurer to subrogation to the collateral rights of the insured, certain conflicting considerations come into play. To permit the insured to keep the proceeds of both obligations offends public policy which frowns upon placing an insured in a position to profit by a loss which he may be tempted to cause himself or by carelessness fail to prevent. On the other hand, to give the insurer the benefit of the collateral obligation through subrogation ignores the plain terms of the insuring agreement and provides the insurer with a windfall. Its premiums are assumed to represent the fair equivalent of the obligation it contracted to incur without knowledge of the existence of collateral remedies." *Board of Trustees, etc. v. Cream City Mutual Ins. Co.,* 255 Minn. 347, 96 N.W.2d 690, 696 (Sup. Ct. 1959).

. . . .

This court submits that the fallacy of the so-called Wisconsin Rule is well illustrated by the following hypothetical example suggested in the dissenting opinion in *Paramount Fire Ins. Co. v. Aetna Casualty & Surety Co.,* 163 Tex. 250, 353 S.W.2d 841 at p. 846 (Sup. Ct. 1962):

"Suppose the vendor and purchaser had entered into a contract providing for $5,000.00 cash payment, the balance to be paid in monthly instalments of $125.00 each due on the 10th day of each successive succeeding month. This would require 82 months, or approximately seven years, to pay the deferred payments. Vendor could not be forced to take his balance in one lump sum. He could insist on the monthly payments as set out in the contract in order to earn the interest. Under the majority holding Paramount's liability would not be known until the last payment had been made."

In the instant case, the State did not take title until nearly five months following the fire. The delay might well have been even longer. Should the determination of an insured's loss in the vendor-vendee-insurer context be made to await the outcome of such matters? The insurer is not being damaged by being compelled to pay the insured who is owner as of the date of the fire. Its premiums are assumed to represent the fair equivalent of the obligation it contracted to incur without knowledge of the existence of collateral remedies. And the evil of the chance possibility of an ultimate collection by the vendor of the full purchase price from his vendee and also the insurance payment for the damage sustained does not outweigh the disruptions and harassments closely associated with delays in settlement of fire loss claims.

In dealing with the problem at hand, some courts have recognized a theory of constructive trust whereby the vendor-insured can collect for the loss from the insurance company but only so as to hold the payment in trust for his vendee, who is owner of the property in equity under the doctrine of equitable conversion. *Dubin Paper Co. v. Insurance Co. of North America*, 361 Pa. 68, 63 A.2d 85, 8 A.L.R.2d 1393 (Sup. Ct. 1949); and see Godfrey, "Some Limited-Interest Problems," 15 Law & Contemp. Prob. 415 (1950). The issue may perhaps turn on whether the contract of sale requires the vendee to obtain fire insurance. *Raplee v. Piper*, 3 N.Y.2d 179, 164 N.Y.S.2d 732, 143 N.E.2d 919, 64 A.L.R.2d 1397 (Ct. of App. 1957).

The doctrine of equitable conversion is in force in this State. And in a suit for specific performance brought by a vendee against his vendor, the constructive trust theory has been applied so as to entitle the vendee to the proceeds of an insurance policy placed on the property by the vendor. But this court expresses no opinion as to the applicability of the theory when the suit, as here, is only between the vendor-insured and the insurer. The question of disposition of the insurance proceeds once they are in plaintiffs' hands is not now before the court. The only point to be emphasized is that any equitable title in the vendee cannot be set up as a defense by the fire insurer in a suit brought against it on its contract with the vendor.

It is concluded therefore that defendant's motion for summary judgment is denied. Plaintiffs' motion for partial summary judgment on specific legal issues is granted. The matter may proceed accordingly to trial of the remaining issues.

Plaintiffs are directed to submit an order in conformity with this opinion within ten days consented to as to form or settled upon notice.

VOGEL v. NORTHERN ASSURANCE CO.

219 F.2d 409 (3rd Cir. 1955)

GOODRICH, CIRCUIT JUDGE.

This is an appeal from a decision in an insurance case. With a stipulated loss of $12,000 the plaintiff finds himself in the happy possession of a judgment against two insurance companies which aggregates $15,000. The insurance companies, quite naturally, appeal.

The whole question is one of Pennsylvania law. The property insured against fire was located in Pennsylvania; the insurance policies were written and delivered in Pennsylvania. Our sole problem is to determine as best we can the Pennsylvania law which governs this situation.

The undisputed facts present a question with all the tantalizing niceties of the type which examiners pose to law students. Indeed, the problem of the case can be posed in the form of a hypothetical examination question. Here it is:

S, a seller of real property, (in the actual case a man named Shank) agrees to sell the land to V, the vendee, for $15,000. (The vendee's real name in this case is Vogel so the initials fit happily.) S then takes out fire insurance on the property in the amount of $6,000; V does likewise but in the amount of $9,000. Before S conveys the property to V a fire occurs, damaging the house on the land to the extent of $12,000. V goes ahead and completes his part of the purchase agreement and receives a deed from S. Following this, S assigns to V all of his rights against the insurance company under the policy. V then sues both S's insurer (Northern Assurance Company, Ltd.) and his own insurer (Mount Joy Mutual Insurance Company). Was the district court correct in giving judgment against each company even though the total recovery exceeds the stipulated loss by $3,000?

We start the analysis with the well-settled rule in Pennsylvania, derived from English law, that when a contract to sell land is made the equitable ownership passes forthwith to the buyer. The seller's "title" which he retains until final conveyance is but a "security title" and the risk of loss or advantage of gain is borne by the buyer.

The seller with this security title may take out fire insurance to protect his interest. The Pennsylvania decisions say unequivocally that as between the seller and the insurance company the seller is the owner of the property. Of course, upon the performance of the contract of sale, the seller no longer has an insurable interest. The Pennsylvania cases demonstrate very clearly, however, that a seller of real estate, having taken out fire insurance, can collect from the insurance company under the policy for a loss occurring prior to the date of settlement. The reason assigned is that the rights and liabilities of the parties to the insurance contract become fixed when the loss occurs. It is not valid argument, according to these authorities, that the seller has suffered no loss because the vendee has later completed the contract of sale and paid the seller.

So far, so good. Is the insurance money thus collected by the seller his own to do with as he pleases? May he use it to buy himself a new car, give it to a favorite grandchild or otherwise dispose of it as people do who have some extra money? In this particular case S, instead of collecting the money, assigned his rights against the insurance company to V. The district judge indicates that he thinks that S was under no obligation to do this. *See Vogel v. Northern Assur. Co., D.C. E.D. Pa.* 1953, 114 F. Supp. 591. If that were so and this insurance money, or the claim to it, belonged to S free and clear, then his gift of the insurance proceeds to V, or to anybody else, would certainly be none of the insurance company's business. It would simply be a case where a man is allowed to do what he pleases with his own.

We think the district court was mistaken on this point because under Pennsylvania law the seller becomes the trustee of the property and rights incident thereto and holds them in trust for the vendee. The most recent case in Pennsylvania which involved this point directly is *Dubin Paper Co. v. Insurance Co. of North America, [*361 Pa. 68, 63 A.2d 85, 8 A.L.R.2d 1393 (1949)]. In the *Dubin* case the loss occurred prior to the date of settlement of the contract of sale. The vendee having performed his contract, the seller upon receiving checks from his insurance companies to cover the fire loss returned them to the insurance companies. Then the vendee brought an action in equity against the insurance companies and the seller to compel the insurance companies to pay the proceeds to the seller and to have the court declare that the seller hold the proceeds as trustee for the plaintiff. The problem was discussed at length by Chief Justice Maxey. The conclusion was that the action was well brought and that the plaintiff was entitled to the relief for which he prayed.

This decision clearly shows that the insurance money which S collects from the insurance company after he has been paid by the vendee is not his to keep or spend but in equity belongs to the vendee. As we read the *Dubin* and earlier Pennsylvania cases no other conclusion is possible. So, in this particular instance, when V had complied with the terms of the contract of sale, the proceeds due on the insurance which S had taken out was something to which V was equitably entitled. That means that in this case V (Vogel) may clearly maintain his action against the insurance company which was the insurer on S's contract.

Northern makes two arguments with considerable plausibility. One is that the insurance which S takes out covers only the security title which he has. If he gets his money from the vendee he suffers no loss and should not be allowed to recover anything against the insurance company. Northern also argues that it is entitled to subrogation to the insured's right to the extent that the insured has a claim over and above the amount of his loss. Both of these arguments are pretty good. But in this case the federal court is bound to apply state law as best it can. The state law has been settled, and firmly settled, against Northern's arguments by the series of decisions which we have already cited above.

Then we pass to the claim of V against his insurer. This insurance policy was taken out by V himself in the amount of $12,000, but contains a three-fourths value clause. There is no doubt that a vendee who has made a contract of sale to buy land can himself take out insurance. This is only common sense; if the vendee bears the risk of loss he certainly has a risk which he can insure against. What is there, then, to prevent V from recovering against the insurance company for the loss which it is agreed took place?

Mount Joy argues that it is excused from paying because there was in the policy a place for the noting of other insurance and the insured gave Mount Joy no information on this. Therefore, it says, this provision being one to guard against fraud in over insurance, it does not have to pay anything. As pointed out by the district judge, however, these policies were taken out on different interests. S took out a policy to protect his interest as seller; V took out a policy to protect his interest as an equitable owner. The settled interpretation of the "other insurance" clause is that the other insurance must be "on the same interest and subject, and against the same risk." 3 Richards on Insurance 1667 (5th ed., Freedman, 1952). The district court was correct in holding the other insurance clause inapplicable.

Furthermore, it is to be pointed out that what S assigned to V was not an insurance policy. He assigned to V his claim against the insurance company for a loss which had already taken place and which left him with a claim against the insurance company. And under the Pennsylvania cases which we have set out above that claim was for the face of the policy, not for the protection of S's security title.

This brings us out to an affirmance of a judgment for $15,000, $3,000 more than the loss. This, it is true, seems incongruous in view of the often stated generalization that fire insurance is indemnity insurance. Vance on Insurance § 14 (3d ed., 1951); 1 Richards on Insurance 3. The incongruity, if there is one, reaches clear back to 1853 in the settled rule in Pennsylvania that the seller can recover fully against the insurance company for a loss occurring between the time of the agreement and final settlement even though the buyer has taken title according to the terms of the contract. We have no doubt that the ingenuity of insurance counsel will draft a provision whereby total recovery can be limited to actual loss if that is an object to be desired. And if this Court has failed in its examination of Pennsylvania law on the subject, it will be compelled to take the course over.

The judgment of the district court will be affirmed.

NOTES

1. *Evaluating the rules.* The *Wolf* and *Vogel* cases involve executory contracts for the sale of realty. Which is better—the New York rule or the Wisconsin rule—from the standpoint of: (1) the parties to the contract of sale; (2) the insurer; and (3) the public? In considering this question, it should be observed that there are several principles, and possible corollaries, at work in the court decisions.

First, it is said that property insurance is a personal contract between the insured and insurer and is not for the benefit of third-parties. Another way to state this is that the insurance does not run with the property.

Second, the time of loss is customarily the point at which the existence of an insurable interest is tested. A possible corollary of this principle is that losses should be measured as of the date of physical harm, i.e., loss, and that the insurer's liability and any rights of the insured to recover are determined at that time. Thus, events subsequent to the time of loss are irrelevant.

Third, another principle involves the idea that the insurer agreed, in return for a premium, to indemnify against loss and that it is a windfall if the insurer does not have to pay for damage to property which is the subject of the insurance. Thus, the insurer should pay someone for the loss.

Finally, there is the principle of indemnity which means the insurer should only pay for actual loss sustained that is not otherwise compensated.

Which principles are sacrificed under the New York rule? The Wisconsin rule? Does the *Vogel* case completely accommodate the competing principles? Why should the seller in *Wolf* collect insurance proceeds if the full purchase price for the property has been paid? Is it relevant that the vendee in *Wolf* probably only wanted the land for a highway and would have torn the buildings down anyway? *See P. R. DeBellis Enterprises, Inc. v. Lumbermen's Mutual Casualty Co.,* 77 N.J. 428, 390 A.2d 1171 (1978) (criticizing *Wolf* for applying policy language too literally and holding that events subsequent to casualty may be significant in determining insured's interest).

2. *Is there a better approach?* Is there a better method of approaching or resolving the insurance problems under executory contracts for the sale of realty? Should insurance proceeds simply be allocated to the party who bears the risk of loss, regardless of whose interest the insurance was purchased to protect? Should each insurer pay its own insured's loss, with the assertion of subrogation rights to follow after these payments?

3. *Indemnity revisited.* When both vendor and vendee have insurance, as was the case in *Vogel,* the issue has some different dimensions. Does the result in *Vogel* square with the principle of indemnity? If not, how should this problem be resolved? Is the rationale for the constructive trust approach still present where both the vendor and vendee have insured their own interests? *See Paramount Fire Insurance Co. v. Aetna Casualty and Surety Co.,* 163 Tex. 250, 353 S.W.2d 841 (1961) (vendor suffers no loss, vendor's insurer has no obligation, and loss falls on vendee's insurer). Should the insurer for the vendor and the insurer for the vendee be required to prorate coverage in proportion to the value of the interests of the vendor and vendee at the date of the loss? *See id.* (Griffin, J., dissenting). If the vendor's insurer pays proceeds to vendor, does the vendor's insurer have a subrogation right against the vendee, the effect of which would fall on the vendee's insurer? *See State Farm General Insurance Co. v. Stewart,* 288 Ill. App. 3d 678, 681 N.E.2d 625 (1997) (no).

4. *Lease-purchase agreements.* Assume that, instead of a sales contract for realty, L enters a contract to lease real property to T, with the latter having an option to purchase. T takes possession and prior to any exercise of the

option to purchase, a fire destroys the improvements on the property. The lease is silent as to any obligation to repair or restore the premises. If T has taken out fire insurance, may T recover the full damage to the improvements or just the value of the use of the improvements for the unexpired term of the lease? Should the answer depend on whether T exercises her option to purchase after the fire? *See Kelly v. Iowa Valley Mutual Insurance Ass'n,* 332 N.W.2d 330 (Iowa 1983).

5. *Involuntary sales.* In *Wolf,* the vendor and vendee successfully negotiated a sale of the property; if that had not occurred, the implication in the court's opinion is that the State would have obtained the property by asserting its powers of eminent domain. If the property had been destroyed while a condemnation proceeding was pending, would the outcome in the case have been different?

A condemnation proceeding is an example of an involuntary or forced sale. There are other kinds of forced sales, such as those that occur under foreclosure proceedings for debts arising from private loans secured by the property. If the owner of property is delinquent in paying taxes, a forced sale can occur through foreclosure proceedings. In all of these situations, it is important to understand where the risk of loss rests because there usually is an executory period before title and possession are completely and finally transferred.

Because these types of transactions are usually governed by detailed statutes, there is no substitute for familiarizing oneself with the law of the particular jurisdiction in order to understand where the risk of loss lies at any point in the process. For example, would you advise a condemnee client to maintain insurance in force until the proceedings are completed if the condemnor has an interim right to abandon the proceedings and relinquish the property to the condemnee? In *Insurance Co. of N. Am. v. Alberstadt,* 383 Pa. 556, 119 A.2d 83 (1956), Alberstadt owned premises which she insured through Empire Mutual. She failed to pay her taxes, however, and she saw her property sold at a sheriff's sale to Patterson, who promptly insured the property with INA. After the sale but before the buyer paid the sheriff the amount of his bid (and before the period of redemption expired), a fire damaged the property. Because Alberstadt held legal title to the property at the time of the fire, the court held that she was entitled to recover the amount of the damage from Empire. The fact that she had an unexercised right of redemption was not enough, however, for her to be allowed to retain the proceeds, which were deemed to belong to the equitable owner of the property, Patterson. The buyer, however, was not entitled to collect under both policies in full, as the court reasoned that this would violate the principle of indemnity. Thus, Patterson's recovery was limited to the amount of the loss, which was ordered to be paid by both insurers in the proportion of the amounts of their respective policy limits. Note that *Vogel* was decided by the Third Circuit one year before *Alberstadt.* Did the federal court correctly guess the law of Pennsylvania? *See St. Paul Fire & Marine Insurance Co. v. Insurance Placement Facility,* 687 F. Supp. 172 (E.D. Pa. 1988).

Risk of Loss, the UCC, and Goods

With regard to the risk of loss under executory contracts conveying personal property, there is good news and bad news. The good news is that there is no equivalent doctrine of equitable conversion. The bad news is that the old common law rule (which was easy to state, but hard to apply) under the Uniform Sales Act that placed the risk of loss on the party having legal title to the goods has been displaced by a much more complicated, albeit a more just, system under the Uniform Commercial Code.

The pertinent provisions are found in sections 2-509 and 2-510. Absent some agreement to the contrary, the placement of the risk of loss first depends on whether there is a breach of the contract of sale. If neither party has breached, the fact situations are divided into three basic categories. First, when the parties have entered into a contract calling for goods to be shipped by carrier, the Code makes a distinction between "shipment" and "destination" contracts. The Code gives detailed definitions of shipping terms which determine which type of contract is involved, but, in short, a shipment contract requires only that the seller deliver the goods to the carrier in order to shift the risk of loss to the buyer. Conversely, a destination contract leaves the risk of loss on the seller until the carrier delivers the goods to the purchaser. Thus, the Code creates a consistent principle on risk of loss which applies in the absence of the parties' express agreement about allocation of risk. Both the second and third categories cover situations where delivery is to be made without a carrier, i.e., directly from the seller to the buyer. The second deals with the situation in which goods are held by a bailee to be delivered without being moved. Essentially, the risk of loss here is placed on the party who has control over the bailee. The third category is a catch-all provision for nonbreach cases and turns on whether the seller is a merchant. If so, the risk passes to the buyer upon actual receipt of the goods; otherwise, the risk passes to the buyer on tender of delivery.

If there is a breach of the sales contract (which need not be related to the risk of loss), three categories also are utilized, but essentially the risk of loss is placed on the breaching party absent a contrary agreement. There is, however, one big exception. To the extent the nonbreaching party has insurance that covers the casualty loss, the breaching party gets the benefit of the insurance. To this extent the nonbreaching party bears the risk of loss. Moreover, the casualty insurer is denied a right of subrogation based on the sales contract to keep the loss from being shifted to the breaching party.

The provisions allocating the risk of loss in nonbreach situations are designed to place the loss on the party most likely to have insured or prepared against the loss. This is accomplished, in the main, by putting the risk on the party having possession or control over the goods. The provisions with regard to breach situations where the risk of loss is placed in part by utilizing the nonbreaching party's insurance seems to depart from the basic approach of risk allocation under the nonbreach situations and has been severely criticized.

For several years, the National Conference of Commissioners on Uniform State Laws and the American Law Institute have been engaged in a joint project to revise Article 2 of the U.C.C. Earlier drafts of the new Article 2 made some changes in the risk of loss provisions summarized above in breach situations. The summer 2000 draft, however, proposed essentially the same framework as described above; whatever finally emerges from the revision process is unlikely to make major changes. Moreover, this project is not slated for completion until 2001, at the earliest, and it will be some time thereafter before the state legislatures adopt the revised version.

How does all of this compare with the cases dealing with allocation of risks in executory contracts for sale of realty?

For a more detailed discussion of the subject of risk of loss under the U.C.C., see William H. Lawrence & William H. Henning, Understanding Sales and Leases of Goods 169–85 (1995); James J. White & Robert S. Summers, Uniform Commercial Code 178–90 (5th ed. 1999).

[b] Mortgagors and Mortgagees

NATIONWIDE MUTUAL INSURANCE CO. v. HUNT
327 S.C. 89, 488 S.E.2d 339 (1997)

Toal, Justice:

The primary issue in this insurance contract dispute is Nationwide Mutual Insurance Company's ("Insurance Company") appeal of the directed verdict in favor of First Citizens Bank ("Mortgagee") on the issue of breach of contract. We affirm.

FACTUAL/PROCEDURAL BACKGROUND

In March 1992, Robbin T. Hunt ("Hunt") obtained a $7,000 loan from Mortgagee. This was a third mortgage on Hunt's property. In early February 1993, she obtained another loan from Mortgagee; this one was for $5,000. Later in the same month, Hunt was issued a policy of fire insurance on her house by Insurance Company. On April 12, 1993, Hunt's property was destroyed by fire.

Insurance Company commenced this action against Hunt and Mortgagee, seeking a declaratory judgment that it was not liable under the fire insurance policy. Hunt and Mortgagee separately counterclaimed for breach of contract and bad faith refusal to pay insurance claim. The case was tried. The trial court directed a verdict on Mortgagee's counterclaim for breach of contract and entered judgment in the amount of $10,300. The remaining issues went before the jury, which found that Insurance Company had proven Hunt had made fraudulent representations regarding material issues in her application for fire insurance and that Insurance Company had proven Hunt engaged in intentional acts that caused a loss by fire or civil arson. The jury further found that Mortgagee had not proven that Insurance Company had acted in bad faith in handling the fire insurance benefit claim.

Insurance Company now appeals the directed verdict in favor of Mortgagee. The primary issue before the Court is whether Mortgagee may recover under the insured's fire insurance policy, despite the insured's acts of fraud, intentional concealment, and misrepresentation. Mortgagee has cross-appealed, arguing that the trial court erred in not instructing the jury as to the relevance of the directed verdict in Mortgagee's favor. Moreover, it disputes the court's denial of its motion for J.N.O.V. or, in the alternative, a new trial.

LAW/ANALYSIS

A. COVERAGE FOR MORTGAGEE

Insurance Company argues that because the fire insurance policy was obtained through fraud, intentional concealment, and misrepresentation by Hunt, the policy was void ab initio, and there was no coverage for Mortgagee. We disagree. Insurance Company cites the following language from the policy:

> The entire policy will be void if, whether before or after a loss, you have:
>
> a. intentionally concealed or misrepresented any material fact or circumstance;
>
> b. engaged in fraudulent conduct; or
>
> c. made false statements;
>
> relating to this insurance.

It argues that because the entire policy would be void under this provision, Mortgagee's interest would likewise be extinguished.

The law is well settled on the question of whether a mortgagee may recover on an insurance policy where there has been misconduct by the insured. A mortgagee's ability to recover largely depends on the type of mortgagee clause used in the insurance contract. There are two major categories of mortgagee clauses: (1) loss-payable and (2) standard clauses. A loss-payable (or open mortgage) clause typically declares that the loss, if any, is payable to a mortgagee as its interest might appear. The standard (or union or New York mortgage) clause uses language similar to the loss-payable, but further stipulates that, as to the interest of the mortgagee, the insurance shall not be invalidated by certain specified acts of the insured, which continue as grounds of forfeiture against him. The following is an example of a standard clause:

> [T]his insurance, as to the interest of the mortgagee only, shall not be invalidated by any act or neglect of the mortgagor or the owner of the within described property, nor by any foreclosure or other proceedings or notice of sale relating to the property, nor by any change in the title or ownership [of] the property, nor by the occupation of the premises for purposes more hazardous than are permitted by this policy, provided, that in case the mortgagor or owner shall neglect to pay any premium due under this policy, the mortgagee shall, on demand, pay the same.

5A John A. Appleman A. Jean Appleman, Insurance Law & Practice § 3401 (1970 & Supp.1997).

Under loss-payable clauses, it has been held that an insured's misconduct bars recovery by the mortgagee. On the other hand, if the contract includes a standard clause, then the interests of the mortgagee in the proceeds of the policy will not be invalidated by the misconduct of the insured. *See* D.E. Evins, Annotation, *Fraud, False Swearing, or Other Misconduct of Insured as Affecting Right of Innocent Mortgagee or Loss Payee to Recover on Property Insurance,* 24 A.L.R.3d 435 (1969 & Supp.1996).

The difference between the two types of clauses has been explained in this way: The loss-payable clause merely identifies the person who may collect the proceeds. Insurance Law & Practice § 3401. Under such a clause, the mortgagee stands in the insured's shoes and is usually subject to the same defenses; however, with the standard form, the mortgagee may become liable to pay the premium to the insurance company, and in return, is freed from policy defenses which the company may have used against the insured. *Id.* Thus,

> the modern decisions are unanimous, and the earlier decisions virtually so, in holding that a mortgagee under a standard mortgage clause may (where not guilty himself of any breaches of policy conditions) recover from the insurer for a loss sustained by the mortgaged property, even though the risk be excluded from the policy coverage, where any act of the mortgagor has caused or contributed to the loss as resulting from an excluded risk; and even though as between the mortgagor-insured and the insurer there is no coverage because of some default by the mortgagor.

Ingersoll-Rand Fin. Corp. v. Employers Ins. of Wausau, 771 F.2d 910, 913 (5th Cir.1985), *cert. denied,* 475 U.S. 1046, 106 S.Ct. 1263, 89 L.Ed.2d 573 (1986); *see also Foremost Ins. Co. v. Allstate Ins. Co.,* 439 Mich. 378, 486 N.W.2d 600, 602–03 (1992) (Under the standard clause, "a lienholder is not subject to the exclusions available to the insurer against the insured because an independent or separate contract of insurance exists between the lienholder and the insurer."); *Equality Sav. & Loan Ass'n v. Missouri Property Ins. Placement Facility,* 537 S.W.2d 440, 441 (Mo.Ct.App.1976) (Standard mortgage clause "has been interpreted to mean that such insurance is not invalidated by any act or neglect on the part of the mortgagor before, at the time of, or after the policy is issued."); *National Commercial Bank & Trust Co. v. Jamestown Mut. Ins. Co.,* 70 Misc.2d 701, 334 N.Y.S.2d 1000, 1001 (N.Y.Sup.Ct.1972) ("A fire insurance contract endorsed with the standard mortgagee clause creates an independent contract for the insurance of the mortgagee's interest."); *Aetna Life & Casualty Co. v. Charles S. Martin Distrib. Co.,* 120 Ga.App. 133, 169 S.E.2d 695, 696 (1969) (Under a New York standard mortgagee clause, the fact that insured had wilfully and fraudulently burned her property in order to collect the insurance thereon, does not bar mortgagee's claim to the proceeds of the policy.).

South Carolina cases are very much in line with the approach of the majority of jurisdictions. In *Orenstein v. New Jersey Ins. Co.,* 131 S.C. 500, 512, 127 S.E. 570, 574 (1925), we concluded that "In standard or union form of loss payable clause the mortgagee is entitled to full protection, and no act or neglect of the insured can prejudice his rights." In *Prudential Ins. Co. v. Franklin Fire Ins. Co.,* 180 S.C. 250, 185 S.E. 537 (1936), which involved the construction of a New York standard form of mortgagee clause attached to a policy of fire insurance, the Court declared that "The mortgage clause constitutes an independent agreement between the insurance company and the mortgagee." *Prudential,* 180 S.C. at 253, 185 S.E. at 538. More recently, in *Fort Hill Federal Savings & Loan Association v. South Carolina Farm Bureau Insurance Company,* 281 S.C. 532, 316 S.E.2d 684 (Ct.App.1984), the Court of Appeals considered a policy containing a standard mortgagee clause. The insured gave the insurance company a bad check for the premium, and by separate action, it was determined that the insurance company was absolved of liability to the insured. As to the insurance company's liability to the mortgagee, the insurance company argued that the mortgagee named in the standard mortgagee clause was simply a third-party beneficiary of the contract between the insured and the insurance company. It further contended that the contract was "void *ab initio*" as to mortgagee because of insured's failure to pay the premium.

The Court of Appeals rejected this argument, writing, "Even though the policy might be void *ab initio* as to the [insured] because of nonpayment of the premium, it remained viable as to [mortgagee] until cancelled in accordance with the mortgagee cancellation clause." *Id.* at 537, 316 S.E.2d at 687. The opinion reasoned that the "mortgagee in this state occupies a unique position; his status is separate from the mortgagor and this status is so independent that no act or neglect by the mortgagor can derogate this status provided that if the mortgagor fails to pay the premium, the mortgagee will on demand." *Id.* at 537, 316 S.E.2d at 687–88. The Court of Appeals explained that

> in South Carolina we do not fully accept the majority rule that a standard mortgagee clause creates a distinct and independent insurance contract. . . . A mortgagee's rights under a fire insurance policy are dependent upon the existence of a secured debt owed the mortgagee by the mortgagor-insured; to this extent the mortgagee cannot be independent of the insured.

Id. at 537, 316 S.E.2d at 687. However, the opinion continued by explaining the difference between South Carolina's approach and that of the majority:

> [T]here is, in reality, only a semantic difference in the South Carolina rule and the majority rule that the mortgagee clause creates a distinct and independent contract. Our court wisely reserves certain conditions and subrogation rights, but absent these considerations, our rule vests the mortgagee with a status which includes all of the rights incident to an independent and separate contract and the insured can do nothing either by act or neglect which will divest him of these rights other than payment in full of the mortgage indebtedness.

Id. at 538–39, 316 S.E.2d at 688. We agree with the Court of Appeals that there is no substantive difference between the majority rule and the rule in South Carolina.

The contract between the insured Hunt and Insurance Company contains a standard mortgagee clause:

> If a mortgagee is named in this policy, any loss payable under Coverage A or B will be paid to the mortgagee and you, as interests appear. If more than one mortgagee is named, the order of payment will be the same as the order of precedence of the mortgages.
>
> If we deny your claim, that denial will not apply to a valid claim of the mortgagee, if the mortgagee:
>
> > a. notifies us of any change in ownership, occupancy or substantial change in risk of which the mortgagee is aware;
> >
> > b. pays any premium due under this policy on demand if you have neglected to pay the premium; and
> >
> > c. submits a signed, sworn statement of loss within 60 days after receiving notice from us of your failure to do so. Policy conditions relating to Appraisal, Suit Against Us and Loss Payment apply to the mortgagee.
>
> If we decide to cancel or not to renew this policy, the mortgagee will be notified at least 10 days before the date cancellation or nonrenewal takes effect.

Insurance Company argues that this provision is not a standard clause because it does not contain precisely the same wording of such clauses, specifically, ". . . the interest of the mortgagee only, shall not be invalidated by any act or neglect of the mortgagor or the owner. . . ." We disagree. The present clause, with its wording "If we deny your claim, that denial will not apply to a valid claim of the mortgagee. . . .," is substantially the same as the wording of typical standard clauses. It would elevate form over substance to adopt Insurance Company's argument. Our conclusion is buttressed by the fact that Insurance Company's policy was specially written in simple language. The policy begins with the following introductory statement:

> Now—Fire insurance protection you can count on in a policy you can understand.
>
> You now have a different kind of insurance policy. One that's readable, understandable, straightforward.

One of the distinguishing features of standard clauses is that they require the mortgagee to pay premiums on the policy if the insured fails to do so. Such clearly is the case here: "denial [of insured's claim] will not apply to a valid claim of the mortgagee, if the mortgagee. . .pays any premium due under this policy on demand if [insured] ha[s] neglected to pay the premium. . . ." Although its wording is not precisely the same as typical standard clauses, the clause in dispute here is clearly a standard clause. Thus, Mortgagee has an independent status which authorizes recovery by it, even though recovery is precluded as to Hunt.

Insurance Company further argues that paragraph 3 of the contract declares that the entire policy is void if there is intentional concealment, fraudulent conduct, or false statements by the insured, and as such, this provision trumps the mortgage clause. This provision is clearly directed toward Hunt, the insured. To apply it to Mortgagee as well would render the mortgagee clause of the contract a nullity. This argument must also be rejected because it would in effect overrule the majority rule discussed above, which states that mortgagee may recover under standard mortgagee clauses despite the insured's misconduct.

Insurance Company raises other arguments including that Mortgagee was aware of a substantial change in risk. This argument was not raised below and is thus barred. Even if it were preserved, factual support for this argument has not been offered. Insurance company has not presented any evidence that Mortgagee was aware of a "substantial change in risk" after the policy was issued. Insurance Company further argues that Hunt was agent of Mortgagee; therefore, the voiding of her policy would be binding on the principal Mortgagee. This argument is without merit. As discussed above, the standard mortgagee clause creates an independent contract for the insurance of the mortgagee's interest; accordingly, denial of Hunt's claim has no effect on that of Mortgagee.

. . . .

CONCLUSION

Based on the foregoing, we AFFIRM both on the appeal of Insurance Company and Mortgagee's cross-appeal.

FINNEY, C.J., and MOORE, WALLER and BURNETT, JJ., concur.

NOTES

1. *Nature of secured creditor's interest.* The *Hunt* case provides an introduction to insurable interests in secured transactions and the development of what is known as the "New York standard mortgage clause," sometimes referred to as the "Union mortgage clause." If an owner of property has not encumbered the property in any way, she may be the only person that has an insurable interest. On the other hand, if the property is mortgaged or otherwise secures a debt, it should be clear that the secured creditor also has an interest that ought to be insurable. What is the nature of the risk faced by the creditor? If the owner-debtor buys property insurance against certain perils and the policy merely provides that upon loss the insurer will pay the secured creditor "as its interest may appear," is the creditor adequately protected? For example, what if the insured-mortgagor intentionally sets the property on fire to collect the insurance? Should the result be any different where the insured-mortgagor defaults on the premium payments? See generally John W. Steinmetz, Stephen E. Goldman & Daniel F. Sullivan, *The Standard Mortgage Clause in Property Insurance Policies*, 33 Tort & Ins. L. J. 81 (1997).

2. *Legal effect of standard mortgage clause.* The court in *Hunt* discussed whether the standard mortgage clause created a "separate" or "independent" contract of insurance for the mortgagee. What does it mean to say that the mortgagee's rights are "dependent" upon the existence of a secured debt?

What does it mean to say that the mortgagee's rights are "independent" from those of the mortgagor? For example, if the insurer cancels the mortgagor's coverage but fails to notify the mortgagee about this cancellation, does this revive the mortgagor's canceled coverage? The vast majority of cases say "no." *See Economy Fire & Casualty Co. v. Hughes,* 271 Ill. App. 3d 1009, 649 N.E. 2d 561 (1995).

3. *Rebuild or repay?* Suppose homeowner purchases a home in 1998, paying 20 percent down and financing the remainder through a loan with Friendly Bank. Homeowner purchases an owner-mortgagee policy with a standard mortgage clause from Reliable Insurer to cover both the interests of the homeowner and those of the mortgagee. When the home is totally destroyed by fire in 2000, homeowner wishes to use the proceeds of the insurance to rebuild and to keep the terms of the original loan and mortgage in place. Friendly Bank wishes to have the proceeds used to repay the loan, with any excess being paid to homeowner. Who prevails? *See Savarese v. Ohio Farmers' Insurance Co.,* 182 N.E. 665 (N.Y. App. Div. 1932) (mortgagee has absolute right to proceeds); *Cottman Co. v. Continental Trust Co.,* 182 A. 551 (Md. 1936) (mortgagor has right to use proceeds of insurance to rebuild or replace damaged property).

4. *Ramifications of foreclosure.* When a mortgagor falls behind in repaying the debt owned the mortgagee, the mortgagee ordinarily has a right to foreclose on the insured property to satisfy the mortgage debt. What if after foreclosure the property is destroyed? What if the property is destroyed before the foreclosure is completed? Consider the next case.

NATIONWIDE MUTUAL FIRE INSURANCE CO. v. WILBORN
291 Ala. 193, 279 So. 2d 460 (1973)

HEFLIN, CHIEF JUSTICE.

This is an appeal from a final decree rendered by the Circuit Court of Calhoun County, Alabama, in Equity, denying appellant-respondent's (Nationwide) motion for a rehearing and fixing the amount of damages at $26,105. Appellee-complainant, Ethel Wilborn (Wilborn), filed a bill seeking a declaration of her rights of recovery for a fire loss to a residence on which fire insurance policies had been issued by Nationwide, and appellee-respondent, State Farm Fire and Casualty Insurance Company (State Farm). In addition to the two insurance companies mentioned above, Wilborn joined Robert and Katie Stewart (Stewarts) and the First National Bank of Anniston, Alabama (First National), as parties respondent. Of the four original respondents, only the two insurance companies have appeared in this appeal. At the time the State Farm policy was issued the Stewarts held an equitable interest in the insured property; however, it is not contested that they have no interest in this litigation. First National, although originally joined as a party respondent because it appeared as mortgagee in the Nationwide policy, has consented to the declaratory relief sought by Wilborn.

The chain of events which gave rise to this controversy began on March 27, 1970, when Wilborn and the Stewarts entered into a contract whereby the Stewarts agreed to buy, and Wilborn agreed to sell, certain property known as 21 Mont Camille Drive in Anniston for a purchase price of $27,500. The Stewarts were obligated, as a part of the agreement, "to keep the property insured. . .in an amount not less than $25,500, loss payable to the party of the first part [Wilborn] as his interest may appear." Pursuant to this provision the Stewarts took out a policy of fire insurance with State Farm in the amount of $27,500, which went into effect on April 20, 1970. The State Farm policy contained what is known as the New York Standard Mortgage Loss Payable clause, usually referred to as the New York Standard Mortgage clause naming Wilborn as mortgagee, which clause reads as follows:

> "12. Mortgage Clause-Coverage A only: (This entire clause is void unless name of mortgagee (or trustee) is inserted in the Declarations) Loss, if any, under this policy, shall be payable to the mortgagee (or trustee), named on the first page of this policy, as interest may appear, under all present or future mortgages upon the property herein described in which the aforesaid may have an interest as mortgagee (or trustee), in order of precedence of said mortgages, and this insurance as to the interest of the mortgagee (or trustee) only therein, shall not be invalidated by any act or neglect of the mortgagor or owner of the within described property, nor by any foreclosure or other proceedings or notice of sale relating to the property, nor by any change in the title or ownership of the property, nor by the occupation of the premises for the purposes more hazardous than are permitted by this policy; provided, that in case the mortgagor or owner shall neglect to pay any premium due under this policy, the mortgagee (or trustee) shall, on demand, pay the same."

Wilborn, prior to April 20, 1970, had procured on the same premises through Nationwide, a fire policy which also contained the New York Standard Mortgage clause naming First National, the institution through which Wilborn had originally financed the construction of the house in question, as mortgagee.

The sale of the insured property was cancelled on May 26, 1970, for reasons not here pertinent, and the Stewarts were relieved of any further liability to the vendor, Wilborn. On July 2, 1970, the fire loss made the basis of this suit occurred. Wilborn's bill sought recovery for this loss. The trial court rendered its amended final decree on September 3, 1971, declaring that "no coverage for the loss made the subject of this suit existed under the policy of insurance issued by State Farm" and that "Wilborn have and recover of Nationwide . . ., the sum of $28,795." The court's decree of November 4, 1971, denying Nationwide's motion for a rehearing, affirmed its former decree of September 3, 1971, except as to the amount of damages, which was reduced to $26,105. It is from this decree that Nationwide has appealed.

The principal point of dissension in the instant case is presented by Nationwide's assignment of error number 5 under which it argues that the trial court erred in holding that no coverage existed under the State Farm policy. Nationwide maintains that the New York Standard Mortgage clause in the State Farm policy constitutes a separate contract between State Farm and Wilborn, which is enforceable in favor of Wilborn, who occupied, in effect, the position of mortgagee, notwithstanding the fact that her interest in the insured property had increased or ripened into full ownership prior to the fire loss.

The question thus presented is whether the mortgagee may recover insurance proceeds under a policy containing a New York Standard Mortgage clause after the mortgage debt has been fully satisfied by foreclosure or otherwise.

From the language of the New York Standard Mortgage clause it is clear that the parties contemplated the possibility of foreclosure and that protection should be afforded the mortgagee or its assigns. The concept was that the insurance should follow the property. In Alabama there have developed two distinct (and distinguishable) lines of cases. One line allows the insurance to follow the property past foreclosure and may be classified as the "loss after foreclosure" concept. The other line of cases makes a difference if the debt owing to the mortgagee has been fully satisfied by foreclosure or otherwise following loss. This can be classified as the "foreclosure after loss" principle.

The first line of cases applies where the foreclosure occurs prior to the loss, and allows the mortgagee to recover the proceeds under the policy. *Continental Insurance Company of New York v. Rotholz*, 222 Ala. 574, 133 So. 587 (1931). In that case, Rotholz brought suit against Continental. The policy contained the New York Standard clause in which Rotholz was designated as mortgagee.

Within the policy coverage time and prior to the loss by fire the mortgagee, Rotholz, foreclosed and purchased the property at the foreclosure sale. The defendant, insurer, contended that there had been a change of ownership or occupancy by virtue of the mortgagee's foreclosure and purchase of the property at the sale; that the policy provided that the policy should be void in the event that the mortgagee fail to notify the insurer of such a change of ownership or occupancy; that no such notice was given, and, hence, the policy was void. This court, in answering these contentions and allowing recovery by the mortgagee, commented on the nature of the New York Standard Mortgage clause as follows:

> ". . . the New York Standard clause operates to create a *separate and independent* insurance of the mortgagee's interest in the property, and his acquisition of title to the insured property is generally regarded as an increase of interest rather than a change of ownership." (Emphasis added)

The fact that the mortgage debt had been satisfied prior to suit did not preclude recovery by the mortgagee under the policy where the loss occurred subsequent to satisfaction of the mortgage debt. The *Rotholz* holding was reaffirmed in *Hartford Fire Insurance Co. v. Aaron*, 226 Ala. 430, 147 So. 628 (1933), by way of dicta.

In *Rotholz*, the mortgagee had foreclosed prior to the fire loss and immediately before the loss in question occupied the position of owner, not mortgagee. The former mortgagee, the owner at the time of loss, had an insurable interest in protecting his property from loss by fire. The elevation of the mortgagee to the position of owner by foreclosure prior to the fire loss did not affect the operation of the New York Standard Mortgage clause which provided that:

> ". . . this insurance [the separate and individual insurance provision of the New York Standard clause], as to the interest of the mortgagee (or trustee) only therein, shall not be invalidated by. . .any foreclosure . . . ."

This provision has the effect of transferring the payment of the proceeds in the event of a fire loss to the owner where the mortgagee has foreclosed prior to the loss. Other jurisdictions which have considered the issue have interpreted this clause in the same manner as this court did in *Rotholz*. Where there is a New York Standard Mortgage clause the rationale of these cases protects the mortgagee after foreclosure or other change of ownership or title. In other words, the insurance follows the property even if foreclosure has occurred before loss.

Where, on the other hand, the loss precedes the foreclosure, the rule is different since the mortgagee has an election as to how he may satisfy the mortgage indebtedness by two different means. He may look to the insurance company for payment as mortgagee under the New York Standard Mortgage clause and may recover, up to the limits of the policy, the full amount of the mortgage debt at the time of the loss. In this event he would have no additional recourse against the mortgagor for the reason that his debt has been fully satisfied.

The second alternative available to the mortgagee is satisfaction of the mortgage debt by foreclosure. If the mortgagee elects to pursue this latter option, and the foreclosure sale does not bring the full amount of the mortgage debt at the time of the loss, he may recover the balance due under the insurance policy as owner. If the foreclosure does fully satisfy the mortgage debt, he, of course, has no additional recourse against the insurance company, as his debt has been fully satisfied. *Aetna Ins. Co. v. Baldwin Co. Building & Loan Association,* 231 Ala. 102, 163 So. 604 (1935).

The plaintiff in *Baldwin County* brought suit against Aetna on a policy containing a New York Standard Mortgage clause, in which it was named as mortgagee. The plaintiff-mortgagee had foreclosed and become the purchaser of the property *after* the fire loss made the basis of the suit. The New York Standard Mortgage clause contained in the policy was identical, in all material aspects, to the clause in *Rotholz*. The issue presented was stated as follows: ". . . whether plaintiff was shown to have a right to recover the amount of the loss thus insured, continuing up to the time of the beginning of the suit, or whether his right terminated by the foreclosure sale in which the plaintiff was the purchaser at the full amount of the debt."

This court in *Baldwin County* distinguished between satisfaction of the mortgage debt before the loss, and satisfaction of the mortgage debt *after* the loss, stating that in the former case, the mortgagee had been allowed recovery, while in the latter, the mortgagee has been denied recovery under the policy in the event of *full* satisfaction at foreclosure. The rule of law enunciated in *Baldwin County* may be stated as follows: Anyone designated as mortgagee in the New York Standard Mortgage clause forfeits his right to recover, under the policy, the amount of loss insured against, by foreclosure and purchase at the foreclosure sale or other *full* satisfaction of the mortgage debt, where such satisfaction occurs subsequent to the loss in question.

The rationale stated in *Baldwin County* is that at the time of, and immediately after the fire loss, plaintiff-mortgagee is the creditor of the owner, the plaintiff-mortgagee having had security for that debt in the form of a mortgage on the property and a claim for the loss on the insurance policy. *But in no event is the plaintiff-mortgagee due to collect more than the debt secured.* If the owner-debtor had paid plaintiff-mortgagee voluntarily, all of the plaintiff's rights and remedies would have immediately terminated, and he could not have proceeded further to enforce any feature of his security. When a mortgagee forecloses and at the sale he collects the *full* amount of his debt, he is no longer a creditor, as his debt is paid. The rationale and holding of *Baldwin County* appears to be in the mainstream of judicial thought throughout the country.

Thus the status of the Alabama law relative to the effect of foreclosure on the mortgagee's right of recovery, under the policy, for damages as a result of injury to the mortgaged property, was clearly divisible into the two lines of cases discussed above. In the "foreclosure prior to loss" situation (*Rotholz*) the foreclosure (or other change or increase of ownership or change of title as contemplated by the loss payee clause) occurs in the context of the insured property existing in its undamaged condition and the satisfaction of debt takes into account the value of such property in its undamaged condition prior to loss and the need for the insurance to follow the property. In the "foreclosure after loss" situation (*Baldwin County*) the foreclosure occurs in the context of the insured property having been damaged and the satisfaction of the debt takes into account the damaged condition of the property at the time of such foreclosure. In the former situation (foreclosure prior to loss), the value of the undamaged property at the time of foreclosure is an incident to the satisfaction of the debt; while in the latter (foreclosure after loss), to allow recovery of insurance proceeds by the mortgagee after full satisfaction of the debt would amount to mortgagee's unjust enrichment.

It appears that these two lines of cases have established a general rule and an exception to the general rule where a policy contains a New York Standard Mortgage clause. The general rule is that this loss payee clause affords protection to the mortgagee as his interest may appear before or after foreclosure or other methods of change of ownership or title or other mediums of increased ownership of the mortgage property and the insurance follows the property; the exception to this general rule being that if the mortgage indebtedness is fully satisfied *after* loss by foreclosure or otherwise, then the insurance company is no longer liable to the mortgagee.

This court, therefore, holds that the mortgagee was covered by the State Farm policy at the time of the loss made the basis of this suit, as owner. This holding is further supported by the plain language of the policy itself which provides that "this insurance as to the interest of the mortgagee (or trustee). . .shall not be invalidated. . .by any foreclosure or other proceedings or notice of sale relating to the property, nor by any change in the title or ownership of the property. . . ."

. . . .

Having determined that at the time of the fire loss to Wilborn's property there were in force in her favor two policies of insurance on the burned dwelling, the question becomes whether Nationwide is entitled to a 12/23 apportionment of the amount fixed as damages. [Both policies contained substantially similar clauses requiring any loss be prorated on the basis of the policy limits if there is other insurance.]

If the policies of two insurance companies are in force at the date of the loss and the status of the two insurers is that of insurers of the same property of the same insured against the same hazard, they are each proportionately and severally liable for the loss at the ratio which the amount of their respective policies bears to the whole insurance covering the property against the perils involved. *Louisville Fire & Marine Insurance Co. v. St. Paul Fire & Marine Insurance Co.*, 252 Ala. 532, 41 So. 2d 585 (1949).

State Farm contends that the two policies did not insure the "same insured" as required under *Louisville Fire & Marine*. It reasons that the loss, under Nationwide's policy, up to $18,889.44, was payable to First National under the loss-payable clause; whereas, State Farm's liability, if any, is solely to Wilborn as mortgagee. This argument is at odds with the evidence in this case, which made clear the fact that there was nothing due the bank under its mortgage at the time of the trial of the case, hence, the bank was not entitled to any portion of the proceeds of either of the two policies.

This court, therefore, holds that the Wilborn property was covered by two insurance policies against the hazard of fire, and that Nationwide and State Farm must share the liability on a pro rata basis. Nationwide is liable for 30,000/57,500(12/23) of the loss; and State Farm is liable for 27,500/57,500(11/23) of the loss. The plaintiff is further entitled to interest.

This cause is reversed and remanded with instructions for the trial court to enter a final decree for the plaintiff in accordance with this opinion.

Reversed and remanded with instructions.

MERRILL, HARWOOD and FAULKNER, JJ., concur.

COLEMAN, J., concurs in the result.

NOTES

1. *Was State Farm on the risk?* Do you agree with the court that State Farm had coverage in effect at the time of the fire in *Wilborn*? Is canceling a sales contract the same thing as a foreclosure?

2. *Just what is being insured?* Assume that Barnes purchases a building from Sierra for $200,000, paying $20,000 from his own money and the balance of $180,000 from a loan obtained from Acme Finance Co. To receive the loan, Acme requires that Barnes mortgage the property and carry fire and extended coverage insurance with a New York standard mortgage clause, with Acme named as the payee. Subsequently, an accidental fire completely destroys the building. At the time of the fire, Barnes owes Acme a balance of $80,000 on

the loan, and the latter demands and receives this amount from the insurer. Is the insurer subrogated to Acme's rights on the debt owed by Barnes? If not, what happens to the debt?

Suppose that for a year after the fire, Barnes continues to make payments to Acme on the debt, thereby reducing the amount of the debt to $70,000. At that time, Acme learns of the fire and seeks to recover under the policy. How much should it recover? *See Jones v. Wesbanco Bank Parkersburg,* 194 W.Va. 381, 460 S.E.2d 627 (1995).

3. *Effect of foreclosure sale on amount of insurance proceeds.* It is worth noting, given that litigation over the issue still arises under the New York standard mortgage clause, that a mortgagee may extinguish its insurable interest by bidding in the full amount of the debt at a foreclosure sale after the loss. For example, assume under the hypothetical in note 2 above that Barnes defaults on the loan after the fire. As explained in *Wilborn,* Acme may choose to claim against the insurer for the debt or foreclose on the property. If Acme chooses to foreclose, and a third party buys the property at the foreclosure sale for less than the debt, Acme may claim the balance of the debt from the insurer. However, if Acme bids on the property and ultimately has the high bid, the debt is still reduced by the amount of the bid just as if a third party had bid the amount. Consequently, even if the property is not really worth what the mortgagee were to bid, the mortgagee will not be allowed by most courts to collect the difference between what the property is worth and the debt from the insurer. Under the majority rule, absent some agreement with the insurer, the mortgagee can only seek the insurance proceeds for the difference, if any, between the winning bid and the debt. See *American Fire and Indemnity Co. v. Weeks,* 693 So. 2d 1386 (Ala. 1997); National Farmers Union Property & Casualty Co., 669 So. 2d 767 (Miss. 1996); *Benton Banking Co. v. Tennessee Farmers Mutual Insurance Co.,* 906 S.W.2d 436 (Tenn. 1995); *Whitestone Savings & Loan Ass'n v. Allstate Insurance Co.,* 28 N.Y.2d 332, 321 N.Y.S.2d 862, 270 N.E.2d 694 (1971); but *see Wilson v. Glancy,* 913 P.2d 286 (Okla. 1995); *Georgia Farm Bureau Mutual Insurance Co. v. Brewer,* 413 S.E.2d 770 (Ga. App. 1991). Why would a mortgagee knowingly ever bid more than the property is worth? If a mortgagee is unaware of prior damage to property when it makes its bid at the foreclosure sale, should the mortgagee be entitled to reformation of the foreclosure contract in order to reduce the price it paid for the property? To rescission of the foreclosure sale? *See Chrysler First Financial Services Corp. v. Bolling,* 608 So. 2d 734 (Ala. 1992); *Fireman's Fund Mortgage Corp. v. Allstate Insurance Co.,* 838 P.2d 790 (Alaska 1992).

If the mortgagee's interest is extinguished, can the mortgagor then recover from the insurer the full policy limits? Or should the mortgagor's recovery be limited to the amount of the mortgagor's interest in the property at the time of the loss? *See Lee v. Royal Indemnity Co.,* 108 F.3d 651 (6th Cir. 1997).

4. *Assignments.* It is common for real estate lenders to sell loans to third parties. Such transactions are assignments; note that property insurance policies are personal contracts and, as such, do not run with the land. Moreover, an insured cannot assign a property insurance policy to a third party, unless the insurer consents to the assignment. If a mortgagee assigns

its interests to a third party in exchange for a consideration and the property is then destroyed, can the mortgagee still collect proceeds? What if the property is destroyed, and then the assignment occurs? Does it matter in the latter case whether the assignment is accompanied by a payment from assignee to assignor-mortgagee? *See CLS Mortgage, Inc. v. Bruno,* 86 Wash. App. 390, 937 P.2d 1106 (1997); *Amboy National Bank v. Somers,* 930 F. Supp. 1053 (D.N.J. 1996).

[c] Lessors and Lessees

CITIZENS INSURANCE CO. v. FOXBILT, INC.
226 F.2d 641 (8th Cir. 1955), 53 A.L.R.2d 1376 (1957)

SANBORN, CIRCUIT JUDGE.

This is an appeal from a judgment in favor of Foxbilt, Inc., an Iowa corporation (appellee), in an action brought by it in the District Court of Polk County, Iowa, to recover for a fire loss to certain property covered by an Iowa Standard Fire Insurance Policy issued by the Citizens Insurance Company of New Jersey (appellant) on July 21, 1951, for the term of three years. The Insurance Company removed the case to the United States District Court for the Southern District of Iowa on the ground of diversity of citizenship and amount in controversy. 128 F. Supp. 594. The case was submitted upon a stipulation of facts

The policy, so far as pertinent, provided that the Company

> "does insure Foxbilt, Inc. and legal representatives, to the extent of the actual cash value of the property at the time of loss, but not exceeding the amount which it would cost to repair or replace the property with material of like kind and quality within a reasonable time after such loss,. . .against all Direct Loss By Fire, Lightning And By Removal From Premises Endangered By The Perils Insured Against In This Policy, Except As Hereinafter Provided, to the property described hereinafter . . . ."

The coverage of the original policy, by an endorsement dated January 19, 1953, was, for an additional premium, extended to include, among other items of property located at 5041/2 Grand Avenue, Des Moines, Iowa:

> Item C. And Improvements and Betterments to buildings, except to buildings owned by the insured or while located on the premises of any manufacturing plant owned or controlled by the insured. This Company agrees to accept and consider the insured in the event of loss in the position of sole and unconditional owner of such Improvements and Betterments, any contract or lease the insured may have made to the contrary notwithstanding.

Liability was limited to $75,000.

The insured occupied, for office purposes, the building at 5041/2 Grand Avenue under a lease, by the terms of which it agreed, at its own expense, to do such remodeling, decorating and redecorating as might be needed. The lease ran from April 1, 1952, to November 30, 1955. It contained, among others, the following provisions:

"15. That if during the time of this lease the said premises are destroyed or partially destroyed by fire or other casualty so as to render the same wholly unfit for occupancy and if they shall be so badly damaged that they cannot be repaired within ninety (90) days from the happening of such damage in compliance with the laws of the State of Iowa and the City ordinances of the City of Des Moines, then this lease shall cease and become null and void from the date of such damage or destruction; and if said premises shall be so damaged but shall be repairable within ninety (90) days from the happening of such damage, then the rent shall not run or accrue while repairs are being made, and the Lessor shall repair the same with all reasonable speed and the rent shall commence immediately after the said repairs shall be completed. If said premises shall be so slightly injured by fire or other casualty as not to render the same unfit for occupancy, then the Lessor agrees that the same shall be repaired with reasonable promptness and in that case the rent accrued or accruing shall not cease or terminate."

On September 6, 1953, while the insurance was in force, property of the insured in the leased building, together with improvements and betterments, was partially destroyed by a fire. As a result of the fire, the insured property was damaged to the extent of $57,720.16.

The Insurance Company paid the insured, on account of its liability under the policy, $40,000, and offered to pay an additional $2,695.87, which the Company contended was the entire balance due the insured for the fire loss sustained. The $40,000 payment related to loss of or damage to property other than the insured improvements and betterments.

Subsequent to the fire, the improvements and betterments which were destroyed, damaged or injured by the fire and for which the Insurance Company has made no payment to the insured, were completely restored by the lessor of the building, at her expense, under the terms of the lease between the insured and the lessor.

The fire had rendered the leased premises unfit for occupancy. The insured moved its offices temporarily to other leased premises. The damaged building at 504 1/2 Grand Avenue was restored by the lessor so that it could be reoccupied on December 18, 1953. The insured then reoccupied the building. The insured paid no rent to the lessor from September 6 to December 17, 1953.

The parties agreed that if the insured was entitled to recover for the loss of improvements and betterments, the judgment should be for $14,906.22 with interest from January 5, 1954, but that if the insured was not entitled to recover for such loss the judgment should be for $2,695.87 with such interest and costs as the court might deem proper.

The insured contended that, by the terms of the contract of insurance and under the applicable law of Iowa, the Insurance Company was liable for the damage caused by the fire to the improvements and betterments, regardless of the fact that they had been subsequently restored at the expense of the lessor of the building. The Insurance Company claimed that, since the insured had suffered no pecuniary loss on account of the damage to the improvements and betterments, the insured was not entitled to recover for such damage.

The District Court concluded that, under the stipulated facts and the applicable Iowa law, the Insurance Company was, by the terms of its policy, liable to the insured for the damage caused by the fire to the improvements and betterments, despite the fact that the lessor had restored them without expense to the insured.

This Court is not an appellate court of the State of Iowa and establishes no rules of law for that State. The question for review in a case such as this is not whether the trial court has reached a correct conclusion, but whether it has reached a permissible one.

If the Insurance Company had, in the instant case, desired a definitive ruling upon the question of its liability under Iowa law, it should not have removed this action, but should have submitted its defense to the District Court of Polk County, Iowa, and should then have appealed to the Supreme Court of Iowa in the event of an adverse decision. Having invoked the jurisdiction of the federal District Court, the Insurance Company can prevail, upon appeal, only if it can demonstrate that the determination of that court was induced by a clear misconception of the local law or a clear misapplication of it to the evidentiary facts.

It is conceded that the Supreme Court of Iowa has not as yet decided the question which the District Court was called upon to decide. That it may be problematical whether the Iowa Supreme Court would reach the same conclusion in a similar case is of no help to the Insurance Company on this appeal. If the question decided was a doubtful question of Iowa law as to which there can be a justifiable difference of opinion, the judgment must be affirmed.

Under the law of Iowa, a fire insurance policy is a contract of indemnity by which the insurer agrees to indemnify the insured against loss or damage to the insured property by fire, not exceeding the amount of the insurance. Liability under the policy attaches on the happening of the loss.

The measure of damages under Iowa law, in the event of loss, is ordinarily the difference between the fair market value of the insured property immediately before the fire and its fair market value immediately thereafter, not exceeding the face amount of the policy nor the cost of repair and replacement.

Since the liability of the insurer is for indemnity against loss to property and attaches on the happening of the loss and since the amount of the liability is determinable as of that time, it reasonably can be argued that the subsequent repair or restoration of the insured property by a third party without cost to the insured cannot relieve the insurer of its accrued liability. That is the law in some of the states.

In the case of *Alexandra Restaurant, Inc. v. New Hampshire Insurance Co. of Manchester,* 272 App. Div. 346, 71 N.Y.S.2d 515, which is closely analogous to the instant case, a lessor had restored, under a lease, after a fire, improvements which the lessee had insured against loss by fire. The Supreme Court of New York, Appellate Division, held that, under the law of that State, the fact that the lessor had restored the improvements did not affect the insurer's liability under its policy. In support of its decision, the court cited: *Foley v. Manufacturers' & Builders Fire Ins. Co.,* 152 N.Y 131, 46 N.E. 318, 43 L.R.A. 664; *Savarese v. Ohio Farmers' Ins. Co.,* 260 N.Y. 45, 182 N.E. 665, 91 A.L.R. 1341; *Tiemann v. Citizens' Insurance Co.,* 76 App. Div. 5, 78 N.Y.S. 620; *Rosenbloom v. Maryland Insurance Co.,* 258 App. Div. 14, 15 N.Y.S.2d 304. The rulings in those cases are discussed in the opinion. The *Alexandra Restaurant* case was affirmed by the Court of Appeals of New York, 297 N.Y. 858, 79 N.E.2d 268. It is apparent that, under the law of New York, the rights of an insurer and the insured under a fire insurance policy are established as of the time of the fire and loss, and that the fact that the insured has ultimately recouped his loss from another source does not relieve the insurer of its liability.

There are also cases in other states which tend to support the views of the District Court in the instant case.

. . . .

There is, however, respectable authority opposed to what, for convenience, may be called the New York rule.

In 44 C.J.S., Insurance, § 224, p. 933, it is said:

"Fire insurance is a personal contract with insured, and not a contract in rem, its purpose being not to insure property against fire, but to insure the owner of the property against loss by fire."

In 45 C.J.S., Insurance, § 915, p. 1010, the text reads as follows:

"Since a contract for insurance against fire ordinarily is a contract of indemnity, as discussed *supra* § 14, insured is entitled to receive the sum necessary to indemnify him, or to be put, as far as practicable, in the same condition pecuniarily in which he would have been had there been no fire; that is, he may recover to the extent of his loss occasioned by the fire, but no more, and he cannot recover if he has sustained no loss."

. . . .

Appleman, in Insurance Law and Practice, Vol. 6, § 3861, pages 207–208, says:

". . . If the damaged property is restored or repaired by a mortgagor or lessee, neither the mortgagee [citing *Friemansdorf v. Watertown Ins. Co.,* C.C. Ill. 1879, 1 F. 68] nor the lessor [*citing Ramsdell v. Insurance Co. of North America,* 1928, 197 Wis. 136, 221 N.W. 654] would be entitled to recover from the insurer. A few cases have reached a contrary conclusion [*citing Pink v. Smith, 1937, 281 Mich. 107, 274 N.W. 727; Savarese v. Ohio Farmers' Ins. Co. of LeRoy, Ohio, 1932, 260 N.Y. 45, 182 N.E. 665, 91 A.L.R. 1341*]."

Enough has been said, we think, to show that the question submitted to the District Court in the instant case was and is a doubtful question of Iowa law. The Iowa Supreme Court, were this case before it, might adopt the rule which prevails in New York or it might conclude that the rule contended for by the

Insurance Company is the better one. The Insurance Company has not demonstrated, and we think it would not be possible to demonstrate, that the conclusion reached by the District Court was not a permissible one or that it was based upon a misapplication or misconception of the applicable law of Iowa.

While the restoration by the lessor of the betterments and improvements covered by the policy has resulted in a windfall to the insured, the Insurance Company, for a substantial premium voluntarily undertook to indemnify the insured for loss to the betterments and improvements caused by fire. Such a loss did occur, and we think it reasonably may be believed that, under the terms of the policy, construing them most favorably to the insured, the Insurance Company was bound to pay the insured what the Insurance Company would have to pay had the betterments not been restored by the lessor of the building.

The judgment appealed from is affirmed.

NOTES

1. *Leases and related situations.* Although there are few cases involving lessors and lessees and their respective rights to recover on a property insurance policy for damage which the other has replaced or repaired, the issue has come up in other contexts. In *Gustafson v. Central Iowa Mutual Insurance Ass'n,* 277 N.W.2d 609 (Iowa 1979), 7 A.L.R.4th 484 (1981), the insureds purchased three steel buildings which were warranted by the manufacturer to be replaced if they were directly damaged by snow or wind within five years. The buildings were insured, among other risks, against wind storm. The buildings were destroyed by a tornado and the manufacturer replaced them free of charge to the insureds. The insurers contended there was no actual loss to the insureds and denied liability. The Supreme Court of Iowa, in a suit by the insureds on the policies, adopted the New York rule, holding "that an insurance company accepting and retaining premiums for the coverage of loss that occurred should not be relieved of liability on the basis of contractual relations between the claimant and third parties, and. . .determination of loss should not be postponed to some future unspecified date . . . ." *Id.* at 613.

The Court listed those cases which have followed the New York and the Wisconsin rules in various contexts:

> Many jurisdictions have found the *Foley-Alexandra* [New York rule] reasoning sound. Compare these decisions with *DeBellis Enterprises, Inc. v. Lumbermens' Mutual Casualty Co.,* 77 N.J. 428, 390 A.2d 1171 (1978) (fire insurer's liability not relieved by redemption of property from insured tax sale purchaser) and *and* [sic] *Montgomery v. First National Bank,* 265 Or. 55, 508 P.2d 428 (1973) (fire insurer's liability not relieved by owner repair of secured, insured party's property) and *Aetna Casualty and Surety Co. v. Cameron Clay Products, Inc.,* 151 W. Va. 269, 151 S.E.2d 305 (1966) (fire insurer's liability not relieved by existence of executory contract to convey upon buyer's performance

of conditions precedent) and *Rutherford v. Pearl Assurance Co.*, 164 So. 2d 213 (Fla. App. 1964) (fire insurer's liability not relieved by secured sale of property by insured) and *Koppinger v. Implement Dealers Mutual Insurance Co.*, 122 N.W.2d 134 (N.D. 1963) (fire insurer's liability not relieved by secured sale of property by insured) and *Hughes v. Potomac Insurance Co.*, 199 Cal. App. 2d 239, 18 Cal. Rptr. 650 (1962) (flood insurer's liability not relieved by flood control district's repair of damaged home) and *Board of Trustees v. Cream City Mutual Insurance Co.*, 255 Minn. 347, 96 N.W.2d 690 (1959) (fire insurer's liability not relieved by secured sale of property by insured) and *New England Gas and Electric Association v. Ocean Accident and Guarantee Corp.*, 330 Mass. 640, 116 N.E.2d 671 (1953) (property insurer's liability not relieved by free replacement of damaged machine) and *Heidisch v. Globe and Republic Insurance Co.*, 368 Pa. 602, 84 A.2d 566 (1951) (fire insurer's liability not relieved by condemnation under eminent domain where title had not yet passed) and *Plate Glass Underwriters' Mutual Insurance Co. v. Ridgewood Realty Co.*, 219 Mo. App. 186, 269 S.W. 659 (1925) (plate glass insurer's liability not relieved by landlord's obligation to make repairs.)

. . . .

Other courts which have followed the Wisconsin rule include *Paramount Fire Insurance Co. v. Aetna Casualty and Surety Co.*, 163 Tex. 250, 353 S.W.2d 841 (1962); *Glens Falls Insurance Co. v. Sterling*, 219 Md. 217, 148 A.2d 453 (1959); and *Beman v. Springfield Fire and Marine Insurance Co.*, 303 Ill. App. 554, 25 N.E.2d 603 (1940).

Id. at 612–13.

2. *Insurer's right of subrogation.* Another context involves the right of the landlord's property insurer to be subrogated to any cause of action of the landlord against a tenant for damage to the leased premises. Even if the lease and insurance arrangements do not explicitly treat the tenant as a named or additional insured, the majority of modern authorities, absent an express agreement to the contrary, hold that a tenant is an implied co-insured, along with the landlord, in which case the insurer has no right of subrogation. *See Community Credit Union v. Homelvig*, 487 N.W.2d 602 (N.D. 1992) (citing authorities and following majority rule). A minority of courts have held that the landlord's insurer may subrogate against the tenant in the absence of language in the lease exculpating the tenant from negligence or expressly obligating the landlord to provide insurance. *See, e.g., Newbauer v. Hostetter*, 485 N.W.2d 87 (Iowa 1992). Yet another approach is found in *Bannock Building Co. v. Sahlberg*, 126 Idaho 545, 887 P.2d 1052 (1994), where the court stated that whether a lessee is a coinsured under the lessor's fire policy is to be determined on case-by-case basis, focusing on the terms of the lease agreement to determine the parties' reasonable expectations regarding who would bear risk of loss for damage to the leased premises. What arguments are there for treating a tenant as a co-insured under the landlord's insurance policy?

3. *Comparing results in leases versus sales of real property.* Would you agree that the courts in the realty lease cases are following essentially the same

rules that are being applied in the more modern cases involving executory contracts for the sale of land?

4. *Automobile rentals.* One of the most common forms of leases of chattels today involves automobile rentals. Consider the following.

BERMAN & BOURNE, RENTERS COPE WITH AUTO COVER WOES,

National Underwriter: Property & Casualty/Employee Benefits Ed., May 4, 1987, at 24, col. 4. *

Few consumers pay as much attention to insurance coverage on rental cars as they do to insuring their own cars.

Today, with many changes in car rental company practices over the past few years, this can be a serious mistake.

Consumers can find themselves stuck with enormous bills for damages to rental cars if they do not fully understand the terms of the rental contract, the insurance provided by the rental company, and the relevant coverage under their own automobile insurance.

Also at risk are insurance agents who advise their automobile insurance clients. A failure to provide proper advice about rental car coverage can produce adverse reactions ranging from ill will to costly and time consuming errors and omissions claims.

The issue of rental car insurance coverage is fraught with such potential for financial loss because of two interacting factors.

First, car rental contracts vary, not only among rental companies, but sometimes among locations of the same company as well.

Second, automobile insurance policies differ from company to company. There are also variations in policy forms as approved in different states.

These differences are creating confusion and coverage gaps in rental car insurance with respect to liability and physical damage coverages, and to personal and commercial automobile policies.

Here, however, we will focus only on the issue of collision coverage for rental cars rented by individuals.

Car rental companies have made three major changes in their contracts that affect the renter's vulnerability to collision damage:

• Making the renter responsible for more of the collision damage loss;

• Including conditions and restrictions that can void the collision damage waiver (CDW); and,

• Increasing the cost of CDW.

Not many years ago, a rental customer who declined the CDW would be responsible only for the first few hundred dollars of damage to the car. More recently, the common limitation was $1,500, then $2,500.

Today, the four major car rental companies — Hertz, Avis, National and Budget—all make the renter responsible up to the full value of the car. With other rental companies the renter's responsibility can range anywhere from $1,500 to full value.

Conditions in the rental contract can affect the amount of the renter's responsibility.

One major rental company's contract, for example, limits the renter's responsibility to $3,000, but amends this to full value if the renter drives the car "unsafely."

Typically, car rental contracts prohibit these activities: allowing a driver not named in the contract to drive; taking the car out of the state without the permission of the rental company; driving on unpaved roads; exceeding the speed limit; engaging in a speed contest; using the car for towing or pushing; and driving under the influence of alcohol or drugs.

Violating these conditions will void the CDW — even though the renter has paid for it—and make him responsible for the full damage to the car.

When the charge for a CDW was only a couple of dollars a day, no one paid much attention to it. Now that the CDW fee ranges from $6.95 to $10 or more per day, more rental car customers are asking whether they really need it.

When a car is rented for a day or two, the CDW charges may not seem substantial, but for rentals of a week or more, the charge can even exceed the basic rental rate.

When the daily charge for CDW is annualized, the resulting figure can far exceed the annual premium most insurance companies would charge for collision insurance.

This fact, along with the high pressure tactics used by some car rental company personnel to get customers to accept the CDW, has attracted the attention of many insurance regulators and consumer advocates.

More than a few car rental agents are obviously motivated to get renters to accept the CDW, and consumers frequently complain that they generally don't take the time to explain CDW completely.

Often, rental agents don't always know how the CDW differs from collision insurance, and thus may not provide as complete protection as insurance.

Even representatives of the rental companies have admitted that their agents often don't or can't take the time to adequately explain the CDW to a customer.

There is some evidence that car rental companies are trying to address this problem. A brochure from National Car Rental, for example, does a good job of explaining what CDW is and the fact that the customer has the option of accepting or declining it.

The brochure also points out that the customer's personal automobile insurance may cover collision damage to a rental car.

But it also includes some scary language implying that the renter may have his insurance rates increased or his policy canceled if he files a claim for damage to a rental car.

It concludes by encouraging consumers to purchase the CDW option, saying: "Isn't the peace of mind worth the charge?"

Obviously, some customers are not so sure it is, or they would not be asking their agent or insurance company representative whether they should accept the CDW when renting a car.

To properly answer this question, one needs to understand not only the current situation in car rental contracts, but also how the various automobile insurance policy forms respond (or don't respond) to claims for damage to rental cars.

Until the ISO's Personal Automobile Policy (PAP) standard form was revised in early 1986, it covered damage to rental cars under the liability policy. If damage was caused by the insured's negligence, the liability coverage would respond.

A special provision also made the liability coverage apply if damage wasn't caused by the insured's negligence. But it was limited to $1,000 in most states. On the standard form no deductible would apply in either instance.

The April 1986 edition of the PAP treats damage to rental cars under the renter's physical damage coverage. The same Comprehensive and Collision coverage which the insured carries on his own car(s) extends to any car he rents.

Of course, the Collision deductible stated in the policy applies to damage to rental cars as well.

This revision reflects the view that a rental car is most often a substitute for the renter's own car, and that his insurance should respond to damage to the rental car in the same way.

Other major automobile insurers, including State Farm, Allstate, GEICO and USAA, also cover damage to rental cars under the renter's physical damage coverage.

The many non-ISO forms in use, however, vary greatly. Some may cover damage to rental cars under the renter's liability insurance; some under his physical damage insurance; and others may not cover it at all.

Because of revisions through the years, there is even a wide variation in ISO forms. Some companies in certain states still use the [F]amily Automobile [Policy], others, the original PAP, and still others the April 1986 edition of the PAP.

Even where the policy intends to cover damage to rental cars, the language still can present problems. In some instances coverage can depend on whether the insurance company considers a rented car to be a "temporary substitute vehicle."

There is also a question as to how much the insurer will pay if a rental car is totalled and has a higher value than the insured's own car.

While ISO has stated that the intent of their policy is to provide ACV coverage up to the full value of the rental car, the language of the policy doesn't state this unequivocally.

Additionally, depending on the language of the rental contract, the customer may assume liability by signing the rental agreement.

If this is the case, his personal insurance policy may not respond if it excludes coverage for contractual liability.

An even greater potential danger is that rental company practices regarding damaged returned cars could lead to unintended violations by the renter of the terms of his personal automobile coverage.

The rental company may assess the damage and make the renter pay for it immediately, then proceed to have the car repaired.

The renter is then left to seek recovery from his insurance company. However, the renter's policy undoubtedly contains provisions requiring him to notify the company in the event of a loss and to cooperate in the investigation and settlement of the claim.

Even though the insured was prevented by the car rental company from complying, his insurer could conceivably deny the claim.

In the absence of clear, unequivocal policy language spelling out the terms of coverage, insurance companies have several "outs" if they choose to deny a claim.

One has to wonder whether the insurers are content to leave the question of the extent of rental car coverage under their policies without a clear answer.

. . . .

NOTES

1. *Car rental update.* Although some aspects of automobile rental agreements have changed since the above essay was published, the insurance issues are not materially different. The daily cost of a CDW now runs between $9 and $25 per day. Consumers Union, *Navigating the Fast Turns of Car-Rental Insurance*, Consumers Reports Travel Letter, April 2000, at 1, 8. About 60 percent of all auto insurance policies cover rentals, and millions of other drivers receive rental car coverage from their credit card agreements, assuming the credit card is used to reserve and pay for the rental. But this means that many insurance policies do not cover rental cars; indeed, if the insured has dropped collision and comprehensive coverage because her car is an old one, she will not have that coverage for her rental car. See *id.* Moreover, some credit cards provide only limited coverage. Some cards do not provide coverage for "expensive" or "exotic" cars, including the popular sport utility vehicles, and for coverage while driving in other countries. See *id.* at 11. CDW is not the only insurance that is available when renting a vehicle. Rental car companies also offer supplemental liability insurance ("SLI"), personal accident insurance ("PAI"), and personal effects coverage ("PEC"). One study estimated that insurance increases the cost of daily car rentals by 46 percent. *Id.* at 1 (citing study by U.S. Public Interest Research Group).

2. *Coverage under PAP.* Assume you own a small, economy car which is worth about $5,000, but while on a trip you take advantage of ABC Rental

Car Co.'s special weekend rate and rent a $50,000 luxury car. You do not purchase the Collision Damage Waiver. If your insurance policy is the same as the Personal Auto Policy in Appendix E and you are carrying full coverage for damage to your own car, would you be covered for the full value of the rented car if you were to "total" it?

3. *Unconscionability and reasonable expectations.* You will probably be glad to know that some courts have held certain aspects of the "fine print" mentioned in the article above that unduly limit or narrow the benefits of a CDW agreement to be unenforceable on grounds of unconscionability. *See, e.g., Davis v. M.L.G. Corp.,* 712 P.2d 985 (Colo. 1986); *Val Preda Leasing, Inc. v. Rogriquez,* 540 A.2d 648 (Vt. 1987). Other courts have refused to construe the limiting language of the CDW to deprive the lessee of the benefits that would be reasonably expected by a purchaser. *See, e.g., Automobile Leasing & Rental, Inc. v. Thomas,* 679 P.2d 1269 (Nev. 1984). Is it relevant that car-rental counter agents are usually paid commissions for selling optional coverage? See Travel Letter, *supra,* at 1.

4. *Is the CDW insurance?* As indicated in note 6 following the *GAF* case in § 1.02, courts have been reluctant to hold that the CDW constitutes insurance for state regulatory purposes. Does payment of the CDW daily charge look like insurance to a consumer? In the meantime, the National Association of Insurance Commissioners has drafted model legislation on the subject. The first model act was adopted in 1986 and not only declared that the CDW constituted a form of insurance subject to the jurisdiction of the state insurance regulator, but also required the rental car agents who sold it to be licensed by the state. This action resulted from a number of reported abuses: high rates, hard-sell and scare tactics used upon consumers, failure to advise customers of alternatives to the CDW, exclusions from coverage, and deceptive advertising practices regarding rental rates. In 1988, the NAIC's industry advisory committee reported that the 1986 model act did not correct most of the abuses recognized, and that changing the law of bailment would be a better regulatory approach. The NAIC was persuaded to issue a new model act in 1988, and this act simply prescribes the type of CDW limitations that rental car companies may include in their leases and subjects them to a fine for violations of the act. See IV NAIC, COLLISION DAMAGE WAIVER MODEL ACT, Model Laws, Regulations and Guidelines 728-1 to -3 (1996). As of 1999, only two states had adopted the model, although at least 26 other states had some kind of related regulation for CDWs. *Id.* at 728-5 to -8. New York banned the sale of the CDW in 1989, N.Y. Gen. Bus. Law § 396-z.4 (Consol. 1999), and legislatures in several other states have put a cap on the fee. *See, e.g.,* Cal. Civ. Code § 1936(i) (Deering 1999); Neb. Rev. Stat. § 482.3165 (2000).

5. *Bailments and the "in trust or on consignment" clause.* At least one insurance problem that arises under bailments of goods and related arrangements deserves mention. It involves the "held in trust or on consignment or for storage" clause contained in commercial property insurance policies. Assume Mary places personal property in storage with Acme Moving & Storage, Inc. and, while in storage, the property is destroyed by fire caused by an Act of God. The storage contract is silent on the issue of Acme's responsibility, but Acme has a commercial property insurance policy that covers all of its real

and personal property. As to personal property of others that is on the premises and "held in trust or on consignment or for storage," the policy says that it covers such property "provided that the Insured is legally liable therefor." Does the policy cover Mary's property or only the legal liability of Acme, if any, for the fire? Since the fire occurred through no fault of Acme, and if Mary has no insurance of her own, it may be that her only potential source of indemnification is Acme's insurance policy. How should the issue be resolved? *See United States v. Globe & Rutgers Fire Insurance Co.,* 104 F. Supp. 632 (N.D. Tex. 1952).

[d]   Life Tenants, Remaindermen, and Tenants at Will

MORRIS v. MORRIS

274 Or. 127, 544 P.2d 1034 (1976)

McALLISTER, JUSTICE.

This is an action for a declaratory judgment to determine the right to fire insurance proceeds as between the life tenant Alta F. Morris and the remainderman A.L. Morris.

The facts were stipulated. The defendant, Alta F. Morris, is the life tenant of a farm in Wasco County. Her son, A.L. Morris, the plaintiff, is the remainderman. The defendant, Alta F. Morris, purchased fire insurance from Oregon Mutual Insurance Company insuring a farmhouse on the farm for $15,000, the full value thereof. All premiums on the policy were paid by Alta F. Morris and she is the only insured named in the policy. On March 10, 1973 the farmhouse was totally destroyed by fire. The fire was not caused by or contributed to by the negligence of defendant.

On April 27, 1973 before Oregon Mutual had paid the proceeds of the policy, plaintiff informed Oregon Mutual of his interest in the property. Defendant Alta F. Morris received all the proceeds of the policy and has not used the proceeds to reconstruct the farmhouse or to restore the property to its former condition, nor has she offered to reimburse the plaintiff for the loss resulting from the loss of the farmhouse.

The trial court found in favor of plaintiff against defendant Alta F. Morris, but found for Oregon Mutual. Both the plaintiff and defendant Alta F. Morris have appealed.

Plaintiff contends, and defendant denies, that a portion of the fire insurance proceeds, which Alta F. Morris received, belongs to plaintiff as remainderman. The only issue is whether plaintiff is entitled to any portion of the insurance proceeds.

It is the general rule that a life tenant is entitled to all the proceeds for a loss if the life tenant has procured the insurance policy in his own name and for his own benefit and has paid the premium from his own funds. The general rule is not changed by the fact that the insurance is for the full value of the property rather than only for the value of the life tenant's interest in the property. Annotation, Life Tenant — Insurance—Remainderman, 126

A.L.R. 336, 345 et seq.; 51 Am. Jur. 2d 416, Life Tenants and Remaindermen, § 158; Restatement of Property, § 123(2).

In the Annotation in 126 A.L.R. the annotator, at page 345, states the rule thus:

> "It is clearly the general rule that where a life tenant insures the property in his own name and for his own benefit and pays the premiums from his own funds, he is, at least in the absence of a fiduciary relationship between him and the remainderman existing apart from the nature and incidents of the tenancy itself, or of an agreement between him and the remainderman as to which of them shall procure and maintain insurance, entitled to the proceeds of the insurance upon a loss; and the fact that the insurance was for the whole value of the fee is not generally regarded as affecting the right of the life tenant to the whole amount of the proceeds, although a contrary view has occasionally been taken."

Converse v. Boston Safe Deposit & Trust Co., 315 Mass. 544, 53 N.E.2d 841, 843 (1944), is typical of the cases holding in accord with the general rule. We quote from that case:

> "Where, as here, there is nothing to show that Mrs. Converse was required by the terms of her mother's will creating her life estate or by any agreement with the plaintiff to obtain fire insurance in his behalf, she was not bound to obtain such insurance either for her own benefit or for that of the plaintiff. A life tenant or a remainderman may obtain insurance upon his own interest and for himself alone. A remainderman has no claim upon the proceeds of fire insurance received by a life tenant from insurance obtained by a life tenant who was under no obligation to him to carry insurance, where the policies were obtained by the life tenant in his own name, at his own expense and for his sole benefit. A remainderman has no interest in contracts of insurance in which he was not a party and which were not obtained for his protection. The fact that the property was insured by the life tenant for its full value is not enough to show that he intended to cover the interest of the remainderman. If a life tenant, who has insured for his own benefit, receives from the insurers more than the value of the life tenancy, that is a matter between the parties to the contracts of insurance and creates no claim in favor of the remainderman in the excess paid over the value of the life tenancy in the property. The underlying principle is that fire insurance policies are personal contracts providing for the payment of indemnity to the insured in case of loss, and the amount received does not stand for nor represent the property damaged or destroyed although the measure of indemnity depends upon the determination of the value of the interest of the insured in the property covered by the policies. In a word, the money received by a life tenant from his own contracts of insurance belongs to him, and he cannot be compelled to hold the money as though it were substituted for the property or as though it were the proceeds of the property. . . ."

Plaintiff has cited three cases from other jurisdictions, but, upon examination, we find those cases are inapposite and do not support his position.

Although there are no Oregon cases directly on point, our decisions in analogous situations are in accord with the general rule. In *Miller v. Gold Beach Packing Co.,* 131 Or. 302, 282 P. 764, 66 A.L.R. 858 (1929), the tenant of a building secured a fire insurance policy covering the building. The building was destroyed by fire and the tenant declined to use the insurance proceeds to rebuild. The lessors brought an action to recover the value of their interest in the estate as remaindermen. This court said:

"... The courts, which have reached the conclusion that the remainderman is entitled to no interest in insurance money obtained by a tenant upon a policy of insurance procured by him without any agreement between the two that he should obtain protection for both, premise their holdings upon the following grounds: (1) The tenant as well as the remainderman has an insurable interest. (2) The tenant is under no obligation to insure the property for the benefit of the remainderman. (3) The contract of insurance, which either obtains, is personal to him, and the other has no interest in it. (4) If the tenant obtains from the insurance company more than the value of his estate, the remainderman does not thereby become entitled to the surplus, because the contract of insurance does not undertake to indemnify him. (5) The tenant is neither required to rebuild nor to provide a fund to take the place of the building upon its destruction. (6) The proceeds of the fire insurance contract are not proceeds of the destroyed building; they come to the tenant from a third party as the result of a contract for indemnity. (7) The insurable estates of the tenant and the remainderman are separate and distinct; they are not united or merged under the contract of insurance, and hence the latter affords the remainderman no basis for any relief. (8) The amount of the insurance policy obtained by the tenant and the amount ultimately collected is for the determination of the tenant and the insurer; it does not affect the remainderman. (9) If a tenant in obtaining a policy of insurance, or in obtaining a settlement, places an excessive value upon his interest in the property, his act does not constitute him the agent of the remainderman so that the latter becomes entitled to any part of the insurance money." 131 Or. at 308–309, 282 P. at 766.

The court concluded that the contract for insurance was personal, the tenant was not the lessors' agent or trustee, and there was no rule of law which authorized giving any surplus beyond the tenant's fair compensation to the lessors. "They were strangers to the contract of insurance, and must now be content to remain strangers to its fruits." 131 Or. at 313, 282 P. at 768.

. . . .

The judgment of the trial court is reversed with instructions to enter judgment for defendant Alta F. Morris. This disposition of the main issue makes it unnecessary to consider plaintiff's cross-appeal.

NOTES

1. *Majority and minority rules. Morris* is representative of the majority approach. In *Ellerbusch v. Myers,* 683 N.E.2d 1352 (Ind.App. 1997), the court, in the course of endorsing the majority rule, described the approaches followed by other courts:

> [A] minority of courts has concluded that a life tenant is entitled to all of the insurance proceeds only when the policy of insurance merely covers the life tenant's interest. Under this view, if the life tenant recovers insurance proceeds that exceed the value of the life estate, then the tenant most hold the excess in trust for the benefit of the remaindermen. Yet another minority rule holds that insurance proceeds collected by the life tenant, regardless of the amount, stand in place of the destroyed property and must be used to rebuild the property. If the property cannot be rebuilt, the life tenant must invest the proceeds for the benefit of the remaindermen, in which case the life tenant would be entitled to any interest earned on the fund during his life.

683 N.E.2d at 1354–55.

2. *Effect of life tenant's death after loss.* In *Home Insurance Co. v. Adler,* 269 Md. 715, 309 A.2d 751 (1973), the insured died in the fire that damaged the house in which she held a life estate, the death occurring approximately nineteen minutes after the fire began. The insurer paid for the personal property lost in the fire, but refused to pay for the fire damage to the house, maintaining that the insured's insurable interest terminated at the moment of death and, therefore, no pecuniary loss was suffered by the insured in the case. The Maryland Court of Appeals held that the insurer's liability attached at the moment the fire started and that it was liable to pay the life tenant's estate the full damage to the house up to the policy limits without regard to the length of time she lived after the fire began. Would the result have been the same if the life tenant had been killed instantly by an explosion that destroyed the house?

If a life tenant is obligated to make repairs to the house if it is damaged under the rules of the law of property, does it make sense to give the proceeds to the executor of the estate? Presumably, if the repairs are not made, the remaindermen would bring an action for waste against the estate. Does it not make more sense to give the proceeds to the remaindermen, who have a stake in making sure repairs are done properly (or who bear the consequences of the repairs not being made at all)? In *In re Estate of Jackson,* 508 N.W.2d 374 (S.D. 1993), the life tenant-insured died one month after a hail storm damaged the house in which she lived. The trial court held that the property insurance proceeds were the property of the life tenant's estate, but the Supreme Court of South Dakota reversed, holding that the life tenant had an obligation to repair damage that occurred before her death, and therefore the remaindermen, rather than the life tenant's estate, were entitled to the proceeds. Yet if the estate was deemed to hold the proceeds in constructive trust for the benefit of the remaindermen, why was there anything wrong with the trial court's decision?

3. *Tenants at will.* In *Liverpool & London & Globe Insurance Co. v. Bolling,* 176 Va. 182, 10 S.E.2d 518 (1940), Henry Bolling and his son, Clarence, conducted a general mercantile business in a building owned by Henry. Clarence was married to Anne, but they divorced. As part of the property settlement, Anne received the stock of merchandise and thereafter she carried on the business. It was undisputed that Anne did not own the building in which the business was housed, but that Henry had told her "she could have it as long as she wanted it," and that she did not pay any rent for using the building. Although it was disputed, the jury found that Anne explained the situation to the insurer's agent when she purchased insurance on the building. Did Anne have any interest in the building that was insurable? If so, what theory of insurable interest would be needed to support her claim? (Insurable interest requirements for property were discussed in § 2.02[2].

[3] Causation

Every insurance policy includes language of causation somewhere in its text. A typical property insurance policy might state that "the policy insures against all direct loss caused by" specified perils. Exclusions in the policy might state that losses caused by other perils are not covered. Moreover, the subject of causation is not limited to property insurance policies. A liability policy might state that coverage exits if the liability is caused by certain acts, or that no coverage exists if the loss is caused by other designated acts. In accidental death policies, the question of coverage will turn upon whether death was caused by an accident or some nonaccidental cause. Policy language with respect to causation might appear to be straightforward, but the seemingly simple text often disguises extremely complex and difficult questions. See Robert H. Jerry, II, Understanding Insurance Law § 67[a], at 482 (2d ed. 1996).

Where causation is an issue in an insurance coverage case, the typical fact pattern involves a loss caused by a combination of covered and excluded, or covered and noncovered, causes. How then does one determine whether the loss is covered? Collection and analysis of facts is extremely important; but once the forces that operate to produce the loss are documented, one must determine which of the causes have legal significance for purposes of coverage and which do not. This issue is commonly referred to as one of "concurrent causation," although it is not uncommon to find references to a "chain of causation" in some cases, particularly where the contributing causes occur in a series, with each cause producing another, which in turn produces another, and so on.

Through the years, numerous scholars and commentators have articulated frameworks for analyzing causation problems. See, *e.g.*, Edwin W. Patterson, Essentials of Insurance Law 199-235 (1935) (probably the most widely known framework); Edwin W. Patterson, Essentials of Insurance Law 226-71 (2d ed. 1957) (an elaboration of the framework in the first edition); Robert E. Keeton, Insurance Law: Basic Text 306–19 (1971) (a framework which draws heavily upon Patterson); William C. Brewer, Jr., *Concurrent Causation in Insurance Contracts*, 59 Mich. L. Rev. 1141 (1961); Robert H. Jerry, II, Understanding Insurance Law § 67, at 361–64 (1987) (a framework which draws heavily upon Brewer by referencing two dimensions of causation, dominance and remoteness); R. Dennis Withers, *Proximate Cause and Multiple Causation in First-Party Insurance Cases*, 20 Forum 256 (1985); Robert H. Jerry, II, Understanding Insurance Law § 67 (2d ed. 1996) (a "dual-filter" framework, which elaborates on the framework of the 1987 edition). For better or worse, "[n]one of these frameworks. . .has had any apparent sustained influence on the development of the law of causation, and the terminology offered in each has not become a part of the legal vocabulary." Jerry, *supra*, at 484.

There are essentially three "models" or "views" one can have of causation. Under the "liberal" approach (i.e., liberal in the sense that coverage is viewed expansively), one could take a package of concurrent causes and assert that as long as any one of the concurrent causes is a covered peril, the loss is covered. Under the "conservative" approach, one could take the same package and assert that as long as any one of the concurrent causes is an excluded peril, the loss is not covered. A "middle ground" approach would examine the package of concurrent causes and ask which of the causes is the most "important" in some legal sense—i.e., which of the causes is "efficient," or "proximate," or "dominant," or some other rubric which connotes that "this cause is a 'big deal,' and the others are not."

In resolving a causation problem, the starting place is the language of the contract. Different policies have different language; this is one area where individual insurers will customize otherwise standardized forms, and where the standard language changes periodically. In *McDonald v. State Farm Fire and Casualty Co.,* 119 Wash. 2d 724, 837 P.2d 1000 (1992) (en banc), the policyholders' home was insured under a policy that covered the property in the event of "accidental direct physical loss," subject to a number of specific exclusions, the most pertinent of which were a "foundation cracking" exclusion, an "earth movement" exclusion, and a "faulty workmanship and materials" exclusion (the precise text of which are set forth in the margin *). The

---

* The "foundation cracking exclusion" stated:

We do not insure for loss to the property described in Coverage A either consisting of, or directly and immediately caused by, one or more of the following: . . .

i. settling, cracking, shrinking, bulging, or expansion of pavements, patios, foundation, walls, floors, roofs or ceilings; . . . ."

The "earth movement exclusion" stated:

We do not insure under any coverage for loss (including collapse of an insured building or part of a building) which would not have occurred in the absence of one or more of the following excluded events. We do not insure for such loss regardless of: a) the cause of the excluded event; or b) other causes of the loss; or c) whether other causes acted concurrently or in any sequence with the excluded event to produce the loss: . . . .

b. Earth Movement, meaning any loss caused by, resulting from, contributed to or aggravated by earthquake; landslide; mudflow; sinkhole; erosion; the sinking, rising, shifting, expanding, or contracting of the earth. . . ."

The "faulty workmanship and materials exclusion" stated:

We do not insure under any coverage for loss consisting of one or more of the items below: a. conduct, act, failure to act, or decision of any person, group, organization or

home had been built in 1984 on a hill overlooking an inlet. Following heavy rains less than two years later, the ground (or "fill") on the uphill side of the house slid away, causing the foundation of the house to crack and tilt downhill. The insurer denied the claim, citing the policy exclusion for earth movement and any loss resulting from earth movement. After $27,000 worth of repairs, another round of heavy rains the next year caused the loss to recur. The insurer again denied coverage, and the insureds sued. The insureds' soil engineers opined that the "cause of the 1987 damage to the house was the faulty design and construction of the filled area near the foundation with unsuitable fill materials." 837 P.2d at 1002–03.

Whom do you think should have prevailed in *McDonald*? No matter how you answer the question, you would have had more than one judge in your company. The trial judge entered a summary judgment for the insurer. The Court of Appeals reversed, reasoning that the "ensuing loss" clause in the exclusion was a grant of coverage for loss caused by faulty materials and construction, and that the foundation cracking and earth movement exclusions were attempts to limit coverage in violation of the "efficient proximate cause rule" approved in *Graham v. Public Employees Mutual Insurance Co.*, 98 Wash. 2d 533, 538, 656 P.2d 1077 (1983), a case which appears *infra*. The Supreme Court reinstated the trial court's judgment, reasoning that "the State Farm homeowners' policy does not cover loss caused by defective construction or materials and the ensuing losses of foundation cracking and earth movement." 837 P.2d at 1006.

As this quick look at *McDonald* suggests, the lawyer who undertakes to search for perfect clarity in the law of causation should pack for a long journey. "Because causation as a theory or doctrine is elusive, inconsistent outcomes in the cases must be expected, and these differing outcomes will often turn on subtle factual distinctions . . . . Perhaps the most useful exercise, then, to help garner an understanding of causation issues in insurance law is to construct a framework for discussing causation issues, a framework on which fact patterns will be hung and analyzed during the process of determining whether a loss was caused by a covered risk or some other risk outside the coverage." Jerry, *supra*, at 483. Can such a framework be constructed out of the following cases?

---

governmental body whether intentional, wrongful, negligent, or without fault; b. defect, weakness, inadequacy, fault or unsoundness in:

. . . .

(2) design, specifications, workmanship, construction, grading, compaction;

(3) materials used in construction or repair; or . . . . of any property (including land, structures, or improvements of any kind) whether on or off the residence premises. However, we do insure for any ensuing loss from items a. and b. unless the ensuing loss is itself a Loss Not Insured by this Section.

GRAHAM v. PUBLIC EMPLOYEES MUTUAL INSURANCE CO.

98 Wash. 2d 533, 656 P.2d 1077 (1983)

DORE, JUSTICE.

This appeal arises from a dispute which erupted between two insurance companies and their insureds following the May 18, 1980 explosion of Mt. St. Helens. The early pyroclastic flows from the eruption, along with hot ash and debris, began melting the snow and ice flanking the mountain and the broken glacial ice blocks within the Toutle River valley. This water, combined with torrential rains from the eruption cloud, existing ground water, water displaced from Spirit Lake, and ash and debris, created mudflows which began moving down the valley shortly after the eruption began. This process continued throughout the day of May 18.

At some point, a large mudflow developed in the upper reaches of the south fork of the valley from the Toutle and Talus glaciers. The mudflow gouged and filled the land into new forms as it moved, damaging or destroying many homes within its path. Approximately 10 hours after the eruption began, the appellants' homes, 20–25 miles away from Mt. St. Helens, were destroyed by a mudflow or a combination of mudflows preceded by water damage from flooding.

At the time of the eruption, homeowners insurance policies issued by Public Employees Mutual Insurance Company (hereafter PEMCO) to appellants Graham and Campbell, and a policy issued by Pennsylvania General Insurance Company (hereafter PGI) to appellants Fotheringill were in effect. All three policies provided in pertinent part as follows:

SECTION 1—EXCLUSIONS

We do not cover loss resulting directly or indirectly from:

. . . .

> 2. Earth Movement. Direct loss by fire, explosion, theft, or breakage of glass or safety glazing materials resulting from earth movement is covered.

> 3. Water damage, meaning:

> a. flood, . . .

Of the seven exclusions listed in the PEMCO policy, "earth movement" is the only one not specifically defined in the policy.

Prior to March 1980, PEMCO utilized insurance forms containing this exclusionary language:

This policy does not insure against loss:

. . . .

> 2. caused by, resulting from, contributed to or aggravated by any earth movement, including but not limited to earthquake, volcanic eruption, landslide, mudflow, earth sinking, rising or shifting;

unless loss by fire, explosion or breakage of glass constituting a part of the building(s) covered hereunder, including glass in storm doors and storm windows, ensues, and this Company shall then be liable only for such ensuing loss, but this exclusion does not apply to loss by theft;

This language was deleted by PEMCO in an overall effort to simplify the policy language.

The homeowners filed claims against the insurance companies under their homeowners policies, but the insurance companies rejected their claims on the basis that the damage was excludable as "earth movement" in the form of mudflows or a combination of earth movement and water damage. The Grahams and Campbells then commenced this action against PEMCO in Cowlitz County Superior Court. On April 10, 1981, the trial court granted PEMCO's motion for summary judgment, dismissing the homeowners' complaint. Meanwhile, the Fotheringills instituted a suit against PGI in the same court. On April 29, 1981, the trial court, after hearing argument virtually identical to that of the Graham case, granted PGI's motion for summary judgment, dismissing the Fotheringills' complaint.

For the purpose of ruling on the summary judgment motion, the trial court assumed the movement of Mt. St. Helens to be an "explosion" within the terms of the insurance policies. The trial court noted this issue was a factual issue to be determined by a jury. We agree, as the true meaning of "explosion" in each case must be settled by the common experience of jurors. Because direct loss from an explosion resulting from earth movement is not excluded from coverage, the jury must also determine the factual issue of whether the earth movements were caused by the earthquakes and harmonic tremors which preceded the eruption.

If the jury determines the volcanic eruption was an explosion resulting from earth movement, it will then be necessary to reach the issue of whether the loss was a direct result of the eruption. The trial court held that the causation analysis of *Bruener v. Twin City Fire Ins. Co.*, 37 Wash. 2d 181, 222 P.2d 833 (1950) precluded the plaintiffs' claims.

In *Bruener,* the insured's vehicle skidded on icy pavement and collided with an embankment. The insurance policy contained a collision exclusion to the comprehensive coverage. This court held that the loss was a "collision" for insurance purposes, reasoning as follows at 183–84, 222 P.2d 833:

> In tort cases, the rules of proximate cause are applied for the single purpose of fixing culpability, with which insurance cases are not concerned. For that purpose, the tort rules of proximate cause reach back of both the injury and the physical cause to fix the blame on those who created the situation in which the physical laws of nature operated. The happening of an accident does not, in itself, establish negligence and tort liability. The question is always, why did the injury occur. Insurance cases are not concerned with why the injury occurred or the question of culpability, but only with the nature of the injury and how it happened.

The *Bruener* court expressly overruled *Ploe v. International Indem. Co.,* 128 Wash. 480, 223 P. 327 (1924), a case involving a driver who lost control of an automobile while rounding a curve on a mountain road. The car left the highway and traveled 25 feet before striking a stump along the road. Holding that the insurer was not liable, the court characterized the proximate cause of the accident to be the skidding of the car and not the collision with the stump. *Ploe, at* 483, 223 P. 327. The court reasoned that the destruction of the car was imminent from the time it left the highway, whether it struck the stump or not. In overruling the *Ploe* decision, the *Bruener court,* 37 Wash. 2d at 185, 222 P.2d 833 replaced this proximate cause analysis with one of "direct, violent and efficient cause".

In *Dickson v. United States Fidelity & Guar. Co.,* 77 Wash. 2d 785, 466 P.2d 515 (1970), the plaintiff's boom crane was insured under a policy which excluded coverage for latent defects. The boom crane was damaged when earth, collapsing onto an "H" beam that was being removed, caused a sudden stoppage of the hoist. This stoppage put an increase in load on the boom structure, causing a defective weld to break and the boom to collapse. This court affirmed the trial court's ruling that the earth collapse was the external and responsible cause of the failure of the weld and the collapse of the boom, stating at 793, 466 P.2d 515:

> The trial court regarded the collapsing earth as the external and responsible cause of the failure of the weld and the collapse of the boom. He did not thereby rule in contradiction to our rule on insurance causation, as set forth in *Bruener v. Twin City Fire Ins. Co.,* [37 Wash. 2d 181, 222 P.2d 833 (1950)] wherein we stated that, for the purposes of insurance litigation, the responsible cause of a loss is that which is the "direct, violent and efficient cause of the damage."

In reviewing the foregoing cases, we conclude the immediate physical cause analysis is no longer appropriate and should be discarded. The *Bruener* rule is an anomaly, inconsistent with the rule in the majority of other jurisdictions.[1] We have defined "proximate cause" as that cause "which, in a natural and continuous sequence, unbroken by any new, independent cause, produces the event, and without which that event would not have occurred." Where a peril specifically insured against sets other causes in motion which, in an unbroken sequence and connection between the act and final loss, produce the result for which recovery is sought, the insured peril is regarded as the "proximate cause" of the entire loss.

It is the efficient or predominant cause which sets into motion the chain of events producing the loss which is regarded as the proximate cause, not necessarily the last act in a chain of events. The mechanical simplicity of the *Bruener* rule does not allow inquiry into the intent and expectations of the

---

[1] 18 G. Couch, *Insurance* § 74:693 (2d ed. 1968) states the majority rule as:

"When loss is sustained by the insured it is necessary that the loss be proximately, rather than remotely, caused by the peril insured against."

parties to the insurance contract. We now specifically overrule the *Bruener* case.[2]

The determination of proximate cause is well established in this state. As a general rule, the question of proximate cause is for the jury, and it is only when the facts are undisputed and the inferences therefrom are plain and incapable of reasonable doubt or difference of opinion that it may be a question of law for the court.

In the present case, the mudflows which destroyed the appellants' homes would not have occurred without the eruption of Mt. St. Helens. The eruption displaced water from Spirit Lake, and set into motion the melting of the snow and ice flanking the mountain. A jury could reasonably determine the water displacement, melting snow and ice and mudflows were mere manifestations of the eruption, finding that the eruption of Mt. St. Helens was the proximate cause of the damage to appellants' homes. This issue is not a question of law but a question of fact, to be determined by the trier of facts.

Conclusion

The *Bruener* decision is hereby overruled. We remand to the trial court for a jury determination of whether the movement of Mt. St. Helens was an "explosion" within the terms of the insurance policies; whether that "explosion" was preceded by earth movement, and whether appellants' damages were proximately caused by the eruption of Mt. St. Helens on May 18, 1980.

ROSELLINI, STAFFORD, UTTER, WILLIAMS, and PEARSON, JJ., concur.

BRACHTENBACH, CHIEF JUSTICE (dissenting).

In its ardor to explain the relationship of proximate cause to insurance law the majority strays from the basic issues presented by this case. First, what are the express terms of the policy? Second, are any of those terms ambiguous? Third, if the terms of the policy are unambiguous, would application of those terms result in coverage? The majority fails to apply such a step by step analysis. Consequently, it neglects a clear provision of the policy that requires that we affirm the trial court's grant of summary judgment. I therefore dissent.

. . . .

The obvious flaw in the majority's opinion is that it improperly applies the terms of the policy to the chain of events. The facts of this case reveal the following possible chain of events which should result in a denial of coverage regardless of proximate cause analysis. As suggested by the majority, on May 18, 1980, earthquakes and moving lava caused earth to move, which caused an eruption (explosion?), which caused earth movement in the form of mudflows. The majority concludes that the exclusion operates to exclude the initial earth movement which preceded the eruption but that the exception

---

[2] In *Frontier Lanes v. Canadian Indem. Co.,* 26 Wash. App. 342, 346, 613 P.2d 166 (1980), the Court of Appeals read *Bruener v. Twin City Fire Ins. Co.,* 37 Wash. 2d 181, 222 P.2d 833 (1950) to require that a loss could be attributed to vandalism or malicious mischief only if "the immediate physical cause of that loss was the vandalistic or malicious act itself or an instrumentality employed directly by the wrongdoer to carry out that act". We decline to follow the *Frontier* analysis insofar as it is inconsistent with our holding in the present case.

for explosion contained in the exclusion brings the incident back within the potential terms of the policy. But if that result is correct, the majority neglects a necessary additional inquiry — that is—should the earth movement exclusion be applied a second time to exclude coverage for mudflows? This last question presents strictly a legal issue involving the proper interpretation of policy terms. I submit that the only logical resolution of this issue is that the earth movement exclusion must be considered a second time. This answer requires, unfortunately, that we deny coverage. To do otherwise, however, would be to use proximate cause analysis to circumvent the clear terms of the policy. In addition, the majority appears to stop its inquiry at a point on the causation chain where coverage would be provided. The majority's analysis requires that we ignore clear provisions in the insurance contract. This we cannot 'do. . . .

The interpretation I suggest is necessary to give effect to the expectations that the parties had at the time they contracted for insurance coverage. I would therefore deny coverage and affirm the trial court.

DOLLIVER and DIMMICK, JJ., concur.

NOTES

1. *A mountain shrinks.* It is difficult to appreciate the sheer magnitude of the eruption of Mt. St. Helens. The May 1980 eruption killed 57 people, and the blast of rock off the top and side of the mountain removed 1,313 feet from the mountain's height. One estimate placed the monetary damage at $2.7 billion. Smithsonian Institution Scientific Event Network, Global Volcanism 1975-85 354 (1987). Yet Mt. St. Helens is hardly an anomaly; it is but one of several active (i.e., "hot") mountains in the Cascade Mountain range. California's Lassen Peak erupted in 1914, and several other mountains have been active since 1800, including Mt. Baker and Mt. Rainier in Washington, Mt. Hood in Oregon, and Mt. Shasta and Cinder Cone in California. If Mt. Rainier were to erupt, the homes of approximately 50,000 people could be affected by mudflows. See generally Stephen L. Harris, Fire & Ice: The Cascade Volcanoes (rev. ed. 1980).

Under the pre-1980 policy form, how would the case have been decided? What do you suppose were the insurer's objectives in the 1980 policy revision? Did the insurer properly assess the risk posed by volcanoes on the west coast?

2. *What else is at stake here?* The west coast's exposure to earthquakes is well known. The 1906 San Francisco earthquake is legendary, but large earthquakes have rocked the west coast in recent years. The most memorable are the 6.9 (Richter Scale) earthquake in San Francisco in 1989 and the 6.8 earthquake in Northridge (north of Los Angeles) in 1994. The Northridge earthquake was the second most damaging natural disaster in U.S. history, exceeded only by Hurricane Andrew in southern Florida in 1992. The 6.8 earthquake in Kobe, Japan in 1995 killed 5,200 people and caused, by one estimate, $82.4 billion in damage (only $2.5 billion of which was insured). See *1995 Claims Total $150 Billion,* Bus. Ins., Mar. 11, 1996, at 17. The U.S.

Geological Survey released a study in October 1999 that gives the San Francisco Bay area a 70 percent change of a 6.7 earthquake before 2030. One study by Stanford University scientists estimated that if an earthquake similar to the 1906 San Francisco episode struck the same area today, fatalities could reach 8,000 and total damages could reach $225 billion. See Ruth Gastel, ed., *Earthquakes: Risk and Insurance Issues*, Ins. Issues Update (Insurance Information Institute), Nov. 1999.

Many people are surprised to learn that the west coast is not the only area in the U.S. with this kind of vulnerability. Three of the largest earthquakes in the history of North America (and the largest known earthquake in the continental U.S.) occurred in the Missouri boot heel and extreme northeast Arkansas during the winter of 1811–12 (the so-called "New Madrid seismic zone"). All had magnitudes greater than 8.0, the landscape of the area was drastically changed, the Mississippi River reversed its flow for several hours, and people were awakened as far away as Pittsburgh, Pennsylvania and Norfolk, Virginia. Aftershocks continued until 1817. Otto Nuttli, *The Central Mississippi Valley Earthquakes of 1811–12*, in Proceedings of the Symposium on The New Madrid Seismic Zone 33–63 (1984). One study estimates the probability of a significant damaging earthquake in this area (i.e., a 6.3 on the Richter Scale) within the next 15 years at 40–63 percent, and within the next 50 years at 86–97 percent. The probability of a cataclysmic earthquake (8.0 or stronger) within the next 50 years is small, but not de minimis — between 2.7 and 4.0 percent. Arch C. Johnston & Susan J. Nava, *Recurrence Rates and Probability Estimates for the New Madrid Seismic Zone,* 90 J. of Geophysical Res. 6737 (1985). A more recent study casts doubt on the likelihood of a cataclysmic New Madrid earthquake, but the researchers do not disagree with the U.S. Geologic Survey's estimate that the odds of a 6.0 earthquake in this area within 40 years are 90 percent. See Karl Mueller et al., *Fault Slip Rates in the Modern New Madrid Seismic Zone,* 286 Science 1135 (1999). At the bottom line, earthquakes have occurred in 39 states during the 1900s and have caused damage in all states; it is estimated that 90 percent of the nation's population live in areas that are "seismically active." See Gastel, *supra.*

The greatest risk of most earthquakes may be, ironically, not the damage caused by earth movement, but the losses caused by resulting fires when natural gas lines (and water lines used to fight the fires) break. If earthquake is an excluded peril but fire loss is covered, the causation issue rears its head. The insurance industry sought to have this problem addressed with proposed legislation introduced in the California legislature in the early 1980s; these bills addressed concurrent causation in general terms. When it became clear that these reforms had no prospect of enactment, the industry sought legislation which was enacted and codified as Cal. Ins. Code. § 10088 (Deering 1999). This section provides:

> Notwithstanding the provisions of Section 530, 532, or any other provision of law, and in the absence of an endorsement or an additional policy provision specifically covering the peril of earthquake, no policy which by its terms does not cover the peril of earthquake shall provide or shall be held to provide coverage for any loss or damage when

earthquake is a proximate cause regardless of whether the loss or damage also directly or indirectly results from or is contributed to, concurrently or in any sequence by any other proximate or remote cause, whether or not covered by the policy. The term "policy" as used in this section includes all policies of any nature, including, but not limited to, business and commercial forms providing coverage against loss due to damage to the property of the insured. Nothing in this section shall operate to affect the provisions of Section 2071 or preclude an insurer from specifically providing coverage for direct loss caused by explosion, theft, or glass breakage resulting from an earthquake.

What effect would this statute have had if it had been the law in Washington at the time of the eruption of Mt. St. Helens? Does this statute help or hurt insureds in California? Suppose a forest fire in California has moved into a valley, damaging homes. Then, by coincidence, an earthquake occurs in the valley, causing further damage. Some homes, weakened by fire, would not have collapsed in the earthquake but for the fire. What consequences does the statute have for losses in these circumstances? See generally Michael E. Bragg, *Concurrent Causation and the Art of Policy Drafting: New Perils for Property Insurers,* 20 Forum 385 (1985).

3. *Filtering the causes.* If one rejects either the conservative or liberal approaches (see the textual material preceding *Graham*), one must apply some kind of filter that assesses the relative significance of the causes. Do the descriptions "moving," "direct," "prime," "predominant" or "dominant," "efficient," and "proximate" connote different things?

If "direct" means the last cause prior to the loss, should the insurer have prevailed under the reasoning that a "mudflow," i.e., earth movement, was the "direct" cause of the loss? Does the court's proximate cause test trump policy language? Should it? Alternatively, does "direct" imply something else? How could the "explosion," i.e., eruption, be a "direct" cause of the loss? What exactly did the majority and the dissent disagree about?

4. *Shifting policy language I.* Compare the pre-1980 policy language, the policy language in *Graham,* and the policy language in *McDonald*, quoted in the introductory note. How did the language change? "Shifting winds carried ashclouds [from Mt. St. Helens] in almost every direction, drifting as far as Spokane, Washington, 300 miles distant." Harris, *supra,* at 15. What other fallout do you perceive from Mt. St. Helens?

Examine the language in the Homeowners Policy in Appendix C at "Section I-Exclusions," Paragraphs 2 and 3. Does this language resolve the issue considered in *Graham?*

5. *Shifting judicial attitudes.* Compare the causation approaches in *Ploe, Bruener*, and *Graham.* Are these changes simply another example of the eternal path of the law, or do you see more fallout from Mt. St. Helens?

6. *What trumps—court-made rule or policy language?* Should an insurer be allowed to contract around the causation test favored by courts in any particular jurisdiction? Or should the causation doctrine trump whatever the insurer puts in the policy? A number of courts have treated the efficient

proximate cause rule as immutable, and have condemned insurers' efforts to override the rule with policy language seeking to implement the "conservative" approach to causation. *See, e.g., Safeco Insurance Co. v. Hirschmann,* 112 Wash. 2d 621, 773 P.2d 413 (1989); *Howell v. State Farm Mutual Insurance Co.,* 218 Cal. App. 3d 1446, 267 Cal. Rptr. 708 (1990). But other courts disagree. *See, e.g., Findlay v. United Pacific Insurance Co.,* 129 Wash. 2d 368, 917 P.2d 116 (1996) (distinguishing, and limiting, *Hirschmann*); *State Farm Fire & Casualty Co. v. Slade,* 747 So. 2d 293 (Ala. 1999); *Front Row Theatre, Inc. v. American Manufacturers Mutual Insurance Co.,* 18 F.3d 1343 (6th Cir. 1994); *State Farm Fire and Casualty Co. v. Bongan,* 925 P.2d 1042 (Alaska 1996). The court in *Schroeder v. State Farm Fire & Casualty Co.,* 770 F. Supp. 558, 561 (D. Nev. 1991) stated the point succinctly: "[T]he parties could, as they did, contract out of the efficient proximate cause doctrine without violating public policy."

Should the presence (or lack) of a statute codifying a causation rule matter on the "what trumps" question? *See Alf v. State Farm Fire and Casualty Co.,* 850 P.2d 1272 (Utah 1993). The existence of two causation statutes in the California Insurance Code is arguably a basis for distinguishing the causation precedents in that jurisdiction. *See Garvey v. State Farm Fire and Casualty Co.,* 48 Cal. 3d 395, 770 P.2d 704, 257 Cal. Rptr. 292 (1989) (en banc).

7. *The Patterson causation framework.* The textual material before *Graham* mentioned that of the various frameworks offered to conceptualize causation, the most famous is the one developed by Professor Edwin W. Patterson. The essence of his framework can be discerned from the following excerpt from the 1957 edition of his treatise.

> Insurance contracts contain two types of provisions limiting the insurer's liability in terms of causation. The one embraces the limitations upon the *consequences* of the insured event . . .; the other includes restrictions upon the *causes* of the insured event. Provisions of the latter type are commonly called *exceptions,* and the causes to which they refer may be called *excepted causes.* The latter are to be distinguished from *excluded events,* which are often referred to in the contract as not falling within the definition of the insured event. In marine-insurance contracts (Lloyds form), the clause, "warranted free of capture, seizure," etc., excludes these events from the broader clause "perils of the sea." These distinctions are useful in analyzing the language of contracts and applying the analysis to claims made under contracts. [emphasis in original.]

E.W. Patterson, Essentials of Insurance Law 249 (2d ed. 1957).

Judge Robert E. Keeton explained Patterson's system in the following manner, which explanation is summarized here: What Patterson calls an "excepted cause" restriction is really an "inconclusive" clause. An inconclusive clause does not necessarily mean the insured cannot recover; instead, it simply means that the insured cannot recover where there is only one cause and the clause preempts coverage for damage from that cause. If there is another cause of the damage which is covered by the policy, the insured can recover. Keeton labeled Patterson's "excluded event," for which there is no coverage because the event itself is eliminated from the risk transferred, as a "conclusive" clause. As Keeton explained, every incident is at once a cause, event, or consequence, depending on the perspective one chooses to take. Thus, the legal effects given to certain clauses depend on how one categorizes the incident. Nonetheless, as Patterson argued, and Keeton agreed, the framework is helpful if only to ensure consistent treatment of like clauses. See Robert E. Keeton & Alan I. Widiss, Insurance Law § 5.5(a) (Student ed. 1988). For additional discussion of the Patterson framework, see Robert H. Jerry, II, Understanding Insurance Law § 67[e][1] (2d ed. 1996).

8. *Shifting policy language II.* As the foregoing materials suggest, insurers continue to revise and tweak policy language on causation to accomplish their underwriting objectives. How far would you let insurers go in this regard? Consider the next case.

MURRAY v. STATE FARM FIRE AND CASUALTY CO.
203 W.Va. 477, 509 S.E.2d 1 (1998)

STARCHER, Justice.

The appellants and defendants below, State Farm Fire and Casualty Company ("State Farm") and Allstate Insurance Company ("Allstate"), appeal an order of the Circuit Court of Jackson County granting summary judgment to several homeowners in a dispute concerning policy exclusions in two home-owners' insurance policies. The policyholders' homes were damaged by rocks falling from the highwall of a 40-year old abandoned rock quarry situated next to the homes. The policyholders' insurance carriers denied coverage, claiming that the applicable insurance policies excluded losses caused by "landslides" and "erosion." The circuit court concluded that the policies did not exclude from coverage losses caused by "rockfalls" and "weathering," and that the plaintiffs' losses were the result of those events. The circuit court held that the plaintiffs were entitled to coverage under the policies.

After reviewing the record, we conclude that questions of material fact exist concerning whether coverage exists under both policies. We reverse the circuit court's order granting summary judgment and remand the case for trial.

I.

Factual Background

The plaintiff-appellees in this case-Robert and Janet Murray, Bernie and Julie Rees, and Robert Withrow-are the owners of three adjacent properties on Spring Street in Ripley, West Virginia. The plaintiffs' homes were con-structed on their properties in the 1970's. Immediately adjacent to the rear of the three houses is a man-made highwall standing nearly 50 feet high. This vertical highwall is the result of quarrying operations conducted in the 1950's. The highwall is allegedly located on property owned by defendant-appellee Robert B. Harris.

On February 22, 1994, several large boulders and rocks fell off the highwall and onto the houses owned by plaintiffs Murray and Withrow, causing extensive damage. The house owned by plaintiffs Mr. and Mrs. Rees was not damaged by rocks. However, firemen compelled all three families to leave their homes because of the possibility that additional rocks could fall, and turned off all electricity and water. An engineer who examined the highwall several days later concluded that further rockfalls would "continue to occur, some with potentially disastrous results."[1] None of the three families has lived in their homes since February 22, 1994.[2]

Several engineers and geologists examined the property and highwall in the following weeks. Each gave, to some extent, an opinion that what occurred on Spring Street was primarily a "rockfall" and not a "landslide," because no "sliding" was involved: a layer of shale supporting a layer of sandstone "weathered," removing support for the sandstone, and sandstone blocks broke loose and dropped onto the plaintiffs' homes.[3] One expert said that he thought

---

[1] The March 2, 1994 report from engineer Eric G. Denemark to Mr. Rees stated:

Looking at the highwall from the Church Street end up to and past the Withrow's yard, there is evidence of other past rockfalls. We feel that this wall is inherently unstable and that these events will continue to occur over time. Immediately behind the Withrow home a large block is already wedged off the sandstone unit and sits, precariously and temporarily, on what is left of the underlying shale. This is an extremely dangerous situation that, in our opinion, places the Withrow home at immediate risk.

The situation behind your home has not advanced quite as far. . . . It is only a matter of time before it too will fail resulting in a rockfall similar to that which occurred last week.

Another factor perhaps worthy of consideration, is that, typically, small pieces of rock will "spall" off the wall sporadically but relatively continuously. . . . While the potential for structural damages is minimal, a relatively small fragment, grapefruit-size for example, can easily inflict a serious or fatal injury should it strike a person or animal. You may want to consider this when contemplating letting your children or pets play near the highwall. We would consider anywhere in the backyard to be potentially dangerous.

[2] The Rees allege that after moving from their home they were unable to afford the mortgage payments. They were forced to convey the property back to the bank holding the deed of trust. The bank then moved the house and relocated it to another site.

As to the remaining houses, a letter from the City of Ripley Building inspector states that:

Presently the houses are unsightly, unsafe, and are creating a health hazard. We are requesting they be torn down and removed from their location. We feel it would be unsafe to repair or rebuild either house at their present site. The city will not issue any building permit for rebuilding or repairing either house without first having the rockfall stabilizing and secured.

[3] Hobart M. King, an expert hired by the City of Ripley, stated in a letter to the mayor that:

Because the distinction between a rockfall and a landslide is sometimes important for insurance purposes, I made special effort to determine what had happened. . . .

Mr. King discussed this distinction in his deposition testimony:

A: In a landslide, what you have is a mass [of] rock or soil that is sliding over an underlying surface. That sliding takes place across a plane. There is a plane or a surface of failure at the base of the moving material. When I was looking at what had happened in Spring Street, there was no surface of failure along which sliding occurred. Sandstone blocks had fallen from the higher elevation above that

of a rockfall as "almost a vertical displacement free-falling through the air off of a cliff, a highwall, an escarpment." However, several of the experts conceded that rock falls are considered to be a type of landslide, and are accepted as a sub-category of a landslide; and they further agreed that erosion contributed to the moving of the rocks in the instant case.

Furthermore, there is evidence in the record that negligent construction of the highwall behind the plaintiffs' residences, namely the cutting of the rock face at a near vertical angle, contributed to the rockfall. Expert George A. Hall indicated that "the design of the cut-slope on Spring Street did not meet standards which you would reasonably and normally expect for civil engineering purposes of designing cut-slopes." He also said that had proper civil engineering techniques been used when the highwall was created, the danger of a fall like the one that occurred would not be present.

Plaintiffs Murray and Rees filed claims for the losses to their homes with their homeowner's insurance carrier, defendant State Farm. Plaintiff Withrow filed a similar claim with his insurance carrier, defendant Allstate. Insurance agents notified the plaintiffs that State Farm and Allstate would not cover the losses, citing to numerous policy provisions and exclusions, including an exclusion for losses caused by landslide or erosion.

The plaintiffs then filed the instant lawsuit against defendants Allstate and State Farm alleging breach of contract and bad faith. The plaintiffs also sued defendant Harris for nuisance, trespass, and failing to protect the plaintiffs' property from the "dangerous, artificial manmade condition existing on the defendant's property[.]" Defendant State Farm filed a counterclaim against the plaintiffs seeking a declaratory judgment regarding State Farm's obligations under its policies.

The plaintiffs and defendants State Farm and Allstate filed motions for summary judgment concerning coverage under the disputed insurance policies. Through a letter ruling on January 3, 1997 and a subsequent order on March 17, 1997, the circuit court granted summary judgment to the plaintiffs. The circuit court held that the rockfall "is a loss covered under the plaintiffs' respective insurance policies." The court also held that whether the plaintiffs' damages were caused by a rockfall, and the extent of those damages, were issues to be determined by a jury.

State Farm and Allstate now appeal the circuit court's order.

. . . .

III.

Discussion

Defendants Allstate and State Farm provided the plaintiffs with "all-risk" homeowner's insurance policies.[4] Under an all-risk policy, recovery is allowed

---

shale layer that I previously discussed was underneath the sandstone. So, those two reasons would be why I would call that a rockfall. . . .

   Q: Would you agree that a rockfall is a type of landslide?

   A: No. Slide[s] take place over a surface of failure. A fall occurs when a piece of the earth has broken away and falls independently, no sliding involved.

[4] Allstate insured Mr. Withrow's home under a "Deluxe Homeowners Policy" which provided

for all losses arising from any fortuitous cause, unless the policy contains an express provision excluding the loss from coverage.

Both Allstate and State Farm contend that the losses suffered by the plaintiffs are barred from coverage by express policy provisions excluding losses resulting from "earth movement, including but not limited to. . .landslide. . .[or] erosion[.]"

The defendants challenge the circuit court's order on four grounds. First, both defendants challenge the circuit court's summary judgment order finding that coverage existed under the policies because the plaintiffs' losses were the result of a "rockfall" caused by "weathering," and not excluded by policy provisions regarding "landslide" and "erosion." Second, both defendants argue that the earth movement exclusions are clear and unambiguous, and should therefore not be construed but instead applied to exclude coverage for the plaintiffs. Third, defendant State Farm argues that even if the earth movement exclusion could be construed as ambiguous, an extensive "lead-in" clause in its policy clarifies any ambiguity and excludes any coverage as to plaintiffs Murray and Rees. Lastly, both defendants argue that the plaintiffs cannot recover for the total loss of their homes due to the potential for a future rockfall, but can only recover for the actual physical damage sustained.

We address these arguments in turn.

A.

The Circuit Court's Summary Judgment Order

We first address the circuit court's order. While the circuit court's letter ruling and subsequent order are less than perfectly clear, it appears that the circuit court concluded that the boulders that damaged the plaintiffs' homes arose from a "rockfall" rather than a "landslide." Based in part upon the expert testimony in the record, the circuit court construed the policy language strictly against the insurance carriers and found that "the language therein did not include or contemplate a rockfall[.]" The circuit court further referred to expert testimony, apparently to hold that the rockfall was the result of "weathering" as opposed to "erosion," and that the plaintiffs were therefore covered under their homeowners' policies.

Defendants Allstate and State Farm first contend that the circuit court erred in finding that a "rockfall" is not included within the definition of "landslide." The defendants cite to *Dupps v. Travelers Ins. Co.,* 80 F.3d 312 (8th Cir.1996), where the court, addressing a landslide triggered by a sinkhole, stated that "[t]he ordinary meaning of the term 'landslide' includes rocks falling down a bluff. . . . [T]he only reasonable interpretation of the policy prohibits recovery for rocks which have fallen. . . ." 80 F.3d at 314. Similarly, the court in Syllabus Point 4 of Olmstead v. Lumbermens Mut. Ins. Co., 22 Ohio St.2d 212, 259 N.E.2d 123 (1970) concluded that "[t]he common ordinary

---

that Allstate would pay for any "sudden and accidental physical loss to the property described in the Dwelling Protection Coverage, except as limited or excluded by this policy." The State Farm Homeowners Policy (Special Form 3) provided to the Murrays and Rees indicates that the policy "insure[s] for accidental direct physical loss to the property described in Coverage A except as provided in SECTION 1-LOSSES NOT INSURED."

meaning of the word 'landslide' is a sliding down of a mass of soil or rock on a steep slope."

We agree with the defendants that the circuit court erred. We hold that the plain, ordinary meaning of the word "landslide" in an insurance policy contemplates a sliding down of a mass of soil or rock on or from a steep slope.

Allstate and State Farm also argue that the circuit court erred in concluding that "weathering" is different from "erosion," and therefore any loss resulting from weathering is not excluded from coverage. The *Dictionary of Geological Terms* defines "erosion" as "the group of processes whereby earth or rock material is loosened or dissolved and removed from any part of the earth's surface," specifying that it includes the processes of "weathering, solution, corrosion and transportation." The *American Heritage Dictionary* also includes within its definition of erosion the "natural processes, including weathering, dissolution, abrasion, corrosion and transportation, by which material is removed from the earth's surface."

We again agree that the circuit court erred. We hold that the plain, ordinary meaning of the word "erosion" in an insurance policy contemplates a natural process that includes weathering, dissolution, abrasion, corrosion and transportation whereby material is removed from the earth's surface.

Applying these definitions to the circuit court's order, it is clear that the circuit court's granting of partial summary judgment to the plaintiffs was incorrect. A naturally-occurring "rockfall" is included within the common definition of "landslide," and the process of "weathering" to rock is included as a component of the natural process of erosion. We further hold that the circuit court erred in finding that as a matter of law coverage existed under the policies by applying these definitions. However, as discussed below substantial questions of fact remain to be resolved concerning the existence of coverage.

B.

Earth Movement Exclusion

Both insurance policies in this case contain exclusions for "earth movement." The policy issued by Allstate excludes coverage for any loss resulting from:

> 2. Earth movement, including, but not limited to, earthquake, volcanic eruption, landslide, subsidence, mud flow, sinkhole, erosion, or the sinking, rising, shifting, expanding, bulging, cracking, settling or contracting of the earth. This exclusion applies whether or not the earth movement is combined with water.

Similarly, the policy issued by State Farm excludes coverage for losses resulting from:

> b. Earth Movement, meaning the sinking, rising, shifting, expanding or contracting of earth, all whether combined with water or not. Earth movement includes but is not limited to earthquake, landslide, mudflow, sinkhole, subsidence and erosion.

When a policyholder shows that a loss occurred while an insurance policy was in force, but the insurance company seeks to avoid liability through the operation of an exclusion, the insurance company has the burden of proving the exclusion applies to the facts in the case. "Where the policy language involved is exclusionary, it will be strictly construed against the insurer in order that the purpose of providing indemnity not be defeated."

Both of the earth movement exclusions in this case refer to "earth movement" including, but not limited to "earthquake," "volcanic eruption," "landslide," "subsidence," "mud flow," "sinkhole," "erosion," "sinking," "shifting," or "settling." None of these terms is further defined in the insurance policies. The defendant insurance companies argue that the facts in this case show that the rocks and earthen debris that fell on the plaintiffs' homes constitute a "landslide" caused by "erosion," an event within the earth movement exclusions.

The plaintiffs, however, argue that the facts show the damage to their homes was caused by the negligent creation of the highwall in the 1950's and its negligent maintenance by defendant Harris today, two events that would be covered by the policies.

On the one hand, the exclusions cited in the defendants' policies could bar coverage for solely *natural* events such as earthquakes, volcanic eruptions, and sinkholes. On the other hand, the same exclusions refer to events which could be *man-made*, such as subsidence or earth movement caused by equipment or a broken water line. Or, as alleged in this case, earth movement could be caused by *both man and nature* over a period of time, such as landslides, mudflows, or the earth sinking, shifting, or settling. Because the policy language is reasonably susceptible to different meanings, we believe that the earth movement exclusions in the insurance policies at issue are ambiguous, and must have a more limited meaning than that assigned to it by the defendants.

The majority of courts that have considered earth movement exclusions have found them to be ambiguous. Having found the clause to be ambiguous, courts have used two methods of policy construction to examine whether coverage exists or is excluded under the earth movement exclusion. First, courts have applied two doctrines of construction, *ejusdem generis* and *noscitur a sociis*, to limit the application of the earth movement exclusion to natural, catastrophic events, rather than man-made events.

Second, courts have examined the particular causes of the loss presented by the policyholder, and although an excluded event (such as earth movement) may have been a concurring or contributing cause of a loss, courts have allowed policyholders to recover under an insurance policy if the proximate cause of the loss was an event insured by the policy.

We believe that both approaches are applicable in this case.[8] . . . . We therefore examine exclusions in the instant case using the same two approaches.

---

[8] While every insurance policy must be analyzed based upon its own language, numerous courts faced with analogous policy language have reached nearly identical conclusions. A clear majority of courts continue to find earth movement exclusions ambiguous, and limited in application only to naturally-occurring catastrophic events such as earthquakes. However, a few jurisdictions have concluded that earth movement exclusions are not ambiguous, and apply to absolve the insurance company from any liability under the policy regardless of the cause or type of earth movement.

First, having determined that the earth movement exclusions at issue in this case are ambiguous, we apply the construction principles of *ejusdem generis* and *noscitur a sociis*. Under the doctrine of *ejusdem generis*, "[w]here general words are used in a contract after specific terms, the general words will be limited in their meaning or restricted to things of like kind and nature with those specified." The phrase *noscitur a sociis* literally means "it is known from its associates," and the doctrine implies that the meaning of a general word is or may be known from the meaning of accompanying specific words. The doctrines are similar in nature, and their application holds that in an ambiguous phrase mixing general words with specific words, the general words are not construed broadly but are restricted to a sense analogous to the specific words.

In the seminal case of *Wyatt v. Northwestern Mutual Ins. Co. of Seattle*, 304 F.Supp. 781 (D.Minn.1969), the district court considered a summary judgment motion where an insurance company sought, through the operation of an earth movement exclusion, to avoid liability for losses caused by the negligence of a contractor excavating land adjacent to the policyholder's home. While holding that the exclusionary language was intended to remove from coverage losses resulting from natural causes and natural phenomena, such as earthquakes, the court concluded that questions of fact remained as to whether the movement of earth that damaged the policyholder's house was caused by the actions of third parties. The court reasoned that the earth movement exclusion was created by insurance companies

. . . to relieve the insurer from occasional major disasters which are almost impossible to predict and thus to insure against. There are earthquakes or floods which cause a major catastrophe and wreak damage to everyone in a large area rather than one individual policyholder. When such happens, the very basis upon which insurance companies operate is said to be destroyed. When damage is so widespread no longer can insurance companies spread the risk and offset a few or the average percentage of losses by many premiums. Looking at the special exclusionary clause in the policy here in question, it seems to cover situations where one single event could adversely affect a large number of policyholders. . . . All of these are phenomena likely to affect great numbers of people when they occur.

This gives some force to the view that the various exclusions were not intended to cover the situation as here where "earth movement" occurred under a single dwelling, allegedly due to human action of third persons in the immediate vicinity of the damage.

304 F.Supp. at 783. We believe that similar reasoning underlies the exclusions in this case.

Examining the exclusionary terms used by Allstate and State Farm in their context, and applying the rule that ambiguities must be resolved in favor of the insured, we conclude that both earth movement exclusions must be read to refer only to phenomena resulting from natural, rather than man-made, forces.

Therefore, when an earth movement exclusion in an insurance policy contains terms not otherwise defined in the policy, and the terms of the exclusion relate to natural events (such as earthquakes or volcanic eruptions), which events, in some instances, may also be attributed to a combination of natural and man-made causes (such as landslides, subsidence or erosion), the terms of the exclusion must be read together and limited to exclude naturally-occurring events rather than man-made events.

The second approach consistently taken by courts in construing insurance policies is that for coverage to exist under an insurance policy, policyholders are required to prove that the efficient proximate cause of the loss was an insured risk.[9] . . . .

. . . .

The scope of coverage under an all-risk homeowner's policy includes all risks except those risks specifically excluded by the policy. A majority of jurisdictions use the "efficient proximate cause" doctrine [10] in adjudicating coverage issues for all-risk insurance policies, where both a covered and a non-covered peril contribute to a loss. [11] When a loss is caused by a combination of covered and specifically excluded risks, the loss is covered if the covered risk was the proximate cause of the loss. . . .

We hold that, when examining whether coverage exists for a loss under a first-party insurance policy when the loss is caused by a combination of covered and specifically excluded risks, the loss is covered if the covered risk was the efficient proximate cause of the loss. No coverage exists for a loss if the covered risk was only a remote cause of the loss, or conversely, if the excluded risk was the efficient proximate cause of the loss. The efficient proximate cause is the risk that sets others in motion. It is not necessarily the last act in a chain of events, nor is it the triggering cause. The efficient

---

[9] As one court indicated, the efficient proximate cause rule is "a rule of construction because certain consequences follow from the terms of the contract and from a legal policy applicable to the situation. Insurers cannot circumvent the rule by redefining causation." *Sunbreaker Condominium Association v. Travelers Ins. Co.*, 79 Wash.App. 368, 375 n. 8, 901 P.2d 1079, 1082 n. 8 (1995) (citations omitted).

[10] Courts use varying terms such as "proximate cause," "efficient proximate cause," "efficient cause," "predominant cause" or "moving cause." As one court grappling with the meaning of the efficient proximate cause doctrine noted,

> Regardless of the name of the doctrine or number of adjectives within it, the law requires a decision as to what event will be held accountable as the cause of the loss. . . . Given the weight of authority, [and] the similarity if not identicalness of efficient proximate cause to proximate cause. . . .the Court finds that the predominating cause of the loss is the appropriate standard.

Pioneer Chlor Alkali Co., Inc., v. National Union Fire Ins. Co. of Pittsburgh, Pa., 863 F.Supp. 1226, 1231 (D.Nev.1994). The court went on to say in a footnote that:

> Although perhaps containing an unnecessary adjective, and not at all making the doctrine more clear, the Court will use the majority term "efficient proximate cause." To invent a new term would only add to the confusion in this legal nebula where case precedents filled with the legal jargon of efficient proximate cause offer little guidance in the doctrine's application and result.

Id., n. 6. We believe this reasoning is equally applicable to the instant case.

[11] By one commentator's count, 34 jurisdictions (including West Virginia in *LaBris v. Western National Ins. Co.*, 133 W.Va. 731, 59 S.E.2d 236 (1950)) have adopted some form of concurrent or proximate cause analysis in examining coverage under first-party and/or third-party insurance policies. *See* F. MacLaughlin, *Third-Party Liability Policies: The Concurrent Causation Doctrine and Pollution Exclusions*, 24 Brief 20, 22–23 (1995).

proximate cause doctrine looks to the quality of the links in the chain of causation. The efficient proximate cause is the predominating cause of the loss.[12]

One more point is made clear by courts considering the problem of concurrent risks: the question of which event was the efficient proximate cause of the loss is generally a question of fact.

After reviewing the record, we conclude that substantial questions of material fact remain for jury resolution. The earth movement exclusions apply to exclude naturally occurring risks. The plaintiffs argue that the evidence currently in the record suggests that the rocks fell from the quarry highwall due to its negligent vertical construction in the 1950's, and its negligent maintenance by the current owner. These risks facially appear to be covered by the language in both policies. Conversely, the defendants argue that the plaintiffs' losses are the result of the excluded event of a landslide caused by another excluded event, erosion. We believe that whichever of these events was the efficient proximate cause of the plaintiffs' losses is a question for the finder of fact.

C.

State Farm's Lead-In Clause

State Farm contends in its reply brief that a "lead-in" clause in the "Losses Not Insured" section of its policy precludes coverage to plaintiffs Murray and Rees, and excludes coverage for all forms of earth movement, regardless of whether resulting from natural or man-made causes. The State Farm lead-in clause states:

---

[12] An example of the efficient proximate cause doctrine in action is *Frontis v. Milwaukee Ins. Co.*, 156 Conn. 492, 242 A.2d 749 (1968). The policyholder owned the Frontis building, a four-story building sharing a common wall with an adjoining building. A fire in the adjoining building destroyed the building, requiring its demolition and removal. The only fire damage caused to the Frontis building was a broken window. However, without the lateral support of the adjoining building, the shared common wall could no longer support the Frontis building, requiring the removal of the third and fourth floors of the Frontis building.

The court in *Frontis* was asked to address whether the removal of the top two floors of the Frontis building was a "direct loss by fire" within the meaning of an insurance policy. The court concluded that the loss was covered, holding that a fire can be the proximate, dominant, active and efficient cause of a loss even if the fire starts outside the insured premises and never extends to them in the form of combustion. 156 Conn. at 497, 242 A.2d at 752.

Another example is *Brian Chuchua's Jeep, Inc. v. Farmers Ins. Group*, 10 Cal.App.4th 1579, 13 Cal.Rptr.2d 444 (1992). The policyholder purchased earthquake insurance. An earthquake damaged an underground gasoline tank, and leaking gasoline damaged the soil. The insurance carrier refused coverage for the gasoline clean-up costs citing a pollution exclusion. The court determined that because the risk of earthquake was insured against, if "the trier of fact determines the earthquake was the efficient proximate cause of the leakage, the cleanup expenses will be covered." 10 Cal.App.4th at 1583, 13 Cal.Rptr.2d at 446. Insurance companies sought to have *Brian Chuchua's Jeep* "depublished" by the California Supreme Court arguing its publication would compromise their pollution exclusions because it "mandates an analysis of whether, despite the exclusion, the cause of the loss is covered." The Court refused to depublish the opinion. *See Third-Party Liability Policies: The Concurrent Causation Doctrine and Pollution Exclusions*, 24 Brief 20, 43 (1995).

. . . .

SECTION I—LOSSES NOT INSURED

*   *   *   *   *   *

2. We do not insure under any coverage for any loss which would not have occurred in the absence of one or more of the following excluded events. We do not insure for such loss regardless of: (a) the cause of the excluded event; or (b) other causes of the loss; or (c) whether other causes acted concurrently or in any sequence with the excluded event to produce the loss; or (d) whether the event occurs suddenly or gradually, involves isolated or widespread damage, arises from natural or external forces, or occurs as a result of any combination of these:

The policy then goes on to list numerous occurrences that are excluded, including the previously discussed "earth movement."

State Farm uses unique language in the "Losses Not Insured" section of its policy (which includes the earth movement exclusion), language not employed by other insurance companies in standard all-risk insurance policies. As one court recently recognized in construing an earth movement exclusion,

. . . State Farm adopted language peculiar to itself, and one of plaintiffs' [insurance] experts describes State Farm as a "deviated company" which employs its own language and is "known in the industry as ones who try to push earth movement as broadly as they can."

Winters v. Charter Oak Fire Ins. Co., 4 F.Supp.2d 1288, 1292 (D.N.M.1998).

The court in *Cox v. State Farm Fire & Cas. Co.,* 217 Ga.App. 796, 459 S.E.2d 446 (1995) considered State Farm policy language nearly identical to that at hand and held the lead-in clause to be ambiguous. The policyholders in *Cox* alleged that their home had been damaged by vibrations from explosions, and that explosions were a covered peril under their homeowner's policy. As in this case, State Farm in that case denied coverage under the earth movement exclusion, and argued that man-made earth movement was excluded by the lead-in clause which expanded the exclusion to cover "natural or external forces." The court stated that:

Because "external" is not defined in the policy, we must give the word its usual and common meaning. As we have found no definition of the word that means anything other than apart, beyond, exterior or connected to the outside (see Webster's Third New International Dictionary), we cannot define the word to include a concept of non-natural or man-made forces as State Farm would have us do. Therefore, we must interpret this provision as excluding coverage arising from natural forces from beyond or outside the property.

217 Ga.App. at 797, 459 S.E.2d at 448 (citation omitted).

We believe a similar analysis applies here. The policy language at issue in this case does not define the term "external," and we must therefore give the word its "plain, ordinary meaning." We can find no definition for "external" that means anything other than outside, apart, or beyond, and we cannot define the word to include man-made forces as State Farm would have us do. As with the court in *Cox*, we interpret the provision as excluding from coverage natural risks arising from beyond or outside the property.

State Farm also argues that its lead-in clause operates to defeat the efficient proximate cause doctrine, and argues that if earth movement in any way contributes to a loss, regardless of the proximate cause, then under the lead-in clause the entire loss is excluded from coverage under the all-risk policy. The plaintiffs, however, argue that such a construction reaches a result contrary to the reasonable expectations of policyholders. We agree with the plaintiffs' argument.

"With respect to insurance contracts, the doctrine of reasonable expectations is that the objectively reasonable expectations of applicants and intended beneficiaries regarding the terms of insurance contracts will be honored even though painstaking study of the policy provisions would have negated those expectations." Syllabus Point 8, National Mut. Ins. Co., *supra*.[13]

As in the instant case, where third-party negligence is alleged to be the proximate cause of a loss, we believe a policyholder could reasonably expect to be covered under State Farm's policy. Only through a painstaking review of the lengthy "Losses Not Included" section would a policyholder discover the language suggesting that, because the negligence occurred in conjunction with an excluded event, the loss would not be covered. "Insureds with all-risks insurance likely have heightened expectations because of the comprehensive nature of the coverage and the greater premium rates. These expectations would not often be given effect if recovery was denied whenever an exception or exclusion contributed to the loss." R. Fierce, *Insurance Law-Concurrent Causation: Examination of Alternative Approaches*, 1985 S.Ill.U.L.J. 527, 544 (1986).

An example of the overbreadth of State Farm's position was suggested by the court in *Wyatt v. Northwestern Mut. Ins. Co. of Seattle*, 304 F.Supp. at 783, which stated:

> It seems hard to contend that the insurance policy meant to exclude all earth movements, for it is difficult to distinguish between a situation where a piece of heavy equipment breaks loose and hits a house causing serious damage and a situation where that equipment instead hits only an embankment next to a house but causes the earth to move and thereby damages the house. Certainly not all earth movements, or at least those where some human action causes such are included in the exclusion.

However, applying State Farm's interpretation of its policy to the fact pattern proffered by the court in *Wyatt,* there would be no coverage. We believe such an interpretation clearly goes against the reasonable expectations of the parties.

---

[13] "Before the doctrine of reasonable expectations is applicable to an insurance contract, there must be an ambiguity regarding the terms of that contract." Syllabus Point 2, *Robertson v. Fowler,* 197 W.Va. 116, 475 S.E.2d 116 (1996). As noted previously, the policy language at issue in the State Farm policy is subject to several interpretations, and is therefore ambiguous.

. . . .

Our examination of the State Farm lead-in clause leads us to a similar conclusion. As indicated previously, when an insurance carrier chooses to insure against a loss proximately caused by a particular peril, it may not rely on the mere concurrence of an excluded peril to deny coverage. The excluded peril must itself be the efficient proximate cause of the loss. Because State Farm's lead-in clause conflicts with the reasonable expectations of the parties, it should be construed to allow coverage for losses proximately caused by a covered risk, and deny coverage only when an excepted risk is the efficient proximate cause of the loss.[14] We therefore decline to follow these latter jurisdictions.

D.

Whether the Plaintiffs Suffered a "Direct Physical Loss" To Their Property

As indicated previously, the Allstate policy provides coverage for any "sudden and accidental loss to the property," while the State Farm policy "insure[s] for accidental direct physical loss to the property[.]" Defendants

---

[14] We acknowledge that jurisdictions are in conflict over the effect of the State Farm lead-in clause in landslide cases. At least two jurisdictions hold the clause has no effect on limiting coverage: California (*Howell v. State Farm Fire & Cas. Co.*, 218 Cal.App.3d 1446, 267 Cal.Rptr. 708 (1st Dist.1990)); and Georgia (*Cox v. State Farm Fire & Cas. Co.*, 217 Ga.App. 796, 459 S.E.2d 446 (1995)). At least five jurisdictions hold that the lead-in clause is enforceable: Alaska (*State Farm Fire & Cas. Co. v. Bongen*, 925 P.2d 1042 (Alaska 1996)); New York (*Kula v. State Farm Fire & Cas. Co.*, 212 A.D.2d 16, 628 N.Y.S.2d 988 (N.Y.A.D.1995)); Utah (*Alf v. State Farm Fire & Cas. Co.*, 850 P.2d 1272 (Utah 1993) and *Village Inn Apartments v. State Farm Fire & Cas. Co.*, 790 P.2d 581 (Utah App.1990)); Nevada (*Schroeder v. State Farm Fire & Cas. Co.*, 770 F.Supp. 558 (D.Nev.1991)); and Arizona (*Millar v. State Farm Fire & Cas. Co.*, 167 Ariz. 93, 804 P.2d 822 (1990)).

We question the holdings of these latter jurisdictions, as they found the earth movement policy language to be unambiguous and clear, and suggested that the policyholder's reasonable expectations were more in line with being a "fervent hope usually engendered by loss." *Millar*, 167 Ariz. at 97, 804 P.2d at 826. These latter jurisdictions also suggest that the policyholder and insurance company freely negotiated and defined the scope of coverage, and intended to exclude the efficient proximate cause doctrine. Such a position is contrary to the position we have taken in our case law that "[i]nsurance contracts are notoriously complex. . .and border on the status of contracts of adhesion. Under this view the insured and insurer do not stand in *pari causa*, and therefore, the insured's assent to the agreement lacks completeness in relation to that of the insurer." *Bell v. State Farm Mut. Auto. Ins. Co.*, 157 W.Va. 623, 628–29, 207 S.E.2d 147, 150–151 (1974) (citations omitted). As we said in *National Mut. Ins. Co. v. McMahon & Sons, Inc.*, 177 W.Va. 734, 741–42 n. 6, 356 S.E.2d 488, 495–96 n. 6 (1987):

> While this rule may equitably be enforced with regard to a contract negotiated at arm's length between parties of reasonably equivalent bargaining power and signed by each, it would be unfair to apply the general rule in the case of the modern insurance contract. These policies are contracts of adhesion, offered on a take-it-or-leave-it basis, often sight unseen until the premium is paid and accepted, full of complicated, almost mystical, language. "It is generally recognized the insured will not read the detailed, cross-referenced, standardized, mass-produced insurance form, nor understand it if he does." *C & J Fertilizer, Inc. v. Allied Mutual Insurance Co.*, 227 N.W.2d 169, 174 (Iowa 1975); accord, 3 Corbin on Contracts § 559 (1960); Keeton, [*Insurance Law Rights at Variance with Policy Provisions*,] 83 Harv.L.Rev. [961] at 968 [1970]. The majority rule is that the insured is not presumed to know the contents of an adhesion-type insurance policy delivered to him, 7 *Williston on Contracts* § 906 B (1963), and we hereby adopt the majority view.

Allstate and State Farm do not dispute the fact that the plaintiffs' losses were "sudden" and "accidental." Instead, the defendants argue that as a matter of law the insurance carriers cannot be held responsible for the total loss of the plaintiffs' property. The defendants essentially contend that while their policies might cover the actual physical damage to the Murray and Withrow homes, the policies do not cover any losses occasioned by the potential damage that could be caused by future rockfalls.

. . . .

. . .[I]n *Hughes [v. Potomac Ins. Co.*, 199 Cal.App.2d 239, 18 Cal.Rptr. 650 (1st Dist.1962)], the policyholders awoke one morning to discover 30 feet of their backyard had washed into a creek, leaving their home standing on the edge of a newly-formed 30-foot cliff. The landslide deprived the house of subjacent and lateral support essential to the stability of the house. An insurance adjuster concluded that the house sustained only $50.00 in damage, but that the cost of a retaining wall and fill to support the dwelling was $19,000.00. The insurance carrier denied coverage contending its policy only insured the physical damage to the dwelling. The court rejected this argument and found the appellant insurance carrier liable for the entire loss to the use of the property. The court stated:

> To accept appellant's interpretation of its policy would be to conclude that a building which has been overturned or which has been placed in such a position as to overhang a steep cliff has not been "damaged" so long as its paint remains intact and its walls still adhere to one another. Despite the fact that a "dwelling building" might be rendered completely useless to its owners, appellant would deny that any loss or damage had occurred unless some tangible injury to the physical structure itself could be detected. Common sense requires that a policy should not be so interpreted in the absence of a provision specifically limiting coverage in this manner. Respondents correctly point out that a "dwelling" or "dwelling building" connotes a place fit for occupancy, a safe place in which to dwell or live. It goes without question that respondents' "dwelling building" suffered real and severe damage when the soil beneath it slid away and left it overhanging a 30-foot cliff. Until such damage was repaired and the land beneath the building stabilized, the structure could scarcely be considered a "dwelling building" in the sense that rational persons would be content to reside there.

199 Cal.App.2d at 248–49, 18 Cal.Rptr. at 655.

We believe similar reasoning is applicable to the case at hand. The policies in question provide coverage against "sudden and accidental loss" and "accidental direct physical loss" to property. "'Direct physical loss' provisions require only that a covered property be injured, not destroyed. Direct physical loss also may exist in the absence of structural damage to the insured property."

The properties insured by Allstate and State Farm in this case were homes, buildings normally thought of as a safe place in which to dwell or live. It seems undisputed from the record that on February 22, 1994 all three of the plaintiffs' homes became unsafe for habitation, and therefore suffered real damage when it became clear that rocks and boulders could come crashing down at any time. The record suggests that until the highwall on defendant Harris' property is stabilized, the plaintiffs' houses could scarcely be considered "homes" in the sense that rational persons would be content to reside there.

We therefore hold that an insurance policy provision providing coverage for a "sudden and accidental loss" or an "accidental direct physical loss" to insured property requires only that the property be damaged, not destroyed. Losses covered by the policy, including those rendering the insured property unusable or uninhabitable, may exist in the absence of structural damage to the insured property.

IV.

Conclusion

We reverse the circuit court's summary judgment ruling that found as a matter of law that coverage existed under the Allstate and State Farm policies. Because we find substantial questions of material fact in the record concerning the existence of coverage, we remand the case for further proceedings to determine whether the plaintiffs sustained a loss, and whether that loss was proximately caused by the covered risk of third-party negligence, or proximately caused by the excluded natural events of a landslide or erosion.

Reversed and remanded.

[Appendices supplied by the court omitted.]

. . . .

NOTES

1. *Different judicial views.* The court in *Murray* candidly acknowledged that its views on causation (and interpretation of the specific text) were not followed by all courts. One of the cases cited by the court, *State Farm Fire and Casualty Co. v. Bongen,* 925 P.2d 1042 (Alaska 1996), takes the opposite view on almost every issue considered in *Murray.* As a homeowner contemplating the purchase of insurance, which approach would you prefer govern the policy you purchase?

2. *Reasonable expectations revisited.* West Virginia follows (or at least followed in the principal case) the "strong form" of the reasonable expectations doctrine. See § 3.02[4], *supra.* Would the case have been decided differently if West Virginia adhered to the "weak form" of the doctrine?

3. *Automobiles and causation.* As discussed in more detail in § 6.05, *infra,* there are two different types of automobile property insurance. *Collision* insurance is for losses caused by collision, with exclusions for loss caused by fire, theft, hail, windstorm, vandalism, flood, etc. *Comprehensive* insurance is for loss caused by perils other than collisions. In theory, the coverages dovetail; if an insured has both kinds of insurance, which is often the case, a loss resulting from concurrent causes raises no coverage question—one of

the kinds of insurance covers the loss, even if it is hard to determine which one.

The situation changes if an insured has collision or comprehensive coverage, but not both, and a loss is caused by multiple causes. Suppose, for example, while the insured is driving the covered vehicle, a sudden hailstorm smashes out the windshield; this causes the driver to lose control of the vehicle and hit a tree. The windshield can be replaced under the comprehensive coverage; but is the damage to the rest of the vehicle covered under the comprehensive or the collision coverage? If a conservative (or perhaps even a middle-ground) approach to causation is followed, the exclusion for hail damage may take the entire loss outside of the collision coverage. Under the comprehensive coverage, there is also a question whether the hailstorm was the proximate cause of all of the loss. If the insured has either collision or comprehensive coverage but not both, the answers to these difficult questions are important. *See, e.g., Western Leasing, Inc. v. Occidental Fire & Casualty Co.,* 268 Or. 426, 521 P.2d 352 (1974); *Providence Washington Ins. Co. v. Proffitt,* 150 Tex. 207, 239 S.W.2d 379 (1951); *Mammina v. Homeland Insurance Co.,* 371 Ill. 555, 21 N.E.2d 726 (1939); *Fogarty v. Fidelity & Casualty Co.,* 122 Conn. 245, 188 A. 481 (1936); *Gargallo v. Nationwide General Insurance Co.,* 598 N.E.2d 1219 (Ohio Ct. App. 1991); *Allison v. Iowa Mutual Insurance Co.* 258 S.E.2d 489 (N.C. Ct. App. 1979).

4. *Other situations.* The causation issue can arise in virtually endless other situations, implicating all kinds of property, personal, and liability coverages. *See, e.g., SCAC Transp. (USA) Inc. v. Atlantic Mutual Insurance Co.,* 652 F. Supp. 1091 (S.D.N.Y. 1987) (cargo, partially damaged by covered risks of bad stacking and vandalism, is confiscated by Iranian Customs Authority, an excluded risk); *Lorenzo v. State Farm Fire & Casualty Co.* 736 P.2d 51 (Haw. 1987) (considering whether insured's work loss benefits under no-fault auto insurance could be withdrawn when insured suffers disabling heart attack unrelated to prior auto accident); *Orman v. Prudential Insurance Co. of Am.,* 296 N.W.2d 380 (Minn. 1980) (insured under accidental death policy suffers non-fatal brain hemorrhage, which causes her to lose consciousness, which causes her to fall in bathtub, where she drowns).

5. *The last word?* Should legislatures intervene and draft statutes that resolve causation issues once and for all? If so, if you were a member of the legislature, how would you draft the statute? How would you ensure that your draft would have broad support from insurers, consumers, and regulators?

[4]   Trigger of Coverage in Progressive Loss Situations

PRUDENTIAL-LMI COMMERCIAL INSURANCE v. SUPERIOR COURT

51 Cal. 3d 674, 798 P.2d 1230, 274 Cal. Rptr. 387 (1990)

Lucas, Chief Justice.

Petitioner Prudential-LMI Commercial Insurance (Prudential) and real parties in interest (plaintiffs), each seek review of a Court of Appeal decision issuing a writ of mandate directing summary judgment in favor of Prudential. The action involves progressive property damage to an apartment house owned by plaintiffs and insured over the years by successive insurers, including Prudential. We granted review to address three issues: (i) when does the standard one-year limitation period (hereafter one-year suit provision) contained in all fire policies (pursuant to Ins. Code, § 2071)[1] begin to run in a progressive property damage case; (ii) should a rule of equitable tolling be imposed to postpone the running of the one-year suit provision from the date notice of loss is given to the insurer until formal denial of the claim; and, (iii) when there are successive insurers, who is responsible for indemnifying the insured for a covered loss when the loss is not discovered until several years after it commences? The last issue can be resolved by placing responsibility on (a) the insurer insuring the risk at the time the damage began, (b) the insurer insuring the risk at the time the damage manifested itself, or (c) all insurers on the risk, under an allocation (or exposure) theory of recovery.

. . . .

As we explain further below, we emphasize that our holding is limited in application to the first party progressive property loss cases in the context of a homeowner's insurance policy. As we recognized in *Garvey v. State Farm Fire & Casualty Co.* (1989) 48 Cal. 3d 395, 405–408, 257 Cal. Rptr. 292, 770 P.2d 704, there are substantial analytical differences between first party property policies and third party liability policies. Accordingly, we intimate no view as to the application of our decision in either the third party liability or commercial liability (including toxic tort) context.

BACKGROUND

1. *The Policy*

Plaintiffs, as trustees of a family trust, built an apartment house in 1970-1971 and insured it with four successive fire and extended coverage property insurers between 1971 and 1986. Prudential insured the risk between October 27, 1977, and October 27, 1980. It issued an all-risk homeowner's policy which insured against "ALL RISKS OF DIRECT PHYSICAL LOSS except as hereinafter excluded." . . . .

. . . .

The policy contained several standard provisions adopted from the "California Standard Form Fire Insurance Policy" and section 2071, entitled "Requirements in case loss occurs." The provisions in relevant part required the insured to: "give written notice. . .without unnecessary delay, protect the property from further damage. . .and within 60 days after the loss, unless such time is extended in writing by this company, the insured shall render to this company a proof of loss, signed and sworn to by the insured, stating the knowledge and belief of the insured as to the following: the time and origin of the loss, [and] the interest of the insured and all others in the property. . . ."

. . . .

Plaintiffs' policy also contained the standard one-year suit provision first adopted by the Legislature in 1909 as part of the "California Standard Form

---

[1] All further statutory references are to the Insurance Code unless otherwise noted.

Fire Insurance Policy." (See §§ 2070, 2071.) It provided: "No suit or action on this policy for the recovery of any claim shall be sustainable in any court of law or equity unless all the requirements of this policy shall have been complied with, and unless commenced within 12 months next after inception of the loss." With this background in mind, we turn to the facts underlying this claim.

2. *The Facts*

While replacing the floor covering in an apartment unit in November 1985, plaintiffs discovered an extensive crack in the foundation and floor slab of the building. In December 1985, they filed a claim with their brokers who immediately notified Prudential and the other companies that had issued insurance policies on the property during plaintiffs' period of ownership. Prudential conducted an investigation of the claim, which included an examination under oath of plaintiffs in February 1987. Prudential concluded the crack was caused by expansive soil that caused stress, rupturing the foundation of the building. In August 1987, shortly before receiving formal written notice that their claim had been denied under the policy's earth movement exclusion, plaintiffs sued Prudential, the four other insurers that had insured the property between 1971 and 1986, and their insurance brokers or agents, alleging theories of breach of contract, bad faith, breach of fiduciary duties and negligence.

Prudential sought summary judgment,. . .contending there was no evidence any loss was suffered during its policy period and hence it could not be required to indemnify plaintiffs. Prudential observed that carpeting had been installed in 1982, covering the area later damaged, but asserted that at the time of installation (nearly two years after Prudential's coverage had ended), plaintiffs observed no damage or evidence of cracking. Prudential also claimed that because plaintiffs filed suit 20 months after filing their claim, the action was barred by the standard one-year suit provision contained in its policy, pursuant to section 2071.

The court denied the motion in its entirety, stating that triable issues existed as to whether. . .the damage occurred during the policy period, and when the crack first appeared. Prudential sought a writ of mandate to review the denial of the motion, arguing only that the action was time-barred because plaintiffs failed to comply with the policy's notice-of-claim requirement and one-year suit provision.

The Court of Appeal issued a peremptory writ of mandate directing the trial court to vacate its order denying the insurer's summary judgment motion and to enter another order granting the relief requested. In so holding, the court adopted a "delayed discovery" rule: The one-year suit provision begins to run when damage to property is sufficient to put a reasonable person on notice of the possibility of property loss. It determined that a delayed discovery rule must be applied to the policy requirement that a claim be made without unnecessary delay. The court explained that to rule otherwise would require claimants to pursue their rights under the policy even if still "blamelessly ignorant" of the objective facts underlying the claim.

Thus, the policy requirement of notice of loss without unnecessary delay, and the further provision calling for the commencement of suit within 12 months from the "inception of the loss," were relaxed in cases of continuous and progressive loss by the application of a delayed discovery rule. The court based its reasoning on the fact that progressive property loss can occur and cause damage long before its discovery by the insured.

After adopting the delayed discovery rule, however, the Court of Appeal held that plaintiffs were nonetheless too late in filing their action under the one-year suit provision. The court explained that although factual issues remained unresolved as to whether plaintiffs' failure to earlier discover the damage to the property was reasonable, the issue need not be resolved because plaintiffs failed to bring their action on the policy within the limitations period of 12 months after "a reasonable person" would have been placed on notice of property damage.

Next, the Court of Appeal noted that in property cases involving progressive loss, the period over which the damage took place may have occurred within one or several policy periods. The court reasoned that because it is often difficult to detect progressive property loss and such damage may occur over several policy periods without detection, equity demands an apportionment of damages between those insurers on the risk during the entire period the damage progressed. The court discussed two cases we examine further below: *Home Ins. Co. v. Landmark Ins. Co.,* (1988) 205 Cal. App. 3d 1388, 253 Cal. Rptr. 277 (*Home Ins. Co.*), and *California Union Ins. Co. v. Landmark Ins. Co.* (1983) 145 Cal. App. 3d 462, 193 Cal. Rptr. 461 (*California Union Ins. Co.*). As stated above, both plaintiffs and Prudential seek review on the one-year suit provision and successive insurer issues. . . .

DISCUSSION

[The court held, after discussing the issue at length, that the one-year suit provision begins to run on the date of the "inception of the loss," defined as "that point in time when appreciable damage occurs and is or should be known to the insured, such that a reasonable insured would be aware that his notification duty under the policy has been triggered." It also held that this limitation period should be equitably tolled from the time the insured files a timely notice, pursuant to policy notice provisions, to the time the insurer formally denies the claim in writing. (These issues will be examined in a subsequent chapter dealing with the requirements for processing insurance claims. See § 8.01[3], *infra.*) The court then went on to address the trigger issue in first-party property damage cases.]

. . . .

5. *Progressive Loss Rule*

We next examine allocation of indemnity between successive first party property insurers when the loss is continuous and progressive throughout successive policy periods, but is not discovered until it becomes appreciable, for a reasonable insured to be aware that his notification duty under the policy has been triggered. Although the Court of Appeal here held that plaintiffs' claim was time-barred under section 2071, it observed in dictum that apportionment of damages between all insurers who insured the risk during the time of the development of the injury would be the "equitable result." The court based its reasoning on a line of cases applying the "continuous exposure theory" of loss allocation, which apportions payment between those insurers whose policies insured the risk during the period from the date when damage first occurred to the date of its discovery by the insured.

The foregoing theory was first announced in the context of a third party construction defect case (*Gruol Construction Co. v. Insurance Co. of North America* (1974) 11 Wash. App. 632, 524 P.2d 427), and more recently found application in cases involving asbestos bodily injury. (*Ins. Co. North America v. Forty-Eight Insulations* (6th Cir. 1980) 633 F.2d 1212; *Keene Corp. v. Ins. Co. of North America* (D.C. Cir. 1981) 667 F.2d 1034.) In 1983, the Court of Appeal relied on these cases to conclude that apportionment of liability among successive insurers was the only equitable method for determining which carrier should pay in a third party property damage case, when the loss (leakage from a swimming pool) continued over two separate policy periods. (*California Union Ins. Co., supra,* 145 Cal. App. 3d 462, 193 Cal. Rptr. 461.)

Prudential argues that even assuming the applicable one-year suit provision does not bar suit, it should not be responsible for any covered loss, because plaintiffs presented no evidence that a loss was suffered during the period of its policy term (October 27, 1977, to October 27, 1980). It also asserts that because its policy period ended in 1980—five years before the damage was allegedly discovered by plaintiffs — it should not be responsible for indemnification of any covered loss. Prudential asks the court to adopt a "manifestation rule" of property coverage that fixes liability for first party property losses solely on the insurer whose policy was in force at the time the progressive damage became appreciable or "manifest." (*See Home Ins. Co., supra,* 205 Cal. App. 3d 1388, 253 Cal. Rptr. 277.) In discussing both the manifestation and continuous exposure theories, we keep in mind the important distinction that must be made in a causation analysis between first party property damage cases and third party liability cases. (*Garvey v. State Farm Fire & Casualty Co., supra,* 48 Cal. 3d 395 at p. 406, 257 Cal. Rptr. 292, 770 P.2d 704.)

The Manifestation and Exposure Theories

The first case to discuss a manifestation theory in the first party property context was *Snapp v. State Farm Fire & Cas. Co.* (1962) 206 Cal. App. 2d 827, 831–832, 24 Cal. Rptr. 44 (*Snapp*). The *Snapp* court was called on to resolve the insurer's contention that its homeowner's policy did not cover a loss to the insured residence resulting from the movement of unstable fill. The homeowner's policy was written by State Farm for a three-year term commencing in 1956 and consisted of the "California Standard Form Fire Insurance Policy" and an endorsement extending the coverage to insure against property loss.

The loss "materialized" and thus became "ascertainable" during State Farm's policy period and continued to progress after the policy term expired. State Farm first argued that because the instability of the fill made the resulting earth movement "inevitable," the loss was not a "fortuitous" event, and hence not covered under the policy. State Farm relied, in part, on sections 22 and 250, which codify the "loss-in-progress rule" and provide that an insurance contract indemnifies only against contingent or unknown events

(§ 22), and any such contingent or unknown event may be insured against subject to the limitations of the Insurance Code (§ 250).[7]

The court rejected this argument, however, and held that although the loss may have been "inevitable," such inevitability did not alter the fact that "at the time the contract of insurance was entered into, the event was only a *contingency* or *risk* that might or might not occur within the term of the policy." [italics in original].

State Farm next asserted that even assuming it was responsible for the loss, its liability became "terminable" on the date its policy expired and therefore it was not liable for the "continuing damage or loss" after expiration. In rejecting State Farm's argument, the *Snapp* court noted that the question of whether the insurer was liable for the loss was a legal rather than factual issue. The court held, "[t]o permit the insurer to terminate its liability while the fortuitous peril which materialized during the term of the policy was still active would not be in accord either with applicable precedents or with the common understanding of the nature and purpose of insurance; it would allow an injustice to be worked upon the insured by defeating the very substance of the protection for which his premiums were paid." Thus the court determined, "once the contingent event insured against has occurred during the period covered, the liability of the carrier becomes contractual rather than potential only, and the sole issue remaining is the sole extent of its obligation, and it is immaterial that this may not be fully ascertained at the end of the policy period." The court concluded the date of "materialization" of a loss determines which carrier must provide indemnity for a loss suffered by the insured, and the carrier insuring the risk at the time the damage is first discovered is liable for the entire loss.

Next, in *Sabella v. Wisler* (1963) 59 Cal. 2d 21, 25, 27 Cal. Rptr. 689, 377 P.2d 889 (*Sabella*), the insurer claimed that damage to the insured's residence was not fortuitous and thus not covered because "the damage occurred as a result of the operation of forces inherent" in the underlying soil conditions (including uncompacted fill and defective workmanship in the installation of a sewer outflow that ultimately broke). *Sabella* rejected the insurer's contention that the loss was "not fortuitous and hence not a 'risk' properly the subject of insurance." Relying on *Snapp*, *Sabella* held that even if it were inevitable that the damage would have occurred at some time during ownership of the house, the loss was covered because such loss was a contingency or risk at the time the parties entered into the policy.

The next California case to address the problems arising in progressive property damage cases presented the issue of which carrier should indemnify insureds for a loss that occurred over two separate policy periods. In *California Union Ins. Co., supra,* 145 Cal. App. 3d 462, 193 Cal. Rptr. 461, a third party liability insurance case, the insureds installed a swimming pool during

---

[7] The loss-in-progress rule codifies a fundamental principle of insurance law that an insurer cannot insure against a loss that is known or apparent to the insured. The public policy rule is premised on the view that: To hold the insurer liable for a progressive and continuing property loss that was discovered before the carrier insured the risk "would be to impose upon the insurer a guaranty of the good quality of the [property insured] . . ., which liability under the policy the insurer had not assumed."

Landmark Insurance Company's policy period. The pipes to the pool (and possibly the pool itself) began to leak during Landmark's policy period and continued to leak during the term of the subsequent insurer, California Union. Repairs which the parties believed corrected the leakage were made during Landmark's policy term. Nonetheless, because the underlying cause of the damage had not been discovered, the repairs were ineffective and additional damage occurred after California Union insured the risk.

Because the case involved liability policies, the Court of Appeal relied on three out-of-state liability cases that had apportioned payment between successive insurers when the damage or injury had continued during the separate policy periods. One case involved construction damage (*Gruol Construction Co. v. Insurance Co. of North America, supra,* 11 Wash. App. 632, 524 P.2d 427), and the others involved asbestos related bodily injury (*Ins. Co. of North America v. Forty-Eight Insulations, supra,* 633 F.2d 1212; *Keene Corp. v. Ins. Co. of North America, supra,* 667 F.2d 1034).

The *California Union Ins. Co.* court determined that it was faced with a "one occurrence" case, involving continuous, progressive and deteriorating damage, notwithstanding the fact that new damage occurred to the pool after certain repairs had been made, and held both insurers jointly and severally liable for the damages. It reasoned that in a third party liability case "involving continuous, progressive and deteriorating damage," the carrier insuring the risk when the damage first becomes apparent remains responsible for indemnifying the loss until the damage is complete, notwithstanding a policy provision which purports to limit coverage to losses occurring within the parameters of the policy term. (*See* Hook, *Multiple Policy Period Losses and Liability Under First Party Policies* (1985) Tort & Ins. L.J. 393, 395 [hereafter Hook].)

In *Home Ins. Co.,* the sole issue was "which of two first party insurers is liable for the loss from continuing property damage manifested during successive policy periods."[8] Home insured the Hotel del Coronado against property damage for the period September 1, 1980, through October 1, 1986. The concrete facade of portions of the structure "first began to visibly manifest deterioration in the form of. . .'spalling' (cracking and chipping)" in or about December of 1980. The spalling continued after it was first discovered by the insured and became progressively worse over time, extending through the expiration of Home's coverage and the inception of the Landmark policy. Although the damage was initially discovered in the first of the two policy periods, and continued through both policy periods, apparently it was impossible to determine the extent of damage occurring during each period, and thus the amount of coverage owed by each insurer could not be determined. In a subsequent declaratory relief action, the trial court determined that under the manifestation and loss-in-progress rules, Home was solely at risk.

---

[8] *Home Ins. Co.,* , was decided before *Garvey v. State Farm Fire & Casualty Co., supra,* 48 Cal. 3d 395, 406, 257 Cal. Rptr. 292, 770 P.2d 704, and thus did not distinguish between policy language used in the first or third party context. As noted by the present Court of Appeal (the same court that decided *Home Ins. Co.*), the distinction is an important one. The Court of Appeal herein thus noted that *Home Ins. Co.* must be limited to its facts because, in failing to distinguish between first and third party issues, it was admittedly "not a case for all purposes."

The Court of Appeal affirmed, holding that the "date of manifestation determines which carrier must provide indemnity for a loss suffered by its insured." (*Home Ins. Co., supra,* 205 Cal. App. 3d at p. 1392, 253 Cal. Rptr. 277.) The court rejected Home's reliance on *California Union, supra,* 145 Cal. App. 3d 462, 193 Cal. Rptr. 461, for the proposition that the loss-in-progress rule is inapplicable to claims for continuing and progressive property damage. . . . . Thus, the *Home Ins. Co.* court reasoned, *California Union* should not be applied to the property damage case before the court. Accordingly, the court held that "as between two first party insurers, one of which is on the risk on the date of first manifestation of property damage, and the other on the risk after the date of the first manifestation of damage, the first insurer must pay the entire claim."

Because *California Union Ins. Co.* addressed a third party liability question, its analysis necessarily differed in many respects from the one we undertake here. As one court observed, in first party cases applying the rule finding coverage only on actual occurrence of injury, no damage or injury of any kind has taken place until manifestation; the cause instead lies dormant until it later causes appreciable injury. (*Ins. Co. of North America v. Forty-Eight Insulations, supra,* 633 F.2d 1212, 1222, fn. 18.) By contrast, when damages slowly accumulate, the exposure theory should apply. As Hook observes, "The issue of continuous and progressive losses has not arisen frequently in the context of first party cases (perhaps because homeowner's policies were [originally drafted] to cover only sudden damage such as fire and windstorm, and not gradual damage such as settlement)." (Hook, *supra,* at p. 398.) Other commentators have warned against confusing first and third party issues. "Applying the terminology that has grown up around bodily injury [liability] insurance coverage cases in the context of coverage for property damage implies that the considerations are identical and obscures the real differences between the two types of problems." (Arness & Eliason, *Insurance Coverage for Property Damage in Asbestos and Other Toxic Tort Cases* (1986) 72 Va. L. Rev. 943, 973, fn. 108.) Accordingly, and because the issue of whether an allocation or exposure theory should apply in the third party property damage liability context is not before the court, we leave its resolution to another date.

As stated by the *Home Ins. Co.* court, the manifestation rule in the first party context "promotes certainty in the insurance industry and allows insurers to gauge premiums with greater accuracy. Presumably this should reduce costs for consumers because insurers will be able to set aside proper reserves for well-defined coverages and avoid increasing such reserves to cover potential financial losses caused by uncertainty in the definition of coverage."

Based on the reasoning set forth in *Snapp, Sabella* and *Home Ins. Co.,* we conclude that in first party progressive property loss cases, when, as in the present case, the loss occurs over several policy periods and is not discovered until several years after it commences, the manifestation rule applies. As stated above, prior to the manifestation of damage, the loss is still a contingency under the policy and the insured has not suffered a compensable loss. (*Snapp, supra,* 206 Cal. App. 2d at pp. 831–832, 24 Cal. Rptr. 44.) Once the loss is manifested, however, the risk is no longer contingent; rather an event has occurred that triggers indemnity unless such event is specifically excluded under the policy terms. Correspondingly, in conformity with the loss-in-progress rule, insurers whose policy terms commence after initial manifestation of the loss are not responsible for any potential claim relating to the previously discovered and manifested loss. Under this rule, the reasonable expectations of the insureds are met because they look to their present carrier for coverage. At the same time the underwriting practices of the insurer can be made predictable because the insurer is not liable for a loss once its contract with the insured ends unless the manifestation of loss occurred during its contract term.

One final question must be addressed regarding the application of a manifestation rule of coverage in progressive loss cases: how does the rule relate to our rules of delayed discovery and equitable tolling announced above? We have previously defined the term "inception of the loss" as that point in time when appreciable damage occurs and is or should be known to the insured, such that a reasonable insured would be aware that his notification duty under the policy has been triggered. We conclude that the definition of "manifestation of the loss" must be the same. Under this standard, the date of manifestation and hence the date of inception of the loss will, in many cases, be an issue of fact for the jury to decide. When, however, the evidence supports only one conclusion, summary judgment may be appropriate. For example, when the undisputed evidence establishes that no damage had been discovered before a given date (i.e., no manifestation occurred), then insurers whose policies expired prior to that date could not be liable for the loss and would be entitled to summary judgment. The litigation can then be narrowed to include only the insurers whose policies were in effect when the damage became manifest.

CONCLUSION

Based on the principles discussed above, we conclude plaintiffs should be allowed to amend their complaint to allege that their delayed discovery of the loss at issue was reasonable, and that they timely notified Prudential of the loss without unnecessary delay following its manifestation. If it is found that plaintiffs' delayed discovery of the loss was reasonable, then the rule of equitable tolling would operate to toll the one-year suit provision from the date the insured filed a timely notice of loss to Prudential's formal denial of coverage. Whether Prudential must then indemnify plaintiffs for any covered claim under the policy necessarily depends on whether that insurer was the carrier of record on the date of manifestation of the loss. Although it appears from the present record that manifestation of loss occurred in November 1985, after Prudential's policy had expired, we note that plaintiffs have joined other insurers in the litigation. Therefore, in the absence of conclusive evidence, we decline to speculate concerning the date manifestation of loss occurred. The decision of the Court of Appeal is reversed and the cause remanded for proceedings consistent with our opinion.

MOSK, BROUSSARD, PANELLI, EAGLESON, KENNARD and ARABIAN, JJ., concur.

NOTES

1. *"Trigger" issue.* One of the issues addressed in *Prudential-LMI* is commonly referred to as the "trigger of coverage" issue. Essentially, the inquiry involves the question of what has to take place during any particular policy period to actuate the insurer's obligations under the contract. If the insurer's obligation in *Prudential-LMI* was to indemnify the insured for property damage caused by fire and the apartment house was damaged by fire on January 1, 1979, would there be any problem in deciding which policy was triggered? So what was the source of the difficulty under the actual facts and the prior court decisions in the case?

2. *Trigger test in progressive harm cases.* In a case involving progressive damage under a first-party property damage policy, as the court points out, the trigger issue could be resolved in at least three different ways. The test could be one of (1) when the damage actually begins to take place, (2) when the damage is discovered or should have been discovered, or (3) a combination of the first two, in which case one would focus on the period from the time damage began through the time the damage is or should have been discovered. Do you agree with the court's choice of trigger in *Prudential-LMI*?

3. *Trigger for different purposes?* Would it be logical in a progressive injury case to have one trigger — say the second choice—for notice and the one-year suit provision and a different trigger—say the first or third choice—for determining which insurer or insurers have to indemnify the insured?

4. *First-party versus third-party coverage.* The *Prudential-LMI* court makes it quite clear that the trigger adopted for a first-party property damage policy may not be appropriate for a third-party (liability) policy. Why would there be any need to consider a different trigger in the latter situation? This question will receive further attention in § 5.02[2][c], *infra*.

[5] Jointly Owned Property and Illegal Acts of Co-insured

KULUBIS v. TEXAS FARM BUREAU UNDERWRITERS INSURANCE CO.

706 S.W.2d 953 (Tex. 1986)

WALLACE, JUSTICE.

This is a suit on a fire insurance policy. Betty Kulubis sued Texas Farm Bureau Underwriters Insurance Company for the proceeds of a policy after her estranged husband intentionally burned the couple's mobile home. The trial court rendered judgment for Texas Farm and the court of appeals, with one justice dissenting, affirmed that judgment. 699 S.W.2d 287. We reverse the judgment of the court of appeals and render judgment for Betty Kulubis.

Betty and John Kulubis were married in 1971. Her parents subsequently gave them a mobile home upon which they purchased a homeowners insurance policy from Texas Farm. Both Betty and John were named insureds in the policy. In 1982, Betty filed suit for divorce. After being served with the divorce citation, John set fire to the mobile home, destroying it and all of the personal property inside. He then unsuccessfully attempted suicide. It is uncontroverted that Betty had no knowledge of nor did she participate in the destruction of the mobile home.

The court of appeals denied recovery to Betty based upon *Jones v. Fidelity & Guaranty Insurance Co.,* 250 S.W.2d 281 (Tex. Civ. App.—Waco 1952, writ ref'd). Betty asks us to reconsider the holding in *Jones* inasmuch as a majority of the states that have addressed the issue have abandoned that rule and now permit recovery under the facts of this case.

The *Jones* decision was based upon a holding that co-insureds under an insurance policy covering jointly owned property acquire joint rights and obligations under the policy. Therefore, the illegal acts of one of the co-insureds prevent recovery by the other co-insured. At the time this court adopted the *Jones* rule it was the traditional rule in the United States. The *Jones* court cited *Monaghan v. Agricultural Fire Insurance Co.,* 53 Mich. 238, 18 N.W. 797 (1884); *Kosior v. Continental Insurance Co.,* 299 Mass. 601, 13 N.E.2d 423 (1938); *Bowers Co. v. London Assurance Corp.,* 90 Pa. Super. 121 (1926); and *Bellman v. Home Insurance Co.,* 178 Wis. 349, 189 N.W. 1028 (1922).

In 1942, the New Hampshire Supreme Court first permitted recovery by a co-insured in Betty Kulubis' position. *Hoyt v. New Hampshire Fire Insurance Co.,* 29 A.2d 121, 92 N.H. 242 (1942). That court reasoned that the proper test to be applied was what a reasonable person would have understood the fire insurance policy to mean. The court then held that an innocent victim of a co-insured's illegal act in destroying the jointly owned property would reasonably expect to be covered by the policy.

Between 1974 and 1985, sixteen other states adopted the test set out in *Hoyt.* We note that of the four jurisdictions relied on in *Jones,* two of them have adopted the test in *Hoyt,* and a third, Pennsylvania, has questioned the rule.

We will examine the reasoning supporting the *Jones* decision along with the reasoning of those jurisdictions which have rejected the *Jones* rule to determine if this court will continue to follow *Jones.* As stated above, the basis of *Jones* was that fraudulent losses are generally excepted from coverage of fire insurance contracts upon the grounds of public policy and morals. *Jones* at 281–82. Put another way, public policy dictates that a wrongdoer should not benefit from his wrongdoing. This led the court to hold that a joint owner who illegally destroys property could not benefit from his illegal act and, because his co-owner/co-insured was mutually obligated under the policy, the innocent victim of the illegal destruction was also barred from recovery. *Id.* at 282.

The reasoning adopted by the states that follow the *Hoyt* rule is also based on public policy. In *Morgan v. Cincinnati Insurance Co.,* 411 Mich. 267, 307 N.W.2d 53 (1981), the Michigan Supreme Court, in overruling *Monaghan,* held that public policy requires that an innocent co-insured be permitted to recover based upon the insured's reasonable expectations. The Wisconsin Supreme Court in *Hedtcke v. Sentry Insurance Co.,* 109 Wis. 2d 461, 326 N.W.2d 727 (1982), in overruling *Bellman,* also followed the policy of not punishing the innocent victim for the wrongs of another.

Other policy considerations we must consider are: (1) prevention of fraud upon the insurance company; (2) prevention of unjust enrichment by the insurance company; and (3) refusal to impute the criminal acts of the wrongdoer to an innocent victim.

We hold the more enlightened reasoning dictates that the illegal destruction of jointly owned property by one co-insured shall not bar recovery under an insurance policy by an innocent co-insured. A trial court is uniquely situated to make the determination of the co-insured's innocence, and, unless there is a finding of lack of innocence, the co-insured shall be permitted to recover.

We hold that this test will best protect the insurance company from fraud while assuring that the insurance company will not be unjustly enriched. It will also permit an innocent victim whose property has been destroyed to collect under an insurance policy for a loss reasonably expected to be covered. This test also avoids the imputation of criminal action to an innocent victim.

Texas courts are faced with an additional problem in this situation because we are a community property state. It is not necessary for us to address that particular problem at this time inasmuch as the mobile home in question was a gift to Betty and John and as such an undivided one-half interest was the separate property of each of them. We are not to be understood as holding that an innocent spouse is barred from recovering under an insurance policy covering community property. We do not have that fact situation before us and therefore do not address the problem of how to compensate the innocent spouse and yet not permit benefit to the wrongdoing spouse. That problem will be addressed when and if it is presented to us.

In this case, Betty Kulubis was the owner of a one-half interest in the mobile home and the personal property which was destroyed by her husband. She is therefore entitled to recover one-half of the stipulated amount of the loss of $21,000 plus prejudgment and post-judgment interest as well as attorney's fees as found by the trial court.

The judgment of the court of appeals is reversed and judgment is rendered for Betty Kulubis.

NOTES

1. *Erosion of old rule.* As pointed out in *Kulubis,* there was a time when courts refused to permit any recovery in a case where one co-insured commits fraud or intentionally destroys the insured property. This was based primarily on one of two reasons: (1) the property was owned by the co-insureds in an indivisible manner or (2) the wrongdoing of one co-insured should be imputed to an innocent co-insured. The first worked to deny coverage where the property was held in joint tenancy, tenancy by the entireties, or as community property because there was, according to the courts, an indivisible obligation

on the part of the insureds not to violate the policy. The second reason could be invoked to prevent a co-insured from benefitting from another co-insured's wrongdoing, for example, where they were married. More recently courts have been persuaded that the claim of an innocent co-insured should not be so easily defeated and have rejected the idea that the manner in which the property is held or that imputation of fault should provide the governing rule. *See, e.g., Howell v. Ohio Casualty Insurance Co.,* 124 N.J. Super. 414, 307 A.2d 142 (1973); *Error v. Western Home Insurance Co.,* 762 P.2d 1077 (Utah 1988).

2. *A more technical approach.* In rejecting the old rule, some courts, for the reasons relied on in *Kulubis,* have employed an analysis that favors coverage for the innocent co-insured, unless the policy clearly prohibits coverage. Other courts have employed a more technical approach by closely examining the policy language to determine the rights of the parties. For example, the New York Standard Fire Policy (1943 edition), see Appendix A, provides:

> This entire policy shall be void if, whether before or after a loss, *the* insured has wilfully concealed or misrepresented any material fact or circumstance concerning this insurance or the subject thereof, or the interest of *the* insured therein, or in case of any fraud or false swearing by *the* insured relating thereto.
>
> . . . .
>
> This Company shall not be liable for loss by fire or other perils insured against in this policy caused, directly or indirectly, by:. . .neglect of *the* insured to use all reasonable means to save and preserve the property at and after a loss. [Emphasis added.]

The technical approach has led to somewhat different interpretations, but not always to different results. Some courts have read the reference to "the" insured to be an expression of intent by the legislature, in adopting the standard form, to protect innocent co-insureds from the loss of coverage because of policy violations by a co-insured. *See, e.g., Morgan v. Cincinnati Insurance Co.,* 411 Mich. 267, 307 N.W.2d 53 (1981); *Hogs Unlimited v. Farm Bureau Mutual Insurance Co.,* 401 N.W.2d 381 (Minn. 1981). Other courts have concluded that the language is ambiguous in that it is not clear whether the rights and obligations of the insureds are joint or several under the policy. Thus, they also construe the policy language in favor of the innocent co-insured. *See, e.g., Steigler v. Insurance Co. of North America,* 384 A.2d 398 (Del. 1978).

3. *Insurers' reactions.* The rejection of the old rule denying coverage caused some insurers to change the policy language to refer to "an" or "any" insured, instead of "the" insured, to make it clear that the wrongful conduct of any insured would defeat coverage for all insureds unless other policy provisions prevented this result. With this change, some insurers have been successful in defeating coverage, as the plain language then denies coverage to the innocent co-insured. *See, e.g., Utah Farm Bureau Insurance Co. v. Crook,* 980 P.2d 685 (Utah 1999); *Noland v. Farmers Ins. Co.,* 892 S.W.2d 271 (Ark. 1995); *Tyler v. Fireman's Fund Insurance Co.,* 841 P.2d 538 (Mont. 1992); *Dolcy v. Rhode Island Joint Reinsurance Ass'n,* 589 A.2d 313 (R.I. 1991). Other courts, however, have refused to enforce the new language on the basis that it detracts from the statutorily prescribed coverage under the New York Standard Fire

Policy. *See, e.g., Watson v. United Services Automobile Ass'n,* 566 N.W.2d 683 (Minn. 1997); *Borman v. State Farm Fire & Casualty Co.,* 446 Mich. 482, 521 N.W.2d 266 (1994); *Osbon v. National Union Fire Insurance Co.,* 632 So. 2d 1158 (La. 1994); *Fireman's Fund Insurance Co. v. Dean,* S.E.2d 436 (Ga. App. 1994).

What if the policy language is not prescribed by statute? Is there another basis to argue that an innocent co-insured should still be entitled to recover even if the policy refers to "an" or "any" insured?

4. *Domestic abuse and public policy.* Should insurers be allowed to deny coverage to innocent victims of domestic abuse when a co-insured destroys the jointly owned property? How should "abuse" be defined? See Deborah S. Hellman, *Is Actuarially Fair Insurance Pricing Actually Fair?: A Case Study in Insuring Battered Women,* 32 Harv. C.R.-C.L. L. Rev. 355 (1997).

The NAIC has drafted a series of model acts for victims of domestic abuse for different lines of insurance (*e.g.,* health; life; disability), and one of the models, which was drafted in 1997 and amended in 1998, pertains to property insurance. See *Unfair Discrimination Against Subjects of Abuse in Property and Casualty Insurance Model Act,* in V NAIC, Model Laws, Regulations and Guidelines 898-1 (1999). The model states that it is "unfairly discriminatory" for an insurer to "fail to pay losses arising out of abuse to an innocent first party claimant to the extent of such claimants' legal interest in the covered property if the loss is caused by the intentional act of an insured." A number of states have statutes on domestic abuse, but they vary with respect to lines of insurance affected and many details. Yet it is fair to say that an increasing number of states are enacting statutory "innocent spouse" exceptions to the no coverage rule. *See, e.g.,* Neb. Rev. Stat. § 44-7406 (Michie 2000); Md. Code Ann Ins. § 27-504 (1999); S.D. Codified Laws § 58-18B-27 (Michie 2000); Tex. Ins. Code Ann. art. 21.21-5 (West 2000). To take one example, Wash. Rev. Code § 48.18.550 (2000) authorizes insurers to exclude coverage caused by the intentional or fraudulent act of "an" or "any" insured. However, the exclusion

> shall not apply to deny an insured's otherwise-covered property loss if the property loss is caused by an act of domestic abuse by another insured under the policy, the insured claiming property loss files a police report and cooperates with any law enforcement investigation relating to the act of domestic abuse, and the insured claiming property loss did not cooperate in or contribute to the creation of the property loss.

Of all of the cases involving the intentional destruction of property by a co-insured, the overwhelming majority involve one spouse trying to hurt the other. But this is not the only situation where the issue can arise. Should it make any difference in the result in these cases if the insured property is owned by business partners and one of the co-insured partners commits arson?

5. *Calculating the innocent co-insured's recovery.* What if the mobile home in *Kulubis* had constituted community property? Should the result be any different? *See Texas Farmers Insurance Co. v. Murphy,* 996 S.W.2d 873 (Tex. 1999) (holding that there is no public policy against allowing an innocent

spouse to recover one-half of the policy benefits when community property is intentionally destroyed by other spouse, assuming the contract permits recovery); *Federated American InsuranceCo. v. Strong,* 102 Wash. 2d 665, 689 P.2d 68 (1984) (holding that to the extent the property is community property, the insurer must reimburse the innocent spouse one-half the damages). In other words, if the innocent co-insured's interest in jointly-owned property is to be protected, how is that interest to be valued? For example, with respect to jointly owned property, should the innocent co-insured spouse be compensated at 100 percent of the loss (up to the policy limits)? At 100 percent of the loss up to 50 percent of the policy limits? At 50 percent of the loss up to 100 percent of the policy limits? At 50 percent of the loss up to 50 percent of the policy limits? What public policy does your answer further — making sure arsonists/abusers do not benefit from their crimes, or making sure innocent co-insureds are not punished?

§ 4.06 Marine Insurance

Precisely when and where the commercial practice of insurance began is uncertain, but the roots of commercial insurance must be in the primitive arrangements that developed to deal with the risks of ancient maritime commerce in the Mediterranean and Aegean Seas.* See I James A. Joyce, A Treatise on the Law of Insurance of Every Kind 1–4 (1917). Written evidence of risk-sharing arrangements dates to the maritime practices of the Babylonians, as recorded in the Code of Hammurabi (c. 2250 B.C.E.). The Phaenicians probably inherited and refined these practices (c. 1600-1000 B.C.E.), the Greeks took them to a high degree of sophistication in the maritime law of Rhodes (c. 916 B.C.E.), and the Romans borrowed heavily from Greek practices, as the essential elements of Rhodian law are stated in the Code of Justinian. As ancient as these arrangements are, it is probable that multilateral risk-distribution practices date to whenever the first traders boarded a boat and set off sell their wares in a distant market:

> We must constantly remember that in the old times, for perhaps thousands of years, the merchants or owners of cargo used, almost of course, to sail with their wares from port to port like pedlars. In these little vessels, mostly navigating the Mediterranean or Aegean Sea, where storms quickly spring up and subside, occasions would be frequent where shipwreck could only be averted by lightening the ship of portions of her cargo, a measure which, however beneficial to the rest, might to one man on board mean ruin. His consent to such a sacrifice could only be bought by a promise—first express, then customary and taken for granted—that when, or if, the ship came safe to shore, all who had profited by his loss would pay their share to make it good.

---

* This note is derived from an unpublished manuscript: Robert H. Jerry, II, The Communitarian Values of Insurance (unpub. man., Aug. 30, 1999). © 1999 by the author. Reprinted with permission.

Richard Lowndes, The Law of General Average: English and Foreign 2–3 (4th ed. 1888). These practices, which have survived fundamentally intact to modern times, were predicated on an *ex ante* allocation of the risk of uncertain loss. The mutual benefits of this risk-distribution arrangement were so obvious that it became the functional equivalent of an implied term in all maritime shipping ventures.

Evidence of modern commercial insurance practices can be found at least by the 13th century; by this time, the custom of making mutual contracts of insurance was widespread in the maritime states of Italy. See William R. Vance, Handbook on the Law of Insurance 10–11 (3d ed. 1951). By the 14th and 15th centuries, mutual and nonmutual insurance was understood and practiced throughout Europe; by the 14th century, a commercial practice of insuring maritime risks on a nonmutual basis had developed. See C.F. Trenerry, The Origin and Early History of Insurance 243–82 (1926). The exact details of the evolution from agreements among traders on a voyage to commercial risk transfer and distribution are obscure, but at some point it probably became apparent that pooling the risks of many voyages could more effectively distribute risk than simply pooling the risks among the shippers on one voyage. The emergence of commercial insurance also had something to do with how the ancient merchant financed his trading enterprise. By as early as the fifth and fourth centuries B.C.E., it was common for traders to work primarily with borrowed funds. See Lionel Casson, Ancient Trade and Society 26 (1979). The traders needed money to purchase goods and rent space on a vessel; if they used their own funds for these purposes (and many traders had little), they risked financial ruin if the voyage failed. It was natural, then, to think of using borrowed funds, but the consequences of being unable to pay a useless loan in the event of disaster was severe. In ancient Greece, the trader (or if he did not survive the voyage, his heirs) might become slaves upon the loan's foreclosure. To deal with this problem, the "bottomry loan" arrangement emerged, under which the lender took full responsibility for the loss of the ship or cargo. Such loans were accompanied by very high rates of interest (perhaps as much as 100 percent), but functionally the loan served as both an investment in the business (successful completion of the voyage would promise a handsome return) and insurance against the risk of loss. In other words, the high interest rate reflected the fact that the loan also functioned as both investment and insurance; if the cargo or ship disappeared, was destroyed in a storm, or was captured by pirates, the merchant did not have to repay the loan. At some point, entrepreneurs in the Italian maritime states must have come to realize that the insurance aspects of the bottomry loan could be separated from the loan's investment purpose, and the commercial practice of insurance would be one result of this separation.

The ancient maritime practices, which are the cradle of the modern commercial insurance business, remain quite visible in the modern marine insurance business. The cases which follow provide a brief synopsis of marine coverages for cargoes and vessels, respectively. As the cases suggest, marine insurance policies have several specific provisions which have changed little over the centuries. They now carry with them an extensive body of interpretive law which pours content into the customary provisions.

SHAVER TRANSPORTATION CO. v. TRAVELERS INDEMNITY CO.

481 F. Supp. 892 (D. Or. 1979)

SKOPIL, CIRCUIT JUDGE, Sitting by Designation:

This is an action to recover on a marine cargo policy issued by the defendant, The Travelers Indemnity Company (Travelers). The subject matter of marine insurance claims is "maritime" and within the admiralty jurisdiction of the federal courts.

FACTS

Shaver Transportation Company (Shaver), a barge company, contracted with Weyerhaeuser Company (Weyerhaeuser) to transport caustic soda from Weyerhaeuser plants to a buyer of the soda, GATX. Following the terms of the agreement, Shaver arranged for marine cargo insurance with Travelers. Several different "coverages" were discussed. Shaver decided on Free from Particular Average and "standard perils" provisions supplemented with "specially to cover" clauses.

Shaver loaded the first shipment of caustic soda on one of its barges and transported it to the consignee, GATX. GATX refused delivery. The soda had been contaminated with tallow. It was unfit for GATX's purposes. The parties agreed that contamination occurred as Shaver was loading the caustic soda aboard the barge. The barge had previously carried a load of tallow, and Shaver had not thoroughly cleaned the barge input lines.

The barge was returned to Shaver's dock. The cargo was heated to prevent the caustic soda from solidifying. A report of the contaminated cargo was made to the defendant through its insurance brokers, Johnson and Higgins (J & H). Shortly thereafter J & H notified Shaver that the contamination did not represent a recoverable loss under the defendant's marine open cargo policy.

Shaver continued to store the soda on board the barge. Shaver investigated possible on-shore storage facilities and finally contracted with a chemical salvage company for removal of the liquid. Because of the caustic nature of the cargo, Shaver incurred expenses in storage, including the cost of heating the soda and repair to corroded boilers and pipes. Weyerhaeuser lost the value of the shipment, offset partially by the salvage value. Shaver and Weyerhaeuser notified Travelers that they claimed under the marine cargo insurance policy and tendered abandonment of the cargo to Travelers. Travelers refused the tender and denied liability under the policy.

ISSUES

Although the plaintiffs request recovery under several theories, there is only one major issue in the case:

> Are the losses incurred by the plaintiffs the consequences of an insured event under the marine cargo insurance policy?

If the losses are not insured against, no recovery is possible. If coverage is afforded, I must determine which expenses are covered under the policy.

Plaintiffs have meticulously examined the policy and argue for recovery under several theories.

Theories of Recovery

I. *Recovery Under Perils of the Sea Clause and Free from Particular Average Clause*

The Perils clause,[1] almost identical to ancient perils provisions dating back several hundred years, defines the risks protected by the policy. In addition to a long list of "perils of the sea", the clause concludes with "and all other perils, losses, and misfortunes, that have or shall, come to the hurt, detriment, or damage to the said goods and merchandise". Plaintiff argues that the "forced" disposition of the caustic soda was like jettison (an enumerated peril) and is covered by the concluding language of the clause. That language has been interpreted to include only perils that are similar to the enumerated perils.

Whether or not I conclude the forced disposition was a type of jettison, plaintiffs are unable to show an insurable loss due to jettison. The loss—contamination of the cargo—occurred at the time of loading. The disposition of the cargo caused no loss to plaintiffs but rather an offset against previous losses. Plaintiffs cannot recover under the Perils clause of the policy.

The term "jettison" also appears in the Free from Particular Average clause.[2] If jettison did occur, this clause affords coverage regardless of the amount of cargo damage. However, I find that a jettison did not occur in this instance. Jettison is the act of throwing overboard from a vessel a part of the cargo, in case of extreme danger, to lighten the ship.[3] The orderly unloading and sale of the cargo to a chemical salvage company is not "jettison". Plaintiff cannot recover under the Free from Particular Average clause.

II. *Recovery Under Warehouse-to-Warehouse Clause; Marine Extension Clause; Shore Coverage Clause*

These clauses augment the Perils clause by defining the scope of the coverage intended. However, with the exception of the shore coverage, these clauses do not define the nature of the risks covered by the policy but merely define where physically the coverage extends.

To recover under either the Warehouse-to-Warehouse[4] or the Marine

---

[1] (Clause 39) "Touching the adventures and perils which the said Assurers are contented to bear, and take upon themselves, they are of the seas and inland waters, man of war, fires, enemies, pirates, rovers, assailing thieves, jettisons, letters of mart and countermart, reprisals, taking at sea, arrests, restraints and detainments of all kings, princes of people of what nation, condition or quality soever, barratry of the master and mariners, and all other perils, losses and misfortunes, that have or shall come to the hurt, detriment or damage to the said goods and merchandise, or any part thereof."

[2] (Clause 12B) "Other shipments covered hereunder are insured:

"Free of Particular Average unless caused by the vessel and/or interest insured being stranded, sunk, burst, on fire or in collision with another ship or vessel or with ice or with any substance other than water, but liable for jettison and/or washing overboard, irrespective of percentage."

[3] Black's Law Dictionary (4th ed. 1966); Gilmore & Black, The Law of Admiralty, § 5-10 (2d ed. 1975).

[4] (Clause 9) "This insurance attaches from the time the goods leave the Warehouse and/or Store

Extension clause[5] the plaintiffs must show that an insured peril existed and the damage was proximately caused by that peril. Although the parties disagree, the weight of authority indicates plaintiffs bear the burden of proving coverage. Plaintiffs have not met that burden.

The shore coverage clause[6] provides coverage for enumerated risks occurring on shore. Plaintiffs argue that contamination while loading is a shore accident. However, since the contamination occurred within the barge's intake lines, the incident arose "on board". Therefore shore coverage does not apply. Even if it were to apply, contamination of cargo is not within the enumerated risks covered by the shore coverage clause.

---

at the place named in the policy for the commencement of the transit and continues during the ordinary course of transit, including customary transhipment if any, until the goods are discharged overside from the overseas vessel at the final port. Thereafter the insurance continues whilst the goods are in transit and/or awaiting transit until delivered to final warehouse at the destination named in the policy or until the expiry of 15 days (or 30 days if the destination to which the goods are insured is outside the limits of the port) whichever shall first occur. The time limits referred to above to be reckoned from midnight of the day on which the discharge overside of the goods hereby insured from the overseas vessel is completed. Held covered at a premium to be arranged in the event of transhipment, if any, other than as above and/or in the event of delay in excess of the above time limits arising from circumstances beyond the control of the Assured."

[5] (Clause 10) "This policy is extended to cover all shipments which become at risk hereunder in accordance with the following clauses . . .

"I. This insurance attaches from the time the goods leave the warehouse at the place named in this policy. . .and continues until the goods are delivered to the final warehouse . . . .

"II. This insurance specially to cover the goods during

(i) deviation, delay, forced discharge, reshipment and transhipment,

(ii) . . . .

. . . .

"IV. This insurance shall in no case be deemed to extend to cover loss, damage, or expense proximately caused by delay or inherent vice or nature of the subject-matter insured.

. . . .

Nothing in the foregoing shall be construed as overruling the F.C.&S. clause or as extending this insurance to cover any risks of war . . . ."

[6] (Clause 13) "Including while on docks, wharves or elsewhere on shore and/or during land transportation, risks of collision, derailment, fire, lightning, sprinkler leakage, cyclones, hurricanes, earthquakes, floods, the rising of navigable waters, or any accident to the conveyance and/or collapse and/or subsidence of docks and/or structures, and to pay loss or damage caused thereby, even though the insurance be otherwise F.P.A."

III. *Recovery of Extraordinary Expenses Under Landing and Warehousing Clause*[7] ; *Extra Expenses Clause*[8] ; *Sue and Labor Clause*[9]

Under these provisions the insured is entitled to recover expenses associated with losses incurred as a result of an insured peril. For reasons outlined in Paragraph I, I find that the losses suffered by plaintiffs were not caused by a peril covered by the policy. Recovery under these provisions is therefore precluded.

IV. *Recovery Under Inchmaree Clause*

The purpose of the Inchmaree clause[10] is to expand the coverage of the policy beyond the perils provision. Federal law, 46 U.S.C. § 192 (Harter Act), and 46 U.S.C. § 1304(2)(a) (Carriage of Goods by Sea Act), allows a vessel owner to become exempt from liability for fault or error in navigation or management of the ship. In contrast, the shipowner must retain liability for negligence in the care and custody of the cargo. The Inchmaree clause is intended to provide coverage to a cargo owner when a loss is due to error in navigation or management of the vessel since the carrier is exempt from liability. Plaintiffs argue the contamination was the result of an error in management and therefore covered under the Inchmaree clause. Defendant naturally urges the court to find the loss caused by fault in the care and custody of the cargo.

The United States Supreme Court has addressed the distinction between error in management and error in care of cargo but has not articulated a clear test. *Oceanic Steam Navigation v. Aiken,* 196 U.S. 589, 25 S. Ct. 317, 49 L. Ed. 610 (1905). The Ninth Circuit, noting that no precise definitions exist, advocates a case-by-case determination using the following test:

> "If the act in question has the primary purpose of affecting the ship, it is 'in navigation or in management'; but if the primary purpose is

[7] (Clause 20) "Notwithstanding any average warranty contained herein, these Assurers agree to pay landing, warehousing, forwarding or other expenses and/or particular charges should same be incurred, as well as any partial loss arising from transhipment. Also to pay the insured value of any package, piece or unit totally lost in loading, transhipment and/or discharge."

[8] (Clause 38) "Where, by reason of a peril insured against under this policy, extra expenses are incurred to destroy, dump or otherwise dispose of the damaged goods, or where extra expenses are incurred in discharging from the vessel and/or craft and/or conveyance, such expenses will be recoverable in full in addition to the damage to the insured interest."

[9] (Clause 40) "In case of any loss or misfortune, it shall be lawful and necessary to and for the Assured, his or their factors, servants and assigns, to sue, labor and travel for in and about the defense, safeguard and recovery of the said goods and merchandise, or any part thereof without prejudice to this insurance; nor shall the acts of the insured or insurers, in recovering, saving and preserving the property insured, in case of disaster, be considered a waiver or an acceptance of abandonment; to the charges whereof the said Assurers will contribute according to the rate and quantity of the sum herein insured."

[10] (Clause 24) "This insurance is also specially to cover any loss of or damage to the interest insured hereunder, through the bursting of boilers, breakage of shafts or through any latent defect in the machinery, hull or appurtenances, or from faults or errors in the navigation and/or management of the vessel by the Master, Mariners, Mates, Engineers or Pilots; provided, however, that this clause shall not be construed as covering loss arising out of delay, deterioration or loss of market, unless otherwise provided elsewhere herein."

to affect the cargo, it is not 'in navigation or in management'." *Grace Line, Inc. v. Todd Shipyards Corporation,* 500 F.2d 361, 374 (9th Cir. 1974).

Using this test, I find that the contamination of the cargo in this case was caused by fault in the care, custody, and control of the cargo. The Inchmaree clause will not provide coverage for plaintiffs' losses under the facts of this case.

V. *Recovery Under Negligence Clause*

The Negligence clause [11] provides coverage against losses due to enumerated perils caused by the unseaworthiness of the vessel. To recover under this clause plaintiffs must show that the barge was unseaworthy. This unseaworthiness must then cause a loss through one of the enumerated perils: "sinking, stranding, fire, explosion, contact with seawater, or by any other cause of the nature of any of the risks assumed in the policy".

"Seaworthiness" depends on such factors as the type of vessel, character of the voyage, reasonable weather, navigational conditions, and type of cargo. A vessel is unseaworthy if she is not reasonably fit to carry cargo she has undertaken to transport. I find Shaver's barge unseaworthy as a result of improper loading of cargo.

Plaintiffs must demonstrate that the unseaworthiness of the barge caused a loss to cargo by one or more of the enumerated perils. Since contamination is not an enumerated peril, plaintiff urges coverage under the doctrine of *ejusdem generis* [12] by suggesting the barge was in imminent danger of sinking. Although there is evidence that the caustic soda would have eventually corroded through the barge and caused it to sink, the process would have taken three to five years. This possibility is too far removed to find coverage under a provision providing for loss due to sinking. No recovery is possible under the Negligence clause of this policy.

---

[11] (Clause 21) "The Assured are not to be prejudiced by the presence of the negligence clause and/or latent defect clause in the bills of lading and/or charter party and/or contract of affreightment. The seaworthiness of the vessel and/or craft as between the Assured and Assurers is hereby admitted, and the Assurers agree that in the event unseaworthiness or a wrongful act or misconduct of shipowner, charterer, their agents or servants, shall, directly or indirectly, cause loss or damage to the cargo insured by sinking, stranding, fire, explosion, contact with seawater, or by any other cause of the nature of any of the risks assumed in the policy, the Assurers will (subject to the terms of average and other conditions of the policy) pay to an innocent Assured the resulting loss. With leave to sail with or without pilots, and to tow and assist vessels or craft in all situations and to be towed."

[12] Ejusdem generis is a rule of construction. Where general words are used in a contract after specific terms, they are to be confined to things of the same kind or class as the things previously specified.

VI. *Recovery Under General Average Clauses*[13] (Clause 35) "General Average and Salvage Charges are payable in full irrespective of comparison between the insured and contributory values."

General average is a venerable doctrine of maritime law that dates back 2,800 years.[14] The doctrine provides that when a portion of ship or cargo is sacrificed to save the rest from a real and substantial peril, each owner of property saved contributes ratably to make up the loss of those whose property has been sacrificed. General average contribution exists independently of marine insurance and is owed even in the absence of cargo insurance. However, cargo owners typically insure themselves against possible obligation arising from a general average situation. This policy contains such protection.

The United States Supreme Court in *Barnard v. Adams*, 51 U.S. (10 How.) 270, 13 L.Ed. 417 (1850), described three events that created a general average situation: (1) A common danger to which ship, cargo, and crew were all exposed and which is imminent and apparently inevitable; (2) A voluntary sacrifice of a part for the benefit of the whole; and (3) Successful avoidance of the peril. Modern law has eased the requirement of imminency and requires only that a peril be real and substantial.

Two classes of general average exist: those which arise from sacrifices of part of ship or cargo made to save the whole adventure, and those which arise out of extraordinary expenses incurred for the joint benefit of ship and cargo. Expenditures made by the carrier to avert a peril must be made in good faith.

To require a general average contribution, there must first be a general average situation. Plaintiffs assert that the imminent sinking of the barge is a general average situation that requires contribution from the cargo owners. Defendant contends that no real peril existed and any alleged loss occurred at the time of contamination.

Did a general average situation exist? "Mere incidents of the voyage" not giving rise to extraordinary common danger to vessel or cargo do not require general average sacrifices. To create a general average situation there must be "fair reason to regard a vessel in peril", and the peril must be "real and substantial". Although there was evidence of corrosion due to the nature of the cargo that would have eventually caused the barge to sink, no real and substantial peril existed.

Plaintiffs have incurred extraordinary expenses as a result of the contamination of the cargo. Nevertheless, I find that under the circumstances of this case no general average situation existed.[15] Sacrifices where there is no peril present no claim for contribution.

---

[13] (Clause 21) "General Average, Salvage and Special Charges, as per foreign custom, payable according to foreign statement, and/or per York-Antwerp Rules and/or in accordance with the contract of affreightment, if and as required; or, failing any provision in or there be no contract of affreightment, payable in accordance with the Laws and Usages of the Port of San Francisco."

[14] See generally Gilmore & Black, The Law of Admiralty, § 5-1 (2d ed. 1975).

[15] A respected authority has urged the courts to be "vigilant to see that the extension by analogy of the principle of general average does not encroach upon the equally valid and more important principle that the shipowner is under a duty to employ whatever means are needful to fill his contract of carriage, even though difficulties of various sorts may result in its costing him more than liked". Gilmore & Black, The Law of Admiralty, § 5-11 at 767 (2d ed. 1975).

Even assuming that a peril existed, defendant claims that contribution cannot be requested when the vessel owner was at fault in creating the situation. Vessel owners have long placed in bills of lading a provision incorporating the protections of the Harter Act, 46 U.S.C. §§ 190-196, and Carriage of Goods by Sea Act, 46 U.S.C. §§ 1300-1315. This provision, known as the Jason clause [16] entitles shipowners to contribution notwithstanding negligence in creating the general average situation. However, the shipowner must comply with 46 U.S.C. § 1303(1)(a) requiring due diligence to make the vessel seaworthy.

The burden of proving "due diligence" to make the vessel seaworthy falls on the vessel owner. I find that Shaver did not meet this burden. Shaver failed to properly clean or inspect the barge's input lines. Thus if I assume that a peril existed, contribution from the cargo owner (in this case, insurance proceeds) cannot be requested. Shaver failed to use due diligence to make the barge seaworthy.

Conclusion

Plaintiffs suggest a number of theories of recovery under the marine cargo insurance policy. None is suited to this case. I am aided in my construction of this policy by one additional fact. Shaver *rejected* insurance coverage costing more but expressly covering the risks of contamination of cargo. I conclude that the plaintiffs did not believe contamination was covered under the policy. Plaintiffs' present attempt to include this type of loss within the coverage of the policy is an afterthought.

Judgment shall be entered for the defendant.

This opinion shall constitute findings of fact and conclusions of law pursuant to Fed. R. Civ. P. 52(a).

INLAND RIVERS SERVICE CORP. v. HARTFORD FIRE INSURANCE CO.

66 Ohio St.2d 32, 418 N.E.2d 1381 (1981)

On Saturday, April 21, 1973, a barge owned by Inland Rivers Service Corporation, appellant, and designated the MCB-1558, carried 1,426 tons of gravel up the Ohio River from Patriot, Indiana, to a landing terminal in Cincinnati. On April 21 or 22, while moored with other barges, the MCB-1558 sank, carrying its cargo with it to the bottom of the Ohio River. Appellant filed a claim against its marine insurance carrier, Hartford Fire Insurance Company, appellee, which the latter refused to pay.

Appellant filed an action in the Court of Common Pleas of Hamilton County against appellee, seeking recovery under the "perils of the sea" clause of its marine insurance contract. Appellant argued that the sinking was caused by

---

[16] Named after the United States Supreme Court decision holding the clause valid. The Jason, 225 U.S. 32, 32 S. Ct. 560, 56 L. Ed. 969 (1912).

a hole punctured in the river side of the barge below the water line. Although appellant was unable to identify who or what caused the hole, it offered evidence to show that the hole was caused by an external instrumentality and that it may have resulted from bridge construction work downstream. Appellee asserted that the loss was caused by bad bottomry and neglect, and therefore was not within the coverage of the insurance policy. The case was argued to the trial court without the intervention of a jury, and, at the conclusion of the evidence, that court entered judgment in favor of appellant in the amount of $25,146 plus six percent interest from September 28, 1973. The trial court found that the insurance policy was in effect on the date of the loss and that the MCB-1558 was a constructive total loss. The court also found "[t]hat at the inception of the policy the vessel was in a seaworthy condition, by stipulation, and thereafter, during the currency of the policy, the insured exercised due diligence to keep the vessel seaworthy, and in all respects fit, tight and properly manned, equipped and supplied, and is entitled to recovery against the defendant, Hartford." The court further stated "[a]s to the cause of the sinking, in this court's mind it still remains unresolved, and unanswered."

Upon appeal, the Court of Appeals modified the judgment of the trial court by deleting the award of damages against appellee. The Court of Appeals held that appellee was entitled to a judgment in its favor due to appellant's failure "to present evidence of probative force sufficient to prove by a preponderance that the loss was caused by a peril or risk covered by the policy." The Court of Appeals held further that appellant's evidence "utterly failed to prove what or who caused the puncture in the hull, the most likely point of entry of the water."

The cause is now before this court pursuant to the allowance of a motion to certify the record.

PER CURIAM.

The cause before us concerns recovery for a loss under a "perils of the sea" clause of a marine insurance policy.

This clause reads, in relevant part: "Touching the adventures and perils which this company is contended to bear and take upon itself, they are of the waters named herein, fire, lightning, earthquake, assailing thieves, jettisons, barratry of the master and mariners and all other like perils that shall come to the hurt, detriment or damage of the vessel named herein."

Marine insurance policies have long insured against various "adventures and perils" which may befall vessels and cargo. Usually included among those risks are perils "of the seas" or "of the waters." Coverage extends to fortuitous losses occurring through extraordinary action of the sea. Extraordinary action of the wind and waves is a sea peril, as are collision, foundering, stranding, and striking on rocks and icebergs. Gilmore & Black, The Law of Admiralty (1975 ed.), at pages 72–73. Even damage to a moored vessel by its striking a sharp object constitutes a peril of the sea where it results from extraordinary and unforeseen factors and not from the inherent weakness of the vessel itself. Annotation, 85 A.L.R.2d 446, 448. Ordinary wear and tear on a vessel is not, however, contemplated as a peril of the sea. 11 Couch on Insurance 434, Section 43:112.

It is undisputed that one seeking to recover on an insurance policy generally has the burden of proving a loss and demonstrating coverage under the policy. The issue in the instant case is whether, under a "perils of the sea" clause, the insured sustains this burden by merely showing that the probable cause of a leak (which results in a loss) is external to the vessel, or whether the insured must also show exactly who or what caused the leak.

Paragraph six of the syllabus in *Western Insurance Co. v. Tobin* (1877), 32 Ohio St. 77, reads as follows: "When a steamboat is shown to have been seaworthy at the time she was insured, and no intervening circumstance occurs to render her unseaworthy, her seaworthiness is presumed to continue; but when, during the life of the policy, she springs a dangerous leak, without apparent cause, a new presumption arises—that of unseaworthiness; yet, as this new presumption is not a conclusive one, the owners are not required, to entitle them to recover for the loss, to show the identical cause of her loss, but may show a probable cause."

Applying *Tobin, supra,* to the instant case, we conclude that the record shows that the barge was seaworthy when it was insured and that no intervening circumstance arose to render it unseaworthy. The record further shows that the barge sprang a dangerous leak without apparent cause, thus raising a rebuttable presumption that it was unseaworthy when it sank. To overcome that presumption, the appellant needed to show a probable cause of the loss by a peril of the sea. This burden could be satisfied by showing that the loss probably resulted from a fortuitous cause *external* to the barge. However, appellant had no burden to prove exactly who or what may have caused the dangerous leak.

The record reveals that appellant offered expert evidence that a hole found in the side plate of the barge, below the water line, had been "punched in" by an instrumentality external to the vessel, and that the hole was the cause of the sinking. We find this evidence to be sufficient to support the trial court's finding that appellant overcame the presumption of unseaworthiness and carried its burden of persuading the finder of fact that the loss resulted from a covered "peril of the sea."

For the foregoing reasons, the judgment of the Court of Appeals is reversed.

Judgment reversed.

WILLIAM B. BROWN, PAUL W. BROWN, SWEENEY, LOCHER, HOLMES and CLIFFORD F. BROWN, JJ., concur.

CELEBREZZE, CHIEF JUSTICE, dissenting.

Emulating Sherlock Holmes, who once solved a crime based on the dog that did *not* bark[,] the majority inferentially reasons that a peril of the sea caused the sinking of the barge based on what was *not* proved at trial. Unlike the famous fictional detective, however, the majority floats far off course on their voyage of analyzing the burden of proof in marine casualty litigation. I cannot sign aboard for this cruise and must, therefore, respectfully register my dissent.

Initially, it should be noted that the phrase "peril of the sea" has been defined as:

"Perils of the sea embrace all kinds of marine casualties, such as shipwreck, foundering, stranding, collision, and every specie of damage done to the ship or goods at sea by the violent action of the winds or waves. *They do not embrace all losses happening on the sea,* or a peril whose only connection with the sea is that it arises aboard ship, or all damage of which the sea is the cause, but only those perils which are of the sea." (Emphasis added.) 45 C.J.S. Insurance § 854, at pages 934–935. *See, also,* Gilmore & Black, The Law of Admiralty (1975 ed.), at pages 72–73.

It is a universal principle of insurance and maritime law that the insured has the burden of proving, by a preponderance of the evidence, that the damage to the vessel was caused by an insured risk, i.e., a peril of the sea.

While the presumptions of *Western Insurance Co. v. Tobin* (1877), 32 Ohio St. 77, may shift the burden of producing evidence back and forth between the parties, the burden of proof, also known as the burden of persuasion, remains with the insured throughout the trial. The burden of proof does not shift to the insurer to prove that the loss was caused by something other than a peril of the sea.

Applying the foregoing principles to the facts at bar, it is evident that the record harbors two fundamental flaws. First, a review of the transcript unveils the following colloquy between the trial judge and plaintiff's-appellant's counsel:

"At this time, the Court is still unaware of what caused the sinking of the barge, *I don't think the burden is upon you to show me what caused it to sink.*"

This statement vividly demonstrates to me that the trial court misperceived the burden of proof in this case and improperly relieved the insured of this burden by assigning it, instead, to the insurer. This, by itself, in my estimation, constitutes reversible error.

The second flaw relates to the following statement by the trial judge, *the finder of fact* in this case:

"We can go into great lengths to find out what caused it [the hole in the barge]. . . . The thing before the Court is that the barge did sink and it ended up on the bottom 25 to 50 feet down, and that's where we are right now. What caused it I don't know, and I don't think you know. *I don't think anyone knows at this point.*" (Emphasis added.)

Apparently, the evidence presented after this remark did not shed any light on the cause of the sinking.

Moreover, when announcing his final decision on December 20, 1977, the trial judge stated:

"As to the cause of the sinking, in this Court's mind it still remains unresolved, and unanswered."

It seems to me that if the finder of fact could not conclude what caused the hole or the sinking, then the insured, the party with the burden of proof, did not succeed in demonstrating, by a preponderance of the reliable, probative and credible evidence, the probability, or even possibility, that such sinking was caused by a peril of the sea, a covered risk. Evidently, the finder of fact felt that the connection between the construction vessels upstream, the alleged peril of the sea, and the sinking was much too tenuous.

My reading of the trial judge's comments illustrates that he not only believed that the barge owner had not demonstrated that the sinking was caused by a peril of the sea, but also, that, in his mind, it was equally plausible that the sinking was caused by a leak within the barge itself, by bad bottomry or by some other non-covered risk.

Thus, construing the trial judge's comments about the conflicting expert testimony and all the evidence in a light most favorable to the barge owner, we have, at most, a case that is "in equipoise." Much like in baseball where "a tie goes to the runner," an insurance case in equilibrium "goes to the insurer" when the insured fails to meet its burden of proof.

I am fully cognizant of the fact that the insured, in cases like this, does not have to prove the exact cause of the sinking or offer into evidence the precise submerged object that might have caused the sinking. See Annotation, 31 A.L.R. 1378. I dissent on the basis that the finder of fact and a unanimous Court of Appeals, though rendering different judgments, concluded that the evidence did not preponderate in favor of attributing the sinking to a covered risk. Since the trial judge was in a better position than we are to evaluate the conflicting evidence and credibility of the witnesses, I submit that it is more appropriate to defer to his analysis of the competing inferences.

The record in this case is voluminous. The pleadings, transcript, exhibits and appendices occupy the better part of a file cabinet. After a long trial and a fully-developed appeal, the finder of fact and a unanimous Court of Appeals concluded, in essence, that the barge sank in some unknown manner, by some unknown object, at some unknown time. We sit as an appellate court with a limited scope of review; we do not sit as a roving band of claims adjusters with Ouija boards. How this court can, eight years after the sinking of this barge, substitute its judgment for the finder of fact and conclude that the sinking was, indeed, caused by a covered risk, remains, to me, an existential mystery.

NOTES

1. *Choice of law.* Admiralty jurisdiction is granted to the federal judicial power under Article III of the U.S. Constitution. *See* U.S. Const., art. III, § 2, cl. 1. As Justice Blackmun wrote in *East River S.S. Corp. v. Transamerica Delaval, Inc.,* 476 U.S. 858 (1986), "[w]ith admiralty jurisdiction comes the application of substantive admiralty law." *Id.* at 864. From these two points, one might assume that a uniform federal common law would be applied to marine insurance matters. Surprisingly, the Supreme Court held in *Wilburn Boat Co. v. Fireman's Fund Insurance Co.,* 348 U.S. 310 (1955), that in the field of marine insurance law, state law, instead of federal maritime law, would be applied where there is no judicially established federal admiralty

rule on the issue or any reason to fashion one. See *id.* at 316–21. Thus, in *Wilburn Boat*, the Court held that there was no established federal admiralty rule on the effect of a breach of warranty in a marine insurance policy, there was no basis for fashioning a federal rule, and the state law of Texas applied. See *id.* at 321. How important is it that there be a consistent, uniform body of marine insurance law? Under the law of *Wilburn Boat*, when is a federal rule "established"? When is it appropriate for a federal court to "fashion" a federal rule? In determining the state rule, is the applicable law state marine insurance law, or may nonmarine insurance law principles be considered? Few Supreme Court decisions have been so widely and consistently criticized as *Wilburn Boat*. For a sampling of the critique and some suggested solutions, see Thomas J. Schoenbaum, *Marine Insurance*, 31 J. Mar. L. & Com. 281 (2000); Michael F. Sturley, *Restating the Law of Marine Insurance: A Workable Solution to the Wilburn Boat Problem*, 29 J. Mar. L. & Com. 41 (1998); Joel K. Goldstein, *The Life and Times of Wilburn Boat: A Critical Guide*, 28 J. Mar. L. & Com. 395 (Part I), 555 (Part II) (1997).

2. *Utmost good faith.* One of the rules which appears to have been firmly established before *Wilburn Boat* and therefore not subject to modification by differing state approaches is *uberrima fides*, which refers to the insured's duty of utmost good faith in making disclosures to the underwriter. This rule ratchets up the insured's duty to make disclosures beyond those that would be required under common law rules of fraud, misrepresentation, and concealment. An oft-quoted statement of the rule comes from *Sun Mutual Insurance Co. v. Ocean Insurance Co.,* 107 U.S. 485 (1882):

> The assured will not be allowed to protect himself against the charge of an undue concealment by evidence that he had disclosed to the underwriters, in *general* terms, the information that he possessed. Where his own information is specific, it must be communicated in the terms in which it was received. . . . It is the duty of the assured to place the underwriter in the same situation as himself; to give to him the same means and opportunity of judging of the value of the risks; and when any circumstance is withheld, however slight and immaterial it may have seemed to himself, that, if disclosed, would probably have influenced the terms of the insurance, the concealment vitiates the policy.

107 U.S. at 510–11. How is this rule intertwined with the development of the law of warranty, misrepresentation, and concealment? See the textual material at the beginning of § 3.02[1][a], *supra.* For more discussion of *uberrima fides* in marine insurance, see John P. Kavanagh, Jr., *"Ask Me No Questions and I'll Tell You No Lies": The Doctrine of Uberrimae Fidei in Marine Insurance Transactions*, 17 Tul. Mar. L. J. 37 (1992); Mitchell J. Popham & Chau Vo, *Misrepresentation and Concealment in Marine Insurance Contracts: An Analysis of Federal and State Law Within the Ninth Circuit*, 11 U.S.F. Mar. L. J. 99 (1999).

3. *Loss calculations.* The concept of average is unique to marine insurance, but the concept of coinsurance is not. Property insurers early on borrowed the concept of coinsurance from marine insurance in order to encourage insureds

to purchase larger amounts of coverage on pieces of property. For more discussion, see § 2.02[7][b], *supra*.

4. *Inland marine insurance.* Insurers of marine risks found it natural to extend their operations to other business activities. Initially, marine insurance covered shipping in international waters; it was a small and logical step for marine insurers to cover ships and cargoes in inland waterways and lakes— hence the term "inland marine insurance." Gradually the business of these insurers extended to any cargo that moved, and to any instrumentality of shipping (such as piers, bridges, and tunnels) and to any vessel on which goods are shipped (*e.g.*, aircraft, trucks, etc.) See Robert H. Jerry, II, Understanding Insurance Law § 13A[a], at 25 (2d ed. 1996).

5. *For further reading.* As stated in the introductory note, these materials only provide a brief introduction to the special field of marine insurance. If your are inclined to learn more about this subject, here are some useful places, in addition to the other materials cited in these notes, to pursue your inquiry: Graydon S. Staring & George L. Waddell, *Marine Insurance*, 73 Tul. L. Rev. 1619 (1999) (part of a symposium on *Admiralty Law at the Millennium*); *Symposium: Marine Insurance*, 66 Tul. L. Rev. 257–509 (1991).

Chapter 5

COMMON THIRD-PARTY COVERAGES AND RECURRING ISSUES

"At one time, it was contended that liability insurance was illegal because it tended to make the insured careless of the safety of others. The validity of such insurance has been universally upheld, however, even though it covers liability for injuries caused by violations of traffic laws. A person can lawfully insure against liability for the willful or even criminal acts of his employees, in which he does not participate. Probably, insurance against civil liability due to the operation of a motor car would not cover a case of willful murder by the insured . . . ." —Professor Edwin W. Patterson, in Essentials of Insurance Law 48-49 (1935)

"A rumor, published in the book *Hollywood Trivia*, has it that 'Abbott and Costello once took out a $100,000 insurance policy with Lloyd's of London that stipulated payment if any of their audience should die of laughter.' In reality, however, no record of such policy exists in the files, a spokesperson for [Lloyd's] said in 1989."—Abbott & Costello Fun Facts, www.city-net.com/abbottandcostellofc/facts.html(quoting Stephen Cox & John Lofflin, The Official Abbott & Costello Scrapbook (1990))

Liability insurance is designed to protect individuals and legal entities, such as corporations, partnerships, and associations, against tort and some other forms of legal obligations to pay money damages. Corporate organizations include private nonprofit institutions and governmental entities, as well as the usual forms of commercial organizations. Unincorporated associations may also purchase liability insurance.

Liability insurance is a relatively recent development in the insurance business, having come into existence as the exposure to monetary awards became more formidable during the latter part of the nineteenth century. Its rapid growth parallels societal changes in modern countries, particularly the myriad kinds of accident-producing activities spawned by the industrial revolution and growth in public and private transportation. Initially and for sometime thereafter, the primary, if not the only, interest protected was the economic well-being of the insured. The early forms of insurance were designed to indemnify the insured only against losses actually incurred through liability to third parties. If the insured did not pay because of insolvency or other reasons, the insurer owed nothing since the insured suffered no actual out-of-pocket loss. However, in modern times there has been more of a concern with providing compensation to accident victims. Thus, most policies today are true liability policies in that they protect the insured against the *responsibility* for damage to third parties regardless of the insured's own ability to pay for the harm. One also might observe that in some instances, the system has been reversed so that the insurance now is primarily for the benefit of the accident victim. No better illustration of this shift can be found than the compulsory automobile liability insurance laws that most states have now adopted. These are explored in § 6.02, *infra*.

In addition to protecting the insured against responsibility for damage to third parties, a second extremely important component of liability insurance is the insurer's promise to defend the insured against the claims of third parties brought against the insured. Essentially, this commitment serves as "litigation insurance." The insured, whether an individual or a business entity, has a risk that third parties might sue the insured for damages, even by making frivolous or unfounded claims against the insured. Even when the insured is completely confident of defeating the third party's claims, the cost of defending against such claims can be very high. Obviously, the fees of the attorney providing the defense will probably be the most significant expense, although other expenses, such as deposition expenses and the costs of expert witnesses can also be quite large. The insurer's promise to designate and pay for an attorney to defend the insured is of great value to the insured. But, as with paying for any damages the insured is found to owe third parties, the insurer is obligated to provide a defense only if the claim is within coverage. The duty to defend has its own complexities and sometimes its own special problems, and these will be given more attention in § 8.02, *infra*. The current chapter will focus on the risks covered and interests protected by liability insurance.

There are different kinds of liability insurance. In § 4.05, we examined, among other things, the property insurance coverage provided by homeowners insurance. We begin this chapter by returning to homeowners insurance for the purpose of studying the liability protection afforded by the typical homeowners form. In other words, the homeowners policy contains both first-party property coverage on the described premises and contents as well as a general-purpose liability policy for the named insured and additional insureds. A renters policy will be structured the same way, except that the property portion will cover the insured's personal belongings, since there are no owned premises to be covered. Excluded from coverage under these policies will be liabilities that arise out of the use of automobiles, the insured's business activities, the insured's service as a director or officer of a corporation, etc. For these "special" purposes, an insured might purchase a special-purpose coverage, such as automobile liability insurance as part of the insured's coverage of automobile-related risks (see *e.g.*, Appendix E), or directors and officers ("D & O") insurance. For business or commercial liability risks, the insured will purchase a separate policy. Except for highly specialized risks, most of these forms will be, or will closely resemble, the Commercial General Liability Policy (the "CGL"), which is fairly described as a general-purpose liability policy for businesses (see Appendix B). Some businesses may also need a special-purpose coverage, such as environmental impairment liability ("EIL") insurance, in addition to the general liability form. Some policy provisions are unique to the particular form mentioned, particularly the special-purpose forms. Generally speaking, however, many legal principles are applicable to liability insurance generally, regardless of the particular form (although one must always be alert to the language of particular forms which can alter the significance of any given rule in a particular situation).

In this chapter, we will consider issues that commonly arise under the homeowners form, issues that commonly arise under the CGL, and then will conclude with a review of some recurring issues that cut across both kinds of coverage.

§ 5.01   Personal Liability Coverage under the Homeowners Policy

[1]   The Nature of the Coverage

Personal liability coverage, as noted above, is bundled with property coverage in a homeowners (or renters) insurance policy. This does not mean, however, that the insured is only covered for liability that arises at the described premises (as would be the case if, for example, the insured negligently constructed a swing set for her children in the backyard and this negligence proximately resulted in injury to a neighbor's child who was using the swing set). The insured might be liable for negligence anywhere the insured goes for a host of reasons; the liability policy provides protection when the insured is away from home as well. On the other hand, the insured is covered for *all* possible liabilities. For example, the insurer does not provide coverage for damages caused by the insured's breach of most kinds of contractual relationships with other parties. (Why not? See the Homeowners Policy in Appendix C. In what circumstances might the consequences of a breach of contract be covered?) The coverage is circumscribed in other important respects as well. Consider the next case.

STANLEY v. AMERICAN FIRE & CASUALTY CO.
361 So. 2d 1030 (Ala. 1978)

ALMON, JUSTICE.

This is an action for declaratory judgment to determine coverage under a homeowner insurance policy issued to Mark Stanley. The trial court ruled there was no coverage because the policy "clearly and unambiguously excluded coverage for any loss related to business pursuits on the insured premises."

Alicia Schofield, who was just over one year of age, was injured when she fell backwards on a bed of hot coals in the Stanley home fireplace. At the time of the incident, Mrs. Stanley was in the kitchen preparing lunch for herself, her own children, and the other children for whom she was baby-sitting.

For several months prior to this Mrs. Stanley kept the children of various friends and neighbors in her home during the day. She cared for eight different children, but no more than five at the same time. Mrs. Stanley received three dollars per day for each child as compensation.

At issue is the following policy exclusion:

"This policy does not apply:

"1. Under Coverage E—Personal Liability and Coverage F—Medical Payments to Others . . . .

"d. to bodily injury or property damage arising out of business pursuits of any insured except activities therein which are ordinarily incident to non-business pursuits."

The trial court ruled that in caring for children Mrs. Stanley was engaged in a "business pursuit" within the meaning of the policy exclusion. The judgment, however, lacks any reference to whether the injury arose out of "activities therein which are ordinarily incident to non-business pursuits," the exception to the exclusion. Our inquiry is directed to the exception.

The above provision, both exclusion and exception, have been the subject of several court decisions in other jurisdictions. The provision does not lend itself to clarity, resulting in a split of opinion over whether it is ambiguous, with the consensus being that it is poorly worded. *See Crane v. State Farm and Cas. Co.,* 5 Cal. 3d 112, 95 Cal. Rptr. 513, 485 P.2d 1129 (1971);; and *Gulf Ins. Co. v. Tilley,* 280 F. Supp. 60, 64-65 (N.D. Ind. 1967); *aff'd,* 393 F.2d 119 (7th Cir. 1968).

The *Crane* and *Tilley* cases deal with substantially the same question as we have here and conclude the activity there was within the exception to the exclusion, resulting in coverage.

In *Tilley,* the exclusionary clause was held inoperative where baby care was furnished for consideration, and the baby sustained burns when she overturned a coffee percolator. The district trial court assumed that the child care was a business pursuit, but characterized insured's coffee brewing for herself and a guest as an activity not connected with baby care, thus ordinarily incident to non-business pursuits. This analysis is questionable. The baby was burned because of the condition on the premises, and the baby's own activity. The business of child care contemplates the exercising of due care to safeguard a child of tender years from household conditions and activities; and, any activity of the insured in this regard from which injury results cannot logically be called an activity ordinarily incidental to a non-business pursuit. In other words, the activity referred to is a failure to supervise rather than making coffee for a third party. Undertaking the business relation of child care for compensation is certainly not ordinarily incident to the conduct of a household.

In *Crane* the Supreme Court of California reasoned that "indeed, it is difficult to conceive of an activity more ordinarily incident to a noncommercial pursuit than home care of children." We agree with the general [assertion], but disagree with their conclusion that child care for pay is ordinarily a non-business pursuit. It should be remembered that we are not here dealing with a temporary or casual keeping of children, but rather with a more permanent arrangement for an agreed upon compensation. The Supreme Court of California in *Crane* reversed the Court of Appeals. The Court of Appeals' decision is styled the same and appears in 14 Cal. App. 3d 727, 92 Cal. Rptr. 621. It is our view that the Court of Appeals' decision is better reasoned and more properly analyzes the other cases cited than does the opinion of the Supreme Court of California. The facts are strikingly similar to the ones before us. In view of the similarity we will quote liberally from their opinion:

" 'Babysitting' is an occupation in which the babysitter has the responsibility of keeping her infant charges entertained and protected from harm and even mischief. (*Tropical Coach Lines, Inc. v. King (*1962 Fla. Sup. Ct.) 147 So. 2d 318, 319.)

"The term 'babysitting' perhaps is inaptly used to describe the contract for day care for children involved here. In ordinary parlance, the 'babysitter' is one employed as a matter of convenience by parents to stay with a child or children, so that they may for a few hours seek their pleasure, or tend to affairs external to the home. This differs from day-in, day-out child care for an indefinite period, as here.

" 'Business' in its broad sense embraces anything about which a person may be busy, and in its usual sense, signifies an undertaking or calling for gain, profit, advantage or livelihood. While 'business pursuit' in some contexts is synonymous with 'business,' it more accurately denotes a continued, extended or prolonged course of business or occupation. Child care for compensation as evidenced in this case was much more than a casual accommodation, and was properly found to be a 'business pursuit' under the terms of the policy exclusion. (*Mansfield v. Hyde (*1952) 112 Cal. App. 2d 133, 137-138, 245 P.2d 577; *Long v. City of Anaheim (*1967) 255 Cal. App. 2d 191, 197, 63 Cal. Rptr. 56; *cf. Dorrell v. Norida Land & Timber Co.* (1933) 53 Idaho 793, 27 P.2d 960, 963, reviewing definitions; *Fadden v. Cambridge Mutual Fire Insurance Co. (Sup. Ct.* 1966) 51 Misc. 2d 858, 274 N.Y.S.2d 235, 241; *Home Insurance Company v. Aurigemma (Sup. Ct.* 1965) 45 Misc. 2d 875, 257 N.Y.S.2d 980, 985. These New York trial court cases involve the same exclusionary clause here considered.)

"It has been held in a variety of contexts that a single day's act, or single transaction does not qualify as a business. We need not explore the ramifications of these definitions, in view of the continuity of the services here contracted for and performed, according to the evidence. The present case does not involve casual babysitting, a temporary arrangement for an hour, a day or an evening, for the convenience of parents. It seems clear that while an individual instance might involve a business arrangement, such would lack the continuity of a 'business pursuit.' " 92 Cal. Rptr. at 622.

We are in accord with the several authorities that the exclusionary provision is poorly worded and could have been written with more specificity. Yet when applied to these facts we do not find it ambiguous.

Two questions become pertinent. First, did the injury arise out of a business pursuit? We hold that it did. Second, did the injury arise out of an activity which is ordinarily incident to a non-business pursuit? The activity referred to is not preparing lunch, which would ordinarily be incident to a non-business pursuit, but rather to the failure to properly supervise a young child. Supervising children on a regular basis for compensation is ordinarily a business pursuit.

We are therefore of the opinion that the business exclusion is applicable and the judgment of the trial court is correct.

The judgment is affirmed.

Affirmed.

TORBERT, C.J., and BLOODWORTH, FAULKNER and EMBRY, JJ., concur.

NOTES

1. *The purpose and nature of homeowners coverage.* The homeowners policy in *Stanley* is one of a variety of policies designed for owners and occupiers of land which provide liability coverage in addition to the usual first-party coverages regarding fire, extended coverage, and allied lines. Like auto policies, many owner's and occupier's policies also provide medical payments coverage. There are specific policies designed for landlords, tenants, and owners of property other than homes. In addition to the basic liability coverages for bodily injury and property damage under these policies, one can purchase endorsements to extend the coverage to other types of personal injury. Finally, "umbrella" policies are available which permit an insured to purchase liability coverage in excess of the primary coverage under an owner's or occupier's policy, and in excess of the primary coverage under an auto liability policy. Thus, an insured may arrange for fairly complete protection for tort liability with substantial monetary limits by coordinating coverages and limits. In these times, the prevailing wisdom is that most people are well advised to purchase a complete package with substantial limits. A contrary view reasons that high liability limits attract lawsuits, and that one should purchase sufficient liability insurance to protect one's assets. How would one protect future earnings?

2. *The structure of the homeowners policy.* A widely-used version of the homeowners policy appears in Appendix C. Note that "Section II—Liability Coverages" describes what coverage the insurer is willing to provide, and then a set of exclusions in "Section II—Exclusions" cuts against this grant of coverage. Is there any doubt about the existence of an "occurrence" or "accident" in *Stanley*?

In 2000, the ISO announced a major overhaul of its homeowners form, the first major revision of the form since 1991. As of June 2000, the new form had been filed with regulators in seven states in the Midwest and Northeast, and the ISO hoped to have it filed in 47 or 48 states by the end of 2000. See Robert W. Mitchell, *ISO Unveils New Homeowners Policy Plan*, Nat'l Underwriter (Prop.-Cas.), June 19, 2000, at 10. One early report indicated that the new form would revise the definition of and some aspects of the coverage for home business liabilities. See David Reich-Hale, *ISO Tinkering With Homeowners Coverage*, Nat. Under. (Prop.-Cas.), Jan. 10, 2000, at 8.

3. *"Bodily injury" and "property damage."* These terms are defined in the policy. See Appendix C. In most settings, the definitions present no particular difficulties. What if, however, the victim alleges an emotional distress damage in the absence of a physical injury? Is this type of loss within the ambit of "bodily injury"? For example, in *Vigna v. Allstate Insurance Co.*, 686 A.2d 598 (Me. 1996), a building contractor brought a breach of contract action against

the insured homeowners, alleging the insureds' failure to pay for renovations that the contractor made to the insureds' home. A separate count of the complaint alleged "emotional pain and suffering" as a result of his reasonable reliance on the insureds' promises to pay. Is this claim within the coverage? Compare *Vigna* with *Moore v. Continental Casualty Co.,* 746 A.2d 1252 (Conn. 2000).

4. *The logic of a business pursuits exclusion.* Why are insurers interested in excluding liabilities arising out of business activities from the homeowners coverage? If you were a homeowner, would you prefer the exclusion?

As the *Stanley* opinion acknowledges, courts have divided when applying the business pursuits exclusion. See generally David J. Marchitelli, Annotation, *Construction and Application of "Business Pursuits" Exclusion Provision in General Liability Policy,* 35 A.L.R.5th 375 (1996). Does the fact that courts continue to disagree about the meaning of the exclusion indicate that the exclusion is ambiguous? See *State Farm Fire & Casualty Co. v. Reed,* 873 S.W.2d 698 (Tex. 1993)(held, home day care center's failure to maintain fence through which toddler gained access to swimming pool and drowned came within exception to business pursuits exclusion). Most recent decisions are in accord with the reasoning in *Stanley,* but there are notable exceptions—such as *Reed* — to the contrary. As for *Reed,* if the insured's supervision of the child was so lax as to permit the toddler to escape to a swimming pool area, why is this negligence not within the business pursuits exclusion? See *State Farm Fire and Casualty Co. v. Vaughan,* 968 S.W.2d 931 (Tex. 1998) (business pursuits exclusion barred coverage for day care operator's alleged negligence in leaving child in closet unsupervised and then leaving the premises).

5. *Sexual harassment in the workplace and "business pursuits."* If a third-party sues the insured for sexual harassment alleged to have occurred in the workplace, is the claim excluded from coverage by the business pursuits exclusion? Is harassment a business pursuit? Is it ordinarily incidental to non-business pursuits? *Compare Zimmerman v. Safeco Insurance Co.,* 605 N.W.2d 727 (Minn. 2000) (exclusion in homeowners policy applied to claims of former employee against employer, and claim was not within exception to exclusion); *Armed Forces Insurance Exchange v. Transamerica Insurance Co.,* 88 Haw. 373, 966 P.2d 1099 (Haw. Ct. App. 1998) (acts of sexual assault and harassment alleged by victims of employee's conduct when entering homes under pretext of conducting home inspections for employer held within exclusion to coverage), with *State Farm Fire and Casualty Co. v. Burkhardt,* 96 F. Supp.2d 1343 (M.D. Ala. 2000) (business pursuits exclusion from umbrella policy's personal injury coverage did not apply to invasion of privacy claim arising out of workplace sexual harassment). If you were counsel for the insurers in these cases, what argument would you make apart from the business pursuits exclusion?

6. *The exclusion for automobiles.* Absent some exclusionary provision in a homeowners policy, the liability coverage language would extend to the insured's auto accidents. Thus, the homeowners policy attempts to avoid duplicating this coverage by excluding most accidents involving the ownership, maintenance, or use of a motor vehicle. This attempt to the two types of policies has produced a substantial amount of litigation. Under the language

in the homeowners policy in Appendix C, would the insured have coverage in the following situations?

a. Homeowner is working on his car, which is parked on an incline next to the curb in front of his home. As a result of Homeowner's negligence in failing to block the wheels, Neighbor, who is assisting Homeowner, is injured when the car rolls over him while he is underneath the car removing a rusted-out tailpipe. Is Homeowner covered under the policy for the injury caused Neighbor? For a case with similar facts, see *State Farm Mutual Automobile Insurance Co. v. Roberts,* 166 Vt. 452, 697 A.2d 667 (1997).

b. Homeowner's daughter is riding her motorized minibike in her backyard when she negligently runs over Neighbor's three-year-old child who toddles into the yard. Assuming Homeowner's daughter is an insured under the policy, is she covered?

c. Homeowner is riding as a passenger in Neighbor's car while Neighbor is behind the wheel on a Los Angeles freeway. As a prank, Homeowner shoots a rubber band at Neighbor. Homeowner, however, misjudges the striking power of the rubber band, which causes intense pain when it hits Neighbor in the eye. As a result, Neighbor loses control of the car and causes a thirty-five-car pileup on the freeway. Neighbor sues Homeowner. Is Homeowner covered under the policy? *See West American Insurance Co. v. Silverman,* 378 So. 2d 28 (Fla. App. 1980).

d. While visiting a friend at the friend's house, Homeowner leaves her automobile parked in the driveway. When entering the house, Homeowner leaves her purse just inside the front door, with the keys visibly and prominently hanging from a strap. Friend's three-year-old, unnoticed by Friend or Homeowner, takes the keys, gets into Homeowner's car, and manages to disengage the parking brake, move the gearshift from "park" to "neutral," and turn the ignition switch enough to enable the car to roll down the driveway's incline and into the street, where the car strikes a pedestrian and another car, causing injury and damage. Homeowner is a defendant in these lawsuits. Is Homeowner covered?

e. Insured is a passenger in friend's vehicle. The teen boys are "cruising," when they stop at a traffic light. Also stopped at the light in the adjacent lane and next to the vehicle is Victim's van, being driven by Victim. Without any provocation, Insured suddenly rolls down his vehicle's window, and makes obscene gestures, yells obscenities, shakes his fists, spits on the Victim's van, and yells threats, all at the direction of Victim and in a violent manner. While Insured does this, the driver of the vehicle revs the engine and rocks it back and forth. Insured's intent is to frighten Victim, and he succeeds. Victim, who takes Insured seriously and thinks he may be under the influence of drugs or alcohol, tries to get away, but in doing so the van hits a curb and Victim suffers bodily injury. Does the Insured's behavior fall within the automobile exclusion? *See United Services Automobile Ass'n v. Morgan,* 23 Kan. App. 2d 987, 939 P.2d 959 (1997). For a similar situation, *see Allstate Insurance Co. v. Johnston,* 194 Ariz. 902, 984 P.2d 10 (1999) (insured, while riding in pickup and acting as if he had a gun, causes driver of another car to lose control, crash, and injure plaintiff passenger).

Note that an insured will be liable for damages to the plaintiff in the underlying tort action only if tort law imposes a liability. But remember that the insured is nevertheless interested in the insurer providing a defense to any groundless claim within coverage, which is one of the benefits provided by a liability policy. The insurer's "duty to defend" receives more attention in § 8.02.

7. *Negligent entrustment of an automobile.* There have been many cases involving a homeowner's negligent entrustment of a motor vehicle to a third party, who in turn causes injury to someone else. Where the entrustee's negligence arises out of the maintenance, operation, or use of the motor vehicle, is the homeowner-entrustor covered despite the exclusionary language for motor vehicles in the standard homeowners policy? See the exclusionary language in the policy in Appendix C. There is a fairly even split in the authorities, but the more modern cases have favored the insurer. *See e.g., Taylor v. American Fire and Casualty Co.,* 925 P.2d 1279 (Utah 1996) (no coverage under homeowners policy for negligent supervision claim); *Aetna Casualty and Surety Co. v. Home Insurance Co.,* 44 Mass. App. Ct. 218, 689 N.E.2d 1355 (1998) (same); *Great Central Insurance Co. v. Roemmich,* 291 N.W.2d 772 (S.D. 1980) (discussing cases on both sides). Compare *Columbia Mutual Insurance Co. v. Neal,* 992 S.W.2d 204 (Mo. Ct. App. 1999) (automobile exclusion did not apply to wrongful death claim brought by mother of deceased child against insureds, grandparents of the child, for negligent supervision of child who was run over by car, owned by grandparents but being operated by third party, on grandparents' property). Is this trend surprising if policies have the exclusionary language of the form in Appendix C?

8. *The "derivative liability" issue.* The question on negligent entrustment of an automobile in the prior note is representative of a question that can arise in a number of contexts. The common fact pattern involves bodily injury or property damage to a third party, the direct cause of which appears to be subject to an exclusion (*e.g.,* use of an automobile). Some other cause, however, is alleged to contribute to the loss, and the victim (and the insured) argue that this contributing cause (*e.g.,* the parents' negligent failure to supervise their child's use of the automobile). These cases do not always involve cars or the automobile exclusion. *See e.g., Jones v. Horace Mann Insurance Co.,* 937 P.2d 1360 (Alaska 1997)(motorized vehicle exclusion barred coverage for alleged negligent entrustment of snowmobile to child and alleged negligent supervision of child); *Cambridge Mutual Fire Ins. Co. v. Perry,* 692 A.2d 1388 (Me. 1997)(daughter sued father for alleged sexual abuse and mother for alleged negligent supervision in failing to protect her from father; held, intentional acts exclusion did not bar negligent supervision claim); *C.P. v. Allstate Insurance Co.,* 996 P.2d 1216 (Alaska 2000) (parents of child allegedly physically and sexually assaulted by adult son of insureds sued insureds for negligent supervision; held, homeowners policy's criminal and intentional act exclusions did not exclude coverage); *Austin Mutual Insurance Co. v. Klande,*

563 N.W.2d 282 (Minn. Ct. App. 1997)(failure to supervise child and allowing motorcycle with hot engine and muffler to fall on child).

9. *The "other premises" exclusion.* Another important exclusion in the standard homeowners policy excludes liability for damages "arising out of any premises, other than an insured premises, owned, rented, or controlled by any insured." In *National Farmers Union Property and Casualty Co. v. Western Casualty and Surety Co.,* 577 P.2d 961 (Utah 1978), the insured, who was the Captain of the "Sheriff's Mounted Posse of Weber County," was conducting a practice drill for the posse on county property. The main gate to the property was left open, and while the drill was underway, a horse escaped the property, ran onto the adjacent main highway, and was there struck by a vehicle in which the plaintiff was a passenger. The plaintiff sued for his injuries, contending that the insured, "as Captain of the posse, knew or should have known the gate was left open from the time the first posse member entered, until after the last posse member left," and further that the insured "was negligent in his failure to supervise the activities of the posse members on the grounds of the organization and was negligent in his failure to close the main gate or see to it the gate was closed during drills, so horses could not escape from the posse grounds." The liability carriers for the horse's owner and the posse settled, but the insured's homeowners insurer denied coverage under the "other premises" exclusion set forth at the beginning of this paragraph. Was the insured covered? *See also Sea Insurance Co. v. Westchester Fire Insurance Co.,* 51 F.3d 22 (2d Cir. 1995); *Lanoue v. Fireman's Fund Amercian Insurance Co.,* 278 N.W.2d 49 (Minn. 1979), overruled on other grounds by *American Standard Insurance Co. v. Le,* 551 N.W.2d 923 (Minn.1996).

Suppose an insured homeowner remodels the family room and installs a new electric outlet. The following year, the homeowner sells the house to home buyer. Five years later, the home buyer is fatally electrocuted when using a "wet vac" in the family room while it is plugged into the referenced outlet. By this time, the insured homeowner lives in a new house, which is insured by a policy which excludes from coverage any bodily injury or property damage "arising out of the ownership or rental to any insured of any premises other than an insured premise." Naturally, the previously owned house is not insured under the homeowner's current policy. The spouse of the decedent sues homeowner, alleging that the death was caused by homeowner's negligent installation of the outlet. Is the homeowner covered for this potential liability? *See Tacker v. American Family Mutual Insurance Co.,* 530 N.W.2d 674 (Iowa 1995).

10. *The "care, custody, and control" exclusion.* Another exclusion in the typical homeowners form provides that the personal liability coverage under the policy does not apply "to property damage to property occupied or used by the Insured or rented to or in the care, custody or control of the Insured or as to which the Insured is for any purpose exercising physical control." Assume that Jones owns a power saw but does not have room for it at his apartment. Jones asks Homeowner's permission to leave the saw in Homeowner's garage and tells Homeowner to feel free to use it and that he, Jones, would like to come over and use it from time to time. Homeowner agrees, but never has any occasion to use the saw. Jones, however, uses the saw several times

a month. Homeowner negligently damages the saw while attempting to move it to another part of the garage. Is Homeowner covered? *See generally* Donald M. Zupanec, Annotation, *Scope of Clause Excluding from Contractor's or Similar Liability Policy Damage to Property in Care, Custody, or Control of Insured,* 8 A.L.R.4th 563 (1981).

[2] Intentionally-caused Loss

There are, as one would expect, many other exclusions in the standard homeowners form, exclusions too numerous to discuss in detail in a basic insurance law course. One, however, that must be considered is the exclusion for bodily injury or property damage caused intentionally by the insured. Does this exclusion implicate the fundamental requirement of fortuity? Does this exclusion have any relevance to the homeowners policy's *grant* of coverage in the occurrence clause (or equivalent coverage provision)? Does it matter whether the results of intended conduct turn out to be different from what the insured expected? Consider the next two cases and the notes which follow them.

AMCO INSURANCE CO. v. HAHT

490 N.W.2d 843 (Iowa 1992) (en banc)

HARRIS, JUSTICE.

An insurer brought this declaratory judgment action to test its contention that there is no coverage for liability in a wrongful death claim. The insured, an eleven-year-old child, deliberately struck another child with a thrown baseball after becoming irritated in a neighborhood game. According to the trial court's findings the insured intended to hurt the second child, but not to cause him bodily injury. The question concerns an exclusion for liability for bodily injury expected or intended by the insured. The district court found that the exclusion did not apply and we agree.

Plaintiff AMCO Insurance Company issued Henry and Kathryn Haht a homeowners insurance policy. The Hahts' son (Chris) was an insured under the policy. Chris reached his eleventh birthday nine days after the neighborhood baseball game in which the incident occurred.

There was ample evidence to support these trial court findings: On June 9, 1988, Chris, his younger brother Travis, and two neighborhood friends, Matt Lottman and Mike Carrigan, were playing "lob ball," or "workup" in Chris's backyard in Sutherland, Iowa. The game included someone pitching, someone batting, and the others fielding. After about an hour an argument developed (not surprisingly) over who should pitch. Matt, who had been in the field, wanted to pitch. Chris, who was batting, wanted Travis to pitch. Matt threw the baseball at Travis, who was pitching, hitting him in the leg. Some arguments and some pushing and shoving developed, but the game continued. After some period of time, Matt announced that because he could not pitch he was quitting and threw his glove to the ground. Chris, who happened to have the ball, threw it in Matt's direction. The ball struck Matt in the temple and Matt tragically died as a result of the injuries he received. Matt Lottman's parents (defendants Lottman) have filed a petition. . .seeking damages from Chris for the wrongful death of Matt. . . . AMCO issued [a] homeowners policy . . . to Chris's parents [for the period in question]. The Lottmans and Hahts contend the policy covers Chris and his alleged liability for the wrongful death of Matt. AMCO disagrees, contending the actions of Chris were intentional and hence excluded under the following language of the policy: "COVERAGE E—Personal Liability and Coverage F—Medical Payments to Others do not apply to bodily injury or property damage: a. which is expected or intended by the insured; . . . ."

The policy defines bodily injury as "bodily harm, sickness or disease, including required care, loss of services and death that results." The policy defines occurrence as "an accident, including exposure to conditions, which results, during the policy period, in: a. bodily injury; . . . ."

I.

General principles are not disputed. Where insurance policies "are ambiguous, require interpretation, or are susceptible to two equally proper constructions, the court will adopt the construction most favorable to the insured." This principle of construction is necessary because insurance policies are in the nature of adhesion contracts. Additionally, "[a]n insurer, having affirmatively expressed coverage through broad promises, assumes a duty to define any limitations or exclusionary clauses in clear and explicit terms." Also, "[a] contract of insurance should be interpreted from a viewpoint of an ordinary [lay] person, not a specialist or expert." Therefore, "[w]hen words are left undefined in a policy [they will not be given] a technical meaning. Rather [they will be given] their ordinary meaning, one which a reasonable person would understand them to mean." Lastly, where parties disagree as to the meaning of terms, there is an objective test to determine whether the terms are ambiguous: "Is the language fairly susceptible to two interpretations?"

II.

By its terms the exclusion clause operates to prevent insurance coverage for an insured's personal liability for bodily injury in two situations: (1) where the insured expected bodily injury; and (2) where the insured intended bodily injury. We first consider AMCO's contention that the exclusion was triggered because Chris expected bodily injury.

We have defined the term "expected," as used in exclusionary clauses of insurance policies. We said the term "denotes that the actor knew or should have known that there was a substantial probability that certain consequences will result from his actions." *Weber v. IMT Ins. Co.*, 462 N.W.2d 283, 287 (Iowa 1990). Substantial probability requires the indicators to be "strong enough to alert a reasonably prudent [person] not only to the possibility of the results occurring but the indications also must be sufficient to forewarn [that person] that the results are highly likely to occur." *Id.*

There is no evidence Chris knew or should have known Matt's death would result from the thrown ball. The tragic consequence here was, by all accounts, entirely unexpected. Chris plainly did not intend this tragic injury to Matt.

III.

The much closer question is presented on AMCO's claim that Chris intended bodily injury to Matt. We, like courts elsewhere, have explored what sort of intent will trigger an intentional injury exclusion. We adhere to the majority view, under which the exclusion is triggered where the insured intended both (1) to do the act which caused the injury, and (2) to cause some kind of bodily injury. *Altena v. United Fire and Casualty Co.*, 422 N.W.2d 485, 488 (Iowa 1988). The intent to cause the injury may be either actual or inferred. *Id.* Intent may be inferred from the nature of the act and the accompanying reasonable foreseeability of harm. *Id.* In addition, "once intent to cause injury is found, it is immaterial that the actual injury caused is of a different character or magnitude than that intended." *Id.*

AMCO thinks the facts here qualify for exclusion under our *Altena* holding. Chris and his parents defend against the exclusion clause by contending Chris's intent to "hurt" Matt, a mere matter of playground bickering, did not rise to the level of intent to bodily injure him, as contemplated in *Altena*. It was on this point that Chris prevailed in district court and with the court of appeals majority.

We think Chris's point is well taken. An eleven-year-old boy, animated by an obscure playground snit, lacks the same capacity to formulate an intent to injure that is possessed by an adult, or even a youth of more maturity. In this respect the present case differs from those from other jurisdictions, cited in support of AMCO. *See Pachucki v. Republic Ins. Co.*, 89 Wis. 2d 703, 278 N.W.2d 898 (1979) (a youth old enough to be employed in a print shop); *Iowa Kemper Ins. Co. v. Stone*, 269 N.W.2d 885 (Minn. 1978) (a sixteen-year-old youth).

Chris and his parents can also rely on a direct defense on the basis of the wording of the policy, which differs from that in *Altena*. The exclusion in *Altena* was addressed to "any act committed by . . . the insured with intent to cause personal injury." *Altena*, 422 N.W.2d at 486. The exclusion involved here is not addressed to the insured's act. Rather, AMCO's exclusion is addressed to "bodily injury . . . intended by the insured." The target of this language is the injury specifically intended by the insured.

We in no way retreat from our holding in *Altena*; we merely hold it does not apply on this policy in these special circumstances. To apply *Altena* here would grossly overemphasize the vague, uncertain meanderings in the mind of an eleven-year-old child involved in a playground spat. The exclusion does not apply and the district court was correct in so holding.

DECISION OF COURT OF APPEALS AND JUDGMENT OF DISTRICT COURT AFFIRMED.

All Justices concur except SNELL, J., and McGIVERIN, C.J., and SCHULTZ, J., who dissent.

SNELL, JUSTICE (dissenting).

I respectfully dissent.

The majority has reached a result that would not be expected or intended from the language of the insurance policy. In fact, the policy language clearly states an exclusion from coverage that embraces this case.

Coverage E excludes personal liability to others for "bodily injury" expected or intended by the insured. The majority's analysis transforms this exclusion language to "death" expected or intended by the insured. Of course, the tragic death of Matt was not expected or intended by anyone. But to assign this as the reason that exclusionary insurance coverage does not apply subverts the policy principles cited by the majority.

The policy construction should not turn on whether death was expected or intended. "Bodily injury" is defined in the policy itself to include "bodily harm" as well as death. Bodily harm obviously has a broader scope than just the ultimate harm of death. The construction by the majority so narrows the policy exclusion that it would virtually have no application.

In a death case little short of murder would be excluded. If the insured intended to kill but succeeded only in maiming the victim, coverage would apply because the injury was not specifically intended by the assailant. In a less extreme case, the exclusion would not prevent coverage if the assailant intended to break the victim's arm but broke his leg instead. Such an interpretation totally changes the purpose of homeowners insurance covering accidents.

The policy exclusion does not depend on how severe or how tragic were the consequences of the act. The exclusion applies because the trial court found that harm was intended by the insured to another. The principles enunciated in *Altena v. United Fire and Casualty Co.*, 422 N.W.2d 485, 488 (Iowa 1988), apply to deny coverage. An insurer is entitled to rely on them in gauging the risk of its insurance underwriting.

The majority distinguishes this case from *Altena* because the exclusion in the AMCO homeowners policy issued to the Hahts excluded damages for "bodily injury . . . intended by the insured." The majority adopts the view that the exclusion applies only when the insured has the specific intent to cause the type of injury suffered. This test would apply in all cases where the intentional injury exclusion clause in an insurance policy has language similar to the AMCO policy. In *Altena*, we expressly rejected that view in favor of the majority rule, noting our decision in *McAndrews v. Farm Bureau Mutual Insurance Co.*, 349 N.W.2d 117 (Iowa 1984), in which we denied coverage to an insured who injured the victim in self defense under an exclusion for "bodily injury which is either expected or intended from the standpoint of the insured." We did not distinguish the policy language in *McAndrews* when we examined that decision in *Altena*. In fact, in *Altena* we relied extensively on cases that interpreted exclusion clauses with language identical or similar to the AMCO policy. See *Altena*, 422 N.W.2d at 488-89. We cited these decisions from other jurisdictions to support the majority rule that the intent to act and the intent to cause some kind of bodily injury are sufficient to deny insurance coverage. The language in the AMCO policy does not direct that we now adopt a different view.

In *Pachucki v. Republic Insurance Co.*, 89 Wis. 2d 703, 278 N.W.2d 898 (1979), the Supreme Court of Wisconsin denied coverage for the insured's intentional acts under a policy exclusion for "bodily injury. . .which is either expected or intended from the standpoint of the insured." The insured struck the victim, injuring his eye, with a "greening pin" which he had projected with a rubber band. The court found that the insured intended to strike the victim's body with the pin and intended to inflict no greater harm than a "sting" to the victim. The Wisconsin court held that recovery must be barred under the intentional tort exclusionary sections of the applicable insurance policies because the insured intended to act and to inflict injury; it was immaterial that the resulting injury was different in character or magnitude from the injury that was intended. *Id.* at 904.

The Supreme Court of Minnesota has examined similar exclusion language in *Iowa Kemper Insurance Co. v. Stone,* 269 N.W.2d 885 (Minn.1978). In that case, the insured intentionally struck the victim with the buckle of his belt which he had wrapped around his hand. The blow caused the victim to suffer from a continuing epileptic condition. The homeowners insurance policy in the name of the insured's father provided that there would be no coverage for "bodily injury . . . caused intentionally by or at the direction of the insured." The Supreme Court of Minnesota determined that there would be no coverage. The Court stated:

> The "intent" required to exclude coverage is neither the "intent to act" nor the "intent to cause the specific injury complained of." Rather, it is the "intent to cause bodily injury" even if the actual injury is more severe or of a different nature than the injury intended.
>
> . . . .
>
> The rule is well-established and well-reasoned, consistent with the reasonable expectations of the parties to the insurance contract and the public policy against "licensing" intentional and unlawful harmful acts. In the instant case, the direct and inferential evidence permits only one conclusion: [the insured] intended to injure [the victim]. The district court's conclusion to that effect was clearly correct; coverage was therefore properly excluded.

Id. at 887.

In *Youngwirth v. State Farm Mutual Automobile Insurance Co.,* we set out principles applicable to intent of the parties in insurance contracts. A second principle auxiliary to the determination of intent is that the language of insurance contracts must be given its common and ordinary meaning and must be construed as popularly understood. We have said: ". . . the words, terms, and provisions of insurance contracts, and particularly clauses limiting or excluding liability on the policy, must be given a practical, reasonable and fair interpretation. . . . Such words must be given their plain, ordinary, and popular meaning and not peculiar or technical meanings." 258 Iowa 974, 978, 140 N.W.2d 881, 884 (1966);.

The majority has carved out of the policy an exception to the policy exclusion concerning eleven-year-olds injuring someone in a playground argument. Nothing in the policy remotely suggests the creation of this idea. While compassion for parties suffering tragic injuries has a rightful place in law it should not negate the clear meaning of language already fixed by our jurisprudence. An insurer is entitled to have some idea of what it is insuring.

Christopher Haht intended to hit and cause bodily injury to Matt Lottman. The fact that the injury was more severe than Christopher intended is not a consideration under the principles we adopted in *Altena*. Coverage should be denied.

McGIVERIN, C.J., AND SCHULTZ, J., join this dissent.

————————

Nationwide Insurance v. Board of Trustees of the University of Illinois, 116 F.3d 1154 (7th Cir. 1997). The insurer sought a declaratory judgment that it was not required to defend or indemnify insured with respect to the University of Illinois's lawsuit against the insured, based on damage caused when the insured and others set fire to the Astroturf in the football stadium at the Champaign-Urbana campus, causing in excess of $600,000 in damages. The homeowners policy had been issued to the insured's parents in Pennsylvania, and excluded property damage "which is expected or intended by the insured." The Seventh Circuit, in an opinion by Judge Rovner, upheld the district court's summary judgment for Nationwide, under the reasoning that the claim was not covered because applicable Pennsylvania law would "deem the damage resulting from [the insured's] actions expected or intended."

"Sometimes common sense prevails, even in the law. This is one of those occasions.

"   . . . .

"Both Zavalis and the University's Board of Trustees have appealed the district court's judgment, but the Trustees are not properly before us. They are not parties to the underlying insurance contract, and although as the victims of Zavalis' alleged wrongdoing they have an obvious interest in the question of indemnification (which the district court did not reach), they have no interest in whether Nationwide must supply Zavalis with a defense. . . . . (Ironically, the Trustees seem to be handling Zavalis' defense quite nicely on their own: rather than writing his own appellate brief, Zavalis has simply joined the Trustees' brief; so although the Trustees' appeal has been dismissed, Zavalis has the benefit of the arguments they made.)

"   . . . . an insured 'expects or intends' the injury in question when he acts with an intent or a conscious awareness that damage will result. The insured may not 'expect or intend' the damage when the actual result is an injury wholly different in kind from the type he anticipated would occur; and the magnitude of the resulting harm is one factor that can be considered in that assessment. Yet, the mere fact that the actual damage is more severe than the insured anticipated does not, by itself, necessarily establish that he did not 'expect or intend' it. Judge Baker found that '[p]ouring lighter fluid on Astroturf and setting it aflame could only be interpreted as intending some kind of damage.' Based on the record before him, then, he perceived no way in which the University's claim against Zavalis might be covered by his parents' insurance policy in view of the exclusion for intentional property damage. He accordingly concluded that Nationwide had no duty to defend Zavalis in the Illinois suit.

"On appeal, Zavalis does not take issue with the notion that if he intended to set fire to some portion of the Astroturf, the resulting damage was 'expected or intended' even though far more of the turf burned than he planned on. He instead quarrels with the premise that he intended to burn any part of the Astroturf. We took this as a given in the prior appeal, but in that respect Zavalis claims that we jumped the gun. We did not have Zavalis' deposition in the state court action before us at that time, and there Zavalis testified that it was never his intent for the Astroturf to burn; rather, he and his colleagues thought that the lighter fluid alone would burn, leaving only a residue of soot on the portions of the Astroturf to which it had been applied—spelling out the letters 'F-O-O' —which would be visible on television or from the bleachers. In fact, Zavalis recalled, he and his friends had tried the same thing on a concrete sidewalk earlier, and had caused no damage (actually, they couldn't get the lighter fluid even to ignite); and to Zavalis, the Astroturf itself felt like concrete, so he thought the results would be equally harmless. Even after the letters 'F-O-O' were ablaze on the field (the flames reaching from eight to eighteen inches into the air), the three young men didn't think they had done any damage to the playing surface. On the contrary, by Zavalis' account, they left the stadium believing nothing was seriously wrong, tossed the lighter fluid bottle into a Port-a-Potty on their way out, and went home to bed, confident they had done no real harm even as they heard the wail of fire engines a short while later. As Zavalis sees things, then, the district court either should have granted summary judgment in his favor for want of any evidence that he intended the Astroturf to burn or, at the very least, it should have found that there was a dispute of material fact on this question and denied Nationwide's own motion for summary judgment.

"In their effort to bring intentional acts within the coverage of insurance policies, insureds and their victims find themselves creatively alleging that the insured 'carelessly and negligently failed to refrain from avoiding' his victim (read: repeatedly stabbed him with a four-inch blade), *Allstate Ins. Co. v. Carioto,* 194 Ill.App.3d 767, 141 Ill.Dec. 389, 391, 551 N.E.2d 382, 384 (1990), 'negligent[ly], careless[ly] and/or reckless[ly]' 'struck' his victim (read: poked her eye out with a broomstick), *Nationwide Mut. Ins. Co. v. Yaeger,* 1994 WL 447405, *2 (E.D.Pa. Aug.19, 1994), aff'd. without published op., 60 F.3d 816 (3d Cir.1995), or '[a]ccidentally, negligently or inadvertently' committed a 'trespass' (read: shot his victim four times in the chest at close range with a nine-millimeter automatic), *Germantown Ins. Co. v. Martin,* 407 Pa.Super. 326, 595 A.2d 1172, 1173 (1991).

"Zavalis' artful (if less extravagant) spin on his own actions fits comfortably within this genre, and to no greater degree of success. The undisputed (and inescapable) fact is that Zavalis did intend to damage the Astroturf. Whether he meant to actually scorch the Astroturf (to 'brand' it, as the University alleges in its complaint) or merely to leave a layer of soot on the turf that could be cleaned away later as if he had used a giant washable Crayola marker, common sense tells us that his purpose was to damage the field nonetheless. Damage need not be permanent to constitute 'damage,' and defacement certainly qualifies as damage even if is easier and less costly to rectify than several hundred square feet of incinerated Astroturf. What is more, Zavalis meant to inflict that damage by means of fire. We may assume, as Zavalis steadfastly maintains, that he meant only for the lighter fluid to burn, not the Astroturf itself. There might be some quibbling with the plausibility of that plan. The very purpose of an accelerant like lighter fluid is, through its own combustion, to cause other things with a higher flash point (charcoal, for example) to burn; little if any soot is likely to be left behind if the accelerant fails in that purpose. But this may be putting too fine a point on the matter for three college students whose primary beverages that day had been beer, punch laced with Triple Sec and/or Everclear, Tequila Sunrises, and Alabama Slammers. The important point is that Zavalis and his accomplices did intend for there to be a fire-by Zavalis' account, he simply did not intend for the fire to spread beyond the accelerant and to engulf the Astroturf. But this leaves him no better off than the young vandal who meant only to set a fire within the confines of several boxes of books and ended up causing $1.3 million in damage to a school building. *City of Newton v. Krasnigor,* 404 Mass. 682, 536 N.E.2d 1078, 1082 (1989). For that matter, as Nationwide argues, Zavalis is really no different from the insured who when he took a swing did not expect to break his victim's nose. *State Farm Fire & Casualty Co. v. Levine,* 389 Pa.Super. 1, 566 A.2d 318, 320 (1989).

"Aleck Zavalis and his companions most likely had no idea when they sallied forth into the wee hours of that September morning in 1989 that someone would make a federal case out of their prank. Then again, they probably did not anticipate that their little escapade would cost the University more than half a million dollars, either. The principle is as important as the price tag. Nationwide need not supply Zavalis with a defense if the University's complaint against him does not comprehend an injury within the coverage of his parents' insurance policy. Here, Zavalis literally played with fire; and although the resulting harm was far beyond what he expected, 'this [was][a] harm controlled by the insured, and it is this harm which the companies should not be forced to insure against.' *Elitzky,* 517 A.2d at 988. Nationwide is entitled to a declaration that it is not obligated to defend Zavalis against the University's Illinois suit. We therefore affirm Judge Baker's grant of summary judgment in favor of Nationwide."

NOTES

1. *An implied exclusion?* If there is no intentional injury exclusion in a liability policy, should the court hold that it is nevertheless against public policy to insure against such acts? *See Isenhart v. General Casualty Co. of Am.,* 233 Or. 49, 377 P.2d 26 (1962). What connections do you see between the principle of fortuity and the intentional injury exclusion? The first question posed will hardly ever arise, given that such exclusions are standard fare in all liability policies.

2. *Where's the occurrence?* If there is no coverage in the first instance, is the intentional injury exclusion even relevant? Do you agree that there was an "occurrence" in *Haht*? Was there an "accident," and hence an "occurrence," in *Nationwide*? In *Frankenmuth Mutual Insurance Co. v. Masters,* 460 Mich. 105, 595 N.W.2d 832 (1999), the insured and his employee intentionally set fire to inventory in their store. They did not intend or expect that the fire would get out of control and damage adjoining buildings. The court held that

the collateral damage was not "accidental" as defined in the homeowners and CGL policies at issue, and there was accordingly no "occurrence" which could trigger coverage in the first instance. 460 Mich. at 107. Whose perspective should be used to determine whether an accident has occurred—the insured's or the victim's?

3. *Evolving policy language.* Although the intentional injury exclusion is standard fare, the text of the exclusion has had various permutations through the years. One early version provided that "an assault and battery shall be deemed an accident unless committed by or at the direction of the insured." Would the presence of this language have changed the result in *Haht?* In what kind of case might it make a difference? See Restatement (Second) of Torts §§ 13, 18, and 21 (definitions of assault and battery).

In many older homeowners policies (but also in some recent ones), it was common for the policy to contain a coverage-granting provision (the insurer will "pay all damages which the insured becomes legally obligated to pay because of bodily injury to any person . . . caused by an occurrence to which this insurance applies"), followed by an exclusion for "bodily injury or property damages caused wilfully, intentionally or maliciously by or at the direction of the insured." While this may on its face appear to separate the intent issue from the coverage issue, "occurrence" was usually defined as an "accident," which puts the question of intent into play, as the previous note indicates.

The configuration of provisions in older policies has been superseded in many modern policies by the adoption of new exclusionary language or by a revised definition of "occurrence" promulgated by the Insurance Services Office in 1966. The operative language is the same in both provisions. "Occurrence" is defined to mean "an accident, including injurious exposure to conditions, which results, during the policy period, in bodily injury or property damage neither expected nor intended from the standpoint of the insured." The exclusion simply says that the policy does not apply "to bodily injury or property damage which is either expected or intended from the standpoint of the insured."

4. *What is "intent"?* Restatement (Second) of Torts § 8A defines "intent" to mean that "the actor desires to cause consequences of his act, or that he believes that the consequences are substantially certain to result from it." The comment goes on to explain that where the probability factor decreases and the chances that the consequences will ensue become less than a substantial certainty, the actor's conduct falls outside the definition of "intent." The conduct then should be classified as reckless or even just negligent. How do the clauses containing the exclusionary language described above comport with the Restatement's definition of "intent"?

If the insured is convicted of a crime for which intent is an element, and if the insured is subsequently sued by the victim in a civil proceeding for injuries suffered, does the homeowners policy provide coverage? Does it matter if the insured pleads guilty in lieu of going to trial in the criminal proceeding? *See State Farm Fire and Casualty Co. v. Fullerton,* 118 F.3d 374 (5th Cir. 1997).

5. *One rule: Intent to act and to cause the harm that resulted.* A few courts, when asking whether the harm was "caused intentionally," ask whether the

insured (a) intended his or her act and (b) intended to inflict the specific kind of harm that resulted. *See Norris v. State Farm Fire & Casualty Co.,* 16 S.W.3d 242 (Ark. 2000); *Preferred Mutual Insurance Co. v. Gamache,* 426 Mass. 93, 686 N.E.2d 989 (1997); *Physicians Insurance Co. of Ohio v. Swanson,* 569 N.E.2d 906 (Ohio 1991). Is this a good standard for compensating victims? For deterring tortious conduct? How does such a test stack up against the fortuity requirement? How does this standard affect the insurer's chances of getting a summary judgment?

6. *Another rule: Intent to act plus results that are natural and probable consequences.* At the other end of the continuum, some courts, borrowing from tort law and criminal law doctrines, ask wl ether (a) the insured intended his act, and (b) the damages or injuries which resulted are the natural and probable consequences of the insured's act. *See Ohio Casualty Insurance Co. v. Horner,* 583 N.W.2d 804 (N.D. 1998); *St. Paul Insurance Cos. v. Talladega Nursing Home, Inc.,* 606 F.2d 631 (5th Cir. 1979). If a court states, as many have done, that a person "is presumed to intend the natural and probable consequences of his or her acts," does that mean that the insured loses coverage if he or she intentionally acts but has *no* intent regarding the consequences of his or her act?

How is the test, as articulated, any different from the test for negligence in tort law? If the negligent acts are excluded from coverage under liability policies, what is left?

In *Horner, supra,* the insured, a 16-year-old, used a slingshot to propel a quarter-sized rock at a pedestrian from his location in a moving vehicle, and the court held that he was not covered for the resulting liability. 583 N.W.2d at 807-08. Is *Horner* distinguishable from a child placing a smoke bomb in an apartment, which in turn starts a fire which causes great damage? How would the court in *Haht* decide these cases? Should the court indulge the presumption and deny coverage, or put the burden on the insurer to prove that the child understood the consequences of the act? *Compare West Bldg. Materials, Inc. v. Allstate Insurance Co.,* 363 So. 2d 398 (Fla. App. 1978) with *Allstate Insurance Co. v. Steinemer,* 723 F.2d 873 (11th Cir. 1984).

7. *Yet another rule: Intent to act plus intent to cause some kind of harm.* In most jurisdictions, the rule is one that sits between the two rules discussed in the preceding notes. Under the majority view, the insured must have intended both the act *and* to cause some kind of injury or damage. The fact that the precise kind of injury or damage that results differs from what was intended does not prevent the exclusion from applying. *See e.g., Lewis v. Allstate Insurance Co.,* 730 So. 2d 65 (Miss. 1999); *Allstate Indemnity Co. v. Lewis,* 985 F. Supp. 1341 (M.D. Ala. 1997); *Allstate Insurance Co. v. Dillard,* 859 F. Supp. 1501 (M.D. Ga. 1994).

How does the intent plus some-kind-of-harm test apply in the facts of *Haht*? How would this test apply to the child's use of the smoke bomb, as described in the preceding note? *See Unigard Mutual Insurance Co. v. Argonaut Insurance Co.,* 579 P.2d 1015 (Wash. Ct. App. 1978). If the insured sets fire to a building that he mistakenly believes to be an abortion clinic, should the owner of the destroyed building be able to obtain the benefit of the insured's liability policy? *See American Family Mutual Insurance Co. v. Mission Medical Group,* 72 F.3d 645 (8th Cir. 1995).

8. *When is injury or damage "expected" by the insured?* What is the difference between "expected" and "intended"? Is it possible for injury or damage to be one but not the other? If "intent" connotes "desire" and "expected" connotes "foreseeability," what *degree* of awareness is necessary to make a result "expected"? *See Honeycomb Systems, Inc. v. Admiral Insurance Co.,* 567 F. Supp. 1400 (D. Me. 1983). When discussing identical language found in the CGL, Professor Kenneth Abraham has observed that the word "expected" involves three separate issues: the degree of probability of harm; the amount of the insured's awareness of the probability; and the extent to which deviation in the kind of harm that results from the insured's expectation will be tolerated. Kenneth S. Abraham, Environmental Liability Insurance Law 132 (1991). Does this tempt one to conclude that "expected" means the same thing as "intended" and leave it at that? *See State Farm Fire & Casualty Co. v. Muth,* 207 N.W.2d 364 (Neb. 1973).

Suppose the insured admits intentionally kicking open a locked door of a restroom stall in order to deliver a "wake-up call"to the stall's occupant, a co-worker with whom he had ongoing disagreements. The door, however, swings open violently and hits the co-worker, causing injury. The insured did not intend any offensive contact or physical injury. Is the insured covered? *See Blue Ridge Insurance Co. v. Puig,* 64 F. Supp. 2d 514 (D. Md. 1999).

9. *Practical jokers; kids will be kids.* Everyone knows at least one practical joker, perhaps someone like the insured in the *Nationwide* case. In that case, the link between setting fire to the stadium carpet and the property damage was hard to miss. When the joker intends the act but exercises incredibly poor judgment by disregarding less obvious risks of injury, is the joker covered by her liability policy when the prank goes awry? *See Millers Mutual Insurance Co. v. Strainer,* 663 P.2d 338 (Mont. 1983) (employee, as a joke, squirts smoke into coworker's respirator). Should the intelligence or maturity of the insured matter? For example, have you ever dropped pumpkins from overpasses of interstates, making the seeds and pulp splash onto the sides of moving cars and trucks? Such conduct is patently stupid, but if a teenager does this in disregard of the obvious dangers and without intent to hurt anyone, and if the teen misjudges the drop and sends the pumpkin through a car's windshield with tragic consequences, is the teenager's act (assume the teenager is an insured) covered by a liability policy? *See Vermont Mutual Insurance Co. v. Dalzell,* 218 N.W.2d 52 (Mich. Ct. App. 1974). If a fraternity pledge is injured during a hazing incident and he sues the fraternity members involved, are the members covered by their policies of homeowners insurance? *See Auto-Owners Insurance Co. v. American Central Insurance Co.,* 739 So. 2d 1078 (Ala. 1999). What if the passenger in a vehicle while joking grabs the steering wheel and turns it suddenly, thereby causing an accident in which others are injured? *See Harrison v. Tomes,* 956 S.W.2d 268 (Mo. 1997).

10. *A robbery gone awry.* In *Continental Western Insurance Co. v. Toal,* 309 Minn. 169, 244 N.W.2d 121 (1976), a group of individuals, including the insureds, attempted an armed robbery at a bowling alley. Although they did not specifically intend to shoot anyone during the robbery, they did intend

to threaten people with guns and use them if necessary. During the course of the robbery, one of the robbers, who was not an insured, shot and killed an employee. The employee's widow brought a wrongful death action against all of the participants on the theory of joint venture, and the insurers commenced a declaratory judgment action to determine their obligation to the insureds. The Minnesota court, in construing the "expected or intended" language, said that intent may be established by proof of an actual intent to injure or when the character of an act is such that an intention to inflict injury can be inferred as a matter of law. Given that standard, are the insureds covered? *See also Landry v. Leonard,* 720 A.2d 907 (Me. 1998); *Ohio Casualty Insurance Co. v. Henderson,* 189 Ariz. 184, 939 P.2d 1337 (1997).

11. *Contrarian cases; using the victim's perspective.* A few cases have taken the position that the perspective of the tort victim should be utilized in determining whether there was an accident or occurrence under liability insurance, in lieu of the orthodox rule that the matter should be approached from the insured's perspective. *See e.g., Tomlin v. State Farm Mutual Automobile Liability Insurance Co.,* 95 Wis. 2d 215, 290 N.W.2d 285 (1980). *See also* Annot., *Liability Insurance: Assault as an "Accident," or Injuries Therefrom as "Accidentally" Sustained, Within Coverage Clause,* 72 A.L.R.3d 1090 (1976). Where the insured and injured person are the same, as in first-party policies of life and health and accident insurance, the Wisconsin analysis produces the correct result. But are cases dealing with those types of first-party insurance authority for the proposition that an intentional tortfeasor should be protected by third-party liability insurance simply because the injury is fortuitous from the perspective of the tort victim?

Some of the cases relied on by the Wisconsin court in *Tomlin* appeared to involve vicarious responsibility for intentionally caused injuries. *See Fox Wisconsin Corp. v. Century Indemnity Co.,* 219 Wis. 549, 263 N.W. 567 (1935). Is there any violation of public policy in permitting liability coverage for an employer who is vicariously responsible for the intentional torts of an employee, so long as the harm is fortuitous as to the employer, i.e., the employer did not direct the employee to intentionally harm someone or otherwise participate in the wrongdoing? How about the liability of parents for the intentional acts of their children in circumstances where a parent was negligent in supervising or controlling the child? *Compare Unigard Mutual Insurance Co. v. Argonaut Insurance Co.,* 20 Wash. App. 261, 579 P.2d 1015 (1978), with *Allstate Ins. Co. v. Steele,* 74 F.3d 878 (8th Cir. 1996), and *Chacon v. American Family Mutual Insurance Co.,* 788 P.2d 748 (Colo. 1990) (en banc). Does the "by or at the direction" and the "not intended or expected" language contemplate coverage for those intentional tort situations where a parent's or an employer's liability is imposed for the mere negligence of the parent or employer or where it is imposed solely on a vicarious basis? The latter can occur with parents under so-called "malicious mischief" statutes. *See* Ariz. Rev. Stat. Ann. § 12-661 (West 1992 & Supp. 1999).

12. *Contrarian cases and the objective of victim compensation.* Some courts have held that it is against public policy to indemnify an insured who intentionally inflicts harm, even if the policy does not contain exclusionary language, but that it does not violate any public policy to compel the insurer

to pay the damages suffered by an innocent intentional tort victim, as long as the insured does not benefit. In *Ambassador Insurance Co. v. Montes,* 76 N.J. 477, 388 A.2d 603 (1978), the insured intentionally set fire to a building that he owned, and an infant perished in the fire. A wrongful death action was brought against the insured. In holding that there was coverage, the court relied primarily on first-party insurance cases where there was more than one insured under the policy and only one insured intentionally caused the loss. In those cases, the courts held that an innocent insured could recover. Are those cases relevant to third-party liability insurance situations? Does the *Montes* opinion stand third-party insurance on its head in viewing the tort victim as an insured? In *Montes,* the insurance policy in evidence did not contain any definition of "occurrence" or any exclusionary language as to intentional acts. A later case seems to limit *Montes* to the situation where the policy is silent and casts some doubt on future applications. *See Allstate Insurance Co. v. Malec,* 104 N.J. 1, 514 A.2d 832 (1986).

13. *More hard issues.* In the all-too-common and always tragic circumstances where an adult sexually molests a child, is the adult's civil liability excluded from coverage pursuant to the principles outlined above? Should the urge for victim compensation in such cases cut in favor of construing the exclusion narrowly (and coverage broadly)? Does mental incapacity or insanity present any special problems? What about incapacity caused by voluntary intoxication or drug abuse? Consider the next case.

WILEY v. STATE FARM FIRE & CASUALTY CO.

995 F.2d 457 (3d Cir. 1993)

ROSENN, CIRCUIT JUDGE.

In this diversity case, we are called upon to predict whether Pennsylvania law would obligate an insurer under its homeowner's insurance policy to provide coverage for damages incurred by an insured in the sexual molestation of his minor niece. Prior to the commencement of the present action, the insured, Floyd Wiley, Jr. (Floyd), pled guilty in 1988 in a state court of Pennsylvania to one count of indecent assault and one count of corrupting the morals of a minor.

The plaintiffs, Dennis and Elaine Wiley, as parents and next of friend of the minor (the Wileys), citizens of Ohio, then filed the instant civil suit against Floyd, a citizen of Pennsylvania, in the United States District Court for the Western District of Pennsylvania to recover money damages for bodily harm resulting from their daughter's molestation in 1986. The complaint alleged negligent infliction of personal injury, as well as intentional tort.

Floyd tendered defense of the civil action to State Farm Fire and Casualty Co. (State Farm) under the homeowner's policy it issued to him. State Farm accepted the defense subject to a reservation of rights to contest coverage on the ground that Floyd's conduct fell within a standard homeowner's policy coverage exclusion for bodily injury "intended or expected" by an insured (the intended harm exclusion).[1] The proper construction of this clause is at the heart of the insurer's defense and is the sole issue on appeal. The parties eventually stipulated to Floyd's culpability, the value of the Wileys' claim should they prevail, and the filing of a declaratory judgment action against State Farm to determine the applicability of the homeowner's policy to the Wileys' claim. Upon the filing of the declaratory judgment action, the plaintiffs dismissed the suit against Floyd.

Both parties filed motions for summary judgment. The district court denied the Wileys' motion and entered judgment granting State Farm's motion. The Wileys timely appealed. We affirm.

I. BACKGROUND

In July 1986, Floyd sexually molested his minor niece, then age 13, while she was a visitor at his home. It was undisputed for purposes of summary judgment that Floyd, an admitted alcoholic at the time of these incidents of sexual misconduct, was intoxicated during these episodes. Although the district court found no Pennsylvania law directly on point, it determined that courts in other jurisdictions infer an intent to harm as a matter of law from acts of child molestation and rape, which intent precludes insurance coverage. It also found that other courts consider the sexual molestation of children to be a criminal offense for which public policy precludes a claim that no harm was intended. For these reasons, the court predicted that the Pennsylvania Supreme Court would hold Floyd's sexual abuse of the minor excluded from coverage under his homeowner's policy with State Farm. *Wiley v. State Farm Fire & Cas. Co.*, No. 89-421, slip op. at 2-4, 1992 WL 503433 (W.D.Pa. Feb. 24, 1992).

On appeal, the Wileys contend that the district court erred . . . (2) in finding that Pennsylvania public policy insulates the insurer from liability to victims of sexual molestation when the insured's actions are found to be criminal, regardless of the actual existence or non-existence of an intent to harm.

II. DISCUSSION

. . . .

B. APPLICABILITY OF THE INFERRED INTENT RULE WHEN THE INSURED ASSERTS AN ABSENCE OF SUBJECTIVE INTENT TO HARM

The inferred intent rule allows a court to infer an actor's intent from the nature and character of his or her acts. *See e.g., Fireman's Fund Ins. Co. v.*

---

[1] The policy provided in pertinent part, in Section II, Coverage L, for the payment of a claim against an insured for damages because of bodily injury or property damage to which coverage applies and for which the insured is legally liable. Section II, Coverage M, provided for the payment of necessary medical expenses incurred or medically ascertained as a result of an accident causing bodily injury. The exclusions provision of Section II, however, provided: 1. Coverage L and Coverage M do not apply to: a. bodily injury or property damage which is expected or intended by an insured. . . . One court has pointed out that it is preferable to consider the issue of initial coverage before addressing the issue of exclusion. *Western Nat'l Assurance Co. v. Hecker,* 43 Wash. App. 816, 719 P.2d 954, 958 n. 2 (1986). The issue of initial coverage is not raised by the parties to this appeal, however, and we therefore do not address it.

Hill, 314 N.W.2d 834, 835 (Minn.1982). Courts applying the inferred intent rule generally do so to establish conclusively the existence of intent to harm as a matter of law. *See e.g., State Farm Fire & Cas. Co. v. Abraio,* 874 F.2d 619, 623 (9th Cir. 1989) (applying California law) ("there is an irrebuttable presumption of intent to harm supplied as a matter of law in child molestation cases"). Once established, this conclusive presumption of intent to harm results in a determination as a matter of law that, notwithstanding the insured's assertion of an absence of subjective intent to harm, an insurer has no obligation under a policy containing a standard intended harm exclusion to provide coverage for bodily injury to a child sexually abused by an insured adult. *Id.* at 623.

In adjudicating general liability insurance cases, as opposed to those exceptional cases involving sexual child abuse, Pennsylvania courts presently follow the intermediate appellate court decision of *United Services Automobile Association v. Elitzky,* 358 Pa. Super. 362, 517 A.2d 982 (1986), *appeal denied,* 515 Pa. 600, 528 A.2d 957 (1987). Applying well-settled standards of insurance contract interpretation, the *Elitzky* court first determined that, as used in the standard intended harm exclusion, "intentional and expected are synonymous." 517 A.2d at 986, 991. The court then stated:

> We hold that an intended harm exclusionary clause in an insurance contract is ambiguous as a matter of law and must be construed against the insurer. We hold that such a clause excludes only injury and damage of the same general type which the insured intended to cause. An insured intends an injury if he desired to cause the consequences of his act or if he acted knowing that such consequences were substantially certain to result. [*Id.* at 989.]

In Pennsylvania, then, it is not sufficient that the insured intended his actions; rather, for the resulting injury to be excluded from coverage, the insured must have specifically intended to cause harm. Additionally, in cases that do not involve sexual child abuse, Pennsylvania has adopted a general standard for determining the existence of this specific intent that looks to the insured's actual subjective intent.

In the context of general liability insurance cases, this subjective standard is not uncommon. *See e.g., Continental W. Ins. Co. v. Toal,* 309 Minn. 169, 244 N.W.2d 121, 124-25 (1976) (intended harm exclusion inapplicable unless insured acts with intent to cause bodily injury). As the district court noted in this case, however, Pennsylvania has not decided the appropriate standard for determining the existence of an insured's intent to harm in the specific context of liability insurance cases involving intentional acts of child molestation. In this particular context, *Elitzky's* subjective standard for determining intent to harm is considered the minority rule. *See Whitt v. DeLeu,* 707 F. Supp. 1011, 1015 & n. 7 (W.D. Wis. 1989) (discussing cases adopting subjective test as taking minority approach).

If the Pennsylvania Supreme Court would apply this minority rule in the case of an insured's sexual child abuse, Floyd's assertion that he subjectively intended no harm, standing alone, would raise a genuine issue of triable fact as to Floyd's mental state at the time he sexually abused his niece. The court's grant of summary judgment rejecting any obligation on State Farm's part to provide coverage for the minor's bodily harm would then have been error. If, however, the Pennsylvania Supreme Court would adopt and apply the inferred intent rule in the exceptional case of sexual child abuse by an insured adult, as the district court predicted it would, then the district court did not err in granting summary judgment.

Although no federal appeals court has previously attempted to interpret Pennsylvania law in the specific context of sexual child abuse by an insured adult who claims to have had no subjective intent to harm the abused child, the district court in the instant case is not the first court to have predicted the Pennsylvania Supreme Court's adoption of the inferred intent rule. In *Foremost Insurance Co. v. Weetman,* 726 F. Supp. 618, 621-22 (W.D. Pa. 1989), *aff'd without op.,* 904 F.2d 694 (3d Cir. 1990), the court predicted Pennsylvania's adoption and application of the inferred intent rule after determining that "[a] majority of the courts have held that in liability insurance cases involving sexual abuse of children, the intent to cause injury can be inferred as a matter of law." 726 F. Supp. at 620. The court noted further that "there is an apparent shift in minority jurisdictions toward the majority view." *Id.* at 621.

The *Weetman* court correctly observed that the majority of jurisdictions to have considered the question of which standard to use in cases of an insured's sexual abuse of a child had adopted the inferred intent rule. This has remained true over the intervening years, even as the number of courts to have faced the question has increased; further, the trend noted in *Weetman* for minority jurisdictions to convert to the majority approach continues to grow.

. . . .

Many courts have discussed the circumstances under which it may be appropriate to infer intent to harm from the character of the act committed. . . .

. . . .

To summarize our survey of these and other analogous cases, we acknowledge that the overwhelming majority of courts considering the issue of an insurer's obligation to provide coverage for damages caused by an insured adult's intentional sexual abuse of a child have concluded that the insured's intent to harm will be inferred as a matter of law despite the insured's assertion that he or she subjectively did not intend to harm the child. These courts have so held regardless of whether the sexual abuse was "nonviolent" or unaccompanied by penetration. They have so held despite the result of denying the victim another source of compensation and without displacing a subjective or objective intent standard in other categories of liability insurance cases.

Further, the majority courts have supported their adoption of the inferred intent rule by noting that the state's proscription of sexual contact between an adult and a minor is a clear indication that such contact is inherently injurious to the victim; that criminalization of such conduct additionally serves to place the insured on notice of "the societal understanding that the harm from such conduct is inseparable from its performance," [*Allstate v.] Mugavero,* 581 N.Y.S.2d [142] at 146, 589 N.E.2d [365] at 369 [(N.Y. 1992)];

that the harm to the victimized child is no less serious when the abusive adult's subjective intentions are purportedly "benign," *id.*; and that, as a matter of insurance contract interpretation based on the expectations of the parties to the contract, "[t]he average person purchasing homeowner's insurance would cringe at the very suggestion that he was paying for [coverage for liability arising out of his sexual abuse of a child]. And certainly he would not want to share that type of risk with other homeowner's policy holders." *Rodriguez by Brennan v. Williams,* 42 Wash. App. 633, 713 P.2d 135, 137-38 *aff'd en banc,* 107 Wash. 2d 381, 729 P.2d 627 (1986).

Finally, the minority approach has been criticized as "logically untenable," [*Western National Assur. Co. v.*] *Hecker,* 719 P.2d [954] at 960 [(Wash. App. 1986)], with one court noting that "a completely subjective test would virtually make 'it impossible to preclude coverage for intentional [injuries] absent admissions by insureds of specific intent to harm or injure. Human nature augurs against any viable expectation of such admissions.'" [*Horace Mann Ins. Co. v.*] *Leeber,* 376 S.E.2d [581,] at 586 [(W. Va. 1988)] (alteration in original) (citation omitted). Assertions by insured adults that they did not intend the harm resulting from their intentional sexual misconduct with minors have been described as "def[ying] logic," *Landis [v. Allstate Ins. Co.],* 546 So. 2d [1051] at 1053 [(Fla. 1989)]; "little short of absurd," *Mutual of Enumclaw v. Merrill,* 102 Or. App. 408, 794 P.2d 818, 820 (1990); and "fl[ying] in the face of all reason, common sense and experience," [*CNA Ins. Co. v.*] *McGinnis,* 666 S.W.2d [689], at 691 [(Ark. 1984)].

In surveying out-of-state authority on this issue, the Supreme Court of California distilled the majority courts' view:

> [O]ther courts have relied in large part on a realistic view of child molestation. The view was well put by a Florida justice: ". . . I am absolutely unwilling to deny the foreseeability of injury to a child who is subjected to sexual abuse. It defies human response and sensitivity to conclude that the inevitable product of the sexual molestation of a child is not intended. That conduct inescapably inspires some response in the minor victim. Whether the response is a precocious excitation of libido, an utter revulsion or simply confusion, the child suffers grave psychological injury. . . . The damage [the child in this case] suffered flowed just as surely from [the insured's] criminal acts as if he had taken his fist or a club and struck her in the face." [*J.C. Penny Cas. Co. v.*] *M.K.,* 278 Cal. Rptr. [64,] at 74-75, 804 P.2d [689,] at 699-700 [(Cal. 1991)] (quoting *Zordan v. Page,* 500 So. 2d 608, 613 (Fla. Dist. Ct. App. 1986) (Frank, J., dissenting), overruled by *Landis,* 546 So. 2d 1051).

We believe a rule holding that harm to children in sexual molestation cases is inherent in the very act of sexual assault committed on a child, regardless of the motivation for or nature of such assault, and that the resulting injuries are, as a matter of law, intentional represents an enlightened and perceptive view of the evolving law. We therefore predict that the Pennsylvania Supreme Court, if called upon to decide the issue, would adopt the inferred intent rule in liability insurance cases involving an insured adult's intentional sexual abuse of a child to raise a conclusive presumption of the insured's intent to harm the victim, regardless of the insured's assertion of a subjective lack of intent to harm.

C. APPLICABILITY OF THE INFERRED INTENT RULE WHEN THE INSURED ASSERTS AN INCAPACITY TO FORM AN INTENT TO HARM

Although a majority of courts have adopted and applied the inferred intent rule in cases where the insured merely asserts a subjective intent not to harm the minor victim of his or her sexual abuse, see *supra* section II.B., a different and more subtle issue is raised when the insured asserts an incapacity to form the requisite intent.[2] There are fewer cases addressing this legal and factual twist, both in the context of general liability insurance cases and in the exceptional context of sexual child abuse cases, and the courts' responses to this issue have been mixed.

Court treatment of the issue has evolved along three basic lines:

1. Some courts look first to the nature and character of the act committed. They reason that if the nature and character of the act are such that an intent to harm may be inferred, as in cases involving the insured's acts of sexual child abuse, then any question of the inability to form the intent to harm, whether it arises out of alleged mental disease or defect or voluntary intoxication, is immaterial in resolving the insurer's obligation to provide coverage. The insured's subjective intent to harm in such context is wholly irrelevant.

2. Some courts hold that, as a matter of law, an insured may never assert a lack of capacity to form intent caused by voluntary intoxication as a defense to the application of an intended harm exclusion, regardless of the act committed. These courts essentially reason that evidence establishing that the insured was under the influence of intoxicants "is of no consequence, for the law must not permit the use of such stimuli to become a defense for one's actions." *Hanover Ins. Co. v. Newcomer,* 585 S.W.2d 285, 289 (Mo. Ct. App. 1979).

3. Other courts maintain, however, that where an incapacity to form intent to harm is alleged, that incapacity may render unintentional any harm caused by the insured so that such an incapacity must be considered by a factfinder when resolving the issue of the existence of intent to harm.

The second approach outlined above, which rejects consideration of voluntary intoxication in all liability insurance cases, is inapplicable under existing Pennsylvania precedent because the Pennsylvania intermediate court has already announced that intoxication is indeed to be considered in general liability insurance cases when resolving the issue of subjective intent. *Stidham v. Millvale Sportsmen's Club,* 421 Pa. Super. 548, 618 A.2d 945, 952 (1992). However, the Pennsylvania courts have not spoken on the need to consider intoxication in the exceptional context of sexual child abuse cases. We are therefore left to determine which of the other approaches referred to above Pennsylvania would adopt.

---

[2] The incapacity to form intent is often more specifically labelled a lack of or deficiency in mental capacity to form intent, whether due to mental disease or defect or voluntary intoxication by alcohol and/or drugs.

. . . .

As mentioned above, the Pennsylvania Superior Court has recently discussed Pennsylvania's law of intent in the context of general liability insurance cases interpreting the intended harm exclusion. *Stidham*, 421 Pa. Super. 548, 618 A.2d 945. In *Stidham*, the insured became voluntarily intoxicated and suffered an alcoholic blackout. In this condition, he shot and killed the victim, a man he had never met and to whom he had never spoken. In discussing the insurer's obligation to defend and indemnify its insured under a homeowner's policy in a civil suit brought by the victim's estate, the superior court stated:

> For purposes of the insurance policy provision excluding coverage for expected or intended injuries by the insured, "an insured intends an injury if he desired to cause the consequences of his act or if he acted knowing that such consequences were substantially certain to result." *United Serv. Auto. Ass'n v. Elitzky,* [358 Pa. Super. 362], 517 A.2d 982, 989 (Pa. Super. 1986), *appeal denied,* [515 Pa. 600], 528 A.2d 957 (Pa. 1987). Moreover, imbibed intoxicants must be considered in determining if the actor has the ability to formulate an intent.

The court in *Stidham* rendered its opinion after the district court decision in the instant case. However, we do not believe that the district court would have been bound in this case by *Stidham's* admonition that intoxication must be considered in determining the existence of intent under an intended harm exclusion any more than it was bound earlier by *Elitzky* in applying a subjective standard to the intent question. Both *Stidham* and *Elitzky* are general liability insurance cases in which there was no determination that the nature and character of the insured's acts were such that his intent to harm could be inferred. We interpret *Stidham's* enunciated rule on voluntary intoxication to be a specific manifestation of *Elitzky's* subjective intent standard, i.e., where a subjective standard is applicable to the intent question, then voluntary intoxication, if alleged, must be considered in the resolution of that issue. The *Stidham* rule, however, does not extend beyond general liability insurance cases to mandate application of the third approach outlined above.

The first approach offers the better rule because in exceptional cases such as sexual child abuse, where the insured's conduct is both intentional and of such a nature and character that harm inheres in it, that conduct affords a sufficiently clear demonstration of intent to harm subsuming any need for a separate inquiry into capacity. Once it is determined, strictly by examining the nature and character of the act in question, that it is appropriate to apply the inferred intent rule, then the actor's actual subjective intent to harm or capacity to form that intent becomes irrelevant. At that point, it does not matter whether a subjective intent existed or why it did or did not exist. Once subjective intent is deemed irrelevant, an actor who is unable to form the intent to harm is indistinguishable from one who could have formed the intent but claims he or she did not.

We therefore predict that the Pennsylvania Supreme Court, if called upon to decide the issue, would apply the inferred intent rule in liability insurance cases involving sexual child abuse where the insured asserts an incapacity of any sort to form an intent to harm.

III. CONCLUSION

. . . .

In affirming the district court's prediction that the Pennsylvania Supreme Court would adopt and apply the inferred intent rule to the present case, we accept the court's implicit ruling that Floyd intended harm to the minor as a matter of law. "Where the intent to injure is inferred as a matter of law from the nature of the acts committed, the subjective . . . intent of the insured to cause injury is irrelevant." [*Allstate Ins. Co. v.*] *Roelfs,* 698 F. Supp. [815,] at 820-21 nn. 6-7 [(D. Alaska 1987)]. Therefore, Floyd's assertions concerning his lack of subjective intent to harm, even to the extent they are grounded in an alleged inability to formulate such intent, are irrelevant to the matter at hand and do not create a genuine issue of material fact precluding summary judgment in favor of State Farm.

Having established the existence of the intended harm exclusion in Floyd's homeowner's policy and Floyd's intent to harm his minor niece as a matter of law through application of the inferred intent rule, State Farm merits judgment as a matter of law; it is under no obligation to provide coverage for bodily harm caused by Floyd's sexual abuse of the minor.

Accordingly, the judgment of the district court will be affirmed. [3]

NOTES

1. *Where is the occurrence?* How can a sexual assault be an "occurrence"? Or an "accident"? *See Allstate Insurance Co. v. S.F.,* 518 N.W.2d 37 (Minn. 1994).

2. *Implications for other cases.* The obvious question is to what other kinds of cases the reasoning in *Wiley* might be applied. If someone points a gun at someone else and fires it, is it appropriate to infer intent to injure? If someone gets hurt with the insured's gun while the insured is participating in an armed robbery, is it appropriate to affirm intent to injure? If an adult shakes a baby to the point of inflicting the condition of "shaken baby syndrome," is it appropriate to infer intent to injure? *See Farm Bureau Insurance Co. v. Witte,* 594 N.W.2d 574 (Neb. 1999) (yes, regardless of insured's subjective intent).

In cases where an adult sexually assaults, abuses, or exploits a minor, *Wiley* represents the overwhelming majority view. For other recent examples, *see TBH v. Meyer,* 716 A.2d 31 (Vt. 1998); *Pettit v. Erie Insurance Exchange,* 349 Md. 777, 709 A.2d 1287 (1998). What about the situation where a child sexually assaults another child? On this question, the courts appear to be evenly split. *See Fire Insurance Exchange v. Diehl,* 450 Mich. 678, 545 N.W.2d

---

[3] Because we affirm based on the intended harm exclusion in Floyd's insurance contract, we do not address the question whether Pennsylvania public policy would also preclude insurance coverage under the facts of this case.

602 (1996); *Allstate Insurance Co. v. Steele,* 74 F.3d 878 (8th Cir. 1996); *Country Mutual Insurance Co. v. Hagan,* 298 Ill.App.3d 495, 698 N.E.2d 271 (1998) (discussing cases on both sides of the issue).

The number of insurance law cases involving sexual abuse or assaults—particularly of children — has increased in recent years, reflecting a very sad and tragic aspect of our society. For more discussion of the insurance issues which can arise in such situations, see David S. Florig, *Insurance Coverage for Sexual Abuse or Molestation,* 30 Tort & Ins. L.J. 699 (1995).

3. *Implications for cases involving only adults.* If the victim of sexual misconduct is an adult instead of a child, should the rule of inferred intent apply? If not, what are the ramifications in the sexual abuse situation of Pennsylvania's requirement that the intentional act exclusion applies only when the insured intends to inflict harm? What are the chances that an insurer will obtain a summary judgment on the intent to harm issue? This circumstance makes the public policy issue, not decided in *Wiley,* an extremely important one to insurers. For subsequent developments in Pennsylvania, *see* *Teti v. Huron Insurance Co.,* 914 F. Supp. 1132 (E.D. Pa. 1996).

On what circumstances should the application of the inferred intent rule depend? If an insured intentionally engages in unprotected sex with a consensual partner and negligently (i.e., unintentionally) transmits genital herpes to him or her, is the resulting damage caused "intentionally"? *Compare* *State Farm Fire & Casualty Co. v. S.S. & G.W.,* 858 S.W.2d 374 (Tex. 1993) with *R.W. v. T.P.,* 528 N.W.2d 869 (Minn. 1995). In some jurisdictions, it is a crime for a person who knows he or she is afflicted with HIV to have sexual intercourse without informing the other person of the condition and securing his or her consent. Is this factor relevant? *See Allstate Insurance Co. v. Myers,* 951 F. Supp. 1014 (M.D. Fla. 1996). If your answer is that the inferred intent rule should not apply whenever the sexual act is consensual, does your answer change if the plaintiff alleges being victimized by "unconsenting sexual acts"? *See State Farm Fire and Casualty Co. v. Brooks,* 43 F. Supp. 2d 695 (E.D. Tex. 1998). See generally Daniel C. Eidsmoe & Pamela K. Edwards, *Sex, Lies, and Insurance Coverage? Insurance Carrier Coverage Defenses for Sexually Transmitted Disease Claims,* 34 Tort & Ins. L. J. 921 (1999).

Sexual harassment claims can implicate the "business pursuits" exclusion if the harassment occurs in the workplace. But the intentional injury exclusion has relevance as well. *See Commercial Union Insurance Co. v. Sky, Inc.,* 810 F. Supp. 249 (W.D. Ark. 1992); *State Farm Fire & Casualty Co. v. Company, Inc.,* 654 So. 2d 944 (Fla. Dist. Ct. App. 1995). For a discussion of the issue in the context of one set of widely publicized allegations, see Richard C. Giller, *One Attorney's Opinion Regarding Coverage for the Claims Asserted by Paula Jones Against President Clinton,* 2 BNA Ins. Coverage Lit. Rpt. 261 (1996).

As in-house counsel for an insurer, would you recommend any modification in policy forms given the recent increase in lawsuits alleging damage or injury from sexual conduct (and misconduct)?

4. *Diminished capacity.* Is the criminal standard for insanity the appropriate one to use for determining whether an insured is capable of intentional conduct? *Compare Ruvolo v. American Casualty Co.,* 189 A.2d 204 (N.J. 1963),

with *Economy Preferred Insurance Co. v. Mass,* 242 Neb. 842, 497 N.W.2d 6 (1993).

If an insane person understands the physical nature and consequences of the act, is the act intentional for purposes of liability insurance? If the exclusion's purpose is to deny economic protection to persons who commit intentional wrongs, how is this purpose served if the actor cannot appreciate the significance of his or her conduct? *See Lititz Mutual Insurance Co. v. Bell,* 352 Md. 782, 724 A.2d 102 (1999); *Prasad v. Allstate Ins. Co.,* 644 So. 2d 992 (Fla. 1994); *Johnson v. Insurance Co. of N. Am.,* 350 S.E.2d 616 (Va. 1986). See generally Catherine A. Salton, *Mental Incapacity and Liability Insurance Exclusionary Clauses: The Effect of Insanity Upon Intent,* 78 Cal. L. Rev. 1027 (1990).

As the court in *Wiley* indicates, the law on whether intoxication vitiates the capacity to form the intent necessary to trigger the intentional act exclusion is unsettled. Should doubts in this area be resolved by considering the interests of victims? Is the public interest served by a rule that makes coverage more probable the more intoxicated the insured can prove himself to be? *See Dolan v. State Farm Fire & Casualty Co.,* 573 N.W.2d 254 (Iowa 1998); *Republic Insurance Co. v. Feidler,* 193 Ariz. 8, 969 P.2d 173 (Ariz. App. 1998).

[3] Defense of Self and Others

In most of the cases in the preceding subsection, the insured's conduct fell below, for one reason or another, some kind of commonly accepted norm of behavior. Picture now an insured who is not a deviant, a boor, or one possessing impaired judgment. The insured witnesses a stranger committing an unprovoked, violent assault upon a member of his family. The insured rushes to the scene and inflicts disabling injuries on the perpetrator to the precise degree necessary to protect the family member. Later, the perpetrator sues the insured for injuries suffered at the hands of the insured. Is the insured covered under his or her liability policy? Consider the next case.

TRANSAMERICA INSURANCE GROUP v. MEERE
143 Ariz. 351, 694 P.2d 181 (1984)

FELDMAN, JUSTICE.

Lynne Edward Meere (defendant) petitions this court for review of the majority decision of the court of appeals (*Transamerica Insurance Group v. Meere,* 143 Ariz. 433, 694 P.2d 263 (1983)), which affirmed a summary judgment in favor of Transamerica. The trial court had determined that Transamerica was not required to defend Meere in a civil action and that the homeowner's policy issued by Transamerica to Meere did not potentially provide liability coverage for Meere. . . . We granted review in this case and in *Fire Insurance Exchange v. Berray,* 143 Ariz. 429, 694 P.2d 259 (1983) to settle a conflict in the court of appeals' decisions (*see* Rule 23(c)(4)) concerning the impact of the intentional injury exclusion on an insurer's duty to defend an action brought by a third party for assault when the insured has raised the affirmative claim of the privilege of self-defense.

FACTS

In an appeal from summary judgment the evidence is viewed in the light most favorable to the party against whom summary judgment was taken. Viewed in that light, the facts are as follows.

On March 27, 1980, at about 12:30 a.m., Meere and a friend, Leon Ivey, were leaving Lindy's, a bar in Florence, Arizona. Outside Lindy's, Meere and Ivey were confronted by several off-duty employees of the Arizona State Prison. Meere alleges that he was quite apprehensive because he had been informed by a captain at Arizona State Prison that a rumor was circulating among the guards that Ivey and Meere, both ex-police officers, were under-cover investigators of narcotics flow into the prison. One of the guards, Dennis Pruitt, approached Meere. Meere and Pruitt exchanged words. Pruitt then struck Meere, knocking him to the ground; Meere put up his hands, said "I don't want to fight," and was struck again by Pruitt. The two then exchanged blows. The fight ended when Meere knocked Pruitt to the ground and kicked Pruitt as he attempted to get up and come at Meere again. Pruitt lost partial use of an eye as a result of this fight.

Pruitt brought a tort action against Meere. His complaint reads, in part:

III

That on or about March 27, 1980, at approximately 12:30 a.m., Dennis R. Pruitt was struck in the face, his eye and other areas of his body by Lynne Edward Meere . . . .

. . . .

VIII

The aforesaid acts of defendants were grossly negligent and outra-geous acts done with reckless disregard of the rights of plaintiffs and as a result thereof, said defendants should be made to respond in punitive damages . . . .

Transamerica insures Meere against tort liability. It brought this declara-tory judgment action against Meere and Pruitt to establish that it had no duty to defend or indemnify Meere against Pruitt's tort action. Its complaint alleges that

. . . defendant Lynne Edward Meere intentionally struck with his hands and feet the defendant Dennis Pruitt in the face and about the body . . . .

In his answer to the declaratory judgment action Meere denied that allegation. When asked "upon what facts do you base your denial of our allegation that you intentionally struck Mr. Pruitt," Meere responded as follows:

Well, from the statement that you're making right there, I would say that it would be the fact the I intentionally did it. As far as I'm concerned, I was defending myself. It was a self-defense situation. And I was warding off an attack. And I was fearful of [for] my life.

Meere deposition, p. 16. Meere also stated "I did not intentionally strike him. I mean, it was self-defense." Meere stated that he was also fearful because "the fight came to me. I didn't go to it." Meere deposition, p. 20. He had no intention of seriously injuring Pruitt.

The thrust of Meere's deposition testimony is that he used only the force he though was necessary to repulse a persistent attack by Pruitt while he and Ivey were partially surrounded by several aggressive off-duty prison guards, one of whom they believed was armed with a gun. It is uncontested, however, that Meere intended to strike the blow that injured Pruitt.

At the time of the fight, the Transamerica homeowner's policy insuring Meere contained the following exclusion:

> Personal liability coverage does not apply to bodily injury, personal injury, or property damage, (A) which is expected or intended by the insured . . . .

Transamerica relied on this exclusion in seeking the declaratory judgment of noncoverage. The trial court granted summary judgment on this basis and the court of appeals affirmed. We reverse the judgment of the trial court and vacate the opinion of the court of appeals.

I—CHARACTERIZATION OF ISSUE

The basic question is whether the insured's subjective intent to cause or not to cause injury is relevant where the act producing injury was intentional but committed in self-defense. Is the insured bound by the natural and probable consequences of his immediate act of striking the blow, even though he may establish that he had no underlying or basic intent to injure the victim? The majority of the court of appeals held:

> Meere's statements that he did not intend to seriously injure Pruitt or cause the loss of his eyesight, though relevant to his subjective intent or motive, are immaterial to determine whether the exclusion applies. . . . We therefore find that the bodily injury to Pruitt was 'intended' by Meere within the meaning of the policy exclusion.

Transamerica Insurance Group v. Meere, 143 Ariz. at 435, 694 P.2d at 265. Division II of the court of appeals had previously reached a similar conclusion in *Lockhart v. Allstate Insurance Co.,* 119 Ariz. 150, 579 P.2d 1120 (1978). A majority of a different department of Division I reached the opposite conclusion in *Fire Insurance Exchange v. Berray, supra,* holding that an act committed in self-defense was not within the intentional exclusion from liability coverage.

Those who espouse the view that an intentional act committed in self-defense falls within the exclusion base their position on *Steinmetz v. National American Insurance Co.,* 121 Ariz. 268, 589 P.2d 911 (App. 1978) and *Clark v. Allstate Insurance Co.,* 22 Ariz. App. 601, 529 P.2d 1195 (1975). Both cases hold that where the insured intentionally commits an act calculated to cause some injury, he will not be permitted to deny an intent to injure nor be allowed to evade the scope of the exclusionary clause by pleading that the resultant injury "is different either in character or magnitude from the injury that was intended." *Steinmetz,* 121 Ariz. at 271, 589 P.2d at 914. However, neither

Steinmetz nor *Clark* was a self-defense case. In both cases it was assumed or presumed from the performance of the act that the insured intended to inflict an injury. That assumption is proper in both *Steinmetz* and *Clark* because the insured, acting without justification or privilege, committed an act bound to cause *some* injury. It is, therefore, of no consequence that he may have intended a different or lesser injury. The exclusion applies whenever the insured intends to injure.

But the issue before us requires a definition of "intent"; does a person acting in self-defense, or with other justification, really "intend" to injure even though he acts in a manner quite likely or even certain to cause some injury? Where, unlike *Steinmetz* and *Clark,* there is some justification or privilege connected with the insured's intentional act, do we deal with basic intent or simply with immediate intent—the natural consequences of the act?

We find authority from other states in conflict. *See* Annot., 2 ALR 3d 1238 (1965). The annotation summarizes the divergence of opinion as follows:

> The courts have generally held that injury or damage is "caused intentionally" within the meaning of an "intentional injury exclusion clause" [only] if the insured has acted with the specific intent to cause harm to a third party, with the result that the insurer will not be relieved of its obligations . . . unless the insured has acted with such specific intent. Under this view, it is not sufficient that the insured's intentional, albeit wrongful, act has resulted in unintended harm to a third person; it is the harm itself that must be intended before the exclusion will apply. There is, however, some authority for the proposition that such a clause will operate to relieve a liability insurer of its duty to indemnify an insured whose intentional act has caused harm to a third person where the nature or character of the act is such that an intent to cause harm is thereby inferred as a matter of law.

Id. at 1241 (footnote omitted).

Steinmetz and *Clark* seem to fit within what the annotation scope note indicates to be the minority view. Some of the cases on the supposed majority and minority sides of the question resolve the issue on the fictional basis of the "intent of the parties." *See e.g., Patrons-Oxford Mutual Insurance Co. v. Dodge,* 426 A.2d 888 (Me. 1981) (holding the clause ambiguous and to be construed against the insurer because it fails to specify whether the intent referred to is the objective intent which accompanied the immediate act of striking the blow or the "actual subjective intention" which motivated the insured's conduct). Of course, a finding of ambiguity is the easy way out since it permits the court to create its own version of the contract and to find, or fail to find, ambiguity in order to justify an almost predetermined result. This is an approach which we have abandoned. We believe the proper methodology is to determine the meaning of the clause—where it is susceptible to different constructions—by examining the purpose of the exclusion in question, the public policy considerations involved and the transaction as a whole. We proceed, therefore, to analyze these factors.

II—PUBLIC POLICY, BUSINESS POLICY AND EXCLUSIONS FOR INTENTIONAL INJURY IN INSURANCE POLICIES

Insurance policies are purchased "as protection against calamity." *Noble v. National American Life Insurance Company,* 128 Ariz. 188, 189, 624 P.2d 866, 867 (1981). The "business" principle here is that an insured seeks the safety of insurance against risks that are outside his control and the insurer agrees to cover for a premium based on actuarial calculations of the random occurrence (risk) of such events in a given population. This principle is the basis for the "intentional exclusion" and, according to Appleman, is central to the purposes of insurance:

> The intentional exclusion is necessary to the insurer to enable it to set rates and supply coverage only if losses under policies are uncertain from the standpoint of any single policyholder, and if a single insured is allowed through intentional or reckless acts to *consciously* control risks covered by policy, *the central concept of insurance is violated.*

7A Appleman, Insurance Law and Practice, § 4492.01 at 21 (1979) (emphasis supplied). Thus, as a matter of contract, it seems proper to conclude that the clause is designed by the insurer to exclude indemnification when the insured suffers a loss resulting from the exercise of his own volition; the exclusion applies because the insured is assumed to have controlled the risk.

From a non-contractual standpoint, the cases have taken the position that the clause also articulates a public policy which forbids contracts indemnifying a person against loss resulting from his own willful wrongdoing. *Gray v. Zurich Insurance Co.,* 65 Cal. 2d 263, 54 Cal. Rptr. 104, 419 P.2d 168 (1966). These principles of contractual "intent" and public policy coincide; the provision is designed to prevent an insured from acting wrongfully with the security of knowing that his insurance company will "pay the piper" for the damages. That design is not served by interpreting the provision to exclude coverage in self-defense situations where the insured is not acting by conscious design but is attempting to avoid a "calamity" which has befallen him.

Of course, one may strike a blow in self-defense, with an intent to injure as a tactic of defense. We turn, therefore, to examine the question of whether, in such a context, the relevant intent is that which accompanies the immediate act or the purpose which underlies the insured's basic conduct.

A. THE CONCEPT OF SELF-DEFENSE

Examination of self-defense as a concept of tort law is helpful in determining how to interpret an insurance policy which indemnifies against tort damages and contains an exclusionary clause for injuries "expected or intended" by the insured. In discussing the evolution of the concept of fault in tort law, Prosser offers some important historical insights.

> Originally the man who hurt another by pure accident, or in self-defense, was required to make good the damage inflicted. "In all civil acts," it was said, "the law doth not so much regard the intent of the actor, as the loss and damage of the party suffering." There was . . . a rule, undoubtedly supported by the general feeling in the community, that "he who breaks must pay."

Prosser, Handbook on the Law of Torts § 75 at 492 (4th ed. 1971) (footnotes omitted). As social policy and community sentiment, much of this may still be true today, but modern tort law does seek to characterize the behavior of the actor as either blameworthy or morally faultless. In tort law, therefore, there is usually a need to distinguish between negligence and intent. This is a matter of "line drawing."

> [T]he *mere knowledge and appreciation of a risk,* short of substantial certainty, *is not the equivalent of intent. The defendant who acts in the belief or consciousness that he is causing an appreciable risk of harm to another may be negligent,* and if the risk is great his conduct may be characterized as reckless or wanton, but it is not classed as an intentional wrong. In such cases the distinction between intent and negligence obviously is a matter of degree. Apparently the line has been drawn by the courts at the point where the known danger ceases to be only a foreseeable risk which a reasonable man would avoid, and becomes a substantial certainty.

Prosser, *supra,* § 8 at 32 (emphasis supplied).

This understanding of "intent" and "negligence" has particular relevance for understanding the "privilege" of self-defense in tort law. One may use only reasonable force (which, of course, might injure the aggressor) to prevent harm to his person. Prosser, *supra,* § 19 at 108.

> The defendant is not privileged to inflict a beating which goes beyond the real or apparent necessities of his own defense. If he does, he is committing *a tort as to the excessive force,* and it is entirely possible that each party may have an action against the other.

Id. at 109-10 (emphasis supplied). The tort of "excessive force" in the course of self-defense is apparently "nonintentional tortious conduct," to use the phrase of the California court in *Gray v. Zurich, supra.* By using this term the California court seems to be balancing the scales to fix minimal blame on one who overreacts in self-defense because it implicitly recognizes that the mental state induced in one repulsing an attack is different from that of the attacker (who commits an "intentional tort"). *Id.* Thus, tort law recognizes an inherent distinction in the quality of "intent." The attacker commits an intentional tort; the defender, though he strikes intentionally, may not act with wrongful intent. This distinction is a recognition in tort law that the basic or underlying intent of the actor is more important in characterizing the conduct than the immediate intent accompanying the act which produced the injury.

B. ANALYSIS OF CASE LAW

Meere claimed in his deposition that, while he "intentionally" struck Pruitt, his purpose was only to defend himself. Meere desired no harm to Pruitt but sought only to prevent harm to himself. As we have noted, in such a case the word "intent" operates at different levels and has different connotations. However, Transamerica argues that Meere's subjective intent is of no moment because one is held to have intended the natural and probable consequences of his act, whatever they are and regardless of actual subjective feeling. We have recognized that

> [A]n act may be so certain to cause a particular injury that the intent to cause the harm is inferred as a matter of law and the subjective intent of the actor is immaterial.

Farmers Insurance Company of Arizona v. Vagnozzi, 138 Ariz. 443, 449, 675 P.2d 703, 709 (1983).

This statement in *Vagnozzi* is based on the holdings in *Steinmetz v. National American Insurance Co., supra* and *Clark v. Allstate Insurance Co., supra.* Both of these cases, however, are easily distinguished. In *Clark,* for instance, the intentional blow was entirely unprovoked. Clark came to his fight; Meere's fight "came to him." Clark may be presumed to have had the detached reflection which is not expected of a person faced with an uplifted fist or with an unprovoked attack. Under the *Steinmetz-Clark* rule the insured is conclusively presumed to have intended to injure when he commits an act calculated to cause some injury. However, we also recognized in *Vagnozzi* that the *Steinmetz-Clark* rule is not applicable in all cases.

> The presumption that a person intends the ordinary consequences of his voluntary actions, used in determining responsibility for the consequences of voluntary acts, has no application to the interpretation of terms used in insurance contracts.
>
>   . . . .
>
> . . . [the insured] stated in his deposition that he intended to hit Vagnozzi but also stated he did so in order to knock Vagnozzi out of the way and pursue the ball. The policy definition of "accident" as an event resulting in injury [neither] expected or intended by the insured makes the subjective intent of the insured a question of fact to be determined after listening to the testimony. The two interpretations which can be drawn from [the insured's] testimony create enough question as to his intent that the *Steinmetz* exception does not apply. For purposes of determining that a resulting injury was so certain to occur that the actor intended the harm as a matter of a law, we find that intentionally throwing an elbow in an attempt to get the ball during a heated basketball game is distinguishable from deliberately punching a person in the face. Whether the injury was the intended result of [the insured's] act or whether the act constituted negligent or grossly reckless conduct is a matter upon which reasonable minds can differ.

Vagnozzi, 138 Ariz. at 449-50, 675 P.2d at 709-10.

We believe the blow struck in self-defense is analogous to that struck in an attempt to get to the basketball. In both cases the insured must be aware that his act possibly or even probably may cause injury. In neither case does the insured necessarily have a primary desire to injure the victim. The unprovoked blow, such as that struck in *Steinmetz* or *Clark,* however, is different. The *unprovoked* (unprivileged) act of striking someone in the face with a fist is an unequivocal manifestation of a basic purpose or desire to cause some injury and the law will not allow the insured to evade the applicability of the exclusions by protestations of innocence. The blow was volitional, the event was in the control of the insured, and no accident or calamity beyond his control occurred. The law presumes he intended the result which was the natural consequence of his intentional act. In summary, in *Clark* and *Steinmetz,* the insured controlled the loss and thus fell within the category of risks which both the insurance contract and public policy consider uninsurable. In the case at bench, however, there is evidence from which the finder of fact may decide that Meere was confronted with a risk over which he had little control. His blow may not have been the result of a cognitive process, and his action may not have been "voluntary." Although his act was intentional, and its natural consequence was to cause injury, his basic desire or purpose may not have been to injure. The *Steinmetz-Clark* presumption does not apply.

Substantial authority supports such an analysis. The Nebraska Supreme Court, after analyzing a number of cases concluded:

> The cases, as evidenced by those already cited, point out that when one acts in self-defense the actor is not generally acting for the purpose of intending any injury to another but, rather, is acting for the purpose of attempting to prevent injury to himself. It can easily be said that such act, though resulting in bodily injury to another, was neither expected nor intended within the terms of the policy . . . . An injury resulting from an act committed by an insured in self-defense is not, as a matter of law, an expected or intended act . . .

Allstate Insurance Company v. Novak, 210 Neb. 184, 192-93, 313 N.W.2d 636, 640-41 (1981).

Analogous situations exist in which inquiry into the insured's basic subjective intent has not been limited to cases of sports injury, where some degree of force is to be expected, or to cases of self-defense. It extends to other situations in which the insured acted intentionally but did not control the risk. For instance, where the insured commits an intentional act causing injury but lacks the mental capacity to act "rationally," the clause does not apply because its application would be "inconsistent with a primary purpose for incorporating intentional injury exclusions . . ., *i.e.,* to preclude individuals from benefiting financially when they deliberately cause injury." *Globe American Casualty Co. v. Lyons,* 131 Ariz. at 339-40, 641 P.2d at 253-54. Where the insured intentionally injures the victim because of mistaken identity, the clause does not apply. *Curtain v. Aldrich,* 589 S.W.2d 61 (Mo. App. 1979) (the insured beat a "burglar" over the head with a crowbar, only to find that the "burglar" was his brother-in-law; the court held that if the jury found a case of mistaken identity and further found that there was no specific intent to injure the brother-in-law, the exclusion would not be applicable even though the insured intentionally struck blows intending to injure a burglar).

Case authority to the contrary exists. *See e.g., Home Insurance Company v. Neilsen,* 165 Ind. App. 445, 450, 332 N.E.2d 240 (1975). We believe, however, that when the factors involving public policy and the purpose of the contractual exclusion are considered, the proper interpretation of the clause in question is that it excludes indemnification or coverage when the insured intentionally acts *wrongfully* with a purpose to injure. When he acts wrongfully, he commits an intentional tort by performing an act designed to inflict injury. He will not be allowed under such circumstances to deny a basic intent demonstrated by his acts. *Steinmetz, supra; Clark, supra.* Nor will he be allowed to escape from the exclusionary clause by claiming that he did not intend the precise injury—in character or magnitude—that in fact occurred. However, if the insured can show facts which might establish that he acted with privilege (as in a sports injury case, for instance) or under claim of right recognized by law (as in self-defense), he will be permitted to explain his subjective intent, and it will be for the fact finder to determine whether he had an underlying purpose to injure. The basic question is whether the conduct which led to the blow was intentionally wrongful from the viewpoint of the law of torts. Such an interpretation comports with the intent of the exclusionary clause in a policy which insures against tort damages; it is consistent both with the public policy which forbids indemnification against wrongful acts and with the better reasoned authority.

. . . .

Thus, if the trier of fact determines that Meere was the aggressor and acted wrongfully by striking Pruitt without legal justification, the basic intent to injure will be presumed and the exclusion will apply. *Steinmetz, supra.* If the finder of fact determines that Meere's conduct was not intentionally wrongful, but that he acted instead in self-defense with no basic purpose to injure, the exclusion will not apply. Of course, in such circumstances one would expect that the judgment in the tort case will be in Meere's favor, and Transamerica's purse will be spared. If the jury finds that Meere acted in self-defense with no basic desire or intent to harm Pruitt, but negligently used force greater than necessary in self-defense, Meere may be liable for damages to Pruitt. In such an event, the true situation is one of negligence. *Gray v. Zurich, supra. It is the only real exposure for Transamerica and it is, we believe, within the coverage of the policy and not within the exclusion.*

Since the complaint alleges facts which may be within the policy coverage, the insurer is obligated to assume the defense. Of course, further discovery may reveal uncontested facts which obviate the self-defense theory which Meere has raised. If these facts plainly take the case outside policy coverage, there is no duty to defend.

We hold, therefore, that the court erred in granting summary judgment to Transamerica. The judgment of the trial court is reversed, the opinion of the court of appeals is vacated, and the case is remanded for further proceedings not inconsistent with this opinion.

GORDON, V.C.J., and HAYS and CAMERON, JJ., concur.

HOLOHAN, CHIEF JUSTICE, dissenting.

The resolution of this case by the majority is actually a decision by the court based on policy to distribute the consequences of the loss on an insurance company. I come to this conclusion because a reading of the majority opinion shows that it is not based on logic. The decisions from other jurisdictions collected in 2 A.L.R.3d 1238 *et seq.* present a variety of approaches to the problem. The majority of this court reject the decisions which find the insurance exclusion in this case ambiguous.

The issue of whether self-defense was excluded from coverage under an insurance policy containing language similar to that in this case was decided in *Lockhart v. Allstate Ins. Co.,* 119 Ariz. 150, 579 P.2d 1120 (App. 1978). Review was denied by this court.

The exclusion in *Lockhart* read: "to bodily injury or property damage which is either expected or intended from the standpoint of the Insured." *Id.,* 119 Ariz. at 151, 579 P.2d at 1121. Construing the language of the exclusion the court stated:

> The insurance policy excludes coverage for an intentional act of the insured which was intended to cause injury or which could be expected to cause injury. The question of self-defense presents an issue of motive or justification for an intentionally caused harm but does nothing to avoid the inference of intent to harm that necessarily follows Lockhart's deliberate shooting at Owes.

Id., 119 Ariz. at 152, 579 P.2d at 1122 (citation omitted). This court, however, distinguishes the intent involved in an intentional act and that in self-defense, and concludes that the intent of the actor is more important in characterizing the conduct than the immediate intent accompanying the act which produces the injury. 143 Ariz. at 357, 694 P.2d at 187. While this may be an interesting philosophic conclusion, it does nothing to change the plain meaning of the policy exclusion. At one time this court stated that an insurance company had the right to limit its liability and to impose conditions and restrictions upon its contractual obligations not inconsistent with public policy. That position is effectively overruled with today's decision.

Not being satisfied with changing self-defense into a non-intentional act, the majority concludes that the exclusion does not apply even if the defense of self-defense is not available because greater force was used than necessary. The "greater force than allowed by self-defense" has now become negligence.

What the court has done in this case is to mandate insurance coverage whenever an insured contends his intentional acts were done in self-defense; further, the insurance company must now defend and pay the judgment up to policy limits even if the insured exceeds the limits of legitimate self-defense.

The decision by the majority is neither supported by logic nor good policy, and I dissent.

Auto-Owners Insurance Co. v. Harrington, 455 Mich. 377, 565 N.W.2d 839 (1997). Brian Tew resided with the neighbor of the Harringtons, the insureds. The Harringtons had seen Tew act aggressively and erratically; their nephew, who was visiting them on August 1, 1989, told them that Tew had said he could kill the nephew with his bare hands. About 11:00 p.m. that day, Tew shot an automatic weapon into a nearby lake and threatened "to kill someone." At that point, James Harrington, who had been alarmed about Tew's behavior during the day and was feeling frightened about Tew's threats to harm someone, retrieved his twelve-gauge shotgun from his garage.

Marion Harrington subsequently saw Tew scaling up the Harringtons' garage and approaching the window where she and her children were.

Harrington assumed that Tew still had the automatic weapon and planned to use it to harm his wife and children. Tew was unarmed. Harrington got his shotgun, aimed it at Tew, and shot him in the stomach. Tew died of his wounds. The county prosecutor brought no charges against Harrington.

Tew's father filed a wrongful death action against the Harringtons. The Harringtons' homeowners' insurer brought a declaratory judgment action seeking a determination that it owed no duty to defend the insureds against the wrongful death claim. The policy excluded coverage for "bodily injury or property damage expected or intended by an insured person." The trial court granted a summary judgment for the insureds. A divided Court of Appeals reversed, holding that the intentional acts exclusion applied, and the Supreme Court affirmed. in a 4-3 decision.

"In this case, the Court of Appeals found that the exclusion language regarding expected or intentional injury was unambiguous. We agree. In fact, this Court has repeatedly held that the 'intended or expected' language that is used in the policy exclusion is 'clear and unambiguous' as applied to a variety of similar factual contexts.

"We further agree with the Court of Appeals that this language requires a subjective inquiry into the intent *or expectation* of the insured. In this case, the policy's use of the word 'expected' broadens the scope of the exclusion because 'expected' injuries are the 'natural, foreseeable, expected, and anticipated result of an intentional act.' We have, therefore, stated that this 'intended or expected' language bars coverage for injuries caused by an insured who acted intentionally despite his awareness that harm was likely to follow from his conduct. "In other words, coverage is precluded if the insured's claim that he did not intend or expect the injury 'flies in the face of all reason, common sense and experience.' "

"In his deposition testimony, Harrington admitted that he intentionally pointed his gun at Tew and intended to shoot him, hoping to stop Tew's advance toward the bedroom window. From these admissions, the Court of Appeals majority correctly inferred that Harrington certainly was aware or 'knew that intentionally shooting at Brian would result in serious bodily harm or death.' We agree and find that Harrington intended, or at least expected, that bodily injury would result from shooting Tew; moreover, we find that any conclusion to the contrary would 'fl[y] in the face of all reason, common sense and experience.'

"In so holding we acknowledge that certain other jurisdictions have found that an insured's intentional act taken in self-defense does not constitute intentional conduct. *See Transamerica Ins. Group v. Meere,* 143 Ariz. 351, 694 P.2d 181 (1984). However, our holding today is consonant with the majority of state court's that have similarly refused to create a self-defense exception to the intentional-act exclusion. Moreover, it is true to the plain wording of the exclusion. Indeed, while the Harringtons argue that acts taken in self-defense are not 'intentional' because they are reactionary and a justifiable response to unwarranted aggression, this reasoning fails because the exclusion does not qualify the injuries excluded from coverage with terms such as 'wrongful' or 'unjustified.' Rather, the plain language of the policy exclusion indicates that it only distinguishes injuries that are either 'intended or expected' from those that are purely accidental, meaning unintended or unexpected.

"To except injurious action taken in self-defense from the intentional-acts exclusion would impermissibly disregard the clear language of the exclusion in the contract between insurer and insured. We refuse to do so in this case and find that the exclusion is unambiguous and that the injuries caused by Harrington were intentional, or at least expected, and therefore clearly excluded from indemnification coverage, even if taken in self-defense.[9] . . ..

NOTES

1. *A split in the cases.* Courts are split on the issue presented in *Meere* and *Harrington*, just like the judges in those cases. See generally James L. Rigelhaupt, Jr., Annotation, *Acts in Self-Defense as Within Provision of Liability Insurance Policy Expressly Excluding Coverage for Damage or Injury Intended or Expected by Insured*, 34 A.L.R.4th 761 (1984). The weight of recent authority, however, appears to rest with the no coverage answer given by the dissenting judges in *Meere* and the majority in *Harrington*. For other recent cases, *see Cooperative Fire Insurance Ass'n of Vermont v. Bizon*, 693 A.2d 722 (Vt. 1997) (exclusion applies against claim that insured shot burglars in self-defense); *Nationwide Mutual Fire Insurance Co. v. Mitchell*, 911 F. Supp. 230 (S.D. Miss. 1995) (exclusion applies where 16-year-old son inflicted injury on woman, ex-wife of his stepfather, who moved toward and pushed his mother during domestic dispute); *Stoebner v. South Dakota Farm Bureau Mutual Insurance Co.*, 598 N.W.2d 557 (S.D. 1999) (reversing summary judgment and remanding for trial because of disputed fact issue over whether insured intended to inflict harm or to defend herself); *Safeco Insurance Co. v. Tunkle*, 997 F. Supp. 1356 (D. Mont. 1998)(shooting of intruder in self-defense is "occurrence" and is not an intentional act under intentional act exclusion).

2. *The scope of the privilege.* The privilege of self-defense is limited to the use of force which reasonably appears to be necessary for protection against the threatened injury. Whether the force used is reasonable is viewed from the perspective of the person being attacked. See Dan B. Dobbs, The Law of Torts § 72 (2000). Where the defendant acts with the knowledge that the force employed is beyond that necessary to defend, this is clearly a battery and should be excluded from liability coverage under standard clauses. On the other hand, the defendant may not act with such knowledge but may still be judged to have exceeded the privilege, because the force used is more than that which would have been reasonable when viewed from the defendant's perspective. In the latter case, even though a battery is committed, should

---

[9] In affirming the decision of the Court of Appeals, we note that policy concerns also weigh in favor of finding that the 'expected or intended' language does not include intentional acts taken in self-defense. The interests to be balanced include, on the one hand, compensation to persons injured and in compliance with the contract between insured and insurer, and, on the other hand, the interest of the people of this state in refusing to compensate or indemnify the intentionally injurious acts of another, whether legally excused in the criminal or civil context or not.

there be coverage for the defendant under the language of a standard liability policy such as that in *Meere*?

Meere involved a claim of defense of oneself, and *Harrington* involved a claim of defense of family. Should the distinction matter? What if the insured, a shopper at a mall, uses his gun to stop an armed robbery in progress, and inflicts a fatal wound on the robber? What if the insured has that intention, but accidentally shoots a bystander who steps into the line of fire?

3. *The scope of the remedy for exceeding the privilege.* Assuming that a defendant-insured is found to have exceeded the privilege of self-defense, should he or she be liable for all of the harm inflicted, or just that caused by the excessive force? How about the liability insurer — what should it have to pay?

4. *Problem: Wedding memories that last a lifetime.* Insured was employed (for a $300 fee) as a disc jockey for a wedding reception held at fashionable country club. Insured had a full-time job, but for a number of years he conducted his DJ business on the side. He had printed cards with a business name, and he declared income on his tax return from DJ activities in the range of $5000 to $7000 annually. On the day of the reception, he set up his own equipment, stacking his loudspeakers next to the dance floor. During the reception, he had several alcoholic beverages. At one point, he was approached by an obstreperous and intoxicated guest who was upset because he had forgotten to play a requested song. The guest threw a punch at the insured, who retaliated in what he said was self-defense. The guest was not deterred; in the scuffle that ensued, one of the insured's speakers became dislodged, fell, and struck plaintiff, a wedding guest not involved in the scuffle, on the head, causing bleeding, bruising, and a concussion. Plaintiff incurred medical expenses and lost $5,000 in wages for the work she missed due to her injuries. Plaintiff sued the insured, alleging that he had been negligent in "the placement, use and supervision of the stereo equipment" and "in his physical conduct." Does the insured's homeowners policy provide coverage for these claims? For a very similar case, *see Luneau v. Peerless Insurance Co.,* 750 A.2d 1031 (Vt. 2000).

§ 5.02   The Commercial General Liability Policy

[1]   The Nature of the Coverage

The Commercial General Liability Policy (commonly referred to as the "CGL") provides general liability insurance for businesses. The CGL has gone through several revisions since it was first marketed in 1941. Major revisions of the form occurred in 1947, 1955, 1966, 1973, and in 1986. The most recent iterations of the CGL appear in Appendix B. (Appendix B(1) is the "occurrence" version of the form, and Appendix B(2) is the "claims made" version of the form. The distinction will be examined later in this section; although the distinction is important, most aspects of the two forms are identical). Speculation abounds that another major revision of the CGL may occur in the next few years. As originally conceived, the CGL's purpose was to provide general liability coverage to a commercial insured regardless of the nature of the insured's business, although for many years the customary practice (one which is no longer followed) was to supplement the CGL form with provisions drafted for particular kinds of businesses. One of the 1986 revisions was to change the name of the form from "Comprehensive General Liability Policy" to "Commercial General Liability Policy." Why do you suppose the name change occurred? For a brief history of the evolution of the CGL, see the portion of the court's opinion in *Montrose Chemical Corp. v. Admiral Insurance Co.,* 10 Cal. 4th 645, 924 P.2d 878, 42 Cal. Rptr. 2d 324 (1995), which appears in subsection (B)(2)(c), *infra.* For more detailed discussions of this history from the perspectives, respectively, of an associate general counsel for an insurer and a policyholder attorney, see George H. Tinker, *Comprehensive General Liability Insurance — Perspective and Overview,* 25 Fed. of Ins. Couns. Quar. 217 (1975), and Eugene R. Anderson, *History of Disputed Provisions of the 1966 Standard Form Comprehensive General Liability Insurance Policy, Drafting History, Sales History, and Historical Review of Commentators,* 369 PLI/Lit 203 (1989).

[2]   The Insuring Agreement

[a]   The Meaning of "Occurrence"

In the "occurrence" CGL in Appendix B(1), the first few paragraphs of "Section I—Coverages" contains the "Insuring Agreement." It reads in part as follows:

1. Insuring Agreement

   a.   We will pay those sums that the insured becomes legally obligated to pay as damages because of "bodily injury" or "property damage" to which this insurance applies. We will have the right and duty to defend the insured against any "suit" seeking those damages. . . ..

   b.   This insurance applies to "bodily injury" and "property damage" only if:

      (1)   The "bodily injury" or "property damage" is caused by an "occurrence" that takes place in the "coverage territory"; and

      (2)   The "bodily injury" or "property damage" occurs during the policy period.

· · · ·

Several phrases in the basic agreement have been the subject of considerable litigation. After a close reading of the insuring agreement, which phrases seem most important?

Perhaps the most important word in the insuring agreement, with the possible exception of "insured," is "occurrence." This is the event which triggers coverage; in the absence of an occurrence, the CGL provides nothing. The meaning of this important term in the CGL is examined in the next case.

GATX LEASING CORP. v. NATIONAL UNION FIRE INSURANCE CO.

64 F.3d 1112 (7th Cir. 1995)

RIPPLE, CIRCUIT JUDGE.

GATX was sued by TCR and Arco under various theories of liability for damages related to the loss of petroleum stored by TCR and Arco in a GATX facility. In dealing with this suit, GATX incurred significant attorneys' fees and settlement costs. Consequently, GATX filed a declaratory judgment action against Nation [sic] Union Fire Insurance Company, alleging that National Union had a duty to defend and to indemnify GATX under both a general liability policy and a related umbrella policy. The district court granted judgment on the pleadings to National Union. For the reasons contained herein, we affirm.

I

BACKGROUND

A. Facts

Amarco Petroleum, Inc. ("Amarco") operated a petroleum product terminal storage and transfer facility near Houston, Texas. GATX was a secured creditor of Amarco, and had leased separately virtually all of the plant assets at the facility to Amarco. In November 1983, GATX filed an involuntary petition in bankruptcy against Amarco. GATX terminated the equipment lease prior to the filing of the bankruptcy petition and assumed possession of the facility assets.

Two customers of the facility, Arco Chemical Company ("Arco") and Texas City Refining ("TCR"), considered not renewing their agreement because of Amarco's apparent insolvency. Around that time, officers of GATX conferred with Arco and TCR regarding a continuing agreement. GATX wanted the facility operations to continue in order to protect the value of the facility assets, as well as to maintain the revenue derived from the facility's use. To that end, GATX acquired the exclusive use of the name "Amarco Petroleum, Inc." to ensure continuity of business. Further, GATX assured Arco and TCR that, if they continued to use the facility and renewed their petroleum products storage agreements, GATX would be responsible for facility operations. Arco and TCR renewed their storage agreements on the assurances that GATX would be responsible for the continuing control and operation of the facilities.

In June 1985, Arco and TCR discovered that vast quantities of their stored products were missing, and TCR found that further quantities of its fuel had been degraded by the unauthorized addition of foreign chemical substances. This discovery was not made until 1985, Arco and TCR submit, because GATX and its employees had, both orally and in writing, represented that their inventories were consistent with the quantities of product originally delivered for storage, and had conspired to hide the thefts of the product.

Following the discovery of the missing petroleum products, Arco filed claims, and TCR intervened, against GATX and several GATX entities,[1] among others, alleging breach of contract, breach of guarantee, negligence, fraudulent inducement and misrepresentation, and conversion. GATX requested that National Union Fire Insurance Company of Pittsburgh, Pennsylvania ("National Union") defend and indemnify it with respect to the lawsuits, but National Union declined. Eventually, GATX settled with Arco for the sum of approximately $300,000, and with TCR for $500,000. GATX estimated that its defense costs, including attorneys' fees, that led up to the settlement totalled $450,000.

On January 24, 1994, GATX filed a declaratory judgment action against National Union, contending that National Union had a duty to defend and to indemnify GATX for the Arco and TCR legal actions under two policies issued to Amarco, effective June 14, 1984: the Primary Policy, No. EHA 940-9398 RA, and the Umbrella Policy No. EHA 940-9399. These policies stated that National Union, on behalf of Amarco or any other insured, would recompense all amounts to which Amarco or any insured became legally obligated due to "property damage" caused by an "occurrence." Because GATX had leased equipment to Amarco which comprised the "principal facilities," GATX was named as an additional "person insured" under the primary policy.

B. District Court Proceedings

National Union moved for judgment on the pleadings. See Fed.R.Civ.P. 12(c). The district court granted the motion. The court first determined that Texas substantive law applied. The court then held that, under the terms of the insurance agreements, GATX could not allege any "property damage" caused by an "occurrence." . . . .

II

ANALYSIS

1.

[In an omitted portion of the opinion, the court held that the law of Texas applied.]

2.

We now turn to the general principles of Texas law that must guide our analysis. GATX submits that the theft and contamination of the Arco and TCR petroleum products in storage at the GATX facility was an "occurrence" for purposes of the National Union insurance policy, and that therefore National Union had a duty to defend GATX, the insured.[7] . . . .

---

[1] Arco sued GATX and its subsidiary, GLC Petroleum services. TCR intervened against the same defendants and two other entities affiliated with GATX: GATX Leasing Corporation and GATX Terminals Corporation. We refer to all the GATX entities collectively as "GATX."

[7] National Union's duty to defend is also contingent on whether the theft, conversion, and adulteration of the petroleum products is classified as "property damage" under the terms of the primary and umbrella insurance policies. The district court held that the theft or conversion is not, while the contamination of TCR's petroleum was. We need not consider this issue on review because we conclude that GATX did not allege an "occurrence" under the terms of the insurance policies.

As a general rule, under Texas law, insurance contracts are interpreted under the same rules of construction as standard contracts. However, if the insurance policy is susceptible to more than one reasonable interpretation, any ambiguity will be resolved by adopting a construction that favors the insured. "Not every difference in the interpretation of an insurance policy amounts to an ambiguity," however. *Maryland Casualty Co. [v. Texas Commerce Bancshares]*, 878 F. Supp. [939] at 941 [(N.D.Tex. 1995)]. Although the insured and insurer likely may take conflicting views of coverage, neither conflicting expectations nor dialectics are sufficient to create an ambiguity.

3.

With the principles of Texas law that we have just set forth in mind, we now turn to the facts of the case before us. We first examine the pertinent insurance policies. The primary policy defined an "occurrence" as:

> [A]n accident, including continuous or repeated exposure to conditions, which results in bodily injury or property damage neither expected nor intended from the standpoint of the insured[.]

R.1-1, Ex.A. In the umbrella policy, the term "occurrence" is defined as:

> [A]n event, including continuous or repeated exposure to conditions, which result in Personal Injury or Property Damage during the policy period, neither expected nor intended from the standpoint of the insured[.] *Id.*

An examination of the pleadings in the underlying litigation makes clear that the plaintiffs in that case sought recovery against GATX for theft, conversion, and contamination of petroleum products. We also note that, in this appeal, GATX does not ask us to review the analysis of the district court regarding whether the petroleum loss and contamination represents "property damage" under the terms of the insurance policies. Our task on review is to determine solely whether the facts, as alleged in the underlying complaint, can be characterized as an "occurrence" that triggers National Union's duty to defend GATX.

Our review of the relevant case law makes clear that, when harm to property is caused by the intentional act of one party, it cannot be characterized as "accidental" or an "event" causing an "occurrence" under an insurance policy. This result is correct even if the insured allowed the intentional act only through its negligence.[9] This basic principle recognizes the reality that

---

[9] The district court correctly noted that, "[a]lthough the two policies contain somewhat different language, the differences are not material. GATX attempts to distinguish the 'accident' language in the Primary Policy from the 'event' language in the Umbrella Policy. Whether 'occurrence' is defined specifically to include an 'accident' or not, an 'occurrence' must still be accidental."

A leading treatise defines "accident" as:

> an unusual or unexpected event, happening without negligence; chance or contingency; happening by chance or unexpectedly; an event from an unknown cause or an unexpected event from a known cause.

11 Couch on Insurance § 44:288 at 443 (2d ed. 1982). Such language indicates that the substitution of "event" for "accident" is irrelevant. Further support is also found in the fact that since 1940, the insurance industry has used a standard general liability policy. This standard policy, the Comprehensive General Liability Policy, was most recently modified in 1972 so that "occurrence"

the risk of accidental loss or damage to property is fundamentally different from the risk of loss from intentional acts of the insured. Texas has recognized this fundamental distinction. It has also made clear that, when the volitional act of the insured is predicated on an act of negligence, the principle remains intact. In *Argonaut Southwest Ins. Co. v. Maupin*, 500 S.W.2d 633 (Tex. 1973), the Supreme Court of Texas held that an insurer was not required to defend an insured under terms of a policy that provided for the defense of the insured against claims arising out of an "accident."[11] In *Maupin*, the insured removed "borrow material" from property after receiving permission for removal from the current tenant. The actual property owner sued the insured on theory of trespass. The court stated that, even though it could be argued that the insured did not intend to injure the property owner, the damage that occurred resulted from the intentional removal of "borrow material." *Id.* at 635. The court noted that:

> Where acts are voluntary and intentional and the injury is the natural result of the act, the result was not caused by accident even though that result may have been unexpected, unforeseen and unintended. There was no insurance against liability for damages caused by mistake or error. The cause of the injury was not an accident within the meaning of this policy. *Id.* (quoting *Thomason v. United States Fidelity & Guar. Co.*, 248 F.2d 417 (5th Cir. 1957)). Thus, the Supreme Court of Texas, in considering an insurance policy very similar to the policy at issue here, concluded, in essence, that despite the negligence of the insured, who was unaware of the true owner of the property from which material was taken, the ensuing damage was not an event that could be characterized as an "occurrence" for purposes of invoking the policy's duty to defend.

In *Red Ball Leasing, Inc. v. Hartford Accident & Indem. Co.*, 915 F.2d 306, 309-10 (7th Cir. 1990), in the course of interpreting Indiana law, we looked for support to the Texas decision and held that an insured's deliberate and contemplated act of repossessing trucks did not become an "accident" under the relevant insurance policy simply because the insured's negligence prompted the act.[12] In *Red Ball*, the insured, who was in the business of selling and leasing trucks, improperly repossessed some trucks. We held that

---

now means "an accident, including continuous or repeated exposure to conditions, which result in bodily injury or property damage neither expected nor intended from the standpoint of the insured." See John A. Appelman, 7A Insurance Law and Practice P 4491 at 3, P 4492 at 15 (Rev. ed. 1979);. The standard liability policy language is sufficiently close to the language contained in the umbrella policy that we believe that there exists no real difference in meaning between the two.

[11] In relevant part, the provisions of the insurance policy at issue in Maupin:

> The word 'occurrence' as used herein shall mean either (a) an accident, or (b) in the absence of an accident, a condition for which the insured is responsible which during the policy period causes physical injury to or destruction of property which was not intended.

500 S.W.2d at 634 n. 1.

[12] The policy at issue in Red Ball defined an "occurrence" as: an accident, including continuous or repeated exposure to conditions, which results in . . . property damage neither expected nor intended from the standpoint of the insured. Red Ball, 915 F.2d at 307-08 (emphasis removed).

such an incident was not an "accident" covered under the relevant casualty policy even though the insured mistakenly believed it had a right to repossess the trucks because its accounting system erroneously indicated that the buyer had defaulted on payments. The crux of our analysis relied on the fact that the insured's decision to repossess the trucks was intentional. We concluded:

> A volitional act does not become an accident simply because the insured's negligence prompted the act. Injury that is caused by negligence must be distinguished from injury that is caused by a deliberate and contemplated act initiated at least in part by the actor's negligence at some earlier point. The former injury may be an accident. . . . However, the latter injury, because it is intended and the negligence is attenuated from the volitional act, is not an accident. *Id.* at 311. If the damage at issue resulted from a volitional act, we have held that such a situation does not constitute an "occurrence" for purposes of insurance policy interpretation. See *Id.* at 309-11 & nn. 1-4 (collecting cases).

The plaintiffs in the underlying action included in their complaint an allegation that GATX had supervised its personnel in a negligent manner and therefore permitted the theft. The district court therefore examined several cases that, in the view of GATX, require that National Union defend it on this claim and therefore on the entire action. We note initially that these cases cannot be considered controlling. None are based on the law of Texas . . . . Other federal courts, also obliged to discern the course that the Supreme Court of Texas would follow, have concluded that a claim such as the one before us would not be considered independent, but rather interdependent, of the claim of intentional misconduct. In *Old Republic Ins. Co. v. Comprehensive Health Care Assocs., Inc.*, 786 F. Supp. 629 (N.D. Tex. 1992), *aff'd*, 2 F.3d 105 (5th Cir. 1993), former employees brought suit against their employer and its employee alleging sexual harassment, discrimination, and negligent hiring. The court, considering a declaratory judgment action involving a duty to defend, cited the Texas Supreme Court case *Maupin* favorably and held that the employee allegations did not constitute an "occurrence." The court stated

> [T]he Court is not persuaded by the argument that the allegations are severable and, therefore, insurers owe a separate and distinct duty to defend [the employer]. To the contrary, each and every allegation arises out of the alleged acts of sexual harassment. Finding a separate and distinct duty to defend [the employer] would necessarily require proof of the underlying sexual harassment. The allegations are not mutually exclusive; rather they are related and interdependent. Without the underlying sexual harassment there would have been no injury and obviously, no basis for a suit against [the employer] for negligence. *Id.* at 633.

Similar reasoning was employed by the Fifth Circuit in *Columbia Mut. Ins. Co. v. Fiesta Mart, Inc.*, 987 F.2d 1124 (5th Cir. 1993). In *Fiesta Mart*, the court held that the insurer did not owe a duty to defend an insured in an underlying suit based on a theory of negligence because the insured's negligence was related to, interdependent on, and inseparable from, the intentional fraudulent activity of a financial corporation to which the insured leased "vendor locations." The court stated that, without the volitional fraudulent act of the financial corporation, which the insured had allowed to conduct business on its premises, there would have been no basis for suit against the insured.

GATX's complaint presents no factual basis that can be characterized as an "occurrence" to invoke National Union's duty to defend. The loss and damage to the petroleum products alleged by TCR and Arco resulted from volitional acts of employees of the storage facility. As such, given the relevant Texas law, we cannot, as a matter of law, separate the negligent act of GATX from the intentional acts of the storage facility employees for purposes of construing the relevant insurance provisions. Accordingly, we affirm the district court's conclusion that, as a matter of Texas law, GATX "cannot establish that TCR and Arco sued for 'property damage' that was caused by an 'occurrence.' "

. . . .

NOTES

1. *Evolving policy language.* The first CGL policies used the phrase "caused by accident." The term "accident" served several purposes. It distinguished between intentionally caused harm, which was not covered, and inadvertently caused harm, which was covered. Also, the accident had to occur during the policy period before there was coverage. In some respects, the term "accident" was problematic. If a liability-producing event is not sudden, forceful, and violent (consider, for example, a slow, gradual deterioration of a storage tank and/or a continuous seepage of a toxic substance from the tank, which in small quantities is harmless but eventually accumulates to a point at which a recognizable harm exists), is the event an "accident"? And did it refer to the negligent act or omission rather than to the moment when injury or destruction takes place? Litigation over these questions prompted the substitution in the 1966 CGL revision of the phrase "caused by occurrence" for "caused by accident." "Occurrence" was defined to mean "an accident, including injurious exposure to conditions, which results during the policy period, in bodily injury or property damage neither expected nor intended from the standpoint of the insured." In 1973 the phrase "injurious exposure to conditions" was changed to "continuous or repeated exposure to conditions." Until 1986, "occurrence" was defined in accordance with the policy definition referred to in *GATX Leasing*.

The 1986 CGL revision changed the definition of occurrence to the following: " 'Occurrence' means an accident, including continuous or repeated exposures to substantially the same general harmful conditions." The "neither expected nor intended" phrase was removed from the definition of occurrence and placed in an exclusion with virtually identical phrasing. For examples of cases where the 1986 revision was at issue, *see Federated Mutual Insurance Co. v. Grapevine Excavation Inc.,* 197 F.3d 720 (5th Cir. 1999); *Macon Iron & Paper Stock Co., Inc. v. Transcontinental Insurance Co.,* 93 F.Supp.2d 1370 (M.D.Ga. 1999); *Nationwide Prop. & Casualty Insurance Co. v. Eryo Hearing Aid Serv.,*

Inc. 895 F.Supp. 85 (E.D. Pa. 1995). For more on this history, *see Montrose Chemical Corp. v. Admiral Insurance Co.,* 897 P.2d 1 (Cal. 1995), which appears as a principal case in § 5.02[2][c], *infra.*

2. *A first glimpse at "claims made" coverage. GATX Leasing* involved the occurrence version of the CGL. We will take up claims made coverage in § 5.02[4], *infra,* but it is worth taking a moment at this early juncture to understand how the claims made form differs from the occurrence form. When you compare the Insuring Agreement in the "occurrence" form in Appendix B(1) to that which is in the "claims made" form in Appendix B(2), the differences are in paragraph 1(b) and paragraph 1(c). Paragraph 1(a) and paragraph 1(b)(1) are identical. In the form in GATX Leasing and under the occurrence form in Appendix B(1), the bodily injury or property damage must occur during the policy period. After you read the language in the claims made form (Appendix B(2)) in paragraphs 1(b)(3) and 1(c), how would you describe the difference between the coverages? Note that the definition of "occurrence" is still important in the claims made form.

3. *Is* Maupin *correct?* The court in *GATX Leasing* relied heavily on the 1973 Texas supreme court decision in *Maupin.* The theory of liability in *Maupin* was trespass, a kind of intentional tort, and the court concluded there was no occurrence. What if the trespasser does not know that the entry will cause harm? Must the trespasser know of both the unlawful entry and the resulting harm?

Franklin Outdoor Advertising Company constructs billboards on highways; it often leases the land on which its structures are erected. In *Franklin v. Western National Mutual Insurance Co.,* 574 N.W.2d 405 (Minn. 1998), Franklin, the CGL insured, became involved in a dispute with the Laudenbachs, one of its lessors, who wanted to sell a portion of the leased property to a third party and claimed a right to terminate the lease and require Franklin to remove the billboard. When Franklin brought a declaratory judgment action to determine its rights under the lease, the lessors counterclaimed for trespass, alleging Franklin's intentional refusal to remove its sign despite the lessors' demand that it do so. Franklin asked its insurer to defend the counterclaim. Is this claim covered by the CGL?

In the area of torts involving property, consider the tort of nuisance. Under modern law, legal responsibility for a nuisance may be based on intentional conduct, negligent conduct, or strict liability. Is a nuisance an "occurrence"? *See Millard Warehouse Inc. v. Harford Fire Insurance Co.,* 204 Neb. 518, 283 N.W.2d 56 (1979).

4. *Fortuity revisited.* Can a trespass ever be fortuitous? Is a nuisance based on intentional conduct fortuitous? This is particularly important in the environmental damage cases, which have dominated CGL litigation during the 1980s and 1990s. The essence of the problem is this: Suppose a firm intentionally stores hazardous wastes in sealed, supposedly water-and air-tight drums, and intentionally buries them in a pit lined with special materials to prevent (it was thought) any substances from leeching into adjacent groundwater supplies. The wastes, however, escape all of these safeguards and pollute the water. Does the damage result from an "occurrence"? In particular, is the damage "accidental"? After all, should the firm have realized

when the wastes were stored that drums and even carefully constructed pits do not last forever? If the eventual failure of the pollution-prevent devices is certain, how is the damage "fortuitous"? *See Waste Management of Carolinas, Inc. v. Peerless Insurance Co.,* 340 S.E.2d 374 (N.C. 1986).

Suppose a recycler of scrap metal purchases railroad cars from a third party, unaware that the seller lacks good title to the cars. The recycler cuts up the cars for scrap metal and resells the metal. Thereafter, the true owner of the cars sues the recycler for conversion of stolen property, etc. The recycler seeks coverage under its CGL. Has a fortuitous loss occurred? Has there been an "accident" or "occurrence" within the meaning of the CGL? *See Mindis Metals, Inc. v. Transportation Insurance Co.,* 209 F.3d 1296 (11th Cir. 2000).

Whether an insured's sexual abuse of third parties is covered by the homeowners form was considered in § 5.01[2], *supra*. If the abuser's (or alleged abuser's) employer is sued for negligent employment, supervising, placement, and/or training of the employee, in circumstances where the employee is alleged to have committed acts of abuse on third parties, does the employer have coverage under the CGL? *See American Employers Insurance Co. v. Doe 3B,* 165 F.3d 1209 (8th Cir. 1999) (alleged negligent supervision of priest); *Evangelical Lutheran Church in America v. Atlantic Mutual Insurance Co.,* 169 F.3d 947 (5th Cir. 1999) (similar circumstances); *American Guarantee and Liability Insurance Co. v.* 1906 Company, 129 F.3d 802 (5th Cir. 1997) (predicting Mississippi law regarding employee's surreptitious videotaping of models in dressing room at photography studio).

5. *Trigger of coverage.* What if an insured changes CGL insurers every year? The definition of "occurrence" obviously contemplates some situations where the loss occurs over a long period of time. If the temporal nature of the loss appears to cross through multiple policy periods, the question will arise as to which policy or policies is "on the risk," i.e., which policies are "triggered." This issue is discussed in § 5.02[2][c], *infra*.

6. *Other parts of the insuring agreement.* If no occurrence exists, the analysis is over, but if an occurrence is found, the analysis is barely underway. Other provisions in the basic insuring agreement may be implicated, depending on the circumstances.

7. *Other parts I: "to which this insurance applies."* This phrase recognizes that there are specific kinds of exposures covered by the CGL as well as specific exclusions to the affirmative grants of coverage. The company's obligation only extends to liability to which the insurance applies, not all liabilities imaginable. *See Friar v. Statutory Trustees of Kirkwood Sports Ass'n,* 959 S.W.2d 808 (Mo. App. 1997) ("to which this insurance applies" limits coverage for bodily injury or property damage).

8. *Other parts II: "as damages."* The term "damages" is not defined in the CGL. If a complaint seeks only equitable relief, should there be coverage under policy language like that in *GATX Leasing,* assuming the insured's conduct constituted an accident or occurrence? *Compare Doyle v. Allstate Insurance Co.,* 1 N.Y.2d 439, 136 N.E.2d 484, 154 N.Y.S.2d 10 (1956) with *Aetna Casualty & Surety Co. v. Hanna,* 224 F.2d 499 (5th Cir. 1955), 53 A.L.R.2d 1125 (1957) and *Desrochers v. New York Casualty Co.,* 99 N.H. 129, 106 A.2d 196 (1954).

The question of what constitutes "damages" has been litigated in almost every major environmental liability insurance case. Under the federal Comprehensive Environmental Response, Compensation and Liability Act of 1980 ("CERCLA"), 42 U.S.C. § 9601 et seq., commonly known as the "Superfund Act," the Environmental Protection Agency (EPA) may order clean-up of toxic waste sites or spills and may even order an abatement of environmental threats prior to the occurrence of any damage. *See* 42 U.S.C. § 9607(a). Are these so-called "response costs" to be considered "damages" for purposes of CGL coverage? At first, courts that addressed the issue were sharply divided, but most courts have now concluded that "damages" includes government-ordered "response costs." *See e.g., Farmland Industries, Inc. v. Republic Insurance Co.,* 941 S.W.2d 505 (Mo. 1997); *Ryan v. Royal Insurance Co. of Am.,* 916 F.2d 731 (1st Cir. 1990) (PRP letter must "demand" and not "request" cleanup to constitute "damages"); *Avondale Industries, Inc. v. Travelers Indemnity Co.,* 887 F.2d 1200 (2d Cir. 1989), *reh'g denied,* 894 F.2d 498 (1990), *cert. denied,* 496 U.S. 906 (1990); *Morton International, Inc. v. General Accident Insurance Co. of Am.,* 629 A.2d 831 (N.J. 1993), *cert. denied,* 512 U.S. 1245 (1994).

What if the insured voluntarily cleans up a toxic waste site under threat of government-ordered response costs? Are those expenses "damages" under the CGL? Can it be said that the insured is "legally obligated to pay" those expenses? *Compare Weyerhauser Co. v. Aetna Casualty & Surety Co.,* 874 P.2d 142 (Wash. 1994), with *City of Edgerton v. General Casualty Co. of Wis.,* 517 N.W.2d 463 (Wis. 1994). See generally Jordan S. Stanzler & Charles A. Yuen, *Coverage for Environmental Cleanup Costs: History of the Word "Damages" Under CGL Policies,* 16 Colum J. Envtl. L. 73 (1991).

In assessing the outcomes of these cases or their usefulness as controlling precedent, one must take care to notice which version of the CGL is being interpreted and applied. When the CGL's pollution exclusion was modified in 1986 (a subject that receives more attention in § 5.02[3][c], *infra*), the revised CGL included a provision that excluded "[a]ny loss, cost, or expense arising out of any governmental direction or request that you test for, monitor, clean up, remove, contain, treat, detoxify or neutralize pollutants." (See ISO CGL Policy, CG 00 02 11 85). The most recent iteration of the CGL handles this situation somewhat differently (see paragraph f(2) in the pollution exclusion in the form in Appendix B.) Does the new form have the effect of implementing the majority judicial approach in the contract between insured and insurer?

Should it matter if the EPA-ordered clean-up occurs on the insured's own property? The EPA may be concerned about imminent injury to adjacent property owned by third parties or to a nearby city water supply. Note that if the insured did nothing and the pollution did eventually cause damage to third parties, those third parties could sue the insured in tort. Note also that the CGL is a *liability* policy; consistently with this purpose, CGL policies have long contained a so-called "owned property exclusion," which excludes damage to property either "owned or occupied by the insured" and to property under the "care, custody or control" of the insured. *Compare State Department of Environmental Protection v. Signo Trading International, Inc.,* 612 A.2d 932

(N.J. 1992) (no coverage due to owned-property exclusion), with *Aetna Casualty & Surety Co. v. Dow Chemical Co.,* 28 F. Supp. 2d 448 (E.D. Mich. 1998) (on-site clean-up is not barred by owned property exclusion if there is threat that contaminants in the insured's soil will migrate to groundwater or to property of others); *Diamond Shamrock Chemicals Co. v. Aetna Casualty & Surety Co.,* 554 A.2d 1342 (N.J. Super. Ct. 1989) (insurer denied summary judgment on basis of owned property exclusion because fact issue remained as to whether dioxin contamination on insured's property posed immediate threat to others). Suppose a homeowner's yard has an old, tall tree that leans ominously over a neighbor's house. If the homeowner were to ask her liability insurer to bear the expense of cutting down the tree in order to avoid damage to the neighbor's house should the tree fall (as seems likely, at least eventually), what response do you suppose the insurer would make? Does it matter who owns the groundwater that is being cleansed?

9. *Other parts III: "suits."* The issues raised in the foregoing note also implicate another term in the insuring agreement—"suits." Is a letter from the EPA notifying the insured that it is a responsible party for pollution a "suit"? If no complaint has been filed, how can there be a "suit"? Is there a difference between a "suit" and a "claim"? Should the fact that the EPA has alternative remedial options, not all of which involve the initiation of litigation, matter when it comes to how the policy is interpreted? Courts are divided on this issue. *See e.g., Foster-Gardner, Inc. v. National Union fire Insurance Co.,* 18 Cal. 4th 857, 959 P.2d 265, 77 Cal. Rptr. 2d 107 (1998) (EPA order notifying insured that it was a responsible party was not a "suit," and insurer did not owe duty to defend); *Michigan Millers Mutual Ins. Co. v. Bronson Plating Co.,* 445 Mich. 558, 519 N.W.2d 864 (1994) (term "suit" may encompass some nonjudicial proceedings); *Compass Insurance Co. v. City of Littleton,* 984 P.2d 606 (Colo. 1999) (coercive EPA action initiated by potentially responsible party letters are "suits" covered by CGL policies). See generally Mark S. Dennison, Annotation, *What Constitutes "Suit" Triggering Insurer's Duty to Defend Environmental Claims—State Cases,* 48 A.L.R.5th 355 (1997).

10. *Other parts IV: "bodily injury."* For coverage to exist under the CGL, either "bodily injury" or "property damage" must result from an occurrence. "Bodily injury" is usually defined to mean bodily injury, sickness, or disease, including death. See the definitions in the policies in Appendices B, C, and E. Note that the definitions in the homeowners form and the CGL policy are different; are the distinctions material?

Is an emotional injury, by itself, a bodily injury? *Compare National Casualty Co. v. Great Southwest Fire Insurance Co.,* 833 P.2d 741 (Colo. 1992), with *Lavanant v. General Accident Insurance Co. of Am.,* 584 N.E.2d 744 (N.Y. 1992). What if the emotional injury produces physical manifestations? *See Garvis v. Employers Mutual Casualty Co.,* 497 N.W.2d 254 (Minn. 1993). Does emotional distress with accompanying physical manifestations produced by a noncovered economic loss constitute "bodily injury"? *See Keating v. National Union Fire. Insurance Co.,* 995 F.2d 154 (9th Cir. 1993); *Waller v. Truck Insurance Exchange,* 11 Cal. 4th 1, 900 P.2d 619, 44 Cal. Rptr. 2d 370 (Cal. 1995).

Is the insurance policy definition of bodily injury coextensive with the tort definition for personal injury? For discussion of this issue in the context of an automobile liability policy, *see McNeill v. Metropolitan Property & Liability Insurance Co.,* 420 Mass. 587, 650 N.E.2d 793 (1995), in § 6.01, *infra.*

11. *Other parts V: "property damage."* Beginning in 1966, the CGL form in widespread use limited "property damage" to mean destruction of, injury to, or loss of the use of *tangible* property. See the definitions of property damage in the policies in Appendices B, C, and E. If this is the definition, would harm caused exclusively to intangible economic interests and property rights—such as lost profits, loss of goodwill, loss of anticipated benefits of a bargain, or loss of an investment—be covered? *See Travelers Insurance Cos. v. Penda Corp.,* 974 F.2d 823 (7th Cir. 1992). Assuming that tangible property is involved, must there be actual physical harm to the property? Or is it sufficient that the damage is only the loss of use of tangible property? *See Aetna Casualty & Surety Co. v. General Time Corp.,* 704 F.2d 80 (2d Cir. 1983).

12. *Other coverages in the CGL.* Section I of the CGL sets forth the various "coverages," and is divided into three parts. (See Appendix B.) Coverage A is for "bodily injury and property damage liability"; most of the case law involves issues that arise under Coverage A. Related to Coverage A is Coverage C, which is for "medical payments" arising out of accidents in which third parties suffer bodily injury.

Coverage B is for "personal and advertising injury." The term "personal injury" is often used to refer to bodily injuries, but when used in connection with commercial liability insurance coverage, it has a special meaning. In this context, it typically refers to three categories of intentional torts: (1) false arrest, malicious prosecution, or willful detention; (2) libel, slander, or defamation of character; and (3) invasion of privacy, wrongful eviction, or wrongful entry.

"Advertising injury" typically refers to publication offenses, misappropriation of ideas, and infringement of copyright or trademark offenses. These two areas of potential liabilities are combined in a the "personal and advertising injury" coverage of the CGL. "Personal and advertising injury" is defined in the CGL as "injury, including consequential 'bodily injury', arising out of one or more of the following offenses," after which follows a list which includes, among others, false arrest, malicious prosecution, wrongful eviction, slander, libel, invasion of privacy, using another's advertising idea in one's own advertisement, and infringement upon another's "copyright, trade dress or slogan" in one's advertisement. (See the definition in Appendix B.)

Coverage B in the 1998 CGL form (see Appendix B) is substantially revised from the 1986 iteration of Coverage B. The 1998 definition deletes some offenses that were covered by the 1986 CGL, and the 1998 CGL has some new exclusions and revisions in others. The effect of the revision should be to moot some disputes over what constitutes "advertising" under the earlier form. Language in the 1973 CGL excluding coverage for "trademark infringement" was generally enforced, but revisions in the 1986 CGL led to some (but not all) courts finding coverage for such claims under the revised CGL. The 1998 revision provides coverage for "trade dress" infringement in an advertisement, but not for trademark infringement. For more discussion of the personal injury and advertising coverage, see Bruce Telles, *Insurance Coverage for Intellectual Property Torts,* 602 PLI/Lit 629 (April 1999); Lawrence O. Monin, *ISO*

Advertising and Personal Injury 1998 Revisions: Major Surgery or Just a Band-Aid Fix?, 4 Mealey's Emerging Ins. Disp. 24 (Aug. 19, 1999).

13. *Other specialty coverages.* "Errors and omissions" policies are generally purchased by attorneys, physicians, and other professions. These receive more attention in § 5.02[4], *infra*. Firms in the entertainment business, newspapers, and other media enterprises usually purchase coverage tailored to those industries. Patent infringement claims are not covered by the CGL, so some insurers offer specialty coverage for patent and other intellectual property claims. See generally Telles, *supra* (cited in the prior note). Coverage for other types of injuries, such as civil rights violations, also may be obtained under special policies or endorsements.

14. *The Y2K non-event.* Many observers expected a cataclysm on January 1, 2000 when computers world-wide were predicted to malfunction, but this, as we all now know, did not occur. The CGL has no express exclusion for Y2K liabilities, and this led to considerable concern in the industry about exposure for possible losses, which it now appears will not occur anywhere near the magnitudes some feared. Businesses spent, however, billions of dollars upgrading computer software and equipment to avoid future problems attributed to the so-called "millennium bug," and some of these firms are now seeking coverage under the reasoning that the expense was incurred in order to mitigate what would have been a covered loss. See Joanne Wojcik, *Y2K bug is still biting*, Bus. Ins., July 17, 2000, at 1 (listing and discussing Y2K coverage cases being litigated). For discussion of the insurance coverage issues potentially raised by Y2K, see Jeffrey W. Stempel, *A Mixed Bag for Chicken Little: Analyzing Year 2000 Claims and Insurance Coverage*, 48 Emory L.J. 169 (1999); Bruce Telles, *The Year 2000 Problem and Insurance Coverage*, 602 PLI/Lit 687 (April 1999), Kirk Pasich, *Insurance Coverage for the Year 2000 Problem*, SE64 ALI-ABA 27 (Jan. 13, 2000). Nevertheless, the rapid development of e commerce and Internet business portends a new era of information-based commercial liability, and insurance policies and companies will adapt to this new environment with new and revised coverages. In fact, more insurers are offering new kinds of policies that are specifically designed to cover e-commerce risks. See Roberto Ceniceros, *Web risks spur changes in insurance coverage*, Bus. Ins., Feb. 7, 2000, at 1.

15. *Counting the occurrences.* If a business owner covered by a CGL is unfortunate enough to have one light fixture fall from the ceiling and hit one customer in the head, she can safely conclude that there has been one occurrence. Many situations do not play out so neatly. Consider the next case.

[b]   Multiple Losses and the Number of Occurrences

HOME INDEMNITY CO. v. CITY OF MOBILE
749 F.2d 659 (11th Cir. 1984)

JAMES C. HILL, CIRCUIT JUDGE:

The sole issue presented in this case is the meaning of the term "occurrence" as used in a comprehensive, general liability insurance policy issued by plaintiff/appellant Home Indemnity Company (Home) to the defendant/appellee City of Mobile (City).

This case arose as a result of over 200 lawsuits filed against the City of Mobile after major rains on April 13, 1980, May 16-17, 1980 and May 5-6, 1981. During and following these rains, overflows occurred at various points in the surface water drainage system maintained by the City, and extensive flood damage resulted. In suits filed in state court, property owners alleged that the City was liable for the flood damage due to its negligence in the planning, construction, operation, and maintenance of its surface water drainage system.

Prior to the flooding, Home issued to the City an insurance policy indemnifying the City against property damage liability up to $100,000 for any one occurrence.[1] The City apparently sought this policy to protect itself from potential liability as a result of 1975 Alabama legislation which partially waived sovereign immunity, permitting damage recoveries against governmental entities up to $100,000 for property damage "arising out of any single occurrence." Ala. Code § 11-93-2.

The terms of the policy issued by Home provide that:

> The Company will pay on behalf of the insured all sums which the insured shall become legally obligated to pay as damages because of (a) bodily injury or (b) property damage to which this insurance applies, caused by *an occurrence* (emphasis added).

This per occurrence limit is defined as follows:

> The total liability of the company for all damages because of all property damage sustained by one or more persons or organizations as a result of *any one occurrence* should not exceed the limit of property damage liability stated in the schedule as applicable to *"each occurrence."*

"Occurrence" is defined in the policy as an accident, including continuous or repeated exposure to conditions, which results in bodily injury or property damages neither expected nor intended from the standpoint of the insured. In addition, the policy states that:

> for the purpose of determining the limit of the company's liability, all bodily injury and property damage arising out of the continuous or repeated exposure to substantially the same general conditions shall be considered as arising out of *one occurrence.*

In November, 1980, Home filed this suit in federal district court seeking a declaratory judgment as to the meaning of the term "occurrence" in the policy. Home argued (and still contends) that each separate rainfall and consequent flooding is "one occurrence;" and that since there were three separate rainfalls that resulted in flooding, it is liable for only three "occurrences." The City and the numerous flood victims maintained (and still maintain) that "occurrence" should be defined in terms of the resulting damage

---

[1] The City's yearly premium payments on this policy for 1981 and 1982 were approximately $307,000.

to each claimant's property, so that each incident of flooding to the property of each individual property owner is an "occurrence."

The district court issued its final order interpreting the policy on December 1, 1982, and entered a final judgment for the defendants based on that order on November 3, 1983. The court held that the term "occurrence" as used in this policy means "the occurrence of events or incidents for which the City is liable," stating further that the policy extends $100,000 in coverage to the City "for each occurrence which results in the City becoming legally obligated to pay damages for property damages." The court noted that what creates liability against the City is not the rainfall and flooding itself, but the "intervening negligence of the City" in constructing or maintaining its drainage system. Home brought this appeal from that judgment.

We agree with the above statements of the district court, although we clarify any portions of the court's order which could be construed as indicating that the damages to each individual property owner are separate "occurrences."

This court is bound by Alabama law in interpreting this insurance contract. We must give to the terms of the policy the meaning intended by the parties to the policy. *United States Fire Insurance Co. v. Safeco Insurance Co.,* 444 So. 2d 844, 846 (Ala. 1983).

In the recent case of *United States Fire Insurance,* the Alabama Supreme Court adopted the "cause" theory of analyzing the meaning of an "occurrence" in an insurance policy, rather than the "effect" or "result" theory. In that case, water had leaked through the roof of a building, damaging the merchandise of the lessee occupying the building. Subsequently, the lessee sustained additional damages by rainfall when the roofing company working on the roof failed to effectively cover a portion of the roof on which it was working. The lessor had two insurance policies: one providing primary coverage for losses up to $100,000 per occurrence; and a second, "umbrella" policy covering excess losses. The definition of "one occurrence" in the primary insurance policy was identical to the definition in our present case.[2] The primary insurer refused to pay more than $100,000, asserting that all of the water damage resulted from one "occurrence."

The issue presented to the Alabama Supreme Court was whether the additional damage caused by the later rainfall, resulting from the roofing company's negligence, was part of a single occurrence as defined by the insurance policy. The court first set out the applicable standard—"[a]s long as the injuries stem from one proximate cause there is a single occurrence." 444 So. 2d at 846. Thus, a single occurrence may result in multiple injuries to multiple parties over a period of time; but if one cause is interrupted and replaced by another intervening cause, the chain of causation is broken and more than one occurrence has taken place. *Id.* at 846-47. Based on the facts of the case, the court then determined that two separate occurrences had taken place, because the additional damage was caused by a "separate, intervening

---

[2] Under the heading "LIMITS OF LIABILITY," the policy provided that:

> For the purpose of determining the limit of the company's liability, all bodily injuries and property damage arising out of continuous or repeated exposure to substantially the same general conditions shall be considered as arising out of one occurrence.

cause" (the negligence of the roofing crew) rather than the prior condition of the roof. *Id.* at 847. In addition, the two instances of water damage were found to be easily distinguishable in time and space; and one event did not cause the other. *Id.* In sum, the initial water damage was caused by the "occurrence" of the leaky roof, and the later damage was caused by the "occurrence" of the negligence of the roofing crew.

Although it did not deal with Alabama law, *Maurice Pincoffs Co. v. St. Paul Fire and Marine Insurance Co.*, 447 F.2d 204 (5th Cir. 1971), is another instructive case. In *Pincoffs*, the Pincoffs company imported 110,000 pounds of canary seed which was sold to various dealers who then sold the seed to bird owners. The seed was contaminated and killed many birds. St. Paul provided primary liability insurance coverage with a single occurrence limit of $50,000 and an aggregate limit of $100,000. The definition of the term "occurrence" in the policy was nearly identical to the definition in the policy issued to the City of Mobile. The district court thought that it was the contamination of the seed that was the occurrence to which the policy referred, because it was contaminated seed that caused the damage. However, the Fifth Circuit reversed, stating:

> We think that the "occurrence" to which the policy must refer is *the occurrence of the events or incidents for which Pincoffs is liable.* It was the sale of the contaminated seed for which Pincoffs was liable. . . . Pincoffs received the seed in a contaminated condition and did not itself contaminate the seed. However, it was not the act of contamination which subjected Pincoffs to liability. If Pincoffs had destroyed the seed before sale, for instance, there would be no occurrence at all for which the insured would be liable. But once a sale was made there would be liability for any resulting damages. It was the sale that created the exposure to "a condition which resulted in property damage neither expected nor intended from the standpoint of the insured," under the definition of the policy. *And for each of the eight sales made by Pincoffs, there was a new exposure and another occurrence.* *Id.* at 206 (emphasis added).

Like the *Pincoffs* case, our present case involves general liability insurance coverage where the insurer need pay a claim only after the City of Mobile has been held liable for negligently causing damage. As *United States Fire Insurance* indicates, Alabama law requires us to look to the proximate cause of the damages in interpreting an "occurrence." Therefore, we agree with the district court that, under Alabama law, the "occurrence" to which this policy refers is the "events or incidents for which the City is liable;" that is, a single "occurrence" encompasses all damage proximately resulting from each incident or series of incidents of negligence which create the City's liability for flooding.

Under this standard, it is obvious that neither the appellant nor the appellees are correct in their interpretation of "occurrence." The rainfall and flooding itself were not the "occurrences," since those were Acts of God for which the City is not liable; it is the intervening negligence of the City in maintaining its water drainage system which creates the City's liability. Likewise, "occurrence" does not refer to the flooding damages sustained by each individual property, since that interpretation improperly focuses on the effects of the events leading to liability, rather than on the cause of those events.

We hold that each discrete act or omission, or series of acts or omissions, on the part of the City of Mobile which caused water to flood and damage properties instead of draining properly is a single "occurrence" within the terms of the insurance policy. Thus, if on account of the City's negligence a drain on one street was blocked so that water flooded ten houses on that street, that would be one "occurrence" with a limit of $100,000 applicable to the total damage done to the ten houses. If, at some other location, on account of negligence on the part of the City, a storm sewer spilled over or broke open so that water flooded one house, that would be another occurrence with a total of $100,000 coverage available for the claims arising out of the damage to that house. If, on the other side of the City, on account of the City's negligence, water flooding caused damage to 100 houses, that would be a third "occurrence" and there would be $100,000 in coverage applicable to all property damage proximately resulting from that negligent act.

This interpretation should enable the parties to return to state court to sort out their specific claims. We note that at this stage in the proceedings there apparently has not yet been any determination of negligence or liability against the City of Mobile for flood damages. Once the City's liability to individual property owners is determined, the appropriate court can apply general proximate cause principles to ascertain each "occurrence" for which the Home Indemnity Company must reimburse the City.

As interpreted in this opinion, the judgment of the district court is

Affirmed.

NOTES

1. *Cause theory versus effect theory.* Looking at the "effects" of the liability-creating conditions to determine the number of occurrences will usually increase the number of occurrences. Most courts, like the court in *Home Indemnity*, ask how many "causes" produced the multiple losses. In many situations, however, this is only the beginning of the analytical difficulties, as *Home Indemnity* illustrates.

2. *Counting the causes.* The court in *Home Indemnity* says that each discrete act or omission, or series of acts or omissions, is an occurrence. What supports this conclusion? What are the other possible answers? Has the court selected the best of these alternatives?

Consider, for example, *American Red Cross v. Travelers Indemnity Co.,* 816 F. Supp. 755 (D.C.D.C. 1993). The insured was sued for allegedly distributing HIV-contaminated blood. Under cause analysis, how many occurrences? One, i.e., the insured's general, negligent practice of handling blood products? Or more than one? Is each decision involved in handling blood (i.e., whether to screen a donor, whether to test the blood, etc.) an occurrence? Is each shipment of contaminated blood an occurrence? Is each *packet* of contaminated blood in a shipment a separate occurrence? What factors help decide such cases?

The court in *Home Indemnity* relied on *Pincoffs*, which involved the insured's sale of contaminated bird seed to eight dealers who in turn sold the feed to 100 bird owners, each of whom filed a claim for damages. Is *Pincoffs* decided correctly? *See Champion International Corp. v. Continental Casualty Co.,* 546 F.2d 502 (2d Cir. 1976), *cert. denied,* 434 U.S. 819 (1977); *Industrial Steel Container Co. v. Fireman's Fund Insurance Co.,* 399 N.W.2d 156 (Minn. Ct. App. 1987). Is it possible to distinguish contaminated bird seed from the contaminated blood involved in the *American Red Cross* case, *supra*?

What if a manufacturer ships a plaster ingredient that is appropriate only for use on the exterior of houses, and not on the interiors, but the packages of the ingredient contain no warning label such as "for exterior use only." The direct recipient of the product knows of the limitation, but contractors who purchase the product from the first buyer do not. The product is used in the interior of 28 homes, with property damage resulting. How many occurrences? One, i.e., the failure to warn? Twenty-eight, given the 28 incorrect uses? Or some number in between? *See Chemstar, Inc. v. Liberty Mutual Insurance Co.,* 41 F.3d 429 (9th Cir. 1994), *cert. denied,* 517 U.S. 1219 (1996).

3. *Policy limits and deductibles.* It would be a mistake to assume that the insured is always benefitted by a finding of multiple occurrences. Suppose the City's liability were established at $100,000, and assume that the City's policy had a $10,000-per-occurrence deductible. If ten occurrences were found to have created the $100,000 liability, the insurer would be obligated for no portion of the loss.

Suppose that the City's policy had an aggregate limit of $1 million, a per-occurrence limit of $100,000, and a $10,000-per-occurrence deductible. Assume total damages in excess of $1 million. For each occurrence up to the aggregate limit, the insured gets an additional $90,000 in coverage. After the aggregate limit is reached, would each additional occurrence cost the insured $10,000 in coverage? What if there were 100 occurrences?

If you were counsel to an insurance company, would you recommend that it use "per-claim" deductibles as opposed to "per-occurrence" deductibles?

4. *The "unifying directive."* Since 1966, the CGL has contained some kind of language purporting to make (to quote the 1973 CGL) "repeated exposure to substantially the same general conditions" to be "considered as arising out of one occurrence." The language has come to be known as the "unifying directive." The concept is incorporated directly into the definition of "occurrence" in the 1986 CGL (see Appendix B).

Does this language solve the problem presented by the multiple loss cases? What is the meaning of the phrase "the same general conditions" or, to quote the 1986 CGL, "the same general harmful conditions"? Did the court in *Home Indemnity* fail to give enough attention to the unifying directive?

5. *Pattern of conduct cases.* Where a pattern of conduct causes injury to one or more persons, determining the number of occurrences can be difficult. Suppose, for example, a pattern of company decision-making leads to discriminatory employment practices. Is the company-wide policy one occurrence? Is each distribution of the policy to company offices an occurrence? Is each act of discrimination an occurrence? *See Appalachian Insurance Co. v. Liberty*

Mutual Insurance Co., 676 F.2d 56 (3d Cir. 1982); *Transport Insurance Co. v. Lee Way Motor Freight,* 487 F. Supp. 1325 (N.D. Tex. 1980). If the insured's pattern of sexual misconduct causes injury to one person over a period of time, is the pattern "one occurrence," or is each separate act of misconduct an "occurrence"? What if there are multiple victims of the same insured's repeated misconduct? *Compare Lee v. Interstate Fire & Casualty Co.,* 826 F. Supp. 1156 (N.D. Ill. 1993), with *Society of the Roman Catholic Church of the Diocese of Lafayette and Lake Charles, Inc. v. Interstate Fire & Casualty Co.,* 26 F.3d 1359 (5th Cir. 1994).

6. *Counting occurrences in other kinds of liability insurance.* Although business practices lend themselves to the multiple occurrence problem, the same issue periodically arises in other kinds of liability insurance, including homeowners or automobile insurance. Most auto accidents are discrete, single-occurrence events, but some multiple-car automobile accidents can raise the issue, particularly if the loss-producing events transpire over many seconds or minutes. *See e.g., Bush v. Guaranty National Insurance Co.,* 848 P.2d 1057 (Nev. 1993) (car-child accident); *Olsen v. Moore,* 202 N.W.2d 236 (Wis. 1972)(auto crossing median and hitting two vehicles in two different lanes); *Voigt v. Riesterer,* 523 N.W.2d 133 (Wis. Ct. App. 1994) (auto accident with three to five minutes between two impacts).

[c] Trigger of Coverage in Progressive Loss Cases

MONTROSE CHEMICAL CORP. v. ADMIRAL INSURANCE CO.

10 Cal. 4th 645, 913 P.2d 878, 42 Cal. Rptr. 2d 324 (1995)

LUCAS, CHIEF JUSTICE.

[Editors' note: The facts are summarized in the excerpt from this case that appears in § 2.01[2], *supra.* After reviewing the facts, the court began by summarizing its prior decision in *Prudential-LMI Com. Ins. v. Superior Court,* 51 Cal. 3d 674, 274 Cal. Rptr. 387, 798 P.2d 1230 (1990); this case appears in § 4.05[4], *supra.* The *Montrose* court then observed that it had expressly reserved the question of what allocation rules "should apply in third-party liability insurance cases involving continuous or progressively deteriorating damage or injury."] In this case we address the issue reserved in *Prudential-LMI.* . . . .

TRIGGER OF COVERAGE IN THIRD PARTY PROGRESSIVE LOSS CASES

As noted, Admiral moved for summary judgment in the trial court on grounds that it had no duty to defend or indemnify Montrose in the Levin Metals cases because the circumstances which trigger coverage, within the meaning of the coverage clauses in its policies, did not occur during the policy periods . . . . Having convinced the trial court, but not the Court of Appeal, Admiral seeks to renew these claims [in this court]. . . . .

1. *Preliminary considerations: distinguishing third party liability insurance from first party property insurance.*

To properly analyze the trigger of coverage issues presented in this case, it is necessary to first clearly distinguish between third party liability insurance, the type of coverage here at issue, and coverage under a first party property insurance policy, such as the standardized homeowners policy in issue in *Prudential-LMI, supra*, 51 Cal. 3d 674, 274 Cal. Rptr. 387, 798 P.2d 1230.

As we observed in both *Garvey [v. State Farm Fire & Casualty Co.* (1989) 48 Cal. 3d 395,] 399, fn. 2, 257 Cal. Rptr. 292, 770 P.2d 704, and *Prudential-LMI, supra*, 51 Cal. 3d at pp. 698-699, 274 Cal. Rptr. 387, 798 P.2d 1230, a first party insurance policy provides coverage for loss or damage sustained directly by the insured (*e.g.*, life, disability, health, fire, theft and casualty insurance). A third party liability policy, in contrast, provides coverage for liability of the insured to a "third party" (*e.g.*, a CGL policy, a directors and officers liability policy, or an errors and omissions policy). In the usual first party policy, the insurer promises to pay money to the insured upon the happening of an event, the risk of which has been insured against. In the typical third party liability policy, the carrier assumes a contractual duty to pay judgments the insured becomes legally obligated to pay as damages because of bodily injury or property damage caused by the insured.

The difference in the nature of the risks insured against under first party property policies and third party liability policies is also reflected in the differing causation analyses that must be undertaken to determine coverage under each type of policy. (*Garvey, supra*, 48 Cal. 3d at p. 406, 257 Cal. Rptr. 292, 770 P.2d 704.) " 'Property insurance . . . is an agreement, a contract, in which the insurer agrees to indemnify the insured in the event that the insured property suffers a covered loss. Coverage, in turn, is commonly provided by reference to causation, *e.g.*, "loss caused by . . ." certain enumerated perils. [¶] The term "perils" in traditional property insurance parlance refers to fortuitous, active, physical forces such as lightning, wind, and explosion, which bring about the loss.' " (*Ibid.*, quoting Bragg, *Concurrent Causation and the Art of Policy Drafting: New Perils for Property Insurers* (1985) 20 Forum 385, 386-387.) In contrast, " *'the "cause" of loss in the context of a property insurance contract is totally different from that in a liability policy.'* " (*Garvey, supra*, 48 Cal. 3d at p. 406, 257 Cal. Rptr. 292, 770 P.2d 704, italics in original.) "[T]he right to coverage in the third party liability insurance context draws on traditional tort concepts of fault, proximate cause and duty. This liability analysis differs substantially from the coverage analysis in the property insurance context, which draws on the relationship between perils that are either covered or excluded in the contract. *In liability insurance, by insuring for personal liability, and agreeing to cover the insured for his own negligence, the insurer agrees to cover the insured for a broader spectrum of risks.*" (*Id.* at p. 407, 257 Cal. Rptr. 292, 770 P.2d 704, italics added.)

The parties' expectations may also differ depending upon the type of coverage sought. First party property coverage is typically purchased in an amount sufficient to cover the insured's maximum potential loss (*e.g.*, fire insurance typically covers the value of the property insured). Hence, there is no reason for a first party insured to look to more than one policy in the event of loss (the policy in effect at the time of the fire). Third party liability coverage differs substantially. As the Court of Appeal below observed, "at best, the insured makes an educated guess about its potential exposure to third parties. At worst, the insured's best guess falls far short of the mark."

Yet another distinction between the two types of insurance coverage is that third party CGL policies do not impose, as a condition of coverage, a requirement that the damage or injury be discovered at any particular point in time. Instead, they provide coverage for injuries and damage caused by an "occurrence," and typically define "occurrence" as an accident (or sometimes a "loss"), including a "continuous or repeated exposure to conditions," that results in bodily injury or property damage during the policy period. The standardized CGL policy language (like the language in Admiral's policies) will be reviewed in greater detail below. As will be seen, nothing about this language suggests a manifestation or discovery requirement as a prerequisite for triggering coverage.

Another important difference between first and third party policies is that first party insurance policies require the insured to bring any action against the insurer within 12 months after "inception of the loss." Before an action is filed under such a policy, there must be a dispute between the insured and insurer. Before there can be a dispute, the insured must (or reasonably should) know it has suffered a "loss." By contrast, third party liability policies do not include a 12-month limitations period in which the insured must bring an action against the insurer (although the policies may contain express notification requirements). It is the damaged or injured third party who initiates the action against the insured. If coverage is ultimately established, it is the insurer that in turn must indemnify the insured for "all sums which the insured shall become legally obligated to pay." Hence, there is no "inception of the loss" language in a standard CGL policy, and, as will become apparent, no corollary need to apply the definition of "inception of the loss" that this court articulated in *Prudential-LMI, supra*.

Unfortunately, some courts have failed to draw these critical distinctions when discussing coverage issues under first and third party insurance policies. In the third party liability insurance context, some reported cases have muddied the waters by seemingly failing to distinguish between disputes arising between an insured and insurer, and actions among several CGL carriers that seek a judicial declaration allocating a loss already paid out to the insured under one or more such policies. In suits between an insured and an insurer to determine coverage, interpretation of the policy language and, in the case of ambiguous policy language, the expectations of the parties, will typically take precedence. The existence of excess or "secondary insurance" policies, "other insurance" clauses, or similar policy language decreeing the manner of apportionment of liability under multiple policies may also factor into the coverage analysis.

In contrast, where two or more CGL carriers turn to the courts to allocate the cost of indemnity for a paid loss, different contractual and policy considerations may come into play in the effort to apportion such costs among the insurers. The task may require allocation of contribution amongst all insurers on the risk in proportion to their respective policies' liability limits (such as deductibles and ceilings) or the time periods covered under each such policy.

Reported cases whose analyses fail to take these distinctions into account, although purporting to clarify or settle an underlying "trigger of coverage" issue, may shed more darkness than light on the matter.

The proper analysis and resolution of a trigger of coverage issue may also depend on whether the CGL policy in issue insures against liability to third parties for bodily injury, property damage, or both. As will be shown, the coverage clauses in Admiral's policies do not distinguish between the nature of the underlying harm (bodily injury or property damage) that triggers the insured's liability coverage. Accordingly, Montrose and Admiral appear to agree that under a plain reading of that unambiguous aspect of the policy language, whatever be the circumstances (or timing of the circumstances) that will potentially trigger liability coverage under the policies, coverage will apply uniformly under such circumstances whether the claims be for bodily injury, or property damage, alleged in the underlying third party lawsuits.

Finally, the proper resolution of a trigger of coverage issue in any given case may turn on whether the court is addressing underlying facts involving a single event resulting in immediate injury (*e.g.*, an explosion causing instantaneous bodily injuries and destruction of property), a single event resulting in delayed or progressively deteriorating injury (*e.g.*, a chemical spill), or a continuing event (referred to in CGL policies as "continuous or repeated exposure to conditions") resulting in single or multiple injuries (*e.g.*, exposure to toxic wastes or asbestos over time). Significantly, in the present case we are dealing both with claims of continuous or progressively deteriorating bodily injury (the Newman v. Stringfellow lawsuit), and progressively deteriorating property damage (the Stringfellow and Levin Metals cases), all arising from continuous or repeated exposure to hazardous waste contamination over time, allegedly including the periods when Admiral's policies were in effect.

With these considerations in mind, we turn next to the express language of the contracts of insurance here in issue, looking first to the relevant principles of insurance policy interpretation that must govern our construction of the contested provisions.

2. Admiral's policy language and the applicable rules of interpretation.

Insurance policies are contracts and, therefore, are governed in the first instance by the rules of construction applicable to contracts. Under statutory rules of contract interpretation, the mutual intention of the parties at the time the contract is formed governs its interpretation. Such intent is to be inferred, if possible, solely from the written provisions of the contract. The "clear and explicit" meaning of these provisions, interpreted in their "ordinary and popular sense," controls judicial interpretation unless "used by the parties in a technical sense, or unless a special meaning is given to them by usage." If the meaning a layperson would ascribe to the language of a contract of insurance is clear and unambiguous, a court will apply that meaning.

. . . .

Turning to the express policy language, Admiral contracted with Montrose to "pay on behalf of the insured all sums which the insured shall become legally obligated to pay as damages because of . . . *bodily injury, or* . . . *property damage to which this insurance applies,* caused by an occurrence. . . ." (Italics added.) "[P]roperty damage to which this insurance applies" is defined in Admiral's policies as "(1) physical injury to or destruction of tangible property *which occurs during the policy period*, including the loss of use thereof at any time resulting therefrom. . . ." (Italics added.) "Bodily injury" to which the insurance applies is defined as "bodily injury, sickness or disease sustained by any person *which occurs during the policy period*, including death at any time resulting therefrom." (Italics added.) We find no ambiguity in this language; it clearly and explicitly provides that the occurrence of bodily injury or property damage during the policy period is the operative event that triggers coverage.

Furthermore, "occurrence" is defined in Admiral's policies as "an accident, *including continuous or repeated exposure to conditions*, which results in bodily injury or property damage neither expected nor intended from the standpoint of the insured." (Italics added.) When read together with the aforementioned clauses defining covered bodily injury and property damage, this policy language unambiguously distinguishes between the causative event—an accident or "continuous and repeated exposure to conditions"—and the resulting "bodily injury or property damage." It is the latter injury or damage that must "occur" during the policy period, and "which results" from the accident or "continuous and repeated exposure to conditions." In this case, it is the third party litigants' bodily injuries and property damage, which are alleged to have been continuous or progressively deteriorating throughout Admiral's policy periods, and which allegedly resulted from the continuous and repeated exposure to toxic chemicals for which the insured, Montrose, is an allegedly responsible party, that triggers potential coverage under the policies in question.

3. Settled case law, and the drafting history of the standardized CGL policy language, confirm that coverage is triggered by damage or injury occurring during the policy period.

Admiral contends that to read its CGL policies as providing that coverage is triggered when damage or injury occurs within the policy periods as a result of an "occurrence" is to "ignore the policy language and confuse the consequences of the occurrence with the occurrence itself, i.e., the event that 'resulted' in damage." Admiral in essence urges that coverage under a CGL policy is established at the time of the "occurrence" (i.e., the precipitating act or event) [which] first gives rise to appreciable damage or injury, and that policies that commence after an "occurrence" and some consequent appreciable damage or injury cannot be on the risk for progressive damage or injury that occur during such subsequent policy periods.

California courts have long recognized that coverage in the context of a liability insurance policy is established at the time the complaining party was actually damaged. In *Remmer v. Glens Falls Indem. Co.* (1956) 140 Cal. App. 2d 84, 295 P.2d 19 (*Remmer*), the court was asked to interpret the definition of "occurrence" as that term was used in a CGL policy. The precise issue in *Remmer* was whether the act of defectively grading and filling a lot constituted the sole occurrence giving rise to coverage under the policy's "one occurrence" provision, or whether subsequent injury (an alleged maintenance of a nuisance on the graded lot adjoining the third party claimants' property) also triggered liability coverage under the policy. Relying on cases from California and other jurisdictions, the *Remmer* court formulated the following rule: "The general rule is that the time of the occurrence of an accident within the meaning of an indemnity policy is not the time the wrongful act was committed, but the time when the complaining party was actually damaged." (*Id.* at p. 88, 295 P.2d 19.)

The *Remmer* formulation, which distinguishes between a wrongful act and the injurious result of that act, and holds that the triggering of liability coverage under a CGL policy is established at the time the complaining third party was actually damaged, has been embraced by such noted experts as Appleman (7A Appleman, Insurance Law & Practice (1979 rev.) § 4501.03, p. 256) and Couch (11 Couch, Insurance (2d ed. 1982) § 44:8, p. 194.) It can be found in American Jurisprudence Second (43 Am. Jur. 2d (1982 rev.) Insurance, § Ê243, p. 324), has been accepted by the courts of many other states, and has been cited by federal courts interpreting the law of still other states. Indeed, as stated by the Idaho Supreme Court, "This rule is followed in every jurisdiction that has considered the issue except Louisiana."

Although the Court of Appeal concluded that potential coverage was triggered under Admiral's policies by damage or injury occurring during the policy periods, the court did not trace this longstanding interpretation of how liability coverage is triggered under a CGL policy to the rule formulated in *Remmer*. Instead, the court independently looked to the drafting history of the standard CGL policy language for support for its conclusion that no reasonable construction, other than that described above, could be placed on the insurance industry's use of such policy language.

Admiral contends that evidence of the drafting history of the standardized CGL policy provisions and definitions, and available interpretative materials, are irrelevant and should not have been considered by the Court of Appeal in construing the language of its CGL policies issued to Montrose. Most courts and commentators have recognized, however, that the presence of standardized industry provisions and the availability of interpretative literature are of considerable assistance in determining coverage issues. Such interpretative materials have been widely cited and relied on in the relevant case law and authorities construing standardized insurance policy language. As one court has suggested, "where two insurers dispute the meaning of identical standard form policy language—the meaning attached to the provisions by the insurance industry is, at minimum, relevant." On the other hand, as another court has observed, "[w]hile insurance industry publications are *helpful* in understanding the scope of coverage insurers are trying to delineate in any given policy, they are by no means dispositive." In this case, we find the drafting history relevant in evaluating Admiral's argument that, from a public policy standpoint, the insurance industry will be harmed by the adoption of a continuous injury trigger that the industry assertedly never anticipated would be applied to these policies.

Standard CGL policy language was revised by insurance industry drafters in several important respects starting in 1966. Prior to that year, third party general liability policies covered bodily injuries and damages caused by "accidents." In 1966, the National Bureau of Casualty Underwriters and the Mutual Insurance Rating Board, the predecessor organizations to the

Insurance Services Office (ISO),[13] changed the standard form policy from an "accident-based" to an "occurrence-based" format. It is reasonable to infer that the insurance industry knew precisely what the change entailed.

In comments addressing the question of coverage under the new CGL policies for progressive personal injury or property damage resulting over an extended period of time, one of the drafters explained that "in some exposure type cases involving cumulative injuries it is possible that more than one policy will afford coverage." (Elliott, *The New Comprehensive General Liability Policy*, in Liability Insurance Disputes (PLI, Schreiber edit. 1968), pp. 12-3– 12-5; see also Obrist, *The New Comprehensive General Liability Insurance Policy—A Coverage Analysis* (Defense Research Inst. Monograph 1966) p. 6 [same]; Nachman, *The New Policy Provisions for General Liability Insurance* (1965) 18 CPU Annals 197, 200 [same].)

By 1966, the insurance industry was also demonstrating its awareness of potential coverage issues involving continuous or progressively deteriorating bodily injury and property damage. Richard H. Elliott, then secretary of the National Bureau of Casualty Underwriters, wrote the following regarding the adoption of the occurrence-based CGL policy, which standard form policy retained the term "accident" within its definition of occurrence: "The new policy will afford coverage on an 'occurrence' basis. 'Occurrence' is defined as 'an accident, *including injurious exposure to conditions, which results, during the policy period, in bodily injury and property damage* neither expected nor intended from the standpoint of the insured.' Note that this definition includes the word 'accident.' This has been done in order to clarify the intent with respect to time of coverage and application of policy limits, particularly in situations involving a related series of events attributable to the same factor. Under such circumstances only one accident or occurrence is intended *as far as the application of policy limits is concerned.* For example, the liability of a contractor arising out of the derailment of ten or twelve freight cars as a result of a collision with a piece of his equipment is intended to be subject to one application of the occurrence limit of the policy. *Retention of the word 'accident' is limiting in this sense and no other.*" (Elliott, *The New Comprehensive General Liability Policy*, in Liability Insurance Disputes, *supra*, at p. 12-5, italics added.)

Secretary Elliott's comments leave little doubt that the definition of "occurrence" in the newly drafted standard form CGL policy was intended to provide coverage when damage or injury resulting from an accident or "injurious exposure to conditions" occurs during the policy period. The term "accident" was left in the definition of occurrence for the purpose of circumscribing the policy limits applicable to each occurrence. The drafters did not intend to require that an "accident" in the literal sense, *e.g.*, a sudden precipitating event, occur during the policy period in order to trigger potential coverage for ensuing damage or injury. "The reference to 'injurious exposure to conditions

---

[13] ISO is a non-profit trade association that provides rating, statistical, and actuarial policy forms and related drafting services to approximately 3,000 nationwide property or casualty insurers. Policy forms developed by ISO are approved by its constituent insurance carriers and then submitted to state agencies for review. Most carriers use the basic ISO forms, at least as the starting point for their general liability policies.

[resulting in] . . . bodily injury [or property damage]' eliminates any require-ment that the injury result from a sudden event. Although it is most common that an injury takes place simultaneously with the exposure, there are many instances of injuries taking place over an extended period of time before they become evident [for example, the slow ingestion of foreign substances or the inhalation of noxious fumes]. In these and similar cases, the definition of 'occurrence' identifies the time of loss for purposes of applying coverage—the injury must take place during the policy period."

As these materials demonstrate, the drafters of the standard occurrence-based CGL policy, and the experts advising the industry regarding its interpretation when formulated in 1966, contemplated that the policy would afford liability coverage for all property damage or injury occurring during the policy period resulting from an accident, or from injurious exposure to conditions. Nothing in the policy language purports to exclude damage or injury of a continuous or progressively deteriorating nature, as long as it occurs during the policy period. Nor is there any basis for inferring that an insured's understanding and reasonable expectations regarding the scope of coverage for damage or injury occasioned during the effective period of an occurrence-based CGL policy would have been otherwise.

We have shown how the clear and explicit language of Admiral's policies supports the conclusion that potential coverage is triggered by the occurrence of bodily injury or property damage during the policy periods, as a result of an accident or the "continuous or repeated exposure to conditions." We next review the relevant reported decisions, from California, the federal courts, and other state courts, that have sought to construe the industry-standardized CGL policy language to determine how continuous injury or damage triggers potential coverage under such policies. As will be seen, the weight of authority, consistent with our own interpretation of Admiral's express policy language, is that bodily injury and property damage that is continuous or progressively deteriorating throughout successive CGL policy periods, is potentially covered by all policies in effect during those periods.

4. Survey of case law and authorities discussing triggering of coverage under CGL policies where injury or damage is continuous over successive policy periods.

The issue of trigger of coverage in continuous injury or damage cases has been explored by many courts. Courts have recognized several "triggers" as a means of identifying the nature and timing of damage or injury that will give rise to liability coverage under an occurrence-based CGL policy. The courts have generally viewed the *timing* of damage or injury under occurrence-based CGL policies in four ways: at the date of exposure to the injurious or damage-causing event or conditions; at the date of the first occurrence of "injury in fact"; at the date of manifestation or discovery of the damage or injury; and over the continuous period from exposure through manifestation and beyond, where the damage or injury is ongoing, continuous, or progres-sively deteriorating throughout a policy period or successive policy periods. At this point it will be helpful to briefly outline the various trigger theories formulated by the courts.

The exposure (or continuous exposure) trigger. This trigger of coverage theory, first applied in cases involving asbestos-related bodily injuries, focuses on the date on which the injury-producing agent first contacts the body. The exposure theory apportions the cost of indemnity among those insurers whose policies were in effect from that point in time onward. In effect, under this theory, damage or injury is deemed to commence from the first contact of the injury-producing agent with the injured party. The leading case espousing this trigger of coverage analysis is the Sixth Circuit's decision in *Ins. Co. of North America v. Forty-Eight Insulations* (6th Cir. 1980) 633 F.2d 1212, clarified (1981) 657 F.2d 814, cert. den. (1981) 454 U.S. 1109, 102 S. Ct. 686, 70 L. Ed. 2d 650 (*Forty-Eight Insulations.*) The court in *Forty-Eight Insulations* found that the covered occurrence of injury commenced with the immediate contact of an asbestos fiber with the lungs, even though the progressive disease typically took some 20 years to develop. The court reasoned that because of the cumulative and progressively deteriorating nature of the disease, it had to be distinguished from the ordinary accident or injury situation, and further, that because the injury is a continuing one, the insurers who furnished comprehensive general liability policies would expect the scope of their policies' coverage to parallel the applicable theory of liability.

The manifestation (or manifestation of loss) trigger. This trigger of coverage, which, as already explained, was adopted by this court in the first party property insurance context in *Prudential-LMI, supra,* 51 Cal. 3d 674, 274 Cal. Rptr. 387, 798 P.2d 1230, holds the insurer insuring the property at the time appreciable property damage first becomes manifest solely responsible for indemnification to the insured. For purposes of applying the rule, the time at which the property damage becomes manifest (also the point of "inception of the loss") is "that point in time when appreciable damage occurs and is or should be known to the insured, such that a reasonable insured would be aware that his notification duty under the policy had been triggered." (*Id.* at p. 699, 274 Cal. Rptr. 387, 798 P.2d 1230.)

. . . .[15]

The continuous injury (or multiple) trigger. Under this trigger of coverage theory, bodily injuries and property damage that are continuous or progressively deteriorating throughout successive policy periods are covered by all policies in effect during those periods. The timing of the accident, event, or conditions *causing* the bodily injury or property damage, *e.g.*, an insured's negligent act, is largely immaterial to establishing coverage; it can occur before or during the policy period. Neither is the date of discovery of the damage

---

[15] We are aware of only one appellate court decision that has adopted the manifestation trigger of coverage for bodily injuries in the context of third party liability insurance. In *Eagle-Picher Industries v. Liberty Mut. Ins. Co.* (1st Cir. 1982) 682 F.2d 12, the United States Court of Appeals for the First Circuit concluded on the evidence before it that the injury resulting from inhalation of asbestos fibers did not "occur" until the symptoms of the disease asbestosis had manifested themselves. The asbestos manufacturer had no insurance prior to 1968, the period when most of the exposure took place. The manufacturer's CGL insurance coverage began when the number of claims began accelerating. As was the case in *Forty-Eight Insulations, supra,* 633 F.2d 1212, the court in *Eagle-Picher*, in adopting the manifestation trigger, made clear its intention to interpret the policies in a manner that would afford and maximize coverage on the particular facts of that case. The *Eagle-Picher* case therefore stands as somewhat of an aberration.

or injury controlling: it might or might not be contemporaneous with the causal event. It is only the *effect*—the occurrence of bodily injury or property damage during the policy period, resulting from a sudden accidental event or the "continuous or repeated exposure to conditions"—that triggers potential liability coverage. The appellate cases in which this trigger of coverage was developed are discussed in greater detail below.

The injury-in-fact trigger. Under an injury-in-fact trigger, coverage is first triggered at that point in time at which an actual injury can be shown, retrospectively, to have been first suffered. This rationale places the injury-in-fact somewhere between the exposure, which is considered the initiating cause of the disease or bodily injury, and the manifestation of symptoms, which, logically, is only possible when an injury already exists. In the context of continuous or progressively deteriorating injuries, the injury-in-fact trigger, like the continuous injury trigger, affords coverage for continuing or progressive injuries occurring during successive policy periods subsequent to the established date of the initial injury-in-fact. However, the injury-in-fact trigger, unlike the exposure trigger, when applied in asbestos cases excludes from coverage the period from initial exposure to the date on which the injury-in-fact was first suffered.[16]

As already indicated, in the case before us, Montrose urges our adoption of a continuous injury trigger of coverage. Admiral in turn, in its briefs, urges us to apply a manifestation trigger of coverage. At oral argument, however, counsel for Admiral appeared to deviate from this position, arguing instead that an injury-in-fact trigger, and not a manifestation trigger, should be applied. We shall give Admiral the benefit of the doubt and consider which, if any, of the recognized trigger of coverage theories should be applied here. The precise question, of course, is what result follows *under the language of the policies of insurance to which the parties agreed, including the standardized definitions that were incorporated into those policies.* As will be seen, most courts that have analyzed the issue have found the continuous injury trigger of coverage applicable to the standard occurrence-based CGL policy.

[In a discussion that is too lengthy to include here, the court went on to consider a number of California and federal cases construing the language of the CGL policy and concluded that the continuous injury trigger should apply in the case *sub judice.*]

5. Various practical and policy considerations further support adoption of the continuous injury trigger of coverage for the third party claims of continuous or progressively deteriorating damage or injury brought under the CGL policies in this case.

---

16 . . . . Unlike the manifestation trigger, however, the injury-in-fact trigger acknowledges that actual injury may "occur" before it has become manifest or been discovered. Under [this] approach, coverage is triggered by " 'a real but undiscovered injury, proved in retrospect to have existed at the relevant time . . . irrespective of the time the injury became [diagnosable].' " That is, after an injury has been diagnosed, it may be inferred, from evidence establishing the "gestation period" and the stage to which the illness has advanced, that the harm or "injury-in-fact" actually began sometime earlier. . . . Because we do not here face the unique facts of asbestos-related bodily injury claims, we deem it appropriate that trigger of coverage questions specifically involving asbestos claims be left for decision, in the first instance, on an appropriate record in a case in which they are squarely presented.

. . . .

Our conclusion that the continuous injury trigger of coverage should be applied to the third party CGL policies in this case is also in conformity with several important policy considerations. In *Prudential-LMI, supra*, 51 Cal. 3d at page 699, 274 Cal. Rptr. 387, 798 P.2d 1230, we observed, as one policy reason favoring adoption of the manifestation trigger of coverage in first party property insurance cases, that "the underwriting practices of the insurer can be made predictable because the insurer is not liable for a loss once its contract with the insured ends unless the manifestation of loss occurred during its contract term." Admiral here suggests that the general policy favoring the predictability of underwriting practices and reserves will be negatively affected by adoption of a continuous injury trigger in the third party CGL insurance context. We disagree. A number of factors undercut Admiral's concerns.

First, leaving aside the availability of excess (multiple) policies or "other insurance" clauses, and absent express policy language decreeing the manner of apportionment of contribution among successive liability insurers, the courts will generally apply equitable considerations to spread the cost among the several policies and insurers.

Second, in establishing reserves for the standard form occurrence-based CGL policies which replaced accident-based policies in 1966, the insurance industry, as we have shown, was fully aware of the intended scope of coverage of the new policies, coupled with the specific provision providing coverage for continuous or repeated exposure to conditions causing property damage or bodily injury. Indeed, the drafting history of the standard occurrence-based CGL policy reflects that not only did the drafters understand the term occurrence to mean an accident or exposure to injurious conditions *resulting in the occurrence of damage or injury during the policy period*, they specifically considered and *rejected* the suggestion that language establishing a manifestation or discovery trigger of coverage be incorporated into the standard form CGL policy. Among the reasons relied on for rejecting the incorporation of such limitations into the standard definitions in the coverage clauses were several stated equitable concerns: the difficulty of applying such limitations or requirements in cases of continuing damage or injury over the course of successive policy periods, the uncertainty of who would bear the burden of a discovery requirement (i.e., the insured or third party claimants), the arbitrariness, from the carrier's perspective, of telescoping all damage in a continuing injury case into a single policy period, and the fear that policyholders could be disadvantaged by such an approach. In short, the insurance industry is on record as itself having identified several sound policy considerations favoring adoption of a continuous injury trigger of coverage in the third party liability insurance context.[23]

Finally, we agree with Montrose that application of a manifestation trigger of coverage to an occurrence-based CGL policy would unduly transform it into

---

[23] One commentator has suggested that, "because it encourages all insurers to monitor risks and change [sic] appropriate premiums, the continuous trigger rule appears to be the most efficient doctrine for toxic waste cases." (Note, *Developments in the Law—Toxic Waste Litigation, supra*, 99 Harv.L.Rev. at p. 1581.)

a "claims made" policy. Claims made policies were specifically developed to limit an insurer's risk by restricting coverage to the single policy in effect at the time a claim was asserted against the insured, *without regard to the timing of the damage or injury*, thus permitting the carrier to establish reserves without regard to possibilities of inflation, upward-spiraling jury awards, or enlargements of tort liability after the policy period.[24] The insurance industry's introduction of "claims made" policies into the area of comprehensive liability insurance itself attests to the industry's understanding that the standard occurrence-based CGL policy provides coverage for injury or damage that may not be discovered or manifested until after expiration of the policy period. That understanding is clearly reflected in the higher premiums that must be paid for occurrence-based coverage to offset the increased exposure. We agree with the conclusion of the Court of Appeal below that to apply a manifestation trigger of coverage to Admiral's occurrence-based CGL policies would be to effectively rewrite Admiral's contracts of insurance with Montrose, transforming the broader and more expensive occurrence-based CGL policy into a claims made policy.

We therefore conclude that the continuous injury trigger of coverage should be applied to the underlying third party claims of continuous or progressively deteriorating damage or injury alleged to have occurred during Admiral's policy periods. Where, as here, successive CGL policy periods are implicated, bodily injury and property damage which is continuous or progressively deteriorating throughout several policy periods is potentially covered by all policies in effect during those periods.

. . . .

CONCLUSION

Although we have determined that the continuous injury trigger of coverage should be applied in this case, . . . we hasten to add that resolution of [this issue] in Montrose's favor would appear not to mark the end of the coverage-related inquiries in this complex litigation.

We do not herein purport to reach the merits of whether coverage under Admiral's policies for the injury and damage alleged in the five underlying lawsuits against Montrose can ultimately be established. Whether the damages and injuries alleged were in fact "continuous" is itself a matter for final determination by the trier of fact. Nor do we determine the effect, if any, of any exclusions contained in Admiral's policies on the duty to defend or the

---

[24] "Claims made" policies beneficially permit insurers more accurately to predict the limits of their exposure and the premium needed to accommodate the risk undertaken, resulting in lower premiums than are charged for an occurrence-based policy. "Claims made" coverage arose more than 20 years ago, initially in the field of professional liability insurance, because underwriters were concerned that occurrence-based coverage was adversely affecting the underwriting process. Because the injury and negligence giving rise to a malpractice claim is often not discoverable until years after the negligent act or omission, professional liability insurance carriers, in an effort to reduce their exposure to an unpredictable and lengthy "tail" of lawsuits, shifted to the "claims made" policy. The "claims made" concept was subsequently extended into the field of general liability coverage, and in 1986 ISO issued both a revised standard form occurrence-based CGL policy (now referred to as a *commercial* general liability policy) and a new standard form CGL "claims made" policy.

ultimate issue of coverage, or reach the merits of any affirmative defenses to coverage that might be available to Admiral.

. . . .

The judgment of the Court of Appeal is affirmed, and the matter remanded for further proceedings consistent with the views expressed herein.

Mosk, Kennard, Arabian, George and Werdegar, JJ., concur.

Baxter, Justice, concurring.

. . . .

NOTES

1. *Evolution of the CGL policy (reprise).* As discussed in § 3.04[1], *supra,* the early forms of liability insurance limited coverage to injury or damage "caused by accident." The term "accident" served several purposes. It distinguished between intentionally caused harm, which was not covered, and inadvertently caused harm, which was covered. It also provided a reference point for establishing certain mechanics of the insurance, such as notice and cooperation requirements and application of policy limits, and measuring certain time periods, such as the policy-period provisions. With regard to the latter, the accident had to occur during the policy period for coverage to exist.

The term "accident," however, was ambiguous in several respects. For example, did it include gradual deterioration or repeated exposure to deleterious substances the culmination of which eventually resulted in harm? And did it refer to the negligent act or omission rather than to the moment when injury or destruction takes place? Thus, the term proved to be problematic for insurers—and for insureds too for that matter—and the liability insurance industry set out to develop new policy language. As the *Montrose* court points out, after many years of work, a standard provision was adopted in 1966 which utilized the word "occurrence." "Occurrence" was defined to mean "an accident, including injurious exposure to conditions, which results during the policy period, in bodily injury or property damage neither expected nor intended from the standpoint of the insured." In 1973 the phrase "injurious exposure to conditions" was changed to "continuous or repeated exposure to conditions." Policies, such as the comprehensive general liability policy (CGL), utilized the 1966 and 1973 language and are known as occurrence policies. These policies have generated an unprecedented amount of litigation, in large part because these are the policies that are called into play when businesses are accused of pollution or being involved in mass torts such as some of the drug and pharmaceutical cases.

2. *Triggering event.* Assume that the standard "occurrence" policy language applies in the following case. A negligently repairs the brakes on his own auto. He later sells the auto to B and B is seriously injured when the brakes fail. In the meantime, A cancels his auto policy. Would A be covered under the standard language if the brake failure and injuries to B take place after the policy is canceled? What if the brake failure and injuries occur a week before

A cancels his policy, but B lingers on and finally dies from complications several months after the policy is canceled. Would A have coverage in the latter case, and, if so, for how much of the damages?

3. *Comparing insuring clauses.* As Justice Mosk points out, the CGL occurrence policy is the one that was in issue in *Montrose.* How does the insuring clause in the CGL policy compare to the insuring clause in *Prudential-LMI* in § 4.05[4]? Does the difference in language dictate the difference in result in the two cases or does the result turn more on the nature of the underlying risk that is being transferred to the insurer? *See Guaranty National Insurance Co. v. Azrock Industries, Inc.,* 211 F.3d 239 (5th Cir. 2000) (approving different trigger theory for first-party and third-party coverages).

4. *Timing of harm.* If an insured under consecutive CGL policies suddenly causes bodily harm or property damage that is confined to one policy period, of the four triggers that are mentioned in the cases — exposure, manifestation, continuous, and injury-in-fact — which do you believe pays the greatest fidelity to the "occurrence" language in the CGL policy? Should a different result obtain if the harm or damage is progressive and indivisible and is sustained over a number of years where the consecutive CGL policies are in effect? What if the policies are issued by different insurers?

5. *Allocation of proceeds of successive policies.* In a continuous or progressive harm case where multiple successive CGL policies are on the risk because the court adopts either the injury in fact or the continuous trigger test, how should the damages that are assessed against the insured be allocated among the policies? Does the language of the CGL policy address this issue? What if the period in question covers ten years and the insurer in year 3 is insolvent? What if, instead, the insured had decided not to buy any insurance in year 3? How should these events affect the issue of allocation? Needless to say, issues such as these have resulted in a vast amount of litigation. For more discussion, see Barbara C. Neff, ed., Understanding Allocation (1999); Jeffrey W. Stempel, *Domtar Baby: Misplaced Notions of Equitable Apportionment Create a Thicket of Potential Unfairness for Insurance Policyholders,* 25 Wm. Mitchell L. Rev. 769 (1999).

6. *The "new" CGL policy.* Does the language of the insuring and related clauses of the 1998 iteration of the CGL (see Appendix B) solve the trigger issue addressed in *Montrose?* How about the issues raised in notes 2 and 5, above?

7. *After coverage come exclusions.* Finding an "occurrence" is not, of course, the end of the analysis. The CGL contains numerous exclusions to coverage; these can be found in the sample forms in Appendix B. It is impossible in a basic insurance course to cover them all; this is regrettable, for many have a rich accompaniment in the case law. The next section considers some of the more significant exclusions.

[3]　Exclusions From Coverage

[a]　Intentionally-caused Loss

CAPITOL INDEMNITY CORP. v. BLAZER

51 F. Supp. 2d 1080 (D. Nev. 1999)

PRO, District Judge.

. . . .

This is a Summary Judgment Motion [filed by the insurer, Capitol Indemnity] to determine an insurer's obligation to indemnify or defend the insured against suit pursuant to the terms and provisions of an insurance policy. The insurer also seeks to recover all costs incurred in the investigation and defense of the underlying suit. Adjudication of the summary judgment motion requires the Court to interpret the insurance policy and decide the following two questions: (1) whether the incidents giving rise to the insured's liability constitute an "occurrence" under the policy, and (2) if so, whether the exclusion provisions of the policy nevertheless preclude coverage in this case.

The Court finds that while this case involves an "occurrence," as defined by the insurance policy, the exclusion provisions preclude coverage. Therefore, the insurer has no duty to defend or indemnify the insured with respect to the underlying suit. . . .

II. Factual Background

On January 23, 1997, Peter Banach ("Banach"), Buddy Simpson ("Simpson") and David Lawrence Shaw ("Shaw"), were patrons of a tavern known as the Bird Off Paradise Lounge ("Lounge"), owned and operated by Robert A. Blazer, Jr. ("Blazer"). While at the Lounge, Banach and Simpson committed assault and battery upon Shaw. As a result, Shaw allegedly suffered serious bodily injuries, including a total loss of vision in his left eye. Banach and Simpson were subsequently found guilty of criminal assault and battery.

Shaw filed a civil complaint against Banach, Simpson, Blazer, the Lounge, and the bartender working the night of the assault, Tina Petruccio ("Petruccio"). The Complaint states five claims for relief, sounding in both intentional tort and negligence. Shaw seeks medical and related expenses, general and punitive damages, costs and attorneys fees.

Blazer maintained a commercial general liability policy with Capitol Indemnity Corporation ("Capitol Indemnity") which was effective at the time of the assault and battery. The policy provides coverage for bodily injury only if it is caused by an "occurrence." The policy, in turn, defines an "occurrence" as an "accident." In addition, the policy contains various exclusionary provisions which bar coverage in particular instances, even where the event may qualify as an "occurrence."

First, the Assault and Battery Exclusion precludes coverage for " 'bodily injury' . . . arising out of *assault, battery* or *assault and battery.*" Second, the Liquor Liability Exclusion precludes coverage for " 'bodily injury' . . . for which any insured may be held liable by reason of causing or contributing to the intoxication of any person . . . or any statute, ordinance, or regulation relating to the sale, gift, distribution or use of alcoholic beverages." Third, the insurance does not apply to " 'bodily injury' . . . expected or intended from the standpoint of the insured."

. . . .

To determine Capitol Indemnity's entitlement to summary judgment, this Court must answer the following questions about the policy provisions: (1) Does an intentional assault and battery constitute an insurable "occurrence" as defined by the policy? (2) If so, do the assault and battery and liquor liability exclusion provisions preclude coverage for Blazer's liability? (3) If coverage is precluded, is Capitol Indemnity entitled to reimbursement of its expenses incurred in the investigation and defense of Shaw's claims?

A. Applicable Law

A federal court, sitting in diversity, must apply state law in construing an insurance policy. Accordingly, this Court must construe the policy as a Nevada state court would if presented with the same question. . . . .

An insurance company's duty to defend and/or indemnify its insured arises from the provisions of the insurance policy. "The insurer must defend any lawsuit brought against its insured which potentially seeks damages within the coverage of the policy."

"An insurance policy is to be judged from the perspective of one not trained in law or in insurance, with the terms of the contract viewed in their plain, ordinary and popular sense." Ambiguous terms in an insurance policy will be construed in favor of the insured and against the insurer.

On the other hand, when contract language is clear and unambiguous, a court cannot, under the guise of interpretation, distort the plain meaning of the contract. Accordingly, Nevada courts will enforce unambiguous policy provisions that exclude coverage.

Any attempt to restrict insurance coverage must be done clearly and explicitly. In particular, an insurer, wishing to restrict the coverage of a policy, should employ language which clearly and distinctly communicates to the insured the nature of the limitation.

B. Intentional Harms as a Covered Occurrence

"The analysis of [a policy] exclusion begins with determining whether the act in question is covered by the policy, that is, whether it constituted an accident or occurrence as required under the policy; absent coverage, the applicability of [a policy] exclusion is irrelevant." In the present case, the policy only provides coverage for bodily injury caused by an "occurrence," which is defined as an "accident." Thus, the initial question before this Court is whether an intentional tort, like assault and battery, constitutes an "accident" under the policy.

The policy does not define "accident." Nor does the Assault and Battery Exclusion specifically assert that assault and battery is not an accident. The Court is aware of only one Nevada decision, *Catania v. State Farm Life Ins. Co., Inc.*, 95 Nev. 532, 598 P.2d 631 (1979), which divines a layperson's plain and ordinary interpretation of the term "accidental" in the context of insurance policies. In *Catania*, the court discussed whether the insured's death was accidental for the purposes of an accidental death insurance policy, where the insured died from the effects of a self-inflicted heroin injection. In construing the term "accidental," as it was understood by the average man, the court stated that "[o]ne paying the premium for a policy which insures against 'death by accidental means' intends to . . . insure against the fortuitous, the unintentional, and the unexpected, that which happens through mishap, mischance or misjudgment." *Id.* at 632 (quoting *Knight v. Metropolitan Life Ins. Co.*, 103 Ariz. 100, 437 P.2d 416, 420 (1968)). In concluding that the insured's death was accidental, the court held that "where an insured dies as the result of an intentional or expected act or event, but did not intend or expect death to result, the death is 'accidental' within the contemplation of that term, as utilized in a policy such as the one before us." *Id.* at 633.

Thus, it is important to note that the *Catania* court interpreted the term "accidental" from the perspective of the insured as to whether the result of his actions was accidental, rather than looking to the intentional nature of the means. Since the insured did not intend to die, his death was accidental in the context of his insurance policy, even though his death was proximately caused by an intentional act.

Here, there is no reason to believe that the term "accident" would take on a different meaning, to the ordinary person, merely because of its transference to the context of a commercial liability policy. . . . .

. . . .

Therefore, the Court must examine whether Blazer, the insured in this case, expected or intended Shaw's resulting bodily injuries. In this regard, Capitol Indemnity has submitted no evidence indicative of any intent or expectation of injury on Blazer's part. Barring the submission of such evidence, this Court can not, at this time, summarily adjudicate the matter in Capitol Indemnity's favor. *See Catania*, 598 P.2d at 633 (holding the issue of whether insured's death was expected or intended, and therefore not accidental, to be a question of fact).

C. Exclusion Provisions

Nonetheless, even if Shaw's injuries were accidental, and therefore an "occurrence" under the policy, they may be uninsurable under the exclusionary provisions. In order for the Court to determine whether the exclusionary provisions preclude coverage in this case, the Court must decide if the provisions clearly and unambiguously bar coverage for Shaw's injuries, even where his injuries were inflicted by third parties.

1. Assault and Battery Exclusion

Capitol Indemnity's Assault and Battery Exclusion provides: "This insurance does not apply to bodily injury, property damage, or personal injury arising out of *assault, battery*, or *assault and battery*." The policy defines "assault" as "a willful attempt to offer with force or violence to harm or hurt a person without the actual doing of the harm or hurt." "Battery" is defined as "any battering or beating inflicted on a person without his or her consent." "Assault and Battery" is defined within the policy to include such acts as "the ejection or exclusion with force or violence or attempt thereof, of any person of the premises by the insured and his/her/its employees or agents."

Depending upon the precision of the language used, such exclusions may bar coverage for negligence claims brought against an insured commercial host for alleged negligence related to an assault or battery committed against the plaintiff by an unrelated third party. See 7A J. Appleman, *Insurance Law and Practice* § 4492.01 (Supp.1998). The more complete and precise the form of the exclusion, the less likely the court is to find the provision ambiguous. *Id.* Therefore, in order to prevail on summary judgment, Capitol Indemnity must have clearly and distinctly communicated to Blazer the nature of any restrictions or limitations of coverage. Moreover, the Court will construe any ambiguities in Blazer's favor.

On occasion, courts have reviewed provisions similar to those in the present case. *See e.g., Hermitage Ins. Co. v. Dahms,* 842 F.Supp. 319 (N.D.Ill.1994);[2] *Berg v. Schultz,* 190 Wis.2d 170, 526 N.W.2d 781 (Ct.App.1994).[3] The significant factor in determining that these provisions unambiguously excluded coverage for the negligence actions, filed against the commercial host as a result of personal injuries suffered at the hands of a third party, was that the insurance policy provisions excluded claims "arising out of" or "caused by" the assault and/or battery.

In order for a claim or injury to "arise out of" an assault and battery, a causal connection must be established. *Compare Mt. Vernon Fire Ins. Co. v. Creative Hous., Ltd.,* 93 F.3d 63, 66 (2d Cir.1996)(requiring "but for" causation) and *Hermitage,* 842 F.Supp. at 324 (same) with *Ross v. City,* 408 N.W.2d 910, 912 (Minn.Ct.App.1987) (requiring only a general causal connection) and *Essex Ins. Co. v. Fieldhouse, Inc.,* 506 N.W.2d 772, 776 (Iowa 1993)(acknowledging that the "overwhelming weight of authority in jurisdictions that have interpreted . . . assault and battery exclusions involving assault and battery committed by a third party" looks for a causal connection between the claims against the insured and the assault and battery).

The *Mt. Vernon* decision is particularly helpful in clarifying the scope of this "arising out of" terminology. In *Mt. Vernon,* the Second Circuit Court of Appeals reviewed a policy which excluded claims "based on" assault and battery. However, it certified two questions to the New York Court of Appeals in order to clarify the scope of "based on" and "arising out of" terminology in the realm of third-party assault and battery. First, the New York Court of Appeals determined that "no significant difference exists between the phrases "based on" and "arising out of" and that neither phrase is ambiguous." Second, it discussed whether assaults committed by the insured's employees should be discussed differently from assaults committed by unrelated persons.

The New York Court of Appeals decided that "the crucial inquiry is not who perpetrated the assault, but rather whether the cause of action would not exist 'but for' assault." As a result, the Second Circuit Court of Appeals reversed

---

[2] The *Hermitage* exclusion provided that "bodily injury or death alleged to have been caused by ASSULT [sic] AND/OR BATTERY shall not be deemed an accident or occurrence under the Policy and no coverage shall apply hereunder." 842 F.Supp. at 322.

[3] The *Berg* policy provided, "This insurance does not apply to 'bodily injury' or 'property damage' or 'personal injury' arising out of Assault and/or Battery." 526 N.W.2d at 782.

the district court's earlier determination that the exclusionary clause was ambiguous, concluding that "because [the insured] would be unable to maintain claims for [negligence] 'but for' the assault upon her, under New York law, her claims are 'based on' assault and battery and therefore excluded from coverage under the insurance policy."

While the Nevada Supreme Court has not precisely addressed the clarity and scope of such "arising out of" terminology in the context of assault and battery exclusions, it has previously followed a policy of broad inclusive interpretation of such provisions. *See Hernandez v. First Fin. Ins. Co.,* 106 Nev. 900, 802 P.2d 1278, 1280 (1990) (finding no insurer duty to defend against negligent hiring claim where policy barred coverage of "any . . . omission in connection with the prevention" of assault and battery). In light of this policy, this Court believes that the Nevada Supreme Court, if confronted with the question *sub judice*, would apply the same inclusive definitions crafted in the *Berg, Hermitage,* and *Mt. Vernon* decisions and bar coverage. Pursuant to this "but for approach, 'it is immaterial whether the assault was committed by the insured or an employee of the insured on the one hand, or by a third party on the other.' " *Id.* (quoting *Mt. Vernon Fire Ins. Co. v. Creative Hous., Ltd.,* 88 N.Y.2d 347, 645 N.Y.S.2d 433, 668 N.E.2d 404, 407 (1996)). Instead, the Court must take a broader perspective and look to the resulting injuries which give rise to the cause of action against the insured. Here, none of Shaw's claims could have arisen absent the commission of the tortious assault and battery and the resulting physical injuries. Hence, any absence of references to third parties will not, as Blazer contends, render the Assault and Battery Exclusion ambiguous.

Our conclusion, denying coverage to Blazer under the insurance policy, is consistent with the manner in which other courts have handled this particular policy exclusion. Blazer has failed to provide any persuasive case law to contradict these findings. . . . . Therefore, the Assault and Battery Exclusion applies and Capitol Indemnity has no duty to defend or indemnify Blazer with respect to any of the claims in the underlying action as a matter of law.

2. Liquor Liability Exclusion

While the Assault and Battery Exclusion alone will preclude coverage as to all of Shaw's claims against Blazer, the liquor liability provisions of the policy would also bar coverage of many of those same claims. The Liquor Liability Exclusion prohibits coverage for " 'bodily injury' . . . for which any insured may be held liable by reason of [c]ausing or contributing to the intoxication of any person . . . or [a]ny statute, ordinance or regulation relating to the sale, gift, distribution or use of alcoholic beverages." Although neither side contests the clarity or prominence of this exclusion, many courts have found similarly worded exclusions to be unambiguous. Capitol Indemnity and Blazer do, however, dispute the applicability of these provisions to Shaw's third and fourth claims for relief.

The Nevada Supreme Court has never discussed the applicability or scope of a liquor liability exclusion. However, most other courts in determining the scope of liquor liability exclusions have made the distinction between (a) allegations arising directly out of or dependent upon the sale of alcohol, the service of alcoholic beverages, or the causing of a person's intoxication, and (b) allegations based in more general theories of negligence which could arise in contexts completely unrelated to alcohol. *See Interstate Fire & Casualty Co., Inc. v.* 1218 *Wisconsin, Inc.,* 136 F.3d 830, 835 (D.C.Cir.1998); *J.A.J., Inc. v. Aetna Casualty and Sur. Co.,* 529 A.2d 806, 808 (Me.1987); *Paradigm Ins. Co. v. Texas Richmond Corp.,* 942 S.W.2d 645, 651 (Tex.App.1997, writ denied).

A comparison of the *Paradigm* and *J.A.J.* cases illustrates this distinction. Both cases included allegations that the insured negligently allowed the patron to leave the bar in an intoxicated state. However, in *Paradigm*, the court barred the plaintiff's claims from coverage under the policy's liquor liability exclusion because they "arose out of" the business of serving alcohol or were linked to causing the tortfeasor's intoxication. In contrast, the *J.A.J.* court did not bar the plaintiff's claims because they were "unaffected by alcohol consumption" and could have been based in theories arising out of the insured's knowledge that the patrons were developing an antagonistic relationship likely to result in violence.

The important factor which reconciles the different results is the nexus between the allegations and the consumption of alcohol. For example, in *Paradigm*, the intoxicated patron caused an automobile accident and injured a third party who then sued the bar for failing to prevent the intoxicated patron from leaving the bar and driving in an intoxicated state. The theory behind the plaintiff's claims against the bar necessarily depended upon the patron's intoxicated state; therefore, the claim was logically barred from coverage under the plain language of the exclusion. In contrast, the intoxicated patron in *J.A.J.* left the bar, whereupon he was assaulted. The plaintiff's claims against the bar did not depend upon the patron's intoxicated state because they could have been based on the theory that the bar negligently allowed the patron to leave the bar, despite knowing of the antagonistic attitudes of the parties waiting for him outside the premises. In essence, one claim could only be brought upon an establishment serving or selling alcohol and the other could be brought against any establishment on general negligence grounds.

This Court is confident that Nevada would adopt the same analysis in light of the vast majority of cases which have adopted and/or followed this precedent. Therefore, in applying these principles to the present case, the allegations within the third and fourth claims for relief which have a direct nexus to the sale or service of alcohol or the causing or contributing to any person's intoxication are barred by the Liquor Liability Exclusion. In contrast, those allegations which could arise in non-alcohol related contexts will survive.

. . . .

In summary, the Liquor Liability Exclusion bars coverage for those claims which have a close nexus to the sale or service of liquor and/or the causing or contributing to the intoxication of any person. The Court must emphasize, however, that even those claims which are not excluded under the Liquor Liability Exclusion are nonetheless barred from coverage by the Assault and Battery Exclusion.[5]

---

[5] Although the parties also dispute the applicability of the Expected or Intended Injury Exclusion, the Court finds it unnecessary to explore the matter, given the completely preclusive effects of the Assault and Battery Exclusion and, to a lesser extent, those of the Liquor Liability Exclusion.

. . . .

V. Conclusion

The assault and battery of Shaw could be an "occurrence" under the insurance policy. However, Capitol Indemnity has no duty to defend or indemnify Blazer, Petruccio, or the Lounge as to Shaw's claims because coverage is completely precluded by the Assault and Battery Exclusion and, to a lesser extent, the Liquor Liability Exclusion. Furthermore, Capitol Indemnity is not entitled to reimbursement of expenses incurred because it has not presented any evidence of a reservation of the right to reimbursement.

IT IS THEREFORE ORDERED that Capitol Indemnity's Motion for Summary Judgment is GRANTED in part and DENIED in part.

The Motion is GRANTED with respect to Capitol Indemnity's request for declaratory relief finding that it has no duty to defend or indemnify Blazer against any of Shaw's claims.

. . . .

NOTES

1. *Different policy language.* Note that the CGL forms in Appendix B do not have an "assault and battery" exclusion as such. But many commercial liability forms do have such an exclusion, and they are quite common in liability policies issued to taverns, restaurants, and other businesses where alcoholic beverages are served and rowdiness might otherwise be anticipated from time to time. The precise wording of the clause often varies from policy to policy, as the principal case suggests, and these differences can be very significant when applied to specific circumstances. One formulation, for example, provides that the insurer has no obligation to pay for damages "arising out of an assault or battery, provoked or unprovoked, committed by an insured or by an employee or agent of the insured(s)." What does this exclusion add to the preclusive effect of the intentional act exclusion (i.e., for " 'bodily injury' . . . expected or intended from the standpoint of the insured")? Before you answer the question, review the definition of "insured" in the CGL in Appendix (B) ("Section II—Who is an Insured"). When the assault and battery exclusion extends to acts committed by the insured and its employees and agents, the exclusion has a different reach than the exclusion which was at issue in *Capitol Indemnity*. In such circumstances, courts have generally held the exclusion applicable, even though the victim's complaint alleges only negligence. *See e.g., Century Transit Systems, Inc. v. American Empire Surplus Lines Ins. Co.,* 42 Cal. App. 4th 121, 49 Cal. Rptr. 2d 567 (1996) (suit by two men who were beaten by cab driver as they attempted to film a political demonstration by gay rights activists); *Schexnayder v. Fed Ventures,* 625 So. 2d 530 (La. Ct. App. 1993) (suit by club, i.e., tavern, patrons against manager and employees arising out of alleged excessive force in ejecting patrons from club). But there are broader formulations, as *Capitol Indemnity* shows, and these exclusions have engendered no small amount of litigation. See generally Kimberly J. Winbush, Annotation, *Validity, Construction, and Effect of*

Assault and Battery Exclusion in Liability Insurance Policy at Issue, 44 A.L.R.5th 91 (1996).

2. *Fortuity revisited.* As a matter of tort law, the extent to which businesses owe a duty to their customers to protect them from random criminal acts in their parking lots presents a very difficult question. Whether the acts are foreseeable presents one set of problems, and the extent to which businesses should be expected to invest in precautions presents another. Needless to say, judicial answers to these questions are not always consistent. See Dan B. Dobbs, The Law of Torts § 324 (2000). If tort liability does exist, should it be insurable? If two supermarket customers get into a fight over a parking space in the parking lot, and if the party on the losing end of this encounter sues the supermarket for negligent supervision of the lot and failure to provide proper security, would you disagree that the claimed damage is fortuitous from the perspective of the supermarket? If you think the damage is fortuitous, why are some insurers so eager to exclude coverage for such losses? *See Burlington Ins. Co. v. Mexican American Unity Council, Inc.*, 905 S.W.2d 359 (Tex. App. 1995) (suit by resident of youth home alleging negligence in allowing her to leave premises, in circumstances where she was physically and sexually assaulted outside the premises). If the jurisdiction in which the insured resides recognizes only a very limited tort duty in this situation, does the coverage in the insurance policy with respect to parking lot assaults matter?

3. *The "intentional act" exclusion.* The court in *Capitol Indemnity* ultimately declined to reach the issue of how this exclusion might apply to the circumstances presented in that case. If the court had decided that question (i.e., assume the policy had neither a liquor liability nor an assault and battery exclusion), how should it have ruled?

In § 5.01[2], the intentional act exclusion in the context of homeowners coverage was examined. The problems that can arise in that context are no different from those that can arise in the commercial setting. Note, however, that the "Expected or Intended Injury" exclusion in the CGL in Appendix B appends a sentence that is not found in the homeowners form in Appendix C: "This exclusion does not apply to 'bodily injury' resulting from the use of reasonable force to protect persons or property." Should this sentence be added to the exclusion in the homeowners form? What difference would it make?

4. *Bars and taverns.* It should come as no surprise that bars and taverns provide the venue for many of the more interesting cases in this area. The tort duty issues are not simple in this setting either. See Joan Teshima, *Tavernkeeper's Liability to Patron for Third Person's Assault*, 43 A.L.R.4th 281 (1986). The policy in *Capitol Indemnity* had a separate exclusion that addressed many of the foreseeable kinds of liquor-related liabilities. Notice that the CGL in Appendix B has a "liquor liability" exclusion as well. If the insurer includes a liquor liability exclusion in the policy, why does it also need an assault and battery exclusion?

5. *The role of public policy.* Assume that Nevada has a state law titled "Private Tavern Regulatory and Licensing Law," the purpose of which is to "require qualifying criteria for bar and tavern owners, so as to prevent unqualified individuals from operating bars and taverns in a manner that injures

the public." Assume further that the law requires tavern owners to take training, secure a license, and purchase a general liability policy in the amount of at least $500,000. What effect, if any, should such a law have upon the court's analysis in *Capitol Indemnity*? *See Hickey v. Centenary Oyster House*, 719 So. 2d 421 (La. 1998) (divided court upholding assault and battery exclusion with respect to customer who was shot by armed robber in parking lot of restaurant, notwithstanding presence of licensed security guard).

6. *Pollution cases.* Whether a loss is intentional or accidental is particularly difficult in the environmental damage cases. Those are discussed in § 5.02[3][c], *infra.*

[b] The "Business Risk" Exclusions

KNUTSON CONSTRUCTION CO. v. ST. PAUL FIRE AND MARINE INSURANCE CO.

396 N.W.2d 229 (Minn. 1986) (en banc)

KELLEY, JUSTICE.

Appellant Knutson Construction Company (Knutson), a general contractor, purchased comprehensive general liability insurance policies (CGL) with a completed operations and broad form property damage endorsement (BFPD) from respondent insurance companies: St. Paul Fire and Marine (St. Paul Fire), St. Paul Mercury Insurance Company (Mercury), and United States Fire Insurance Company (USF). During the policy periods, Knutson was the general contractor on a project to erect a large apartment complex. Years after completion of the project, the owner sued Knutson alleging extensive damage to the project building due to a breach of contract, negligence, and other claims. After St. Paul Fire and USF had declined to defend or indemnify it, Knutson commenced this declaratory judgment action alleging coverage under the policies. Relying on *Bor-Son Building Corp. v. Employers Commercial Union*, 323 N.W.2d 58 (Minn. 1982), the trial court granted summary judgment motions made by the insurers. The court of appeals affirmed. *Knutson Construction Co. v. St. Paul Fire and Marine Insurance Co.*, 366 N.W.2d 738 (Minn. App. 1985). We affirm.

Respondent St. Paul Fire had issued Knutson comprehensive general liability policies with a broad form property damage endorsement, including completed operations, from January 1, 1973, through March 1, 1979. USF had issued virtually identical policies from March 1, 1979, through March 1, 1982.

In June 1973, Knutson contracted with Gateway Investors, Ltd. (Gateway) to construct, as general contractor, a 16-story building called Rivergate Apartments. Knutson contracted to furnish all materials and to perform all the work according to drawings and specifications prepared by architects and engineers under contract with Gateway.[3] Knutson additionally agreed to

---

[3] Knutson Companies, Inc., parent corporation of Knutson Construction Co., was a general partner of Gateway Investors, Ltd., Rivergate project owner, at the time the contract was signed. Knutson Companies, Inc. sold all but one-tenth of one percent of its partnership interest in

correct any defects due to faulty materials or workmanship appearing within one year of the date of substantial completion of the project.

Construction began in 1973 and ended in 1975. Knutson subcontracted with independent contractors and suppliers to provide much of the labor and material for the project, including caulking and sealing, installation of windows, prefabricated brick masonry panels, plumbing, heating, ventilating and air conditioning work. Gateway contracted directly with a manufacturer for supply of the windows. Architects hired by Gateway supervised the project.

Rivergate was certified as complete on May 22, 1975. Four years later, during the winter of 1979-1980, the owner of the Rivergate Apartments found excessive cracks, staining and spalling (chipping) on the exterior brick work of the building. Further examination revealed individual bricks and some prefabricated brick panels were loosening and steel connectors in contact with the brick panels and mortar were corroding. The owners considered these structural defects a substantial threat to the safety of Rivergate residents and passersby. Other problems alleged since completion of the building involve the heating and air conditioning systems and difficulty with the windows which allegedly failed to seal out air and moisture or to open and close properly.

Gateway, and its managing general partner, Sentinel Management Company, sued Knutson Construction Company, among others, in March, 1981, to recover building repair costs.[4] The complaint alleges Knutson breached its construction contract by using defective materials and employing improper methods, not complying with project specifications, not performing in a professional, workmanlike manner and generally "failing to construct and complete a sound durable structure." Knutson was also charged with negligence, breach of warranty and misrepresentation in relation to the building's masonry work, heating, air conditioning and window installation.

After St. Paul Fire and USF declined to defend that suit, Knutson commenced this declaratory judgment action. The trial court held and the court of appeals agreed that *Bor-Son* was dispositive and both courts ruled in favor of the respondent policy insurers.

On appeal to this court, Knutson asserts that the courts below erred because of existence of factual and legal differences distinguishing the contractor's undertaking in *Bor-Son* as compared to Knutson's undertaking in the Rivergate project. Factually, Knutson contends the major difference is that *Bor-Son* arose out of a "turnkey" project, one in which the owner had no involvement until the project was completed and the contractor-developer gave the owner

---

Gateway to LandTech Management Corp. on December 19, 1974, effective January 1, 1975. The sale agreement lists the principal asset of Gateway as land upon which the Knutson Construction Company is constructing a 269-unit high-rise apartment according to specifications entitled Elderly Housing Project for Knutson Development Company. The agreement further states the project is under a construction contract "pursuant to which Knutson Construction has agreed to provide all materials and perform all work of construction for a fixed price of $3,628,983." *Id.* LandTech later changed its name to Sentinel Management Company, and became the managing general partner in Gateway and a co-plaintiff in the underlying action to this case.

[4] Others named as defendants in the complaint and amended complaint include the project's architects and engineers, subcontractors, suppliers of materials and the company which issued the performance bond.

a key to turn in the door, whereas in this case, Knutson contends, the general contractor had less control and overall responsibility for the project. Knutson notes Gateway retained the project architect who prepared the plans and specifications and that it contracted directly with the supplier of the windows. Thus, Knutson concludes the Rivergate project, unlike the project in *Bor-Son*, cannot be regarded as the sole work or product of Knutson. Implicit in this assertion is the contention that the general contractor cannot control risks of defective workmanship by its subcontractors.

Respondents reply that the fact that *Bor-Son* involved a turnkey project is without significance. As in *Bor-Son*, they assert, Knutson bore the ultimate contractual responsibility to provide all labor and materials for the Rivergate project. They conclude, therefore, Knutson had "effective control" over the project, including the work of subcontractors such that Knutson was ultimately accountable for delivering a defect-free building to Rivergate.

Striking factual similarities exist between *Bor-Son* and this case. Both involved housing projects in which each owner hired a supervising architect for its project. In both cases, each general contractor was contractually bound to furnish materials and work for the project. In each case, the general contractor agreed to correct any defects due to faulty materials or workmanship appearing within a year of the building's completion. Both general contractors were sued by owners for damage to the buildings allegedly caused by the use of defective materials and workmanship. As in *Bor-Son*, the owner here, Rivergate, sought only costs for correcting defects in the building itself. No third party claims involving injuries or other property damages were involved in either underlying action commenced by the owners. Additionally, the comprehensive general liability insurance policies in both declaratory judgment actions are substantially identical. In both instances, the policies contain BFPD endorsements and completed operation endorsements. It is therefore apparent that both courts below correctly concluded that the relevant facts of this case are indistinguishable from those in *Bor-Son*.

Is there a legal distinction between the two cases? Respondents contend that the legal issues presented in this case cannot be distinguished from our *Bor-Son* holding. In *Bor-Son*, we held the standard CGL policy does not cover contractual claims to repair building defects caused by faulty materials and workmanship. We delineated the difference between contractual business risks, assumed by the general contractor, and risks of tort liability to third parties, assumed by the insurer, as follows:

> "The risk intended to be insured is the possibility that the goods, products or work of the insured, once relinquished or completed, will cause bodily injury or damage to property other than to the product or completed work itself, and for which the insured may be found liable. The insured, as a source of goods or services, may be liable as a matter of contract law to make good on products or work which is defective or otherwise unsuitable because it is lacking in some capacity. This may even extend to an obligation to completely replace or rebuild the deficient product or work. This liability, however, is not what the coverages in question are designed to protect against. The coverage is for tort liability for physical damage to others and not for

contractual liability of the insured for economic loss because the product or completed work is not that for which the damaged person bargained." 323 N.W.2d at 63 (quoting [Roger C.] Henderson, *Insurance Protection for Products Liability and Completed Operations— What Every Lawyer Should Know*, 50 Neb. L. Rev. 415, 441 (1971)). Because all the damages claimed by HRA arose out of Bor-Son's breach of contract (that is, faulty workmanship and defective materials), there was no coverage under the CGL policy.

Id.

Respondents note that the business risk arising out of contract, and assumed by Knutson as general contractor, as well as the kind and nature of damage claimed by Gateway and Sentinel, as owners, is identical to the damages claimed by the HRA in *Bor-Son*. They urge that we adhere to the rule in *Bor-Son* because it is consistent with the underwriting intent of comprehensive general liability policies. They assert abandonment of the *Bor-Son* rule, which would result in transferring the loss due to faulty construction from the contractor, who has engaged to complete a structure in a good workmanlike manner, to the CGL insurer would serve to encourage substandard construction, or even fraud, which would be against the public policy of the state. Respondents argue that risk of loss to work itself caused by poor workmanship or the contractor's use of inferior materials should rest with the contractors who can control those risks by completing projects in a workmanlike manner, whereas the CGL insurer is in no position to reduce such risks. The insurers aver that to impose such risks on the CGL insurer will make the cost of CGL insurance prohibitive because, in effect, the policy will become a performance bond.

On the other hand, appellant Knutson argues that even if it be conceded that the underlying facts in *Bor-Son* and the instant case are indistinguishable, *Bor-Son* has no precedential value because it did not consider relevant provisions in the CGL policy as modified by the BFPD endorsement. In essence, Knutson claims that the BFPD endorsement modifies the "work performed" exclusion of the CGL policy, Exclusion T, thereby granting coverage to the general contractor for claims arising out of the work which the contractor engaged to perform.[5]

---

[5] The St. Paul Fire policy, as well as the USF policy, contained exclusions from coverage. In particular, they contained exclusions (p), (s) and (t):

(p) To property damage.

(1) To property owned or occupied by or rented to the Insured, or except with respect to the use of elevators, to property held by the Insured for sale or entrusted to the Insured for storage or safekeeping;

(2) Except with respect to liability under a written sidetrack agreement or the use of elevators to:

(a) Property while on premises owned by or rented to the Insured for the purpose of having operations performed on such property by or on behalf of the Insured;

(b) Tools or equipment while being used by the Insured in performing his operations;

(c) Property in the custody of the Insured which is to be installed, erected or used in construction by the Insured;

(d) That particular part of any property, not on premises owned by or rented to the Insured;

An analysis of the issue commences with the consideration of elementary insurance principles. In exchange for the payment of a premium, an insurer assumes certain risks that otherwise would be the obligation of the insured. In order to have predictable and affordable insurance rates, the insurers' assumptions of risk are usually limited to those beyond the "effective control" of the insured. That principle applies to the CGL insurance policy.[6]

In every construction project, the owner and contractor incur risks or exposure to loss. Some of these risks can be shifted to insurers—others cannot. The owner has the risk that the contractor will fail to properly perform his contractual obligations. This risk can be shifted by the owner either securing, or requiring the contractor to provide, a performance bond.[7] The owner likewise has the risk the project may be destroyed by fire, explosion or the like during construction. The contractor may have a similar risk. Either or both may shift that risk to an insurer by acquiring a builder's risk policy. Again, such losses are generally beyond the effective control of either the contractor or the owner. Finally, the owner has the risk of being subject to claims of third parties who claim to have sustained property damage or personal injury as the result of the project being defectively constructed. The contractor is likewise subject to this risk. The owner's risk, however, is usually derivative since the claims usually arise from defective workmanship or materials used by the contractor. This risk of third party personal injury or property damage claim due to defective workmanship or materials may be shifted by the contractor purchasing a comprehensive general liability insurance policy to protect against loss to third persons or their property during the course of the work or, if a completed operations endorsement is paid for, thereafter. However, in addition to and apart from those risks, the contractor likewise has a contractual business risk that he may be liable to the owner

---

(1) Upon which operations are being performed by or on behalf of the Insured at the time of property damage arising out of such operations; or

(2) Out of which any property damage arises; or

(3) The restoration, repair or replacement of which has been made or is necessary by reason of faulty workmanship thereon by or on behalf of the insured;

(s) To property damage to the Named Insured's products arising out of such products or any part of such products.

(t) (Broad Form Property Damage Endorsement)

With respect to the completed operations hazard, to property damage to the work performed by the Named Insured arising out of the work or any portion thereof, or out of materials, parts or equipment furnished in connection therewith.

[6] See G.H. Tinker, *Comprehensive General Liability Insurance—Prospective In Overview*, 25 Fed'n Ins. Coun. Q., 217, 224 (1975) wherein the author explains the purpose of the CGL policy as follows:

It is not the function of the CGL policy to guarantee the technical competence and integrity of business management. The CGL policy does not serve as a performance bond, nor does it serve as a warranty of goods or services. It does not ordinarily contemplate coverage for losses which are a normal, frequent or predictable consequence of the business operations. Nor does it contemplate ordinary business expense, or injury or damage to others which results by intent or indifference.

[7] If the contractor defaults, the owner can look to the surety for indemnification of the cost of repairs or completion of the work. Even so, the ultimate responsibility rests with the contractor who is liable to the surety who has indemnified the owner or completed the work. Therefore, even though the owner can shift the risk over which he has no "effective control," the contractor cannot.

resulting from failure to properly complete the building project itself in a manner so as to not cause damage to it. This risk is one the general contractor effectively controls and one which the insurer does not assume because it has no effective control over those risks and cannot establish predictable and affordable insurance rates. Nonetheless, appellant urges us in this case to hold that by the purchase of a CGL policy, a contractor shifts to the insurer this business risk which it effectively controls. Unlike the surety on a performance bond, a CGL insurer has no recourse against a contractor for the employment of defective materials or shoddy workmanship on the construction project.

Even though it cannot be conclusively demonstrated that adoption of appellant's proposed holding would promote shoddy workmanship and the lack of exercise of due care, undoubtedly it would present the opportunity or incentive for the insured general contractor to be less than optimally diligent in these regards in the performance of his contractual obligations to complete a project in a good workmanlike manner. To accept the appellant's contention would be to provide the contractor with assurance that notwithstanding shoddy workmanship, the construction project would be properly completed by indemnification paid to the owner by the comprehensive general liability insurer. In and of itself, the incentive for the contractor to fairly and accurately bid a contract in order to secure the job would be removed. Even if such result would not always be inevitable, the possibility of such consequences, in our view, is incompatible with the general public policy concerning the relationship between contractors and owners. Those policy reasons were best articulated in *Centex Homes Corp. v. Prestressed Systems,* 444 So. 2d 66 (Fla. App. 1984):

> It is well established that the purpose of comprehensive liability insurance coverage is to provide protection for personal injury or property damage caused by the product only and not for the replacement or repair of the product. [citations omitted] The policy reasons for this result are obvious. If insurance proceeds could be used to pay for the repairing and/or replacing of poorly constructed products, a contractor or subcontractor could receive initial payment for its work and then receive subsequent payment from the insurance company to repair and replace it. [citations omitted] Equally repugnant on policy grounds is the notion that the presence of insurance obviates the obligation to perform the job initially in a workmanlike manner.

Id. at 66-67.

An exclusion in the CGL policy clearly excludes coverage for damage or injury to this project which is expected or intended by the insured. But liability for damage to the project itself encompasses much more than intentional acts of contractor misdoings. No matter how diligently and how assiduously a contractor attempts to control the workmanship and materials used on the project, when, in spite of those efforts, the projects fall short, the consequences of the failure is endemic in a commercial undertaking. *Weedo v. Stone-E-Brick,* 81 N.J. 233, 405 A.2d 788 (1979).[8] Recognizing these well-established

---

[8] The New Jersey court explained the risk as follows:

The insured-contractor can take pains to control the quality of the goods and services

insurance principles, we held in *Bor-Son* that claims for damage to the project itself were not covered under the contractor's comprehensive general liability policy. We there labeled claims of this type as "business risk." *Bor-Son Building Corp. v. Employers Commercial Union*, 323 N.W.2d 58, 61 (Minn. 1982). Even though an examination of the CGL policies in this case, as well as the policy in *Bor-Son*, will reveal no exclusions specifically designated as "business risk," in insurance law the scope of the phase is well understood. As explained in an article by G.H. Tinker, entitled *Comprehensive General Liability Insurance—Prospective and Overview*, 25 Fed'n Ins. Coun. Q. 217, 224 (1975):

> "Business Risks," then, are those risks which management can and should control or reduce to manageable proportions; risks which management cannot effectively avoid because of the nature of the business operations; and risks which relate to the repair or replacement of faulty work or products. These risks are a normal, foreseeable and expected incident of doing business and should be reflected in the price of the product or service rather than as a cost of insurance to be shared by others.

In the policies at issue here, such "business risk" type exclusions can be found, for example, in exclusions "P," "S" and "T" of the St. Paul Fire policies.[9] These exclusions generally operate to exclude coverage for claims arising out of the insured's product when the claim for relief seeks replacement or repair of damages to the product itself. Therefore, absent other considerations, we reaffirm our holding in *Bor-Son* that the CGL policy does not provide coverage for claims of defective materials and workmanship giving rise to a claim for damage to the property itself which is the subject matter of the construction project.

But does the existence of the BFPD endorsement in these policies, as appellant contends, operate to provide coverage that would otherwise be excluded under the CGL policy for the claims made by Rivergate? Consistent with *Bor-Son*, we hold it does not.

Appellant asserts that we did not address the BFPD endorsement in *Bor-Son*, and therefore "the entire analysis of the opinion and all the authority it cites is outdated, obsolete, and of no application." Appellant is in error. We did consider Knutson's BFPD contention and there rejected it. The issue was raised in the *Bor-Son* briefs as well as in the petition for rehearing. We rejected that claim in *Bor-Son* because the general contractor was fully responsible for all phases of the project—even though there it had subcontracted all of the work on the project. Here, Knutson retained portions of the

---

supplied. At the same time he undertakes the risk that he may fail in this endeavor and thereby incur contractual liability whether express or implied. The consequences of not performing well is part of every business venture; the replacement or repair of faulty goods and works is a business expense, to be borne by the insured-contractor in order to satisfy customers.

Id., 405 A.2d at 791.

[9] Exclusion "P" is the "owned or occupied" exclusion; Exclusion "S" is the "products" exclusion; and Exclusion "T" is the "work performed" exclusion.

work for itself. Nevertheless, in both instances, the structure became the contractor's product.[12]

Notwithstanding our rejection of similar assertions raised in *Bor-Son*, appellant Knutson argues that the removal of the words "or on behalf of" in the work performed exclusion from the BFPD exclusion expands coverage to include coverage for the claims now being asserted against Knutson by Rivergate.

In some construction projects, the general contractor has overall responsibility in control of the construction of the building. In *Bor-Son* that exclusive control and responsibility was considered decisive. On other construction projects, the so-called general contractor has something less than overall control of the work of subcontractors. Here, however, as in *Bor-Son*, Knutson, by contract, undertook to furnish all materials and labor. It had responsibility for all construction work — its own as well as its subcontractors. It had "effective control" over all project work and materials, including those provided by subcontractors. When the completed project is turned over to the owner by the general contractor, all of the work performed and materials furnished by subcontractors merges into the general contractor's product—a product it has contracted to complete in a good workmanlike manner. Thereby it incurred the business risk of liability arising from its failure to fulfill that contractual obligation. Thus, whether the work was "done by" or "on behalf of" the general contractor is irrelevant to the analysis. The completed product is to be viewed as a whole, not as a "grouping" of component parts.[13] The CGL policy excludes damage to the product for the exact public policy reasons hereinbefore discussed. Slight difference in wording in the work performed exclusion in the BFPD endorsement does not affect this exclusion.

We are not alone in this analysis. This precise issue was addressed in *Tucker Construction Co. v. Michigan Mutual Insurance Co.*, 423 So. 2d 525 (Fla. App. 1982). There, as in this case, a general contractor by contract agreed to build a building. The general contractor hired a soil-testing firm which recommended a method of installing the foundation. Sometime after completion of the structure, its floor began to settle. The general contractor blamed the settling on the work and services performed by the subcontracting soil-testing firm. The general contractor submitted a claim to its insurer which had written a CGL policy providing coverage for property damage including completed operations and BFPD coverage. The completed operations coverage

---

[12] Appellant Knutson argues the building was not a "product" within the meaning of the product exclusion. Consistent with the majority of the courts which have addressed the issue, we held in *Bor-Son* that the buildings were a "product." 323 N.W.2d at 63. Supportive of this conclusion are *S.W. Forest Indus., Inc. v. Pole Bldgs., Inc.*, 478 F.2d 185 (9th Cir. 1973) (industrial building); *Home Indem. Co. v. Miller*, 399 F.2d 78 (8th Cir. 1968) (completed home a contractor's product); *Constr. Corp. v. Charter Oak Fire Ins. Co.*, 66 A.D.2d 315, 414 N.Y.S.2d 385 (1979) (school building a product); *Zanco, Inc. v. Michigan Mut. Ins. Co.*, 11 Ohio St. 3d 114, 464 N.E.2d 513 (1984) (defects in condominium complex came under products exclusion); *Haugan v. Home Ind. Co.*, 86 S.D. 406, 197 N.W.2d 18 (1972) (products exclusion, among others applies to defectively built aircraft hanger and office building). Contra, *see Johnson v. Nat'l Union Fire Ins. Co. of Pittsburgh*, 56 Misc. 2d 983, 289 N.Y.S.2d 852 (1968) and *Kissel v. Aetna Casualty & Sur. Co.*, 380 S.W.2d 497 (Mo. App. 1964) both of which, however, involved third party claims.

[13] Of course, the general contractor may have a remedy for contribution, indemnity or otherwise against subcontractors who breached contracts.

contained the same exclusion at issue in this case—that is, the words "or on behalf of" contained in the CGL policy had been omitted, and, as in this case, the omission resulted from a substitution of an exclusion containing the words "work performed by the named insured." There, as here, the general contractor argued its CGL policy containing the identical BFPD and completed operation endorsement provided coverage because the building defects were caused by the subcontractor. In rejecting that assertion, the court stated:

> The deletion of the phrase relating to subcontractors in the exclusion in the completed operations policy makes sense because the insured contractor has presumably accepted the subcontractor's work as his own (at least so far as its potential tort liability is concerned), and has turned the completed work over to the owner by the time such a completed operations policy is operative. In effect the applicable exclusion provides that the "completed operations" hazard coverage does not apply "to property damage to work performed by the named insured arising out of such work or any portion thereof." The words "work performed by" in this context in the policy mean the same as "the restaurant constructed by" the insured and was intended to exclude coverage of the insured's contractual liability for damages to the "work" caused by the insured's neglect or failure to complete and deliver the completed "work" in accordance with his contractual undertaking with the owner.

Id. at 528. Thus, it appears the Florida court followed the same analysis as this court utilized in *Bor-Son*. The result is that, regardless of the BFPD and completed operation endorsement, the general contractor ordinarily may not pass on to its CGL insurer the risk that the contractor may be called upon to repair defective work or replace defective materials which it, the general contractor, is, by contract solely responsible for.[14]

The trial court and the court of appeals correctly held that *Bor-Son* precluded coverage to Knutson against Rivergate's claims. Accordingly, we affirm.[15]

NOTES

1. *Business risks versus insurable risks.* As the principal case indicates, the CGL is designed to cover liabilities incurred in the operation of a business, not losses that are in the nature of "negative profits." What do the business risk exclusions have to do with fortuity?

---

[14] Appellant Knutson and the dissenter in the court of appeals rely on *S.W. Louisiana Grain, Inc. v. Howard A. Duncan, Inc.,* 438 So. 2d 215 (La. App. 1983) which held the modified language in the BFPD endorsement when viewed alongside the completed work exclusion created an ambiguity, and therefore construed it against the insurers so as to afford coverage. When considered in connection with the allocation of construction risks and principles of insurance, we can ascertain no perceived ambiguity. . . .

[15] We do not address the issue of whether the warranty exceptions in the policies (St. Paul Fire (g) and USF(a)) are applicable because not briefed by appellant.

Do the court's comments about moral hazard hold water? If providing coverage for "business risks" would lead to more shoddy work, does it follow that providing protection against tort liability caused by shoddy work would also encourage more shoddy work? Instead of moral hazard, does the distinction between business risks and insurable risks have something to do with the frequency with which the type of loss occurs?

2. *Defective work by subcontractors.* In *O'Shaughnessy v. Smuckler Corp.,* 543 N.W.2d 99 (Minn. App. 1996), a case with facts similar to *Knutson,* *Knutson* was deemed not to be controlling because of differences in the language of the applicable policy. The court held that the explicit language of the post-1986 CGL covered property damage to the insured's work, for which the insured was liable, when the damaged work or work out of which the damage arose was performed on the insured's behalf by a subcontractor. The court questioned the avowed rationale of the business risk exclusions when the contractor's liability is based on faulty work of a subcontractor. After quoting from *Knutson,* the court stated:

> We note that this rationale is less applicable to a claim by a general contractor for the defective work of its subcontractor. A general contractor has minimal control over the work of its subcontractors by definition, and the fact that the general contractor receives coverage will not relieve the subcontractor of ultimate liability for unworkmanlike or defective work. In such a case, an insurer will have subrogation rights against the subcontractor who performed the defective work. Presumably, the Business Risk Doctrine will preclude the subcontractor from recovering from its own insurer. Thus, the goal of the Business Risk Doctrine would still be achieved because ultimate responsibility for poor workmanship would lie with the one who performed it.

543 N.W.2d at 102. Do you agree with the court's assumption that the general contractor only has "minimal control" over the work of subcontractors? In *Blaylock & Brown Construction, Inc. v. AIU Insurance Co.,* 796 S.W.2d 146 (Tenn. App. 1990), the court read the CGL quite differently in the course of holding that the CGL did not cover damage to a house allegedly caused by improper work performed by the subcontractor:

> [T]he named insured is the general contractor and work performed by the insured must necessarily be such work as the named insured is required to perform under the construction contract. How the insured performs the work is a matter for its decision in the exercise of sound business practice. The contractor can employ subcontractors or use employees to do the work, but in the end, when the work is completed, all the work called for by the contract on the part of the contractor must be deemed to be work performed by the contractor. We hold that the language of the policy excludes liability coverage for the plaintiffs for damage to the property constructed pursuant to the contract.

796 S.W.2d at 154. Courts have continued to disagree about the proper resolution of this issue. *See e.g., Schwindt v. Underwriters at Lloyd's of*

London, 81 Wash. App. 293, 914 P.2d 119 (1996) (agreeing with *Knutson* and *Blaylock*); *Fireguard Sprinkler Systems, Inc. v. Scottsdale Insurance Co.,* 864 F.2d 648 (9th Cir. 1988) (rejecting *Knutson*); *Stratton & Co., Inc. v. Argonaut Insurance Co.,* 469 S.E.2d 545 (Ga. App. 1996)(agreeing with *Fireguard Sprinkler* and rejecting *Knutson* and *Blaylock*); *Green Construction Co. v. National Union Fire Insurance Co.,* 771 F. Supp. 1000 (W.D. Mo. 1991) (agreeing with *Fireguard Sprinkler* and rejecting *Knutson*).

3. *Evolving structure of the CGL.* The early CGL was a basic liability form to which numerous endorsements were added depending on the nature of the insured's business and the insured's particular needs. As Professor Henderson explains in the following passage, endorsements might be added in response to the emergence of new forms of liability:

> The development of insurance protection for products liability, denominated "Products Hazard" coverage, has paralleled the development of the modern rules for products liability. . . . Prior to the expansion of the common law theories of liability for injuries arising from unreasonably dangerous products, there was not much need for such insurance coverage. The manufacturer could only be sued for negligence, and this alone was an insurmountable burden for the plaintiff in many cases. Even if the plaintiff could marshal the necessary evidence, there was the privity barrier. Thus, the greatest risk that a manufacturer suffered, aside from employer's liability, was for injuries to third persons arising out of conditions or activities on or near his premises and for operations away from such premises but related thereto. Insurance protection for such risks was readily available in the form of what is now called "Premises and Operations" coverage. This coverage, as indicated, however, applied only to injuries occurring on, or adjacent to, the described premises, and during the progress of operations away from the premises. If the injury occurred away from the premises and after operations had been completed, there was no coverage.

> . . . [W]ith the fall of the privity requirement and development of strict products liability, a new coverage was in order. This coverage, products hazard coverage, was supplied by simply adding to the existing premises and operations coverage a provision for injuries caused by products away from the premises and after the insured had relinquished possession of them. At the same time, and usually under the same paragraph entitled simply "Products Hazards" or "Products Hazards (Including Completed Operations)," coverage was provided for operations that had been completed or abandoned and which had taken place away from the described premises.

> . . . [T]his coverage [had] to be specifically purchased by the insured by so electing on the face of the policy or by purchasing an endorsement which either add[ed] the coverage to or delete[d] the exclusion of the coverage under the basic policy.

Roger C. Henderson, *Insurance Protection for Products Liability and Completed Operations,* 50 Neb. L. Rev. 415, 417-18 (1971). *

Thus, prior to 1986, the CGL excluded coverage for completed operations, and no coverage existed unless the insured specifically purchased an endorsement adding the coverage. (For a discussion of the pre-1986 structure of the policy in the context of a claim against a contractor, *see Frontier Insulation Contractors, Inc. v. Merchants Mutual Insurance Co.,* 667 N.Y.S.2d 866, 690 N.E.2d 866 (N.Y. 1997) (discussing products hazard exclusion).) But the endorsement proved so popular that the 1986 revision incorporated the coverage into the general form. When this occurred, many of the particular provisions of the endorsement were amended, but the general nature of the coverage remained the same. See generally Gregory G. Schultz, *Commercial General Liability Coverage for Faulty Construction Claims,* 33 Tort & Ins. L. J. 257 (1997); Robert J. Franco, *Insurance Coverage for Faulty Workmanship Claims Under Commercial General Liability Policies,* 30 Tort & Ins. L. J. 785 (1995). Changes in wording can have, however, momentous consequences, as the preceding note attests; in dealing with a question of coverage in this area, careful attention must be given not only to the language of the policy but also to what precise provisions were at issue in any prior case offered as authority on any particular issue.

4. *Contract breaches and business risks.* Under the definition of "property damage" in the 1986 CGL, if after the insured-contractor builds a townhouse the roof collapses by reason of inept construction, injuring a third party's property, does the CGL provide coverage for the liability to the third party? (Yes.) If the third party were the owner of the premises and sued the insured for contractual liability, would the CGL provide coverage? (No.) For insights into the answers to the two questions, ask whether a breach of contract is an "occurrence," and whether a contract breach falls within the definition of "property damage." Having said all of this, does it make sense to draw a distinction for coverage purposes between the "breach" and the "result of the breach"?

What if the roof collapse described above causes a properly-constructed roof in an adjacent townhouse (which, though it shares a common wall, was built by a different contractor) to collapse? For coverage to exist, must there be "derivative damage" from the breach of contract? *See Maryland Casualty Co. v. Reeder,* 221 Cal. App. 3d 961, 270 Cal. Rptr. 719 (1990).

5. *Incorporating defective products into other products.* If the insured is engaged in the business of building engines and the insured's poor workmanship in building a particular engine (*e.g.,* faulty construction of the cooling system) results in damage to the engine, the damage to the engine is not covered. Assume, however, that the insured's business is to build radiators, which third parties incorporate into their own engines. If the insured's shoddy workmanship in building radiators leads to damage to third parties' engines, is this loss "property damage" within the meaning of the CGL? *See Yakima Cement Products Co. v. Great American Insurance Co.,* 93 Wash. 2d 210, 608 P.2d 254 (Wash. 1980). See generally Lorelie S. Masters & Richard P. Lewis, *The Incorporation Doctrine: "Incorporating" Historic Coverage into the 1973 CGL Form,* 17 Ins. Lit. Rptr. 452 (1995).

6. *"Products."* What is a "product" anyway? The current CGL excludes coverage for " 'property damage' to 'your product' arising out of it or any

portion of it." The term "your product" is defined as "a. Any goods or products, other than real property, manufactured, sold, handled, distributed or disposed of by: (1) You . . .; or b. Containers (other than vehicles), materials, parts or equipment furnished in connection with such goods or products." When a contractor builds a house or a building, is the resulting structure a "product"? *Compare Schwindt v. Underwriters at Lloyd's of London,* 81 Wash. App. 293, 914 P.2d 119 (1996) (medical building constructed by contractors is a product), with *Maryland Casualty Co. v. Reeder,* 221 Cal. App. 3d 961, 270 Cal. Rptr. 719 (1990)(insured contractor's product was not entire condominium project); *Green Construction Co. v. National Union Fire Insurance Co.,* 771 F. Supp. 1000 (W.D. Mo. 1991) (dam constructed by insured was "work" but was not "product" within meaning of exclusion for "injury to product"). Services, i.e., the providing of labor only, presumably cannot be a "product." *See Rhone-Poulenc Rorer Inc. v. Home Indemnity Co.,* 832 F. Supp. 114 (E.D. Pa. 1993); *Underwriters at Interest v. SCI Steelcon,* 905 F. Supp. 441 (W.D. Mich. 1995); *Hartford Mutual Insurance Co. v. Moorhead,* 578 A.2d 492 (Pa. Super. 1990). One commentator offered this view: "This [i.e., the products] exclusion is intended to bar coverage for any of the products or personal property brought onto the job by the contractor and intended to remain on the jobsite. This exclusion is not intended to bar coverage for claims arising from the insured's products, but coverage for the products themselves." Franco, *supra,* at 798-99.

7. An Assessment. It is easy after exploring the nuances of the business risk exclusions to lose sight of the forest. The CGL is designed to cover fortuitous liabilities, not replace, repair, or reimburse poor work performed by contractors. How well have the forms drafted by the insurance industry functioned to make this distinction? Obviously, much remains unsettled. But before you conclude that the contest between the construction industry and the insurance industry is a battle unlike any other, consider the materials in the next subsection.

[c] The Pollution Exclusion

No single exclusion has had more prominence in insurance litigation than the pollution exclusion. Indeed, it is arguable that the insurability of liabilities for environmental damage is the most prominent *corporate* litigation issue of the last couple of decades. This issue is so vast that an entire course could be devoted to it alone; indeed, entire treatises are devoted to this particular topic. See generally Kenneth S. Abraham, Environmental Liability Insurance Law (1991); Tod I. Zuckerman & Mark C. Raskoff, Environmental Insurance Litigation: Law and Practice (1992). For a brief introduction to the coverage issues implicated by the pollution exclusion, consider the next two cases.

CHARTER OIL CO. v. AMERICAN EMPLOYERS' INSURANCE CO.

69 F.3d 1160 (D.C. Cir. 1995)

Stephen F. Williams, Circuit Judge:

In the early 1970s Independent Petrochemical Corporation ("IPC"), a wholly-owned subsidiary of plaintiff Charter Oil, was in the business of selling petrochemical products. As a courtesy to a customer, it arranged on several occasions for the disposal of waste oil by a St. Louis waste oil hauler, Bliss Oil, understanding that Bliss would take the oil to a waste disposal site. In fact, after Bliss Oil's president tasted the oil to check its suitability for other uses and found the flavor fit, Bliss sprayed it as a dust suppressant at various locations throughout Missouri. The sprayings occurred over a period of at least two months, with each spraying lasting about 30-40 minutes. The waste oil turned out to contain dioxin, a chemical compound alleged to cause harm to humans, animals, and plants.[1] The discharge of the dioxin-contaminated oil gave rise to claims against IPC by the federal government, the State of Missouri, and over 1,600 private plaintiffs, the latter seeking in aggregate $4 billion in compensatory damages and the same amount in punitive damages. IPC entered into settlements covering all of the claims and is now in bankruptcy. Its outstanding obligations include over $100 million owed to the federal government for clean-up of various sites in Missouri.

Charter and its affiliates (including IPC) sued several primary and excess insurers that had issued comprehensive general liability policies to them over the 1971-1983 period, seeking a declaratory judgment that these policies obliged the insurers to provide indemnification for all obligations arising out of Bliss's spraying activities. Each of the policies at issue contains one of four forms of pollution exclusion; three of the forms, on which the parties have focused, create an exception to the exclusion—i.e., affirmatively cover—harm from pollution releases that are "sudden and accidental." The first form (termed the "domestic insurers' exclusion" by the district court) provides:

> [This insurance does not apply to] [b]odily injury or property damage arising out of the discharge, dispersal, release or escape of smoke, vapors, soot, fumes, acids, alkalis, toxic chemicals, liquids or gases, waste materials or other irritants, contaminants or pollutants into or upon land, the atmosphere or any watercourse or body of water, *but this exclusion does not apply if such discharge, dispersal, release or escape is sudden and accidental.*

The second and third forms (the "London exclusion" and the "INA exclusion") are identical in all relevant respects. The fourth form, contained in policies issued by defendant Travelers, replaces the "sudden and accidental" language with a requirement that the discharge of pollutants be neither "expected" nor "intended."

In the decision under review here, the district court granted the insurers' motion for summary judgment on claims governed by Missouri law. *Independent Petrochemical Corp. v. Aetna Casualty & Sur. Co.*, 842 F. Supp. 575 (D.D.C. 1994). The court's key ruling was that the phrase "sudden and accidental" is unambiguous and means "unexpected, unintended, and abrupt." *Id.* at 579-80. This appeal followed. We affirm, rejecting Charter's contentions that the phrase "sudden and accidental" is sufficiently ambiguous to allow recovery for the injury from Bliss's sprayings and that representations made to state

---

[1] The issue whether dioxin causes cancer in humans is highly controversial. *See e.g.*, Richard Stone, "Panel Slams EPA's Dioxin Analysis," 268 Science 1124 (May 26, 1995) (reporting critique by the EPA's Science Advisory Board).

insurance regulators when insurers introduced the pollution exclusion create a public policy bar to its enforcement as interpreted by the district court.

Although all parties agree that Missouri law controls, we have no ruling from the Missouri courts interpreting "sudden and accidental." Other circuits have certified questions to state supreme courts concerning the interpretation of the pollution exclusion, but that solution is not available here because the Missouri Supreme Court declines to answer questions certified to it by federal courts.

I.

A. "Sudden and Accidental."

Charter argues, first, that the phrase "sudden and accidental" is facially ambiguous and thus, under standard principles of insurance law and specifically those of Missouri, should be interpreted to embrace rather than exclude coverage. Second, it argues that even if the phrase is not facially ambiguous, extrinsic evidence reveals a "latent ambiguity," which (unless clearly resolved by extrinsic evidence in favor of the insurer) again requires an interpretation favoring coverage.

1. Facial Ambiguity.
a. The Anti-redundancy Canon.

Charter says that "sudden" is ambiguous in that it may be interpreted to mean either "unexpected and unintended" (the interpretation favored by Charter) or "unexpected, unintended, and abrupt" (the interpretation favored by the insurers and adopted by the district court). In support of its position, Charter points to dictionary definitions of "sudden" that emphasize the element of unexpectedness and downplay or ignore that of abruptness. *E.g.*, Webster's Third New International Dictionary 2284 (1981) (listing, as the first definition of "sudden," "happening without previous notice or with very brief notice: coming or occurring unexpectedly: not foreseen or prepared for"). The district court rejected Charter's interpretation, relying heavily on the Eighth Circuit's construction of Missouri law in *Aetna Casualty & Sur. Co. v. General Dynamics Corp.*, 968 F.2d 707 (8th Cir. 1992). There the court held that the word "sudden," when joined with "accidental," imposes a requirement of temporal abruptness. *Id.* at 710. To rule otherwise, it said, would render "sudden" superfluous in the phrase "sudden and accidental," since "accidental" already imposes a requirement of unexpectedness. *Id.* Missouri law requires that all terms of an insurance contract be given meaning; thus, "sudden" cannot mean merely unexpected. *General Dynamics*, 968 F.2d at 710. Rather, under Missouri law's dictate that policy language be given its plain meaning, "sudden" must mean "quick" or "abrupt." *Id.*

Under the "home circuit" rule of *Abex Corp. v. Maryland Casualty Co.*, 790 F.2d 119, 125-26 (D.C. Cir. 1986), we "defer to the local circuit's view of the law of a state in its jurisdiction when that circuit has made a reasoned inquiry into state law, unless we are convinced that the court has ignored clear signals emanating from the state courts." . . . General Dynamics therefore controls our interpretation of "sudden and accidental" unless we conclude that the court "clearly misread" Missouri law. *Abex*, 790 F.2d at 126. As rulings in this very litigation show, our deference under *Abex* is not slavish. Thus, in

Independent Petrochemical Corp., 944 F.2d at 944-47 (D.C. Cir. 1991), we refused to defer to the Eighth Circuit's conclusion that the term "damages" in the standard-form comprehensive general liability policy did not include environmental clean-up costs. We noted that the Eighth Circuit's decision was at odds with every other case applying the rules of insurance contract interpretation in force in Missouri, and we concluded that the decision presented the "rare" case in which *Abex* deference was not warranted. *Id.* at 945, 946.

The present appeal does not present such a case. First, the *General Dynamics* court's determination that "accidental" includes an element of unexpectedness, 968 F.2d at 710, is based on many cases so deciding, in Missouri and elsewhere. Charter has not pointed to any Missouri case interpreting "accidental" in a way that excludes the unexpected.

General Dynamics's use of the anti-redundancy canon is also consistent with Missouri caselaw. Charter points out that the cases applying the anti-redundancy canon all involve potentially redundant clauses, not individual words. Indeed, for the drafters of language excluding coverage for damages arising out of the "discharge, dispersal, release or escape" of "smoke, vapors, soot, fumes, acids, alkalis, toxic chemicals, liquids or gases, waste materials or other irritants, contaminants, or pollutants" to argue against redundancy of individual words in insurance policies may seem odd — although, of course, it is possible that over a broad set of applications each word may add a critical element. In any event, we agree with defendants that in the context of the simple pairing, "sudden and accidental," as distinguished from a laundry list of terms ("discharge, dispersal, release or escape"), application of Missouri's anti-redundancy canon is not a "clear misreading" of Missouri law. As the Tenth Circuit said in concluding under Utah law that "sudden" had a meaning distinct from that of "accidental": "Dictionaries may indicate each word has several overlapping meanings. We cannot use only the redundant definitions, however." *Hartford Accident & Indemnity Co. v. United States Fidelity & Guaranty Co.*, 962 F.2d 1484, 1489 (10th Cir. 1992). Indeed, if the effect of the rule that ambiguities are construed against the insurer were to force the interpreter always to choose the redundant meaning from among a dictionary's offerings, it would be quite difficult for insurance policies to exclude members of a set of closely related circumstances. ("Abrupt" wouldn't work here, for example, as Webster's Third New International includes "unexpected" as one of its meanings.) The congruence of *General Dynamics* with other decisions applying the anti-redundancy canon in interpreting "sudden and accidental" stands in sharp contrast to the Eighth Circuit's departure from other courts' conclusions in the decision to which we declined to accord *Abex* deference.

Having determined that "sudden" must mean something other than "unexpected," the *General Dynamics* court went on to hold that the term's "plain meaning" is "abrupt." 968 F.2d at 710. We find no "clear misreading" of Missouri law in this second interpretive step. Under that law, the language of an insurance policy is to be given "the meaning that would ordinarily be understood by the layman who bought and paid for the policy." *Robin v. Blue Cross Hosp. Serv., Inc.*, 637 S.W.2d 695, 698 (Mo. 1982) (en banc) (internal quotation marks and citation omitted). Other courts applying this interpretive canon to the "sudden and accidental" language have concluded with the *General Dynamics* court that "sudden" means "abrupt." . . . .

Further, even apart from the redundancy problem, reading "sudden" to mean only unexpected presents serious difficulties. In advocating that reading, for instance, the Supreme Court of Georgia reasoned: "[O]n reflection one realizes that, even in its popular usage, 'sudden' does not usually describe the duration of an event, but rather its unexpectedness: a sudden storm, a sudden turn in the road, sudden death." *Claussen v. Aetna Casualty & Sur. Co.,* 259 Ga. 333, 380 S.E.2d 686, 688 (1989). The instances cited seem unconvincing. A "sudden turn" connotes an abrupt change in direction, one that might still be described as "sudden" by a driver who had traveled the road many times and knew to expect the turn. Likewise, the other two usages seem likely in fact to apply only where the event is abrupt—a spike in an imaginary graph rather than a gentle slope—and any unexpected character seems in large part merely a typical concomitant of the event's being abrupt. A sudden death presumably refers to the process itself (not the moment when, say, the heart stops or brain waves cease, a moment that will always be more or less instantaneous), and is implicitly contrasted to a lingering death (as from most forms of cancer); the death is, then, of short duration. And while "sudden storms" may in common parlance usually arise abruptly, they also typically end quickly; we doubt if Noah referred to the rain that necessitated his ark as a "sudden storm," no matter how abruptly it may have started.

b. Purpose of Policy Term.

Putting canons aside, Missouri courts in interpreting insurance contracts look to the underlying commercial or legal purpose sought to be achieved by a policy term. And the "abruptness" interpretation of "sudden" fits well with what is at least a plausible business purpose for the restriction of coverage to "sudden and accidental" releases. That restriction may serve as a back up to the requirement under standard "occurrence" policies that the harm be "unexpected and unintended," denying coverage for damages that may have been expected or intended, or at least are more likely to be such, but which cannot readily be proven as such. See Kenneth S. Abraham, Environmental Liability Insurance Law 153 (1991). Discharges of long duration seem more likely than ones of short duration to be part of the insured's ordinary operations and hence more likely to produce harm that is expected or intended by the insured (where avoidance of the harmful discharge would be costly). Such long-term discharges, characteristically (though not always) expected and avoidable, were likely the model of pollution-causing activity in the late 1960s and early 1970s, before the initiation of intensive federal regulation of waste storage and management in 1980. See Comprehensive Environmental Response, Compensation and Liability Act of 1980 ("CERCLA"), Pub.L. No. 96-510, 94 Stat. 2767 (codified as amended at 42 U.S.C. §§ 9601-9675). The impossibility of pinpointing every instance of expected or intended harm means that in the absence of an additional requirement that the discharge be abrupt, the insured would recover in some situations in which it in fact expected or intended the harm. Yet both insured and insurer have an incentive, at the contracting stage, to rule out such liability. If a policy allows recovery for discharges that expectedly or intentionally generate liability, insureds will be tempted (at the margin) to engage in harm-generating (or reckless) behavior, i.e., will be subject to "moral hazard." To the extent that the moral hazard is not constrained, total compensable losses will be increased by a number of reasonably avoidable losses, and premiums, of course, will rise with them. Thus, the imposition of an abruptness requirement may plausibly be viewed as aimed at controlling moral hazard and thereby benefitting both parties.

Of course, suddenness is only an imperfect mechanism for identifying harm that the insured neither expected nor intended. Here, the suddenness of Bliss's discharge presumably has little if any bearing on whether the resulting harm was expected or intended by Charter. By definition, however, a proxy only approximates the underlying item of interest. The absence of a perfect fit therefore provides no basis for refusing to apply the proxy or for distorting its meaning.[2]

c. Historical Interpretation.

Charter argues that Abex deference to General Dynamics is unjustified in light of the courts' historic interpretation of "sudden and accidental" language in boiler and machinery policies, and indeed two courts have been persuaded that the language acquired an established meaning in the boiler and machinery context. *See New Castle County v. Hartford Accident & Indemnity Co.,* 933 F.2d 1162, 1197 (3rd Cir. 1991) ("The phrase 'sudden and accidental' was not new to the insurance industry. For many years, it had been used in the standard boiler and machinery policy, and the courts uniformly had construed the phrase to mean unexpected and unintended.") (footnotes and citations omitted). But Charter and the courts adopting that argument rely on only two cases. Two hardly make a massive trend, and in fact each of the two cases has a significant vulnerability as authority. The first, *New England Gas & Elec. Ass'n v. Ocean Accident & Guarantee Corp.,* 330 Mass. 640, 116 N.E.2d 671, 680 (1953), involved an event of very brief duration, rendering the interpretation of "sudden" immaterial to the result. The court specifically rejected the notions that the insured's spindle, over its final 75 minutes of operation, "was merely undergoing only slow and gradual structural changes" and that its cracking "was gradual and not sudden." The second case, although rejecting a requirement of limited duration, actually used reasoning that

---

[2] Abraham, *supra,* at 153-55, also suggests that a requirement of sudden onset—as distinguished from a requirement of limited duration—might help to control moral hazard. His argument seems to be that a sudden onset, or "boom," alerts all to the occurrence of the discharge and thus allows the insurer to enforce a duty to mitigate on the part of the insured. In contrast, when a discharge begins gradually it will be difficult to enforce any duty to mitigate, and that duty will be subject to moral hazard. A requirement of sudden onset might help to control this moral hazard problem. *Id.* We are somewhat skeptical of this analysis. First, enforcement of a duty to mitigate would seem to require complex knowledge about a wide range of factors other than simply the onset of the discharge, such as the costs and benefits of each possible corrective measure. Second, even in terms of identifying the onset, we suspect that in many cases the insured's failure to take action in response to a discharge that begins with a whimper rather than a bang would be due to its ignorance of the event rather than to its shirking the duty to mitigate. If the set of cases in which insureds would fail to mitigate gradually-beginning discharges of which they are aware is small, then coverage of harms resulting from such discharges would not create any significant moral hazard problem.

resonates with the discussion of moral hazard above, and thus supports rather than undermines the *General Dynamics* result: It seems to us that the risk to the insurer would be the same, whether a break was instantaneous or began with a crack which developed over a period of time until the final cleavage occurred, as long as its progress was undetectable [sic]. On the other hand, the insured should not be permitted to proceed recklessly and hold the insurer liable for damage if it had been forewarned of a possible break and could have taken steps to forestall it or avoid an interruption of business resulting therefrom. *Anderson & Middleton Lumber Co. v. Lumbermen's Mutual Casualty Co.*, 53 Wash. 2d 404, 333 P.2d 938, 940-41 (1959) (emphasis added). The court thus saw a relationship between abruptness and the insured's lack of capacity to prevent an accident but failed to notice that an independent requirement of abruptness might serve the parties' basic goals. In short, the boiler and machinery policy precedents provide almost no support for Charter's preferred analysis.

2. Latent Ambiguity.

Charter argues that even if "sudden and accidental" is not facially ambiguous, the insurers' prior claims behavior and representations made to state insurance regulators reveal a latent ambiguity in the phrase. Latent ambiguity can arise where language, clear on its face, fails to resolve an uncertainty when juxtaposed with circumstances in the world that the language is supposed to govern. *See AM Int'l, Inc. v. Graphic Management, Inc.*, 44 F.3d 572, 575 (7th Cir. 1995). Thus, for example, the contract in *Raffles v. Wichelhaus*, 2 H. & C. 906, 159 Eng. Rep. 375 (Ex.1864), which called for the shipment of goods on the ship Peerless, was "[c]lear as a boll" on its face, 44 F.3d at 575, but desperately ambiguous when it turned out there were two or more ships of that name. Evidence of the state of the world to which a contract is to be applied is necessarily admissible to reveal a latent ambiguity, as Missouri courts clearly recognize. Once the latent ambiguity is thus established, a broader range of extrinsic evidence may be admitted to resolve it, including (in Missouri) otherwise inadmissible evidence of the circumstances surrounding the parties' entry into the contract, and of the behavior of the parties with respect to similar contracts. While we do not read these cases as indicating that Missouri allows such a broad range of extrinsic evidence to establish an ambiguity, we will assume it does, for even under that assumption Charter's extrinsic evidence is inadequate.

Charter first points to evidence of the payment by certain (unspecified) defendants of the initial claims against Charter and its affiliates arising out of Bliss's spraying. The insurers paid, in aggregate, $2.8 million, a tiny fraction of Charter's ultimate liability. J.A. 999. Charter argues that the payment of the initial claims places a practical construction on the parties' agreement, one that the defendants are not now free to ignore. The defendants respond that the decision by an individual claims representative to pay a single claim or a small number of claims should not, without more, bind the insurer to an interpretation under which the insured is covered for all similar claims. (A fortiori, one insurer's claims behavior should not bind other insurers.) We agree with the defendants. A contrary holding would require that an insurer, before paying modest claims such as the initial claims by Charter here, conduct an investigation in far greater depth than the amount at stake would justify, simply to avoid the risk of massive exposure down the road. . . .

The second sort of extrinsic evidence proffered by Charter concerns representations made to insurance regulators (and contemporaneous internal memoranda) regarding the scope of the pollution exclusion. Again we assume that such evidence might in some circumstances establish a latent ambiguity in the pollution exclusion, but we find that none of the evidence proffered rises to the level of suggesting material inconsistency between the representations or internal memoranda and the policy language as interpreted in *General Dynamics*.

In this category Charter points first to the insurers' representation that the newly introduced pollution exclusion merely "clarified" existing coverage. The insurers stated in various fora that because damages from pollution tended to be expected or intended and thus excluded from coverage by virtue of the threshold requirement for coverage under standard occurrence policies, the effect of the pollution exclusion was merely to "clarif[y] th[e] situation so as to avoid any question of intent." J.A. 5067F; see also J.A. 5024-5025 (testimony of David E. Kuizenga) (interpreting insurers' explanation of the pollution exclusion); J.A. 5069A-5069B (testimony of James C. Schmitt) (stating that a coverage-reducing exclusion would have encountered substantial regulatory resistance in Missouri in 1970). According to Charter, this evidence demonstrates that the "sudden and accidental" language in the pollution exclusion, even if clear on its face, was not interpreted or understood to impose conditions beyond the traditional "unexpected and unintended" requirement. But the addition of "clarifying" language necessarily implies some element of change; presumably some cases, whose classification was in doubt before the change, can afterwards be classified with certainty. Moreover, in the context of insurance policies, where ambiguous language is construed against the insurer, a clarification that yields any wins for the insurer (out of the set of formerly ambiguous cases) represents a slight curtailment of the former theoretically available coverage. And here the emphasis is properly on theoretical availability. The record evidence, undisputed by Charter, shows that pollution claims were far less common and far less broad in scope in the era in which the pollution exclusion was drafted than they are today. *e.g.*, Supplemental Appendix at 414 (affidavit of Frank Ovaitt). Furthermore, as we noted above, the classic image of pollution in that era was the steady emission of pollutants into the air or a stream, not the kind of ground contamination that CERCLA and parallel developments made crucial. See, *e.g.*, J.A. 2128, 2174, 2176 (script of speech delivered November 11, 1965 by the Secretary of the Hartford Insurance Co., entitled "Implications of Coverage for Gradual Injury or Damage" (1965)) (using, as an illustration of gradual harm, "the discharge of corrosive material into the atmosphere or watercourses"). Against this backdrop, the insurers' statement that damages from pollution tended to be expected or intended and thus exempt from coverage under standard occurrence policies seems entirely plausible. While the expansion of liability for environmental harm in subsequent decades may have greatly increased the scope of "pollution damages" and reduced the likelihood of such damages being expected or intended, these later developments cannot convert the insurers' 1970 statements into misrepresentations.

Charter likewise fails to show how an internal statement by Aetna's in-house counsel, expressing reluctance to concede any reduction in coverage as a result of the pollution exclusion, supports the conclusion that the insurers' representations to regulators were deceptive. The counsel stated that Aetna did not want to concede any reduction in coverage as a result of the exclusion "because this is tantamount to admitting that all such cases are now covered, whereas some of them may not be covered." J.A. 5060. Though the meaning is obscure, it appears quite consistent with the insurers' position that the language change was one of clarification. Charter also points to a statement by the Aetna counsel that "[t]here may be a hue and cry because there will be no reduction in premium, despite the fact that coverage would appear to be cut back. . . ." *Id.* This statement appears in a list of "industry public relations" issues related to the filing of the pollution exclusion, and it is immediately followed by the statement that Aetna did not want to concede any reduction in coverage. Charter has not explained how an industry public relations concern about coverage "appear[ing]"—most plausibly to insurance regulators or policyholders—to be cut back is inconsistent with the representation of the exclusion as a "clarification" of existing coverage. Further, no premium reduction would have been likely for a linguistic change "for an exclusion where there was little or no loss experience" because of the limited scope of pollution liability at the time the exclusion was developed. Ovaitt Affidavit, Supplemental Appendix at 414.

Charter points finally to statements appearing in what it calls "insurance industry" publications, such as an item in the May 1971 issue of F.C. & S. Bulletins. See J.A. 2136, 2425-26. Without some reason to believe that any of the defendants is responsible for these statements—and Charter provides none—they appear to be only the view of some third party. Even if they provided an unequivocal reading of the pollution exception—and they don't— Charter does not explain why we should regard them as material.

Closely related to Charter's latent ambiguity contention is its argument that the insurers' statements to regulators require the court to strike down the exclusion (as interpreted in *General Dynamics*) on grounds of public policy. The district court rejected Charter's argument, relying again on *General Dynamics*, which the district court described as "implicitly reject[ing]" an analogous argument explicitly made by the insured in that case. *Independent Petrochemical Corp.*, 842 F. Supp. at 582. But since the *General Dynamics* court did not explicitly address the public policy argument, it cannot clearly be said to have made a "reasoned inquiry" into Missouri law on the subject, as required for deference under *Abex*. See 790 F.2d at 125.

Charter has not pointed to any articulated policy of the Missouri legislature or the Missouri courts calling for judicial invalidation of contracts on the type of grounds urged by Charter, i.e., alleged misconduct of insurers before state regulators, as opposed to a substantive conflict between state public policy and a contract's terms. It is conceivable, of course, that Missouri courts would accept such a theory. We find it unnecessary to decide whether they would as a general matter, however, because Charter has failed to establish any convincing inconsistency between the representations and the language of the pollution exclusion as interpreted in General Dynamics.

B. "Suddenness" of Bliss's Discharge.

Because the pollution exclusion as interpreted in *General Dynamics* denies coverage unless the discharge of pollutants is abrupt, we must determine whether Bliss's discharge of dioxin-contaminated oil satisfied this requirement. Clearly, if the discharge is defined as the aggregate of Bliss's oil-spraying activities, then it was not abrupt; Charter concedes that the spraying took place over a period of at least two months. It argues that each spraying session, taking about 30-40 minutes, should be viewed as a distinct discharge, and that, so viewed, the discharges were abrupt. The logical consequence of this argument, however, is that spraying in, say, 30-minute increments over a two-month period with five-minute breaks between each increment would satisfy the suddenness requirement, whereas constant spraying over the same two-month period would not. We cannot conceive of any sensible basis for such a distinction. As Charter itself acknowledges, the rationale for excluding coverage when the polluting activity is undertaken repeatedly in the course of ordinary business operations is that the resulting harm is less likely than otherwise to be unexpected and unintended. As our discussion of moral hazard above suggests, suddenness serves as a proxy for harm that is truly unexpected and unintended, and the presence or absence of periodic breaks in an activity occurring over an extended period has little or no bearing on that likelihood. Thus we see no basis for disaggregating the spraying sessions.

As noted above, suddenness is only a proxy for harm that is unexpected and unintended, and here Charter presumably neither expected nor intended the harm that resulted from Bliss's spraying. Again, however, the inevitable imperfections in a proxy's fit are no basis for refusing to apply it. Thus we conclude that Bliss's discharge of dioxin-contaminated oil was not "sudden."

C. Coverage under the Travelers Policies.

As we mentioned at the start, the policies issued by defendant Travelers did not contain the "sudden and accidental" language but instead preserved coverage for discharges that were neither "expected" nor "intended." As to those policies the duration of Bliss's spraying activity does not bar coverage. Rather, Charter should recover if the discharge of the dioxin-contaminated oil was neither expected nor intended. The district court treated this requirement as identical to the "accidental" requirement in the other policies, *Independent Petrochemical Corp.*, 842 F. Supp. at 577, 584-85 & n. 14, and Charter does not dispute that characterization on appeal.

The district court ruled that Bliss's discharge was not accidental, 842 F. Supp. at 584-85, citing significant case authority in support of that view, though no cases from Missouri itself. Charter did not dispute the district court's ruling in its opening brief, and, perhaps as a result, the defendants' briefs devoted only fairly limited attention to the issue. Charter's reply brief addressed the issue quite seriously, arguing that the discharge was accidental under Missouri law because Bliss was unaware that the material he was discharging contained dioxin. Even then, Charter was unable to adduce any Missouri case from which its proposed conclusion would follow inescapably. Because Charter's strategy may well have "sandbagg[ed]" the insurers by denying them any chance to respond to the specifics of Charter's argument, we deem the issue waived.

. . . .

The district court's grant of summary judgment for the defendants is

Affirmed.

NOTES

1. *The origin of the 1973 exclusion.* When the CGL was modified in 1966 to cover "occurrences," the term "occurrence" was defined as "an accident, including continuous or repeated exposure to conditions." This change made clear the policy's purpose to cover not just sudden, unexpected events but also long-term exposures to harmful conditions or substances which caused damage during the policy's term. Given this expansion of coverage in 1966, it would seem that the emergence of the pollution exclusion in 1973 was either an effort to constrict coverage or to make the policy's coverage conform to what the industry intended when occurrence-based coverage was created in 1966. The language of the 1973 exclusion at least implies that the exclusion was designed to remove coverage for releases of pollutants which were not "sudden and accidental." Whether this was the purpose of the exclusion has been much debated; in any event, the meaning of "sudden and accidental" has been much debated as well. For a succinct history of the evolution of the pollution exclusion, *see American States Insurance Co. v. Koloms,* 177 Ill.2d 473, 687 N.E.2d 72, 79-81 (1997).

2. *Three questions.* The first question that must be asked and answered is whether there has been an "occurrence." If there has been no occurrence, there is no coverage, so the question of the exclusion's relevance or applicability will not arise. Was there an "occurrence" in *Charter Oil?* How could there be an "accident" when intentional spraying was involved?

The second question is whether the exclusion applies, i.e., was the injury or damage caused by one of the named materials in connection with one of the four events (i.e., discharge, dispersal, release, or escape).

If the exclusion applies, a third question must be considered: does the exception to the exclusion apply? That is, was the event "sudden and accidental"? If so, there is coverage, and the exclusion does not apply. If not, there is no coverage because, although an "occurrence" occurred, the exclusion vitiates the coverage.

3. *Sudden and accidental.* For the exception to the exclusion to apply, must the actual movement of the pollutant be "sudden and accidental," or must the harm or damage be "sudden and accidental"? Why would this matter? Does "sudden" have a clear meaning apart from the word "accidental"? If the phrase is ambiguous, what result should follow? In *CPC International, Inc. v. Northbrook Excess and Surplus Insurance Co.,* 144 F.3d 35 (1st Cir. 1998), a railroad engineer moved a group of railroad tank cars while one of them was still attached to a chemical storage tank at a Rhode Island manufacturing faciltity. A hole was torn in the bottom of the tank; the 6,200 gallons of perchlorethylene ("perc") gushed out and bored a four-foot hole in the ground. Five years later, drinking water wells in the vicinity were found to be

contaminated with a variety of perc and perc-related chemicals. The court distinguished *Charter Oil*, indicating that the railroad car accident was "not an instance of attempting to parse a sequence of events in regular polluting activities into component parts and then arguing whether each part is sudden and accidental. Rather, there was a massive, sudden and accidental event in the perc spill and it was up to the jury to decide whether that, or the ongoing pollution, led to the property damage for which indemnification is sought." 144 F.3d at 48. A jury verdict for the insured was affirmed on appeal.

Courts have divided over the significance and meaning of the exception to the exclusion. Compare *New Castle County. v. Hartford Accident & Indemnity Co.,* 933 F.2d 1162 (3d Cir. 1991) (applying Delaware law); *Queen City Farms, Inc. v. Central National Insurance Co.,* 882 P.2d 703 (Wash. 1994)(en banc), with *Mustang Tractor & Equipment Co. v. Liberty Mutual Insurance Co.,* 76 F.3d 89 (1996)(applying Texas law); *Aetna Casualty & Surety Co. v. General Dynamics Corp.,* 968 F.2d 707 (8th Cir. 1992) (applying Missouri law); *Ray Industries, Inc. v. Liberty Mutual Insurance Co.,* 974 F.2d 754 (6th Cir. 1992) (applying Michigan law). But the weight of authority in the recent cases is more sympathetic to the position taken in *Charter Oil.*

4. *Drafting history.* Was the court correct to consider statements made by industry officials at or near the time the 1973 exclusion was drafted and included in policies? Is drafting history even relevant to interpreting standardized forms? Why should industry interpretations of policy language carry *any* weight in setting the contours of coverage? Is what the industry has reason to think insureds would understand more important? How does the parol evidence rule fit into all of this? *Compare Montrose Chemical Corp. v. Admiral Insurance Co.,* 913 P.2d 878 (Cal. 1995)with *Anderson v. Minnesota Insurance Guaranty Ass'n,* 520 N.W.2d 155 (Minn. App. 1994), *rev'd on other grounds,* 534 N.W.2d 706 (Minn. 1995). The court in *Charter Oil* was not particularly impressed with the insured's argument that the insurance industry had misrepresented the nature of the exclusion when it was presented for regulatory approval in the early 1970s. For a different view on this history, *see Morton International, Inc. v. General Accident Insurance Co. of Am.,* 629 A.2d 831, 876 (N.J. 1993), *cert. denied,* 512 U.S. 1245 (1994).

5. *The industry's response.* Millions of dollars have been spent on attorney's fees to litigate the meaning of the 1973 pollution exclusion. Can it be surprising, then, that the industry would introduce a new exclusion? The 1973 exclusion will, however, continue to receive much attention in coverage litigation well into the next century. Why? As time marches on, however, the newer exclusion, which appeared in the 1986 CGL revision (and which has undergone some modifications since), will be invoked in many more situations. Consider, for example, the next case.

STONEY RUN CO. v. PRUDENTIAL-LMI COMMERCIAL INSURANCE CO.

47 F.3d 34 (2d Cir. 1995)

Altimari, Circuit Judge:

Plaintiffs-appellants Stoney Run Company and Larrymore Organization (collectively, "Plaintiffs") appeal from a judgment of the United States District Court for the Northern District of New York (McAvoy, J.), granting defendant-appellee Prudential-LMI Commercial Insurance Company's ("Prudential") motion to dismiss two claims for relief in Plaintiffs' complaint. Plaintiffs sought a declaration that Prudential was obliged to defend and/or indemnify them in connection with three civil actions filed against Plaintiffs for damages due to carbon monoxide poisoning in their apartment buildings. The district court dismissed the two claims for relief on the grounds that they fell unambiguously within a "pollution exclusion" clause contained in the policies issued by Prudential to Plaintiffs. Because we conclude that under New York law, the pollution exclusion clause at issue does not unambiguously apply to the underlying civil actions, we reverse the judgment of the district court.

BACKGROUND

Stoney Run Company is a partnership that owns the Stoney Run Apartments, a real estate complex in Kingston, New York. Larrymore Organization is a Virginia corporation that acts as the real estate agent for Stoney Run. Prudential issued two general commercial liability policies to Plaintiffs in connection with the Stoney Run Apartments. During the effective dates of these policies, several tenants at the Stoney Run Apartments were killed or injured by the inhalation of carbon monoxide emitted into their apartments due to a faulty heating and ventilation system.

Subsequently, three civil actions were commenced against Plaintiffs by the injured persons or their legal representatives [for death or injury due to defendant's negligence.] . . . .

Prudential declined to defend or provide coverage for [two of the actions, the Gruner and Schomer claims]. . . . Prudential relied on the following exclusion clause contained in its policies:

> This insurance does not apply to: (f)(1) "Bodily injury" or "property damage" arising out of the actual, alleged or threatened discharge, dispersal, release or escape of pollutants: (a) [a]t or from premises you own, rent or occupy[.] Pollutants means any solid, liquid, gaseous or thermal irritant or contaminant, including smoke, vapor, soot, fumes, acids, alkalis, chemicals and waste. Waste includes materials to be recycled, reconditioned or reclaimed.

This clause (hereinafter the "pollution exclusion clause") is a standard industry clause used in general commercial liability policies.

. . . .

Plaintiffs now appeal the district court's dismissal of the claims for relief in their complaint relating to the [two] actions.

DISCUSSION

The sole issue on appeal is whether the claims for relief alleged in the [two] actions fall unambiguously within the pollution exclusion clause under New York law. Prudential argues that the district court correctly held that the injuries caused by carbon monoxide poisoning clearly fell within the pollution exclusion clause: there was a "discharge, dispersal, release or escape" of carbon monoxide, a "pollutant," "at or from the premises" owned by Plaintiffs. Plaintiffs, on the other hand, contend that the district court should have considered the purpose of the pollution exclusion clause in determining whether or not the clause was subject to another reasonable interpretation. The purpose of this standard clause, Plaintiffs maintain, is to exclude coverage only for environmental pollution, not damages due to routine commercial hazards such as a faulty heating and ventilation system. We conclude that the pollution exclusion clause at issue is ambiguous as applied to the [two] actions because it is reasonable to interpret that clause as applying only to environmental pollution.

We review de novo the district court's grant of Prudential's motion to dismiss. Under New York law, an insurer's duty to defend is "exceedingly broad." An insurer must defend a claim whenever the complaint suggests a reasonable possibility of coverage, regardless of the merits of the action. *See Fitzpatrick v. American Honda Motor Co.,* 78 N.Y.2d 61, 571 N.Y.S.2d 672, 673-74, 575 N.E.2d 90, 91-92 (1991).

An insurer, however, may negate coverage by virtue of an exclusionary clause if the insurer establishes that the clause "is stated in clear and unmistakable language, is subject to no other reasonable interpretation, and applies in the particular case." *Continental Casualty Co. v. Rapid-American Corp.,* 80 N.Y.2d 640, 593 N.Y.S.2d 966, 972, 609 N.E.2d 506, 512 (1993). When construing an insurance policy, the tests applied are "common speech" and the "reasonable expectation and purpose of the ordinary businessman." *Ace Wire & Cable Co. v. Aetna Casualty & Surety Co.,* 60 N.Y.2d 390, 469 N.Y.S.2d 655, 658, 457 N.E.2d 761, 764 (1983). Any ambiguity is to be construed against the insurer, particularly when the ambiguity is in an exclusionary clause. An exclusionary clause, moreover, can be ambiguous in one context and not in another.

As a threshold matter, we believe that it is appropriate to construe the standard pollution exclusion clause in light of its general purpose, which is to exclude coverage for environmental pollution. New York courts have consistently considered this purpose in determining whether an insurer is obliged to defend. In *Continental Casualty,* for example, the Court of Appeals considered an insurer's duty to defend actions for personal injuries suffered by assorted contractors who were exposed to asbestos products. The pollution exclusion clause before the court, which differs slightly from the one we now consider, applied to the discharge, dispersal, release, or escape of irritants, contaminants, or pollutants "into or upon land, the atmosphere or any water course or body of water." The court held that the pollution exclusion clause did not apply, stating that the term "atmosphere" was ambiguous as applied to the inhalation of asbestos. See 593 N.Y.S.2d at 972-73, 609 N.E.2d at 512-13. The court then noted that "[a]mbiguity is further revealed by examining the purpose of the clause, meant to exclude coverage for environmental pollution." *Id.* at 973, 609 N.E.2d at 513. In addition, the court stated that terms such as "discharge" and "dispersal" were terms of art of environmental law used in reference to injuries caused by "disposal or containment of hazardous waste." *Id.*

Subsequent decisions of New York courts have also construed pollution exclusion clauses as applying only to environmental pollution. For example, in *Karroll v. Atomergic Chemetals Corp.,* 194 A.D.2d 715, 600 N.Y.S.2d 101 (1993), the court held that the pollution exclusion clause did not apply to injuries suffered by a bulldozer operator who was accidentally sprayed with sulfuric acid. In so holding, the court stated that the clause could be "reasonably interpreted to apply only to instances of environmental pollution." *Id.,* 600 N.Y.S.2d at 102.

Prudential claims that *Continental Casualty* is inapplicable because that decision interpreted a different pollution exclusion clause. In contrast, Prudential argues, the clause in this case refers more broadly to the discharge of pollutants at or from the premises owned by the insured. *See Oates v. State of New York,* 157 Misc. 2d 618, 597 N.Y.S.2d 550, 553 (Ct. Cl. 1993)(injuries suffered by child due to insured's negligent failure to remove lead paint from apartment falls within pollution exclusion clause; court notes that "only reasonable interpretation [of clause] is that it 'is just what it purports to be — absolute' ") (citations omitted). We reject this argument.

Although the Court of Appeals in *Continental Casualty* did base its decision in part on the ambiguous term "atmosphere," it also clearly relied on the general purpose of the pollution exclusion clause. Moreover, in its discussion of this purpose, the Court of Appeals relied on two decisions construing pollution exclusion clauses nearly identical to the clause in the case at bar. *See West Am. Ins. Co. v. Tufco Flooring East, Inc.,* 104 N.C. App. 312, 409 S.E.2d 692, 699 (1991) (court concludes that change in language of pollution exclusion clause was not intended "to expand the scope of the clause to nonenvironmental damage" and that "a discharge into the environment is necessary for the clause to be applicable"); *Atlantic Mut. Ins. Co. v. McFadden,* 413 Mass. 90, 595 N.E.2d 762, 764 (1992) ("We conclude that an insured could reasonably have understood the provision at issue to exclude coverage for injury caused by certain forms of industrial pollution, but not coverage for injury allegedly caused by the presence of leaded materials in a private residence.").

Prudential also argues that *Continental Casualty* and the cases Plaintiffs rely upon are distinguishable because the alleged damages in those cases resulted from direct contact with useful products, such as asbestos, chemicals, or lead paint, intentionally placed into areas where they caused harm. By contrast, Prudential argues, carbon monoxide is a toxic byproduct without a useful purpose that unintentionally was released into the Stoney Run Apartments.

Even if several of the cases cited by Plaintiffs do involve so-called direct contact with useful products, courts have not focused on this distinction as the basis for their decisions. The issue remains whether the pollution exclusion clause unambiguously includes injuries caused by exposure to carbon monoxide within an apartment. As set forth above, a reasonable interpretation of the pollution exclusion clause is that it applies only to environmental pollution, and not to all contact with substances that can be classified as pollutants. We hold that the release of carbon monoxide into an apartment is not the type of environmental pollution contemplated by the pollution exclusion clause.

An examination of the manner in which other jurisdictions interpret pollution exclusion clauses further bolsters our conclusion that the clause is ambiguous as applied to the facts presented on this appeal. Two courts addressing nearly identical factual situations have deemed pollution exclusion clauses ambiguous. In a recent decision, the United States Court of Appeals for the Tenth Circuit held that a standard pollution exclusion clause did not exclude coverage for injuries tenants sustained due to carbon monoxide emissions from a faulty wall heater. *See Regional Bank of Colo., N.A. v. St. Paul Fire and Marine Ins. Co.,* 35 F.3d 494 (10th Cir. 1994). The court found the exclusion clause ambiguous, reasoning that

> [w]hile a reasonable person of ordinary intelligence might well understand carbon monoxide is a pollutant when it is emitted in an industrial or environmental setting, an ordinary policyholder would not reasonably characterize carbon monoxide emitted from a residential heater which malfunctioned as "pollution." It seems far more reasonable that a policy holder would understand the exclusion as being limited to irritants and contaminants commonly thought of as pollution and not as applying to every possible irritant or contaminant imaginable. *Id.* at 498.

Similarly, another court held that a standard pollution exclusion clause did not apply to injuries caused by carbon monoxide emissions from a leaking gas heater in a home. *See Thompson v. Temple,* 580 So. 2d 1133, 1135 (La. Ct. App. 1991) ("intent of the insurance industry in adding pollution exclusion clauses . . . was to exclude coverage for entities which knowingly pollute the environment over a substantial period of time").

We need not decide the precise scope of the pollution exclusion clause contained in Plaintiffs' policies. Instead, we need only determine whether the clause is ambiguous as applied to the facts of this case and subject to no other reasonable interpretation than the one advanced by Prudential. As noted above, the pollution exclusion clause can be reasonably interpreted as applying only to environmental pollution. A reasonable policyholder might not characterize the escape of carbon monoxide from a faulty residential heating and ventilation system as environmental pollution. Accordingly, we find the pollution exclusion clause ambiguous as applied to the [two] actions.

CONCLUSION

Because the pollution exclusion clause is ambiguous as applied to the facts presented, we reverse the judgment of the district court to the extent that it granted Prudential's motion to dismiss the [two] actions. The district court is directed to enter judgment consistent with this opinion.

NOTES

1. *How absolute is "absolute"?* The pollution exclusion at issue in *Stoney Run* is the version found in the 1986 CGL. How does it differ from the 1973 pollution exclusion? Is its meaning absolutely clear with respect to environmental damage? The answer most courts have given is yes. *See United States Liability Insurance Co. v. Bourbeau,* 49 F.3d 786 (1st Cir. 1995); *Park-Ohio Industries, Inc. v. Home Indemnity Co.,* 975 F.2d 1215 (6th Cir. 1992); *Western World Insurance Co. v. Stack Oil, Inc.,* 922 F.2d 118 (2d Cir. 1990). What if the environmental damage results when a tanker truck carrying toxic materials overturns and a spill results? What if a container of toxic materials falls off a truck and spills? *See Red Panther Chemical Co. v. Insurance Co. of State of Pa.,* 43 F.3d 514 (10th Cir. 1994).

2. *Too broad or too specific?* In one sense, the 1986 exclusion is more specific, in that it takes off the table the difficult "sudden and accidental" issue and it gives a seemingly precise list of items that constitute "pollutants." In another sense, the 1986 exclusion is broader because the sum total of items listed in the definition of "pollutants" represents a fairly large slice of the earth and its atmosphere; for example, lots of things can be an "irritant" in a particular context. Because the exclusion seems to pull in different directions simultaneously, courts have not found it easy to apply in all settings. One court described the situation this way: "Unfortunately, despite the abundance of opinions construing the exclusion, courts have not reached a clear consensus as to its proper interpretation. This is true even within the fairly rare context of carbon monoxide poisoning. Some courts have construed the exclusion in favor of the insured, holding that the exclusion is vague and ambiguous. . . . Other courts, however, have denied coverage on the grounds that the exclusion is plain an unambiguous. . . . Still other courts have largely ignored the language of the exclusion and have found coverage on the basis of the reasonable expectations of the insured. . . . Meanwhile, courts have also considered the exclusion in the context of other types of 'pollutants.' They, too, have failed to achieve a consistent interpretation of the clause." *American States Insurance Co. v. Koloms,* 177 Ill.2d 473, 687 N.E.2d 72, 78 (1997). Although the *Koloms* court ultimately came down on the side of coverage in a situation where tenants suffered carbon monoxide poisoning due to a faulty furnace in their building, a number of courts have disagreed with this position. *See e.g., Assicurazioni Generali v. Neil,* 160 F.3d 997 (4th Cir. 1998) (applying Maryland law; no coverage in case where hotel guests suffered carbon monoxide poisoning); *Longaberger Co. v. United States Fidelity & Guaranty Co.,* 31 F. Supp. 2d 595 (S.D. Ohio 1998), *aff'd,* 201 F.3d 441 (6th Cir. 1999) (table) (no coverage for carbon monoxide poisoning of tenant); *Essex Insurance Co. v. Tri-Town Corp.,* 863 F. Supp. 38 (D. Mass. 1994) (no coverage for injuries from a carbon-monoxide emitting Zamboni machine at hockey game); *Bernhardt v. Hartford Fire Insurance Co.,* 648 A.2d 1047 (Md. Ct. App. 1994), *cert.*

granted (Md. 1995), *appeal dismissed prior to oral argument,* 659 A.2d 296 (Md. 1996) (no coverage for injury to tenants from build-up of carbon monoxide).

Is the kind of liability incurred by the insured in *Stoney Run* the reason the insured purchased liability insurance in the first place? Imagine the same exclusion being included in a homeowners policy; would the insured have a reasonable expectation of coverage if she were sued for negligent maintenance of a basement heater that malfunctioned and caused the death due to carbon monoxide poisoning of an overnight visitor? Would you describe this event as "the guest died in an accident" or "the guest was killed by a pollutant"? *See Western Alliance Insurance Co. v. Gill,* 426 Mass. 115, 686 N.E.2d 997 (1997) (restaurant customer exposed to carbon monoxide fumes released by tandoori ovens at Indian restaurant). Why should the commercial policy be treated differently? Yet if an insured does not like the absolute constriction of coverage required by the strict language of the exclusion and approved by state insurance departments, is the insured's proper recourse to the legislature, which could be asked to ban the absolute exclusion? Is this a good idea? What would you put in its place?

3. *Lead paint and other situations.* Did the court in *Stoney Run* deal with the lead paint cases adequately? Is lead paint contamination distinguishable from carbon monoxide contamination? Courts have divided on the question of whether the chipping, flaking, or deterioration of lead-based paint into dust or fumes is a "discharge, dispersal, release, or escape" within the meaning of the pollution exclusion clause. *See e.g., Peace v. Northwestern National Insurance Co.,* 228 Wis.2d 106, 596 N.W.2d 429 (Wis. 1999) (no coverage; citing cases on both sides); *United States Liability Insurance Co. v. Bourbeau,* 49 F.3d 786 (1st Cir. 1995) (no coverage); *Byrd v. Blumenreich,* 317 N.J.Super. 496, 722 A.2d 598 (1999)(absolute pollution exclusion does not bar coverage for child's ingestion of flaking and peeling lead paint chips).

Exposure to carbon monoxide and dust from lead paint chips are two prominent categories of injury that have prompted debate over the scope of the 1986 pollution exclusion. There are, of course, other examples. *See e.g., Garfield Slope Housing Corp. v. Public Service Mutual Insurance Co.,* 973 F. Supp. 326 (E.D.N.Y. 1997) (alleged injury due to fumes from new hallway carpet in apartment); *Meridian Mutual Insurance Co. v. Kellman,* 197 F.3d 1178 (6th Cir. 1999) (fumes from toxic chemical used by construction contractor to seal floor of school). Should the pollution exclusion's field of operation be confined to "traditional" environmental damage? Does the text of the absolute pollution exclusion forbid this interpretation?

4. *Another approach.* Environmental liabilities are but one, albeit an extremely important, example of "long-tail" claims. A policy written many years ago may be invoked years, even a few decades, later for a currently-assessed liability. Of course, the premiums collected by the insurer years ago are not even close to being sufficient to pay for liabilities imposed presently, particularly when no one could foresee years ago the new kinds of liability that would be imposed. Is this not, however, the reason one purchases liability insurance? Regardless, insurers, particularly in the 1980s, actively marketed the claims-made CGL, the current version of which appears in Appendix B(2).

Many regulators were not enthusiastic, and insureds tended to prefer occurrence coverage. Most CGL policies are now occurrence policies, but one should not discount the possibility of more claims-made coverage being written in the future. Moreover, claims-made coverage remains the norm in several discrete commercial areas, with professional liability insurance (such as lawyers malpractice insurance) being prominent among them. This kind of coverage is explored in more detail in the next subsection, and professional liability policies will provide the grist for this inquiry.

[4] Claims-made Coverage

SPARKS v. ST. PAUL INSURANCE CO.
100 N.J. 325, 495 A.2d 406 (1985)

STEIN, J.

In this case, as in *Zuckerman v. National Union Fire Ins. Co.,* 100 N.J. 304, 495 A.2d 395 (1985), which the Court also decides today, we consider the enforceability of certain coverage limitations contained in a "claims made" professional liability insurance policy issued by appellant St. Paul Insurance Company (St. Paul). The trial court and the Appellate Division refused to enforce the policy provision limiting coverage to claims and potential claims reported to St. Paul during the policy period. We granted the insurance company's petition for certification, 99 N.J. 211, 491 A.2d 706 (1984), in order to resolve the apparent conflict between the unreported Appellate Division decision in this case and the Appellate Division decision in *Zuckerman, supra,* 194 N.J. Super. 206, 476 A.2d 820 (1984), enforcing a similar provision in the "claims made" policy at issue in that case.

I

The material facts are not in dispute. In November, 1978, respondents, John and Carolyn Sparks, retained A. Raymond Guarriello, a New Jersey attorney, to represent them in connection with the sale of their residence. That transaction resulted in litigation between respondents and the prospective purchasers. In the course of that litigation, apparently due to Guarriello's negligence, Mr. and Mrs. Sparks failed to answer interrogatories. This resulted in an order entered in mid-October, 1979, suppressing the Sparks' answer and counterclaim. A default judgment for specific performance was entered against Mr. and Mrs. Sparks in February, 1980, and a money judgment for $18,899.08 was entered against them in May, 1981. It is not disputed that Guarriello's negligence was the proximate cause of the judgments against Mr. and Mrs. Sparks.

On November 6, 1976, appellant, St. Paul, issued Guarriello a one-year professional malpractice policy that was renewed for successive one-year periods, terminating on November 6, 1979. On September 27, 1979, St. Paul issued a substitute policy for one additional year that was to take effect on November 6, 1979. Guarriello failed to pay the premium and appellant sent Guarriello a notice canceling the substitute policy, effective January 21, 1980.

Between June and August of 1980, substituted counsel for respondents notified St. Paul of the underlying facts and demanded that the insurance company provide malpractice coverage with respect to Guarriello's negligence.

The policy issued to Guarriello in 1976 was denominated a "claims made" policy. A "Schedule" attached to the declaration page of the policy bore the following notice:

TO OUR POLICYHOLDERS

This is a "claims made" Coverage Form. It only covers claims arising from the performance of professional services *subsequent to the retroactive date indicated* and then only to claims first made within the provisions of the Policy while this Coverage Form is in force. No coverage is afforded for claims first made after the termination of this insurance unless and to the extent that Reporting Endorsements are purchased in accordance with Condition 3 of this Coverage Form. Please review the Policy carefully. [Emphasis added.]

The retroactive date set forth in the policy was November 6, 1976, the same date as the effective date of coverage. Therefore, unlike the standard "claims made" policy that was involved in our decision in *Zuckerman, supra*, 100 N.J. at 307-309, 495 A.2d 395, St. Paul's policy provided no retroactive coverage whatsoever during its first year. In that year, the coverage provided by the policy applied only to errors and omissions that occurred during the policy year and were reported to the company within the policy year. During the two renewal years beginning November 6, 1977 and November 6, 1978, the policy afforded "retroactive" coverage for negligence that occurred subsequent to November 6, 1976.

In April, 1981, St. Paul rejected respondent's demand that it provide coverage for Guarriello's malpractice since the company received notice of the claim after the termination of the second renewal policy in November, 1979 and after the January, 1980 cancellation of the replacement policy for nonpayment of the premium.[1] In June, 1981, Mr. and Mrs. Sparks obtained a $42,968.08 judgment against Guarriello based upon his malpractice.

The present action commenced in October, 1981. Mr. and Mrs. Sparks sought a declaratory judgment that the liability insurance policy issued by St. Paul was valid and enforceable to pay the judgment obtained against Guarriello. In August, 1983, St. Paul's motion for summary judgment was denied and in September, 1983, summary judgment was granted in favor of Mr. and Mrs. Sparks. That judgment was affirmed by the Appellate Division, which held "claims made" policies to be unenforceable as violative of public policy.

II

In our decision in *Zuckerman, supra*, 100 N.J. at 309-313, 495 A.2d at 398-400, we summarized the origins of "claims made" or "discovery" liability

---

[1] Although St. Paul's Notice of Cancellation stated that it would be effective January 21, 1980, the insurance company now maintains that its effect was to cancel the replacement policy *ab initio* as of November 6, 1979. As discussed *infra* at 415-416 & n. 5, the effective date of the cancellation is not material.

policies and emphasized the distinction between such policies and the more traditional "occurrence" policies. That distinction warrants reiteration in view of the unusual provisions of the policy issued to Guarriello by St. Paul:

> [T]here are two types of Errors and Omissions Policies: the "discovery" policy and the "occurrence" policy. In a discovery policy the coverage is effective if the negligent or omitted act is discovered and brought to the attention of the insurance company during the period of the policy, no matter when the act occurred. In an occurrence policy the coverage is effective if the negligent or omitted act occurred during the period of the policy, whatever the date of discovery.

[*Samuel N. Zarpas, Inc. v. Morrow,* 215 F. Supp. 887, 888 (D.N.J. 1963).]

Another court characterized "claims made" policies as "provid[ing] unlimited retroactive coverage and no prospective coverage at all," as distinguished from "occurrence" policies which "provide unlimited prospective coverage and no retroactive coverage at all." *Brander v. Nabors,* 443 F. Supp. 764, 767 (N.D. Miss.), *aff'd,* 579 F.2d 888 (5th Cir. 1978).

The distinction between the two types of policies has also been described in terms of the peril insured:

> In the "occurrence" policy, the peril insured is the "occurrence" itself. Once the "occurrence" takes place, coverage attaches even though the claim may not be made for some time thereafter. While in the "claims made" policy, it is the making of the claim which is the event and peril being insured and, subject to policy language, regardless of when the occurrence took place.

[S. Kroll, "The Professional Liability Policy 'Claims Made,'" 13 Forum 842, 843 (1978).]

In *Zuckerman, supra,* 100 N.J. at 311-313, 495 A.2d at 399, we discussed in detail the significant social utility of the "claims made" policy that has led to its supplanting the occurrence policy in the professional liability field. We noted that since the insurance company that issues an "occurrence" policy is exposed to a "tail"—that is, the lapse of time between the occurrence and the date on which the claim is made—there is considerable difficulty in accurately calculating underwriting risks and premiums with respect to perils that typically lead to long tail exposure. Moreover, claims asserted in the fields of professional malpractice, products liability, and environmental law often present the added difficulty of determining precisely when the actuating event "occurred" for the purpose of defining coverage. From the standpoint of the insured, there is the danger of inadequate coverage in cases in which claims are asserted long after the error or omission occurred, because inflationary factors lead to judgments that are higher than those originally contemplated when coverage was purchased years earlier.

From the insurer's perspective, the clear advantage derived from a "claims made" policy is the limitation of liability to claims asserted during the policy period. This limitation enables insurers to calculate risks and premiums with greater precision. Although "claims made" policies provide coverage for errors and omissions occurring prior to the policy's inception, the elimination of exposure to claims filed after the policy expiration date enables companies to issue these policies at reduced premiums. J. Parker, "The Untimely Demise of the 'Claims Made' Insurance Form? A Critique of *Stine v. Continental Casualty Co.*," 1983 Det. C.L. Rev. 25, 73.

In *Zuckerman,* we observed that Courts throughout the country have upheld the validity of "claims made" policies. Although "claims made" policies have regularly been challenged on public policy grounds, the vast majority of courts that have considered these challenges have enforced the policies as written. [2]

The courts that have declined to enforce "claims made" policies have based their decisions on special factual circumstances. *J.G. Link & Co. v. Continental Cas. Co.,* 470 F.2d 1133 (9th Cir. 1972), *cert. denied,* 414 U.S. 829, 94 S. Ct. 55, 38 L. Ed. 2d 63 (1973) (policy covered claims made during policy period but due to certain ambiguities in policy language, court could not determine if policy was intended to provide "occurrence" or "claims made" coverage); *Gyler v. Mission Ins. Co.,* 10 Cal. 3d 216, 514 P. [2d] 1219, 110 Cal. Rptr. 139, (1973) (policy insuring against "claims which *may* be made" during the policy period found to be too ambiguous to allow enforcement of "claims made" coverage limitation) (emphasis added).

We also reviewed in *Zuckerman, supra*, the commercial utility of "claims made" policies and scrutinized the terms of the policy at issue in that case. We concluded that there were "no considerations of public policy that would inhibit . . . enforcement of the 'claims made' policy issued to appellant [Zuckerman]." Similarly, we would not hesitate to enforce St. Paul's policy in this case if it comported with the generally accepted expectations of "claims made" insurance. The coverage provided by St. Paul's policy, however, materially diverges from customary "claims made" coverage in terms of its retroactive protection. It provides neither the prospective coverage typical of an "occurrence" policy, nor the retroactive coverage typical of a "claims made" policy. During the first policy year, coverage was limited to acts of malpractice that occurred, were discovered, and were reported to the insurance company during the same year. Although there was slight retroactive coverage during the second and third renewal years of the policy, the retroactive coverage was significantly more limited than that contemplated in the standard "claims made" policy.

III

Jones v. Continental Cas. Co., 123 N.J. Super. 353, 303 A.2d 91 (Ch. Div. 1973), is the only reported case in which a "claims made" policy was invalidated because of its lack of retroactive coverage. Jones was a professional engineer who was insured against errors and omissions under a policy that took effect in February, 1965, and was renewed annually until its termination in April, 1970. In August, 1971, a contractor sued Jones for malpractice based upon engineering services he had performed during the policy period. Jones' insurance carrier declined coverage because it did not receive notification of the claim during the policy period. Jones, seeking to compel coverage, sued the carrier.

---

[2] For a more complete list of cases enforcing "claims made" policies, see *Zuckerman, supra,* 100 N.J. 313-314, 495 A.2d at 400.

The retroactive coverage provided for in Jones' policy was unusual in that it was limited "to errors, omissions or negligent acts which occur[red] . . . prior to the effective date of this policy *if . . . insured by this Company under [a] prior policy.*" *Id.* at 356, 303 A.2d 91 (emphasis added). The court concluded that this retroactive coverage impermissibly inhibited plaintiff's freedom of contract because he would be deprived of coverage if he did not continue to renew his policy with the same insurance company. The court also held that the total absence of prospective coverage violated this State's public policy in favor of extending time for making a claim or bringing suit for latent injuries. Accordingly, the court declined to enforce the coverage limitations in defendant's policy, concluding, on public policy grounds, that such limitations were inconsistent with the plaintiff's "reasonable expectations" of coverage and that plaintiff's notice to defendant was sufficiently timely to invoke coverage under the policy.

Other state and federal courts confronted with "claims made" policies providing limited or no retroactive coverage have declined to follow *Jones.*[3] But at least one proponent of "claims made" policies has acknowledged the unique limitations of the coverage afforded by the "claims made" policy in *Jones:*

> Indeed, the *Jones* [*sic*] policy was peculiarly narrow in its coverage; it required the insured to have been covered by prior policies issued *only* by the insurer as a condition precedent to being covered for errors and omissions accruing prior to the effective date of the policy. . . . Consequently, because the insured did not have prior policies with CNA, the *Jones* policy afforded the insured coverage only for acts occurring during the term of insurance and then only if the policy was maintained; in effect, it only provided "occurrence" coverage without the prospective benefits of the same.

[J. Parker, *supra,* 1983 Det. C.L. Rev. at 36 n. 38.]

Similarly, in *Brander v. Nabors, supra,* 443 F. Supp. 764, a federal district court in Mississippi considered a "claims made" policy that provided no retroactive coverage but afforded prospective coverage for a three-year period beyond the policy expiration date. Although, in the context of that policy, the court found no necessity for retroactive protection, it conceded that a more significant problem would be presented by a policy affording neither prospective nor retroactive coverage:

> We would be confronted with a more serious question of public policy if a "claims made" policy with neither a period of retroactive coverage nor a period of prospective coverage, but requiring notice to the insured within the policy period, were involved; in that event, the insurance coverage would be effective only for the time premiums are paid, and during which notice of the claim would have to be given to the insurer. Such a policy would necessitate closer scrutiny from the

---

[3] The cases rejecting *Jones* reasoned that because unambiguous provisions of the policies clearly restricted retroactive coverage, and premiums were presumably reduced to reflect the limited protection, there was no basis on which to invalidate the limitations on coverage. Other cases have enforced "claims made" policies that afforded significantly limited or no retroactive coverage without expressly discussing that issue.

standpoint of what period of coverage is reasonable in light of public policy. That precise issue is, however, not before us, and we express no opinion as to the validity of a policy structured on such narrow grounds.

[*Id.*, 443 F. Supp. at 773.]

IV

Although it is a well-established principle that insurance contracts will not be enforced if they violate public policy, the application of that principle has been limited in order that freedom of contract is not impaired unreasonably:

> "[P]ublic policy" is that principle of law which holds that "no person can lawfully do that which has a tendency to be injurious to the public or against public good . . ." even though "no actual injury" may have resulted therefrom in a particular case "to the public." It is a question of law which the court must decide in light of the particular circumstances of each case.
>
> . . . .
>
> . . . Men of "full age and competent understanding" have the "utmost liberty of contracting." Contracts so freely and voluntarily made, in the absence of express or implied prohibition, are sacred and are enforced by courts of justice. And courts do "not lightly interfere with this freedom of contract." Lord Jessel, in *Printing Registering Co. v. Sampson,* 19 Eq. 462, 465; 21 E.R. Co. 696, 699 (cited in *Driver v. Smith, supra ([89 N.J. Eq.] at p. 359 [104 A. 717]). Or in the words of the late Mr. Justice Butler, "The principle that contracts in contravention of public policy are not enforceable should be applied with caution and only in cases plainly within the reasons on which the doctrine rests." Twin City Pipe Line Co. v. Harding Glass Co., supra, 283 U.S. 353 (at p. 356 [51 S. Ct. 476, at p. 477, 75 L. Ed. 1112 (1931)]); 75 L. Ed. 1116.*

[*Allen v. Commercial Cas. Ins. Co., supra,* 131 N.J.L. at 477-478, 37 A.2d 37.]

The doctrine that courts do not lightly interfere with freedom of contract must be applied cautiously and realistically with regard to complex contracts of insurance, since such contracts are highly technical, extremely difficult to understand, and not subject to bargaining over the terms. They are contracts of adhesion, prepared unilaterally by the insurer, and have always been subjected to careful judicial scrutiny to avoid injury to the public.

For example, in *Gaunt v. John Hancock Mut. Life Ins. Co.,* 160 F.2d 599 (2d Cir.), *cert. denied,* 331 U.S. 849, 67 S. Ct. 1736, 91 L. Ed. 1858 (1947), Judge Learned Hand rejected an insurance company's contention that the language set forth on a receipt for a life insurance premium postponed commencement of coverage until the insurer approved the application:

> An underwriter might so understand the phrase, when read in its context, but the application was not to be submitted to underwriters; it was to go to persons utterly unacquainted with the niceties of life insurance, who would read it colloquially. It is the understanding of such persons that counts; and not one in a hundred would suppose

that he would be covered, not "as of the date of completion of Part B," as the defendant promised, but only as of the date of approval.

[*Id.* at 601 (footnote omitted).]

The recognition that insurance policies are not readily understood has impelled courts to resolve ambiguities in such contracts against the insurance companies.

This recognition has also led courts to enforce unambiguous insurance contracts in accordance with the reasonable expectations of the insured. . . .

. . . .

The interpretation of insurance contracts to accord with the reasonable expectations of the insured, regardless of the existence of any ambiguity in the policy, constitutes judicial recognition of the unique nature of contracts of insurance. By traditional standards of contract law, the consent of both parties, based on an informed understanding of the terms and conditions of the contract, is rarely present in insurance contracts. W.D. Slawson, "Standard Form Contracts and Democratic Control of Lawmaking Power," 84 Harv. L. Rev. 529, 539-41 (1971); R. Keeton, Insurance Law 350-52 (1971). Because understanding is lacking, the consent necessary to sustain traditional contracts cannot be presumed to exist in most contracts of insurance. Such consent can be inferred only to the extent that the policy language conforms to public expectations and commercially reasonable standards. See W.D. Slawson, *supra,* 84 Harv. L. Rev. at 566; R. Keeton, *supra*, at 350-52. In instances in which the insurance contract is inconsistent with public expectations and commercially accepted standards, judicial regulation of insurance contracts is essential in order to prevent overreaching and injustice. R. Keeton, *supra*, at 350-52; R. Keeton, "Insurance Law Rights at Variance with Policy Provisions," 83 Harv. L. Rev. 961, 967 (1970). One commentator has stated the principle as follows:

> The objectively reasonable expectations of applicants and intended beneficiaries regarding the terms of insurance contracts will be honored even though painstaking study of the policy provisions would have negated those expectations.

[R. Keeton, *supra*, at 351; R. Keeton, *supra,* 83 Harv. L. Rev. at 967.]

We find that the contract of insurance sold by St. Paul to Guarriello does not conform to the objectively reasonable expectations of the insured with respect to the scope of the insured and is violative of the public policy of this State. Although we held today in *Zuckerman v. National Union Fire Ins. Co., supra,* 100 N.J. 304, 495 A.2d 395 (1985), that a "claims made" policy that fulfills the reasonable expectations of the insured with respect to the scope of coverage is valid and enforceable, the policy at issue here is substantially different from the standard "claims made" policy. Indeed, St. Paul's policy combines the worst features of "occurrence" and "claims made" policies and the best of neither. It provides neither the prospective coverage typical of an "occurrence" policy, nor the "retroactive" coverage typical of a "claims made" policy. During the first year that the policy was in force, it provided no retroactive coverage for occurrences prior to the effective date of the policy. Thus, it afforded the insured only minimal protection against professional liability claims. Only claims asserted during the policy year, based on negligence that occurred during the policy year, and that were subsequently communicated to the company during the policy year were under the umbrella of coverage.

The realities of professional malpractice, however, suggest that it would be the rare instance in which an error occurred and was discovered with sufficient time to report it to the insurance company, all within a twelve-month period. The victims of professional malpractice are frequently unaware of any negligence until their injury becomes manifest long after the error or omission was committed.

Our review of the use of "claims made" policies in the professional liability field demonstrates that a policy that defines the scope of coverage so narrowly is incompatible with the objectively reasonable expectations of purchasers of professional liability coverage. We assume that there are vast numbers of professionals covered by "claims made" policies who are unaware of the basic distinction between their policies and the traditional "occurrence" policy. However, those professionals covered by "claims made" policies who do understand how their policies differ from "occurrence" policies would expect that in return for the loss of prospective coverage provided by "occurrence" policies, they would be afforded reasonable retroactive coverage by their "claims made" policies. A leading proponent of "claims made" coverage has characterized this *quid pro quo*—the relinquishment of prospective coverage in return for retroactive coverage—as *"the essential* trade-off inherent in the concept of 'claims-made' insurance." S. Kroll, *supra,* 13 Forum at 854 (emphasis added); *see* J. Parker, *supra,* 1983 Det. C.L. Rev. at 27 & n. 3.

We do not decide in this case the precise standard by which the reasonableness of retroactive coverage is to be measured. We hold, however, that where there has been no proof of factual circumstances that would render such limited retroactive coverage both reasonable and expected,[4] a "claims made" policy that affords no retroactive coverage whatsoever during its initial year of issuance does not accord with the objectively reasonable expectations of the purchasers of professional liability insurance. The fact that subsequent renewals of that policy provide minimal retroactive coverage, *i.e.,* to the effective date of the original policy, does not cure the significant deficiency inherent in the underlying policy.

To enforce policies that provide such unrealistically narrow coverage to professionals, and, derivatively, to the public they serve, would in our view cause the kind of broad injury to the public at large contemplated by the doctrine that precludes the enforcement of contracts that violate public policy. Put another way, were we to uphold the validity of St. Paul's policy in this case, the likely result would be the perpetuation in the professional liability insurance market of "claims made" policies offering comparably limited coverage. Because insurance contracts are contracts of adhesion, the terms of which are not customarily bargained for, courts have a special responsibility

---

[4] "Claims made" policies with no retroactive coverage might be appropriate in certain contexts. For example, such policies might properly be offered at a reduced premium to the professional in his very first year of practice, or to the professional who changes from "occurrence" to "claims made" protection. Nothing in the record before us suggests that this is such a case.

to prevent the marketing of policies that provide unrealistic and inadequate coverage.

Because in our view the policy sold by respondent is not a true "claims made" policy, we hold that the provisions in the policy that limit coverage to claims asserted only during the policy period are unenforceable. In view of its peculiar, absolute limitations on retroactive coverage, we construe the policy, despite its denomination, as one analogous to an "occurrence" policy. We therefore impute into the policy's provisions a right of prospective notification in order that the policy, as construed by us, provide a scope of coverage commensurate with the reasonable expectations of the insured as to "occurrence" policy coverage. Thus construed, we hold that the actual notice afforded to St. Paul by the attorneys for respondents between June and August, 1980 was furnished as soon as possible under the circumstances.[5] We follow in this limited and special factual setting the doctrine of *Cooper v. Government Employees Ins. Co.,* 51 N.J. 86, 237 A.2d 870 (1968), and find that there is no necessity to consider whether the insurance company is exposed to prejudice if the notice has been provided within a reasonable time. We emphasize, as we noted in *Zuckerman, supra,* 100 N.J. at 323-324, 495 A.2d at 405-406, the total inapplicability of the *Cooper* doctrine to a true "claims made" policy, but we apply its principle here because of our conclusion that this policy should be construed as a traditional "occurrence" form rather than as a "claims made" policy.

Accordingly, we hold that under these circumstances, the claim asserted by respondents against Guarriello, to the extent that it is based upon negligence that occurred during the policy period, is within the coverage afforded by appellant's policy. The notice to appellant between June and August, 1980, is sufficient to invoke that coverage. Accordingly, we modify and affirm the judgment of the Appellate Division and remand the matter to the trial court to consider, in accordance with the principles set forth in this opinion, any unresolved issues with respect to the specific coverage afforded by St. Paul's policy for the money judgment recovered against Guarriell.[6] We do not retain jurisdiction.

---

[5] New attorneys for Mr. and Mrs. Sparks were substituted in place of Guarriello on April 8, 1980. They provided St. Paul with official notice of the claim against Guarriello between June and August, 1980. Under the circumstances, we cannot say that the timing of such notice was unreasonable.

We are cognizant that had St. Paul's policy contained adequate retroactive coverage, Mr. and Mrs. Sparks would not have been afforded coverage. See *Zuckerman, supra,* 100 N.J. 304, 495 A.2d 395. An alternative construction of the policy would impute into it reasonable retroactive coverage and sustain the enforceability of the notice requirement. We reject this approach. It would be inequitable to hold an insurance policy void as against public policy and yet, when deciding between two plausible constructions of that policy, adopt the construction that is favorable to the drafter of the offensive document.

[6] This Court has not ruled previously that "claims made" policies without adequate retroactive coverage are contrary to the public policy of this State. In note 4, *supra,* we referred to the narrow circumstances in which such policies might be appropriate and valid. Accordingly, on remand the trial court should not be precluded from considering evidence tending to prove that the terms of this policy were specifically understood and bargained for by Guarriello and that, although a policy with adequate retroactive coverage was available to him from St. Paul, he specifically elected to purchase this policy with no retroactive coverage in the first year. Our holding is based

For modification and affirmance — CHIEF JUSTICE WILENTZ and JUSTICES CLIFFORD, HANDLER, POLLOCK, O'HERN, GARIBALDI and STEIN—7.

Opposed—None.

NOTES

1. *Claims-made versus occurrence policies.* What are the advantages and disadvantages of the claims-made policy form in comparison with the occurrence form? Examine the professional liability claims-made form in Appendix F. Does it run afoul of the rule in *Sparks*? (For your information, in the original Specimen reproduced in the Appendix, the text of the "Important Notice" blocks on pages 1 and 2 is printed in red letters.)

2. *The logic of* Sparks. Would an earlier retroactive date in the insured's policy have changed the fact that the claim was made after the policy's expiration? Note that the problem concerning the court was not the "tail" of the claims, but was instead the "nose." When would an insured need coverage for claims arising out of occurrences prior to the effective date of the claims-made coverage? If, for example, the insured is switching from occurrence to claims-made coverage, would not the prior occurrence policy(ies) cover any pre-claims-made policy claims? Is the concern over the retroactive coverage much ado about nothing? See Richard D. Catenacci, *Sparks Revisited: Sparks v. St. Paul Insurance Co.,* 23 Tort & Ins. L.J. 707 (1988).

If the real issue is one of unfair surprise to the insured about the nature of the coverage, what is there for one to be unfairly surprised about? In *Concord Hospital v. New Hampshire Medical Malpractice Joint Underwriting Ass'n,* 633 A.2d 1384 (N.H. 1993), the court said that "the layperson of average intelligence does not know what 'claims made' refers to and cannot be expected to read crucial provisions into the term." 633 A.2d at 1386. Should the fact that Mr. Guarriello was an attorney matter? Or should only attorneys who had a course in insurance law be the ones expected to understand their policies?

3. *The "notice prejudice" rule.* In § 8.01[1], *infra,* we explore the insured's obligation to give notice of a loss, including the rule that has developed in many states that forecloses the insurer from denying coverage in the absence of some showing of prejudice on account of the late notice. Why does this general proposition not control the issue presented in *Sparks*? In *Lexington Insurance Co. v. Rugg & Knopp, Inc.,* 165 F.3d 1087 (7th Cir. 1999), the insurer, which had issued a claims-made policy to the insured contractor, brought a declaratory judgment seeking a determination that it was not

---

on the record before us and on the assumption that, had any such evidence existed, it would have been offered in opposition to the motion for summary judgment.

If such evidence is offered, and the trial court concludes that the evidence is sufficient to prove that although insurance contracts are normally contracts of adhesion, good faith bargaining in this instance took place between the parties; that the terms of this policy were specifically bargained for and understood by [Guarriello]; and that the policy was purchased by him in preference to a policy with adequate retroactive coverage, the trial court would then be justified in enforcing the policy as written.

obligated to provide coverage for losses arising out of the contractor's incompetent performance of a construction contract due to the insured's late notice. In rejecting the insurer's position, the court observed that "[t]he cases cited by Lexington in support of the proposition that claims-made policies should not be subject to a notice-prejudice rule do not even address by analogy the situation involved in Wisconsin, where there is an unambiguous statute squarely on point . . . . What the insurer may not do under any sort of policy, whether claims-made or occurrence, is to refuse liability for payment merely because of late notice. That is Wisconsin public policy as determined by the legislature." 165 F.3d at 1093-94. Did the Wisconsin legislature intend to alter this aspect of the claims-made form? In *Lexington Insurance Co. v. St. Louis University*, 88 F.3d 632 (8th Cir. 1996), the insurer fared better: "Both [occurrence and claims-made] policies require the insured to promptly notify the insurer of possible covered losses. With a claim made policy, however, that notice is not simply part of the insured's duty to cooperate. It defines the limits of the insurer's obligation—if there is no timely notice, there is no coverage . . . . [E]xcusing tardy notice 'would alter a basic term of the insurance contract.' " 88 F.3d at 634. *See also Home Insurance Co. of Illinois v. Adco Oil Co.*, 154 F.3d 739 (7th Cir. 1998) (under Illinois law, claims-made policy provided no coverage for claim first reported to insurer after expiration of policy).

4. *The nature of professional liability insurance.* The policy in *Sparks* (and in the policy in *Hoyt*, which follows these notes) involves a kind of "errors and omissions" coverage, or what is more commonly referred to as professional liability or malpractice insurance. Most lay people have a casual understanding of medical and legal malpractice insurance; it is less well known that such coverages are also common in the professions of dentistry, accounting, engineering, pharmacy, and architecture. Insurance agents and brokers can also obtain errors and omissions coverage. These policies are generally limited to providing coverage for liability arising from those acts involving the performance or rendition of services customarily performed by the particular profession. For example, if a patient slips and falls in the waiting room of a doctor's office due to the negligence of the doctor's employees, the doctor's malpractice policy would not cover the claim. It could be covered, however, under a policy providing liability insurance for premises and operations. *See Foremost Insurance Co. v. Hartford Insurance Group*, 385 So. 2d 110 (Fla. App. 1980).

In some situations, it is difficult to determine exactly what services are customarily performed by a profession, and this is particularly true with regard to the legal profession. Consider the definition of "legal services" in the Lawyers Professional Liability Policy in Appendix F. If a lawyer is entrusted with funds that the client has withdrawn from a savings account and is instructed to invest the funds in instruments that earn more interest, is the lawyer providing "professional services"? What if the lawyer organizes a limited partnership for the purpose of investing in real estate, does the legal work for the partnership, and solicits his existing clients' participation in the partnerships? If the lawyer is later sued by the clients because the investment fails to produce income, is the lawyer's potential liability covered by the policy? Are these kinds of entrepreneurial activities different from preparing the clients' tax returns? *Compare Continental Casualty Co. v. Burton,* 795 F.2d 1187 (4th Cir. 1986) (applying Virginia law), with *General Accident Insurance Co. v. Namesnik,* 790 F.2d 1397 (9th Cir. 1986) (applying Arizona law). For a case involving what constitutes "professional services" of an accountant, *see Bancroft v. Indemnity Insurance Co. of N. Am.,* 203 F. Supp. 49 (W.D. La.), *aff'd,* 309 F.2d 959 (5th Cir. 1962).

What if the attorney acts as a trustee and also serves as the attorney for the trust, a not uncommon situation? One court, in construing a clause providing coverage for liability "arising from the performance of professional services" and which described "fiduciary activi[ties]" as within the scope of "professional services," held that it was required "to fictionalize the insured as two personae — the Trustee and the Attorney—and then to determine if the insured's actions would render him legally responsible as an Attorney to the fictional Trustee," and, further, that the inquiry must proceed along two lines. The court must inquire first whether the acts for which the insured was responsible were performed in his role as an attorney and, second, whether the acts were such that an attorney would be legally liable for their commission. *Transamerica Insurance Co. v. Keown,* 451 F. Supp. 397, 401 (D.N.J. 1978).

If the attorney-insured is serving as a guardian (a kind of fiduciary capacity) and is a defendant in a lawsuit in which the attorney's discharge from this capacity is sought, must the malpractice insurer provide a defense? In *Felice v. St. Paul Fire & Marine Insurance Co.,* 42 Wash. App. 352, 711 P.2d 1066 (1985), the attorney's malpractice policy covered amounts the attorney was legally required to pay to compensate others for loss resulting from legal or notary services that were provided or should have been provided and defined "legal services" to include those performed while serving in a fiduciary capacity, such as guardian. The court held that there was no coverage for an action to discharge the attorney-insured as a guardian, as the relief sought was that of removal of the attorney as guardian rather than money damages.

Malpractice policies typically exclude coverage for dishonest, fraudulent, criminal, or malicious acts or omissions. Not surprisingly, such exclusions have been the subject of much litigation. *Compare Conner v. Transamerica Insurance Co.,* 496 P.2d 770 (Okla. 1972)(holding that there was a duty under the legal malpractice policy to defend the attorney-insureds who allegedly engaged in fraudulent, deceitful, and dishonest conduct such as false affidavits, forgery, and deliberate misrepresentations), with *St. Paul Insurance Co. v. Bonded Realty, Inc.,* 578 S.W.2d 191 (Tex. Civ. App.), *aff'd,* 583 S.W.2d 619 (Tex. 1979) (holding that there was no coverage under real estate agent's errors and omissions policy where insured agent was found to have violated the Texas Deceptive Trade Practices-Consumer Protection Act by making representations which were known by the insured to be false). In *Brooks, Tarlton, Gilbert, Douglas & Kressler v. U.S. Fire Insurance Co.,* 832 F.2d 1358 (5th Cir. 1987), the court held that the exclusion in question did not operate to preclude coverage where the client alleged that her attorneys violated their ethical obligations, reasoning that these claims amounted only to constructive fraud, which is not the same as a "fraudulent" act under the policy language. The court said that the latter requires dishonesty of purpose or intent to deceive, whereas the former involves a breach of some legal or equitable duty that the law declares to be fraudulent because of its tendency to deceive others, to violate confidence, or to injure public interest.

5. *Directors and officers liability insurance.* Another important kind of claims-made coverage is directors and officers liability insurance. The typical "D&O" policy has two major parts. The directors and officers portion provides coverage for losses suffered by directors and officers for which the corporation does not provide indemnification. The "company reimbursement" portion provides coverage for claims for which the company does provide indemnity. See generally Joseph P. Monteleone and Nicholas J. Conca, *Directors and Officers Indemnification and Liability Insurance: An Overview of Legal and Practical Issues*, 51 Business Lawyer 573, 587-588 (1996).

Under the "company reimbursement" coverage, insurers can be expected to insist that the corporation properly grant indemnification, meaning that the indemnification be required by statute, corporate charter, or applicable bylaw. See *Id.* at 588. Under the coverage provided directly to directors and officers, policy language will state, in effect, that the coverage extends to individual directors and officers only for claims that relate to their acts or omissions in their capacities as directors and officers, and not in other capacities (such as a stockholder or an attorney for the corporation). *See Continental Copper & Steel Industries v. Johnson,* 491 F. Supp. 360 (S.D.N.Y. 1980), *aff'd,* 647 P.2d 161 (2d Cir. 1981). Also, the D&O policy does not provide coverage for the corporation in circumstances where a plaintiff recovers damages against the corporation itself.

The contours of the D&O policy's coverage can easily create a situation where a complex of claims against directors, officers, and a corporate entity produces a mix of covered and noncovered or excluded claims against a mix of covered and noncovered parties. This gives rise to an issue of "allocation," meaning that a determination must sometimes be made as to what portion of defense costs and a judgment or settlement must be paid by the D&O carrier. How this allocation should occur has been a subject of frequent litigation in recent years, particularly with respect to the issue of covered and noncovered parties. *See e.g., Safeway Stores, Inc. v. National Union Fire Insurance Co.,* 64 F.3d 1282 (9th Cir. 1995); *Caterpillar, Inc. v. Great American Insurance Co.,* 62 F.3d 955 (7th Cir. 1995); *Piper Jaffray Cos., Inc., v. National Union Fire Insurance Co.,* 38 F. Supp. 2d 771 (D. Minn. 1999).

6. *What constitutes a "claim"?* Since a "claim" is the critical event in a claims-made policy, it becomes important to know whether a "claim" has been made at all in order to determine when it was made. The meaning of the word "claim" arises in a variety of policy contexts, but it is not always defined in the policy. Even the CGL, although it provides that a claim is deemed to have been made when written notice of a claim is received by the insured or insurer, fails to define the operative word. See Appendix B(2) (claims-made form). Compare the professional liability claims-made form in Appendix F, where "claim" is defined. Because the claims-made form has less history than the occurrence form, there are relatively fewer cases defining the word "claim"; but as this form is put in more frequent use, one surely can anticipate that the meaning of "claim" will be a fruitful source of litigation where there is

no unambiguous policy definition. For example, *compare Employers Insurance of Wausau v. Bodi-Wachs Aviation Insurance Agency, Inc.,* 39 F.3d 138 (7th Cir. 1994), holding that a claim was not made under a professional liability claims-made policy until the insured was actually sued for damages, with *Berry v. St. Paul Fire & Marine Co.,* 70 F.3d 981 (8th Cir. 1995), holding that lawyer's letter to an insured that referred to client's "product liability claim" and to attorney's lien, and that advised insured to forward letter to its insurer, qualifies as a claim. *See also Walker v. Larson,* 727 P.2d 1321 (Mont. 1986). This issue receives more attention in the next case and the notes which follow.

HOYT v. ST. PAUL FIRE & MARINE INSURANCE CO.
607 F.2d 864 (9th Cir. 1979)

Before MERRILL and TRASK, CIRCUIT JUDGES, and EAST,[*] DISTRICT JUDGE.

MERRILL, CIRCUIT JUDGE:

Appellant Hoyt appeals the district court's grant of summary judgment and dismissal of his action for declaratory judgment against appellee, his professional liability insurance carrier. Hoyt, a lawyer, sought coverage benefits in regard to a malpractice action pending against him in state court.

On April 27, 1973, appellee issued a one-year "Lawyer's Professional Liability Policy" for Hoyt's firm. Paragraph "G" contained the following clause:

> This policy applies within the United States of America, its territories or possessions or Canada to professional services performed for others (a) during the policy period *(b) prior to the effective date of the Policy if claim is made or suit is brought during the policy period* and providing the Insured, at the effective date of the Policy, had no knowledge or could not have reasonably foreseen any circumstance which might result in a claim or suit. (emphasis added).

The renewal policy, effective on April 27, 1974, did not contain the "if claim is made" provision of the expired policy.

The events leading up to the malpractice claim arose out of a will drawn by Hoyt for Constance Cope in 1962, in which Cope exercised a general power of appointment given to her by her mother's will. Cope died on November 29, 1973. On January 7, 1974, Hoyt received a letter from an attorney in La Jolla, California, who was handling Cope's estate. The letter informed Hoyt of Cope's death and requested Hoyt to sign a "Certificate of Subscribing Witness to Will," which he did. The next communication Hoyt received from the attorney was a letter dated April 5, 1974. In part the letter stated:

> I am enclosing a copy of Mrs. Cope's will dated January 30, 1962, which I believe you prepared for Mrs. Cope. I'm also enclosing a copy

---

[*] Honorable William G. East, Senior United States District Judge of the District of Oregon, sitting by designation.

of the Constance Maria Gummey will dated February 10, 1920. In article SIXTH of Mrs. Cope's will, she exercises the general Power of Appointment granted to her under the Gummey Will, Article FIFTH. As I read section 2041 of the Internal Revenue Code, property subject to a general power of appointment created on or before October 21, 1942, (as in this case) is includible in the gross estate of the holder of the power only if the holder exercises the power by will. Since the disposition of the Trust assets in failure of exercise of the power was equally among Mrs. Cope's sons and since Mrs. Cope exercised the power to provide an equal disposition among her sons, *I wonder what the point was in having her exercise the power in her will. It seems as though it has simply created substantial additional tax in her estate which could have been avoided had she said nothing about the power, in her will. Any thought or information you have on this point would be greatly appreciated.* (emphasis added).

Hoyt responded on April 11, 1974, stating in part:

I am aware of the potential risks involved in exercising powers and I would assume that the banks that were handling her parents' estates would have reviewed the Will of January 30, 1962, and pointed out the undesirable features reexercising the power of appointment.

Hoyt did not hear from the attorney again until September 4, 1974. In the interim, the professional liability policy issued by St. Paul expired on April 27, 1974. In his letter of September 4, the attorney for the Cope estate accused Hoyt of gross negligence in preparing the will and made demand upon him for "all sums paid or which may hereafter become due or payable by the estate of Constance Marie Cope or the beneficiaries of the Constance M. Gummey trust on account of United States estate taxes and California inheritance taxes attributable to the inclusion of the Gummey trust assets in the Cope taxable estate." Hoyt responded denying liability.

Upon receipt of a summons and complaint on May 20, 1975, Hoyt notified his local insurance agent, Robert Rissi, and forwarded all the documents to appellee. Thereafter, on June 3, 1975, Rissi notified Hoyt by letter that the insurance company was accepting the case and that it had been referred to a Phoenix attorney for defense.

On July 15, 1975, Rissi wrote Hoyt denying coverage and instructed the company attorney to withdraw from Hoyt's defense. Hoyt retained independent counsel as defense counsel in the state court malpractice action. The retained counsel recommended that Hoyt seek a United States district court declaratory judgment, and thereupon sought a stay of the state court proceedings pending the outcome of such declaratory judgment action. This diversity action was filed on December 15, 1976, pursuant to the Federal Declaratory Judgment Act, 28 U.S.C. § 2201. After discovery had been substantially completed, both parties moved for summary judgment. The district court granted appellee's motion and dismissed the action on April 8, 1977.

The question presented is whether the April 5, 1974, letter from the attorney in the Cope estate was a claim within the "if claim is made" clause of the 1973 policy. If it was, Hoyt was covered by the terms of the 1973 policy. If it was not, since the professional services were not performed within the policy period of either the 1973 or the 1974 policy, Hoyt was without coverage.

In our judgment the letter of April 5, 1974, did not constitute a claim. It was a request for information and explanation. If Hoyt was put on notice of any kind it was only that a claim might be expected to follow if the estate attorney was not satisfied with the explanation. In our view an inquiry cannot be transformed into a claim or demand depending in each case on the reasonable expectations of the insured — whether he should reasonably have been satisfied that the explanation would be accepted as justification for the questioned conduct or should reasonably have expected that it would not. Such a rule would firmly write uncertainty of coverage into every policy.

It is argued that *J. G. Link & Co. v. Continental Casualty Co.*, 470 F.2d 1133 (9th Cir. 1972), *cert. denied*, 414 U.S. 829, 94 S. Ct. 55, 38 L. Ed. 2d 63 (1973), should be read to hold that that is in truth the case—that the word "claim" in this context is inherently ambiguous and that the policy should be construed against the insurer. We do not so read that case. There an architect suffered suit and judgment for negligent design and construction of a funeral home, resulting in a squeaking floor — a condition that could well prove an embarrassment to such an establishment. He was insured by an architect's errors and omissions policy that provided (as does the policy here) that claim must be made on the insured within the policy period. No claim in the form of a demand was made until suit was brought after expiration of the policy period. However, the defect had been called to the architect's attention during the policy period.

This court there read two provisions of the policy as related to each other: (1) The "if claim is made" clause; (2) The provision that notice be given to the insurer when claim was made. The latter provided that "[A]s soon as practicable after *receiving information as to his alleged errors*, omission or negligent acts" the insured should give notice to the company. 470 F.2d at 1135 (emphasis added). From this the court concluded that the receipt of information *could* constitute a claim requiring notice, but that the "if claim is made" clause was ambiguous because the kind and extent of information needed to trigger the duty to give notice was not spelled out: "[T]he nature of the information required to secure coverage is far from clear." *Id.* at 1137.

In the instant case the policy's notice clause also serves to cast light on the meaning of the "if claim is made" clause. Condition C(2) of the policy reads:

> If claim is made or suit is brought against the Insured, the Insured shall immediately forward to the Company every demand, notice, summons or other process received by him or his representative.

Thus, the "claim" contemplated is unambiguously in the nature of a demand or notice.

We conclude that the 1973 policy did not provide coverage.

. . . .

Judgment affirmed.

EAST, SENIOR DISTRICT JUDGE, dissenting:

I respectfully dissent from the conclusions reached by the majority . . . .

It is well recognized under Arizona law that any ambiguities in an insurance contract are construed against the insurer and in favor of the insured. Hoyt points out that the phrase "if claim is made" is not defined anywhere in the policy. He, therefore, urges that St. Paul is responsible for any inherent ambiguity in the meaning and consequences of that term and must be prepared to defend and answer any claim against an insured that arguably comes within the policy's provisions. Hoyt maintains the April 5th letter was within a broad definition of the meaning of a "claim"; *i.e.,* a mere notice that there may have been some negligence on his part in rendering a legal service.

While I do not fully subscribe to Hoyt's expansive definition of a "claim," I do agree with Hoyt's contention that a claim of professional malfeasance was made against him through the content of the April 5th letter well within the policy period. The April 5th letter clearly asserts a claimed financial loss to the Cope estate resulting from a questioned professional practice by Hoyt. It would be foolhardy for any reasonable attorney to interpret Henry's polite request for Hoyt's thinking or information on the matter as other than a claim to justify the challenged professional practice or pay up. Hoyt's response of April 11 acknowledged the risk involved and sought to place the blame elsewhere.

The majority attempts to distinguish the rationale of this Court's opinion in *J. G. Link & Co. v. Continental Casualty Co.,* 470 F.2d 1133 (9th Cir. 1972), *cert. denied,* 414 U.S. 829, 94 S. Ct. 55, 38 L. Ed. 2d 63 (1973), from the facts here. I am convinced that the rationale of *J. G. Link & Co.* dictates a reversal of the District Court's summary judgment. The majority's attempt to distinguish the holding in *J. G. Link & Co.* is based solely upon their reading of the April 5th letter. I read that letter as an explicit notice of a "defect" in Hoyt's professional advice and product. Only a naive attorney and his insurer would think the adverse assertion would evaporate with the coming dawn. The letter was sufficient to elicit Hoyt's lame excuse of April 11.

St. Paul did not raise the defense of untimely notice of the claim made. The District Court did not reach that issue nor should we. If the majority does not wish to squarely meet and disagree with the rationale of *J. G. Link & Co.,* they should seek a reversal of that precedent.

NOTES

1. *Policy considerations.* Aside from the obvious differences in coverage provided under the claims-made form and the occurrence form, are there policy considerations based on sheer mechanics? For example, for certain coverages under a CGL policy, there must be bodily injury or property damage to trigger an occurrence policy; in comparison, there must be a claim to trigger a claims-made policy. The laws of nature pretty well govern how and when the former occurs, but what about the vicissitudes involving how and when a claim is made? The California lawyer's choice of words in *Hoyt* proved to be crucial. Was he just being nice or what? Would it be possible to draft policy language to avoid these problems?

2. *The insurers' view.* For a discussion of the meaning of "claim" in a variety of insurance policy contexts, see James W. Morris, Rufus G. Coldwell & Ann Adams Webster, *Is There a "Claim" in a Claims-Made Policy?,* 29 For the Defense, No. 2, Feb. 1987, at 15. There the authors contend:

> Judicial interpretations of the meaning of the word "claim" are remarkably consistent, given the variety of policy contexts in which the definitional issue arises. Their principal teaching can be summarized thus: a "claim" *is* an express demand for specific remedy (by specific compensation or specific corrective action) of existing injury allegedly caused by the insured's wrongful conduct. The cases also teach that a claim *is not:* the incident or conduct that gives rise to a claim; a third party's calling attention to an alleged wrong and a loss, and demanding information or an explanation; nor even something the insured himself considers a claim or potential claim, without an express demand for specific remedy of existing injury.

> "Claim" must be objectively identifiable and may not be left to subjective guesswork or *post hoc* manipulation by one side or the other in ensuing coverage litigation. Under the objective test for "claim," two essential elements must exist:

> (1) identifiable, existing injury to a third party; (2) an express demand by the third party that his injury be redressed.

Do you agree with the authors that both of the elements enumerated must exist?

3. *Reporting requirements.* In addition to requiring the claim to be made within the policy's period of coverage, most claims-made policies require that the claim be *reported* to the insurer during the policy's period as well. In § 8.01, *infra*, one of the themes of the cases is that courts tend not to hold insureds to the precise letter of an insurance policy's deadlines in connection with claims processing, although there are notable exceptions in the case law. Most courts, however, apply the reporting requirement in claims-made policies literally, and have upheld unambiguous reporting deadlines. *See e.g.*, *DiLuglio v. New England Insurance Co.,* 959 F.2d 355 (1st Cir. 1992); *Esmailzadeh v. Johnson and Speakman,* 869 F.2d 422 (8th Cir. 1989). But *see Doctors' Co. v. Insurance Corp. of Am.* 864 P.2d 1018 (Wyo. 1993). Are courts acting inconsistently with respect to these two issues? Or are the issues distinguishable? Some states have statutes or regulations requiring a 30-day or 60-day period after the policy's termination during which claims can be reported. *See, e.g.,* 40 Pa. Cons. Stat. Ann. § 3405 (1992); Ark. Stat. § 23-79-306(b) (1995). What is the rationale for extending the reporting period after a policy's termination date?

§ 5.03 Other Recurring Issues

[1] Coverage for Punitive Damage Liability

FIRST BANK (N.A.)–BILLINGS v. TRANSAMERICA INSURANCE CO.

679 P.2d 1217 (Mont. 1984)

GULBRANDSON, JUSTICE.

The United States District Court for the District of Montana has certified two questions to this Court for instructions concerning Montana law.

First Bank Billings has been named a defendant in three wrongful repossession cases . . . . Transamerica has undertaken the defense of First Bank, but has reserved its rights under its insurance contract with the bank and has denied any coverage for punitive damages under this contract. Transamerica argues that the public policy of Montana forbids such coverage. On motion of First Bank, the United States District Court has certified the following questions to this Court:

(1) Does the public policy of Montana permit insurance coverage of punitive damages?

(2) If the public policy of Montana does not *generally* permit insurance coverage of punitive damages, would it nevertheless permit coverage for punitive damages for which a banking corporation is or could be held liable by reasons of the acts of its employees?

For the reasons stated below, we conclude in response to the first question that insurance coverage of punitive damages is not a violation of public policy. Thus, we need not address the substance of the second question.

Counsel for First Bank have presented ten considerations in support of permitting insurance coverage of punitive damages. Transamerica has mounted a strong challenge to all of these considerations. We recognize that there is considerable authority supporting the positions of both parties. See generally Annot., 16 ALR 4th 11 (1982) (comparing and contrasting different views on liability insurance coverage as extending to liability for punitive or exemplary damages). We note, however, that most of the important decisions, as well as the major arguments of the parties, emphasize three primary considerations as ultimately dispositive of the questions before us. These are (1) public policy as expressed in constitutions and statutes; (2) the purpose of punitive damages; and (3) the circumstances under which punitive damages become available to aggrieved plaintiffs. Although we address these matters separately in this opinion, we recognize that they are interrelated to a high degree, and we therefore are careful not to sever the important ties that bind them together.

Before proceeding to the critical issues, we must first address a disagreement between the parties concerning the focus of our review. First Bank has urged this Court to center on what it claims are the "blanket terms" of the insurance contract, wherein Transamerica agrees to "pay on behalf of the insured all sums which the insured shall be legally obligated to pay as damages because of personal injury or advertising injury to which this insurance applies . . ." First Bank inferentially asks this Court to answer the certified question in light of this contract language. Specifically, we are asked to decide whether public policy bars coverage even when the contract supposedly provides indemnification for "all sums" arising from liability.

We reject the approach suggested by First Bank. Transamerica correctly notes that the certified questions forwarded by the Federal District Court do not call for an interpretation of contract language. We are asked only to decide whether public policy permits or bars coverage of punitive damages, regardless of the contract language. We leave the threshold issue of contract interpretation for the Federal District Court to decide. For similar reasons, we also decline to review allegations by First Bank that Transamerica is attempting to "wriggle out" of its negotiated insurance contract. That, too, is a matter for decision by the District Court.

. . . .

Sources of Public Policy in Montana

"Public policy is that principle of law which holds that no citizen can lawfully do that which has a tendency to be injurious to the public or against public good." Public policy is typically found "in the constitution and the laws and the course of administration." In determining the public policy of this state, legislative enactments must yield to constitutional provisions, and judicial decisions must recognize and yield to constitutional provisions and legislative enactments. Judicial decisions are a superior repository of statements about public policy only in the absence of constitutional and valid legislative declarations.

Public Policy as Expressed in the Constitution and Statutes

We find nothing in the Montana Constitution declaring a public policy on the question before us. We therefore turn to relevant statutes and case law construing the same.

Prior to adoption of this state's comprehensive insurance code, Sections 33-1-101 et seq., MCA, the law of Montana provided that "[a]n insurer is not liable for a loss caused by the willful act of the insured; but he is not exonerated by the negligence of the insured, or of his agents or others." Section 40-604, R.C.M.1947 [repealed 1959]. This statute was based on Cal. Ins. Code Section 533 (West 1972), which has been construed to prohibit insurance coverage of punitive damages in most instances in California. Section 40-604 is no longer law in Montana, having been repealed upon adoption in 1959 of the insurance code. Transamerica argues that repeal "does not mean that the legislature intended to bless the sins of cheats, frauds, and oppressors, and absolve them from wrongdoing." While there is some truth in this assertion, we conclude that not even Transamerica would argue that a repealed statute has a life beyond the grave. If there is a public policy against permitting coverage, it must flow from an existing statute.

Our attention is also directed to the punitive damages law, Section 27-1-221, MCA, which provides that:

> [i]n any action for a breach of an obligation not arising from contract where the defendant has been guilty of oppression, fraud, or malice, actual or presumed, the jury, in addition to the actual damages, may give damages for the sake of example and by way of punishing the defendant.

There is nothing in this statute amounting to an express statement on the public policy issue before us. Nevertheless, Transamerica reasons syllogistically that, because punishment is an explicit aim of applying punitive damages, and because punishment, to be such, must cause its recipient to suffer, there can be no punishment if a defendant is permitted to, in effect, "shift" the financial burden of the imposed punishment to his or her insurance carrier. Transamerica thus concludes that a public policy against coverage emanates from the concept of punishment as embodied in the statute. This is the conclusion reached by courts in some states with the same or similar punitive damage laws. Although we are impressed with the reasoning behind Transamerica's argument, we reject it, for reasons discussed *infra,* as an inaccurate expression of the practical consequences of applying punitive damages law in some cases in Montana.

Transamerica also directs our attention to Section 28-11-302, MCA, which provides that "[a]n agreement to indemnify a person against an act thereafter to be done is void if the act be known by such person, at the time of doing it, to be unlawful." Transamerica reasons that, because insurance is a contract of indemnity, Section 28-11-302 operates as an express policy against coverage for tortious acts warranting imposition of punitive damages. We reject this interpretation.

Modern insurance contracts typically provide coverage for a host of tortious activities, with the assurance that the insured will be indemnified at least for compensatory damages arising from unlawful conduct by the insured; *e.g.,* libel and slander, malicious prosecution, etc. Even Transamerica would not argue that Section 28-11-302 erects a bar to liability insurance for compensatory damages, be they awarded for ordinary negligence or malicious, fraudulent or oppressive conduct. The need to reduce financial risks and promote economic stability in modern society has rendered this statute applicable only to conduct defined as criminal.

In summary, we find no express policy by the legislature on the subject of insurance coverage for punitive damages. Although reasoned arguments can be made for reading some kind of prohibition into the language of the punitive damages statute, we decline to do so without first examining judicial construction of that statute and then considering the practical consequences of awarding punitive damages.

Public Policy in Light of Judicial Decisions

As noted above, a major aim of awarding punitive damages is punishment of the defendant for oppressive, fraudulent or malicious conduct. We have also recognized that an award of punitive damages can serve as a deterrent to like conduct by other individuals. Whether both goals will be served adequately by permitting insurance coverage of punitive damages has been the principal concern of courts that have already addressed the coverage question.

Several courts have followed the lead of the Court of Appeals of the Fifth Circuit and have concluded that the mutual goals of punishment and deterrence are defeated if coverage is permitted. In *Northwestern Nat'l Cas. Co. v. McNulty* (5th Cir. 1962), 307 F.2d 432, Circuit Judge John Minor Wisdom made this oft-quoted observation:

> Where a person is able to insure himself against punishment he gains a freedom of misconduct inconsistent with the establishment of sanctions against such misconduct. It is not disputed that insurance against criminal fines or penalties would be void as violative of public policy. The same public policy should invalidate any contract of insurance against the civil punishment that punitive damages represent.
>
> The policy considerations in a state where . . . punitive damages are awarded for punishment and deterrence, would seem to require that the damages rest ultimately as well as nominally on the party actually responsible for the wrong. If that person were permitted to shift the burden to an insurance company, punitive damages would serve no useful purpose. Such damages do not compensate the plaintiff for his injury, since compensatory damages already have made the plaintiff whole. And there is no point in punishing the insurance company; it has done no wrong. In actual fact, of course, and considering the extent to which the public is insured, the burden would ultimately come to rest not on the insurance companies but on the public, since the added liability to the insurance companies would be passed along to the premium payers. Society would then be punishing itself for the wrong committed by the insured.

307 F.2d at 440-41. For similar views, *see Harrell v. Travelers Indem. Co.* (1977), 279 Or. 199, 567 P.2d 1013, 1022 (HOLMAN, J., dissenting).

Upon reflection, we grant the intellectual appeal of Judge Wisdom's reasoning, and recognize that it has been both praised and followed in other jurisdictions. Nevertheless, we find that this reasoning does not address the substance of punitive damages law as applied in Montana. To determine public policy concerning insurance coverage of punitive damages solely on deductive conclusions like those articulated by Judge Wisdom "is to lean upon a slender reed."

Oregon Supreme Court Justice Hans Linde correctly observed in his concurring opinion in *Harrell, supra,* that "[a] court-made public policy against otherwise lawful liability insurance can be defended, not *because* the purpose of punitive damages is always deterrence and *because* insurance will always destroy their deterrent effect, but only *when* these considerations apply." (emphasis his). 279 Or. 199, 567 P.2d at 1029. Empirical observation informs us that many kinds of willful and wanton conduct are never successfully deterred by punitive damage awards. This is especially true in automobile accident cases. *See, e.g.,* the discussion in *Lazenby v. Universal Underwriters Ins. Co.* (1964), 214 Tenn. 639, 383 S.W.2d 1, concerning the failure of civil and criminal sanctions to deter wrongful conduct on the highways. We have few doubts that the deterrent impact is minimal in cases involving other types of tortious conduct. This leaves punishment as perhaps the only effectively realizable goal of awarding punitive damages. However, as will be pointed out in the discussion *infra,* punishment in the context of punitive damages may come as a wholly unanticipated aspect of one's conduct, thus weakening the case against permitting insurance coverage of all punitive damage awards.

In the instant dispute, First Bank fears that its insurance contract with Transamerica will become virtually worthless if it is exposed to punitive damage awards without the possibility of coverage. The Bank also claims that such a fine line exists between conduct justifying imposition of punitive damages and conduct not justifying such damages that permitting coverage is not in violation of public policy. Both arguments warrant serious attention.

The contract issued by Transamerica to First Bank is not unlike many insurance agreements. It includes coverage for false arrest, detention, or imprisonment, malicious prosecution, wrongful entry or eviction, libel and slander, racial or religious discrimination, and wrongful repossession. All of these torts give rise to claims for punitive damages; on this there is no dispute. In many cases involving these torts, actual damages may be minimal, but the punitive damages extremely high. Indeed, many claims for relief are not made financially worthwhile without the prospect of recovering punitive damages. See *[Harrell], supra,* 279 Or. 199, 567 P.2d at 1029 (LINDE, J., concurring). Assuming that coverage was deemed contrary to public policy, and in the event of minimal, if any compensatory damages, an insured facing a significant award of punitives would receive little solace from what would amount to a worthless insurance policy.

The "fine-line" problem raised by First Bank also suggests that a public policy against coverage would have less than desirable results, especially where the defendant is again assessed a particularly large punitive damage award. A consistent theme running through cases holding that public policy does not forbid insurance coverage is that juries and judges typically award punitives for a broad range of conduct not often described as willful or wanton, but as merely reckless or unjustifiable. When combined with the possibility that different fact finders in similar fact situations may reach differing conclusions as to the availability of punitive damages, the argument for denial of coverage becomes difficult to sustain. First Bank also emphasizes, and not without good reason, that a defendant may be subject to a punitive damage award for conduct not considered or known to be wrongful prior to imposition of the award. In these instances, forbidding coverage after the fact may work an injustice to unsuspecting defendants.

We have recently attempted to come to grips with the problem of uncertainty in the area of punitive damages. In *Owens v. Parker Drilling Co., (Mont.* 1984), 676 P.2d 162, 41 St. Rep. 66, this Court acknowledged the expanded availability of punitive damage awards based on concepts like gross negligence, recklessness and unjustifiability. With respect to presumed malice as a ground specified in Section 27-1-221, MCA, for imposing exemplary or punitive damages, this Court adopted the following standard:

When a person knows or has reason to know of facts which create a high degree of risk of harm to the substantial interests of another, and either deliberately proceeds to act in conscious disregard of or indifference to that risk, or recklessly proceeds in unreasonable disregard of or indifference to that risk, his conduct meets the standard of willful, wanton, and/or reckless to which the law of this State will allow imposition of punitive damages on the basis of presumed malice.

Owens, supra, 676 P.2d 162, 41 St. Rep. at 69. Although we have described this standard as "more definitive and perhaps more stringent than those of the past," *Owens, supra*, 676 P.2d 162, 41 St. Rep. at 69, we acknowledge that [fact finders] may still wrestle with concepts like recklessness and reasonableness, such that defendants may not know that their conduct constituted presumed malice until after trial, and that a defendant in one case may never know the sting of punitive damages while another defendant in a similar case may be faced with financing a sizeable award. Similarly, we have yet to work out a definitive standard for "oppression" within the meaning of Section 27-1-221.

Even though we are further down the road to refining the concept of punitive damages than are many other state courts, the law is still in such a state of flux as to warrant caution on the issue of whether public policy prohibits coverage of punitive damages in all cases. We therefore decline the opportunity to define limits for insurance coverage of punitive damages. Insurance companies are more than capable of evaluating risks and deciding whether they will offer policies to indemnify all or some conduct determined by judges or juries to be malicious, fraudulent or oppressive. A likely response to this opinion by some carriers may be the drafting of specific exclusions of coverage of punitive damages. However, the fact that some individuals may be willing to pay higher premiums for such coverage may convince carriers to extend coverage in some situations. It is conceivable that a combination of different approaches by insurance companies may result in a delineation of the limits of coverage better than anything this Court could establish.

Conclusion

We find that providing insurance coverage of punitive damages is not contrary to public policy. Transamerica admittedly has set forth a strong argument in support of an opposite holding, but we find the consequences of adopting that position unacceptable. The problems posed by insurance coverage of punitive damages are unquestionably like those inherent in the Gordian Knot. Unlike Alexander the Great, however, we cannot make a clean slice through our version of the Knot, in order to unravel all the aspects of the question before us, without working an injustice to many policy holders. Alexander dealt only with an inanimate object; we deal with people. Use of the judicial sword therefore is inappropriate in this case. Here, we must "untie" the knot, painstaking as the process may be. Until such time that the law of punitive damages is more certain and predictable, or until the legislature alters the law of punitive damages or expressly declares a policy against coverage in all cases, we leave the decision of whether coverage will be permitted to the insurance carriers and their customers.

SHEA, HARRISON and SHEEHY, JJ., and GORDON R. BENNETT, DISTRICT JUDGE,* CONCUR.

MORRISON, J., SPECIALLY CONCURS AND WILL FILE A SPECIAL CONCURRENCE LATER.

NOTES

1. *The law of punitive damages.* Before the question of the insurability of punitive damages can even arise, state or federal law must allow punitive damages to be awarded. Almost all states allow such damages, but this is an area where many changes are occurring. At least half the states have enacted one or more kinds of regulatory limitations on the award of such damages, including caps on punitive damage awards, requiring a portion of the award to be paid to the state, bifurcating the liability phase of a trial from the punitive damages phase, requiring a heightened standard of proof for the recovery of punitive damages (usually requiring that such damages be proved by "clear and convincing" evidence, and requiring proportionality between compensatory and punitive damage awards. See Jane Mallor & Barry S. Roberts, *Punitive Damages: On the Path to a Principled Approach?,* 50 Hastings L.J. 1001 (1999). The amount of damages that can be awarded has federal constitutional dimensions as well. *See BMW of North America, Inc. v. Gore,* 517 U.S. 559 (1996). See generally Dan B. Dobbs, Law of Remedies §Ê3.11 (2d ed. 1993).

2. *What is going on here?* Liability for injuries intentionally inflicted are already excluded pursuant to the intentional act exclusion. How is it, then, that an insurer can ever be called on to pay punitive damages? See generally Alan I. Widiss, *Liability Insurance Coverage for Punitive Damages?,* 39 Villanova L. Rev. 455 (1994).

3. *Why not exclude coverage for punitive damages?* Could insurers avoid all the fuss by putting a clear exclusion in the policy stating that punitive damage liability is not covered? Why are such exclusions uncommon? Where the liability insurance policy specifically excludes punitive damages, courts have enforced the policy as written. *See e.g., Rummel v. St. Paul Surplus Lines Insurance Co.,* 123 N.M. 767, 945 P.2d 985 (1997); *Cassel v. Schacht,* 140 Ariz. 495, 683 P.2d 294 (1984).

The court in *First Bank* addressed the single issue of whether it was against public policy to permit insurance against punitive damages. It is a separate issue as to whether the language of the particular insurance contract covers punitive damages. The Supreme Court of Montana sidestepped that issue, but most modern courts have not been reticent to hold that, absent a specific exclusion, such damages are covered. *See e.g., Collins & Aikman Corp. v. Hartford Accident & Indemnity Co.,* 335 N.C. 91, 436 S.E.2d 243 (1993); *J.T. Brown v. Marey,* 124 Wis. 2d 426, 369 N.W.2d 677 (Wis. 1985); *Greenwood Cemetery, Inc. v. Travelers Indemnity Co.,* 238 Ga. 313, 232 S.E.2d 910 (1977). But *see Hartford Casualty Insurance Co. v. Powell,* 19 F. Supp. 2d 678 (N.D.

---

*Sitting for HASWELL, C.J.

Tex. 1998) (predicting that Texas Supreme Court would not allow coverage). These cases typically involve the standard policy language that the insurer agrees to pay "all sums which the insured shall become legally obligated to pay as damages because of bodily injury . . . and property damage." The courts emphasize the words "all sums," but is there arguably a problem regarding awards of punitive damages under the balance of the clause? See the dissenting opinion in *Southern Farm Bureau Casualty Insurance Co. v. Daniel,* 246 Ark. 849, 440 S.W.2d 582 (1969).

4. *The public policy issue and liability vicariously imposed.* Approximately forty-five states have addressed the public policy issue, and about two-thirds of these jurisdictions are in accord with the view of the Montana Supreme Court. Of the jurisdictions which do not allow insurability, approximately two-third of those recognize an exception for damages assessed solely because of vicarious responsibility; in the remaining one-third, the answer is unclear. See Barry S. Ostrager & Thomas R. Newman, Handbook on Insurance Coverage Disputes § 14.06 (10th ed. 2000) (chart summarizing precedents in all states and territories); Lorelie S. Masters, *Punitive Damages: Covered or Not?,* 55 Bus. Law. 283 (1999). Should the vicarious liability exception exist if the jurisdiction imposes such liability only if the principal has some degree of complicity in the conduct which created the liability? For further discussion of the public policy issues, see Tom Baker, *Reconsidering Insurance for Punitive Damages,* 1998 Wis. L. Rev. 101.

5. *Other kinds of "punitive" damages.* Should statutory multiple damages (*e.g.,* treble damages) under a dog-bite statute be covered under the liability policy? Such damages were treated as punitive damages and held covered in *Cieslewicz v. Mutual Service Casualty Insurance Co.,* 84 Wis. 2d 91, 267 N.W.2d 595 (1978). Should monetary sanctions imposed on attorneys under Rule 11 or Rule 37 of the Federal Rules of Civil Procedure and similar state rules be insurable? *See* Thomas M. Hamilton, H. Anne McKee & David H. Levitt, *Insurability of Monetary Sanctions Under Attorney Errors and Omissions Policies,* 54 Def. Couns. J. 520 (1987).

Where an insured is entitled to punitive damages against an uninsured or underinsured motorist, should the insured be entitled to collect such damages from the uninsured or underinsured motorist insurer? Courts have given different answers, although the weight of recent authority, primarily in the uninsured motorist context, answers the question in the negative. *Compare Kentucky Central Insurance Co. v. Schneider,* 15 S.W.3d 373 (Ky. 2000) (no); *State Auto Insurance Co. v. Risovich,* 204 W. Va. 87, 511 S.E.2d 498 (1998) (no); *Siggelkow v. Phoenix Insurance Co.,* 109 Nev. 42, 846 P.2d 303 (1993) (no); *Shuamber v. Henderson,* 579 N.E.2d 452 (Ind. 1991) (no); *Santos v. Lumbermens Mutual Casualty Co.,* 556 N.E.2d 983 (Mass. 1990) (no); with *Jones v. State Farm Mutual Automobile Insurance Co.,* 610 A.2d 1352 (Del. 1992) (yes); *Sharp v. Daigre,* 555 So. 2d 1361 (La. 1990) (yes); *Stewart v. State Farm Mutual Automobile Insurance Co.,* 104 N.M. 744, 726 P.2d 1374 (1986) (yes).

6. *Evidentiary considerations.* In cases where punitive damages are assessable, evidence of the defendant's wealth or financial resources is generally admissible in order for the trier of fact to determine the appropriate amount

of damages. Dan B. Dobbs, *supra* Note 1. Should the fact that the defendant has liability insurance that covers punitive damages be admissible?

7. *Personal liability insurance.* Although the insurability of punitive damages issue is, for obvious reasons, more significant in commercial situations, the issue can arise with respect to personal liability insurance, such as the homeowners policy. When personal liability is involved, should the answers be different?

[2] "Other Insurance" Provisions in Liability Insurance

CARRIERS INSURANCE CO. v. AMERICAN POLICYHOLDERS' INSURANCE CO.
404 A.2d 216 (Maine 1979)

[This case appears in § 2.03[5], *supra.*]

NOTES

1. *For what purpose?* If "other insurance" clauses in liability policies are not designed to prevent overinsuring, what are they designed to do and why? See generally Susan Randall, *Coordinating Liability Insurance*, 1995 Wis. L. Rev. 1339.

2. *Determining primacy.* As the court in *Carriers* indicates, in the jurisdictions that do not follow the *Lamb-Weston* doctrine there are a number of variations on how to determine which policy is primary and which is secondary. Consider the test articulated in *Integrity Mutual Insurance Co. v. State Automobile & Casualty Underwriters Insurance Co.*, 307 Minn. 173, 174, 239 N.W.2d 445, 446 (1976):

> The approach of the Minnesota court has traditionally been more complex than the *Lamb-Weston* doctrine. In *Federal Ins. Co. v. Prestemon*, 278 Minn. 218, 231, 153 N.W.2d 429, 437 (1967), we stated that the better approach is to allocate respective policy coverages in light of the total policy insuring intent, as determined by the primary policy risks upon which each policy's premiums were based and as determined by the primary function of each policy. The Minnesota courts examine the policies and determine whether the insurers are concurrently liable on the risk, or one is primarily liable and another only secondarily liable. If they are concurrently liable, each must pay a pro rata share of the entire loss. On the other hand, if one insurer is primarily liable and the other only secondarily, the primary insurer must pay up to its limit of liability, and then the secondary insurer must pay for any excess up to its own limit of liability. In addition, some coverages may be neither primary nor secondary, but tertiary in their application.

> The nub of the Minnesota doctrine is that coverages of a given risk shall be 'stacked' for payment in the order of their closeness to the

risk. That is, the insurer whose coverage was effected for the primary purpose of insuring that risk will be liable first for payment, and the insurer whose coverage of the risk was the most incidental to the basic purpose of its insuring intent will be liable last. If two coverages contemplate the risk equally, then the two companies providing those coverages will prorate the liability between themselves on the basis of their respective limits of liability.

Does the Minnesota rule make any sense? Is this an area which is ripe for legislative preemption?

3. *Self-insurance as "other insurance."* If an firm chooses to self-insure instead of purchasing liability insurance, should the self-insured retention be treated as "other insurance" for the purpose of offsetting a liability insurer's responsibility? On the general issue of whether self-insured retentions constitute "insurance," most courts have answered the question in the negative. *See e.g., St. John's Regional Health Center v. American Casualty Co.,* 980 F.2d 1222 (8th Cir. 1992); *Hillsborough County Hospital & Welfare Board v. Taylor,* 546 So. 2d 1055 (Fla. 1989). Should a different answer be given when compulsory auto liability insurance is involved? Should businesses that have the financial means to self-insure their own fleets of automobiles be able to escape the obligation to contribute to the reimbursement of injuries suffered by third parties? *See Hillegass v. Landwehr,* 499 N.W.2d 652 (Wis. 1993). It is not difficult to imagine how this issue might arise. Suppose insured, who owns his own vehicle and has purchased liability insurance for that vehicle, leases a car in a jurisdiction with a statute that makes the lessor jointly and severally liable with its lessee in the event the lessee operates the vehicle negligently and causes injury to a third person. If the lessor chooses to self-insure, should the lessor be made to contribute to a judgment arising out of the lessee's operation of the leased automobile under the reasoning that the self-insurance is "other insurance"?

4. *Contracting around "other insurance" problems.* In the materials on warranty in § 3.02[1][d], *supra,* one of the issues considered was to what extent insurers should be allowed to use coverage provisions to circumvent warranty regulation. Would you allow insurers to use a similar technique to circumvent judicial regulation of "other insurance" provisions? Consider the next case.

FREMONT INDEMNITY CO. v. NEW ENGLAND REINSURANCE CO.

168 Ariz. 476, 815 P.2d 403 (1991) (en banc)

CORCORAN, JUSTICE.

In this case we must settle another conflict between two separate insurance policies containing similar "other insurance" provisions. Claims under each policy arise from the same alleged incident of legal malpractice. New England Reinsurance Company petitions for review of the court of appeals' decision holding that Fremont Indemnity Company's policy excludes coverage for the conduct in question.

We granted review . . . to determine whether language in both policies may be construed to allow only one insurer to benefit by the fortuitous existence of the other insurer's coverage. Our decision turns on whether the terms and conditions of both policies invoke the rules governing conflicting insurance clauses, and not whether policy provisions are set forth in a clear and unambiguous fashion. Therefore, we decline New England's invitation to examine Fremont's policy for inherent inconsistencies or ambiguities.

Because we believe that the competing policies, when read in their entirety, contain mutually repugnant "other insurance" clauses, we vacate the court of appeals' decision and affirm the trial court's ruling apportioning primary coverage on a pro rata basis. . . .

Factual and Procedural History

In May 1985, the Insured, an attorney, was sued by a former client seeking damages for legal malpractice allegedly committed in 1982. The conduct at issue was covered by two "claims made" professional liability policies:[1] (1) a policy issued by New England to the law firm that employed Insured in 1982; and (2) a policy issued by Fremont to the law firm in which Insured became a partner after 1982. Each policy provided $2,000,000 in coverage and was in effect when the Insured sought coverage for the alleged malpractice. New England's policy period ran for a one-year period beginning October 1984, and Fremont's policy was in effect from November 1984 to November 1985.

New England denied coverage, but Fremont agreed to defend Insured with a reservation of rights. After settling the claim for $70,000, Fremont agreed to pay the $9,000 difference between the deductibles required under each policy. Because the New England policy contains a $10,000 deductible, Fremont apparently believed it was liable for the first $10,000 of the settlement, subject to its own $1,000 deductible. Fremont also agreed, without prejudice to its own claim of no coverage, to share one-half of the remaining balance of $61,000 with New England. New England agreed to pay one-half of the defense costs.

Fremont then sued New England, arguing that its liability is limited to the difference between the New England and Fremont deductibles and, pursuant to an "other insurance" provision, the excess over the coverage of the New England policy. Because Fremont already had paid the $9,000 difference in deductibles and New England's policy limit exceeds the amount of the settlement, Fremont claimed New England is liable for the entire $61,000.

After hearing cross-motions for summary judgment, the trial court found that Fremont's policy is ambiguous concerning coverage and that the "other insurance" provisions of each policy are mutually repugnant. The trial court therefore held that each policy provides primary coverage on a pro rata basis. Because both policies provide the same amount of coverage, each insurer was

---

[1] "A 'claims made' policy is one whereby the carrier agrees to assume liability for any errors, including those made prior to the inception of the policy as long as a claim is made during the policy period." *Chamberlin v. Smith,* 72 Cal.App.3d 835, 845 n. 5, 140 Cal.Rptr. 493, 498-99 n. 5 (1977).

ordered to pay one-half of the settlement after required deductibles and one-half of the defense costs.

A divided court of appeals reversed, finding that the Fremont policy is not ambiguous and excludes liability except for Fremont's share of the cost of the defense and the deductible required by the New England policy. Judge Livermore dissented because he believed that the policies contain mutually repugnant excess clauses.

Discussion

1. Other Insurance Clauses and Mutual Repugnancy

"Other insurance" clauses seek "to limit or eliminate coverage under the policy in the event the insured has other insurance available." A. Windt, Insurance Claims and Disputes: Representation of Insurance Companies and Insureds § 7.01, at 386 (2d ed. 1988). In *State Farm Mut. Auto. Ins. Co. v. Bogart*, we mentioned that "other insurance" clauses fall into 3 general categories: (1) excess clauses, which provide coverage only for amounts due after all other available insurance is exhausted; (2) pro rata clauses, limiting liability to the proportion that the insurer's policy limit bears to the aggregate of other available limits; and (3) escape clauses, which state that an otherwise applicable policy will afford no coverage at all if other insurance is available. 149 Ariz. 145, 147, 717 P.2d 449, 451 (1986).

Assuming the insured has access to additional coverage, uncontested "other insurance" provisions are enforced and reduce the insurer's liability accordingly. When more than one policy contains an "other insurance" provision, however, courts must resolve the resulting battle of semantics over which clause, if any, will be given effect over the other. To do this, courts must ask whether the competing "other insurance" provision is contradictory and, if so, how mutually repugnant provisions should be resolved. See Windt, § 7.01, at 387–88.

Arizona follows the general rule of prorating the risk between contradictory "other insurance" provisions. For instance, in (Harbor Ins. Co. v. United Services Auto. Ass'n), the Arizona Court of Appeals held that "where two policies cover the same occurrence and both contain 'other insurance' clauses, the [other] insurance provisions are mutually repugnant and must be disregarded. Each insurer is then liable for a pro rata share of the settlement or judgment." 114 Ariz. 58, 63, 559 P.2d 178, 183 (App.1976). This court later explained that no other rule is possible because, "if a court were to give literal effect to each of the [other insurance] clauses, each policy would be cancelled out. . . ." *Bogart,* 149 Ariz. at 148, 717 P.2d at 452.[2] Further, we simply cannot solve the circular riddle caused by conflicting clauses "by picking up one policy, and reading it with the result which would be opposite to that reached if the other policy were first in order." *Id.*; at 149, 717 P.2d at 453.

---

[2] "This result occurs because the 'other insurance' clauses are triggered only when the other insurance is 'available' or 'collectible.' Before one reads the other insurance clause in the second policy that policy is 'available,' so that the clause in the policy being read is triggered and the first policy becomes 'unavailable.'" *Bogart,* 149 Ariz. at 148 n. 1, 717 P.2d at 452 n. 1.

2. Interpretation

In this case, a divided court of appeals declined to prorate liability because it believed that the Fremont policy, unlike the New England policy, contains an unambiguous exception to coverage in addition to an "other insurance" provision. This alleged exception in the Fremont policy is found in Insuring Agreement III and states:

> This policy applies to acts, errors, omissions or personal injuries which occur anywhere in the world:
>
> . . . .
>
> (B) prior to the effective date of the Policy, provided that:
>
> . . . .
>
> (2) there is no other valid and collectible insurance available to the Insured for any such prior act, error, omission or personal injury. . . .

After concluding that the terms and conditions of Fremont's policy are clear and unambiguous, the majority elected to enforce Fremont's Insuring Agreement III before giving effect to the "other insurance" provision contained in the New England policy, thereby relieving Fremont of its obligation to provide primary coverage.

In support of its reasoning, the court of appeals cited *Chamberlin v. Smith,* 72 Cal.App.3d 835, 140 Cal.Rptr. 493 (1977), in which the California Court of Appeal refused to prorate malpractice liability between two competing insurance companies that placed "other insurance" clauses in the conditions sections of their respective policies. One insurer was required to bear the entire loss because the other insurer included an additional "other insurance" clause in its insuring agreements. *Id.* at 847-50, 140 Cal.Rptr. at 500-02. According to the court in *Chamberlin,* this second "other insurance" clause operated as "an exception from coverage," regardless of the existence of "other insurance" language in the competing policy.[3] *Id.*

We disagree with the majority's conclusion and its reliance on Chamberlin for two important reasons. First, Insuring Agreement III of Fremont's policy contains an "escape from" rather than an "exception to" liability. By definition, an exception or exclusion provides that there is no coverage regardless of the existence of other insurance. *See e.g., Industrial Indem. Co. v. Goettl,* 138 Ariz. 315, 318, 674 P.2d 869, 872 (App.1983) (exclusion is intended to negate all coverage for specific injuries or conduct). An escape clause, in contrast, provides that "a policy which would otherwise cover the loss will afford no coverage at all in the event that there is other insurance available." *Bogart,* 149 Ariz. at 147, 717 P.2d at 451.

Thus, Fremont's alleged exception is actually a textbook escape clause, and we cannot agree with the theory implied in Chamberlin that such a clause is transformed into an exception simply because of its location in an insuring

---

[3] The court also reasoned that competing "other insurance" clauses should not be reconciled if the "error or omission occurs during the life of one policy, and the claim is made during the life of another." *Chamberlin,* 72 Cal.App.3d at 848, 140 Cal.Rptr. at 500-01. The present dispute, however, does not involve *successive* attorney malpractice policies, and neither the Fremont policy nor the New England policy was in effect at the time of Insured's alleged malpractice.

agreement as opposed to another portion of a policy. As a general rule, insurers cannot gain an advantage merely by rearranging "other insurance" provisions. Windt, § 704, at 404–05 n. 69.

Second, we agree with Judge Livermore's dissent that the Fremont and New England policies contain mutually repugnant "other insurance" clauses. To discern the actual effect of some policies, we cannot read "other insurance" clauses in isolation. The Fremont policy, for example, contains not one, but two "other insurance" clauses, and we must analyze them together in order to read the policy as a whole and "give a reasonable and harmonious meaning and effect to all its provisions."

The escape clause in Fremont's Insuring Agreement III, therefore, must be read in conjunction with the "other insurance" language contained in Fremont's Condition II, which states:

> [W]ith respect to professional services rendered prior to the effective date of this Policy, the insurance hereunder shall apply only as excess insurance over any other valid and collectible insurance and shall then apply only in the amount by which the applicable limit of liability of this Policy exceeds the sum of the applicable limit of liability of all such other insurance.

This excerpt from Condition II is properly defined as an excess clause, and provides coverage only after all other available insurance has been exhausted. When coupled, Insuring Agreement III and Condition II resemble a composite escape and excess clause, sometimes referred to as a contingent excess clause. The gist of the hybrid escape-excess clause is to permit escape if the loss is less than any other insurance protection and to provide excess insurance if its coverage exceeds the other valid insurance.

Careful inspection of the New England policy reveals only one relevant "other insurance" clause.[4] Condition B of the New England policy provides:

> B. Other Insurance: This policy shall, subject to the terms, conditions and limitations of this insurance, be in excess of any other valid and collectible insurance available to the Insured, whether such other insurance is stated to be primary, pro rata, contributory, excess, contingent or otherwise, unless such other insurance is written only as a specific excess insurance over the limits of liability provided in this policy.

This condition, like Condition II in the Fremont policy, is a true excess clause designed to provide coverage only for the liability above the maximum coverage of all other available insurance.

Although a combined escape-excess clause and a true excess clause may not automatically cancel themselves out, we believe such clauses are sufficiently repugnant to require proration. The purpose of each is to render coverage

---

[4] We note that Insuring Clause A of the New England policy contains a provision similar to the escape clause in Fremont's Insuring Agreement III. New England's escape clause, however, applies only if there is a *prior* policy or policies which provide insurance." (Emphasis added.) Because the inception date of the New England policy precedes that of the Fremont policy, the escape clause in Insuring Clause A is inapplicable.

secondary to that of any other policy and, in the event such "other insurance" covers the entire loss, eliminate liability altogether. In terms of effect, then, Fremont's composite escape-excess clause and New England's true excess clause are indistinguishable. The combined escape-excess clause simply expresses what the true excess clause implies—no coverage if other insurance provides adequate protection, but excess coverage if other insurance is insufficient.

By inquiring whether the terms and conditions of the Fremont policy are sufficiently clear and unambiguous to be enforced as written, the majority in the court of appeals misses the mark. The critical point is that both policies, by virtue of their respective "other insurance" provisions, provide the same degree of coverage if other available insurance exists. When pitted against each other, the policies promote a circuitous debate in which each insurer, claiming that its policy must be read first, refuses to pay at all.[5]

Because nothing in the record compels a finding that one "claims made" policy should be favored over the other without resort to arbitrary criteria, we are placed in the unenviable position of having to untie a virtual "Gordian knot" of insurance coverage. Following the advice of Alexander the Great, we believe that the best way out of such a predicament is simply to draw a sword and cut the knot. This result does not: (1) arbitrarily assign an order of priority to the policies; (2) deprive the Insured of any coverage; (3) give a windfall to one insurer at the expense of another; (4) encourage litigation that is ultimately detrimental to the insurance-buying public; or (5) delay settlements. Our decision also comports with the "growing weight of authority" construing escape devices as mutually repugnant to general excess clauses. Accordingly, we hold that both Fremont and New England are obligated to pay their pro rata share of the settlement pursuant to the mutual repugnancy rules explained in *Bogart*.

Disposition

Because we find no compelling reason to favor one policy over the other, we vacate the court of appeals' opinion and affirm the trial court's decision to prorate the loss, after required deductibles and equal shares of defense costs, on the basis of one-half to Fremont and one-half to New England.

GORDON, C.J., FELDMAN, V.C.J., and CAMERON and MOELLER, JJ., concur.

NOTES

1. *Implications of mobility in the market for lawyers.* As a law student, you probably have some sense of characteristics of the lawyer "labor market." When you take your first employment after law school, you will want to

---

[5] If we read Fremont's policy first, we must find it inapplicable because its escape device is triggered by the New England policy, making New England the sole primary carrier. However, if we read the New England policy first, its excess provision is triggered by the existence of the Fremont policy. New England would then escape liability because the limits of the Fremont policy exceed the amount of the loss, thereby negating the need for excess coverage.

acquire coverage under a professional liability policy; at this juncture, you presumably have had no opportunity commit acts of malpractice in the past for which claims might be filed against you. Suppose you take a job with a law firm, but then a few years later you desire to change your geographic location or pursue what you think is a better opportunity with another firm. You will obtain malpractice insurance with your new position, but in a claims-made environment, there is a possibility that you will be sued while employed by your new employer for acts or omissions you committed under your previous employment. Which insurance policy should be expected to provide coverage for this claim? What is an "optimal" package of insurance coverages for claims that might be asserted against you?

2. *The insurer's perspective.* If the general principle is that prior policies should cover prior acts of negligence, how should the insurer structure its policies to achieve that result? Is there anything wrong with an insurer issuing a claims-made form explicitly stating that no coverage is provided for acts or neglect occurring prior to the policy's effective date? Is such a provision different from an "other insurance" clause? If so, how? If the Fremont Indemnity policy had been the same form as that which appears in Appendix F, how would the case have been decided?

3. *A split in the cases.* As the court acknowledges, judicial opinion on the issue presented in *Fremont Indemnity* is divided. In addition to the *Chamberlin* decision discussed by the court, *see American Continental Insurance Co. v. Phico Insurance Co.,* 132 N.C. App. 430, 512 S.E.2d 490 (1999); *Smith v. Neumann,* 289 Ill. App. 3d 1056, 682 N.E.2d 1245 (1997); *Planet Insurance Co. v. Ertz,* 920 S.W.2d 591 (Mo. App. 1991); *Evanston Insurance Co. v. Affiliated FM Insurance Co.,* 556 F. Supp. 135 (D. Conn. 1983).

4. *Statutory regulation.* Many financial responsibility and compulsory liability insurance statutes specifically recognize that the policy may provide for the prorating of the insurance thereunder with other valid and collectible insurance. *See, e.g.,* Ariz. Rev. Stat. Ann. § 28-4010 (West 1998). The specific language of the statute in question is usually determinative and must be consulted, especially regarding the enforceability of other insurance clauses in uninsured motorist coverage. *See Westhoff v. American Interinsurance Exchange,* 250 N.W.2d 404 (Iowa 1977).

[3]   Causation Issues in Third Party Insurance

STATE FARM MUTUAL AUTOMOBILE INSURANCE CO. v. PARTRIDGE
10 Cal. 3d 94, 514 P.2d 123, 109 Cal. Rptr. 811 (1973)

TOBRINER, JUSTICE.

The instant case presents a somewhat novel question of insurance coverage: when two negligent acts of an insured one auto-related and the other non-auto-related constitute concurrent causes of an accident, is the insured covered under both his homeowner's policy and his automobile liability policy, or is coverage limited to the automobile policy? State Farm Insurance Company (State Farm), the insurer which issued both policies at issue in this case,[1] brought this declaratory judgment action requesting a determination as to which one, or both, of its policies afforded coverage for the accident in question.

In the trial court the insurer, relying on an exclusionary provision in the homeowner's policy which withheld coverage for injuries "arising out of the use" of a motor vehicle, contended that coverage was only available under the automobile liability policy. Defendants,[2] on the other hand, argued that since two independent negligent acts, one covered by the homeowner's policy and one by the automobile policy, jointly caused the accident, coverage should be afforded by both policies. After a non-jury trial, the court agreed with defendants and entered judgment holding the insurer liable under both policies. State Farm appeals from that judgment.

As discussed below, we have concluded that the trial court decision, finding liability under both insurance policies, should be affirmed. Initially, we shall point out that coverage is unquestionably available under the automobile liability policy since the instant accident bore some causal relationship to the use of the insured vehicle. Thereafter, we shall explain that although the homeowner's policy excluded injuries "arising out of the use" of an automobile, such exclusion does not preclude coverage when an accident results from the concurrence of a non-auto-related cause and an auto-related cause. The comprehensive personal liability coverage of the homeowner's policy affords the insured protection for liability accruing generally from non-auto-related risks. Whenever such a non-auto risk is a proximate cause of an injury, liability attaches to the insured, and coverage for such liability should naturally follow. Coverage cannot be defeated simply because a separate excluded risk constitutes an additional cause of the injury. We therefore conclude that the trial court properly found that coverage is available under both of the policies in question.

We begin our analysis with a brief review of the facts of the case, which are not in dispute. The circumstances resulting in the accident at issue reveal an instance of what can only be described as blatant recklessness. Wayne Partridge, the named insured of the two insurance policies issued by State Farm, was a hunting enthusiast who owned a .357 Magnum pistol. Prior to the date of the accident, Partridge filed the trigger mechanism of his pistol to lighten the trigger pull so that the gun would have "hair trigger action"; the trial court specifically found this modification of the gun to be a negligent act, creating an exceptionally dangerous weapon.

On the evening of July 26, 1969, Partridge and two friends, Vanida Neilson and Ray Albertson, were driving in the countryside in Partridge's four-wheel drive Ford Bronco. With Vanida sitting between them in the front seat, Partridge and Albertson hunted jackrabbits by shooting out of the windows

---

[1] The polices were actually issued by two separate corporate entities, State Farm Mutual Automobile Insurance Company and State Farm Fire and Casualty Company, but for convenience we shall refer to the insurers as simply "State Farm" or "the insurer."

[2] The insurer joined both Wayne Partridge, the insured, and Vanida Neilson, the injured individual, as defendants in the declaratory judgment action. For convenience, we shall refer to these parties as either "defendants" or "the insured."

of the moving vehicle; Partridge was using his modified.357 Magnum. On the occasion in question here, Partridge spotted a running jackrabbit crossing the road, and, in order to keep the rabbit within the car's headlights, Partridge drove his vehicle off the paved road onto the adjacent rough terrain. The vehicle hit a bump, the pistol discharged and a bullet entered Vanida's left arm and penetrated down to her spinal cord, resulting in paralysis. At the time of the accident, Partridge was either holding the gun in his lap or resting it on top of the steering wheel pointed at Vanida.

Thereafter, Vanida filed a personal injury action against Partridge seeking damages of $500,000. During settlement discussions between Vanida and State Farm, a controversy arose as to whether coverage was available under both Partridge's automobile liability policy and his homeowner's policy, or, if under just one policy, which one; the automobile policy contained a $15,000 limit, the homeowner's policy a $25,000 limit. Pursuant to these negotiations, State Farm agreed immediately to pay Vanida $15,000 and to institute the present declaratory judgment action to determine which of the policies provided coverage for the accident in question. Both parties agreed to be bound by the final determination (including appeal) in this action, and, as part of the settlement, Vanida agreed not to pursue further her action against Partridge,[3] the insurer, in turn, agreed to pay the full amount of all insurance policies found applicable, waiving any right to contest the monetary value of Vanida's damages.

State Farm then commenced the present action, setting out in its complaint the undisputed facts related above, and attaching the two relevant insurance policies issued to Partridge. The "Automobile Policy" contains a typically broad coverage or insuring clause, affording coverage for bodily injuries "caused by accident arising out of the . . . use . . . of the owned motor vehicle."[4] The "Homeowner's Policy," in addition to affording the normal coverage against fire and theft, contains a common comprehensive "personal liability" provision, which generally covers the named insured for all personal liability not falling within specific exclusionary provisions of the policy.[5] The broad coverage clause of this "personal liability" section is followed by a lengthy list of "exclusions"; the exclusionary clause relevant to this case excludes coverage for "bodily injury . . . arising out of the . . . use of . . . any motor vehicle," but excepts

---

[3] The record does not disclose the reason for Vanida's agreement to this condition, but the trial court surmised that the most probable explanation was that any personal judgment against Partridge would be uncollectible.

[4] The coverage clause of the "Automobile Policy" provides in relevant part: "[The company] agrees . . . [t]o pay on behalf of the insured all sums which the insured shall become legally obligated to pay as damages because of (A) bodily injury sustained by other persons . . . caused by accident arising out of the ownership, maintenance or use, including loading or unloading, of the owned motor vehicle. . . ."

[5] The coverage clause of the "Personal Liability" section of the "Homeowner's Policy" provides in relevant part: "This Company agrees to pay on behalf of the Insured all sums which the Insured shall become legally obligated to pay as damages because of bodily injury or property damage, to which this insurance applies, caused by an occurrence." "Occurrence" is defined broadly by the policy as "an accident, including injurious exposure to conditions, which results, during the policy term, in bodily injury or property damage."

from this exclusion injuries arising from non-registered vehicles kept exclusively on the "residence premises."[6]

As noted above, State Farm contended that because the use of the car played some causal role in the accident in question, the injuries "arose out of the use of the car" within the meaning of the homeowner's exclusionary provision, and thus that only the automobile policy provided coverage for the injuries. Defendants claimed, in response, that both the filing of the trigger mechanism and the negligent driving were concurrent causes of the accident, and argued that under such circumstances both policies were applicable.

The trial court first found that the insured, Partridge, had been negligent both in modifying the gun by filing its trigger mechanism and in driving his vehicle off the paved road onto the rough terrain, and that these two negligent acts were independent, concurrent proximate causes of Vanida's injuries. The court then concluded that both policies issued by State Farm to Partridge applied to the accident and that Vanida was entitled to recover under both.

The court's reasoning is clearly revealed in its memorandum opinion: "In the Court's opinion each of the policies affords different coverage for distinct and different acts of negligence of the insured which resulted in injuries to a third person. [¶] It should make no difference that Partridge was the owner-driver and insured under the automobile liability policy and was also the insured under the homeowner's liability policy. There were two separate, distinct and different acts of negligence committed by Partridge, one of which was entirely disconnected with the use of a motor vehicle and the other while using a motor vehicle . . . [B]oth proximately and concurrently contributed to [Vanida's] injuries and therefore both policies should afford coverage." State Farm now appeals from this decision.

On this appeal we begin from the established rule that since the underlying facts are not in dispute " 'it is the duty of the appellate court . . . to make its own independent determination of the meaning of the language used in the instrument[s] under consideration.' [Citations.]" We turn first to the automobile liability policy.

As noted above, the insuring clause of the automobile liability policy provided the typical coverage for bodily injuries "arising out the . . . use . . . of the insured automobile." Past California cases have established beyond contention that this language of "arising out of the use," *when utilized in a coverage or insuring clause of an insurance policy*, has broad and comprehensive application, and affords coverage for injuries bearing almost any causal relation with the vehicle. As the Court of Appeal observed in *St. Paul Fire & Marine Ins. Co. v. Hartford Acc. & Indem., Co.* (1966) 244 Cal. App. 2d 826, 831, 53 Cal. Rptr. 650, 654: "When employed in a public liability policy without restriction, words such as "use" or "using" have comprehensive scope. [Citations.]" Although our cases have not yet defined with absolute precision the

---

[6] The applicable exclusionary clause reads: "This policy does not apply: 1. Under Coverage E — Personal Liability . . . (a) To Bodily Injury or Property Damage Arising Out of the Ownership, Maintenance, Operation, Use, Loading or Unloading of: . . . (2) Any Motor Vehicle Owned or Operated By, or Rented or Loaned to, any Insured; But this subdivision (2) does not apply to bodily injury or property damage occurring on the residence premises if the motor vehicle is not subject to motor vehicle registration because it is used exclusively on the residence premises or kept in dead storage on the residence premises . . . ."

requisite causal connection necessary to invoke such a coverage clause,[7] we have no doubt that in the instant case the role played by the use of the car—constituting a substantial, and indeed, a proximate cause of the accident—was certainly sufficient to bring the present accident within the coverage of the automobile policy.[8] Neither party questions this conclusion.

The controversy in this case, instead, focuses solely upon the applicability of the homeowner's policy to the instant accident. The insurer, pointing to the exclusionary clause of the homeowner's policy which denies coverage for injuries "arising out of the . . . use . . . of a motor vehicle," contends that since, as we have just determined, the instant accident "arose out of the use" of the vehicle for purposes of the automobile policy, the homeowner's policy necessarily excludes the accident. Emphasizing that the language of the homeowner's exclusionary clause is nearly identical to the language of the automobile policy's coverage clause, and that the same insurer drafted and issued both policies, State Farm argues that the policies were intended to be mutually exclusive and that no overlapping coverage can be permitted. For the reasons discussed below, we cannot agree.

Initially we point out that the insurer overlooks the fact that although the language in the two policies is substantially similar, past authorities have made it abundantly clear that an entirely different rule of construction applies to exclusionary clauses as distinguished from coverage clauses. Whereas coverage clauses are interpreted broadly so as to afford the greatest possible protection to the insured, exclusionary clauses are interpreted narrowly against the insurer. These differing canons of construction, both derived from the fundamental principle that all ambiguities in an insurance policy are construed against the insurer-draftsman, mean that in ambiguous situations an insurer might be found liable under both insurance policies.

In view of the above approach the fact that an accident has been found to "arise out of the use" of a vehicle for purposes of an automobile policy is not necessarily determinative of the question of whether that same accident falls within a similarly worded exclusionary clause of a homeowner's policy. As one commentator has recently observed: "It is clear that the expression 'use of an automobile' has different meanings under different circumstances and that, whenever possible, the courts will apply an interpretation which gives, but never takes away, coverage for the 'use' of an automobile, thereby causing automobile and non-automobile liability policies to overlap, notwithstanding

---

[7] The California cases uniformly hold that the "use" of an automobile need not amount to a "proximate cause" of the accident for coverage to follow. Some minimal causal connection between the vehicle and an accident is, however, required. "Although the vehicle need not be, in the legal sense, a proximate cause of the injury, the events giving rise to the claim must arise out of, and be related to, its use." The cases have not further refined the minimum requisite "causal connection" threshold but under the established authorities the automobile policy clearly covered the accident in the instant case.

[8] Our conclusion that the automobile policy provides coverage for the "shooting" accident in the instant case does not conflict with a long line of cases finding no automobile coverage for somewhat similar hunting accidents. In all such cases the courts have specifically noted that there was *absolutely no* causal relationship between the accidental firing of the gun and the use of the automobile. Whenever circumstances reveal that the insured vehicle did bear some, albeit slight, causal connection with the shooting accident, courts have generally permitted recovery under automobile liability policies.

the exclusion against the 'use' of an automobile in most non-automobile liability policies." (Marcus, Overlapping Liability Insurance (1967) 16 Def. L.J. 549, 556.)

Although liability under the homeowner's policy could possibly be predicated upon the ambiguity of the exclusionary clause in the context of the instant accident, we need not rely upon this ground. The basis for such liability in this case is far stronger. Here the "use" of Partridge's car was not the sole cause of Vanida's injuries but was only one of two joint causes of the accident. Thus, even if we assume that the connection of the car with the accident is the type of non-ambiguous causal relationship which would normally bring the exclusionary clause into play, the crucial question presented is whether a liability insurance policy provides coverage for an accident caused jointly by an insured risk (the negligent filing of the trigger mechanism) and by an excluded risk (the negligent driving). Defendants correctly contend that when two such risks constitute concurrent proximate causes of an accident, the insurer is liable so long as one of the causes is covered by the policy.

In issuing the homeowner's policy to Partridge, State Farm agreed to protect the insured against liability accruing from non-auto-related risks. The insurer does not deny that Partridge's negligence in filing the trigger mechanism of his gun was a risk covered by the homeowner's policy; thus, if the gun had accidently fired while the insured was walking down the street or running through the woods, the insurer admits that any resultant damage would clearly be covered by the policy. The insurer contends, nonetheless, that coverage is foreclosed here because the present accident arose out of the use of an automobile.

In the instant case, however, although the accident occurred in a vehicle, the insured's negligent modification of the gun suffices, in itself, to render him fully liable for the resulting injuries. Under these facts the damages to Vanida are, under the language of the homeowner's coverage clause, "sums which the Insured . . . [became] legally obligated to pay" because of the negligent filing of the trigger mechanism; inasmuch as the liability of the insured arises from his non-auto-related conduct, and exists independently of any "use" of his car, we believe the homeowner's policy covers that liability.

A hypothetical may serve to explain further our conclusion in this regard. If, after negligently modifying the gun, Partridge had lent it to a friend who had then driven his own insured car negligently, resulting in the firing of the gun and injuring the passenger, both Partridge and his friend under traditional joint tortfeasor principles would be liable for the injury. In such circumstances, Partridge's personal liability would surely be covered by his homeowner's policy, and his friend's liability would be covered by automobile insurance. When viewed from this perspective, it can be seen that State Farm is presently attempting to escape liability under the homeowner's policy simply because, in the instant case, both negligent acts happened to have been committed by a single tortfeasor. In our view, this coincidence cannot defeat the insurer's obligation to indemnify the insured for liability arising from non-automobile risks.

In *Brooks v. Metropolitan Life Ins. Co.* (1945) 27 Cal. 2d 305, 163 P.2d 689 this court faced a somewhat similar problem of determining insurance coverage in a case involving a multiplicity of causes. In *Brooks*, an insured, afflicted with debilitating cancer, was covered by an accident policy which excluded "injury . . . [or] death . . . caused wholly or partly, directly or indirectly, by disease or mental infirmity . . . ." (27 Cal. 2d at p. 306, 163 P.2d at p. 690.)[9] The insured died in a fire, and the insurer sought to escape liability by establishing that a healthy individual would not have perished and thus that the insured's infirm condition did contribute to his death. While acknowledging that the insured's condition did contribute to his death, our court rejected the insurer's contention that coverage was unavailable simply because one of two joint causes of the death was an excluded risk. Chief Justice Gibson, writing for a unanimous court, declared that under such circumstances "the presence of preexisting disease or infirmity will not relieve the insurer from liability *if the accident is the proximate cause of death . . .* [R]ecovery may be had even though a diseased or infirm condition appears to actually contribute to cause the death if the accident sets in progress the chain of events leading directly to death, or if it is the prime or moving cause." (27 Cal. 2d at pp. 309–310, 163 P.2d at p. 691; emphasis added.) The court accordingly permitted recovery under the policy.

The rationale of the *Brooks* decision equally applies to the instant case. Here, as in *Brooks,* an insured risk (the modification of the gun) combined with an excluded risk (the negligent use of the car) to produce the ultimate injury. Although there may be some question whether either of the two causes in the instant case can be properly characterized as *the* "prime," "moving" or "efficient" cause of the accident[10] we believe that coverage under a liability insurance policy is equally available to an insured whenever an insured risk constitutes simply a concurrent proximate cause of the injuries.[11] That

---

[9] The exclusionary clause in *Brooks* was thus much broader than the provision at issue in the instant case, for the present policy gives absolutely no indication that coverage afforded for liability accruing from a covered risk is to be withdrawn whenever an excluded risk constitutes an additional cause of the injury. In *Brooks*, however, despite the breadth of the language of the exclusionary clause, the court still held the policy applicable where the insured risk constituted the proximate cause of the injury.

[10] In *Sabella v. Wisler* (1963) 59 Cal. 2d 21, 31-32, 27 Cal. Rptr. 689, 695, 377 P.2d 889, 895, the court, quoting 6 Couch on Insurance (1930) section 1466, restated the *Brooks* principle in terms of "efficient cause": " '[I]n determining whether a loss is within an exception in a policy, where there is a concurrence of different causes, the efficient cause—the one that sets others in motion — is the cause to which the loss is attributed, though the other causes may follow it, and operate more immediately in producing the disaster.' " In *Sabella,* although damage to an insured dwelling resulted from "settling," an excluded risk, the court found that the settling, in turn, had resulted directly from leakage from a broken sewer pipe, an insured risk; on these facts the "efficient cause" terminology was useful, because the court could find that the break in the pipe "set the other cause," settling, "in moti

In the [instant] case, however, the "efficient cause" language is not very helpful, for here both causes were independent of each other: the filing of the trigger did not "cause" the careless driving, nor vice versa. Both, however, caused the injury. In traditional tort jargon, both are concurrent proximate causes of the accident, the negligent driving constituting an intervening, but non-superseding, cause of the accident. If committed by separate individuals, both actors would be joint tortfeasors fully liable for the resulting injuries. Moreover, the fact that both acts were committed by a single person does not alter their nature as concurrent proximate causes.

[11] Our conclusion that coverage is available whenever an insured risk constitutes a proximate cause of an accident, even if an excluded risk is a concurrent proximate cause, is consistent with Insurance Code sections 530 and 532, as authoritatively construed in *Sabella v. Wisler* (1963)

multiple causes may have effectuated the loss does not negate any single cause; that multiple acts concurred in the infliction of injury does not nullify any single contributory act.

The case of *Hughes v. Potomac Ins. Co.* (1962) 199 Cal. App. 2d 239, 18 Cal. Rptr. 650supports this conclusion. In *Hughes* the trial court found that a landslide was caused by ground water from rainfall, a covered risk, rather than by overflow from a river, an excluded risk. The Court of Appeal affirmed, declaring that even if the trial court had erred in finding the ground water to be the sole source of the landslide, the insurer would still be liable for " '[i]t has been held that when two causes join in causing an injury, one of which is insured against, the insured is covered by the policy . . . .' *Zimmerman v. Continental Life Ins. Co.* (1929) 99 Cal. App. 723, 726, 279 P. 464, 465.)"

In the instant case the trial court specifically found that Partridge's negligence in filing the trigger mechanism of his gun constituted a proximate cause of Vanida's injuries. Applying the above principles, we conclude that the trial court properly found the homeowner's policy applicable to the accident.

. . . .

In sum, in purchasing two separate insurance policies from State Farm, the insured obtained coverage for liabilities arising from different sources. Under the homeowner's policy, the insurer agreed to protect the insured against liability arising generally from non-auto-related risks; under the automobile policy the insurer guaranteed indemnity arising from auto-related risks. Since the injury and the insured's liability in the instant case resulted from both auto-related and non-auto-related causes, the insurer is liable under both policies. The trial court properly concluded that coverage was available under both the automobile policy and the homeowner's policy.

The judgment is affirmed.

WRIGHT, C.J., and MOSK, and BURKE, JJ.

CLARK, JUSTICE (dissenting).

I dissent.

The language of the exclusion clause of the homeowner's policy, "arising out of the . . . use . . . of a motor vehicle," is clear and unambiguous when applied

---

59 Cal. 2d 21, 27 Cal. Rptr. 689, 377 P.2d 889 (discussed in fn. 10, *supra*), Section 530 provides that "[a]n insurer is liable for a loss of which a peril insured against was the proximate cause, although a peril not contemplated by the contract may have been a remote cause of the loss; but he is not liable for a loss of which the peril insured against was only a remote cause." Section 532 provides that "[i]f a peril is specially excepted in a contract of insurance and there is a loss which would not have occurred but for such peril, such loss is thereby excepted even though the immediate cause of the loss was a peril which was not excepted."

In interpreting these two sections in light of one another, the *Sabella* court rejected the insurer's contention that coverage was unavailable whenever an excluded risk constituted a "but for" cause of an accident. The *Sabella* court declared: "[I]f section 532 were construed in the manner contended for by defendant insurer, where an excepted peril operated to any extent in the chain of causation so that the resulting harm would not have occurred 'but for' the excepted peril's operation, the insurer would be exempt even though an insured peril was the proximate cause of the loss. Such a result would be directly contrary to the provision in section 530, in accordance with the general rule, for liability of the insurer where the peril insured against proximately resulted in the loss." (59 Cal. 2d at p. 33, 27 Cal. Rptr. at p. 696, 377 P. 2d at p. 896.)

to the facts of this case. Neither statute nor public policy precludes giving effect to the exclusion clause before us, and it should be enforced in accordance with the reasonable expectations of the parties.

. . . .

Because the negligent driving of an automobile was found to have been a direct and proximate cause of the accident, this occurrence comes within the express language of the exclusion clause, which negates coverage. In no way does the contract indicate the exclusion clause will be rendered inapplicable by the circumstance that there were other nonexcluded causes of the accident. The clause manifests the intent of the parties to exclude coverage by the homeowner's policy for accidents caused by [high]-risk, auto-related activity, and the rates were no doubt fixed and paid accordingly. Foreseeing the possibility of car-related negligence actions, the prudent person seeks the coverage of an automobile liability policy—this the insured did. This court should not now add to the homeowner's policy, in the guise of construction, a provision nullifying the exclusion clause in cases of concurrent proximate causation. Such provision would be consistent neither with the contract as written nor with the reasonable expectations of the parties.

Although section 530 of the Insurance Code mandates coverage when the insured peril is the proximate cause of the accident and the excluded peril is a remote cause, neither statute nor public policy precludes giving effect to an exclusion clause when the causes are independent, concurrent and proximate. To the contrary, section 532 of that code reflects a policy of effectuating exclusion clauses in cases similar to this. Within the limits of *Sabella v. Wisler* (1963) 59 Cal. 2d 21, 27 Cal. Rptr. 689, 377 P.2d 889[12] (See ante, p. 818 of 109 Cal. Rptr., p. 130 of 514 P.2d, fn. 11), the section requires that, in cases of concurrent causation when the excepted peril is a "but for" cause and the immediate cause of the loss was a nonexcepted peril, the exclusion clause will be controlling.[13]

Two cases in particular are relied on by the majority as factually and legally similar to this one. In *Brooks v. Metropolitan Life Ins. Co.* (1945) 27 Cal. 2d 305, 163 P.2d 689, in which a cancer patient succumbed to accidental injuries in part because of his existing condition, the court found the excluded cause was remote, stating: "[R]ecovery may be had even though a disease or infirm condition [the excluded risk] appears to actually contribute to cause the death if the accident [the insured risk] sets in progress the chain of events leading directly to death, or if it is the prime or moving cause." (*Id.*, at pp. 309–310, 163 P.2d at 691.) In Sabella v. Wisler, *supra*, the insured risk (rupture of a sewer line) was the efficient proximate cause, the one setting the excluded cause (subsidence) in motion.

---

[12] *Sabella* says, in effect, that because of a conflict with section 530, section 532 is inoperative where a "but for" cause is too remote to be regarded as proximate. *Sabella* does not say that section 532 conflicts with section 530 when it is applied to exclude coverage of an occurrence concurrently and proximately caused by an excluded peril.

[13] The broad language, "It has been held that when two causes join in causing an injury, one of which is insured against, the insured is covered by the policy . . ." (*Hughes v. Potomac Ins. Co.* (1962) 199 Cal. App. 2d 239, 244, 18 Cal. Rptr. 650, 653; *Zimmerman v. Continental Life Ins. Co.* (1929) 99 Cal. App. 723, 726, 279 P. 464), is contrary to section 532 (even as construed in *Sabella v. Wisler, supra)* and should not be relied on in this case.

In both cases coverage was properly allowed, for certainly an insured may reasonably expect that remote, incidental, or dependent causes will be disregarded in determining his coverage. However, in the instant case, the excluded cause was not remote, incidental, or dependent, but rather was direct, proximate, and independent; and, as the majority appears to concede, it can hardly be said the risk insured against by the homeowner's policy was the "prime," "moving," or "efficient" cause.

Under the circumstances, we should give effect to the exclusion clause in accordance with the obvious expectations of the parties.

I would reverse the judgment.

MC$ESC;COMB, J., concurs.

NOTES

1. *A "leading case."* *Partridge* has been described as a "leading case" on concurrent causation in other decisions. *See Vanguard Insurance Co. v. Clarke,* 475 N.W.2d 48 (Mich. 1991); *Warrilow v. Norrell,* 791 S.W.2d 515 (Tex. Ct. App. 1989); *Mission National Insurance Co. v. Coachella Valley Water Dist.,* 258 Cal. Rtpr. 639 (Cal. Ct. App. 1989). It has been an influential precedent in many other decisions as well.

2. *First-party versus third-party insurance.* In the materials on property insurance, we considered what kind of causation rule should be applied for first-party property losses. See § 4.05[3], *supra.* Should the first-party rules be applied to liability insurance, or vice versa? In *Garvey v. State Farm Fire and Casualty Co.,* 48 Cal.3d 395, 770 P.2d 704, 257 Cal.Rptr. 292 (1989)(en banc), the court held that it was inappropriate to apply the rule of *Partridge* to a first-party claim for property damage. The court explained:

> The following quotation summarizes the distinction that must be drawn: "Property insurance . . . is an agreement, a contract, in which the insurer agrees to indemnify the insured in the event that the insured property suffers a covered loss. Coverage, in turn, is commonly provided by reference to causation, *e.g.,* 'loss caused by . . .' certain enumerated perils. [¶] The term 'perils' in traditional property insurance parlance refers to fortuitous, active, physical forces such as lightning, wind, and explosion, which bring about the loss. *Thus, the 'cause' of loss in the context of a property insurance contract is totally different from that in a liability policy.* This distinction is critical to the resolution of losses involving multiple causes. [¶] Frequently property losses occur which involve more than one peril that might be considered legally significant. If one of the causes (perils) arguably falls within the coverage grant — commonly either because it is specifically insured (as in a named peril policy) or not specifically excepted or excluded (as in an "all risks" policy)—disputes over coverage can arise. The task becomes one of identifying the most important cause of the loss and attributing the loss to that cause." ([Michael E.] Bragg, [Concurrent Causation and the Art of Policy

Drafting: New Perils for Property Insurers, 20 Forum 385, 386-87 (1985)], italics added.)

> On the other hand, the right to coverage in the third-party liability insurance context draws on traditional tort concepts of fault, proximate cause and duty. This liability analysis differs substantially from the coverage analysis in the property insurance context, which draws on the relationship between perils that are either covered or excluded in the contract. In liability insurance, by insuring for personal liability, and agreeing to cover the insured for his own negligence, the insurer agrees to cover the insured for a broader spectrum of risks.

770 P.2d at 710. The court also thought that the comparison between premium charged and coverage provided was relevant:

> In the property insurance context, the insurer and the insured can tailor the policy according to the selection of insured and excluded risks and, in the process, determine the corresponding premium to meet the economic needs of the insured. On the other hand, if the insurer is expected to cover claims that are outside the scope of the first-party property loss policy, an "all-risk" policy would become an "all-loss" policy. (Friedman, Concurrent Causation: The Coverage Trap (1985) 86 Best's Rev.: Prop./Casualty 50, 58.) In most instances, the insured can point to some arguably covered contributing factor. As we shall discuss, if the rule in *Partridge* were extended to first-party cases, the presence of such a cause, no matter how minor, would give rise to coverage.
>
>   . . . [T]he reasonable expectations of the insurer and the insured in the first-party property loss portion of a homeowner's policy—as manifested in the distribution of risks, the proportionate premiums charged and the coverage for all risks except those specifically excluded—cannot reasonably include an expectation of coverage in property loss cases in which the efficient proximate cause of the loss is an activity expressly excluded under the policy. Indeed, if we were to approve of the trial court's directed verdict, we would be requiring ordinary insureds to bear the expense of increased premiums necessitated by the erroneous expansion of their insurers' potential liabilities.

Id. at 711. Do you agree that these differences justify two different sets of causation rules? Do tort rules ordain the liability of insurers? What if in *Partridge* there had been two tortfeasors—a vehicle driver, who had only a homeowner's policy, and a "trigger-filer," who only had an automobile policy?

3. *Characterizing the loss.* The court described the causes as concurrent. Could the causes be viewed as sequential? If so, does that make one cause "dependent" on the other?

Should the "concurrent causation" rule be limited to situations where each cause is truly independent of the other? If so, was that the situation in *Partridge*? Did not the bouncing of the vehicle start the chain of causation that led to the injury? Does it then follow that the operation of the vehicle was the predominant, efficient cause of the loss?

Exactly what is the disagreement between the majority and the dissent? Is Justice Clark not correct that the injury "arose out of the use" of the automobile? Why is he then not correct that this conclusion is determinative on the coverage question under the homeowners policy?

4. *Coordinating the coverages.* In *Partridge*, State Farm issued both the homeowners and the automobile policies. This is no doubt the usual situation, given that most consumers will probably use the same company for both kinds of coverage. Indeed, there are often advantages to doing so; if one wants "umbrella" liability coverage over both the homeowners and the automobile coverage, the chances of failing to maintain adequate underlying coverage are reduced if one insurer sells all of the different pieces of insurance. In facts like those presented in *Partridge*, it is unlikely that State Farm would have taken the position that there was no coverage under *any* policy.

Suppose, however, that ABC Insurance Company sold the auto policy, and XYZ Insurance Company sold the homeowners. Given the risks posed by firearms, would you, if you were a commissioner of insurance, allow ABC to exclude coverage under the auto policy if the alleged injury involved, either directly or indirectly, the use of a firearm? If you would, what are the consequences if XYZ inserted a provision in the policy that excluded coverage if the use of an automobile contributed to the loss, either directly or indirectly, in any manner? Should State Farm be able, if it desires, to create policy language in its two forms that accomplish the same result as the language in ABC's and XYZ's hypothetical policies?

5. *Derivative liability.* If the tortfeasor in *Partridge* had been a minor, who was an insured under his parents' homeowners policy, and if the vehicle in which he and the passenger were riding was an all-terrain recreational vehicle that was not specifically covered by any other insurance policy, how would you have pleaded the case? In *Mailhiot v. Nationwide Mutual Fire Insurance Co.*, 740 A.2d 360 (Vt. 1999), the passenger who was injured in an accident involving an all-terrain vehicle being operated by the insureds' son sued the parents for negligent supervision. Should the concurrent causation doctrine apply in this instance? *See also State Farm Mutual Automobile Insurance Co. v. Roberts*, 166 Vt. 452, 697 A.2d 667 (1997).

Chapter 6

AUTOMOBILE INSURANCE: COMMON
COVERAGES AND RECURRING ISSUES

"Before the advent of motor vehicles, death or serious injury in accidents on the public highway was a rarity; now it is a commonplace. But the people are not more careless now than then; in fact they are more careful, because more fearful. The increase in accidents is due to the danger *inherent* in the operation of motor vehicles by and among people of average human frailty. It is not preventable by any practical means yet devised. But perhaps the resulting monetary loss may be spread over the motoring class most responsible therefor, partially for their own benefit but with some corresponding benefits to the non-motoring class least responsible. . . . A motor vehicle accident compensation act seems desirable *if it can be made workable*; but can it?"— Ernest C. Carman, a "member of the Minneapolis Bar," in *Is a Motor Vehicle Accident Compensation Act Advisable?*, 4 Minn. L. Rev. 1, 12–13 (1919)

Humankind has invented machines more dangerous than the automobile; also, there are many kinds of machines that are used by more people than automobiles. (Examples of the latter may not leap to mind, but we suggest that the television is one, and the cooking stove and the telephone may be two others.) But when one asks what machine is the most widely used *and* the most dangerous, automobiles (and related motorized vehicles) have no competition. Since the first traffic death in 1899, more than 30 million people have died in motor vehicle crashes worldwide, a number roughly equal to the population of the state of California.[*]

According to national transportation statistics, 41,345 people perished and over 3.1 million personal injuries were suffered in the 6.3 million auto accidents that occurred in the United States in 1999. Motor vehicle crashes are the leading cause of death for young people (i.e., age 1 to 34), and one person dies in an auto accident every 13 minutes. According to the U.S. Department of Transportation, the total societal cost of motor vehicle accidents exceeds $150 billion annually. Although these numbers viewed in isolation are of stunning magnitude, the good news is that the number of fatalities has actually *declined* from the 56,300 highway deaths that occurred in 1972. In terms of fatalities per miles driven, the decline has been extraordinary—from 2.68 deaths per 100 million miles driven in 1983 to 1.50 deaths in 1999, the

---

[*] The data in this introductory note comes from three sources: Insurance Information Institute: The Fact Book 2000 (1999); Ruth Gastel, ed., *Auto Safety and Crashworthiness*, Insurance Issues Update (Insurance Information Institute), June 2000; 1999 National Transportation Statistics provided by the U.S. Department of Transportation (www.bts.gov/btsprod/nts); and the Highway Loss Data Institute of the Insurance Institute for Highway Safety (www.highwaysafety.org/safety_facts).

lowest ever. This decline is no doubt attributable to fewer drunk drivers (due to heightened public awareness and enforcement of driving-under-the-influence laws), more statutes which restrict young drivers and screen elderly drivers, increased use of seat belts and child-safety restraints, safer vehicles (including the widespread usage of air bags), and a population with a greater percentage of more mature, safer drivers. In other words, mechanisms other than insurance are extraordinarily important in dealing with the risk of injury and damage from automobile accidents. But with automobiles occupying center-stage in the world of injurious and damaging accidents, it should come as no surprise that automobile insurance is extremely important to our society—even if no account is taken of the fact that the automobile is the first or second most important asset on many, and perhaps most, personal balance sheets.

In automobile insurance, one finds considerable variety in the language of particular forms used by particular companies. As part of the trend toward more readable and understandable policy forms, the Insurance Service Office (ISO) introduced new automobile insurance policies in the late 1970s. The Personal Auto Policy (PAP) was designed to replace earlier policies—the Family Automobile Policy and the Special Auto Policy—as the standard form for insuring personal autos and certain types of nonbusiness trucks. A copy of the PAP is contained in Appendix E. The Business Auto Policy (BAP) was designed by ISO to cover commercial automobiles and other automobiles not eligible to be insured under the PAP. It replaces the Basic Auto Policy and the Comprehensive Auto Liability Policy. Another personal auto policy form was developed by the National Association of Independent Insurers (NAII); it is called the "Family Car Policy." Many insurance companies that belong to the NAII use this policy instead of the PAP developed by ISO.

A sample of a recent version of the Personal Auto Policy is set forth in Appendix E. Note that the policy has four distinct coverages: Part A is the liability coverage, which provides protection for the insured's own liability for bodily injury or property damage caused to third parties. Part B is the medical payments coverage (sometimes also called "PIP benefits," which refers to "personal injury protection" benefits), which is essentially a first-party insurance coverage for medical and hospital expenses incurred as a result of an automobile accident. When first-party benefits extend to lost wages, disability benefits, and the cost of replacing services normally performed by the injured person (e.g., household services), it is common to refer to the coverage as "PIP benefits." Part C provides uninsured motorist protection: this coverage protects the insured in case she suffers bodily injury (not property damage) at the hands of an uninsured motorist, who by definition lacks liability insurance which would otherwise compensate the insured. Underinsured motorist protection is closely related to uninsured motorist coverage; it is provided by a separate endorsement. Finally, Part D provides first-party property coverage for the insured vehicle, and this coverage has two parts, collision and comprehensive.

Which of these coverages the insured has depends, of course, on which the insured chooses to purchase. State statutes in almost all states require the owner of a motor vehicle to purchase minimum amounts of liability coverage, so almost every insured will have the Part A coverage. Medical payments and uninsured motorist protect is required in some states, and required to be offered to the insured in some others. Underinsured motorist coverage is required in only a few states, but is required to be offered in others. First-party property coverage is optional in all states; many insureds drop such coverage if their vehicle is old, and basically self-insure against the risk of the car's destruction due, for example, to weather perils, theft, etc., and to collisions in which either the insured is at fault or the tortfeasor is uninsured. (For a listing of what kind of coverage is required in each state, visit the Insurance Information Institute website at www.iii.org/individuals/auto/autopolicy.html.)

Each of the parts of the automobile policy receives attention in the sections which follow, but in the first section we examine the nature of the risk covered by the automobile insurance policy.

§ 6.01 The Nature of the Risk Covered

McNEILL v. MARYLAND INSURANCE GUARANTY ASSOCIATION

48 Md. App. 411, 427 A.2d 1056 (1981)

LISS, JUDGE.

Appellee, Maryland Insurance Guaranty Association, filed a declaratory judgment action in the Superior Court of Baltimore City seeking a determination of automobile liability coverage under an insurance policy issued by the bankrupt Maryland Indemnity Insurance Company (hereinafter MIIC) to its policyholder, Evelyn Watkins. Appellant, Charlie McNeill, answered the bill for declaratory judgment, and the parties agreed to submit the case on a stipulated statement of facts. That statement reads as follows:

> On September 2, 1975, Maryland Indemnity Insurance Company issued Policy No. A58318 to Evelyn Watkins for a 1968 Dodge Coronet, Serial No. WP46F8A2379106. That policy was in effect on December 12, 1975.
>
> On December 12, 1975, Charlie McNeill could not start his motor vehicle; whereupon he requested his friend, Evelyn Watkins, to bring her car to his location so that he could "jump-start" or "hot-shot" his car. Evelyn Watkins authorized Edward Hill to take her car to the aid of Charlie McNeill and he did so.
>
> Charlie McNeill connected the cables to the batteries of both cars and the Watkins car engine was running at all times, all at the explicit direction of Charlie McNeill. Charlie McNeill then took off one or more of the battery caps from the battery located in his vehicle. At this time, Edward Hill, who was not in any of the vehicles but was standing in the area as an observer, lit a match causing the battery in the McNeill vehicle to explode resulting in Charlie McNeill being seriously injured.

Negligence and the absence of contributory negligence are admitted and, therefore, are not at issue. The Maryland Insurance Guaranty Association, representing the bankrupt insurer Maryland Indemnity, has filed the Declaratory Judgment action seeking determination of whether coverage may be afforded on the above policy to the claimant McNeill.

At oral argument before this Court the panel of judges hearing this case inquired whether the jumper cables were connected to both cars at all times pertinent; *i.e.,* whether the cables remained connected uninterruptedly from the time they were originally connected until the time the battery exploded. Counsel for the parties were unable to answer this question at argument. Several days later, however, a letter was received in which both parties stipulated that the answer to the query was "yes." Furthermore, the letter (signed by both parties) represented to the panel:

Counsel also wish to bring to the Panel's attention, a clarification on the role of the match in causing the battery to explode. Counsel would agree that the lighting of a match which has absolutely nothing to do with the use or operation of a motor vehicle caused the explosion and . . . it is further necessary to point out that the lighting of the match caused an explosion not in the Watkins car, but in McNeill's car. It was McNeill's battery that exploded and it was caused by a match.

Counsel, of course, disagree as to whether appellant's injuries given the factual situation in its totality, "arose out of . . . the use of the insured's vehicle."

We have accepted the added stipulation of the parties as an additional portion of the appellate record.[1]

The Watkins vehicle was covered by the aforementioned policy which provided in pertinent part:

Coverage A—Bodily Injury Liability; . . .

To pay on behalf of the insured all sums which the insured shall become legally obligated to pay as damages because of:

A. bodily injury, . . .

arising out of the ownership, maintenance or use of the owned automobile . . . .

The trial judge, after consideration of the agreed statement of facts and memoranda of law submitted by the parties, held that the injury sustained by appellant did not arise out of the "ownership, maintenance or use" of the Watkins automobile and that MIIC was not liable to appellant under the terms of the Watkins policy. From this judgment, McNeill appeals.

---

[1] In fairness to the trial court we point out that the judge did not have before him the additional facts elicited by the query of the panel on appeal. We, of course, cannot speculate as to whether the additional information would have affected the trial court's conclusion. We have concluded that we should not avail ourselves of the provisions of Maryland Rule 1071 which permits a remand to the trial court under these circumstances; rather, in the interest of judicial economy of time, we choose to dispose of the issue raised by this appeal.

The sole issue to be determined by this appeal is whether the injury sustained by the appellant was caused by an accident arising out of the "ownership, maintenance or use" of the Watkins vehicle.

The standard adopted by the Court of Appeals in the interpretation of provisions of an insurance policy where the disputed provision is susceptible to more than one construction is that the provision must be "liberally construed in order to promote . . . recovery for innocent victims of motor vehicle accidents." "Ownership, maintenance or use clauses" do not limit recovery solely to injuries that are caused by direct physical contact with the insured vehicle; nor is it necessary that the damages be directly sustained or inflicted by the operation of the motor vehicle.

Appellant contends that it is sufficient to establish liability and coverage where there is a substantial nexus between the injury sustained and the use of the motor vehicle as contemplated by the insurance carrier and the insured.

Appellee argues that an automobile liability policy which provides coverage for accidents arising out of the "use" of a covered vehicle does not insure the owner of the vehicle unless it is shown that there is a causal connection between the use of the automobile and the accident, or the creation of the condition which caused the accident.

The Court of Appeals, in *Frazier v. Unsatisfied Claim and Judgment Board,* 262 Md. 115, 277 A.2d 57 (1971) had before it a factual situation in which a child of five years was a passenger in the rear seat of an open convertible vehicle which was being operated by the child's mother. An unidentified vehicle proceeding in the opposite direction passed the convertible and a lighted firecracker was thrown from the unidentified vehicle into the rear seat of the convertible. Distracted by the occurrence, the mother lost control of her car and struck a tree, severely injuring her child. The trial court concluded as a matter of law that the injuries did not arise out of the ownership, maintenance and use of the unidentified automobile. In reversing the trial court, the Court of Appeals held:

> 8 Blashfield, Automobile Law & Practice § 317.1 at 5–6 (Lewis ed. 1966); 7 Appleman, Insurance Law & Practice § 4317 at 144–6 (1942) and an Annotation, 89 A.L.R.2d 150 would seem to support the proposition that whether an injury is or is not within the coverage provided by an automobile insurance policy may well turn on the question whether the use of an automobile is directly or merely incidentally causally connected with the injury, even though the automobile itself may not have proximately caused the injury. Compare, for example, *National Indemnity Co. v. Ewing,* 235 Md. 145, 200 A.2d 680 (1964) (recovery allowed plaintiff, who fell from insured's car, and was injured while being escorted back to car on foot) and *Mullen v. Hartford Accident & Indemnity Co.,* 287 Mass. 262, 191 N.E. 394 (1934) (injury sustained from slipping on oil leaking from car held to be within provisions of policy) with *Commercial Union Ins. Co. of New York v. Hall,* 246 F. Supp. 64 (E.D.S.C. 1965) (no liability to plaintiff, whose way was blocked by insured's car and was then assaulted by insured) and *Kraus v. Allstate Ins. Co.,* 258 F. Supp. 407 (W.D. Pa.

1966) *aff'd* 379 F.2d 443 (3d Cir. 1967) (insurer not liable to pedestrians when insured detonated dynamite in his car). [262 Md. at 118, 277 A.2d 57.]

. . . .

From our reading of the briefs submitted by the parties we find no appreciable dispute between the parties as to the applicable principles of law governing this case. Both sides concede that a causal relationship or connection must exist between an accident and the ownership, maintenance and use of the insured vehicle in order for coverage to be provided under the policy provision. They further agree that absent such a causal connection of relationship, recovery will be denied. The problem arises as to the application of the law to the facts of the instant case.

Appellee relies heavily upon *Plaxco v. United States Fidelity & Guaranty Co.*, 252 S.C. 437, 166 S.E.2d 799 (1969), where an action was also sought in declaratory relief. The issue in *Plaxco* was whether the use by an insured of his automobile battery to crank the engines of his airplane by connecting the batteries with jumper cables constituted a use of an automobile within the meaning of the automobile liability insurance policy providing coverage arising out of the ownership, maintenance or use of any automobile. In *Plaxco,* the plaintiff drove his automobile to the airport for the purpose of making a trip in his airplane. The plane battery was either dead or too weak to start the engine so he drove his automobile to the left wing and connected the batteries of the plane to the auto by use of a jumper cable. When this was done he entered the plane, started the engine and engaged the brakes and alighted to disconnect the jumper cables, leaving the airplane engine running. After the plaintiff disconnected one of the cables from the automobile battery, and while attempting to disconnect the other, the airplane brakes failed to hold and struck another aircraft. The court held that the accident did not result from the use of plaintiff's automobile, when it stated:

> The accident in question did not result from the use of plaintiff's automobile. The only connection between the automobile and the airplane was the use of the automobile battery to start the airplane engine. This purpose had been completed when the airplane moved forward, after the brakes failed to hold. We find nothing in the facts or circumstances to show a causal connection between the use of the automobile battery as a source of power to start the airplane engine and the subsequent forward movement of the airplane. As stated by the trial judge, "the power source was coincidental only." The facts show that the accident resulted from the use of the airplane and not the insured automobile. [252 S.C. at 441, 166 S.E.2d 799.]

We conclude that the facts in *Plaxco* are distinguishable from the case at bar. The use of the Watkins vehicle was clearly a use which was or should have been contemplated and anticipated by the insurance carrier and the owner of the vehicle. It is not unusual that an insured might on occasion be required to use his vehicle to charge the battery of another vehicle. At the time the explosion took place, the Watkins vehicle was still being used in an activity permitted by her policy. The additional stipulation makes it clear that the Watkins vehicle was still attached by the jumper cables to McNeill's vehicle at the time Watkins' driver negligently threw the match. McNeill's activity in unscrewing the battery caps was entirely consistent with an effort to determine whether the battery had sufficient fluid and charge to permit McNeill's car to operate without being attached to the jumper cables. The lighting of the cigarette by Watkins' driver was not an intervening or independent cause, as was the failure of the airplane brakes in *Plaxco*. We conclude that this case on its facts is governed by *Merchants Co. v. Hartford Accident and Indemnity Co.,* 187 Miss. 301, 188 So. 571 (1939), where the Court held:

> In examining the cited cases, it will be observed that some of them proceed as if the automobile liability policy had expressly required that the injury for which the insurer could be held must be the proximate result of the use of the automobile truck. And if the policy here before us contained that express language, it might be that liability under the St. Paul Company policy in the present case would be denied on the ground that the proximate cause of the injury was the technically separable fact of the failure to remove the poles from the road. But we are in accord with the ruling expressed in *Panhandle Steel Products Co. v. Fidelity Union Cas. Co. [Tex. Civ. App.,* 23 S.W.2d 799] . . . that an insurance contract such as we have here does not require that the injury must be the proximate result, in the strict legal sense of that term, of a negligent act which happened in the actual use or operation of the truck; and, on the other hand, we would not assent to a contention that the policy liability would extend to something distinctly remote, although within the line of causation.
>
> Our conclusion, under a policy such as is here before us, is that where a dangerous situation causing injury is one which arose out of or had its source in, the use or operation of the automobile, the chain of responsibility must be deemed to possess the requisite articulation with the use or operation until broken by the intervention of some event which has no direct or substantial relation to the use or operation,—which is to say, that the event which breaks the chain, and which, therefore, would exclude liability under the automobile policy, must be an event which bears no direct or substantial relation to the use or operation; and until an event of the latter nature transpires the liability under the policy exists. [188 So. at 572.]

Appellee would, in effect, have us adopt the strict rules of direct and proximate cause in order to deny coverage. This, in light of the opinions by the Court of Appeals which we have cited, we decline to do. Under the facts in this case we conclude that there was a causal relationship between the use of the Watkins vehicle to start McNeill's automobile and that the explosion was caused by the careless throwing of the match by Watkins' driver which ignited the fumes released when the battery caps were unscrewed. We find that at the time this occurred the Watkins vehicle was being "used" as contemplated by the Watkins liability insurance policy.

Judgment reversed, costs to be paid by appellee.

FARM BUREAU MUTUAL INSURANCE CO. v. EVANS

7 Kan. App. 2d 60, 637 P.2d 491 (1981)

ABBOTT, JUDGE:

This is an appeal by two automobile liability insurance carriers from an order granting summary judgment against them holding that the respective policies issued by them provided coverage for the accident in question.

The determinative issue in this case is whether liability for bodily injury caused by the throwing of a lighted firecracker (M-80) from the rear of a parked station wagon "arose out of the use of an automobile" so as to be covered under the automobile liability insurance policies in issue.

On April 28, 1979, a going-away party was being held for David and Karen Evans. The party was held in a large, open field. Several bonfires were going; keg beer was available. It started to rain and turn cold. Damon Rose (not a party to this action), at his wife's request, parked the Roses' station wagon so that the back seat was facing a bonfire. The Rose station wagon has three seats, the back one of which faces the rear of the station wagon. The tailgate was open. Mike Ehinger was sitting in the middle of the back seat facing the fire. Kathy Rose and Danny Ireland were beside him. It is alleged that Ehinger, with the aid of Rose and Ireland, lit an explosive device known as an M-80 and threw it out of the rear of the station wagon. It landed in a glass of beer held by Karen Evans. When it exploded, Karen Evans received extensive damage to her hand and a number of puncture wounds to her body from the shattered glass.

The Evanses are plaintiffs in a personal injury action brought against Kathy Rose, Mike Ehinger and Danny Ireland for Karen's personal injuries sustained as a result of the explosion. Farm Bureau Mutual Insurance Company, Inc., insures the Rose automobile and Farmers Insurance Company, Inc., insures an automobile owned by Mike Ehinger. Both policies provide coverage for bodily injury "arising out of the ownership, maintenance or use" of the insured vehicle.

The question before the trial court was whether the two policies provided coverage for Mike Ehinger, Danny Ireland and Kathy Rose, or any of them, with regard to claims made against them by the Evanses. The trial court determined that there was coverage because the automobile was being used as shelter, a reasonable incident of its use and one reasonably contemplated by the parties to the insurance contract.

The policy provision in question is mandated by the legislature. K.S.A.1980 Supp. 40-3107(b). As an automobile liability coverage clause, it is to be interpreted broadly to afford the greatest possible protection to the insured. In the case before us, the trial court found the vehicle was being "used" within the meaning of the coverage clause because of its use as a shelter. But mere use of a vehicle, standing alone, is not sufficient to trigger coverage. Thus, even though the vehicle was being used within the meaning of the automobile liability policies, the question remains whether that use is so remote from the negligent act that it can be said there was no causal relationship between the use of the car and the injuries sustained.

Kansas has construed the word "use" in connection with automobile liability policies on three occasions: *Alliance Mutual Casualty Co. v. Boston Insurance Co.,* 196 Kan. 323, 411 P.2d 616 (1966); *Esfeld Trucking, Inc. v. Metropolitan Insurance Co.,* 193 Kan. 7, 392 P.2d 107 (1964); *United States Fidelity & Guar. Co. v. Farm Bureau Mut. Ins. Co.,* 2 Kan. App. 2d 580, 584 P.2d 1264. None of these cases is exactly in point, but language found in *Esfeld* indicates Kansas follows the majority rule that there must be some causal connection between the use of the insured vehicle and the injury. In *Esfeld,* the court stated: "In determining the coverage of a policy such as our present one a court must consider whether the injury sustained was a natural and reasonable incident or consequence of the use of the vehicle involved for the purposes shown by the declarations of the policy though not foreseen or expected." 193 Kan. at 11, 392 P.2d 107.

The general rule in other jurisdictions is that "arising out of the use" of a vehicle requires the finding of some causal connection or relation between the use of the vehicle and the injury. Stated another way, an injury does not arise out of the "use" of a vehicle within the meaning of the coverage clause of an automobile liability policy if it is caused by some intervening cause not identifiable with normal ownership, maintenance and use of the insured vehicle and the injury complained of. The provision, however, imparts a more liberal concept of a causation than "proximate cause" in its traditional, legal sense.

We need not decide whether a different result might be reached if the vehicle had been in motion at the time. Some courts have held that if a vehicle is moving and the speed of the car contributed to the impact of a thrown missile, such would be a sufficient causal connection. Likewise, the mere throwing of the contents of an ashtray or other trash normally found in a vehicle could constitute a use. The throwing of an explosive device from a car, however, has generally been held to be so remotely connected with the use of the vehicle that it is not causally related to the injury.

The use of the Roses' vehicle did not causally contribute to Karen's injuries anymore [sic] than it would have if one of the occupants under the facts present in this case had shot her with a firearm. The fact that the M-80 was lit inside the vehicle and the defendants might have had difficulty lighting it if no shelter had been available is so remote that it does not furnish the necessary causal relationship between the use of the car and her injuries. We see no more difference in the use of the vehicle here under the facts present than if the owner of the vehicle had been outside the car and in order to avoid the rain had held the device under the car or stood on the "leeward" side of it to light the device.

Having concluded the trial court erred in determining that the insurance policies in question provided coverage, we deem the remaining issues moot.

Reversed with directions to enter judgment for the insurance carriers on their motions for summary judgment.

NOTES

1. *The essence of the coverage.* If an automobile is being driven when an accident occurs, does the loss automatically arise out of the "ownership, maintenance, or use" of the vehicle? What if the victim is standing on the bed of the insured's truck as the truck is slowly driven past a row of apple trees, and the victim falls out of the truck while trying to reach for an apple? If the truck were stationary when the fall occurred, does the answer change? What if the insured fell from the truck because he had placed a stepladder in its bed, and failed to properly secure the ladder? *See Leverette v. Aetna Casualty & Surety Co.,* 276 S.E.2d 859 (Ga. Ct. App. 1981).

Generally speaking, people purchase a homeowners (or renters) policy to cover their general personal liabilities except for liabilities arising out of the use of automobiles, and automobile liability policies are purchased to provide insurance for the automobile-related risks. When the insured negligently operates his or her car and crashes into another in a garden-variety automobile accident, the automobile is being "used" as an automobile. People, however, put their automobiles to many kinds of uses, some of them quite innovative, and the question often arises whether the loss arises out of the automobile's "ownership, maintenance, or use."

Although liability coverage under standard automobile policies is limited to bodily injury or property damage "arising out of the ownership, maintenance or use" of the insured's automobile, note that coverage is also extended to the insured's operation or use of a non-owned automobile, but under somewhat narrower circumstances. This receives more attention in § 6.02[3] of this Chapter, *infra*.

2. *Ownership, maintenance, or use?* Each term in the coverage provision applies to distinct risks notwithstanding the possibility of overlap in some situations. The first two terms are the narrower of the three and have produced less litigation than that under the term "use."

Note that both *McNeill* and *Evans* involve the liability coverages of the automobile policy. The "ownership, maintenance, or use" issue also arises in connection with the uninsured and underinsured coverages, which are discussed in § 6.03, *infra*. Notice the different language in the insuring agreement of each of the coverages in the Personal Auto Policy in Appendix E. Why do the medical payments and first-party property coverages not raise this issue? Some policies, however, use "ownership, maintenance or use" language in connection with the first-party medical payment coverage.

a. *Ownership.* One may be liable as an owner of an automobile under the common law "family purpose" doctrine or by virtue of an owner-consent statute. *See* Dan B. Dobbs, The Law of Torts § 340 (2000). The term "ownership" in the policy applies to these situations as well as any other where mere ownership is the basis for imposing liability, vicarious or otherwise.

If the insured has sold his vehicle under a conditional sales agreement and retains title for security purposes until the last payment is made, is the insured the "owner" of the vehicle for insurance purposes? *See Beatty v. Western Pacific Insurance Co.,* 445 P.2d 325 (Wash. 1968). It has become very common in recent years for people to lease vehicles for multi-year terms instead of purchasing the vehicle with borrowed funds and making payments on a promissory note. Standard policy language treats vehicles leased under long-term arrangements as the equivalent of owned vehicles.

b. *Maintenance.* The unqualified term "maintenance" applies to anyone who negligently injures a third party as a result of servicing, repairing, or otherwise maintaining the vehicle, but standard policies generally exclude coverage for those who are in the business of furnishing such services. Thus, your friendly auto mechanic does not get the benefit of your coverage when he negligently repairs your brakes. However, you or your retired neighbor would be covered if either or both of you did so. If an insured is assaulted by third parties while changing a tire, do the insured's injuries arise out of the maintenance of the vehicle? *See Blish v. Atlanta Casualty Co.,* 736 So.2d 1151 (Fla. 1999) (yes).

c. *Use.* The term "use," as illustrated in *McNeill* and *Evans,* has produced a substantial amount of litigation, as might be imagined given all that transpires in and around the automobile in our society.

Do you agree with the *McNeill* court that Hill was "using" Watkins' car when he lit the match that caused the battery in McNeill's car to explode? Would it be important to know whether the charging of the McNeill battery by the Watkins' car created the situation where an explosion could occur, i.e., whether the chemical process involved in charging a battery in this manner produces more combustible fumes than are otherwise emitted by a battery? Depending on the answer, would it have behooved one of the attorneys to make sure that information on the subject was introduced at trial or contained in the stipulation?

If McNeill was "using" Watkins' car, were Ehinger and his pals "using" the Rose vehicle in the *Evans* case? What is the difference?

3. *Use and the "transportational function."* Some courts ask whether the vehicle is being used in its "transportational function." The focus, then, is on whether the motor vehicle is being used "as a motor vehicle," to be distinguished from being used as "a housing facility of sorts, as an advertising display (such as at a car dealership), as a foundation for construction equipment, as a mobile public library, or perhaps even when a car is on display in a museum." *McKenzie v. Auto Club Insurance Ass'n,* 458 Mich. 214, 580 N.W.2d 424 (1998) (insured is nonfatally asphyxiated while sleeping in camper attached to pickup truck). But do you agree that a vehicle is solely a device for getting from one place to another? Can it not also be used (and expected to be used) as a device for shelter (*e.g.,* the so-called "car campers")? Anyone who has spent time on a farm knows that farming vehicles are put to many different uses. If an insured uses a pick-up truck to pull a rope that lifts a wooden platform via a pulley system, the rope breaks, and the platform falls on someone causing injury, does the loss "arise out of the use" of the truck? *See Lawver v. Boling,* 238 N.W.2d 514 (Wis. 1976). How would the court in *Evans* have decided the farm truck and the pulley case?

People also use vehicles to transport things, including pets. If a dog is being transported by a car and it bites a passenger while the car is moving (or getting ready to move), does this injury arise out of the use of the vehicle? If the vehicle is stopped and parked while Rover rests inside it, a child opens the door and gets in the car, and Rover bites the child, does this injury arise out of the use of the vehicle? See *Keppler v. American Family Mutual Insurance Co.*, 588 N.W.2d 105 (Iowa 1999); *Farmers Union Cooperative Insurance Co. v. Allied Property and Casualty Insurance Co.*, 569 N.W.2d 436 (Neb. 1997).

4. *Vehicles and firearms*. Cars and trucks are dangerous enough, but many people have demonstrated through the years that one can multiply risk exponentially by using a car and a gun at the same time. This mix of uses has produced a large number of perplexing cases where the meaning of the term "use" was the issue.

Can you reconcile the following two cases? In *Kohl v. Union Insurance Co.*, 731 P.2d 134 (Colo. 1986), a claimant-bystander's injuries were held to be causally related to the insured-defendant's use of his jeep. In *Kohl*, the accidental discharge of a rifle occurred while insured was lifting the rifle out of the jeep's gun rack while the jeep was parked preparatory to unloading the rifle and safely storing it for journey home from hunting trip). In *Azar v. Employers Casualty Co.*, 178 Colo. 58, 495 P.2d 554 (1972), the claimant-passenger's injuries were held not to be causally related to defendant-driver's use of the car in which both were riding while hunting rabbits. In *Azar*, the defendant stopped the car, prepared to fire his shotgun through the window, but changed his mind and accidentally discharged the gun while bringing it back into the car.

What about these two cases? In *Fidelity & Casualty Co. v. Lott*, 273 F.2d 500 (5th Cir. 1960), the insured was held to be "using" his car when he rested his rifle on the top of the car for better aim and fired. The bullet struck the curvature of the roof, deflected downward, and killed a passenger). But in *Norgaard v. Nodak Mutual Insurance Co.*, 201 N.W.2d 871 (N.D. 1972), the insured was held not be "using" his car when he used the roof as a gun rest, fired, and killed a passenger whom he did not see alighting from the car.

Some courts have attempted to articulate a test in car-gunshot accidents which distinguishes a situation in which a vehicle is the mere "situs" of an accident from one in which the vehicle itself or permanent attachments to the vehicle causally contribute in some way to produce the injury. See, e.g., *Thornton v. Allstate Insurance Co.*, 425 Mich. 643, 391 N.W.2d 320 (1986). How helpful is this test? Do you think the cramped physical quarters of the car contributed significantly to the accident in *Azar*? Did the autos in *Lott* and *Norgaard* causally contribute in some way to produce the injuries?

5. *Vehicles as launching pads*. *Evans* puts the "car as launching pad" issue in play. Judge Abbott acknowledged but did not address the complication that would arise if the car had been in motion. Where objects, such as eggs or beer mugs, are thrown from a moving vehicle, does this constitute a "use" within the automobile liability coverage clause? See *National Am. Insurance Co. v. Insurance Co. of N. Am.*, 74 Cal. App. 3d 565, 140 Cal. Rptr. 828 (1977), and *Odom v. Deltona Corp.*, 341 So. 2d 977 (Fla. 1977). Should a distinction be

made between throwing the "usual stuff" out of cars (such as apple cores, sticks, and trash) and tossing out inherently dangerous objects (such as fireworks)?

Is firing a gun (i.e., launching a bullet) from inside a vehicle to be handled under the same principles? Given the recent increase in gun-related violence committed from inside moving vehicles (*e.g.*, drive-by shootings), is it fair to suggest that these kinds of events involve "expected" uses of vehicles, at least for the purpose of insurance coverage? *See, e.g., State Farm Mutual Automobile Insurance Co. v. Bookert,* 337 S.C. 291, 523 S.E.2d 181 (1999) (insured not entitled to UIM benefits for injuries from gunshots fired from a vehicle); *Farmers Texas County Mutual Insurance Co. v. Griffin,* 955 S.W.2d 81 (Tex. 1997) (victim of drive-by shooting did not allege "auto accident" within meaning of liability policy); *Lexie v. State Farm Mutual Automobile Insurance Co.,* 251 Va. 390, 469 S.E.2d 61 (1996) (held, no causal connection between two separate drive-by shooting incidents and use of vehicles for purposes of UM coverage). For additional discussion, see Charles W. Benton, Annotation, *Automobile Insurance Coverage for Drive-By Shootings and Other Incidents Involving the Intentional Discharge of Firearms from Moving Motor Vehicles,* 41 A.L.R.5th 91 (1996).

What about injuries suffered by the insured-driver during a carjacking? *See Bourne v. Farmers Insurance Exchange,* 534 N.W.2d 491 (Mich. 1995) (insurer not obligated to pay no-fault benefits to insured for injuries suffered during carjacking). See generally Diane L. Schmauder, Annotation, *No-Fault Insurance Coverage for Injury or Death of Insured Occurring During Carjacking or Attempted Carjacking,* 42 A.L.R.5th 727 (1996).

Insights into these questions can be gained by reviewing the majority and dissenting opinions in *Pemco Insurance Co. v. Schlea,* 817 P.2d 878 (Wash. Ct. App. 1991), where the majority held that the abduction and rape of the insured in an automobile her assailant had taken from a co-worker did not arise out of the "use" of the vehicle. The majority reasoned that "[k]idnapping, assault, and rape are not motoring risks against which the parties intended to insure." 817 P.2d at 880. The dissent had a different view: "While using a vehicle as a means of transporting a victim and as a place to commit a rape is not either a 'reasonable,' or 'traditional' use of an automobile, it is . . . a use nonetheless." *Id.*

How about throwing objects *inside* a moving vehicle? *See United Servs. Automobile Ass'n v. Aetna Casualty & Surety Co.,* 75 A.D.2d 1022, 429 N.Y.S.2d 508 (1980). Even well-behaved children sometimes forget the rules for inside-the-car behavior.

6. *Other forms.* Some motor vehicle policies use a slightly different wording. They provide coverage for liability arising out of the "ownership, maintenance or use, including loading or unloading" of the vehicle. Does the "loading and unloading" language really add anything to the word "use"? The "loading and unloading" language has produced some surprisingly broad legal interpretations under the comprehensive general liability and basic auto policies, and steps were taken in drafting the business version of the automobile policy to limit this language to activities more directly involved in the actual or immediate loading and unloading process.

If a passenger is bitten by the insured's dog as the passenger is getting out of the insured's car, does the injury arise out of the "unloading" of the vehicle? *See Hartford Accident & Indemnity Co. v. Civil Service Employees Insurance Co.,* 108 Cal. Rptr. 737 (Cal. Ct. App. 1973). Does it matter whether the dog was in the car at the time of the bite, as opposed to running across the lawn to meet his prey? If the former, is it customary to expect vehicles to be used to transport pets, which means the unloading issue need not even be reached? If the victim is already out of the car at the time of the bite, is the process of "unloading" already over, so that the insurance does not provide coverage? *See Shoreland Early Childhood Center v. Alexander,* 616 N.E.2d 274 (Ohio Ct. App. 1992).

7. *Other more-or-less common situations.* As one might predict, the situations in which insureds become liable to third parties and a motor vehicle is somewhere in the picture are virtually infinite. Consider the following:

a. Do altercations between people who have just been involved in auto accidents "arise out of the ownership, maintenance, or use" of the vehicle? *See Foss v. Cignarella,* 482 A.2d 954 (N.J. Super. Ct. 1984)(insured sideswiped plaintiff when passing on left by driving on median; plaintiff's vehicle bumped insured's as both stopped; insured emerged from vehicle in rage and stabbed plaintiff who was still in car with window partially down); see also *Allstate Insurance Co. v Gillespie,* 455 So. 2d 617 (Fla. Dist. Ct. App. 1984) (assault on insured, who was sitting in car, by person who was enraged by manner in which insured was driving; insured produced gun, which discharged and injured attacker, and attacker sued insured); *Morosini v. Citizens Insurance Co. of Am.,* 461 Mich. 303, 602 N.W.2d 828 (1999)(insured's vehicle was struck from behind by another motorist in minor accident; when insured left his vehicle to inspect damage, other motorist assaulted and injured insured).

b. What if the victim falls from a moving vehicle while trying to resist the amorous advances of the driver? *See Chapman v. Allstate Insurance Co.,* 211 S.C.2d 876 (S.C. 1975).

c. If the insured accidentally slams the door on a passenger's hand, causing injury, is the loss covered? Are you entirely comfortable covering such claims if the victim is a member of the insured's family? *See Coletrain v. Coletrain,* 121 S.E.2d 89 (S.C. 1961).

d. The insured uses his covered vehicle to transport tools to an intersection. He stops the car and turns it off. He takes the tools out of the car, and uses them to remove (i.e., steal) a stop sign at the intersection, which he places in his car along with the tools. He drives off with his loot. Later, a motorist is killed at the intersection because of the stop sign's removal. The heirs of the decedent bring a negligence action against the insured. Does the auto liability policy provide coverage for the death? *See Molitor v. Davidson,* 978 P.2d 294 (Kan.Ct.App. 1999). If the court adheres to the precedent of *Evans,* what result?

8. *Problem: The case of the very bad break.* On July 4, Howard asked Green to help him attempt to pull his boat and boat trailer across a beach by hauling it with Howard's car. Green lent Howard a nylon rope, two shackles, and a pulley. Green hitched the pulley to a telephone pole. Green stayed at the

trailer with Spiro in order to help guide the boat and trailer in the proper direction at the time it was to be towed. Howard attached one shackle to the rear bumper of his car and the other shackle to the trailer, thereby attaching the line to both the car and the trailer. Howard started the car and began to go forward. At that time Spiro and Green held onto the tongue of the trailer in order to guide it in the proper direction. When Howard started to move his car, the line tightened and, a few seconds later, slackened. The shackle attached to the rear bumper of his car broke and a fragment struck and fatally injured Paul, a lifeguard who was about 50 feet away. At no time did Green drive the car. Howard's boat and trailer were registered to him. The trailer was designed for use with a private passenger motor vehicle, and was not being used during this incident for business purposes with another type of motor vehicle.

The facts in this problem are exactly those in *Liberty Mutual Insurance Co. v. Agrippino,* 375 Mass. 108, 375 N.E.2d 702 (1978). The Massachusetts court held that there was no coverage under the auto policy actually issued to Green. Assume, however, that Green has an automobile policy in the form of the policy in Appendix E. If Paul's estate sues Green, does Green have any coverage under this policy?

---

§ 6.02 Compulsory Liability Insurance

[1] The Nature of the Coverage

ODUM v. NATIONWIDE MUTUAL INSURANCE CO.

101 N.C. App. 627, 401 S.E.2d 87,
cert. denied, 329 N.C. 499, 407 S.E.2d 539 (1991)

JOHNSON, JUDGE.

This action arises out of an auto accident which occurred on 16 June 1987 when a car driven by Robert McPhaul, husband of the insured, Arnetta McPhaul, crossed the center line and collided with a car driven by Clifton Oxendine. Mrs. McPhaul was a passenger in the car driven by Robert. Both Arnetta McPhaul and Clifton Oxendine died of injuries sustained in the wreck. Following Nationwide's denial of coverage, plaintiffs brought suit to collect under a motor vehicle liability insurance policy issued to Arnetta McPhaul.

. . . .

Nationwide answered plaintiffs' complaint and counterclaimed, alleging that Arnetta McPhaul made fraudulent and intentional misrepresentations on her insurance application which rendered the policy void ab initio. Nationwide moved for summary judgment on the ground that there was no genuine issue of material fact and the insurance policy was void ab initio as a matter of law. By judgment dated 8 December 1989, Judge Farmer denied Nationwide's motion for summary judgment and decreed that the insurance policy was in full effect and that defendant Nationwide was bound by the terms and conditions of the policy. Nationwide appeals.

The parties stipulate to the following facts:

Nationwide issued a motor vehicle liability insurance policy to Arnetta McPhaul for a 1979 Datsun owned by her. The stated policy limits for bodily injury liability were $50,000 each person and $100,000 each accident. As of the day of the accident, 16 June 1987, the premium charged on that policy was paid current. On that day, at about 6:30 a.m., Arnetta McPhaul was riding as a passenger in the Datsun which was driven by her husband, Robert. The Datsun collided with a vehicle operated by Clifton Oxendine. Both Arnetta McPhaul and Clifton Oxendine died as a result of their injuries.

In her application for insurance, Mrs. McPhaul represented that she was divorced, that she was the sole driver in her household and that no driver in her household had any convictions or motor vehicle offenses in the last five years. Her signature was witnessed by the Nationwide agent taking the application, who informed her that by law she was required to list her husband on the application if she was married and that her signature on the application was an attestation that the information on the application was true.

It is further stipulated that Vonzell McPhaul, Robert's brother, knew that as of 5 August 1986, Robert and Arnetta had been married for about nine years and that on 16 June 1987, the day of the accident, they were living together as man and wife; that the vehicle registered in Arnetta's name was a family vehicle which was often driven by Robert and that on the morning of the accident Robert was driving himself and Arnetta to work, as he regularly did. It is further stipulated that on 25 March 1985 Robert McPhaul was convicted of driving while impaired.

The parties stipulate that it is Nationwide's customary practice when writing automobile insurance policies to order driving records for all drivers listed on a new application and if the record should reveal a conviction for driving while impaired within five years of the date of the application, Nationwide automatically and without exception cedes the insurance risk to the reinsurance facility. Had Mrs. McPhaul listed Robert as her husband, Nationwide would have discovered his conviction and automatically ceded the insurance.

Finally, the parties stipulate that Nationwide was notified of the accident and subsequently conducted an investigation during which it became aware that the vehicle was operated by Robert McPhaul, husband of Arnetta McPhaul, and that having such knowledge, Nationwide tendered payment of $939.00 pursuant to the collision coverage provided to Arnetta McPhaul.

. . . .

Defendant Nationwide contends that the trial court erred in ruling that, despite Mrs. McPhaul's deliberate and material misrepresentations, the policy was not void ab initio but was in full effect. Nationwide argues in the alternative, that the misrepresentations render the policy void as to Mrs. McPhaul even though it is valid as to the injured third party. . . .

The issue on appeal is whether the insurer on an automobile liability policy can avoid liability after an injury has occurred on the ground that the policy was procured by the insured's deliberate and material misrepresentations on the application.

Neither party made a distinction in its arguments between the minimum mandatory coverage required by G.S. § 20-279.21(b)(2) (1989) (bodily injury: $25,000 per person, $50,000 per accident) and the larger amount of coverage under the liability policy at issue in this case ($50,000 per person, $100,000 per accident). Such a distinction is important to a proper resolution of this appeal.

First, Nationwide argues that G.S. § 58-3-10 applies to the automobile liability policy at issue and thus a material misrepresentation on an application form constitutes a defense to recovery under the policy. As to the statutory amount of coverage required by G.S. § 20-279.21, we disagree.

General Statutes § 58-3-10, adopted in 1901, falls within Chapter 58, Insurance, article 3, General Regulations for Insurance. As an earlier and more general statement of insurance law, it is superseded with respect to automobile liability insurance by Chapter 20, Motor Vehicles, specifically by article 9A, The Motor Vehicle Safety and Financial Responsibility Act of 1953, and article 13, The Vehicle Financial Responsibility Act of 1957. Chapter 20 represents a complete and comprehensive legislative scheme for the regulation of motor vehicles and as such, its insurance provisions regarding automobiles prevail over the more general insurance regulations of Chapter 58. The 1953 Act, found at G.S. §§ 20-279.1 to 20-279.39, applies to drivers whose licenses have been suspended and relates to the restoration of driver's licenses while the 1957 Act, found at G.S. §§ 20-309 to 20-319, applies to all motor vehicles owners and relates to vehicle registration. The two Acts are complementary and are to be construed in *pari materia* so as to harmonize them and give effect to both.

Chapter 20 requires, *inter alia*, the following with regard to liability insurance. No self-propelled motor vehicle shall be registered in this state unless the owner has financial responsibility as provided in article 13. G.S. § 20-309(a). Financial responsibility shall be a liability insurance policy or other approved form as defined in Chapter 20, article 9A. G.S. § 20-309(b). An owner's policy of liability insurance shall insure against loss from the liability imposed by law for damages arising out of the ownership, maintenance or use of the vehicle because of bodily injury, in the amounts of $25,000 per person, and $50,000 per accident, because of injury to or death of two or more persons in any one accident. G.S. § 20-279.21(b)(2). General Statutes § 20-279.21(f) expressly provides:

> Every motor vehicle liability policy shall be subject to the following provisions which need not be contained therein: (1) Except as hereinafter provided, the liability of the insurance carrier *with respect to the insurance required by this Article shall become absolute whenever injury or damage covered by said motor vehicle liability policy occurs;* said policy may not be canceled or annulled as to such liability by any agreement between the insurance carrier and the insured after the occurrence of the injury or damage; *no statement made by the insured*

or on his behalf and no violation of said policy *shall defeat or void said policy* (emphasis added).

Although we can find no North Carolina case which deals specifically with the effect of G.S. § 20-279.21(f)(1) in a situation involving a misrepresentation made in the application for insurance, there are several North Carolina cases which have interpreted the impact of § 20-279.21(f)(1) on the liability of insurance carriers when an insured violates a provision of the policy. The seminal case is *Swain v. Insurance Co.,* 253 N.C. 120, 116 S.E.2d 482 (1960), where the insurance contract provided that the insured, in the event of suit against him, must forward immediately to the insurer "every demand, notice, summons or other process received by him" and must cooperate with the insurer in defending the suit. *Swain,* 253 N.C. at 127, 116 S.E.2d at 487. The insured violated this provision and the insurance company pleaded this violation as a defense to recovery under the policy by an injured third party who had obtained a default judgment against the insured. The Court found:

> The manifest purpose of the 1957 Act [is] to provide protection, within the required limits, to persons injured or damaged by the negligent operation of a motor vehicle; and, in respect of a "motor vehicle liability policy," to provide such protection notwithstanding violations of policy provisions by the owner subsequent to accidents on which such injured parties base their claim.

Swain, 253 N.C. at 126, 116 S.E.2d at 487. The Court further found that "to bar recovery from an insurer on account of such a policy violation would 'practically nullify the statute by making the enforcement of the rights of the person intended to be protected dependent upon the acts of the very person who caused the injury.'" *Id.,* quoting *Lott v. American Fidelity & Cas. Co.,* 161 S.C. 314, 159 S.E. 635 (1931). *Accord, Jones v. Ins. Co.,* 270 N.C. 454, 155 S.E.2d 118 (1967) (failure of insured to give notice of suit to insurer as required by policy is no defense against default judgment in favor of injured third party); *see also, Insurance Co. v. Roberts,* 261 N.C. 285, 134 S.E.2d 654 (1964) (primary purpose of compulsory motor vehicle liability insurance is to compensate innocent victims therefore no reason why injured third party's rights to recover from insurance carrier should depend upon whether the conduct of its insured was intentional or negligent). The *Swain* and *Jones* decisions specifically concerned violations of insurance policy provisions with regard to notice, the violation of which occurred after the injury had occurred and after the liability of the insurer had become absolute. These decisions were based upon the legislative purpose for mandatory vehicle liability insurance (to protect innocent victims) and the words of the statute ("the liability of the carrier . . . shall become absolute whenever injury . . . occurs . . . and no violation of said policy shall defeat or void said policy," G.S. § 20-279.21(f)(1)). We find that this analysis demands a similar result when the defense asserted is fraud in the application for insurance. Subsection (f)(1) of G.S. § 20-279.21, quoted above in part, provides that the insurer's liability becomes absolute whenever injury occurs, and "no statement made by the insured . . . shall defeat or void said policy." Every policy is subject to this provision whether it is expressly stated in the contract or not. G.S. § 20-279.21(f) ("Every motor vehicle liability policy shall be subject to the following provisions which need not be contained therein[.]"). This result is strengthened by the recognition that the legislature included at subsection (h) a provision by which insurers could recoup losses for which they became obligated solely by operation of the statute. Subsection (h) of G.S. § 20-279.21 states:

> Any motor vehicle liability policy may provide that the insured shall reimburse the insurance carrier for any payment the insurance carrier would not have been obligated to make under the terms of the policy except for the provision of this Article.

See, Insurance Co. v. Webb, 10 N.C. App. 672, 179 S.E.2d 803 (1971). We note that the insurance policy at issue in this case was not included in the record and defendant Nationwide has not pleaded this clause in any counterclaim for recoupment.

We find, however, that the holding above, that fraud in an application for motor vehicle liability insurance is not a defense to the insurer's liability once injury has occurred, applies only to the statutory minimum amount. In the case *sub judice*, the stated policy limit was greater than the statutory minimum and as to that amount, the above analysis does not apply.

The distinction between the mandatory amount of coverage required by statute (see G.S. § 20-279.21(b)(2)) and any amount in excess of that, is found in G.S. § 20-279.21(g):

> Any policy which grants the coverage required for a motor vehicle liability policy may also grant any lawful coverage in excess of or in addition to the coverage specified for a motor vehicle liability policy and such excess or additional coverage shall not be subject to the provision of this Article. With respect to a policy which grants such excess or additional coverage the term "motor vehicle liability policy" shall apply only to that part of the coverage which is required by this section.

The effect of this distinction was recognized in *Swain,* 253 N.C. at 127, 116 S.E.2d at 487–88. As explained in *Swain,* the 1957 Act changed the law with respect to the compulsory amount such that a violation of a policy provision was not a defense to liability of the insurer, but as to any amount in excess of that, a policy provision requiring notice to the insurer would be enforced as written and a violation was a valid and complete defense. The *Swain* Court pointed to *Muncie v. Ins. Co.,* 253 N.C. 74, 116 S.E.2d 474 (1960), as being a statement of the applicable law as to coverage "in excess of or in addition to the coverage specified for a motor vehicle liability policy." *Muncie* involved an accident which occurred prior to the effective date of the 1957 Act. An injured third party sued the insurer to collect on a judgment against the insured. The insurer plead as a defense the violation of a policy provision requiring the insured to give the insurer timely notice of the accident. The Court held that the constitutional guaranty of freedom of contract required that the policy provision be enforced as written. Thus, the violation of the notice provision in the policy by the insured was a complete defense both as to the insured and the injured third party.

We therefore hold that as to any coverage in excess of the statutory minimum, the insurer is not precluded by statute or public policy from asserting the defense of fraud. Such a defense, if successful, would insulate the insurer against liability as to both the insured, Arnetta McPhaul, and the injured third party, Mr. Oxendine. *Muncie,* 253 N.C. 74, 116 S.E.2d 474.

. . . .

In summary, we find that as to the mandatory amount of motor vehicle liability insurance coverage required by G.S. § 20-279.21, fraud in an application for insurance is not a defense to the insurer's liability once injury has occurred, but as to any amount of coverage in excess of the statutory minimum, fraud is a defense under common law or contract law principles.

Therefore, we modify the decision of the court below in that we affirm summary judgment for plaintiffs, finding the insurance policy valid, but only to the extent of the mandatory amount of coverage. As to the amount in excess, we find that there exist genuine issues of material fact.

We modify and affirm in part the judgment below, and remand for further proceedings not inconsistent with this opinion.

Modified and affirmed in part and remanded.

EAGLES AND PARKER, JJ., CONCUR.

NOTES

1. *The compulsory liability insurance landscape.* As of January 1, 2001 (barring repeals, which are highly unlikely), 47 states and the District of Columbia require every person registering a motor vehicle in the state to purchase liability insurance in at least a specified minimum amount. (The three exceptions are New Hampshire, Tennessee, and Wisconsin.) See Ruth Gastel, ed., *Compulsory Liability Insurance,* Insurance Issues Update (Insurance Information Institute), April 2000. This requirement can sometimes be satisfied if the insured (usually a business) shows that it has sufficient assets to cover the specified minimum. The specified minimums are likely to be "bodily injury per person," "bodily injury per occurrence," and "property per occurrence." Thus, a person who purchases "25/50/10" in liability limits will have $50,000 in limits available to reimburse victims for bodily injury in any one accident, regardless of the number of people injured; however, the insurer will pay no single victim more than $25,000. The insured would have $10,000 in coverage available to pay for property damage caused by the insured. Problems involving policy limits are given more attention in § 6.02[5] of this Chapter, *infra.*

With liability insurance being required almost everywhere in the United States, why is it that there are so many uninsured motorists? It is estimated the about 15 percent of all vehicles nationwide are not covered by a liability insurance policy, and in some locales, the estimate is as high as 30 percent. This is true despite penalties in many states that include driver's license or license plate confiscation, impounding of vehicles, fines, and jail time. See *id.* If you lived in one of the states where liability insurance is not required, would you operate a vehicle without liability insurance? Why or why not?

2. *Financial responsibility requirements.* The compulsory liability insurance requirements usually connect to, or dovetail with, financial responsibility requirements, which exist in all states. These requirements compel owners of motor vehicles to demonstrate financial responsibility in some way. In most states, the demonstration must be "pre-accident," meaning that the owner must demonstrate financial responsibility for any future accidents. This can be accomplished, ordinarily, by a certificate of insurance, depositing cash or securities with a governmental entity, posting a bond, or some equivalent act. In a few states, the showing of financial responsibility is not required until after the owner's vehicle is involved in an accident; if at that time the owner cannot establish his or her responsibility, the vehicle's registration or perhaps the owner's license to drive may be suspended. Is it fair to assume that the pressure associated with losing one's vehicle registration or license to drive will be sufficient to induce owners to demonstrate responsibility after an accident has occurred?

3. *What is North Carolina's public policy?* The court in *Odum* makes clear that the purpose of compulsory liability insurance is to protect third parties. To the extent of the statutory minimums, Nationwide cannot assert a fraud defense, and the rationale has to do with North Carolina's policy of protecting third parties. Why does this public policy "end" when amounts exceeding the statutory minimums are implicated? Is it the public policy of North Carolina to help accident victims as long as they are not helped "too much"?

4. *Fortuity, compensating victims, and intentional wrongs.* It should come as no surprise that automobile insurance, like other kinds of insurance, is meant to compensate for accidental, fortuitous losses. If an insured intentionally inflicts loss on another person, one would think that the intentional act exclusion would apply to eliminate the insured's liability insurance coverage. (Whether the insured acted intentionally so as to trigger the exclusion would involve issues similar to those that arise in connection with the intentional act exclusion in the homeowners coverage, which was discussed in § 5.01[2], *supra.*). Does the logic of *Odum*, however, extend to intentional torts? In other words, suppose the insured, while driving his insured car, takes offense at the behavior of a pedestrian and deliberately strikes the pedestrian with the vehicle, causing serious injury. If the pedestrian sues the insured for wilful, wanton, reckless, and negligent behavior that caused the pedestrian's injuries, must the insured's liability carrier provide coverage? *See State Farm Mutual Automobile Insurance Co. v. Wertz,* 540 N.W.2d 636 (S.D. 1995); *Wheeler v. O'Connell,* 9 N.E.2d 544 (Mass. 1937).

If you are inclined to enforce the intentional act exclusion to deny coverage, does your analysis change if domestic abuse is involved? In *State Farm Mutual Automobile Insurance Co. v. Martin,* 660 A.2d 66 (Pa. Super. Ct. 1995), the insured, while intoxicated, drove to the rented home where his wife, from whom he was separated, was living, drove his truck into the rear of his wife's vehicle, drove across the lawn when his wife came out of the house and struck her, and then drove his truck into the wall of the house three times. Should other well-behaved insureds who belong to the same risk pool in which the insured in *Martin* belonged contribute premiums to pay for these kinds of liabilities?

In a different twist on the fortuity issue, consider *Nygaard v. State Farm Insurance Co.,* 591 N.W.2d 738 (Minn.Ct.App. 1999), where the insured deliberately drove her car into the path of an 18-wheel tractor-trailer in a successful suicide attempt. The truck's driver was injured. Must the insured's liability insurer provide coverage to the decedent's estate for the benefit of the injured truck driver? Was there an "accident" in these circumstances? Whose perspective matters?

5. *Reimbursing the insurer.* The court in *Odum* mentioned Nationwide's right to reimbursement, a right it had apparently waived by failing to assert it. Does this make the insured-tortfeasor a mere debtor and the insurer a guarantor? Does this arrangement violate the rule that the insurer cannot have subrogation against its own insured?

6. *Reforming the system.* Do you support additional efforts to increase the number of motorists who purchase liability insurance? Think about your own automobile insurance; in what ways do you subsidize uninsured motorists? Note that a governmental agency must administer and enforce the compulsory insurance system, and this has costs. Does the existence of liability insurance encourage victims of accidents to sue negligent drivers more often and to inflate the amounts claimed as damages in accidents? The poor are disproportionately represented among the uninsured motorist population; if reformers succeed in forcing the purchase of liability insurance by uninsureds (or keeping uninsured motorists off the roads), what other effects do you foresee on the poor? Would you support reducing the minimum coverages that must be purchased so that premiums would decline and more people could therefore afford the coverage? California has recently launched such a program in Los Angeles and San Francisco, two cities where premiums have typically been the highest in the state and where the percentage of uninsured motorists exceeds the statewide figure of 25 percent. See J.C. Howard, *Low-Cost Auto Plan Takes Test Drive in Calif.,* Nat'l Underwriter (Prop.-Cas.), July 17, 2000, at 6.

Would you support "no-pay, no-play" legislation? The idea is that a person who does not purchase liability insurance is prohibited from suing other drivers for non-economic damages, such as pain and suffering. *See, e.g.,* Cal. Civ. Code § 3333.4(a) (West 1997); La. Rev. Stat. § 32:866(A)(1) (West Supp. 2000). If you like the idea, would you support taking away the victim's ability to sue the tortfeasor for *any* kind of loss if the victim has failed to purchase all of the mandated automobile coverages? *See, e.g.,* N.J. Stat. Ann. § 39:6A-4.5 (West 1990 & Supp. 2000) (injured person who fails to maintain medical expense benefits coverage mandated by statute has no cause of action for economic or noneconomic loss sustained as a result of an accident while operating an uninsured vehicle). No-fault, as an alternative to the liability system, will be considered at the end of this Chapter in § 6.06.

[2] Omnibus Coverage

It should now be evident that the interests protected in modern liability insurance include both the insured and the person who is injured by the insured's conduct. Indeed, in some kinds of liability insurance, most notably compulsory automobile liability insurance, the principal interest protected is that of the auto accident victim. Thus, the label "third party" insurance exists in the insurance vocabulary because of the coverage's obvious beneficial significance for victims of legal wrongs. Yet liability insurance is purchased by an individual or entity that is concerned about its potential legal liability. Consequently, the starting place to determine whose interests are protected under any kind of liability insurance, including automobile insurance, policy involves determining "who" is the insured.

One could say that the starting place for determining "who" is the insured is to inspect the declaration sheet for the purpose of finding out who is the "named insured." The question of who is the named insured rarely arises; the few cases that do exist tend to involve a mistake in designation or a misunderstanding between insurer and insured about what a particular designation means (as would be the case when, for example, there is a disagreement about which part of a corporate entity is within the coverage). In personal insurance, the next "who is the insured" question might involve asking whether the person who seeks coverage is a resident relative of the insured or a member of the insured's household (depending on what precise language the policy uses to designate persons entitled to coverage).

In automobile insurance, the question of who is a named insured and a resident relative of the named insured is not limited to the liability coverage. This question can also be relevant to the medical payments coverage and the uninsured and underinsured motorist protections. Because this issue cuts across different coverages, we take it up in § 6.07[1], *infra*, as one of the "recurring issues" in automobile insurance.

In this section, we take up another set of "who is insured" issues that arise under the liability coverage of the automobile insurance policy. In the notes, we will point out when some of the questions have counterparts in other lines of liability insurance. As you might expect, automobile liability insurance gives rise to many issues as to who is insured. This, no doubt, is due to the role that the automobile plays in our society and the attempts of the insurance industry to respond to that phenomenon. Thus, this subsection is necessarily only a modest attempt to raise a few of the more common issues concerning who it is that is protected under the basic automobile liability policy. More extensive treatment of this and other types of liability insurance is necessarily left to the treatises and other works on the subject.

ODOLECKI v. HARTFORD ACCIDENT & INDEMNITY CO.

55 N.J. 542, 264 A.2d 38 (1970)

PROCTOR, J.

This case concerns the question of coverage under the omnibus clause of an automobile liability insurance policy. The policy was issued by the defendant, Hartford Accident & Indemnity Company (Hartford) to Mrs. Kathryn

Zylka, and covered her automobile which was involved in a collision on July 7, 1964. The omnibus clause was of standard form and provided in pertinent part that coverage under the policy was extended to the named insured, her spouse, and "any person while using the automobile . . . provided the actual use of the automobile is by the named insured or such spouse or with the permission of either."

The facts are not in material dispute. Mrs. Zylka, the owner of the insured vehicle, gave her teenage son, Michael, general permission to use the car when he returned home from college for his summer vacation. She also told him not to let anyone else drive the car. This admonition was repeated on several occasions when he used the car. On the night of July 7, 1964, Michael was using the car for a social visit to a neighbor's house. While there he permitted his friend, the plaintiff, Douglas Odolecki, to borrow the car in order that the latter might pick up his girlfriend. On his way to a hospital where the girl worked, Odolecki was involved in an accident with another car which resulted in the filing of several personal injury actions against him.

After receiving notice of the accident, the defendant-insurer informed the plaintiff that he was not covered by the policy issued to Mrs. Zylka since he was not operating the vehicle with the "permission" of the named insured or her spouse as required by the policy. The plaintiff filed the present action to have himself declared an additional insured. Sitting without a jury, the trial court held that the Zylka policy did not cover the plaintiff as an additional insured because Mrs. Zylka had never given him permission to use the car, because she had expressly prohibited her son from giving permission to others to use the car, and because the use of the car was not within the use granted by Mrs. Zylka to her son. In denying plaintiff relief the trial judge relied principally on this Court's decision in *Baesler v. Globe Indemnity Co.*, 33 N.J. 148, 162 A.2d 854 (1960). Plaintiff appealed to the Appellate Division, and pending argument there, we granted certification on our own motion.

Baesler, upon which the trial court relied, is virtually identical with the present case. There, the named insured bought a car for the exclusive use of his nephew with the stipulation that the car not be used by others. Despite this admonition, the nephew permitted a friend to use the automobile for a social engagement, and while the friend was driving he had an accident in which his passenger was injured. The passenger recovered a judgment for personal injuries against the friend-driver, and the latter, claiming to be an additional insured, sued the insurer of the named insured to recover the amount of the judgment. In a four to three decision, this Court held that the plaintiff was not covered by the policy which the defendant had issued. The Court noted the general rule that, ordinarily, a permittee is not authorized to allow another to use an insured vehicle on the basis of his own permission to use it and that therefore there could be no coverage under the standard omnibus clause. *Id.* at 151, 162 A.2d 854. Since we adhered to this rule at that time, it followed, *a fortiori,* that when there was an express prohibition by the named insured, and no other countervailing factor, the second permittee could not claim a greater right than he could in the absence of such a prohibition. The plaintiff concedes that under *Baesler* he is not entitled to qualify as an additional insured, but he argues that our decisions since *Baesler* have eroded the holding in that case to the point where it no longer represents the law of this state. The validity of this contention depends upon an analysis of these post-*Baesler* decisions.

In the term of court following *Baesler,* we decided Matits v. Nationwide Mutual Ins. Co., 33 N.J. 488, 166 A.2d 345 (1960). There we dealt with the related question of whether the original permittee was an additional insured when she substantially deviated from the scope of the named insured's permission. In that case the husband of the named insured lent his wife's car to a neighbor so that the latter could visit her sick mother in a nearby town. After the visit, the permittee drove in a direction away from the named insured's home and alternately visited two bars over a period of several hours. On the way home, she was involved in a collision with another car.

We were called upon to decide whether the permittee's deviation vitiated the named insured's initial permission so as to deprive her of coverage under the standard omnibus clause of the policy issued by the defendant insurer. The law of New Jersey pertaining to coverage when a permittee deviated from the scope of permission was then unclear. Other jurisdictions had adopted one of three views. The first is the liberal or "initial permission" rule which allows coverage if a person has permission to use the automobile irrespective of any deviations from the scope of permission so long as it remains in his possession. The second view, the moderate or "minor deviation" rule, allows coverage only where the deviation from the scope of the permissive use does not constitute a gross violation. Finally, the strict or "conversion" rule denies coverage for *any* deviation from the time, place, or purpose specified. For a discussion of these rules, see generally 7 Appleman, Insurance Law and Practice, §§ 4366, 4367, 4368, and cases cited therein.

In *Matits,* we adopted the initial permission rule. It was our view that the minor deviation and conversion rules, which made coverage turn on the scope of permission given in the first instance, rendered coverage uncertain, fostered unnecessary litigation, and did not comport with New Jersey's legislative policy of assuring an available fund for the innocent victims of automobile accidents. *See* Motor Vehicle Security-Responsibility Law, N.J.S.A. 39:6-23 to 60; Unsatisfied Claim and Judgment Fund Law, N.J.S.A. 39:6-61 to 91; Motor Vehicle Liability Security Fund Act, N.J.S.A. 39:6-92 to 104. Accordingly, we held that if a person is given permission to use a motor vehicle in the first instance, *any* subsequent use short of an unlawful taking while it remains in his possession, is a permissive use within the standard omnibus clause in an automobile liability insurance policy regardless of any restrictions given by the named insured. Therefore, the permittee was an additional insured under the policy issued by the defendant insurer.

In a dissenting opinion, Justice Hall contended that the minor deviation rule was the only sound approach to the problem. He expressed the belief, however, that the Court's adoption of the initial permission rule undermined the holding of *Baesler* since it rendered irrelevant any actions by a permittee subsequent to the grant of original permission. He reasoned that the majority's holding made it impossible for an insured to restrict a grant of permission, and therefore that the result in *Baesler* was irreconcilable with that in *Matits.*

Our holding in *Matits* has since been reaffirmed in *Small v. Schuncke,* [1] 42 N.J. 407, 201 A.2d 56 (1964) and *Selected Risks Insurance Co. v. Zullo,* 48 N.J. 362, 225 A.2d 570 (1966). Now we must decide whether initial permission is unrestrictable in terms of second permittees as well as in terms of scope of deviations.

We had already indicated in *Baesler* that in certain circumstances a prohibition of a loan to a second permittee could be ineffective regarding insurance coverage. There we noted that if, for example, a father gave his son the use of the family car for a social engagement and the son turned over the wheel to a fellow occupant despite his father's admonitions to the contrary, there might be coverage. 33 N.J. at 153–154, 162 A.2d 854. This dictum later became our holding in *Indemnity Ins. Co., etc. v. Metropolitan Cas. Ins. Co. of N. Y.,* 33 N.J. 507, 166 A.2d 355 (1960), decided the same day in *Matits.* There the named insured lent her car to an employee for the purpose of driving several customers on a business inspection. The employee was specifically instructed not to let anyone else drive the car. While returning from the inspection the employee allowed a passenger to drive and the car was involved in an accident. We held that the passenger-second permittee was covered since the car was being used for the purpose permitted by the named insured. Thus, it was possible for a second permittee to qualify as an additional insured notwithstanding the original permittee's violation of the named insured's instructions.

In *Matits*, and the subsequent cases in which we continued to follow the initial permission rule, we emphasized the importance of minimizing litigation of omnibus clause coverage. We were concerned with the continuing problem of determining factually the scope of permission given by the named insured. In order to alleviate the problem we adopted the rule that once permission was given to use a car on the highways, the person giving permission could not bar coverage by restricting the time, place, or purpose for which the car could be used. Clearly, the same kind of litigation results from a rule which inquires into the named insured's permission regarding the use of the car by persons other than his initial permittee. The question again depends upon the scope of the permission. Instead of what the named insured said regarding the time, place, and purpose of the permissive use, a court must examine what was said regarding other drivers. This kind of inquiry is precisely what we sought to avoid in *Matits.*

Thus, *Baesler* is not consistent with our announced policy of limiting litigation which turns on petty factual distinctions, particularly where these distinctions bear so little relationship to the subject of insurance coverage in the named insured's own mind. A named insured's admonitions to his permittee regarding the use of the vehicle by other drivers is rarely if ever intended to restrict the scope of insurance coverage. Moreover, as Chief Justice Weintraub pointed out in his dissent in *Baesler:* "A named insured untutored in law and fearful that his consent might lead to his own liability for damages

---

[1] Interestingly, *Small* involved a second permittee as well as a deviation from the scope of permission. However, the insurer conceded that if the first permittee was covered under the omnibus clause at the time of collision, the second permittee was also covered. 42 N.J. at 412, 201 A.2d 56.

in excess of the policy limits (indeed by statute in some jurisdictions he would be so liable) may well be tempted to invent a claim that he prohibited others to drive or to convert a precatory request into a binding prohibition." 33 N.J. at 159, 162 A.2d at 860–861. We add that the fear of insurance policy cancellations might well have the same effect.

A second and more important policy is that of assuring that all persons wrongfully injured have financially responsible persons to look to for damages. *Matits v. Nationwide Mutual Ins. Co., supra,* 33 N.J. at 495–496, 166 A.2d 345. In other words, a liability insurance contract is for the benefit of the public as well as for the benefit of the named or additional insured. The Legislature's desire to implement this policy is demonstrated by our financial responsibility laws cited above. In *Selected Risks Ins. Co. v. Zullo, supra,* we discussed the importance of these statutes and held that an insurer could not depart from the omnibus coverage described in N.J.S.A. 39:6-46(a) which contained substantially the same language we construed in *Matits. Id.* 48 N.J. 369, 225 A.2d 570. Thus, insurers were required to draw policies which conformed with the initial permission rule.

Although the above policy considerations would seem to dictate a departure from *Baesler,* we are urged that the language of the omnibus clause precludes coverage for a prohibited second permittee. More specifically, defendant argues that the words "provided the actual use of the automobile is by the named insured . . . or with [her] permission" could not include use by Odolecki since Mrs. Zylka had told her son not to let anyone else drive the car. We fail, however, to see the distinction between a case where a first permittee exceeds the scope of permission in terms of time, place, or purpose, and a case where he exceeds the scope of permission in terms of use of the vehicle by another. Once an owner voluntarily hands over the keys to his car, the extent of permission he actually grants is as irrelevant in the one case as in the other. And as *Matits* and its progeny indicate restrictions are irrelevant in scope cases. The spurious nature of this distinction was pointed out by Cohen & Cohen in their article, "Automobile Liability Insurance: Public Policy and the Omnibus Clause in New Jersey," 15 Rutgers L. Rev. 155, 168 (1961). We think that once the initial permission has been given by the named insured, coverage is fixed, barring theft or the like. There is no claim of such an unlawful taking in the present case.

Accordingly, we hold that plaintiff was an additional insured within the terms of the policy issued to Mrs. Zylka by the defendant insurer. *Baesler v. Globe Indemnity Co., supra, is no longer the law of this state.*

Reversed.

For reversal: CHIEF JUSTICE WEINTRAUB, and JUSTICES JACOBS, FRANCIS, PROCTOR, HALL, SCHETTINO and HANEMAN—7.

For affirmance: None.

NOTES

1. *Persons insured.* The question of who is insured under the liability coverages of a personal automobile policy has several potential dimensions.

If the person seeking coverage is named in the appropriate space on the declaration page of the policy, this person is a "named insured"; few problems arise with these designations, apart from mistaken designations and other misunderstandings. There are two other important groups of people that may be covered. The first is resident relatives of the household of the named insured and others using the insured automobile. The "resident relative" designation is given more attention in § 6.07[1], *infra*, of this Chapter. The second group is those persons operating the vehicle with the permission of the named insured or the spouse of the named insured. The latter designation is referred to as "omnibus" coverage and is explored in this subsection.

2. *Modern trend.* The modern trend has been to adopt the "initial permission" or liberal interpretation rule. *See Commercial Union Insurance Co. v. Johnson,* 294 Ark. 444, 745 S.W.2d 589 (1988) (citing authorities which have adopted and rejected this position).

3. *Is there a better approach?* The relevant language in the policy in *Odolecki* still appears in many policies, and when permission is an issue under other policy forms, the court's analysis is still pertinent. But is this the only way to handle the issue? What if the policy covered anyone using the insured vehicle, but then excluded coverage for any person who uses the vehicle "without a reasonable belief that that person is entitled to do so"? By the same token, the policy could extend coverage to the named insured and resident relatives when they are driving *any* vehicle, subject to an exclusion for operating a vehicle "without a reasonable belief that that person is entitled to do so"? How would the issue in *Odolecki* be resolved under a policy structured in this manner? Before you answer these questions, consider the next case.

CLOSE v. EBERTZ
583 N.W.2d 794 (N.D. 1998)

Sandstrom, Justice.

American Economy Insurance Co. (American) appealed a summary judgment awarding Clifford Close $50,000 and Millie Close $10,000 in their garnishment action to collect insurance proceeds for personal injuries under an automobile liability policy issued to John Ebertz. We hold the entitlement exclusion under the policy excluding coverage to "any person" using an auto without a reasonable belief the person is entitled to do so applies to a "family member" of the insured. Because the Closes do not dispute the trial court's ruling John Ebertz's son, Dominic Ebertz, was driving the vehicle at the time of the accident without his father's express or implied permission, we further hold the policy provides no coverage. We reverse the summary judgment and remand for entry of summary judgment in favor of American.

I

On October 1, 1992, American issued an automobile policy to John Ebertz for a 1979 Ford van. On October 12, 1992, John Ebertz's 15-year-old son,

Dominic Ebertz, skipped school, took the van, and went riding around Devils Lake with a friend while his father and stepmother were at work. Dominic Ebertz had no drivers license, and he and his friend returned the van to the home before his parents returned for lunch. The boys hid in the van until the parents returned to work.

The boys, with Dominic Ebertz at the wheel, continued driving around Devils Lake during the afternoon. When an off-duty police officer attempted to stop the boys, Dominic Ebertz fled. During the chase, Dominic Ebertz entered an intersection and collided with a vehicle driven by Randy Holtz. The collision caused the Ebertz van to veer into a vehicle driven by Clifford Close, which was approaching the intersection from the opposite direction. Clifford Close suffered serious injuries in the accident. Dominic Ebertz was charged with unauthorized use of the vehicle.

Clifford Close and his wife, Millie Close, sued Dominic Ebertz, John Ebertz, and Randy Holtz to collect damages for Clifford Close's personal injuries. Millie Close also sought damages for loss of consortium. The Closes alleged John Ebertz was liable under the family car doctrine or under the doctrine of negligent entrustment. The court granted summary judgment dismissing John Ebertz, concluding neither doctrine applied because Dominic Ebertz was not using the van with his father's express or implied permission. The Closes and Randy Holtz reached a settlement agreement. The Closes were awarded a default judgment against Dominic Ebertz in the amount of $168,131.82.

The Closes then brought a garnishment action against John Ebertz's insurance company, American. American claimed the entitlement exclusion in the policy excluding coverage to "any person" using an auto without a reasonable belief the person is entitled to do so applied to "family members." Because Dominic Ebertz used the van without John Ebertz's express or implied permission, American asserted there was no coverage under the policy. The Closes did not challenge the trial court's earlier ruling Dominic Ebertz used the van without his father's permission, but argued the policy language was ambiguous and should be interpreted to provide coverage under the circumstances.

Both parties moved for summary judgment. The trial court concluded the "any person" language in the policy did not include "family members," and ruled the policy provided coverage. Judgment was entered against American awarding Clifford Close $50,000, the per person limit under the policy, and Millie Close an additional $10,000 on her loss of consortium claim.

. . . .

II

. . . .

A

John Ebertz's American automobile policy's "Part A-Liability Coverage" says:

Insuring Agreement

> A.   We will pay damages for "bodily injury" or "property damage" for which any "insured" becomes legally responsible because of an auto accident. . . .

B. "Insured," as used in this Part, means:

1. You or any "family member" for the ownership, maintenance or use of any "auto" or "trailer."

2. Any person using "your covered auto."

A "family member" is defined in the policy as "a person related to you by
blood, marriage or adoption who is a resident of your household. This includes
a ward or foster child."

The policy contains nine exclusions, including the following:

Exclusions

A. We do not provide Liability Coverage for any person:

* * *

8. Using an "auto" without a reasonable belief that person is
entitled to do so.

The term "any person" is not defined in the policy. The trial court noted
the undefined term "any person" is used both in the introductory Paragraph
A to the Exclusions and in Paragraph B.2 of the "Insuring Agreement" defining
an insured as "[a]ny person using 'your covered auto.'" The court reasoned
the "undefined term 'any person' could reasonably be interpreted to mean any
'insured' or as simply a reference to the second category of insureds i.e. 'any
person using your covered auto' as described in B-2 of the Insuring Agreement." The court further reasoned because "the provision can be reasonably
interpreted in either way, it is ambiguous and must be interpreted . . . against
[American], who could have eliminated the ambiguity through a more careful
choice of terms. . . ." The court therefore held the exclusion of "any person"
did not include a "family member," and ruled the American policy provided
coverage for the Closes' injuries arising from the October 12, 1992, accident.

B

The interpretation of an insurance policy is a question of law, fully reviewable on appeal. This Court reviews the trial court's interpretation by independently construing and examining the insurance policy. We look first to the
language of the insurance contract, and if the language is clear on its face,
there is no room for construction. If coverage hinges on an undefined term,
we apply the plain, ordinary meaning of the term in interpreting the contract.
Although insurance policies are contracts of adhesion, and we will resolve
ambiguities in favor of the insured when appropriate, we will not strain the
definition to provide coverage for the insured.

The question whether an entitlement exclusion in an automobile policy
applies to members of the family of the named insured has generated a fairly
substantial amount of litigation. *See* Annot., *Application of Automobile
Insurance "Entitlement" Exclusion to Family Member*, 25 A.L.R.5th 60 (1994).
Construing policy language indistinguishable from the language at issue here,
a minority of courts have determined the "any person" language of the
exclusion does not include a "family member," and there is coverage under

circumstances comparable to this case. The majority of courts, however, have concluded the "any person" language unambiguously includes a "family member," and there is no coverage under these circumstances.

The reasoning underlying the minority view is the phrases "any person" and "family member" in the policy define mutually exclusive classes, so an exclusion for "any person" does not include family members but means any person other than a family member. The minority view is also based on the conclusion the policy language is ambiguous and should be resolved against the insurer. Some minority-view courts also rely on the reasonable expectation of the insured that family members will be protected when operating a covered family vehicle even without permission, and conclude the family member's disobedience is a family matter to be dealt with internally.

The reasoning underlying the majority view is the term "any person" is unambiguous, with no technical or restricted definition in the policy, and should be given its common meaning to include any person, including a "family member." The majority-view courts reject arguments an ambiguity is created merely because one part of the policy establishes general coverage while the other part establishes specific exclusions. The majority reason policy exclusions should be logically construed to include the named insured and family members, those "persons" typically covered, because it would be pointless for the policy to exclude coverage for "persons" not covered by the policy in the first place. The majority also reason, while the entitlement exclusion does not contain an exception for the named insured or a "family member," certain other policy exclusions, while pertaining generally to "any person," contain specific exceptions for the named insured or any "family member." These courts have observed if the exclusion for nonpermissive use does not apply to the named insured or a family member, neither would any other policy exclusion, including the one for intentional torts, because all of the exclusions refer to "any person." The majority-view courts argue the minority view's reasonable expectations and public policy arguments merely create coverage the insured has not paid for and the insurer has not agreed to provide.

C

We believe the reasoning of the majority is sound, and we, therefore, hold the American policy excludes coverage for the Closes' injuries under the circumstances. Several considerations lead us to this conclusion.

First, the "Insuring Agreement" of the policy distinguishes between the named insured and family members, and any other person, to provide coverage for the named insured and family members while driving either the covered vehicle or a borrowed vehicle. The "Insuring Agreement" thus limits coverage for any other person to those instances in which the other person is driving a covered vehicle.

Second, there is nothing ambiguous about the phrase "any person" used in the American policy exclusions section. Because the phrase "any person" has no technical meaning and is not defined in the policy, we give the phrase its plain, ordinary meaning. "Any" is defined as "unlimited in amount, quantity, number, time, or extent." *Webster's Third New International Dictionary*, at p. 97 (1971). Thus, "any person" must be construed to mean all persons, including family members.

Third, there are nine exclusions listed in the American policy applicable to "any person." Exclusion A.6 states American will not provide liability coverage for "any person:"

6. While employed or otherwise engaged in the "business" of:
    a. selling;
    b. repairing;
    c. servicing;
    d. storing; or
    e. parking;

vehicles designed for use mainly on public highways. This includes road testing and delivery. This exclusion (A.6.) does not apply to the ownership, maintenance or use of "your covered auto" by:

    a. you;
    b. any "family member"; or
    c. any partner, agent or employee of you or any "family member."

Obviously, if "any person" did not include family members, there would be no need to specifically except family members from exclusion A.6. The specific exception of family members from exclusion A.6, but not from exclusion A.8, strongly implies family members are included in exclusion A.8.

Fourth, if the exclusion for nonpermissive use does not apply to family members, none of the other eight exclusions would apply to family members because all exclusions apply to "any person." Adopting the minority view would arguably result in allowing coverage for insureds and their family members for intentional torts under exclusion A.1 of the American policy. There is a strong public policy in North Dakota precluding an insured from being indemnified for losses caused by the insured's intentional or willful conduct.

Finally, because the term "insured" under the "Insuring Agreement" is defined as including the named insured as well as any "family member" using "any 'auto,'" whether it is the covered auto or not, adopting the minority view would allow coverage for a car thief under his own policy or under the policy of a family member with whom he resides, not only when stealing the family car, but when stealing any car. This result is untenable and contrary to public policy.

The Closes rely on the dissenting opinion in [*Hartford Insurance Co. of the Midwest v.] Halt,* 646 N.Y.S.2d [589 (N.Y.App.Div. 1996)] at 596–97(Callahan, J., dissenting), in which the New York Supreme Court, Appellate Division, Fourth Department, overruled its earlier decision in *Paychex, Inc. v. Covenant Ins. Co.,* 156 A.D.2d 936, 549 N.Y.S.2d 237 (4 Dept.1989), which had adopted the minority view. The dissent in *Halt,* 646 N.Y.S.2d at 596, focuses on "the many disputes caused by these provisions and the different resolutions in various jurisdictions" to support a conclusion of ambiguity. However, we are not persuaded disagreement among courts over the proper interpretation of an insurance policy automatically means there is ambiguity requiring coverage.

The dissent in *Halt,* 646 N.Y.S.2d at 597, also stresses the 1989 *Paychex* decision placed New York insurers on notice its policy was considered ambiguous, but the insurers did nothing to revise the policy language. While this argument may have some force in New York, it carries little weight in North Dakota. Indeed, this Court had never addressed the issue and the majority of courts have not followed the *Paychex* line of reasoning.

We conclude, as a matter of law, the entitlement exclusion to the American automobile policy excluding coverage to "any person" using an auto without a reasonable belief the person is entitled to do so applies to a "family member" of the insured. Because the Closes do not challenge the trial court's ruling Dominic Ebertz was driving the vehicle at the time of the accident without his father's express or implied permission, we conclude the insurance policy provides no coverage for the Closes' injuries resulting from the October 12, 1992, accident.

. . . .

IV

We reverse the summary judgment and remand for entry of summary judgment in favor of American.

VANDE WALLE, C.J., NEUMANN, MARING and MESCHKE, JJ., concur.

NOTES

1. *Implications.* In the policy in *Odolecki,* the named insured and household residents were covered, plus anyone using the vehicle with the permission of the named insured or the named insured's spouse. Does the introduction of the "reasonable belief" exclusion signal insurers' desire to reduce this coverage? Did the court in *Close* give insufficient attention to North Dakota's public policies as reflected in its requirement that all drivers have liability insurance, or show financial responsibility, as a condition to registering a vehicle? *See* N.D. Cent. Code § 26.1-41-02 (1995). Was the court too hasty in saying what is good for New York is not good for North Dakota?

The next subsection of these materials discusses "drive other cars" (or "DOC") coverage, referring to the coverage provided by the liability policy when the named insured is driving someone else's vehicle. The "reasonable belief" exclusion certainly has the effect of placing an outer limit on this coverage. To take an extreme example, if the named insured steals someone else's car and then injures a third-party while driving the stolen vehicle away, the named insured has no coverage. As *Close* indicates, however, the policy text has other implications.

2. *"Look, ma—no driver's license!"* That was the situation in *Close.* Does it follow that whenever a person is operating a vehicle without a valid driver's license (either because the driver is underage or because the license has been suspended or revoked) that person is using the vehicle "without a reasonable belief that [he] is entitled to do so"? *See Craig v. Barnes,* 710 A.2d 258 (Me. 1998) (insured's fiancee, who owned vehicle but had no driver's license, lacked

reasonable belief in entitlement to use vehicle; held, no coverage); *Farm and City Insurance Co. v. Gilmore,* 539 N.W.2d 154 (Iowa 1995)(unlicensed teenager had reasonable belief that he was entitled to drive vehicle after being asked to do so by insured's brother who had lawful possession of vehicle; held, coverage).

Some policies have exclusions for named insureds and permissive users who do not have a valid driver's license. In *Adams v. Thomas,* 729 So.2d 1041 (La. 1999), the Supreme Court of Louisiana struck down the clause as contravening the state's statutory omnibus clause and the public policies of the state cutting in favor of protecting accident victims. If your liability insurance premiums would decline if no coverage were extended to unlicensed drivers, would your support the exclusion?

If a member of the insured's household has a poor driving record (imagine a person with multiple DWI convictions, several prior accidents and moving violations, and some history of driving without a valid license), should the insurer be allowed to issue the policy with an endorsement that excludes coverage for a particular named person? This kind of exclusion and related provisions receives more attention in § 6.02[4] of this Chapter, *infra*.

3. *Other policy forms.* Another form places the "reasonable belief" limitation in the coverage provisions. For example, the policy at issue in *Midwest Casualty Insurance Co. v. Whitetail,* 596 N.W.2d 341 (N.D. 1999), listed the classes of insureds (*e.g.*, "you," "relative or resident using your insured car"; etc.) and then added this clause: "However, no person shall be considered an insured person if the person uses your insured car without having your permission." The court held that the permissive use clause was unambiguous and excluded coverage "to any person driving the insured car without the owner's permission," including the insured's adult son. 596 N.W.2d at 344. *See also Lobeck v. State Farm Mutual Automobile Insurance Co.,* 582 N.W.2d 246 (Minn. 1998) (upholding "consent" and "permission" clauses in two policies).

4. *The permittee's permittee revisited.* Is the "reasonable belief" exclusion to be applied to whomever is driving the car at the time of the accident? If a parent gives permission to a licensed child to drive the family car, and this child gives permission to an unlicensed sibling to drive the car, does the exclusion apply? What if the parent has told the licensed child not to let anyone else drive the car, but the second permittee, also a licensed driver, does not know this? In *Rutgers Casualty Co. v. Collins,* 158 N.J. 542, 730 A.2d 833 (1999), the Supreme Court of New Jersey held that if the passenger had initial permission to drive, the reasonableness of the driver's belief was irrelevant in circumstances where the passenger had extended permission to the driver. Is this result supported by the policy text, or is it an effort to protect accident victims? For comparison, *see State Farm Mutual Automobile Insurance Co. v. Ragatz,* 571 N.W.2d 155 (S.D. 1997), where the court upheld the insurer's denial of coverage when the owner's son, who had permission to drive the car provided he did not let anyone else drive it, gave permission to a friend and roommate who was driving the car at the time of the accident.

5. *The current PAP.* Look at the PAP in Appendix E. How would *Close* be decided if the current version of the PAP were at issue?

6. *Problems of liability coverage while driving a rented car.* Short-term lessees of rental cars should have their own liability insurance, but car rental companies will also have coverage, inasmuch as they are at risk of suit whenever one of their cars is being operated by a lessee. If you have rented a vehicle, you probably know that you are asked who will be driving the vehicle, and sometimes you are charged an extra fee if there is an additional driver. You are also probably aware that lessees sometimes let third parties drive rental cars without having obtained permission for this use from the rental car company. Can an insurer which issues a liability policy to an auto rental company disclaim responsibility for a person operating a rented vehicle with the lessee's permission but in violation of the rental agreement between the lessee and the rental company? One treatise gives this answer: "[A]n individual who rents a vehicle does not have authority to delegate permission to drive the vehicle to a third person who is not named on the rental agreement, given an express prohibition in the rental agreement that no un-named driver operate the vehicle. Even in light of policy restrictions, however, under certain circumstances, implied authority to delegate to a second permittee may exist." 8 Couch on Insurance § 112:80 (3d ed. 1999). Obviously, the cases are not entirely consistent. In *Motor Vehicle Accident Indemnification Corp. v. Continental National American Group Co.,* 35 N.Y.2d 260, 319 N.E.2d 182, 360 N.Y.S.2d 859 (1974), the court held that the rental company's insurer's restrictions on nonpermissive users violated the public policy of New York, and that the rental company would be deemed to have given "constructive consent" to such users: "[T]hese considerations of sound public policy will prevent the evasion of the liability of one leasing cars for profit (and, in turn, his insurer) via the attempted device of restrictions on or conditions of use which run counter to the recognized realities [of the car rental business] and, in a measure, disguise the transaction." 319 N.E.2d at 185. To the same effect is *Metropolitan Property and Casualty Insurance Co. v. Hertz Corp.,* 981 P.2d 1091 (Colo. 1999) (en banc). Some states have achieved the same result by enacting statutes for auto rental companies regarding liability insurance for the drivers of their rented cars. *See, e.g.,* Ariz. Rev. Stat. § 28-2166 (1998); Del. Code Ann. tit. 21 § 6102 (1995); Wis. Stat. Ann. § 344.51 (West 1999).

If the lessee commits in the rental agreement to comply with applicable laws, and then proceeds to drive the car while intoxicated (in violation of law) with the result that a third-party is injured, is this deviation from the scope of permission a "material" one which renders the loss outside the lessor's liability insurer's coverage? *See Liberty Mutual Insurance Co. v. Thomas,* 333 Ark. 655, 971 S.W.2d 244 (1998) (coverage). What if the rental agreement has an exclusion for "driving while intoxicated"? *See Budget Rent-a-Car Systems, Inc. v. Ricardo,* 85 Haw. 243, 942 P.2d 507 (1997) (coverage). What if the lessee agrees in the rental agreement not to drive the car in a particular location (*e.g.,* a public road that is particularly dangerous), the lessee violates this provision, and injures a third party in a collision? *See Budget Rent-A-Car Systems, Inc. v. Coffin,* 82 Haw. 351, 922 P.2d 964 (1996) (no coverage). Can you identify a principle which reconciles the cited cases?'

7. *The "commercial omnibus" coverage.* Most of the insurance issues arising in the cases contained thus far in this section involve the type of automobile liability policy that is marketed to individuals. Of course, businesses also need

liability insurance, and the ISO has developed the Business Auto Policy (BAP), which is specially designed for commercial and similar operations that utilize motor vehicles. The formats of the Personal Auto Policy (see Appendix E) and the BAP are different, but in some respects the coverages are similar. For example, both provide coverage for liability arising out of the ownership, maintenance, or use of the vehicle, including loading and unloading the vehicle. For more on issues that can arise under the "commercial omnibus" coverage, see the next case.

LIBERTY MUTUAL INSURANCE CO. v. AMERICAN EMPLOYERS INSURANCE CO.

556 S.W.2d 242 (Tex. 1977)

SAM D. JOHNSON, JUSTICE.

American Employers Insurance Company sought a declaratory judgment that a policy issued by Liberty Mutual Insurance Company to U.S. Plywood required Liberty to defend Homette Corporation, American's insured. The trial court rendered a judgment that Liberty's policy created a duty to defend Homette. The court of civil appeals affirmed. 545 S.W.2d 216. We reverse and render judgment that Liberty has no obligation to defend Homette.

The sole question is whether the evidence supports the conclusion of the courts below that a truck and flatbed trailer were "borrowed" by Homette under the provisions of a comprehensive automobile liability insurance policy issued by Liberty to U.S. Plywood, a division of Champion International Corporation. Liberty issued a policy to U.S. Plywood which provided coverage for bodily injuries suffered as a result of a loading or an unloading of a vehicle owned by U.S. Plywood. The coverage was limited to employees of U.S. Plywood and lessees or "borrowers" of vehicles owned by U.S. Plywood. [1]

---

[1] The policy provided:

"The company will pay on behalf of the insured all sums which the insured shall become legally obligated to pay as damages because of Coverage A bodily injury or Coverage B property damage to which this insurance applies, caused by an occurrence and arising out of the ownership, maintenance or use, including loading and unloading, of any automobile,. . .

" . . . .

"PERSONS INSURED. Each of the following is an insured under this insurance to the extent set forth below:

"(a) the named insured;

" . . . .

"(c) any other person while using an owned automobile or a hired automobile with the permission of the named insured, provided his actual operation or (if he is not operating) his other actual use thereof is within the scope of such permission, but with respect to bodily injury or property damage arising out of the loading or unloading thereof, such other person shall be an insured only if he is:

"(1) a lessee or borrower of the automobile, or

"(2) an employee of the named insured or of such lessee or borrower;

Don Dragoo, an employee of U.S. Plywood, delivered a load of plywood decking to a plant owned by Homette. After parking the vehicle, Dragoo removed the nylon webbing used to secure the six-foot stacks of Novadeck, a type of plywood decking. Homette's employees began to unload the decking, using forklifts to unload about twenty sheets at a time. Dragoo was standing on the side of the truck opposite from that on which the unloading was begun. Dragoo was not aiding the unloading in any manner. He was merely rolling up the webbing used to secure the decking on the delivery truck when several sheets of the decking struck and killed him.

Subsequently, Dragoo's widow sued Homette, alleging negligence on the part of Homette, its agents, or its employees which proximately caused Dragoo's death. American, Homette's insurance carrier, then sought a declaratory judgment that, under the policy issued by Liberty to U.S. Plywood, Liberty had a duty to defend Homette. American asserted that Homette had "borrowed" U.S. Plywood's vehicle in order to unload it and, thus, Homette came within the protection of the policy as a "borrower" of U.S. Plywood's vehicle. The trial court, sitting without a jury, rendered judgment for American. The court filed findings of fact[2] and conclusions of law that Dragoo was not engaged in "unloading" the truck at the time of his death, that Homette exercised no control over the movement of Dragoo or the truck, that Dragoo's death occurred while the truck was being "unloaded," and that Homette had "borrowed" the truck for the purpose of unloading it.

The court of civil appeals defined "borrower" as "someone who has, with permission of the owner, temporary possession and use of the property of another for his own purposes." 545 S.W.2d 216 at 223. That court concluded that Homette met these requirements and therefore was a "borrower." Although we agree with the court of civil appeals' general definition of

---

"   . . . .

"When used in this policy . . . 'automobile' means a land motor vehicle, trailer, or semi-trailer designed for travel on public roads (including any machinery or apparatus attached thereto) . . . ."

The policy does not define "borrower." Neither party contends that the "lessee" requirement applies.

[2] The trial court, in the pertinent findings of fact, stated:

"   . . . .

"4. It was understood and had been the practice in the past that upon the arrival of U.S. Plywood's truck on Homette's premises, Homette employees would unload the truck;

"5. Such was the situation on the date in question;

"6. While on the premises of Homette, Dragoo drove U.S. Plywood's truck to the unloading area of Homette;

"7. Homette employees were standing by at such time to unload the truck. Upon Dragoo's arriving at the unloading area, he removed the bindings that retained the decking to the bed of the truck and then stood beside the truck while employees of Homette, using a forklift, began unloading the cargo;

"   . . . .

"9. At no time during the proceedings did any employees of Homette exercise any control over the movement of Mr. Dragoo or the truck;

"   . . . .

"11. At the time of his death, Dragoo was not engaged in 'unloading' the truck; . . . ".

"borrower," we do not agree that Homette falls within it because there is no evidence that Homette had possession of the truck and trailer rig.

We base our holding on recent changes in coverage afforded by automobile liability insurance. Prior to the addition of the loading and unloading endorsement of the automobile liability policy neither the automobile policy nor the standard liability policy defined which insurer had liability coverage for injuries sustained upon the premises of one who was insured under a general liability policy during the loading and unloading of a vehicle not owned or hired by the general liability insured. This question was settled by the later addition of the loading and unloading clause: the automobile liability insurer would provide coverage for injuries sustained as a result of negligence in the loading and unloading of the vehicle. The inclusion of the loading and unloading clause expanded the coverage of the policy from that afforded by the phrase "ownership, maintenance or use . . . of any automobile." Texas has adopted the broader majority view that "loading and unloading" embraces not only the immediate transfer of the goods to or from the vehicle, but also the complete operation of transporting the goods between the vehicle and the place from or to which they are being delivered. *Travelers Insurance Co. v. Employers Casualty Co.*, 380 S.W.2d 610 (Tex. 1964). Under the complete operation approach the coverage provided by a loading and unloading clause extended to a broad group of persons who were not employees of the owner of the vehicle; the only requisite for coverage was that they were using (unloading) the truck with the consent of the owner. *Travelers Insurance Co. v. Employers Casualty Co., supra, at 614.*[3]

General rules of construction lead us to conclude that the policy exclusion for persons who were unloaders but not "borrowers" of the vehicle was intended to limit the insurer's liability for injuries resulting from acts of these nonemployees of the owner of the vehicle. The purpose of an exclusion is to take something out of the coverage that would otherwise have been included in it. An interpretation that gives a reasonable meaning to all provisions is preferable to one that leaves a portion of the policy useless, inexplicable, or creates surplusage. The inquiry then becomes whether, given the limiting effect that the exclusion was intended to have, the court of civil appeals correctly analyzed the evidence in the present case.

The evidence in the record reflects that Dragoo parked the truck and Homette then began to unload. Homette's employees did not move the truck on this occasion nor is there evidence that U.S. Plywood consented on any other occasion to the movement of the truck by Homette's employees. There is no evidence that Homette's employees had ever in the past moved a U.S. Plywood truck as part of the unloading operation. There is no evidence that Homette's employees had ever instructed Dragoo to move the truck from one location to another. There is no evidence who had the keys to the truck at the time of the accident. The only evidence in the record is the statement by

---

[3] For example, in *Travelers Insurance Co. v. Employers Casualty Co., supra, the automobile liability carrier for Capitol Aggregates, Inc., a company which delivered concrete to a construction jobsite, was required to pay the amount of a settlement entered into between the beneficiaries of workers killed in an accident and Borders Steel Erection Company. The workers were employed by the general contractor on the job and were killed when a crane, owned by Borders and used to unload Capitol's trucks, buckled and fell.*

the sales manager of U.S. Plywood that Homette had express or implied permission to unload the decking. It is impossible to conclude from this statement that Homette had sufficient possession to be a "borrower." The only contact Homette's employees had with the truck was to drive up to it with forklifts and remove the decking. If, as American argues, this was enough to bring Homette within the policy, the "borrower" requirement would be meaningless because one would need only to be an unloader to also be a "borrower." We decline to adopt American's construction of the policy. While unloading is a "use" of the vehicle, the conjunction "and" in the definition of "borrower" indicates that one must also have possession of the vehicle to be a "borrower." Possession connotes the right to exercise dominion and control over the truck and trailer. There is no evidence that Homette had this right.

The court of civil appeals cited a number of cases that involved insurance policies containing "borrower" language. For various reasons these cases are not dispositive of the instant case . . . .

In conclusion, we do not find the cases cited by the court of civil appeals persuasive. We hold that merely proving one had the right to remove goods from a truck is not evidence one was a "borrower" of the truck. There must be evidence of possession. The record in this case discloses no such evidence.

The judgments of the trial court and the court of civil appeals are reversed and judgment is rendered declaring that Liberty Mutual Insurance Company is not obliged to defend the suit.

BARROW, J., not sitting.

NOTES

1. *The "loading and unloading" problem.* The "loading and unloading" aspect of the motor vehicle coverage has spawned considerable litigation under the Personal Auto Policy as well as the Business Auto Policy. Some of these issues were raised in § 6.01 of this Chapter (see note 6 following *Evans, supra*). A particular problem arose in the commercial context, however, under facts similar to those found in *Liberty Mutual*. Essentially, the issue is one of whose policy applies—the one on the motor vehicle, or the general liability policy of the business to whom the goods are being delivered. To resolve the problem under earlier language in the commercial motor vehicle policy (which did not contain the refinements found in the Liberty Mutual policy in the principal case), courts usually resorted to one of two tests—either the "coming to rest" doctrine or the "completed operations" doctrine. Under the former approach, the unloading process includes only the actual moving of the goods from the vehicle until they first come to rest. When the goods have begun to move toward their final destination, independent of the motor vehicle, the vehicle is no longer connected with the process of unloading. Consequently, there is no coverage under the vehicle policy after the goods have come to rest. Unloading under the "completed operations" doctrine, however, expands coverage to include all the operations necessary to effect a completed delivery.

As the court explains in *Liberty Mutual*, the "completed operations" doctrine worked to extend coverage to many people who were not employees of the owner of the vehicle and to situations that had little to do with risks associated with the vehicle. For example, there could be coverage for the conduct of a forklift driver, who works for the recipient of the goods, when she negligently stacks the goods and the goods fall over on a salesman visiting some time after the truck leaves the premises. Eventually, the motor vehicle policies were amended to contain the language found in the Liberty Mutual policy that was issued to U.S. Plywood to curb what some motor vehicle insurers thought were overly expansive judicial interpretations.

2. *The best laid plans of mice and men.* Of course, even the newer forms do not resolve all questions. *See, e.g., Kennedy v. Jefferson Smurfit Co.,* 147 N.J. 394, 688 A.2d 89 (1997) (addressing whether shipper's negligent selection of defective pallet during loading was part of "use" of tractor-trailer; answering question in affirmative, and holding that shipper qualified as additional insured under omnibus provision of trailer owner's policy). Furthermore, even with respect to the loading-unloading issue, it seems, at least from some insurers' perspectives, that nothing ever works out exactly as planned. Subsequent to the change in policy language, several courts held that the attempt to restrict coverage under the loading and unloading coverage conflicts with the liability coverage requirements of the particular state's compulsory motor vehicle insurance laws. *See, e.g., Mission Insurance Co. v. AID Insurance Co.,* 120 Ariz. 220, 585 P.2d 240 (1978) (holding policy restrictions conflict with statute that requires coverage for ownership, maintenance, or use because "use" includes more expansive definition of loading and unloading); *Amery Motor Co. v. Corey,* 46 Wis. 2d 291, 174 N.W.2d 540 (1970) (holding policy restrictions conflict with statutorily required omnibus clause). However, the Arizona legislature changed the result in *Mission* in 1982 when it enacted legislation prescribing liability coverages for certain commercial motor vehicles, coverages which do not include complete permissive user (omnibus) coverage. *See Wilshire Insurance Co. v. Home Insurance Co.,* 179 Ariz. 602, 880 P.2d 1148 (Ct. App. 1994).

For more discussion and other cases dealing with the virtually endless fact patterns arising under the "ownership, maintenance, or use" language, including loading and unloading, of a motor vehicle liability insurance policy, see Robert H. Jerry, II, Understanding Insurance Law § 136A (2d ed. 1996).

3. *Employees with wanderlust.* Just as personal automobile insurers and insureds must deal with the problem of drivers who operate vehicles in ways and places without permission, commercial automobile insurers and insureds have similar problems. Employees do not always follow directions, and they do not always use the vehicles in the manners their employers intended. As with personal automobiles, the issues will be whether the employee is using the vehicle within the scope of the permission, whether the employee has committed a material or immaterial deviation, whether the initial permission is broad enough to cover the actual use, etc. *See, e.g., Warner Trucking, Inc. v. Carolina Casualty Insurance Co.,* 686 N.E.2d 102 (Ind. 1997) (holding that insurer had no duty to provide coverage for individual liability of driver who violated company rules by operating truck after consuming alcohol earlier in the day; fact issue existed precluding summary judgment on whether employee was acting within scope of employment for purposes of vicarious

liability claim against employer); *Mid-Continent Casualty Co. v. Everett,* 340 F.2d 64 (10th Cir. 1965) (bus driver operating bus in wrong direction on his route while intoxicated deemed outside scope of permission).

[3] Nonowned Automobile Coverage

FARMERS INSURANCE CO. v. USF&G CO.
13 Wash. App. 836, 537 P.2d 839 (1975)

McINTURFF, CHIEF JUDGE.

This is a declaratory judgment action brought by Farmers Insurance Co. of Washington (Farmers) seeking an interpretation of the term "owner" as used in the nonowned automobile clause in their policy. The trial court held that the word "owner" would include one who has possession of a vehicle; and that since the driver had permission of the one in possession of the vehicle to drive it, under the policy he had permission of the owner. Farmers appeals.

In 1971 defendant Swanneck consigned his 1965 Oldsmobile for the purpose of sale to defendant Kroske, who operated a used car business. Other than his desire to have the automobile sold, Swanneck expressed nothing regarding its use by Kroske. Subsequently, Kroske loaned Swanneck's automobile to defendant Linda Warn to use temporarily while her automobile was being repaired. Kroske expressed no restrictions to Warn regarding its use. Warn used Swanneck's car to go to a birthday party and while there became too inebriated to return home. She asked defendant Haabey to drive her car home. While returning the automobile to Warn's home, Haabey, accompanied by the defendant Hensley, had an accident in which Hensley was seriously injured. Hensley made a claim against Haabey—who was insured by Farmers—for his injuries.

The "ownership, maintenance or use" clause in Haabey's policy, relating to liability, provided that Farmers would pay all damages the insured becomes legally obligated to pay arising out of the "ownership, maintenance or use, . . . of the described automobile or a non-owned automobile."[1]

The policy defined the term *"insured"* within the nonowned automobile clause to include:

> (b) with respect to a non-owned automobile,
>
>   (1) the named insured or relative, and
>
>   (2) any other person or organization not owning or hiring such automobile if legally responsible for its use by the named insured or a relative, but only in the event such named

---

[1] The "ownership, maintenance and use" clause is designed to protect the named insured against all claims for damages arising out of the operation of any owned or nonowned automobile. *McMichael v. American Ins. Co.,* 351 F.2d 665, 668 (8th Cir. 1965); 12 G. Couch, Insurance § 45:67 at 155–56 (2d R. Anderson ed. 1964) [hereinafter cited Couch on Insurance]. To fall within the coverage provided by this clause, title to the automobile legal or equitable is not necessary; legal possession or responsibility for its use is sufficient where there are no questions regarding the formalities of title transfer. Couch on Insurance § 45:62, at 151.

> insured or relative is legally liable for the occurrence; pro-
> vided the actual use of the non-owned automobile by the
> persons in (1) and (2) above is *with the permission of the
> owner.*

(Italics ours.)

The broad issue is whether the permission provision was intended to include situations where the insured is driving an auto unaware that he is doing so without the "permission of the owner."

Farmers contends that the word "owner" as used in the insurance policy does not mean any person who has possession of the vehicle but means the title owner. It is emphasized that the terms of the contract are not ambiguous and the language is plain. Farmers further argues that the term "owner" generally applies to one having a proprietary interest beyond that of a mere bailee in the context of an automobile insurance policy. It is claimed that the word "owner" as used in the framework of an automobile liability insurance policy is the same as the statutory definition of "owner" in RCW 46.04.380. Finally, Farmers urges that the court is legislating by interpreting the term.

We are concerned primarily with the nonownership clause. Its purpose is to add to, rather than reduce, the coverage provided by other provisions of the policy. The clause provides the insured coverage during infrequent or occasional use of a nonowned automobile. The permission provision of the nonownership clause was added to restrict coverage in the aftermath of two cases[6] in which children of the named insureds stole automobiles and the insureds were held liable under the nonowned auto coverage as a result of the accidents. Thus the permission requirement was designed specifically to preclude coverage where a stolen automobile was involved or where the insured had reason to know that he did not have the permission of the title owner to drive the automobile.

A purchaser of liability insurance does not contemplate driving a nonowned car without the permission of the owner. The average person purchasing such insurance and the insurer recognize the insured's need to be protected in situations where he is driving another's automobile in the honest belief that he has the owner's permission. The coverage is intended to protect drivers who are uncertain whether another's automobile is covered by insurance. Although the purposes of the "ownership, use and maintenance" clause and the "nonownership" clause are similar, there exists an inconsistency as nothing relating to permission is stated in the former. If parts of the same writing are inconsistent, they should be construed so as to harmonize with one another.

We must determine whether the term "owner" is ambiguous. If the language of a contract is not ambiguous its meaning and the intent of the parties are to be determined from its language alone, without resort to other rules of construction. A written instrument is ambiguous when its terms are uncertain or capable of being understood in more than one manner. The term is not defined in the policy. The term is, however, a *nomen generalissimum* and its

---

[6] *Home Indemnity Co. v. Ware*, 285 F.2d 852 (3d Cir. 1960); *Sperling v. Great Am. Indemnity Co.*, 7 N.Y.2d 442, 199 N.Y.S.2d 465, 166 N.E.2d 482 (1960).

meaning should be gathered from the context in which it is used. The term may have many meanings depending upon the circumstances in which it is used.

73 C.J.S. Property § 13(c) at 188 (1951) defines the term "owner" as applied to personal property to include the following:

> the person to whom a chattel belongs; the person who has the possession and control of a chattel; the person in possession and control of any article of personalty; one who has power of disposition, care, control, and management; one in possession, having care, control, and management; one having the right to possession and control; the person in whom legal title is vested.[13]

We find that the word "owner" is ambiguous and the average person may assign it to a wide variety of connotations other than the technical one, *i.e.,* title owner, urged by plaintiff. Referring to the rules of construction, we note with particular emphasis that any ambiguities in an exclusionary clause must be construed most favorably to the insured; that language in insurance policies is to be interpreted in a manner in which it would be understood by the *average* man, and not in a technical sense; that an interpretation most favorable to the insured must be applied if the policy is fairly susceptible to two different interpretations, even though a different or technical meaning may have been intended by the insurer; and that insurance policies should be construed to maximize coverage in a fashion consonant with fairness to the insurer.

Aside from the fact that an ambiguity in the term is present there are other practical considerations to be weighed in reaching our decision. First, the insurer is not providing coverage for any risk not anticipated; we are not dealing with a stolen automobile, nor one which was loaned to another contrary to the express desire of the owner. Mr. Haabey has paid premiums to Farmers to be protected against liability for injuries arising out of his use of a nonowned automobile. Secondly, it would not be workable for the driver of a nonowned automobile to determine in all instances whether he had the express or implied permission of the title owner, legal or equitable, to drive the car. Although there is authority to the contrary,[19] we choose to follow the rationale adopted in *Carlsson v. Pennsylvania Gen. Ins. Co.,* 214 Pa. Super. 479, 257 A.2d 861 (1969), where the owner of the automobile had loaned it to his son with the express restriction that it be operated in the Pittsburgh area. In spite of this prohibition, the son took the car to another town and loaned it to a friend. The friend while driving the automobile was involved in an accident and he sought to recover under his father's automobile policy.

---

[13] The fact that the word "owner" may have different meanings in different contexts has been recognized by our court. *See Smith v. Craver,* 89 Wash. 243, 247, 154 P. 156 (1916) (a mortgagor in possession is an owner).

[19] *Phillips v. Government Emp. Ins. Co., [258 F. Supp. 114 (E.D. Tenn. 1966)] (the term "owner" means title owner and is not ambiguous); *Civil Serv. Emp. Ins. Co. v. Roberts,* 10 Ariz. App. 512, 460 P.2d 48 (1969); *see Bright v. Ohio Cas. Ins. Co.,* 444 F.2d 1341 (6th Cir. 1971); *Jones v. Indiana Lumbermen's Mut. Ins. Co.,* 161 So. 2d 445 (La. App. 1964); *cf. State Farm Mut. Auto. Ins. Co. v. Mohan,* 85 Ill. App. 2d 10, 228 N.E.2d 283 (1967) (policy required permission of the owner or one in lawful possession); *State Auto. Mut. Ins. Co. v. Williams,* 268 Md. 535, 302 A.2d 627 (1973) (policy required permission of the owner or one reasonably believed to be the owner).

The *Carlsson* court concluded that the insurance company was liable and stated at page 866, 257 A.2d at page 866:

> We find, therefore that the insurance company in referring to the consent of the "owner" in non-owned automobile coverage included therein the consent of the possessor of the automobile, so long as the borrower reasonably believes that the possessor is the owner or has the permission of the owner to lend the automobile to third persons. [20]

In view of the rules of construction and our determination that the term "owner" is ambiguous as used in Farmers policy, we find that the term may include both the title owner, legal or equitable, as well as the possessor of the automobile so long as the one driving the auto reasonably believes that he has the permission of the owner to drive the vehicle. To hold otherwise would necessitate inquiry concerning who was the owner each time the car of another was driven, absent knowledge to the contrary. One could never have the secure knowledge that he was driving with permission of the owner. He would always be driving the car of another at his peril.

Farmers contention that the definition of owner in RCW 46.04.380 is controlling lacks merit. That title concerns the motor vehicle code and does not deal with insurance which is found in RCW 48.

Finally, it is urged that the court by so holding would be legislating. The legislature has not defined the term "owner" within the insurance code and the insurance policy does not define it. Hence, it is incumbent upon the court to interpret the meaning of that term, keeping in mind the many rules of construction enunciated in this opinion.

The remaining assignments of error, not argued in the brief, will not be considered.

Judgment of the superior court is affirmed.

GREEN, J., concurs.

MUNSON, J., concurs in the result.

NOTES

1. *Comparing the PAP.* Would the same result obtain under the language of the Personal Auto Policy (PAP) in Appendix E? As noted in the prior subsection, the "reasonable belief" exclusion has much to do with the coverage for driving nonowned cars.

Assume Friend is going out of town for a few days and leaves his car keys with Parent, who is Friend's neighbor. Parent has a 17-year-old child residing in her household who takes the keys and uses Friend's car, during which time

---

[20] Accord, *State Farm Mut. Auto. Ins. Co. v. Zurich American Ins. Co.,* 118 N.J. Super. 84, 286 A.2d 517, 523 (1972) (quoting with approval). We note that the *Carlsson* opinion was in part based upon a state statute requiring that in order for a policy of insurance to be valid it must insure motor vehicles not owned by the insured. We have no similar statute in the state of Washington. We also note that the opinion was based upon *Phillips v. Government Emp. Ins. Co.,* 258 F. Supp. 114 (E.D. Tenn. 1966), *rev'd* 395 F.2d 166 (6th Cir. 1968).

the child negligently runs over Plaintiff. Is the child covered under Parent's policy, assuming it is like the one in Appendix E? Is there any basis upon which Parent could be vicariously liable in tort for her child's negligence? What if Plaintiff sues alleging Parent was negligent in not securing the keys so that the child could not take the car and that Parent knew, from prior experience, that her child was likely to do so and drive irresponsibly? In either case, is there any coverage for Parent under the PAP?

2. *Furnished for "regular use" exclusion.* Another fertile source of litigation stems from the fact that the nonowned auto coverage, often referred to as the "Drive-Other-Cars" (DOC) coverage, does not apply to an auto that is furnished to the named insured or a member of the named insured's household for the "regular use" of such person. See "Part A—Liability Coverage" of the policy in Appendix E. For example, if Nancy leaves her car with Joan for the summer while Nancy tours Europe, and Joan's son, Dave, uses the car several times a week to run errands, would Joan's Personal Auto Policy cover Dave while he is driving Nancy's car? *See Farm Bureau Mutual Insurance Co. v. Nikkel,* 460 Mich. 558, 596 N.W.2d 915 (1999). What is the purpose of the exclusion, and is it justified?

3. *Public policy.* Courts have been highly skeptical of exclusions from uninsured or underinsured motorist coverage based on the fact that the insured is using a nonowned car not insured under the policy. Note that the Personal Auto Policy in Appendix E has no such exclusion. Why do you suppose courts are hostile to such exclusions? *See Prudential Insurance Co. v. Martinson,* 589 N.W.2d 64 (Iowa 1999) (exclusion which purported to negate UIM coverage while insured occupied a nonowned vehicle held invalid); *Blazekovic v. City of Milwaukee,* 234 Wis.2d 587, 610 N.W.2d 467 (2000) (exclusion from UM coverage while city firefighter used non-owned emergency vehicles in connection with her employment was invalid). But courts are not so concerned when the exclusion takes away liability insurance coverage for the insured's use of a nonowned vehicle owned by another resident in the household. Why should this be so? *See American Family Mutual Insurance Co. v. Livengood,* 970 P.2d 1054 (Mont. 1998) (roommate no. 1, who insured her own car, causes injury to third party when driving roommate no. 2's insured car)..

[4]   Family Exclusion and Similar Clauses

NATIONAL COUNTY MUTUAL FIRE INSURANCE CO. v. JOHNSON
879 S.W.2d 1 (Tex. 1993)

Hightower, Justice.

This cause involves the validity of a family member exclusion in a Texas automobile liability policy. . . . .

While driving his truck, Johnson collided with another automobile. Johnson's wife, a passenger in the truck, was injured in the collision and later brought suit against her husband seeking compensation for her injuries.

Johnson requested that National County unconditionally defend him in the suit and National County refused. Instead, National County contended that the family member exclusion[1] in the policy precluded coverage for the claim by Johnson's wife and offered to defend Johnson subject to a reservation of its rights to deny coverage and payment of any judgment rendered against him. Johnson filed a declaratory judgment to determine his rights under the policy and National County filed a counterclaim for declaratory relief asking the court to determine the validity of [the] family member exclusion.

The trial court rendered judgment for Johnson holding the family member exclusion invalid and National County liable for Johnson's defense and coverage under the policy. . . . . The court of appeals affirmed the trial court's decision. . . .

I.

National County argues that the family member exclusion is a valid exclusion which is consistent with the public policy underlying the Texas Motor Vehicle Safety-Responsibility Act. We disagree.

The Texas Motor Vehicle Safety-Responsibility Act (the Act) originated in 1951 and was enacted for the benefit of "all citizens of this state." Acts 1951, 52 Leg. p. 1227, ch. 498. Amendments to the Act in 1982 effectively mandate automobile liability insurance by requiring "[p]roof of ability to respond in damages for liability, on account of accidents . . . arising out of the ownership, maintenance or use of a motor vehicle." TEX. REV. CIV. STAT. ANN. art. 6701h § 1(10) (Vernon Supp.1993).[2] In addition, the statute requires that

> no motor vehicle may be operated in this State unless a policy of automobile liability insurance in at least the minimum amounts to provide evidence of financial responsibility under this Act is in effect *to insure against potential losses which may arise out of the operation of the vehicle.*

Id. § 1A(a) (emphasis added). This section of the Act makes it clear that the legislature's purpose in amending the Act was to protect claimants from losses by requiring all drivers to be responsible for damages arising out of their use of an automobile.[3]

---

[1] The exclusion . . . provides "We do not provide Liability Coverage for you or any *family member* for bodily injury to you or any *family member.*"

[2] Effective January 1, 1986, the statutorily required minimum liability amounts are "Twenty Thousand Dollars ($20,000) because of bodily injury to or death of one person in any one accident, and, subject to said limit for one person, Forty Thousand Dollars ($40,000) because of bodily injury to or death of two (2) or more persons in any one accident, and Fifteen Thousand Dollars ($15,000) because of injury to or destruction of property of others in any one accident." TEX. REV. CIV. STAT. ANN. art. 6701h § 1(10) (Vernon Supp.1993). . . .

[3] Section 21(b) of the Act, which concerns proof of financial responsibility for the future, also requires liability insurance which will pay "all sums which the insured shall become legally obligated to pay as damages arising out of the ownership, maintenance or use of such motor vehicle." TEX. REV. CIV. STAT. ANN. art. 6701h s 21(b) (Vernon Supp. 1993). Although not applicable in this case because the record fails to indicate that Johnson's policy was proof of financial responsibility for the "future," this section further demonstrates the Act's prevailing theme of protection of all claimants from those damages arising out of the use of a motor vehicle.

This court has recognized that the public policy behind the Texas Motor Vehicle Safety-Responsibility Act is to protect all potential claimants from damages resulting from automobile accidents.

There is no question in our minds that the compulsory insurance requirement of the Texas motor vehicle safety law implies that all potential claimants for damages resulting from automobile accidents are intended as beneficiaries of the statutorily required automobile liability coverage. *See* the Texas Motor Vehicle Safety-Responsibility Act, TEX. REV. CIV. STAT. ANN. art. 6701h, §§ 1(10). 1A.2(b), 5 and 32(f) (setting out the definitions and mandatory minimum liability requirements for automobile insurance as well as the fines and penal sanctions for failure to have general automobile liability coverage.) *Dairyland County Mut. Ins. v. Childress,* 650 S.W.2d 770, 775 (Tex. 1983).

We must consider whether the family member exclusion is consistent with the legislative purpose of ensuring that every motor vehicle is covered by an automobile liability policy that will protect all claimants against losses which arise out of the operation of the vehicle. We hold that it is not.

"When the Legislature specifies a particular extent of insurance coverage any attempt to void or narrow such coverage is improper and ineffective." Actions by the State Board of Insurance must be consistent with, and in furtherance of, expressed statutory purposes. If the Board approves a clause which conflicts with the statute, the Board's approval is ineffective. Here, the Board's approval of the family member exclusion[4] results in a situation in which a claimant for damages resulting from an automobile accident is not allowed to recover damages under an automobile liability insurance policy that the legislature statutorily requires to protect such claimants from losses. The exclusion prevents a specific class of innocent victims, those persons related to and living with the negligent driver, from receiving financial protection under an insurance policy.[5] Such a result is clearly contrary to the express legislative mandate. The Board's action in approving a family member exclusion providing for such scenarios is inconsistent with the statutory purpose of the Act, and thus their approval of the exclusion is ineffective.[6]

---

[4] Apparently the purpose of the family member exclusion was to protect insurers from being victimized by fraudulent or collusive lawsuits between members of the same family. Annot., *Validity, Construction, and Application of Provision of Automobile Liability Policy Excluding from Coverage Injury or Death of Member of Family or Household of Insured,* 46 A.L.R.3d 1024, 1029–32 (1972). However, this court has rejected this argument. *Whitworth v. Bynum,* 699 S.W.2d 194, 197 (Tex.1985) ("We refuse to indulge in the assumption that close relatives will prevaricate so as to promote a spurious lawsuit.")

[5] The family member exclusion creates an inequity by stripping family members of coverage under an automobile liability policy but allowing coverage for everyone else.

> [T]here is something wanting in a system of justice which permits strangers, friends, relatives and emancipated children to recover for injuries suffered as a result of their driver's negligence but denies this right to the driver's spouse and minor children who are also passengers in the same vehicle.

Immer v. Risko, 56 N.J. 482, 267 A.2d 481, 488 (1970).

[6] The dissent protests that the court abrogates a contractual provision of an insurance policy. However, this court and several courts of appeals have previously declared clauses or provisions in insurance policies invalid.

The majority of jurisdictions with mandatory insurance laws hold family member exclusions invalid because they are contrary to public policy.[7] Seven of those jurisdictions hold that the exclusion is only invalid up to the statutorily required minimum liability amounts and valid above those minimum amounts. Two additional jurisdictions reach that same conclusion, but do so because of express language in their financial responsibility statutes which addresses coverage in excess of the statutorily required minimums. Of the remaining jurisdictions which hold the exclusion invalid, six specifically refuse to limit recovery to the minimum amounts required by statute and instead allow recovery for the amounts of coverage provided by the policy. Six more jurisdictions hold that family member exclusions are invalid but do not determine whether recovery is limited to the statutorily required minimum liability amounts. We join those jurisdictions which reason that because the family member exclusion violates public policy, the provision is completely void.

The family member exclusion makes drivers uninsured for claims against them by their own family members, despite the statutorily mandated requirement that all drivers carry liability insurance to "to respond in damages for liability on account of accidents" and "ensure against potential losses which may arise out of the operation of the vehicle."[12] Thus, we hold that the family member exclusion is completely void because it conflicts with the Texas Motor Vehicle Safety-Responsibility Act as well as with the public policy underlying the Act. Accordingly, we affirm the judgment of the court of appeals.

DOGGETT, GAMMAGE and SPECTOR, JJ., join in this opinion.

Concurring and dissenting opinion by CORNYN, J.

Dissenting opinion by ENOCH, J., joined by PHILLIPS, C.J., and GONZALES and HECHT, JJ.

CORNYN, JUSTICE, concurring and dissenting.[1]

While I agree with the plurality that the family member exclusion ("exclusion") is invalid, I differ both as to the reason why, and, thus, the degree to which, this exclusion is invalid. The legislative mandate that every automobile operator carry liability insurance cannot be contravened, and the exclusion

---

[7] The dissent overlooks the fact that of the 25 jurisdictions with mandatory automobile insurance laws which have considered the validity of family member exclusions, 21 jurisdictions found that family member exclusions are invalid because they are contrary to public policy.

[12] Under the dissent's analysis, one would be unable to acquire automobile liability coverage for injuries one family member causes another to the same extent as coverage obtainable against third parties. Hence, if a family purchased liability coverage with limits of $300,000, family members would not be protected for injuries caused to each other. Under the concurrence's analysis, one would be unfairly restricted in family member liability coverage to no more than the statutorily required minimum amount. Hence, if a family purchased liability coverage with limits of $300,000, family members would only be protected up to $20,000 for injuries caused to each other.

[1] Justice Hightower's opinion is on behalf of a plurality of the court, only. Therefore, the views I express in this concurring and dissenting opinion determine the scope of the court's judgment: As a result, the family member exclusion is invalid only to the extent it conflicts with the Texas Safety Responsibility Act, TEX. REV. CIV. STAT. ANN. art. 6701h § 1(10) (Vernon Supp.1993), that is, to the statutorily-imposed minimum limit of automobile liability insurance imposed by the Act.

is unenforceable for that reason. As the basis under which I find this exclusion to be invalid is a statutorily-imposed minimum limit of automobile liability insurance, it follows that the exclusion should only be held invalid up to this statutory minimum. I would, therefore, hold that an insurer's liability is fixed at the minimum limits mandated by statute.

Because this exclusion has the effect of rendering an operator uninsured as to certain potential injured parties (i.e., family members), the plurality concludes that this exclusion violates both (1) public policy, as well as (2) the statutory requirement of minimum liability insurance. Respecting the second justification, however, honors the first as well because the legislative will as to the "public policy" in this area has been expressed by the statutorily-required minimum liability insurance requirement. The source, logic, and credibility of any other public policy to which the plurality ostensibly defers is questionable.

According to the plurality, the majority of jurisdictions with mandatory insurance laws have held family member exclusion clauses invalid because they are contrary to public policy. In this "majority," however, there is very little precise explanation as to what a general holding as "against public policy" means.

The legislature has expressed the relevant public policy in this area, and in its judgment an operator of a motor vehicle must have liability insurance at a certain minimum level. The plurality points to no other public policy implicated. The legislature has not said that family members should receive greater coverage than other members of the public, yet by totally invalidating these exclusions and allowing recovery up to the total amount of the policy, the plurality is divining new public policy that has nothing to do with the compulsory insurance law of the state. It is not for this court to evaluate the public policy implications of mandatory insurance coverage; the legislature has already done that.

I would, therefore, hold these exclusions invalid because they conflict with Texas' compulsory liability insurance statute. I would declare them to be invalid only up to the minimum amount of mandated liability insurance.

ENOCH, JUSTICE, dissenting.

With the stroke of a pen, the Court rips the family member exclusion endorsement out of every automobile liability insurance policy in this state. By this act, the Court creates contingent obligations for every insurance company which has a policy in force in this state, obligations for which these companies have neither assessed the risks nor charged and collected premiums. To do this, the Court asserts that a statute, enacted at a time when the common law of Texas did not recognize intra-family tort actions, dictates today, that an insurance policy provision which excludes coverage for intra-family tort liability is invalid and against public policy. I respectfully dissent.

The Court holds that Texas Personal Auto Policy Endorsement 575, the family member exclusion, is void because it conflicts with the Texas Motor Vehicle Safety-Responsibility Act ("the Act") which requires that all motor vehicles operated in the state have at least a minimum amount of liability insurance coverage. In coming to this conclusion, the Court fails to acknowledge that this statute came into effect in 1982, at a time when Texas common law prohibited tort actions between family members. The statute is completely silent about extending the protections of the act to family members. Not until this Court's decision in *Price v. Price*, 732 S.W.2d 316 (Tex. 1987), did Texas permit lawsuits between spouses arising out of automobile accidents. Ignoring ten years of legal history, the Court jumps to the conclusion that the family member exclusion, promulgated in 1987 (no doubt prompted by this Court's holding in Price), is in conflict with the statute and against public policy. To the contrary, the legal history firmly supports the conclusion that the promulgated rules of the Insurance Commission allowing the exclusion of family members from the mandatory liability insurance provisions are consistent with the purposes of the statute and are not in derogation of the public policy underlying the Act.

The Texas Motor Vehicle Safety-Responsibility Act requires persons to obtain at least the minimum required liability insurance in order to operate a motor vehicle in the state. The Act seeks to assure that someone is financially responsible for each automobile on the road for any "potential losses which may arise out of the operation of that vehicle." The question in this case is whether the family member exclusion is inconsistent with the stated policy in the statute that there be financial responsibility for the operation of a motor vehicle. The Court's answer to this question is troublesome in two respects.

I.

The Court abrogates a contractual provision. Adopted in 1987, the family member exclusion provides that the insurer will "not provide Liability Coverage for you or any family member for bodily injury to you or any family member." This exclusion is a mandatory endorsement to the Texas Personal Auto Policy. Regardless, the endorsement excluding family members is a contractual term. Of immediate concern is that invalidating the family member exclusion allows coverage for the insured's misfeasance without the insured having paid for the coverage. Of greater concern, however, is that absent constitutional infirmity of the statute, or clear violation of statutory authority by the Board, this Court should not abrogate the express provisions of the insurance contract. In this case there is no constitutional challenge to the Act, and it is surely questionable that a statute enacted in 1982, five years prior to this Court's decision in Price, and which was silent on intra-family tort liability, clearly dictates that the Board cannot promulgate a family exclusion for automobile liability insurance policies.

II.

The Court is ill equipped to evaluate public policy implications of mandatory insurance. The Texas Legislature and the State Board of Insurance are the proper fora to determine the public policy of Texas as it relates to automobile insurance coverage. And, the Board of Insurance's promulgation of the family member exclusion is entitled to weight. The legislature amended the Act in 1989 and 1991, after the family member exclusion was promulgated, and failed to address the family member exclusion. Since the legislature did not address the exclusion, the Texas Board of Insurance's promulgation of Endorsement 575 should be given great deference. The family member exclusion is neither in conflict with the Act nor against the public policy of this state as expressed through the statute.

The Court relies, however, on language in *Dairyland* which purports to identify third parties as the intended beneficiaries of the Texas Motor Vehicle Safety-Responsibility Act. However, that case did not address the effect of the family member exclusion which specifically denies coverage to an identifiable class of persons which the insurance was never intended to cover. The *Dairyland* case merely addressed Texas' motor vehicle safety laws in the context of whether a judgment creditor in an automobile liability case could sue the insurer for attorneys' fees under the insuring agreement. The coverage question was based upon a non-owner's endorsement for which the insured had specifically contracted. *Dairyland* is inapplicable to this case.

Furthermore, the rationale in *Dairyland* does not apply to family member circumstances. First, where a family member is the adverse party, the insured does not have the same incentive to assist the insurer in its defense. This not only compounds defense costs, but compounds the difficulty of estimating the risk being insured. Second, the family member, as part of the household, is in a position to know or inquire about insurance coverage. The household is in a position to know that the exclusion exists and to make other suitable insuring arrangements if they choose to do so. As an example, the household could be covered under the insured's group health or other first party medical insurance. Finally, automobile liability policies must include personal injury protection for a member of the insured's household, unless the insured rejects that coverage in writing. Interestingly, by invalidating the family member exclusion in the insuring agreement, the Court allows Johnson to obtain coverage, neither contracted nor paid for, in addition to alternate coverage expressly provided for by another statute.

It is inconceivable that the legislature intended to force consumers to purchase liability insurance to cover a judgment of a family member given that at the time the legislature enacted the Texas Motor Vehicle-Responsibility Act family members could not obtain a judgment for injuries caused by the negligent driving of another family member. While intra-family tort immunity was later abolished for automobile cases by judicial intervention, that in and of itself does not automatically adjudge the family member exclusion in an insurance policy to be invalid as against public policy. Nor does it mean that insurance companies must be forced to sell or consumers must be forced to buy liability insurance to cover their family.

On a final note, the Court has not evaluated, nor does it have the resources to evaluate, the impact of this decision. We should refrain from affecting the public policy of our state in this manner. Subject to constitutional review, the better policy is to allow the State Board of Insurance or the legislature, both with much greater resources, the wide latitude necessary to evaluate the social benefits and economic costs associated with a state wide, system wide change in mandated insurance coverage.

III.

Today, the Court abrogates an express contractual provision without fully evaluating the public policy implications. I cannot join the Court's opinion.

I would reverse the judgment of the court of appeals and render that Mr. Johnson take nothing from National County Mutual Fire Insurance Company or Consumers County Mutual Insurance Company.

PHILLIPS, C.J., and GONZALEZ and HECHT, JJ., join in this dissenting opinion.

NOTES

1. *Evaluating the opinions.* In a subsequent opinion, the Texas Supreme Court made it clear that *Johnson* invalidated the family member exclusion only to the extent that the Texas Safety Responsibility Act requires motorists to carry minimum liability limits. *Liberty Mutual Fire Insurance Co. v. Sanford,* 879 S.W.2d 9 (Tex. 1994). Other courts have made the same distinction between statutorily mandated liability limits and coverage beyond those limits. *See, e.g., Pribble v. State Farm Mutual Automobile Insurance Co.,* 933 P.2d 1108 (Wyo. 1997); *Smalls v. State Farm Mutual Automobile Insurance Co.,* 678 A.2d 32 (D.C. 1996). With which of the opinions in *Johnson* do you agree?

See also Nichols v. Anderson, 837 F.2d 1372 (5th Cir. 1988), in which the court held that the insurer was only liable for $25,000, the minimum limit required under the Arkansas statute, rather than the policy limit of $100,000, where a radius exclusion clause was determined to be void as against public policy. (Radius clauses are discussed in note 3 following *Hall v. Amica Mutual Insurance Co.* in § 6.07[2] of this Chapter, infra).

2. *Scope of the exclusion.* The exclusion in *Johnson* pertains only to family members. Who would you expect to be included within any definition of "family member" that you might find in the policy? See the "Definitions" section in the Personal Automobile Policy in Appendix E. Some policies have used a broader exclusion that not only applies to claims of family members but eliminates liability coverage for a claim of any member of the household of the named insured. *See Meyer v. State Farm Mutual Automobile Insurance Co.,* 689 P.2d 585 (Colo. 1984). Is either the family exclusion or the household exclusion clause broader than the intra-family immunity doctrine which, until relatively recently, barred suits by one member of a family against another member of the family for negligently caused injuries? As to the latter, see Dan B. Dobbs, The Law of Torts §§ 279-80 (2000). If so, is there justification for the present language or should insurers only be permitted to exclude coverage for claims by the members of a family that were barred by the intra-family immunity doctrine?

3. *Majority rules.* The majority rule appears to be that both the family and household exclusions violate the standard financial responsibility act or compulsory liability insurance statute to the extent of statutorily prescribed minimums, but are enforceable beyond the minimums. *See, e.g., State Farm Mutual Automobile Insurance Co. v. Mastbaum,* 748 P.2d 1042, 1043 (Utah 1987) ("The vast majority of cases . . . have held that household exclusions or analogous exclusions are enforceable with respect to policy amounts in

excess of the statutory minimum"); *Nation v. State Farm Insurance Co.,* 880 P.2d 877 (Okla. 1994) (exclusion void as to minimum amount of statutorily-mandated coverage). Martin J. McMahon, Annotation, *Validity, Under Insurance Statutes, of Coverage Exclusion for Injury or Death of Insured's Family or Household Members,* 52 A.L.R.4th 18 (1988).

4. *The "named insured" exclusion.* Given the majority approach with respect to the household exclusion, should the same result obtain if the policy contains a named insured exclusion, i.e., an exclusion that says it does not provide coverage for a claim by a named insured in the policy? This type of exclusion operates in basically two kinds of situations. In the first, the named insured is injured while a passenger in her own vehicle; the driver is not an insured, but is driving the vehicle with the named insured's permission. The named insured wants to recover from his own insurer on account of the permissive driver's negligence, but is prevented from doing so by the named insured exclusion. In the second situation, two individuals are co-insureds under the same policy; the named insured exclusion operates to prevent one co-insured from recovering proceeds based on the liability of the other, as would be the case where one co-insured is driving and the other is a passenger. *See Farmers Insurance Exchange v. Dotson,* 913 P.2d 27 (Colo. 1996); *State Farm Mutual Automobile Insurance Co. v. Falness,* 178 Ariz. 281, 872 P.2d 1233 (1994); *New York Underwriters Insurance Co. v. Superior Court,* 104 Ariz. 544, 456 P.2d 914 (1969), 46 A.L.R.3d 1057 (1972).

5. *The "named driver" exclusion.* Some financial responsibility acts and compulsory liability insurance statutes expressly permit exclusion of a named driver. This usually is accomplished by an endorsement which simply lists the name of the person who is not to be afforded coverage. *See Garza v. Glen Falls Insurance Co.,* 105 N.M. 220, 731 P.2d 363 (1986). However, where the statute is silent, there are cases holding that such attempts run afoul of the purpose of the statute which is to protect the public and that named driver exclusions are void. *See Farmers Insurance Exchange v. Dotson,* 913 P.2d 27 (Colo. 1996); *Iowa Mutual Insurance Co. v. Davis,* 752 P.2d 166 (Mont. 1988).

6. *Exclusions in nonmandated policies.* If there is no statutory prescription or proscription which applies to a policy, the family, household, and named insured exclusion clauses are usually enforced as written. This is typically the result with respect to, for example, homeowners insurance, farm or ranch liability policies, and other liability insurance coverages. *See, e.g., Page v. Mountain West Farm Bureau Mutual Insurance Co.,* 2 P.3d 506 (Wyo. 2000); *Kentucky Farm Bureau Mutual Insurance Co. v. Thompson,* 1 S.W.3d 475 (Ky. 1999)(noting that prior precedent striking down household exclusion in automobile insurance (*Lewis v. West American Insurance Co.,* 927 S.W.2d 829 (Ky. 1996) was irrelevant); *Commercial Union Insurance Co. v. Alves,* 677 A.2d 70 (Me. 1996); *Patrons Mutual Insurance Ass'n v. Harmon,* 240 Kan. 707, 732 P.2d 741 (1987). *See also Reinsurance Association of Minnesota v. Hanks,* 539 N.W.2d 793 (Minn. 1995) (upholding intra-family bodily injury exclusion in noncustodial parent's multi-peril farm policy and denying coverage for injuries sustained by insured's minor daughter in lawn mowing accident). Are there any other arguments, besides the one based upon statutory invalidation, that could be used in trying to persuade a court that the exclusion in a homeowners

or a multi-peril farm policy should not be enforced? *See Dechert v. Maine Insurance Guaranty Ass'n,* 711 A.2d 1290 (Me. 1998); *Mutual of Enumclaw Insurance Co. v. Roberts,* 128 Idaho 232, 912 P.2d 119 (1996).

7. *What to do about the curious jury?* In a case where a family member is permitted to sue another family member in tort for damages that are covered under a liability insurance policy, should the jury be informed that there is insurance coverage and the defendant-insured's attorney is being provided by the insurer? Who would want this information brought to the jury's attention? *See Myers v. Robertson,* 891 P.2d 199 (Alaska 1995).

[5] Per-Person and Per-Occurence Policy Limits

IN THE MATTER OF MOSTOW v. STATE FARM INSURANCE COS.

88 N.Y.2d 321, 668 N.E.2d 392 (1996).
[This case appears in § 3.02[2], supra.]

NOTES

1. *General principles.* A "per person" (or "each person") limit designates the maximum amount that an insurer will pay for bodily injury to any one person. If several persons are injured in an occurrence, the "per person" limit applies to each one. A "per occurrence" limit designates the maximum amount that an insurer will pay for all covered bodily injury losses from a single occurrence, regardless of the number of persons who suffer injury (or who suffer property damage). An "aggregate limit" designates the maximum amount that an insurer will pay for all covered losses during the policy period. Personal automobile policies typically do not have an aggregate limit; these are more common in commercial liability and professional malpractice policies.

Most personal automobile policies have separate limits for bodily injury and property damage liability. These policies are known as "split limits" policies. If a policy is described as "100/300/50," that means that the per person bodily injury limit is $100,000, the per occurrence bodily injury limit is $300,000, and the separate property damage limit is $50,000. If the policy is a "single limit" policy, there will be one limit for each occurrence: a bodily injury loss to any one person is covered up to $300,000, a property damage loss is covered up to $300,000, or any combination of bodily injury and property damage losses to one or more persons is covered up to a limit of $300,000. See Constance M. Luthardt, Barry D. Smith & Eric A. Wiening, Property and Liability Insurance Principles (3d ed. 1999), at 9-29 to 9-30. This is how per person and per occurrence limits have been applied in many cases for many years. *See, e.g., Standard Accident Insurance Co. v. Winget,* 197 F.2d 97 (9th Cir. 1952), 34 A.L.R.2d 250 (1954); *Mannheimer Brothers v. Kansas Casualty & Surety Co.,* 149 Minn. 482, 184 N.W. 189 (1921).

To test your understanding of how these limits interact, assume that Jane has a personal auto policy (like that in Appendix E) with split limits of 100/300/50. Jane is liable for a covered automobile accident which causes $250,000 in bodily injury damages to Dave, the driver of the other car, and $120,000 in bodily injury damages to Mary, a passenger in Dave's car. The damage to Dave's car amounts to $20,000. What will Jane's insurer pay in connection with these liabilities? What if Jane's policy had a single limit of $300,000 instead of the split limits?

Suppose the insurer in the preceding example managed to settle Dave's bodily injury claim for $70,000. Does that mean an extra $30,000 is available for Mary? When multiple claimants are present whose total claims greatly exceed the per occurrence limit, does a claimant run any risks by not engaging the insurer in settlement negotiations when other claimants are doing so?

2. *What went wrong in* Mostow? The drafter's intent, as described in the preceding note, was not implemented in *Mostow*. Why not? If you were the insurer, how would you change future iterations of the policy?

3. *Multiple losses from a single "accident" or "occurrence" revisited.* In § 5.02[2][b], *supra,* the issue of multiple losses from a single "occurrence" was considered in the context of the CGL policy. The same issue can, of course, arise here. For example, assume that Driver stops off after work for a few beers and, upon leaving the tavern, sideswipes an oncoming vehicle, injuring Occupant, and careens into Pedestrian. Driver then attempts to flee the scene and several blocks away runs a stop sign, injuring Motorist. Are there one, two, or three accidents or occurrences? What difference would it make under a policy with split limits of 10/20/5 if the victims suffered bodily injury damages as follows: Occupant, $7,500; Pedestrian, $15,000; and Motorist, $10,000? *See Arizona Prop. & Casualty Insurance Guaranty Fund v. Helme,* 153 Ariz. 129, 735 P.2d 451 (1987), 64 A.L.R.4th 651 (1988).

Some liability policies or endorsements thereto contain a deductible for each claim made against the insured. In *Atlas Underwriters, Ltd. v. Meredith-Burda, Inc.,* 231 Va. 255, 343 S.E.2d 65 (1986), 60 A.L.R.4th 977 (1988), the insured defendant damaged approximately forty vehicles owned by employees of the plaintiff while spray painting two water towers on the plaintiff's property. Plaintiff paid its employees for the damage and took assignments of their claims against the defendant insured. The liability policy in question contained a $250 deductible "per claim" and only one of the vehicles sustained damage in excess of this amount. Does "claim" mean the plaintiff's claim in the aggregate based on the forty assignments so that the deductible would apply only once or should it still apply to each of the forty assigned claims?

4. *Post-judgment interest.* There is a split of authority on how to handle post-judgment interest. Currently, the majority holds that the language ". . . the company shall . . . pay . . . all interest accruing after the entry of judgment . . ." means the interest is calculated on the entire amount of the judgment, even if the judgment exceeds the policy limits. *Allegheny Airlines v. Forth Corp.,* 663 F.2d 751, 755 (7th Cir. 1981). However, once the insurer "has paid, tendered or deposited in court, such part of such judgment as does not exceed the limit of the company's liability thereon," the duty of the insurer to pay interest, and, therefore, its liability for such ceases. *Knippen v. Glens Falls*

Insurance Co., 564 F.2d 525, 529 (D.C. Cir. 1977). As to any unpaid balance of the judgment, the insured is liable for this amount, plus any interest accruing on the unpaid balance. If the latter is true, why should the insurer be liable for interest on that portion of the judgment in excess of policy limits prior to tender or payment into court? *See also Grimes v. Swaim,* 971 F.2d 622 (10th Cir. 1992) (pointing out that some courts have construed the policy language in *Allegheny* to require that the insurer pay or tender the accrued interest as well as the policy limits in order to stop its obligation to pay interest).

5. *Pre-judgment interest.* To the extent pre-judgment interest is awarded for claims involving bodily injury and property damage, should the interest be treated as part of the "damages" and therefore be subject to the "per person" and "per accident" policy limits or should it be treated like post-judgment interest and be payable in addition to the applicable limits? If the insurance industry proposed to amend certain policies, such as personal auto and home-owners forms, to clarify that pre-judgment interest is not to be treated the same as post-judgment interest, but is to be considered as damages and therefore subject to the "per person" and "per accident" limits, should the insurance regulator of the state approve or disapprove such forms? Examine the policy in Appendix E on this question.

6. *Other defense costs.* The costs of defending the claim are typically not subject to the per person or per occurrence limits. These aspects of the liability policies receive attention in § 8.02, *infra.*

7. *Applying the limits.* If one person suffers bodily injuries and a second person suffers emotion distress or loss of consortium damages, is the second person's damages subject to a second "per person" limit? Consider the next case.

McNEILL v. METROPOLITAN PROPERTY LIABILITY INSURANCE CO.

420 Mass. 587, 650 N.E.2d 793 (1995)

Before WILKINS, ABRAMS, O'CONNOR and GREANEY, JJ.

ABRAMS, JUSTICE.

The plaintiff's daughter was involved in an accident while a passenger in an automobile driven by John Desjardins. The plaintiff, Ronald C. McNeill, arrived at the accident scene and witnessed his daughter's injured state. His daughter died from her injuries two days later. As a result, the plaintiff suffered emotional distress which exacerbated his diabetic condition and led to his developing an ulcer.[1]

---

[1] The defendant accepts the plaintiff's assertion that these physical conditions were causally related to the emotional distress he suffered as a result of the accident.

The plaintiff, as administrator of his daughter's estate, brought a wrongful death action against Desjardins. He also brought an action against Desjardins on his own behalf for negligent infliction of emotional distress. At the time of the accident, Desjardins was insured under a policy issued by the defendant. The policy provides optional bodily injury liability coverage in the amount of $100,000 "per person" and $300,000 "per accident."

The policy is a standard personal automobile insurance policy. It provides: "The most we will pay for injuries to one or more persons as a result of bodily injury to any one person in any one accident is shown on the Coverage Selections Page as the 'per person' limit. Subject to this limit, the most we will pay for injuries to two or more people as the result of bodily injury to two or more people in any one accident is shown on the Coverage Selections Page as the 'per accident' limit."[2]

The wrongful death claim was settled for the policy's $100,000 "per person" limit. The defendant contended that both claims were subject to a single "per person" limit of $100,000. The plaintiff filed a complaint for declaratory judgment seeking a declaration that his claim for negligent infliction of emotional distress triggered a second "per person" limit, entitling him to seek another $100,000. The parties each filed motions for summary judgment. The judge denied the plaintiff's motion and allowed the defendant's motion, declaring that the plaintiff's claims are subject to a single "per person" limit of $100,000. The plaintiff appealed. We granted the defendant's application for direct appellate review. We affirm.[3]

. . . .

The "per person" limit, limits to $100,000 the policy's coverage for "injuries to one or more persons as a result of bodily injury to any one person in any one accident." "This language is clear and unambiguous." *Santos v. Lumbermens Mut. Casualty Co.,* 408 Mass. 70, 79, 556 N.E.2d 983 (1990). It applies the "per person" limit to injuries to more than one person where the injuries result from bodily injuries to the same person in the same accident. See *id.*

The wrongful death claim sought recovery for an injury (i.e., the plaintiff's daughter's death) resulting from bodily injury to the plaintiff's daughter in the accident. While the emotional distress claim seeks recovery for a different injury (i.e., the plaintiff's emotional distress), this injury also was the result of the daughter's bodily injury in the accident. It is his daughter's injuries, and her resulting death which caused the plaintiff the emotional distress for which he seeks relief. As the motion judge noted, the plaintiff's emotional distress claim "is a by-product of and entirely dependent upon the bodily injury to his daughter." The claims thus are subject to the same "per person" limit.

The plaintiff's physical ailments do not warrant a separate "per person" limit. While they may constitute "bodily injury," they are the result of the plaintiff's emotional distress, not its cause. The plaintiff's argument that his emotional distress was a bodily injury received in the accident is flawed

---

[2] The policy defines the word "we" as "the company issuing th[e] policy," namely, the defendant.

[3] The only issue on appeal is whether both claims are subject to the same "per person" limit. It is not disputed that the plaintiff's emotional distress claim is covered by the policy and that this claim is independent of the wrongful death claim.

because emotional distress is not a bodily injury. *Allstate Ins. Co. v. Diamant,* 401 Mass. 654, 656, 518 N.E.2d 1154 (1988) (" 'Bodily injury' . . . encompasses only physical injuries to the body and the consequences thereof"). *See Sullivan v. Boston Gas Co.,* 414 Mass. 129, 138 n. 9, 605 N.E.2d 805 (1993), citing *Allstate Ins. Co. v. Diamant, supra* ("We have . . . construed the words 'bodily injury' in an insurance policy to exclude the coverage of mental pain . . .").[4]

The plaintiff argues that, because the emotional distress claim is independent of the wrongful death claim and seeks recovery for injuries to a different person than the wrongful death claim, it should not be subject to the same "per person" limit as the wrongful death claim. The policy limits coverage for all claims resulting from bodily injury to one person in one accident. Here, all claims result from the plaintiff's daughter's injury in the single accident, and thus they are subject to the $100,000 "per person" limit.

Our decision is bolstered by the fact that the policy language at issue was created to prevent the type of interpretation urged by the plaintiff. In *Bilodeau* [*v. Lumbermens Mut. Cas. Co.,* 392 Mass. 537,] 538, 543, 467 N.E.2d 137, we held that under the then standard automobile insurance policy, a claim for loss of consortium was entitled to a separate "per person" limit from the underlying claim for bodily injuries in the accident. The "per person" limit limited the amount paid "for injuries to any one person as a result of any one accident." *Id.* at 540, 467 N.E.2d 137. To eliminate the effect of this decision, the commissioner changed the "per person" limit in the standard policy to the language at issue in the present case. *Santos, supra* at 79, 556 N.E.2d 983. In *Santos,* we held that, under this new language, consortium-like claims are subject to the same "per person" limits as the bodily injury claims, as they result from the same bodily injury in the accident. *Id.*

Judgment affirmed.

NOTES

1. *Massachusetts background.* In *Bilodeau v. Lumbermens Mutual Casualty Co.,* 392 Mass. 537, 467 N.E.2d 137 (1984), 46 A.L.R.4th (1986), referred to in *McNeill,* the Supreme Judicial Court of Massachusetts was asked to decide whether the state-prescribed automobile liability policy provided separate bodily injury limits for a consortium claim. Unlike most jurisdictions that faced the issue, the Massachusetts court held that the particular policy language regarding the "per person" bodily injury limit did not require that the consortium claim and the bodily injury claim be treated as one injury. For example, assume that Husband suffers serious head injuries in an auto accident negligently caused by Driver and sustains $140,000 in damages. Driver has an auto liability policy providing $100,000 in coverage for each person injured and $300,000 for each accident. In addition to Husband's tort

---

[4] The fact that an essential element of a claim for negligent infliction of emotional distress is "physical harm manifested by objective symptomatology," *Payton v. Abbott Labs,* 386 Mass. 540, 557, 437 N.E.2d 171 (1982), does not make such emotional distress a bodily injury. This requirement exists for evidentiary purposes and is not related to the classification of injuries as bodily injuries for insurance purposes.

claim, Wife files a claim for loss of consortium, demanding $50,000. How much could Husband and Wife recover under the *Bilodeau* rule?

After the *Bilodeau* decision, the Massachusetts Commissioner of Insurance exercised his authority to change the language of the prescribed policy, thereby bringing it within the rule applied by most jurisdictions—the rule in *McNeill*. *See McGovern v. Williams,* 741 S.W.2d 373 (Tex. 1987) (citing cases following majority and minority views).

2. *Wrongful death and survival claims.* In *McNeill,* there was no issue about the wrongful death claim arising out of bodily injury, but just how does the "per person" limit work in that type of case? Just to make it a little more interesting, what if there is, in addition to the wrongful death claim, a claim on behalf of the deceased under a survival statute? Assume Tom Jones is seriously injured in an auto accident and lingers on in the hospital until he finally dies from the injuries. A survival action on behalf of the deceased, Jones, and a wrongful death action on behalf of his six children are brought seeking damages of $100,000 and $500,000, respectively. Assume the applicable policy limits are $300,000 per person and $600,000 per accident for bodily injury. How would these limits apply in Massachusetts assuming the rule in *Bilodeau* governed the outcome? What would be the result under *McNeill*? How should the limits apply under the policy in Appendix E? *See Lumley v. Farmers Insurance Co.,* 716 S.W.2d 455 (Mo. App. 1986).

3. *Derivative versus independent claims.* Does the question of whether the consortium claim is to be governed by the "per person" limit applicable to the individual claiming physical injury turn on whether the former claim is derivative or independent from the latter claim? Most states treat the consortium claim as a derivative claim, which means that any defense that is good against the individual suffering bodily injury is good against the consortium claimant. If the claim is independent, it matters not that the individual suffering bodily injury is at fault or otherwise barred from pursuing a claim. It just so happens that Massachusetts is one of the few jurisdictions that says a consortium claim is an independent claim belonging to the spouse or child of the physically injured person. *See Feltch v. General Rental Co.,* 383 Mass. 603, 421 N.E.2d 67 (1981).

4. *"Bodily injury" revisited.* Do you agree with the court's conclusion in *McNeill* that the emotional distress claim does not constitute "bodily injury"? Essentially, a wrongful death claim is one for economic loss in most jurisdictions and a consortium claim involves injury to a relationship. So, what is the nature of a claim for emotional distress? Compare the definitions of "bodily injury" in the liability provisions of the policies in Appendices B, C, and E. If the emotional distress claim in *McNeill* does not constitute "bodily injury," would there be any coverage at all for McNeill's claim under the liability policy carried by Desjardin, so that there was no need to even discuss the policy limits issue? For more on the meaning of "bodily injury," see note 10 following *GATX Leasing Corp. v. National Union Fire Insurance Co.,* 64 F.3d 1112 (7th Cir. 1995) in § 5.02[2][a], *supra.*

[6]   Property "Rented To" or "In Charge Of" the Insured

SECURITY MUTUAL CASUALTY CO. v. JOHNSON
584 S.W.2d 703 (Tex. 1979)

POPE, JUSTICE.

Herman Johnson and Timothy Johnson sued their insurer, Security Mutual Casualty Company, to recover the amount of a judgment rendered against Timothy Johnson for damages to a pickup truck driven by Timothy. Trial was to a jury and judgment was rendered for the Johnsons. The court of civil appeals affirmed the judgment of the trial court. 575 S.W.2d 107. We reverse the judgments of the courts below and render judgment that plaintiffs take nothing.

Eugene George was employed by W. H. McColm and had permission to drive home from work every night a pickup truck owned by McColm and to keep the truck at his home over weekends. George was allowed to use the truck for both business and pleasure. Timothy Johnson was a friend of Eugene George and his brother, Paul George. There was testimony that Eugene permitted Paul and Timothy to use the pickup frequently, requiring only that they replace the gasoline; that Timothy had been using the truck for a year and a half before the accident; and that Timothy believed the pickup belonged to Eugene.

On the night of the accident, Timothy and Paul were taking Paul's cousin home. Paul did not have a driver's license, so Timothy was driving the pickup. The accident occurred when Timothy collided with a lamp pole, causing damage to the truck.

McColm filed suit against Timothy Johnson and recovered a judgment for $2,131. At the time of the collision, Herman Johnson, Timothy's father, had a policy of personal injury and property damage liability insurance with Security Mutual. The policy did not include collision or comprehensive coverage. Security Mutual refused to defend Timothy or to pay the judgment. The Johnsons filed this suit against Security Mutual to recover the amount of the judgment.

Part I—Liability, of the policy of insurance in effect at the time of the accident, provided for payment on behalf of the insured of all sums for which the insured shall become legally obligated to pay as damages because of bodily injury and property damage arising out of ownership, maintenance, or use of the owned automobile or any non-owned automobile. Persons insured with respect to a non-owned automobile are defined as the named insured and any relative, but only with respect to a private passenger automobile or trailer, provided the actual operation is with the permission or reasonably believed permission of the owner and within the scope of such permission. Liability under these provisions is further governed by the following exclusion:

This policy does not apply under Part I:

. . . .

(i) to injury or destruction of (1) property owned or transported by the insured or (2) property rented to or *in charge of the insured* other than a residence or private garage; [Emphasis added.]

Security Mutual contends policy coverage is excluded because Timothy Johnson was "in charge of" the automobile at the time of the collision.

Terms used in an insurance contract are given their ordinary and generally accepted meaning unless the policy shows the words were meant in a technical or different sense. *Guardian Life Insurance Co. of America v. Scott,* 405 S.W.2d 64 (Tex. 1966). Generally, the criterion for determining whether property is "in charge of" the insured within such an exclusion is the insured's right to exercise dominion or control over the property. *Maryland Casualty Company v. Golden Jersey Creamery,* 389 S.W.2d 701, (Tex. Civ. App.—Corpus Christi 1965, writ ref'd n.r.e.); 13 Couch, Insurance 2d § 45:946 (1965).

The term has been interpreted by many jurisdictions. The majority finds the term unambiguous and applicable to "property" in charge of the insured, including motor vehicles. We follow those jurisdictions that regard "property in charge of the insured" to include the pickup truck driven by Timothy Johnson.

We view the facts of this case to establish that at the time of the accident, Timothy Johnson was "in charge of" the property and, therefore, liability was excluded. Timothy Johnson had sole control of the pickup at the time of the collision and was the only person present with an operator's license. To the ordinary person, one is "in charge of" personal property when he has possession of it, has the right to exercise dominion and control over it, and is actually exercising physical control over it. At the time of the collision, Timothy was driving the truck and in our view the ordinary meaning of the words used in the exclusionary clause leaves no doubt that coverage is excluded.

Normally, a liability policy does not cover damage to the insured's property or property within his control. If an insured desires coverage on property that he owns or that is in his charge, he must secure collision or comprehensive coverage and pay an additional premium. There was no collision coverage in effect at the time of the accident and it cannot be asserted that such coverage was expected under the provisions of the liability policy.

The judgments of the courts below are reversed and judgment is rendered that plaintiffs take nothing.

NOTES

1. *One of the mysteries of life?* Why would an insurer except from the exclusionary language a residence or private garage? If Eugene George were renting his home and he negligently drove the pickup into the garage wall, would he have coverage under a policy like that in Appendix E in a suit by the landlord against him? What if the landlord left a riding lawnmower in the garage which George used to mow the lawn and George negligently ran into it with the pickup? Why the distinction?

2. *Subrogation rights.* Assume that the pickup truck in *Johnson* was a personal vehicle of W. H. McColm and that he carried collision coverage under a policy like that in Appendix E. If his insurer, after paying McColm under the facts of the *Johnson* case, attempted to assert a right of subrogation by bringing a negligence suit against Timothy, would the suit be permitted?

3. *Coverage for rental cars.* Notice that the exclusionary clause in the principal case would eliminate any liability coverage for tortious damage to a rental car driven by the insured. Had Eugene George carried collision and comprehensive coverage under an auto policy like that in Appendix E, would damage to a car rented and driven by him be covered under these first-party coverages? *See also* the Berman & Bourne essay in § 4.05[3][c], *supra*.

4. *When is property "in charge" of insured?* The issue of whether property is in charge of the insured, so that the exclusion is triggered, arises in various types of liability insurance policies. For example, in *Eisenbarth v. Hartford Fire Insurance Co.*, 840 P.2d 945 (Wyo. 1992) a farm-ranch liability policy excluded coverage for damage to property in the "care, custody or control of the insured." The insured, a farmer, entered into an agreement allowing a neighboring rancher to board cattle on the insured's corn stalks for 60 days. Under the agreement, the insured was obligated to maintain the cattle in a fenced area, allow them to feed upon the corn stalks, provide supplemental feed if the corn stalks froze, provide the cattle with salt and minerals at the rancher's expense, conduct a daily count of the cattle and locate any cattle not accounted for, and watch the cattle for signs of illness. During the period of the agreement, some of the cattle became sick and died. The rancher sued and a jury found that the insured-farmer was 60 percent at fault and the rancher was 40 percent at fault in causing the death of the cattle. The trial court entered summary judgment for the insurer on the basis of the exclusion, but the Wyoming Supreme Court reversed, holding that the matter involved a question to be resolved by the trier of fact:

> While not determinative of the issue here presented, th[e] jury [in the suit by the rancher against the insured-farmer] apparently found at least joint responsibility and some level of joint care, custody or control. The question then is what are the limits of the exclusion intended by the "care, custody or control" language in the Hartford policy. Must [the insured] have total care, custody or control (100%) in all decisions affecting the livestock? What is the effect of minimal or joint care, custody or control? What level of "care, custody or control" calls the exclusion to play? Does it mean any level, some level, or complete "care, custody or control?" It would have been a simple matter for the writer of the insurance contract to clearly state that care, custody or control of its insured, no matter how slight, would exclude coverage if that was the intent of the parties. Having failed to do so, we hold that total (not shared) care, custody or control is necessary for the exclusion to apply. Whether there was total care, custody or control in [the insured] is a genuine issue of material fact which precludes application of the exclusion as a matter of law.

840 P.2d at 950. For a similar clause in the liability section of the homeowners form, see "Section II—Exclusions," par. 2(c), in Appendix C.

---

§ 6.03   Uninsured and Underinsured Motorist Insurance

[1]   The Nature of the Coverage

Uninsured motorist (often called "UM") coverage was developed by the insurance industry in the 1950s as a response to gaps in the traditional tort liability-compensation system. The hit-and-run driver is one obvious kind of gap. A post-accident financial responsibility system might keep uninsured drivers off the road, but such a system does little to help the victim of an uninsured driver's first accident. Charitable immunities have been substantially eroded through the years (sometimes only to the extent of the charity's liability insurance), but early on these immunities were problematic for some accident victims as well.

Initially, UM coverage was offered only in the amounts specified in the financial responsibility law of the state. However, there followed a series of steps in which legislatures began to require, first, that it be offered; second, that the insurance policy be deemed to include it unless the insured refuses it in writing; and, finally, in some states, that the coverage be a mandated part of an auto liability policy that the insured is required to carry. Statutes typically require that coverage be provided or offered in an amount equal to the financial responsibility laws of the particular state, but some statutes require that an amount "at least" as high as that amount be provided or offered. 1 Alan I. Widiss, Uninsured and Underinsured Motorist Insurance § 2.12, at 46–47 (rev. 2d ed. 1999).

Is uninsured motorist insurance a first-party coverage or a third-party coverage? A fair answer is that it is elements of each. UM insurance is a kind of first-party insurance in the sense that the insured looks to her own insurer for reimbursement of the insured's own loss. But UM insurance retains elements of the tort liability system, because the insured must establish than an uninsured third-party was responsible for the insured's loss, meaning that the insured must establish the uninsured motorist's liability in tort. If the insurer can establish that no tort occurred, the insured does not recover. In a sense, then, it is as if the insured purchases a contingent liability insurance policy for the benefit of some unknown third-party tortfeasor; if the third-party injures the insured and has no insurance, the UM coverage will provide the coverage the tortfeasor might have (indeed, should have) purchased, but the proceeds end up being paid to the insured-victim. Needless to say, the hybrid nature of UM insurance is a breeding ground for complexities.

Underinsured motorist insurance, a separate coverage (and often called "UIM" insurance), was developed in the 1980s as a complement to uninsured motorist coverage. Whereas UM coverage applies when the tortfeasor has no auto liability insurance at all or less than that legally required to pay the loss, UIM coverage applies when the tortfeasor carries enough insurance to meet any legal requirements, but the amount is insufficient to pay the full loss.

There are essentially two distinct models of UIM insurance. Under one approach, if the tortfeasor lacks sufficient liability insurance to reimburse the victim's loss, the victim can recover UIM benefits from her own insurer measured by the difference between the victim's own higher liability limits and the tortfeasor's lower liability limits. This kind of statute is not so much interested in fully compensating the victim for her own loss, but rather seeks to ensure that the victim-insured has resort to coverage at least as extensive as the victim's own liability insurance. In a sense, this is a "gap-filling" coverage. With the UIM gap-filler, an insured with high UM limits who is injured by a torfeasor with minimum liability limits might recover less than an insured with the same coverage who is injured by an uninsured motorist. Another way to view this kind of system is that it caps the victim's UIM recovery at the amount of UM benefits. For an example of this kind of system, see Kan. Stat. Ann. § 40-284(b) (1993).

A different approach to UIM coverage makes the insured's liability coverage an add-on to the tortfeasor's liability coverage, up to the amount of the victim's loss. Because this is an "excess coverage" approach as opposed to a "gap-filling" or "topping-off" approach, it has the potential to do a better job of victim compensation, but it should cost more as well. For an example of this kind of system, see Ark. Code Ann. § 23-89-209 (Michie 1999).

There is a multivolume treatise devoted to the subject of uninsured (and underinsured) motorist insurance. For more information on the subject, see Alan I. Widiss, Uninsured and Underinsured Motorist Insurance (2d rev. ed. 1999).

[2] Judicial Regulation

LOWING v. ALLSTATE INSURANCE CO.

176 Ariz. 101, 859 P.2d 724 (1993) (en banc)

MARTONE, JUSTICE.

We are asked to decide whether an unidentified accident-causing motorist is "uninsured" within the meaning of the Uninsured Motorist Act, A.R.S. § 20-259.01, and thus whether an insurance policy that does not provide coverage for bodily injury caused by such motorists, unless physical contact occurred between the motorist and the insured, fails to comply with the statute. We answer both of these questions in the affirmative and therefore overrule our previous rulings to the contrary in *Balestrieri v. Hartford Accident & Indem. Ins. Co.*, 112 Ariz. 160, 540 P.2d 126 (1975)and *State Farm Mut. Auto. Ins. Co. v. Brudnock*, 151 Ariz. 268, 727 P.2d 321 (1986).

I. BACKGROUND

A. *Horvath v. Continental Casualty*

Lewis Horvath and three of his children sustained injuries when Horvath swerved his car to avoid another car attempting to pass a truck in a no-passing zone on a curve. Though Horvath's action prevented a head-on collision, he was forced off the road. The driver of the other car, whose identity remains unknown, did not stop.

Because Horvath's uninsured motorist insurance covers only those accidents caused by unknown motorists who actually "hit" the insured's vehicle, his insurance carrier, Continental Casualty, refused to cover Horvath's losses.[1] Horvath sued, seeking a declaration that the policy limitation is contrary to the requirements of A.R.S. § 20-259.01, Arizona's Uninsured Motorist Act, and thus void. The trial court granted Continental's motion to dismiss, and the court of appeals affirmed based on this court's holding in *Balestrieri* that such provisions are valid. We granted Horvath's petition for review.

B. *Lowing v. Allstate Ins. Co.*

Paula Lowing sustained injuries when Salvatore Gentile, the owner and driver of the vehicle in which she was a passenger, swerved to avoid colliding with a vehicle that ran a stop sign. Gentile's car missed the other vehicle, but left the roadway and overturned. The other vehicle did not stop, and its driver was never identified. Gentile's uninsured motorist insurance carrier, Allstate, refused to cover Lowing's damages because its policy limits coverage to cases in which there is actual physical contact with the unknown accident-causing vehicle.[2] Gentile sued, seeking a declaration that the policy limitation is void under A.R.S. § 20-259.01. The trial court granted Allstate's motion for summary judgment and the court of appeals affirmed based on the *Balestrieri* line of cases. We granted Lowing's petition for review and consolidated it with the *Horvath* case.

II. ANALYSIS

A. Does A.R.S. § 20-259.01 require coverage of unidentified motorists?

The first question we must answer is one of statutory interpretation: does A.R.S. § 20-259.01 require coverage of unidentified motorists in addition to known motorists who are demonstrably uninsured? "The primary principle of statutory interpretation is to determine and give effect to legislative intent." *Wyatt v. Wehmueller,* 167 Ariz. 281, 284, 806 P.2d 870, 873 (1991). The best and most reliable index of a statute's meaning is its language. That language,

---

[1] The policy reads, in relevant part:

> We pay damages which you or any other covered person are legally entitled to recover from the owner or operator of an uninsured or underinsured motor vehicle or boat because of bodily injury: 1. Sustained by you or any covered person; and 2. Caused by a motor vehicle or boat accident.

CNA's Universal Security Policy Deluxe, at 23 (Exhibit A to Complaint). Twenty-six pages later, in the definitions section of the policy, "uninsured motor vehicle or boat" is defined as:

> a land motor vehicle or boat or trailer of any type:
>
> *
>
> c. Which is a hit-and-run motor vehicle or boat whose operator or owner cannot be identified and which hits: (1) You or any covered person; (2) A motor vehicle which you or any covered person are occupying; or (3) Your motor vehicle or boat.

Id. at 49.

[2] The insurance policy defines an "uninsured auto" as, inter alia, "[a] hit and run motor vehicle which causes bodily injury to a person insured by physical contact with the insured or with the vehicle occupied by that person. The identity of the operator and owner of the vehicle must be unknown."

where clear and unequivocal, controls the statute's meaning unless it leads to absurd or impossible results. Where, instead, the statute's language is subject to different interpretations, the court is free to consult other sources of legislative intent such as the statute's context, historical background, consequences, spirit and purpose. Section 20-259.01(A) states:

> No automobile liability or motor vehicle liability policy . . . shall be delivered or issued for delivery in this state . . . unless coverage is provided in the policy . . . for the protection of persons insured who are legally entitled to recover damages from owners or operators of uninsured motor vehicles because of bodily injury. . . .

In *Balestrieri*, we upheld a physical contact requirement against a public policy challenge based on what the court perceived to be the "plain language" of § 20-259.01. We reasoned that the statute requires coverage of injuries caused by "uninsured motorists" and that "uninsured" means those motorists we know are uninsured, not unidentified motorists who may or may not be uninsured. 112 Ariz. at 163, 540 P.2d at 129. Therefore, the statute does not require coverage of damages caused by any unidentified accident-causing motorist, whether "hit and run" or "miss and run." *Id.*

In reality, however, we cannot apply the "plain language" of the statute because we cannot know which unidentified motorists are uninsured and which are not. We must instead presume either that unidentified motorists are insured or that they are uninsured. If we presume the former, some persons injured by uninsured motorists will go uncompensated. If we presume the latter, some persons injured by insured motorists will recover from their uninsured motorist insurance carrier. Neither situation is contemplated by the literal language of the statute. The statute does not address the unidentified motorist issue. It is therefore ambiguous, and we must consult other sources to determine which of the two interpretations is more in line with legislative intent.

The purpose of § 20-259.01 is, broadly speaking, to "close the gap in protection under the Safety Responsibility Act, A.R.S. § 28-1101 et seq.", *Calvert v. Farmers Ins. Co. of Arizona,* 144 Ariz. 291, 294, 697 P.2d 684, 687 (1985), and protect people who are injured by financially irresponsible motorists, *id.* at 295, 697 P.2d at 688. Section 20-259.01 is remedial in nature and should be liberally construed in order to effectuate its purpose. *Id.* at 294, 697 P.2d at 687. Exclusions and limitations on coverage are generally invalid unless contemplated by the statute. *Id.*

Interpreting the statute to require coverage of damages caused by unidentified motorists advances its protective goal; interpreting it in a way that does not require such coverage frustrates that goal. It is unlikely that the legislature intended to protect the injured person from an uninsured motorist responsible enough to stop and be identified but not from a motorist, insured or not, irresponsible enough to cause an accident and then flee.

In *Porter v. Empire Fire and Marine Ins. Co.,* 106 Ariz. 274, 475 P.2d 258 (1970), we held that an insured who recovers less than the statutory minimum amount of coverage from a negligent motorist because the negligent driver's liability insurance is split among multiple claimants may recover the balance (i.e., up to the statutory minimum) from his or her uninsured motorist coverage. The rationale of the case was that, although the negligent motorist purchased some liability insurance, he or she is functionally uninsured as to the injured person because insurance is not available up to the minimum amount required by statute. Because the Uninsured Motorist Act was designed to make available to all persons injured by negligent motorists a certain minimum amount of compensation, the motorist was uninsured within the meaning of the act.

Likewise, unidentified motorists are functionally uninsured as to the persons they injure because they have no insurance that is in fact available and collectible. In *Balestrieri*, we attempted to reconcile our holding with *Porter* by noting that "in both [cases] the injured party maintains the burden of establishing the fact that the negligent motorist was uninsured." 112 Ariz. at 163–64, 540 P.2d at 129–30. But an insured will never know, and can never prove, whether an unidentified negligent motorist is insured. What is important in the two cases is not which party has the burden of proof, but who is considered uninsured. In *Porter* an insured motorist with too little insurance to compensate an injured party up to the minimum statutory limits is considered uninsured. When we held in *Balestrieri* that an unidentified motorist is presumed to be insured until the plaintiff proves otherwise, we departed from the spirit of the earlier case.[3]

Thus, interpreting "owners or operators of uninsured motor vehicles" to include unidentified motorists is consistent with the general purpose of the statute, and with this court's construction of the statute. But there is more. [The court reviewed the history of A.R.S. § 20-259.01 and concluded that "the legislature specifically intended the statute to include the unidentified motorist."]

. . . .

We thus hold that an unidentified accident-causing motorist is an "owner or operator of an uninsured motor vehicle" within the meaning of § 20-259.01, and that the statute requires every automobile liability policy delivered or issued for delivery in Arizona to provide coverage for bodily injury caused by such motorists.

B. Is the physical contact requirement void as against public policy?

The policies at issue in this case do provide coverage for some unidentified accident-causing drivers: those that actually "hit" or have "physical contact" with the insured or the vehicle occupied by the insured. Having concluded that

---

[3] One might argue that, if we apply the rationale of Porter to the instant case, we would have to hold that the person injured by an unidentified driver can only recover from his or her insurer up to the minimum amount required by the financial responsibility act even if he or she had purchased greater uninsured motorist protection. This is not the case, however. In Porter the negligent motorist did in fact have insurance; the only problem was that it was split between several claimants. Had the court allowed the plaintiff in that case to recover up to the limits of his uninsured motorist coverage (which might, after all, have been over the statutory minimum) it would have turned uninsured motorist coverage into a form of underinsured motorist coverage. It makes sense that we refused to do so. In the instant case, however, the same rationale does not apply. From the viewpoint of the injured party, the unidentified accident-causing motorist is wholly uninsured and the injured party should be able to recover up to the limits of his or her uninsured motorist coverage.

§ 20-259.01 requires coverage of damages caused by unidentified motorists, the question becomes whether the contact limitation violates the statute. We conclude that it does. Exceptions to coverage are not generally permitted unless expressly allowed by statute. The physical contact requirement, by arbitrarily excluding a class of people from coverage, directly conflicts with what we have determined to be the public policy of protecting people who are injured by financially irresponsible motorists.

The physical contact requirement flows from the language of the policy—not the language of our statute, and is wholly unrelated to the question of being "uninsured in fact." Our knowledge of the "insured" status of a hit and run driver is no better than our knowledge of the "insured" status of a miss and run driver. In either case, the unknown motorist is uninsured as to the injured party—there is no coverage available. The whole purpose of uninsured and underinsured motorist coverage is to allow a prudent person to protect himself or herself against the universe of risks. To exclude miss and run drivers from the definition frustrates the purpose of the statute.

Commentators agree that the physical contact requirement was created by insurance companies to prevent fraudulent claims by insureds who negligently damage their vehicles and invent a "phantom" vehicle in an attempt to recover from their insurer. The contact requirement, however, is both too broad and too narrow to accomplish this goal. *See DeMello v. First Ins. Co. of Hawaii,* 55 Haw. 519, 523 P.2d 304, 310 (1974). As one commentator noted, if twenty witnesses will swear that an accident occurred as claimed by the injured insured, it is simply arbitrary to deny coverage in the absence of physical contact under the rubric of fraud prevention. *Brown v. Progressive Mut. Ins. Co.,* 249 So. 2d 429, 430 (Fla. 1971). Conversely, if there are no witnesses to an insured's own negligence, he or she can easily claim physical contact when there was none, and create the evidence to corroborate such a claim. *See Anderson v. State Farm Mut. Auto. Insurance Co.,* 133 Ariz. 464, 470, 652 P.2d 537, 543 (1982) (Feldman, J., concurring).

We therefore conclude that the physical contact requirement of the policies is not an authorized exception to the coverage required by the statute. It is therefore void as against public policy.

C. Stare Decisis

We have dealt with the merits of the issue as though this were a case of first impression. Of course it is not. In *Balestrieri,* we upheld the physical contact requirement, and have since refused two invitations to overrule that case.

. . . .

. . . While we should and do pay appropriate homage to precedent, we also realize that we are not prisoners of the past. In this case, there are compelling reasons to overrule precedent. . . . We conclude that this is another instance in which a departure from precedent is warranted.

. . . [B]y overruling *Balestrieri* we return to the policy expressed in *Porter* of evaluating the status of the financially irresponsible motorist from the viewpoint of the injured insured. [Further,] the facts of these cases demonstrate that the *Balestrieri* interpretation is unjust. As one commentator noted:

An alert, athletic pedestrian who barely manages to avoid contact with such a car by leaping through a plate glass window receives the unkindest cuts of all for his efforts, but cannot qualify. Snubbed, too, is the driver who miraculously manages to steer his car off the highway and thus avoid a collision with an oncoming vehicle traveling in the wrong lane, but in so doing effects a rather abrupt stop against an unyielding bridge abutment.

McGlynn v. Safeco Insurance Co. of America, 216 Mont. 379, 701 P.2d 735, 739 (1985)(quoting 55 Ill. Bar J. 143, 147 (1966)). In contrast, a less alert pedestrian or driver would recover. Finally, by overruling *Balestrieri* we join the view of a leading commentator in the field. See Alan I. Widiss, 1 Uninsured and Underinsured Motorist Insurance § 9.7 at 484–85 (2d ed. 1990). In short, although we have a healthy respect for stare decisis, we will not be bound by a rule with nothing more than precedent to recommend it. *See Streitweiser v. Middlesex Mut. Assurance Co.,* 219 Conn. 371, 593 A.2d 498 (1991)(court overruled prior precedent and held that the Connecticut uninsured motorist statute requires coverage of damages caused by unidentified motorists).

. . . .

IV. CONCLUSION

We hold that unidentified accident-causing drivers are uninsured within the meaning of A.R.S. § 20-259.01. Therefore, insurers issuing automobile liability policies within this state must provide coverage for damages caused by these drivers. Physical contact requirements, by restricting coverage to only those unidentified drivers who actually hit the insured, are in conflict with the statute and are void. By so holding, we overrule our prior decisions to the contrary, The memorandum decision of the court of appeals in *Lowing* is vacated. That part of the memorandum decision in *Horvath* that relates to the physical contact requirement is vacated. In both cases the judgments of the superior court are reversed and the cases are remanded to the superior court for proceedings consistent with this opinion.

FELDMAN C.J., MOELLER V.C.J., AND ZLAKET, J., CONCUR.

CORCORAN, JUSTICE, SPECIALLY CONCURRING: [opinion omitted.]

NOTES

1. *Some examples of some complexities.* Virtually every state has at least the equivalent of a few volumes of its reports filled with cases sorting out the complexities of UM and UIM coverage. For a taste of the complexities, assume that the automobiles of *A,* who has the uninsured and underinsured motorist coverages set out in Appendix E, and *B,* who is the negligent cause, collide.

a. If *B* has a personal liability policy that covers his negligent acts in general, but no automobile liability policy, is *B* uninsured? *See State Farm Mutual Automobile Insurance Co. v. Taylor,* 725 P.2d 821 (Mont. 1986).

b. If *B* has an applicable auto liability policy, but the insurer is insolvent and in receivership, is *B* uninsured?

c. What if *A* is not carrying collision coverage under his policy and *B* has no insurance? Can *A* collect for the physical damage to his car caused by *B* under *A*'s uninsured motorist coverage?

d. If *A*'s underinsured motorist coverage is in the amount of $100,000 for bodily injury to one person and *B* has $15,000 in liability coverage which is available to pay for *A*'s injuries, assuming *B*'s coverage complies with the applicable state law and that *A*'s damages for bodily injury were $110,000, how much can *A* collect from his own insurance company?

e. Assume further in (d) that there was a pedestrian injured and that the pedestrian was entitled to a portion of *B*'s insurance, so that *A* received only $5,000 from *B*'s liability insurer. How much can *A* now collect from his own insurer? *See American States Insurance Co. v. Estate of Tollari,* 362 N.W.2d 519 (Iowa 1985).

2. *The hit-and-run conundrum.* "Several state statutes require that the insured's vehicle have a 'physical contact' with the hit-and-run driver. Other state statutes reject the physical contact requirement. A third group of state statutes require that uninsured motorist coverages provide protection for the victims of hit-and-run drivers, but the statutes do not specifically require or proscribe physical contact as a prerequisite to coverage. In these states, courts have been asked to interpret the statutes, and the courts have reached divergent results. Courts in at least eighteen states have declared that the statutes do not require physical contact and that policies requiring such contact are contrary to the statute and are void as against public policy. In at least fifteen other states, courts have declined to follow this reasoning and have upheld policies in which the insurer has limited uninsured motorist coverage to situations where the physical contact is evident." Robert H. Jerry, II, Understanding Insurance Law § 134[b][4], at 868 (2d ed. 1996). The case law is so voluminous that it supports three recent ALR annotations by David J. Marchitelli on the "physical contact" requirement; these can be found at 77 A.L.R.5th 319 (2000), 78 A.L.R.5th 341 (2000), and 79 A.L.R.5th 289 (2000).

If you were a legislator, would you support a statute that required hit-and-run UM coverage in the absence of physical contact, provided the insured has at least one disinterested witness willing to substantiate the insured's version of the accident? In *Hamric v. Doe,* 201 W.Va. 615, 499 S.E.2d 619 (1997), the Supreme Court of West Virginia interpreted that state's statute, which requires a physical contact (*see* W.Va.Code § 33-6-31(e)(iii) (Supp. 2000), as being satisfied if independent, disinterested third-party testimony showed that the vehicle would have struck the insured but for the insured's evasive action. Even if this answer makes sense, is it appropriate for a court to fashion it, as opposed to leaving the issue to the legislature?

3. *Other kinds of impacts.* In the following situations, assume the insured has uninsured motorist coverage and that the insured suffers bodily injury in the described incidents. Is the insured covered?

a. The insured hits a piece of vehicular debris lying in the roadway (such as a tire fragment, a muffler, etc.), and has an accident as a result of this contact. incident? *See Theis v. Midwest Security Insurance Co.,* 232 Wis.2d 749, 606 N.W.2d 162 (2000)(truck leaf spring); *State Farm Mutual Automobile*

Insurance Co. v. Norman, 446 S.E.2d 720 (W. Va. 1994)(semi-truck tire); *All-state Insurance Co. v. Killakey,* 580 N.E.2d 399 (N.Y. 1991)(tire and rim). What if the debris is nonvehicular (such as, for example, a barrel that has fallen off the back of a truck, or a piece of ice)? In either case, is it essential that the insured (or some disinterested party) see the debris fall off some other vehicle? Is the case easier if the debris falls off the vehicle and is still in motion at the time of the impact with the victim's car? *See Dehnel v. State Farm Mutual Automobile Insurance Co.,* 231 Wis.2d 14, 604 N.W.2d 575 (Wis.App. 1999)(ice); *Government Employees Insurance Co. v. Goldschlager,* 355 N.Y.S.2d 9 (N.Y. App. Div. 1974)(detached wheel). In *Bauer v. Government Employees Insurance Co.,* 61 F.Supp.2d 514 (E.D.La. 1999), the court made an "Erie guess" at Mississippi law: "Mississippi law does not allow recovery under a UM policy for contact with debris in the roadway unless there is a 'complete, proximate, direct and timely relationship' between an unidentified vehicle and the injury to the insured." 61 F.Supp.2d at 519. Does this test clear the air?

b. An unknown motorist's vehicle kicks up a piece of debris (like a rock or fragment of a car) and propels it through the insured's windshield, causing an accident? *Compare Hill v. Citizens Insurance Co.,* 403 N.W.2d 147 (Mich. Ct. App. 1986), with *Masler v. State Farm Mutual Automobile Insurance Co.,* 894 S.W.2d 633 (Ky. 1995). Should a distinction be drawn between an object which was a piece of the unidentified vehicle or which was projected by that vehicle, and an object which originates from an occupant of the unidentified vehicle? *See Wills v. State Farm Insurance Co.,* 222 Mich.App. 110, 564 N.W.2d 488 (1997) (answering question posed in affirmative). Is the case easier if the unknown motorist hits a second car, which in turn is propelled into the insured's car? *See Hoyle v. Carroll,* 646 S.W.2d 161 (Tenn. 1983).

c. An uninsured motorist is driving a car on an interstate highway, runs out of gas, leaves his vehicle and starts walking to a gas station; the path he chooses to walk, however, is the middle of a traffic lane. The insured swerves to miss the uninsured pedestrian, but loses control and is seriously injured in the ensuing accident. Does the accident "arise out of the use" of the uninsured motorist's automobile? *See Aryainejad v. Economy Fire & Casualty Co.,* 278 Ill. App. 3d 1049, 663 N.E.2d 1107 (1996).

d. Insured, a bicycle commuter, is injured when a passing truck grazes a portfolio strapped to the rear carrier of the bicycle he is riding. *See General Accident Insurance Co. v. Gladstone,* 260 A.D.2d 855, 687 N.Y.S.2d 830 (N.Y.App.Div. 1999).

Can you articulate a principle that provides consistent results across all of these situations?

4. *Occupancy.* Another key phrase in most uninsured motorist policies connects insureds to the coverage through the concept of "occupancy." In the Personal Auto Policy in Appendix E, Part C, the term "insured" includes "[a]ny other person 'occupying' 'your covered auto.'" Note that the same phrase appears in the Medical Payments Coverage (Part B), and that the named insured and "family members" are covered while "occupying" a motor vehicle or while in the status of a pedestrian. Is someone "occupying" a vehicle when she is getting out of it? *See Olsen v. Farm Bureau Insurance Co. of Neb.,* 259 Neb.

329, 609 N.W.2d 664 (2000)(yes). When a child is crossing the traffic lanes en route to getting on a school bus, is the student "occupying" the bus? *See Newman v. Erie Insurance Exchange,* 256 Va. 501, 507 S.E.2d 348 (1998) (no, but student was "using" the bus). Is it necessary to be in physical contact with a vehicle to be occupying it? *See Tropf v. American Family Mutual Insurance Co.,* 558 N.W.2d 158 (Iowa 1997) (yes; insured who had exited insured vehicle after it was involved in two-car crash and then was injured when lunging out of path of another vehicle, was not occupying the insured vehicle at time of injury). See generally Jacqueline G. Slifkin, Annotation, *Automobile Insurance: What Constitutes "Occupying" Under Owned-Vehicle Exclusion of Uninsured-or Underinsured Motorist Coverage of Automobile Insurance Policy,* 59 A.L.R.5th 191 (1998).

5. *Fortuity and accidental loss revisited.* Whether the liability portion of the automobile policy should cover losses that are nonfortuitous in some sense was considered earlier. (See § 6.02[1], note 4, *supra*). In uninsured motorist insurance and the medpay coverages, similar problems arise. Consider the following: Susan is a passenger in Mark's vehicle when it collides with Richard's vehicle; Richard is negligent and uninsured. While the police are investigating the accident, a police officer invites Susan to get in a police car, about 120 feet away from the accident, to warm up (the weather is cold) until the police are ready to interview her. While Susan stands by the vehicle, Richard shoots and kills her. Does Susan's uninsured motorist policy provide coverage for her wrongful death? *See General Accident Insurance Co. of Am. v. Olivier,* 574 A.2d 1240 (R.I. 1990). Has Susan died in an "accident"? (Note the language of the "Insuring Agreement" in Part C of the Personal Auto Policy in Appendix E.) Is it not correct that an intentional assault on an insured who does not provoke or intend the injuries is an "accident"? *See Abraham v. Raso,* 183 F.3d 279 (3d Cir. 1999) (under New Jersey law, in deciding whether accident occurred, courts should look at event from tort victim's perspective); *Wendell v. State Farm Mutual Automobile Insurance Co.,* 293 Mont. 140, 974 P.2d 623 (1999) (to same effect); but *See Landry v. Dairyland Insurance Co.,* 166 Vt. 634, 701 A.2d 1035 (1997) (insured's brother, while riding in insured's car, was hit by tire iron thrown by tortfeasor from side of road; held, no coverage because no accident). But what if the policy provides uninsured motorist benefits for injuries suffered in *"motor vehicle* accidents"? *See Blackman v. Wright,* 716 A.2d 648 (Pa.Super.Ct. 1998).

How would the rationale for your answer in Susan's case (above) apply to the facts of *Fox v. Country Mutual Insurance Co.,* 327 Or. 500, 964 P.2d 997 (1998)? Vincent, a high school student, decided to wreck his pickup in order to collect the insurance proceeds. Fox, Vincent's friend, agreed to be present. Fox told a witness shortly before the incident that he would be a lookout; Vincent testified that Fox changed his mind before the wreck and decided to ride in the truck, thinking that the seat belt would save him. Fox's heirs argued that the record supported the inference that Fox wanted out of the truck before the crash, but Vincent did not let him out. Whatever really happened, Vincent intended to crash the truck, Fox was a passenger in the truck at the time of the crash, Fox did not intend to cause any injury to himself in the crash, and Fox died. Was Fox's death in this intentional wreck "caused by accident" for purposes of UM coverage?

6. *Conflicts of interest.* In § 8.02[3], *infra*, the potential for conflicts of interest between insurer and insured in the liability insurance situation are explored. Uninsured motorist coverage has its own potential for conflict. Suppose an insured is injured by an uninsured motorist, but the insurer believes that the insured's claim is invalid. The insurer may find itself in the position of resisting the insured's claim. One court gave this analysis:

> [A]n insurer providing uninsured motorist coverage to an insured involved in an accident may intervene in an action to determine the liability of an uninsured motorist. The insurer should be "permitted to raise all defenses to [the allegations of the uninsured motorist's negligence]—both affirmative and negative—which the defendant . . . could have raised had [the defendant appeared]." To focus on the resulting litigation between the intervenor and its insured on the question of the uninsured motorist's negligence, and to alleviate the potential conflicts of interest which arise as a consequence of the insurer's intervention, . . . an intervening insurer may be required to provide independent legal counsel to its insured or to reimburse its insured for reasonable legal expenses incurred in defending against the insurer's intervention. The provision of counsel or reimbursement of expenses should be directly related to litigation of the issue of the uninsured motorist's negligence and the damages resulting from that negligence and should not implicate collateral issues relating to the insurer's intervention.

Chatterton v. Walker, 938 P.2d 255, 262 (Utah. 1997). In first-party property insurance, an insurer might end up contesting the insured's claim as well, but no one suggests that the insurer must provide the insured with an attorney. Why is uninsured motorist coverage any different?

Most courts allow the insurer's contractual liability to be litigated in the same action where the uninsured tortfeasor's tort liability is litigated. This eliminates the need for two separate actions, thereby eliminating redundant proceedings. *See, e.g., Fetch v. Quam,* 530 N.W.2d 337 (N.D. 1995); *Heisner v. Jones,* 184 Neb. 602, 169 N.W.2d 606 (1969). But the judicial view on this question is not unanimous. For more information, see Francis M. Dougherty, Annotation, *Right of Insurer Issuing "Uninsured Motorist" Coverage to Intervene in Action by Insured Against Uninsured Motorist,* 35 A.L.R.4th 757 (1985).

---

§ 6.04 First-Party Medical Coverage

One of the most important developments in automobile insurance in recent decades was the emergence in the 1970s of mandatory first-party medical payment coverage, which provides first-party protection against medical expenses incurred as a result of an automobile accident. During the 1970s,

15 states mandated the purchase of first-party medical payment protection (sometimes called "MedPay" or "medical payments insurance") and four states mandated that such coverage be offered to purchasers of auto insurance. By 1974, insurers in all states were offering first-party medical payments coverage as an option. Robert H. Joost, Automobile Insurance and No-Fault §§ 1.1, 1.9 (2d ed. 1992). When first-party benefits extend to lost wages, disability benefits, funeral benefits, the cost of replacing services normally performed by the injured person (*e.g.*, household services), and other economic losses, it is common to refer to the coverage as "PIP benefits." Subrogation issues that surround this type of coverage were examined in § 2.03[4], *supra*. Because health insurance provides similar coverage, does it make any sense to offer medical payments coverage as an add-on to an automobile liability insurance policy? When first-party medical payment coverage is combined with limitations on the right to sue in tort for reimbursement of these expenses, one has the makings of a true no-fault system; this is discussed in § 6.07, *infra*. In non-no-fault jurisdictions, the medical payments coverage should be understood as an add-on to the other protections provided by the automobile policy.

RELIANCE MUTUAL LIFE INSURANCE CO. v. BOOHER
166 So. 2d 222 (Fla. Dist. App. 1964), 10 A.L.R.3d 458 (1966)

SMITH, CHIEF JUDGE.

The plaintiff-appellee, Thelma W. Booher, brought an action for a declaratory judgment and other relief, requesting that the Court determine whether or not the defendant insurance company is liable for certain medical expenses incurred by her as a result of injuries she suffered in an automobile accident. The insurance policy in question insured the plaintiff against loss due to medical expense resulting from accidental bodily injury and it contained the following proviso: "provided that such expense shall be incurred within 52 weeks from the date of such injury." The trial court found that the quoted proviso was susceptible of more than one meaning or interpretation, and it construed the proviso to mean that if the expenses were brought on, occasioned, or caused within 52 weeks from the date of injury, then the liability for such expenses arose within the time limit. On this premise the court entered judgment for the plaintiff, from which the insurance company appeals. The plaintiff has filed cross assignments of error.

The facts essential to decision are not in dispute. The plaintiff received facial injuries in an automobile accident on October 4, 1959. The original emergency operation could only suture the "flaps" down. The plaintiff's face was disfigured as a result of the accident. She consulted a plastic surgeon, who advised that further operations could not be commenced until the flesh had begun settling and had partially healed. In May of 1960, plaintiff "engaged or employed the surgeon to perform the necessary reconstructive surgery." Operations were performed on May 17, 1960, for which the plaintiff was hospitalized through May 21; on November 22, 1960, for which the plaintiff was hospitalized through November 24; and finally on July 26, 1961. In the trial court the insurance company contended that it was not liable for any of the reconstructive surgery because it was not a necessary service and because the expenses of such surgery were not incurred within the 52-week time limit. On appeal, however, the insurance company contends only that the court erred in its interpretation of the time limit provision of the policy. It is urged that the court, in interpreting the policy, in effect re-wrote the parties' contract so that the insurance company would be liable for all expenses no matter when incurred, if the necessity for the expenses manifested itself within 52 weeks from the date of the injury. The insurance company contends that this interpretation is entirely outside the language of the policy and that the lower court's construction is neither reasonable nor equitable. The parties state that they have been unable to find any decision in Florida construing such a provision in an insurance policy, and our independent research has disclosed none. With respect to the general rules governing the construction of insurance contracts, the parties are in agreement. Terms in an insurance policy which are ambiguous, equivocal or uncertain, to the extent that the intention of the parties is not clear and cannot be ascertained by the application of ordinary rules of construction, are to be construed strictly and most strongly against the insurer; however, if the language is clear and unambiguous the court should give the language its natural meaning.

We find that the words "provided that such expense shall be incurred within 52 weeks from the date of such injury" are clear and unambiguous. "Incur" is defined by Webster as follows: "To meet or fall in with, as something inconvenient or harmful; become liable or subject to; to bring down upon oneself; as, to *incur* debt, danger, displeasure, penalty, etc." As used in the insurance policy here involved, the words contained in the proviso mean that the insured must have actually paid or must have become liable for the payment of such expense within 52 weeks from the date of the injury which necessitated the expense. The plaintiff's engagement of the services of the surgeon to perform the necessary reconstructive surgery, although admittedly made during the 52-week period, was not the incurring of an expense at that time, for at that time the fees of the surgeon were neither understood nor agreed upon. The first operation was performed within the 52-week period, and the expense of that operation with resultant hospitalization was incurred prior to the termination of the 52-week period. At the time of the expiration of the 52-week period the plaintiff had not incurred any expenses for medical services to be rendered in the future. An expense is the same as a debt, and it has been incurred when liability for payment attaches. A contingent expense has been incurred when the contingency upon which the payment depends has occurred. The plaintiff's engagement of the services of the surgeon for his future services constituted a contingent promise to pay for his services, and the expense was not incurred until the contingency occurred, which was the surgeon's performance of the services.

Provisions agreeing to pay for loss incurred by medical expenses within a fixed period of time from the date of the accident or injury necessitating the medical expense are contained in many types of insurance policies.[1] There are several decisions construing such provisions. *Drobne v. Aetna Casualty & Surety Co., Ohio App.* 1950, 115 N.E.2d 589; *Maryland Casualty Company v. Thomas, Tex. Civ. App.* 1956, 289 S.W.2d 652; *Herold v. Aetna Life Insurance Co., Tex. Civ. App.* 1935, 77 S.W.2d 1060; *Pilot Life Insurance Company v. Stephens,* 1958, 97 Ga. App. 529, 103 S.E.2d 651; *Czarnecki v. American Indemnity Company,* 1963, 259 N.C. 718, 131 S.E.2d 347; *Kirchoff v. Nationwide Mutual Insurance Company,* 1963, 19 A.D.2d 638, 241 N.Y.S.2d 185. These decisions must be examined in the light of the language of each policy and the facts in each case. When so examined, the conflicts become more apparent than real. For instance, in the *Drobne* and *Thomas* cases, the insured *employed or engaged* the doctor's services by a binding contract before the expiration of the policy's period of limitation and *paid in advance* or *became obligated to pay* for medical care. On this basis, the expenses in each case were found to have been incurred prior to the expiration of the fixed period. By contrast, in the Herold, Stephens and Czarnecki cases, there had been no contractual employment or prepayment during the period of time specified in the policy. In the Kirchoff case, the company's liability was further restricted because the policy contained an explicit definition of the term "incurred" as meaning the date upon which the service or purchase giving rise to the charge occurred.

The decisions in cases involving the time of injury, the time of performance of the medical services, and the time of termination of the policy, which decisions are surveyed in the Annotation, 75 A.L.R.2d 876, are not applicable here, because the question of the liability of an insurer for expenses incurred after termination of a policy containing no express provisions concerning liability after termination is separate and distinct from the question of limitations clearly and expressly provided in policies such as the one in the case at bar.

In an insurance policy the parties are at liberty to make such contract as they deem advantageous—unless restricted by statute. Our attention has not been called to any statute requiring insurance companies to obligate themselves to pay all medical expenses incurred on account of accidental injury which occurred during the effective time of the policy. We see no difference between a contractual agreement fixing a time limit and one fixing a total dollar limit of liability. The very language to which the plaintiff consented when she accepted the policy prohibits her recovery for any of the medical expenses incurred by the operations which were performed on November 22, 1960 and July 26, 1961.

Although the plaintiff's testimony was itemized as to the expenses of each operation, the court entered judgment in an amount substantially less than the total. This was a result of the court's finding that the surgeon's fees were excessive. The amount of the surgeon's fees was fixed by the court in one sum for all three operations; therefore, we are unable to direct the entry of a judgment for a specific amount and we will thus remand the cause for a new trial, at which time the court can also again consider the amount of the award

---

[1] For example, the medical payment provisions of an automobile liability insurance policy; accidental death or dismemberment provision in a life insurance policy; accident and health insurance policies; and specialized types of insurance policies, such as maternity.

for attorney's fees for the plaintiff. The amount of such attorney's fees need not be determined solely on the amount of the judgment recovered by the plaintiff. We find the other factors considered by the court to be proper in determining a reasonable attorney's fee to be allowed to the plaintiff.

. . . .

The judgment is reversed with directions to grant the defendant a new trial.

WARREN, LAMAR, ASSOCIATE JUDGE, concurs.

WHITE, J., dissents.

WHITE, JUDGE (dissenting).

The policy clause under consideration reads as follows:

> "Provided, however, that the company's maximum liability for medical, surgical and/or hospital bills shall not exceed a maximum of Three Thousand Five Hundred Dollars ($3,500.00) and provided that such expense shall be *incurred* within fifty-two (52) weeks from the date of such injury." (emphasis added)

The plaintiff's need for treatment arose when she was injured, causing her to seek such therapeutical and surgical services as would be reasonably necessary. She engaged professional services with the understanding that successive stages of reconstructive surgery would be required, and these services were engaged within the policy limitation of fifty-two weeks on the incurring of such expense. The plaintiff's obligation to pay for the impending services when and if performed was, as I see it, clearly incurred within the time limited, even though it was not then feasible to reduce the entire expenses to a sum certain until after completion of the needed surgery. This, rather than the "contingent" obligation thesis, strikes me as the only interpretation truly compatible with the rule governing the construction of policies written by paid insurers.

I would affirm the judgment in its entirety.

NOTES

1. *Clever lawyering.* The 52-week time period in which medical expenses had to be incurred to qualify for reimbursement under a policy like that in *Booher* creates a real problem for people sustaining certain types of injuries. For example, facial injuries to a child may require medical procedures that cannot be performed until the child's bone and other facial structures mature, particularly injuries to the jaw. It may take several years to perform skin grafts and other types of plastic surgery. Dental work can also present problems. If you were approached by a client with this type of problem, could you devise some arrangement to collect the policy benefits even though the medical procedures could not actually be performed within the time period required in the policy? For more discussion, see Charles W. Davis, Annotation, *When is Medical Expense "Incurred" Under Policy Providing for Payment of Medical Expenses Incurred Within Fixed Period of Time from Date of Injury*, 65 A.L.R.5th 649 (1999).

2. *What to do?* At the time *Booher* was decided, the standard medical payments provision in an auto policy required that covered medical expenses be incurred within one year of the accident which necessitated the treatment. Does the medical payments coverage in the Personal Automobile Policy in Appendix E take care of the problem in *Booher*? If not, do you have any ideas how the problem could be remedied without exposing the insurer to questionable claims many years after the policy has terminated? If one has other forms of health coverage that cover all types of accidents and sickness, why even buy medical payments coverage if the auto insurance industry persists in imposing a time period in which the medical expenses have to be incurred?

3. *Temporal limits compared.* In the section on accidental death and dismemberment insurance (*see* § 4.02[2], *supra*), we considered whether a provision in such a policy requiring the death or dismemberment to occur within a stated period (*e.g.*, 90 days) of the accident or occurrence to be within the coverage violated public policy. If one is inclined to the minority view that such provisions are unenforceable on the grounds that they violate public policy, is it possible for one to adhere to that position and yet agree with the holding in *Booher*? Or is trying to maintain both positions simultaneously inherently inconsistent?

---

§ 6.05　First-Party Property Coverage

ALLISON v. IOWA MUTUAL INSURANCE CO.
343 N.C. App. 200, 258 S.E.2d 489 (1979)

HEDRICK, JUDGE.

[Plaintiff sought to recover $8,500 under a "general automobile liability" policy for damage to his dump truck when the bridge on which the truck was traveling collapsed. The insurer's policy provided comprehensive insurance coverage on the truck, but did not provide collision coverage. The truck, a two-ton dump truck, was carrying a load of gravel; it was stipulated that as the truck proceeded across a bridge, "said bridge collapsed and the plaintiff's truck slid into the river or creek running under said bridge and turned on its right side, therein damaging said vehicle." The truck was repaired at a cost of $8,500, and the insured sought reimbursement for all of this sum from the insurer. Except for paying $111 to repair the windshield, the insurer refused to pay the claim "taking the position that said damage was caused by collision and was not covered under . . . the aforesaid policy. . . ." The trial judge entered judgment for the plaintiff in the amount of $8500, and the insurer appealed.]

Defendant's exceptions to each of the trial judge's conclusions of law present for review the single question of whether the court erred in entering judgment for plaintiff. The question is not whether plaintiff's truck was covered under the policy. It was. Rather, the question is whether the event which gave rise to the damage is excluded from the kind of loss for which the policy provides protection.

Defendant argues that the collapse of the bridge resulting in damage to plaintiff's truck was an accident by collision and that the occurrence was therefore excluded from coverage since the plaintiff had not insured this vehicle against loss by collision. Plaintiff, on the other hand, contends that the collapse of the bridge did not constitute a collision and asserts that the policy includes such an occurrence under its provisions for comprehensive coverage. The relevant inquiry for this Court is thus refined into determining whether the trial judge erred in concluding that the accident occasioned by the collapse of the bridge was not a "collision" within the meaning of the policy which provides in pertinent part as follows:

> 1. The company will pay for loss to covered automobiles: COVERAGE O— COMPREHENSIVE *From any cause except collision*; but, for the purpose of this coverage, breakage of glass and loss caused by missiles, falling objects, fire, theft or larceny, windstorm, hail, earthquake, explosion, riot or civil commotion, malicious mischief or vandalism, water, flood, or (as to a covered automobile of the private passenger type) colliding with a bird or animal, shall not be deemed loss caused by collision. . . . (Emphasis added.)

Elsewhere the policy defines "collision" to mean "(i) collision of a covered automobile with another object or with a vehicle to which it is attached, or (ii) upset of such covered automobile. . . ."

The principles of law with respect to the interpretation and construction of insurance policies are firmly established. As with any contract, the ultimate goal is to divine the parties' intentions at the time the policy was issued. Where the policy defines a term, that definition must be used. Conversely, nontechnical words which are not defined "are to be given the same meaning they usually receive in ordinary speech, unless the context requires otherwise." *Grant v. Emmco Insurance Co.,* 295 N.C. 39, 42, 243 S.E.2d 894, 897 (1978). Moreover, if the meaning of language "*or the effect of provisions* is uncertain or capable of several reasonable interpretations," *Woods v. Nationwide Mutual Insurance Co.,* 295 N.C. at 506, 246 S.E.2d at 777 (emphasis added), such ambiguity will be resolved in favor of the insured and against the insurance company since, as it is said, the company chose the language.

In the instant case, although the policy sets out three types of occurrences that are deemed to constitute a collision, the term itself is not defined. The word is popularly understood, however, to mean a striking together of two objects. "The term denotes the act of colliding; striking together; violent contact. . . . (It) implies an impact or sudden contact of a moving body with an obstruction in its line of motion, whether both bodies are in motion or one stationary. . . ." Black's Law Dictionary 330 (4th ed. 1968).

In 7 Am. Jur. 2d, Automobile Insurance § 65 (1963), it is said:

> While the ground of a highway is considered an "object" within the meaning of a collision insurance policy, it is generally held that contact

of an automobile with the roadbed itself does not constitute a "collision" with an object within the meaning of the term as used in a collision insurance policy.

Furthermore, in a case which presents strikingly similar facts to the case at bar, the Florida Supreme Court held that the giving way of the roadbed over which the plaintiff's car was traveling, resulting in the car's sliding down into the soft sand under the road and getting stuck, was not a collision within the popular and usual meaning of the term. *Aetna Casualty & Surety Co. v. Cartmel,* 87 Fla. 495, 100 So. 802 (1924).

With reference to defendant's contention that the event giving rise to the damage in this case was a "collision", we have carefully considered each case upon which defendant purports to rely and find only one of them to be worthy of comment. Our Supreme Court held, in *Morton v. Blue Ridge Insurance Co.,* [255 N.C. 360, 121 S.E.2d 716 (1961)], that a collision, within the meaning of that term as used in the policy being construed there, resulted when the plaintiff's automobile suddenly rolled backwards into a canal. The car had been backed down a launching ramp to launch a boat from a trailer hooked to the rear of the car. While the driver and passengers were lowering the boat into the water, the unattended and previously stationary car suddenly rolled into the water. When the insurance company refused to honor his claim, plaintiff brought suit, and the Court held that the car's striking of the water in the canal and of the bottom of the canal was a collision, entitling plaintiff to recover under the collision provisions of the policy.

We find this case to be readily distinguishable on its facts. The impetus for the accident in *Morton* was obviously occasioned by the manner in which the vehicle was being used. Although there was no evidence regarding what caused the car to suddenly roll backwards, the driver had driven it onto and parked it on the ramp, thereby initiating the chain of events that culminated in the collision of his car with the bottom of the canal. Conversely, in the present case, there is plainly no element of driver control. Nothing the operator of the truck did can be said to have set in force the succeeding events. The collapse of the bridge, and that occurrence only, engendered the consequent accident and damage. We think the cases are clearly distinguishable and find the *Morton* case to be inapposite.

In the case at bar, we hold that the collapse of the bridge upon which plaintiff's truck was being operated, resulting in the truck's sliding down into the river or creek underneath the bridge and thereby being damaged, was not a "collision" either within the usual meaning of the term or as contemplated by the policy and the parties. Since it is not disputed that the policy provides coverage for losses arising from all causes except collision, it follows that the losses suffered under the circumstances here are covered, and the company is liable on plaintiff's claim. Thus, in the conclusions and judgment of the trial judge, we find no error.

Affirmed.

Clark and Harry C. Martin, JJ., Concur.

NOTES

1. *The nature of the coverage.* If the insured's vehicle is destroyed in an accident caused by the negligence of a third party, that third party (or the third party's liability insurer) will pay for the insured's property damage. There are many situations, however, where the insured's car or truck may be damaged and no third party is responsible. The auto accident where the insured is at fault is one obvious example. Hailstorms, falling trees, vandals, and thieves are other common perils, to name a few. The insured has an obvious interest in insuring her own property against these kinds of losses. Because it is so common to purchase vehicles with borrowed funds, the lender is likely to have a security interest in the vehicle, and the lender is likely to insist that the owner acquire and maintain insurance against such perils as well.

As *Allison* makes clear, collision coverage and comprehensive coverage address distinct perils. The coverages are meant to dovetail, and if the insured purchases both of them, the insured is unlikely to confront any problem in having his or her loss indemnified by the insurer. If, however, the insured purchases one coverage but not the other, cases like *Allison* can arise.

2. *Sorting out the borderline situations.* Is *Allison* decided correctly? Should comprehensive coverage apply whenever a vehicle is not being operated, and collision coverage apply whenever a vehicle is being operated? If a tree falls on a car while the car is being operated, should the fact of the vehicle's operation make a difference in whether the loss is under the collision or comprehensive coverage? Or should the focus be on whether the "risk" is operational, i.e., a tree falling on a car is "non-operational" and therefore the resulting loss is covered under the comprehensive coverage, whether or not the car is moving?

3. *The limits of comprehensive coverage.* The insured is driving his eight-year-old Audi when smoke begins to pour out of the dashboard. When he pulls over and opens the hood, he sees that wires in the engine compartment have begun to melt. The immediate crisis is ended when he disconnects the battery cables, and pulls some fuses and relays. After being towed to a garage, he learns that his car has suffered extensive damage. He contacts his insurer, but is told that electrical breakdowns are not covered by his policy. The insured's coverage is that contained in Appendix E, and he argues that the list of causes of damage that are considered "other than collision" is not an exclusive list. Is the insured correct, and, if so, is the insured covered? *See Mack v. Acadia Insurance Co.,* 709 A.2d 1187 (Me. 1998). What if the "hot wires" had caused a fire in the engine compartment?

4. *Other kinds of "theft."* Under the policy in Appendix E, would an insured be covered if she was the innocent purchaser of a stolen vehicle and the vehicle were repossessed by its true owner? *See Western Farm Bureau Insurance Co. v. Carter,* 127 N.M. 186, 979 P.2d 231 (1999). Some policies have had exclusions for losses that occur due to an insured's voluntary surrender of custody, possession, or title of a vehicle, as would be the case where the

insured allows a third party to test-drive the vehicle when contemplating its sale and the person absconds with it. Are such exclusions justified? Needless to say, the decisions in this area are difficult to reconcile; much depends on the law of theft in the particular jurisdiction, the specific policy's language, and the circumstances of the loss. See generally Christopher H. Hall, Annotation, *What Constitutes Theft Within Automobile Theft Insurance Policy— Modern Cases*, 67 A.L.R.4th 82 (1989).

5. *The "after market parts" litigation.* When the insurer repairs your car pursuant to the first-party coverages, exactly what are the insurer's obligations? When a part on your car wears out or is damaged in an accident, auto repair shops have two choices for the kind of replacement part that will be installed—either original equipment manufacturer ("OEM") parts (meaning parts made by the manufacturer of the automobile or its approved licensee), or generic, after-market parts not associated with the manufacturer ("non-OEM" parts). Non-OEM parts are not to be confused with used parts; if you have replaced a dead car battery with a battery you purchased from a department store or a car parts store, you used a non-OEM part, even though it was brand new. (If you purchased the battery at the service department of the car dealer that sold you the car, you used an OEM part.) Non-OEM parts are cheaper than OEM parts, but some consumer groups and persons in the auto repair trade (and, predictably, manufacturers of OEM parts) have claimed that non-OEM parts are of inferior quality and, depending on the part, are sometimes less safe. In February 1999, Consumers Union published its own study in *Consumer Reports*, which concluded that the quality of non-OEM parts varies widely, and that the quality of some were poor. In the wake of this study, at least 14 lawsuits were filed against different insurers. See *Suits blast insurers for mandating generic auto parts*, Denv. Post, Aug. 25, 1999, at CO3. On the other hand, insurers claim that OEM parts are over-priced; one insurance industry study found that the cost of rebuilding a 1999 Toyota Camry LE with OEM parts would be $101,335, four times the retail price of the vehicle. See Amanda Levin, *OEM Auto Parts Overpriced, Ins. Study Says*, Nat'l Underwriter (Prop. & Cas.), Sept. 6, 1999, at 4.

When a car is damaged in a collision, some insureds want OEM parts, under the reasoning that using non-OEM parts reduces the value of the car. About 34 states now require insurers to notify their policyholders that non-OEM parts will be used in repairs; in most of these states, the statute or regulation is based on an NAIC model regulation. *After Market Parts Model Regulation*, in V NAIC, Model Laws, Regulations and Guidelines 891-1 (1997). Minnesota prohibits insurers from requiring non-OEM parts. *See* Minn. Stat. Ann. § 72A.201.6(7) (West 1999 & Supp. 2000). Until recently, insurer practices varied. State Farm consistently required (until 1999, for reasons discussed below) the use of non-OEM parts. Some insurers will install OEM parts if the insured pays the difference between the cost of the non-OEM and the OEM part. Others pay for OEM replacement parts.

It is fair to say that insurers are now more cautious about encouraging the use of non-OEM parts. In October 1999, an jury in Illinois found State Farm liable for $1.2 billion in damages (including $730 million in punitive damages) in a class action lawsuit which alleged that State Farm's practices in using non-OEM parts constituted a breach of contract and consumer fraud. The plaintiffs claimed successfully that the use of non-OEM parts did not restore their vehicles to their pre-accident quality. The insurer contested this point on the merits, and argued that the use of non-OEM parts kept premiums lower for insureds. The verdict, which is now on appeal, is controversial; class action certification issues are the predominate questions in this stage of the appeal. See *State Farm Still Waiting to Hear from Plaintiffs in Aftermarket-Parts Verdict Appeal*, Best's Ins. News, June 20, 2000 (2000 WL 4086659). But the issue remains a live one, and not just with respect to State Farm. In May 2000, the state of Florida sued an insurer for allegedly requiring insureds to use non-OEM parts (see *Florida Sues Auto Insurer over "Inferior" Crash Parts*, Fed. & St. Ins. Week, May 30, 2000 (2000 WL 20101435)). In November 1999, a lawsuit seeking a class action was filed in Illinois against several insurers, alleging a conspiracy in creating and funding the "Certified Automotive Parts Association" (CAPA), which is the organization that certifies the quality of non-OEM parts. See generally Ruth Gastel, ed., *Auto Safety and Crashworthiness*, Insurance Issues Update (Insurance Information Institute), June 2000; Margaret Mannix, *Bumper stumper: real or generic?*, U.S. News & World Rpt., Oct. 18, 1999, at 99. If insurers are correct that non-OEM parts save insureds money and that auto manufacturers have unnecessarily inflated the prices of OEM parts, should insurers be prevented from contracting with insureds to repair vehicles with non-OEM parts?

---

§ 6.06 No-Fault Insurance

ROBERT H. JERRY, II, UNDERSTANDING INSURANCE LAW
§ 132, at 851–55 (2d ed. 1996). [*]

[4] [Observations on the Traditional Liability System]

Few would seriously suggest that the traditional liability system is perfect. No enforcement mechanism can assure that 100 percent of the motorists in any given state have liability insurance, even if it is compulsory. Uninsured and underinsured motorist benefits can help fill these gaps, but because UM and UIM coverage allows an insured to recover from his or her own insurer to the extent the insured could recover in tort against the uninsured (or underinsured) motorist, valid defenses to the insured's claim will prevent the insured from receiving compensation for his or her loss.

To some extent, MedPay benefits can help when liability insurance falls short (and MedPay benefits are important for the circumstance where the

---

insured causes his or her own injury and there is no other responsible party). This, however, only serves to raise another issue: the traditional liability system requires risk-averse people to "double insure." One must purchase liability insurance to protect oneself from the consequences of one's own negligence, and the cost of this coverage will be, in theory, a function of the likelihood that the insured will cause someone else a loss. But it is not possible to rely on other people to do the same; thus, it is also necessary to purchase sufficient first-party coverage to guard against being injured by someone else, and the cost of this coverage will be a function of how many people in one's vicinity are probably driving without coverage.

One of the important reasons this system survives in so many jurisdictions is that it is understood by most people. Auto accidents are almost always the result of someone's negligence, and the notion that the negligent party should be responsible for the loss is a powerful one, as is the related idea that "my premiums" should not be determined by the poor driving habits of other people. Yet it is no small irony that in the American legal system the idea that an injured party should be reimbursed for loss without regard to his or her fault is actually more important than the fault-based mechanism for recovering damages found in tort law. All first-party insurance is essentially "no-fault" coverage: an individual who negligently starts a fire that burns down his or her house recovers under the individual's own fire insurance policy; a person whose negligent operation of his or her auto results in a one-car accident will be covered for both the personal injury and property damage, assuming the person purchased the correct coverages; a person who incurs medical expenses because of deliberate (*e.g.*, excessive smoking or drinking) or negligent (*e.g.*, standing on the top step of a ladder and falling off) acts is protected by his or her health insurance. Overall, the number of situations in which an individual looks to a third party as his or her primary source of relief is actually quite small relatively to all compensable losses that occur in our society.

[b] Add-on No-Fault

In eleven jurisdictions (in addition to the true no-fault states discussed below), statutes require that insureds be given an opportunity to purchase first-party no-fault benefits that provide compensation for economic loss suffered as a result of an auto accident. These statutes do not limit the right to sue in tort. However, individuals who recover no-fault benefits cannot recover those benefits a second time in a lawsuit against the tortfeasor.[6] In some of these jurisdictions, the insurer has a subrogation right against the tortfeasor to the extent of the payment of first-party benefits.[7] Where a subrogation right does not exist, the assumption is that the system will produce some cost savings in circumstances where a person's losses are less than the amount of no-fault coverage; obviously, such a person has no incentive to bring a suit against the tortfeasor. In two of the eleven jurisdictions, the motorist is required to purchase the no-fault benefits; in the other nine states, the purchase of the benefits is optional.

---

[6] [Robert H.] Joost, [Automobile Insurance and No-Fault (2d ed. 1992)], at §§ 2:19, 5.01; [Ruth] Gastel, *No-Fault Auto Insurance*, Insurance Information Institute III Abstracts (April 1995).

[7] [Joost], *supra*, § 5.01.

[c] True No-Fault

During the 1970s, sixteen states mandated no-fault benefits and established thresholds for the right to bring a tort action against the person causing the injury. The amount of the benefits varied, as did the thresholds. All of the plans but one had monetary thresholds; under these plans, if the injured party had medical expenses above a certain amount, the person could sue a third party in tort, but if the expenses were below the threshold, the person could not pursue a tort remedy. Some of the plans combined a monetary threshold with a verbal threshold, under which a person could also sue if he or she suffered an injury of a particular type (such as a broken weight-bearing bone, permanent disfigurements, etc.).

Through the years, some states modified their no-fault laws, and some statutes were repealed. As of 1995, thirteen states and Puerto Rico have true no-fault laws, meaning statutes that mandate the purchase of first-party benefits and place some restrictions on tort suits. Five of the thirteen states use verbal thresholds for the right to sue in tort, and the remainder use a monetary threshold. Also, three of the states, as discussed below, allow motorists to reject the limitation on tort actions and thereby retain the right to sue for injuries suffered in automobile accidents.

While it can be said that twenty-three states, the District of Columbia, and Puerto Rico are no-fault jurisdictions, only ten of these jurisdictions unconditionally require that all the motorists in the state surrender the right to sue in tort. Three states make the limitation on the right to sue in tort possible, but do not require it. In the remaining jurisdictions, the first-party no-fault benefits are optional, and the right to sue in tort is not affected, except to the extent that a person who collects first-party benefits cannot recover the same benefits twice.

As for the thirteen true no-fault jurisdictions, the extent to which the tort system is replaced with no-fault principles depends on the level of the thresholds. Some states adopted relatively low thresholds in their statutes; for example, in the 1973 Kansas statute, the victim must have suffered an injury that caused medical expenses of at least $500 to be incurred or that consisted "in whole or in part of permanent disfigurement, a fracture of a weightbearing bone, a compound, comminuted, displaced or compressed fracture, loss of a body member, permanent injury within reasonable medical probability, permanent loss of a bodily function or death."[15] The thresholds were in the alternative, and the monetary threshold was relatively easy to meet. Moreover, many states did not increase their thresholds for many years, and a decade or more of inflation substantially eroded their impact. For example, it was not until 1987 that Kansas raised its threshold to $2000. At the opposite extreme is a state like Hawaii, where the threshold, called the "medical rehabilitation limit," is adjusted annually and which was set at $10,000 in 1992.[16] Obviously, a high threshold prevents a relatively larger number of tort claims from being litigated.

The kinds of benefits that no-fault policies provide on a first-party basis vary from state to state, but most benefits fall into one of five categories: (1) the

---

[15] Kan. Stat. Ann. § 40-3117 (1974).

[16] *See* Haw. Rev. Stat. § 431:10C-308.

insured's loss of income, wages, or earnings; (2) the value of personal services that the insured would ordinarily have performed for his or her family; (3) the survivors' loss, based on the income, wages, or earnings that a deceased insured would have provided; (4) medical, health-related, and rehabilitation expenses; and (5) funeral expenses. These benefits are commonly called "personal injury protection" benefits, or "PIP benefits."

All no-fault statutes permit insurers to insert some exclusions in the policies. For example, only injuries "arising out of the use" of a vehicle need be covered, and benefits are payable only to "covered persons." A common exclusion eliminates coverage for persons who failed to purchase a required policy in circumstances where the policy would have provided coverage for the injury in question. The obvious purpose of such an exclusion is to encourage people to purchase no-fault coverage and to prevent the insurance industry generally from having to reimburse losses for which additional premiums should have been collected. Statutes also routinely permit exclusions for injuries suffered while intentionally attempting to inflict injury on another, while fleeing the police, while under the influence of alcohol, etc.

Most no-fault statutes also give the insurer that pays no-fault benefits a subrogation right against the tortfeasor. Thus, if the insured's injuries are sufficiently serious that the insured has an action in tort against the third-party who caused the injury, the insurer is entitled to be reimbursed out of the insured's recovery to the extent the judgment duplicates PIP benefits paid. In situations where subrogation is available and is asserted, the burden of paying the no-fault benefits actually falls on the tortfeasor's liability insurer. If the insured's injuries are such that no action in tort can be brought against the third-party, the insurer has no subrogation right—since the insured has no right against the tortfeasor to which the insurer can be subrogated.

Most no-fault statutes do not mandate first-party coverage for property damage. Currently, only Michigan and Delaware require the insurer to issue no-fault coverage for property damage caused by their insured motorists arising out of the use, operation, or maintenance of the vehicle. Thus, for the most part, American no-fault is limited to personal injury losses.

The constitutionality of no-fault statutes has been challenged in several states on a variety of grounds, usually due process and equal protection. With only a very few exceptions, courts have upheld no-fault statutes against these constitutional challenges.

[d] Choice systems

Nothing precludes putting a no-fault and traditional tort system side-by-side in the same state, as discussed in more detail below. No state currently has an ambitious choice system in place, but three states (Kentucky, New Jersey, and Pennsylvania) give motorists the opportunity to surrender their right to sue in tort in exchange for lower premiums or higher benefits. In Kentucky, the statute requires each motorist to purchase no-fault insurance unless the motorist affirmatively rejects no-fault and the limitation on tort suits; however, any motorist rejecting no-fault must maintain minimum amounts of liability insurance.[22] Under the New Jersey statute, each

---

[22] Joost, [supra] § 8.22.

automobile owner must maintain specified no-fault coverage. However, each owner then is asked to choose between (a) retaining the right to sue in tort for all accidental injuries, and (b) giving up the right to sue in tort unless the injury is "serious," as defined in the statute (i.e., the verbal threshold). If no choice is made, the insured is treated as having elected the verbal threshold.[23] The Pennsylvania statute is like the New Jersey statute, except that the option which surrenders a portion of the right to sue in tort (called the "limited tort option" as opposed to the "full tort option") can sue for all medical and other economic losses, but cannot claim pain and suffering unless the injuries fall within the statute's definition of "serious injury" or other described condition.[24]

NOTES

1. *No-fault update.* At 2000, the "count of the states" as set forth in the foregoing excerpt remains unchanged. See Ruth Gastel, ed., *No-Fault Auto Insurance*, Ins. Issues Update (Insurance Information Institute), July 2000. In the late 1990s, bills were considered in Congress that would create a choice system nationwide, except that states could amend or opt out of the system. Supporters estimated that "The Auto Choice Reform Act" would save $30 to $45 billion nationwide. According to 1999 data compiled by RAND's Institute for Civil Justice, motorists in the average state could expect to save about 45 percent of medical payments premiums and about 21 percent of the total auto insurance premium if half of the state's motorists opted for the no-fault alternative. See Robert H. Joost, Automobile Insurance and No-Fault § 1.2H, at 56 (2d ed. 1992 & supp. 1999); Gary T. Schwartz, *Auto No-Fault and First-Party Insurance: Advantages and Problems*, 73 S. Cal. L. Rev. 611 (2000); Jeffrey O'Connell et al., *The Comparative Costs of Allowing Consumer Choice for Auto Insurance in All Fifty States*, 55 Md. L. Rev. 160 (1996); Robert R. Detlefsen, *Escaping the Tort-Based Auto Accident Compensation System: The Federal Auto Choice Reform Act of 1997*, 17 J. Ins. Reg. 186 (1998). Insurers, however, were divided in their support for the plan, and a November 1998 public opinion survey by the Insurance Research Council showed that only one in four would opt for the no-fault alternative, even with a significant premium savings. See Gastel, *supra*. Despite the attention that the federal initiative received, why do you suppose public interest in no-fault alternatives seemingly waned in recent years?

2. *First-party medical payments.* Add-on no-fault is not "true no-fault" because the tort liability system is not affected. But it may be fair to assert that the emergence of mandatory first-party medical payment coverages during the 1970s is more important than the more widely discussed and debated true no-fault proposals. In the 1970s, 15 states mandated the purchase of first-party medical payment protection (sometimes called "Med-Pay" or "medical payments insurance") and four states mandated that such coverage be offered to purchasers of auto insurance. By 1974, insurers in all

---

[23] *Id.*, § 8.23.

[24] *Id.*, § 8.24.

states were offering first-party medical payments coverage as an option. Robert H. Joost, Automobile Insurance and No-Fault §§ 1.1, 1.9 (2d ed. 1992). Because health insurance provides similar coverage, does it make any sense to offer medical payments coverage as an add-on to an automobile liability insurance policy?

When first-party medical payment coverage is combined with limitations on the right to sue in tort for reimbursement of these expenses, one has the makings of a true no-fault system. In most true no-fault plans, however, the first-party benefits are broader: MedPay usually covers only medical and hospital expenses, but the "Personal Injury Protection" or "PIP" benefits of no-fault ordinarily also include disability benefits, funeral benefits, and other economic losses in addition to medical and hospital expenses.

3. *"Arising out of the ownership, maintenance, and use" revisited.* No-fault benefits purport to cover the insured wherever he or she may be, whether a driver, an occupant, or a pedestrian, but the loss must have some connection to the use of an automobile. In *Bredemeier v. Farmers Insurance Exchange,* 950 P.2d 616 (Colo.Ct.App. 1998), the plaintiff, while walking through a parking lot at night, tripped and fell over a speed bump, suffering injury. Several disinterested witnesses testified that a vehicle owned and insured by Larson was parked in the lot in such a manner as to block the light from a fixture on a nearby building that otherwise would have illuminated the speed bump. It was not the purpose of the light to illuminate the speed bump, but it was undisputed that but for the manner in which the Larson vehicle was parked, the light would have incidentally illuminated the speed bump. Is the plaintiff entitled to PIP benefits under the Larson policy? The court said that "PIP benefits are not triggered simply because an injury takes place in or around a vehicle." 950 P.2d at 618. "[I]t is generally held that there must be a causal relation or connection between the injury and the use of the vehicle in order for the injury to come within the meaning of the phrase 'arising out of the use' of a vehicle." *Id.,* quoting *Azar v. Employers Casualty Co.,* 178 Colo. 58, 495 P.2d 554, 555 (1972). Was the plaintiff's injury "close enough" to the Larson's car and policy? *See also Tyrrell v. Farmers Insurance Co. of Wash.,* 140 Wash.2d 129, 994 P.2d 833 (2000)(insured who slipped during middle of night when getting out of camper affixed to pickup truck was not injured in a "motor vehicle accident").

In no-fault, as opposed to liability insurance, are there more reasons to construe "use" and its companion terms more narrowly? *See Thornton v. Allstate Insurance Co.,* 391 N.W.2d 320 (Mich. 1986) (taxi driver shot by passenger while car in motion; held, injuries not covered by no-fault policy); *Morosini v. Citizens Insurance Co. of Am.,* 461 Mich. 303, 602 N.W.2d 828 (1999)(held, insured not entitled to PIP benefits for injuries suffered when he was assaulted by driver of another auto after minor traffic accident); compare *Ganiron v. Hawaii Insurance Guaranty Ass'n,* 744 P.2d 1210 (Haw. 1987)(insured, while driving car, shot by occupant of another moving vehicle; held, injuries covered by no-fault policy). Much depends on the language of the no-fault statute. *See, e.g.,* Uniform Motor Vehicle Accident Reparations Act, 14 U.L.A. 35 (1990), § 1, at 42–43 (injuries covered by act are limited to those arising out of the maintenance or use of a motor vehicle "as a motor vehicle").

How would the quoted language from the Uniform Act apply to some of the uses of automobiles you have encountered in these materials? If a couple are parked with the motor running on "lovers' lane" and die from carbon monoxide poisoning due to a leak in the exhaust system, would no-fault benefits be provided in a jurisdiction that has adopted the Uniform Act? *See Spisak v. Nationwide Mutual Insurance Co.*, 478 A.2d 891 (Pa. Super. 1984). How would the Uniform Act apply to the situation in *Bredemeier*?

4. *Pay at the pump?* In California and several other states in the 1990s, some reformers pushed for and some legislatures considered a novel kind of no-fault proposal. The idea was to add a surcharge to the price of gasoline (in the vicinity of 25 cents a gallon) which would be used to pay for economic losses suffered in auto accidents without regard to fault. Tort liability for auto accidents would be eliminated. Supporters argued that the plan would eliminate the problem of the insureds subsidizing the uninsureds, since everyone would pay for the insurance with each gallon of gas purchased. Negligence was not completely removed from the system; bad drivers would pay a surcharge beyond the gasoline charge. No jurisdiction has opted for pay-at-the-pump. If you were a legislator, would you support such a plan? Why or why not? For further discussion, see J. Daniel Khazzoom, *Pay-at-thePump Auto Insurance: Review of Criticisms and Proposed Modification*, 18 J. Ins. Reg. 448 (2000); Douglas Berg, et al., *Pay-at-the-pump Auto Insurance: Could It Work?*, 47 CPCU J. 140 (1994) (favoring proposal); Richard A. Stohlman, *Pay-at-the-pump is No Panacea*, 48 CPCU J. 72 (1995) (opposing proposal); Stephen D. Sugarman, *Auto Insurance Reform: Should We "Pay at the Pump"?*, 5 Am. Enterprise 20 (1994) (favoring proposal).

5. *Political realities.* Is there any chance that a political majority can be mustered in any state to implement an aggressive, comprehensive no-fault system? Does that fact impel more serious consideration of the choice alternatives? Should everyone at least have the option to trade his or her right to a trial by jury for an insurer's promise of immediate, full compensation of all economic loss suffered in an auto accident, regardless of who is at fault?

If no-fault makes sense in the automobile situation, should it be applied in other settings, such as medical accidents and medical malpractice? What about products liability? If many of the perceived problems of the tort liability system devolve from the failure of a substantial number of accident victims to get full compensation for their economic losses, is expanded use of no-fault a path out of the forest? See Richard C. Ausness, *An Insurance-Based Compensation System for Product-Related Injuries*, 58 U. Pitt. L. Rev. 669 (1997); Derry Ridgway, *No-Fault Vaccine Insurance: Lessons from the National Vaccine Injury Compensation Program*, 24 J. Health Pol. Pol'y & L. 59 (1999).

---

§ 6.07 Other Recurring Issues

[1] Named Insureds and Residents of the Same Household

USAA CASUALTY INSURANCE CO. v. HENSLEY
465 S.E.2d 791 (Va. 1996)

HENRY H. WHITING, SENIOR JUSTICE

. . . .

I.

[Mr. and Mrs. Hoang lived in Saudi Arabia with their four children. There being no further education available to the children after the ninth grade, the Hoangs sent their two oldest children, Paul and George, to live with Mrs. Hoang's mother in Virginia.]

George ate, slept, and kept his belongings at his grandmother's house, and he spent all but one of his vacations there. While living in his grandmother's house, George assisted around the house by running errands, cleaning parts of the house, mowing the lawn, and cooking. He worked in the Centreville area during the summer of 1992, using his grandmother's address for employment and tax purposes.

Excluding the 1991-92 school year, when his parents sent him to a military academy in Front Royal, and a vacation to various cities in the United States with his parents in 1992, George lived continuously in his grandmother's house. He never visited his parents in Saudi Arabia after he came to Virginia.

George talked on the telephone frequently and corresponded infrequently with his parents in Saudi Arabia while he was living in Virginia. Mrs. Hoang returned from Saudi Arabia to her mother's house several times a year for visits of several days each to oversee her two sons' activities. She and her husband continued to support George and pay his educational expenses while he was in Virginia.

[In July 1992, Mrs. Hoang purchased a Volvo automobile, primarily for Paul and George to use in Virginia, and insured it with USAA Casualty Insurance Company (USAA). She listed herself as the named insured and listed herself, her husband, Paul, and George as the operators. She also advised USAA that the insured vehicle was to be principally garaged at the grandmother's house and that each operator had a Virginia driver's license. Shortly after buying the Volvo and the USAA insurance, Mrs. Hoang traded the Volvo for an Oldsmobile automobile, and USAA transferred coverage to the Oldsmobile.]

In November 1992, Michelle [George's aunt] asked George to take her Porsche automobile (covered by a separate USAA liability policy issued to

Michelle) to a filling station to be refueled. While driving the Porsche to the filling station, George collided with a car driven by Michael Steven Hensley.

Hensley was injured in the collision and brought a personal injury action against George. Hensley also brought this declaratory judgment action against USAA, Mrs. Hoang, Michelle, and George to obtain a declaration that the USAA policy on Mrs. Hoang's Oldsmobile provided additional liability coverage to George in the personal injury action beyond the coverage provided by the USAA policy on the Porsche.

Upon attaining the age of 18 and after the accident, George registered to vote in Virginia and applied for admission to a state university, where he was accepted as an in-state student and charged the reduced tuition rate for Virginia residents.

. . . . [T]he trial court entered a declaratory judgment in conformity with Hensley's request. USAA appeals.

II.

We resolve the issue in this appeal by considering the pertinent language in the USAA policy on the Oldsmobile. Liability coverage for the operation of a non-owned automobile is provided to the named insured or "any relative" of the named insured. And a "relative" is defined in the policy as "a relative of the named insured who is a resident of the same household." (Emphasis added.)

USAA argues that, because George was a resident of his grandmother's household in Centreville, he was not a resident of the same household as his mother. Thus, USAA argues that George was not a relative as defined in the policy. On the other hand, the other parties successfully contended in the trial court, and contend on this appeal, that George qualified as a relative under the policy definition because he was a resident of his mother's household in Saudi Arabia. We agree with USAA.

III.

We have considered similar policy language in a number of other cases. In doing so, we said:

> The meaning of "resident" or "residence", a prolific source of litigation, depends upon the context in which it is used. . . . Here, we must interpret the meaning of "resident", when followed by "of the same household". The word "household", . . . connotes a settled status; a more settled or permanent status is indicated by "resident of the same household" than would be indicated by "resident of the same house or apartment".

Allstate Ins. Co. v. Patterson, 231 Va. 358, 361, 344 S.E.2d 890, 892 (1986)(quoting *State Farm Mut. Auto. Ins. Co. v. Smith*, 206 Va. 280, 285, 142 S.E.2d 562, 565–66 (1965)). Continuing, we also said:

> Whether the term "household" or "family" is used, the term embraces a collection of persons as a single group, with one head, living together, a unit of permanent and domestic character, under one roof; a "collective body of persons living together within one curtilage, subsisting

in common and directing their attention to a common object, the promotion of their mutual interests and social happiness".

And, as we noted in Patterson, a person's intent is important in determining whether he qualifies as a resident of a household. However, since George was an unemancipated minor at the time of the accident, we must also consider his parents' intent in this determination. *See* Code § 16.1-334 (unemancipated minor cannot establish his own residence); *see also* Code § 16.1-333 (parent must consent to minor's emancipation); *Brumfield v. Brumfield,* 194 Va. 577, 581–82, 74 S.E.2d 170, 173–74 (1953)(intent of parent determines whether minor is emancipated), overruled on other grounds by *Smith v. Kauffman,* 212 Va. 181, 183 S.E.2d 190 (1971). Here, there is no evidence of an intent on the part of George or his parents that he would return to Saudi Arabia to rejoin their household there. On the contrary, the evidence indicates that his parents intended that George become a part of his grandmother's household until they returned from Saudi Arabia. There is no evidence that George left any of his belongings in Saudi Arabia, that he maintained a room in his former residence there, that he ever returned to visit, or that he had anything more than telephone and mail contact with his parents while they were in Saudi Arabia.

After George came to live with his grandmother, his parents saw him only in Virginia and on their vacation in the summer of 1992. His parents supplied George with a car titled in Virginia and registered at his grandmother's address, and they permitted him to get a Virginia driver's license. Furthermore, George was allowed to spend his vacations in Virginia, work there during the summer, and apply for admission to a Virginia university as a Virginia resident. Additionally, George's parents must have known that George was more than a mere boarder at his grandmother's house, as evidenced by his activities in contributing to the common burdens associated with the operation of a household.

Even though George testified that his grandmother's house was not his "home," the extended period of his residence there with no apparent intention on his or his parents' part for him to return to his parents' home in Saudi Arabia, as well as his activities at his grandmother's house, gainsay this conclusion. Instead, we think this evidence indicates that George was living with his relatives in a unit of permanent and domestic character, subsisting in common, in which each household member, including George, participated in the promotion of their mutual interests and social happiness. Under these facts and circumstances, we conclude that reasonable persons could not differ in concluding that, at the time of the collision, George was a member of his grandmother's household in Virginia, and was no longer a member of his mother's household in Saudi Arabia. Accordingly, we think that the trial court erred in concluding that Mrs. Hoang's USAA policy on the Oldsmobile provided additional coverage against George's possible liability to Hensley.

Therefore, we will reverse the trial court's judgment and enter final judgment in this Court declaring that George was not covered by Mrs. Hoang's USAA policy when he operated his aunt's Porsche and collided with Hensley.

Reversed and final judgment.

NOTES

1. *Persons insured.* The issue of who is insured under the liability coverages of a personal automobile policy may be divided into several parts. If the person seeking coverage is actually named in the appropriate space on the declaration page of the policy, this person is a "named insured" and few problems arise outside of mistakes involving the intentions of the parties to the contract. There are two other important groups of people that may be covered. The first is resident relatives of the household of the named insured. Whatever definition the policy uses for including resident relatives in the coverage will be relevant in some way to three coverages in the automobile policy: the liability coverage; the medical payments coverage; and the uninsured (and underinsured) motorist coverage. The second group of covered persons is those using the insured automobile with the permission of the named insured or the spouse of the named insured. The latter is referred to as "omnibus" coverage and was explored in the materials in this Chapter on the automobile policy's liability coverage (*see* § 6.02[2], *supra*). This subsection addresses problems regarding named insureds and resident relatives of the named insured's household.

2. *Who is a "named insured"?* Who was the named insured in *Hensley?* Mrs. Hoang listed her husband and her two sons, as well as herself, as principal operators of the Volvo, and in turn the Oldsmobile. What was the purpose of doing so if it was not to also make these individuals named insureds? If Mrs. Hoang had come to you for advice about buying liability insurance in connection with the car she was planning to provide her two sons, what could you have told her so that the result in *Hensley* might have been avoided?

3. *The problem of children away from home.* The issue of residency arises fairly frequently with regard to children of a named insured who are living away from home. For example, consider the facts of *Morgan v. Illinois Farmers Insurance Co.,* 392 N.W.2d 37, 38–39 (Minn. App. 1986):

> Appellant Charlotte Morgan was involved in an automobile accident with an uninsured motorist on November 4, 1981, while she was driving the vehicle of her roommate, Claire Donaldson. She was 21 years of age at the time, did not own her own vehicle, and did not have her own insurance policy.
>
> Appellants Albert and Dona Morgan, parents of Charlotte Morgan, had purchased automobile insurance from respondent Illinois Farmers Insurance Co. The insurance policy included uninsured motorist coverage for resident relatives of the named insureds, appellants Albert and Dona Morgan. After the accident, in which Charlotte Morgan was badly injured, Albert and Dona Morgan applied to Illinois Farmers for uninsured motorist benefits. The insurance company denied coverage, claiming Charlotte Morgan was not a "resident relative" of her parents household.

Charlotte Morgan graduated from high school in 1978 and attended college during portions of the next six years. She took another residence when she began college, although she returned to live in her parents' home from time to time. She received some mail at her parents' home, kept many of her possessions there, and still had a bedroom there. She spent virtually all weekends and holidays with her parents. She received financial support from her parents, was claimed as a dependent on her parents' 1980 and 1981 tax returns, and had her own key to her parents' home.

Charlotte Morgan moved to Salem, Massachusetts for six months in 1980, but returned to Minnesota in November 1980 when her father suffered a heart attack. She enrolled at the University of Minnesota in December 1980 and lived either with her parents or her grandparents until July 1981 when she moved into an apartment with Claire Donaldson. Because Charlotte Morgan did not have her own car, she would drive either a vehicle of her father's or her roommate's vehicle. While recuperating from her injuries late in 1981, Morgan again stayed with her parents for several weeks.

By virtue of Minnesota Stat. § 65B.43, subd. 5, the policy in question provided coverage for a relative of the named insured who "resides in the same household with the named insured if that person usually makes his home in the same family unit, even though he temporarily lives elsewhere." In construing this provision, the court held Charlotte Morgan was covered. *Id.* at 39. Do you agree? *See also Carbon v. Allstate Insurance Co.,* 719 So.2d 437 (La. 1998) ("resident relative" included unmarried dependent child temporarily living away from home under divorced parents' joint legal custody arrangement). See generally Carolyn Kelly MacWilliam, Annotation, *Who is "Member" or "Resident" of Same "Family" or "Household" Within No-Fault or Uninsured Motorist Provisions of Motor Vehicle Insurance Policy,* 66 A.L.R.5th 269 (1999).

Would there be coverage for Charlotte Morgan under the facts stated if her parents had a policy like that in Appendix E?

4. *The problem of the nonresident spouse.* The spouse of a named insured is not automatically covered under the standard personal automobile liability policy, i.e., the spouse has to be a resident of the named insured's household, too. See Appendix E. Is a spouse of a named insured covered if the spouse "moves out" during a period of marital strife? *See Gordinier v. Aetna Casualty & Surety Co.,* 154 Ariz. 266, 742 P.2d 277 (1987); *Hawaiian Insurance & Guaranty Co. v. Federated America# Insurance Co.,* 13 Wash. App. 7, 534 P.2d 48 (1975), 93 A.L.R.3d 407 (1979). How does the policy in Appendix E handle the "moving out" situation?

5. *The problem of the resident roommate.* At what point do two or more unmarried persons residing together become a household? *See Shivvers v. American Family Insurance Co.,* 256 Neb. 159, 589 N.W.2d 129 (1999).

6. *Multiple residencies?* Would it be possible for an individual to be a resident of more than one household for purposes of an auto liability insurance policy? *See Pellegrino v. State Farm Insurance Co.,* 167 Misc. 2d 617, 639 N.Y.S.2d 668 (N.Y. Sup. Ct. 1996).

7. *Uninsured motorist coverage.* Assume that Randy is a senior in high school and a resident of his parent's household. His parents have a policy like that in Appendix E. Randy is injured while riding as a passenger in his friend's car when it is involved in a collision with another vehicle. Neither of the drivers carry any insurance. Is Randy covered under his parent's uninsured motorist coverage? Does it make any difference which driver was negligent? Would it make any difference if Randy was a pedestrian instead of a passenger?

[2] Geographical and Other Physical Location Limitations

Most examples of insurance policy provisions which attempt to limit the risks transferred on the basis of geographical or physical location of persons, property, or events are found in automobile insurance. There are, however, examples in other lines of insurance. Before taking up the issue in automobile insurance, it is worth pausing to consider geographical and physical location limitations in other kinds of insurance.

In life and accidental death insurance, limitations based on physical location are rare. Some older policies did exclude coverage, usually for accidental death, under an aviation clause that said there was no coverage "while" the insured was "in or on" a device for aerial navigation. See C.T. Drechsler, Annotation, *Construction and Application of Provisions of Life or Accident Policy Relating to Aeronautics,* 17 A.L.R.2d 1041, 1058–1059, clauses 27 and 29 (1951). Modern forms speak in terms of death or accidents "resulting" from aviation activities, which narrows the former exclusion considerably. (See the Accidental Death Benefit provisions in the sample life insurance policy in Appendix G.)

Geographical location is not usually relevant in modern indemnity-type health insurance forms, such as group contracts for hospitalization and medical expenses. Policies purchased by major companies usually cover the insureds on a world-wide basis, but it would be prudent to check the master contract when an extended trip outside the United States is planned. The rise in managed care arrangements has significantly changed the health insurance landscape, and inherent in the nature of many of these health care plans are de facto geographic limitations. These inhere in the requirements of many plans that the subscriber to the health care plan and his or her dependents receive medical care from a network of physicians and hospitals in the locale in which the insured resides. Exceptions are typically made for emergency care required when the insured is out of the service area, but non-emergency care is provided by the plan only from network health care providers. Point-of-service plans give the insured more choice with respect to providers, but the cost to the patient to use non-network providers is customarily much higher. Some employers, such as large universities, which provide both indemnity and health service contracts on an optional basis for their employees, have standard arrangements so that employees may switch from a service contract, such as with an HMO, to an indemnity carrier when the individual will be outside the provider area for an extended period.

As for property insurance, the coverage for buildings and fixtures is usually described in terms of location in that the policy declaration page calls for an address or other location identifier. There often is coverage for personal property that is located on the premises. This is what one would expect to find in a standard homeowners policy and also in some commercial policies. A more restrictive condition based on location may be found in policies that are issued to jewelers, many of which require that the jewelry be stored in a certain type of safe during the time that the store is not open for business. Coverage under a Jewelers' Block Policy may also depend on whether the jewelry is located in a display case, window, or other area of the store during business hours. *See Charles, Henry & Crowley, Co. v. Home Insurance Co.,* 349 Mass. 723, 212 N.E.2d 240 (1965). There are examples in ocean marine insurance where the coverage may be conditioned upon the location of the vessel, *e.g.*, that it will not go into certain waters. *See Certain Underwriters at Lloyd's v. Montford,* 52 F.3d 1201 (9th Cir. 1995). Other examples could be cited, but the essential point is that the location of the property may be determinative when it comes to coverage under certain policies.

Beyond the liability coverage of automobile policies, there are other types of liability policies which also contain limitations on risks based on physical location. For example, the premises and operations coverage and the products hazard and completed operations coverage in the Comprehensive General Liability (and the more recent Commercial General Liability) policy turn in some instances on whether the accident took place on or off the insured's premises. See Roger C. Henderson, *Insurance Protection for Products Liability and Completed Operations,* 50 Neb. L. Rev. 415, 419–20 (1971). The "on and off premises" distinction also applies to some aspects of liability coverages contained in the various property owners' policies, often involving the use of certain vehicles off the premises. *See, e.g., Herzog v. National American Insurance Co.,* 2 Cal. 3d 192, 465 P.2d 841, 84 Cal. Rptr. 705 (1970) (use of motor bike "away from the premises or the ways immediately adjoining" under homeowners policy); *Bankert v. Threshermen's Mutual Insurance Co.,* 110 Wis. 2d 469, 329 N.W.2d 150 (1983) (use of motorcycle "away from the premises or the ways immediately adjoining" under farm owners' policy); and *Scherschligt v. Empire Fire & Marine Insurance Co.,* 662 F.2d 470 (8th Cir. 1981) (use of automobile "away from the premises or the ways immediately adjoining" under a Farmers Comprehensive Personal Insurance policy). Notice that the personal liability coverage under the homeowners policy in Appendix C does not contain a territorial limitation, for example to the United States and Canada, as does the auto policy in Appendix E. Why would an insurer be willing to insure against personal liability under a homeowners policy on a world-wide basis, but not under an auto policy?

Automobile insurance provides most examples of geographical or physical location limitations. Consider the cases which follow.

JULIAN v. JOHNSON
438 So. 2d 503 (Fla. Dist. App. 1983)

ORFINGER, CHIEF JUDGE.

This is an appeal from a final judgment awarding appellees, plaintiffs below, personal injury protection (PIP) benefits under a policy of insurance issued to appellant Ronald J. Julian by Allstate Insurance Company (Allstate) in the State of Massachusetts. We reverse.

Appellees Johnson and Parris filed suit against Julian and Allstate, alleging in substance, that on the day in question Julian was operating a motor vehicle owned by one Larry Corbin, bearing Massachusetts license plates, with Corbin's knowledge and consent, and while so operating the motor vehicle in Holly Hill, Florida, carelessly and negligently caused it to collide with plaintiffs, then pedestrians, as a result of which plaintiffs suffered permanent injury. Count I of the complaint requested recovery of tort damages. Count II alleged that the driver Julian had a policy of insurance with Allstate, issued in the state of Massachusetts, which provided PIP benefits "in accordance with the terms of the policy"; that plaintiffs had demanded such benefits but that payment thereof had been refused. PIP benefits under the policy were demanded in this count.

The liability claims (Count I) were ultimately settled and the issues of PIP coverage were presented to the trial court without a jury on the following stipulated facts:

A. At the time of the accident which is the subject of this claim for personal protection benefits under an Allstate automobile insurance policy issued to Ronald J. Julian, Ronald J. Julian was not driving his own car but was driving a car owned by Larry Corbin.

B. The plaintiffs, Robert Johnson, Jr., and Richard Parris, were Florida residents at the time of this accident.

C. The plaintiffs were pedestrians at the time of this accident.

D. Allstate Insurance Company issued a policy to Ronald J. Julian in the Commonwealth of Massachusetts, according to Massachusetts law, and at a time when Ronald J. Julian was a resident of the Commonwealth of Massachusetts.

E. The policy provides personal injury protection benefits to Ronald J. Julian and others, but the provision of such benefits is subject to any and all provisions, limitations, exclusions governing the payment of such benefits.

The issues remaining to be determined by the court were set forth by the parties as follows:

A. Whether personal injury protection coverage, and the benefits thereunder, are available to the plaintiffs or whether such coverage is excluded by the terms, language and provisions of said policy.

B. If coverage is provided to plaintiffs, what is the amount of coverage available to plaintiffs?

On the basis of the stipulated facts and the insurance policy and medical bills stipulated into evidence, the trial court entered judgment for Johnson in the amount of $10,000, and for Parris in the amount of $1360.64. Allstate contends that the insurance policy issued to Julian does not provide coverage for the PIP damages awarded, and we agree.

The insurance policy in question is a Massachusetts policy, issued to a Massachusetts resident (Julian) and covering an automobile registered in Massachusetts, owned by Julian. The insured automobile is not the automobile driven by Julian at the time of the accident in question. The policy is an "easy to read" contract written exclusively for the Massachusetts automobile owner. It is divided into two parts: compulsory insurance required under Massachusetts law of all automobiles registered in Massachusetts and optional insurance coverage which provides additional coverage not found under the compulsory section, but which is not required by the State of Massachusetts.

The compulsory insurance section is divided into four parts: bodily injury to others; personal injury protection; bodily injury caused by an uninsured auto; and damage to someone else's property. The most significant provision of these four to the facts of the instant case is part two on PIP coverage which provides in pertinent part:

> We will pay the benefits described below to you and other people injured or killed in auto accidents. For any one accident, we will pay as many people as are injured, but the most we will pay for injuries to any one person is $2,000. This is the most we will pay no matter how many autos or premiums are shown on the Coverage Selections page.
>
> . . . .
>
> We will pay PIP benefits to or for:
>
> 3. Any pedestrian, including you, if injured by your auto in Massachusetts, or any Massachusetts resident who, while a pedestrian, is struck by your auto outside of Massachusetts.

It is clear that no PIP coverage is provided to appellees under the quoted portion of the policy and the stipulated facts here. But, say appellees, there is optional coverage under the policy providing both additional bodily injury coverage to others and additional medical payment coverage, which portion of the policy has this provision:

> Some other states and Canadian provinces require visiting autos to have higher amounts of bodily injury or property damage coverage than you may have purchased. But, if you have purchased any coverage at all under this Part, we will automatically provide the required higher coverage.

Thus, appellees contend that if the defendant or insured vehicle was taken out of Massachusetts to another state, or to Canada, then the policy issued in Massachusetts would conform to the minimum PIP requirements of that state.

We cannot put new language into this contract and make it apply to PIP coverage when by its very terms, the extension applies only to bodily injury coverage and property damage coverage. These coverages are clearly distinct from PIP coverage under the policy terms.

Appellant contends that we have a "choice of law" problem here and that we should apply Massachusetts law, because the policy fully complies with the law of that state. Appellee says that choice of law is not involved here because this case is "simply an interpretation of an insurance policy to decide whether or not the policy conforms to the minimum statutory insurance requirements of the State of Florida on the date of the accident."

Florida public policy, as expressed by its statutory law, does not support the judgment, because the Florida statutory requirements for PIP coverage, by their very terms, do not require *Florida* PIP coverage under the facts of this case. Section 627.731, Florida Statutes (1981), applies the No-Fault Act to motor vehicles "registered in this state." The vehicle here was registered in Massachusetts. The No-Fault Act requires that the *owner* of the vehicle have insurance coverage, not the driver. Section 627.733(2), Florida Statutes (1981), requires that non-resident owners of motor vehicles which have been physically present in the state for more than 90 days during the preceding 365 days shall thereafter maintain security as required by law. The stipulated facts do not show this out-of-state vehicle to have been in this state during such period. Finally, section 627.736(1), Florida Statutes (1981), says:

> *Every insurance policy complying with the security requirements of s. 627.733* shall provide personal injury protection providing for payment of all reasonable expenses incurred for necessary medical, surgical, x-ray, dental, and rehabilitative services, including prosthetic devices; necessary ambulance, hospital, and nursing services; and funeral and disability benefits to the named insured, relatives residing in the same household, persons operating the insured motor vehicle, passengers in such motor vehicle, and other persons struck by such motor vehicle and suffering bodily injury while not an occupant of a self-propelled vehicle, all as specifically provided in subsection (2) and paragraph (4)(d), to a limit of $10,000 for loss sustained by any such person as a result of bodily injury, sickness, disease, or death arising out of the ownership, maintenance, or use of a motor vehicle . . . [Emphasis supplied].

Since neither the subject vehicle nor the appellant driver were required to have the PIP coverage under section 627.733(2), then section 627.736(1), likewise does not apply. Therefore, even if we apply Florida law, that law does not provide for PIP coverage under the stipulated facts.

Plaintiffs have their remedy under usual tort principles, which they have already exercised. They were not entitled to PIP benefits as well, so the judgment is erroneous and is reversed, with directions to enter judgment for appellants.

Reversed and Remanded.

DAUKSCH AND COWART, JJ., concur.

NOTES

1. *Auto liability policies.* Standard automobile liability insurance policies contain a territorial restriction which usually consists of "The United States

of America, its territories or possessions, or Canada, or while such vehicle is being transported between ports thereof," or similar language. Some policies also extend certain coverages to "such accidents and loss in Mexico within fifty miles of the United States boundary." Very few policies, as a matter of course, provide world-wide coverage. Why would an automobile liability insurer want to restrict coverage to that in the quoted language? If some insurers are willing to provide coverage in Mexico within fifty miles of the United States boundary, why would they not be willing to provide it throughout Mexico?

2. *No-fault auto insurance.* The coverage at issue in *Julian* is no-fault automobile insurance, which was addressed in the previous section of this Chapter. Would there be any problems in compelling insurers to afford no-fault auto insurance benefits on a world-wide basis? What will happen from the standpoint of claims processing when an insured is confined to a Turkish hospital for treatment for injuries sustained in an automobile accident in Turkey?

3. *Uninsured and underinsured motorist coverage.* Uninsured and underinsured motorist coverage typically have a territorial limitation similar to that found in the liability coverage mentioned in note 1 above. This territorial limitation has been challenged at times as being void. See the following case.

HALL v. AMICA MUTUAL INSURANCE CO.

538 Pa. 337, 648 A.2d 755 (1994)

Before Nix, C.J., and Flaherty, Zappala, Papadakos, Cappy, Castille and Montemuro, JJ.

Flaherty, Justice.

This case involves questions regarding the scope of review of statutory arbitration awards [and] public policy affecting territorial limitations on Pennsylvania automobile insurance coverage . . . .

Appellee Hall, the insured, was injured while operating a motor vehicle in Barbados, an independent country in the West Indies, when he was forced off the road by a phantom vehicle, causing him to strike a tree. He suffered catastrophic physical injuries, including permanent paralysis. Appellee was insured under three Amica insurance policies, with a combined total of $3,000,000 in uninsured motorist coverage.

Appellee's claim for uninsured motorist benefits was denied by appellant Amica Insurance Company on the basis of the policies' territorial limitation, which clearly and unambiguously limited the territory of coverage to the United States, its territories and possessions, Puerto Rico, and Canada. Appellee invoked the policies' arbitration clause, . . . [a]rbitrators were selected and a hearing took place. Appellee moved for partial summary judgment seeking a declaration that the territorial limitation in the Amica policies was unenforceable pursuant to Gerardi v. Harleysville Insurance Co., 293 Pa.

Super. 375, 439 A.2d 160 (1981). The arbitrators granted the motion, declared the limitation invalid, then awarded $3,000,000 in uninsured motorist benefits.

[Appellant sought review of the arbitration award in the court of common pleas and that court held it did not have jurisdiction to review the award of the arbitrators, but, even if it did, it would hold, as the arbitrators did, that the territorial limitation clause is invalid and unenforceable as a contravention of public policy. Appellant appealed to the Superior Court, which reversed the trial court's holding that it lacked jurisdiction to review the arbitration award, but affirmed the alternative holding that the territorial limitation was contrary to public policy and therefore unenforceable. The Superior Court affirmed the judgment of $3,000,000, and the parties appealed to the Supreme Court of Pennsylvania. The Supreme Court first held that a court has the power to review an arbitration award under these circumstances and then proceeded to address the public policy issue.]

Inasmuch as the arbitrators' decision is reviewable, we must decide whether the lower tribunals were correct in holding the territorial limitation clause of appellants' insurance contract to be unenforceable as against public policy. The two courts relied primarily on the seminal case of *Gerardi v. Harleysville Insurance Co., supra,* together with the more recent case *Serefeas v. Nationwide Insurance Co.,* 338 Pa. Super. 587, 488 A.2d 48 (1985), both of which support the holding of the arbitration panel, the trial court, and the Superior Court.

The holding of *Gerardi* had two major bases. First, subsection (e) of the uninsured motorist act sets forth three instances where the coverage required by the act does not apply; the three exceptions do not include territorial limitations; and the statutory construction act provides that "[e]xceptions expressed in a statute shall be construed to exclude all others." 1 Pa. C.S. § 1924. The Superior Court quoted this court to the effect that the uninsured motorist statute "mandates a floor of minimum protection to be afforded to the owner/operator of a motor vehicle within the Commonwealth. The legislature has permitted enhancement of that minimum protection, but we believe the statute does not permit a diminution of that protection below the statutory limits."

This rationale in *Gerardi* is not persuasive. It provides an illustrative example of the logical fallacy of *petitio principii*. The syllogism representing this rationale may be stated thus: the statute requires worldwide uninsured motorist coverage; the statute authorizes three exceptions but does not authorize a territorial limitation; explicit exceptions exclude all other exceptions; therefore the statute requires worldwide coverage. The reasoning is valid only if one starts with the conclusion. Unless the statute requires worldwide coverage, a territorial limitation is not an exception, the rule of statutory construction, *expressio unius est exclusio alterius*—expression of one exception excludes all others—does not come into play, and the logic breaks down entirely.

Gerardi represents an anomaly in the genre of statutory construction cases: though it repeatedly quotes rules of statutory construction, it neglects to quote the language of the statute purportedly being construed. The critical portion of the statute, subsection (e) provides:

> (e) The coverage required by [the uninsured motorist act] does not apply:
>
> (1) To property damage sustained by the insured.
>
> (2) To bodily injury sustained by the insured with respect to which the insured or his representative shall, without the written consent of the insurer, make any settlement with or prosecute to judgment any action against any person who may be legally liable therefor.
>
> (3) In any instance where it would inure directly or indirectly to the benefit of any workmen's compensation carrier or to any person qualified as a self-insurer under any workmen's compensation law.

As the subsection states, the legislature was listing permissible exceptions to *the coverage required by the statute*. If the legislature did not intend to require worldwide coverage, it would not be expected to list territorial limitations as exceptions to the coverage required by the statute. An example might help to illustrate the point. If the statute had explicitly required worldwide uninsured motorist coverage but listed as an exception that an insurer might exclude such coverage in countries subjected to trade sanctions by the U.S. government, then the limitation set forth in the Amica policy at issue would contravene the statute by virtue of 1 Pa.C.S. § 1924. The *Gerardi* majority conceded, however, that the statute did not explicitly mandate any specific territorial scope of coverage, but by assuming that *worldwide* coverage was required, it was able to discover a logical path to the conclusion that worldwide coverage was *required*. This defect in logic was noted by Judge Hester, dissenting.

That the *Gerardi* majority did not find it necessary to quote the statutory language being interpreted was perhaps due to its heavy reliance on its second rationale, which was to examine the spirit of the act, rather than its words, to ascertain and effectuate the intention of the General Assembly, as mandated by 1 Pa. C.S. § 1921(a). The court quoted *Sands v. Granite Mutual Insurance Co.,* 232 Pa. Super. 70, 80, 331 A.2d 711, 716 (1974): "The purpose of the uninsured motorist law is to provide protection to innocent victims of irresponsible drivers," adding that "any conditions or restrictions in an insurance policy which are held to be in derogation of the legislative purpose of the uninsured motorist law are void as against public policy," quoting *Brader v. Nationwide Mutual Insurance Co.,* 270 Pa. Super. 258, 263, 411 A.2d 516, 519 (1979).

Circular reasoning is again evident in this second rationale of the *Gerardi* majority. If we accept that the "purpose of the uninsured motorist law is to provide protection to innocent victims of irresponsible [uninsured] drivers," then an uninsured motorist policy which fails to provide any protection to the innocent victims of irresponsible uninsured drivers would contravene the legislative purpose and offend public policy. But unless one begins with the point at issue, namely that the purpose of the uninsured motorist law is to protect the victims of uninsured drivers *everywhere in the world*, there is no reason to conclude that an insurance policy providing uninsured motorist coverage within clearly defined territorial limits violates the legislative purpose of the statute or contravenes any public policy. The Amica insurance clause clearly protects the innocent victims of irresponsible uninsured drivers in the United States, its territories and possessions, Puerto Rico, and Canada; in so doing, it clearly effectuates the purpose of the statute. Whether it violates public policy by excluding accidents in Barbados is the ultimate question in the case and its solution is not advanced by the circular reasoning of *Gerardi*.

The rationale of *Serefeas v. Nationwide Insurance Co., supra*, to some extent tracks the reasoning employed in *Gerardi*. It was construing the language of the No-fault Motor Vehicle Insurance Act, 40 P.S. § 1009.101 et seq., repealed by Act of February 12, 1984, P.L. 26, No. 11, s 8(a), effective October 1, 1984.[25] It rejected, in conclusory fashion, the principle that when a statute is interpreted by the agency charged with its enforcement or administration, its interpretation should be given great weight and should be disregarded only if the interpretation is clearly erroneous. The Pennsylvania Insurance Commission, responsible to implement the statute, has promulgated regulations permitting the territorial limitation at issue in this case. *See* 31 Pa.Code §§ 63.3(a), 63.2 (requiring coverage only "within the United States, its territories, and Canada.") The form of the policy issued by Amica was submitted to and approved by the insurance commissioner. We regard this factor as a significant one.

Public policy is more concrete than a general desideratum which presumably supports the legislation in question and thus forms part of the legislature's intention. Public policy is more than a vague goal which may be used to circumvent the plain meaning of a statute. Both the United States Supreme Court and this court have been unequivocal in this regard.

> Public policy is to be ascertained by reference to the laws and legal precedents and not from general considerations of supposed public interest. As the term "public policy" is vague, there must be found definite indications in the law of the sovereignty to justify the invalidation of a contract as contrary to that policy. . . . Only dominant public policy would justify such action. In the absence of a plain indication of that policy through long governmental practice or statutory enactments, or of violations of obvious ethical or moral standards, the Court should not assume to declare contracts . . . contrary to public policy. The courts must be content to await legislative action.

---

[25] *Gerardi* and *Serefeas, supra*, arose under the now-repealed No-fault Act; this case falls under the legislation which replaced the No-fault Act—the Motor Vehicle Financial Responsibility Law, Act of Feb. 12, 1984, P.L. 26, No. 11, § 3, effective Oct. 1, 1984, codified at 75 Pa.C.S. § 1701 et seq., specifically subchapter C, Uninsured and Underinsured Motorist Coverage. Section 1731 provided:

> (a) General rule.—No motor vehicle liability insurance policy shall be delivered or issued for delivery in this Commonwealth, with respect to any motor vehicle registered or principally garaged in this Commonwealth, unless uninsured motorist and underinsured motorist coverages are provided therein or supplemental thereto *in amounts equal to the bodily injury liability coverage.* . . .

75 Pa.C.S. § 1731(a) (Emphasis added). The statute thus required uninsured motorist coverage which was coextensive with liability coverage and was silent as to territorial limitations. The uninsured motorist law was subsequently amended again in 1990, [to make it optionable.]

Muschany v. United States, 324 U.S. 49, 66–67, 65 S. Ct. 442, 451, 89 L. Ed. 744, 756 (1945) (footnotes and citations omitted).

> It is only when a given policy is so obviously for or against the public health, safety, morals or welfare that there is a virtual unanimity of opinion in regard to it, that a court may constitute itself the voice of the community in so declaring. There must be a positive, well-defined, universal public sentiment, deeply integrated in the customs and beliefs of the people and in their conviction of what is just and right and in the interests of the public weal. . . . Only in the clearest cases, therefore, may a court make an alleged public policy the basis of judicial decision.

Mamlin v. Genoe, 340 Pa. 320, 325, 17 A.2d 407, 409 (1941).

It would be easy to state a public policy in the forbidden sense of "general considerations of supposed public interest," to elevate it to the status of unstated statutory language, thence to hold that an agency interpretation or insurance contract provision which is perfectly consistent with the plain words of the statute nonetheless violates the judicially perceived public policy and is therefore unenforceable. Although uninsured motorist coverage serves the purpose of protecting innocent victims from irresponsible uninsured motorists, that purpose does not rise to the level of a public policy overriding every other consideration of statutory construction.[26] Not to lose sight of the forest for the trees, we quote the obvious: "[T]he policy of liberal interpretation of the [uninsured motorist law] is not limitless, a proverbial House that Jack Built. . . . [T]here is a correlation between the premiums paid by the insured and the coverage a claimant could reasonably expect to receive."

Moreover, Amica argues that it contracted and collected a premium to insure its customer against loss due to uninsured motorists in a clearly stated territory; it did not contract to cover its customer throughout the world including places where uninsured motorist risk is entirely unknown or the known risk is unacceptably high, regardless of a country's traffic rules and regulations, traffic patterns, insurance requirements, even where no motor vehicle insurance is required at all. If uninsured motorist coverage were extended worldwide, the rates of Pennsylvania insurers would necessarily reflect the increased scope of the risk as well as the increased difficulty and expense involved in the investigation of claims. In addition, motorists who do not drive in foreign countries would be required to subsidize the additional

---

[26] 75 Pa.C.S. § 1731(a) provides:

> *(a) Mandatory offering.*—No motor vehicle liability insurance policy shall be delivered or issued for delivery in this Commonwealth, with respect to any motor vehicle registered or principally garaged in this Commonwealth, unless uninsured motorist and underinsured motorist coverages are offered therein or supplemental thereto in amounts as provided in section 1734 (relating to request for lower limits of coverage). *Purchase of uninsured motorist and underinsured motorist coverages is optional.* Act of 1990, Feb. 7, P.L. 11, No. 6, § 9, effective July 1, 1990. (Emphasis added.) The fact that a Pennsylvania motorist need not purchase uninsured motorist coverage even within the state of Pennsylvania undermines the argument that public policy in favor of protection against uninsured motorists has such force, dominance, and universality that insurers *must* offer worldwide uninsured motorist coverage and *cannot* include any territorial limitations in an uninsured motorist policy.

costs of underwriting the risk to those who do. We do not think the uninsured motorist law contains an indication of public policy which is clear enough to void a plain, unambiguous territorial limitation clause in an insurance contract.

All these considerations cast grave doubt on the conclusion that public policy mandates that Pennsylvania auto insurers provide worldwide uninsured motorist coverage to their customers. "Only in the clearest cases . . . may a court make an alleged public policy the basis of judicial decision." *Mamlin v. Genoe, supra,* 340 Pa. at 325, 17 A.2d at 409. This is obviously not the clearest of cases, so it is beyond judicial authority to declare the lucid territorial limitation of the Amica insurance contract to be void as against public policy. Summary judgment for Amica Mutual Insurance Company should have been granted.

. . . .

The order of the Superior Court is reversed.

PAPADAKOS, J., concurs in the result.

MONTEMURO, J., is sitting by designation.

NOTES

1. *Does the territorial restriction violate public policy?* Although the challenge to the territorial restriction in the uninsured motorist coverage in *Hall* was not successful, at least two courts of last resort have held that the territorial scope of the uninsured motorist coverage must be coextensive with that of the liability coverage. *See Bartning v. State Farm Fire & Casualty Co.,* 162 Ariz. 344, 783 P.2d 790 (1989); *Mission Insurance Co. v. Brown,* 63 Cal. 2d 508, 47 Cal. Rptr. 363, 407 P.2d 275 (1965). These decisions were reached on the grounds that the uninsured motorist coverage was mandated by the particular state's compulsory automobile insurance statute and that the coverage was designed to put the insured in the same position as if the uninsured tortfeasor had purchased the minimum liability insurance that also was required. Therefore, if the liability coverage is in effect in Mexico, then the uninsured motorist coverage is similarly in effect. Any attempt to restrict uninsured motorist coverage to a territory less than that for the liability coverage would be void because it conflicts with the public policy underlying the statutes.

In a similar vein, New York's highest court has held that a policy which expressly limited uninsured motorist coverage to accidents occurring in New York would be deemed amended to provide uninsured motorist coverage for an accident that occurred in another state in which uninsured motorist coverage was mandatory. *See American Transit Insurance Co. v. Abdelghany,* 80 N.Y.2d 162, 589 N.Y.S.2d 842, 603 N.E.2d 947 (1992). See generally Philip White, Annotation, *Validity of Territorial Restrictions on Uninsured/Underinsured Coverage in Automobile Insurance Policies,* 55 A.L.R.5th 747 (1998).

Since *Bartning* was decided, the Arizona legislature has made uninsured motorist coverage optional. What effect might this have on the decision? Is there still a basis for arguing that uninsured motorist coverage must be coextensive with the territorial provision in the liability coverage?

2. *Driving in Mexico? Better plan ahead.* One U.S. company provides the following warning on the cover page of its automobile policy:

> Unless you have automobile insurance written by a Mexican insurance company, you may spend many hours or days in jail, if you have an accident in Mexico. You should secure insurance coverage from a company licensed under the laws of Mexico to write such insurance in order to avoid penalties and complications under the laws of Mexico, including the possible impoundment of your automobile.

State Farm Mutual Automobile Insurance Company form 9803.5. No such warnings are made about driving in Canada, leaving one to wonder what all the fuss is about with respect to the United States' southern neighbor.

In a nutshell, the problem is this: Although some policies provide that the liability, medical payments, and physical damage coverages apply in Mexico within fifty miles of the United States border, Mexican officials do not recognize U.S. insurance companies. Unless insurance is carried with an insurance company licensed under the laws of Mexico, it is as if there is no insurance at all as far as Mexico is concerned. In addition to the fact that U.S. companies are presently not able to qualify for a Mexican license, an automobile in Mexico is considered a "dangerous instrumentality" and strict liability is the rule. In fact, in Mexico an automobile accident is considered a criminal offense, and all parties may be detained until authorities determine who is responsible. Unlike U.S. law where one is presumed innocent until proven guilty, the law of Mexico is based on the Napoleonic Code, which presumes guilt until innocence is proved. Once blame is affixed, that person's automobile will remain impounded until the damages are paid. What's one to do? You can obtain a Mexican insurance policy by dialing a toll-free number and charging a policy to a credit card; per-day coverage is approximately $20. But even this may not be enough if an ensuing accident involves personal injury or death. In that event, the driver may be jailed until the authorities assess fault, and the responsible driver may remain incarcerated until restitution to the victims and a fine is paid. See Joanne Wojcik, *RIMS 1998: If You're Driving to Mexico, Make Sure You're Covered*, Bus. Ins., Apr. 20, 1998, at T16. It may be that the position of the Mexican government will eventually change under the North American Free Trade Agreement, but the prudent motorist driving in Mexico would be well advised to heed this warning, unless, of course, one is not averse to the risk of spending one's vacation in a jail.

3. *Radius clause.* Another type of territorial restriction is found in a clause that is relatively common in some types of motor vehicle policies designed for trucking businesses. One such clause, known as a "radius" clause or endorsement, reads as follows:

> It is agreed that the insurance with respect to the automobile described above or designated in the policy as subject to this endorsement does not apply, if regular or frequent trips of the automobile

exceed a 300 mile radius of the limits of the city or town where such automobile is principally garaged as stated in the policy, to any bodily injury or property damage which occurs during any such trip, or return therefrom, other than bodily injury or property damage which occurs during the use of such automobile for personal, pleasure or family purposes on a trip beyond such radius.

See Moss v. Mid-America Fire & Marine Insurance Co., 103 Idaho 298, 647 P.2d 754 (1982). The radius clause is an attempt to limit the risk transferred to the insurer on the basis of geographical location. Why would an insurer want to restrict coverage in this manner?

There has been much litigation over the meaning of the words "regular or frequent," as used in the radius clause. For example, in *Moss* the insured made 135 commercial hauling trips. Of these, thirteen were outside the 300 mile radius provision. On the last of the thirteen trips, the insured was involved in an accident. The trial court ruled in favor of the insurer on a motion for summary judgment that the thirteen trips were "regular or frequent" as a matter of law. On appeal, the Idaho Supreme Court, in a split decision, reversed and remanded for further proceedings. Two justices decided that the issue was one for the trier of fact, two justices decided that the trial court was correct in granting the insurer's motion for summary judgment, and the fifth justice concurred with the first two only for the purpose of reversing the decision of the trial court so that the trial court might consider granting the insured's motion for summary judgment on the issue. Would the public be better served by a policy provision strictly confining the coverage to the prescribed area and eliminating the "frequent or regular" use language?

4. *Does the radius clause violate compulsory insurance statutes?* A few courts have held that certain radius clauses violate the compulsory automobile liability insurance statute of the particular jurisdiction. *See, e.g., Equity Mutual Insurance Co. v. Spring Valley Wholesale Nursery, Inc.,* 747 P.2d 947 (Okla. 1987).

Chapter 7
EFFECTING, MODIFYING, AND TERMINATING COVERAGE

"The creation and enforcement of insurance contracts impinge at every turn upon the public interest and vitally affect the social and economic welfare of individuals."—Bertram Harnett (Lecturer in Law at Columbia University School of Law, and later a Justice of the New York Supreme Court) & John V. Thornton (Lecturer in Law at Columbia), in *Interest in Property: A Socio-Economic Reevaluation of a Legal Concept*, 48 Colum. L. Rev. 1162, 1162 (1948)

§ 7.01 Authority to Contract

As a general rule insurance contracts are issued by corporations, but there are exceptions, such as those underwritten by individuals through Lloyd's of London. Of course, corporations and other organizations, as well as people, buy insurance. In the great majority of these situations, the contracting parties never see or deal with each other directly. Most often, the parties deal through agents, brokers, and other intermediaries. Thus, the role of these intermediaries and the law governing the relationships are quite important to the parties. The most important body of law governing these relationships is that of agency. This section introduces some of the fundamental rules regarding the principal-agent relationship and concomitant legal problems in the context of insurance marketing.

[1] Principal-Agent Relationship

NUNLEY v. MERRILL
513 So. 2d 582 (Miss. 1987)

HAWKINS, PRESIDING JUSTICE, for the Court:

Truman Nunley has appealed from a summary judgment rendered by the circuit court of Prentiss County in favor of the defendants Independent Fire Insurance Company and Vanguard Underwriters Insurance Company in a suit by Nunley to recover for a fire loss of his home. We agree with the circuit court that Nunley had no policy of insurance with either company and affirm.

FACTS

Vassar Insurance Agency, Inc. (Vassar), of Booneville was established by John Vassar in 1955. He and Charles Bolton were the licensed agents for

Independent Fire, and in 1980 Vassar sold his interest in the local agency to Bolton. On December 16, 1982, Independent Fire terminated authority of Bolton and Vassar to represent it. During that month a representative of Independent Fire went to the agency in Booneville to recover its policy forms, and according to the company call sheet record no forms were found. Thereafter, Bolton moved away, and Barbara Merrill, who had been secretary-treasurer of the agency, assumed ownership, and conducted all of its business.

Nunley is a retired resident of Tishomingo. Before his retirement, he was self-employed and did logging and pulpwood work.

In early November, 1983, Nunley had gone to the Vassar agency in Booneville and discussed with Merrill the possibility of acquiring homeowners' insurance on his home. Either at that time or in February, 1984, after securing the information necessary to write a policy, Merrill received the premium for the policy in cash and told Nunley that she would get the policy for him. She did not at any time tell him the name of the company that would issue the policy, and he never asked.

Sometime in February, 1984, Nunley received a policy on an Independent Fire insurance form through the mail. This policy was later destroyed in the fire. A copy of the policy (which presumably came from the bank that held the mortgage on Nunley's home) provided coverage on Nunley's home beginning February 21, 1984. In the space provided for the signature of the authorized representative, "Vassar Insurance Company, Inc." was typed.

On April 2, 1984, Nunley drove into Booneville to run some errands. Around 10:30 or 11:00 a.m., he went by Merrill's office to discuss insurance coverage of his trucks and other equipment. Nunley testified that he made his insurance payments on the trucks around the first of each month. Nothing was mentioned during this discussion regarding Nunley's homeowner coverage. After Nunley left Merrill's office, Merrill called Pearl River Insurance Managers (Pearl River) at approximately 11:00 a.m in an attempt to bind coverage through Vanguard Underwriters for Nunley's home. Pearl River was the general agent of Vanguard Underwriters.

After Nunley left Merrill's office, he returned to his home in Tishomingo County to discover his house had been destroyed by a fire of undetermined causes. Tishomingo Fire Department reports show that they received the call at 9:10 a.m. on April 2, 1984. Nunley notified Merrill that afternoon, and Merrill reportedly told him that his loss "was being taken care of."

Merrill filled out a loss report on either the afternoon of the fire loss or the next morning and mailed it to Pearl River. The report indicated that she was notified of the loss at 4:30 p.m. on April 1, 1984. Merrill claimed that this was an error and she did not think that she was trying to back date the insurance. In addition, Nunley's application for homeowner's coverage was filled out by Merrill on April 2, but had been dated April 1. Merrill stated that she made another error.

The Vanguard Underwriters policy was issued on April 5, 1984. The policy states the inception date as April 2, 1984, and had been antedated to 12:01 a.m. of that day.

Both insurance companies refused to pay Nunley's claim, and the circuit court complaint was filed September 26, 1984, against both companies and Merrill individually.

Independent Fire denied liability based upon the fact that Merrill was not and never had been a licensed agent for it, and had no authority, actual or apparent to represent it. A. Wayne Smith, assistant vice-president of the company, made an affidavit that Independent Fire had no knowledge that the policy had been issued, and no premium had been received by the company.

However, on January 7, 1985, Independent Fire did mail a "special notice" to Nunley informing him that his coverage would expire on the policy anniversary. Nunley argued that this was a sufficient "notice" to create a factual issue as to whether Independent Fire had knowledge that the policy had been issued. In response, Independent Fire averred that the special notice resulted from a computer error, setting out by affidavit that when a suit was filed the law required the company to establish a loss reserve for the pending claim. Independent Fire averred further the policy information and reserve information were routinely entered into the company's computer, which automatically prepared and mailed a routine notice of expiration to the named insured, in this case Nunley.

Based on the facts before it by affidavit and deposition, the circuit court granted summary judgment in favor of Independent Fire under our holding in *Resolute Insurance Co. v. State,* 290 So. 2d 599 (Miss. 1974), the Court finding that Merrill had no authority to issue the Independent Fire policy.

The lower court granted summary judgment to Vanguard Underwriters based on the rulings of this Court that property which has already been destroyed by fire cannot be covered by a fire insurance policy.

Feeling aggrieved by these rulings, Nunley appeals to this Court.

Law
A. *Summary Judgment Regarding Independent Fire*

Nunley contends the issue of Merrill's actual or apparent authority is a material issue of fact that should be resolved by trial on the merits, not by summary judgment. Nunley also argues that the "special notice" mailed to him on January 7, 1985, by Independent Fire created an issue of fact as to Independent Fire's knowledge that Nunley's policy had been issued.

The case of *Resolute Insurance Co. v. State,* 290 So. 2d 599 (Miss. 1974), is closely on point and is virtually indistinguishable from the instant case. In that case, the son of a deceased agent for Resolute Insurance Company came into possession of various numbered, blank powers of attorney which he used to make bail bonds for four persons who were arrested and incarcerated. The deceased agent's son procured the release of the four prisoners, and upon the subsequent failure of the principals to appear as required by the bond, forfeiture on the bonds was sought. The insurance company sought to vacate the judgment on the grounds that the bonds had not been executed with the knowledge, consent and authority of the insurance company. However, final judgment was taken on the bonds, and the insurance company appealed. This Court reversed the judgment of the trial court denying the insurance company's petition to vacate the judgment on the bond.

This Court found the following uncontradicted facts regarding the question of agency:

> The John Wilson who called and arranged for the release of the prisoners was the son of a former agent of Resolute Insurance Company. The elder John Wilson died in August of 1971, and *soon after his death an attorney from Resolute Insurance Company was sent to Augusta, Georgia, to gather all papers and documents pertaining to Resolute Insurance Company.* Evidently, the four powers of attorney and qualifying power of attorney were acquired by the son, John Wilson, without the knowledge of Resolute. The son was never an agent for Resolute, nor was he ever a licensed bondsman in Georgia or in Mississippi. [Emphasis added]
>
> . . . .
>
> It is evident from the testimony in this case that John S. Wilson, Jr., was not the agent of Resolute Insurance Company at the time he signed the bonds and filed the power of attorney . . . .

290 So. 2d at 601.

In the instant case, Barbara Merrill never filed a certificate of authority for Independent Fire and therefore was not a licensed agent. The policy forms in her office had been in the possession of the previous owners who were licensed agents. Independent Fire also sent a representative to gather the policy forms which could not be found. Accordingly, the lack of an agency relationship between Merrill and Independent Fire is obvious.

Nunley contends there remains a material issue of fact as to whether Merrill had apparent authority. The *Resolute* Court dealt with the issue of apparent authority simply by stating: "A good deal of authority has been cited on the law of agency in this case as to the apparent authority of any agent, none of which is applicable since no agent or agency is involved herein." 290 So. 2d at 603. Since there is no agency relationship between Merrill and Independent Fire, this Court also need not consider Merrill's apparent authority.

Nunley next charges that Independent Fire should be estopped from denying that they issued the policy since they obtained a benefit from the issuance of the policy. This Court likewise dealt with this issue in the *Resolute* case, where we stated:

> We must bear in mind that the record in this case shows conclusively that the insurance company had no knowledge that the son of their deceased agent had obtained possession of the various powers of attorney furnished his father by the insurance company.

Nunley attempts to show Independent Fire had knowledge of the facts by pointing to the "special notice" sent by Independent Fire to Nunley in January of 1985. It should be noted that when this notice was sent, Independent Fire had denied any liability and affidavits had been filed stating Independent Fire had no knowledge of the policy issuance. Based on the affidavits of Vice President Smith that Independent Fire received no premium for the policy, we find that the lower court justifiably relied on the explanation of Independent Fire concerning the special notice. There is nothing in this record to suggest this "special notice" was anything more than Independent Fire deposed it was. Merrill obviously knew she had no contract with Independent Fire, or she would not have been scurrying about on April 2 attempting to secure coverage with Vanguard.

Based on the documentary evidence, affidavits, and depositions submitted by Independent Fire, we conclude that no material issue of fact existed since it was undisputed that Merrill was never an agent of Independent Fire when she purportedly issued the policy.

B. *Vanguard*

Nunley thought he had a fire insurance policy with Independent Fire. Merrill knew that he did not. Nunley made no request of Merrill to secure other insurance.

Ordinarily, a policy of insurance issued after a loss is not a valid policy.

This Court has held, however, that where at the time of an application for insurance there has been a loss but neither the applicant nor the insurer knew of this fact a recovery may be had on a policy subsequently issued, which was antedated so as to include the time at which the loss occurred. Yet, such a rule presupposes there was a contract, a meeting of the minds of the parties.

There was no meeting of the minds of the parties in this case. Nunley made no application for insurance on April 2, 1984. The Indiana Supreme Court faced a similar case to this in *Celina Mutual Casualty Co. v. Baldridge,* 213 Ind. 198, 10 N.E.2d 904 (1937). On July 19, 1930, Baldridge thought he had insurance on his car with a company called American States Insurance Company (which later cancelled the policy for nonpayment of premium, although he had paid the local agent). After his car was damaged, the local agent, a Mrs. Brishaber, informed Baldridge that she had insured him on July 19 with Celina Mutual Casualty Company. The Indiana Supreme Court had this to say:

> [I]t is sufficient that on July 19th, when Mrs. Brishaber says she undertook to cancel his policy and procure him a new one in the appellant company, she had no authority to act for him, and he had no knowledge of her action. . . .
>
> To create a contract of insurance there must be an agreement between the insurer and the insured. There must be a meeting of the minds. . . . There was no contract made on July 19th, because appellee had not authorized or requested the issuance of insurance, and had no knowledge that a contract with appellant was contemplated. . . .
>
> "An agent of an insurance company has no authority to insure property already destroyed; and a policy written and intended as a substitute for a subsisting policy in another company, but not delivered, and of which the assured has no knowledge until after the property is destroyed by fire is not a valid contract of insurance." [Citations omitted]
>
> A direction authorizing an insurance agent to procure a policy of insurance is exhausted by the procuring of one policy, and confers no

authority to afterwards cancel and procure other or different policies. [Citations omitted]

In *Clark v. Insurance Co. of North America* (1896) 89 Me. 26, 34, 36, 35 A. 1008, 1011, 35 L.R.A. 276, it is said:

"The contract of insurance is to be tested by the principles applicable to the making of contracts in general. The terms of the contract must have been agreed upon. This necessarily implies the action of two minds, of two contracting parties. If it is incomplete in any material particular, or the assent of either party is wanting, it is of no binding force. . . .

"In this case, the action of the agent in the transaction relative to the attempted change of risk to the defendant company was entirely ex parte. If we assume that he was acting with authority from the company, it was then no more than a proposition which had not been made known to the plaintiff. To give it validity required his knowledge and his consent. At the time of the loss, knowledge had not been conveyed to him, and his acceptance had not been given. The rights and liabilities of the parties are to be determined by their legal status at the time of the loss. It is inconceivable that the defendant company can be held liable for indemnity against loss when no contract for indemnity existed at the time the loss occurred."

. . . .

It seems clear that there never was a contract between the appellant and the appellee, or ever a thought of such a contract, except in the mind of the local agent, until after the property to be insured was destroyed. There can be no contract without knowledge of the contracting parties. . . .

We do not have the question before us of whether Merrill has any rights against Vanguard. Also, Nunley's cause of action against Merrill remains unaffected by this decision, the circuit court having rendered a Rule 54(b) final judgment only as to Independent Fire and Vanguard. Rule 54(b) Mississippi Rules of Civil Procedure.

We do hold no insurance contract of any kind was ever entered into as between Nunley and Vanguard.

The judgment of the circuit court is accordingly affirmed.

Affirmed.

Caldwell v. American National Insurance Co., 456 F.2d 1368 (8th Cir. 1972). Messerschmidt, an agent of the American National Insurance Company, solicited Elmer Caldwell for a "term 65" life insurance policy. Elmer submitted an application for the policy on January 3, 1969, and paid the first month's premium. He failed, however, to complete his medical examination within the 40-day post-application period prescribed by the insurer. He was so notified, and the insurer refunded the premium payment. Thereafter, Messerschmidt obtained a second premium payment from Elmer to "reopen the file." This time, Elmer completed the medical examination. Three months later, on July 9, 1969, Messerschmidt had Elmer sign an American National form requesting reconsideration of his application. No policy was issued, however, and Elmer died on July 28, 1969. Rosetta Caldwell, Elmer's widow, sued the insurer on an alleged oral contract to insure Elmer's life made between the Caldwells and American National's agent, Messerschmidt. Rosetta contended that the "the agent's representations that Caldwell would be covered by insurance when the application was filled out, the premium paid and the medical examination completed constituted an oral agreement to insure Caldwell, binding appellee [the insurer] to its terms." The trial court dismissed appellant's claim under Fed. R. Civ. P. 41(b), and the Eighth Circuit affirmed in a per curiam opinion.

The trial court held that the appellant failed in her burden of proving the existence of an oral contract to insure; that Messerschmidt was nothing more than a soliciting agent, in contrast to a general agent, and with neither actual nor apparent authority to orally bind the appellee to a contract of insurance; and that the deceased had no right to rely on the representations as to the existence of coverage since (1) the application provided that in the absence of a conditional receipt being tendered no coverage ensued until the policy was issued (no policy was issued); (2) the appellant and decedent, having received an "Important Notice to Applicant," which clearly stated no coverage was in effect and that the premium was being refunded, were put on notice that their file was closed and no insurance existed; and (3) the "Declaration of Insurability" in which Caldwell reapplied for coverage, plainly stated no coverage existed under the first application and would not until the policy was issued. The trial court also held that there were no representations concerning the existence of insurance after the reapplication was signed on July 9, 1969, and further that the lapse of time between July 9 and August 26, the date of rejection by appellee, was not an unreasonable period of time for the company to reconsider the file and to accept or reject the reapplication.

"It is clear that the soliciting (life insurance) agent could not orally enter into and bind his principal to a contract for insurance.[1] The trial court, in its findings, held that Messerschmidt did not have such authority.

"In any event, a thorough review of the entire record convinces us that the trial court's findings are supported by substantial evidence and are not clearly erroneous. *See* Fed. Rules Civ. Proc. Rule 52."

---

[1] He was, however, authorized to issue a conditional or binding receipt which would have provided interim coverage in this case when (1) the application was completed; (2) the first premium paid; and (3) the required medical examination was completed if the applicant was insurable.

Binders or conditional receipts of this type, which do not require final "Home Office" approval, appear to create interim coverage effective whenever the required medical examination is completed, assuming the applicant is insurable. This temporary contract of insurance would, of course, be subject to a condition subsequent—rejection of the application by the insurance company—assuming such occurs prior to the applicant's death.

Here, though the agent was firmly convinced he had tendered Caldwell a binder, the appellant denied that he had and argued to such effect, apparently for the reason that the binder limited appellee's liability for interim coverage to $50,000, whereas, the oral contract, if established, would have provided accidental death coverage of $75,000. The trial court found that no binder had been issued.

NOTES

1. *Actual authority: express and implied.* The agent-principal relationship involves the power of the former to affect the legal relationship of the latter with third parties. This power may be *express*; that is, it may arise from an agreement whereby the agent is expressly authorized to act on behalf of the principal. In the world of insurance, this agreement is usually in writing, but it could be oral. The agent-principal relationship also may be *implied* from the acts of the parties even though there is no express agreement. Whether the relationship is express or implied, the agent must reasonably believe she has the authority to act on behalf of the principal. Finally, implied authority also may be incidental to express authority because it is not always possible to cover every detail of the agent's power in the agreement. Whether the agent's authority is explicit or implicit, this authority constitutes *actual authority* and is to be distinguished from *apparent authority*. (The Restatement of Agency treats the distinction as one between authority, without the modifier "actual," and apparent authority, but many courts use the term "actual authority" to make the distinction.) If the agent has neither actual nor apparent authority, as a general rule the agent cannot bind the insurer. *See, e.g., Hallas v. Boehmke and Dobosz, Inc.,* 239 Conn. 658, 686 A.2d 491 (1997); *Northern Assurance Co. of Am. v. Summers,* 17 F.3d 956 (7th Cir. 1994) (applying Indiana law).

2. *Apparent authority.* It is clear in *Nunley* that Ms. Merrill did not have actual authority to bind Independent Fire Insurance Company to a contract of homeowners insurance. Did she have apparent authority to do so? The court said that it did not have to consider whether Merrill had apparent authority to bind Independent Fire because there was no agency relationship. Does the court have apparent authority confused with implied actual authority? Consider the following comments from Restatement (Second) of Agency § 8 (1958):

> a. Apparent authority results from a manifestation by a person that another is his agent, the manifestation being made to a third person and not, as when authority is created, to the agent. It is entirely distinct from authority, either express or implied. The power to deal with third persons which results from it may, however, be identical with the power created by authority[,] as it is where the principal's statements to the third person are the same as to the agent and are similarly interpreted. On the other hand, the power may be greater or smaller than that resulting from authority. If it exists, the third person has the same rights with reference to the principal as where the agent is authorized. In the relation between principal and agent, however, apparent authority differs from authority, in that the one having it may not be a fiduciary, may have no privilege to exercise it and may not even know he has it. Although normally it results from a prior relation of principal and agent, this is not necessarily the case. . . . The rules of interpretation of apparent authority are,

however, the same as those for authority, substituting the manifestation to the third person in place of that to the agent.

  . . . .

    b. The manifestation of the principal may be made directly to a third
person, or may be made to the community, by signs, by advertising,
by authorizing the agent to state that he is authorized, or by continuously employing the agent. . . .

Do you agree with the reasoning of the court in *Nunley* as to why Ms. Merrill
also lacked apparent authority? On the other hand, do you agree with the
result? For a case in which the life insurer was held to have extended apparent
authority to a sales agent lacking actual authority to bind coverage, *see*
Rickborn v. Liberty Life Insurance Co., 321 S.C. 291, 468 S.E.2d 292 (1996).

    3. *What about Vanguard?* Why didn't Nunley's original request for insur-
ance survive so that Merrill's attempt to place coverage with Vanguard
through the Pearl River agency actually result in an effective contract of fire
insurance? The court said that Nunley did not apply for insurance on April
2, 1984, but was there any time limit on the application that he made with
Merrill either in November 1983 or February 1984? Neither Nunley or Merrill,
much less Pearl River or Vanguard, knew that a fire loss had already taken
place when Merrill called Pearl River; is this enough to meet the fortuity
requirement?

    4. *Authority created by ratification or estoppel.* Although there in fact may
be no actual or apparent authority, agency authority may be recognized or
created in other ways. For example, A may be bound by the unauthorized acts
of B if A, with full knowledge of the facts, chooses to approve and adopt, i.e.,
ratify, the acts of B. For discussion of this possibility in the insurance context,
see Fuller v. Eastern Fire & Casualty Insurance Co., 240 S.C. 75, 124 S.E.2d
602 (1962); *A.I. Credit Corp. v. Providence Washington Insurance Co.*, 96 Civ.
7955 (AGS), 1998 U.S. Dist. LEXIS 17102, at *1 (S.D.N.Y. Oct. 29, 1998). In
addition, an insurer may be estopped to deny a principal-agency relationship
under some circumstances even though there is no actual or apparent
authority created in the agent. See Restatement (Second) of Agency § 8B
(1958).

    5. *Authority depending on type of insurance.* The type of insurance often
dictates the scope of authority of agents who market the insurance for
insurers. Life insurers exercise considerable home office control because their
contracts are typically for long periods of time, the danger of adverse selection
is more acute, and the insurer may not cancel the policy unilaterally. Unlike
health insurers who can contract around adverse selection problems by
excluding preexisting illnesses and related conditions, the object of the life
insurance contract—a type of "all risk" insurance against premature death—
makes it more difficult to deal with this problem by contract. Thus, life
insurers usually use soliciting agents who are authorized to do only what the
name implies—to solicit applications from prospective insureds. The applications do not constitute contracts of insurance, but technically are offers to buy
insurance from the insurers. This marketing technique allows the insurer to
employ underwriting standards that tend to be much more individualized as

far as the particular company is concerned due to competition and other factors. This calls for greater centralization of underwriting control in the home office as compared to other forms of insurance.

Property and casualty insurance, by way of contrast, involve contracts for a much shorter period, six months being typical for personal auto insurance and one year for a homeowners policy. Also, the insurer is not faced with a book of business that it will have to live with for the indefinite future. The adverse selection problem, although it exists, is not as severe as in life insurance. There are incentives against illegally destroying one's property for gain and subjecting oneself to personal injury that do not exist where a person discovers a terminal illness or other serious risk to life and would like to provide life insurance for loved ones. It also is the case that the need for immediate coverage generally is much more acute for the subjects of property and casualty insurance, and the causation problems are much more easily dealt with under this type of contract than in life insurance contracts. In addition, there is usually a provision for unilaterally canceling a property and casualty contract within a certain period of time if the home office disapproves. Finally, property and casualty insurers use much more objective rating factors, and less discretion is exercised in the decision to insure. Thus, agents for property and casualty insurers typically are empowered with much broader authority to bind their respective principals and routinely enter contracts with prospective insureds that provide immediate coverage prior to submitting the applications to the home office.

6. *Authority created by statute.* A principal-agent relationship may also be the product of legislation. A classic example of this occurred around the end of the nineteenth century. Prior to this time, few states attempted to regulate the relationship between those who represented insurance companies and consumers. Consequently, as the courts began to impose the law of agency on these relationships, the insurers responded with disclaimers in their applications and policies aimed at negating the legal responsibilities imposed by judicial decisions. As one court explained:

> The courts long ago decided [to apply] to the relation between the insurance companies and their agents the well-settled rule of agency that all acts performed and all knowledge acquired by an agent in the conduct of the business of his agency are the acts and knowledge of the principal. After this doctrine had been established, the insurance companies, in order to evade it and escape liability for the acts and knowledge of their agents in the due prosecution of the business of their agencies, inserted in their applications and policies a provision to the effect that the persons soliciting or taking the application should be deemed the agent of the insured, and not of the insurer. . . .

New York Life Insurance Co. v. Russell, 77 F. 94, 105 (8th Cir. 1896). The contractual provisions resulted in insurers being able to shield themselves from acts of those who were, all except in name, their agents. As usually happens when things become so lopsided, this led to cases of hardship and injustice, and eventually to legislation when a number of states enacted statutes establishing a statutory standard of agency that could not be altered by an insurance policy or application. *See Continental Ins. Co. v. Chamberlin,* 132 U.S. 304 (1889).

Many states still have statutes that provide that any person who transacts specified kinds of insurance business — such as soliciting or procuring an application for life insurance—for a company shall in all matters relating to the application and the policy issued in consequence thereof be regarded as the agent of the insurer. *See Almerico v. RLI Insurance Co.,* 716 So. 2d 775 (Fla. 1998) (discussing requirements to create statutory agent under Florida law); *Paulson v. Western Life Insurance Co.,* 292 Or. 38, 636 P.2d 935 (1981).

7. *Dual agency.* A person can be an agent for two persons at the same time so long as the fact of the dual agency is revealed to both principals and they consent. *Anfinsen Plastic Molding Co. v. Konen,* 68 Ill. App. 3d 355, 386 N.E.2d 108 (1979). *See also Etheridge v. Atlantic Mutual Insurance Co.,* 480 A.2d 1341 (R.I. 1984). Insurance brokers (including the so-called "independent agent") have actual authority from multiple insurers, although the actual authority is likely to be more limited than with agents who represent one company exclusively. Note, too, that the intermediary can be an agent for both the insured and the insurer. To the extent the intermediary is an agent for the insured, acts by the intermediary cannot be imputed to the insurer. *See, e.g., General Accident Insurance Co. of Am. v. American National Fireproofing, Inc.,* 716 A.2d 751 (R.I. 1998).

8. *Brokers.* An insurance broker is a person who solicits and negotiates contracts of insurance and, in the trade, is normally thought of as the agent of the insured. This is true even though the broker is compensated through a commission from the insurer. While this is still the case in England, *see, e.g., Edinburgh Assur. Co. v. R.L. Burns Corp.,* 479 F. Supp. 138 (C.D. Cal. 1979), a number of American jurisdictions have passed statutes declaring that under certain circumstances a broker is the agent of the insurer, *see, e.g., Fryar v. Employers Insurance of Wausau,* 94 N.M. 77, 607 P.2d 615 (1980).

9. *Problem.* Assume that Smith calls on Jones in an attempt to have Jones complete an application for life insurance to be submitted to the Heavenly Insurance Company. In the process of completing the application, Smith reads Jones the questions and fills in the answers as Jones responds. One question inquires if the applicant has sought medical treatment in the past five years. Jones says he went to the doctor twice in the last year for back pain. The doctor prescribed some medicine which he takes regularly and he gets along "pretty well." Smith says that is not what the question is getting at and that the ailment has to be serious. Smith then writes in "no" for the answer. Upon completing the application, Smith tells Jones that the insurance will take effect upon the date Jones signs the application if Jones submits the first year's premium at the time the application is mailed to the home office. Jones signs the application and pays the premium. The application, however, clearly states that no insurance will be in force unless and until the application is approved at the home office and the policy is delivered to the applicant while in good health. In fact, the only authority possessed by Smith is to solicit applications on behalf of Heavenly, which the latter will consider but has no obligation to approve. As it turns out, Jones has pancreatic cancer and dies before the home office passes on the application.

If the common law regarding principal-agent relationships governs, is Heavenly bound by the acts of Smith so that it has to pay the benefits under the policy applied for? *See Ellingwood v. N.N. Investors Life Insurance Co.,* 805 P.2d 70 (N.M. 1991).

How would you analyze the problem if Smith were acting as an agent for Jones, i.e., if Smith were a broker or so-called "independent agent"? *See St. Paul Surplus Lines Insurance Co. v. Feingold & Feingold Insurance Agency, Inc.,* 427 Mass. 372, 693 N.E.2d 669 (1998).

10. *Conditional receipts.* In an attempt to compete more favorably in the market for prospective insureds, many life insurers have come to use conditional receipts. These vary in language with the particular company, but the type described in footnote 1 of *Caldwell* is not uncommon. The soliciting agent is authorized under certain circumstances to bind the insurer to coverage through the use of this type of receipt. However, as explained, this usually results only in temporary insurance while the home office considers the applicant for a permanent policy. There are other types of conditional receipts that are more problematic because they do not clearly provide interim coverage. These will be examined more closely in connection with *Grandpre v. Northwestern National Life Insurance Co.,* 261 N.W.2d 804 (S.D. 1977), which is taken up in § 7.02[1][b], *infra.*

11. *Caveat I: The facts of the case matter.* All of this is what one generally would expect to find when dealing with agents who sell the respective types of insurance. Of course, there are exceptions, and, in the final analysis, the authority of the agent is limited by the power delegated or other action taken by the principal, unless modified by statute. As in any occupation or profession, neither competence nor ethical behavior is spread evenly among its members. Given the fact that there are thousands of agents operating under different types of authority and that they do all kinds of things, within and without their express authority, insurance marketing has been a fertile ground for litigation. In fact, the issues raised in this section are anything but atypical.

12. *Caveat II: The implications of the Internet.* At 2000, the Internet is having a noticeable impact on how insurance products are marketed. Some insurers have direct sales through the Internet, many web sites provide insurance quotes, and many brokers are using the web to gain new customers. As a percentage of transactions, web-based insurance marketing is in its infancy, but some of the pioneers in this field predict that within ten years as much as 80 percent of personal insurance and 60 percent of small-business commercial insurance will be purchased on-line. See Lisa S. Howard, *Internet Reshaping U.S. Insurance Sales,* Nat'l Underwriter (Prop.-Cas.), Aug. 7, 2000, at 13. A fair prediction is that courts and regulators will seek to apply existing legal principles to this new environment. How this will work remains to be seen; stay tuned.

[2]   Agency Problems in Group Insurance

PAULSON v. WESTERN LIFE INSURANCE CO.
292 Or. 38, 636 P.2d 935 (1981)

Peterson, Justice.

The rapid growth of group insurance in the United States has given rise to a number of cases in which the principal issue is whether the employer-policyholder, in the administration of the policy, is the agent of the insurer, of the insured worker, or the agent of neither. That issue, among others, is involved in this case.

The Facts

Roof & Floor Components, Inc., (hereinafter referred to as "employer" or as "policyholder") is a Salem concern that, in 1974, applied to the defendant for a "group insurance policy" that would provide its employees life insurance benefits, hospital expense benefits, supplemental accident expense benefits, and major medical expense benefits. The policy was issued and became effective on February 7, 1974. It provided for optional coverage of a worker's spouse and specified unmarried children.

The plan covered different classes of employees. A Class I employee qualified for personal coverage and dependents coverage without proof of insurability if application for coverage was made within 30 days following the first day of employment. Plaintiff was a Class I employee. Defendant issued a brochure, which the plaintiff never saw prior to the dispute which gave rise to this case, but which is nonetheless relevant. It provided:

> "When you enroll for benefits for your eligible dependents more than 31 days after you are initially eligible, it is necessary that satisfactory evidence of insurability be furnished to the insurance company. Benefits will be effective when approved by the insurance company. You will be notified as to the effective date."
>
> " . . . .
>
> "If you enroll when initially eligible, merely complete an enrollment form authorizing necessary salary/payroll deduction and return it to your supervisor."
>
> "Should you wish to enroll more than 31 days after your initial eligibility date for benefits on your eligible dependents, it is necessary that evidence of insurability satisfactory to the insurance company be furnished. Special forms are available for this purpose. Benefits for you and your dependents will be effective when approved by the insurance company."[2]

---

[2] The brochure contained a provision to the effect that the brochure was "not a part of the insurance contract. Your coverage is fully explained by your certificate. You should read it carefully and then place it in the pocket at the back of this booklet for safekeeping."

Reference is made to the brochure because it, more than the policy itself, sets forth the legal effect of the policy in understandable terms. The brochure also reflects the insurer's opinion as to the legal effect of the policy and it also sets forth some policy practices which, as will be seen below, are relevant.

The brochure also contained provisions relating to the duties of the insurer and the employer:

"The Insurance Company will perform the following functions:

1. Maintain records of all employees and dependents insured by the program.

2. Determine the eligibility of individual claimants for receipt of benefits.

3. Process claims for benefits.

4. Authorize the payment of benefits.

5. Make payments of benefits to beneficiaries.

6. Make determination on appeal of claim denials.

"The Plan administrator [the employer] will perform the following functions:

1. Receive and remit contributions for the program.

2. Maintain records of all employees and dependents insured.

3. Select the Insurance Carrier."

The insurance policy contained these provisions:

"Data Required from Policyholder [the employer]: The policyholder shall furnish periodically to the Company such information relative to individuals becoming insured, changes in amounts of insurance, and terminations of insurance as the Company may require for the administration of the insurance under this policy. The Company shall have the right to inspect any records of the Policyholder which relate to the insurance under this policy at any reasonable time.

"Clerical Error: The Policyholder's failure, due to clerical error, to report the name of any individual who has qualified for insurance under this policy or to report the name of any individual whose classification has been changed shall not deprive such individual of insurance under this policy or affect the amount of insurance to which he is entitled; nor shall the Policyholder's failure to report the termination of insurance for any individual continue such insurance beyond the date of termination determined in accordance with the provisions of this policy."

The insurer provided the employer with enrollment forms and claim forms which, as necessary, were given to the employees by the employer. Claim forms, after they were filled out, were normally mailed to the insurer by the employee.

The plaintiff came to work for the employer on June 23, 1976. His medical insurance then in effect—with another carrier—remained effective until October 1, 1976. Prior to going to work for the employer, he talked to the owner of the business, a Mr. Largest, about the company health insurance. Mr. Largest told the plaintiff that he could elect coverage for himself and for his dependents any time in the first six months of employment without any evidence of insurability required. Paulson therefore decided to keep his other coverage in effect "until it ran out" and then apply for coverage with the employer's carrier. Accordingly, on September 1, 1976, he received and filled out an application for coverage which was sent to the defendant, with appropriate premiums.

On November 3, 1976, the defendant wrote to the employer advising the employer that because the application was not made ". . . within the eligibility period as specified in your policy, evidence of insurability is required." A form was enclosed for Mr. Paulson to execute and return.

After this letter was received, Mr. Largest went "back and forth for about two weeks" with the company's agent, without resolution of the matter. Plaintiff was then advised of the problem. At about the same time, plaintiff's daughter became ill, and he incurred substantial medical expenses to treat the illness. The plaintiff's claim for payment of these medical expenses was denied on the ground that the policy was not in effect.

The plaintiff thereafter filed this action against the defendant, alleging that on September 1, 1976, the defendant entered into an insurance contract with the plaintiff which, on November 25, 1976, was ". . . in effect or should have been in effect." The defendant filed an answer admitting its corporate status and denying the remainder of the plaintiff's complaint. The answer also contained an affirmative defense, which is not otherwise relevant to this opinion. The plaintiff's reply denied the affirmative allegations of the defendant's answer, and affirmatively alleged that plaintiff had relied upon the "statements by the Plaintiff's employer," and that the defendant was estopped from denying coverage.

On trial, at the conclusion of all the evidence, the defendant moved for a directed verdict on several grounds, one being that ". . . Largest was not acting as [the insurer's] agent . . . and the court should rule as a matter of law that he was not. . . ."

. . . . After extended argument, the trial court granted the defendant's motion for directed verdict, saying:

> "The evidence shows me that the acts of the employer, in this case, Mr. Largest, are nothing more than keeping a supply of application forms, claim forms, brochures, withholding premiums and terminating coverage when the employment ceases and such. It is merely ministerial and nothing indicates to me that Mr. Largest was given any authority, apparent or actual, to actually represent the insurance company as agent in any respect."

The Court of Appeals, 47 Or. App. 376, 613 P.2d 1115 in a two-line per curiam opinion, affirmed, citing *Bowes v. Lakeside Industries, Inc.*, 297 Minn. 86, 209 N.W.2d 900 (1973).

"Insurer-Administered Plans" Vis-à-Vis "Employer-Administered Plans"

The defendant asserts:

> "The majority rule is that the employer-master policyholder is not the agent of the insurer in a group insurance context. *Boseman v. Connecticut General Life Ins. Co.*, 301 U.S. 196, 57 S. Ct. 686, 81 L. Ed. 1036 (1937); *Duvall [Duval] v. Metropolitan Life Ins. Co.*, 82 N.H.

543, 136 A. 400, 50 A.L.R. 1276 (1927). This longstanding rule is still the majority rule. . . ."

Many courts and commentators also discuss cases such as this in terms of a "majority rule" and "minority rule." See cases cited and discussion in D. Gregg, *Group Insurance: Agency Characterization of the Master Policy-holder*, 46 Wash. L. Rev. 377 (1971), and R. Borst, *Group Policyholder as Agent of Insurer or Group Member*, Vol. 14, No. 2, Federation of Insurance Counsel Quarterly 11 (1963). Our analysis of the decisions convinces us that many courts, even though they purport to apply a "majority rule" or a "minority rule," actually base their decision upon the facts relating to the division of functions between the insurer and the employer-policyholder, and that any "majority" or "minority" rule is more apparent than real. It is more correct to say that when the plan is exclusively administered by the insurer, as a matter of law no agency relationship exists between the insurer and the employer. But if the employer performs all of the administration of the policy, an agency relationship exists between the insurer and the employer, as a matter of law. Between these two extremes, as the division of functions becomes less separate, or to put it another way, as the employer assumes responsibility for more administrative or sales functions which are customarily performed by an insurer, a question of fact will arise as to the agency relationship between the insurer and the employer. A comparison of two decisions illustrates the point.

Elfstrom v. New York Life Ins. Co., 67 Cal. 2d 503, 63 Cal. Rptr. 35, 432 P.2d 731 (1967), is often cited as representing the minority view. In that case, one Elfstrom was the president and majority stockholder of a corporation. His daughter, a student, had worked for the corporation on a part-time basis. Before leaving on an extended trip, Elfstrom instructed his bookkeeper, Mrs. Still, "to be sure that Brenda was covered." Brenda was then going to college. At the request of Mrs. Still, Brenda signed an enrollment card, Mrs. Still filled in the blanks, and reported to the defendant that Brenda was added as an insured under the group policy.

One of the eligibility requirements of the defendant's policy was that the employee work at least 32 hours a week, and that the employee had completed six months of continuous employment as an eligible employee. Brenda met neither requirement, but she was unaware of any attempt to misrepresent her status to the insurer.

Shortly thereafter, Brenda died of aplastic anemia, and the defendant denied coverage. Her beneficiaries sued the insurer, claiming that Mrs. Still was the insurer's agent. The opinion of the California Supreme Court contains an extensive discussion of the growth and development of group insurance, the purposes of group insurance, and the administration of group insurance. The opinion described employer-administered plans and insurer-administered plans as follows:

"The administration of a group policy may be handled either by the insurer itself on the basis of information furnished to it by the employer or, as in the present case, by the employer. If the insurer administers the policy, the employer periodically submits to the insurer the names of its employees and other information relevant to coverage. The preparation of accounting records and changes of beneficiary, as well as other details are handled in the insurer's offices. Ordinarily, an employee who becomes eligible for insurance is required to sign an acceptance card authorizing payroll deductions and indicating his choice of beneficiary. The company then sets up an accounting record for the employee and prepares his certificate of insurance. Other duties of administration include the termination of an employee's insurance upon notice from the employer, adjustment of benefits and premiums as the employee's classification changes, and the recording of changes of beneficiaries. [Citing authorities.]

"Under an employer-administered plan the employer performs these functions, sometimes resulting in a saving in premiums. The only records regularly exchanged between the employer and the insurer are those pertaining to the calculation and payment of premiums, usually in terms of the number of lives insured, the amount of insurance in force, and specification of changes. These functions are performed by the employer under the direction of the insurance company, which ordinarily provides service visits by a representative to check on the administration of the plan, examine the employer's records, lend assistance to the employer in improving administrative practices, and promote the enrollment of additional employees in the plan. [Citing authorities.]" 63 Cal. Rptr. 35, 432 P.2d at 735–736.

Justice Mosk, the writer of the opinion, referred to the two lines of authority, stating that they were "hopelessly in conflict" (63 Cal. Rptr. 35, 432 P.2d at 736). The court held, as a matter of law, that the employer was the agent of the insurer in administering the group insurance policy because the employer performed virtually all of the tasks incident to the administration of the policy, under the supervision of the insurer. As to the defendant's assertion that the employer was the agent of the employee, the court said:

"The most persuasive rationale for adopting the view that the employer acts as the agent of the insurer, however, is that the employee has no knowledge of or control over the employer's actions in handling the policy or its administration. An agency relationship is based upon consent by one person that another shall act in his behalf and be subject to his control. (*Edwards v. Freeman* (1949) 34 Cal. 2d 589, 592, 212 P.2d 883.) It is clear from the evidence regarding procedural techniques here that the insurer-employer relationship meets this agency test with regard to the administration of the policy, whereas that between the employer and its employees fails to reflect true agency. The insurer directs the performance of the employer's administrative acts, and if these duties are not undertaken properly the insurer is in a position to exercise more constricted control over the employer's conduct." 63 Cal. Rptr. 35, 432 P.2d at 738. (Footnotes omitted.)

The case cited by the Court of Appeals, *Bowes v. Lakeside Industries, Inc.*, 297 Minn. 86, 209 N.W.2d 900 (1973), typifies the type of case often cited as representative of the majority rule. In that case one Bowes was the employer's (*Lakeside*) national sales manager. During the period of time he was so employed, he was covered by the company's group health and life insurance program issued by the defendant California Life Insurance Company. Bowes left the company to form his own company to act as sales representative for 19 toy manufacturers, including his previous employer.

The group life insurance issued by California Life to Lakeside required, as a condition of eligibility, that the employee be a "full-time employee." When Bowes left Lakeside, he said he wished to continue his insurance coverage. Lakeside's personnel director agreed that there was still a close relationship, and that there would be "no problem in continuing his coverage so long as he [Bowes] was willing to pay the full amount of the premiums." 209 N.W.2d at 901. Bowes did so, thereafter died, and California Life refused to pay benefits to Bowes' widow.

The plaintiff sued California Life, contending that Lakeside was its agent to administer the group policy, and was therefore bound by Lakeside's declaration that Bowes was eligible for coverage. As to this, the Minnesota court held:

> ". . . We are aware of a developing trend, best exemplified by *Elfstrom v. New York Life Ins. Co.,* 67 Cal. 2d 503, 63 Cal. Rptr. 35, 432 P.2d 731 (1967), recognizing that group insurance policies may be employer-administered as distinguished from insurer-administered, in which case the employer may be deemed to act as agent for the insurer. The instant case, however, does not invite adoption or adaptation of the *Elfstrom* doctrine. The insurance policy considered in *Elfstrom* was deemed 'employer-administered' because the insurer had delegated extensive duties to the employer, including enrolling employees, adding and deleting dependents, terminating and reinstating insurance, reporting details of coverage, indicating the amounts of premiums paid, issuing certificates of insurance, and determining eligibility for coverage. The California Life-Lakeside policy, as the trial court in effect found, was 'insurer-administered' because Lakeside, the named 'policyholder,' had only the limited function of supplying data as to the persons within the insured group and remitting premiums for their coverage. Lakeside's records were subject to examination by the insurer, and all other records were maintained by the insurer.
>
> "The crucial determination made by the employer in *Elfstrom* was that an unquestioned employee was 'full-time' within the meaning of the policy arrangements. The more basic question in the instant case was whether the so-called employee was an employee at all. Lakeside's action in undertaking to accommodate Bowes' desire for continuance of inexpensive group life insurance benefits was contrary to the plain terms of the policy *and patently adverse to the interests of the insurer which the asserted agent is supposed to represent.* Important to both the contractual claim against California Life and the fraud claim against Lakeside is the found fact that both Bowes and Segal of Lakeside understood, as well they should, that Bowes' insurable status was doubtful and that the insurer, not the insured, would ultimately make the determination." (Footnote omitted; emphasis added.) 209 N.W.2d at 901–902.

The Minnesota court held, as a matter of law, that the employer was not the agent of the carrier because the program was "insurer-administered," and because the employer ". . . had only the limited function of supplying data . . . and remitting premiums." 209 N.W.2d at 902.

It appears to us that *Elfstrom* and *Bowes* are neither inconsistent with each other nor do they reflect the application of different rules. Rather, they reflect the application of this rule: In the performance of a function delegated by the insurer to the employer, the employer is deemed to be the agent of the insurer.

In *Bowes,* the insurer was held not liable because the employer's designated responsibilities did not include the determination of coverage of employees. In *Elfstrom,* however, the court held the insurer liable because the employer had been expressly charged with the performance of the function of enrolling eligible employees ". . . under the direction of an agent of [the insurer]." 63 Cal. Rptr. 35, 432 P.2d at 736.

The essence of the plaintiff's claim herein is that Largest told him that he had six months within which to qualify for coverage for himself and his dependents without proof of insurability; that he relied upon Largest statements and deferred filing his application for coverage; that had he known the true facts, he would have applied for and been issued coverage for himself and his dependents without proof of insurability, which insurance would have been in effect at the time of his daughter's illness.

In the normal two-party insurance transaction, the insurer performs a variety of tasks such as solicitation of the insured, which often includes discussions with the potential insured as to cost of coverage, the benefits, the exclusions, insurability, and other aspects of the insurance policy; the delivery of an application for insurance, sometimes involving assistance with the preparation of the application itself; the processing of the application; the issuance of the insurance policy or certificate of insurance; collecting premiums; and processing claims, including the delivery of claim forms and the handling of the claim after receipt.

By the defendant's express admission in its brochure, some of these tasks were to be performed by the employer, including the receipt and remittance of contributions for the program, and maintenance of records of all insured employees and dependents. Although the contract between the insurer and the employer is silent as to such things as enrollment forms, claim forms, and the like, there is evidence that the insurer expected the employer to distribute application forms to the employees, to receive and forward the application forms to the carrier, and to deliver claim forms to the employees. In this case, when the carrier wrote to the employer regarding the plaintiff's coverage, the insurer relied upon the employer to assist in obtaining evidence of insurability.

The policy itself contains provisions respecting the employer's responsibility, which include periodically furnishing "such information relative to individuals becoming insured . . . as the company may require for the administration of the insurance under this policy." In addition, the policy expressly provides that the insurer remains liable for the employer's errors, in specified respects.

The plaintiff asserts that there is evidence to support a finding that the employer was the agent of the insurer for other purposes, as well—that if the employer is given the responsibility to deliver application forms to the employees, it is not unlikely that the employee might have questions as to the coverage, particularly when the brochure was not given to the employee at the time the application was delivered. We agree. The trier of fact could well find that the employee reasonably believed that the employer was authorized to answer such questions. See Restatement of Agency (Second) 32, § 8, and *Elfstrom v. New York Life Ins. Co., supra,* 63 Cal. Rptr. 35, 432 P.2d at 738.[3] We very much doubt that the insurer would deny that the employer had no right to correctly answer questions regarding the coverage. If true representations are within the employer's authority or apparent authority, in the absence of notice to the employee, the trier of fact could hold the insurer responsible for innocent misrepresentations made by the employer, such as were apparently made in this case. Restatement of Agency (Second) 384, § 162.

In *Beeson v. Hegstad,* 199 Or. 325, 330, 261 P.2d 381 (1953), it is stated that "[i]t is elementary that express authority given an agent to do certain things carries with it the implied authority to do all other things reasonably incident to and necessary for carrying out the objectives of the agency." The evidence shows that the employer had express authority to perform specified acts, and the defendant, in its policy, expressly made itself liable for the employer's failure to perform some of those acts. In addition, the evidence shows that the employer had other responsibilities in the administration of the program. If an employer is charged with the performance of functions incident to the administration or sales of insurance which are commonly performed by the insurer, it is proper to say that the employer is the insurer's agent for those purposes. If there are other functions for which the employer has no responsibility it is equally logical to say that the employer is not the insurer's agent for those purposes.

Here there is evidence, both direct and indirect, that the employer performed some functions incident to the initiation of coverage by employees, which duties included the distribution, receipt and forwarding of applications for insurance and was expressly charged by the insurer with responsibility for ". . . [furnishing] to the Company . . . information relative to individuals becoming insured . . . ." Specific limitations on the employer's duties and responsibilities are not set forth in the policy.

We cannot say, as a matter of law, that the authority to distribute enrollment forms, applications, and claim forms did not carry with it the implied authority to answer questions regarding deadlines for filing such forms. Nor can we say, as a matter of law, that it was unreasonable for the plaintiff to

---

[3] Compare this language from *Elfstrom v. New York Life Ins. Co.,* 67 Cal. 2d 503, 63 Cal. Rptr. 35, 432 P.2d 731, 738 (1967):

"The most persuasive rationale for adopting the view that the employer acts as the agent of the insurer, however, is that the employee has no knowledge of or control over the employer's actions in handling the policy or its administration. An agency relationship is based upon consent by one person that another shall act in his behalf and be subject to his control. . . .

". . . Nevertheless, it would be inconsistent with the actual relationship of the parties and would do violence to the traditional concept of agency to hold that the employees rather than the insurer control and direct the employer's acts in administering a policy of group insurance. . . ."

look to Mr. Largest for such information. The trial court erred in directing a verdict for defendant.

. . . .

Reversed and remanded to the trial court for trial.

[The dissenting opinion of Justice Tanzer is omitted.]

NOTES

1. *Unique nature of group insurance.* Group insurance contracts present some unique problems as to agent and principal relations, as *Paulson* illustrates. This is because there is a third actor in addition to the usual two. The group representative contracts for the benefits, but is not the insured. The insureds, on the other hand, usually have little to say about the package of benefits and even less to say about how the program is to be administered. At the same time, the insurer depends on the group representative to do certain things in order to achieve the marketing efficiency and other cost savings that make group insurance so attractive. It is obvious that the group representative occupies a position that may have a negative as well as a positive impact on both the insurer and the insureds. Should traditional principal-agent rules apply? For a recent treatment of the issue (with citations to other authorities), *see Middleton v. Russell Group,* 126 N.C. App. 1, 483 S.E.2d 727 (1997).

2. *Dual role of group representative.* Is it conceivable that under the same group arrangement the group representative—for example, an employer— could be the agent of the insureds for some purposes and the agent of the insurer for other purposes? Assume that an employer represents to some of its employees that the group policy provides $1 million in coverage for inpatient psychiatric care when the policy, in fact, limits psychiatric benefits to $10,000. As a result of this representation, a number of employees enroll in the group program. Is there anything about the nature of this situation that would lead you to say that the representations of the employer should or should not be binding on the group insurer? What if, in another case, the employer loses the enrollment card of an employee who signs up for group health insurance and the employee's name is never transmitted to the group insurer as an enrollee. The employee contracts AIDS before the error is discovered, and the open enrollment period has expired. Is the nature of this problem different from that in the first case? Does it call for different treatment? How would these cases be resolved under the reasoning in *Paulson?* Are you satisfied that the *Paulson* approach is the best one, or is there a better way?

3. *Clerical errors.* Is the "Clerical Error" provision in the group contract in *Paulson* broad enough to adequately protect against all group representative mistakes? Is there any better way to protect against the inevitable errors and mistakes of employers that are bound to occur occasionally in effecting and terminating coverage for employees? How about a provision in the master contract that would place the responsibility for inadvertent errors on the

insurer? Should this type of provision also include the type of "error" where the group representative mistakenly misrepresents some aspect of coverage under the group contract? Try your hand at drafting such a provision and then *see All States Life Insurance Co. v. Tillman,* 226 Ala. 245, 146 So. 393 (1933).

4. *A problem of interpretation.* Suppose the policy of employer-provided group life insurance states that "notice of the claims can be submitted at the Insurer's office or to any authorized agent of the Insurer." The policy also states that the notice must be submitted no later than 31 days after the death of the covered employee. On the last day on which a claim can be submitted, the beneficiary of a deceased certificate holder submits a claim to the employer's office. The employer forwards the claim to the insurer, where it arrives two days later. Is the notice timely? *See Golt v. Aetna Life Insurance Co., No.* 99-459, 2000 Mont. LEXIS 161, at *1 (Mont. June 13, 2000).

5. *Competency to contract for insurance.* The authority or power of a prospective insured to enter into a contract of insurance is seldom questioned. However, some people, such as minors, do labor under disabilities. Thus, a number of states have adopted statutes that remove the disability of minors above a certain age to enter into contracts of life insurance. Compare the following statutes:

a. *Arizona Revised Statutes* (1999)

§ 20-1106. Capacity to contract for insurance; minors

A. Any person of competent legal capacity may contract for insurance.

B. A minor not less than fifteen years of age as of his nearest birthday may, notwithstanding his minority, contract for life or disability insurance on his own life or body, for his own benefit or for the benefit of his father or mother, spouse, child, brother, sister or grandparents. The minor shall, notwithstanding his minority, be deemed competent to exercise all rights and powers with respect to or under any contract of life or disability insurance on his own life or body, as though of full legal age, and may surrender his interest therein and give a valid discharge for any benefit accruing or money payable thereunder. The minor shall not, by reason of his minority, be entitled to rescind, avoid or repudiate the contract, nor to rescind, avoid or repudiate any exercise of a right or privilege thereunder, except that the minor, not otherwise emancipated, shall not be bound by any unperformed agreement to pay, by promissory note or otherwise, any premium on such an insurance contract.

b. *McKinney's Consolidated New York Insurance Laws Annotated* (McKinney 1985)

§ 3207. Life insurance contracts by or for the benefit of minors; on the lives of minors, limitations on amount

(a) A minor above the age of fourteen years and six months shall be deemed competent to enter into a contract for, be the owner of, and exercise all rights relating to, a policy of life insurance upon the life of the minor or upon the life of any person in whom the minor has an insurable interest, but the beneficiary of such policy may be only the minor or the parent, spouse, brother, sister, child or grandparent of the minor.

. . . .

Which statute do you prefer?

§ 7.02 Effecting Coverage

[1] Binders, Conditional Receipts, and Good Health Provisions

[a] Property and Casualty Insurance

STATEWIDE INSURANCE CORP. v. DEWAR
143 Ariz. 553, 694 P.2d 1167 (1984)

FELDMAN, JUSTICE.

Robert and Irene Dewar (Dewar) petition for review of a judgment entered in a declaratory judgment action in which Statewide Insurance Company (Statewide) sought an adjudication that Loren Desotell (Desotell) was not covered for damages which he had inflicted upon Dewar in an automobile accident. The trial court entered summary judgment against Dewar; the court of appeals affirmed by majority opinion. *Statewide Insurance Corporation v. Dewar*, 143 Ariz. 576, 694 P.2d 1190 (1983). We granted review to settle the narrow issue of whether a binder for automobile liability insurance covers the prospective insured for an accident occurring between the time coverage is bound and the application for insurance is rejected . . . .

FACTS

On February 18, 1977 Desotell met with Reuben Frank, an agent of Statewide, to purchase automobile insurance. Desotell and Frank had not done business before. Desotell completed an application for insurance on a standard form prepared by Statewide. The application states in bold face type in the upper right hand corner that

> [u]nless otherwise agreed, insurance will become effective at 12:01 a.m. of day following date of postmark[.] Application will not be accepted for coverage bound unless complete in every detail and signed.

Desotell completed and signed the application. He gave Frank a check for $67.00—the premium for the first two months of the policy. Frank bound coverage as of 1:30 p.m. on February 18, 1977 and so noted in the lower left corner of the application. The parties had no discussion with regard to the terms on which the check was given by Desotell and accepted by Frank. In his affidavit Frank stated that he "presumed the check would be paid when presented to the bank" and that he and Desotell "had no agreements as to when or in what manner to negotiate the check." The only writing evidencing the check transaction is the combination of application and binder. It contains no language concerning the mode of payment, nor does it condition the existence of coverage under the binder in any way.

Desotell's check was presented to his bank for payment on February 22, 1977, the next banking day. Desotell claims that on that date he had $1,400 in his checking account. However, this balance consisted primarily of checks drawn on out-of-town banks and these had not yet cleared. The bank dishonored Desotell's check and returned it to Statewide with the notation "uncollected funds." Statewide received the notice of dishonor on February 28, 1977 and sent the following note to Desotell:

> The check for your automobile insurance with our company is returned herewith. This check was uncollectable from the bank, who (sic) returned it to us marked "insufficient funds".[1]

> It is now impossible for us to issue automobile insurance for you and must ask that you contact your agent, Reuben E. Frank, . . . if other arrangements are necessary.

On March 1st Desotell and Dewar were involved in the automobile accident in which Irene Dewar was injured. On either March 2nd or March 3rd Desotell received the message quoted above.

Mrs. Dewar evidently sustained serious injuries; her medical expenses allegedly exceed $30,000. Dewar sued Desotell; Statewide disclaimed coverage for Desotell, leaving him "uninsured" with respect to the Dewar claim. Dewars made a claim under the uninsured motorist provisions of their insurance policy and were paid $15,000 by their insurer, Continental Casualty Co. As subrogee, and in Dewar's name, Continental brought an action against Desotell for recovery of the uninsured motorist payment. *See* A.R.S. § 20-259.01(G). Desotell claimed that he was covered by Statewide with respect to this action, and the declaratory judgment action by Statewide against Desotell and Dewar followed.

The present argument, at least in part, is between the two insurers. Having paid $15,000 under its uninsured motorist coverage, Continental argues that Statewide should have paid the loss under the binder for liability coverage issued to Desotell. All parties acknowledge that the liability policy for which

---

[1] It should be noted at this point that, as established by the affidavit of an officer of the bank, there is a significant difference between "uncollected funds" and "insufficient funds." Desotell's check was returned to Statewide marked "uncollected funds," not "insufficient funds," as was indicated in Statewide's notice of 2/28/77. The notation "uncollected funds" means that funds have been deposited in the account but that the bank has not yet collected the funds. The notation "insufficient funds" means "that there are inadequate funds in the relevant account to cover the check." The significance of this distinction, as noted in an affidavit of record, is that the usual process followed where checks are not honored because of "uncollected funds" is resubmittal of the check to the bank rather than return to payor.

There is nothing in the record, nor any allegation by Statewide, that Desotell knowingly or intentionally paid the $67.00 premium with a check which he knew or suspected would not be honored by the bank. On the record before us and the trial court, this is not a case in which the named insured attempted to obtain insurance without paying the premium, and Statewide has made no allegation to that effect.

Desotell applied was not issued, so that if there is coverage by Statewide it can be based only on the binder. Two issues are raised by the facts. The first is whether the binder went into effect or whether it was void because dishonor of the check was either a failure of consideration or a condition subsequent. If the binder did go into effect, the second issue is whether the coverage bound was terminated prior to the time of the accident.

Both sides moved for summary judgment. Both sides agreed that there was no disputed issue of fact. Each claims that it was entitled to judgment as a matter of law. The trial court found for Statewide. In pertinent part, its judgment reads as follows:

> The document issued by . . . Statewide . . . was an application for insurance on behalf of defendant Loren J. Desotell;

> That automobile liability insurance coverages insuring the said defendant Loren J. Desotell did not go into effect until payment of the required premium;

> That payment of the required premium was never made; . . .

Dewar appealed. Conceding that Desotell's policy had never been issued and that coverage under that policy never went into effect, Dewar argued, nevertheless, that coverage had been effected under the binder issued at the time the check for the premium payment on the policy was delivered to the agent. Dewar contends that such coverage did not terminate until the day after the accident, when Desotell received the message from Statewide informing him of the dishonor of the check and consequent rejection of his application for insurance. The majority of the court of appeals rejected this reasoning and stated "that when the check is dishonored there is a failure of consideration, relieving the other party from liability . . . ." 143 Ariz. at 577–578, 694 P.2d at 1191–92. Characterizing Dewar's argument as "a rather ingenuous legal theory [relating] to some imagined 'special' law pertaining to insurance binder contracts" (*id.* at 578, 694 P.2d at 1192), the court held that where the agent has "required the actual present payment of the premium as consideration for the extension of binder coverage" (*id.* at 579, 694 P.2d at 1193) neither the binder coverage nor the policy coverage goes into effect until the payment required has actually been made. We do not disagree with this portion of the court's legal analysis, but find it inapplicable to the uncontroverted facts of this case.

Nature of a Binder

Binders have been referred to as contingently accepted applications for insurance. *Turner v. Worth Ins. Co.,* 106 Ariz. 132, 134, 472 P.2d 1, 3 (1970). A binder is simply a contract made in contemplation of the issuance of a later, formal agreement of insurance. The binder incorporates by implication all the terms of the policy to be issued. *Id.* at 133, 472 P.2d at 2. Thus, the binder is a contract of temporary insurance, effective as of the date agreed upon by the parties, issued and in effect pending investigation of the risk and until a formal policy is written. *Id.* Consideration for the binder is the insured's promise to purchase the policy. No other or independent consideration is required, *although, of course, parties may agree on conditions* for issuance of the binder. *Rutherford v. John O'Lexey's Boat & Yacht Ins.,* 118 Ariz. 380, 576 P.2d 1380 (App. 1980); 12A Appleman, *Insurance Law and Practice,* § 7228, at 154–55 (1981). As a matter of public policy, however, the insurer is not allowed to make the binder effective only on the condition that the policy is subsequently issued, since this would place the insurer in a position to destroy the utility of the binder by refusing to issue the formal policy when it discovers that a loss has occurred while the binder was supposedly in effect. *Turner v. Worth,* 106 Ariz. at 536, 472 P.2d at 5; *Rutherford v. John O'Lexey's,* 118 Ariz. at 382, 576 P.2d at 1382.

Turner and *Rutherford* are worth comparing. In *Turner,* the parties expressed an intent that the binder issue as temporary insurance and we held that such intent could not be nullified by the insurer's argument of an unexpressed, implied condition permitting it to later nullify the binder by refusing to issue the permanent policy. 106 Ariz. at 136, 472 P.2d at 5. In *Rutherford,* there was an agreement that the binder be issued on the explicit condition that the insured post his application and check on the next business day. 118 Ariz. at 382, 576 P.2d at 1382. Both cases, therefore, stand for the well-recognized proposition that binders are separate contracts of temporary insurance and come into effect in accordance with the intent of the parties. This, indeed, is one area of the law of insurance where the law has always recognized that the expressed intent of the parties governs and the "deal is dickered."[2]

With these principles in mind, we turn to the facts of the case at bench. The affidavit indicated that Frank "presumed" that the check would be good and that the insurance would be effective on that condition. On the other hand, it was Desotell's "understanding" that he had immediate coverage under the binder and he had funds in the bank. There was no discussion of the check nor any statement made with respect to whether the giving and acceptance of the check would constitute payment of the premium and discharge the debt (leaving the creditor only with the right to secure payment of the check), or whether the giving of the check was a conditional payment, becoming absolute upon the check being honored. *See* H. Bailey, *Brady on Bank Checks,* § 4.4 at 4–9 (5th Ed. 1979). The agent stated in this supplemental affidavit that the issuance of the binder pending the writing of the policy was "predicated upon [the] check in payment of the [policy] premium due being good." However, this was not the deal which the agent made with the insured, nor the intent expressed in the papers the agent prepared at the time of the transaction. The only thing expressed at the time of the transaction was the agent's notation, in his own handwriting, that the binder would be effective as of 1:30 p.m., February 18. At best for the insurer, the affidavit indicates only that the agent had an *unexpressed* understanding different from that which he wrote at the time of the transaction. The affidavits, carefully avoid stating that the agent manifested his "presumption" or his "predicate" for issuing the binder by expressing it in any way. We do not believe that unexpressed intent of either party may be given effect over their expressed

---

[2] One reason for this, no doubt, is that a binder is usually issued orally or in memo form. The law implies adoption of the "usual clauses." 12A *Appleman, supra,* § 7232. What is in controversy usually is existence, effective date, or limits — all matters of specific contract rather than standardized forms.

intent. The rule is that "it is not the undisclosed intent of the parties with which we are concerned, but the outward manifestations of their assent." *Isaak v. Massachusetts Indemnity Life Ins. Co.,* 127 Ariz. 581, 584, 623 P.2d 11, 14 (1981). The parties here did make an outward manifestation of their intent. The portion of the application concerning the effective date of the binder was not a printed provision in a previously prepared form. It was, rather, a blank to be filled in. That blank, filled in by Statewide's agent, explicitly provided that coverage would be bound and go into effect immediately.[3] There is no indication here that the parties bargained for a different deal or had agreed upon a different effective date. In the absence of such evidence the expressed intent of the parties should govern. *Isaak v. Massachusetts, supra.* Upon completion of the form, the insured would have left the office justifiably assuming he was bound and covered pending consideration of his application for issuance of the permanent policy. If the insurer had intended to make the effective date of the binder conditioned upon the check being honored or upon any other event, it should not have made the binder effective immediately or should have provided for some condition in the binder. *Cullotta v. Kemper Corp.,* 78 Ill. 2d 25, 31, 34 Ill. Dec. 306, 309, 397 N.E.2d 1372, 1375 (1979); *Dairyland Ins. Co. v. Kankelberg,* 368 F. Supp. 996, 998 (D.C. Or. 1973); *Bartleman v. Humphrey,* 441 S.W.2d 335, 343 (Mo. 1969).

Bartleman, supra, is instructive. It holds that the insurer has the right to treat the check as conditional payment, making the insurance effective immediately, or to make issuance and effectiveness of the binder conditional on the check being paid. The intent of the parties in this respect is controlling. *Id.* at 343–44. In *Kankelberg, supra,* the policy to be issued contained an express provision conditioning the effectiveness of the insurance on the payment of the premium, but the binder provided for immediate coverage. The court held that the insurance granted by the binder came into existence and was effective, even though the check was later dishonored because payment was stopped.

Cullotta, supra, discusses three lines of authority. One, which it describes as a majority, holds that the check issued for payment of the premium acts as an absolute satisfaction of the obligation to pay the premium, leaving the policy effective and the insurer free to pursue its remedies under negotiable instruments law. *Id.* 78 Ill. 2d at 29, 34 Ill. Dec. at 308, 397 N.E.2d at 1374. Some courts "have focused on the question of whether the insurer intended the acceptance of the check to be absolute or conditional." A third rule views the "determinative issue as one of waiver" if it is "found that the insurer intended to accept the premium check as absolute payment." *Id.*

---

[3] The provision appears as follows:

I warrant this information to be true and correct, and understand that the company is relying thereon in rating and issuance of this policy. I understand that misrepresentation on my part will void the proposed insurance contract. I have read the foregoing statement and declare it to be true. It is the responsibility of the agent to be certain that this application is received by Statewide.

APPLICANTS SIGNATURE

AGENTS SIGNATURE

COVERAGE BOUND

DATE 2/8 TIME 1:30 PM

PREMIUM FINANCE CONTRACT ON REVERSE SIDE

The result under both approaches is that, absent fraud on the part of the insured, once the insurer accepts the check without evidencing an intent to do so conditionally, it can no longer exercise its right to declare the policy lapsed due to nonpayment, even though the check is later dishonored.

Id. at 29–30, 34 Ill. Dec. at 308–09, 397 N.E.2d at 1374–75 (emphasis supplied).

Thus, the cases do not turn upon the attempt of the judge to read the minds of the parties and determine what they must have meant with regard to the effective date of insurance in those cases where payment of the policy premium is demanded at the time the binder is issued, and where that payment is made by check. Rather, the cases turn, as they should, on the expressed intent of the parties with regard to the effective date of the binder. The agent's unexpressed presumptions cannot be used to contradict the plain meaning of what was expressed and agreed upon. *Turner v. Worth, supra.* Here, the parties did agree upon an effective date for the binder, though not for the policy. The agreement was not set forth in some pre-printed form which was neither read nor understood. It was, rather, written into a blank provided for that purpose. In the absence of any claim of mistake or fraud, we must assume that the parties meant just what they said, that the coverage bound would be effective as of 1:30 p.m. on February 18, 1977. By agreement, Desotell had insurance as of that moment. By decisional law (*Turner v. Worth Ins. Co., supra*), and by statute (A.R.S. § 20-1120(B)), the binder would terminate on the issuance of the policy.

Upon dishonor of the check given for the policy premium, Statewide had several options. First, it could have presented the check again for payment; second, it could have proceeded to issue the policy and enforced the insured's promise to pay by action on the check. *See* A.R.S. § 44–2550. Finally, it could have refused the application for insurance and cancelled coverage under the binder—retaining the right to collect for any temporary coverage that it had already extended under the binder. It cannot contend that no insurance ever existed under the binder. *Dairyland Ins. Co. v. Kankelberg,* 368 F. Supp. at 998. We hold, therefore, that coverage under the binder became effective in accordance with the terms contained therein and was not voided *ab initio* when the check was later dishonored.[4]

---

[4] In reaching this decision we do not create a "special law" of contracts pertaining to insurance binders as feared by the court of appeals. The same fundamental law of contracts applies to both binders and insurance policies. We simply recognize that the binder and the policy are two different contracts. One is a contract for temporary insurance and the other is the contract for permanent insurance. This distinction is recognized by case law and statute. *See* A.R.S. § 20–1120 and § 28–1170. A.R.S. § 20–1120 distinguishes the binder from the policy and states that the binder shall not be valid beyond the date on which the policy is issued. A.R.S. § 28–1170 requires that a binder ". . . issued pending the issuance of a motor vehicle liability policy shall be deemed to fulfill the requirements for such a policy." A.R.S. § 28-1170(K). *See also Greene v. Commercial Union Ins. Co.,* 136 Ga. App. 346, 347–48, 221 S.E.2d 479, 481 (1975). Because we resolve the issue of effectiveness on a contract basis, according to the expressed intent of the parties, we need not reach issues which may be raised under the financial responsibility laws.

When Was Notice of Termination Effective

Statewide's notice of rejection of the application for insurance was mailed to Desotell the day before the accident and received by him the day after that accident. Under A.R.S. 20-1120(B), a binder terminates on issuance of the policy applied for or within ninety days, whichever is sooner. By decisional law, the general rule is that a rejection of the application for insurance terminates the binder. This is because the binder is temporary insurance granted until the company acts upon the application. 12A Appleman, *supra*, § 7227 at 145–151. It is also generally recognized that the notice of rejection or refusal, with its implicit termination of the binder, is effective only when received by the insured. *State Farm Mutual Auto Ins. Co. v. Collins*, 75 Ga. App. 335, 341, 43 S.E.2d 277, 282 (1947); *Smith v. Westland Life Ins. Co.*, 15 Cal. 3d 111, 121, 123 Cal. Rptr. 649, 656, 539 P.2d 433, 440 (1975) (life insurance); Annot., *Temporary Automobile Insurance*, 12 A.L.R.3d 1306 (1967). We adopt this principle, which seems generally recognized in the cases, as the law of Arizona. Any other rule would either leave the insurer with an unacceptable risk for up to ninety days or leave the expectant insured unaware that his application has been rejected and that he is driving while uninsured. Such a situation would be contrary to the principles which we expressed in *Schecter v. Killingsworth*, 93 Ariz. 273, 280 n. 3, 380 P.2d 136, 141 n. 3 (1963).

Resolving the notice issue on these grounds, we need not examine the interplay between A.R.S. § 20-1631, which limits the grounds for which an insurer can cancel or fail to renew a policy which has been in effect for sixty days; A.R.S. § 20-1632, which specifically addresses the issue of notice to insureds and contains no distinction between ordinary policies and binders; and A.R.S. § 28-1170(K), which states that "[a] binder issued pending the issuance of a motor vehicle liability policy shall be deemed to fulfill the requirements for such a policy."

We hold, therefore, that because Desotell had not yet received notice that his application had been rejected, the binder which went into effect on the date set forth in the application was still in effect at the time of the accident. Desotell was insured by Statewide at that time for the agreed limits of the binder. The terms of coverage were those terms customarily contained in Statewide policies.

The trial court erred in granting summary judgment to Statewide and denying summary judgment to Dewar. The judgment of the trial court is reversed, the opinion of the court of appeals is vacated and the cause is remanded to the superior court for further proceedings consistent with this opinion.

GORDON, V.C.J., and HAYS and CAMERON, JJ., concur.

HOLOHAN, CHIEF JUSTICE, dissenting.

It seems basic to me that people must pay for what they purchase whether it be goods, automobiles, or insurance. A check given in payment of goods is accepted with the expectation that the check will be honored by the bank. Our commercial code recognizes that payment by check is conditioned and does not act as payment unless honored by the bank. A.R.S. § 44-2359.

The court's opinion adopts a line of authority which holds that payment for insurance is different from the usual transaction and different rules apply.

The majority opinion of the Court of Appeals in this case appears to me to present the more sensible legal position. I adopt the opinion of the majority in the Court of Appeals and dissent from the opinion of this court.

The opinion of this court has not advanced any sound policy reason against treating payment by check as a conditional payment which voids a binder or insurance policy if the check is dishonored by the bank.

The acceptance of a check as conditional payment does no violence to the concept of insurance protection. The honoring of the check is a condition subsequent to the creation of the insurance contract. The majority in this court recognizes the legality of conditions subsequent in an insurance binder when it cites with approval *Rutherford v. John O'Lexey's Boat & Yacht Ins., Ltd.,* 118 Ariz. 380, 576 P.2d 1380 (App. 1978). The insurance binder in *Rutherford* was effective provided the insured submitted a completed application on July 9. The insured had an accident on July 8, and he failed to submit the completed application on the 9th. The denial of coverage by the insurance company was upheld.

It seems consistent to hold that the insurance policy in this case was subject to the condition subsequent that the insured's check in payment be honored by his bank.

The majority in this court rely mainly on two cases. *Bartleman v. Humphrey,* 441 S.W.2d 335 (Mo. 1969), and *Cullotta v. Kemper Corp.,* 78 Ill. 2d 25, 34 Ill. Dec. 306, 397 N.E.2d 1372 (1979). Although a federal district court case is also cited, I doubt that the majority means to place much reliance on a decision by a federal trial court. In any event, the cited cases support the proposition that the classification of the acceptance of a check as absolute or conditional payment is determined according to the facts and circumstances surrounding the transaction and is a question of fact to be determined by the trier of fact.

Unfortunately, the majority in this case ignores its cited cases and proceeds to decide the disputed issues in the case. The fact that the binder had an effective date was found to be conclusive proof that the check was not accepted conditionally.

In both *Bartleman* and *Cullotta* an insurance policy had been issued in each instance and checks processed as cash premiums, but those courts held that proof of the insurer's intent at time of acceptance is an issue to be submitted to the trier of fact. The rule in Arizona has been that even if the facts of a case are not in dispute, the inferences to be drawn from those facts may be in dispute. If different inferences can be drawn from the facts, the issues may not be resolved by summary judgment, and the issues must be submitted to the trier of fact.

The evidence presented by the insurance company was that the transaction involved an application for insurance for a two month period. The applicant was not a regular customer, and there was no intention to extend credit to him. Payment was required for the entire two month policy. The affidavit of the agent handling the transaction was to the effect that the applicant, not being a regular customer, was given a binder pending issuance of the policy "predicated upon his check in payment of the premium due being good upon presentation to his bank." In light of these facts it appears to me that different conclusions could be reached from a consideration of all the facts, and this court, following its cited authority, should have remanded the case for trial.

NOTES

1. *Current practice of binding coverage.* The *Dewars* case illustrates the current practice of property and casualty insurers to "bind" or effect coverage on a temporary basis while the application for a policy to cover the standard time period, for example six months or one year, is reviewed by those having authority to issue such policies.

2. *Oral binders.* At one time it was not uncommon for certain types of insurers to bind coverage orally. Of course, this assumes that the insurance agent is authorized to bind the insurer through an oral agreement. *See Gulbrandson v. Empire Mutual Insurance Co.,* 251 Minn. 387, 87 N.W.2d 850 (1958); *Parks v. State Farm General Insurance Co.,* 231 Ga. App. 26, 497 S.E.2d 575 (1998). Some insurers still employ such practices. Should the law treat oral binders for temporary coverage differently from oral agreements to insure generally? Would your answer depend on the type of insurance involved?

3. *Validity of oral contracts of insurance.* Absent a statutory prohibition or a limitation in the charter of the insurer, oral contracts of insurance are enforceable as a general rule at common law. *Whitehall v. Commonwealth Casualty Co.,* 125 Neb. 16, 248 N.W. 692 (1933). Statutory prohibitions are not common, but where they exist they tend to apply to permanent contracts of life and health and accident insurance. *See, e.g., First Protection Life Insurance Co. v. Compton,* 335 S.E.2d 262 (Va. 1985). Why would there be legislative prohibitions on these types of contracts and not on others such as property and casualty insurance? Also, why would a legislature prohibit oral permanent contracts but not oral temporary contracts or binders?

For there to be a valid oral contract of insurance, there must be a sufficient designation of the insurer by the agent. If the agent is a company agent (an employee of the insurer) and writes for only one insurer, there is little problem as to designation. However, if the agent is an independent agent and writes for more than one company, an appropriate overt act or manifestation by the agent to place the coverage with a particular company is indispensable. *See Julien v. Spring Lake Park Agency, Inc.,* 283 Minn. 101, 166 N.W.2d 355 (1969), 35 A.L.R.3d 815 (1971); *Milwaukee Bedding Co. v. Graebner,* 182 Wis. 171, 196 N.W. 533 (1923).

In addition to a sufficient designation, there must be agreement on enough particulars as to the coverage for there to be an effective contract, oral or written. Many of the details may be supplied in the policy form, rate book, and other sources which the parties clearly intend to incorporate into the agreement. *First Protection Life Insurance Co. v. Compton,* 335 S.E.2d 262 (Va. 1985). But there are cases where the necessary elements are sufficiently lacking for there to be a valid contract. *See Young v. White,* 551 S.W.2d 12 (Ky. App. 1977).

4. *Mandated coverages versus mandated offerings.* Many jurisdictions now require motor vehicle owners to carry liability insurance with certain minimum limits for bodily injury and property damage. Some of these jurisdictions also mandate that uninsured motorist coverage, up to the minimum bodily injury limits for third-party liability, be included in the policy. Others only require that the uninsured motorist coverage be offered, with the insured having the option to decline it or to select lower limits. With regard to underinsured motorist coverage, the statutes usually follow the latter pattern—it has to be offered, but it may be rejected. The same requirement to offer, with the option to reject, may apply to coverage in excess of the minimum limits for uninsured motorist coverage. In the remaining jurisdictions, uninsured and underinsured motorist coverages are purely optional in the same way one may choose to either buy or not buy medical payments, physical damage, or towing coverage. See generally Robert H. Jerry, II, Understanding Insurance Law § 134 (2d ed. 1996).

The question of exactly what coverages are included in an oral contract of insurance may become more complicated where a statute mandates that certain coverages be offered to an insured with the insured having the option to reject. For example, what if Dick calls his insurance agent and requests that the latter orally bind coverage on his new motorcycle. Dick says he wants the required liability coverages, and physical damage coverages. Agent agrees to do so, but tells Dick to come by as soon as he can to complete and sign an application for a permanent policy. In the meantime, Dick's wife, Beth, is injured by an underinsured motorist while she is riding the motorcycle. The insurer with which coverage is bound admits that there might be underinsured motorist coverage in effect if the agent had not offered Dick the option of buying it when he came to complete the application, but denies that any such coverage exists under the oral binder. Assuming that the statute requiring that underinsured motorist coverage be offered merely says that such coverage is to be offered when a motor vehicle policy is "delivered or issued for delivery in this state," if you represented the insurer, what arguments could you make? *See Anderson v. Vrahnos,* 149 Ill. App. 3d 251, 500 N.E.2d 110 (1986).

[b] Life Insurance

GRANDPRE v. NORTHWESTERN NATIONAL LIFE INSURANCE CO.
261 N.W.2d 804 (S.D. 1977)

MORGAN, JUSTICE (on reassignment).

The plaintiff appeals from a judgment for the defendant after a trial to the court in an action which she brought as beneficiary to recover upon a temporary contract of life insurance upon her husband's life. We affirm.

The case was submitted to the trial court on stipulated facts and therefore we review the same by our own reading of the stipulated facts without any presumption that the trial court saw or heard the witnesses. The facts as stipulated establish that on March 13, 1970, Elwood N. Caufield, an agent for defendant, and Glen Scott, a broker for defendant, went to the Stanley E. Grandpre (Grandpre) residence near Conde, South Dakota, and solicited an application for insurance. At that time, Grandpre (age 54) completed an application for a $10,000 life insurance policy; gave Caufield a check for $43.71, which represented the full initial premium for the policy applied for and executed a Master Account Plan Request and Agreement. In return, Grandpre received a premium deposit receipt and was advised by Caufield that a physical examination would be required to complete the application. Caufield made arrangements for a physical examination of Grandpre by Dr. Saxton, which took place at the Huron Clinic in Huron, South Dakota, on March 18. Defendant received Dr. Saxton's report on March 20. After examining the report, defendant's underwriting department requested more information from Dr. Lenz (also of the Huron Clinic) who had taken an electrocardiogram of Grandpre in 1968. The information from Dr. Lenz was received on April 3, 1970, and was sent on to one of defendant's staff physicians for review. The staff physician discovered minor irregularities and he recommended that a current electrocardiogram be obtained for examination by a heart specialist.

In the meantime, defendant ordered and received on April 2, 1970, a Retail Credit Report which stated that Grandpre was "presently hospitalized in St. John's Hospital in Huron, South Dakota, as he reportedly had a stroke on March 29, 1970, about 11 o'clock at night." He was rushed to the hospital and wasn't expected to survive as "known to local sources." The defendant immediately mailed a request for a medical history of Grandpre to St. John's Hospital.

Defendant received a medical report on Grandpre directly from St. John's Hospital on April 9, 1970. The report revealed prior hospitalizations in July 1967 and March 1968, for "GI hemorrhage, probably duodenal ulcer" and in October 1968, for "upper GI hemorrhage." Because of Grandpre's ulcer history, defendant determined that he was not insurable on a standard basis and Grandpre's application was declined on Friday, April 10, 1970. On April 13, defendant issued a draft for $43.71, which represented a return of the premium deposit. On April 14, defendant wrote to Caufield declining Stanley Grandpre's application, enclosing the draft. On April 15, Caufield telephoned defendant's underwriting department to communicate the fact that Stanley Grandpre had died on April 9, 1970. On May 5, 1970, Caufield attempted to deliver defendant's draft to plaintiff who refused to accept. On May 14, 1970, defendant mailed the draft to plaintiff, but plaintiff has not cashed it.

Appellant urges that the deposit receipt provided coverage from the date of the application (the completion of the medical exam as per No. 3) unless the coverage was actually rejected (notice sent and received) prior to the date of the decedent's death (assignments of error Nos. 2 and 3).

Both parties agree that the condition as set out in the deposit receipt was a condition subsequent and the trial court so held.

The issue we must decide is whether a contract of insurance arose immediately upon receipt by defendant of the premium and completion of the required medical examination of Grandpre, subject to the right of defendant to terminate the agreement by notification to the applicant during his lifetime if it concluded that Grandpre was not an insurable risk, as appellant contends, or whether the premium deposit receipt created a contract of insurance to become effective as of the date of application only after the respondent insurance company determined Grandpre satisfied the condition of being an insurable risk, as a condition subsequent which if not satisfied would void retroactively all previous temporary coverage.

The determination of this issue turns on the interpretation of the language of the premium deposit receipt. It should be noted that due to the uniqueness and variation of each insurance company's conditional receipt or binder, the precedent evolved from this case may well be limited.

The conditional receipt is a sales device instituted by the life insurance industry whereby a life insurance company would warrant coverage upon payment of the initial life insurance premium at the time of application and the satisfaction of various conditions precedent to coverage. These conditions may include insurability, actual acceptance by the company and delivery and receipt of the policy. The purpose of this sales device was to correct the disadvantageous situation that was present due to the necessary interval between the time a policy of insurance is applied for and the time it is issued. A lack of coverage during this interval before issuance of the policy, which may extend for days or weeks, is disadvantageous to the applicant in that he may suffer an illness or accident that will make him uninsurable. It is also disadvantageous to the insurer in that the insurance company runs the risk that the applicant may change his mind and buy from a competitor or may decline insurance altogether, in either event it incurs a net loss for the expenses of investigating and processing the application. The conditional receipt remedies these problems by requiring an initial premium which is usually forfeited if the applicant revokes his desire for the insurance while the company is determining the insurability of the applicant. It also usually provides temporary insurance to the applicant while the company is determining the applicant's insurability and consequently, any subsequent change in the applicant's condition (i.e., death or his becoming uninsurable) will not result in lack of coverage if the company has determined that he was insurable *at the time of the application.* (emphasis added)

The premium deposit receipt that Grandpre received is similar to that of a conditional receipt as stated above. After stating that payment had been received from Grandpre "as premium deposit for proposed insurance," the frontside of the receipt also contained the following language: "IMPORTANT: This receipt does not provide any insurance until after its conditions are met." (see Appendix A) The terms and conditions on the back of the receipt provided that if (1) the full initial premium is paid, (2) any required physical examination is completed, and (3) the company is satisfied that the applicant is an insurable risk under the company's rules and standards for the policy, the policy would become effective as of the application date, which was defined as "the latest of the date of Part I, the date of Part II, or the date of completion of the last of all medical examinations required, if any." (see Appendix B)

The receipt here in question would be classified as the type generally referred to as the "insurable" type rather than approval type. As stated in *Cliborn v. Lincoln Natl. Ins. Co.,* 332 F.2d 645 (10th Cir. 1964) the "insurable" type is usually interpreted as providing:

That the insurance would be in force if at the date the application is completed, the applicant be in good health, *be a risk acceptable under the company rules on the plan of insurance applied for and at the rate of premium paid.* (emphasis added)

Since the application is not subject to the approval or acceptance by the company as provided in the "approval" type receipt, it is not necessary to discuss the authorities considering the approval type of receipt.

The courts have generally construed conditional receipts with satisfaction provisions similar to the defendant's in one of three ways: (1) The condition of insurability must be met before any contract of insurance exists, i.e., condition precedent;[4] or (2) the condition of insurability, if not met, retroactively destroys any temporary insurance coverage which may have existed, i.e., condition subsequent (trial court's and defendant's position); or (3) temporary insurance coverage exists subject to termination by the company only upon notice to applicant. (plaintiff's position).

In support of appellant's position a number of jurisdictions have held that the conditional receipt gives rise to an interim contract of insurance, said insurance being terminable upon the company's good faith determination that the applicant is uninsurable and notification of the applicant of this decision. These decisions are usually based on the premise that the conditions as set forth in the conditional receipt are ambiguous and uncertain and therefore must be most strongly construed against the insurer, and where provisions are susceptible to different interpretations, the interpretation which will sustain the policy should be adopted. In this light those courts have adopted the interpretation of the premium deposit receipt as providing a temporary contract for life insurance immediately upon execution of the application, payment of the premium and the completion of the medical examination. Consequently, the provision in the receipt that the company be satisfied that the insured be acceptable at the date of the application creates only a right of the insurer to terminate the contract if the company becomes dissatisfied with the risk before a permanent policy is issued or a loss incurred.[5] Accepting this interpretation, the insurance company would be liable for they did not terminate the policy until after the applicant had died and thus had not given the applicant personal notice of termination.

However, that is not the case in this situation. The trial court found and we agree, that the language within the premium receipt is not ambiguous. This court has held that a contract of insurance is to be construed liberally in favor of insured and strictly against the insurer only when the language of the contract is ambiguous and susceptible of more than one interpretation. Thus, the insurance contract's language must be construed according to its plain and ordinary meaning. It does not permit the court to make a forced

---

[4] We will not discuss the condition precedent question any further since as previously mentioned both parties and the trial court have addressed the conditional receipt as a condition subsequent.

[5] *Toevs v. Western Farm Bureau Life Ins. Co.,* 1971, 94 Idaho 151, 483 P.2d 682; *Service v. Pyramid Life Ins. Co.,* 1968, 201 Kan. 196, 440 P.2d 944; *Jones v. John Hancock Mutual Life Insurance Co.,* 416 F.2d 829 (6th Cir. 1969); *Metropolitan Life Insurance Co. v. Wood,* 302 F.2d 802 (9th Cir. 1962); *Ransom v. The Penn Mutual Life Ins. Co.,* 1954, 43 Cal. 2d 420, 274 P.2d 633; *Gaunt v. John Hancock Mutual Life Ins. Co.,* 160 F.2d 599 (2d Cir. 1947).

construction or a new contract for the parties. There is stated on the front of the receipt in boldface letters "IMPORTANT: This receipt does *NOT* provide any insurance until after its conditions are met." (emphasis added). We feel that the plain and ordinary meaning of the words involved in the conditions would alert any ordinary person to understand what had to be completed before the temporary or interim insurance would be effective. Even the fact that the conditions of the receipt were on the back of the form has not persuaded courts to find such terms and receipts ambiguous.

Since we can find no ambiguity in the receipts, we apply a strict contractual construction in holding that the receipt clearly means that a contract of insurance is to be effective as of the date that the applicant signed the application, paid the premium deposit, or completed the physical examination, whichever occurred later, conditioned however upon the subsequent finding by the insurer of the applicant's insurability as of such date. This interpretation means that, if and when the company has made a good faith determination that the condition has not been satisfied and the applicant is uninsurable, this determination would retroactively defeat all previous existing temporary insurance coverage, i.e., insurability is a condition subsequent. We feel that this construction clearly expresses the intention of the parties.

The insurance company is not receiving a premium without assuming any risk. It is assuming the risk that if something unrelated to insurability had happened to Grandpre subsequent to the application date and regardless of whether the company accepted or rejected the policy, the insurance company would be liable if Grandpre had been insurable at the date of application, as defined. The insurance industry is a risk industry, operated on a supposedly sound actuarial basis. The conditions that must be met to attain insurance coverage were reasonable and were very clearly stated in the receipt. We cannot expect the insurers to write their contracts in the language of children's primers, "see the dog run, run dog run" style.

The obvious advantage that the applicant acquired was that if the insurance company made a determination that he was insurable at the date of the application, he would be covered during the interim period in case something would happen to his health.[11]

With respect to the question of insurability at the date of application it is important to notice that the receipt specifically provided:

> . . . shall be satisfied that each person proposed for insurance under the policy applied for was on the Application Date insurable under the Company's rules and standards for the policy in the amount and on the form applied for and for the premium specified in Part I.

This type of clause has usually been interpreted to mean the applicant must meet an objective standard of insurability, and that this standard is the company's own standard for the plan, the amount and the benefits applied for

---

[11] Other advantages that would accrue to the applicant would be: (1) The insurable applicant who dies prior to the completion of the company's evaluation of the application is protected; (2) the policy would sooner become incontestable; (3) the policy would earlier reach maturity with corresponding acceleration of dividends and cash surrender; (4) if the insured's birthday was between "completion" and "approval" the premium would be computed at a lower rate; (5) when the policy covers disability, the coverage dates from "completion."

and at the rate applied for. Based on this standard of insurability, Grandpre, at the time of application, was not insurable. Affidavits by the company officers and the stipulation of facts, point No. 8 show that the application was made on the standard basis but, because of Grandpre's ulcer history, defendant had determined that he was not insurable on a standard basis. Counsel for the plaintiff had stipulated to this fact. The company had a right to decline issuance of policy even though applicant may have been eligible for different or rated policy.

This is not to say that the insurer's officers could defeat the applicant's right to temporary insurance by arbitrarily refusing to form an opinion of the applicant's insurability until after applicant's death. They must prove at trial that at the commencement of interim coverage they had determined that applicant was an uninsurable risk in the amount and form applied for. It must be shown that the determination by the officers of the applicant's insurability at the time of his application must have been made in good faith and was not an arbitrary act. If a reasonably prudent and careful officer, acting in good faith, would on available evidence find that applicant was insurable for the type of insurance applied for, that insurance policy would be effective from the application date, thus allowing the insurance proceeds to go to the beneficiary. In examining the record we find that the insurer proceeded expeditiously and in good faith in determining that Grandpre was uninsurable in the amount and form applied for. The ulcer condition did not happen subsequent to the application date and therefore would have necessitated a change from the policy applied for.

We distinguish this case from *Duerksen v. Brookings Life & Casualty,* 84 S.D. 20, 166 N.W.2d 567 (1969) in which this Court held that the period of effective insurance was from the date the policy is accepted by the company, not the date of application, even though in that case the policy was back dated to the date of application. In the instant case the policy specifically states:

> insurance under the terms and conditions of each policy applied for shall become effective *as of the application date* regardless of the occurrence after the application date of death or change of insurability
>
> . . . .

A literal reading of Grandpre's policy demonstrates that the policy is effective at the application date, whereas, in *Duerksen* there is no mention that there was a relation back clause within the contract. In *Duerksen* the insurance company back dated the policy on their own volition. *Duerksen* can still be good law for policies that do not include within the policy a relation back clause as was found in *Grandpre.* Also, the insurance policy in *Duerksen* was of the type conditioned upon acceptance *and delivery* which stated that the insurance company would not incur any obligation or would not go into effect *until it was accepted* by the insured. Therefore, a contract of insurance did not arise until the point of acceptance in *Duerksen* by the specific contractual agreement.

We therefore affirm the holding of the trial court.

DUNN, C.J., and WOLLMAN, J., concur.

ZASTROW and PORTER, JJ., dissent.

Appendices to follow.

APPENDIX A   APPENDIX B

Detach only if deposit of the full initial premium for each policy is made at time of completion of Part I.

PREMIUM DEPOSIT RECEIPT

Received from _____, the following:

Life insurance premium deposit .... $ _____
Health insurance premium deposit .... $ _____
Total deposit .... $ _____
_____ as premium deposit for proposed insurance on _____

IMPORTANT: This Receipt does not provide any insurance until after its conditions are met.

for which Part I of an application bearing the same number as this receipt is this date made to Northwestern National Life Insurance Company, Minneapolis, Minnesota.

The terms and conditions on the other side hereof are a part of this receipt.

_____   ____, 19 __   _____
Place and Date   (over)   Agent

No 156327

IMPORTANT: This Receipt does not provide any insurance until after its conditions are met.

THE PAYMENT ACKNOWLEDGED BY THIS RECEIPT IS MADE AND RECEIVED SUBJECT TO THE FOLLOWING CONDITIONS:

(As used herein, "Application Date" shall mean "the latest of the date of Part I, the date of Part II, or the date of completion of the last of all medical examinations required, if any.")

A. (1) If the amount received by the Company's agent on the date of this receipt is the full initial premium for each policy applied for in Part I; and

(2) If the medical examinations, if any, required by the Company are completed; and

(3) If the Company at its Home Office shall be satisfied that each person proposed for insurance under the policy applied for was on the Application Date insurable under the Company's rules and standards for the policy in the amount and on the form applied for and for the premium specified in Part I;

then, but only after such conditions are met, insurance under the terms and conditions of each policy applied for shall become effective as of the Application Date regardless of the occurrence after the Application Date of death or change of insurability of any person proposed for insurance; provided, however, that the maximum amount of insurance upon the Life Proposed which may take effect under this paragraph A shall be $200,000 of life insurance and $50,000 accidental death benefit reduced by the respective amounts of ordinary life insurance and accidental death benefit (1) in force in the Company on the Application Date on the Life Proposed, and (2) applied for in the Company on the Life Proposed under an outstanding Premium Deposit Receipt bearing a lower number than this Receipt.

B. Except as provided under paragraph A above, no insurance shall take effect, including insurance in excess of the maximum limits as specified in paragraph A above, unless and until a policy or policies is issued and delivered to the Owner and the full initial premium paid, all while there has been no change in the insurability of any person proposed for insurance from the date of this application.

C. If the conditions set forth in paragraph A(1) above are met, but if 45 days after the date of this receipt any of the other conditions in paragraph A above have not been met, the application shall be deemed declined. If the Company declines to issue a policy or issues a policy other than as applied for which is not accepted, the amount paid will be refunded. There shall be no liability on account of this receipt if any check or draft is not honored upon presentation for payment by the Company. No agent is authorized to waive or modify the provisions of this receipt.

ZASTROW, JUSTICE (dissenting).

The majority holds that the premium deposit receipt is of the "insurable" type and not the "approval" type of conditional receipt. However, that interpretation ignores the very language of condition No. 3, i.e.:

> *"If the Company at its Home Office shall be satisfied* that each person proposed for insurance under the policy applied for was on the Application Date insurable under the Company's rules and standards for the policy in the amount and on the form applied for and for the premium specified in Part I; *then but only after such conditions are met,* insurance under the terms and conditions of each policy applied for shall become effective as of the Application Date regardless of the occurrence after the Application Date of death or change of insurability of any person proposed for insurance . . . ."

It is only too clear that the temporary insurance does not become effective until the company is satisfied with the proposed insured; whereupon, a policy will be issued which relates back to the application date. This is the strict construction view adopted by some jurisdictions. The rationale behind these holdings is simply that as a matter of strict contract law the language of the receipt clearly expresses the intention of the parties. Annot., 2 A.L.R.2d 987, 43 Am. Jur. 2d, Insurance, § 220-225; 44 C.J.S. Insurance § 230a(3).

However, I agree with the Nevada Supreme Court's statements in *Prudential Insurance Company of America v. Lamme,* 1967, 83 Nev. 146, 425 P.2d 346 that:

> "[A]n insurance policy is not an ordinary contract. It is a complex instrument, unilaterally prepared, and seldom understood by the assured. The same is equally true of the conditional receipt. The parties are not similarly situated. The company and its representatives are expert in the field; the applicant is not. A court should not be unaware of this reality and subordinate its significance to strict legal doctrine. (citation omitted) Nor should a court be obliged to overlook the obvious advantage to the company in obtaining payment of the premium when the application is made. It is a device to avoid the possibility that the applicant will change his mind and revoke his application, or deal with a rival company."

425 P.2d at 347.

If there was to be no contract of insurance until the company was satisfied as to the applicant's insurability, and a policy issues thereon, it would seem entirely immaterial to the insured whether the contract related back to the date of the application or not. If he lived until the application was approved and a policy issued, it would not matter whether he had been insured during the interim between the date of the application and the date of issuance of the policy. On the other hand, if he died before the application was approved and the policy issued, his beneficiary would derive no benefit from the insurance if a "rejection in good faith" is made by the company.

Though the underwriters may be aware that certain advantages exist which could justify construing the premium deposit receipt in this way, the ordinary applicant would not be aware of those advantages. As Judge Learned Hand stated in *Gaunt v. John Hancock Mutual Life Ins. Co.,* 1947, 2 Cir., 160 F.2d 599:

> "An underwriter might so understand the phrase, when read in its context, but the application was not to be submitted to underwriters; *it was to go to persons utterly unacquainted with the niceties of life insurance, who would read it colloquially. It is the understanding of such persons that counts;* and not one in a hundred would suppose that he would be covered, not 'as of the date of completion of Part B,' as the defendant promised, but only as of the date of approval. Had that been what the defendant meant, certainly it was easy to say so; and had it in addition meant to make the policy retroactive for some purposes, certainly it was easy to say that too. To demand that persons wholly unfamiliar with insurance shall spell all this out in the very teeth of the language used, is unpardonable. It does indeed some violence to the words not to make actual 'approval' always a condition, and to substitute a prospective approval, however inevitable, when the insured has died before approval. *But it does greater violence to make the insurance 'in force' only from the date of 'approval;' for the ordinary applicant who has paid his first premium and has successfully passed his physical examination, would not by the remotest chance understand the clause as leaving him uncovered until the insurer at its leisure approved the risk; he would assume that he was getting immediate coverage for his money.*"

160 F.2d at 601–602; cert. den., 331 U.S. 849, 67 S. Ct. 1736, 91 L. Ed. 1858 (emphasis supplied)

The chief objective of a relation back provision would be to enable the insurance company to collect premiums for a period during which there was in fact no insurance and, consequently, no risk.

It would appear that the majority's interpretation of the premium deposit receipt as a condition subsequent is clearly contrary to the plain meaning of the language used in the receipt. At the very least, it certainly indicates that the terms and conditions of the receipt are ambiguous.

In construing the premium deposit receipt, we keep in mind the rules of interpreting insurance contracts that any uncertainty or ambiguity must be [construed] most strongly against the insurer, and where provisions are susceptible to different interpretations, the interpretation which will sustain the policy should be adopted. Therefore, I would adopt the interpretation of the premium deposit receipt as providing a temporary contract for life insurance immediately upon execution of the application, payment of the premium and the completion of the medical examination. The provision that the company be satisfied that the insured be acceptable at the date of the application creates only a right of the insurer to terminate the contract if the company becomes dissatisfied with the risk before a permanent policy is issued.

. . . .

It would not have to be decided whether rejection would have been effective without notice to the applicant since rejection did not occur prior to his death, but, in fact, happened one day after his death. The temporary insurance contract upon Grandpre's life was still in effect at the time of his death and the insurance company is liable.

PORTER, JUSTICE (dissenting).

I would hold that defendant insurer was under a duty to explicitly inform Grandpre that he had no life insurance coverage until such time in the future as insurer, at its home office, might approve issuance of the policy applied for. . . .

When the insurer's representatives solicited Grandpre they could readily have taken his application without any advance premium. Instead, for reasons important to the company and to its financial advantage, they sought and obtained from Grandpre the sum of $43.71 and in return gave him a premium deposit receipt. Appendixes A and B. Unless otherwise informed by [an] insurer, a reasonable man in the position of Grandpre could understand that collection of this initial premium afforded him interim or temporary coverage until the insurer at some time in the future issued or declined to issue the policy. The principle of honoring reasonable expectations properly applies under these circumstances. Keeton, Insurance Law § 6.3(a) (1971). "It is important to note, however, that the principle of honoring reasonable expectations does not deny the insurer the opportunity to make an explicit qualification effective by calling it to the attention of a policyholder at the time of contracting, thereby negating surprise to him." *Keeton, supra*, at 352.

If the premium were not collected with the application, Grandpre could not reasonably understand that he was afforded interim coverage. Since it was collected, the insurer was left with the obligation to express to Grandpre the fact of his non-coverage in a manner it could reasonably expect a layman to understand. The medium chosen by insurer—its premium deposit receipt— would not be readily understood by most laymen. (Reference to the reverse side of the receipt might cause many lawyers to consider the preceding sentence an understatement.) The front side, Appendix A, is in larger type than the back side, Appendix B. The reasonable layman, observing on the front side, "IMPORTANT: This Receipt does not provide any insurance until after its conditions are met," upon turning to the reverse side would likely be unable to gain any understanding, much less a clear or explicit understanding, from the fine print conditions there. Moreover, reference on the reverse side to "Part I" and "Part II" in effect required Grandpre to consult two additional documents not placed in his possession, the completed application (Part I) and the subsequently completed doctor report of examination (Part II).

The insurer prepared all the forms used and unilaterally dictated all steps of the transaction. If under the procedure chosen by insurer, the objectively reasonable expectation of the lay applicant arising from that procedure is not to be met, the insurer should be chargeable. Thus, under the circumstances here, I would hold that insurer, as a matter of law, afforded coverage from the time of collection of the premium and delivery of the premium deposit receipt, Appendixes A and B.

I would also avoid the serious impracticalities which may well result from allowing retroactive coverage where the insurer's home office decision may not infrequently be made with knowledge that an applicant has died.

I concur in the dissenting opinion of Justice Zastrow as a further basis for reversal.

Rohde v. Massachusetts Mutual Life Ins. Co., 632 F.2d 667, 668–669 (6th Cir. 1980): "An application for life insurance is an offer to purchase a policy and the insurer must accept before a contract exists. During the time the offer is outstanding and unaccepted the applicant has the power to revoke the offer. Such revocation would not only deny the insurer the right to accept and complete a sale, but also would be likely to cause the insurer to lose the expense of processing and investigating an application.

"Insurers discourage or prevent the revocation of offers by use of conditional receipts or 'binders' that give the insurer the option of ultimately accepting or rejecting the offer while making the offer irrevocable by conditionally accepting it. The most straightforward of these binders accept the offer and, as consideration for the applicant's promise to purchase insurance, create immediate insurance for the applicant while reserving a right of the insurer to cancel all insurance after an opportunity to investigate the application.

"The more prevalent form of binder, however, seeks to make the applicant's offer irrevocable without giving the applicant interim insurance in exchange. *See* 7 *Williston on Contracts,* § 902A, pp. 197–203 (3d ed. 1963). In this form insurance is promised to begin as of the date of the application or receipt subject to the qualification that the application must first be accepted or approved before any coverage begins. With these two provisions standing side-by-side in the binder, all that the applicant actually receives in exchange for his promise to purchase is the possibility of interim insurance. If the insurer does not approve the application, then no coverage ever exists. Of course, by the time the insurer approves or rejects, it will be likely to know whether the applicant has incurred a covered loss and can exercise its option to reject. Thus, the possibility of interim coverage is largely illusory under this type of binder. Recognizing that such binders are confusing to applicants and that applicants generally would be unlikely to enter such bargains if they actually understood them, courts have tended to find that binders that condition liability on 'approval' of the insurer are ambiguous and that the parties to such contracts actually intend interim insurance as consideration for the applicants' promises to purchase insurance if the insurer approves."

NOTES

1. *Use of conditional receipts in selling life insurance.* The opinions in *Grandpre* and *Rohde* discuss two types of conditional receipts — "insurable" receipts and "approval" receipts—used by insurers that sell life insurance. According to the courts, what is the purpose of a conditional receipt?

2. *Distinguishing types of receipts.* Some insurers, as indicated in *Rohde,* use a form of receipt that clearly provides temporary insurance while the

application is pending. There is nothing conditional about it, except that it expires once the insurance applied for is either issued or disapproved. This is the intent of the parties and few issues arise. A conditional receipt, however, is quite different because there is no insurance until a particular condition or conditions are met. What conditions must be met under the two types of conditional receipts discussed in *Grandpre* and *Rohde?* Is it correct to describe the insurance that comes into existence once the condition or conditions are satisfied as temporary insurance?

3. *Benefits of conditional receipts.* What are the benefits of conditional receipts to the life insurance applicant? It should be obvious that the insurable type provides more benefits to the applicant than the approval type, but are there sufficient benefits under the approval type to justify its use by life insurers?

4. *Termination of temporary insurance created under conditional receipts.* The dissenting opinions in *Grandpre* took the position that there was temporary coverage under the conditional receipt in question until the insurer rejected the applicant, but did not decide whether notice of rejection to the applicant was required. *Prudential Insurance Co. of Am. v. Lamme,* 83 Nev. 146, 425 P.2d 346 (1967), cited by the first dissent, recognized that a conditional receipt created temporary insurance and held that it remained in effect until actual notice of rejection of the application was communicated to the applicant. Several years later, the Supreme Court of California added another condition for termination. It held that the insurer also had to tender the premium back to the applicant. *Smith v. Westland Life Insurance Co.,* 15 Cal. 3d 111, 539 P.2d 433, 123 Cal. Rptr. 649 (1974). Finally, the Supreme Court of Pennsylvania added another twist. In *Collister v. Nationwide Life Insurance Co.,* 479 Pa. 579, 388 A.2d 1346 (1978), *cert. denied,* 439 U.S. 1089 (1979), the court held that use of a conditional receipt, coupled with a premium payment, creates a temporary contract of life insurance that stays in effect until the insurer gives notice that the application has been rejected and returns the premium. Further, the court held that in those situations where the circumstances indicate that the insurer did not intend to provide interim coverage, the insurer has the burden to prove by clear and convincing evidence that the applicant had no reasonable basis for believing that she was purchasing immediate coverage. All three of these cases—*Lamme, Smith,* and *Collister*—adopted the reasonable expectations doctrine espoused by the second dissent in *Grandpre.* Does this mean that the doctrine, which was discussed in § 3.02[4], *supra,* has more appeal with respect to binders than it does with respect to the insurance policy?

5. *Insurer's defenses revisited.* If the insurer has a good defense to coverage under the policy (*e.g.,* the insured materially misrepresented facts on the application), does this defense apply with equal force to the binder? *See Riner v. Allstate Life Insurance Co.,* 131 F.3d 530 (5th Cir. 1997) (applying Texas law; insurer cannot rely on misrepresentations in application to defeat coverage under temporary receipt unless application is attached to binder). Should it?

6. *Delivery and "delivery while in good health" conditions.* Still other insurers use a receipt form that conditions coverage on delivery of the policy

to the applicant. In some instances, this type of form requires that the policy be delivered while the applicant is in good health. These requirements are an attempt to reserve on behalf of the insurer a right to reject until the last moment. Aside from the fairness issue, a requirement of "delivery" of an insurance contract has the potential of raising all the issues inherent in that condition that have arisen regarding delivery of deeds, goods, and the like. For example, *Compare Pruitt v. Great Southern Life Insurance Co.*, 202 La. 527, 12 So. 2d 261 (1942), 145 A.L.R. 1427 (1943) (requiring actual delivery) and *Wanshura v. State Farm Life Insurance Co.*, 275 N.W.2d 559 (Minn. 1978) (finding constructive delivery sufficient). As to what constitutes "good health," consider the following case.

[c] Delivery in Good Health Requirements

METROPOLITAN LIFE INSURANCE CO. v. DEVORE
66 Cal. 2d 129, 424 P.2d 321, 56 Cal. Rptr. 881 (1967),
30 A.L.R.3d 376 (1970)

Mosk, Justice.

Metropolitan Life Insurance Company (hereinafter Metropolitan) brought an action to cancel or rescind a 15-year mortgage term life insurance policy issued to Charles Devore. The complaint alleged that Metropolitan's liability was conditioned on Devore's "continued insurability" at the time the policy was delivered, that Devore was not in good health at the time of delivery and was aware of this fact, and that he had concealed material matters relating to his health in his application for insurance. Devore died after this action was filed and subsequently his widow and beneficiary of the policy, Josephine Devore, brought suit to recover death benefits. The two actions were consolidated for purposes of trial and the court, sitting without a jury, found against Metropolitan and in favor of Mrs. Devore.

On September 2, 1959, Charles Devore executed Part A of a written application for insurance. The questions in this part did not relate to his medical history. At the end of Part A, the application provided, "The Company shall incur no liability under this application until a policy has been delivered and the full first premium specified in the policy has actually been paid to and accepted by the Company during the lifetime and continued insurability of the applicant, in which case such policy shall be deemed to have taken effect as of the date of issue as recited therein. . . ."

On September 21, 1959, Devore submitted to a medical examination by a doctor of Metropolitan's choice. During the examination, the doctor filled in Parts B and C of the application. Part B, which was signed by Devore, consisted of his answers to a series of questions relating to his medical history, and Part C was the doctor's report on the physical examination given to Devore. In Part B the following questions and answers appear:

"4. Have you ever had or been treated for or sought advice concerning . . . any disease of the blood or blood vessels? [A] No.

"5. (a) Have you ever been a patient in or visited a hospital, clinic, dispensary or sanitorium for observation, examination or treatment? [A] Yes. Appendectomy 5 yrs ago. Good Samaritan hosp. Portland, Ore, Dr. Chauncey.

"(b) Have you ever had or been advised to have a surgical operation? [A] Yes. [Same as answer to (a).]

"(c) Have you ever been advised to modify or restrict your eating, drinking or living habits because of any health condition? [A] No.

"(d) Do you have periodic physical examinations or check-ups? [A] Yes—Dr. Thorner Beverly Hills.

"(e) Have you ever had an electro-cardiogram or X-ray examination or any laboratory examinations or tests? [A] Yes. 1 yr ago. Routine exam Dr. Thorner ch. X-ray EKG neg.

"(f) Have you consulted any physician, healer or other practitioner within the past 5 years for any reason not mentioned above? [A] No."

Devore's application was sent to Metropolitan's headquarters in San Francisco, and after an investigation Metropolitan discovered that Devore had a history of dyspepsia or indigestion in 1953 and a possible cardiospasm or pylorospasm in 1959 (a spasm of the muscles at the inlet or outlet of the stomach). Metropolitan asked Devore to report to its doctor again and at this interview on October 14, he stated that he had experienced occasional attacks of indigestion, that in 1952 he had been advised by a physician to refrain from eating fatty foods, and that the tests given at that time were negative.

On October 10, 1959, Devore went to Dr. Thorner, his own physician, for a routine physical examination. On that date Dr. Thorner took an electrocardiogram, which was found to be normal, but he requested Devore to return on October 19. Another electrocardiogram, taken on the 19th after exercise, showed an abnormality. The doctor diagnosed Devore's condition as arteriosclerotic heart disease, but did not convey this information to Devore. The evidence with regard to Devore's condition and his knowledge of it will be discussed in more detail hereinafter. Dr. Thorner suggested that Devore be admitted to the hospital "for rest and medication to prevent trouble" and Devore entered the hospital on October 21, 1959, remaining there until he was discharged on October 26. After his discharge, he continued under Dr. Thorner's care until he died of heart disease on January 10, 1962. Witnesses for Metropolitan testified that the company would not have issued a policy if it had known about Dr. Thorner's diagnosis and treatment of Devore's heart condition.

Metropolitan approved the issuance of a policy to Devore on November 12, 1959, and issued a policy on an "intermediate" basis, which required a higher premium than would be applicable for a man of Devore's age who was in average health. The policy was delivered to him on November 30, at which time he paid a full year's premium. He also executed a document entitled "Application Amendment," which stated in part:

"The undersigned hereby amends the application for Life insurance made to your Company on the date stated above — By changing the classification to Intermediate. By correctly stating the amount of insurance as $20,000. By requesting that the policy issued bear date of issue of September 1, 1959. By answering 'No' to Question 9 (b), Part B, reading: 'Have you during the past five years been associated with any person suffering from tuberculosis?' These amendments and declarations are to be considered as a part of the said application and subject to the agreements, covenants, and statements therein contained. The said application, together with these amendments, is to be considered as the basis of and as a part of the contract of insurance. *The said application, as amended, is correct and true, and I hereby ratify and confirm the statements therein made as of the date hereof.*" (Emphasis added.)

[The court affirmed the finding of the trial court that Devore had not concealed material matters relating to his health either in the original or the amended application for insurance. The court then went on to consider the issue of good health.]

We next reach the question whether the contract of insurance ever became effective because Metropolitan insists that when the policy was delivered on November 30, Devore was no longer insurable. It will be recalled that the application provides that Metropolitan shall incur no liability until a policy has been delivered and the premium paid during the continued insurability of the applicant.

Brubaker v. Beneficial etc. Life Ins. Co., 130 Cal. App. 2d 340, 278 P.2d 966 (1955), guides us in construing a provision of this type.[6] In *Brubaker,* the insured applied for a policy in March 1952. The application stated that the policy issued should not take effect unless and until the full first premium had been paid and the policy delivered to the insured during his "good health." The company issued a policy, which was delivered on April 11. Subsequently, it was discovered that the insured had cancer, a condition which antedated the application for and delivery of the policy. The insurance company claimed that the delivery of the policy during the good health of the insured was a condition precedent to its liability, and that this condition was not met.

The court in *Brubaker* adopted the view prevailing in a majority of jurisdictions that the insurer, having the advantage of a medical examination and dealing with an insured apparently in good health and acting in good faith, will not be permitted to avoid the contract if it should develop after delivery of the policy that the insured had actually been afflicted with serious pathology. The opinion states, "The majority of the cases . . . have taken the position that such a provision relates only to changes in the condition of the insured occurring after the making or acceptance of the application for the policy and before its date, issuance, or delivery, at least where in connection with the application there was an examination of the insured by a physician representing the insurer." (130 Cal. App. 2d at p. 345, 278 P.2d at p. 968.) The court

---

[6] Both parties cite and quote from *American Nat. Ins. Co. v. Herrera* (1963) 211 Cal. App. 2d 793, 27 Cal. Rptr. 641, but distinguish it from the present case on the ground that the rule stated there relates to a situation where the insurer does not require the applicant to submit to a medical examination. The *Herrera* case itself distinguishes *Brubaker* on this ground, and the discussion which follows will be confined to a situation in which, as here, the insurer's doctor examines the applicant prior to the issuance of the policy.

concluded that it would be unfair to hold a policy void where an insured had complied with every provision of the contract merely because, lurking undetected within his anatomy, was some pathology which would in the future prove fatal.

Metropolitan concedes that California follows the majority rule and that no difference in result here would be justified merely because the words "continued insurability" rather than "continued good health" are used in the policy.

The parties are at odds, however, regarding application of the *Brubaker* rule. Metropolitan contends that Devore's good health changed in the interval between the time he applied for the policy and its delivery, because he was diagnosed as suffering from arteriosclerotic heart disease, whereas Mrs. Devore claims that there was no change during that period because his heart disease, if any, antedated the time of application.

Metropolitan's position is sound in this instance. The "change" in the *Brubaker* rule refers to a change of the health of the insured which has manifested itself before the time of delivery. Although in that case the disease antedated the application for the policy, the court's holding was based on the fact that the seriousness of the insured's illness was not evident until after the policy had been delivered. Other cases following the majority rule also turn on the question whether the "change" in health became manifest before delivery or issuance, and factually they involved situations, like *Brubaker,* in which the insured's disease actually existed before [issuance] or delivery of the policy.

In the present case, there can be no doubt that, before delivery of the policy, Devore's doctor determined that he was suffering from arteriosclerotic heart disease. That the diagnosis indicated some change in Devore's physical condition, i.e., the manifestation of a previously latent disease, cannot be doubted.[7] However, the trial court also found that at the time the policy was delivered Devore considered himself to be in good health and had no knowledge of any condition such as would lead him or any reasonable person to believe his life or health was endangered. Metropolitan argues that the "continued insurability" clause of the policy operates to avoid liability even if Devore was not aware of any change in his health. No authority is cited except for the distinguishable cases mentioned in the margin, holding that an insurer may rely on such a provision if the insured himself is not aware that his health has materially worsened between the time of application and delivery although a stranger to the contract of insurance has acquired such knowledge.[8] One case from a jurisdiction following the majority rule involved

---

[7] We need not discuss Mrs. Devore's contention that Devore's heart condition was so mild that it could not be viewed as constituting a material change in his health. As shall appear, we conclude that the "good health" clause is applicable only where the insured himself has knowledge that his good health has been materially affected in the interim between application and delivery, and here the evidence supports the trial court's conclusion that Devore did not have such knowledge. It may also be noted that the trial court found that there was no material change in Devore's condition between application and delivery. This finding appears to be based on the fact that whatever heart disease Devore suffered from antedated the time of his application.

[8] Although Metropolitan purports to cite a number of cases for this view, they all involved jurisdictions in which the minority rule was followed, requiring the insured to actually be in good health on the day of issuance or delivery. Obviously, where this is the rule, the knowledge of the insured is immaterial.

a situation in which a physician, between the time of application and delivery, determined that the insured was suffering from heart disease but did not communicate this fact to him. (*Madsen v. Metropolitan Life Ins. Co.* (1959) 90 R.I. 176, 156 A.2d 203.) It was there held that the insurer could not rely on a "good health" provision because the *insured* had no knowledge of his heart ailment prior to the time the policy was delivered.

It is clear from the reasoning employed in *Brubaker* that the purpose of the majority rule is to prevent the insurer from relying on the "good health" provision where an applicant for insurance believes in good faith that he is healthy on the effective date of the policy. It is patently unfair to charge him with the uncommunicated knowledge of a third person under such circumstances. In sum, a "good health" provision does not bar recovery where the applicant believes in good faith that his health has not materially changed between the time of application and delivery. However, he cannot rely on the fact that a disease predated the application where the latent condition becomes manifest before delivery and he has knowledge of its seriousness.

Metropolitan then contends that, even if Devore's own knowledge of the state of his health is material, the evidence does not support the trial court's finding that Devore did not believe and had no reasonable cause to believe that there had been a material change in his good health. The testimony in the present case, when viewed in the light most favorable to the trial court's findings, indicates the following:

Devore consulted Dr. Thorner on October 10, 1959, for the purpose of a routine examination, pursuant to his practice to undergo regular physical checkups. At the October 10 visit Dr. Thorner found no evidence of disease and an electrocardiogram performed on that date was normal. However, Devore appeared to be nervous and, in answer to a question which the doctor routinely asked patients who came in for examination, Devore stated that he felt "a little pressure in the chest if he rushes." Devore returned on October 19 and, at that time, an electrocardiogram was performed after exercise. On the basis of this test the doctor made a diagnosis of arteriosclerotic heart disease secondary to coronary insufficiency. The condition was very mild. Although the doctor did not recall his specific statements to Devore, he routinely advised patients who were overweight, as Devore was, not to overeat and to avoid excitement and unusual physical exertion. He also told Devore that he had mild hardening of the arteries (a condition which in the doctor's opinion did not indicate serious heart disease) and that he should go into the hospital for rest and medication to prevent trouble. In the hospital, Devore was placed on a medicine known as Dicumerol which, he was told, was prescribed to "thin his blood." Electrocardiograms performed during his hospital stay and thereafter were normal.

In a deposition given by Devore before his death and introduced into evidence, he stated that Dr. Thorner had told him the October 19 electrocardiogram was a little different than the previous one, conveying the idea that it was not a normal test, and that he needed a complete rest. While he was in the hospital Dr. Thorner told him that he had a little hardening of the arteries. Mrs. Devore testified that during her husband's hospital stay he did not complain of any difficulties and conducted his business affairs from the telephone in the hospital corridor. After discharge, he continued under the care of Dr. Thorner, visiting him about once a week for the first month and less frequently thereafter. He continued to take Dicumerol. He worked a regular eight-to-ten-hour day, appeared vigorous and healthy, and remained active in various civic organizations until the day of his death more than two years later.

We cannot say that the evidence is insufficient to support the trial court's finding that Devore could reasonably believe that he was in good health and insurable at the time the policy was delivered to him.

The judgment is affirmed.

TRAYNOR, C.J., and PETERS, TOBRINER, BURKE and PEEK, JJ., concur.

MCCOMB, JUSTICE (dissenting).

. . . .

NOTES

1. *Test for determining good health.* Does the court in *Devore* adopt an objective or a subjective test for deciding whether the applicant was in good health? Are you persuaded that the court reached the right result? In *Harte v. United Benefit Life Insurance Co.*, 66 Cal. 2d 148, 424 P.2d 329, 56 Cal. Rptr. 889 (1967), the applicant for a life insurance policy was diagnosed by his family physician as having inoperable cancer between the time of application and delivery of the policy. The applicant had been examined before the diagnosis by a physician employed by the insurer, but the cancer was not discovered at that time. The family physician informed the applicant's wife, but not the applicant. He was never informed. The court followed the *Devore* rule, holding that it is the insured's own knowledge of the state of his health which is decisive rather than the uncommunicated knowledge of a third party. Even though the wife was the beneficiary, there was no evidence of fraud or bad faith on her part because, among other reasons, there was no indication she was aware of the "good health" clause.

Other courts, however, have not been as generous towards applicants and have enforced a good health clause as a condition that had to be satisfied without regard to the knowledge of the applicant. *See, e.g., Ruwitch v. William Penn Life Assurance Co. of America*, 966 F.2d 1234 (8th Cir. 1992) (applying Missouri law). But compare *Hardester v. Lincoln National Life Insurance Co.*, 52 F.3d 70 (4th Cir. 1995) (applying federal common law in interpreting health policy governed by ERISA). See also Robert H. Jerry, II, Understanding Insurance Law § 34[c] (2nd ed. 1996). In many cases where the good health clause is at issue, the misrepresentation defense is as well. Why? *See Kioutas v. Life Insurance Co. of Va.*, 35 F. Supp. 2d 616 (N.D. Ill. 1998).

2. *Applications that do not require medical examinations.* In footnote 6 of *Devore*, the court reserved judgment on the issue regarding the situation where the insurer did not require a medical examination. If the insurer in *Devore* had not required a medical examination, should it make any difference

in the result? What arguments would you make for the insurer and what response would you make for the insured? Which side has the better of the issue?

3. *Regulation of conditional receipts.* If you, as the state commissioner of insurance, had the power to approve or disapprove policy forms, would you prohibit insurance companies from using any of the conditional receipts that you have encountered in this section? Why? For a collection of different conditional receipt clauses used by various insurers, see C.T. Drechsler, Annotation, *Temporary Life, Accident, or Health Insurance Pending Approval of Application or Issuance of Policy,* 2 A.L.R.2d 943, 960–962 nn. 7–9 (1948). See also Comment, *Life Insurance Receipts: The Mystery of the Non-Binding Binder,* 63 Yale L.J. 523 (1953-54).

[2] Insurer's Duty to Act on Application

CONTINENTAL LIFE & ACCIDENT CO. v. SONGER
124 Ariz. 294, 603 P.2d 921 (Ariz. Ct. App. 1979), 18 A.L.R.4th 1099 (1982)

CONTRERAS, JUDGE.

This appeal and cross-appeal present a substantial number of issues concerning the legal remedies available to a medical insurance applicant whose injury occurs prior to the date the application is either accepted or rejected by the insurance company's home office. The issues arose out of an action brought by appellees and cross-appellants David and Nancy Songer (Songers) against appellant and cross-appellee Continental Life and Accident Company (Continental), two other insurance companies, and two insurance agents. The action involves an effort to recover damages including benefits allegedly due under a medical insurance policy.

The complaint filed by plaintiffs was framed in three counts. Count One alleged the existence of a medical insurance contract and requested damages for the medical expenses payable under the policy, for mental distress, and punitive damages. Count Two alleged negligence on the part of the agents and Continental in processing the application for medical insurance and sought damages for the medical expenses payable under the policy and for mental distress. Count Three was based on a theory of estoppel and sought damages only in the amount that would be payable under the terms of the policy.

After summary judgment was granted in favor of all defendants except Continental and one of its agents, the case proceeded to trial. The jury returned a general verdict against Continental only, and assessed damages in the sum of $4,000. Judgment was entered in the amount of the verdict, together with attorneys' fees in the amount of $2,000 and costs. The trial court denied Continental's motion for a new trial or for judgment notwithstanding the verdict. In addition, the court denied the Songers' motion for a new trial on the issue of punitive damages. Continental has appealed the judgment against it and the denial of its post-trial motions. Coextantly, the Songers have cross-appealed from the denial of their motion for a new trial on the issue of punitive damages.

With the exception of the testimony concerning a "binder," the facts giving rise to the Songers' action are not in substantial dispute. In the summer of 1973, the Songers were planning an extended visit to the Island of Ponape.[1] Anticipating difficulties they might encounter in procuring insurance coverage once they left the States, the Songers wanted to obtain medical insurance before departure which would cover them on their trip. With these thoughts in mind, on August 6, 1973, they discussed major medical coverage with insurance agents, including an agent of Continental, and began to fill out an application. In the course of filling out the application, Nancy Songer mentioned that she had been advised by one of her physicians that she had an "innocent" heart murmur. Arrangements were made for her to have a medical examination, which she promptly received. After her medical examination, on August 13, 1973, the agents returned to complete the application. On that date, David Songer signed the completed application, gave the Continental agent a check in the amount of $133 for the first six months' premium, and received a receipt signed by the agent.

The record reflects a sharp conflict in the testimony concerning the contemporaneous statements by Continental's agent regarding the effective date of coverage and the conditions and terms affecting that coverage. The Songers testified that, during their discussion with the agents, they were assured there was a "binder," and that they were immediately covered unless and until they heard otherwise from the company. Although Continental's agent admitted he used the word "binder" in both meetings, he claimed that he intended the term to be taken in its slang sense rather than in the sense which imparts a legal significance and obligation on the part of Continental. The agent testified that he did not tell the Songers that there was immediate coverage, but instead explained to them that coverage would begin as of the date of application if the application was later accepted by the company.[3]

Approximately one week after the application was submitted and the check received by Continental, the Songers left for the Island of Ponape. After being gone from the United States for about 60 days, and since the Songers had not heard anything from Continental about their application, Nancy Songer wrote a letter to her mother, Mrs. Knowles, asking her to inquire into the matter. On the day she received the letter—October 23, 1973—Mrs. Knowles phoned Continental's agent and asked the reason for the delay of over two months. The agent replied that the delay was due to the fact that Continental was having difficulty in obtaining necessary medical records from Mrs. Songer's doctor, apparently because the records were filed under her maiden

---

[1] For the benefit of those as unfamiliar as this court as to the location of Ponape, it is an island in the Pacific in the grouping known as Micronesia east of the Phillipine [sic] Islands. Ponape is 176 square miles and had an estimated population of 21,000 in 1971. 13 Encyclopedia Britannica, 826–36 (1974).

[3] The written terms of the Application for Health Insurance provided, in part, that "the insurance applied for will not become effective until this application has been accepted by the Company at its Home Office."

name. On October 24, 1973, this problem was resolved and the doctor's office forwarded the necessary information to Continental.

On October 30, 1973, Mrs. Songer was involved in a motor vehicle accident on the Island of Ponape and was severely injured. A few days later, Continental gave written notice that the Songers' application for medical insurance was being declined for medical and other reasons. This notice was by means of a letter written and mailed on November 3, 1973, by Continental's agent to Mrs. Knowles. Accompanying the notice was a refund check from Continental dated October 29, 1973. The Songers never endorsed the check or accepted the refund.

The appellant's primary contention on appeal is that it was error for the trial court to submit to the jury certain instructions which misstated the law regarding temporary insurance contracts and erroneously allowed the jurors to consider oral representations to vary or contradict the written terms of the insurance application and receipt. Additionally, appellant contends that there was no legal or evidentiary basis for the submission of the case on a theory of negligence with the accompanying negligence instructions. Appellant also asserts that the instructions on damages were erroneous because they allowed consideration of elements of damage which were improper under the theory of the case as presented and were not supported by the evidence. Finally, appellant argues that it was error for the trial court to deny appellant's motion for a directed verdict.

The Songers, on the other hand, contend that the case was properly submitted on the theories presented and that the instructions were proper and were supported by the evidence. In their cross-appeal, they raise several additional issues concerning the instructions with respect to punitive damages. Basically, they contend that the trial court erred in refusing to instruct on the issues of reckless disregard, willful and wanton conduct, and intentional infliction of mental suffering. The cross-appellants ask that they be granted a new trial on these issues alone.

The numerous issues raised in this appeal and cross-appeal can be considered and better understood by discussing those issues under the headings of (1) the insurance contract theory; (2) the negligence theory; and (3) the damages.

[Discussion of the insurance contract theory has been omitted. The court found that there was no ambiguity in the written application, that the parol evidence rule necessarily barred consideration of the oral representations of the agent, and reversed for a new trial.]

We have specifically held that there was reversible error in submitting this case to the jury on the temporary oral contract theory and, ordinarily, we would not address the parties' other contentions. However, since this case is being reversed and remanded for a new trial, we feel compelled to discuss what may be the "law of the case" in the superior court if the issues and evidence remain substantially the same as presented here. Thus, for the guidance of the court and counsel, we will discuss the issues of negligence and damages, particularly the issue as to whether, in Arizona, an insurance company can be held liable for negligent delay in processing an application.

Appellees here argue that the tort theory of liability for "negligent delay" by an insurance company in the processing of an application should be recognized in Arizona and that the jury was correctly instructed as to the legal standards by which to judge appellant's conduct on the issue of negligence. Appellant, on the other hand, contends that it was error to submit the case and instruct the jury on negligence because neither Arizona case law nor the evidence presented at trial support submission of the case on this theory.

The "negligent delay" theory, generally stated, is that an insurance company is under a duty to act upon an application for insurance within a reasonable period of time, and a violation of this duty, with resultant damages, subjects the company to liability for negligence. In reviewing the case law from other jurisdictions on the question of whether an insurer may be so liable in tort, we find there is an almost even division of authority. *See* Annot., 32 A.L.R.2d 487 (1953 & Supp. 1977).

There are no cases in Arizona which have expressly accepted or rejected the "negligence delay" concept. We do, however, note that this court has very recently held that Arizona does recognize a cause of action in tort for the alleged bad faith refusal of an insurer to pay a claim of its own insured. *Noble v. National American Life Insurance Co.,* 1 CA-CIV 4006 (filed June 28, 1979). The holding in *Noble* was predicated on the recognition that an insurer under Arizona case law has a duty "to deal fairly with its insured." This duty is "imposed by law by virtue of the contractual relationship but [is] independent of its terms." Although *Noble* is distinguishable from the instant case in that there was no question as to the existence of an insurance contract in *Noble,* we are of the opinion that a similar duty of dealing fairly should be imposed in situations where, as here, there may be some question as to the existence of a contract for insurance and the insurer unreasonably delays in processing the application after having accepted the payment of a premium. *See* J. Appleman, 12 Insurance Law and Practice § 7226, at 330 (1943 & Supp. 1979 at 311).

Resolution of the negligence theory advanced by appellees in the instant case was left open by our supreme court in the case of *New York Life Insurance Co. v. Lawrence,* 56 Ariz. 28, 104 P.2d 165 (1940). In *Lawrence,* a complaint was filed, on the tort theory only, by the administrator of the estate of a woman who had died prior to the time any action was taken on her application for life insurance. The court, in holding that the company violated no duty owed to the applicant, based its decision on the fact that the company had rejected the policy within the 60-day time period expressly stated in the application. The *Lawrence* court limited its decision to the particular facts of that case, stating that "under the facts of this case it is not necessary for us to consider what the correct general rule is if there is no agreement between the parties as to how long the insurer may have to consider the application." *Id.* at 34, 104 P.2d at 167.

After reviewing and studying cases from other jurisdictions, it is our opinion that in the absence of an express provision in the application as to the length of time an insurer has to consider the application, the insurer is under a duty to act upon an application for insurance within a reasonable period of time and a violation of this duty with resultant damages subjects the insurer to liability for negligence. We agree with "[t]he more liberal, and probably the better rule . . . that an insurance company obtaining an application for insurance is under a duty to accept it or to reject it within a reasonable time, and is liable if it delays unreasonably in acting thereon." J. Appleman, *supra* at 326–27.

Our express recognition of the negligent delay theory is in accord with and justified by the precepts of individual consumer protection and the public interest. Because insurance companies are licensed and regulated by the state, they are part of an industry which is affected by the public interest. As a result, they can and should be held to a broader legal responsibility than are parties to purely private contracts. This is especially true in cases where the insurance carriers have solicited and obtained an application for insurance, and have received payment of a premium.

In addition, and since insurance companies unilaterally prepare the applications and set forth the conditions for acceptance, the parties are not in an equal bargaining position. There must, in all fairness, be some degree of correlative consumer protection. We are of the opinion that an insurance company which retains an application for medical insurance that does not contain a provision as to the time within which the application must be acted upon, and also retains payment of a premium, may be held liable in damages if it fails to either accept or reject the application within a reasonable period of time. It is generally the rule that the determination of what constitutes a reasonable time is a question for the jury. In the instant case, then, the jury was properly instructed as to the legal standard by which to judge appellant's conduct on the issue of negligence, and specifically whether Continental acted within a reasonable time.[8]

DAMAGES

The final questions for our consideration relate to the extent and measure of damages to which an insurer may be held liable where it has been determined that the insurer has negligently delayed in processing an application. We address the questions raised by the parties regarding damages primarily for the guidance of court and counsel in the new trial. It must be kept in mind, though, that our conclusions, in part, are based upon the evidence in the present record.

The general rule is that the amount of damages recoverable for negligent delay in passing upon an application for insurance cannot exceed the amount

---

[8] Although not discussed in the briefs, we note that the instant case was submitted to the jury on a third theory — estoppel. Our review of the cases which have considered this theory in situations factually similar to this one leads us to the conclusion, consistent with this opinion, that it is permissible to instruct the jury to consider the estoppel theory as an adjunct to a claim for negligent delay by an insurance company. The general rule of applicability is perhaps best stated by Appleman.

> "By failure to act upon an application duly made, the period of delay may be so unreasonable as to estop the insurer from denying liability. A retention of the application and premium payment for an unreasonable and unwarranted length of time may raise an inference of acceptance. Of course, the question of how long the insured may rely on a presumption of acceptance depends on the facts of each case."

J. Appleman, *supra* at 328–29.

of insurance applied for or the amount of benefits which the applicant would have received had there been an actual contract of insurance. Annot., 32 A.L.R.2d § 28 at 536 (1953). The cases so holding generally predicate their conclusions on the traditional concept that nonpayment and delay in paying benefits is strictly classified as a breach of contract action and because an insurance policy is a contract to pay money only, recovery is limited to the amount due plus legal interest. This rule has also been justified on the ground that it provides a simple, direct and certain measure of damages. But simplicity and directness should not justify the hardship or economic losses which can be caused by such a rule. In a very realistic sense, the certainty of this rule can result in insurance carriers taking unfair advantage of their policyholders or prospective policyholders since the carriers can rest secure with the knowledge that their maximum liability exposure is limited to the contractual amount due plus legal interest. However, we are of the opinion that damages need not be restricted solely to the amount which would have been paid if a contract of insurance had existed.

We have previously stated that an insurer is under a good faith duty to deal fairly with the applicant for insurance and to act upon the application within a reasonable time. Our finding of such duty rests upon the dual propositions that an insurance company is affected with the public interest, and that the parties to an application are not in an equal bargaining position. The good faith duty arises from the insurer's relationship to the public in general, and to an applicant in particular, and is not dependent upon a specific finding that there is a contract. Rather, it is in the nature of an implied or quasi-contract between the applicant and insurer that the latter will act upon the application within a reasonable time. Since we view the liability discussed above not as being dependent on a finding of a contract, but as being analogous to that in tort actions, we are of the opinion that the general rules with respect to damages in a negligence action should apply.

As a general rule, a plaintiff in a tort action is entitled to recover such sums as will reasonably compensate him for all damages sustained by him as the direct, natural and proximate result of such negligence, provided they are established with reasonable certainty. Since this rule is applicable in the instant case, the Songers, upon retrial and provided liability is established, are entitled to recover the damages which were directly caused by the conduct of Continental.

In their cross-appeal, the Songers question whether they were entitled to an instruction regarding recovery for intentional infliction of emotional distress. Under Arizona law, which does recognize the tort of intentional inflic-tion of emotional distress,[9] one may recover such damages "only where the defendant's acts are 'so outrageous in character and so extreme in degree, as to go beyond all possible bounds of decency, and to be regarded as atrocious, and utterly intolerable in a civilized community.'"

---

[9] Arizona recognizes the tort as it is set forth in The Restatement (Second) of Torts § 46(1) (1965). Section 46(1) provides:

"One who by extreme and outrageous conduct intentionally or recklessly causes severe emotional distress to another is subject to liability for such emotional distress, and if bodily harm to the other results from it, for such bodily harm."

Although there is clearly a question as to whether Continental was negligent in failing to act upon the Songer application for more than 80 days, we find no evidence in the present record that Continental committed an act which could be classified as "extreme and outrageous." It is the duty of the court (rather than the jury) to determine, in the first instance, whether the acts complained of can be considered extreme and outrageous so as to substantiate a claim for relief. Under the present state of the record, we agree with the trial court's determination that there was insufficient evidence of extreme and outrageous conduct necessary to support a claim for intentional infliction of emotional distress. Barring production of such evidence at the new trial, it is our opinion that the trial court would not be in error in refusing to so instruct the jury.

Finally, the question is presented of whether punitive damages may be awarded, or for that matter, even considered in actions of this nature. It is the well established rule that punitive damages may be awarded in tort actions where the conduct of the wrongdoer is wanton, reckless or shows spite or ill will or where there is a reckless indifference to the interests of others. With respect to this question, we adopt and incorporate our previous statements regarding the question of consideration of damages for the intentional infliction of emotional distress. We further note that our review of the present record discloses that there is no evidence of wanton conduct or reckless indifference on the part of Continental, and thus there was a lack of sufficient evidence which would have supported an instruction on the issue of punitive damages. For the reasons stated, this case is reversed and remanded for retrial.

WREN, P.J., and DONOFRIO, J., concur.

NOTES

1. *Insurer's duty to act on application.* As noted in *Songer,* courts have reached different results on whether an insurer has a duty to act promptly on an insured's application for insurance. For example, in *Usher v. Allstate Insurance Co.,* 300 Minn. 52, 218 N.W.2d 201 (1974), the Supreme Court of Minnesota held that there is no legal duty on the part of a health insurance company to accept or reject an application for insurance and that mere delay on the part of the company in passing upon the application cannot be construed as an acceptance which would support either an action for breach of contract or one sounding in tort. A similar split in the authorities can be found with regard to applications for life insurance. *See, e.g., Royal Maccabees Life Insurance Co. v. Peterson,* 139 F.3d 568 (7th Cir. 1998) (recognizing duty to act promptly and vacating summary judgment for insurer where insurer believed applicant was insurable six days before death, but did not issue policy until seven days after death); *Duffie v. Bankers' Life Ass'n,* 160 Iowa 19, 139 N.W. 1087 (1913)(recognizing a tort duty to act promptly or without undue delay on a life insurance application); *Watkins v. Coastal States Life Insurance Co.,* 118 Ga. App. 145, 162 S.E.2d 788 (1968) (because application for insurance is an offer, there can be no tort action for delay in responding to offer).

See also Kristine Cordier Karnezis, Annotation, *Liability Of Insurer For Damages Resulting From Delay In Passing Upon An Application For Life Insurance,* 1 A.L.R.4th 1202 (1980).

What should the rule be with regard to applications for permanent property and casualty insurance where there is no temporary binder? Is the argument for recognizing a duty stronger or weaker under these types of insurance as compared to life and health insurance? See 3 Eric Mills Holmes, Holmes's Appleman on Insurance § 12.1 (2d ed. 1998).

2. *Agent's duty to procure coverage.* Although there may be some question whether an insurer has a duty, either in contract or tort, to consider and promptly act on an application for insurance, the law is clear that an agent who undertakes to procure coverage may be liable for failing to do so. The liability may be imposed under a contract theory for breaching a promise to procure the insurance as well as under a tort theory for a wrongful failure to do so. *See Keller Lorenz Co. v. Insurance Associates Corp.,* 98 Idaho 678, 570 P.2d 1366 (1977). As to the standard of care owed by an agent under the tort duty, the agent must use reasonable diligence in attempting to place the coverage and must seasonably notify the client if unable to obtain the insurance. *Havas v. Carter,* 89 Nev. 497, 515 P.2d 397 (1973), 64 A.L.R.3d 394 (1975). Of course, liability for breach of contract to procure is not based on fault—the issue is simply whether the agent performed her promise. See generally Robin Cheryl Miller, *Liability of Insurance Agent or Broker on Ground of Inadequacy of Liability-Insurance Coverage Procured*, 60 A.L.R.5th 165 (1998).

Suppose the agent recommends, at the time of renewal, that the insured delete a particular coverage on the ground that it is not needed. The insured agrees. The insured then suffers a loss that would have been covered but for the deletion. Should the insured be able to succeed in a claim for negligent failure to procure insurance? Is the appropriate theory breach of the "duty to advise"? *See Hobbs v. Midwest Insurance, Inc.,* 253 Neb. 278, 570 N.W.2d 525 (1997).

3. *Failed procurement and misrepresentation.* If the insured ends up with coverage but not the kind of coverage he expected, the insured may allege not only that the agent failed to procure the proper coverage but that the agent's negligently misrepresented the scope of the coverage that was procured. If the insured fails to read the policy when it was delivered, should this eliminate the insured's misrepresentation claim? *See Butcher v. Truck Insurance Exchange,* 77 Cal. App. 4th 1442, 92 Cal. Rptr. 2d 521 (Cal. Ct. App. 2000) (insured's failure to read policy procured by agent does not preclude insured's negligent misrepresentation action against agent for misrepresenting scope of policy agent procured). If it does, how can an insured ever hold the agent responsible for negligent misrepresentation? *See Small v. King,* 915 P.2d 1192 (Wyo. 1996)(insured who read policy and understood it could not claim that agent misrepresented coverage). Assuming the insured has some kind of duty to read, can there be circumstances where the agent's conduct will excuse the insured's nonsatisfaction of the duty? *See Rollins Burdick Hunter of Utah, Inc. v. Board of Trustees of Ball State University,* 665 N.E.2d 914 (Ind. Ct. App. 1996).

Whether the agent's actions or representations with respect to the coverage are binding on the *insurer* will depend on the agent's authority. *See, e.g., American States Insurance Co. v. Natchez Steam Laundry,* 131 F.3d 551 (5th Cir. 1998) (applying Mississippi law; agent's oral representations can, if relied upon, modify coverage; but agent's representations that CGL covered sexual harassment could not modify plain language of policy excluding such coverage); *Maville v. Peerless Insurance Co.,* 141 N.H. 317, 686 A.2d 1165 (1996) (general agent had authority to reduce policy limits upon insured's request).

4. *Causation.* In order to recover for a failure to procure, must the prospective insured prove that a policy substantially as applied for would have been issued but for the default of the agent? What if coverage like what the insured claims she expected is available nowhere in the market at any price? Does it matter whether the cause of action is one for breach of contract or negligence? If causation is an issue, must the proof show that an insurer which the agent had authority to bind would have issued the policy or just that it was more probable than not that the insured would have obtained the type of policy or coverage applied for from some insurer? *See Bayly, Martin & Fay v. Pete's Satire,* 739 P.2d 239 (Colo. 1987) (holding, in negligent failure to procure case, it is incumbent upon claimant to prove that such coverage was generally available in the insurance industry). But *see Lovett v. Bradford,* 676 So. 2d 893 (Miss. 1996) (trial court was not required to give jury instruction that insured had to prove insurance was available elsewhere in order to prove that agent's negligence in completing application was cause of insured's loss); *Wood v. Newman, Hayes & Dixon Insurance Agency,* 905 S.W.2d 559 (Tenn. 1995) (holding agent's failure to provide notice of diminished coverage in renewal policy was cause in fact of insured's uncovered loss notwithstanding fact that original coverage was not available in insurance markets at time of renewal). Does the same issue arise and would the plaintiff have the same burden under the tort theory relied on in *Songer*?

In the same vein, if the agent fails to procure the correct coverage but the insurer pays the claim anyway, is the insured damaged? *See Mashburn v. Meeker Sharkey Financial Group, Inc.,* 339 Ark. 411, 5 S.W.3d 469 (1999).

5. *Respondeat superior.* Is it important in a failure to procure case whether the insurance agent is a broker, independent agent, or company agent? *Compare Monarch Insurance Co. v. Siegel,* 625 F. Supp. 693 (N.D. Ind. 1986) with *State Farm Life Insurance Co. v. Fort Wayne National Bank,* 474 N.E.2d 524 (Ind. App. 1985).

6. *Defenses and damages.* As an attorney preparing to file a case based upon an agent's failure to procure insurance, should you be concerned about possible defenses that may be available to the agent or insurer, depending on the theories of liability that you plead? Would it make any difference if, instead of a complete failure to procure any coverage, the agent procured coverage that was materially different from that promised? See John D. Ingram, *What Are Insurance Producers' Duties to Their Clients?,* 57 Defense Counsel J. 61, 64-65 (Jan. 1990). What about the measure of damages that would be available under contract as compared to tort? With regard to the latter issue, what did the *Songer* court have to say?

7. *Agent's duty to third parties.* In *Flattery v. Gregory,* 397 Mass. 143, 489 N.E.2d 1257 (1986), the court considered whether an insurance agent owes to a traveler on the highway, injured by the negligent driving of another, a duty to fulfill the agent's pre-accident promise to the negligent driver to obtain optional liability coverage on the latter's motor vehicle. The plaintiff-traveler sued the insurance agent on two theories: (1) negligent failure to procure and (2) breach of contract. The agent had obtained a policy providing coverage for $20,000 per person and $40,000 per accident, the minimum liability limits required under Massachusetts law. The plaintiff-traveler alleged that the insurance agent promised to obtain $100,000/300,000 limits for the negligent driver, but failed to do so and that the agent was liable to the plaintiff. The trial court dismissed these claims. How would you rule, and why, if you were on the Supreme Judicial Court of Massachusetts? Would you reach the same result if the agent had failed to procure *any* insurance for the negligent driver? For other cases considering the issue of an agent's liability to a third party, *see Jones v. Hyatt Insurance Agency, Inc.,* 356 Md. 639, 741 A.2d 1099 (1999) (alleged promise to secure automobile liability insurance); *Quigley v. Bay State Graphics, Inc.,* 427 Mass. 455, 693 N.E.2d 1368 (1998) (alleged promise to secure property insurance); *Rae v. Air-Speed, Inc.,* 386 Mass. 187, 435 N.E.2d 628 (1982)(agent promised to procure statutorily-required workers compensation insurance); *Ferguson v. Cash, Sullivan and Cross Insurance Agency, Inc.,* 831 P.2d 380 (Ariz. Ct. App. 1992).

[3]   Insurance Agent's Duty to Advise

NELSON v. DAVIDSON
155 Wis. 2d 674, 456 N.W.2d 343 (1990)

BABLITCH, JUSTICE.

The plaintiffs in these consolidated cases were involved in auto accidents where the negligent party had insufficient insurance to cover the damages. Prior to the accidents, both plaintiffs had obtained insurance coverage from State Farm Mutual Automobile Insurance Company (State Farm), but each lacked underinsured motorist (UIM) coverage. We accepted certification to determine whether an insurance agent owes an affirmative duty to advise its insureds of the availability or advisability of underinsured motorist (UIM) coverage. We conclude that absent special circumstances they do not. We therefore affirm the decisions of the circuit courts granting summary judgments in favor of the defendants.

Gloria Brunckhorst Nelson (Nelson) was involved as a passenger in a one-car accident in River Falls on October 14, 1982. Nelson and her former husband had purchased casualty insurance coverage from State Farm through its agent, Paul Davidson (Davidson), for two cars with coverage to begin in 1980 and 1981. Nelson alleges by affidavit that she relied exclusively on Davidson for auto insurance information and that he offered advice to her on at least two occasions. Nelson also claims that she requested "the best coverage" available with respect to motor vehicle insurance, and that she was assured by one of Davidson's employees that she had the best coverage. Davidson denies that Nelson or her former husband ever discussed or requested underinsured motorist coverage, and further that he never held himself out as an insurance advisor, consultant, or specialist.

Rachel Pritchard (Pritchard) and her former husband Lynn were involved in a two car collision while riding with their daughter in Michigan on December 28, 1983. The Pritchards had purchased automobile insurance from State Farm agent, Henry Baier (Baier), since 1969. Prior to that time, they insured their automobiles with State Farm through Baier's predecessor. Lynn Pritchard made all decisions regarding auto insurance purchases for the family, and on at least one occasion purchased uninsured motorist coverage in excess of the limits mandated by statute. The Pritchards allege that they expected State Farm and its agents would provide them with reasonable and timely information and counsel regarding their family's automobile insurance requirements.

State Farm began marketing underinsured motorist (UIM) coverage in Wisconsin in January, 1982. At about that time, the company mailed a pamphlet to all Wisconsin insureds informing them about the availability of UIM coverage. These inserts were sent with semiannual premium renewal notices as premiums became due in 1982. The pamphlet contained the following section regarding the availability of UIM coverage:

Also New Coverage Available—Coverage W

To protect you from damages caused by underinsured motor vehicles, State Farm now offers Coverage W—Underinsured Motor Vehicle Coverage. Here's how Coverage W works: If the other driver is at fault in an accident and damages for injuries to you and your passengers exceed the amount that you receive from that driver's insurance company, your Underinsured Motor Vehicle Coverage takes over, up to the limits you choose.

The plaintiffs allege that they have no recollection of receiving the pamphlet, although they concede they may have. It is undisputed that neither party attempted thereafter to communicate with the other regarding the availability or scope of UIM coverage.

The plaintiffs subsequently commenced this suit for damages, alleging State Farm and its agents were negligent in failing to adequately inform them of the availability of UIM coverage. The defendants moved for summary judgements [sic] of dismissal, primarily on the ground that they had no duty to inform their insureds of the availability of UIM coverage, nor to recommend certain policy limits. In the alternative, the defendants argued that in any event they mailed notices of the availability of UIM coverage to all Wisconsin policyholders in early 1982, prior to the accidents.

The trial courts granted summary judgments in favor of the defendants and dismissed the actions. The trial courts concluded that an insurance agent has no affirmative duty under Wisconsin law to inform the insured about available coverages, or to review existing coverage to determine whether coverage is adequate.

We accepted certification of the consolidated cases specifically to resolve whether an insurance agent has an affirmative duty to inform the insured regarding the availability of UIM coverage. We affirm the decisions of the trial courts granting summary judgment in favor of the defendants.

In Wisconsin, a plaintiff alleging a negligence cause of action is required to plead the four traditional elements of a tort: 1) a duty on the part of the defendant; 2) a breach of that duty; 3) a causal connection between the conduct and the injury; and 4) an actual loss or damage as a result of the injury. Therefore, in order for liability to exist in the present case, it must first be shown that the defendants had an affirmative duty to advise clients of the availability of UIM coverage.

This court on a number of occasions has discussed the somewhat elusive concept of "duty." In *Ollerman v. O'Rourke Co., Inc.,* 94 Wis. 2d 17, 27, 288 N.W.2d 95 (1980), we pointed out that the question of duty presents an issue of law, and that when the court resolves a question of duty the court is essentially making a policy determination. Furthermore, we made clear in *Walker v. Bignell,* 100 Wis. 2d 256, 265, 301 N.W.2d 447 (1981), that the imposition of liability in a given situation is a question of policy whether the liability is regulated by the notion of duty, or whether liability is cut off after all the elements of negligence have been established, as more recent cases of this court have stated.

The plaintiffs refer us to no cases decided by a Wisconsin court holding that an insurance agent possesses an affirmative duty to advise a client regarding the availability or advisability of insurance coverage. Rather, they rely principally upon several cases from other jurisdictions holding that insurance agents have a duty to advise clients concerning the kind and extent of desired coverage, and to choose the appropriate insurance for the client. For example, in *Sobotor v. Prudential Property & Cas. Ins. Company,* 200 N.J. Super. 333, 491 A.2d 737, 742 (1984), the court stated that the inequality between the average purchaser of insurance and the insurance agent entitles the client, "untutored in the intricacies of insurance," to a broad measure of protections, including all information pertinent to the risk and desired coverage before the contract is issued. In *Dimeo v. Burns, Brooks & McNeil, Inc.,* 6 Conn. App. 241, 504 A.2d 557, 559 (1986), the court stated that insurance is a specialized field with specialized knowledge and experience, and an agent has the duty to advise the client about the kind and extent of desired coverage and to choose the appropriate insurance for the client.

However, the vast majority of other jurisdictions hold that the general duty of care which an insurance agent owes a client does not include the obligation to advise of available coverages. These courts conclude that while it may be good business for an insurance agent to make such suggestions, and perhaps inquire into financial circumstances, the failure to do so does not constitute either negligence or breach of contract for which an insurer must answer in damages. Nor is the insured under an obligation to respond to the agent's questions. The seminal case on the issue, *Hardt v. Brink,* 192 F. Supp. 879, 880 (W.D. Wash. 1961), states:

> Clearly, the ordinary insurance solicitor only assumes those duties normally found in any agency relationship. In general this includes

the obligation to deal with his principal in good faith and to carry out his instructions. No affirmative duty to advise is assumed by the mere creation of an agency relationship.

Jurisdictions following this rule have delineated strong policy considerations which weigh against the imposition of any liability for failing to advise or provide plaintiffs with coverage. For instance, in *Dubreuil v. Allstate Ins. Co.,* 511 A.2d 300, 302 (R.I.1986), the court observed that imposing liability on insurers for failure to advise clients of available coverage would remove any burden from the insured to take care of his or her own financial needs and expectations in entering the marketplace and choosing from the competitive products available. The court stated that adopting such a rule would transform insurance companies from a competitive industry "'into personal financial counselors or guardians of the insured, a result we believe goes well beyond anything required by law or dictated by common sense.'" *Id.* (quoting *Gibson v. Government Employers Insurance Co.,* 162 Cal. App. 3d 441, 451–52, 208 Cal. Rptr. 511 (1984).

Similarly, in *Suter v. Virgil R. Lee & Son, Inc.,* 51 Wash. App. 524, 754 P.2d 155, 157 (1988), the court stated that ordinarily the insured knows the extent of his personal assets and his ability to pay better than the insurance agent. Thus, the court concluded it is the insured's responsibility to advise the agent of the insurance he wants, including the limits of the policy to be issued. *Id.* (citing *Jones v. Grewe,* 189 Cal. App. 3d 950, 234 Cal. Rptr. 717, 721 (1987), review denied, May 14, 1987.)

These courts have also noted the negative consequences to the insurance industry which would follow from liability. For example, the obvious extension of the rule advocated by the plaintiffs would subject insurance carriers to liability for failing to advise their own clients of every possible insurance option, or even an arguably better package of insurance offered by a competitor. Furthermore, the creation of a duty to advise could afford insureds the opportunity to insure after the loss by merely asserting they would have bought the additional coverage had it been offered. *See Polski v. Powers,* 221 Neb. 361, 377 N.W.2d 106 (1985); *Blonsky v. Allstate Ins. Co.,* 128 Misc. 2d 981, 491 N.Y.S.2d 895 (1985).

In the present case, the plaintiffs acknowledge the majority rule that generally an insurance agent does not have an affirmative duty to advise a client regarding the availability or adequacy of coverage. Nevertheless, they argue that a duty to advise clients as to the availability of insurance may arise when a statutory obligation or a special relationship arises between agent and buyer.

Regarding a statutory obligation, the court in *Pabitzky v. Frager,* 164 Cal. App. 3d 401, 210 Cal. Rptr. 426 (1985), stated that there is no duty on the part of an insurer to do more than to call the attention of the customer to the statutory requirements. In Wisconsin, the legislature has long taken an active role in determining which insurance coverages must be provided or offered by insurance companies. The public policy of Wisconsin, as currently articulated by the legislature in sec. 632.32(4), Stats, encompasses mandatory uninsured motorist and medical payment coverages. The legislature has considered mandatory UIM coverage during its last three sessions, including the most recent session.

To date, the statutory duty expressed by the legislature does not encompass mandatory UIM coverage, and we hesitate to interfere in determining an area of broad public policy in which the legislature has assumed such an active role. If the defendants were found liable to the plaintiffs for failure to advise in the present case, the express and limited public policy of the state, established solely by the legislature on the dates the policy was issued and the injuries occurred, would be expanded by the judiciary. We conclude that if such a duty is to be imposed on the defendants, it should be imposed as a statutory one and not an implied judicial one.

It is more difficult to derive any absolute rule from the caselaw as to the requirements of a "special relationship." However, it is apparent that something more than the standard insured-insurer relationship is required in order to create a special relationship obligating the insurer to advise the policy-holder concerning his or her insurance coverage. *Bruner v. League General Ins. Co.*, 164 Mich. App. 28, 416 N.W.2d 318 (1987). Some courts require an express agreement, or a long established relationship of entrustment from which it clearly appears the agent appreciated the duty of giving advice, and compensation for consultation and advice was received apart from the premiums paid by the insured. *See, e.g., Sandbulte v. Farm Bureau Mutual Ins. Co.*, 343 N.W.2d 457 (Iowa 1984); *Gibson*, 162 Cal. App. 3d at 448–49, 208 Cal. Rptr. 511; *Nowell v. Dawn-Leavitt Agency, Inc.*, 127 Ariz. 48, 617 P.2d 1164, 1168 (Ariz. App. 1980); *Fleming v. Torrey*, 273 N.W.2d 169 (S.D. 1978). Other courts hold that a special relationship may be shown by an insurance agent who holds himself or herself out as being a highly-skilled insurance expert, coupled with the insured's reliance on the expertise of the agent to the insured's detriment. *See Hardt*, 192 F. Supp. at 881.

In the present case, the plaintiffs failed to set forth any facts that could establish such a relationship. The record does not indicate that State Farm or its agents expressly contracted to assume the duties of advisor or consultant, nor is there any evidence that the agents held themselves out as specialists or as highly skilled insurance experts. Moreover, neither agent received additional compensation for consultation or advice.

Pritchard alleges that she and her former husband expected State Farm and its agents would provide them with reasonable and timely information and counseling regarding their family's automobile insurance needs. However, as the defendants correctly point out, there is not even a mention of any representation made by the defendants that they would provide advice, much less on an ongoing basis. The mere allegation that a client relied upon an agent and had great confidence in him is insufficient to imply the existence of a duty to advise. The principal-agent relationship cannot be so drastically expanded unilaterally.

Nelson claims that she requested "the best coverage" available with respect to automobile insurance, and that she was assured by one of the agent's employees that she had the best coverage. However, there is no evidence that Nelson requested that such advice be continued on an ongoing basis, and there is no indication that State Farm offered UIM coverage at the time of these requests. Indeed, Nelson did not even go so far as to contact the agent after the 1982 pamphlet introducing UIM coverage was mailed to all State Farm policyholders in Wisconsin. We decline to impose upon the agent an ongoing duty under these circumstances to advise an insured regarding coverage for an indefinite period of time.

Accordingly, we affirm the decisions of the trial courts granting summary judgment to the defendants. We conclude that an insurance agent has no affirmative duty under existing Wisconsin law, absent special circumstances, to inform an insured concerning the availability or advisability of UIM coverage.

Judgments affirmed.

NOTES

1. *Duty to inform or advise regarding insurance needs.* The *Nelson* case spells out the majority rule regarding the duty of an insurance agent to inform or advise a prospective insured of insurance needs. For other examples, *see Harts v. Farmers Insurance Exchange,* 461 Mich. 1, 597 N.W.2d 47 (1999) (no duty to advise absent a special relationship, which was not present); *Gordon v. Spectrum, Inc.,* 981 P.2d 488 (Wyo. 1999) (absent special relationship, no continuing duty to advise exists; held, no duty to advise former client, where policy period has expired, of liability insurer's insolvency); *Macabio v. TIG Insurance Co.,* 87 Haw. 307, 955 P.2d 100 (1998) (agent owed no duty to make unsolicited call on insureds to inform them of change in stacking law relevant to UIM coverage);

Do you think that the courts have drawn the scope of the duty too narrowly? Is it really true that an agent would be unfairly burdened if a duty to inform or advise were recognized, at least with regard to the type of insurance sought by the prospective insured? For example, if the prospect were seeking homeowners coverage, the range of information or advice about such policies is not unlimited. The insurance industry has developed standard forms and is it too much to ask that the agent be knowledgeable enough to explain the different types of forms — say the difference between a specified risk and an all risk form—and the basic differences in coverages? How about for automobile insurance, for which there are also standard forms? If the agent represents a company that does not use the standard forms, shouldn't the agent be able to explain how the policy differs from the standard form? On the other hand, would it be too easy, after an uncovered or inadequately covered loss, for an insured to allege that she would have purchased the missing coverage but for the agent's failure to inform or advise her about it? Moreover, would the recognition of a broader duty place the courts on a slippery slope that would have no workable footholds so that far more cases would end up going to the jury than would be desirable?

2. *Insurance as a type of chattel.* As mentioned in § 1.03, *supra,* one authority on contracts has opined that an insurance contract may be viewed as a special form of chattel that the public has come to purchase just like an appliance

or other goods, really not knowing anymore about how it works than most chattels that are purchased. See 7 Samuel Williston, A Treatise on the Law of Contracts § 900, at 34 (3d ed. Jaeger 1963). Does the rule in *Nelson* complement this idea by saying that insurers have no more of an obligation to explain how a particular policy works than a manufacturer of a hair dryer?

3. *Minority rule.* A few jurisdictions have adopted a broader duty to inform or advise, but it is not clear how far the courts are willing, or will be permitted, to go in this direction. For example, the *Nelson* court cites the *Sobotor* case for the proposition that New Jersey has adopted a rule that imposes a duty on insurers to inform the insured of "all information pertinent to the risk and desired coverage before the contract is issued." *Sobotor* was one of a number of New Jersey decisions that dealt with an insurer's duty to inform or advise an insured about the availability of underinsured motorist coverage, but this line of decisions was mostly nullified in 1993 when the New Jersey legislature acted, as one court described it, "to put an immediate end to this explosion of litigation by providing blanket immunity [to insurance agents and insurers] except in cases of willful, wanton, or gross negligence." *Strube v. Travelers Indemnity Co.,* 277 N.J. Super. 236, 243, 649 A.2d 624, 627 (N.J. Super. Ct. App. Div. 1994). However, outside the area of underinsured motorist coverage, the rule in New Jersey that an insurer or insurance agent owes a duty to the insured to act with reasonable skill and diligence in informing and advising an insured appears to be alive and well. In *Brill v. Guardian Life Insurance Co. of America,* 142 N.J. 520, 666 A.2d 146 (1995) the Supreme Court of New Jersey reaffirmed this rule in holding that an insurance broker was negligent as a matter of law for failing to inform a prospective insured that immediate coverage was available through a temporary binder. For another recent case following the minority view, *see Southwest Auto Painting and Body Repair, Inc. v. Binsfeld,* 904 P.2d 1268 (Ariz. Ct. App. 1995).

4. *Cross-currents with the insured's duty to read.* If the insured understands the limitations of the coverage after reading it, does the acquired knowledge destroy the insured's claim that the agent negligently failed to give proper advice? *See Small v. King,* 915 P.2d 1192 (Wyo. 1996). If the answer is "yes," what if the agent fails to explain a limitation in a policy's coverage and the insured would have understood the limitation *if* she had taken the time to read the policy? Does the insured's failure to read the policy insulate the agent from liability? Is the proximate cause of the insured's loss in that event her failure to read the policy, as opposed to the agent's failure to explain? *See Dahlke v. John F. Zimmer Insurance Agency, Inc.,* 245 Neb. 800, 515 N.W.2d 767 (1994), *on appeal after remand,* 252 Neb. 596, 567 N.W.2d 548 (1997). The answers to these questions turn in no small way on whether an insured has a duty to read the policy. Does the recognition of a duty to read fit better with the majority or minority rule with respect to the duty to advise? Assuming the insured has some kind of duty to read, can there be circumstances where the agent's conduct will excuse the insured's nonsatisfaction of the duty? *See Rollins Burdick Hunter of Utah, Inc. v. Board of Trustees of Ball State University,* 665 N.E.2d 914 (Ind. Ct. App. 1996).

5. *Defenses.* If a duty to inform or advise is recognized, either under the exceptions to the majority rule noted in *Nelson* that involve a statutory

obligation or a special relationship or because the jurisdiction follows a minority view, under what circumstances might an agent or insurer have an affirmative defense, and what would the defense be?

6. *"Vanishing premium" life insurance.* One of the most hotly litigated issues in recent years involves a product called "vanishing premium" life insurance. In the 1980s, life insurers offered and agents marketed new products with the sales pitch that the cash value created by the initial premium payments would grow to a point that the premium would be paid out of ongoing earnings (i.e., would "vanish") within five to ten years. Ten years later, many insureds were told that their premiums had not vanished, and that they would need to continue to make premium payments. Predictably, lawsuits were filed — typically class actions—against almost every major insurance company. The role that agents played in the marketing of these policies has figured prominently in these lawsuits. Some of the suits have settled, the outcomes in others has been mixed, courts have divided on the class certification issues, and some of the suits are still pending. For a summary of the issues in the vanishing premium lawsuits, see Daniel R. Fischel & Robert S. Stillman, *The Law and Economics of Vanishing Premium Life Insurance*, 22 Del. J. Corp. L. 1 (1997).

7. *Respondeat superior.* It should be noticed that the agent in each case in *Nelson* was employed by State Farm Mutual Automobile Insurance Company and, therefore, each was a company agent. A company agent only represents one insurer, whereas an independent agent may represent a number of different insurers. If there is a duty to inform or advise regarding insurance needs, would any particular insurer be liable for a breach of the duty by an independent agent? What if a broker breaches the duty?

§ 7.03 Modification and Termination of Coverage

Insurance policies, like all contracts, have temporal constraints. They provide coverage, i.e., the risk is transferred, only for certain periods of time. These periods vary with the type of insurance. For example, as explained in § 1.05[3], individual life insurance contracts may cover the whole life of the *cestui que vie* or just a period of years. Health and accident insurance may be written the same way. Property and casualty insurance, on the other hand, is usually written for a term of one year, although it has become common for auto insurers to write policies only for a six-month period. At one time fire policies, including homeowners policies, were written for a three-year period, but now they are written for annual periods only. Why have insurers reduced the periods for which they are willing to write auto and fire policies?

Although an insurance policy may be in effect and, therefore, legally binding on the insured and insurer for a specified period, it is always possible for the parties to mutually agree to modify or cancel the policy. Neither party, however, can unilaterally modify or terminate the coverage unless the policy authorizes such action. *See, e.g., Krebs v. Strange,* 419 So. 2d 178 (Miss. 1982)(unilateral attempt by insurer to modify policy invalid); *Markel v. Travelers Insurance Co.,* 510 F.2d 1201 (10th Cir. 1975) (policy still in force where insurer had not agreed to insured's cancellation request prior to loss). Unless there is a breach, the contract is in force until it expires by its own terms.

Modification of an existing contract can be a two-edged proposition, involving the termination of existing provisions as well as the creation of new provisions. The power of intermediaries to effect these changes depends on the authority of such persons and raises the same principal-agent issues explored in § 7.01 of this Chapter, *supra*. For example, as to the issue of cancellation, one should not assume that the authority of an agent to sell or bind insurance coverage carries with it the authority to cancel the coverage. *See, e.g., Markel v. Travelers Insurance Co., supra.*

Even though an insurance contract is effective only for specific time periods, it is common practice for an insurer to renew the policy for subsequent periods each time that it expires. If the coverage provisions of the renewal policy are substantially the same as the expired policy, few problems arise as long as the insured keeps the policy in force by paying the premiums. On the other hand, what if the insurer fails to bring material reductions in coverage or benefits to the attention of the policyholder? Does the insured have the responsibility to read the policy to determine if any material changes have been made? *See Aetna Insurance Co. v. Lythgoe*, 618 P.2d 1057 (Wyo. 1980).

In addition to the termination of coverage through expiration of the policy period, a policy may lapse or coverage may otherwise cease upon the occurrence of certain events. If the owner of a house or car sells the property, the policy may no longer be in effect simply because the insured has no insurable interest. This kind of lapse is rather straightforward compared to other situations. More problematic examples may be found in the New York Standard Fire Policy (1943 ed.) which, unless modified by written endorsement, provides that there is no coverage "while the hazard is increased by any means within the control or knowledge of the insured; or while a described building, whether intended for occupancy by owner or tenant, is vacant or unoccupied beyond a period of sixty consecutive days . . . ." See Appendix A. There also is case law for the proposition that, absent a policy provision extending coverage, an automobile liability policy lapses on the death of the named insured. *Wilkins v. Inland Mutual Insurance Co.*, 253 F.2d 489 (4th Cir. 1958). However, modern auto policies frequently extend protection to (1) the named insured's surviving spouse, if a resident of the same household; (2) the named insured's legal representative, but only while acting within the scope of such duties; and (3) any person having proper temporary custody of the vehicle, until the legal representative is appointed and qualified. *See Oroian v. Allstate Insurance Co.*, 62 Md. App. 654, 490 A.2d 1321 (1985). See also Annotation, *Automobile Insurance: Coverage As Extending Beyond Death of Named Insured*, 30 A.L.R.3d 1047 (1970). Does the auto policy in Appendix E speak to this point?

Group insurance contracts present some unique issues regarding modification and termination of coverage similar to those that were explored in § 7.01. The group contract may expire or be modified or terminated by the insurer and the policyholder; this has an obvious effect on certificate holders when it happens. In other cases, the certificate holder may lose his or her eligibility for coverage even though the policy continues in force without any change. Does the certificate holder have any rights in these situations? Consider the following materials.

[1]   Group Coverage

GUARDIAN LIFE INSURANCE CO. OF AMERICA v. ZERANCE

505 Pa. 345, 479 A.2d 949 (1984)

LARSEN, JUSTICE.

This appeal involves a declaratory judgment action filed by appellee, Frances M. Zerance, guardian of the estate of Nicholas A. Zerance (insured), seeking judicial construction of a group medical benefits insurance policy issued pursuant to a group plan by the appellant, Guardian Life Insurance Company of America (Guardian Life). The policy in question provided for, inter alia, medical and health benefits coverage for employees of Middletown East End Warehouse Company (Middletown) who qualified under the group plan. We are asked to construe the group insurance policy to determine whether the appellant properly terminated the insured's disability benefit payments as of December 31, 1979. The controversy arose in the following background.

In 1974, Nicholas A. Zerance was an employee of Middletown. He was insured under the group insurance policy issued by Guardian Life. On February 16, 1974, the insured became disabled due to certain after-effects of surgery. As a result of the disability, he has required extensive medical and nursing care on a continuing basis. The medical and nursing expenses necessitated by his disability were covered under the Guardian Life group medical policy from February 16, 1974 until December 31, 1979.

In November, 1978, appellee, Frances M. Zerance, as guardian of the insured, was informed by Middletown that the insurance coverage would be terminated on November 30, 1978. On November 30, 1978, Middletown cancelled its group policy with Guardian Life effective December 1, 1978. The appellant continued to pay medical and nursing expenses for the insured until December 31, 1979. At that time, pursuant to the terms of the policy, all benefits were terminated. The policy provisions under which benefit payments were discontinued provide as follows:

"Termination of Your Insurance.

"The group policy provides that your insurance will terminate upon the earlier of: (a) The date the group policy terminates or is amended to terminate insurance on the class or classes of employees to which you belong or (b) The date your employment terminates. This means that the date you cease to be actively at work on a full time basis with your employer, except that under certain circumstances specified in the Group Policy, your employment may be deemed, for the purposes of the insurance, to continue for a limited period after such cessation.

In addition, if you fail to make the required contribution, when due, for any benefits for which you are required to contribute, such benefits will terminate at the end of the period for which you made the last required contribution.

"Coverage after Termination.

"If this insurance terminates for any reason (other than for non-payment of premium or because of exhaustion of the total benefit after age 65) and on such date of termination you or your dependent are totally disabled and under the care of a physician, coverage pertaining solely to the injury or sickness which caused the total disability will be extended during the uninterrupted continuance of such total disability subject to all limitations and provisions of this major medical expense coverage. Covered charges which would otherwise be payable for complications of pregnancy shall also be paid after termination of insurance provided the pregnancy had its inception prior to the date of the termination of insurance.

"This extension of insurance shall terminate on the earliest of the following occurrences: (a) The date these benefits are replaced by another plan providing similar benefits (other than a group policy issued by the Guardian) and under which you or your dependent are a member of the classes eligible; (b) The date total disability ends but in no event beyond the last day of the calendar year next following the calendar year in which your insurance terminated."

The trial court, treating the case as a non-jury civil action, received evidence and concluded that the cancellation of the group insurance was effective and binding on the insured. A verdict was entered in favor of Guardian Life. Appellee's exceptions were denied and judgment was entered in accordance with the verdict. On appeal, the Superior Court reversed, holding that the insured's right to the payment of benefits was vested and the termination provision of the policy may not be construed to divest that right. For the reasons that follow, we reverse the order of the Superior Court and hold that the termination provisions of the Guardian Life group insurance contract are valid and the insured is bound by the language of the policy.

Generally, in group insurance policies, the insurance carrier and the employer are the primary contracting parties and the rights of an insured employee are no greater than as provided by the terms of the policy. Where it is consistent with the provisions of the policy, and notice of the intended cancellation is given to the insured, the employer may cancel the policy and thereby terminate the coverage of the individual employees.

The appellee argues that the insured's right to benefits under the Guardian Life group policy fully vested at the time he became disabled, and the subsequent cancellation of the policy cannot divest that right. The appellee relies on *Turley v. John Hancock Mutual Life Insurance Company*, 315 Pa. 245, 173 A. 163 (1934) as controlling this case. Appellee's reliance on *Turley* is ill-founded.

In *Turley,* the insured died and his widow made a claim for a $1,000.00 insurance benefit under the terms of a group policy. The group insurance provided a death benefit payable in a lump sum in the event of death to the named beneficiary. The policy also provided:

> In the event of total and permanent disability, occurring before the age of 60, ... the . . . . insurance . . . . will become payable to the member himself in a single sum.

> If total and permanent disability occurs after the age of 60, the insurance will be paid only when death occurs.

Id., at 247, 173 A. at 164. The insured became totally and permanently disabled after the age of 60 and subsequently died. The only defense raised to the widow's suit was that the insured had been discharged from his employment prior to his death and he failed to convert the insurance.[7] The defense concluded that because of the insured's discharge and his failure to convert, there was no liability under the policy. The question before the court then was whether the discharge affected the insured's rights as urged by the defendants. In upholding Turley's widow's right to the insurance benefit, we said:

> Undoubtedly this contention would be sound had not a member's substantive right prior thereto become fixed. Turley became totally and permanently disabled when he was a member of the association and an employee of the company. He was unable to continue his employment. When that condition arose he became entitled to the benefit from the insurance to be paid to his beneficiary at death. His rights became vested. True, the benefit was not to be enjoyed until death, but his beneficiary was then to receive it. Rights are vested when the right to enjoyment, present or prospective, has become the property of some particular person or persons as a present interest. Turley was not able to work after being disabled, of course; his rights were fixed and determined . . . when he was forced to leave his work because of disability. It was not the intent and purpose of the "Plan of Protection" to oust a man from the association, as well as from the company, who had become permanently disabled after he was 60. The "Plan of Protection" distinctly says otherwise.

Id. at 249–250; 173 A. at 165. The insurance contract in *Turley* provided that when an insured became totally and permanently disabled, a lump sum benefit vested. The time when payment of that benefit was due depended upon the age of the disabled insured. If the insured was under 60 years of age payment was due immediately to the insured himself. If the insured was over the age of 60 then payment was due upon his death. The total and permanent disability of the insured activated the insurer's obligation to pay the lump sum benefit and vested the insured's right to receive it. Under the terms of the policy, this obligation of the insurer and right of the insured was not dependent upon continuation of the insurance contract.

---

[7] The policy provided that the insurance terminated upon termination of membership in the employees' association unless the insured elected to continue the coverage under the conversion privilege contained in the contract. (When Turley was discharged from his employment, his membership in the Employee's Association terminated).

The issue in the case *sub judice* goes beyond the question of whether the insured's right to benefit payments became vested when he suffered his disability. Indeed, subject to the terms of the policy, the disability of the insured activated his right to receive reimbursement for necessary medical expenses as such expenses were incurred. The question here is whether that right can be terminated by cancellation of the policy.

The clear provisions of the termination clause in question were part of the insurance contract from its inception. Payment of medical benefits to a disabled insured was specifically subject to those provisions. The insured's right to benefit payments can rise no higher than as provided by the terms of the policy. Under the policy, cancellation extinguished the right to benefits, subject to the provisions extending benefits in particular cases. When the insurance terminated for any reason other than non-payment of premium or exhaustion of benefits, the policy provided for "coverage after termination" which extended the insurance coverage until, "the date total disability ends but in no event beyond the last day of the calendar year next following the calendar year in which [the] insurance terminated." Where the policy language is unambiguous, a court cannot adopt a construction which conflicts with the clear meaning of the language. Language in a policy that is clear cannot be interpreted to mean other than what it plainly says. The language in the policy in question is clear and unambiguous and must be enforced as written.

The appellant, Guardian Life followed the policy provisions to the letter, providing benefits from the date of disability until December 31, 1979—the last day of the calendar year which followed the year in which the insurance was cancelled. The appellee argues that the appellant is liable for the payment of benefits until the policy limit of $250,000.00 is exhausted. This monetary limitation, is, however, subject to the termination provisions of the insurance contract. The appellant was liable for benefit payments up to $250,000.00 or until the right to benefits was otherwise terminated. Here, the right to benefits was otherwise terminated by the cancellation of the policy. We may not rewrite the insurance contract, under the guise of judicial interpretation, to expand the coverage beyond that as provided in the policy.

The appellee next argues that if the policy must be construed as terminating the insured's benefits following cancellation of the contract, then the termination provisions are void as against public policy. The provisions in question specifically provide a qualified insured with insurance coverage for a reasonable time after the policy terminates. We can discern no public policy that forbids such provisions.

> Public policy is to be ascertained by reference to the laws and legal precedents and not from general considerations of supposed public interest.

Muschany v. United States, 324 U.S. 49, 65 S. Ct. 442, 89 L. Ed. 744 (1945). In *Mamlin v. Genoe,* 340 Pa. 320, 17 A.2d 407, 409 (1941), Justice Stern, writing for this Court, stated:

> It is only when a given policy is so obviously for or against the public health, safety, morals or welfare that there is a virtual [unanimity]

of opinion in regard to it, that a court may constitute itself the voice of the community in [declaring that policy to be against public policy].

We find no such [unanimity] of opinion against the policy terms challenged in this case. The termination provisions are not obviously against the public health, safety, morals or welfare of the people.

> Only in the clearest of cases . . . may a court make an alleged public policy the basis of judicial decision.

Id. at 409, 17 A.2d at 409. The provisions in question are lawful and not contrary to any public policy of Pennsylvania.

. . . .

The order of the Superior Court is reversed and judgment of the trial court is reinstated.

NOTES

1. *Majority rule.* Where the group insurance contract clearly and unambiguously provides that the insurer or employer may modify or terminate coverage, the majority rule is illustrated by *Zerance.* Besides affecting currently employed insureds, the insurer's or employer's right to modify has been recognized even where the changes affect retired employees who were promised "lifetime" health benefits. *See Gable v. Sweetheart Cup Co., Inc.,* 35 F.3d 851 (4th Cir. 1994), *cert. denied,* 514 U.S. 1057 (1995). But compare *Jensen v. Sipco, Inc.,* 38 F.3d 945 (8th Cir. 1994), *cert. denied,* 115 S. Ct. 1428 (1995) (holding retired employees' rights had vested under health plan). However, according to most cases on the subject, there still is an obligation on behalf of the insurer or employer, at least where it is a contributory plan, to give reasonable notice of modification or termination to the employee. *Ogden v. Continental Casualty Co.,* 208 Kan. 806, 494 P.2d 1169 (1972). See Robert H. Jerry, II, Understanding Insurance Law § 124 (2d ed. 1996).

2. *Exceptions to majority rule.* Some group policies by their terms provide for vesting of benefits and thereby restrict the insurer's right to modify or terminate the coverage. The *Turley* case discussed in *Zerance* is an example. *See also Aetna Life Insurance Co. v. Wilson,* 190 Okla. 363, 123 P.2d 656 (1942). Other cases have prohibited modification of benefits on the ground that there was an ambiguity in the master contract because it did not expressly provide for modification, even though there was an express provision for termination of the contract, *Danzig v. Dikman,* 78 A.D.2d 303, 434 N.Y.S.2d 217 (1980), or that the contract was otherwise ambiguous regarding the power of the insurer and employer to modify or terminate benefits, *Myers v. Kitsap Physicians Service,* 78 Wash. 2d 286, 474 P.2d 109 (1970), 66 A.L.R.3d 1196 (1975). *See also Brown v. Blue Cross & Blue Shield of Miss.,* 427 So. 2d 139 (Miss. 1983)(holding that it would be a violation of public policy to give effect to the insurer's attempted cancellation of a group health contract where the employee and his spouse conceived a child, relying upon the policy in full force and effect, after waiting the required time and were denied any opportunity to obtain insurance elsewhere).

These cases, however, offer little consolation to the employee or other certificate holder in the usual situation where the power to terminate or modify is set out in the policy and notice is properly given. *See, e.g., Solomon v. North American Life and Casualty Insurance Co.,* 151 F.3d 1132 (9th Cir. 1998) (insurer's exercise of right to cancel a group life insurance policy issued to a trust is not a breach of contract or bad faith when insurer acts under termination provision in master policy and individual's certificate and gives proper notice); *Luningham v. Arkansas Poultry Federation Insurance Trust,* 922 S.W.2d 1 (Ark. Ct. App. 1996) (insurer was not required to obtain participant's agreement before modifying terms of the health insurance policy).

Most group insurance programs are offered through the employment setting and are therefore governed by the Employee Retirement Income Security Act of 1974, 29 U.S.C. §§ 1001-1461 ("ERISA"). Although ERISA provides many protections to employees, preventing an employer from modifying or terminating the insurance benefits is not one of them. *See Inter-Modal Rail Employees Ass'n v. Atchison, Topeka, & Santa Fe Railway Co.,* 520 U.S. 510, 513 (1997) ("unless an employer contractually cedes its freedom, . . . it is 'generally free under ERISA, for any reason at any time, to adopt, modify, or terminate [its] welfare pla[n].' "; quoting *Curtiss-Wright Corp. v. Schoonejongen,* 514 U.S. 73, 78 (1995)); *Spacek v. Maritime Association, ILA Pension Plan,* 134 F.3d 283, 293 (5th Cir. 1998) ("strong weight of authority throughout the circuits indicates that, in the area of welfare benefits, which are not subject to ERISA's minimum vesting and accrual requirements, . . . a general amendment provision in a welfare benefits plan is of itself sufficient to unambiguously negate any inference that the employer intends for employee welfare benefits to vest contractually, and thus become unalterable, after the employee retires"); *Chiles v. Ceridian Corp.,* 95 F.3d 1505, 1512 n. 2 (10th Cir. 1996) ("reservation of rights clause allows the employer to retroactively change the medical benefits of retired participants"). The court in *American Federation of Grain Millers, AFL-CIO v. International Multifoods Corp.,* 116 F.3d 976 (2d Cir. 1997), explained it this way:

> Unlike pension plan benefits, the benefits provided by a welfare plan generally are not vested and an employer can amend or terminate a welfare plan at any time. . . . We have explained the reason for this rule as follows:
>
>> With regard to an employer's right to change medical plans, Congress evidenced its recognition of the need for flexibility in rejecting the automatic vesting of welfare plans. Automatic vesting was rejected because the costs of such plans are subject to fluctuating and unpredictable variables. Actuarial decisions concerning fixed annuities are based on fairly stable data, and vesting is appropriate. In contrast, medical insurance must take account of inflation, changes in medical practice and technology, and increases in the costs of treatment independent of inflation. These unstable variables prevent accurate predictions of future needs and costs.
>
> *Moore v. Metropolitan Life Ins. Co.,* 856 F.2d 488, 492 (2d Cir. 1988)

The rule is the same for plans that provide welfare benefits to retirees—retiree welfare benefits are generally not vested, and an employer can amend or terminate a plan providing such benefits at any time.

. . . .

However, . . . if an employer promises vested benefits, that promise will be enforced. However, the circuits disagree as to exactly what language is required to create a promise to vest retiree medical benefits.

All courts agree that if a document unambiguously indicates whether retiree medical benefits are vested, the unambiguous language should be enforced.

However, when the documents are ambiguous as to whether retiree medical benefits are vested, the circuits disagree as to how the documents should be interpreted. . . .

116 F.3d at 979–80. *See also Serrato v. John Hancock Life Insurance Co.,* 31 F.3d 882 (9th Cir. 1994) (state may not require vesting of health insurance benefits in plan governed by ERISA); *McGann v. H & H Music Co.,* 946 F.2d 401 (5th Cir. 1991), *cert. denied,* 506 U.S. 981 (1992)(employer altered group medical plan by reducing benefits for AIDS-related claims from $1 million to $5,000). It should be noted that some disease-specific modifications in health insurance coverage could violate the Americans with Disabilities Act. Thus, there is reason to think that the result in *McGann* does not survive the enactment of the ADA. For more discussion, see Nancy R. Mansfield, *Evolving Limitations on Coverage for AIDS: Implications for Health Insurers and Employers under the ADA,* 35 Tort & Ins. L. J. 117 (1999).

3. *Ramifications of the majority rule.* It should be remembered that health insurance policies usually require that the medical expenses be incurred within the policy period. Thus, when a health policy, group or otherwise, is terminated or modified, the policy usually does not cover subsequently incurred medical expenses for which coverage has been eliminated, even though the onset of the condition that results in the medical expenses took place within the policy period. *See, e.g., Howard v. Blue Cross & Blue Shield of Nebraska,* 494 N.W.2d 99 (Neb. 1992); *Forbau v. Aetna Life Insurance Co.,* 876 S.W.2d 132 (Tex. 1993).

The preexisting condition provision, which has been a common clause in health insurance policies can also create havoc for an insured whose health insurance policy is terminated if the insured fails to take steps to maintain the continuity of coverage. If the insured has developed a condition requiring on-going medical treatment while the policy was in force, a policy that the insured purchases to replace the terminated policy may well exclude coverage for the condition for a designated period of time, or perhaps indefinitely. For more discussion of these conditions and how they are regulated, see § 4.04[4], *supra.*

[2] Conversion and Continuation Rights

AETNA LIFE INSURANCE CO. v. BARNES
361 F.2d 685 (5th Cir. 1966)

JOHN R. BROWN, CIRCUIT JUDGE:

On stipulated facts, the trial Court held the Insurer under a group policy liable to the Employee for total disability benefits. As to that holding we reverse, but remand the case as it is not certain that a possible alternative basis for liability has been factually explored.

The Insurer[1] had issued to the Employer[2] a series of integrated group policies.[3] The Employee[4] had been issued a Certificate of Insurance (note 3, *supra*).

By formal pretrial order, F.R. Civ. P. 16, the parties stipulated that there "are no contested issues of fact . . . and the case is submitted . . . on the stipulations contained in . . ." that order. The stipulated facts as such were few and tersely stated. We repeat, or slightly paraphrase, them without elaboration.

The Employee was "employed by" the Employer "at Fort Worth, Texas and . . . such employment was terminated on" January 26, 1962, "by his employer." During the time the Employee was "employed with [the Employer] and prior to the date of termination," he contracted acute and chronic pancreatitis and gall bladder trouble," and as a result of "such illnesses, he became totally and permanently disabled on February 24, 1962," approximately a month after termination of his employment. But prior to February 24, 1962, "he had not been totally and permanently disabled."

From these abbreviated, but critical, facts two things stand out. First, within approximately a month after termination of employment, the Employee became totally and permanently disabled as a result of illnesses which were active and incurred during employment. But second, although such illness was active during employment, it had not up to date of separation produced total permanent disability.

Although we are not benefited by an opinion of the District Judge in this effort to unravel Texas Insurance law, the conclusions of law based on findings of fact which are nothing more than a repetition of the stipulated facts, reveal quite clearly the District Judge's approach. Thus, he held, the "policy and certificate of insurance covers the total and permanent disability of the [Employee] beginning on February 24, 1962, which was *caused by* and had its *source in* acute and chronic pancreatitis and gall bladder trouble contracted by [him] while he was employed with [the Employer] and prior to the date

---

[1] Aetna Life Insurance Company.

[2] General Dynamics Corporation, at Fort Worth.

[3] The certificate of insurance issued to the Employee referred to them as Group Life Policy No. 4945-R; Group Accidental Death and Dismemberment Policy No. LL-58012; Group Disability Policy No. GS 9091; and Group Hospitalization Expense Policy No. H-3120-R.

[4] John C. Barnes.

of termination with [the Employer]." (Emphasis added). To the Judge the decisive point was the *time* during which the illness had its onset, not the *time* its consequences became totally disabling.

To this the Insurer has a simple, but awesome, answer: this completely disregards the policy. And so it does, for under the policy the critical thing is that the Employee has become totally disabled "while insured under the group policy." It matters not when the illness was first contracted, whether during or before employment. Indeed, the existence of employment is itself secondary for the critical time is spoken of in terms of the time "while [the employee is] *insured* under the group policy."[6] Nevertheless the two are closely intertwined as termination of insurance is defined essentially in terms of termination of employment.[7]

The plain wording of the policy (note 6, *supra*) prevents the application of the District Court's approach. And all of the cases urged here—which presumably persuaded the Court below—confuse the issue of the time at which proof of the existence of total disability must be made with the time at which such disability must exist. Indeed, the policy itself magnifies this distinction[9] as

---

[6] For ease of reference, numbers and letters in brackets are inserted, *e.g.*, [1] [a]:

"[1][a] Upon receipt . . . of satisfactory evidence that the Employee, [b] while insured under the group policy . . . has become totally disabled [c] and that such disability has existed continuously for a period of six months or more [d] and will presumably prevent the Employee for life from engaging in any . . . employment for . . . profit, [e] the Insurance Company will pay to the Employee . . . the amount of insurance in force upon the Employee's life at the time such disability commenced."

[7] As in note 6, numbers in brackets are added for convenience:

"TERMINATION OF INSURANCE"

"[2] The insurance of the Employee will terminate at the earliest applicable time indicated below:

"(a) . . . .

"(b) . . . .

"(c)[i] Insurance of the Employee will automatically cease upon termination of employment (except as provided in the next succeeding paragraph.) [ii] Cessation of active work by the Employee will be deemed termination of employment, except that [iii] if the Employee is absent on account of sickness or injury, [iv] or on account of temporary layoff or leave of absence, employment for group insurance purposes may be deemed to continue [v] while premium payments are continued by the Employer for Insurance of the Employee in accordance with the terms of the group policy.

"[3] If the Employee dies within thirty-one days after termination of employment, and if the Employee was insured under the group policy upon the date of termination of employment, then the amount of insurance for which the Employee was insured upon the date of termination of employment, less the amount of any individual policy issued within said thirty-one days on the life of the Employee in accordance with the conversion privilege described in this Certificate and in force at date of death, will be paid to the beneficiary under the group policy subject to any requirements of the group policy with regard to notice and proof of claim. Such payment will be in lieu of all other benefits with respect to the group life insurance of the Employee."

[9] Following the insuring provision (note 6, *supra*), the policy goes on to provide:

"When claim is made for permanent total disability benefits for the Employee, the Insurance Company will be permitted to examine the Employee at any time before the Employee is admitted by the Insurance Company to be permanently and totally disabled.

"NOTICE OF CLAIM"

do the text authorities[10] so heavily relied on by the Employee.

On the basis of the case as stipulated and tried, the judgment casting the Insurer liable for disability benefits was clearly wrong and must be reversed.

We must, however, deal with some theories which were unearthed largely as a result of a probing exploration from the bench during oral argument. It seemed to us from our recent experience with *John Hancock Mut. Life Ins. Co. v. Schroder,* 5 Cir., 1965, 349 F.2d 406, *affirming* S.D. Tex., 1962, 210 F. Supp. 756, and 1964, 227 F. Supp. 622, that too little attention has been paid to policy provisions which, for one reason or another, purported to keep the policy alive after formal separation from employment.

The first is the theory that the Texas Insurance Code, V.A.T.S.[11] by requiring a 31-day grace period and a mandatory conversion privilege[12] kept the policy alive up through (and beyond) February 24, 1962.

As originally enacted in 1931, the subsection providing for a mandatory conversion privilege recognized that the conversion "policy may or may not contain provisions for disability benefits and provisions for accidental death benefits, at the option of the Company."[13] This section has been successively amended to find its way into the Insurance Code of Texas, Tex. Ins. Code Ann. art. 3.50, § 2 (8), enacted in 1951.[15] By Art. 3.50, § 2(1) of the Code, as

---

"Written notice of claim for the death benefit or permanent total disability benefits provided in the group policy for the Employee shall be given to the Insurance Company at its Home Office within one year after cessation of premium payments for insurance of the Employee; if such notice is not given, the Insurance Company will not be liable for any payment on account of the death or disability of the Employee."

[10] Thus, the Employee ignores altogether the concluding phrase from 3 Appleman, Insurance Law and Practice § 1524: "In the absence of specific policy provisions, proof of disability need not be made during the time the insured is still employed. It is, of course, necessary that the disability be shown to have arisen during the continuance of such employment . . . ." See generally Annot., Time of Disability or Death With Regard to Termination of Coverage Under Group Policy, 68 A.L.R.2d 150, 160 (1959), and Texas cases cited therein.

[11] Tex. Ins. Code Ann. art. 3.50, § 2(1), (8) (1963).

[12]

"CONVERSION PRIVILEGE"

"In case of termination of employment for any reason whatsoever, the Employee will be entitled to have a policy of life insurance issued to him by the Insurance Company without further evidence of insurability, provided:

"(a) the amount of the policy will be in an amount equal to or, at the option of the Employee, an amount less than the amount of the Employee's life insurance under the group policy at the time employment terminated,

"(b) the policy will be upon one of the forms then customarily being issued by the Insurance Company, except Term Insurance,

"(c) the policy will require payment of the premium applicable to the class of risk to which the Employee belongs and to the form and amount of the policy at the Employee's then attained age,

"(d) written application for such a policy and payment of the first premium must be made by the Employee within thirty-one days after termination of employment.

"When an individual policy is issued under the 'Conversion Privilege,' it will be in exchange for all group life benefits under the group policy."

[13] Tex. Laws 1931, ch. 101, § 2(4).

[15] Tex. Laws 1951, ch. 491.

amended and presently in force, the Group Life Policy must afford "a grace period of thirty-one (31) days for the payment of any premium . . . during which grace period the death benefit coverage shall continue in force . . . ." But by § 2(8) the mandatory conversion privilege to be afforded "if the insurance . . . on a person covered under the policy ceases because of termination of employment . . ." is now expressly limited to "an individual policy of life insurance *without disability or other supplementary benefits.*" (Emphasis supplied.) And § 2(10) automatically extending for the 31-day period the insurance provided by the conversion privilege, whether exercised or not,[16] defines the triggering condition "if a person insured under the group policy *dies* during the" 31-day conversion period and restricts the benefits to "the amount of *life insurance* "to which he would have been entitled.

But comprehensive as is this intricate insurance structure and evident as is the Texas concern over the rights of its citizens as nominal assureds under group programs, no aid or comfort comes to the Employee here. First, from 1931 down through the Code, it is clear that Texas distinguishes carefully between group *life* insurance and those other benefits which often are, but need not be, a part of a group life policy. Next, and apart from the mandatory automatic insurance under § 2(10), note 16, *supra*, neither the 31-day grace period for payment of premiums nor the conversion privilege if unexercised has the effect of continuing the insurance in force after termination of employment if by the policy terms that event simultaneously terminates insurance.[18]

The second theory is more plausible and could succeed if factually supported. The heart of this contention is that the Insurer is too preoccupied with termination of *employment* rather than termination of *insurance*. Keeping this distinction carefully in mind, so the argument runs, benefits for total permanent disability occurring after formal separation from employment are nonetheless recoverable if, by reason of the policy terms, the insurance is kept alive after employment.

Of course, the Employee is absolutely right in this theory. It finds express support in the termination of insurance clause, [2] (c) [ii]–[v], (note 7, *supra*), and perhaps other parts of the policy.[19] Under [2] (c) it does state, of course, that the "insurance . . . will automatically cease upon termination of employment." But clause [2] (c) [ii], [iii], [iv] and [v] directly subtract from this sweeping, peremptory generality. Reading all together, merely ceasing active work does not constitute termination of employment if "(c) [ii] cessation of

---

[16] This mandatory coverage is afforded in [3] of the policy, note 7, supra.

[18] This seems to be the generally accepted approach, Annot., 68 A.L.R.2d 8, 116–121 (mandatory conversion privilege), 127 (grace period), as opposed to the minority view urged by the Employee here, *id.* at 125 (mandatory conversion privilege), 131 (grace period).

[19] See, *e.g.*, the insuring clause [1]. Often the disabling condition and cessation of work will coincide. But they need not do so and, indeed, that alone is not enough. Thus under [1][b] the facts must show that during the time the insurance was in force, the employee "has become totally disabled." But under [1][c] the proof must show that such disability "has existed continuously for a period of six months or more." Since this disability is defined as being such as "[1][d] will presumably prevent the Employee for life from engaging in any . . . employment for . . . profit," it is quite likely that in many situations the employee will have been unable to actively work for at least six months.

active work" is due to the employee being "[iii] absent on account of sickness or injury" or "[iv] on account of temporary layoff or leave of absence." In that situation employment for group insurance purposes is "deemed to continue" during such times as "[v] premium payments are continued by the Employer for Insurance of the Employee." Thus, if the Employee ceased active work on January 26 because of sickness, injury, layoff or leave of absence, and if the Employer continued to pay the premiums for him through February 24, his insurance would continue to that time, and he would be entitled to disability benefits because he became totally and permanently disabled while insured under the policy.

On the argument of the case, we had the strong impression that in the presentation of the cause in the trial Court, in the preparation of the stipulation and the development of the legal theories, these policy provisions had been either ignored or their importance underestimated. Of course it is not for us to remake the record or to reject that which the parties by their formal stipulation have proffered to the trial, and now to this Court. But since these policy provisions have such an immediate and perhaps decisive impact, we think that in the administration of justice, the reversal of the judgment on the theories directly presented should not prejudice the right of the Employee to pursue this theory on remand. Especially is this so since the stipulated facts as to the critical element of termination of employment (and hence insurance) are stated in conclusory, not evidential, factual terms.[21] If there is an arguable factual basis for bringing the cessation of active work within [2] (c) [iii] or [iv], then the parties should be afforded an opportunity to withdraw from the stipulation. Of course, as a part of any theory, the facts must also satisfy [2] (c) [v], but considering the manner in which large employers of the kind here involved handle group insurance programs for large bodies of employees, it is not at all unlikely that for this limited 24-day period, the proper premium contributions either were made or the Employer vis-a-vis the Insurer became liable therefor. We think for Texas, as we did for Florida, *Prudential Ins. Co. v. Roberts,* 5 Cir., 1966, 358 F.2d 394 [March 29, 1966], that in determining whether premium payments have been made, the employee's rights are not to be jeopardized by internal bookkeeping-administrative practices adopted for the convenience of the Employer and the Insurer.

Of course, it may be that in the use of these conclusory terms in the stipulated facts the parties recognize that under no arguable basis can termination of insurance be postponed through these policy definitions of termination of employment. That will soon be made known to the trial Court, and in that event the case will be at an end. The case is therefore reversed but remanded for further and not inconsistent proceedings.

---

[21] Thus, it was stipulated that the Employee "was employed by General Dynamics at Fort Worth, Texas, and that such employment was *terminated* on the 26th day of January 1962 by his employer." Again in paragraph 5 it was stipulated that the Employee "contracted" these conditions "while employed with General Dynamics and prior to the date of *termination* with General Dynamics." (Emphasis added.)

Reversed and remanded.

NOTES

1. *Conversion rights.* Many jurisdictions have statutes which require certain group insurers to offer to the insured—the employee or other certificate holder — the right to convert to an individual policy upon termination of the group coverage. The conversion right may vary depending upon whether the policy is canceled or the coverage terminates because a person is no longer eligible for the group insurance. As *Barnes* teaches, this right does not guarantee that the insured will have the same coverage as that under the group contract. *See also Wallace v. Blue Cross Hospital Service, Inc.,* 13 Ill.App.3d 803, 300 N.E.2d 531 (1973), 66 A.L.R.3d 1185 (1975). The insurer is usually required to offer an individual policy customarily marketed by the insurer at standard rates. Although the coverage under the individual policy may not be as extensive as that under the group policy and the cost to the insured may be higher, the right to convert does provide some security for those who might have become uninsurable while covered by the group contract or who might otherwise not be able to purchase insurance.

2. *Notice of right to convert.* Under the statutes mentioned in note 1, notice of the right to convert has to be given to the insured and this obligation is usually imposed on the group insurer, but the group representative or employer may satisfy this requirement. Unfortunately, the notice requirement may be satisfied in most states by including the notice in the certificate or booklet that is provided to the insured upon enrollment, which entails a real risk that the insured will not remember or will not otherwise be apprised of the right to convert when the time comes to do so. Would it be better to require that notice be given both upon enrollment and at the time the plan is terminated or the employee's group eligibility ceases? *See Life Insurance Co. of Arkansas v. Ashley,* 308 Ark. 335, 824 S.W.2d 393 (1992)(holding Arkansas statute required notice at time conversion right arises). If notice is to be given at the time the insured's right to group coverage ends, how should notice be given? Does the last sentence of the statute quoted in the following note adequately deal with the issue of how notice should be given?

3. *Time within which to exercise conversion right.* Group insureds are usually given a statutory period of 31 days to exercise the right to convert to an individual policy, assuming they have been properly notified of the right. What should happen if an insured does not receive proper notice? The National Association of Insurance Commissioners has addressed the issue in a model act governing group life insurance:

> If any individual insured under a group life insurance policy hereafter delivered in this state becomes entitled under the terms of the policy to have an individual policy of life insurance issued without evidence of insurability, subject to making of application and payment of the first premium within the period specified in such policy, and if the individual is not given notice of the existence of the right at least fifteen (15) days prior to the expiration date of the period, then in such

event the individual shall have an additional period within which to exercise the right, but nothing herein contained shall be construed to continue any insurance beyond the period provided in the policy. This additional period shall expire fifteen (15) days after the individual is given the notice but in no event shall the additional period extend beyond 60 days after the expiration date of the period provided in the policy. Written notice presented to the individual or mailed by the policyholder to the last known address of the individual or mailed by the insurer to the last known address of the individual as furnished by the policyholder shall constitute notice for the purpose of this paragraph.

III NAIC, *Group Life Insurance Definition and Group Life Insurance Standard Provisions Model Act, Model Laws, Regulations & Guidelines* 565-1, § 6 (1999). The Model Act also provides that the insured has 31 days after the group policy terminates or the insured ceases to be eligible for group coverage to exercise the right to convert, *id.* at 565–7, 565–8, § 5(H), 5(I), and that if the insured dies within this 31 day period, it will be deemed that the insured had life insurance in the amount "which he would have been entitled to have issued under the individual policy," whether or not application for the individual policy or the payment of the first premium has been made. *Id.* at 565–8, § 5(J). How does all this work?

Assume that neither the insurer or policyholder-employer gives the proper notice to an employee whose employment has been terminated and that the employee dies on the 60th day following termination. Does the estate of the employee or her dependents have any rights under the model act?

The model act or legislation similar to it has been adopted in about forty states. *Id.*, at 565–11 to 565–14.

4. *Right to continue under group coverage after eligibility ceases.* The *Barnes* case and the notes above deal with issues arising under state statutes requiring that conversion rights be contained in certain group contracts of insurance. The right involved is one of switching from a group contract to an individual contract. But what about rights to continue coverage, at least temporarily, under the group contract when the employee or certificate holder is no longer a member of the eligible group? Some states have passed statutes which give certain employees the right to elect to continue coverage under the group policy for limited periods of time. Some of these statutes have extended the right to a spouse of an employee when the spouse loses coverage, for example, due to a divorce. By far, the most significant development in this area has been the enactment of federal legislation requiring continuation coverage for persons covered under most employer-provided health insurance plans in specified situations. This federal law, commonly referred to as "COBRA," was discussed in the notes in § 4.04[1], *supra*.

5. *Notice under individual policies.* The material above deals with rights upon termination of coverage under group contracts. Of course, notice of these rights is a very important facet of a group contract. In contrast, individual contracts of insurance do not contain conversion or continuation rights upon termination. Thus, notice is not a part of the picture. However, the opportunity to renew an individual contract can be very important. Must the insurer give

notice that the policy is about to expire so that the insured might attempt to renew it? Consider the following material.

[3] Expiration and Cancellation

WAYNESVILLE SECURITY BANK V. STUYVESANT INSURANCE CO
499 S.W.2d 218 (Mo. App. 1973), 60 A.L.R.3d 157 (1974)

HOGAN, JUDGE.

Plaintiff Waynesville Security Bank, mortgagee of a "mobile home" owned by one Roy Randolph, brought this action for breach of contract as loss payee in a fire insurance policy issued by defendant Stuyvesant Insurance Company. The loss occurred after the policy had expired; the breach of contract alleged was failure to give the loss payee notice of the expiration of the policy and an opportunity to renew it. The cause was tried to the court on stipulated facts. The court found for the plaintiff and the defendant appeals. Our duty is to determine whether the trial court's judgment represents the proper legal conclusion on the facts stipulated.

From the stipulation of fact, it appears that the policy sued on is a fire insurance policy issued to Mr. Randolph on December 9, 1969. It covers loss or damage to a trailer, or "mobile home", by fire and other specified perils. The policy was endorsed to cover a different trailer in September 1970, but that endorsement is not material to the issues here presented. The term of the policy is typed clearly on its face. The policy contains no provision requiring notice of expiration on the expiration date. The loss payable clause, added by endorsement when the policy was amended, is a "standard" or "union" clause. It provides that the plaintiff's interest "shall not be invalidated by any act or neglect of the . . . Mortgagor or Owner", and further states that "in case the . . . Mortgagor or Owner shall neglect to pay any premium due under [the] policy the Lienholder shall, on demand, pay the same." The insurer reserves the right to cancel the policy upon notice to the lienholder, but the loss payable clause makes no provision for notice of the expiration of the policy, does not mention renewal, and concludes with the provision that "[n]othing herein contained shall be held to vary, alter, waive or *extend* any of the terms, conditions, agreements or limitations of such policy, other than as above stated." (Emphasis added.)

It is stipulated that the policy expired on December 9, 1970, and that it was not thereafter renewed or reinstated. It is further stipulated that no notice of the expiration of the policy was given to the insured or to the plaintiff. The trailer was completely destroyed by fire on December 13, 1970, after the policy had expired. In this court, the defendant claims it was under no obligation to notify the loss payee of the expiration of the policy or afford it an opportunity to renew. The plaintiff claims that the loss payable clause is an independent contract binding the defendant to give notice of the expiration or cancellation of the policy for nonpayment of the premium. Plaintiff emphasizes that the loss payable clause insulates it from the consequences of "any act or neglect of the . . . Mortgagor or Owner", and further maintains that the provision giving it the right to pay any premium due is ambiguous to the extent that it could reasonably be interpreted to require notice of expiration or the insurer's intention not to renew the policy.

Plaintiff's arguments are cleverly contrived but unsound. True, a standard or union mortgage clause operates as an independent contract of insurance between the mortgagee and the insurer which cannot be defeated by a breach of the conditions of the policy on the part of the mortgagor or solely by his act, but because the loss payable clause is endorsed subject to the "terms, conditions, agreements or limitations" of the policy, the insurer's obligation to the plaintiff is no broader than its obligation to the insured, except as specifically stated in the endorsement.

Plaintiff tacitly concedes as much, but asserts that by the terms of the endorsement, it was entitled to notice of cancellation of the policy for nonpayment of the premium. The difficulty with this argument is, in the first place, that the policy was not cancelled during its term. This policy was not a continuing policy, contingent upon payment of premiums as they became due periodically, as were the policies construed in *Mitchell v. Farmers Ins. Exchange,* 396 S.W.2d 647, 650[1] (Mo. 1965), and in *M.F.A. Mut. Ins. Co. v. Quinn,* 259 S.W.2d 854, 859[5] (Mo. App. 1953). The policy period was "12 Months" from "12/9/69" to "12/9/70" with no mention of renewal or of any grace or extension period. This policy was not "cancelled". Plaintiff, in its brief, treats the terms "cancellation" and "termination" as synonyms, but they are not. "Cancellation," as used in insurance law, means termination of a policy period prior to the expiration of the policy period by act of one or all of the parties; "termination" refers to the expiration of the policy by lapse of the policy period. In this case, the policy "terminated" or "expired" by lapse of the policy period. Plaintiff's argument that it did not receive notice of cancellation is therefore wholly without merit.

It is further argued by the plaintiff that the provision in the loss payable clause providing that plaintiff's interest shall not be invalidated by any act or neglect of the mortgagor, and the provision that should the mortgagor neglect to pay any premium due, the mortgagee shall, on demand, pay the premium, are ambiguous and create an inference that the mortgagee will be given notice of the expiration of the policy. This argument is strained and tenuous. The standard or union loss payable clause protects the mortgagee's interest against the [mortgagor's] breach of the *conditions of the policy,* but here there is no provision in the policy requiring the insured to renew it, and the disconnected sentence giving the plaintiff, as mortgagee, the right to pay any premium due if the mortgagor fails to do so is but declarative of the general law. *See* 55 Am. Jur. 2d Mortgages § 268, p. 359 (1971). We do not perceive the ambiguity contended for, and we are not authorized to enlarge the policy by judicial construction.

This brings us to the meritorious question presented: Was plaintiff, as an insured under an independent contract incorporating the policy provisions, entitled to notice of the expiration of the policy and an opportunity to renew it, even though no policy provision required such notice? We think not.

We are aware that in some jurisdictions, statutes have been enacted which contemplate special consideration of the interests of property owners who are exposed to a high degree of risk but are unable to obtain fire insurance through ordinary channels. Thus, it may be that fire insurance policies issued under the so-called FAIR plans require notice of nonrenewal, so the insured may have the opportunity to obtain protection elsewhere. *See* 12 U.S.C.A. § 1749bbb-3(b)(9), and § 379.845, para. 2, R.S. Mo. 1969 V.A.M.S. Other statutes contemplate continuous coverage of particular hazards as a matter of public protection, and therefore require some affirmative indication of the insurer's intention not to renew. See, for example, the statute requiring notice of intention not to renew automobile liability policies construed in *Shore v. Coronet Ins. Co.,* 7 Ill. App. 3d 782, 288 N.E.2d 887, 889[1–4] (1972). In this case, however, there is no statute requiring notice of the expiration of the policy or notice of nonrenewal. There are also cases in which the insurer's custom or course of dealing with a particular insured, such as renewing the policy without request or accepting renewal premiums late without protest have been held to estop the insurer from denying renewal, Annot., 85 A.L.R.2d 1410, 1421–1423, 1424–1432, §§ 9, 12 (1962), but there is no indication here of any such custom or course of dealing. What we are concerned with in this case is the inherent duty of an insurer to give notice of the expiration of a policy in the absence of any policy provision or statute requiring such notice. No question of estoppel or possible waiver is involved.

Counsel frankly admit that they have found no controlling precedent in the decisions of our courts. Neither have we. In *Zeiger v. Farmers' & Laborers' Coop. Ins. Ass'n,* 358 Mo. 353, 214 S.W.2d 426 (1948), the loss payable clause required the insurer to give the mortgagee notice of the mortgagor's failure to pay any premium due, and if the mortgagee desired to continue the insurance in force it was to pay the premium within ten days after such notice. The insurer's failure to give the mortgagee notice was held to be a breach of contract under the loss payable clause, but no such requirement of notice appears in this loss payable endorsement. *Billings v. Independent Mut. Fire Ins. Co.,* 251 S.W.2d 393 (Mo. App. 1952) involved lapse for nonpayment of premium rather than lapse because of expiration of the policy period, and is not authority here. We have been obliged, therefore, to look to decisions from other jurisdictions.

In *Kimball v. Clinton County New Patrons Fire Relief Ass'n,* 23 App. Div. 2d 519, 255 N.Y.S.2d 366 (1965), the plaintiff's buildings were destroyed by fire some nine and one-half months after the stated expiration date of the policy. Plaintiff, who was the named insured, charged the defendant with negligence in failing to give notice of the expiration date of the policy. The court noted that the policy was not cancelled during its term; it contained no provision requiring notice of its expiration at the expiration date, which appeared on the face of the policy, and that there was no requirement of any notice of any assessment not applicable during its term. Rejecting plaintiff's contention that the defendant was estopped to deny renewal, the court held, 255 N.Y.S.2d at 368, that "'[t]he terms of the policy were always within the knowledge of the plaintiff, and if he failed to remember that the policy expired at a certain time before the fire, it was his own negligence, and not defendant's which prevented plaintiff from renewing his policy.'"

In *Kapahua v. Hawaiian Ins. & Guar. Co.,* 50 Haw. 644, 447 P.2d 669 (1968), plaintiff sued the insurer and its agent on the theory that the defendants were negligent in failing to notify her of the expiration date of her policy or to renew her policy automatically. Plaintiff based her case on an implied contractual duty, arising out of trade custom, to notify her that her policy had expired, or to renew it without request. The primary question before the court was one of statutory interpretation, but the court came to the conclusion that the applicable statute merely restated the general insurance law without substantial deviation, and indicated that no duty rested upon an insurer to give an insured notice of the expiration date of his policy, in the absence of a policy provision or statute requiring such notice or unless the insurer had by custom or course of dealing with the particular insured, led him to believe such notice would be given.

Perhaps the most convincing reason why the insurer has no such inherent obligation apart from a policy provision or statute requiring notice of the expiration of the policy is stated in *Norkin v. United States Fire Ins. Co.,* 237 Cal. App. 2d 435, 47 Cal. Rptr. 15 (1965). There the plaintiff sued in tort, alleging among other things that the defendant insurer and several "Doe" defendants had violated a California statute prohibiting "'[t]he suppression of a fact, by one bound to disclose it'" in failing to give plaintiff notice of its intention not to renew plaintiff's automobile liability policy. The court noted that there was no allegation of an express promise to renew, and in sustaining a demurrer to the petition, held, 47 Cal. Rptr. at 17[4]:

> [P]laintiff cites no authority, and we know of none, which requires that an insurance company, a private business, must continue to contract with an insured after the original policy has, by its terms, expired. There being no such obligation, the insurance company here was under no duty to disclose its intentions to plaintiff, assuming that they existed.

These decisions are but illustrative, of course, but they do demonstrate the general principle applicable to this case. No duty rests upon an insurer to notify the insured of the expiration date of his policy, or of its intention not to renew the policy, unless such notice is required by agreement of the parties or by statute, or unless the insurer has by custom or course of dealing with the particular insured led him to believe such notice would be given. Because in this case the duty owed to the plaintiff was no greater than the duty owed to the insured, so far as notice of the expiration of the policy is concerned, defendant was not required to notify the plaintiff that the policy would expire by lapse of the policy period on December 9, 1970. With deference to the trial court, whose judgment we respect, we believe the conclusion drawn from the stipulated facts was clearly erroneous.

Accordingly, the judgment is reversed, with directions to enter a judgment for the defendant.

TITUS, C.J., BILLINGS, J., and GREENE, SPECIAL JUDGE, concur.

STONE, J., not sitting.

NOTES

1. *Notice of policy expiration.* The *Waynesville* case outlines the limited number of situations where the insured has a right to notice that an insurance policy is expiring. Should insurers be required to give notice of expiration, and, if so, for what types of insurance? What should be the consequences if notice is not properly given?

2. *Life insurance grace periods.* Modern life insurance policies and many other kinds of personal insurance policies have a thirty or thirty-one day grace period for the payment of an overdue premium. (See the "grace period" provision in the sample life insurance policy in Appendix G.) In effect, the insurer gives up its right to cancel the policy if the premium is paid within the grace period, and a payment within the grace period is treating as if it were made on time. If the payment is not made within the grace period, the policy lapses as of the date when the premium was due. If the insured dies during the grace period, the overdue premium is paid out of the proceeds owed the beneficiary. Conceptually, the insured is temporally indebted to the insurer for the delinquent premium during the grace period.

Suppose the policy period ends on June 30. On June 25, the insured tells the insurer that the policy should be "canceled effective June 30." If the insurer follows the insured's instructions, and the insured dies on July 10, does the insured have coverage by virtue of the grace period? What if the insured's message is that she "intends not to renew the policy"for the next year? For more discussion, see Robert H. Jerry, II, Understanding Insurance Law § 72 (2d ed. 1996).

3. *Notice of cancellation.* Although an insurer as a general rule has no duty to notify an insured that a policy is expiring according to its own terms, it should be clear that the opposite rule should prevail with regard to any attempt to cancel an existing insurance contract. For one thing, unless the contract provides otherwise, one party may not unilaterally rescind or cancel it. But if this right is reserved in the contract, the contract will usually provide how and when notice must be given. In fact, many states have legislation requiring notice and how it is to be given for certain types of insurance. Most policies, and even the legislation, requiring notice, however, do not require that it actually be received by the insured. It is sufficient that it is duly mailed to the last known address of the insured or the address shown in the policy. *See Government Employees Insurance Co. v. Superior Court,* 27 Ariz. App. 219, 553 P.2d 672 (1976). Does this defeat the purpose of the legislation and should the statute require more than mere mailing to the insured at one of these addresses? If so, what more would you require of the insurer?

4. *Statutory regulation regarding renewal and cancellation.* As indicated in *Waynesville,* many states now have statutes governing renewal of automobile liability policies. This legislation recognizes the hazards involved and the importance of continuous coverage for motorists. Consequently, it also governs the rights and obligations of auto insurers regarding cancellations. In addition, due to concerns about cancellations and nonrenewals of insurance

policies in general, many state legislatures have passed statutes that not only govern the automobile insurance area, but also extend into other areas of individually written insurance policies. Typically, these statutes deal with property and casualty insurance, but other types of insurance may be included. The statutes may vary in substance, but there are some common features.

Some statutes begin with a general provision that prohibits cancellations or nonrenewals solely because of age, race, color, religion, sex, national origin, or ancestry of the insured. Beyond this, a distinction is usually made between policies which have been in effect for a short period and those which have been in effect for longer periods or which have been renewed. For example, if the policy has been in effect for less than 60 days, the insurer may be able to cancel for any reason other than those listed at the beginning of this paragraph. If the policy has been in effect for at least 60 days or is a renewal policy, the insurer is prohibited from canceling or refusing to renew except for certain specified reasons. These reasons usually include failure to pay the premium and fraud in obtaining the policy, but may also include, in the case of automobile insurance, events such as loss of driver's license, permanent disability, and certain criminal convictions associated with driving a motor vehicle. The statutes usually contain provisions detailing how far in advance the insurer must give notice of cancellation or nonrenewal and the consequences of failing to comply with the provision. Finally, the statutes may include provisions requiring the insurer to state the reasons for its action, provisions immunizing the insurer from defamation actions in connection with the obligation to state reasons, and provisions outlining the insured's right to contest the insurer's action through some type of administrative proceeding.

5. *Court imposed restrictions on nonrenewal and cancellation.* Even though the insurance contract may give the insurer the right to cancel, there are cases holding that for public policy reasons it may constitute a breach of contract to fail to renew or to cancel an insurance policy. *See, e.g., L'Orange v. Medical Protective Co.,* 394 F.2d 57 (6th Cir. 1968) (insured under medical malpractice policy stated cause of action for insurer's cancellation due to insured having testified as expert witness in malpractice case against another individual insured by insurer). In fact, several courts have held that an insurer may be guilty of the tort of bad faith for canceling or failing to renew a policy even though it would appear that the insurer had the right to do so. See Roger C. Henderson, *The Tort of Bad Faith in First-Party Insurance Transactions After Two Decades,* 37 Ariz. L. Rev. 1153, 1161 (1995).

6. *Handling post-cancellation late payments.* Suppose the insurer sends a cancellation notice to the insured, indicating that the policy has been cancelled due to nonpayment of premiums. The insured, perhaps having received the cancellation notice (but perhaps not), sends a check for the delinquent premium. If the insurer cashes the check, is the policy reinstated? In the typical scenario, the insured has an accident or suffers a loss shortly after sending in the check, or shortly after the insurer cashes it. In *Brown v. Progressive Gulf Insurance Co.,* No. 1998-CA-01248-SCT, 2000 Miss. LEXIS 36, at *1 (Miss. Feb. 24, 2000), the court held that the insurer was not estopped to deny coverage simply because it administratively processed a late premium

check by cashing it and then issuing a refund check to the insured. The court reasoned that this did not constitute a "formal election" to revive the otherwise canceled policy. *Id.* at *12.

But an insurer that cashes the check runs some risk in doing so. Would *Brown* be decided differently if on four prior occasions the insurer had reinstated the policy when the insured made premium payments that were equally late? Under such circumstances, the insurer may be estopped to deny the existence of coverage or may be deemed to have waived the right to cancel the policy. *See McKeeman v. General American Life Insurance Co.,* 111 Nev. 1042, 899 P.2d 1124 (1995); compare *Hanson v. Cincinnati Life Insurance Co.,* 571 N.W.2d 363 (N.D. 1997). If the insurer simply retains, but does not cash, three monthly checks for the late premium payments after having sent the insured a cancellation notice, is this enough to justify the insured in thinking that the policy has been reinstated? *See Barnett v. Funding Plus of America, Inc.,* 740 So.2d 1069 (Ala. 1999).

7. *Cancellation compared to rescission and reformation.* Needless to say, one should examine the statutes and case law in the particular jurisdiction regarding cancellations and nonrenewals. For example, assume that the insurer has a right to cancel an auto liability policy because there was a fraudulent misrepresentation, but the insured is negligent in causing an accident prior to any attempt by the insurer to cancel. Is the policy to be voided *ab initio*? Is there a difference between the right to cancel under the statute and the common law right of rescission? *Compare Glockel v. State Farm Mutual Automobile Insurance Co.,* 224 Neb. 598, 400 N.W.2d 250 (1987) (holding, at a time when Nebraska did not mandate that motorists carry auto liability insurance, that statutory right to cancel did not foreclose insurer's right to rescind policy *ab initio*) with *Munroe v. Great American Insurance Co.,* 234 Conn. 182, 661 A.2d 581 (1995) and *Erie Insurance Exchange v. Lake,* 671 A.2d 681 (Pa. 1996) (both of which held that cancellation statute abrogated insurer's right to rescind auto liability policy *ab initio* if it would eliminate coverage for innocent third-party claimants). *See also Douglas v. Nationwide Mutual Insurance Co.,* 323 Ark. 105, 913 S.W.2d 277 (1996) (holding insurer may rescind first-party policy *ab initio*, but that it would be a violation of the Arkansas unfair trade practices statute to do so for a liability policy when third-party claims are at issue).

The fact that an insurer may not have a right to rescind a liability policy *ab initio* does not mean that an insurer may not be allowed to seek reformation, even if the result of the reformation is to eliminate coverage for a third-party claim. *See Slaby v. Cox,* 827 P.2d 18 (Kan. 1992).

8. *Problem: Canceling the binder.* On February 1, Alex meets with his agent to renew a policy of property insurance on his home which had lapsed, saying "I want to get some coverage." The agent responds, "Okay." Alex gives the agent a $500 check for the anticipated premium; the agent retains the premium. Alex fills out an application which states below the signature line, "coverage is not provided until this application is approved at the Insurer's home office." At this point, Alex thinks he is covered by a temporary binder from Ace Insurance Co., as per his prior dealings with the agent and the insurer. On February 10, the agent visits Alex, returns the $500 check, and

tells him that the insurer "wouldn't be able to write it [meaning, the coverage]." Parks, angered by the denial, procures coverage from Reliable Insurance Co. later that day. On February 16, a tornado destroys his home. On March 16, Ace Insurance sends Alex a letter notifying him that it had decided to reject his applications; the letter states, *inter alia*, that "the coverage provided under this application and binder is canceled effective April 8. We are not able to issue a policy. We urge you to secure other insurance to prevent any lapse in coverage." Reliable pays for Alex's loss, but Reliable now seeks contribution from Ace, contending that Ace was also on the risk at the time of the loss. Is Reliable correct? For a case with very similar facts, *see Parks v. State Farm General Insurance Co.*, 231 Ga. App. 26, 497 S.E.2d 575 (1998).

Chapter 8

CLAIMS PROCESSES

"The claim professional must harness all of his or her knowledge and expertise to accomplish the objectives of the claim function. He or she must also adhere to the highest degree of ethical conduct. In addition to interacting with other insurance personnel and service providers in a professional manner, the claim professional must deal with public's and regulator's expectations. Insurance companies provide such a vital and necessary service to society that the selling and servicing of insurance is imbued with a public trust."—James K. Markham, Kevin M. Quinley, & Layne S. Thompson, The Claims Environment 27–28 (1993)

§ 8.01 Notice, Proof of Loss, and Other Claims Provisions

Every insurance policy contains a variety of provisions addressing when and how the insured's claims are to be administered. As a practical matter, these provisions elaborate upon both the insurer's and the insured's rights and responsibilities during contract performance.

For example, first-party insurance policies, such as property insurance, have "notice of loss" provisions which, as the name of the clause suggests, require the insured to give notice of losses or accidents within a relatively short period of time after the loss is suffered. First-party policies also have "proof of loss" requirements which instruct the insured to provide a sworn statement to the insurer with detailed information, as requested by the insurer in the proof of loss form, about any claim. Property insurance policies, an important kind of first-party insurance, may contain a provision requiring an appraisal to determine the amount of the loss. Some policies require that certain disputes between the insured and insurer be submitted to arbitration.

Liability insurance policies also have notice of loss provisions. In addition, liability insurance contracts typically contain an important provision requiring the insured to cooperate with the insurer in defending any claims brought against the insured. Both property and liability insurance policies often contain "limitation of action" clauses, which are essentially private statutes of limitations: the insured must assert any claim against the insurer on the policy within a specified period of time, or be barred from a remedy.

Each of these clauses is included in an insurance policy for one or more reasons of benefit to the insurer, or perhaps both the insurer and insured. Not surprisingly, then, insurers usually urge strict enforcement of these provisions, sometimes describing them as conditions which must be met before the insured may bring an action on the policy. From the insured's perspective, however, much can be lost from failure to comply to the letter with one of these provisions; indeed, forfeiture of all coverage for a loss or potential liability is a possible consequence. Generally speaking, courts abhor forfeitures. With many of these clauses, then, the issue for the court is whether strict, literal compliance with the policy's provisions is required, or whether something short of literal compliance is sufficient. Stated otherwise, should the insurer prevail even where an insured's failure to comply works no harm? Consider the following materials.

[1] Notice of Loss

JONES v. BITUMINOUS CASUALTY CORP.

821 S.W.2d 798 (Ky. 1991)

LEIBSON, JUSTICE.

[Bituminous Casualty Corporation, the insurer-respondent, filed a declaratory judgment action in which it sought to establish that it had "no obligation or duty to appear and defend. . .or to indemnify" under a liability policy it issued to Huston Partin and others doing business as S & J Mining Company. The injury giving rise to the insureds' potential liability was suffered by John Jones in an explosion on the mining company's premises on February 7, 1988.]

At one point John Jones had been a partner in the enterprise, but at the time of the explosion he was no longer associated with it. He testified that he was revisiting the premises to check on some equipment and to see when the mine would be reopened. He suffered serious injuries when a fire barrel kept on the premises exploded while in use. At the time of the explosion Huston Partin was either the principal party or the sole owner in S & J Mining Company.

The insurance carrier, Bituminous Casualty, was not notified of the occurrence for six and one-half months. The trial court rendered summary judgment in favor of the insurance carrier, declaring "the policy in question is voided because of the insured's breach of the policy requirement of prompt notice." Jones argued the insurance carrier suffered "no prejudice" from the delay in providing notice, but the trial court made its decision on the basis that prejudice is not required. The Court of Appeals has affirmed. We have accepted discretionary review, and we reverse for reasons that follow.

Huston Partin testified by deposition that he purchased the public liability insurance policy at issue because he was required by government authorities to do so in order to obtain his mining permit. Kentucky Administrative Regulation, 405 KAR 10:030, Sec. 4, requires a public liability insurance policy to cover personal injury and property damage to others, including damage caused by the use of explosives.

The policy in question is designated "Commercial General Liability Coverage." The policy period was from June 11, 1987 to June 11, 1988. Throughout the time span of coverage the partners in S & J Mining changed, continually, except for Huston Partin. John Jones became a partner in December 1987, and remained one until the mine was shut down two weeks before the explosion on February 7, 1988.

According to his deposition, Jones went back to the premises to see if the mine owner, Huston Partin, had any plans to reopen in the near future and to check on equipment owned by a different company, Nan Belle Corporation, where Jones was also employed, which was still located at the mine site. Jones and others who had come to the site to see if the mine was going to be reopened started a fire in a fire barrel located on the premises to provide warmth. Some time later Jones went back to the barrel to poke up the fire and the barrel exploded. His right leg was amputated and his hearing and eyesight were permanently impaired as a result of the explosion. Huston Partin testified by deposition that state and federal investigators had reported the explosion was caused by powder (explosives) in the barrel. Subsequently he was cited by the government as the mine operator for a violation generated by his mishandling of explosives.

John Jones testified that he had no idea as to the cause of the explosion, and for some time thought someone had intentionally tried to blow him up. It was only after completion of the investigation that John Jones considered the explosion might have been an accidental occurrence and the subject of a liability insurance claim.

Huston Partin learned of the explosion and injury to Jones on the day it occurred, but he seems to have been unaware he had insurance that might cover Jones' injury. Thus he failed to notify his insurance carrier of the injury. Indeed, for whatever reason, whether because his financial circumstances render him judgment proof or otherwise, Partin has shown little interest in these proceedings, having failed to respond to his insurance carrier's motion for summary judgment or to appeal the declaratory judgment denying him coverage. Nevertheless, it is quite evident that the real party in interest in the coverage question is Jones, the victim of the explosion.

The insurance carrier, Bituminous Casualty, first became aware of the occurrence through a letter sent to Partin by Jones' attorney, dated August 20, 1988, with a copy to Partin's insurance agent, Energy Insurance Agency, advising Jones intended to pursue a claim. This agency in turn reported the potential claim to Bituminous Casualty on August 24, 1988.

The particular provision in the policy with which we are concerned is in "Section IV — COMMERCIAL GENERAL LIABILITY CONDITIONS." This Section includes multiple, diverse conditions pertaining to obligations of both the insurer and the insured. The one in question is:

"2. Duties In The Event Of Occurrence, Claim Or Suit.

a. You must see to it that we are notified promptly of an 'occurrence' which may result in a claim."

"Section V" of the policy covers "DEFINITIONS" and provides:

"9. 'Occurrence' means an accident, including continuous or repeated exposure to substantially the same general harmful conditions."

The trial court decided this prompt notice clause of the policy was breached by the six and one-half months' delay between the date of the occurrence and the date the occurrence was first reported to the insurance carrier, and further, that this breach was fatal to the coverage without regard to whether the liability insurer sustained prejudice from the delay in giving notice. The trial court cited as authority the view that such "prompt notice" requirements are strictly a matter of contract law, and, as such, "a condition precedent to recovery on the policy." *Reserve Ins. Co. v. Richards, Ky.,* 577 S.W.2d 417, 419 (1979) . . . .

However, although the leading case, *Reserve Ins. Co. v. Richards,* expressed the view that notice is a condition precedent and prejudice from the delay is not material, as Justice Wintersheimer pointed out in his dissent in *Shipley [v. Kentucky Farm Bureau Ins., Ky.,* 747 S.W.2d 596 (1988)], in fact "[i]n *Richards, supra,* the liability carrier did not receive notice until after judgment was entered against the insured which denied the insurance company any opportunity to defend." 747 S.W.2d at 599. The three judge dissent in *Shipley* took the position there was a factual question involving both whether the insured had exercised "reasonable diligence" in providing notice considering the circumstances, and whether the delay in providing notice had prejudiced the insurer.

A recent annotation on the subject in 32 A.L.R.4th 141 addresses the "Modern Status of Rules Requiring Liability Insurer[s] to Show Prejudice to Escape Liability Because of [the] Insured's Failure or Delay in Giving Notice of Accident or Claim, or in Forwarding Suit Papers." It seeks to cover all the more recent cases on this subject from all jurisdictions, including those following a "traditional" view that the "liability insurer need not show that it was prejudiced by an insured's unreasonable and unexcused omission or delay in giving notice," *id.* at 146, and those "representing a modern trend away from the traditional that prejudice to a liability insurer is immaterial" to a new position that "a liability insurer is required to show that it was prejudiced by the insured's omission or delay." *Id.* at 157. Kentucky, citing *Reserve Ins. Co. v. Richards, supra,* is listed among those states still using the so-called "traditional" view.

[While]. . .acknowledging that there are various gradations in adherence to both the "traditional view" and the "modern trend," it suffices to say that a substantial majority now supports the modern trend, holding that an insurer cannot withdraw coverage on the ground that a notice condition has not been met unless the insurer can show that it was prejudiced by the act of the insured. Allowing for certain difficulties in doing the accounting, the ALR Annotation and its Supplement provide cases from some 29 other states now holding that the insurer must show prejudice, and only about 20 still adhering to the view that the presence or absence of prejudice is immaterial. The traditional view has become the minority view, and the view requiring proof of prejudice before invoking a forfeiture now represents the mainstream of American jurisprudence on this subject.

The time has come for Kentucky to reconsider whether failure to provide prompt notice should automatically defeat liability insurance coverage regardless of circumstances . . . .

There are at least four major features in the status of insurance law as it has presently evolved in Kentucky (utilized in varying degrees by the cases from other jurisdictions rejecting the rule of strict contractual construction) which make it unreasonable to follow *Reserve Ins. Co. v. Richards, supra,* in present circumstances. They are:

1) Contracts of Adhesion. Standard form insurance policies such as this are recognized as contracts of adhesion because they are not negotiated; they are offered to the insurance consumer on essentially a "take it or leave it" basis without affording the consumer a realistic opportunity to bargain. As to contracts of adhesion, we stated in *Wolford v. Wolford, Ky.,* 662 S.W.2d 835, 838 (1984): "If the contract has two constructions, the one most favorable to the insured must be adopted . . . . If the contract language is ambiguous, it must be liberally construed to resolve any doubts in favor of the insured . . . ."

A strict forfeiture interpretation of the prompt notice requirement excludes from the equation both the reasons why the insured failed to give prompt notice, such as whether a layman would realize that there was a covered occurrence, and the question whether the insurance carrier suffered any substantial prejudice from the delay. Absent language in the contract clearly spelling out the meaning and parameters of prompt notice and automatic forfeiture consequences, the reach of the term and the consequences are vague. The policy has a latent ambiguity which is subject to the rule of construction that applies to a contract of adherence.

2) The "doctrine of reasonable expectations." In *Woodson v. Manhattan Life Ins. Co. of New York, Ky.,* 743 S.W.2d 835, 839 (1987), we summarized from R.H. Long's "The Law of Liability Insurance," Sec. 5.10B:

> "The gist of the doctrine is that the insured is entitled to all the coverage he may reasonably expect to be provided under the policy. Only an unequivocally conspicuous, plain and clear manifestation of the company's intent to exclude coverage will defeat that expectation."

While recognizing that the policy language clearly imposes a duty on the insured to promptly notify the company, by failing to define prompt notice or to warn of a forfeiture, this result falls beyond the reasonable expectations of the ordinary insurance consumer.

3) Statutory coverage. Huston Partin purchased this policy of public liability insurance because it was required by law in order to obtain a mining permit for the benefit of those who would be exposed to the risk involved by the mining operations. The insurance was required by administrative regulations enacted pursuant to statute, and as such a declaration of public policy. In *Bishop v. Allstate Ins. Co., Ky.,* 623 S.W.2d 865, 867 (1981), we struck down the "household" exclusion clause in an automobile liability insurance contract "to the extent that [such exclusions] dilute or eliminate the minimum coverage requirements of the MVRA." *Bishop v. Allstate* has become a leading case on interpreting policies purchased to provide statutory coverage. We have recently cited and applied it in different but similar circumstances . . . . This case presents a similar problem.

While we recognize that insurance carriers have the right to impose reasonable conditions and limitations on their insurance coverage even where coverage is required by law, nevertheless the question then becomes the reasonableness of the condition as a limitation on public policy as opposed to one of strict contract considerations between private parties where no public interest is involved. Recognizing this, whereas a clause requiring prompt notice is reasonable, and a clause defeating coverage where notice unreasonably delayed causes prejudice to the insurer is appropriate, a clause working a strict forfeiture regardless of prejudice unreasonably interferes with coverage required by mine safety regulations.

4) Premiums. The insurance carrier has argued that such clauses are essential from an actuarial standpoint in order to price the insurance according to the risk. Whereas this argument is valid with reference to imposing on the insurer risks which are unreasonable and unforeseeable, such is not the case with this clause in this policy. Where there has been no prejudice to the insurer from the delay in notice, there has been no increase in the risk. On the contrary, in the absence of prejudice a strict forfeiture clause simply provides the insurance company with a windfall. By adopting a rule requiring proof of prejudice from a delay in notification, all the insurance company is being required to do is to take the risk it was paid to take rather than escape liability for coverage otherwise provided.

Our decision in this case is not without precedent. In *Newark Ins. Co. v. Ezell, Ky.*, 520 S.W.2d 318 (1975), a policy condition pertaining to uninsured motorist coverage required the insured to obtain written consent of the company before prosecuting an action against the uninsured motorist. Absent such consent in advance the judgment could not be enforced against the insurer. We held this condition of the policy should not be subject to "strict enforcement." We stated:

> "In the field of insurance law recognition frequently has been given to the principle that an insurance company may not rely upon a noncompliance by the insured with a condition of the policy if the company has sustained no prejudice by reason of the noncompliance." *Id.* at 321.

This principle was applied because, though the insurance carrier had not been asked nor had it given "written consent" as was specified as a condition of the coverage, the facts showed that the insurance carrier's attorney was aware of the suit in progress against the uninsured motorist and failed to object or to seek to participate in the action.

Thus, Kentucky has already evidenced support for the "modern trend" against strict forfeiture regardless of prejudice in a situation markedly similar to present circumstances. For the reasons stated we overrule *Reserve Ins. Co. v. Richards, Ky.*, 577 S.W.2d 417 (1979), [and other cases in accord with *Richards*].

Two unanswered questions remain: (1) Should the insurance carrier have the burden of proving prejudice from the delay, or should the burden be on the claimant to prove lack of prejudice to the insurance carrier? (2) Should prejudice be measured in terms of actual prejudice or probable prejudice?

There are two reasons for imposing the burden on the insurance carrier to prove prejudice, rather than imposing on the claimant the burden to prove no prejudice resulted. The first is the obvious one: it is virtually impossible to prove a negative, so it would be difficult if not impossible for the claimant to prove the insurance carrier suffered no prejudice. Secondly, the insurance carrier is in a far superior position to be knowledgeable about the facts which establish whether prejudice exists. Indeed, it is difficult to imagine where the claimant would look for evidence that no prejudice exists. Thus we hold that the burden is on the insurance carrier to prove there was in fact some substantial prejudice caused by the delay in reporting the occurrence.

Finally, with reference to whether the insurance company's burden to prove prejudice should be stated in terms of actual prejudice or probable prejudice, we recognize that proof of actual prejudice is an unreasonable burden. We view the question of prejudice in terms of whether it is reasonably probable that the insurance carrier suffered substantial prejudice from the delay in notice. If the evidence on this issue is in conflict, or if reasonable minds could differ as to what the evidence proves in this regard, the issue is one for the trier of fact. The issue is ripe for summary judgment only where the proof is conclusive, or there has been a failure of proof, on this subject.

We reverse the Court of Appeals and the trial court. We vacate the summary judgment and remand this case to the trial court for further proceedings consistent with this Opinion.

LAMBERT, LEIBSON, REYNOLDS, SPAIN, and WINTERSHEIMER, J.J., concur.

STEPHENS, CHIEF JUSTICE, dissenting.

I respectfully dissent.

This Court rewrites the insurance contract by adopting the rule that the insurer, in order to escape liability for coverage, must prove probable prejudice from a delay in notification. Section IV of said contract, clearly and unambiguously requires the insured to promptly notify the carrier of any "occurrence which may result in a claim."

The insured's untimely notice fails to comply with the condition precedent of the contract (Section IV), thus relieving the carrier of liability under the policy, because six and one-half months elapsed between movant's injury and notice to the insurance company of movant's claim. *Richards, supra.*

. . . .

It is jurisprudentially sound to leave departure from our present established rule in *Richards, supra,* to the General Assembly. The majority's new rule based on the concept of prejudice negates the purpose of the contract conditions, rendering them meaningless and in effect rewrites the insurance policy, contrary to the intent of the parties clearly expressed by the language of the contract. This new rule changes legislative and executive policies implicitly expressed by the insurance department's approval of respondent's insurance contract.

. . . .

COMBS, J., joins in this dissent.

[Dissenting opinion by Combs, J., in which Stephens, C.J., joined, omitted.]

NOTES

1. *Advantages of early notice.* Although the court in *Jones* emphasizes the reasons late notice should not cause a forfeiture of coverage, good reasons exist for encouraging early notice. The most obvious of these is encouraging early investigation of losses before relevant evidence becomes lost or disappears. Can you think of others? See Robert H. Jerry, II, Understanding Insurance Law § 81[a] (2d ed. 1996). Does the court's decision in *Jones* sacrifice these benefits? Did the majority err in failing to consider the costs associated with determining whether the insurer has been prejudiced by late notice? Is this one of Chief Justice Stephens' concerns in dissent?

2. *Notice in writing?* Some policies require that the notice to the insurer be in writing. That is how the notice was communicated in *Jones.* It has been held that oral notice is insufficient to satisfy a requirement that the notice be in writing. *See Putney School, Inc. v. Schaaf,* 599 A.2d 322 (Vt. 1991). If the notice in *Jones* had been oral, would it have mattered? How would the insurer have demonstrated prejudice from oral notice?

3. *Manner of notice.* It was, apparently, undisputed that the insurer did not learn of the occurrence until Jones' attorney's letter of August 20, 1988. What if, however, the explosion that injured Jones had been a major mining disaster, with significant loss of life and substantial attendant publicity in national media? Is common knowledge of the disaster enough to constitute "notice"? *See Frankenmuth Mutual Insurance Co. v. Williams,* 645 N.E.2d 605 (Ind. 1995) (insurer could not be said to lack notice of suit where insurer was aware of accusation, had investigated incident, and had sent reservation of rights letter). What if the information received by an insurer about its insured's potential liability is in the nature of "general neighborhood gossip"? *Compare Bantz v. Bongard,* 864 P.2d 618 (Idaho 1993) (information provided to insurer by someone else, other than insured, involved in the accident), with *Allstate Insurance Co. v. Kepchar,* 592 N.E.2d 694 (Ind. Ct. App. 1994) ("general neighborhood gossip"). Jones was the injured victim, not the insured. Should it matter who actually conveys the information about a possible loss to the insurer? Is it prudent or advisable for a victim of a tort to notify the insured's liability insurance carrier?

4. *Agents and notice.* Ivan Insured negligently operates his vehicle and injures a pedestrian. Ivan has a liability policy covering the loss; the policy was secured for the insured by his broker, Anne the Independent Agent, from Reliable Insurance Company. Ivan notifies Anne of the accident. Anne, however, leaves on a six-month cruise the next day without forwarding the notice to Reliable. Does this present any problem for Ivan? *See Met-Coil Systems Corp. v. Columbia Casualty Co.,* 524 N.W.2d 650 (Iowa 1994); *Security Mutual Insurance Co. v. Acker Fitzsimons Corp.,* 293 N.E.2d 76 (N.Y. 1972). If the policy provides that the insured or beneficiary is to give notice to "the insurer or any authorized agent," does it suffice if the beneficiary under a group accidental death policy provided by the decedent's employer gives notice to the employer? *See Golt v. Aetna Life Insurance Co.,* 2 P.3d 841 (Mont. 2000).

5. *Timing issues.* Where notice of "injury," "loss," or "accident" (or whatever is the triggering event in the policy) must be given, from what moment does the time period run? There must be a minimum of knowledge on the part of the insured concerning the event before the notice obligation is triggered. Under first-party coverage, the insured, at a minimum, must be aware that a loss has occurred.

The issue is more complex in liability insurance. Is the triggering event for the obligation to give notice the fact that the insured is aware that he or she has been involved in an accident, or that the insured believes that a tort claim may be filed, or that the insured believes he or she may be liable? Examine Part E ("Duties After An Accident or Loss") in the Personal Auto Policy in Appendix E. The choice can have important consequences. *See D'Aloia v. Travelers Insurance Co.,* 674 N.E.2d 1345 (N.Y. 1995); *Resseguie v. American Mutual Liability Insurance Co.,* 51 Wis. 2d 92, 186 N.W.2d 236 (1971).

Part of the difficulty in liability insurance is that the insured may not be aware at the time of the accident that she is potentially liable. In some kinds of insurance, such as automobile insurance, the potential liability will often be apparent. But in other kinds of insurance, such as malpractice insurance, the insured may be unaware of the insured event until a claim is filed. The insured's reasonable belief that she is not liable may excuse the insured's delay in giving notice to the insurer, but as the court explained in *State v. Glens Falls Insurance Co.,* 134 Vt. 443, 365 A.2d 243 (1976), this exception presupposes more than a cursory investigation, discussion with the claimant, interviewing witnesses, and, according to some cases, consultation with counsel. The court in *Glens Falls* stated:

> The duty to notify arises with the advent of circumstances calculated to instill in the reasonable person belief in the possibility of an impending claim. Reduced to its illogical conclusion, the State's contention would eliminate forever the need for any notice to the insurer, if the prospect of a claim was not apparent at the very time of the occurrence. Even a subsequent notice of claim would not, under this view, trigger the duty. . . . Supervening circumstance cannot, it is true, give rise *retroactively* to a duty to notify; the duty does not arise until circumstances exist which would be a *caveat* to a reasonable person. But when such circumstances arise, the duty to notify arises with them. (Emphasis in original.)

6. *Strict compliance or prejudice?* This question is one of the most important decided by *Jones.* What the court calls the "traditional view" comports with the rule of contract law that express conditions to contract duties must be strictly satisfied. *See, e.g., Steinberg v. Paul Revere Life Insurance Co.,* 73 F. Supp. 2d 358 (S.D.N.Y. 1999), *aff'd,* 210 F.3d 355 (2d Cir. 2000) (applying New York's "no prejudice" rule to late notice under disability policy); *Leadville Corp. v. United States Fidelity & Guaranty Co.,* 55 F.3d 537 (10th Cir. 1995) (applying Colorado law). Typically, however, insurance policies require that notice be given "as soon as practicable," or "forthwith," or, as in the policy in *Jones,* "promptly." Courts have some latitude to determine whether notice is "prompt" or given "as soon as practicable." If a court adheres to the traditional view but measures what is a reasonable time for giving notice as a

relatively long time, is the outcome likely to be much different from that reached in *Jones*?

Many courts have also recognized a variety of extenuating circumstances as excusing the insured's obligation to give notice promptly or within a reasonable time. *See, e.g., Sparacinio v. Pawtucket Mutual Insurance Co.*, 50 F.3d 141 (2d Cir. 1995) (under New York law, labor union's delay in notifying liability insurer excused where union had a reasonable belief that it was not liable and that there was no coverage); *West American Insurance Co. v. Bank of Isle of Wight*, 673 F. Supp. 760 (E.D. Va. 1987) (insured did not know of loss); *Royal-Globe Insurance Co. v. Craven*, 585 N.E.2d 315 (Mass. 1992) (insured excused from 24-hour notice requirement during time insured was in intensive care; but delay for three months after release from hospital was not excused); *Finstad v. Steiger Tractor, Inc.*, 301 N.W.2d 392 (N.D. 1981) (insured did not know of policy's existence). If a court adheres to the traditional view but is particularly generous in recognizing excuses for noncompliance, is the outcome likely to be much different from that reached in *Jones*? *See Argentina v. Otsego Mutual Fire Insurance Co.*, 655 N.E.2d 166 (N.Y. 1995) (171-day delay in giving notice to liability insurer after slip-and-fall accident was excused where incident seemed minor).

The other important way to mitigate the potentially harsh effects of the traditional view is to insist that the insurer suffer prejudice as a result of the lack of notice. Although *Jones* places the burden on the insurer to prove prejudice, some courts have placed the burden on the insured to prove lack of prejudice. *See American Justice Insurance Reciprocal v. Hutchison*, 15 S.W.3d 811 (Tenn. 2000); *Aetna Casualty & Surety Co. v. Murphy*, 206 Conn. 409, 538 A.2d 219 (1988) (listing cases). Where the burden is placed can, obviously, determine who wins. If the burden is placed on the insured to prove lack of prejudice, has the traditional view been retained de facto?

There are many cases, however, where the insured's late notice has not been saved by any of the mitigating doctrines. *See, e.g., Avco Corp. v. Aetna Casualty & Surety Co.*, 679 A.2d 323 (R.I. 1996) (two and one-half year delay in giving notice of liability claims was prejudicial as a matter of law); *Interstate Power Co. v. Insurance Co. of N. Am.*, 603 N.W.2d 751 (Iowa 2000) (three and one-half year delay in giving notice was "unreasonably tardy"); *Deprez v. Continental Western Insurance Co.*, 255 Neb. 381, 584 N.W.2d 805 (1998) (four-year delay in giving notice under uninsured motorist provision of personal auto policy was prejudicial to insurer as a matter of law); *Koski v. Allstate Insurance Co.*, 456 Mich. 439, 572 N.W.2d 636 (1998) (insured's failure to give notice of tort suit until three months after entry of default judgment prejudiced insurer).

7. *What constitutes prejudice?* If the insured fails to give notice of a suit against him or her until after a default judgment has been entered in the plaintiff's favor and the judgment has become final and nonappealable, it seems obvious that the insurer has been prejudiced. Other situations are not so obvious. Is it necessary that the late notice cause the irretrievable loss of a substantial defense? Or is it only necessary that the insurer's ability to defend the claim be diminished? Or is the threshold for prejudice something in between those two tests? *See Weaver v. State Farm Mutual Automobile*

Insurance Co., 936 S.W.2d 818 (Mo. 1997) (affidavit of insurer's claim superintendent stating that uninsured motorist insurer could not get medical records due to one-year delay in receiving notice did not establish prejudice to insurer).

The court in *Jones* held that the insurer's burden was to show a reasonable probability of substantial prejudice, and that insisting that the insurer prove actual prejudice would be an "unreasonable burden." In *Aetna Casualty & Surety Co. v. Dow Chemical Co.,* 10 F. Supp. 2d 800 (E.D. Mich. 1998), the court stated: "An insurer must do more than simply claim that evidence was lost, physically altered, or has otherwise become unavailable and that witnesses have died, disappeared, or their memories have faded. It must establish what is in fact lost by the missing evidence, how this prejudices its position, and why information available from other sources is inadequate." 10 F. Supp. 2d at 813. Which approach is the more appropriate burden to place on the insurer?

8. *Statutory regulation.* Statutes in some states have changed the traditional view. *See, e.g.,* Wis. Stat. Ann. § 631.81 (West 1999) ("failure to furnish such notice or proof [of loss] within the time required by the policy does not invalidate or reduce a claim unless the insurer is prejudiced thereby and it was reasonably possible to meet the time limit"); Mich. Comp. Laws § 500.3008 (2000) (requiring liability policies to contain provision that "failure to give any notice required to be given by such policy within the time specified therein shall not invalidate any claim made by the insured if it shall be shown not to have been reasonably possible to give such notice within the prescribed time and that notice was given as soon as was reasonably possible"). Does the Michigan statute differ materially from the Wisconsin statutes?

Even where the old rule has been changed by statute, a requirement that the insurer show prejudice may apply only to certain types of insurance, such as auto insurance, or only to certain other kinds of claims provisions (covered *infra*), such as the notice and cooperation clauses of a certain type of policy. *See, e.g., Government Employers Insurance Co. v. Harvey,* 278 Md. 548, 366 A.2d 13 (1976) (lack of prejudice irrelevant to six-month proof of loss provision under no-fault statute even though another statute required that auto insurer show prejudice when relying on notice or cooperation clause).

9. *Compulsory insurance.* The court in *Jones* considered it relevant that Huston Partin was required by state statute to purchase liability insurance for his mining operation. No doubt the state required such insurance as a means to protect third-parties who might be injured by the hazards involved in such operations. To the extent an insurer is allowed to disclaim coverage on account of the insured's late notice, who loses?

The court's analogy to automobile insurance, where most states mandate minimum liability coverages, is appropriate. It is common for such statutes to provide that defenses, such as late notice, that would ordinarily discharge the insurer from its obligations cannot be used to prevent the payment of proceeds to injured third parties. *See, e.g.,* Mass. Gen. L. Ann. ch. 175, § 112 (2000) (under motor vehicle liability policy, insurer "shall not deny insurance coverage to an insured because of failure of an insured to seasonably notify an insurance company of an occurrence, incident, claim or. . .a suit. . .unless the insurance company has been prejudiced thereby"); Va. Stat. § 38.2-2201(B)

(2000) (coverages specified in statute shall be payable notwithstanding lack of notice "as soon as practicable. . .except where the failure or refusal prejudices the insurer in establishing the validity of the claim"; to same effect is § 38.2-2204). The insurer might then insist in the insurance policy on a right to reimbursement from the insured for situations where the insurer is required to pay a third-party's loss notwithstanding the insured's failure to give notice of loss or comply with other policy provisions. Whether the insurer can actually obtain reimbursement is, of course, another question altogether.

10. *Uninsured motorist insurance.* Some uninsured motorist coverages contain a particularly short notice provision for "hit-and-run" situations. For example, the policy might require that the accident be reported within twenty-four hours to the police, a judicial officer, or the Commissioner of Motor Vehicles, and that a sworn statement setting out the facts of the accident be filed with the insurer within thirty days. This type of provision was upheld, albeit in a qualified way, in *Allstate Insurance Co. v. Korschun,* 350 So. 2d 1081 (Fla. Dist. Ct. App. 1977), *cert. denied,* 359 So. 2d 1216 (1978). The court emphasized the importance of giving "the police and other interested parties (such as the insurance company) an opportunity to investigate, search and possibly apprehend the hit and run driver," to determine whether "the hit and run vehicle was in fact uninsured," and "to enforce its subrogation rights against a negligent uninsured hit and run motorist." 350 So. 2d at 1081. But the court also explained that the insurer would not be relieved from liability on account of the insured's noncompliance with the statutory notice requirement: "While prejudice to the insurer is presumed in the case of non-compliance with such a notice requirement, the insurer will not automatically be relieved of liability simply by showing that notice was not given within the time provided for in the policy if the insured can demonstrate that the insurer has not thereby been prejudiced." 350 So. 2d at 1082.

11. *A limit on ERISA preemption.* If a group disability policy is provided by an employer to employees, it is a welfare benefit plan governed by ERISA. (See note 10 following *Mahler* in § 2.03[4], *supra.*) If an employee is late in giving the insurer notice of the disability, is the state common law or statutory rule on notice and/or prejudice preempted by ERISA? In *UNUM Life Insurance Co. v. Ward,* 526 U.S. 358, 119 S. Ct. 1380, 143 L. Ed. 2d 462 (1999), the United States Supreme Court held that California's notice-prejudice rule regulated the business of insurance with the meaning of ERISA's savings clause and thereby escaped preemption by ERISA. The Court explained that "the notice-prejudice rule is distinctive most notably because it is a rule firmly applied to insurance contracts, not a general principle guiding a court's discretion in a range of matters," and that "California's insistence that insurers show prejudice before they may deny coverage because of late notice is grounded in policy concerns specific to the insurance industry." 526 U.S. at 372. Because the Court used the case to revisit the criteria for determining whether a state law regulates the "business of insurance" within the meaning of the McCarran-Ferguson Act, *Ward* is an important decision not only for the scope of the McCarran-Ferguson Act but also for the relationship between that Act and ERISA.

[2] Proof of Loss

SIRAVO v. GREAT AMERICAN INSURANCE CO.
122 R.I. 538, 410 A.2d 116 (1980)

WEISBERGER, JUSTICE.

[The insured's home was completely destroyed by fire. She sued her insurers in federal district court on two fire insurance policies, which had been issued to her in conformity with the forms specified by state statutes. The insurers had three defenses: the insured's arson; the insured's misrepresentation of the extent of loss; and the insured's failure to timely file a sworn proof of loss. [2] A general jury verdict was entered for the insurers, and plaintiff appealed. The First Circuit found that all but one of plaintiff's grounds for appeal lacked merit, but that this one ground turned on a question of law that the First Circuit concluded should be answered by the Supreme Court of Rhode Island.]

The United States Court of Appeals for the First Circuit. . .has certified to us the following question of law:

> Does an insured's late filing of the sworn proof of loss, which under the standard form of fire insurance policy, R.I. Gen. Laws § 27-5-3, he is supposed to render within sixty (60) days after the loss, bar the insured's recovery under the policy in the absence of the company's proving prejudice stemming from the insured's failure to comply with the time limits contained in said proof of loss provision?

. . . .

The plaintiff relies on *Pickering v. American Employers Insurance Co.,* 109 R.I. 143, 282 A.2d 584 (1971) to argue that her failure to file the proof of loss

---

[2] Policy provisions concerning notice of loss and filing of proofs of loss are as follows:

> The insured shall give immediate written notice to this company of any loss, protect the property from further damage, forthwith separate the damaged and undamaged personal property, put it in the best possible order, furnish a complete inventory of the destroyed, damaged and undamaged property, showing in detail quantities, costs, actual cash value and amount of loss claimed; *and within sixty (60) days after the loss, unless such time is extended in writing by this company, the insured shall render to this company a proof of loss,* signed and sworn to by the insured, stating the knowledge and belief of the insured as to the following: the time and origin of the loss, the interest of the insured and of all others in the property, the actual cash value of each item thereof and the amount of loss thereto, all encumbrances thereon, all other contracts of insurance, whether valid or not, covering any of said property, any changes in the title, use, occupation, location, possession or exposures of said property since the issuing of this policy, by whom and for what purpose any building herein described and the several parts thereof were occupied at the time of loss and whether or not it then stood on leased ground, and shall furnish a copy of all the descriptions and schedules in all policies and, if required, verified plans and specifications of any building, fixtures or machinery destroyed or damaged. (Emphasis in original.)

The policies also contain the following provision:

> No suit or action on this policy for the recovery of any claim shall be sustainable in any court of law or equity unless all the requirements of this policy shall have been complied with, and unless commenced within twelve (12) months next after inception of the loss.

within sixty days should not bar recovery unless defendants are able to demonstrate that they were thereby prejudiced. In *Pickering,* the plaintiff sought recovery on her automobile liability insurance policy for injuries caused by an uninsured motorist. Among the defenses raised by the insurer was the plaintiff's failure to comply with three provisions included in the policy. Those provisions declared that the giving of notice of a loss and the filing of a sworn written proof of claim should be done "as soon as practicable," while copies of legal process served in the uninsured motorist's suit were to be forwarded to the insurer "immediately."

In *Pickering,* we defined the term "notice" to include such items as the furnishing of a proof of claim and a copy of the summons and complaint. We then held that an insurer could not rely on any of the so-called "notice" provisions of its policy unless it could demonstrate that it had been prejudiced by the lack of notice. . . .

. . . .

Although both notice and proof-of-loss provisions serve a broad common purpose of informing an insurer of the loss for which a claim is made, the two are distinct. The sole purpose of a notice-of-loss provision is to afford the insurer a *seasonable* opportunity for investigation to protect its interests. The purpose of a proof of loss, on the other hand, is to afford the insurer an *adequate* opportunity to protect its interests by facilitating its investigation.

We believe, however, that the distinction does not warrant a refusal to extend *Pickering* to proof-of-loss provisions. *Pickering* required that an automobile insurer show prejudice resulting from an untimely notice of loss. Such prejudice would result from an insurer's inability to conduct any investigation until the time that notice of loss is provided. Without notice of loss, an insurer can conduct no investigation at all. In contrast, an insured's untimely compliance with a proof-of-loss provision may adversely affect the adequacy, but not the existence, of an insurer's opportunity to investigate a claim. The Supreme Court of Wisconsin has noted, "There is no great hurry there [to furnish a proof of loss], such as there is when loss occurs and the insurer must be notified so that it may proceed . . . ." *Britz v. American Insurance Co. of Newark, N.J.,* 2 Wis. 2d 192, 202, 86 N.W.2d 18, 23 (1957). We therefore conclude that logic and reason impel a showing of prejudice, even more forcefully, before a declaration of forfeiture may be based upon an insured's untimely compliance with a proof-of-loss provision. For this purpose, we analogize a proof-of-loss provision to the so-called group of "notice" provisions at issue in *Pickering.*

. . . .

. . . . We therefore apply the *Pickering* rule and hold that an insurer cannot rely on an insured's failure to submit a timely proof of loss under the standard form of fire insurance policy in order to defeat recovery unless the insurer can demonstrate that it has been prejudiced by the late filing.

We thus answer the question certified to us in the negative.

NOTES

1. *Casualty insurance.* Property insurance policies typically require that the insured file within a specified number of days after the loss a written document, normally on a form provided by the insurer, containing considerable detail about the insured's loss and claim. (See, for example, the conditions in the homeowners policy in Appendix C.) Under certain types of standard or union mortgage clauses, the mortgagee, once notified by the insurer that the claim of the insured-mortgagor is being denied, must file a signed, sworn statement of loss within sixty days after receiving the notice. *See Georgia Farm Bureau Mutual Insurance Co. v. First Federal Savings & Loan Ass'n,* 152 Ga. App. 16, 262 S.E.2d 147 (1979). In liability insurance the insured may be asked to submit detailed information about any damaged property within the insured's control.

2. *Life insurance.* In life insurance, a beneficiary will submit to the insurer a proof of loss or "proof of death." This form (including whatever documents are attached to it, such as a death certificate) will seek to establish the fact of the insured's death and the entitlement of the beneficiary to the proceeds. Normally the only time limit for submitting a proof of death is whatever statute of limitations applies to contract actions in the particular locale.

Proving a loss in life insurance rarely raises complex issues; indeed, few events are more unambiguous than death. There are, however, situations in which the content of the proof of loss may be quite significant. If, for example, a claim is made for accidental death benefits in circumstances where the presence of an "accidental" cause is not clear and obvious, the evidence contained in the proof of death will be very important.

Also, if the insured's death is sought to be proved circumstantially (i.e., through absence or disappearance) instead of directly (i.e., through the existence of a dead body), the content of the proof of death will be important. Some policies attempt to deal with the issue with a provision on proof of death based on unexplained absence. In the absence of a controlling policy provision, death might be established by invoking the common law presumption. To invoke the presumption, the plaintiff must allege and prove an unexplained absence for seven years, a diligent search for the *cestui que vie* and circumstances justifying the conclusion that death is the probable reason for the absence. *Borzage v. Metropolitan Life Insurance Co.,* 6 Conn. Cir. Ct. 269, 270 A.2d 688 (1970). Some states have specific statutes addressing the issue.

The National Conference of Commissioners on Uniform State Laws promulgated the Uniform Absence As Evidence of Death and Absentees' Property Act in 1939, which abolishes the common law presumption and puts the issue of whether an absent person is dead to a jury. Only two states have adopted the Uniform Act, however, and one of these states (Wisconsin) omitted the section abolishing the common law presumption. *See* 8A U.L.A. 1 (1993). The Uniform Probate Code contains a provision regarding proof of death based on an absence of five years. This period is, obviously, more favorable to a claimant than the common law presumption, but the language of the Code may limit the statute's reach to probate proceedings. Uniform Probate Code § 1-107, 8 U.L.A. 30 (1998). Should the code provision govern in an action on an insurance contract? *See Branca by Branca v. Security Benefit Life Insurance Co.,* 773 F.2d 1158 (11th Cir. 1985), *modified on other grounds,* 789 F.2d 1511 (1985) (probate provision applies only in probate matters); but *see Carman v. Prudential Insurance Co.,* 748 P.2d 743 (Alaska 1988) (probate provision applicable in proving death in insurance contract dispute). Since these two cases were decided, the code has been amended by eliminating the introductory clause "In proceedings under this Code" from Section 1-107 of the UPC. In addition, Section 1-102 now provides that the Code should be liberally construed to promote its underlying purposes and policies, one of which is "to simplify and clarify the law concerning the affairs of decedents, missing persons, ..." Do these changes cut in favor or against applying the Code to insurance disputes over whether a *cestui que vie* is dead?

3. *Does compliance with proof of loss requirements ever matter?* As *Siravo* suggests, a prejudice requirement is commonly imposed by courts in situations where the insurer seeks to deny coverage for noncompliance with a proof of loss requirement. *See also National Union Fire Insurance Co. v. Federal Deposit Insurance Corp.,* 264 Kan. 733, 957 P.2d 357 (1998). If the proof of loss is deficient on its face, should the insurer be required to notify the insured of the deficiency and give the insured an opportunity to correct it? *See Tennessee Farmers Mutual Insurance Co. v. Wheeler,* 341 S.E.2d 898 (Ga. Ct. App. 1986). Also, many courts have held that the insured need only "substantially comply" with the proof of loss requirement. *See, e.g., Hartfore Fire Insurance Co. v. Himelfarb,* 355 Md. 671, 736 A.2d 295 (1999); *Allstate Insurance Co. v. Charity,* 255 Va. 55, 496 S.E.2d 430 (1998); *Walker v. American Bankers Ins. Group,* 836 P.2d 59 (Nev. 1992); *Canyon Country Store v. Bracey,* 781 P.2d 414 (Utah 1989). Plus, there is the possibility that the insurer might waive or be estopped to assert the requirement. *See Cotton States Mutual Insurance Co. v. Walker,* 232 Ga. App. 41, 500 S.E.2d 487 (1998) (insurer's agent allegedly told insured's spouse that proof of loss needed to be redone, that detailed information had to be provided, and that she "didn't have to be in any big hurry"). After all of this, what is left of the proof of loss requirement?

4. *The timing of substantial compliance.* One answer to the question at the end of the prior note, and a point worth emphasizing, is that the insured must at least substantially comply with the proof of loss requirement *before* an action may be brought on the policy. It is not enough that the insured offers due proof at the trial, nor is it the insurer's general obligation to coax the insured into providing the requisite information. While an insurer may have a duty under particular circumstances to advise a claimant that additional information may be submitted to explain or supplement information previously furnished, and that an insurer's failure to fulfill such a duty constitutes a waiver of the proof of loss requirement, there is no guarantee that a court will conclude that the insurer was obligated to state affirmatively that additional proof might have been submitted. Insureds act at their peril if they assume otherwise. In *Washington v. Metropolitan Life Insurance Co.,* 372 Mass. 714, 363 N.E.2d 683 (1977), there was evidence at trial that would have satisfied the due proof requirement for accidental death benefits, but the evidence was not submitted to the insurer as part of the proof of loss during

the claims process. The Supreme Judicial Court of Massachusetts upheld the trial court's entry of judgment n.o.v. for the defendant-insurer after the jury returned a verdict in the plaintiff's favor. The insurer had denied the claim for accidental death stating that it had not been satisfactorily established, but neither invited nor foreclosed the submission of additional information. The court said the insurer had no duty to do otherwise and that testimony offered at trial does not constitute "due proof." Should more be expected of commercial insureds in filing proofs of loss than homeowners? *See Nathe Brothers, Inc. v. American National Fire Insurance Co.,* 597 N.W.2d 587 (Minn. 1999).

5. *False swearing.* Many property insurance policies contain a clause providing that the policy is void if the insured wilfully conceals or misrepresents a material fact concerning a loss. Absent a statute to the contrary, there is no separate requirement that the insurer show prejudice from the false swearing. Obviously, one place where false swearing is likely to occur is in the proof of loss. False swearing can arise, however, in any aspect of post-loss investigation and processing of the claim. *See Fine v. Bellefonte Underwriters Insurance Co.,* 725 F.2d 179 (2d Cir.), *cert. denied,* 469 U.S. 874 (1984); *Longobardi v. Chubb Insurance Co.,* 582 A.2d 1257 (N.J. 1990). The false swearing defense should be distinguished from a defense that the insured has failed to cooperate by, for example, failing to produce relevant documents. In the latter situation, prejudice from the noncooperation may be required. *See King v. Federal Insurance Co.,* 788 F. Supp. 506 (D. Kan. 1992).

6. *Exaggeration or false swearing?* What if the insured makes a good faith overvaluation the amount of his or her claim? This is, after all, human nature, is it not? Does not everyone think his or her property is worth more than it really is? At some point, an exaggerated valuation becomes false swearing, but the line is not an easy one to draw. *See Auto-Owners Insurance Co. v. Hansen Housing, Inc.,* 604 N.W.2d 504 (S.D. 2000); *Nagel-Taylor Automotive Supplies, Inc. v. Aetna Casualty & Surety Co.,* 402 N.E.2d 302 (Ill. Ct. App. 1980). Some states have passed so-called "anti-technicality statutes" to avoid the problem of distinguishing between deliberately false statements on a proof of loss and an innocent misstatement. Under these statutes, the misrepresentation or false statement made in a proof of loss has no effect unless the insurer proves that the false statements were fraudulently made and the insurer was misled. See Tex. Ins. Code Ann., art. 21.19 (West 1981).

[3] Limitation of Actions

ESTES v. ALASKA INSURANCE GUARANTY ASSOCIATION
774 P.2d 1315 (Alaska 1989)

Compton, Justice.

After fire destroyed his music store, Jack Estes filed a claim with his insurer, Union Indemnity Insurance Company of New York (Union Indemnity). Ten months later, Union Indemnity denied Estes' claim on a number of grounds. One year and seven days after Union Indemnity's denial of his claim, Estes filed suit against it.

When Union Indemnity became insolvent, the Alaska Insurance Guaranty Association (AIGA) assumed Union Indemnity's obligations on its policies. AIGA moved for summary judgment against Estes on the ground that Estes had failed to comply with a policy provision requiring any suit to be filed "within one year after the loss occurs." The trial court granted summary judgment. We reverse.

I. FACTS AND PROCEEDINGS

Jack Estes operated a music store, Estes Music Studio, in Kenai, Alaska. On August 14, 1983, the store and its inventory were destroyed by fire. Soon after the fire, Estes submitted proof of loss to his insurer, Union Indemnity.

Union Indemnity completed its investigation of the loss in January 1984. On June 4, Union Indemnity denied Estes' claim on the grounds that Estes had concealed facts related to the loss, had failed to provide certain documents, and had caused the loss or increased the risk of loss.

Estes did not communicate further with Union Indemnity until March 25, 1985, when Estes' trial attorney, not of the firm that represented Estes during the investigation, wrote to Union Indemnity's attorney asking to be advised of Union Indemnity's position on the claim. There was no response to this letter, and on June 11, 1985, Estes filed a complaint against Union Indemnity. Default judgment was entered against Union Indemnity on October 24, 1985.

[After AIGA assumed Union Indemnity's obligations and succeeded to Union Indemnity's status as defendant in this action, Union Indemnity was dismissed from the action, and the default judgment was set aside.]

AIGA moved for summary judgment on the ground that Estes had failed to comply with a policy provision requiring any suit on the policy to be commenced "within one year after the loss occurs." The trial court granted the motion. Estes appeals.

II. DISCUSSION

On appeal Estes contends that in order to bar his claim for failure to comply with the one-year limit on commencement of suit clause, AIGA must show that it or Union Indemnity was prejudiced by his failure to comply. . . .

. . . .

The multi-peril policy issued to Estes by Union Indemnity includes a five-page list of conditions and definitions. At the bottom of the list's second page, under the heading "Conditions Applicable to Section I," there appears the following provision:

> 15. Suit. No suit shall be brought on this policy unless the insured
> has complied with all the policy provisions and has commenced the
> suit within one year after the loss occurs.

Estes concedes that his suit was not commenced within one year after the loss occurred. But he contends that the limitation provision should be enforced only upon proof by AIGA that AIGA has suffered prejudice as a result of his failure to file suit within the period. Though we have not held heretofore that such proof is required, Estes argues that the reasoning of prior cases supports such a requirement.

. . . .

In *Weaver Bros. v. Chappel,* 684 P.2d 123 (Alaska 1984), we reviewed a policy provision requiring prompt notice of loss. We stated:

> In short, the notice requirement is designed to protect the insurer from prejudice. *In the absence of prejudice, regardless of the reasons for the delayed notice, there is no justification for excusing the insurer from its obligations under the policy.* We recognize the strong societal interest in preserving insurance coverage for accident victims so long as the preservation is equitable for all parties involved.

Id. at 125 (emphasis added).

In *Weaver Bros.,* we reviewed the notice provision under the following standard: Does the application of the notice provision in this case advance the purpose for which it was included in the policy? The question we must now consider is whether the standard adopted in *Weaver Bros.* should be applied to policy clauses that are similar to notice provisions.

A number of courts have adopted the *Weaver Bros.* approach to notice provisions. Of these, some have extended that approach to other policy clauses. Others have chosen not to do so.

. . . .

In *Zuckerman v. Transamerica Insurance Co.,* [133 Ariz. 139,] 650 P.2d [441,] 448 [(1982)], the Arizona Supreme Court held that a contractual modification of the statute of limitations should be enforced only "when the reasons for its existence are thereby served." When enforcement does not serve the reasons for the provision's inclusion in the policy, the insured's reasonable expectation that coverage will not be arbitrarily denied must be given effect. *Id.* In short, the authority of the provision is limited by the reality of the way insurance policies are bought and sold; the effect of the provision is limited by the reasonable expectations of the insured.

We hold that time limit on commencement of suit clauses, notice of loss clauses, proof of loss clauses, and cooperation clauses should all be reviewed on the basis of whether their application in a particular case advances the purpose for which they were included in the policy. Only by so reviewing these clauses can courts satisfy the consumer's reasonable expectation that coverage will not be defeated on arbitrary procedural grounds. Thus, in order to bar Estes' claim for failure to comply with the one-year time limit, AIGA must establish that it suffered as a result of his delay such prejudice as the limit was intended to avoid. Hence, summary judgment was improper, and the judgment of the superior court must be reversed.

. . . .

Like a notice of loss provision, a limitation on commencement of suit clause should be enforced only when its application in a particular case serves the primary purpose for which it was included in the policy: to avoid prejudice. To avail itself of the contractual one-year limit on commencement of suit clause, AIGA must establish that it was prejudiced by Estes' delay in filing suit.

The. . .[superior court's] grant of summary judgment is REVERSED and the case REMANDED for proceedings consistent with this opinion.

MOORE, JUSTICE, dissenting.

I dissent from the majority opinion. The majority rewrites a patently clear clause which has been approved by the legislature, and which has been universally used and enforced in fire insurance policies since 1943. The court's analysis is logically and legally flawed. It unnecessarily creates great uncertainty and ignores precedent of our earlier Alaska Supreme Court decisions, as well as the vast majority of other jurisdictions that have decided this same issue.

. . . .

The majority opinion here does more violence to the clear meaning of this contractual suit limitation clause than any other case in the country to date, excluding those states where such clauses are statutorily prohibited. *Zuckerman*, the only other case to require a showing of prejudice in this context. . .was couched in terms of an estoppel. The majority today, by contrast, announces a rigid rule of law.

The majority has not done its research. It ignores the cases which discuss the public policies served by the suit limitation clause. The majority thus fails to distinguish the suit limitation clause from those clauses designed to protect the insurer from prejudice. A holding of this importance deserves a more thorough analysis.

Prompt notice of claim clauses in insurance policies are designed to avoid prejudice to an insurer in its investigation of accidents. . . .

Suit limitation clauses, by contrast, serve important public policies. Excluding one short-lived Federal District Court case,[3] no court outside Arizona has required an insurer to show prejudice before relying on the contractual suit limitation clause. Eight courts have expressly refused to require such a showing. These courts have all recognized the validity of these clauses and the public policies they serve.

A failure to abide by the limitation of action condition in a policy stands on a much different footing than a non-compliance with the notice provisions. . . . [T]he main purpose underlying the notice stipulations is to safeguard the insurer from prejudice in processing a claim. Therefore, where an insurer's interests have not been harmed by a late notice, the reason for the notice condition is lacking. By contrast, limitation periods on suits are designed to promote justice by preventing surprises through revival of stale claims, to protect defendants and courts from handling matters in which the search for truth may be impaired by loss of evidence, to encourage plaintiffs to use reasonable and proper diligence in enforcing their rights, and to prevent

---

[3] A federal district court in Pennsylvania preceded *Zuckerman v. Transamerica Ins. Co.*, 133 Ariz. 139, 650 P.2d 441 (1982). *ACF Produce, Inc. v. Chubb/Pacific Indem. Group*, 451 F. Supp. 1095, 1098 (E.D.Pa.1978) ("[N]either insurer may avail itself of the limitation of suit clause absent a showing of prejudice"). The Pennsylvania Supreme Court, in *Schreiber v. Pennsylvania Lumberman's Mut. Ins. Co.*, 498 Pa. 21, 444 A.2d 647 (1982), rejected the holding of the district court and held that no showing of prejudice is required before an insurer may rely on the suit limitation clause.

fraud. The presence or absence of prejudice is not, nor should it be, a factor in deciding whether an insurer may effectively assert this defense under the policy. *Zieba [v. Middlesex Mut. Assur. Co.]*, 549 F. Supp. [1318,] 1321 [(D. Conn. 1982)] (citations omitted).

. . . .

It is well known among the insurance industry and the insurance defense bar that legitimate claims are timely filed in all but the most egregious instances, while fraudulent claims are benefitted much more by delay and late filings. This is due to the fading of witness' memories, the loss or disappearance of material evidence, and the death or unavailability of witnesses which accompany the passage of time. Fraudulent claimants are also hesitant to expose themselves to criminal prosecution which may result from the use of discovery pursuant to Alaska Rules of Civil Procedure. By effectively repealing this clause, the majority effectively negates prompt resolution of suspect fire claims which, in my opinion, is contrary to sound public policy reasons for enforcement of the one-year suit limitation clause.

The clause in question is also in the public interest because it helps reduce overall insurance rates. . . .

. . . . The critical inquiry is whether the time limitation affords the insured a reasonable amount of time to file suit once liability has been denied. The 12-month period in question has been in common use since 1943, when codified by the New York legislature. The period of one year from the date of fire has been uniformly upheld as reasonable. Alaskans already have much longer than one year on the basis of *Fireman's Fund Ins. Co. v. Sand Lake Lounge, Inc.*, 514 P.2d 223 (Alaska 1973) [which allows an insured to sue one year from the date the insurer denies liability rather than one year from the date of the event causing the loss].

Many states' legislatures have mandated that fire insurance policies contain the 12-month limitation on suit, in furtherance of the public policies discussed above. Other states merely allow the clauses. A small minority of states expressly prohibit such clauses. [Citing Reader & Polk, The One-Year Suit Limitation in Fire Insurance Policies: Challenges and Counterpunches, 19 Forum 24, 25–27 (1983)].

Like Arizona, Alaska has merely allowed such clauses. However, Alaskan courts have consistently enforced the 12-month clause since at least 1954.

. . . .

The majority clearly mistakes the fundamental purpose of the suit limitation clause and blithely exorcises it out of the insurance contract. In so doing, the majority inexplicably disregards and seriously hampers important public policy reasons for enforcement of the suit limitation clause based upon 35 years of consistent precedent followed by the vast majority of jurisdictions. Why? No notice problems are involved. No ambiguity exists in the suit clause requirement. No unfairness is demonstrated since the insured had 22 months and 7 days after the date of the fire to file a suit against the insurance company. This 1943 fire insurance form has been approved by the insurance commissioner and, implicitly by the legislature. The insured was represented by counsel.

. . . .

In sum, requiring an insurer to show prejudice before relying on the enforcement of the suit limitation clause is simply bad law. Such a result is misguided, misdirected and inappropriate.

NOTES

1. *Suing on the policy.* If an insurer refuses to pay the insured's claim and the insured and insurer are unable to resolve their differences amicably, the insured may assert a claim against the insurer in court. Like any claim any party might have, an insured must bring an action on the policy in a timely manner. State statutes of limitations place an outer limit on the time during which the insured might seek a remedy in court, but many insurers seek to shorten this time period by inserting what are essentially "private statutes of limitations" in their insurance contracts. Contractual limitations periods, like statutes of limitations, seek to cut off stale claims and promote certainty. They are common in first-party insurance, particularly property, health, and disability policies.

2. *Statutory regulation of contractual limitations.* Justice Moore in dissent mentions the presence in some states of statutes that regulate the contractual limitations period in one way or another. Would Justice Moore's position have been stronger if the one-year limitation period had been part of a legislatively-mandated policy form? It seems obvious that a state statute prescribing a particular limitations period must trump a contrary contractual limitations period. But it would seem equally obvious that statutorily mandating the contractual limitations period does not convert the contractual provision into a statute. *See Herman v. Valley Insurance Co.,* 145 Or.App. 124, 928 P.2d 985 (1996). Why should this distinction matter?

Suppose a state statute prohibits a limitations period less than three years. A separate state statute provides for a six-year limitations period for contract actions. Realizing that a two-year contractual limitations period in an insurance policy would be invalid, what is the limitations period? Three years, or six years? *See Bayusik v. Nationwide Mutual Insurance Co.,* 659 A.2d 1188 (Conn. 1995). One way to avoid the issue, which is an important one if the same form is to be used in many different states, is to draft the limitations period as "the longer of two years or the minimum period allowed by state law." Compare *Graingrowers Warehouse Co. v. Central National Insurance,* 711 F. Supp. 1040 (E.D. Wash. 1989) (one year "unless a longer period of time is provided by applicable statute" did not import the six-year statute of limitations for contracts).

Of course, if a general limitations period for contract actions is being applied, an issue of when that period begins to run can arise. Most courts hold that the contract period begins to run when the insurer breaches the contract, but there are other approaches in some jurisdictions. *See, e.g., Grayson v. State Farm Mutual Automobile Insurance,* 114 Nev. 1379, 971 P.2d 798 (1998); *Berkshire Mutual Insurance Co. v. Burbank,* 422 Mass. 659, 664 N.E.2d 1188

(1996) (cause of action for underinsured motorist benefits, and statute of limitations began to run, when insurer breached policy by refusing to submit to arbitration; describing and citing cases for other rules).

3. *Waiver and estoppel.* Justice Moore's dissent leaves little room for doubt about where he stands on the question presented. But can it be doubted that if an insurer leads the insured to reasonably believe that the one-year limitation period will not be enforced, the insurer will subsequently be estopped to assert the provision, or be held to have waived the limitation? If the insurer investigates a claim filed after the limitation period has run, does this conduct, by itself, constitute waiver? *See Federal Deposit Insurance Corp. v. Hartford Accident and Indemnity Co.,* 97 F.3d 1148 (8th Cir. 1996); *Aceves v. Allstate Insurance Co.,* 827 F. Supp. 1473 (S.D. Cal. 1993), *aff'd in part, rev'd in part, vacated in part, dismissed in part, and remanded,* 68 F.3d 1160 (9th Cir. 1995); *Summers v. Auto-Owners Insurance Co.,* 719 N.E.2d 412 (Ind. Ct. App. 1999); *Closser v. Penn Mutual Fire Insurance Co.,* 457 A.2d 1081 (Del. Super. Ct. 1983). Are Justice Moore's concerns as equally pertinent to estoppel and waiver?

4. *Measuring the limitations period.* Justice Moore was equally dismayed by the court's 1973 *Sand Lake Lounge* decision holding that the one-year period should be measured from the date the insurer denies liability rather than from the date of the event causing the loss. The 1943 New York form requires that an action on the policy be commenced within twelve months from the "inception of the loss." Traditionally, this has been interpreted as the time of the event causing the loss, such as the fire or other casualty. *See, e.g., Troutman v. State Farm Fire & Casualty Co.,* 570 F.2d 658 (6th Cir. 1978); *Borgen v. Economy Preferred Insurance Co.,* 500 N.W.2d 419 (Wis. Ct. App. 1993).

Of course, there are many situations where it is difficult to determine when the loss occurred. This led the California Supreme Court in *Prudential-LMI Commercial Insurance v. Superior Court,* 798 P.2d 1230 (Cal. 1990), which appears in § 4.05[4] as a principal case, to approve the so-called "delayed discovery rule." This rule defines "inception of the loss" as "that point in time when appreciable damage occurs and is or should be known to the insured, such that a reasonable insured would be aware that his notification duty under the policy has been triggered." 798 P.2d at 1237.

Sand Lake Lounge represents an approach that has been labeled "equitable tolling." The typical policy gives the insured a specified amount of time to file a proof of loss and contemplates that the insurer will take some time to consider the proof. Therefore, under the logic of this approach, the insured's time to commence the suit should be tolled for the period during which these policy-mandated procedures are being followed. As a practical matter, these procedures are completed when the insurer denies the claim, and the one-year period runs from that moment. *See, e.g., Healthwise of Kentucky, Ltd. v. Anglin,* 956 S.W.2d 213 (Ky. 1997) (one-year policy limitation on bringing suit on group health plan not applied to insureds who followed insurer's internal appeals procedure); *Ford Motor Co. v. Lumbermens Mutual Casualty Co.,* 319 N.W.2d 320 (Mich. 1982). But many cases have refused to toll the limitation period when the insured was not prevented from complying with the provision or simply because of the insurer's investigation of the claim. *See Federal Deposit Insurance Corp. v. Hartford Accident and Indemnity Co.,* 97 F.3d 1148 (8th Cir. 1996) (citing cases). What if the insurer induces or misleads the insured into missing a filing deadline?

5. *Tort claims?* What if the insured's claim against the insurer is a tort claim, not a claim for breach of contract? Must tort claims be brought within the one-year period? If the insurer's duty is imposed by tort law rather than the contract, is the contractual limitations period even relevant? *Compare Hearn v. Rickenbacker,* 400 N.W.2d 90 (Mich. 1987) (contractual limitations period is irrelevant), with *Martin v. Liberty Mutual Fire Insurance Co.,* 293 N.W.2d 168 (Wis. 1980) (contractual limitations period controls time limits for bringing tort claims). Can you imagine a situation in which a plaintiff-insured would prefer to argue that the insurer's bad faith is a breach of contract, and not a tort?

[4]   The Duty to Cooperate

MELLO v. HINGHAM MUTUAL FIRE INSURANCE CO.
421 Mass. 333, 656 N.E.2d 1247 (Mass. 1995)

FRIED, JUSTICE.

[Plaintiffs, Americo and Maria Mello, sued the insurer to recover proceeds the insurer had refused to pay for a fire loss. The insurer] moved for summary judgment alleging that Americo Mello's failure to submit to an examination under oath, as required both by the policy and G.L. c. 175, § 99, Twelfth (1994 ed.), constituted a material breach of the fire insurance policy, thus barring recovery under the policy. The plaintiff asserted that his refusal to submit to the examination was justified because he had become the subject of a criminal investigation for arson in connection with this fire. The plaintiff contends that the privilege against self-incrimination as protected by art. 12 of the Declaration of Rights of the Massachusetts Constitution and the Fifth Amendment to the United States Constitution justifies his refusal to submit to such an examination. [The trial court granted the insurer's motion for summary judgment. Plaintiffs appealed.]

I.

. . . . Hingham issued a policy to the plaintiffs effective September 4, 1992, insuring their residence. On September 25, 1992, a fire of undetermined origin broke out in the plaintiffs' residence. On that day, Hingham received oral notice of loss and commenced an investigation. In addition, the Danvers police and the Massachusetts State police began investigations into what they deemed a suspicious fire. The law enforcement authorities immediately informed Hingham that the plaintiff was a suspect in their respective investigations. Four days later, Hingham sent the plaintiffs notice of the cancellation of their policy, effective October 9, 1992.[2]

---

[2] The policy authorized Hingham's cancellation of the plaintiffs' policy. Such cancellation, however, merely terminated the parties' relationship prospectively and did not affect Hingham's liability to the plaintiffs for the past fire loss.

Pursuant to its investigation, on November 10, 1992, Hingham requested that plaintiff submit to an examination under oath, as required by the policy.[3] He initially agreed to an examination. The plaintiff, however, postponed the examination on two occasions; the first to accommodate his attorney and the second to allow him the opportunity to retain a criminal attorney. On February 23, 1993, Hingham requested that the plaintiff submit to an examination within thirty days. His attorney responded by asking why such an examination was necessary. Hingham, by letter, explained that it required the sworn statement to complete its investigation and determine whether to pay the claim. The plaintiff's attorney responded on March 22, 1993, by asserting the plaintiff's constitutional privilege against self-incrimination.

On March 29, 1993, Hingham demanded that the examination take place before April 30, 1993. The plaintiff declined. On May 3, 1993, Hingham denied coverage for the fire loss.

II.

. . . . [T]he plaintiffs contend that, because the plaintiff was a subject of an on-going criminal investigation concerning the fire, his privilege against self-incrimination, as guaranteed by art. 12 and the Fifth Amendment, excused him from providing a statement under oath to Hingham as required by the insurance policy concerning the circumstances surrounding the fire. . . .

A.

General Laws c. 175, § 99 (1994 ed.), prescribes a statutory form for fire insurance policies. The statute sets out the insured's duty to cooperate in two sentences reprinted in the margin.[4] Prior to our decision in *Johnson Controls, Inc. v. Bowes*, 381 Mass. 278, 409 N.E.2d 185 (1980), the satisfaction of the insured's duties embodied in this cooperation clause was a condition precedent to the insurer's liability under the policy. Thus, the insured's failure to provide notice of loss or a sworn statement of loss within the time period allotted in the policy released the insurer from its obligations under the contract.

---

[3] Although the policy is not part of the summary judgment record, the parties agree that the policy states: "Section I — CONDITIONS. 2. Your Duties After Loss. . . . f. We may reasonably require you to:. . .(3) submit to an examination under oath, while not in the presence of any other insured, and sign the same." This requirement is commonly referred to as the "statement under oath clause," and it has appeared in all standard form Massachusetts homeowners insurance policies since March, 1982, pursuant to G.L. c. 175, § 99. See St. 1981, c. 718, § 2, amending G.L. c. 175, § 99, Twelfth. According to the judge's memorandum, the policy further states that "[n]o action can be brought against [the insurer] unless there has been compliance with the policy provisions."

[4] "The insured shall give immediate written notice to [the insurer] of any loss. . .furnish a complete inventory of the destroyed and damaged property,. . .and the insured shall forthwith render to [the insurer] a signed, sworn statement in proof of loss which sets forth to the best knowledge and belief of the insured the following: the time and cause of the loss, the interest of the insured and of all others in the property, the actual cash value of each item thereof and the amount of loss thereto. . . . The insured, as often as may be reasonably required, shall exhibit to any person designated by [the insurer] all that remains of any property herein described, and submit to examinations under oath by any person named by [the insured][sic], and subscribe the same; and, as often as may be reasonably required, shall produce for examination all books of account, bills, invoices. . .at such reasonable time and place as may be designated by [the insurer]. . . ." G.L. c. 175, § 99, Twelfth (1994 ed.).

In 1980, our decision in *Johnson Controls, Inc. v. Bowes, supra,* "modified the common law in this area by adding prejudice requirements in the contexts of notice provisions." *Darcy v. Hartford Ins. Co.,* 407 Mass. 481, 489, 554 N.E.2d 28 (1990). We reasoned that the notice provision of insurance policies should no longer be strictly construed as a condition precedent to the insurer's liability. *Johnson Controls, Inc. v. Bowes, supra,* 381 Mass. at 282, 409 N.E.2d 185. Instead, the insurer must establish "both that the notice provision was in fact breached and that the breach resulted in prejudice to its position," for its obligations to be discharged. *Id.*

Our decision in *Johnson Controls,* however, affected only the notice provisions of the G.L. c. 175, § 99's duty to cooperate. The second sentence of the statutory provision addresses the insured's responsibilities during the investigation: "as often as may be reasonably required" by the insurer, the "insured. . .shall. . .submit to examinations under oath." The statute contemplates that the insurer, when it determines that an examination is reasonable, may require that the insured submit to such an examination under oath.

It is the law in most jurisdictions that the submission to an examination, if the request is reasonable, is strictly construed as a condition precedent to the insurer's liability. This court agrees with these authorities. In this case, Hingham's request was reasonable, and refusal to submit to an examination may have significantly hampered its ability to investigate the fire and assure itself that the plaintiff had not set the fire. The notification from the Danvers and State police that the plaintiff was being investigated on suspicion of arson understandably raised that concern for Hingham. Therefore, unless the privilege against self-incrimination excuses the plaintiff's failure to comply with Hingham's request, by refusing to submit to its reasonable request for an examination under oath, the plaintiff materially breached the insurance policy, releasing Hingham from its obligations.

The plaintiff, though, asserts that the privilege against self-incrimination excuses his compliance with the statement under oath clause. The privilege is contained in art. 12 and the Fifth Amendment. Article 12 provides that "[n]o subject shall. . .be compelled to accuse, or furnish evidence against himself. . . ." The Fifth Amendment provides that "[n]o person. . .shall be compelled in any criminal case to be a witness against himself." One who invokes the privilege cannot be penalized for that assertion lest the penalty create an impermissible compulsion to testify. "Yet not every undesirable consequence which may flow from the exercise of the privilege against self-incrimination can be characterized as a penalty." *Flint v. Mullen,* 499 F.2d 100, 104 (1st Cir.), *cert. denied,* 419 U.S. 1026, 95 S. Ct. 505, 42 L. Ed. 2d 301 (1974), *quoted in Wansong v. Wansong,* 395 Mass. 154, 157–158, 478 N.E.2d 1270, *cert. denied,* 474 U.S. 1014, 106 S. Ct. 546, 88 L. Ed. 2d 475 (1985).

A person may not seek to obtain a benefit or to turn the legal process to his advantage while claiming the privilege as a way of escaping from obligations and conditions that are normally incident to the claim he makes. This principle holds true particularly where the benefit he seeks is from another private party, who is being asked to make good on its obligation forgoing the countervailing advantages that were part of the bargain. The principle holds true even where the State is also a party to the transaction. In seeking a license, applying for a position, claiming a benefit or even an entitlement, it has never been imagined that a citizen may at one and the same time make a demand on the government and refuse to supply the information that would authenticate it. Even in the situation where the State seeks to compel speech, this court has held that the privilege does not insulate a claimant from being adversely impacted by a decision to remain silent, although the resulting evidence may not itself be introduced in evidence in a subsequent criminal proceeding.

Indeed, even in the criminal process a defendant cannot turn the legal process to his advantage by asserting this privilege. A defendant may not seek to avail himself of his constitutional right to testify in his own behalf in order to offer, for instance, an alibi that only he could know of, without at the same time losing the protection of the privilege and opening himself to cross-examination.

With this as background we turn to the plaintiffs' claim. They argue that the Superior Court's allowance of Hingham's motion for summary judgment imposed an impermissible penalty upon the plaintiff for asserting his privilege against self-incrimination. We disagree. Where the undesirable consequences arise from the claimant's own voluntary actions, the privilege against self-incrimination cannot be used to extricate the claimant from such a dilemma of his own making. The plaintiff voluntarily entered into the contract with Hingham, another private party. Hingham obligated itself to perform duties, some of which were contingent on the plaintiffs' actions. The plaintiffs made a claim against Hingham for coverage, and Hingham asks that the plaintiff keep his part of the bargain even if it may harm his interests in the criminal investigation. A dilemma this may be, but it is not of Hingham's or the Commonwealth's making, anymore than it is a dilemma of the Commonwealth's making when an accused must choose between forfeiting the opportunity to speak in his own behalf and subjecting himself to cross-examination. Thus, it is not by the Commonwealth or by Hingham that the plaintiff "is compelled to. . .furnish evidence against himself," but by his own contractual undertaking.[6] Therefore, we hold that the grant of summary judgment by the Superior Court is a permissible consequence of the plaintiff's assertion of the privilege.

B.

The plaintiffs seek to blunt the force of this argument by two narrower suggestions. First, they propose that the insurer might have waited until the completion of the criminal proceedings — which, after all, did result in a verdict of acquittal in the arson prosecution — before requiring the plaintiff to respond under oath to the insurer's inquiries. This is only a less extreme version of the plaintiffs' principal contention that the insurer's contractual right to the insured's full cooperation must yield to the insured's concerns about self-incrimination. The insurer's contractual right is to determine

---

[6] We attach no significance to the fact that the obligation is imposed as a statutorily prescribed term in a standard policy. This is but a statutory restatement and formalization (in so far as an oath is required) of the general obligation of insureds in many kinds of contracts of insurance to cooperate with the insurer in the investigation and verification of the claim.

promptly — while the evidence and memories are still fresh — the validity of any loss for which it might become liable. The insurer is under a corresponding duty to pay any claim promptly, and if it is later found to have inappropriately delayed or withheld payment, it may significantly increase its own liability. In these circumstances the insurer should not have to delay its investigation for an indeterminate and possibly lengthy period to comport with the interests of the insured.

Second, it has been suggested that the plaintiff's concerns could have been accommodated if the insurer had been content to question only Mrs. Mello under oath, since she had not been told that she was under criminal investigation. Our response to this contention is similar to the one above. The insurer is contractually bound to both the plaintiffs and contractually entitled to pursue its investigation by requesting an inquiry of either. It was free to choose whomever or both of the insureds it believed could assist in that investigation.

Finally, the plaintiffs complain that the insurer and the law enforcement authorities were working "hand-in-glove," suggesting that the insurer's demand under the statute and the policy was a mere pretext for assisting law enforcement authorities with their investigation. The record and the plaintiffs' allegations go no further, however, than to show that the law enforcement authorities and the insurer were aware of each other's investigations and were keeping each other informed of their respective progress. Indeed, there is no support in the record for a suggestion that Hingham was doing anything other than acting reasonably to protect its interests. The insurer, like any citizen who has information relevant to an on-going criminal investigation, has the right (unless there exists a confidential or other special relationship) and sometimes the duty to give law enforcement authorities any information that may be of assistance. If that is all the plaintiffs are complaining about, giving any weight to their complaint on this score would have the unacceptable entailment that the insurer, by pursuing its contractual right, would be disabled from cooperating with law enforcement authorities in ways open to any other citizen.

. . . .

IV.

For the reasons stated in this opinion, the Superior Court's order granting summary judgment for Hingham is affirmed.

So ordered.

––––––––––

NOTES

1. *Policy language.* The language of the policy in *Mello* is typical of property insurance policies. Such policies rarely contain a clause stating "the insured shall cooperate . . .," but usually impose specific obligations on insureds to provide documents, make themselves available for interviews, etc., all of which require the insured's cooperation. It is fair to view the requirement that the insured file a proof of loss as essentially a requirement that the insured

cooperate with the insurer to that extent in processing the claim. Insureds also have a duty to cooperate in third-party insurance; the implications of the duty in this context is taken up in § 8.02[2], *infra*.

2. *What constitutes noncooperation?* Acts of noncooperation run along a continuum ranging from the minor and insignificant to the material, substantial, and prejudicial. Suppose an insured fails to meet with investigators despite repeated requests that he do so. If the insurer's argument is that it could not locate witnesses because of the insured's inaction, but the names of the witnesses were readily available in easily accessible police reports, should the insured lose coverage on account of noncooperation? *See Auto-Owners Insurance Co. v. Rodgers,* 360 So. 2d 716 (Ala. 1978). Is false swearing on a proof of loss a per se breach by the insured of the duty to cooperate?

3. *Must the insurer affirmatively seek the insured's cooperation?* If the insurer must give the insured an opportunity to fix a deficient proof of loss, does it follow that the insurer must take some steps to ask for the insured's cooperation before attempting to assert a defense based on lack of cooperation? In *Watson v. Jones,* 610 P.2d 619 (Kan. 1980), the court stated that the insurer has no defense "if the insurer was not sufficiently diligent in its attempts to secure" the cooperation of the insured or if the insured's lack of cooperation "is found to have occurred through lack of timely effort and diligence on the part of the insurer." 610 P.2d at 623. In *Darcy v. Hartford Insurance Co.,* 554 N.E.2d 28 (Mass. 1990), the court said that the insurer may not disclaim coverage based on a lack of the insured's cooperation unless the insurer had exercised "diligence and good faith" in seeking the insured's cooperation. How much of a burden does this place on an insurer? Is it tantamount to simply requiring the insurer to send a letter to the insured notifying the insured of court dates, hearing times, etc. before being able to assert that the insured's absence at such hearings breaches the duty to cooperate?

4. *Prejudice.* What is the court's position in *Mello* on the issue of whether there is a requirement on the insurer to demonstrate prejudice as a result of the lack of cooperation? Most courts are very explicit in insisting that the insurer establish prejudice as a prerequisite to asserting a noncooperation defense. *See, e.g., Martin v. Travelers Indemnity Co.,* 450 F.2d 542 (5th Cir. 1971); *Darcy v. Hartford Insurance Co.,* 554 N.E.2d 28 (Mass. 1990); *Home Indemnity Co. v. Reed Equipment Co.,* 381 So. 2d 45 (Ala. 1980). Is establishing a *material* lack of cooperation tantamount to showing prejudice?

What constitutes "prejudice?" Is wilful noncooperation (such as a wilful failure to speak to an investigator or to produce documents) per se prejudicial? Must the insurer establish that the insured's failure to cooperate made it more difficult for the insurer to deny the claim? Or simply more difficult to investigate and assess the claim? See Robert H. Jerry, II, Understanding Insurance Law 85[c] (2d ed. 1996).

5. *A problem of timing.* Fire destroys the insured's dwelling, which is covered by a property insurance policy with Reliable Insurance Company. The insured is a "prime suspect." Reliable, while considering the insured's proof of loss, notifies insured that it wants to examine him under oath. Insured refuses. Then, after the one-year limitation period expires, insured sues insurer.

Insurer contends that because the insured refused to appear for the examination under oath, the policy is void. Is complying with a policy provision requiring the insured to submit to such examinations a condition precedent to being able even to file a suit for proceeds? Or is the insured allowed to file suit, with his or her noncompliance having relevance to the validity of the claim? If prejudice is required before the insurer can deny recovery, does the insurer's ability to depose the insured in the lawsuit render irrelevant the insured's refusal to submit to the oral examination before the suit was filed? *Compare Warrilow v. Superior Court,* 689 P.2d 193 (Ariz. Ct. App. 1984) (insured's refusal to submit to examination is breach of policy and forecloses right to recover under policy), with *Thompson v. West Virginia Essential Property Insurance Ass'n,* 186 W. Va. 84, 411 S.E.2d 27 (1991) (insured's refusal to submit to oral examination under oath does not automatically cause loss of coverage), overruled on other grounds, *Light v. Allstate Insurance Co.,* 203 W.Va. 27, 506 S.E.2d 64 (1998).

6. *The self-incrimination argument.* Many insureds have been put to the choice of losing their insurance coverage by refusing to cooperate with the insurer's request for production of documents, or revealing the information and risking the consequences that the information might have in collateral criminal proceedings. On this issue, the holding in *Mello* is squarely in line with the clear weight of authority. *See, e.g., Monticello Insurance Co. v. Mooney,* 733 So. 2d 802 (Miss. 1999); *Tran v. State Farm Fire and Casualty Co.,* 136 Wash. 2d 214, 961 P.2d 358 (1998) (en banc); *United States Fidelity & Guaranty Co. v. Wigginton,* 964 F.2d 487 (5th Cir. 1992); *Pervis v. State Farm Fire & Casualty Co.,* 901 F.2d 944 (11th Cir.), *cert. denied,* 498 U.S. 899 (1990); *Hudson Tire Mart, Inc. v. Aetna Casualty & Surety Co.,* 518 F.2d 671 (2d Cir. 1975). Even if one concedes that no illegal compulsion is involved in forcing an insured to elect between insurance coverage and asserting a Fifth Amendment right not to produce documents and that there is a state action problem in many, if not most, of these cases, are there no public policies inherent in the Fifth Amendment (or similar state constitutional provisions) that might properly be viewed as trumping the insurer's insistence that the insured disclose requested documents or else forfeit coverage? In other contexts, public policy trumps policy language; so why not in this situation?

It would be incorrect to assume, however, that the insurer is entitled to demand that the insured produce personal and financial information irrelevant to the claim. In *Clarke v. Allstate Insurance Co.,* 728 So. 2d 135 (Ala. 1998), the insureds reported that their 1987 Chevy Blazer had been stolen. After a proof of loss was filed, a few weeks later the vehicle was found in a local apartment complex parking lot. Insureds then claimed that the vehicle had been damaged during the time it was stolen. The insurer's adjuster stated that the locks on the Blazer had not been broken, that no electrical wires had been cut, and that whoever had taken the vehicle had done so with a key. A police report indicated that the driver's-side window had been broken from the inside. The court held that the insurer's request for the insured's tax returns, bank statements, and canceled checks for three years before the property loss was "so broad as to be unreasonable on its face." 728 So. 2d at 141. Do you agree with the holding?

7. *Claims processing conditions and warranties.* Now that you have reviewed some of the contractual conditions insurers employ with regard to claims processing, perhaps it is time to revisit the question raised in the last note in § 3.02[1][d]. There we were examining the intricacies of warranties in insurance law and how courts and legislatures have attempted to regulate them. Remember, a warranty is at heart nothing more than a condition which demands strict compliance. If a jurisdiction will only enforce a claims processing condition where the insurer is materially prejudiced, has it achieved the same result that some courts and legislatures wrought when ameliorating the harsh consequences that Lord Mansfield brought about in his opinions dealing with warranties in marine insurance? To the extent that a jurisdiction refuses to require a showing of prejudice with regard to the nonsatisfaction of a claims processing provision, could one argue that relief should nevertheless be granted under any pertinent common law decision or statute regulating warranties because such a claims processing condition is nothing more than a warranty? What would you argue on behalf of the insurer? *See Howard v. Federal Crop Insurance Corp.,* 540 F.2d 695 (4th Cir. 1976). If section 3106 of the New York statute dealing with warranties (set out in § 3.02[1][c]) were to apply, how should the issue be resolved?

[5] Arbitration and Appraisal

ELBERON BATHING CO. v. AMBASSADOR INSURANCE CO.

77 N.J. 1, 389 A.2d 439 (1978), 8 A.L.R.4th 519 (1981)

CONFORD, P.J.A.D. (temporarily assigned).

[Editors' note: The facts of this case, as well as the court's discussion and resolution of the first issue, are in § 2.03[1], *supra.*]

II

We turn to the question whether the failure of the appraisers to deduct depreciation from replacement cost constitutes sufficient cause to set aside the award.

Initially, the trial judge and Appellate Division were correct in approaching the matter of review of the appraisal award from a narrow perspective. It is not in the public interest to encourage litigation over procedures which were designed to resolve disputes without litigation. Thus every reasonable intendment and presumption comes to the support of such awards.

An appraiser, however, can make no legal determinations. The instant appraisers awarded pure replacement cost under a contract and statute which allowed for recovery only to the extent of the "actual cash value." As indicated in Point I above, to the extent that replacement cost is or may be a proper criterion of actual cash value, there must normally be a deduction for depreciation lest the insured receive more than indemnity for his loss. In failing to make such a deduction, the appraisers violated the terms of the policy and committed a mistake of law.

. . . .

There is an alternative justification for setting aside the award. During discussions among the appraisers as to the amount of loss, Thomas, defendant's appraiser, attempted to ascertain such factors as the actual cost to Elberon of effecting the repairs, the actual extent of repairs made, the age of the building, depreciation, the use to which the building had been put and the condition of the building prior to the fire. However, the umpire and the other appraiser refused to attempt to elicit or consider such information.

We have held above that "actual cash value" is to be ascertained by consideration of all relevant evidence. The courts of California and New York have vacated appraisals where the appraisers failed to comply with the applicable standard for ascertaining loss. In *Jefferson Insurance Co. of N.Y. v. Superior Court, supra,* 90 Cal. Rptr. at 611, 475 P.2d at 883, the California Supreme Court vacated an appraisal where the appraisers had considered only replacement cost minus depreciation whereas the California standard was market value. In *Gervant v. New England Fire Ins. Co.,* 306 N.Y. 393, 118 N.E.2d 574 (Ct. App. 1954), it was legal misconduct for an appraiser to consider only evidence as to replacement cost minus depreciation because New York follows the broad evidence rule. *Id.* at 577.

We consequently conclude that the refusal of these appraisers even to consider such factors as those listed above constituted legal misconduct and of itself justifies vacation of the award.[6] Compare *N.J.S.A* 2A:24-8(c), which provides that where arbitrators refuse to hear evidence pertinent and material to the controversy, the court shall vacate the award.

III

Defendant raises the question whether the trial court was required to proceed in this matter under and pursuant to the Arbitration Act, *N.J.S.A.* 2A:24-1 *et seq.* It asserts that if the act was applicable, the award should be vacated because the procedures followed by the appraisers did not conform thereto. We have concluded that the Arbitration Act is not applicable.

A comparison of appraisal and arbitration will be helpful. The purposes of both are the same: to submit disputes to third parties and effect their speedy and efficient resolution without recourse to the courts. To assure minimum judicial intervention, the scope of judicial review of both types of recourse is narrow.

The distinctions are significant. An agreement for arbitration ordinarily encompasses the disposition of the entire controversy between the parties, and judgment may be entered upon the award, whereas an appraisal establishes only the amount of loss and not liability. Arbitration is conducted as a quasi-judicial proceeding, with hearings, notice of hearings, oaths of arbitrators and oaths of witnesses. Appraisers act on their own skill and knowledge, need not be sworn and need hold no formal hearings so long as both sides are given an opportunity to state their positions. Note, "Arbitration or Appraisement?," 8 Syracuse L. Rev. 205, 206 (1957).

---

[6] In some cases a refusal to consider relevant evidence, while improper, might not in itself be cause to set aside an award if the result reached appeared reasonable. Here, however, exclusion of depreciation while applying replacement cost new prevents the result from being reasonable.

The instant policy provision clearly called for an appraisal. That the procedures mandated by the Arbitration Act, *see, e.g.,* N.J.S.A. 2A:24-6, were not followed and that there was no finding with respect to liability tends to indicate that the fact-finders purported to conduct an appraisal. This was entirely proper.

Nothing in the Arbitration Act requires that fire insurance appraisals comply with that statute. Indeed, the word "appraisal" is not found in the act. *See In re Delmar Box Co.,* 309 N.Y. 60, 127 N.E.2d 808, 810–811 (Ct. App. 1955), where the New York court noted the long-prevailing distinctions between appraisals and arbitration, and concluded that any determination that the formal requirements under the Arbitration Act should apply to fire loss appraisals should come from the Legislature. *Id.* at 813. Compare *Jefferson Insurance Company of N. Y. v. Superior Court, supra,* 90 Cal. Rptr. at 610, n. 41, 475 P.2d at 882, n. 41 (under the California Code of Civil Procedure, enforcement procedures respecting arbitration have been made applicable to appraisals). The intention to change a long-established rule or principle is not to be imputed to the Legislature in the absence of a clear manifestation thereof.

Furthermore, since application of the broad evidence rule to appraisals will promote the interchange of information between the appraisers and the parties, one may expect enhancement of the fairness of the procedure without burdening the appraisal with the formalities of arbitration (*e.g.,* oaths, notice of hearings, etc.).

Finally, since arbitrators are entrusted with the broader obligation to determine liability as well as the amount of the award, it is reasonable to require broader procedural safeguards in arbitration. The subject-matter responsibility of appraisers being less, the procedural safeguards attending an appraisal may be lower. However, the Court must correct any erroneous exercise of jurisdiction by an appraiser.

. . . .

If the judge on the remand finds liability on the part of defendant, he shall direct the appraisal procedure to be instituted anew with instructions that the new appraisers make their evaluation of loss based on consideration of all relevant evidence, pursuant to the principles outlined above.

. . . .

NOTES

1. *Appraisal versus arbitration.* As indicated in *Elberon,* appraisals are governed by a different set of rules than arbitrations. While both may be required by the insurance contract, arbitrations also are usually subject to rules and procedures contained in statutes enacted in the particular jurisdiction. Appraisals, on the other hand, usually are governed only by the terms of the contract and any common law that has developed on the subject. An arbitration or appraisal may be mandated by the policy or merely be an option available to be elected by one of the parties. Where mandated, courts have

usually looked upon such methods of dispute resolution with favor and, absent fraud or some other basis to rescind the contract, have upheld the clauses in face of attack. *See, e.g., State Farm Mutual Automobile Insurance Co. v. Broadnax,* 827 P.2d 531 (Colo. 1992); *Hansen v. State Farm Mutual Automobile Insurance Co.,* 112 Idaho 663, 735 P.2d 974 (1987). See generally Robert H. Jerry, II, Understanding Insurance Law § 83 (2d ed. 1996).

2. *Facts, law, and judicial review.* As Professor Widiss has explained, "it is more difficult to successfully attack an arbitrator's decision than it is to secure the reversal of a judgment by either a trial judge or jury." Alan I. Widiss, *Uninsured and Underinsured Motorist Insurance Claims Disputes,* in American Arbitration Ass'n, Insurance ADR Manual 204, 236 (1993). He explains further: "In the century that has followed [*Burchell v. Marsh,* 58 U.S. (How.) 344 (1854)], both courts and commentators have repeatedly stated the basic proposition that the award of an arbitrator cannot be set aside for mere errors of judgment, either as to law or as to fact." *Id.* Bias or conflict of interest is, of course, another matter. See George L. Blum, Annotation, *Setting Aside Arbitration Award on Ground of Interest or Bias of Arbitrators-Insurance Appraisals or Arbitrations,* 63 A.L.R.5th 674 (1998). Whether an arbitrator or appraiser has exceeded the scope of her legal authority is a different matter as well, and this issue is typically subject to review by a court of general jurisdiction.

3. *Examples and other information.* For examples of arbitration and appraisal clauses, see the uninsured motorist provision in the Personal Auto Policy in Appendix E and lines 123–140 in the New York Standard Fire Policy in Appendix A, respectively. For an extensive discussion of arbitration in the insurance context, see American Arbitration Association, Insurance ADR Manual (1993). This volume is a collection of chapters on negotiation, mediation, private judging, court-annexed ADR programs, special masters, and ADR in particular lines of insurance. For a general discussion of ADR, including arbitration, see Edward A. Dauer, Manual of Dispute Resolution (1994).

4. *A duty to inform?* In *Davis v. Blue Cross,* 25 Cal. 3d 418, 158 Cal. Rptr. 828 (1979), the California supreme court held that an insurer breached the duty of good faith and fair dealing when it failed to advise the insureds of their rights under an inconspicuous arbitration clause. *Davis* was "toughened" in *Sarchett v. Blue Shield,* 43 Cal. 3d 1, 729 P.2d 267, 233 Cal. Rptr. 76 (1987), where the court held that the insurer breached the duty of good faith and fair dealing when it failed to timely inform the insured that the health insurance policy contained a provision for peer review and arbitration that the insured could invoke to resolve a dispute over the medical necessity of certain treatment ordered by the insured's physician. Although the policy's review and arbitration provisions were "unambiguous," "clearly set out," [729 P.2d at 273], and "adequately set out with a bold-face heading," [729 P.2d at 277] the court held that the insurer could not passively assume that the insured was aware of his or her rights. Instead, the insurer must take affirmative steps to ensure that the insured is so informed once it is clear to the insurer that the insured disputes the denial of coverage. [729 P.2d at 277.]

Sarchett, however, was read narrowly in *Chase v. Blue Cross of California,* 42 Cal. App. 4th 1142, 50 Cal. Rptr. 2d 178 (1996). In *Chase,* the court stated that the portion of *Sarchett* imposing a duty on the insurer to act affirmatively to ensure that the insured is aware of the arbitration provision was "dictum" and was "apparently occasioned by the egregious conduct of Blue Shield in that case." 50 Cal. Rptr. 2d at 187. Accordingly, the court reasoned that "the insurer does not have an ongoing duty to keep the insured informed of his rights once those rights have been clearly set forth in the policy. However, the insurer may not engage in conduct designed to mislead the insured." *Id.* Where does this leave us?

5. *Anti-arbitration statutes, the FAA, and the McCarran-Ferguson Act.* For a long time, courts were generally hostile to arbitration agreements, but this attitude has undergone significant change in recent years. As the U.S. Supreme Court stated in *Mitsubishi Motors Corp. v. Soler Chrysler-Plymouth, Inc.,* 473 U.S. 614 (1985), "we are well past the time when judicial suspicion of the desirability of arbitration and of the competence of arbitral tribunals inhibited the development of arbitration as an alternative means of dispute resolution." 473 U.S. at 626–627. A number of states have passed statutes, often modeled on the Uniform Arbitration Act, 7 U.L.A. 1 (1997), which make agreements to arbitrate future disputes enforceable. Some of these statutes, however, specifically exempt insurance contracts from the effect of the law or make arbitration agreements unenforceable against insureds. Some other states have separate statutes with either generally-phrased exemptions that are arguably broad enough to take insurance contracts out of the pro-arbitration statutes, or which specifically declare that arbitration clauses in insurance contracts, or certain kinds of insurance contracts, are unenforceable. As many as twenty states have some kind of statute making arbitration unenforceable in the context of uninsured motorist claims. Stephen Lamson, *The Impact of the Federal Arbitration Act and the McCarran-Ferguson Act on Uninsured Motorist Arbitration,* 19 Conn. L. Rev. 241, 248–252 (1987).

Complexity is added to the foregoing picture by the Federal Arbitration Act, which makes agreements to arbitrate future disputes "contained in a contract evidencing a transaction involving commerce. . .valid, irrevocable, and enforceable, save upon such grounds as exist at law or in equity for the revocation of any contract." 9 U.S.C. § 2 (1999). The effect of the FAA on insurance contracts, however, cannot be determined without consideration of the McCarran-Ferguson Act, 15 U.S.C. § 1012(b) (1994), which gives state laws regulating the business of insurance primacy over federal law, unless the federal law is explicitly enacted for the purpose of regulating the business of insurance. *See Lamson, supra,* at 251–75.

When one attempts to put these statutes together, a state anti-arbitration statute of general application is preempted by the FAA, and therefore should not render an arbitration clause in an insurance contract invalid. If, however, a state insurance statute specifically strikes down arbitration clauses in insurance contracts, this statute should be saved from FAA preemption by the McCarran-Ferguson Act. If a state has a general anti-arbitration statute that mentions insurance contracts but the statute is not part of the state's insurance code, is this a statute that regulates the "business of insurance" so as to trigger the "reverse preemption" effect of McCarran-Ferguson? In short, how all of this plays out in particular cases is likely to depend on the precise text of state law. *See, e.g., American Bankers Insurance Co. v. Crawford,* 757 So. 2d 1125 (Ala. 2000) (Alabama's anti-arbitration statute does not "reverse preempt" FAA under provisions of McCarran-Ferguson Act); *DiMercurio v. Sphere Drake Insurance, PLC,* 202 F.3d 71 (1st Cir. 2000) (arbitration clause in insurance policy issued by English insurer to Massachusetts owner of commercial fishing vessel held enforceable). A particularly fertile area for litigation over the effect of these statutes is insurer insolvency; reinsurers and insurers often seek to enforce arbitration provisions, because this will strip jurisdiction from a state insurance commissioner who supervises the liquidation. *See, e.g., Stephens v. American International Insurance Co.,* 66 F.3d 41 (2d Cir. 1995) (anti-arbitration provision in Kentucky rehabilitation and liquidation statute is preserved from FAA preemption by McCarran-Ferguson); *Quackenbush v. Allstate Insurance Co.,* 121 F.3d 1372 (9th Cir. 1997) (arbitration clauses in reinsurance contracts held enforceable with respect to offset obligations owed by insurer to California Insurance Commissioner, as trustee for insolvent reinsureds); *Munich American Reinsurance Co. v. Crawford,* 141 F.3d 585 (5th Cir.), *cert. denied,* 525 U.S. 1016 (1998) (same result with respect to Oklahoma statute governing insurance company delinquency proceedings).

§ 8.02 Dispute Resolution in the Third-Party Context

[1] The Duty to Defend

Robert H. Jerry, II, *The Insurer's Right to Reimbursement of Defense Costs,* **42 Ariz. L. Rev. 13, 17-19 (2000).** [*] As between the duty to defend and the duty to indemnify, the more expansive duty is the duty to defend. The essence of this common assertion is that the insurer is contractually obligated to defend even meritless suits that fall within the policy's coverage. Meritless claims, presumably, will be defeated, which means that the insurer's duty to indemnify such claims will never arise. In that sense, then, the duty to defend is broader: it is triggered in more situations than the duty to indemnify.

Yet in another sense, the common assertion that the duty to defend is broader than the duty to indemnify is misleading. Whatever the differences between the duties, the fact remains that both are directly linked to coverage. This is obvious with respect to the duty to indemnify: the insured need only pay judgments or settlements if the insured's liability arises out of a covered claim. Similarly, the insurer's contractual undertaking is to defend the insured against claims, even ones that are groundless or meritless, *if* the claims are within the scope of the policy's coverage. With respect to any liability insurance product, the insurer defends more claims than it indemnifies; after all, some plaintiffs who sue insureds will lose, and it necessarily follows that insurers will provide indemnification less frequently than they provide defenses. This, however, does not mean that the policy's *coverage* is broader with respect to the insurer's defense obligation, as compared to the

---

[*] Copyright © 2000 by the Arizona Board of Regents. Reprinted by permission. [Editors' note: Footnotes have been deleted from this excerpt.]

insurer's indemnity obligation. The default principle is that an insurer need not defend—let alone indemnify—a claim against its insured that falls outside the policy's coverage.

Examining the conditional nature of the defense and indemnity obligations illuminates the differences between them. Whenever a contract is formed, a set of reciprocal rights and duties is created immediately. The performance of these duties, however, is not always immediately due and owing; this is because it is common for contracting parties to place conditions on performance obligations. Sometimes conditions define the timing of the duty's performance; at other times, a condition's satisfaction or nonsatisfaction will determine whether the duty is ever performed. The insurer's duty to defend, which comes into existence immediately upon the formation of a contract between insurer and insured, is conditioned on, *inter alia*, the filing of a suit against the insured alleging claims *within coverage*. Similarly, the insurer's duty to indemnify comes into existence immediately upon a contract's formation, but it is conditioned on the existence of a judgment against the insured on, or a settlement of, a claim *within coverage*. Thus, the contractual duties of defense and indemnity are coextensive in the sense that the contours of both duties are defined by the coverage provided in the contract; but the condition to the duty to defend will be satisfied in more instances than the condition to the duty to indemnify. This means that the duty to defend will become due and owing in more situations, but this does not alter the essential underlying relationship between the insurer's defense obligation and the existence of coverage.

Beyond the foregoing observations, much remains unclear. . . .

LEDFORD v. GUTOSKI

319 Or. 397, 877 P.2d 80 (1994) (en banc)

UNIS, JUSTICE.

This is an action for defense costs and indemnity brought by Raymond Kuhl as third-party plaintiff against his insurer, Northwest Farm Bureau Insurance Company (Northwest), as third-party defendant. Kuhl was a defendant in an action for malicious prosecution filed by Bill Ledford, in which the complaint (the Ledford complaint) alleged that Kuhl had willfully and maliciously instituted a prosecution of plaintiff because Kuhl "intended to harass, annoy, harm and cause expense to" Ledford and that Kuhl acted "for the purpose of injuring" Ledford.

Kuhl tendered defense of Ledford's claim to Northwest. Kuhl's homeowner's policy provided in part that Northwest would pay "on behalf of an insured for damages resulting from bodily injury or property damage caused by an occurrence, if the insured is legally obligated." The policy defined "occurrence" as "an accident, including continuous or repeated exposure to conditions, which results in bodily injury or property damage neither expected nor intended from the standpoint of the insured." Northwest refused to defend the malicious prosecution claim because, in its view, the Ledford complaint alleged intentional conduct that was outside the policy's coverage.

The malicious prosecution action settled, and Kuhl then filed a third-party complaint against Northwest seeking indemnity and defense costs. The trial court entered summary judgment for Northwest. The Court of Appeals affirmed, holding that Northwest had no duty to defend the claim or to indemnify Kuhl. We allowed Kuhl's petition for review. We affirm the decision of the Court of Appeals on different grounds and affirm the judgment of the trial court.

DUTY TO DEFEND

Whether an insurer has a duty to defend an action against its insured depends on two documents: the complaint and the insurance policy. An insurer has a duty to defend an action against its insured if the claim against the insured stated in the complaint could, without amendment, impose liability for conduct covered by the policy.

In evaluating whether an insurer has a duty to defend, the court looks only at the facts alleged in the complaint to determine whether they provide a basis for recovery that could be covered by the policy: "If the facts alleged in the complaint against the insured do not fall within the coverage of the policy, the insurer should not have the obligation to defend. If a contrary rule were adopted, requiring the insurer to take note of facts other than those alleged, the insurer frequently would be required to speculate upon whether the facts alleged could be proved. We do not think this is a reasonable interpretation of the bargain to defend. It is more reasonable to assume that the parties bargained for the insurer's participation in the lawsuit only if the action brought by the third party, if successful, would impose liability upon the insurer to indemnify the insured." *Isenhart v. General Casualty Co.*, 233 Or. 49, 54, 377 P.2d 26 (1962). An insurer should be able to determine from the face of the complaint whether to accept or reject the tender of the defense of the action.

The insurer has a duty to defend if the complaint provides any basis for which the insurer provides coverage. Even if the complaint alleges some conduct outside the coverage of the policy, the insurer may still have a duty to defend if certain allegations of the complaint, without amendment, could impose liability for conduct covered by the policy. Any ambiguity in the complaint with respect to whether the allegations could be covered is resolved in favor of the insured. We must determine whether the facts alleged in the Ledford complaint may reasonably be interpreted to include conduct within the coverage of Northwest's policy.

The Ledford complaint alleged that Kuhl signed a criminal complaint against Ledford accusing Ledford of committing numerous crimes. The Ledford complaint further alleged that all of the charges against Ledford either were dismissed or resulted in acquittal. The Ledford complaint also alleged that Kuhl acted without probable cause in initiating the criminal prosecution against Ledford because Ledford did not commit the crimes alleged in the criminal complaint and that Kuhl knew that the charges were false. The Ledford complaint also alleged: "[Kuhl] acted maliciously and wilfully in instituting the prosecution of [Ledford] in that [he] intended to harass, annoy, harm and cause expense to [Ledford.]"

Northwest contends that it had no duty to defend because the policy provides coverage only for accidents "which result in bodily injury or property damage neither expected nor intended from the standpoint of the insured," and that the conduct alleged in the complaint falls outside the coverage in that policy because the damage suffered was either intended or expected by Kuhl.

Despite variations in the language of the policies, this court has interpreted various policy provisions excluding insurance coverage for intentionally-caused injuries similarly. Injuries resulting from intentional acts are excluded from insurance coverage when the insured intended to cause the particular injury or harm, as opposed to merely intending the act. For an exclusion from insurance coverage for intentional conduct to apply, "[i]t is not sufficient that the insured's intentional, albeit unlawful, acts have resulted in unintended harm; the acts must have been committed *for the purpose of inflicting the injury and harm* before either a policy provision excluding intentional harm applies or the public policy against insurability attaches." *Nielsen v. St. Paul Companies, supra,* 283 Or. at 281, 583 P.2d 545 (emphasis added).

The Ledford complaint specifically alleged that Kuhl "intended to harass, annoy, harm and cause expense" to Ledford. Those are allegations that Kuhl committed acts outside the coverage of the policy, namely acts committed for the purpose of causing the harm or injury.

Kuhl argues that there are instances in which liability on a malicious prosecution claim can be established even though the defendant did not have a subjective intent to cause harm or injury to the plaintiff. The Court of Appeals rejected Kuhl's argument, inferring a purpose to injure or harm from the general nature of the tort of malicious prosecution. The Court of Appeals stated: "We believe that instituting a criminal proceeding against another for a purpose other than that of achieving justice is, by its nature, an act from which the intent to do harm must necessarily be inferred. When a person purposefully instigates an unfounded criminal proceeding, the natural and ordinary consequence of that act is to cause the accused to incur the expense of defending against the charge, as well as to endure the mental anguish, inconvenience, embarrassment and humiliation that are likely to accompany the prosecution." *Ledford v. Gutoski, supra,* 121 Or. App. [226] at 232, 855 P.2d 196 [(Or. App. 1993)].

Kuhl's argument and the response by the Court of Appeals miss the point in evaluating the duty to defend. In analyzing the duty to defend, a court's focus should be on the conduct alleged in the complaint. Unless the complaint alleges conduct that could be covered by the policy, the duty to defend does not arise. In this case, the Ledford complaint alleged that Kuhl did subjectively intend to cause injury or harm to Ledford. The Ledford complaint did not allege, and without amendment would not permit proof, that Kuhl instituted the criminal action against Ledford for some "malicious" purpose other than to "harass, annoy, harm and cause expense to" Ledford. Because the complaint alleged only that Kuhl subjectively intended to harm or injure Ledford, it is irrelevant whether or not a claim for malicious prosecution could, in theory, be sustained where the defendant did not have a subjective intent to cause harm or injury to the plaintiff. The Ledford complaint alleged only conduct that clearly falls outside the coverage of the policy. Therefore, Northwest had no duty to defend the malicious prosecution action against Kuhl.

DUTY TO INDEMNIFY

Kuhl's third-party complaint also seeks indemnity for the settlement that Kuhl reached with Ledford. The duty to indemnify is independent of the duty to defend. Even when an insurer does not have a duty to defend based on the allegations in the initial complaint, the facts proved at trial on which liability is established may give rise to a duty to indemnify if the insured's conduct is covered.

Northwest argues that it has no duty to indemnify Kuhl because coverage is precluded by the exclusion for intentionally-caused injuries. In order for the exclusion for intentionally-caused injuries to apply, the insured must intend to cause the particular harm or injury. Whether particular conduct is excluded from coverage depends on the subjective intent of the insured, which is a question of fact.

In order for summary judgment to be appropriate on the duty to indemnify, there must be no genuine issue of material fact, and the moving party must be entitled to judgment as a matter of law. In this case, the underlying malicious prosecution action was settled, and no trial was held to determine Kuhl's subjective intent in instituting the criminal prosecution of Ledford. The only evidence before us on this motion for summary judgment is the Ledford complaint, the existence of the settlement, and an affidavit from Kuhl's attorney. The affidavit states that although Kuhl denied instituting the criminal prosecution for a purpose other than to bring Ledford to justice, Kuhl entered into the settlement because "on a cost benefit analysis it made no sense to continue defending and try the case."

Kuhl argues that based on the evidence in the record, summary judgment is inappropriate because a question of fact remains as to his subjective intent in instituting the criminal action against Ledford. Northwest argues that summary judgment is appropriate because, as a matter of law, an intent to harm must be inferred from Kuhl's conduct.

. . . .

The Ledford complaint alleges that Ledford was harmed by being subjected to an unjustifiable criminal prosecution. Liability for instituting an unjustifiable criminal prosecution arises only if a claim for malicious prosecution can be established. One necessary element of a malicious prosecution claim is that the prosecution was instituted by the defendant with "malice," which is defined as any primary purpose other than to bring a person to justice.

The only justifiable primary purpose for bringing a criminal action is to bring a person to justice. A necessary element to establish liability for malicious prosecution is that the defendant acted for some other (i.e., unjustifiable) primary purpose. In other words, every time the defendant is found liable for malicious prosecution, he or she, by definition, has acted with a subjective intent to cause the harm of subjecting the plaintiff to an unjustifiable prosecution. The only reasonable inference that may be drawn from the defendant instituting a criminal prosecution for some primary purpose other than to bring the plaintiff to justice is that the defendant had a subjective intent to cause harm or injury to the plaintiff.

Our conclusion that a subjective intent to harm is a necessary inference from Kuhl's conduct stems from the nature of the tort of malicious prosecution. The subjective intent of the defendant is an element of malicious prosecution. That is not the case with respect to some other intentional torts, such as battery, as to which this court has concluded that the inference of an intent to cause harm does not apply. Those other intentional torts have "lesser included torts," such as negligence, under which liability may be imposed for similar conduct without any subjective intent to cause harm. *See Nielsen v. St. Paul Companies, supra,* 283 Or. at 281, 583 P.2d 545 (trespass and battery); *Snyder v. Nelson, Leatherby Ins., supra,* 278 Or. at 415-416, 564 P.2d 681 (battery).

In order for the duty to indemnify to arise, the insured must be liable for harm or injury that is covered by the policy. The record in this case does not indicate whether Kuhl was in fact liable to Ledford for malicious prosecution. Whether or not Kuhl was in fact liable, however, Northwest has no duty to indemnify. If Kuhl was actually liable for malicious prosecution, there is no duty to indemnify because acts committed with the subjective intent of causing harm or injury are excluded from coverage. On the other hand, if Kuhl was not in fact liable for malicious prosecution, there is no duty to indemnify because Kuhl was not legally obligated to pay money to Ledford. Therefore, because under either circumstance Kuhl was not obligated to pay Ledford for an injury covered by the policy, as a matter of law, Northwest had no duty to indemnify Kuhl for the settlement with Ledford.

The decision of the Court of Appeals is affirmed on different grounds. The judgment of the circuit court is affirmed.

NOTES

1. *Defense and indemnity.* It is often said that the duty to defend is broader than the duty to indemnify. Does the court's decision in *Ledford* suggest that sometimes the duty to indemnify can be broader than the duty to defend? Does this imply a flaw in the court's understanding of the scope of the duty to defend? For more detailed discussion of this question (and other issues), see Ellen S. Pryor, *The Tort Liability Regime and the Duty to Defend,* 58 Md. L. Rev. 1 (1999); Susan Randall, *Redefining the Insurer's Duty to Defend,* 2 Conn. Ins. L. J. 221 (1997).

2. *Selecting the attorney.* The insurer will prefer to select the attorney that will represent the insured even though the insurer understands that the attorney must represent the insured with complete fidelity and may not advance the interests of the insurer to the prejudice of the rights of the insured. Why would the insurer want to do this? This is subject to a significant caveat, as discussed in § 8.02[3] and § 8.02[4], *infra,* that in situations where a conflict of interests exists or arises, the insured becomes entitled to select an attorney of her own choice with the reasonable costs of defense to be paid to the insurer.

Where the insured is given the right to select the attorney, does this create any problems for the liability insurer?

3. *The right to control the defense.* Modern liability insurance forms usually state that the insurer which undertakes the defense has a right to control how the defense is conducted, and courts have reaffirmed this right on many occasions. *See, e.g., McCormack Baron Management Services, Inc. v. American Guarantee & Liability Insurance Co.,* 989 S.W.2d 168, 171 n. 2 (Mo. 1999) (en banc) ("an insurer's obligation to defend is also a right to defend. Depending upon the language of the policy, once an insurer recognizes its right and duty to defend, it usually is afforded control over the litigation to protect its financial interests."); *Farmers Group, Inc. v. Trimble,* 691 P.2d 1138, 1141 (Colo. 1984) (en banc) ("By virtue of the insurance contract, the insurer retains the absolute right to control the defense of actions brought against the insured"); *Kooyman v. Farm Bureau Mutual Insurance Co.,* 315 N.W.2d 30 (Iowa 1982).

Being able to control the defense is important to insurers. If a claim is within the policy limits and there is no deductible, the insurer bears all of the financial risk of the outcome of the litigation; if the insurer will pay any resulting judgment in full, the insurer has an obvious preference to control the defense. Moreover, litigation is expensive; by controlling the defense, the insurer can control its costs. Indeed, the insurer is in a better position to control costs than the insured. The insurer can use its considerable purchasing power to negotiate lower hourly fees to be paid appointed counsel, and efficiencies can be created when the insurer defends many similar claims. To the extent the insurer succeeds in its cost-control efforts, this should reduce insureds' premiums; thus, insureds have reasons to prefer that insurers control the defense of covered claims. Of course, an insured who thinks his or her particular defense is not vigorous may conclude that the insurer's cost-control aims are counterproductive and perhaps even prejudicial to the insured. This resulting tension is explored later in this section.

4. *The case of the embittered law school professor.* A former law professor at the Brooklyn Law School brought five lawsuits against the School, its trustees, and faculty alleging conspiracy to deprive him of his civil rights, to humiliate and humble him, and to cause him loss of employment and mental anguish. These suits were a response to bitter salary disputes between the professor and the School, which culminated in academic charges being brought against the professor, a faculty hearing, and the expulsion in 1975 of the faculty member from his tenured position. The School sued its insurer to recover $315,000 in damages suffered in defending the lawsuits. The insurer declined to defend, asserting that the claimed liabilities were not covered by the policies. On appeal of a summary judgment for the insurer, the Second Circuit referred to the complaint's allegation of "intentional conspiracy," observed that the complaint "is replete with allegations of intentional conduct and injuries," and affirmed the summary judgment. As for the School's contention that there were allegations in the complaint that, if proved, "could result in the insurer's liability for damages resulting from unintentional conduct or intentional conduct producing unintentional injury," the court commented that it could "see no reason why the court should have imagined

what is not in the complaint in order to find liability which was not intended." *Brooklyn Law School v. Aetna Casualty & Surety Co.*, 849 F.2d 788 (2d Cir. 1988).

5. *The "four corners of the complaint."* The starting point for determining whether the insurer owes the insured a duty of defense is the complaint and its allegations. This is sometimes called the "four corners of the complaint" rule. A few recent cases have dubbed this rule the "eight corners" rule under the reasoning that whether a duty to defend exists turns on the four corners of the complaint and the four corners of the policy. *See, e.g., Smith v. Katz*, 226 Wis. 2d 798, 595 N.W.2d 345 (1999); *Two Pesos, Inc. v. Gulf Insurance Co.*, 901 S.W.2d 495 (Tex. Ct. App. 1995); *Mount Vernon Fire Insurance Co. v. Scottsdale Insurance Co.*, 99 Md. App. 545, 638 A.2d 1196 (1994). One court explained the rule as follows: "'The duty to defend is not affected by facts ascertained before suit, developed in the process of litigation, or by the ultimate outcome of the suit.' . . . [T]he court cannot consider anything outside (a) the policy and (b) the pleadings. The effect of this 'eight corners rule' is to minimize uncertainty in assessing a liability insurer's duty, as well as to favor the insured in cases where the merits of the action may be questionable." *Capital Bank v. Commonwealth Land Title Insurance Co.*, 861 S.W.2d 84, 88 (Tex. Ct. App. 1993).

If the Supreme Court in *Ledford* followed a "four corners" approach, what approach did the Court of Appeals follow in its superseded decision? Is there a fundamental difference between the approaches? If the four (or eight) corners rule is the starting point, is it also the ending point? Should an insurer be allowed to escape its obligation to defend by ignoring true facts in circumstances where the plaintiff's attorney failed to draft a good complaint? For consideration of this question (and some others), consider the next case.

FITZPATRICK v. AMERICAN HONDA MOTOR CO.

78 N.Y.2d 61, 575 N.E.2d 90, 571 N.Y.S.2d 672 (1991)

TITONE, JUDGE.

It is well established that a liability insurer has a duty to defend its insured in a pending lawsuit if the pleadings allege a covered occurrence, even though facts outside the four corners of those pleadings indicate that the claim may be meritless or not covered. The issue in this appeal is whether the insurer has a duty to defend in the opposite circumstance, i.e., where the pleadings do not allege a covered occurrence but the insurer has actual knowledge of facts demonstrating that the lawsuit does involve such an occurrence. Under these facts, we hold that the insurer cannot use a third party's pleadings as a shield to avoid its contractual duty to defend its insured.

The plaintiff in the main action, Linda Fitzpatrick, sought recovery for the wrongful death of her husband, John Fitzpatrick, who died on October 31, 1985 while operating a three-wheel all-terrain vehicle. The complaint alleged that the vehicle in question was owned by defendant Frank Moramarco and that Moramarco had given Fitzpatrick permission to use it in connection with the performance of certain yardwork and household chores. According to the complaint, codefendant Cherrywood Property Owners Association (CPOA), the owner of the property on which the accident occurred, had retained Moramarco, and Moramarco, acting as CPOA's agent, had in turn hired Fitzpatrick as an "independent contractor."

In fact, Moramarco was an officer, shareholder and director of an independent concern called Cherrywood Landscaping, Inc. (CLI), which had been retained by CPOA to do landscaping work on CPOA's property. The vehicle involved in Fitzpatrick's accident had been purchased by Moramarco on behalf of CLI for use in its landscaping and gardening business. CLI had also purchased a liability insurance policy from National Casualty Co. (National), which indemnified the corporation against having to pay damages for bodily injury and property damage arising out of its business. While the policy was not an "owner's policy" and Moramarco was not a specifically named insured, the terms of the policy included as "insured persons" "any executive officer, director or stockholder [of the named insured (i.e., CLI)] while acting within the scope of his duties as such."

Shortly after Moramarco was served with papers in the main action, he notified National and requested that the insurer provide him with a defense. National, however, refused, stating that the policy it had issued to CLI did not appear to cover the claim against Moramarco. In subsequent correspondence, Moramarco advised the insurer that the vehicle involved in the Fitzpatrick accident was "owned for and * * * used exclusively for landscaping operations" and that the claims asserted against him in the main action all arose out of activities he undertook for CLI, the named insured. The same circumstances were brought to the insurer's attention in a letter from its own agent in which the company was urged to reconsider its prior decision. Nonetheless, National maintained that it was not required to provide a defense because the complaint did not name CLI, and Moramarco, the named defendant, was not insured as an individual.

Moramarco thereafter commenced a third-party action against National seeking payment of his legal fees in the main action, as well as "judgment over" for any judgment entered against him in the main action. National promptly moved. . .to dismiss the third-party complaint. Relying wholly on the absence of allegations in the Fitzpatrick complaint suggesting that the claim against Moramarco arose in connection with his activities as an officer, shareholder or director of the insured CLI, National argued that it had no duty to defend or indemnify Moramarco under the terms of the policy. In response, Moramarco submitted proof to show that, despite the complaint's inaccuracies, the Fitzpatrick claim actually did involve a covered event.

The Supreme Court denied National's dismissal motion, holding that the question of whether its policy covered the Fitzpatrick accident "must await a plenary trial." The Appellate Division, 159 A.D.2d 548, 552 N.Y.S.2d 413, however, reversed and dismissed the third-party complaint. The court held that the allegations in the complaint are the determinative factor in resolving whether the provisions of an insurance policy have been "activated" in a particular action. Since the Fitzpatrick complaint named Moramarco only in his individual capacity and the insured, CLI, was never even mentioned, the Appellate Division concluded that the existing documentary evidence, i.e., the Fitzpatrick complaint and the National policy, was sufficient to warrant dismissal of Moramarco's third-party claim (see, CPLR 3211[a][1]). This Court granted Moramarco leave to appeal from the Appellate Division order. We now reverse.

This Court has repeatedly held that an insurer's duty to defend its insured arises whenever the allegations in a complaint state a cause of action that gives rise to the reasonable possibility of recovery under the policy. In the present appeal, National asks this Court to hold that the converse is also true. According to National, the complaint allegations are, in all cases, the sole determining consideration and, consequently, an insurer is relieved of the duty to defend whenever the complaint allegations do not on their face set forth a covered cause of action. However, the position National advocates is neither compelled by our prior case law nor consistent with sound legal principles and policies. Accordingly, we reject it.

The rationale underlying the cases in which the "four corners of the complaint" rule was delineated and applied is based on the oft-stated principle that the duty to defend is broader than the duty to indemnify. In other words, as the rule has developed, an insurer may be contractually bound to defend even though it may not ultimately be bound to pay, either because its insured is not factually or legally liable or because the occurrence is later proven to be outside the policy's coverage.

It follows logically from this principle that an insurer's duty to defend is called into play whenever the pleadings allege an act or omission within the policy's coverage. Even where there exist extrinsic facts suggesting that the claim may ultimately prove meritless or outside the policy's coverage, the insurer cannot avoid its commitment to provide a defense, since "[a] complaint subject to defeat because of debatable theories * * * must [nevertheless] be defended by the insured." (*International Paper Co. v. Continental Cas. Co., supra,* 35 N.Y.2d at 326, 361 N.Y.S.2d 873, 320 N.E.2d 619.) Accordingly, the courts of this State have refused to permit insurers to look beyond the complaint's allegations to avoid their obligation to defend and have held that the duty to defend exists "[i]f the complaint contains any facts or allegations which bring the claim even potentially within the protection purchased" (*Technicon Elecs. Corp. v. American Home Assur. Co., supra,* 74 N.Y.2d at 73, 544 N.Y.S.2d 531, 542 N.E.2d 1048). The holdings thus clearly establish that an insurer's duty to defend is at least broad enough to apply when the "four corners of the complaint" suggest the reasonable possibility of coverage.

However, to say that the duty to defend is at least broad enough to apply to actions in which the complaint alleges a covered occurrence is a far cry from saying that the complaint allegations are the sole criteria for measuring the scope of that duty. Indeed, in these circumstances, where the insurer is attempting to shield itself from the responsibility to defend despite its actual knowledge that the lawsuit involves a covered event, wooden application of the "four corners of the complaint" rule would render the duty to defend narrower than the duty to indemnify—clearly an unacceptable result. For that reason, courts and commentators have indicated that the insurer must provide a defense if it has knowledge of facts which potentially bring the claim within the policy's indemnity coverage.

We. . .hold that, rather than mechanically applying only the "four corners of the complaint" rule in these circumstances, the sounder approach is to require the insurer to provide a defense when it has actual knowledge of facts establishing a reasonable possibility of coverage (see generally, 7C Appleman, *op. cit.*, § 4684.01, at 95).[2] This holding fits easily and appropriately within the existing rules governing coverage disputes, which certainly do not require us to extend the "four corners of the complaint" rule to a situation such as this one, where it has not been applied before and, in fact, has no apparent value. Although it has been argued that the "four corners of the complaint" rule has the advantage of certainty, there is no reason to believe that the rule we adopt here will engender any more litigation.

The conclusion we reach here flows naturally from the fact that the duty to defend derives, in the first instance, not from the complaint drafted by a third party, but rather from the insurer's own contract with the insured (*see, e.g.,* 7C Appleman, *op. cit.*, § 4682, at 27 [and authorities cited therein]). While the allegations in the complaint may provide the significant and usual touchstone for determining whether the insurer is contractually bound to provide a defense, the contract itself must always remain a primary point of reference. Indeed, a contrary rule making the terms of the complaint controlling "would allow the insurer to construct a formal fortress of the third party's pleadings * * * thereby successfully ignoring true but unpleaded facts within its knowledge that require it * * * to conduct the * * * insured's defense" (*Associated Indem. Co. v. Insurance Co.,* 68 Ill. App. 3d 807, 816–817, 25 Ill. Dec. 258, 265, 386 N.E.2d 529, 536). Further, an insured's right to a defense should not depend solely on the allegations a third party chooses to put in the complaint. This is particularly so because the drafter of the pleading may be unaware of the true underlying facts or the nuances that may affect the defendant's coverage and it might not be in the insured's (or the insurer's) interest to reveal them.[3]

The principle that an insurer may not rely on the pleadings to narrow the scope of its duty to defend also finds support in the practical realities that prevail under modern pleading rules. As one commentator has observed, "considering the plasticity of modern pleadings, in many cases no one can determine whether the third party suit does or does not fall within the

---

[2] Contrary to the dissenters' assertion (dissenting op., at 73, at 679 of 571 N.Y.S.2d, at 97 of 575 N.E.2d), the above-cited authorities do not uniformly impose on the insurer an obligation to investigate; rather, their holdings on this point are mixed. In any event, the duty we recognize here, i.e., the duty to defend when the facts known to the insurer indicate coverage, does not depend upon, or even imply, a corollary duty to investigate. Indeed, there is nothing in this case, where the insurer was actually notified of the salient facts by both its insured and its own agent, that requires us to create a duty to investigate where none previously existed.

[3] The dissenters' suggestion that, as a result of our ruling, the insured defendant may now be "in the position of dictating the theory of the action" is perplexing. Certainly, it is unlikely that a plaintiff would voluntarily choose an uncovered theory of liability over one that is supported by the facts and could lead to a judgment that is covered by insurance. Accordingly, it is difficult to foresee when a carrier might be called upon "to defend a claim the plaintiff has no intention of asserting."

indemnification coverage of the policy until the suit itself is resolved" (7C Appleman, *op. cit.*, § 4684, at 83). This observation is particularly apt in the context of New York's liberal pleading rules, which permit the pleadings to be amended to conform to the proof at any time, provided that no prejudice is shown.

The facts in this case—where the complaint on its face did not state a covered claim but the underlying facts made known to the insurer by its insured unquestionably involved a covered event—present a clear example. The insurer here refused to defend Frank Moramarco because he was sued, albeit mistakenly, as an employee of CPOA and the owner of the injury-causing vehicle. Had the complaint correctly identified Moramarco as an officer and/or shareholder of the insured CLI, he would have unquestionably been covered for this lawsuit, since the policy provided that "any executive officer, director or stockholder [of CLI] while acting within the scope of his duties as such" was an additional "insured person" under the policy. Further, the insurer promised to "defend any suit against the insured seeking damages on account of * * * bodily injury or property damage" arising out of CLI's landscaping and gardening business–a condition plainly satisfied here. To deny Moramarco an insurance-company sponsored defense under these circumstances merely because the attorney for the plaintiff in the main action accidentally mischaracterized Moramarco's role would be to afford the insurer an undeserved windfall at the expense of its insured.

Indeed, relieving the insurer of its duty to defend is particularly imprudent and counterproductive where, as here, the inaccuracies in the plaintiff's pleadings are likely to become apparent when the true facts are developed on the record and the role of the insured in the incident is fully exposed.[4] At that point, the trial court could well grant a request by the plaintiff to conform the pleadings to the proof, in which event the insurer's core policy obligation to defend Frank Moramarco as an additional insured would unquestionably be triggered. Moramarco should not be required to wait until that point is reached before obtaining an insurance-company sponsored defense, since a "provision for defense of suits is useless and meaningless unless it is offered when the suit arises" (7C Appleman, *op. cit.*, § 4684, at 83).

In sum, application of the "four corners of the complaint" rule in these circumstances is not required by our prior cases and is not even supported by the rationale usually offered in support of the rule. Further, invocation of the rule here and in analogous cases leads to an unjust result, since it exalts form over substance and denies an insured party the benefit of the "litigation

---

[4] Indeed, the parties' submissions to this Court indicate that after the trial court's order denying National's dismissal motion was entered, CLI was added as a party defendant on the complaint and the insurer has undertaken to defend that entity. However, we have neither seen nor been advised of the contents of the amended complaint. Thus, the dissenters' assertion that the complaint in the main action now "include[s] the 'actual facts' regarding ownership and control of the [subject vehicle]" rests on nothing more than sheer speculation. Further, there is no basis for inferring that the "four corners of the complaint" rule has "worked well" in this case. Although CLI is now represented, Moramarco has been forced to retain and pay his own attorney and, as far as may be determined from the present submissions, has yet to be offered relief by the insurer. Manifestly, that result was not within Moramarco's reasonable expectation when he purchased a policy which included CLI's officers and directors as "additional insureds" under precisely these circumstances.

insurance" for which it has paid. These factors militate in favor of a rule requiring the insurer to provide a defense where, notwithstanding the complaint allegations, underlying facts made known to the insurer create a "reasonable possibility that the insured may be held liable for some act or omission covered by the policy" (*Meyers & Sons Corp. v. Zurich Am. Ins. Group, supra,* 74 N.Y.2d at 302, 546 N.Y.S.2d 818, 545 N.E.2d 1206). We therefore hold that National cannot ignore the facts made known to it by its insured and rely instead on the Fitzpatrick complaint alone to assess its duty to defend Moramarco. The third-party complaint by Moramarco seeking payment of his attorney's fees and indemnification in the event that a judgment was entered against him should not have been dismissed.

Accordingly, the order of the Appellate Division should be reversed, with costs, and the motion to dismiss the third-party complaint denied.

ALEXANDER, JUDGE (dissenting).

Because the majority today discards a rule of long standing and, in my view, does so without justification and under circumstances not warranting such a drastic departure from settled precedent, I respectfully dissent.

It is axiomatic that the obligations of a liability insurance carrier to its insured are governed by the terms of the contract of insurance between them and it is only by examining the terms and conditions of that policy that those obligations can be determined with certainty. Obviously, where an insured has been found liable to a third party in respect to a risk covered by the policy, the carrier is obligated to indemnify its insured. Additionally, where the policy so provides, the carrier is obligated to defend its insured against claims asserting risks covered by the policy. Indeed the rule is firmly established that the duty to defend is broader than the duty to indemnify. When the policy contains the insurer's promise to defend the insured, the "liability insurance" is in fact "litigation insurance" as well.

However, this Court has repeatedly held, in a long line of cases, unbroken until now, that the duty of a liability insurer to defend an action brought against an insured is determined by the allegations in the complaint pursuant to which the insured's liability is asserted. "If the facts alleged [in the complaint] raise a reasonable possibility that the insured may be held liable for some act or omission covered by the policy, then the insurer must defend" (*Meyers & Sons Corp. v. Zurich Am. Ins. Group,* 74 N.Y.2d 298, 302, 546 N.Y.S.2d 818, 545 N.E.2d 1206, *supra*).

In determining whether there is a duty to defend however, the Court must compare the allegations of the complaint with the terms of the policy. If those allegations, on their face, are within the compass of the risk covered by the insurance policy, the insurer is obligated to assume the defense of the action.[1]

---

[1] Thus far from being a woodenly applied "'four corners of the complaint rule'" this comparison requirement serves to give certainty and definiteness to the insurer's duty to defend. Indeed the proposition advanced by the majority that the "allegations in the complaint may provide the significant and usual touchstone for determining whether the insurer is contractually bound to provide a defense" abandons any truly objective standard by which to determine whether a duty to defend arises under the contract of insurance, and expresses the majority's intent to substitute an uncertain subjective standard.

Conversely, it logically follows, that if that comparison demonstrates that those allegations are not within the coverage of the policy, the insurance company's duty to defend does not arise. Indeed where it can be determined "that no basis for recovery within the coverage of the policy is stated in the complaint * * * defendant's refusal to defend [may be sustained]." (*Lionel Freedman, Inc. v. Glens Falls Ins. Co.,* 27 N.Y.2d 364, 368, 318 N.Y.S.2d 303, 267 N.E.2d 93, *rearg. denied* 28 N.Y.2d 859, 322 N.Y.S.2d 1029, 271 N.E.2d 236; *Sucrest Corp. v. Fisher Governor Co.,* 83 Misc. 2d 394, 400, 371 N.Y.S.2d 927.)

The underlying negligence complaint of Linda A. Fitzpatrick seeks to recover damages for the wrongful death of her husband John Fitzpatrick which allegedly occurred while he was operating a 1985 Honda ATV all-terrain vehicle. The complaint alleges that Cherrywood Property Owners Association owned the premises where the accident occurred, that the codefendant Frank Moramarco is an employee, agent and/or servant of Cherrywood Property Owners Association, that the offending vehicle was owned by Moramarco and was being operated with the permission and consent of Moramarco and Cherrywood Property Owners Association. The complaint alleges further that Moramarco and "Cherrywood" were negligent and careless in the ownership, operation, maintenance of the premises owned by "Cherrywood" and the ownership, maintenance, use, supervision and control of the 1985 Honda ATV.

The National Casualty policy at issue here, was issued to Cherrywood Landscaping, Inc. and names that entity as the insured. The policy also provides that "any executive officer, director or stockholder (of the named insured) while acting within the scope of his duties as such", is also insured.

A comparison of the allegations of the Fitzpatrick complaint with the provisions of the National Casualty policy demonstrates that the named defendant, Cherrywood Property Owners Association is not an insured under the policy. The insured is Cherrywood Landscaping, Inc.—a completely different corporation. Frank Moramarco is a covered person under this policy only insofar as he is acting within the scope of his activities as an "executive officer, director or stockholder" of Cherrywood Landscaping. The Fitzpatrick complaint alleges Moramarco's liability individually and as an officer, director, agent and/or employee of Cherrywood Property Owners Association. Under settled principles of law therefore since the insured under the policy is not a party to this lawsuit, the event alleged in the complaint is not a covered event under the policy and the carrier's duty to defend does not arise.

Deviating from these settled rules, the majority concludes that notwithstanding that the Fitzpatrick complaint, when compared to the terms of the policy, fails to demonstrate the existence of a covered event, "the insurer must provide a defense if it has knowledge of facts which potentially bring the claim within the policy's indemnity coverage." It should be noted that to support this proposition the majority relies upon cases from other jurisdictions which impose an obligation upon the insurance company to investigate the claim before declining to defend—a requirement that this Court has never before imposed.

The rule which until now has prevailed in this jurisdiction provides certainty in this area of law and is easily applied. By changing the rule, the majority has supplanted certainty with uncertainty; an insurer now will be less clear as to what, if any, investigation it must make into a demand to defend and when it is permissible to decline representation. Concomitantly, the new rule presumably will increase collateral proceedings such as this, to determine whether an insurer in fact has a duty to defend. These collateral proceedings will be made more complicated because courts now will be obligated to look beyond the allegations in the complaint to discover the "actual" facts, or at a minimum whether the insurer "knew" or perhaps even "should have known" of such "actual facts". The rule could also place the insured in the position of dictating the theory of the action, conceivably requiring the carrier to defend a claim the plaintiff has no intention of asserting merely because allegedly there are "facts" which support such a claim.

The majority posits this new rule as being corollary to the established rule that where the allegations of the complaint state a claim within the coverage of the policy, the "insurers [may not] look beyond the complaint's allegations to avoid their obligation to defend." The fact is, however, that under the rule cited by the majority, "the insurance company's duty to defend came into being when it appeared from the allegations in the negligence action that the injury was within the coverage of the policy, and it persisted despite the advice [from the insured] pointing [to] a contrary conclusion" (*Goldberg v. Lumber Mut. Cas. Ins. Co.*, 297 N.Y. 148, 154, 77 N.E.2d 131, *supra* [emphasis added]).

Thus it is clear that under that established rule it is the allegations of the complaint, compared to the policy provisions, that trigger the duty to defend, a duty which persists notwithstanding that liability may ultimately be shown not to exist. This rule gives certainty to the inception of the carrier's duty to defend and is entirely consistent with its obligations under its policy. No satisfactory reason for altering this rule is shown to exist here; thus the order granting summary judgment to the third-party defendant National Casualty Co. should be affirmed.

WACHTLER, C.J. and KAYE and BELLACOSA, JJ., concur with TITONE, J.

ALEXANDER, J., dissents and votes to affirm in a separate opinion in which SIMONS and HANCOCK, JJ., concur.

Order reversed, etc.

NOTES

1. *Groundless versus noncovered claims.* The language sometimes found in liability insurance policies extending the duty to defend to "groundless, false or fraudulent" suits means that the insurer has a duty to defend even though there may be no factual or legal basis for the suit, or even that the claimant's suit is predicated on false or fraudulent grounds. Even if, however, the quoted phrase is not contained in a policy, and newer forms omit the "groundless, false, or fraudulent phrase," the essential nature of the coverage is unchanged: the insurer agrees to defend any claim filed against the insured within the

policy's coverage, regardless of the claim's merit, and even if the claim is specious.

Some policies, such as professional liability or errors and omissions policies, contain an exclusion providing that "[t]his policy does not apply to any dishonest, fraudulent, criminal or malicious act or omission of any insured, partner or employee." The majority view is that the exclusionary language eliminates the insurer's obligation to defend where false or fraudulent conduct is alleged against the insured; that is, such conduct is outside the policy's coverage. This is to be distinguished from allegations that fall within the coverage but which are falsely or fraudulently brought. *See Chipokas v. Travelers Indemnity Co.,* 267 N.W.2d 393 (Iowa 1978); *National Union Fire Insurance Co. v. Shane and Shane Co.,* 605 N.E.2d 1325 (Ohio Ct. App. 1992). But *see Conner v. Transamerica Insurance Co.,* 496 P.2d 770 (Okla. 1972).

2. *The "potentiality" rule.* Many, and perhaps a majority, of courts apply the potentiality (or "possibility of coverage") rule favored by the majority in *Fitzpatrick.* For other examples, *see McCormack Baron Management Services, Inc. v. American Guarantee & Liability Insurance Co.,* 989 S.W.2d 168 (Mo. 1999) (en banc); *Shoshone First Bank v. Pacific Employers Insurance Co.,* 2 P.3d 510 (Wyo. 2000); *Maine Mutual Fire Insurance Co. v. Gervais,* 745 A.2d 360 (Me. 1999). As explained by one court in an oft-quoted passage, the duty to defend "rests primarily on the possibility that coverage exists. This possibility may be remote but if it exists[,] the [insurer] owes the insured a defense." *Spruill Motors, Inc. v. Universal Underwriters Insurance Co.,* 212 Kan. 681, 512 P.2d 403, 407 (1973). Why does the distinction between "four corners" and "potentiality" matter?

3. *Coverage limits as an outer boundary.* The essence of the scope of the duty to defend is coverage. If a plaintiff sues the insured, is the claim one for which, if it were proved and valid, the insurer would pay proceeds on the insured's behalf? If the answer to the question is "yes," the insurer has a duty to defend. A negative answer has different ramifications, as *Ledford* makes clear: if the claim alleged is outside the coverage, the insurer does not have a duty to defend.

The possible illustrations of the foregoing principle in action are virtually endless. Consider, for example, the standard liability policy which protects the insured against awards for bodily injury and property damage. This language is typically held not to provide coverage for pure economic loss that is unassociated with physical injury to the person or to tangible property. Thus, there would be no duty to defend an action seeking recovery for pure economic loss. *See Lamar Truck Plaza, Inc. v. Sentry Insurance,* 757 P.2d 1143 (Colo. App. 1988); *General Insurance Co. of Am. v. Palmetto Bank,* 268 S.C. 355, 233 S.E.2d 699 (1977); *E-Z Loader Boat Trailers, Inc. v. Travelers Indemnity Co.,* 106 Wash. 2d 901, 726 P.2d 439 (1986); *Prudential Property & Casualty Insurance Co. v. Lawrence,* 45 Wash. App. 111, 724 P.2d 418 (1986).

Because the liability policy typically provides coverage for liability imposed on the insured "as damages," suits only for equitable relief would seem to fall in the same category, and many courts have so held. *See, e.g., Aetna Casualty & Surety Co. v. Hanna,* 224 F.2d 499 (5th Cir. 1955); *School District of Shorewood v. Wausau Insurance Cos.,* 488 N.W.2d 82 (Wis. 1992). There is, however, authority to the contrary, usually in circumstances where the court in an equitable action retains the authority to award damages as a remedy. *See Haines v. St. Paul Fire & Marine Insurance Co.,* 428 F. Supp. 435 (D. Md. 1977); *Doyle v. Allstate Insurance Co.,* 1 N.Y.2d 439, 136 N.E.2d 484, 154 N.Y.S.2d 10 (1956). *See also APA-The Engineered Wood Ass'n v. Glens Falls Insurance Co.,* 94 Wash.App. 556, 972 P.2d 937 (1999) (suit "for discovery" under Florida law was equivalent of action for damages, and insurer had duty to defend). Many of the cases favoring the recognition of a duty to defend involve liability coverage for environmental damage. Why should this be so? Does it matter that the Environmental Protection Agency and the equivalent state agencies typically have the authority to compel a party responsible for pollution to clean up a toxic waste site? *See Aetna Casualty and Surety Co. v. Pintlar Corp.,* 948 F.2d 1507 (9th Cir. 1991); *General Casualty Co. of Wisconsin v. Hills,* 209 Wis. 2d 167, 561 N.W.2d 718 (1997).

4. *Disclaiming coverage.* If after the defense is tendered the insurer concludes that the claim is outside coverage and therefore no duty to defend is owed, the insurer needs to disclaim coverage. This is ordinarily accomplished by a written notice to the insured. If the insurer omits one or more grounds for denying coverage from the initial disclaimer, should the insurer be allowed to offer these grounds later as a basis for denying coverage? Most courts answer "yes." *See, e.g., Waller v. Truck Insurance Exchange,* 44 Cal. Rptr. 2d 370, 900 P.2d 619 (Cal. 1995); *Terre Haute First National Bank v. Pacific Employers Insurance Co.,* 634 N.E.2d 1336 (Ind. Ct. App. 1994). But *see Hayden v. Mutual of Enumclaw Insurance Co.,* 95 Wash. App. 563, 977 P.2d 608 (1999); *Armstrong v. Hanover Insurance Co.,* 289 A.2d 669 (Vt. 1971). Does the majority rule countenance unfair surprise?

5. *Who is the insured?* The short answer to the question, "to whom is the duty to defend owed," is "the named insured and any additional insureds." Suppose that Tortfeasor negligently operates Owner's vehicle in a manner that injures Pedestrian. Pedestrian sues Tortfeasor and alleges that Tortfeasor was operating Owner's vehicle with Owner's permission. Tortfeasor submits the claim to Owner's insurer and requests a defense. If Tortfeasor were operating Owner's car with Owner's permission, Reliable would be obligated to provide a defense and indemnify Tortfeasor. Owner, however, claims that Tortfeasor stole the vehicle. Must the insurer provide a defense? *See Colon v. Aetna Life and Casualty Insurance Co.,* 494 N.E.2d 1040 (N.Y. 1985); *Holland American Insurance Co. v. National Indemnity Co.,* 454 P.2d 383 (Wash. 1969). Did the court in *Fitzpatrick* get the answer to this question right?

6. *Ambiguous claims.* If the complaint is ambiguous on a point determinative of coverage, does the insurer have an obligation to defend? Suppose, for example, that the plaintiff sues the insured for negligence, alleging that the insured's actions caused the plaintiff an injury in July or August of 1996. The insured's policy terminated, however, on July 31, 1996. Is the insurer obligated to provide a defense? *See, e.g., Trizec Properties v. Biltmore Construction Co.,* 767 F.2d 810 (11th Cir. 1985); *Howard v. Russell Stover Candies, Inc.,* 649 F.2d 620 (8th Cir. 1981); *Monfils v. Charles,* 216 Wis.2d 323, 575 N.W.2d 728 (Wis. App. 1998). Does the practice of notice pleading matter? Does the insurer

have a duty to investigate the facts to see if coverage might exist? *See Dairy Road Partners v. Island Insurance Co.,* 92 Haw. 398, 992 P.2d 93 (2000).

7. *Discovery of facts negating coverage.* If the insurer undertakes the defense of a claim which is not clearly within or clearly outside the coverage, what is the effect of the discovery of facts that unequivocally and absolutely negate coverage? It is commonly said that an insurer has a duty to defend "until it [can] confine the claim to a recovery that the policy [does] not cover." *See Lee v. Aetna Casualty & Surety Co.,* 178 F.2d 750, 753 (2d Cir. 1949) (opinion by Judge Learned Hand). *See also Meadowbrook, Inc. v. Tower Insurance Co.,* 559 N.W.2d 411, 416 (Minn. 1997) ("an insurer who undertakes an insured's defense under a reservation of rights can withdraw its defense once all arguably covered claims have been dismissed with finality"). How might a "four corners" jurisdiction analyze the problem differently than a "potentiality" jurisdiction? If the insurer must defend whenever there is a "potentiality" of coverage, why should the insurer not be allowed to disclaim the duty when it is clear that there is no potential of coverage? *See Dairy Road Partners v. Island Insurance Co.,* 92 Haw. 398, 992 P.2d 93, 113-14 (2000) (discussing split of authority).

Some courts allow an insurer to disclaim liability only when the relevant facts will not be resolved in the third party's action against the insured. *See, e.g., Hartford Accident & Indemnity Co. v. Aetna Life & Casualty Insurance Co.,* 98 N.J. 18, 483 A.2d 402 (1984). What is the logic of limiting the ability to disclaim in this way?

If, as a general rule, the insurer is allowed to withdraw from the defense, what happens if coverage is absolutely negated on the eve of trial? *See Raymond v. Monsanto Co.,* 329 F. Supp. 247 (D.N.H. 1971). If the insurer can withdraw from the defense, does it necessarily follow that the attorney appointed by the insurer can also withdraw from the defense? Or do different standards apply to the attorney under the reasoning that the relationship between attorney and insured is distinct, at least in some respects, from the relationship between insured and insurer? If the insurer can withdraw but the attorney cannot, who then pays the attorney's fees?

8. *Premature termination of the duty to defend?* The extent to which, if at all, the duty to defend and duty to indemnify are dependent obligations has been a perplexing issue through the years. Much depends on the language of the policy. Since the 1980s, the CGL has read, in pertinent part, as follows: "Our [the insurer's] right and duty to defend end when we have used up the applicable limit of insurance in the payment of judgments or settlements under Coverages A [bodily injury and property damage liability] or B [personal and advertising injury or liability] or medical expenses under Coverage C." The vast majority of courts take note of the words "judgments" and "settlements," and reason that if the insurer has paid out the policy limits pursuant to judgments or settlements, the duty to defend no longer exists. *See, e.g., Utah Power & Light Co. v. Federal Insurance Co.,* 711 F. Supp. 1544 (D. Utah 1989); *Samply v. Integrity Insurance Co.,* 476 So. 2d 79 (Ala. 1985). This means, necessarily, that in circumstances where the plaintiff has a claim against the insured for much more than the policy limits, the insurer cannot tender the policy limits and refuse to defend. Such a payment would not be made pursuant to a "judgment" or "settlement." *See, e.g., Continental Insurance Co. v.*

Burr, 706 A.2d 499 (Del. 1998) (insurer that tendered policy limits in interpleader action against multiple persons injured by insured in accident had not satisfied duty to defend); *California Casualty Insurance Co. v. State Farm Mutual Automobile Insurance Co.,* 185 Ariz. 165, 913 P.2d 505 (Ariz. Ct. App. 1996) (primary insurer not relieved of duty to defend insured by paying policy limits to tort claimant).

9. *The condition of timely notice.* As explored in more detail in the previous section in this Chapter, the insured must notify the insurer in a timely fashion that the event which may give rise to liability has transpired. If the insured fails to do so, the insurer may have a defense to coverage. In automobile insurance, for example, the insured event–an accident—is usually apparent. In other situations, however, the insured event may be much less obvious. Malpractice insurance is a prominent example; sometimes it is not until someone asserts a claim that the insured is aware of information that needs to be reported to the insurer. In any event, in order to invoke the insurer's duty to defend, timely notice of information regarding the triggering event, whether it be an accident or a third-party claim, must be given to the liability insurer.

Notice of the event that creates liability may not, however, be enough to trigger the duty to defend. It may be that formal tender of the defense is required. In *C.J. Duffey Paper Co. v. Liberty Mutual Insurance Co.,* 76 F.3d 177 (8th Cir. 1996), the Eighth Circuit, applying Minnesota law, held that an insurer's receipt of a copy of the complaint against its insured was not sufficient to trigger the duty to defend in circumstances where the insured had not "formally tendered" the defense. Thus, costs of defense incurred prior to the formal tender, which the insurer accepted, were not the insurer's responsibility. Other courts have articulated different, less formal tests. *See, e.g., Towne Realty, Inc. v. Zurich Insurance Co.,* 201 Wis. 2d 260, 548 N.W.2d 64 (1996) (insured's tender is sufficient if insurer is put on notice of claim; insured does not have to specifically request insurer undertake defense); *White Mountain Construction Co. v. Transamerica Insurance Co.,* 631 A.2d 907, 910 (N.H. 1993) ("in order for an insured to tender the defense to the insurer, it need only put the insurer on notice of the claim").

Should pre-tender defense costs be reimbursable by the insurer under a theory of restitution or *quantum meruit? See Nagel v. Kentucky Central Insurance Co.,* 894 S.W.2d 19 (Tex. App. 1994). Note that the CGL provides in the Section IV conditions that "[n]o insureds will, except at their own cost, voluntarily. . .incur any expense, other than for first aid, without our consent." It has been held that defense costs incurred prior to tender of the defense may be nonreimbursable under the "voluntary payment" provision. *See Lafarge Corp. v. Hartford Casualty Co.,* 61 F.3d 389 (5th Cir. 1995); *Faust v. Travelers Insurance Co.,* 55 F.3d 471 (9th Cir. 1995). What is the difference, however, between a "voluntarily" incurred defense cost and an "involuntarily" incurred defense cost? Are defense costs incurred in response to legal process and to protect one's legal interests "involuntary" or "voluntary"? *See Fiorito v. Superior Court,* 226 Cal. App. 3d 433, 277 Cal. Rptr. 27 (Cal. App. 1990).

10. *The duty to defend or prosecute appeals.* Suppose the insurer provides a defense for the insured, and the insured prevails at trial. What if the plaintiff

appeals? *See, e.g., Commerce & Industry Insurance Co. v. Bank of Hawaii,* 832 P.2d 733 (Haw. 1992); *Travelers Indemnity Co. v. East,* 240 So. 2d 277 (Miss. 1970).

What if, however, a judgment adverse to the insured is entered in the trial court? What are the insurer's obligations? It is uniformly accepted that the insurer is not obligated to prosecute appeals where it would be plainly futile to do so. Beyond this principle, there are different tests for the boundary between situations where the insurer must appeal and situations where an appeal is not necessary. *See, e.g., Hawkeye-Security Insurance Co. v. Indemnity Insurance Co.,* 260 F.2d 361 (10th Cir. 1958) (insurer's failure to appeal is breach of duty to defend if failure is fraudulent or in bad faith); *Delmonte v. State Farm Fire and Casualty Co.,* 90 Haw. 39, 975 P.2d 1159, 1169 (1999) ("as a general proposition,. . .the insurer's duty to defend includes a duty to appeal where reasonable grounds for an appeal exist"); *Guarantee Abstract & Title Co. v. Interstate Fire & Casualty Co. Inc.,* 228 Kan. 532, 618 P.2d 1195 (1980) (insurer has duty of good faith and fair dealing, which sometimes requires the insurer to appeal).

Does the "reasonable grounds" test mean that the insurer must appeal whenever there are non-frivolous grounds for doing so? If a judgment is entered against the insured in excess of the policy limits, is the insurer required to appeal? If the judgment is within the policy limits, should the insurer have a right to appeal? Does it matter if a possible outcome of a successful appeal is a new trial which may expose the insured to the risk of an excess judgment? See generally Robert H. Jerry, II, Understanding Insurance Law § 113 (2d ed. 1996).

Whatever test one favors, presumably the same test should be applied to other kinds of post-judgment relief, such a motion for a new trial or a motion for a judgment notwithstanding the verdict. *See Cathay Mortuary (Wah Sang) Inc. v. United Pacific Insurance Co.,* 582 F. Supp. 650 (N.D. Cal. 1985).

11. *Mixed actions: covered and noncovered claims in the same complaint.* If the plaintiff in the underlying action alleges a combination of covered and noncovered claims, must the insurer defend all the claims? Does it matter whether the claims arise out of the same set of facts (i.e., can or cannot be segregated)? *See Imperial Casualty and Indemnity Co. v. State,* 246 Conn. 313, 714 A.2d 1230 (Conn. 1998); *United States Fidelity & Guaranty Co. v. Wilkin Insulation Co.,* 144 Ill. 2d 64, 578 N.E.2d 926 (1991). If a covered claim and a noncovered claim are alleged in the same complaint, what problems might arise in connection with the conduct of the defense (particularly if they arise out of the same set of facts)? This problem will receive more attention in § 8.02[3].

Before taking up that question, however, the next subsection will examine a duty that the insured owes the insurer, which is in many respects reciprocal to the insurer's duty to defend. The insured's duty to cooperate in the first-party situation was examined in § 8.01[4], *supra.* In the third-party situation, what happens if the insured refuses to cooperate with the insurer? If the insurer is given a defense to coverage on account of the insured's lack of cooperation, the ultimate loser may be the person injured by the insured's conduct, assuming the insured is not independently wealthy. Consider the next case.

[2]   The Insured's Obligation to Cooperate

RAMOS v. NORTHWESTERN MUTUAL INSURANCE CO.
336 So. 2d 71 (Fla. 1976)

ROBERTS, JUSTICE.

. . . .

The controlling question in the cause certified to us by the District Court involves whether or not an automobile insurance carrier may still be permitted to avoid liability pursuant to a provision in its contract requiring the insured to give his cooperation in connection with any claim of which the carrier would have responsibility under the contract notwithstanding recent developments in the law. These recent developments referred to include Florida's Financial Responsibility Act,[1] provisions contained in Florida Automobile Reparations Reform Act, and decisions of this Court including *Shingleton v. Bussey*, 223 So. 2d 713 (Fla. 1969).

[Petitioner Mercedes Ramos sued Lawrence Williams and Respondent Northwestern Mutual Insurance Company for damages in connection with injuries suffered in an auto accident in which Williams was allegedly negligent. Northwestern admitted the issuance of the policy of automobile liability insurance to Williams, but alleged as an affirmative defense that the policy did not provide coverage in this case because the accident was not reported by him to his insurer nor did he cooperate with the insurer as required by the terms of the policy. The trial judge granted Northwestern's motion to sever the trial on the coverage issue from the original claim relating to liability and damages. In the underlying tort action, a jury returned a verdict for Ramos and awarded her damages against Williams in the amount of $52,037.

After a non-jury trial on the insurance coverage issues, the trial court entered a judgment in favor of Northwestern, finding no coverage because of the insured's failure to cooperate. Specifically, the trial court found that "NORTHWESTERN received notice of the accident from plaintiff's counsel on December 29, 1969. However, WILLIAMS never contacted NORTHWESTERN, failed to report the accident, failed to notify NORTHWESTERN of his apparent changes of address and, despite efforts of NORTHWESTERN *and*

---

[1] Section 324.011, Florida Statutes, announcing the purpose of the Financial Responsibility Act provides:

> It is the intent of this chapter to recognize the existing rights of all to own motor vehicles and to operate them on the public streets and highways of this state when such rights are used with due consideration for others; to promote safety, and provide financial security by such owners and operators whose responsibility it is to recompense others for injury to person or property caused by the operation of a motor vehicle, so it is required herein that the owner and operator of a motor vehicle involved in an accident shall respond for such damages and show proof of financial ability to respond for damages in future accidents as a requisite to his future exercise of such privileges.

plaintiff's counsel, was never located." Further, the trial court found that Williams "breached the terms of the policy issued by NORTHWESTERN because of his total failure to cooperate. *Further, the breach was material and substantially prejudiced NORTHWESTERN.*" (Emphasis original.) The trial court's conclusions of law continued as follows:

> "It is, therefore, the opinion and judgment of this Court that WILLIAMS was not entitled to coverage under the policy and that NORTHWESTERN was correct in its denial of coverage. The plaintiff relies in part upon the case of *American Fire and Casualty Company v. Collura, Fla.[App.]* 1964, 163 So. 2d 784. Such reliance, however, is misplaced because there the insured notified his carrier of the accident and his whereabouts were known to all parties throughout the proceedings. Further, in considering the issue of cooperation in that case the Second District Court of Appeal stated at page 788:
>
> > In considering the issue of breach of a cooperation clause in an insurance policy, it must always be borne in mind that in order for the company to avoid liability by reason of the insured's breach, the company must show that it has exercised diligence and good faith in bringing about the cooperation of the insured, and that it has in good faith complied with the terms and conditions of the policy. [cases cited] *On the other hand the insured is bound to cooperate with his insurer* and to abide, both in letter and in spirit, with the terms of the contract; or he should *at least* be held to reasonably strict compliance with the terms thereof.
>
> Here, not only did NORTHWESTERN exercise diligence in attempting to locate WILLIAMS but, also, was precluded by WILLIAMS' concealment from "bringing about" his cooperation. Moreover, WILLIAMS totally disregarded his own responsibility in the premises. [Emphases supplied]"

Plaintiff appealed to the District Court of Appeal, Third District, which affirmed the judgment of the trial court although expressly stating that it did so in reliance on past precedent. The District Court opined that the plaintiff made a persuasive argument and but for precedent and this Court's ruling in *Hoffman v. Jones,* 280 So. 2d 431 (Fla. 1973), wherein this Court stated that District Courts should not change law as a matter of public policy, the District Court would have been inclined to reverse the trial court's judgment. Relative to existing precedent, the District Court stated:

> "Under existing Florida law, we conclude that the trial judge's order should be affirmed. *American Fire and Casualty Company v. Vliet,* 148 Fla. 568, 4 So. 2d 862; *American Fire and Casualty Company v. Collura, Fla. App.* 1964, 163 So. 2d 784; *Bordettsky v. Hertz Corporation, Fla. App.* 1965, 171 So. 2d 174; Anno. 60 A.L.R.2d 1146. However, the appellant has made a persuasive argument that because of the modern trend of requiring that motorists carry insurance [§ 627.733, Fla. Stat.; 7 Am. Jur. 2d, Automobile Insurance, §§ 4, 6] insurance

carriers are real parties in interest in automobile accident litigation. *Stecher v. Pomeroy, Fla.* 1971, 253 So. 2d 421; *Godshall v. Unigard Insurance Company, Fla.* 1973, 281 So. 2d 499; *Allred v. Chittenden Pool Supply Inc., Fla.* 1974, 298 So. 2d 361. That, because of the mandatory requirements of the no fault insurance act adopted in recent years in Florida, these older decisions should be ignored and the law should be changed as a matter of public policy and a carrier should suffer the responsibility of finding its insured and, if it could not, it should then be required to respond for any damages within the limits of its policy to the injured innocent party and be left to its remedy by seeking indemnification from its insured."

The District Court concluded that it would certify the matter to this Court as one passing upon a question of great public interest in that it determines that, notwithstanding recent developments in the law, an automobile insurance carrier may still be permitted to avoid liability pursuant to a provision in its contract requiring the insured to give his cooperation in connection with any claim of which the carrier would have responsibility under the contract.

Respondent, Insurance Company, suggests in line with past precedent of this Court and other Florida Appellate Courts, that where an insured has a contractual duty to cooperate with the insurer and there is undisputed evidence that the insured failed to cooperate, thereby breaching his contractual obligation to the substantial prejudice of the insurer in that the insurer was (1) unable to confirm that the vehicle listed was the one involved in the accident, (2) unable to determine the liability situation, (3) unable to determine if there were any passengers in the vehicle in order to obtain their version of the intersectional accident and the existence of injuries inasmuch as the police report indicated no visible injuries, and (4) unable to obtain the insured's cooperation in the defense of the case, an automobile insurance carrier may still be permitted to avoid liability based upon lack of cooperation. Respondent posits that neither Florida Statutes nor recent Florida decisions have abrogated the insured's duty to cooperate. Sub judice, the trial court found that the insured failed completely to cooperate with Northwestern Mutual and found that this breach of the terms of the insurance policy was material and substantially prejudiced Northwestern Mutual. Restating the findings and conclusions of the trial court, the District Court affirmed the final judgment denying coverage.

In light of current public policy as reflected by *Shingleton v. Bussey, supra,* and its progeny, petitioner requests that this Court recede from the Florida decisions which stand for the proposition that an insurer may deny coverage and avoid payment of compensation to the victim of the insured's tort where the insured has been guilty of lack of cooperation which is material and is of such a nature as would substantially prejudice the rights of the insurer, where the insurer has exercised diligence and good faith in seeking to bring about the cooperation of the insured, and where the insurer has in good faith complied with the terms and conditions of the policy.

Relating to petitioner's assertion that the financial responsibility law renders obsolete the defense of prejudicial non-cooperation, the District Court of Appeal, Third District, in *Atlantic National Insurance Co. v. Johnson,* 178

So. 2d 733 (Fla. App. 3, 1965), held that the financial responsibility law does not preclude the insurer from raising the defense of failure to give notice to the insurer for a period of seventeen months after the accident at which time Allstate, the insurer of the other vehicle involved in the accident, notified it.

We are not unmindful of the decisions cited by petitioner, but we adhere to the general philosophy of the precedent set out in *American Fire and Casualty Co. v. Vliet, supra; American Fire and Casualty Co. v. Collura, supra;* and *Bordettsky v. Hertz Corporation, supra. American Universal Insurance Co. v. Stotsberry,* 116 So. 2d 482 (Fla. App. 3, 1959), *Barnes v. Pennsylvania Threshermen & Farmers' Mutual Casualty Insurance Co.,* 146 So. 2d 119 (Fla. App. 3, 1962), *cert. den.* 153 So. 2d 305 (Fla. 1963). We do not feel that the compulsory insurance law or third party beneficiary concept are sufficient justification to recede from that reasoning.

This Court in *American Fire and Casualty Co. v. Vliet, supra,* emphasized that to constitute the breach of a policy, the lack of cooperation must be material and the insurance company must show that it was substantially prejudiced in the particular case by failure to cooperate. Furthermore, as is stated in *Collura, supra,* the insurer must show that it has exercised diligence and good faith in bringing about the cooperation of its insured and must show that it has complied in good faith with the terms of the policy.

Not every failure to cooperate will release the insurance company. Only that failure which constitutes a material breach and substantially prejudices the rights of the insurer in defense of the cause will release the insurer of its obligation to pay. The question of whether the failure to cooperate is so substantially prejudicial as to release the insurance company of its obligation is ordinarily a question of fact, but under some circumstances, particularly where the facts are admitted, it may well be a question of law.

Accordingly, the decision of the District Court is affirmed and the writ is discharged.

It is so ordered.

OVERTON, C. J., and ENGLAND and SUNDBERG, JJ., concur.

ADKINS, J., dissents.

NOTES

1. *Duty or condition or both?* Insurers would prefer to treat the duty to cooperate (and the duty to give timely notice, etc.) as express conditions to the insurer's duty to pay proceeds. In other words, by this analysis the insurer's duty to defend is expressly conditioned on the insured's cooperation; if the cooperation is not forthcoming, the nonoccurrence of the condition has the effect of suspending, and ultimately discharging, the insurer's duty. See Restatement (Second) of Contracts §§ 224, 225. The usual treatment, however, considers the insured's cooperation as a duty the insured owes the insurer. If the insured breaches this duty in a material way, it follows (as is the case with any pair of dependent promises in a bilateral contract, where each side's

duty is constructively conditioned on the other side's performance, see *id.* § 228), that the insurer can suspend its performance, i.e., the performance of its duty to defend. Was petitioner in *Ramos* urging a repeal of these widely accepted principles of contract law?

2. *Why Ramos thought she could win.* The result sought by petitioner may have been novel from the standpoint of the common law, but it is not without support in the precedents. The standard personal automobile liability policy has for some time now contained a clause that accomplishes this result when the policy is certified as proof of financial responsibility by the insurer. A certified policy may be required where the insured previously was involved in an auto accident and was not able through liability insurance or otherwise to compensate a tort victim up to certain required amounts. The same may be true where the insured accumulated a certain number of traffic violations. In order to be able to legally operate a motor vehicle thereafter, proof of financial responsibility must be shown and a certified policy is one way of doing that. The clause precludes the insurer from asserting a policy defense for such things as failure to give timely notice or to cooperate. The insurer must defend the insured and pay any judgment up to the mandatory limits, but thereafter is entitled to seek reimbursement or indemnity from the insured. *See Coburn v. Fox,* 389 N.W.2d 424 (Mich. 1986). The same result also is achieved in some states under compulsory auto insurance statutes. *See, e.g.,* Ariz. Rev. Stat. Ann. § 28-4009(C)(5)(a) & (6) (West 1998 & Supp. 2000).

3. *Direct action statutes.* The fact that the liability insurer agrees to provide a defense and to pay damages on behalf of the insured does not make the insurer a real party in interest to the tort action in most states. Notable exceptions are those few states which have a direct action statute; in these states, the plaintiff can sue the tortfeasor's insurer directly and in the insurer's name. *See, e.g.,* La. Rev. Stat. Ann. § 22:655 (West 2000); Wis. Stat. Ann. § 632.24 (West 1999). For a time, Florida had a judicially-created procedure under which the liability insurer could be made a party to the tort suit, *see Shingleton v. Bussey,* 223 So. 2d 713 (Fla. 1969), but this rule was subsequently overturned by the Florida legislature. Fla. Stat. § 627.4136 (West 1996). Other states have rejected the idea of a judicially-created direct action procedure. *See, e.g., White v. Goodville Mutual Casualty Co.,* 226 Kan. 191, 596 P.2d 1229 (1979).

Why should the insurer care whether it is a named party in the underlying tort action brought by the plaintiff-victim? As a general rule the fact that the insured carries liability insurance is irrelevant to the merits of the tort action and therefore inadmissible. The mere mention of it before a jury by either plaintiff or defendant might be considered prejudicial and may result in a mistrial. *See Deschaine v. Deschaine,* 153 Me. 401, 140 A.2d 746 (1958); *Terry v. Plateau Electric Cooperative,* 825 S.W.2d 418 (Tenn. Ct. App. 1992). Is it not true, however, that liability insurance is so widespread that jurors know, whether the insurer's name is mentioned or not, that an insurer is very likely in the background? Does a direct action procedure make more sense in tort actions arising out of automobile accidents?

4. *Between rocks and hard places.* The fact that the liability insurer may have a defense because the insured has failed in some way to abide by the

terms of the contract can present some real dilemmas for the insurer. There are, however, several options. One is for the insurer to attempt to resolve the issue of whether it owes a duty to defend by bringing a declaratory judgment action. If this option is pursued and the issue is resolved before the trial of the tort action is commenced, the insurer will know whether it has to provide a defense. In the meantime, what should the insurer do? As time passes, evidence may disappear, witnesses' memories may fade, and in general the defense of the tort case may suffer. Thus, should the insurer provide a defense pending the outcome of the declaratory judgment proceeding? What if the trial of the tort case is nearing and preparation is imperative, or what if the tort case is actually called for trial? The insurer has essentially two alternatives: either defend, or refuse to defend. Which is better? If it chooses to defend, how can it protect itself against a claim of waiver or estoppel regarding the policy defense?

Another option is for the insurer to forego an action for declaratory judgment and to confront the basic issue of whether to defend outright by telling the insured a defense either will or will not be provided. Again, is there any way to preserve the policy defense issue where the insurer chooses to defend? What options are available to the insured in this situation?

5. *Insurer's control, insured's cooperation, and conflicting objectives.* If the insured objects to the manner in which the insurer is exercising its right to control the defense, has the insured breached its duty to cooperate? If the insured believes that the insurer is taking too few depositions to prepare an adequate defense, does the insured breach the duty to cooperate if it requests more depositions be taken? What about a demand for more depositions, instead of a request? What if the issue is one of trial strategy? Suppose the insured is concerned about the damage to his or her reputation resulting from media publicity of a long trial, and is objecting to the insurer's "let's-grind-down-the-plaintiff" approach to the case. What are the insured's options? Can the insurer ignore the insured's requests and conduct the litigation as it sees fit? If the insurer withdraws from the defense on the ground that the insured has breached the duty to cooperate, what risks does the insurer run? What if the insurer's assessment of the insured's cooperation, or lack thereof, is later found to be wrong? This theme reappears throughout the next three subsections.

[3]   Conflicts of Interest

GRAY v. ZURICH INSURANCE CO.
65 Cal. 2d 263, 419 P.2d 168, 54 Cal. Rptr. 104
(Cal. 1966) (en banc)

TOBRINER, JUSTICE.

This is an action by an insured against his insurer for failure to defend an action filed against him which stemmed from a complaint alleging that he had committed an assault. The main issue turns on the argument of the insurer that an exclusionary clause of the policy excuses its defense of an action in which a plaintiff alleges that the insured intentionally caused the bodily injury. Yet the language of the policy does not clearly define the application of the exclusionary clause to the duty to defend. Since in that event we test the meaning of the policy according to the insured's reasonable expectation of coverage and since the language of the policy would lead the insured here to expect defense of the third party suit, we cannot exonerate the carrier from the rendition of such protection.

Plaintiff, Dr. Vernon D. Gray, is the named insured under an insurance policy issued by defendant. A "Comprehensive Personal Liability Endorsement" in the policy states, under a paragraph designated "Coverage L," that the insurer agrees "(T)o pay on behalf of the insured all sums which the insured shall become legally obligated to pay as damages because of bodily injury or property damage, and the company shall defend any suit against the insured alleging such bodily injury or property damage and seeking damages which are payable under the terms of this endorsement, even if any of the allegations are groundless, false or fraudulent; but the company may make such investigation and settlement of any claim or suit as it deems expedient." The policy contains a provision that "(T)his endorsement does not apply" to a series of specified exclusions set forth under separate headings, including a paragraph (c) which reads, "under coverages L and M, to bodily injury or property damages caused intentionally by or at the direction of the insured."

The suit which Dr. Gray contends Zurich should have defended arose out of an altercation between him and a Mr. John R. Jones.[1]

Jones filed a complaint in Missouri alleging that Dr. Gray "wilfully, maliciously, brutally and intentionally assaulted" him; he prayed for actual damages of $50,000 and punitive damages of $50,000. Dr. Gray notified defendant of the suit, stating that he had acted in self-defense, and requested that the company defend. Defendant refused on the ground that the complaint alleged an intentional tort which fell outside the coverage of the policy. Dr. Gray thereafter unsuccessfully defended on the theory of self-defense; he suffered a judgment of $6,000 actual damages although the jury refused to award punitive damages.

Dr. Gray then filed the instant action charging defendant with breach of its duty to defend. Defendant answered, admitting the execution of the policy but denying any such obligation. . . . [T]he [trial] court rendered judgment in favor of defendant. We must decide whether or not defendant bore the obligation to defend plaintiff in the Missouri action.

Defendant argues that it need not defend an action in which the complaint reveals on its face that the claimed bodily injury does not fall within the indemnification coverage; that here the Jones complaint alleged that the insured committed an assault, which fell outside such coverage. Defendant

---

[1] Immediately preceding the altercation Dr. Gray had been driving an automobile on a residential street when another automobile narrowly missed colliding with his car. Jones, the driver of the other car, left his vehicle, approached Dr. Gray's car in a menacing manner and jerked open the door. At that point Dr. Gray, fearing physical harm to himself and his passengers, rose from his seat and struck Jones.

urges, as a second answer to plaintiff's contention, that the contract, if construed to require defense of the insured, would violate the public policy of the state and that, indeed, the judgment in the third party suit upholding the claim of an intentional bodily injury operates to estop the insured from recovery. Defendant thirdly contends that any requirement that it defend the Jones suit would embroil it in a hopeless conflict of interest. Finally it submits that, even if it should have defended the third party suit, the damages against it should encompass only the insured's expenses of defense and not the judgment against him.

We shall explain our reasons for concluding that defendant was obligated to defend the Jones suit, and our grounds for rejecting defendant's remaining propositions. Since the policy sets forth the duty to defend as a primary one and since the insurer attempts to avoid it only by an unclear exclusionary clause, the insured would reasonably expect, and is legally entitled to, such protection. As an alternative but secondary ground for our ruling we accept, for purposes of argument, defendant's contention that the duty to defend arises only if the third party suit involves a liability for which the insurer would be required to indemnify the insured, and, even upon this basis, we find a duty to defend.

In interpreting an insurance policy we apply the general principle that doubts as to meaning must be resolved against the insurer and that any exception to the performance of the basic underlying obligation must be so stated as clearly to apprise the insured of its effect.

These principles of interpretation of insurance contracts have found new and vivid restatement in the doctrine of the adhesion contract. As this court has held, a contract entered into between two parties of unequal bargaining strength, expressed in the language of a standardized contract, written by the more powerful bargainer to meet its own needs, and offered to the weaker party on a "take it or leave it basis" carries some consequences that extend beyond orthodox implications. Obligations arising from such a contract inure not alone from the consensual transaction but from the relationship of the parties.

Although courts have long followed the basic precept that they would look to the words of the contract to find the meaning which the parties expected from them, they have also applied the doctrine of the adhesion contract to insurance policies, holding that in view of the disparate bargaining status of the parties we must ascertain that meaning of the contract which the insured would reasonably expect. Thus as Kessler stated in his classic article on adhesion contracts: "In dealing with standardized contracts courts have to determine what the weaker contracting party could legitimately expect by way of services according to the enterpriser's 'calling', and to what extent the stronger party disappointed reasonable expectations based on the typical life situation." (Kessler, Contracts of Adhesion (1943) 43 Colum. L. Rev. 629, 637.)

Professor Patterson, in describing one characteristic consequence of "the conception of adhesion, whether that term is used or not," writes: "The court interprets the form contract to mean what a reasonable buyer would expect it to mean, and thus protects the weaker party's expectation at the expense of the stronger's. This process of interpretation was used many years ago in interpreting (or construing) insurance contracts. * * *" (Fn. omitted; Patterson, The Interpretation and Construction of Contracts (1964) 64 Colum. L. Rev. 833, 858.)

Thus we held in *Steven v. Fidelity & Casualty Co., supra*, 58 Cal. 2d 862, 27 Cal. Rptr. 172, 377 P.2d 284, that we would not enforce an exclusionary clause in an insurance contract which was unclear, saying: "If (the insurer) deals with the public upon a mass basis, the notice of non-coverage of the policy, in a situation in which the public may reasonably expect coverage, must be conspicuous, plain and clear." (58 Cal. 2d at 878, 27 Cal. Rptr. at 182, 377 P.2d at 294.)

When we test the instant policy by these principles we find that its provisions as to the obligation to defend are uncertain and undefined; in the light of the reasonable expectation of the insured, they require the performance of that duty. At the threshold we note that the nature of the obligation to defend is itself necessarily uncertain. Although insurers have often insisted that the duty arises only if the insurer is bound to indemnify the insured, this very contention creates a dilemma. No one can determine whether the third party suit does or does not fall within the indemnification coverage of the policy until that suit is resolved; in the instant case, the determination of whether the insured engaged in intentional, negligent or even wrongful conduct depended upon the judgment in the Jones suit, and, indeed, even after that judgment, no one could be positive whether it rested upon a finding of plaintiff's negligent or his intentional conduct. The carrier's obligation to indemnify inevitably will not be defined until the adjudication of the very action which it should have defended. Hence the policy contains its own seeds of uncertainty; the insurer has held out a promise that by its very nature is ambiguous.

Although this uncertainty in the performance of the duty to defend could have been clarified by the language of the policy we find no such specificity here.[10] An examination of the policy discloses that the broadly stated promise to defend is not conspicuously or clearly conditioned solely on a nonintentional bodily injury; instead, the insured could reasonably expect such protection.

The policy is a "comprehensive personal liability" contract; the designation in itself connotes general protection for alleged bodily injury caused by the insured. The insurer makes two wide promises: "(1.) To pay on behalf of the insured all sums which the insured shall become legally obligated to pay as damages because of bodily injury or property damage, and (2.) the company shall defend any suit against the insured alleging such bodily injury or property damage and seeking damages which are payable under the terms of this endorsement, even if any of the allegations of the suit are groundless,

---

[10] Thus the subject policy affords no clear answer to the following queries: Does the carrier exercise the sole right to determine whether the "suit against the insured alleging such bodily injury" was "caused intentionally by the insured?" When, and under what circumstances, is such determination binding upon the insured? Does the carrier exercise the exclusive power to decide whether "the allegations of the suit are groundless, false, or fraudulent"? When and under what circumstances is such a determination binding upon the insured? Are these matters to be resolved by the pleadings in the third party suit, by the insured's presentation to the insurer of his version of the facts, by the insurer's own investigation of the facts, or by the judgment rendered in the third party suit?

false, or fraudulent": clearly these promises, without further clarification, would lead the insured reasonably to expect the insurer to defend him against suits seeking damages for bodily injury, whatever the alleged cause of the injury, whether intentional or inadvertent.

But the insurer argues that the third party suit must seek "damages which are *payable* under the terms of this endorsement"; it contends that this limitation *modifies* the general duty to defend by confining the duty only to actions seeking damages within the primary coverage of the policy. Under "Exclusions" the policy provides that it "does not apply * * * under coverage L and M to bodily injury * * * caused intentionally by * * * the insured."

The very first paragraph as to coverage, however, provides that "the company shall defend any such suit against the insured alleging such bodily injury" although the allegations of the suit are groundless, false or fraudulent. This language, in its broad sweep, would lead the insured reasonably to expect defense of *any* suit regardless of merit or cause. The relation of the exclusionary clause to this basic promise is anything but clear. The basic promise would support the insured's reasonable expectation that he had bought the rendition of legal services to defend against a suit for bodily injury which alleged he had caused it, negligently, nonintentionally, intentionally or in any other manner. The doctrines and cases we have set forth tell us that the exclusionary clause must be "conspicuous, plain and clear." (*Steven v. Fidelity & Casualty Co., supra*, 58 Cal. 2d 862, 878, 27 Cal. Rptr. 172, 377 P.2d 284.) This clause is not "conspicuous" since it appears only after a long and complicated page of fine print, and is itself in fine print; its relation to the remaining clauses of the policy and its effect is surely not "plain and clear."

A further uncertainty lurks in the exclusionary clause itself. It alludes to damage caused "intentionally by or at the direction of the insured." Yet an act of the insured may carry out his "intention" and also cause unintended harm. When set next to the words "at the direction of the insured" the word "intentionally" might mean to the layman collusive, wilful or planned action beyond the classical notion of intentional tort. This built-in ambiguity has caused debate and refined definition in many courts; in any event, the word surely cannot be "plain and clear" to the layman.

The insured is unhappily surrounded by concentric circles of uncertainty: the first, the unascertainable nature of the insurer's duty to defend; the second, the unknown effect of the provision that the insurer must defend even a groundless, false or fraudulent claim; the third, the uncertain extent of the indemnification coverage. Since we must resolve uncertainties in favor of the insured and interpret the policy provisions according to the layman's reasonable expectations, and since the effect of the exclusionary clause is neither conspicuous, plain nor clear, we hold that in the present case the policy provides for an obligation to defend and that such obligation is independent of the indemnification coverage.

The insurer counters with the contention that this position would compel an insurer "issuing a policy covering liability of the insured for maintenance, use or operation of an automobile * * * to defend the insured in an action for damages for negligently maintaining a stairway and thereby allegedly causing injury to another—because the insured claims that the suit for damages was false or groundless." The "groundless, false, or fraudulent" clause, however, does not extend the obligation to defend without limits; it includes only defense to those actions of the nature and kind covered by the policy. Here the policy insures against "damages because of bodily injury." As we have pointed out, in view of the language of the policy, the insured would reasonably expect protection in an action involving alleged bodily injury. On the other hand the insured could not reasonably expect protection under an automobile insurance policy for injury which occurs from defect in a stairway. Similarly an insured would not expect a defense for an injury involving an automobile under a general comprehensive policy which excluded automobile coverage. We look to the nature and kind of risk covered by the policy as a limitation upon the duty the defend; we cannot absolve the carrier from the duty to defend an insured for loss of the nature and kind against which it insured.[14]

Our holding that the insurer bore the obligation to defend because the policy led plaintiff reasonably to expect such defense, and because the insurer's exclusionary clause did not exonerate it, cuts across defendant's answering contention that the duty arises only if the pleadings disclose a cause of action for which the insurer must indemnify the insured. Defendant would equate the duty to defend with the complaint that pleaded a liability for which the insurer was bound to indemnify the insured. Yet even if we accept defendant's premises, and define the duty to defend by measuring the allegations in the Jones case against the carrier's liability to indemnify, defendant's position still fails. We proceed to discuss this alternative ground of liability of the insurer, accepting for such purpose the insurer's argument that we must test the third party suit against the indemnification coverage of the policy. We point out that the carrier must defend a suit which *potentially* seeks damages within the coverage of the policy; the Jones action was such a suit.

Defendant cannot construct a formal fortress of the third party's pleadings and retreat behind its walls. The pleadings are malleable, changeable and amendable. Although an earlier decision reads: "In determining whether or not the appellant was bound to defend * * * the language of its contract must first be looked to, and next the allegations of the complaints * * *" (*Lamb v. Belt Casualty Co., supra*, 3 Cal. App. 2d 624, 630, 40 P.2d 311, 314), courts do not examine only the pleaded word but the potential liability created by

---

[14] "As to the insured's expectations, it is safe to assume that if the ordinary insurance consumer had thought about them, his expectations would be that the insurer would defend him whenever there was a threat of liability to him and the threat was based on facts within the policy. The insured probably would be surprised at the suggestion that defense coverage might turn on the pleading rules of the court that a third party chose or on how the third party's attorney decided to write the complaint. In some cases the insured might think in terms of his own conduct. The bar owner, for example, might well think that he is insulated from any legal expense arising from injuries to patrons so long as he personally does not intentionally injure someone or tell an employee to do so. To him the possibility of an ambitious claimant who would begin a lawsuit with a charge of intentional injury for the sake of a favorable bargaining position and later be willing to abandon that charge for one of simple negligence might not occur; or if the possibility did occur the insured might not pause to consider whether it would be fatal to part of his insurance coverage. In short, the limits of the phrase "suits alleging such injury," prepared by lawyers, defended by lawyers and authoritatively interpreted by lawyers, are probably not appreciated by the lay insured. And even the more sophisticated insured has no choice in the matter, since the provision is standard." (Comment, [The Insurer's Duty to Defend Under a Liability Insurance Policy], 114 U.Pa.L.Rev. 734, 748 [1966] (fn. omitted).)

the suit. Since the instant action presented the potentiality of a judgment based upon nonintentional conduct, and since liability for such conduct would fall within the indemnification coverage, the duty to defend became manifest at the outset.

To restrict the defense obligation of the insurer to the precise language of the pleading would not only ignore the thrust of the cases but would create an anomaly for the insured. Obviously, as *Ritchie v. Anchor Casualty Co., supra,* 135 Cal. App. 2d 245, 286 P.2d 1000, points out, the complainant in the third party action drafts his complaint in the broadest terms; he may very well stretch the action which lies in only nonintentional conduct to the dramatic complaint that alleges intentional misconduct. In light of the likely overstatement of the complaint and of the plasticity of modern pleading, we should hardly designate the third party as the arbiter of the policy's coverage.

Since modern procedural rules focus on the facts of a case rather than the theory of recovery in the complaint, the duty to defend should be fixed by the facts which the insurer learns from the complaint, the insured, or other sources. An insurer, therefore, bears a duty to defend its insured whenever it ascertains facts which give rise to the potential of liability under the policy. In the instant case the complaint itself, as well as the facts known to the insurer, sufficiently apprised the insurer of these possibilities; hence we need not set out when and upon what other occasions the duty of the insurer to ascertain such possibilities otherwise arises.

Jones' complaint clearly presented the possibility that he might obtain damages that were covered by the indemnity provisions of the policy. Even conduct that is traditionally classified as "intentional" or "wilful" has been held to fall within indemnification coverage. Moreover, despite Jones' pleading of intentional and wilful conduct, he could have amended his complaint to allege merely negligent conduct. Further, plaintiff might have been able to show that in physically defending himself, even if he exceeded the reasonable bounds of self-defense, he did not commit wilful and intended injury, but engaged only in nonintentional tortious conduct. Thus, even accepting the insurer's premise that it had no obligation to defend actions seeking damages not within the indemnification coverage, we find, upon proper measurement of the third party action against the insurer's liability to indemnify, it should have defended because the loss could have fallen within that liability.

We turn to the insurer's second major contention that the contract cannot be read to require the insurer to defend an action seeking damages for an intentional wrong because such an obligation would violate public policy. In support of this argument it relies upon Insurance Code section 533, and Civil Code section 1668.[17]

The contention fails on two grounds. In the first place, the statutes forbid only contracts which indemnify for *"loss"* or *"responsibility"* resulting from wilful wrong-doing. Here we deal with a contract which provides for *legal*

---

[17] Insurance Code section 533 provides: "An insurer is not liable for a loss caused by the wilful act of the insured; but he is not exonerated by the negligence of the insured, or of the insured's agents or others." Civil Code section 1668 provides, in relevant part: "All contracts which have for their object, directly or indirectly, to exempt anyone from responsibility for his own * * * wilful injury to the person or property of another * * * are against the policy of the law."

defense against an action charging such conduct; the contract does not call
for indemnification of the insured if the third party plaintiff prevails. In the
second place, as we pointed out in *Tomerlin v. Canadian Indemnity Co.* (1964)
61 Cal. 2d 638, 648, 39 Cal. Rptr. 731, 737, 394 P.2d 571, 577, the statutes
"establish a public policy to prevent insurance coverage from encouragement
of wilful tort." Thus *Tomerlin* held that if an insurer's obligation to pay a
judgment based on wilful conduct results from an estoppel *after* the conduct,
the obligation could not have previously encouraged the conduct. Similarly,
the present contract does not offend the statute; a contract to defend an
assured upon mere accusation of a wilful tort does not encourage such wilful
conduct.

Nor can we accept defendant's argument that the duty to defend dissolves
simply because the insured is unsuccessful in his defense and because the
injured party recovers on the basis of a finding of the assured's wilful conduct.
Citing *Abbott v. Western Nat. Indem. Co.* (1958) 165 Cal. App. 2d 302, 331
P.2d 997, the insurer urges that if the judgment in a third party suit goes
against the insured it operates as "res judicata or collateral estoppel in the
insured's action or proceeding against the insurer."

We have explained that the insured would reasonably expect a defense by
the insurer in all personal injury actions against him. If he is to be required
to finance his own defense and then, only if successful, hold the insurer to
its promise by means of a second suit for reimbursement, we defeat the basic
reason for the purchase of the insurance. In purchasing his insurance the
insured would reasonably expect that he would stand a better chance of
vindication if supported by the resources and expertise of his insurer than
if compelled to handle and finance the presentation of his case. He would,
moreover, expect to be able to avoid the time, uncertainty and capital outlay
in finding and retaining an attorney of his own. "The courts will not sanction
a construction of the insurer's language that will defeat the very purpose or
object of the insurance." (*Ritchie v. Anchor Casualty Co., supra,* 135 Cal. App.
2d 245, 257, 286 P.2d 1000, 1007.)

Similarly, we find no merit in the insurer's third contention that our holding
will embroil it in a conflict of interests. According to the insurer our ruling
will require defense of an action in which the interests of insurer and insured
are so opposed as to nullify the insurer's fulfillment of its duty of defense and
of the protection of its own interests. For example, the argument goes, if
defendant had defended against the Jones suit it would have sought to
establish either that the insured was free from any liability or that such
liability rested on intentional conduct. The insured, of course, would also seek
a verdict holding him not liable but, if found liable, would attempt to obtain
a ruling that such liability emanated from the nonintentional conduct within
his insurance coverage. Thus, defendant contends, an insurer, if obligated to
defend in this situation, faces an insoluble ethical problem.

Since, however, the court in the third party suit does not adjudicate the
issue of coverage, the insurer's argument collapses. The only question there
litigated is the insured's *liability*. The alleged victim does not concern himself
with the theory of liability; he desires only the largest possible judgment.
Similarly, the insured and insurer seek only to avoid, or at least to minimize,

the judgment. As we have noted, modern procedural rules focus on whether, on a given set of facts, the plaintiff, regardless of the theory, may recover. Thus the question of whether or not the insured engaged in intentional conduct does not normally formulate an issue which is resolved in that litigation.[18]

In any event, if the insurer adequately reserves its right to assert the noncoverage defense later, it will not be bound by the judgment. If the injured party prevails, that party or the insured will assert his claim against the insurer.[19]

At this time the insurer can raise the noncoverage defense previously reserved. In this manner the interests of insured and insurer in defending against the injured party's primary suit will be identical; the insurer will not face the suggested dilemma.

Finally, defendant urges that our holding should require only the reimbursement of the insured's expenses in defending the third party action but not the payment of the judgment. Defendant acknowledges the general rule that an insurer that wrongfully refuses to defend is liable on the judgment against the insured. (*Arenson v. Nat. Auto. & Cas. Ins. Co.* (1955) 45 Cal. 2d 81, 84, 286 P.2d 816; Civ. Code, § 2778.) Defendant argues, however, that the instant situation should be distinguished from that case because here the judgment has not necessarily been rendered on a theory within the policy coverage. Thus defendant would limit the insured's recovery to the expenses of the third party suit.

We rejected a similar proposal in *Tomerlin v. Canadian Indemnity Co.*, *supra*, 61 Cal. 2d 638, 649–650, 39 Cal. Rptr. 731, 394 P.2d 571. In that case, as we have noted, the insurer's obligation to defend arose out of estoppel. The insurer contended that we should apply a "tort" theory of damages to its wrongful refusal to defend. Such a theory, we explained, would impose upon the insured "the impossible burden" of proving the extent of the loss caused by the insurer's breach. As this court said in an analogous situation in *Arenson v. National Auto. & Cas. Ins. Co.* (1957) 48 Cal. 2d 528, 539, 310 P.2d 961, 968: "Having defaulted such agreement the company is manifestly bound to reimburse its insured for the full amount of any obligation reasonably incurred by him. It will not be allowed to defeat or whittle down its obligation on the theory that plaintiff himself was of such limited financial ability that he could not afford to employ able counsel, or to present every reasonable defense, or to carry his cause to the highest court having jurisdiction, * * *. Sustaining such a theory * * * would tend * * * to encourage insurance companies to similar disavowals of responsibility with everything to gain and nothing to lose."

---

[18] In rare cases the issue of punitive damages or a special verdict might present a potential conflict of interests, but such a possibility does not outweigh the advantages of the general rule. Even in such cases, however, the insurer will still be bound, ethically and legally, to litigate in the interests of the insured.

[19] Insurance Code section 11580, subdivision (b)(2) provides that "whenever judgment is secured against the insured * * * in an action based upon bodily injury, death, or property damage, then an action may be brought against the insurer on the policy and subject to its terms and limitations, by such judgment creditor to recover on the judgment."

In summary, the individual consumer in the highly organized and integrated society of today must necessarily rely upon institutions devoted to the public service to perform the basic functions which they undertake. At the same time the consumer does not occupy a sufficiently strong economic position to bargain with such institutions as to specific clauses of their contracts of performance, and, in any event, piecemeal negotiation would sacrifice the advantage of uniformity. Hence the courts in the field of insurance contracts have tended to require that the insurer render the basic insurance protection which it has held out to the insured. This obligation becomes especially manifest in the case in which the insurer has attempted to limit the principal coverage by an unclear exclusionary clause. We test the alleged limitation in the light of the insured's reasonable expectation of coverage; that test compels the indicated outcome of the present litigation.

The judgment is reversed and the trial court instructed to take evidence solely on the issue of damages alleged in plaintiff's complaint including the amount of the judgment in the Jones suit, and the costs, expenses and attorney's fees incurred in defending such suit.

TRAYNOR, C.J., and PETERS, PEEK, MOSK, and BURKE, JJ., concur.

[In a one-sentence dissenting opinion, Justice McComb stated that he would affirm for the reasons set forth in the opinion by Justice Fox for the District Court of Appeal, *Gray v. Zurich Ins. Co.,* 49 Cal. Rptr. 271 (Cal. App. 1966).]

NOTES

1. *A windfall for Dr. Gray?* In the underlying action, Gray was found by the jury to have committed a willful assault on Jones. If you were a member of the pool of insureds which included Dr. Gray, would you have been pleased if the insurer raised your next premium to help pay for Dr. Gray's defense? If you, as the victim of a willful assault, inflicted physical harm on the perpetrator in self-defense, and if you were later sued by the perpetrator for alleged intentionally-inflicted injuries suffered at your hands, would you be pleased if your liability insurer refused to defend you? In this last scenario, suppose you decided that, although you are certain of your defense, the simplest way to be rid of the nuisance suit would be to pay a modest amount in settlement of the claim. (Recall the facts of *Ledford v. Gutoski, supra.*) Does the insurer's argument in *Gray* imply that the insured who settles such an action automatically forfeits coverage?

2. *Defending without a reservation of rights or a nonwaiver agreement.* "A nonwaiver agreement is a contract between the insurer and insured in which the insurer agrees to continue with the defense, while the insured agrees that the insurer shall have the right to contest any issues relating to coverage in the event the insured is found liable in the underlying action. In effect and often in form, it is a reservation of rights letter to which the insured has consented." Robert H. Jerry, II, Understanding Insurance Law § 114[c][3], at 793 (2d ed. 1996). "A reservation of rights notice is simply a unilateral notice sent by the insurer to the insured stating that the insurer reserves the right

to contest coverage despite its undertaking to investigate the claim and defend the insured." *Id.*, at 794.

Where a liability insurer undertakes to defend an insured without a reservation of rights notice or nonwaiver agreement, the insurer may have waived or may be estopped to raise a policy or coverage defense later. *See, e.g., Knox-Tenn Rental Co. v. Home Insurance Co.,* 2 F.3d 678 (6th Cir. 1993); *Peavey Co. v. M/V ANPA,* 971 F.2d 1168 (5th Cir. 1992); *Steptore v. Masco Construction Co.,* 643 So. 2d 1213 (La. 1994). In circumstances where the insurer subsequently asserts that the policy is unenforceable or inapplicable after defending without having secured a nonwaiver agreement or issued a reservation of rights of notice, some courts have held that the insured's right to select independent counsel and to arrange for the initial investigation, settlement negotiations and conduct of the lawsuit creates a conclusive presumption of prejudice where considerable time has elapsed while the insurer has control of the case. *See Safeco Insurance Co. v. Ellinghouse,* 725 P.2d 217 (Mont. 1986); *Transamerica Insurance Group v. Chubb & Son,* 16 Wash. App. 247, 554 P.2d 1080 (1976). *See also Knox-Tenn Rental Co. v. Home Insurance Co.,* 2 F.3d 678 (6th Cir. 1993) (insurer estopped to deny coverage where reservation of rights notice lacked sufficient clarity to notify employee of the reservation).

Why should this be so? Is it reasonable to assume that the attorney appointed by the insurer to defend the insured will conduct the litigation in according with the insurer's interests to the disadvantage of the insured's, and that taking away the insurer's defenses is necessary to deter this conduct? If insurers routinely defend under a reservation of rights whenever there is a possibility that the insurer has a defense to coverage, are insureds any better off? To what extent is the waiver-estoppel rule applied to eliminate unfair surprise?

3. *Covered and noncovered or excluded claims in the same complaint. Gray* presents a difficult issue: when a complaint against the insured alleges both covered and noncovered or excluded claims, how does this combination affect the insurer's duty to defend? How does the court in *Gray* circumvent the conflict of interest issue? Do you agree with the court that no conflict of interest existed? Note that the same issue can arise when the complaint seeks covered compensatory damages and noncovered (in some jurisdictions) punitive damages.

4. *An easier case?* What if the facts which will be determinative of coverage are *not* relevant to the resolution of the tort suit against the insured? Assume, for example, that A takes B's car and while driving it injures C. C alleges A was negligent. B's liability insurer takes the position that A did not have permission to drive the car and that there is no coverage because of an exclusion that withholds coverage for any occurrence while someone is operating the vehicle without a reasonable belief that he or she has permission to do so. Does this situation involve a conflict (even a potential conflict) of interest between insurer and insured? Is there any reason why the insurer should not defend under a reservation of rights? If a defense under reservation is offered, should the insured be compelled to accept it? Is there any rationale under which the result in the underlying tort action would have a collateral

estoppel effect on the coverage issues? Note that counsel appointed by the insurer to defend the insured must not do anything which prejudices the insured's rights on the coverage issue. *See GRE Insurance Group v. Metropolitan Boston Housing Partnership, Inc.*, 61 F.3d 79 (1st Cir. 1995); *Continental Insurance Co. v. Bayless & Roberts, Inc.*, 608 P.2d 281 (Alaska 1980).

A declaratory judgment action could precede the trial of the tort action or even proceed simultaneously with it. If the insurer obtains a declaratory judgment in its favor while the underlying tort action is underway, what are the insurer's options at that point? See Ellen S. Pryor, *The Tort Liability Regime and the Duty to Defend*, 58 Md. L. Rev. 1 (1999).

5. *Self-defense.* Gray alleged in the underlying action that he inflicted injury upon the plaintiff in self-defense. The insurer's contention was that injuries inflicted in self-defense are nevertheless intentional, and are therefore excluded from coverage under the intentional act exclusion. Jurisdictions are split on the merit of the insurer's contention, as discussed in the materials in § 5.01[3]. Suppose the named insured, the named insured's spouse, and their three children are walking in a park when they are attacked by a deranged stranger. The named insured, to protect the family from this attack, inflicts injury on the stranger in self-defense. Stranger later sues the insured for his injuries. Is it "unfair surprise" when the insured discovers (in some jurisdictions) that the insurer will not provide a defense against this meritless claim? If you agree with those jurisdictions that require the insurer to defend, what are the chances that any insured who is alleged to have inflicted injury on a third-party plaintiff will claim self-defense? If the insurer provides a defense where the self-defense claim is bogus, the insured will have received a defense to an excluded claim. Is it a sufficient answer to say that the insurer can later recoup the defense costs expended in the insured's behalf for what later proves to be a claim outside the coverage?

6. *Clarity of the policy.* The court in *Gray* makes much of the policy's ambiguity and the insured's reasonable expectations. If instead of Gray, the insured were a large commercial enterprise with a small army of lawyers that scoured, and sometimes negotiated, the nuances of policy language, would the court's analysis, and perhaps the result of the case, be different?

Does it follow from *Gray* that an insurer could narrow the duty to defend in similar situations through clear policy language? What if the policy stated clearly and unambiguously that whenever the plaintiff's complaint contained any allegation outside the coverage, the insurer would have no duty to defend any claim in the complaint, and the insured's defense to the suit would be his or her own responsibility? Would it matter if policies containing the clear language narrowing the duty to defend were sold at a significant premium reduction?

7. *Strategic pleading.* Suppose your client suffers serious injury in a wanton, unprovoked attack by a neighbor wielding a shovel. You understand that the neighbor lacks personal assets to pay any judgment of significant size. The neighbor does have, however, a homeowners policy and an umbrella policy with combined limits of $1 million. Should you file a complaint against the neighbor on your client's behalf alleging the neighbor's negligence in injuring your client with a shovel? You realize you could never establish a negligence

claim at trial, but you hope to get at least some insurer-funded settlement of the claim. (You think the neighbor might claim, albeit without any foundation, self-defense.) Should you do so? *See Boyles v. Kerr,* 855 S.W.2d 593 (Tex. 1993). For more discussion, see Ellen S. Pryor, *The Stories We Tell: Intentional Harm and the Quest for Insurance Funding*, 75 Tex. L. Rev. 1721 (1997).

8. *Confining the incident to noncovered or excluded claims.* Earlier in § 8.02[1], it was suggested that when the insurer undertakes a defense but the results of investigation and discovery show, unequivocally, that the plaintiff's claim is outside the coverage, the insurer may be entitled to withdraw from the defense. Does this principle imply that the insurer has no duty to defend—or may be obligated *not* to defend—when covered and excluded claims are included in the complaint against the insured? Consider the next case.

BURD v. SUSSEX MUTUAL INSURANCE CO.
56 N.J. 383, 267 A.2d 7 (1970)

WEINTRAUB, C.J.

The defendant carrier issued a Home Owner's policy to plaintiff, Burd, providing him with "Comprehensive Personal Liability Coverage." The ultimate issue is whether the policy covers the liability incurred by Burd when he inflicted shotgun wounds upon August D'Agostino

The shooting incident led to the conviction of Burd for atrocious assault and battery. Thereafter D'Agostino sued Burd for damages. His complaint contained two counts. The first count charged that Burd "did maliciously and intentionally fire a loaded gun at the plaintiff" and as a proximate result "of said negligence," D'Agostino was injured. The second count charged that Burd "did negligently fire a loaded gun at the plaintiff." Burd called upon the carrier to defend the suit but the carrier refused on the ground that the policy expressly excluded coverage of "bodily injury or property damage caused intentionally by or at the direction of the Insured." Burd defended through his own counsel. There was a general verdict for D'Agostino in the sum of $8,500.

Burd then brought the present action against the carrier to recover the amount of D'Agostino's judgment and also the costs incurred in defending that action. D'Agostino was named a party defendant but no relief was sought against him, and he is not a party to the present appeal. Burd and the carrier both moved for summary judgment. Burd prevailed. We certified the carrier's appeal before argument in the Appellate Division.

Burd and the carrier each contended the other was bound by the judgment in a prior proceeding. The carrier urged that Burd was bound by the finding in the criminal case that he intentionally wounded D'Agostino, while Burd contended the carrier had to defend the civil action, and having refused to do so, may not challenge the allegation therein that the injuries were "negligently" inflicted. The trial court held the carrier was thus precluded, and hence did not reach the question whether, if the carrier were free to dispute coverage, Burd would be foreclosed by the criminal conviction from questioning the carrier's position that D'Agostino was intentionally injured within the meaning of the policy exclusion from coverage.

I.

The judgment against the carrier rests upon the premise that the carrier was obligated to defend the suit D'Agostino brought against the insured because the second count of the complaint alleged only "negligence" and thus on its face was beyond the clause excluding coverage for intentional injury. Hence, the insured argues, the carrier, having foregone the opportunity to defend, is estopped to assert the injuries were intentionally caused.

The policy reads:

> LIABILITY: To pay on behalf of the Insured all sums which the Insured shall become legally obligated to pay as damages because of bodily injury or property damage, and the company shall defend any suit against the Insured alleging such bodily injury or property damage and seeking damages which are payable under the terms of this policy, even if any of the allegations of the suit are groundless, false or fraudulent; but the company may make such investigation and settlement of any claim or suit as it deems expedient.

As already stated, the policy provided, under "Special Exclusions," that this coverage did not apply "to bodily injury or property damage caused intentionally by or at the direction of the insured."

The insured says the carrier is obligated to defend an action whenever the complaint alleges a basis of liability within the covenant to pay. That is the general approach. But when coverage, i.e., the duty to pay, depends upon a factual issue which will not be resolved by the trial of the third party's suit against the insured, the duty to defend may depend upon the actual facts and not upon the allegations in the complaint. So, for example, if a policy covered a Ford but not a Chevrolet also owned by the insured, the carrier would not be obligated to defend a third party's complaint against the insured which alleged the automobile involved was the Ford when in fact the car involved was the Chevrolet. The identity of the car, upon which coverage depends, would be irrelevant to the trial of the negligence action.

The sense of the covenant is to defend suits involving claims which the carrier would have to pay if the claimant prevailed in the action. The covenant to defend is thus identified with the covenant to pay. That is the basis of the rule that ordinarily a carrier who defends unsuccessfully may not later deny coverage, absent an express agreement with the insured reserving a right to deny coverage. The obligation to defend "groundless, false or fraudulent" claims does not mean that the carrier will defend claims which would be beyond the covenant to pay if the claimant prevailed. It means only that a carrier may not refuse to defend a suit on the ground that the claim asserted against the insured cannot possibly succeed because either in law or in fact there is no basis for a plaintiff's judgment. . . . In short, the carrier's promise is to defeat or to pay a claim within the policy coverage. . . .

Here the obligation to pay a judgment obtained by the injured party depended upon whether the injuries were intentionally inflicted within the meaning of the exclusionary clause. There may be cases in which the interests of the carrier and the insured coincide so that the carrier can defend such an action with complete devotion to the insured's interest. But if the trial will leave the question of coverage unresolved so that the insured may later be called upon to pay, or if the case may be so defended by a carrier as to prejudice the insured thereafter upon the issue of coverage, the carrier should not be permitted to control the defense. That was the situation in the case at hand. Although both the insurer and the insured would want D'Agostino to fail, yet if D'Agostino should succeed, as it was likely he would, the insured would want the basis to be negligence whereas the carrier would profit if the basis was an intentional injury within the policy exclusion. If plaintiff pressed his claim of negligence, the coverage issue would remain open, for the carrier could hardly insist the injuries were intentionally inflicted. Willfulness is not a defense to a charge of negligence. And if plaintiff sought a judgment for intentional hurt, the carrier could not be expected to resist that basis of liability with the fervor or fidelity of an advocate selected by the insured.

In such circumstances the carrier should not be estopped from disputing coverage because it refused to defend. On the contrary the carrier should not be permitted to assume the defense if it intends to dispute its obligation to pay a plaintiff's judgment, unless of course the insured expressly agrees to that reservation. This is not to free the carrier from its covenant to defend, but rather to translate its obligation into one to reimburse the insured if it is later adjudged that the claim was one within the policy covenant to pay. *See Satterwhite v. Stolz,* 79 N.M. 320, 442 P.2d 810 (Ct. App. 1968).

We think the case comes within *Williams v. Bituminous Casualty Corp.,* 51 N.J. 146, 238 A.2d 177 (1968). There a workmen's compensation petition alleged the accident occurred on a date which was within the period of the policy coverage. The carrier refused to defend because it contended the accident occurred on another day, outside the period of coverage. After the employee obtained an award, the insured sued the carrier. The carrier did not dispute its insured's liability to the third-party claimant as established in the compensation proceeding, but insisted that the liability so established was beyond its coverage notwithstanding that the award in favor of the employee found the accident occurred on a date within the period of policy coverage. In holding the carrier was not precluded by the award, we said, 51 N.J. at 149, 238 A.2d 177, at 179:

> Thus the coverage question does not depend upon an issue material to the litigation between the employee and the employer. The resolution of the employee's claim against the employer would not have settled the coverage problem. More than that, if the Division of Workmen's Compensation somehow accepted the issue in the trial of the employee's claim against the employer, the carrier could not have asserted its position in the employer's name, for a carrier may not so defend an insured as to leave him liable and uncovered. An attorney, engaged by the carrier to defend in the insured's name, could not ethically seek such a result. *See Szabo v. Standard Commercial Body*

Corp., 221 App. Div. 722, 225 N.Y.S. 332 (3d Dept. 1927). That would have been the case here since, if the carrier succeeded in its position that the critical date was the 6th, the employer would have been left with an uninsured compensation liability.

A carrier's contractual right to defend presupposes that if the defense fails, the carrier will pay. *Merchants Indemnity Corp. v. Eggleston,* 37 N.J. 114, 127, 179 A.2d 505 (1962). Hence it is settled that a carrier is estopped to deny coverage of an action it undertakes to defend. This being so, it would be arbitrary to say also that a carrier which declines to incur an estoppel by defending is equally barred from a hearing as to coverage because of a finding made in the suit it could not safely defend. Elementary fairness demands a proceeding in which the differences between the insurer and the insured may be tried. Ideally the injured claimant should be there as well, so that he may also be heard and concluded upon the issue of the carrier's liability.

Whenever the carrier's position so diverges from the insured's that the carrier cannot defend the action with complete fidelity to the insured, there must be a proceeding in which the carrier and the insured, represented by counsel of their own choice, may fight out their differences. That action may, as here, follow the trial of the third party's suit against the insured. Or, unless for special reasons it would be unfair to do so, a declaratory judgment proceeding may be brought in advance of that trial by the carrier or the insured, to the end that the third-party suit may be defended by the party ultimately liable.

In this connection, the insured urges the carrier should be required to seek a declaration of its duty before the trial of the injured party's suit against the insured. But that proposition could lead to unnecessary litigation, for it would compel a lawsuit whenever coverage is denied even though the insured may silently agree with the carrier's position. We think the better course is to leave it to the contenders to decide for themselves if and when to sue.

The insured cites *Gray v. Zurich Ins. Co.,* 65 Cal. 2d 263, 54 Cal. Rptr. 104, 419 P.2d 168 (1966), which the trial court apparently followed. *Gray* also involved a charge of intentional injury. There the insured claimed self-defense but the carrier refused to defend because the policy excluded intentional injuries from coverage. The insured defended the case, unsuccessfully. He thereupon sued for both the amount of the judgment against him and the cost of defense.

The California court held, as one ground for its decision, that the carrier was obligated to defend because under modern pleading an allegation of intentional wrong carries inherently the "potential" of a recovery upon the lesser thesis of a negligent injury. Hence, the court held, the charge on its face came within the policy coverage notwithstanding that ultimately it might be found the injury was intentionally inflicted within the meaning of the express exclusion from coverage. Thus, under *Gray* the carrier must defend every such complaint, whether it be in terms of negligence or of an intentional injury, notwithstanding that in truth the claim, and a plaintiff's judgment thereon, will be beyond the covenant to pay.

The carrier in *Gray* argued that it could not properly have defended the insured since their interests were irreconcilable. The court resolved that problem by holding that in a later action between the carrier and the insured, neither the carrier nor the insured would be bound by the findings in the action against the insured. On that basis the court concluded the carrier could safely have sought the most favorable result for its insured even though its own interests ran the other way, provided, however, that the carrier had properly reserved its right to dispute coverage. On that approach, of course, the carrier was liable for the cost of defense, whatever the outcome of the coverage issue. The court went further, and held that although the carrier could have litigated the issue of coverage in the policy suit (provided it had defended under a reservation of rights), it could not do so because it breached the covenant to defend and therefore must pay also the amount of the judgment against the insured. The approach taken by *Gray* of course differs basically from the approach adopted by our decisions already cited.

It is not clear whether the thesis of *Gray* would be applied by the California court to all coverage problems or whether it is confined to one involving an exclusion of intentional injury. The exclusion of intentional injury is somewhat unique with respect to the problem of coverage. The usual coverage issue depends upon status, time, place, identity of the instrumentality, and the like. But in the case of the exclusion of intentional injuries, the injuries, which otherwise are within the coverage, are excepted therefrom because of a state of mind, and indeed a state of mind which the injured claimant may but need not allege or prove, to prevail against the insured. Since a claimant who charges intentional injury may thus recover even though the intent to injure is not proved, his complaint, on its face, is simultaneously within both the basic covenant to pay and the intentional-injury exclusion from that coverage.

This being so, it follows that if an action charging intentional injury is wholly defeated, the insured can well argue the claim thus found to be "groundless, false or fraudulent" was for bodily injury or property damage within the covenant to pay and did not cease to be such a claim merely because the claimant added the further "groundless, false or fraudulent" allegation of an intent to injure. In that situation the carrier may fairly be required to reimburse the insured for the cost of the successful defense even though the carrier would not have had to pay the judgment if the case had gone against the insured on a finding of intentional injury.

A judgment in favor of the injured party is the eventuality which presents the difficult problem as to whether the carrier should be precluded because it refused to defend a suit it believed to be within the intentional-injury exclusion. But we see no significant difference between that problem and the problem in *Williams v. Bituminous Casualty Corp., supra.* The carrier's obligation to pay will probably not be resolved by a factual determination in the action brought by the injured claimant against the insured, and if perchance that factual determination is made in that suit against the insured, he will not have been represented by counsel of his own choice upon that critical question. And if the coverage issue is not thus decided in the tort action, or if a finding upon it is held not to be binding in the later litigation over coverage, still the carrier's control over preparation and trial of the tort action may well cast the die against the insured. Hence we prefer to apply the approach of *Williams*, i.e., that if a carrier defends an action in the face of a coverage issue, the carrier must pay the judgment (unless the insured expressly agreed to a reservation of that issue), and if the carrier does not defend the tort claim because a plaintiff's verdict will not resolve the coverage problem in the insured's favor or because the carrier cannot defend with complete fidelity to the insured's sole interest, then the carrier may be heard upon the coverage issue in a proceeding upon the policy. And of course if the carrier does not defend, it will have to reimburse the insured for the cost of defense if the tort judgment is held to be within the covenant to pay.

The cases in this area are far from harmonious.

. . . .

The carrier in the case before us was therefore entitled to try the issue whether in truth the injuries inflicted upon D'Agostino were within the exclusion and hence beyond the policy coverage. The summary judgment against the carrier must be reversed.

II.

The remaining question is whether the carrier is entitled to judgment as a matter of law because the insured was convicted on an indictment for atrocious assault and battery.

. . . .

As we noted earlier, D'Agostino was made a party to this suit, although we do not know what position, if any, he took. If D'Agostino asserts a claim against the carrier, he could not be concluded by the judgment of conviction. By statute, N.J.S.A. 17:28-2, an injured claimant has an interest in a liability policy, and is entitled to be heard as to coverage. A claimant's interest is derivative of the insured's (absent a statute providing otherwise) and it is therefore reasonable to admit the judgment of conviction in his suit for whatever evidential worth it may have. But the claimant may not be estopped by a judgment entered in a proceeding begun after he was injured if he was not a party to it. Hence, D'Agostino is not precluded by the criminal conviction.

We could not say collateral estoppel would be appropriate here even as to the insured. Since the record on this appeal did not reveal the issues actually tried in the criminal case, we could not be sure the jury found facts decisive with respect to the insurance controversy.

. . . .

The judgment is reversed and the matter remanded for further proceedings not inconsistent with this opinion.

JACOBS, J. (dissenting).

The insurance carrier in effect refused to participate in the defense of the assured, either with or without reservation. The trial court found that this flat abandonment of the assured violated the broad policy covenant to defend and subjected the carrier to responsibility for the ensuing consequences. In granting summary judgment against the carrier, the trial court accepted pertinent principles recently expressed in the full opinion of the California

Supreme Court in *Gray v. Zurich Ins. Co.,* 65 Cal. 2d 263, 54 Cal. Rptr. 104, 419 P.2d 168 (1966). Since I believe that, under the particular circumstances presented here, application of those principles would more clearly and more justly fulfill the reasonable expectations of the assured in the purchase of his insurance policy with "Comprehensive Personal Liability Coverage," I vote to affirm.

[Editors' note: Justices Francis, Proctor, Hall, Schettino, and Haneman joined Justice Weintraub's opinion.]

NOTES

1. *The tripartite relationship.* Exactly what obligation the insurer owes the insured when a conflict of interest arises is widely and vigorously debated. In sorting out the debate, it is useful to remember that the insurer's obligation to the insured is created by a contract between insurer and insured. When the insurer is obligated to provide a defense, it contracts with an attorney to provide the representation. The contract between insurer and attorney may be formal (i.e., a retainer agreement) or may be informal (i.e., oral and lacking in details). When the attorney appears for and undertakes the defense of the insured, the attorney also establishes her own professional relationship with the insured. This relationship might have its own retainer agreement; the substance of the relationship is also informed by the law of agency, the professional and ethical obligations that attach whenever a lawyer-client relationship is created, and fiduciary considerations. Because the defense of a third-party's claim under a liability policy involves three different relationships (insurer-insured; insurer-attorney; and insured-attorney), the package is often labeled a "tripartite relationship."

The actual defense is undertaken, of course, not by the insurer but by the attorney. When one attempts to answer the question "has the insurer fulfilled its duty to defend," one necessarily looks at the attorney's performance. It does not follow, however, from the conclusion that the attorney has fulfilled her duty to the insured that the insurer has fulfilled its contractual duty to the insured. If, for example, the attorney's authority were limited in the retainer agreement between insurer and insured, the attorney might fulfill all of her obligations to the insurer, but this performance might not be enough to discharge the insurer's duty to the insured. Although the nuances of the tripartite relationship are often unclear in practical application, it would seem that the insured could consent to be represented by appointed counsel without conceding that this appointment fulfills all of the insurer's obligations under the duty to defend. All of this raises difficult issues for the attorney; the most important of these are examined in the next subsection.

2. *Are* Gray *and* Burd *distinguishable?* In both *Gray* and *Burd,* the insured and insurer disagreed over whether the alleged claim was within the coverage. In both cases, the insurer argued that undertaking the defense in those circumstances would create an unacceptable conflict of interest. In each case, the court had a different resolution to the conflict. Can you explain how the

resolutions differ? Are these differing resolutions attributable to different conceptions of the insurer's duty to defend, or are the outcomes attributable to other differences between the two cases?

3. *The implications of* Burd. In *Hartford Accident & Indemnity Co. v. Aetna Life & Casualty Insurance Co.,* 98 N.J. 18, 483 A.2d 402 (1984), the New Jersey Supreme Court reaffirmed *Burd* in a per curiam opinion that quoted and endorsed substantially all of an unpublished Appellate Division decision holding that an insurer is "not only within its rights in refusing to take over the defense" in a conflict situation but is "in fact obligated to follow that course once it denied coverage." 483 A.2d at 407. In a footnote, the court elaborated upon *Burd*:

> The practical effect of *Burd* is that an insured must initially assume the costs of defense itself, subject to reimbursement by the insurer if it prevails on the coverage question. It could be argued that. . .where the trial of the coverage question will simply determine which of two or more insurers must pay rather than possibly result in a finding of no coverage at all, the initial costs of defense should be borne not by the insured, as in *Burd*, but by the insurers, subject to a final allocation of that cost after trial of the coverage question. However, [in this case] the defense. . .was in fact assumed by one of the two insurers,. . .and that proceeding has now been concluded. Therefore, no question of the duty to provide interim financing of defense costs is posed in the current procedural posture of this case.

Id., at n. 3.

Did *Burd* contemplate interim financing of defense costs, or did the court in *Hartford Accident* append something to the opinion in *Burd* that was not there previously? Lower New Jersey courts are, apparently, not certain. In *Morrone v. Harleysville Mutual Insurance Co.,* 283 N.J. Super. 411, 662 A.2d 562 (1995), the court mentioned the possibility that the insurer might be required to finance the costs of defense, subject to a right of reimbursement from the insured, but then added, "Whether this or some other technique is appropriate for handling the insured's defense here is a matter that should, in the first instance, be considered by [the insured and insurer]." 662 A.2d at 421-22. The implication is that the insurer and insured should be able to work this out between themselves. Do you agree that it should be a relatively simple matter to work this out? Then, in *Sands v. CIGNA Property and Casualty Insurance Co.,* 289 N.J.Super. 344, 674 A.2d 169 (1995), the court reversed a summary judgment for an insurer, making an explicit reference to the problem that individual insureds lack the resources to finance the defense of environmental liability litigation. See 674 A.2d at 173. The court in *Trustees of Princeton University v. Aetna Casualty & Surety Co.,* 293 N.J.Super. 296, 680 A.2d 783 (1996), thought that the *Morrone* court misunderstood *Hartford* and that the *Sands* court had made no sense ("The precise holding of *Sands* is difficult to ascertain." 680 A.2d at 790.). The court in *Trustees of Princeton* thought *Burd* fairly straightforward: "[T]he practical effect of the *Burd* rule is that the insured must finance the defense, subject to possible reimbursement from the insurer, not the other way around." 680 A.2d at 789.

Wherever the New Jersey courts finally land, is it realistic to think that insureds are generally able to finance their own defenses? When courts speak of "reimbursing" defense costs, does the term "reimburse" contemplate a one-time payment when the defense is over, or a periodic payment obligation as costs are incurred? *See Village Management, Inc. v. Hartford Accident & Indemnity Co.,* 662 F. Supp. 1366 (N.D. Ill. 1987). Presumably insureds purchase liability insurance to cover eventualities, like large defense costs, that they cannot afford out of their own assets. On the other hand, if insurers advance defense costs to insureds and it is later determined that the claim against the insured was outside the coverage, is it realistic to think that insurers will be able in most situations to recoup defense costs advanced to the insured? If the last question is answered "no," one more question must be asked: is it more unfair to make the entire pool of insureds absorb the additional costs (and hence increased premiums) of providing defenses for noncovered or excluded claims?

4. *A right to reimbursement for costs incurred in defending noncovered claims?* The preceding note suggests the possibility that the insurer which has doubts about coverage but opts to defend under a reservation of rights might later be entitled to reimbursement of defense costs if it is subsequently determined that the claim against the insured was in fact outside the coverage. The common wisdom, at least until recently, has been that an insurer which defends under a reservation of rights is only reserving the right to contest coverage and disclaim the indemnity obligation, but not to recoup litigation costs. *See, e.g., Terra Nova Insurance Co. v.* 900 Bar, Inc., 887 F.2d 1213 (3d Cir. 1989).

If the policy explicitly allows recoupment, is there any reason why the insurer should not be allowed to do so? What if the policy is silent on the issue, but the reservation of rights letter advises the insured that the insurer may seek such reimbursement later? Is the insured's agreement with the terms of the reservation necessary? If so, what if the insured does not agree? What if the insured is silent in response to the reservation of rights letter? *See First Federal Savings & Loan Ass'n v. Transamerica Title Insurance Co.,* 793 F. Supp. 265 (D. Colo. 1992).

Recent cases are divided on the insurer's right to reimbursement of defense costs. In *Buss v. Superior Court,* 939 P.2d 766 (Cal. 1997), the Supreme Court of California held that when an insurer is obligated to defend a mixed action (i.e., an action which alleges both covered and noncovered claims), the insurer is entitled to reimbursement of defense costs incurred in defending noncovered claims, but not in defending potentially covered (and, of course, covered) claims. The court concluded that this result was required by the substantive law of restitution. 939 P.2d at 775-77. The Eighth Circuit, applying Missouri law, held in *Liberty Mutual Insurance Co. v. FAG Bearings Corp.,* 153 F.3d 919 (8th Cir. 1998), that the insurer was not entitled to reimbursement, but the sole allegation in the plaintiff's complaint in the underlying action appeared to be potentially covered, which means *FAG Bearings* is consistent with *Buss.* More recently, however, the Wyoming Supreme Court rejected *Buss* and the reasoning that the law of restitution authorizes the insurer to obtain reimbursement of the costs of defending covered claims. *See Shoshone First*

Bank v. Pacific Employers Insurance Co., 2 P.3d 510 (Wyo. 2000). For more discussion, see Robert H. Jerry, II, *The Insurer's Right to Reimbursement of Defense Costs*, 42 Ariz. L. Rev. 13 (2000); Douglas R. Richmond, *Reimbursing Insurers' Defense Costs: Restitution and Mixed Actions*, 35 San Diego L. Rev. 457 (1998).

5. *Other kinds of conflicts.* The situation presented in *Gray* and *Burd* is not the only kind of conflict that can arise between insured and insurer. How should the following situations be resolved? (For more examples, see Douglas R. Richmond, *Emerging Conflicts of Interest in Insurance Defense Practice*, 32 Tort & Ins. L. J. 69 (1996).)

a. Suppose the insured, who operates a business, negligently injures one of its key customers, who then sues the insured for damages. The insured desires that the insurer settle the claim in order to protect the business relationship the insured has with its customer. The insurer believes the claim is meritless and should be vigorously defended. *See Charter Oak Fire Insurance Co. v. Color Converting Industrial Co.*, 45 F.3d 1170 (7th Cir. 1995).

b. Suppose the insured, a prominent local politician, negligently injures a third party, who sues the insured. Fearing that the adverse publicity will cause her to lose an election she is contesting and otherwise damage her reputation, the insured desires a quick, confidential settlement. The insurer believes the claim is meritless and should be vigorously defended. Cf. *Gibson v. Western Fire Insurance Co.*, 210 Mont. 267, 682 P.2d 725 (1984) (involving physician-insured).

c. Suppose Ron, the insured, is a law student who shares an off-campus apartment with three others. The students car-pool to school, and take turns providing transportation in their own vehicles. One day while Ron is driving, the four have a particularly spirited discussion of the parol evidence rule. Ron becomes distracted and runs a red light; the car is broad-sided, and all four suffer injury. The three passengers sue Ron for negligence. Ron feels guilty about the accident, and is not particularly interested in the insurer's position that the three passengers were not seriously injured, as they allege. *See Dietz v. Hardware Dealers Mutual Fire Insurance Co.*, 276 N.W.2d 808 (Wis. 1979).

d. Suppose a thief steals the insured's car; while driving it away, the thief hits a pedestrian, who is injured. The thief is insolvent, and the insured's auto policy provides no coverage in this instance. (Why?) Pedestrian sues insured under the insured's homeowners policy under the novel theory of "negligent storage of an automobile." Insured desires that a settlement offer by pedestrian be accepted to make the case go away. The insurer wishes to vigorously defend the suit for the purpose of establishing a precedent that the theory of "negligent storage of an automobile" is meritless.

6. *The independent counsel alternative.* In most cases, the plaintiff's claim against the insured will be within the policy limits, and the insurer will have no basis for contesting coverage. In the stereotypical case, the insured is happy to have the insurer providing the defense; indeed, the less the insured can be bothered with the litigation, the better. But not all cases play out so neatly. What if the insured comes to think that counsel appointed by the insurer, who has the insurer as a co-client, will not be able to conduct the defense

impartially? What if the insurer stands to gain a substantial benefit if the insured's interests are not zealously protected in the underlying litigation? It is unquestioned that where there is a conflict of interest between the insurer and insured, the insurer's duty to defend can be satisfied by providing an independent attorney (or by permitting the insured to select one) and paying for the cost of the defense. *Brohawn v. Transamerica Insurance Co.*, 276 Md. 396, 347 A.2d 842 (1975).

The more difficult question is whether an insurer is *required* to follow this course when a conflict arises. Stated otherwise, the question is whether the insurer can fulfill its duty to defend by doing less. The clear weight of recent authority holds that when an irreconcilable conflict arises, the insurer must appoint or allow the insured to select independent counsel whose expenses will be paid by the insurer. *See, e.g., Allstate Insurance Co. v. Campbell*, 639 A.2d 652 (Md. 1994); *White Mountain Construction Co. v. Transamerica Insurance Co.*, 137 N.H. 478, 631 A.2d 987 (1993); *Patrons Mutual Insurance Ass'n v. Harmon*, 240 Kan. 707, 732 P.2d 741 (1987). If the insurer defends under a reservation of rights, is this by itself enough to raise a conflict? *See CHI of Alaska, Inc. v. Employers Reinsurance Corp.*, 844 P.2d 1113 (Alaska 1993) (when insurer defends under reservation of rights, insured has right to independent counsel); *Delmonte v. State Farm Fire and Casualty Co.*, 90 Haw. 39, 975 P.2d 1159, 1172 (1999) (sending reservation of rights letter does not, by itself, require appointment of independent counsel); *Moeller v. American Guarantee and Liability Insurance Co.*, 707 So. 2d 1062 (Miss. 1996) (when defending under reservation, insured must be given opportunity to select independent counsel, with reasonable legal fees to be paid by the insurer). See also 1 Allan D. Windt, Insurance Claims and Disputes § 4.22 (3d ed. 1995).

California has addressed this issue through legislation that defines the respective rights of the liability insurer and the insured when a conflict of interest arises regarding the duty to defend. *See* Cal. Civil Code § 2860 (West 1993). This statute was the California legislature's response to and limitation of a controversial California intermediate appellate court decision which held that whenever there is a potential conflict of interest, it is not sufficient for the insurer to defend the insured under a reservation of rights; instead, the insured is entitled to independent counsel. *See San Diego Federal Credit Union v. Cumis Insurance Society, Inc.*, 162 Cal. App. 3d 358, 208 Cal. Rptr. 494 (1984). The independent counsel required by the *Cumis* decision were labeled "*Cumis*-counsel."

Suppose one accepts the court's reasoning in *Burd* and then insists that the insurer finance on an on-going basis the cost of the defense. Is this tantamount to endorsing the independent counsel alternative?

7. *"Defense-within-limits" policies.* During the 1980s, there was talk of making the defense costs incurred by the insurer subject to the policy limits. A few such policies have been issued by some insurers more recently. A "defense-within-limits" (or "DWL") policy can be structured in different ways, but one formulation would have each dollar of defense costs incurred reduce the coverage available for paying any settlement or judgment by one dollar. Could the inclusion of defense costs within the policy limits of a liability insurance policy produce a conflict of interest situation? See Shaun M. Baldwin, *Legal*

and Ethical Considerations for "Defense Within Limits" Policies, 61 Def. Couns. J. 89 (1994); Daniel Dorsch, *Insurance Defense Costs and the Legal Defense Cost Containment Program: Is the Free Ride Over?,* 53 Ins. Couns. J. 580 (1986).

[4] The Responsibilities of Insurance Defense Counsel

MONTANEZ v. IRIZARRY-RODRIGUEZ

273 N.J. Super. 276, 641 A.2d 1079 (N.J. Super. Ct. App. Div. 1994)

KEEFE, J.A.D.

The principal question presented by this appeal is whether an attorney, assigned by an insurance company to defend an insured in a civil case arising out of a motor vehicle accident, may impeach the insured's credibility on the ground that the attorney was surprised by the insured's testimony. We hold that the attorney may not do so; that his conduct was prejudicial to his client; and that the trial judge's error in permitting the attorney to do so had the capacity to affect the outcome of the trial. Thus, the matter is remanded for a new trial.

Plaintiff, Angelina Montanez, an attorney and wife of defendant Santos Irizarry-Rodriguez, was a passenger in her husband's vehicle on January 23, 1988 when it left the roadway and struck a utility pole.

Plaintiff brought suit against her husband, Cataldi Buick Dealership, General Motors Company, and several John Doe defendants. The complaint, filed by her partner and brother Teofilo Montanez, alleged that the vehicle "sustained a blow-out of a tire[.]" As to Irizarry-Rodriguez, plaintiff alleged that he was careless and negligent in the operation of the vehicle so as to cause it to leave the roadway. The remaining defendants' liability was based upon an alleged defect in the tire. The product liability claims were dismissed prior to trial either voluntarily or by way of summary judgment. Thus, the matter proceeded against Irizarry-Rodriguez on the negligence claim against him.

The matter was tried on all issues. Plaintiff and one of her treating physicians testified at the trial. After plaintiff rested her case, defense counsel called his client Irizarry-Rodriguez as a witness. Defendant, who expressed some difficulty with the English language, testified through an interpreter.

After establishing that the accident happened on the same road that his wife had previously described in her testimony, the following colloquy took place between defense counsel and defendant:

Q: Okay. Around the time the accident happened, did you hear any unusual sounds around your car?

A: Yes.

Q: What did you hear?

A: A small explosion.

Q: Okay. And where did the small explosion seem to be coming from?

A: I can't say for sure, because at the time of the explosion, I was already in the woods.

Q: Did you hear any sounds while you were on Moss Mill Road that were unusual to you?

A: No.

Defense counsel then approached sidebar; announced to the judge that he was "surprised" by his client's testimony; and requested that he be permitted to treat his client as a "hostile witness." Counsel advised the judge that he intended to ask his client questions "pertaining to his bias in this case."

Defense counsel initially advised the judge that "outside this courtroom" defendant told him that the blow-out had occurred on the roadway, whereas his testimony indicated that he did not hear the "explosion" until he was "already in the woods." Defense counsel also represented that his client had given "an oral statement which was recorded," that the statement was given to a representative of the insurance company, and that he might seek leave to call the insurance representative as a "rebuttal" witness. Later, defense counsel advised the judge that he had met with his client prior to trial in his office and had interviewed him with the assistance of an interpreter. He revealed that he had tape-recorded that interview.

The trial judge, accepting at face value counsel's "representation" that defendant's testimony varied from the version he had given the attorney and insurer at an earlier time, permitted defense counsel to treat defendant as a hostile witness over plaintiff's objection.

Thereafter, defense counsel launched into an examination of defendant in a manner that no reasonable person could interpret as being other than an attack on his client's credibility. The questioning focused on the meeting defense counsel had with defendant in his office. The lengthy examination consisted mainly of leading questions by defense counsel testing defendant's recollection of certain topics counsel allegedly discussed with him during the meeting. The following is a brief example of the nature of the inquiry:

Q: Do you remember telling me at the time we met in my office that the explosion that you heard was a loud explosion, do you remember comparing it to a truck backfiring?

The witness: Yes.

. . . .

Q: Okay. Today you said it was a small explosion. In my office you said it was a loud explosion. Why did you give a different answer today?

. . . .

Q: Do you remember telling me in my office that you didn't think this accident was your fault at all?

A: No.

Q: Do you remember telling me that you wanted your wife to get as much money as possible?

A: No.

. . . .

Q: At any time in my office during our interview did you tell me that you were not paying attention when you were driving?

A: Yes.

Q: And at any time in my office did you tell me that you thought this accident was your fault?

A: Yes.

Q: Ask him if he knows what the penalty of perjury is?

A: No, I don't know what punishment or penalty.

Q: Does he understand that—do you understand that is a crime?

A: No.

Q: Ask if—would you like to change any of your answers that you've given up till now?

A: For example, the answers I am giving are the answers I know and the answers I have tried to give, it's an answer to a question he just asked me, that he said to me, that I had said that I would like that my wife would get some money out of her case. She is my wife and she is the one who has suffered all of the injuries. When I said that I wanted my wife to get some money at least to make herself better was because he said to me, my lawyer said to me—

Defense Counsel: Your honor, I'm going to make an objection. I don't think that's responsive to the question.

The Witness: Please, then why wouldn't he—he let me answer the question?

Defense Counsel: Because he's not answering the question.

The Court: Well–

The Witness: I'm just in English too much, but this is a free country.

During the above examination defense counsel apparently placed a tape recorder on the counsel table. Although the jury was never specifically advised that a tape recording of the office interview had been made, that fact was fairly implied by the tape recorder's presence during the examination.

At the end of defendant's direct examination, plaintiff's counsel requested permission to listen to the tape recording of the interview in order to ascertain whether defendant had made statements to his attorney prior to trial that were inconsistent with defendant's proposed trial testimony. Ironically, defense counsel, who had just attacked his client's credibility in front of the jury, denied the request, claiming the attorney-client privilege, with the further irrelevant objection that "[d]iscovery is long over." The judge denied the request and also denied plaintiff's motion for a mistrial.

In summation, defense counsel advised the jury that he had a client who was not "crazy about me as his lawyer[,]" but it was an issue that should not concern them. Thereafter, counsel told the jury that defendant "wants to lose this case and wants his wife to win the case." He admitted that one of his purposes in examining defendant was "to show inconsistencies in testimony he gave here with things he said in the past when he was not here." Finally, although admitting that it was "pretty unusual" for a lawyer to attack his client and that he was "uncomfortable" doing it, he justified his conduct by stating, "that's my job, I had to do it[,]" because defendant "was not credible."

The jury found that defendant was not negligent in response to special interrogatories. Thereafter, a judgment was entered in favor of defendant from which plaintiff now appeals.

On appeal, plaintiff maintained in her brief that the trial judge erred in failing to conduct an Evid. R. 8 (now N.J.R.E. 104) hearing in order to determine whether defendant was in fact a hostile witness. Plaintiff also contended that the trial judge erred by admitting the content of defendant's prior statement as substantive evidence when it did not meet the requirements of Evid. R. 63(1)(a) (now N.J.R.E. 803(a)). Defendant contended in his brief that the prior contradictory statement was not admitted into evidence under Evid. R. 63(1)(a), but, rather, defendant's credibility was impeached pursuant to Evid. R. 20 (now N.J.R.E. 607 and 803(a)(2)).

It became obvious to us upon reviewing the parties' briefs that defense counsel had no reason to impeach his client's testimony were it not for his unexpressed concern that the testimony was going to be harmful to the interests of the insurer who had appointed him to defend the matter. Because neither brief addressed the issue of whether assigned insurance counsel may impeach the credibility of the insured-client when in the course of trial a conflict arises between the client's interests and the interests of the insurer, we asked the attorneys to address the following questions in supplemental briefs:

> If the attorney's primary duty is to his client (the defendant) may he ethically launch into an impeachment of his client's testimony in order to protect the interests of the insurer? Is there an alternative course of action that would protect his client's interest?

In response to our inquiry, insurance counsel defended his actions by relying on R.P.C. 1.6(b) and R.P.C. 3.3(a). In addition, counsel relied upon Evid. R. 20 and the cases of *State v. Johnson,* 216 N.J. Super. 588, 524 A.2d 826 (App. Div. 1987), and *State v. Gallicchio,* 44 N.J. 540, 210 A.2d 409 (1965). Plaintiff maintained, however, that R.P.C. 1.8(b) applies, and claimed that the fraud exception to R.P.C. 1.6 was not satisfied because defense counsel failed to make a prima facie showing of defendant's fraud. Further, plaintiff argued that Evid.R. 20 refers to the impeachment of a witness, not a client, and, in any event, the procedural requirements for neutralizing a witness's testimony set forth in *State v. Johnson, supra,* were not met.

Defendant did not address the second question we posed for supplemental briefing. Plaintiff, however, argues that defense counsel's remedy was either to withdraw from representation of the defendant, or obtain the consent of the insured to proceed notwithstanding the alleged conflict.

The issues that we presented for supplemental briefing are somewhat novel in this jurisdiction. The first question was at least partially answered some time ago by the Court of Errors and Appeals in *Crothers v. Caroselli,* 126 N.J.L. 590, 594, 20 A.2d 77 (E & A 1941). In that case, a defense attorney, who the Court surmised was probably designated by an insurance carrier to represent the defendant, was not allowed to neutralize his client's testimony.

> We hold that it is not at the hands of a party to an action, offering himself as a witness in his own behalf, to cause himself to be contradicted or his testimony neutralized, through prior, oral or written, inconsistent or contrary, statements made by him. [*Id.* at 594, 20 A.2d 77.]

Crothers represents the majority rule. *See Katz v. Ross,* 216 F.2d 880, 884-85 (3d Cir. 1954); *Newman v. Stocker,* 161 Md. 552, 157 A. 761, 763 (1932); *Gass v. Carducci,* 37 Ill. App. 2d 181, 185 N.E.2d 285, 290 (1962); *Spadaro v. Palmisano,* 109 So. 2d 418, 421-22 (Fla. App. 1959).

The rule prohibiting impeachment of an insured by counsel assigned by the insurer is based upon the practical observation that the insured's impeachment is relevant only to an issue between the insured and the insurer, and has no bearing on the only issue in the case at hand, i.e., whether the insured is liable to the plaintiff. Because the insurer is not a party to the case between the plaintiff and the insured, the question whether the insurer will be required to indemnify the insured for the insured's liability cannot be adjudicated in that litigation. See, *e.g., Newman, supra,* 157 A. at 763 ("[The insurance company's] liability to the defendant on a policy of insurance is not being adjudicated in the suit; the only adjudication possible is that upon the liability of the present defendant to the present plaintiff.").

No New Jersey court has specifically addressed the insurer's remedy in the exact context of this case. However, our Supreme Court has acknowledged the possibility of fraud and collusion in tort cases between family members and between hosts and guests, and has suggested two possible remedies for the insurer when the issue arises. The first is intervention by the insurance company in the case between the claimant and the insured, wherein the insurance company would "reveal [its] status in the case, treating the covered defendant-[insured] as a hostile witness in order to attack credibility and show that the husband and wife may be scheming to gain a recovery against the insurance company." *Merenoff v. Merenoff,* 76 N.J. 535, 554, 388 A.2d 951 (1978). The second suggested approach is a "declaratory judgment action following disclaimer. . . ." *Id.* at 555, 388 A.2d 951. However, both approaches envision a situation in which the insurance company has knowledge of the fraud or collusion in sufficient time to act by way of intervention or declaratory judgment before the trial between the claimant and the insured begins.

Merenoff did not anticipate the issue arising as it did here, during trial. Clearly, the insurance company did not have sufficient time to intervene in the subject litigation. Nonetheless, *Merenoff* cannot be read to suggest that assigned counsel for the insured should be permitted to declare a position contrary to the insured-client, and represent the insurance company's interest as if it had intervened. Those jurisdictions that have addressed how the problem should be resolved when it arises during trial have unanimously adopted the view that insurance counsel may not treat the client as a hostile witness in order to vindicate the insurance company's interest. Rather, the insurance company's remedy is by way of separate action after the liability verdict is rendered against the insured. *Katz, supra,* 216 F.2d at 884-85; *Newman, supra,* 157 A. at 763; *Gass, supra,* 185 N.E.2d at 291; *Spadaro, supra,* 109 So. 2d at 421-22. The *Newman* Court concisely stated the rationale for the rule:

> Only another party, treating this defendant as a witness, could be permitted to introduce the contradictory evidence; and the insurer is not a party in this suit, even though it may have employed counsel to defend the suit, having regard to its undertaking to indemnify the defendant. Its liability to the defendant on a policy of insurance is not being adjudicated in the suit; the only adjudication possible is that upon the liability of the present defendant to the present plaintiff. A new claim thereafter, and, if it is resisted, a new suit, would be necessary to adjudicate the liability on the policy. And it would be in that new suit that the insurer would appropriately make the defense on the ground that the insured seeks indemnity for loss from collusive agreement rather than from the liability imposed by law which is the subject of insurance, or on the ground that in violation of a term of the policy the insured has failed to co-operate in the defense, or on any other ground. [*Newman, supra,* 157 A. at 763.]

Thus, the rule that prohibits insurance counsel from impeaching the insured "does not mean that an insurance company must stand helplessly by and see its pockets looted in a case of provable collusion." *Gass, supra,* 185 N.E.2d at 291.

The preference for a separate proceeding is rooted in sound principles of attorney ethics. We acknowledge that the "triadic relationship [of] insurer, insured, and counsel" creates difficult ethical problems. *Lieberman v. Employers Ins. of Wausau,* 84 N.J. 325, 338, 419 A.2d 417 (1980). Nonetheless, it is clear that insurance counsel is required to represent the insured's interest as if the insured hired counsel directly. *Ibid.* Indeed, insurance counsel's loyalty to the insured may actually be paramount. *Ibid.* Permitting insurance counsel to impeach the credibility of an insured places counsel in a position of representing conflicting interests, and actually permits counsel to elevate the insurer's interest over the insured's. Such practice cannot be condoned. *See Williams v. Bituminous Casualty Corp.,* 51 N.J. 146, 149, 238 A.2d 177 (1968) ("An attorney, engaged by the carrier to defend in the insured's name, could not ethically seek. . .a result [which would deny coverage to the insured.]").

The majority view throughout the country is that "when the interest of the insurer and the insured differ, the insurance defense lawyer's ethical duty of undivided loyalty to the client is owed to the insured." Brooke Wunnicke, *The Eternal Triangle: Standards of Ethical Representation by the Insurance Defense Lawyer,* FOR THE DEFENSE February 1989, at 9. See R.P.C. 1.7(b) ("A lawyer shall not represent a client if the representation of that client may be materially limited by the lawyer's responsibilities to another client or to a third person, or by the lawyer's own interests[.] . . ."); *Burd v. Sussex Mutual Ins. Co.,* 56 N.J. 383, 395, 267 A.2d 7 (1970) (An insurance carrier "may not, in the insured's name, so defend as to exculpate the carrier alone.").

Nothing can be more devastating to an insured than to have his or her credibility challenged by assigned insurance counsel. In this case, defendant was left essentially defenseless to his attorney's attack on his credibility. The record discloses that defendant maintained that his testimony in the courtroom was not inconsistent with what he had told his attorney earlier. However, because he was abandoned by counsel, he was unable to advocate that position in a meaningful fashion. Without actual proof that defendant's proposed testimony at trial was, in fact, contradictory to prior statements given to the insurance company or insurance counsel, the jury was nonetheless left with the impression that defendant's attorney believed that defendant was a liar. Moreover, through his examination of defendant, defense counsel placed his own credibility above that of his client's. We conclude that

> [t]he issue of fraud and collusion injected into the trial not only intended to, but did, prejudice the [defendant] in the minds of the jury and caused its attention to be focused upon issues not covered by the pleadings. [*Spadaro, supra,* 109 So. 2d at 421–22.]

Defense counsel's reliance upon R.P.C. 1.6(b) and R.P.C. 3.3(a)(2) and (4) is misplaced. While either rule may permit the lawyer to reveal information gained through the lawyer's representation of the client in certain circumstances, neither rule requires or permits the attorney to represent a conflicting interest hostile to the client's position. The remedy for an attorney in such situations is to disclose the information the attorney believes is required by R.P.C. 1.6(b) and R.P.C. 3.3 to the court, and request permission to withdraw from the litigation pursuant to R.P.C. 1.16. See *Lieberman, supra,* 84 N.J. at 339, 419 A.2d 417 (quoting *Lieberman v. Employers Ins. of Wausau,* 171 N.J. Super. 39, 49-51, 407 A.2d 1256 (App. Div. 1979) ("[W]henever counsel in such cases has reason to believe that the discharge of his duty to the insured would conflict with the discharge of his duty to the insurance carrier, he cannot continue to represent both."). Of course, before withdrawing from representation the lawyer is obliged to give reasonable notice to the client of the grounds for withdrawal. R.P.C. 1.16(d).

In such cases, insurance counsel should ask for a recess when it becomes clear that the insured's testimony is at variance from prior statements. During the recess counsel can explain to the client the consequences of giving testimony which the attorney believes to be untrue. If the client persists in the view that the testimony about to be given is the correct version, counsel should make application to the court for permission to withdraw from representation pursuant to R.P.C. 1.16, assuming counsel's continued belief that the client's testimony is fraudulent.

The court, in turn, is then obligated to ascertain whether a true conflict exists. In such circumstances, more than the mere representation of hostility is required. If a tape recorded statement or other written statement has been given by the insured, those materials should be reviewed by the judge. Perhaps the insured's full testimony, to be given at a N.J.R.E. 104 hearing, should be taken to assist the judge in making a decision on whether a true conflict exists. If the court finds that defense counsel has been placed in a position of conflict, a mistrial must be granted. Of course, none of these procedures were followed in this case. Not even the bare minimum of showing true hostility was evidenced by this record. *See State v. Gallicchio, supra,* 44 N.J. at 547-48, 210 A.2d 409 (The trial judge should, out of the hearing of the jury, decide that there was a prior statement of the witness which is contradictory to his present testimony; that the attorney did not have prior knowledge that the witness would testify contrary to such prior statement; and that the present testimony is harmful in some way).

The judgment under review is reversed and the matter is remanded for a new trial. Present defense counsel should withdraw from the case. We take no position on what procedures should be followed by the insurance company with respect to defendant's continued representation.

NOTES

1. *What happened to the insured's duty to cooperate?* If it can be assumed that the defendant in *Montanez* told an agent of the insurer or the court a false story about the accident at least once, has the insured breached the duty to cooperate? If so, what consequences should follow? Does cooperation embrace a duty on the part of the insured to willingly submit to being impeached at trial if the insurer so instructs? Does the insurance contract between insurer and insured give a different answer than the law of professional responsibility? If so, which body of law—the contract's law or professional responsibility law—takes precedence? For a critique of *Montanez's* answers to these questions, see Charles Silver & Kent Syverud, *The Professional Responsibilities of Insurance Defense Lawyers,* 45 Duke L.J. 255 (1995). For the first part of a detailed study of defense counsel's obligations, see Ellen S. Pryor & Charles Silver, *Defense Lawyers' Professional Responsibilities: Part I — Excess Exposure Cases,* 78 Tex. L. Rev. 599 (2000).

2. *Who is (are) the client(s)?* No one seriously questions that the attorney who appears for the insured in a litigated matter has the insured for a client. But is the insurer also the attorney's client? The weight of authority considers the insurer a client of the attorney, at least at the outset of the representation. Under this view, the insurer and insured are co-clients. *See, e.g., Home Indemnity Co. v. Lane Powell Moss & Miller,* 43 F.3d 1322 (9th Cir. 1995); *The Driggs Corp. v. Pennsylvania Manufacturers' Ass'n Insurance Co.,* 3 F. Supp. 2d 657 (D. Md. 1998), *aff'd,* 181 F.3d 87 (4th Cir. 1999); *Moeller v. American Guarantee and Liability Insurance Co.,* 707 So. 2d 1062 (Miss. 1996); *Mitchum v. Hudgens,* 533 So. 2d 194 (Ala. 1988); *Houston General Insurance Co. v. Superior Court,* 108 Cal. App. 3d 958, 166 Cal. Rptr. 904 (1980).

But there is a significant minority view that concludes that the tripartite relationship (insurer, insured, and attorney) is fraught with potential conflict, and that the insured is, therefore, the sole client of defense counsel from the outset of the representation. See *In re Rules of Professional Conduct and Insurer Imposed Billing Rules and Procedures,* 2 P.3d 806 (Mont. 2000); *Atlanta International Insurance Co. v. Bell,* 475 N.W.2d 294 (Mich. 1991); *First American Carriers v. Kroger Co.,* 302 Ark. 86, 787 S.W.2d 669 (1990). For more discussion, see Charles Silver, *Does Insurance Defense Counsel Represent the Company or the Insured?,* 72 Tex. L. Rev. 1583 (1994); Pryor & Silver, supra (in note 1); Thomas D. Morgan & Charles W. Wolfram, *Lawyers Retained by Liability Carriers to Represent Insureds in the Restatment of the Law Governing Lawyers*, 6 Coverage 44 (Mar.-Apr. 1996).

Obviously, it is important to know who the client is, because it is the client to whom professional responsibilities are owed. The consequences of erring in this area can be enormous given that failure to protect a client's interests can result in liability for malpractice. *See Unigard Insurance Group v. O'Flaherty & Belgum,* 38 Cal. App. 4th 1229, 45 Cal. Rptr. 2d 565 (1995). If the insurer is not one of the defense counsel's clients and if the attorney is outside the insurer's control, does it follow that the insured cannot hold the insurer vicariously liable for the attorney's malpractice? *See State Farm Mutual Automobile Insurance Co. v. Traver,* 980 S.W.2d 625 (Tex. 1998) (insurer is not vicariously liable for malpractice of an independent attorney it selects to defend an insurer); cf. *Atlanta International Insurance Co. v. Bell,* 475 N.W.2d 294 (Mich. 1991) (even though attorney-client relationship did not exist between insurer and attorneys appointed to represent insured, insurer could maintain malpractice action against attorneys under doctrine of equitable subrogation). Does it follow that if the insurer does exercise such control, the insurer should be held vicariously liable to the insured for the attorney's malpractice?

In the preparation of the recently promulgated Restatement (Third) of the Law Governing Lawyers, the American Law Institute grappled with the "who is the client" question. The result of these efforts is reprinted at the end of these notes, and some further comments and questions appear at the end of that excerpt.

3. *Multiple clients, and potential versus actual conflicts.* Whenever an attorney represents multiple clients, there is a potential for conflict. This does not mean, however, that a conflict actually exists or will arise. Indeed, just because multiple clients have divergent interests, it does not follow that the attorney has conflicting interests. "The test is whether there is actual adversity so that the competent representation of one client dictates that the attorney contend for that client which his duty to the other client requires him to oppose. The conflict between the clients may also be recognized by its consequences, that is, the representation of one client is rendered less effective because of the representation of the interests of the other." Ronald E. Mallen & Jeffrey M. Smith, Legal Malpractice § 28.14, at 555 (4th ed. 1996).

What risks and problems can an attorney confront when she has multiple clients in the same matter? Consider the mandate of Disciplinary Rule 5-105(C):

> [A] lawyer may represent multiple clients if it is obvious that the attorney can adequately represent the interest of each and if each consents to the representation after full disclosure of the possible effect of such representation on the exercise of the attorney's independent professional judgment on behalf of each.

Ethical Consideration (EC) 5-15 states that "[a] lawyer should never represent in litigation multiple clients with different interests" and adds that few situations exist where a lawyer "would be justified in representing in litigation multiple clients with potentially differing interests." EC 5-17 identifies "insurer and insured" as a typically recurring situation where "potentially differing interests may appear," and then observes, "Whether a lawyer can fairly and adequately protect the interests of multiple clients in these and similar situations depends upon an analysis of each case." What lessons might the attorney in *Montanez* drawn from EC 5-15 and 5-17?

4. *Irreconcilable conflicts.* What if a irreconcilable conflict arises? Clearly, when an attorney who has undertaken a joint representation finds that the interests of her clients are in irreconcilable conflict, it is not possible for the attorney to ignore the conflict as if nothing has changed. If the lawyer believes the conflict is insurmountable, the lawyer cannot continue with the defense of both clients. *See Hartford Accident & Indemnity Co. v. Foster,* 528 So. 2d 255 (Miss. 1988). Beyond this observation, there is disagreement among courts and commentators. See Symposium, *Liability Insurance Conflicts and Professional Responsibility,* 4 Conn. Ins. L. J. 1-442 (1997); Douglas R. Richmond, *Lost in the Eternal Triangle of Insurance Defense Ethics,* 9 Geo. J. Legal Ethics 475 (1996); Douglas R. Richmond, *Walking a Tightrope: The Tripartite Relationship Between Insurer, Insured, and Insurance Defense Counsel,* 73 Neb. L. Rev. 265 (1994); Robert E. O'Malley, *Ethics Principles for the Insurer, the Insured, and Defense Counsel: The Eternal Triangle Reformed,* 66 Tul. L. Rev. 511 (1991); Geoffrey C. Hazard, Jr., *Triangular Lawyer Relationships: An Exploratory Analysis,* 1 Geo. J. Legal Ethics 15 (1987); John K. Morris, *Conflicts of Interest in Defending Under Liability Insurance Policies: A Proposed Solution,* 1981 Utah L. Rev. 457; Robert H. Jerry, II, Understanding Insurance Law § 114[b][2] (2d ed. 1996).

One answer is that the attorney must withdraw from the representation. *See Lieberman v. Employers Insurance of Wausau,* 419 A.2d 417 (N.J. 1980); *Employers Casualty Co. v. Tilley,* 496 S.W.2d 552 (Tex. 1973). If the attorney withdraws, must the insurer appoint independent counsel? Another answer is that the attorney then assumes a duty of undivided loyalty to the insured. In other words, it is as if the joint-representation, co-client model converts to a one-client model, where the attorney owes absolute allegiance to the insured. *See Point Pleasant Canoe Rental, Inc. v. Tinicum Township,* 110 F.R.D. 166, 170 (E.D. Pa. 1986) ("When conflicts-of-interest arise between an insurance carrier and its insured, the lawyer representing the insured must act exclusively on behalf of, and in the best interests of the insured"); *CHI of Alaska, Inc. v. Employers Reinsurance Corp.,* 844 P.2d 1113, 1117 (Alaska 1993); *Hartford Accident and Indemnity Co. v. Foster,* 528 So. 2d 255, 270 (Miss. 1988); Illinois Advisory Op. 92-02 (1992); Michigan Ethics Op. RI-89 (1991). See generally Charles W. Wolfram, Modern Legal Ethics § 8.4.2 (1986).

5. *Other "lesser" conflicts.* If the lawyer believes the conflict is not insurmountable, can the lawyer continue with the joint representation if the insured consents? Some argue that consent is always required, because dual representation in the insurance context always involves a potential conflict that triggers the need for informed consent before the representation begins. See Stephen L. Pepper, *Applying the Fundamentals of Lawyers' Ethics to Insurance Defense Practice,* 4 Conn. Ins. L. J. 27, 31-41 (1997). Others argue that there is ample opportunity to address potential conflicts at a later time,

and that consent prior to the undertaking of the representation is not routinely needed. See William T. Barker, *Insurance Defense Ethics and the Liability Insurance Bargain*, 4 Conn. Ins. L. J. 75, 87–88 (1997). What if the insured withholds consent?

Determining whether there is a conflict — and then determining whether it is irreconcilable — can itself be a knotty problem, as the materials in the previous subsection indicated. Is the better course for the attorney to err on the side of the insured's interests? How feasible is this answer when the insurer pays the attorney's bills?

Would it be simpler and fairer to have a rule that the attorney appointed by the insurer owes her primary obligation to the insured for all purposes, and that the attorney appointed by the insurer must act against the interests of the insurer whenever the insured's interests differ? What are the advantages and disadvantages of this approach?

6. *Who pays the bill? Who calls the shots? Why should anyone care?* What problems are created if someone other than the client pays the lawyer's bill? MRPC 1.8(f) provides:

> A lawyer shall not accept compensation for representing a client from one other than the client unless:
>
> (1) the client consents after consultation;
>
> (2) there is no interference with the lawyer's independence of professional judgment or with the client-lawyer relationship; and
>
> (3) information relating to the representation of a client is protected as required by rule 1.6.

Clearly, the rule applies to one-client situations where someone else pays the bill. But does the rule apply *only* to that situation? Or does the rule speak more broadly, i.e., does it apply to joint-client or multiple-client representations where one of the clients pays the bill for the others?

If the insured is defense counsel's sole client, is it ethically possible for an insurer to exercise prior approval over counsel's decisions to schedule depositions, retain experts, prepare motions, or conduct research? See *In re Rules of Professional Conduct and Insurer Imposed Billing Rules and Procedures*, 2 P.3d 806 (Mont. 2000); Kent D. Syverud, *The Ethics of Insurer Litigation Management Guidelines and Legal Audits*, 21 Ins. Lit. Rptr. 180 (1999); Douglas R. Richmond, *The Business and Ethics of Liability Insurers' Efforts to Manage Legal Care*, 27 U. Mem. L. Rev. 57 (1997). Do you perceive an analogous issue in the area of health insurance? Are your views about utilization review in health insurance consistent with your views about the relationship between insurer and defense counsel? Need they be?

7. *Staff or "in-house" counsel.* Is there any reason for concern if the insurer uses in-house staff counsel (i.e., employees) to represent insureds? Is there any functional difference between in-house staff counsel and an insurer retaining an outside firm, which has no other clients and relies on the insurer for 100 percent of its billings, to do all of its defense work? *Compare Cincinnati Insurance Co. v. Wills*, 717 N.E.2d 151 (Ind. 1999), *Petition of Youngblood*, 895 S.W.2d 322 (Tenn. 1995), and *In re Allstate Insurance Co.*, 722 S.W.2d

947 (Mo. 1987), with *American Insurance Ass'n v. Kentucky Bar Ass'n,* 917 S.W.2d 568 (Ky. 1996).

8. *Confidential communications.* If the insurer pays the cost of the defense, does this give the insurer an entitlement to communications between the insured and insurer that would otherwise be protected by the attorney-client privilege? The answer depends on the answer to the "who is a client" question. If the insurer is not a client, the lawyer may not reveal confidential information provided by the insured unless the insured authorizes the disclosure. See Model Rules of Professional Conduct 1.6(a) (1994). If the insurer is a co-client with the insured, the insured's communications within the scope of the joint representation are protected from disclosure to third parties, but are not protected from disclosure to the insurer. See Restatement (Third) of The Law Governing Lawyers § 75 (2000); *Goldberg v. American Home Assurance Co.,* 80 A.D.2d 409, 413 (N.Y. App. Div. 1981). If the insured's communications to the lawyer are outside the scope of the joint representation, is the insurer entitled to them?

If an insured, concerned about the loyalty of the attorney appointed by the insurer to provide the defense, retains his or her own separate counsel, are the communications between the insured and separate counsel discoverable by the insurer? Is the work-product of the insured's separately retained counsel discoverable by the insurer?

9. *Subsequent garnishment actions.* Suppose appointed counsel, in the course of providing a defense to the insured in the underlying action, acquires information that tends to establish a defense for the insurer on the question of coverage. Can the same attorney represent the insurer in a subsequent garnishment action brought by the successful plaintiffs in the underlying action? What should the attorney do with the information? If the attorney handles the information improperly, what are the ramifications for the insurer? Does it lose coverage defenses? *See Parsons v. Continental National American Group,* 113 Ariz. 223, 550 P.2d 94 (1976).

10. *Limiting the scope of the attorney's obligations.* Can the insurer limit the scope of the representation that the designated attorney is to provide the insured? For example, can the insurer preclude the attorney from providing advice to the insured on coverage and claims against other insureds? Can the insurer preclude the attorney from advising the insured on settlement offers and settlement negotiations? Is this technique a good way to avoid conflicts of interest?

RESTATEMENT (THIRD) OF THE LAW
GOVERNING LAWYERS (2000)*

§ 134. Compensation or Direction of a Lawyer by a Third Person

(1) A lawyer may not represent a client if someone other than the client will wholly or partly compensate the lawyer for the representation, unless the client consents under the limitations and conditions provided in § 122** and knows of the circumstances and conditions of the payment.

(2) A lawyer's professional conduct on behalf of a client may be directed by someone other than the client if:

(a) the direction does not interfere with the lawyer's independence of professional judgment;

(b) the direction is reasonable in scope and character, such as by reflecting obligations borne by the person directing the lawyer; and

(c) the client consents to the direction under the limitations and conditions provided in § 122.

Comment:

a. Scope and cross-references. This Section applies the general conflicts prohibition of § 121*** to the various situations in which a third person pays a lawyer's fee for representing a client or directs a lawyer's work for a client. The third person might be interested as a relative or friend or have obligations to the client because of indemnification or similar arrangements, or be interested directly in the matter because of a co-client, such as a corporation

---

* Copyright © 2000 by the American Law Institute. Reprinted with permission.

** [Editors' note: Section 122, titled "Client Consent to a Conflict of Interest," provides:

(1) A lawyer may represent a client notwithstanding a conflict of interest prohibited by § 121 if each affected client or former client gives informed consent to the lawyer's representation. Informed consent requires that the client or former client have reasonably adequate information about the material risks of such representation to that client or former client.

(2) Notwithstanding the informed consent of each affected client or former client, a lawyer may not represent a client if:

(a) the representation is prohibited by law;

(b) one client will assert a claim against the other in the same litigation; or

(c) in the circumstances, it is not reasonably likely that the lawyer will be able to provide adequate representation to one or more of the clients.]

*** [Editors' note: Section 121, titled "Basic Prohibition of Conflicts of Interest," provides:

Unless all affected clients and other necessary persons consent to the representation under the limitations and conditions provided in § 122, a lawyer may not represent a client if the representation would involve a conflict of interest. A conflict of interest is involved if there is a substantial risk that the lawyer's representation of the client would be materially and adversely affected by the lawyer's own interests or by the lawyer's duties to another current client, a former client, or a third person.]

sued along with one or more of its employees (see § 131, Comment *e*). The risk of adverse effect on representation of the client is inherent in any such payment or direction. Accordingly, this Section, following the standard rule of the lawyer codes, requires informed consent of the client and imposes limitations on the control that a third person may exercise over the lawyer's work.

While discussion in the following Comments (see Comment *f*) will consider issues of the law governing a lawyer representing an insured person, the relationship between the insured person and the insurer or indemnitor will be controlled by other law, such as the law of insurance or of contract. . . . Issues relating to all such other relationships are beyond the scope of the Restatement.

. . . .

b. Initial client consent. As stated in the Section, under § 122 a client must consent to a lawyer's accepting either a third person's payment of the fee for a client or a third person's direction in a matter. In particular, the client must have knowledge of the circumstances and conditions under which the fee payment or direction is to be provided and any substantial risks to the client thereby created (see § 122, Comment *c*). On consent in insurance-defense representations, see Comment *f* hereto. In an emergency situation in which the lawyer must take action to protect the interests of the client, as in filing an answer to avoid default, the lawyer may take such action even if a conflict appears to exist, but must also promptly take action to address the conflict.

c. Third-person fee payment. This Section accommodates two values implicated by third-person payment of legal fees. First, it requires that a lawyer's loyalty to the client not be compromised by the third-person source of payment. The lawyer's duty of loyalty is to the client alone, although it may also extend to any co-client when that relationship is either consistent with the duty owing to each co-client or is consented to in accordance with § 122. Second, however, the Section acknowledges that it is often in the client's interest to have legal representation paid for by another. Most liability-insurance contracts, for example, provide that the insurer will provide legal representation for an insured who is charged with responsibility for harm to another (see also Comment *f* hereto). . . .

d. Third-person direction of representation. The principle that a lawyer must exercise independent professional judgment on behalf of the client (Subsection (2)(a)) is reflected in the requirement of the lawyer codes that no third person control or direct a lawyer's professional judgment on behalf of a client. Consistent with that requirement, a third person may, with the client's consent and otherwise in the circumstances and to the extent stated in Subsection (2), direct the lawyer's representation of the client. When the conditions of the Subsection are satisfied, the client has, in effect, transferred to the designated third person the client's prerogatives of directing the lawyer's activities (see § 21(2)). The third person's directions must allow for effective representation of the client, and the client must give informed consent to the exercise of the power of direction by the third person. The direction must be reasonable in scope and character, such as by reflecting obligations borne by the person directing the lawyer. Such directions are reasonable in scope and character if, for example, the third party will pay any judgment rendered against the client and makes a decision that defense costs beyond those designated by the third party would not significantly change the likely outcome. Informed client consent may be effective with respect to many forms of direction, ranging from informed consent to particular instances of direction, such as in a representation in which the client otherwise directs the lawyer, to informed consent to general direction of the lawyer by another, such as an insurer or indemnitor on whom the client has contractually conferred the power of direction (see Comment *f*).

. . . .

Just as there are limits to client consent in § 122, there are limits to the restrictions on scope of the representation permitted under this Section. See § 122, Comment *g* (nonconsentable conflicts).

. . . .

e. Preserving confidential client information. Although a legal fee may be paid or direction given by a third person, a lawyer must protect the confidential information of the client. Informed client consent to the third-person payment or direction does not by itself constitute informed consent to the lawyer' revealing such information to that person. Consent to reveal confidential client information must meet the separate requirements of § 62.

. . . .

f. Representing an insured. A lawyer might be designated by an insurer to represent the insured under a liability-insurance policy in which the insurer undertakes to indemnify the insured and to provide a defense. The law governing the relationship between the insured and the insurer is, as stated in Comment *a*, beyond the scope of the Restatement. Certain practices of designated insurance-defense counsel have become customary and, in any event, involve primarily standardized protection afforded by a regulated entity in recurring situations. Thus a particular practice permissible for counsel representing an insured may not be permissible under this Section for a lawyer in noninsurance arrangements with significantly different characteristics.

It is clear in an insurance situation that a lawyer designated to defend the insured has a client-lawyer relationship with the insured. The insurer is not, simply by the fact that it designates the lawyer, a client of the lawyer. Whether a client-lawyer relationship also exists between the lawyer and the insurer is determined under § 14.**** Whether or not such a relationship exists, communications between the lawyer and representatives of the insurer concerning such matters as progress reports, case evaluations, and settlement

---

**** [Editors' note: Section 14, titled "Formation of a Client-Lawyer Relationship," provides:

A relationship of client and lawyer arises when:

(1) a person manifests to a lawyer the person's intent that the lawyer provide legal services for the person; and either

  (a) the lawyer manifests to the person consent to do so; or

  (b) the lawyer fails to manifest lack of consent to do so, and the lawyer knows or reasonably should know that the person reasonably relies on the lawyer to provide the services; or

(2) a tribunal with power to do so appoints the lawyer to provide the services.]

should be regarded as privileged and otherwise immune from discovery by the claimant or another party to the proceeding. Similarly, communications between counsel retained by an insurer to coordinate the efforts of multiple counsel for insureds in multiple suits and such coordinating counsel are subject to the privilege. Because and to the extent that the insurer is directly concerned in the matter financially, the insurer should be accorded standing to assert a claim for appropriate relief from the lawyer for financial loss proximately caused by professional negligence or other wrongful act of the lawyer. Compare § 51, Comment *g*.

The lawyer's acceptance of direction from the insurer is considered in Subsection (2) and Comment *d* hereto. With respect to client consent (see Comment *b* hereto) in insurance representations, when there appears to be no substantial risk that a claim against a client-insured will not be fully covered by an insurance policy pursuant to which the lawyer is appointed and is to be paid, consent in the form of the acquiescence of the client-insured to an informative letter to the client-insured at the outset of the representation should be all that is required. The lawyer should either withdraw or consult with the client-insured (see § 122) when a substantial risk that the client-insured will not be fully covered becomes apparent (see § 121, Comment *c(iii)*).

Illustration:

5. Insurer, a liability-insurance company, has issued a policy to Policyholder under which Insurer is to provide a defense and otherwise insure Policyholder against claims covered under the insurance policy. A suit filed against Policyholder alleges that Policyholder is liable for a covered act and for an amount within the policy's monetary limits. Pursuant to the policy's terms, Insurer designates Lawyer to defend Policyholder. Lawyer believes that doubling the number of depositions taken, at a cost of $5,000, would somewhat increase Policyholder's chances of prevailing and Lawyer so informs Insurer and Policyholder. If the insurance contract confers authority on Insurer to make such decisions about expense of defense, and Lawyer reasonably believes that the additional depositions can be forgone without violating the duty of competent representation owed by Lawyer to Policyholder (see § 52), Lawyer may comply with Insurer's direction that taking depositions would not be worth the cost.

Material divergence of interest might exist between a liability insurer and an insured, for example, when a claim substantially in excess of policy limits is asserted against an insured. If the lawyer knows or should be aware of such an excess claim, the lawyer may not follow directions of the insurer if doing so would put the insured at significantly increased risk of liability in excess of the policy coverage. Such occasions for conflict may exist at the outset of the representation or may be created by events that occur thereafter. The lawyer must address a conflict whenever presented. To the extent that such a conflict is subject to client consent (see § 122(2)(c)), the lawyer may proceed after obtaining client consent under the limitations and conditions stated in § 122.

When there is a question whether a claim against the insured is within the coverage of the policy, a lawyer designated to defend the insured may not reveal adverse confidential client information of the insured to the insurer concerning that question (see § 60) without explicit informed consent of the insured (see § 62). That follows whether or not the lawyer also represents the insurer as co-client and whether or not the insurer has asserted a "reservation of rights" with respect to its defense of the insured (compare § 60, Comment *l* (confidentiality in representation of co-clients in general)).

With respect to events or information that create a conflict of interest between insured and insurer, the lawyer must proceed in the best interests of the insured, consistent with the lawyer's duty not to assist client fraud (see § 94) and, if applicable, consistent with the lawyer's duties to the insurer as co-client (see § 60, Comment *l*). If the designated lawyer finds it impossible so to proceed, the lawyer must withdraw from representation of both clients as provided in § 32 (see also § 60, Comment *l*). The designated lawyer may be precluded by duties to the insurer from providing advice and other legal services to the insured concerning such matters as coverage under the policy, claims against other persons insured by the same insurer, and the advisability of asserting other claims against the insurer. In such instances, the lawyer must inform the insured in an adequate and timely manner of the limitation on the scope of the lawyer's services and the importance of obtaining assistance of other counsel with respect to such matters. Liability of the insurer with respect to such matters is regulated under statutory and common-law rules such as those governing liability for bad-faith refusal to defend or settle. Those rules are beyond the scope of this Restatement (see Comment *a* hereto).

. . . .

NOTES

1. *The history of comment f.* Comment f had a rather tortured drafting history, as demonstrated by the commentary on the section as it was prepared and discussions in the American Law Institute. At the 1996 annual meeting of the membership of the ALI, section 215, the predecessor to section 134, was one of only two sections of the proposed Restatement (Third) that was not approved. After revisions and much debate, the section was approved at the 1998 annual meeting. For a summary of this history by a lawyer who was an active participant in the debate on behalf of the insurance industry, see William T. Barker, *The Tripartite Relationship: Who is the Client and To Whom Does the Attorney Owe Ethical Duties?*, 20 Ins. Lit. Rptr. 729 (1998). To get a flavor of the debate, see the various articles in Symposium, *Liability Insurance Conflicts and Professional Responsibility*, 4 Conn. Ins. L. J. 1-442 (1997), which discuss the issues and cite to various pieces that were written contemporaneously with the debate over what became section 134.

2. *How and when does the insured give consent?* As a general rule, a client must give informed consent if her attorney is going to represent another person in the same matter. Professors Silver and Syverud observe that "[b]ecause attorney-client relationships arise consensually, whether defense counsel has one client or two depends upon the agreement that counsel enters into when retained." Charles Silver & Kent Syverud, *The Professional Responsibilities of Insurance Defense Lawyers*, 45 Duke L.J. 255, 274 (1995). If the

insured must consent to a dual client relationship, when is this consent given? At the time the insured purchases liability insurance? *See Brohawn v. Transamerica Insurance Co.,* 347 A.2d 842 (Md. 1975). If the consent is given when the insured contracts for the coverage, is this consent sufficiently "informed"? Or is it necessary whenever the attorney undertakes the representation to inform the insured that the attorney also has duties to the insurer by virtue of an attorney-client relationship with that party also? American Bar Association Formal Ethics Opinion 96-403 (1996) makes the following point: "We cannot assume that the insured understands or remembers, if he ever read, the insurance policy, or that the insured understands that his lawyer will be acting on his behalf, but at the direction of the insurer without further consultation with the insured." *Id.* at 406.

It seems prudent — and, many would argue, essential under the professional responsibility requirements — for defense counsel to take steps to inform the insured at the outset of the representation about the nature of the representation and to secure the insured's consent. This position was endorsed in Opinion 96-403: "If the lawyer is to proceed with the representation of the insured at the direction of the insurer, the lawyer must make appropriate disclosure sufficient to apprise the insured of the limited nature of his representation as well as the insurer's right to control the defense in accordance with the terms of the insurance contract." *Id.* at 405. How is this to be done? "A short letter clearly stating that the lawyer intends to proceed at the direction of the insurer in accordance with the terms of the insurance contract and what this means to the insured is sufficient to satisfy the requirements of Rule 1.2 in this context. . . . The insured manifests consent to the limited representation by accepting the defense offered by the insurer after being advised by the terms of the representation being offered." *Id.* at 406. Thus, whatever the insurer communicates to the insured, defense counsel's responsibilities to the insured will be defined by the retainer agreement between defense counsel and policyholder.

Should the answer to the question "how does the insured consent" depend on the amount of risk to the insured, meaning that if the claim against the insured is covered by the insurance policy and is less than the policy limits, the consent provided in the insurance policy is adequate, but if the insured has a personal exposure beyond the policy's coverage or limits, more formal consent is required? As the materials in this section suggest, whether the insured's consent is sufficiently informed can be a more difficult question when the plaintiff's complaint against the insured alleges both covered and non-covered claims, or if the insurer is defending under a reservation of right to contest coverage at a later time or to seek reimbursement of defense costs for defending noncovered claims. Should the insured's consent be more "specific" in such cases, as distinguished from the more typical case where there is no contest about coverage and the plaintiff's claim is within the policy limits? See generally Charles Silver & Kent Syverud, *supra,* at 313-31 (1995).

3. *The relationship between rules of professional conduct and the contract between insurer and insured.* Opinion 96-403 stressed that when a dispute arises between the insured and the insurer over how to respond to a plaintiff's settlement offer, defense counsel's responsibilities are controlled by the

lawyer's professional duties, not by the contract between insurer and insured. The opinion specifically stated that such a dispute may require defense counsel's withdrawal; thereafter, the lawyer would be precluded from helping the insurer reach a settlement to which the insured objects by virtue of the "former-client" conflict rule. See *id.* at 5-6.

4. *Did the ALI get it right?* As Professor Nancy Moore has written, "the legal doctrine concerning the ethics of third-party representation is very much in its infancy and. . .neither the judiciary nor the profession itself has seriously confronted some of the important dilemmas commonly presented when a lawyer is paid or otherwise provided by a non-client third party. These dilemmas include the sharing of otherwise confidential information, the ability of the third-party payer to direct at least some aspects of the representation, and questions concerning the 'non-contestability' of some instances of third-party representation." Nancy J. Moore, *Ethical Issues in Third-Party Payment: Beyond the Insurance Defense Paradigm*, 16 Rev. Litig. 585, 588 (1997). Some think that the whole issue is a tempest in a teapot; one lawyer writes, "[a]s everyone knows, this is a hotly debated topic. Frankly, I can't see why." Michael Sean Quinn, *Whom Does the Insurance Defense Lawyer Represent?*, ALI/ABA Continuing Legal Educ., SE64 ALI-ABA 171, 174 (2000). The Montana Supreme Court recently declined to endorse the new Restatement provision: "We decline to recognize a vast exception to the Rules of Professional Conduct that would sanction relationships colored with the appearance of impropriety in order to accommodate the asserted economic exigencies of the insurance market." *In re Rules of Professional Conduct and Insurer Imposed Billing Rules and Procedures*, 2 P.3d 806, 814 (Mont. 2000). Noting that the Restatement section was not yet officially published, the court declined "to join the parties' arguments over the Restatement . . . . More importantly, we are in no way bound by the Restatement in interpreting Montana's Rules of Professional Conduct." *Id.* at 814.

5. *Comparing the Model Rules of Professional Conduct.* How does section 134 square with the Model Rules of Professional Conduct? MRPC 1.2(a) provides that "[a] lawyer shall abide by a client's decisions concerning the objectives of representation, subject to paragraphs (c), (d) and (e), and shall consult with the client as to the means by which they are to be pursued. A lawyer shall abide by a client's decision whether to accept an offer of settlement of a matter. . . .," and MRPC1.2(c) states that "[a] lawyer may limit the objectives of the representation if the client consents after consultation."

What if the lawyer has clients with adverse interests, but the lawyer "reasonably believes the representation will not be adversely affected" and the clients consent after full disclosure? MRPC 1.7 is the "general conflict" rule:

> (a) A lawyer shall not represent a client if the representation of that client will be directly adverse to another client, unless:
>
> > (1) the lawyer reasonably believes the representation will not adversely affect the relationship with the other client; and
>
> > (2) each client consents after consultation.
>
> (b) A lawyer shall not represent a client if the representation of that client may be materially limited by the lawyer's responsibilities to

another client or to a third person, or by the lawyer's own interests, unless:

(1) the lawyer reasonably believes the representation will not be adversely affected; and

(2) the client consents after consultation. When representation of multiple clients in a single matter is undertaken, the consultation shall include explanation of the implications of the common representation and the advantages and risks involved.

Does MRPC 1.7 bless most situations where the attorney appointed by the insurer represents both insured and insurer? If the clients consent, is that enough? See Geoffrey C. Hazard, Jr. & W. William Hodes, The Law of Lawyering: A Handbook on the Model Rules of Professional Conduct § 1.7:301, at 246.1 (1994).

[5] Settlement Obligations

CRISCI v. SECURITY INSURANCE CO.
66 Cal. 2d 425, 426 P.2d 173, 58 Cal. Rptr. 13 (1967)

PETERS, JUSTICE.

In an action against The Security Insurance Company of New Haven, Connecticut, the trial court awarded Rosina Crisci $91,000 (plus interest) because she suffered a judgment in a personal injury action after Security, her insurer, refused to settle the claim. Mrs. Crisci was also awarded $25,000 for mental suffering. Security has appealed.

June DiMare and her husband were tenants in an apartment building owned by Rosina Crisci. Mrs. DiMare was descending the apartment's outside wooden staircase when a tread gave way. She fell through the resulting opening up to her waist and was left hanging 15 feet above the ground. Mrs. DiMare suffered physical injuries and developed a very severe psychosis. In a suit brought against Mrs. Crisci the DiMares alleged that the step broke because Mrs. Crisci was negligent in inspecting and maintaining the stairs. They contended that Mrs. DiMare's mental condition was caused by the accident, and they asked for $400,000 as compensation for physical and mental injuries and medical expenses.

Mrs. Crisci had $10,000 of insurance coverage under a general liability policy issued by Security. The policy obligated Security to defend the suit against Mrs. Crisci and authorized the company to make any settlement it deemed expedient. Security hired an experienced lawyer, Mr. Healy, to handle the case. Both he and defendant's claims manager believed that unless evidence was discovered showing that Mrs. DiMare had a prior mental illness, a jury would probably find that the accident precipitated Mrs. DiMare's psychosis. And both men believed that if the jury felt that the fall triggered the psychosis, a verdict of not less than $100,000 would be returned.

An extensive search turned up no evidence that Mrs. DiMare had any prior mental abnormality. As a teenager Mrs. DiMare had been in a Washington mental hospital, but only to have an abortion. Both Mrs. DiMare and Mrs. Crisci found psychiatrists who would testify that the accident caused Mrs. DiMare's illness, and the insurance company knew of this testimony. Among those who felt the psychosis was not related to the accident were the doctors at the state mental hospital where Mrs. DiMare had been committed following the accident. All the psychiatrists agreed, however, that a psychosis could be triggered by a sudden fear of falling to one's death.

The exact chronology of settlement offers is not established by the record. However, by the time the DiMares' attorney reduced his settlement demands to $10,000, Security had doctors prepared to support its position and was only willing to pay $3,000 for Mrs. DiMare's physical injuries. Security was unwilling to pay one cent for the possibility of a plaintiff's verdict on the mental illness issue. This conclusion was based on the assumption that the jury would believe all of the defendant's psychiatric evidence and none of the plaintiff's. Security also rejected a $9,000 settlement demand at a time when Mrs. Crisci offered to pay $2,500 of the settlement.

A jury awarded Mrs. DiMare $100,000 and her husband $1,000. After an appeal (*DiMare v. Cresci,*[1] 58 Cal. 2d 292, 23 Cal. Rptr. 772, 373 P.2d 860) the insurance company paid $10,000 of this amount, the amount of its policy. The DiMares then sought to collect the balance from Mrs. Crisci. A settlement was arranged by which the DiMares received $22,000, a 40 percent interest in Mrs. Crisci's claim to a particular piece of property, and an assignment of Mrs. Crisci's cause of action against Security. Mrs. Crisci, an immigrant widow of 70, became indigent. She worked as a babysitter, and her grandchildren paid her rent. The change in her financial condition was accompanied by a decline in physical health, hysteria, and suicide attempts. Mrs. Crisci then brought this action.

The liability of an insurer in excess of its policy limits for failure to accept a settlement offer within those limits was considered by this court in *Comunale v. Traders & General Ins. Co.,* 50 Cal. 2d 654, 328 P.2d 198, 68 A.L.R.2d 883. It was there reasoned that in every contract, including policies of insurance, there is an implied covenant of good faith and fair dealing that neither party will do anything which will injure the right of the other to receive the benefits of the agreement; that it is common knowledge that one of the usual methods by which an insured receives protection under a liability insurance policy is by settlement of claims without litigation; that the implied obligation of good faith and fair dealing requires the insurer to settle in an appropriate case although the express terms of the policy do not impose the duty; that in determining whether to settle the insurer must give the interests of the insured at least as much consideration as it gives to its own interests; and that when "there is great risk of a recovery beyond the policy limits so that the most reasonable manner of disposing of the claim is a settlement which can be made within those limits, a consideration in good faith of the insured's interest requires the insurer to settle the claim." (50 Cal. 2d at p. 659, 328 P.2d at p. 201.)

In determining whether an insurer has given consideration to the interests of the insured, the test is whether a prudent insurer without policy limits would have accepted the settlement offer.

---

[1] In the prior litigation plaintiff was sued as "Rosina Cresci."

Several cases, in considering the liability of the insurer, contain language to the effect that bad faith is the equivalent of dishonesty, fraud, and concealment. Obviously a showing that the insurer has been guilty of actual dishonesty, fraud, or concealment is relevant to the determination whether it has given consideration to the insured's interest in considering a settlement offer within the policy limits. The language used in the cases, however, should not be understood as meaning that in the absence of evidence establishing actual dishonesty, fraud, or concealment no recovery may be had for a judgment in excess of the policy limits. *Comunale v. Traders & General Ins. Co., supra,* 50 Cal. 2d 654, 658-659, 328 P.2d 198, makes it clear that liability based [on] an implied covenant exists whenever the insurer refuses to settle in an appropriate case and that liability may exist when the insurer unwarrantedly refuses an offered settlement where the most reasonable manner of disposing of the claim is by accepting the settlement. Liability is imposed not for a bad faith breach of the contract but for failure to meet the duty to accept reasonable settlements, a duty included within the implied covenant of good faith and fair dealing. Moreover, examination of [our prior opinions indicating that bad faith is the equivalent of dishonesty, fraud, and concealment] makes it abundantly clear that recovery may be based on unwarranted rejection of a reasonable settlement offer and that the absence of evidence, circumstantial or direct, showing actual dishonesty, fraud, or concealment is not fatal to the cause of action.

Amicus curiae argues that, whenever an insurer receives an offer to settle within the policy limits and rejects it, the insurer should be liable in every case for the amount of any final judgment whether or not within the policy limits. As we have seen, the duty of the insurer to consider the insured's interest in settlement offers within the policy limits arises from an implied covenant in the contract, and ordinarily contract duties are strictly enforced and not subject to a standard of reasonableness. Obviously, it will always be in the insured's interest to settle within the policy limits when there is any danger, however slight, of a judgment in excess of those limits. Accordingly the rejection of a settlement within the limits where there is any danger of a judgment in excess of the limits can be justified, if at all, only on the basis of interests of the insurer, and, in light of the common knowledge that settlement is one of the usual methods by which an insured receives protection under a liability policy, it may not be unreasonable for an insured who purchases a policy with limits to believe that a sum of money equal to the limits is available and will be used so as to avoid liability on his part with regard to any covered accident. In view of such expectation an insurer should not be permitted to further its own interests by rejecting opportunities to settle within the policy limits unless it is also willing to absorb losses which may result from its failure to settle.

The proposed rule is a simple one to apply and avoids the burdens of a determination whether a settlement offer within the policy limits was reasonable. The proposed rule would also eliminate the danger that an insurer, faced with a settlement offer at or near the policy limits, will reject it and gamble with the insured's money to further its own interests. Moreover, it is not entirely clear that the proposed rule would place a burden on insurers substantially greater than that which is present under existing law. The size of the judgment recovered in the personal injury action when it exceeds the policy limits, although not conclusive, furnishes an inference that the value of the claim is the equivalent of the amount of the judgment and that acceptance of an offer within those limits was the most reasonable method of dealing with the claim.

Finally, and most importantly, there is more than a small amount of elementary justice in a rule that would require that, in this situation where the insurer's and insured's interests necessarily conflict, the insurer, which may reap the benefits of its determination not to settle, should also suffer the detriments of its decision. On the basis of these and other considerations, a number of commentators have urged that the insurer should be liable for any resulting judgment where it refuses to settle within the policy limits.

We need not, however, here determine whether there might be some countervailing considerations precluding adoption of the proposed rule because, under *Comunale v. Traders & General Ins. Co., supra,* 50 Cal. 2d 654, 328 P.2d 198, and the cases following it, the evidence is clearly sufficient to support the determination that Security breached its duty to consider the interests of Mrs. Crisci in proposed settlements. Both Security's attorney and its claims manager agreed that if Mrs. DiMare won an award for her psychosis, that award would be at least $100,000. Security attempts to justify its rejection of a settlement by contending that it believed Mrs. DiMare had no chance of winning on the mental suffering issue. That belief in the circumstances present could be found to be unreasonable. Security was putting blind faith in the power of its psychiatrists to convince the jury when it knew that the accident could have caused the psychosis, that its agents had told it that without evidence of prior mental defects a jury was likely to believe the fall precipitated the psychosis, and that Mrs. DiMare had reputable psychiatrists on her side. Further, the company had been told by a psychiatrist that in a group of 24 psychiatrists, 12 could be found to support each side.

The trial court found that defendant "knew that there was a considerable risk of substantial recovery beyond said policy limits" and that "the defendant did not give as much consideration to the financial interests of its said insured as it gave to its own interests." That is all that was required. The award of $91,000 must therefore be affirmed.

We must next determine the propriety of the award to Mrs. Crisci of $25,000 for her mental suffering. In *Comunale v. Traders & General Ins. Co., supra,* 50 Cal. 2d 654, 663, 328 P.2d 198, 203, it was held that an action of the type involved here sounds in both contract and tort and that "where a case sounds both in contract and tort the plaintiff will ordinarily have freedom of election between an action of tort and one of contract. An exception to this rule is made in suits for personal injury caused by negligence, where the tort character of the action is considered to prevail [citations], but no such exception is applied in cases, like the present one, which relate to financial damage [citations]."[2]

---

[2] *Comunale v. Traders & General Ins. Co., supra,* 50 Cal. 2d 654, 328 P.2d 198, was mainly concerned with the contract aspect of the action. This may be due to the facts that the tort duty is ordinarily based on the insurer's assumption of the defense and of settlement negotiations (see Keeton, Liability Insurance and Responsibility for Settlement (1954) 67 Harv. L. Rev. 1136, 1138-1139; Note (1966), *supra,* 18 Stan. L.

Although this rule was applied in *Comunale* with regard to a statute of limitations, the rule is also applicable in determining liability. Insofar as language in *Critz v. Farmers Ins. Group, supra,* 230 Cal. App. 2d 788, 799, 41 Cal. Rptr. 401, might be interpreted as providing that the action for wrongful refusal to settle sounds solely in contract, it is disapproved.

Fundamental in our jurisprudence is the principle that for every wrong there is a remedy and that an injured party should be compensated for all damage proximately caused by the wrongdoer. Although we recognize exceptions from these fundamental principles, no departure should be sanctioned unless there is a strong necessity therefor.

The general rule of damages in tort is that the injured party may recover for all detriment caused whether it could have been anticipated or not. In accordance with the general rule, it is settled in this state that mental suffering constitutes an aggravation of damages when it naturally ensues from the act complained of, and in this connection mental suffering includes nervousness, grief, anxiety, worry, shock, humiliation and indignity as well as physical pain. The commonest example of the award of damages for mental suffering in addition to other damages is probably where the plaintiff suffers personal injuries in addition to mental distress as a result of either negligent or intentional misconduct by the defendant. Such awards are not confined to cases where the mental suffering award was in addition to an award for personal injuries; damages for mental distress have also been awarded in cases where the tortious conduct was an interference with property rights without any personal injuries apart from the mental distress.

We are satisfied that a plaintiff who as a result of a defendant's tortious conduct loses his property and suffers mental distress may recover not only for the pecuniary loss but also for his mental distress. No substantial reason exists to distinguish the cases which have permitted recovery for mental distress in actions for invasion of property rights. The principal reason for limiting recovery of damages for mental distress is that to permit recovery of such damages would open the door to fictitious claims, to recovery for mere bad manners, and to litigation in the field of trivialities. (Prosser, Torts (3d ed. 1964) § 11, p. 43.) Obviously, where, as here, the claim is actionable and has resulted in substantial damages apart from those due to mental distress, the danger of fictitious claims is reduced, and we are not here concerned with mere bad manners or trivialities but tortious conduct resulting in substantial invasions of clearly protected interests.[3]

Recovery of damages for mental suffering in the instant case does not mean that in every case of breach of contract the injured party may recover such damages. Here the breach also constitutes a tort. Moreover, plaintiff did not seek by the contract involved here to obtain a commercial advantage but to

Rev. 475), and that in Comunale the insurer did not undertake defense or settlement but denied coverage. In any event Comunale expressly recognizes that "wrongful refusal to settle has generally been treated as a tort." (50 Cal. 2d at p. 663, 328 P.2d at p. 203.)

[3] Nor are we here concerned with the problem whether invasion of the plaintiff's right to be free from emotional disturbance is actionable where there is no injury to person or property rights in addition to the inflicted mental distress. (*Cf. Amaya v. Home Ice, Fuel & Supply Co.,* 59 Cal. 2d 295, 29 Cal. Rptr. 33, 379 P.2d 513.)

protect herself against the risks of accidental losses, including the mental distress which might follow from the losses. Among the considerations in purchasing liability insurance, as insurers are well aware, is the peace of mind and security it will provide in the event of an accidental loss, and recovery of damages for mental suffering has been permitted for breach of contracts which directly concern the comfort, happiness or personal esteem of one of the parties.

It is not claimed that plaintiff's mental distress was not caused by defendant's refusal to settle or that the damages awarded were excessive in the light of plaintiff's substantial suffering.

The judgment is affirmed.

TRAYNOR, C. J., and McCOMB, TOBRINER, MOSK and BURKE, JJ., concur.

NOTES

1. *Privilege or duty to settle?* "Liability insurance policies routinely create a contractual duty to defend, but do not by their terms create a duty to settle. Instead, the typical language reserves to the insurer a privilege to settle, or not to settle, as the insurer in the exercise of its discretion sees fit." Robert H. Jerry, II, Understanding Insurance Law § 112, at 761 (2d ed. 1996). For typical language, see the policies in Appendices B and C. The discretion afforded insurers to settle claims by the policy language is considerable; this privilege may extend to permitting the insurer to settle claims without obtaining the insured's consent. *See Caplan v. Fellheimer Eichen Braverman & Kaskey,* 68 F.3d 828 (3d Cir. 1995). Should the insurer have this discretion if the claim is entirely within the deductible? *See, e.g., Shuster v. South Broward Hospital District Physicians' Professional Liability Insurance Trust,* 591 So. 2d 174 (Fla. 1992); *Western Polymer Technology, Inc. v. Reliance Insurance Co.,* 38 Cal. Rptr. 2d 78 (Cal. Ct. App. 1995). What if most, but not all, of the claim is within the deductible? *See United Capitol Insurance Co. v. Bartolotta's Fireworks Co.,* 546 N.W.2d 198 (Wis. Ct. App. 1996) (insurer decides to settle claim for $35,000 in circumstances where deductible is $25,000).

"Notwithstanding the expansive language [in typical liability forms] establishing the insurer's privilege to settle, the insurer's discretion is limited in substantial ways by court-made rules. . . . Although the insurer is entitled to exercise its own judgment, it owes an obligation to the insured to exercise good faith and to maintain a due regard for the insured's interests. Because these obligations may require an insurer in some situations to respond to a settlement offer affirmatively, it is often said that the insurer owes the insured a 'duty to settle.'" Jerry, *supra,* § 113, at 761. The seminal article on the liability insurer's duties regarding settlement is Robert E. Keeton, *Liability Insurance and Responsibility for Settlement,* 67 Harv. L. Rev. 1136 (1954). For a more recent discussion, see Kent Syverud, *The Duty to Settle,* 76 Va. L. Rev. 1113 (1990).

2. *Insured's settlement without insurer's consent.* Ordinarily, the standard liability policy prohibits the insured from settling any claims, voluntarily

assuming a liability, or interfering in a legal proceeding or settlement negotiation without the insurer's consent. Why are insurers interested in imposing such constraints on insureds?

Suppose an insurer is defending an insured under a reservation of rights, and the insured has retained his or her own separate counsel. If the insured, through his or her own separate counsel, settles with the tort victim without the insurer's consent, does this action breach the cooperation clause of the policy? If so, should the insurer be bound by the settlement as to the basis of liability or the amount of the settlement? *See United Services Automobile Ass'n v. Morris*, 154 Ariz. 113, 741 P.2d 246 (1987).

3. *Strict liability for refusal to settle within policy limits?* The duty to settle is not absolute. In other words, an insurer need not respond affirmatively to each and every settlement offer made by a plaintiff. Whether an insurer should be strictly liable for failing to accept offers within policy limits presents a more difficult question. The *Crisci* court did not decide the question; even though no court has adopted such a rule, it continues to be discussed as a possibility. *See Rova Farms Resort, Inc. v. Investor Insurance Co. of Am.*, 65 N.J. 474, 501-02, 323 A.2d 495, 509-10 (1974); *Johansen v. California State Automobile Association Inter-Insurance Bureau*, 538 P.2d 744 (Cal. 1975). In *Asermely v. Allstate Insurance Co.*, 728 A.2d 461 (R.I. 1999), the Supreme Court of Rhode Island approved the following "new rule": "If the insurer declines to settle the case within the policy limits, it does so at its peril in the event that a trial results in a judgment that exceeds the policy limits, including interest. If such a judgment is sustained on appeal or is unappealed, the insurer is liable for the amount that exceeds the policy limits, unless it can show that the insured was unwilling to accept the offer of settlement. The insurer's duty is a fiduciary obligation to act in the best interests of the insured." 728 A.2d at 464. Is the Rhode Island test the functional equivalent of a strict liability rule?

Suppose plaintiff sues insured for a claim covered by a $250,000 liability insurance policy. Plaintiff asserts damages of $300,000. The insurer values the claim at $25,000; the plaintiff offers to settle the claim for $200,000. What considerations are important to the insurer's assessment of whether this offer should be accepted? If the insurer refuses the offer and the case is tried, what are the ramifications of each of the following jury verdicts under a strict liability rule? (a) $15,000; (b) $25,000; (c) $200,000; (d) $300,000.

4. *The "reasonable offer test."* If the duty to settle is not absolute and a strict liability rule is rejected, there is still a need to articulate a standard which distinguishes between settlement offers that must be accepted and offers which can be rejected. Some courts have evoked tort concepts to define this standard, and have ruled that an insurer must respond to settlement offers with "due care." *See, e.g., Maine Bonding v. Centennial Insurance Co.*, 298 Or. 514, 693 P.2d 1296 (1985); *Gray v. Nationwide Mutual Insurance Co.*, 422 Pa. 500, 223 A.2d 8 (1966). As *Crisci* indicates, many courts have approved a "good faith" standard, often pairing it with references to "due care."

Although the terminology of due care and good faith is familiar, the terms themselves have minimal substantive content; more meaning needs to be poured into the ideas. For example, what exactly does "good faith" require? Is it the opposite of "bad faith?" One court addressed the problem in this way:

> Good faith requires the insurer, in handling negotiations for settlement, to treat the conflicting interests of itself and the insured with impartiality, giving equal consideration to both interests. With respect to settlement and trial, an insurance company must, in the exercise of good faith, act as if there were no policy limits applicable to the claim and as if the risk of loss was entirely its own. Bad faith is normally demonstrated by proving that the risks of unfavorable results were out of proportion to the chances of a favorable outcome.

Eastham v. Oregon Automobile Insurance Co., 273 Or. 600, 607, 540 P.2d 364, 367, *rehearing denied,* 273 Or. 610, 542 P.2d 895 (1975).

Are the following elaborations functionally dissimilar, and, if so, how? (a) the test approved in *Crisci*; (b) the insurer must give "equal consideration" to the insured's interests (*see Dairyland Insurance Co. v. Herman,* 124 N.M. 624, 954 P.2d 56 (1997)); (c) the insurer must give "paramount weight" to the insured's interests, even at the expense of its own (*see Lieberman v. Employers Insurance,* 419 A.2d 417 (N.J. 1980)); (d) "an insurer must accept any offer within the limits of coverage that a reasonable party responsible for the entire amount of any subsequent judgment would accept" (quoting Kenneth S. Abraham, Distributing Risk: Insurance, Legal Theory, and Public Policy 191-92 (1986)).

What is the difference between the reasonable offer test and the strict liability test? The reasonable offer test contemplates that an insurer can permissibly reject some settlement offers, and will not necessarily be liable for doing so even if a judgment in excess of the settlement offer (or even the policy limits) is subsequently entered. The strict liability test gives a different answer in some of these situations. Would it not be better, however, to avoid the costs associated with litigating the question of "reasonableness" by favoring a per se rule like that provided by the strict liability alternative?

Whatever test one favors, is the insurer obligated during settlement negotiations to take into account interests of the insured that are not within the policy's coverage? For example, if the insured faces an exposure for punitive damages, must the insurer take this into account in assessing whether it is reasonable to arrange for a settlement within policy limits? If the insured's reputation (an interest not specifically covered by liability insurance) would be damaged by protracted litigation, must the insurer take this into account in deciding whether to accept a settlement offer? *See St. Paul Fire and Marine Insurance Co. v. Convalescent Services, Inc.,* 193 F.3d 340 (5th Cir. 1999) (applying Texas law, holding that insurer in context of settlement negotiations need not consider claims specifically excluded from coverage). If your answer to the foregoing questions is "no," why then is the insurer required to take into account the insured's possible exposure to an excess judgment?

5. *Conflicts revisited.* The potential for disagreement between insurer and insured on settlement is significant. How should the following situations be resolved?

a. Suppose a third party sues the insured for $1 million in damages; the insured's policy limits are $100,000. The third party offers to settle the suit for $95,000. The insured desires that the settlement offer be accepted. The insurer contends that the third party's chances of winning the suit at trial are less than 5 percent, and wants to try the case.

b. Suppose a third party sues a physician for malpractice, alleging $50,000 in damages. The physician's policy has policy limits of $100,000, but the policy contains a per-claim deductible of $5,000. The physician feels strongly that she was not negligent and that the third party was not damaged. The third party offers to settle the claim for $6,000, and the insurer wants to accept this settlement. The physician wants to try the case.

In his classic article on settlement, Judge Robert Keeton (then-Professor Keeton) observed that defense counsel *cannot* represent the insured in settlement; consequently, an insured cannot sue the attorney who negligently advises the insurer to reject a settlement offer. Robert E. Keeton, *Liability Insurance and Responsibility for Settlement*, 67 Harv. L. Rev. 1136, 1169 (1954). Do you agree? *See Hartford Accident & Indemnity Co. v. Foster*, 528 So. 2d 255, 271 (Miss. 1988); *Rogers v. Robson, Masters, Ryan, Brumund & Belom*, 392 N.E.2d 1365 (Ill. App. Ct. 1979), *aff'd*, 407 N.E.2d 47 (Ill. 1980).

6. *Tort or contract (or both)?* Consider what the court in *Crisci* says about the nature of the claim for breach of the duty to settle. Is the duty to settle simply a subset of the duty to defend, in that settling claims is simply one way insurers defend lawsuits against insureds? For courts that use a "due care" or "reasonableness" standard to evaluate whether the insurer has breached the duty to settle, it is perhaps easy to see why the breach of the duty can be said to "sound" in tort, particularly given that the typical liability insurance policy lacks a specific contractual provision imposing the duty.

If the duty to settle comes from the implied obligation of good faith and fair dealing, does it follow that the duty to settle is a tort-based duty? The Restatement (Second) of Contracts § 205 provides that every party to a contract owes the other a duty of good faith and fair dealing in contract performance. If the duty of good faith is a contract duty, does it not follow that a breach of the duty to settle is a contract breach? Is it possible for an insurer to "fail to exercise good faith in responding to a settlement offer" without committing the "tort of bad faith"? (The tort of bad faith receives more attention in § 8.03.) Why does it matter whether the theory of the action is tort or contract?

7. *The $91,000 question.* Whether the theory of Mrs. Crisci's action was tort or contract, once the breach of the duty to settle was found, the insurer was liable for the amount of the judgment against Mrs. Crisci above the policy limits. Why?

If a portion of the judgment above the policy limits had been an award for punitive damages, should the insurer have been responsible for this amount as well? *See PPG Industries, Inc. v. Transamerica Insurance Co.*, 20 Cal. 4th 310, 975 P.2d 652, 84 Cal. Rptr. 2d 455 (1999); *Lira v. Shelter Insurance Co.*, 913 P.2d 514 (Colo. 1996). Does it matter whether the theory of the action is tort or contract?

Suppose the theory of the action for breach of the duty to settle sounds in tort. After the excess judgment is entered, the insurer voluntarily pays the entire amount of the excess judgment. Does this payment then insulate the insurer from a claim that the insurer exercised bad faith in refusing to settle? See David R. Anderson & John W. Dunfee, *No Harm, No Foul: Why a Bad Faith Claim Should Fail When an Insurer Pays the Excess Verdict*, 33 Tort & Ins. L. J. 1001 (1998).

8. *Damages for mental anguish.* Normally, contract law does not award damages for mental anguish. But contract law has long recognized special, exceptional classes of contracts where emotional distress damages can be awarded for the breach of contract, under the reasoning that in these kinds of contracts it is foreseeable at the time of contracting that mental distress will accompany a breach. *See, e.g., Flores v. Baca,* 117 N.M. 306, 871 P.2d 962 (1994); *Wilson v. Houston Funeral Home,* 42 Cal. App. 4th 1124, 50 Cal. Rptr. 2d 169 (1996). Are insurance contracts more like contracts to bury the dead, or more like contracts for the sale of soy beans for future delivery? By allowing Mrs. Crisci to recover in tort, will insurers in the future be inclined to settle claims against insureds for more than the claims are worth, with the consequence that premiums paid by insureds for insurance coverage will increase above optimal levels?

Is all of this a tempest in a teapot? Consider Professor Abraham's insight: "The prospect that liability for noneconomic loss would routinely be imposed in duty-to-settle cases. . .has not materialized. There are only a handful of reported cases in which such liability has been imposed, both around the country and in California itself. The norm in duty-to-settle cases has tended to be an award of economic loss only, measured by the amount of the judgment in excess of policy limits rendered against the policyholder." Kenneth S. Abraham, *The Natural History of the Insurer's Liability for Bad Faith,* 72 Tex. L. Rev. 1295, 1302 (1994). How might one explain the relative paucity of awards for extracontractual, noneconomic loss in duty-to-settle cases? See John H. Bauman, *Emotional Distress Damages and the Tort of Insurance Bad Faith*, 46 Drake L. Rev. 717, 746-49 (1998).

9. *Mechanics of handling settlement offers.* Suppose the plaintiff offers to settle the claim within or at the policy limits. How should the insurer respond? Does the answer change if the insured must pay a deductible? Are the attorney's responsibilities different than the insurer's? *See Rogers v. Robson, Masters, Ryan, Brumund & Belom,* 392 N.E.2d 1365 (Ill. App. Ct. 1979), *aff'd,* 407 N.E.2d 47 (Ill. 1980). At a minimum, the insurer and attorney should keep the insured informed of settlement offers and the progress of negotiations. *See Murach v. Massachusetts Bonding & Insurance Co.,* 339 Mass. 184, 158 N.E.2d 338 (1959). There is authority that the insurer is obligated to take steps to clarify an ambiguous offer from the plaintiff. *See Prosser v. Lueck,* 225 Wis.2d 126, 592 N.W.2d 178 (1999).

When the settlement offer exceeds the policy limits, the problem becomes more complex. At a minimum, the insurer, and the attorney appointed to defend the insured, should take several steps: (a) try (unless obviously futile) to get the settlement offer reduced, as this would benefit the insured; (b) take reasonable steps to determine the facts upon which a decision whether or not to settle can be reached; (c) as noted above, keep the insured informed of any settlement offers received and the progress of settlement negotiations. At the time of the appointment, the insured should have been apprised of the possibility of a liability exceeding policy limits and the insurer's potentially conflicting interest; if this becomes apparent for the first time at the time of the settlement offer, this appraisal should occur at this time. *See Tank v. State Farm & Casualty Co.,* 715 P.2d 1133 (Wash. 1986).

When the insured is sued for a sum in excess of the policy limits, and the insurer and appointed attorney undertake to inform the insured of the insurer's potentially conflicting interest, exactly what should be said to the insured? How would you draft the letter? *See Hartford Accident & Indemnity Co. v. Foster,* 528 So. 2d 255 (Miss. 1988).

10. *Settlement and multiple plaintiffs/multiple claims.* A liability insurer may settle with some claimants in a multiple claims situation even though such settlements deplete or exhaust the policy limits of liability so that the remaining claimants have little or no recourse against the insurer. However, the insurer must act in good faith. *Castoreno v. Western Indemnity Co.,* 213 Kan. 103, 515 P.2d 789 (1973). How would you define the insurer's obligation in such a situation? Where there is a bad faith, discriminatory payment, the insurer may be liable for amounts in excess of the policy limits. *See Hartford Casualty Insurance Co. v. Dodd,* 416 F. Supp. 1216 (D. Md. 1976).

11. *A duty to initiate settlement discussions?* If the plaintiff-tort victim never makes an offer to settle within the policy limits or any offer at all, does this mean that the liability insurer has no obligation to conduct settlement negotiations? *See Coleman v. Holecek,* 542 F.2d 532 (10th Cir. 1976) (applying Kansas law) and *Fulton v. Woodford,* 26 Ariz. App. 17, 545 P.2d 979 (1976). See generally Cindie Keegan McMahon, Annotation, *Duty of Liability Insurer to Initiate Settlement Negotiations,* 51 A.L.R.5th 701 (1997).

[6] Remedying a Breach of the Duty to Defend

NEWHOUSE v. CITIZENS SECURITY MUTUAL INSURANCE CO.
76 Wis. 2d 824, 501 N.W.2d 1 (1993)

WILCOX, JUSTICE.

[The circuit court entered a summary judgment to the insured's assignees; the court concluded that Citizens Security Mutual Insurance Co. (Citizens) breached its duty to defend its insured, Floyd Omann. The judgment awarded Omann's assignees, Robert C. Newhouse and his parents, over $724,000, which represented the amount of a judgment in excess of the policy limits in the Newhouses' underlying personal injury action.

The court of appeals affirmed in part and reversed in part. *Newhouse v. Citizens Security Mut. Ins. Co.,* 170 Wis. 2d 456, 489 N.W.2d 639 (Ct. App. 1992) (*Newhouse II*). In a prior appeal arising out of the underlying personal injury action, the court of appeals held that Floyd Omann had coverage under a homeowners liability policy issued by Citizens with limits of $50,000. *Newhouse v. Laidig, Inc.,* 145 Wis. 2d 236, 426 N.W.2d 88 (Ct. App. 1988) (*Newhouse I*), rev. den. 145 Wis. 2d 912, 428 N.W.2d 559 (1988).

In this action, the Newhouses seek review of that portion of the court of appeals' decision reversing the circuit court's judgment awarding them the full amount of the excess judgment against Omann.] The court of appeals held that the measure of damages for breach of the insurer's duty to defend is the policy limits plus interest together with costs and attorney fees in defending the suit. . . .

The parties raise the following issues for our review: (1) Did Citizens Security Mutual Insurance Company breach a contractual duty to defend its insured, Floyd Omann? (2) What is the proper measure of damages for breach of an insurer's duty to defend? (3) Did the circuit court properly dismiss the Newhouses' tort claims against Citizens? . . . .

We conclude that: (1) Citizens breached its duty to defend its insured, Floyd Omann; (2) a party aggrieved by an insurer's breach of its duty to defend is entitled to recover all damages naturally flowing from the breach; (3) Newhouses' tort claims against Citizens were properly dismissed on summary judgment; . . . .

It is an understatement to describe the facts and procedural history of this case as complex. Fortunately, the facts are undisputed. The present lawsuit is the aftermath of a negligence action brought by Robert Newhouse for injuries he sustained in a tragic farm accident. On October 14, 1983, four-year-old Robert Newhouse was seriously injured when he became entangled in a silo unloader while under the care of his uncles, Timothy and Floyd Omann. The silo and silo unloader were owned by Timothy Omann who rented the farm from his parents. Floyd Omann, Timothy's brother, lived with his parents some distance from the farm. Floyd was at the farm helping Timothy with farm chores on the day of the accident. Floyd was insured under a homeowner's policy issued to his parents carrying a liability limit of $50,000.

At the time of the accident, Robert Newhouse was with Timothy and Floyd who were cleaning out the remaining corn in the bottom of the silo. A clog developed in the silo unloader which required work outside the silo. Timothy and Floyd left Robert in the silo while attending to the problem. The unloader was left running and Robert became entangled in the machinery, resulting in the loss of one leg and serious injury to the other.

On April 1, 1985, Robert Newhouse and his parents commenced a lawsuit against the Omann brothers and others for their alleged negligence in the farm accident. Citizens was not initially named as a defendant. Attorney Don Paul Novitzke filed an answer for Floyd Omann denying liability and then tendered the defense to Citizens.

On January 24, 1986, Citizens commenced an action against its insured, Floyd Omann, seeking a declaratory judgment that its homeowner's policy excluded coverage because the accident did not occur on the insured's premises. Before the circuit court could rule, Robert Newhouse joined Citizens in his negligence lawsuit and Citizens raised the issue of coverage as a defense in that lawsuit as well. Circuit court Judge John G. Bartholomew presided over both actions. On January 12, 1987, Judge Bartholomew issued a declaratory judgment that Citizens' policy did not provide coverage for this accident. There was no appeal from the declaratory judgment. On June 4, 1987, Judge Bartholomew issued an identical no coverage ruling in Robert Newhouse's personal injury action and dismissed Citizens from the lawsuit. The Newhouses and other defendants, except Floyd Omann, appealed the no coverage ruling in the personal injury action.

While the coverage appeal was pending in the court of appeals, Robert's personal injury action proceeded to trial on the merits. Prior to trial, the trial court inquired of Citizens whether it wanted a continuance pending resolution of the coverage appeal and was advised in the negative. The trial began on September 14, 1987. Neither Floyd Omann nor Citizens participated in the personal injury trial. During the course of the trial, each of the defendants settled separately with the Newhouses except Floyd Omann. The trial court dismissed the jury and the case against Floyd Omann was tried without participation by Floyd or Citizens. The trial court apportioned negligence 35% to Floyd Omann, 35% to Timothy Omann and 30% to various machinery manufacturers. Total damages were assessed at $1,281,743.17. On October 15, 1987, judgment was entered against Floyd Omann in the amount of $588,003.70.

On May 17, 1988, the court of appeals decided *Newhouse I*, which held that Citizens' policy provided coverage to Floyd Omann for the negligence alleged in the lawsuit. After the *Newhouse I* decision, Citizens paid its policy limits of $50,000 together with $77,000 interest and costs into the St. Croix county clerks office pending resolution of its petition for review to us which was eventually denied. Citizens also paid Floyd's attorney fees to that point.

Floyd Omann assigned any claims he may have against Citizens to the Newhouses. On August 24, 1989, pursuant to that assignment, the Newhouses commenced the present lawsuit against Citizens. The Newhouses' complaint alleged several causes of action including bad faith, negligence, intentional infliction of emotional stress, and breach of the contractual duty to defend. Citizens filed a third-party claim for contribution against Floyd Omann and his attorney Don Paul Novitzke alleging that their negligence in failing to defend in the personal injury lawsuit increased the damages against Floyd.

The trial court granted summary judgment to the Newhouses on the breach of contract claim and awarded damages in the sum of $724,003.92, representing the full amount of the judgment against Floyd Omann in the underlying personal injury action together with interest and costs. The trial court dismissed the Newhouses' other causes of action. The trial court also found that Citizens' contribution claims against Floyd Omann and Novitzke were frivolous and awarded actual costs and attorney fees.

The court of appeals in *Newhouse II* affirmed the trial court's judgment on all issues except it reversed that part of the summary judgment awarding damages for the full amount of the personal injury judgment against Floyd Omann. The court of appeals concluded that the proper measure of damages for an insurer's breach of its duty to defend is limited to the policy limits plus interest together with costs and the aggrieved party's attorney fees in defending the suit. We granted the Newhouses' petition for review and Citizens' cross-petition for review.

I.

The first issue is whether Citizens breached a contractual duty to defend its insured, Floyd Omann. . . .

. . . .

Citizens argues that it was entitled to rely on the circuit court's decision that no coverage existed under its policy until the court of appeals reversed that decision. Citizens asserts that it was not required to defend Floyd Omann at the liability trial because that trial occurred after the circuit court ruled there was no coverage under Citizens' policy and before the court of appeals reversed that determination. We disagree.

The duty to defend is triggered by the allegations contained within the four corners of the complaint. In the instant case, Floyd Omann was an insured under Citizens' policy. There is no doubt that the allegations against Floyd Omann, if proved, would give rise to liability under the insurance policy. Citizens' duty to defend was triggered by the Newhouses' complaint and became effective when Attorney Don Paul Novitzke tendered Floyd Omann's defense to Citizens.

"An insurer does not breach its contractual duty to defend by denying coverage where the issue of coverage is fairly debatable as long as the insurer provides coverage and defense once coverage is established." *Elliott [v. Donahue]*, 169 Wis. 2d [310,] at 317, 485 N.W.2d 403 [(1992)]. However, when coverage is not determined before a liability trial, the insurer must provide a defense for its insured with regard to liability and damages. *Id.*, 169 Wis. 2d at 318, 485 N.W.2d 403.

In *Elliott*, we clearly stated that the proper procedure for an insurance company to follow when coverage is disputed is to request a bifurcated trial on the issues of coverage and liability and move to stay any proceedings on liability until the issue of coverage is resolved. *Id.* When this procedure is followed, the insurance company runs no risk of breaching its duty to defend.

Citizens did not follow the proper procedure. Citizens refused to accept the circuit court's offer to stay the liability trial until the appeal on the coverage issue was final. Citizens argues that it was entitled to rely on the circuit court's determination that there was no coverage under the policy. However, the circuit court's no coverage determination was not a final decision because it was timely appealed. An insurance company breaches its duty to defend if a liability trial goes forward during the time a no coverage determination is pending on appeal and the insurance company does not defend its insured at the liability trial. When an insurer relies on a lower court ruling that it has no duty to defend, it takes the risk that the ruling will be reversed on appeal.

In cases where a coverage decision is not final before the trial on liability and damages occurs, the insurance company must provide a defense to its insured. *Elliott*, 169 Wis. 2d at 318, 485 N.W.2d 403; *Mowry v. Badger State Mut. Cas. Co.*, 129 Wis. 2d 496, 528-29, 385 N.W.2d 171 (1986). The best approach is for the insurance company to defend under a reservation of rights.

In *Mowry*, the insurance company followed the proper bifurcation procedure, and we held that no breach of the duty to defend occurred. The coverage issue was determined first and coverage was held to apply. The insurance company then provided a defense.

We conclude that Citizens breached its duty to defend Floyd Omann when it failed to provide him with a defense at the liability and damage trial.

II.

Next we must address the proper measure of damages for an insurer's breach of its contractual duty to defend. This is a question of law which this court decides independently and without deference to the lower courts.

The general rule is that where an insurer wrongfully refuses to defend on the grounds that the claim against the insured is not within the coverage of the policy, the insurer is guilty of a breach of contract which renders it liable to the insured for all damages that naturally flow from the breach. *See Thorp Sales Corp. v. Gyuro Grading Co. Inc.,* 111 Wis. 2d 431, 438, 331 N.W.2d 342 (1983); Annotation, *Consequences of liability insurer's refusal to assume defense of action against insured upon ground that claim upon which action is based is not within coverage of policy,* 49 A.L.R.2d 694, 711 (1956 & A.L.R.2d Later Case Service 1987). Damages which naturally flow from an insurer's breach of its duty to defend include: (1) the amount of the judgment or settlement against the insured plus interest; (2) costs and attorney fees incurred by the insured in defending the suit; and (3) any additional costs that the insured can show naturally resulted from the breach.

The controversy in this case focuses on whether the insured is entitled to recover the amount of the judgment against him that exceeded the insurance policy limits. Citizens argues that absent a finding of bad faith, the proper measure of damages is the policy limits plus interest, costs, and attorney fees. The Newhouses argue that Citizens is liable for all consequential damages flowing from the breach which include the excess judgment rendered against Floyd Omann.

We conclude that an excess judgment is properly included in the damages for breach of an insurer's duty to defend, if the excess judgment was a natural or proximate result of the breach. The insurance company must pay damages necessary to put the insured in the same position he would have been in had the insurance company fulfilled the insurance contract. Policy limits do not restrict the damages recoverable by an insured for a breach of the contract by the insurer. *Comunale v. Traders & General Ins. Co.,* 50 Cal. 2d 654, 328 P.2d 198, 201 (1958); *Stockdale v. Jamison,* 416 Mich. 217, 330 N.W.2d 389, 392-93 (1982).

We conclude that when an insurance company fails to follow the proper procedure of requesting a bifurcated trial on the issues of coverage and liability and an excess judgment is rendered against the insured before the coverage issue is finally determined, the excess judgment is a natural and proximate cause of the insurance company's breach of its duty to defend for which it is liable. In the instant case, Citizens failed to accept the trial court's offer of a continuance in the liability trial until the coverage issue was resolved on appeal.

In cases where the coverage and liability issues are not bifurcated, insurance companies can protect themselves by defending under a reservation of rights. In this way the insurer gives up none of its rights should it ultimately be determined that coverage does not exist under the policy.

The court of appeals pointed out that in some jurisdictions the rejection of an offer of settlement is a precondition to recovery in excess of the policy limits. *Newhouse II*, 170 Wis. 2d at 470, 489 N.W.2d 639. While a rejected settlement offer is one factor that can be considered to prove damages in excess of policy limits, we believe other factors may also be considered such as the insurer's refusal to request a continuance in the liability trial. We do not agree with those jurisdictions that require a showing of bad faith before an insurer can be held liable for an excess judgment rendered against its insured. We believe an excess judgment can result from an insurer's breach of its duty to defend in the absence of bad faith.

Citizens failed to accept the trial court's offer of a continuance in the liability trial and breached its duty to defend. We conclude that Citizens is liable for the entire excess judgment rendered against Floyd Omann.

III.

The third issue is whether the circuit court properly dismissed the Newhouses' tort claims alleging negligence, bad faith and intentional infliction of emotional distress. We do not address this issue because we have awarded the full amount of the excess judgment as damages for the breach of contract by Citizens. We affirm the dismissal of the Newhouses' tort claims against Citizens.

. . . .

In conclusion, we reverse that portion of the court of appeals decision limiting damages for Citizens' breach of its contractual duty to defend to the policy limits plus costs and attorney fees. We remand to the circuit court for reinstatement of the original judgment awarding the full excess judgment as damages. We affirm the court of appeals on all other issues.

The decision of the court of appeals is affirmed in part, reversed in part, and remanded.

STEINMETZ, JUSTICE (dissenting.)

The majority concludes that "the excess judgment [in this case] is a natural and proximate cause of the insurance company's breach of its duty to defend." However, the majority does not explain its reasoning for this legal conclusion. Clearly, the child was permanently and severely injured, and the trial court determined the value of those injuries. The record before us does not indicate whether or by how much the trial court's valuation of the child's injuries would have changed had the insurance company's attorney defended Floyd Omann. In short, I see only a deep pocket conclusion by the majority.

. . . .

It would be unethical for a trial judge to award additional damages to an injured party in order to punish an insurance company which failed to defend its insured at trial, when said failure was not in bad faith. Valuation of damages is based exclusively upon the extent of the injuries sustained by the injured party.

. . . .

For the foregoing reasons, I would affirm the court of appeals. Accordingly, I dissent.

NOTES

1. *Attorney's fees and costs incurred in defending the underlying action.* The court of appeals in *Newhouse II* held that the measure of damages for breach of the insurer's duty to defend includes costs and attorney fees incurred in defending the suit. That appellants were entitled to at least this much is indisputable. Why?

Should the insured also recover defense costs incurred before it gave notice of the claim (or tendered the defense) to the insurer? *See Sherwood Brands, Inc. v. Hartford Accident and Indemnity Co.,* 347 Md. 32, 698 A.2d 1078 (1997).

2. *The judgment.* Where the underlying case is tried in circumstances where the insurer has breached the duty to defend, any judgment against the insured that comes within the coverage of the policy, at least up to the policy limits, is recoverable as damages. This is not disputed in *Newhouse* either. The judgment within the policy limits is not, however, a damage, as such, for breach of the duty to defend; when the insurer has a duty to indemnify because the judgment is for a claim within coverage, the insurer must perform that separate duty. Could an insurer breach the duty to defend and then *not* be liable for the resulting judgment against the insured? *See Hamlin, Inc. v. Hartford Accident and Indemnity Co.,* 86 F.3d 93 (7th Cir. 1996).

The real battleground in *Newhouse* concerned the substantial excess judgment. Under well settled principles of contract law, which the court in *Newhouse* acknowledges, damages must naturally and foreseeably arise from the breach. Did the court apply these well-settled principles correctly? Did the insurer's breach of the duty to defend *cause* the excess judgment? Did the insurer's nonparticipation in the underlying action cause Floyd Omann to receive a less effective defense? *See Mesmer v. Maryland Automobile Insurance Fund,* 353 Md. 241, 725 A.2d 1053 (1999) (damages for breach of duty to defend are limited to policy limits and costs of defending the underlying action).

If an attorney appointed by the insurer withdraws from the defense just a few days before trial and without a justification for doing so, is it a natural and foreseeable consequence of this kind of breach of the duty to defend that a larger judgment might be entered against the insured than if the original counsel, who was more familiar with the case, tried it? *See Beckwith Machinery Co. v. Travelers Indemnity Co.,* 638 F. Supp. 1179 (W.D. Pa. 1986).

3. *Insured's settlement.* If the insurer fails to provide a defense when it should, it is foreseeable that the insured will make other arrangements to defend the suit. Is it foreseeable that one of these arrangements might be the

insured's settlement of the third party's claim? Courts have answered this question in the affirmative, making the insurer liable for any reasonable settlement by the insured that comes within the policy coverage and limits. *See, e.g., Bunge Corp. v. London & Overseas Insurance Co.,* 394 F.2d 496 (2d Cir. 1968); *AFCAN v. Mutual Fire, Marine & Inland Insurance Co.,* 595 P.2d 638 (Alaska 1979); *Gladstone v. D.W. Ritter Co.,* 508 N.Y.S.2d 880 (N.Y. Sup. Ct. 1986). A corollary of the latter rule is that the insurer loses the right to invoke the clause prohibiting settlement by the insured without the permission of the insurer. *U.S. Fid. & Guar. Co. v. National Paving & Contracting Co.,* 228 Md. 40, 178 A.2d 872 (1962).

What if the insured settles the claim for an amount in excess of the policy limits? Is the settlement presumed to be the fair value of the claim, or are settlements above the fair value of claims natural and foreseeable consequences of insurers breaching the duty to defend? Does the answer change if the plaintiff in the underlying action offers, before trial, to settle the case for the policy limits, but the insured, who is defending the case through her own counsel, declines the offer, and then at trial the insured decides to settle the case for a sum exceeding the policy limits?

If the insurer does not respond to a settlement offer because it is not defending the action by virtue of its breach of the duty to defend, does it follow that the insurer has breached the duty to settle with all of the attendant consequences (which include liability for any excess judgment)? Or does the insurer not even have a duty to settle when it has not assumed the defense? *See Mesmer v. Maryland Automobile Insurance Fund,* 353 Md. 241, 725 A.2d 1053 (1999); *Farris v. United States Fidelity & Guaranty Co.,* 587 P.2d 1015, 1018-1019 (Or. 1978).

Suppose the claim against the insured has a value of approximately $5,000, but the insured settles the claim for an excessive amount (for example, the policy limits of $100,000). Even though an insurer has wrongfully refused to defend, should it be permitted to contest the reasonableness of the settlement entered into by the insured?

What if the insurer breaches the duty to defend in circumstances where some of the allegations are within coverage, but some are outside coverage? If the insured settles all claims for a lump sum payment, should the insurer be allowed to demonstrate that the only valid claim was one outside coverage and that therefore the insurer has no obligation to pay any portion of the settlement? *See Servidone Construction Corp. v. Security Insurance Co.,* 477 N.E.2d 441 (N.Y. 1985).

4. *Default judgments.* What if the insurer leads the insured to reasonably believe that the insurer will undertake the defense, but the insurer takes no action, and a default judgment in excess of the policy limits is entered against the insured? Does the insured have an obligation to hire his or her own counsel in order to mitigate the damage? What if the insured cannot afford to retain his or her own counsel? Does the insurer's liability for a default judgment in excess of the policy limits depend on whether the insurer knows that the insured lacks the financial means to appoint his or her own counsel?

5. *Insured's attorney's fees in the action against the insurer.* If the insurer breaches the duty to defend, is it a natural and foreseeable consequence of

this breach that the insured will have to hire a lawyer not only to defend the action against the insured but also to prosecute a coverage action against the insurer? Or, like most litigants in U.S. courts, must the insured bear his or her own expenses in vindicating his or her contract rights against the insurer? *Compare Steptore v. Masco Construction Co.,* 643 So. 2d 1213 (La. 1994), with *Cunniff v. Westfield, Inc.,* 829 F. Supp. 55 (E.D.N.Y 1993). If, however, the insurer has acted in bad faith when breaching the duty to defend, the insured should be allowed to recover attorney's fees in prosecuting the coverage action under the settled exception to the American rule which ordinarily requires each party to bear its own expenses in litigation. *See Clark-Peterson Co., Inc. v. Independent Insurance Assoc., Ltd.,* 514 N.W.2d 912 (Iowa 1994); *American States Insurance Co. v. Walker,* 26 Utah 2d 161, 486 P.2d 1042 (1971).

If the insurer brings a declaratory judgment action to establish that the claim against the insured is outside the coverage, the insured will be a defendant in this action. Must the insured bear his or her own attorney's fees in this action? *Compare Atlantic Mutual Insurance Co. v. Judd Co.,* 380 N.W.2d 122 (Minn. 1986), with *Aetna Casualty & Surety Co. v. Pitrolo,* 342 S.E.2d 156 (W. Va. 1986).

6. *Other consequences.* When the insurer breaches the duty to defend, it necessarily follows that the insurer forfeits the right to control the defense of the claim. *See Standard Accident Insurance Co. v. Harrison-Wright Co.,* 207 N.C. 661, 178 S.E. 235 (1935); *Orleans Village v. Union Mutual Fire Insurance Co.,* 133 Vt. 217, 335 A.2d 315 (1975). The breach of the duty to defend being a material breach, it follows that the insurer's breach causes the insurer to lose its right to insist on the insured's compliance with the notice, cooperation, and other claims processing provisions in the policy after the breach. *See, e.g., Milbank Mutual Insurance Co. v. Wentz,* 352 F.2d 592 (8th Cir. 1965); *United Servicess Automobile Ass'n v. Russom,* 241 F.2d 296 (5th Cir. 1957); *Davis v. Criterion Insurance Co.,* 754 P.2d 1331 (Alaska 1988); *Dixie Auto Insurance Co. v. Goudy,* 238 Ark. 432, 382 S.W.2d 380 (1964).

7. *Tort liability?* If the insured's damages for breach of the duty to defend are limited to attorney's fees incurred in defending the suit, litigation costs, and any resulting judgment within the policy limits, what incentive does an insurer have to defend in close cases? Is retaining control of the defense a sufficient incentive for the insurer to defend under a reservation of rights? One answer is to declare the insurer liable for "bad faith" breach of the duty to defend and make the insurer responsible for damages in excess of the policy limits. *See Tibbs v. Great American Insurance Co.,* 755 F.2d 1370 (9th Cir. 1985). Another answer, which has scant judicial support, is to declare that the breach of the duty to defend sounds in tort. *See Smith v. American Family Mutual Insurance Co.,* 294 N.W.2d 751 (N.D. 1980). Is this essentially what the court in *Newhouse* did? Compare *Mesmer v. Maryland Automobile Insurance Fund,* 353 Md. 241, 725 A.2d 1053 (1999) (liability insurer's breach of duty to defend gives rise to a contract action, not a tort action).

8. *Estoppel?* It has been held that if the insurer breaches the duty to defend, the insurer is estopped to deny coverage. *See, e.g., Lloyd's & Institute of London Underwriting Cos. v. Fulton,* 2 P.3d 1199 (Alaska 2000); *Delmonte v. State Farm Fire and Casualty Co.,* 90 Haw. 39, 975 P.2d 1159, 1170 (1999)

(circumstances that give rise to "serious prejudice" to insured may estop insurer to deny coverage, but rule did not apply to facts of instant case); *Novak v. Insurance Adm. Unlimited, Inc.,* 414 N.E.2d 258 (Ill. App. Ct. 1980). If the claims the insurer declined to defend were within coverage, does an estoppel argument add anything? What would an estoppel argument add in a case like *Gray v. Zurich, supra,* where the insured's assault was ultimately found to be intentional and the insured's claim of self-defense was found wanting? Was estoppel the real theory of *Newhouse?* Some courts have rejected the estoppel analysis on the ground that it creates coverage where none exists. *See NAWCAS Benevolent Auxiliary v. Levin,* 162 S.E.2d 738 (Ga. Ct. App. 1968). In *Newhouse,* was coverage created where none existed? Given the availability of mechanisms such as reservation of rights notices and declaratory judgment actions, is it unreasonable to impose an estoppel rule on insurers in these circumstances?

9. *Multiple primary insurers.* Sometimes more than one liability insurer provides primary coverage. Absent an agreement between the insurers as to how the defense will be conducted and expenses shared, can one insurer proceed to defend and then compel another insurer to contribute to the cost later? In *National Indemnity Co. v. St. Paul Insurance Co.,* 150 Ariz. 458, 459, 724 P.2d 544, 545 (1986), the court addressed this issue:

> The authorities are divided on the issue whether one insurance company can compel another insurance company to contribute to the cost of defense of an insured where each insurer has the duty to defend that insured. . . . When an insurer has a duty to defend the insured, there should be no reward to the insurer for breaching that duty. A breach of the obligation to defend should not be encouraged, but the rule which allows an insurer to avoid the costs of defense tends to encourage an avoidance of the insurer's responsibilities.

> Under the principle of equitable subrogation, the insurer which has performed the duty to provide a defense to its insured should be able to compel contribution for a share of the cost of defense from another insurer who had a similar obligation to the same insured but failed to perform it.

10. *Discovery issues.* In an action for bad faith or negligent refusal to defend or settle within policy limits, the insured may be entitled to discover relevant portions of the insurer's claim file, including correspondence and other communications between the insurer and defense counsel. *Henke v. Iowa Home Mutual Cas. Co.,* 249 Iowa 614, 87 N.W.2d 920 (1958). The same may be true under a first-party bad faith claim. *See United Services. Automobile Ass'n v. Werley,* 526 P.2d 28 (Alaska 1974) and *Brown v. Superior Court,* 137 Ariz. 327, 670 P.2d 725 (1983).

[7] The Primary Carrier-Excess Carrier Relationship

COMMERCIAL UNION ASSURANCE CO. v. SAFEWAY STORES, INC.

26 Cal. 3d 912, 610 P.2d 1038, 164 Cal. Rptr. 709 (1980)

BY THE COURT:

We granted a hearing herein in order to resolve a conflict between Court of Appeal opinions in this case and the earlier case of *Transit Casualty Co. v. Spink Corp.* (1979) 94 Cal. App. 3d 124, 156 Cal. Rptr. 360. After an independent study of the issue, we have concluded that the thoughtful opinion of Justice Sabraw (assigned) for the Court of Appeal, First Appellate District, 158 Cal. Rptr. 97, in this case correctly treats the issues, and that we should adopt it as our own opinion. That opinion, with appropriate deletions and additions, is as follows:

This case presents the question of whether an insured owes a duty to its excess liability insurance carrier which would require it to accept a settlement offer below the threshold figure of the excess carrier's exposure where there is a substantial probability of liability in excess of that figure.

Facts:

At all times relevant herein Safeway Stores, Incorporated (hereafter Safeway) had liability insurance coverage as follows:

(a) Travelers Insurance Company and Travelers Indemnity Company (hereafter Travelers) insured Safeway for the first $50,000 of liability.

(b) Safeway insured itself for liability between the sums of $50,000 and $100,000.

(c) Commercial Union Assurance Companies and Mission Insurance Company (hereafter conjunctively referred to as Commercial) provided insurance coverage for Safeway's liability in excess of $100,000 to $20 million.

One Hazel Callies brought an action against Safeway in San Francisco Superior Court and recovered judgment for the sum of $125,000. Thereafter, Commercial was required to pay $25,000 of said judgment in order to discharge its liability under the excess insurance policy.

Commercial, as excess liability carrier, brought the instant action against its insured Safeway and Safeway's primary insurance carrier, Travelers, to recover the $25,000 which it had expended. Commercial alleged that Safeway and Travelers had an opportunity to settle the case for $60,000, or possibly even $50,000, and knew or should have known that there was a possible and probable liability in excess of $100,000. It was further alleged that said defendants had a duty to settle the claim for a sum less than $100,000 when they had an opportunity to do so. Commercial's complaint attempts to state two causes of action against Safeway and Travelers, one in negligence and another for breach of the duty of good faith and fair dealing.

Safeway demurred to the complaint on the grounds of failure to state a cause of action. The court sustained the demurrer with 20 days' leave to amend.

When Commercial failed to amend its complaint, the complaint was dismissed as to Safeway. Commercial now appeals from the judgment of dismissal.

The present case is unusual in that the policyholder, Safeway, was self-insured for liability in an amount below Commercial's initial exposure. While this status may explain Safeway's reluctance to settle, it remains to be determined if the insured owes an independent duty to his excess carrier to accept a reasonable settlement offer so as to avoid exposing the latter to pecuniary harm. [Both of Commercial's theories of recovery, negligence and breach of good faith, depend upon the existence of such a duty.]

It is now well established that an insurer may be held liable for a judgment against the insured in excess of its policy limits where it has breached its implied covenant of good faith and fair dealing by unreasonably refusing to accept a settlement offer within the policy limits (*Crisci v. Security Ins. Co.,* 66 Cal. 2d 425, 429 [58 Cal. Rptr. 13, 426 P.2d 173]; *Comunale v. Traders & General Ins. Co.* (1958) 50 Cal. 2d 654, 661 [328 P.2d 198, 68 A.L.R.2d 883]). The insurer's duty of good faith requires it to "settle within policy limits when there is substantial likelihood of recovery in excess of those limits." (*Murphy v. Allstate Ins. Co.* (1976) 17 Cal. 3d 937, 941 [, 132 Cal. Rptr. 424, 426 553 P.2d 584, 586].)

. . . .

It has been held in California and other jurisdictions that the excess carrier may maintain an action against the primary carrier for [wrongful] refusal to settle within the latter's policy limits (*Northwestern Mut. Ins. Co. v. Farmers Ins. Group* (1978) 76 Cal. App. 3d 1031 [143 Cal. Rptr. 415]; *Valentine v. Aetna Ins. Co.,* 564 F.2d 292; *Estate of Penn v. Amalgamated General Agencies* (1977) 148 N.J. Super. 419 [372 A.2d 1124]). This rule, however, is based on the theory of equitable subrogation: Since the insured would have been able to recover from the primary carrier for a judgment in excess of policy limits caused by the carrier's wrongful refusal to settle, the excess carrier, who discharged the insured's liability as a result of this tort, stands in the shoes of the insured and should be permitted to assert all claims against the primary carrier which the insured himself could have asserted (*see Northwestern Mut. Ins. Co. v. Farmers Ins. Group, supra,* 76 Cal. App. 3d at pp. 1040, 1049–1050, 143 Cal. Rptr. 415). Hence, the rule does not rest upon the finding of any separate duty owed to an excess insurance carrier.

Commercial argues that the implied covenant of good faith and fair dealing is reciprocal, binding the policyholder as well as the carrier (*see Liberty Mut. Ins. Co. v. Altfillisch Constr. Co.* (1977) 70 Cal. App. 3d 789, 797 [139 Cal. Rptr. 91]). It is further contended, in effect, that turnabout is fair play: that the implied covenant of good faith and fair dealing applies to the insured as well as the insurer, and thus the policyholder owes a duty to his excess carrier not to unreasonably refuse an offer of settlement below the amount of excess coverage where a judgment of liability above that amount is substantially likely to occur.

This theory, while possessing superficial plausibility and exquisite simplicity, cannot withstand closer analysis. We have no quarrel with the proposition that a duty of good faith and fair dealing in an insurance policy is a two-way street, running from the insured to his insurer as well as vice versa (*Liberty Mut. Ins. Co. v. Altfillisch Constr. Co., supra,* 70 Cal. App. 3d at p. 797, 139 Cal. Rptr. 91; *Crisci v. Security Ins. Co., supra,* 66 Cal. 2d at p. 429, 58 Cal. Rptr. 13, 426 P.2d 173). However, what that duty embraces is dependent upon the nature of the bargain struck between the insurer and the insured and the legitimate expectations of the parties which arise from the contract.

The essence of the implied covenant of good faith in insurance policies is that "'neither party will do anything which injures the right of the other to receive the benefits of the agreement.'" (*Murphy v. Allstate Ins. Co., supra,* 17 Cal. 3d at p. 940, 132 Cal. Rptr. at p. 426, 553 P.2d at p. 586, quoting from *Brown v. Superior Court* (1949) 34 Cal. 2d 559, 564 [212 P.2d 878]). One of the most important benefits of a maximum limit insurance policy is the assurance that the company will provide the insured with defense and indemnification for the purpose of protecting him from liability. Accordingly, the insured has the legitimate right to expect that the method of settlement within policy limits will be employed in order to give him such protection.

No such expectations can be said to reasonably flow from an excess insurer to its insured. The object of the excess insurance policy is to provide additional resources should the insured's liability surpass a specified sum. The insured owes no duty to defend or indemnify the excess carrier; hence, the carrier can possess no reasonable expectation that the insured will accept a settlement offer as a means of "protecting" the carrier from exposure. The protection of the insurer's pecuniary interests is simply not the object of the bargain.

As [we have] stated: "The duty to settle is implied in law to protect the insured from exposure to liability in excess of coverage as a result of the insurer's gamble—on which only the insured might lose." (*Murphy v. Allstate Ins. Co., supra,* 17 Cal. 3d at p. 941, 132 Cal. Rptr. at p. 426, 553 P.2d at p. 586.) Similar considerations do not apply where the situation is reversed: where the insured is fully covered by primary insurance, the primary insurer is entitled to take control of the settlement negotiations and the insured is precluded from interfering therewith (*see Shapero v. Allstate Ins. Co.* (1971) 14 Cal. App. 3d 433, 437-438 [92 Cal. Rptr. 244], quoting from *Ivy v. Pacific Automobile Ins. Co.* (1958) 156 Cal. App. 2d 652, 659–660 [320 P.2d 140]). Where, as here, the policyholder is self-insured for an amount below the beginning of the excess insurance coverage, he is gambling as much with his own money as with that of the carrier. The crucial point is that the excess carrier has no legitimate expectation that the insured will "give at least as much consideration to the financial well-being" of the insurance company as he does to his "own interests" (*Shapero, supra,* 14 Cal. App. 3d at p. 438, 92 Cal. Rptr. at p. 247), in considering whether to settle for an amount below the excess policy coverage. In fact, the primary reason excess insurance is purchased is to provide an available pool of money in the event that the decision is made to take the gamble of litigating.

With these principles in mind, it becomes clear that the case of *Liberty Mut. Ins. Co. v. Altfillisch Constr. Co., supra,* 70 Cal. App. 3d 789, 139 Cal. Rptr. 91, upon which Commercial bases its argument, is easily distinguishable.

In *Liberty,* the insurance policy contained the standard clauses giving the company the right of subrogation against third parties, plus a provision which expressly prohibited the insured from doing anything which would prejudice such right (*Id.,* at p. 796, 139 Cal. Rptr. 91). The insured leased the equipment covered in the policy to a third party under a contract which effectively released that party from liability for damage, thus cutting off the company's right of subrogation. The court held that the reciprocal covenant of good faith and fair dealing in the insurance policy was breached by the insured, since its act had destroyed "Liberty's expectation of opportunities to subrogate in the event of payment of a loss caused by the negligence of a third party." (P. 797, 139 Cal. Rptr. p. 95.)

In the instant case, whether Commercial could harbor any legitimate expectation that its insured would settle a claim for less than the threshold amount of the policy coverage must be determined in the light of what the parties bargained for. The complaint makes no reference to any language in the policy which would give rise to such expectation. We must therefore ask the question: Did Safeway, when it purchased excess coverage, impliedly promise that it would take all reasonable steps to settle a claim below the limits of Commercial's coverage so as to protect Commercial from possible exposure? Further, did Commercial extend excess coverage with the understanding and expectation that it would receive such favorable treatment from Safeway under the policy? We think not.

At this point, two recent appellate decisions which bear upon this issue, deserve mention.

First, in the case of *Kaiser Foundation Hospitals v. North Star Reinsurance Corp. (*1979) 90 Cal. App. 3d 786 [153 Cal. Rptr. 678], the Court of Appeal for the Second District, Division Five, concluded that the relationship between an insured and primary carrier vis-á-vis the excess carrier was governed by an implied covenant of good faith and fair dealing (p. 792, 153 Cal. Rptr. 678). That decision, however, dealt with a situation where the insured and its primary carrier acted in collusion to wrongfully allocate certain dates of loss so as to maximize the liability of the excess carrier. It appears that the aggravated conduct on the part of the insured and the primary carrier in taking advantage of the excess carrier prompted the Court of Appeal to invoke the basic principles of good faith and fair dealing in order to give proper redress to the excess carrier. It is to be noted that the opinion takes careful pains to emphasize that in speaking of a good faith and fair dealing duty owed by the insured to the excess carrier under these circumstances, it was expressly not amplifying on the nature of such duty: "[W]e make no attempt to define precisely what rights and duties that entails in a case such as this. Such questions are best decided in the light of concrete facts . . ." (p. 794, 153 Cal. Rptr. p. 683).

We acknowledge that equity requires fair dealing between the parties to an insurance contract. We view the *Kaiser* and *Liberty* cases as pointing up a recognition in the law that the insured status as such is not a license for the insured to engage in unconscionable acts which would subvert the legitimate rights and expectations of the excess insurance carrier.

However, we are unable to derive from this sound principle, the precipitous conclusion that the covenant of good faith and fair dealing should be extended to include a "*Comunale* duty" —that is, a duty which would require an insured contemplating settlement to put the excess carrier's financial interests on at least an equal footing with his own. Such a duty cannot reasonably be found from the mere existence of the contractual relationship between insured and excess carrier in the absence of express language in the contract so providing.

We observe that an apparently contrary conclusion has been reached by the Third District in the recent case of *Transit Casualty Co. v. Spink Corp.* [*supra*] 94 Cal. App. 3d 124, 156 Cal. Rptr. 360. [We disapprove that case] insofar as it holds that an insured's duty of good faith and fair dealing to his excess carrier compels him to accept a settlement offer or proceed at his peril where there is a substantial likelihood that an adverse judgment will bring excess insurance coverage into play.

In conclusion, we hold that a policy providing for excess insurance coverage imposes no implied duty upon the insured to accept a settlement offer which would avoid exposing the insurer to liability. Moreover such a duty cannot be predicated upon an insured's implied covenant of good faith and fair dealing. If an excess carrier wishes to insulate itself from liability for an insured's failure to accept what it deems to be a reasonable settlement offer, it may do so by appropriate language in the policy. We hesitate, however, to read into the policy obligations which are neither sought after nor contemplated by the parties. (End of Court of Appeal opinion.)

The judgment is affirmed.

[NEWMAN, JUSTICE, concurred.]

[BIRD, CHIEF JUSTICE, concurred and dissented.]

NOTES

1. *A universal rule.* According to a 1987 decision of the Court of Appeals of Maryland, Arizona was the only jurisdiction (of those where the issue has been raised) to refuse to recognize a cause of action by the excess carrier against the primary carrier for negligence or bad faith failure to settle a claim within the primary limits. *Fireman's Fund Insurance Co. v. Continental Insurance Co.,* 308 Md. 315, 519 A.2d 202 (1987). The Arizona case to which the Maryland court referred was overruled in 1990 in *Hartford Accident & Indemnity Co. v. Aetna Casualty & Surety Co.,* 164 Ariz. 286, 792 P.2d 749 (Ariz. 1990) (en banc). The rule, therefore, is apparently universal.

2. *Insured's duty to excess carrier?* If the primary carrier denies liability and refuses to defend, and the insured then undertakes to defend, does the insured then have an obligation to consider the excess carrier's interest where a settlement offer is made within the primary carrier's limits? *See Employers Mutual Casualty Co. v. Key Pharmaceuticals, Inc.,* 75 F.3d 815 (2d Cir. 1996).

§ 8.03 The Tort of Bad Faith

[1] First-Party Insurance

WHITE v. UNIGARD MUTUAL INSURANCE CO.
112 Idaho 94, 730 P.2d 1014 (1986)

BISTLINE, JUSTICE.

On February 14, 1984, a fire damaged the premises of Nampa Beauty College, owned by Georgeana White. White notified and submitted her claim to her Insurer, Unigard. Arson was suspected, and, subsequently, White and her daughter, Jan Blevins, were charged with arson and insurance fraud. However, at the preliminary hearings the charges were dismissed due to insufficient evidence.

White then demanded settlement of Unigard. Unigard required a sworn statement from White, which she provided. At the request of Unigard, White also made available for inspection various items damaged in the fire. Ultimately, Unigard denied coverage for the loss based upon its belief that White was responsible for the fire. (White's policy excluded coverage in the event of arson or other intentional acts of the insured).

Subsequently, White filed suit in state court. Unigard, a Washington corporation, filed in Federal District Court for the District of Idaho for declaratory relief. Ultimately the state action was removed to the federal court and the two actions were consolidated. Unigard moved for a partial summary judgment as to White's complaint at which time the District Court, pursuant to I.A.R. 12.1(a), certified the following questions concerning Idaho law: (1) does the State of Idaho recognize a tort action, distinct from an action on the contract, for an insurer's bad faith in settling the first party claims of its insured; and (2) is there a private right of action under Idaho's Unfair Claims Settlement Practices Act, Idaho Code § 41-1329 (1977), whereby an insured can sue the insurer for statutory violations committed in connection with the settlement of the insured's claim? The first question we answer in the affirmative and, based on that holding, find that a statutory remedy is neither prescribed nor necessary to assure the effectiveness of Idaho's Unfair Claims Settlement Practices Act, Idaho Code § 41-1329.

I

The first question of law certified by the U.S. District Court of the District of Idaho for review by this Court, pursuant to Idaho Appellate Rule 12.1(a), is whether Idaho recognizes a tort action, distinct from an action on the contract, for an insurer's bad faith in settling the first party claims of its insured.

. . . .

A. *Duty to Settle in Good Faith*

That there is a duty of good faith and fair dealing inherent in every contract is not disputed. Under the common law, "every contract imposes upon each party a duty of good faith and fair dealing in its performance and its enforcement." Restatement (Second) of Contracts § 205 (1979). "[A]ll courts are agreed that the insurer does owe to the insured some duty in this respect." *Hilker v. Western Automobile Insurance Co.,* 204 Wis. 1, 235 N.W. 413, 414 (1931).

The Supreme Court of Montana expressly held in *Lipinski v. Title Ins. Co.,* 202 Mont. 1, 655 P.2d 970 (1983), despite a statutory provision which prohibits the imposition of punitive damages arising from a breach of contract, that "insurance companies have a duty to act in good faith with their insureds, and that *this duty exists independent of the insurance contract and independent of statute."* Id., 655 P.2d at 977 (emphasis added). Such a duty is beyond that which the policy imposes by itself — the duty to defend, settle, and pay — but is a duty imposed by law on an insurer to act fairly and in good faith in discharging its contractual responsibilities. *Gruenberg v. Aetna Ins. Co.,* 9 Cal. 3d 566, 108 Cal. Rptr. 480, 510 P.2d 1032 (1973).

Contrary to some authority, this duty arises not only in the context of third party situations (actions brought as a result of the insurer's failure to settle the claims of third parties within the policy limits of the insured), but also in first party actions (when the insured is personally filing a claim for benefits against the insurer under the policy). As the court in *Gruenberg* stated:

> It is manifest that a common legal principle underlies all of the foregoing decisions; namely, that in every insurance contract there is an implied covenant of good faith and fair dealing. *The duty to so act is imminent in the contract whether the company is attending to claims of third persons against the insured or the claims of the insured itself.* Accordingly, when the insurer unreasonably and in bad faith withholds payment of the claim of its insured, it is subject to liability in tort.

Gruenberg, supra, 108 Cal. Rptr. at 486, 510 P.2d at 1038 (emphasis added).

As the court in *Anderson* noted, "[t]he rationale which recognizes an ancillary duty on an insurance company to exercise good faith in the settlement of third-party claims is equally applicable and of equal importance when the insured seeks payment of legitimate damages from his own insurance company. *That such a duty arises out of the relationship between the contracting parties themselves cannot be doubted." Anderson, supra,* 271 N.W.2d at 375 (emphasis added).

The question before this Court, then, is not whether a duty of "good faith" exists, but rather whether a breach of this duty will give rise to an independent action in tort.

B. Tort of Bad Faith

There has been much confusion in the courts over this precise issue. In *Anderson, supra,* 271 N.W.2d at 374, the court noted that this confusion may be traced to the fact that the tort of bad faith has been referred to by some as a tortious breach of contract. *Id.* at 374. The court was quick to note, however, that:

> [w]hile ["tortious breach of contract"] may be a convenient shorthand method of denominating the intentional conduct of a contracting party when it acts in bad faith to avoid its contract obligations, it is confusing and inappropriate, because it could lead one to believe that the wrong done is the breach of the contract. It obscures the fact that *the bad faith conduct by one party to a contract toward another is a tort separate and apart from a breach of contract per se* and it fails to emphasize the fact that damages may be recovered for the tort and for the contract breach.

Id. at 374 (emphasis added). The court was emphatic in adding that "the tort of bad faith is not a tortious breach of contract. *It is a separate intentional wrong, which results from a breach of a duty imposed as a consequence of the relationship established by contract." Id.* at 374 (emphasis added); accord, *e.g., Rawlings v. Apodaca,* 151 Ariz. 149, 726 P.2d 565, 574–577 (S. Ct. 1986).

. . . .

An action in tort provides a remedy for harm done to insureds though no breach of an express contractual covenant has occurred and where contract damages fail to adequately compensate insureds. While punitive damages are available on contract actions in Idaho, *Linscott v. Rainier National Life Ins. Co.,* 100 Idaho 854, 606 P.2d 958 (1980), the requirement that contract damages be foreseeable at the time of contracting, *Lamb v. Robinson,* 101 Idaho 703, 705, 620 P.2d 276, 278 (1980), in some cases would bar recovery for damages proximately caused by the insurer's bad faith. The measurement of recoverable damages in tort is not limited to those foreseeable at the time of the tortious act; rather they include "[a] reasonable amount which will compensate plaintiff for *all* actual detriment proximately caused by the defendant's wrongful conduct." IDJI 920(1) (1982) (emphasis added). As the California Supreme Court has unanimously held: "The general rule of damages in tort is that the injured party may recover for *all* detriment caused *whether it could have been anticipated or not." Crisci v. Security Ins. Co. of New Haven, Conn.,* 66 Cal. 2d 425, 58 Cal. Rptr. 13, 426 P.2d 173, 178 (1967) (emphasis added). Professor McCormick explains:

> [T]he majority of courts do not use "reasonable foreseeability" as the test of responsibility for particular harmful consequences in tort cases, but hold, on the other hand, that one who commits a wrongful act "is liable for all the direct injury resulting from such act, although such resulting injury could not have been contemplated as a probable result of the act done."

C. McCormick, Handbook on the Law of Damages § 74, p. 265 (1935) (footnote omitted); see also *id.* at § 137, pp. 560–62 (contrasting the basis for compensation in tort and contract cases). Thus, an insured person whose business goes bust as a result of an insurer's bad faith would be able to recover whether the bust was foreseeable or not. For example, an insured who takes out a second mortgage on her business property *after* purchasing her policy, and who could not make her combined payments when the insurer delayed settlement, would recover at tort, but not at contract. To deny an action in tort would deny such recovery and consequently encourage insurers to delay settlement. In contrast, an action in tort will provide necessary compensation for insureds and incentive for insurers to settle valid claims. See Idaho Const., art. 1, § 18 ("[A] speedy remedy [is] afforded for every injury. . . ."). At worst, the availability of an action in tort will add nothing to the liability of insurers.

The *Rawlings* Court aptly observed:

> Because of the disparity in bargaining power and the nature of the contract, the insurer receives both premium and control. *Barrera v. State Farm Mutual Automobile Insurance Co.,* 71 Cal. 2d 659, 79 Cal. Rptr. 106, 117, 456 P.2d 674, 685 (1969). . . . In first-party situations the insurer sets the conditions for both presentment and payment of claims. In both first-and third-party situations the contract and the nature of the relationship effectively give the insurer an almost adjudicatory responsibility. The insurer evaluates the claim, determines whether it falls within the coverage provided, assesses its monetary value, decides on its validity and passes upon payment. Although the insured is not without remedies if he disagrees with the insurer, the very invocation of those remedies detracts significantly from the protection or security which was the object of the transaction. Thus, the insurance contract and the relationship it creates contain more than the company's bare promise to pay certain claims when forced to do so; implicit in the contract and the relationship is the insurer's obligation to play fairly with its insured. *Parsons v. Continental National American Group, supra* [113 Ariz. 223, 550 P.2d 94 (1976)]; *Egan v. Mutual of Omaha Insurance Co.* [24 Cal. 3d 809, 169 Cal. Rptr. 691, 620 P.2d 141 (1979)], *supra.*

Rawlings, supra, 726 P.2d at 570–571 (footnote omitted). Thus, where an insurer "intentionally and unreasonably denies or delays payment" on a claim, and in the process harms the claimant[2] in such a way not fully compensable at contract, the claimant can bring an action in tort to recover for the harm done. *Id.,* 726 P.2d at 572. The availability of an action for bad faith will provide incentive to insurers to honor their implied covenant to the insureds.[3]

C. *The Special Relationship Between Insurer and Insured*

The imposition of liability in tort for bad faith breach of an insurance contract is further warranted when one considers the special relationship which exists between insurer and insured. "The insurance contract has long been recognized as giving rise to a special relationship between insurer and insured

---

[2] Such delay might cause an insured whose business property was damaged to default on payments, or a personally injured insured to forego needed treatment. *Id.* As the *Noble* court observed: "Often the insured is in an especially vulnerable economic position when such a casualty loss occurs." 624 P.2d at 868; accord, *Massey, supra,* 635 S.W.2d at 601.

[3] Contrary to Unigard's assertions, the statutory scheme to regulate the insurance industry fails to provide sufficient incentive. The Department of Insurance has limited means with which to police the insurance industry. Further, in instances of bad faith, the remedies afforded by statute would fail to compensate for damages beyond the policy amounts and attorney's fees occasioned by unreasonable delay. As the Montana Supreme Court has observed, statutes regulating the insurance industry do little to encourage the settlement of large claims unless they are backed up with an action for bad faith. *Klaudt v. Flink,* 202 Mont. 247, 658 P.2d 1065, 1067 (1983) (holding Montana's Unfair Trade Practices Act gives rise to an action in tort).

(*see Manhattan Fire Ins. Co. v. Weill & Ullman,* 69 Va. (28 Gratt.) 389, 26 Am. Rep. 364 (1877)), which requires that the parties deal with each other fairly, honestly, and in good faith (*Germania Ins. Co. v. Rudwig,* 80 Ky. 223, 235 (1882)).″ McCarthy, *Punitive Damages in Bad Faith Cases 3d,* 23 (1983). John G. Holinka, commenting on insurance contracts, noted that it is the unique, "personal" (non-commercial) nature of insurance contracts which justifies the imposition of the duty of good faith and fair dealing. Holinka, *Damages for Mental Suffering Caused by Insurers: Recent Developments in the Law of Tort and Contract,* 48 Notre Dame Lawyer 1303 (1973). The insured-insurer relationship is one "characterized by elements of public interest, adhesion and fiduciary responsibility." *Seaman's Direct Buying Serv. v. Standard Oil,* 686 P.2d 1158, 1166 (Cal. 1984). As Louderback and Jurika noted in *Standards for Limiting the Tort of Bad Faith Breach of Contract,* 16 U.S.F. L. Rev. 187 (1982):

> The adhesionary aspects of the insurance contract, including the lack of bargaining strength of the insured, the contracts standardized terms, the motivation of the insured for entering into the transaction and the nature of the service for which the contract is executed, distinguish this contract [insurance contract] from most other non-insurance commercial contracts. These features characteristic of the insurance contract make it particularly susceptible to public policy considerations.

16 U.S.F. L. Rev. 187, 200–01 (1982). It is in fact these "adhesionary aspects" of the insurance contract which have prompted this court in the past to come to the aid of the insured.

Louderback and Jurika observed that, although the insurance companies cannot be said to be fiduciaries for their insureds in the strict meaning of the term, "under certain circumstances, the insured. . .[has] a right to place [his] trust and confidence in these larger entities." . . .

The defendant concedes that while an action sounding in tort may be applicable in third party situations due to the fiduciary relationship established when the insurer assumes control of the litigation, including the power to settle, it has no merit when the insured is bringing the action himself. This Court addressed this argument, albeit indirectly, in *Sullivan* [*v. Allstate Ins. Co.,* 111 Idaho 304, 723 P.2d 848 (1986)]. In *Sullivan,* Justice Shepard noted correctly that the insured, by initiating a first party law suit against the insurer, *does not* necessarily create an adversarial relationship between himself and the insurer which abrogates the special relationship imposed by the insurance contract. In holding that the trial court was correct in issuing a summary judgment, Justice Shepard stated that "the absence of any showing in the record of bad faith on the part of Allstate in failing to pay the claim submitted by the Sullivans [precluded an action in tort]." *Id.,* 723 P.2d at 851 (Sullivan had alleged outrage, willful breach of contract, and bad faith in refusing to settle a claim made under a policy issued by Allstate). What *Sullivan* teaches, then, is that while there may be an action in tort for the willful breach of an insurance contract and for the insurer's bad faith in failing to promptly settle a valid claim, the outcome of any action will depend upon the particular facts of the case.

Of course the mere failure to immediately settle what later proves to be a valid claim does not of itself establish "bad faith." As indicated earlier, the insured must show the insurer "intentionally and unreasonably denies or delays payment. . . ." *Rawlings, supra,* 726 P.2d at 572. An insurer does not act in bad faith when it challenges the validity of a "fairly debatable" claim, or when its delay results from honest mistakes.

Conclusion

The tort of bad faith breach of insurance contract, then, has its foundations in the common law covenant of good faith and fair dealing and is founded upon the unique relationship of the insurer and the insured, the adhesionary nature of the insurance contract including the potential for overreaching on the part of the insurer, and the unique, "non-commercial" aspect of the insurance contract. Accordingly, we hold that there exists a common law tort action, distinct from an action on the contract, for an insurer's bad faith in settling the first party claims of its insured.

II

The second question of law certified by the U.S. District Court for the District of Idaho to this court. . .is whether a private right of action under Idaho's Unfair Claims Settlement Practices Act, Idaho Code § 41-1329 (1977) (hereinafter "the Act") exists, whereby an insured can sue the insurer for statutory violations committed in connection with the settlement of the insured's claim. Although the courts which have interpreted their own "Unfair Claims Settlement Practices Acts" appear to be divided, there is substantial support for the proposition that "Unfair Claims Settlement Practices Acts" create a private right of action, whereby an insured can sue the insurer for statutory violations committed in connection with the settlement of the insured's claim.

The law of torts today provides a wide "variety of new remedies for newly recognized rights, either outside the traditional tort categories or as subcategories thereof." 74 Am. Jur. 2d, Torts, § 3. In some cases, the law offers remedies for intentionally caused injury to another, even though the wrongdoer's conduct falls outside the traditional pigeon-holes. Restatement (Second) Torts § 870 (1965). In others, statutory law establishes rights, defines wrongs, and implies remedies. *Id.* at § 874A.

According to the Restatement (Second) of Torts § 874A (Tort Liability for Violation of Legislative Provision):

> When a legislative provision protects a class of persons by proscribing or requiring certain conduct but does not provide a civil remedy for the violation, the court may, if it determines that the remedy is appropriate in furtherance of the purpose of the legislation and *needed to assure the effectiveness of the provision,* accord to an injured member of the class a right of action, using a suitable existing tort action or a new cause of action analogous to an existing tort action.

Id. (emphasis added). Under § 874A of [t]he Restatement (Second) of Torts, it is clear that the lack of an express civil remedy in the Insurance Code is not fatal to an insured/plaintiff's tort action. However, based on our discussion and holding in question #1, i.e., that there is a common law duty on the part of insurers to their insured to settle the first party claims of their insured in good faith and that a breach of that duty will give rise to an action in tort, we find that a statutory remedy is neither prescribed nor necessary to assure the effectiveness of Idaho's Unfair Claims Settlement Practices Act, Idaho Code § 41-1329. Thus, we hold that Idaho's Unfair Claims Settlement Practices Act, I.C. § 41-1329, does not give rise to a private right of action whereby an insured can sue an insurer for statutory violations committed in connection with the settlement of the insured's claim.

Costs to Respondent; no award of attorneys fees.

DONALDSON, C.J., and HUNTLEY, J., concur.

BAKES, JUSTICE, concurring as to Part II and dissenting as to Part I:

It has long been the law in this state that non-performance of contractual obligations does not give rise to an action in tort. In *Carroll v. United States,* 107 Idaho 717, 629 P.2d 361 (1984), Justice Huntley, writing for four members of the Court, expressly stated:

> Under Idaho law it is settled that an alleged failure to perform a contractual obligation is not actionable in tort. As Justice Bakes observed in his special concurrence in *Dunbar, supra,* Idaho case law establishes that mere breach of contract does not ordinarily constitute a tort. In *Taylor v. Herbold,* 94 Idaho 133, 483 P.2d 664 (1971), we stated, 'To found an action in tort, there must be a breach of duty apart from the *non-performance* of a contract.' In *Just's, Inc. v. Arrington Construction Co.,* 99 Idaho 462, 583 P.2d 997 (1978), we again acknowledged that 'a tort requires the wrongful invasion of an interest protected by the law, not merely an invasion of an interest created by the agreement of the parties.'. . .Mere non-feasance, *even if it amounts to a willful neglect to perform* the contract, is insufficient to establish a duty in tort.

Id. at 719, 629 P.2d at 363. It is readily apparent that the *sine qua non* of plaintiff's claim against Unigard is the non-performance of a contractual obligation, i.e., failure to pay benefits allegedly due under the contract for which plaintiff has paid premiums. While it has been said that "every contract imposes upon each party a duty of good faith and fair dealing in its performance and its enforcement," Restatement (Second) Contracts, § 205 (1979), such a duty does *not* exist independent of the contract itself. The duty of "good faith and fair dealing" acquires meaning only when considered in the context of the underlying contract. The duty arises *only* in the performance and enforcement of a contract.

Thus, any breach of this duty, which is nothing more than a breach of an implied contractual covenant, gives rise to an action on the contract. It does not give rise to an action in tort. An action in tort lies only for breach of a duty imposed by law apart from a contract, *e.g.,* duty to use ordinary care so as to avoid injury to another. The Court's opinion has failed to grasp this fundamental distinction between tort and contract law. "There is no tort liability for. . .failing to do what one has promised to do in the absence of a duty to act apart from the promise made." Prosser, Torts § 92 (1984). In other words, if the alleged obligation to do or not to do something does not exist except for the contract, then breach of such an obligation is answerable only on a contract theory.

The fact that a contractual covenant, such as a covenant of good faith and fair dealing, is implied does not mean that violation of such gives rise to an action in tort. A covenant of good faith and fair dealing is not a duty that exists independent of the contract. An adequate remedy exists in an action on the contract for breach of the covenant of good faith and fair dealing. There simply is no need for this Court to now create an additional action in tort. If breach of the covenant is so egregious so as to constitute "an extreme deviation from reasonable standards of conduct, performed with an understanding of its consequences," *Linscott v. Rainier National Life Ins. Co.*, 100 Idaho 854, 860, 606 P.2d 958, 964 (1980), then the injured party may properly seek punitive damages for such a "bad faith" breach of a covenant of good faith and fair dealing.

Those jurisdictions which have created the tort of bad faith breach of an insurance contract apparently have done so because those same jurisdictions prohibit an injured party from seeking punitive damages in a contract action for such egregious, bad faith conduct. The leading case relied on by the majority, *Gruenberg v. Aetna Ins. Co.*, 9 Cal. 3d 566, 108 Cal. Rptr. 480, 510 P.2d 1032 (1973), was just such a case. California courts are prohibited from awarding punitive damages in breach of contract actions.

> The statute providing for exemplary or punitive damages authorizes the recovery of such damages *only* in an action for the breach of an obligation *not arising from contract*. Thus, an award of exemplary or punitive damages may not be granted to the plaintiff in an action based on a breach of contract, even though the defendant's breach was willful, fraudulent, or malicious.

23 Cal. Jur. 3d, *Damages* § 121 (1975). Thus, the California Supreme Court in *Gruenberg* had no remedy other than creating the bad faith tort in order to redress the alleged unconscionable actions of the insurance company in that case. Contrary to the law in California, the law in Idaho permits recovery of punitive damages in breach of contract actions. Therefore, the *Gruenberg* rationale is not applicable in this jurisdiction. The same is true in Montana where, as the majority opinion itself recognizes, punitive damages are prohibited in contract actions by statute. That explains why the court in *Lipinski v. Title Ins. Co.*, 202 Mont. 1, 655 P.2d 970 (1983), created the new tort of "bad faith" breach of the duty of fair settlement. However, in Idaho, a party alleging unconscionable conduct on the part of an insurance company in settling a claim may properly seek punitive damages in an action on the contract for such egregious or bad faith conduct. *Linscott v. [Rainier] Natl. Life Ins. Co., supra.* Thus, in Idaho, an action in tort is unnecessary. It adds nothing by way of possible recovery that is not already available by way of an action on the contract.

Plaintiff may sue on the contract and seek damages based on her expectation interest under the contract. Damages based on her expectation interest may be measured by "the loss in the value to [her] of [Unigard's] performance caused by its failure or deficiency, plus any loss, including incidental or consequential, caused by the breach." Restatement (Second) Contracts, § 347 (1981). Plaintiff's alleged damage of loss of credit and foreclosure of her property may be compensable in an action on the contract if such damages were foreseeable, or within the contemplation of the parties, at the time the contract was formed. *Hadley v. Baxendale,* 9 Exch. 341, 156 Eng. Rep. 145 (1854); McCormick, Damages § 137, 138 (1935). Any damages resulting from breach of the covenant of good faith and fair dealing would be recoverable to the extent that the party in breach had reason to foresee that such loss would be the probable result of the breach at the time the contract was made. A foreseeable loss is one which follows from the breach of a contract in the ordinary course of events, or even if not in the ordinary course of events a loss which the party in breach had reason to know would result from a breach of the covenant. Restatement (Second) Contracts § 351 (1981). Accordingly, the plaintiff's contract remedies are adequate and there is no reason for this Court to create another new tort.

. . . .

The action of the Court today is particularly inappropriate given the present public perception that there is a crisis in our tort law system which requires immediate legislative tort law reform. Today's decision can only fan the flames of legislative tort law reform.

SHEPARD, J., concurs.

NOTES

1. *Origins of the action.* The tort of bad faith breach of an insurer's obligation was first recognized by a court of last resort in 1973; the landmark case is *Gruenberg v. Aetna Insurance Co.,* 510 P.2d 1032 (Cal. 1973). Through 2000, at least thirty state courts of last resort have approved the principle that an insurer may be liable under a tort theory for damages to an insured or beneficiary beyond the policy limits. A few additional states have enacted statutes creating a bad faith cause of action. See Barry R. Ostrager & Thomas R. Newman, Handbook on Insurance Coverage Disputes § 12.12[b] (10th ed. 2000); see also Roger C. Henderson, *The Tort of Bad Faith in First-Party Insurance Transactions After Two Decades,* 37 Ariz. L. Rev. 1153, 1153–55 (1995). The quick rise of the action has led to a plethora of practitioner-oriented treatises on the subject and much scholarly commentary. See, *e.g., Symposium on the Law of Bad Faith in Contract and Insurance,* 72 Tex. L. Rev. 1203 (1994) (400-plus page symposium issue); Roger C. Henderson, *The Tort of Bad Faith in First-Party Insurance Transactions: Refining the Standard of Culpability and Reformulating the Remedies by Statute,* 26 U. Mich. J. L. Ref. 1 (1992). For concise summaries of the history of bad faith, see Stephen S. Ashley, *One Hundred Years of Bad Faith,* 15 Bad Faith L. Rpt. 207 (1999); John H. Bauman, *Emotional Distress Damages and the Tort of Insurance Bad Faith,* 46 Drake L. Rev. 717, 732–45 (1998).

2. *Contrarian cases.* A majority of courts considering the issue have recognized the tort of bad faith in the first-party situation, but a good number of

courts have rejected it. *See, e.g., Spencer v. Aetna Life & Casualty Insurance Co.,* 227 Kan. 914, 611 P.2d 149 (1980). What can be said in favor of the minority position? If the state has a statute awarding attorney's fees whenever an insurer's denial of coverage is in bad faith, is it necessary to recognize the common law tort? If the jurisdiction recognizes the tort of outrage, is it necessary also to recognize the tort of bad faith? If a legislature has enacted some kind of statute providing an aggrieved insured with an extracontractual remedy, should this remedy be deemed the exclusive one, and the legislature's failure to approve explicitly a "bad faith remedy" be deemed the final word on the issue? *See Stump v. Commercial Union,* 601 N.E.2d 327 (Ind. 1992); *Howell v. Southern Heritage Insurance Co.,* 448 S.E.2d 275 (Ga. Ct. App. 1994).

3. *Tort versus contract.* The majority and dissenting opinions in *White* illustrate fundamental differences in the standards for awarding damages for breach of contract as compared to tort. Even if one acknowledges these differences, does it necessarily follow that the *amount* of damages Justice Bakes would award for the insurer's conduct differs from the amount Justice Bistline would award?

The tort-plaintiff has a more difficult burden to establish the defendant's wrong than the contract-plaintiff, because the tort-plaintiff must show the breach of a standard of care (i.e., some kind of fault) whereas the contract-plaintiff need only establish a promise and the fact that it was not performed (i.e., fault is irrelevant). Once the tort-plaintiff jumps the higher hurdle, however, the tort-plaintiff will be rewarded with larger damages (generally speaking) than the contract-plaintiff because tort law does not have the same limitations on damages as contract law (e.g., the foreseeability and certainty limitations). But even taking contract law's limitations as they are, does not an insurer foresee at the time of contracting that its breach of a disability or health insurance contract is likely to cause substantial emotional distress and other consequential losses to the insured or beneficiary who was depending on the policy for protection? *See Kewin v. Massachusetts Mutual Life Insurance Co.,* 409 Mich. 401, 295 N.W.2d 50 (1980).

4. *The evolving standard for bad faith liability.* Once it is settled that insurer bad faith is a tort action, the question becomes what kind of insurer misconduct is required to make out the tort. Clearly, it must be more than mere nonperformance of the contract; otherwise, the cause of action belongs in the realm of contract law. Early cases referred to conscious or deliberate wrongdoing, such as where the insurer knows the claim is valid but declines to pay it anyway, perhaps hoping to extort a settlement for less than the contract obligation. *See Gruenberg v. Aetna Insurance Co., supra; Christian v. American Home Assurance Co.,* 577 P.2d 899 (Okla. 1978). This kind of intentional wrongdoing fits easily within the traditional notions of what constitutes a tort.

It was not long, however, before some courts began to view "bad faith" as involving less capricious kinds of insurer behavior. A watershed of sorts was the decision of the Supreme Court of Wisconsin in *Anderson v. Continental Insurance Co.,* 271 N.W.2d 368 (Wis. 1978), where the court held that an insurer could be liable for bad faith not only where it denies a claim knowing that it has no legitimate basis for doing so, but also where it "recklessly" disregards the rights of the insured. Under this test, "[e]ven though an insurer does not actually know that it has no legitimate basis for denying a claim, the insurer may still be liable if there is a high probability that it did not have a reasonable basis and the insurer is either: (1) aware of this fact, or (2) has information that would put a reasonable insurer on notice of this fact. In adding the reckless test, the Wisconsin court moved beyond a mere subjective test to more of an objective test." 1995 Henderson, *supra*, at 1157–58. *Anderson* also recognized a safe harbor of sorts for the insurer; in the court's words, "when a claim is 'fairly debatable,' the insurer is entitled to debate it, whether the debate concerns a matter of fact or law." 271 N.W.2d at 376. This means that when the insured's claim is "fairly debatable," the insurer that denies coverage cannot be held liable for bad faith. *See, e.g., Radecki v. Mutual of Omaha Insurance Co.,* 255 Neb. 224, 583 N.W.2d 320 (1998); *Bushey v. Allstate Insurance Co.,* 670 A.2d 807 (Vt. 1995); *Morgan v. American Family Mutual Insurance Co.,* 534 N.W.2d 92 (Iowa 1995); *First Wyoming Bank, N.A., v. Continental Insurance Co.,* 860 P.2d 1094 (Wyo. 1993). What, though, makes a claim "fairly debatable"? Is an insurer's position on coverage "fairly debatable" if it has some legal support, even if it lacks clear supporting authority? Is the insurer's position on any issue of first impression automatically "fairly debatable"? Is the test simply one of asking whether the insurer has a "reasonable" legal argument?

Currently, the rule in most states conforms to the *Anderson* test, but some other jurisdictions have lowered the hurdle for the tort plaintiff still further: at least two jurisdictions have approved a "gross negligence" test, at least three have extended the tort to mere negligent conduct, and one may have come full circle to an ordinary contract-breach standard, i.e., liability without regard to fault, even though the insurer is reasonably mistaken. *Id.,* at 1158– 1159. Was bad faith ever meant to be the equivalent of "negligent adjustment practices"?

5. *The evolving standard and the role of summary judgment.* What are the chances in the mine-run of these cases that an insurer will be able to secure a summary judgment? As a general proposition, one would expect that an insurer which can show a reasonable basis for its position would be entitled to a summary judgment. For example, if the issue is whether, under an accidental death policy, an insurer's death was caused by accident or by illness, the existence of some evidence tending to show that illness caused the death would not necessarily entitle the insurer to a summary judgment on the coverage issue, but it should arguably be adequate to establish (absent other circumstances) the absence of a material disputed issue on the question of the insurer's good faith. But in *Lucas v. State Farm Fire and Casualty Co.,* 963 P.2d 357 (Idaho 1998), the court ruled that the testimony of a single physician that the insured's injuries were "accidental" and therefore covered under the medical payments provisions of an automobile policy created a triable issue of fact regarding whether the insured's claim was "fairly debatable." See 963 P.2d at 357. Judge Schroeder in dissent stated that this result will "open. . .the flood gates to bad faith claims with scant underpinnings and the potential for oppressive litigation that must ultimately be paid for in insurance rates." 963 P.2d at 361. As an insurance consumer, which side of the issue would you take in *Lucas*?

6. *Unfair claims practices statutes.* The most comprehensive statute dealing with insurer claim practices is the Model Unfair Trade Practices Act, drafted by the National Association of Insurance Commissioners. *"Unfair Trade Practices Act,"* in V National Ass'n of Ins. Comm'rs, Model Laws, Regulations, and Guidelines 880-1 (1999). Every state has adopted either the model or legislation similar to it.

California was one of the few states initially to hold that a private cause of action was created under its version of the model act. *Royal Globe Insurance Co. v. Superior Court,* 23 Cal. 2d 880, 592 P.2d 329, 153 Cal. Rptr. 842 (1979). One remarkable aspect of the decision, which prompted much commotion at the time, was the court's holding that not only the insured but also a third party had a cause of action under the statute. This meant, in effect, that the liability insurer owes duties not only to its own insured but also to the third party who sues the insured. The Supreme Court of California subsequently reversed itself in *Moradi-Shalal v. Fireman's Fund Insurance Cos.,* 46 Cal. 3d 287, 758 P.2d 58, 250 Cal. Rptr. 116 (1988). When executing this about-face move, the court observed that 17 out of 19 states to consider the issue after *Royal Globe* rejected *Royal Globe* either explicitly or implicitly, and even the two remaining states that recognized the private right of action disagreed explicitly with other aspects of *Royal Globe.* 758 P.2d at 63–64, 250 Cal. Rptr. at 121–22. In October 1999, the California legislature returned California law to its *Royal Globe* days, when it enacted two bills that partially restored *Royal Globe* liability. See Richard L. Antognini, *Forward to the Past: California's New-And Old-Bad Faith Statutes,* 22 Ins. Lit. Rptr. 4 (2000). These statutes, however, were short-lived. In California, statutes can be overturned by public referendum, and on November 17, 1999, opponents of the bills presented 1.5 million voter signatures to the Secretary of State, more than enough to require the two bills to be put to a public vote. Thus, California voters had the last word on this issue: in the March 2000 California primary election, approximately 68 percent of the voters decided against implementing the two bills. See Joanne Kochaniec, *Voters reject bad-faith law,* Bus. Ins., Mar. 13, 2000, at 2.

7. *Is coverage necessary?* Can an insurer be liable for bad faith claims processing in a circumstance where the policy provides no coverage? If statutory law obligates insurers to deal with insureds according to prescribed minimum standards, is it necessary for a claim to be within coverage for an insurer to liable to an insured for breach of the duty? If not, what is the remedy for the insurer's breach in a circumstances where coverage does not exist? Is mandating coverage by estoppel appropriate? *See Coventry Associates v. American States Insurance Co.,* 136 Wash.2d 269, 961 P.2d 933 (1998); Douglas R. Richmond, *Truly "Extracontractual" Coverage: Insurer Bad Faith in the Absence of Coverage,* 29 Tort & Ins. L. J. 740 (1994).

In a similar vein, note that the insurer's conduct about which the insured complained in *White* involved the failure to pay benefits under the policy. Is the tort of bad faith limited to benefits-related issues (*e.g.,* destroying evidence relating to the insured's claim for benefits; conditioning payment of an undisputed portion of a claim on settlement of a disputed portion; using undue threats to coerce the insured to settle a claim), or can an insurer be liable for conduct which has little or nothing to do with the decision to pay benefits? Consider the next case.

RAWLINGS v. APODACA

151 Ariz. 149, 726 P.2d 565 (1986)

FELDMAN, JUSTICE.

[Editors' note: The facts and discussion of the insurer's obligation of good faith and fair dealing appear in § 1.03, *supra*.]

2. *Is Breach of an Express Covenant to Pay Claims a Necessary Element of a Cause of Action?*

Having analyzed the interests protected by the implied covenant of good faith, we turn to measure the insurer's conduct in the case at bar. We must begin with a review of Arizona cases to consider the reach of the implied covenant.

A. *Third-Party Cases*

The tort of bad faith developed as a response to insurance adjustment abuses in third-party liability cases. *Crisci v. Security Insurance Co., supra; see also* 16A Appleman, Insurance Law and Practice § 8877 (1981). The early Arizona cases, *Parsons v. Continental National American Group, supra, General Accident Fire & Life Assurance Corp. v. Little,* 103 Ariz. 435, 443 P.2d 690 (1968), and *Farmers Insurance Exchange v. Henderson,* 82 Ariz. 335, 313 P.2d 404 (1957), present typical third-party bad faith situations.

Henderson was the first case in which we addressed the question of an insurer's liability for failure to settle a third-party claim against its insured. Because the insurer rejected three settlement offers despite the strong probability of an adverse verdict, we adopted the "equality of consideration" test to determine whether the insurer had breached its duty of good faith by insufficient consideration of the possibility that refusal to settle might harm the insured. Under this test, with the insurer in sole control of a decision that might result in great damage to the insured, we held that "common honesty" demanded that the insurer give "equal thought to the end that both the insured and the insurer shall be protected." 82 Ariz. at 338, 313 P.2d at 406.

On similar facts in *Little,* we held the insurer had breached its duty of good faith and fair dealing by rejecting the settlement offer and exposing its insured to great harm on the mere chance that it might avoid all liability. 103 Ariz. at 443, 443 P.2d at 698. In both *Henderson* and *Little,* we found a breach of the implied covenant of good faith even though the insurer breached no express covenant of the contract. Nothing in the policy requires the carrier to settle; the policy simply gives the insurer the right to settle if it thinks it best. Also, under the "no action" clause, it requires payment of the claim only if and when a judgment is entered against the insured.

In *Parsons* the policy excluded injuries caused by intentional acts; the attorney therefore rejected numerous settlement offers within the policy limit, and then failed to defend the insured at trial. After judgment was entered for twice the policy limit, the insurer refused to pay, claiming no coverage. We noted the attorney's duty of "undeviating and single allegiance" to the insured. 113 Ariz. at 227, 550 P.2d at 981. Because the lawyer that it provided had actively worked against his client's interest, the insurer was held liable for the entire judgment against the insured. Here again, no express covenant was breached. The company had refused payment of a claim which was not covered. Insurance policies generally give the insurer the right to select counsel and obligate it to provide a defense. They do not require the carrier to provide a defense with "undeviating. . .allegiance" to the insured, yet we held the insurer liable when the attorney failed to do so.

B. *First-Party Cases*

In *Noble v. National American Life Insurance Co., supra,* we recognized the tort of bad faith in first-party cases. In *Noble* the plaintiff had submitted a valid claim for surgical and hospital expenses to her insurance company, which refused to pay. We held that an insurer that intentionally and unreasonably denies or delays payment breaches the covenant of good faith owed to its insured. A failure to pay a claim is unreasonable unless the claim's validity is "fairly debatable" after an adequate investigation. *Id.* In *Sparks v. Republic National Life Insurance Co.,* 132 Ariz. 529, 647 P.2d 1127, *cert. denied,* 459 U.S. 1070, 103 S. Ct. 490, 74 L. Ed. 2d 632 (1982), we reached a similar result in a case where the insurer groundlessly asserted that it had no obligation to continue payments once the policy was terminated. As a result, the claimant had to forego necessary treatment, and suffered serious physical deformities. We held that the fair debatability of the claim cannot be created by the insurer's reliance on ambiguity in the policy, otherwise "insurers would be encouraged to write ambiguous insurance contracts. . . ." 132 Ariz. at 539, 647 P.2d at 1137.

In *Farr v. Transamerica Occidental Life Insurance Co.,* 145 Ariz. 1, 699 P.2d 376 (App. 1984), the court of appeals held that fair debatability cannot be raised where the insurer failed to make an adequate investigation. *Farr,* like *Sparks,* demonstrates that an insurer may be held liable in a first-party case when it seeks to gain unfair financial advantage of its insured through conduct that invades the insured's right to honest and fair treatment.

Thus, in first-party cases also, the insurer's eventual performance of the express covenant — by paying the claim — does *not* release it from liability for "bad faith". The prohibition against challenging a claim unless it is fairly debatable merely expresses the obligation to give equal consideration to the insured's interests. *Gruenberg v. Aetna Insurance Co.,* 9 Cal. 3d at 573, 108 Cal. Rptr. at 485, 510 P.2d at 1037, *cited in Noble v. National American Life Insurance Co.,* 128 Ariz. at 189, 624 P.2d at 867. *See also Tank v. State Farm Fire & Casualty Co.,* 105 Wash. 2d 381, 715 P.2d 1133 (1986) ("an insurance company's duty of good faith [means] an insurer must deal *fairly* with an insured, giving equal consideration *in all matters* to the insured's interests" (emphasis added)).

As we have seen, *Noble, Sparks* and *Farr* are in line with this result. Failure to perform the express covenant to pay the claim is not the *sine qua non* for an action for breach of the implied covenant of good faith and fair dealing. To characterize the cases otherwise, would, in effect, construe them to hold that any breach of the express covenant would give rise to the tort action for bad faith. We hold explicitly that such a result is not permitted. Not every breach of an express covenant in an insurance contract is a breach of the covenant of good faith and fair dealing. Insurance companies, like other enterprises and all human beings, are far from perfect. Papers get lost, telephone messages misplaced and claims ignored because paperwork was misfiled or improperly processed. Such isolated mischances may result in a claim being unpaid or delayed. None of these mistakes will ordinarily constitute a breach of the implied covenant of good faith and fair dealing, even though the company may render itself liable for at least nominal damages for breach of contract in failing to pay the claim.

The cases do not require the insurer to prevent all harm to the insured. As long as it acts honestly, on adequate information and does not place paramount importance on its own interests, it should not be held liable because of a good faith mistake in performance or judgment.

3. *Farmers' Conduct*

Review of Arizona first-party and third-party cases demonstrates that the implied covenant of good faith and fair dealing can be breached even though the company performs its express covenants under the insurance contract. The implied covenant is breached, whether the carrier pays the claim or not, when its conduct damages the very protection or security which the insured sought to gain by buying insurance. *Noble, supra*, at 189, 624 P.2d at 868 (insured has an interest in receiving "protection against calamity."). While the obligation of good faith does not require the insurer to relieve the insured of all possible harm that may come from his choice of policy limits, it does obligate the insurer not to take advantage of the unequal positions in order to become a second source of injury to the insured.

In the case at bench the trial court found that Farmers intentionally pursued a course of conduct designed, for its own benefit, to impede the insureds' claim against the tortfeasor. Thus, although Farmers performed its express covenants, the evidence supports the conclusion that for its own profit Farmers breached its duty to play fairly with its insureds and to give their legitimate interests equal consideration. Those legitimate interests of the insureds arose out of the very event against which Farmers sold protection. The insureds would clearly have been better off without any insurance if by paying $10,000 the insurer could prevent the insureds' recovery of the larger portion of the loss.

Did the Trial Court Err in Considering Expert Testimony to Establish a Duty of Good Faith and Fair Dealing?

During trial plaintiffs' expert witness, James W. Richardson, testified that it is customary in the insurance industry to turn over investigative reports (such as the one denied to Rawlings) to insureds. Mr. Richardson also testified that Farmers had breached industry custom in its attempt to limit its exposure as Apodacas' liability carrier. Defendant argues that such testimony was irrelevant under *Sparks v. Republic National Life Insurance Co., supra.* Sparks held that the "scope of the duty of good faith cannot be delineated by customs of the insurance industry." 132 Ariz. at 539, 647 P.2d at 1137. Because the trial court's findings of fact indicate that the trial court did consider the expert testimony and because defendant claims the judgment against Farmers was based solely on the inadmissible testimony, it argues that the trial court judgment must be reversed.

We disagree. *Sparks* held only that an insurance company could not limit the scope of its duty to the customs of the insurance industry and therefore affirmed the trial court's refusal to instruct the jury that custom was an absolute defense. *Id.* Although compliance with industry custom is not an absolute defense, failure to comply may be relevant to the question of an insurer's alleged bad faith. The trial court therefore did not err in considering such evidence.

Availability of Tort Recovery

Having found that the facts do support the trial court's determination that Farmers breached the implied covenant of good faith and fair dealing, we turn now to inquire whether an action for such breach sounds in tort or in contract.

We have previously noted that the remedy for breach of the implied covenant of good faith is ordinarily on the contract itself. *Wagenseller v. Scottsdale Memorial Hospital,* 147 Ariz. at 383, 710 P.2d at 1038. We remarked, however, that under certain circumstances breach of the covenant may provide the basis for tort claim and noted that tort recovery for breach of the implied covenant is well established in actions brought on insurance contracts but only reluctantly extended to other relationships.

Analysis of the cases does not result in a clear rationale as to when an action for breach of the implied covenant sounds in contract or tort; it "would not be possible to reconcile the results of all cases." W. Prosser & W. Keeton, Law of Torts § 92, at 655 (5th ed. 1984). We agree with the authors' observation:

> Tort obligations are in general obligations that are imposed by law — apart from and independent of promises made and therefore apart from the manifested intention of the parties — to avoid injury to others. By injury here is meant simply the interference with the individual's interest. . .that is deemed worthy of legal protection. . . . [One category is] a large body of intangible interests, both economic and relational.

Id.

Analysis of the cases does lead to the conclusion that a tort action for breach of the implied covenant is more often recognized where the contract creates a relationship in which the law implies special duties not imposed on other contractual relationships. These relationships are "characterized by elements of public interest, adhesion, and fiduciary responsibility." Examples include the implied relational duty of the common carrier to carry his passengers or goods safely. Failure to perform this implied covenant may expose the carrier to liability in tort as well as on the contract of carriage. The law has imposed similar implied covenants on the relationships between innkeeper and guest, physician and patient and attorney and client. In the last two relationships the implied covenant demands reasonable competence, and for its breach the patient or client may maintain an action in either tort or contract. See W. Prosser & W. Keeton, *supra* § 92, at 660–62 (citing numerous cases).

> The principle which seems to have emerged from the decisions in the United States is that there will be liability in tort for misperformance of a contract whenever there would be liability for gratuitous performance without the contract — which is to say, whenever such misperformance involves a foreseeable, unreasonable risk of harm to the interests of the plaintiff.

Id. at 661.

This concept is not a recent development in the law.

> If a defendant may be held liable for the neglect of a duty imposed on him, independently of any contract, by operation of law, a fortiori, ought he to be liable where he has come under an obligation to use care as the result of an undertaking founded on a consideration. Where the duty has its roots in contract, the undertaking to observe due care may be implied from the relationship, and should it be the fact that a breach of the agreement also constitutes such a failure to exercise care as amounts to a tort, the plaintiff may elect, as the common law authorities have it, to sue in case or in assumpsit.

Flint & Walling Manufacturing Co. v. Beckett, 167 Ind. 491, 498, 79 N.E. 503, 505 (1906).

Tort actions for breach of covenants implied in certain types of contractual relationships are most often recognized where the type of contract involved is one in which the plaintiff seeks something more than commercial advantage or profit from the defendant. When dealing with an innkeeper, a common carrier, a lawyer, a doctor or an insurer, the client/customer seeks service, security, peace of mind, protection or some other intangible. These types of contracts create special, partly noncommercial relationships, and when the provider of the service fails to provide the very item which was the implicit objective of the making of the contract, then contract damages are seldom adequate, and the cases have generally permitted the plaintiff to maintain an action in tort as well as in contract. W. Prosser & W. Keeton, *supra,* § 92, at 660–61.

The final important factor which we extract from the cases is that of deterrence. In contractual relationships in which one party primarily has sought protection or security rather than profit or advantage, contract damages not only fail to provide adequate compensation but also fail to provide a substantial deterrence against breach by the party who derives a commercial benefit from the relationship.

> In the first place, they offer no motivation whatsoever for the insurer *not* to breach. If the only damages an insurer will have to pay upon a judgment of breach are the amounts that it would have owed under the policy plus interest, it has every interest in retaining the money,

earning the higher rates of interest on the outside market, and hoping eventually to force the insured into a settlement for less than the policy amount.

Wallis v. Superior Court, 160 Cal. App. 3d at 1117, 207 Cal. Rptr. at 128 (emphasis in original).[4] Thus, we conclude that one of the prime reasons for the recognition of tort actions for breach of the implied obligations raised by certain contractual relationships is that any other rule provides more of an incentive for breach of the contract than for its performance. Certainly, this is often the situation in insurance contracts and, we believe, makes tort remedies appropriate for some types of breach of the duties implied by law in the contractual relationship.

In short, just as some breaches of contractual duties do not implicate the covenant of good faith, some breaches of the implied covenant may not provide the basis for tort recovery, although they may give rise to an action on the express covenant in which contract rules of damages would be applicable. But in special contractual relationships, when one party intentionally breaches the implied covenant of good faith and fair dealing, and when contract remedies serve only to encourage such conduct, it is appropriate to permit the damaged party to maintain an action in tort and to recover tort damages.

In insurance cases we believe the culpable conduct is an intentional act[5] by which the insurer fails to provide the insured with the security and protection from calamity which is the object of the relationship.

The "intent" required here is an "evil hand" — the intent to do the act. Mere negligence or inadvertence is not sufficient — the insurer must intend the act or omission and must form that intent without reasonable or fairly debatable grounds. But an "evil mind" is not required; the insurer need not intend to harm the insured (an issue that arises with respect to the punitive damage question. To be liable for tort damages, it need only to have intended its act or omission, lacking a founded belief that such conduct was permitted by the policy.

The founded belief is absent when the insurer either knows that its position is groundless or when it fails to undertake an investigation adequate to determine whether its position is tenable. In either event, its position is without reasonable basis and subjects it to payment of damages in addition to those traditionally recoverable in a breach of contract action.[6] We do not

---

[4] The English seem to have evolved a similar rule for similar reasons. The English system evidently allows punitive damages for breach of contract where defendant "with a cynical disregard for a plaintiff's rights has calculated that the monetary gain arising out of his wrongdoing will most likely exceed the damages at risk." *See Trans Container Services v. Security Forwarders, Inc.,* 752 F.2d 483, 487 (9th Cir.1985), citing *Rookes v. Barnard,* [1964] A.C. 1129 at 1227. *See also Nicholson v. United Pacific Insurance Co.,* 710 P.2d 1342, 1348 (Mont. 1985).

[5] Again, distinguishing between inadvertence, loss of papers, misfiling of documents and like mischance, negligent or not. *See ante* at 157, 726 P.2d at 573.

[6] We acknowledge, of course, that tort actions for breach of contractually created relationships — such as doctor-patient, lawyer-client, innkeeper-guest — may be maintained even though the defendant's conduct was unintentional. The difference between these and the requirement of intent in "bad faith" cases is attributable to the difference in the covenant implied by law. In the doctor-patient relationship, for example, the law

reach the question of whether the law recognizes tort claims arising out of the insurer/insured relationship and based only upon negligence. *See* Jerry, *Remedying Insurers' Bad Faith Contract Performance: A Reassessment,* 18 Conn. L. Rev. 271, 284–85 (1986). To date Arizona cases have been based only upon a "bad faith" theory.

With this in mind, we turn to examine Farmers' conduct in the case at bench. The evidence supports the trial judge's ultimate factual finding that Farmers attempted to prevent Rawlings' suit against the tortfeasor and that it did so to protect its own financial interests, indifferent to the loss Rawlings would sustain. The evidentiary facts indicate that Farmers pursued this objective by deceit, nondisclosure, reneging on promises, violation of industry custom and deliberate attempts to obfuscate. As noted above, the fact that Farmers paid the claim, while a factor to be considered, is not determinative. What avail was it to Rawlings to recover $10,000 on a $40,000 loss if the company simultaneously destroyed his ability to recover the portion of the loss which was uninsured? The trial court did not err in finding that Farmers committed a tort.

Did the Trial Court Err in Awarding Plaintiffs Compensatory Damages Against Farmers?

Defendant claims that the $1,000 compensatory tort award was "wholly unsupported by any evidence." Defendant argues further that punitive damages may not be awarded absent findings of actual damages.

When, as here, tort damages are recoverable, plaintiff is not limited to the economic damages within the contemplation of the parties at the time the contract was made. *Farr v. Transamerica Occidental Life Insurance Co.,* 145 Ariz. at 6, 699 P.2d at 381. Plaintiff may recover all the losses caused by defendant's conduct, including damages for pain, humiliation and inconvenience, as well as for pecuniary losses. *Id.;* 22 Am. Jur. 2d Damages § 11; Restatement (Second) of Torts § 903. It is undisputed that Rawlings expended his own time and effort trying to obtain the reports. Once that proved unavailing, he then had to retain an attorney to pursue the matter, first with the company, then with the Department of Insurance and finally by filing this lawsuit. The trial judge found that Rawlings sustained damage because (1) they had to hire attorneys to obtain the promised report, (2) they had to spend their own time trying to obtain the report, and (3) they did not receive the report until it was too late to commission their own on-site investigation of the fire. There may be uncertainty as to the amount of damages, but there is none as to the fact that some damage resulted from the wrong. Under some circumstances the finder of fact is given great latitude in fixing the amount. There was no error in the award of compensatory damage. We now turn to the question of whether punitive damages were appropriate.

---

implies an undertaking by the doctor to have and exercise the skill of an average, competent physician. *Harvey v. Kellin,* 115 Ariz. 496, 499, 566 P.2d 297, 300 (1977). Negligence consists of the failure to do so and subjects the doctor to tort liability for the damage resulting therefrom. *Kronke v. Danielson,* 108 Ariz. 400, 499 P.2d 156, 159 (1972).

Punitive Damages

There is some controversy over whether the rule for awards of punitive damages in bad faith tort cases differs from that which exists in other types of tort cases.[7] The argument is advanced that since bad faith is a species of intentional tort, punitive damages are automatically recoverable in every case in which the plaintiff proves that the tort was committed. We reject that contention. In a series of recent cases, our court of appeals has held that punitive damages may not be awarded in a bad faith tort case unless the evidence reflects "something more" than the conduct necessary to establish the tort. *Farr v. Transamerica Occidental Life Insurance Co.,* 145 Ariz. at 7, 699 P.2d at 383 (relying on *Neal v. Farmers Insurance Exchange,* 21 Cal. 3d 910, 148 Cal. Rptr. 389, 582 P.2d 980 (1978)). We agree with the views expressed in *Farr.*

Although the tort of bad faith is founded upon the defendant's intentional conduct, the intent need not be an intent to injure, harm or oppress. It is sufficient to establish the *tort* of bad faith that the defendant has acted intentionally. The jury need not even be instructed on intent. *Sparks,* 132 Ariz. at 538, 647 P.2d at 1136.

However, the species of intentional conduct necessary for recovery of tort damages in a bad faith case may fall short of what is required for a punitive damage award. In this as in other torts, both intentional and unintentional,[8] punitive damages are only recoverable under special circumstances.

> Something more than the mere commission of a tort is always required for punitive damages. There must be circumstances of aggravation or outrage, such as spite or "malice," or a fraudulent or evil motive on the part of the defendant, or such a *conscious and deliberate disregard* of the interests of others that the conduct may be called wilful or wanton. There is general agreement that, because it lacks this element, mere negligence is not enough, even though it is so extreme and egregious to be characterized as "gross," a term of ill-defined content, which occasionally, in a few jurisdictions, has been stretched. . .to justify punitive damages.

W. Prosser & W. Keeton, *supra,* § 2, at 9–10 (emphasis supplied) (citations omitted).

We do not believe that the concept of punitive damages should be stretched. We restrict its availability to those cases in which the defendant's wrongful conduct was guided by evil motives. Thus, to obtain punitive damages, plaintiff must prove that defendant's evil hand was guided by an evil mind. The evil mind which will justify the imposition of punitive damages may be manifested in either of two ways. It may be found where defendant intended to injure the plaintiff. It may also be found where, although not intending to cause injury, defendant consciously pursued a course of conduct knowing that

---

[7] We have recently accepted review and heard argument in two cases in which the issue is presented. *See Linthicum v. Nationwide Life Insurance Co.,* 150 Ariz. 326, 723 P.2d 675 (1986), and *Hawkins v. Allstate Insurance Co.,* No. CV 86 0010-PR.

[8] For example, punitive damages are not recoverable in every fraud case, even though fraud is an intentional tort.

it created a substantial risk of significant harm to others. It has been stated that action justifying the award of punitive damages is "conduct involving some element of outrage similar to that usually found in crime." Restatement (Second) of Torts § 908 comment b; see also W. Prosser & W. Keeton, § 2 at 9. Applying this analogy, punitive damages will be awarded on proof from which the jury may find that the defendant was "aware of and consciously disregard[ed] a substantial and unjustifiable risk that" significant harm would occur. See A.R.S. § 13-105(5)(c), defining criminal recklessness.

Thus, we establish no new category of punitive damages for bad faith cases. Such damages are recoverable in bad faith tort actions when, *and only when,* the facts establish that defendant's conduct was aggravated, outrageous, malicious or fraudulent. Indifference to facts or failure to investigate are sufficient to establish the tort of bad faith but may not rise to the level required by the punitive damage rule. The difference is no doubt harder to articulate in legalistic terms than it is to differentiate on the facts. To obtain tort damages, for instance, plaintiff must prove only that defendant failed to ascertain the true facts and thus acted without or indifferent to the reasonable basis required for denying the claim. To obtain punitive damages, plaintiff must also show that the evil hand that unjustifiably damaged the objectives sought to be reached by the insurance contract was guided by an evil mind which either consciously sought to damage the insured or acted intentionally, knowing that its conduct was likely to cause unjustified, significant damage to the insured. When defendant's motives are shown to be so improper, *or* its conduct so oppressive, outrageous or intolerable that such an "evil mind" may be inferred, punitive damages may be awarded. Restatement (Second) of Torts § 908(2).

Of course, what is intolerable and what motives are truly evil may in many cases be determined at least in part by the type of relationship of the parties. Thus, conduct justifying the award of punitive damages in bad faith tort cases may often be categorized. The court of appeals' thoughtful opinion in *Farr, supra,* covers most of the categories which occur to us. The court mentions such things as fraudulent conduct and "deliberate, overt and dishonest dealings," "oppressive conduct" and "insult and personal abuse." 145 Ariz. at 8–9, 699 P.2d at 383–84. No doubt there are other motives and categories of conduct which evince an "evil mind" and neither this opinion nor *Farr* can be considered all-inclusive.

We turn, again, to the case before us. The trial judge's conclusion of law number 6 was that "Farmers' conduct. . .was intentional and warrants the imposition of punitive damages." No specific findings were made to support this conclusion. For this we do not fault the trial judge, because this case was tried before the decision in *Farr, supra,* and at a time when it may have been assumed that punitive damages could always be recovered for the "intentional tort" of bad faith. The trial judge may or may not have applied the appropriate standards which must be met before punitive damages may be recovered. Those standards are now delineated in *Farr* and this opinion.

In our view, it is better that the punitive damage issue be reexamined by the trial judge under the guidelines laid down in *Farr* and this opinion. We do not suggest any particular disposition. Having heard the evidence, the trial judge is in the best position to consider whether or not it persuades him that Farmers' motive or conduct evinced the "evil mind" which must exist to allow the award of punitive damages. The trial judge may, in his discretion, reopen to take additional evidence on the question of motive and conduct in so far as punitive damages are concerned.

Summary

A covenant of good faith and fair dealing is implied in every contract to prevent each party from impairing the right of the other to receive the benefits which flow from the contract and the relationship it creates. The covenant of good faith and fair dealing may be breached even though the express covenants of the contract are fully performed. For an insured, one of the implied objects of the policy is the protection, security and peace of mind that come from having purchased protection from the economic consequences of catastrophe. Thus an insurer who damages an implied object of the insurance relationship by failing to give its insured equal consideration may breach the implied covenant even though it provides the expressly promised protection.

The breach of contractual covenants ordinarily sounds in contract. However, because of the special relationship between an insurer and its insured, the insured may maintain an action to recover tort damages if the insurer, by an intentional act, also breaches the implied covenant by failing to deal fairly and honestly with its insured's claim or by failing to give equal and fair consideration to the insured's interests.

Finally, if in addition the insured demonstrates that the insurer acted with the evil mind described above, then plaintiff may recover punitive damages.

. . . The judgment is affirmed on all issues except that of punitive damages and is remanded for further proceedings not inconsistent with this opinion.

GORDON, V.C.J., and HAYS and CAMERON, JJ., concur.

HOLOHAN, CHIEF JUSTICE, dissenting.

In *Noble v. National American Life Insurance Co.,* 128 Ariz. 188, 624 P.2d 866 (1981), and in *Sparks v. Republic National Life Insurance Co.,* 132 Ariz. 529, 647 P.2d 1127, *cert. denied,* 459 U.S. 1070, 103 S. Ct. 490, 74 L. Ed. 2d 632 (1982), this court set forth the elements of the tort of "bad faith." Whatever wrong the insurance company committed in this case, it is not the tort of "bad faith."

The rights and obligations of the parties in this case were established by the contract of insurance. The record is clear that the insurance company paid the insured's claim timely and in the amount required by the policy. The majority opinion has yet to demonstrate that there is any provision in the insurance policy which required the insurer to do more than it did. Even applying the so-called "expectations" concept to the insurance contract, there is nothing presented which would indicate that the insured had any belief that the insurance contract required the insurance company to do anything more than pay the amount of the claim.

What the facts of the case demonstrate is that there were representations and promises by the insurance company to the insured which were independent and unrelated to the obligations of the insurance contract. The conduct of the insurer in failing to furnish the report of its investigation, as promised, or otherwise assisting the insured in proving a claim against a third party may be actionable, but not under the tort of "bad faith." There is no Arizona authority which supports the majority's position that this course of dealing is a part of the contract of insurance.

The Court of Appeals, in my judgment, was correct when it stated:

> Assuming, without deciding, that the action of the insurer in the case at bench may have been actionable under another theory, such as fraud or misrepresentation, we do not find that it comes within the limited definition of the tort of "bad faith" as defined in *Noble* and subsequent cases. Nor do we find it appropriate to extend the tort of "bad faith" to fit this situation.

Rawlings v. Apodaca, 151 Ariz. 180, 188, 726 P.2d 596, 604 (App. 1986). I agree with the reasoning in the opinion of the Court of Appeals, and I, therefore, dissent from the opinion of this court.

NOTES

1. *Are customary practices "rights"?* If the expert testimony in *Rawlings* that it is customary to turn over investigative reports to an insured upon request is accurate, does it follow that the insured has a right to the report? If the report involves the liability of another of the insurer's insureds, what right, if any, does the other insured have to maintain the report's confidentiality?

2. *The purpose of the policy.* Is there a difference between bad faith failure to pay benefits and bad faith claims processing? If the insurer engages in bad faith claims processing but pays the claim's full value anyway, should the insured have a bad faith remedy? *See Deese v. State Farm Mutual Automobile Insurance Co.,* 172 Ariz. 504, 838 P.2d 1265 (1992). If the insurer pays a property damage claim after a protracted effort to prove that the insureds committed arson, could the insurer be held liable for bad faith? Does it depend on how the insurer handles the claim? *See State Farm Fire & Casualty Co. v. Simmons,* 963 S.W.2d 42 (Tex. 1998); *Powers v. United Services Automobile Ass'n,* 114 Nev. 79, 962 P.2d 596 (1998).

How were the Rawlings damaged by the insurer's failure to provide the investigative report? To justify a tort remedy, presumably there must have been some kind of damage to an interest protected by the social controls found in the law of tort. If the Rawlings had lost their case against the Apodacas for lack of the investigative report, would that have constituted a consequential, extracontractual harm? Is it enough to constitute bad faith that the insurer impede the insured's recovery, even if the insured ultimately recovers under the policy?

3. *Explanation and advice.* If an insured is ignorant of policy rights or benefits, is it bad faith for the insurer to fail to point these out to the insured? In *Thomas v. Northwestern National Insurance Co.,* 292 Mont. 357, 973 P.2d 804 (1998), the court held that when an insurer issues a renewal policy, it

has an affirmative duty to provide adequate notice of changes in coverage, and that breach of the duty may give rise to liability for bad faith. Citing its prior opinion in *Story v. City of Bozeman,* 242 Mont. 436, 791 P.2d 767 (1990), the court indicated that the common law tort of bad faith can be pursued in the contractual setting only if there is a "special relationship" between the contracting parties, but the court was satisfied that such a relationship exists between an insurer and insured. 973 P.2d at 810. Does this suggest a test along the lines of "silence plus something more," which could be met if the insurer's silence is combined with, for example, an affirmative act whereby the insurer attempted to deceive the insured? *See MFA Mutual Insurance Co. v. Flint,* 574 S.W.2d 718 (Tenn. 1978). Does it make a difference whether the insured is represented by counsel? *See Miller v. Keystone Insurance Co.,* 636 A.2d 1109 (Pa. 1994). See generally Alan I. Widiss, *Obligating Insurers to Inform Insureds About the Existence of Rights and Duties Regarding Coverage for Losses,* 1 Conn. Ins. L. J. 67 (1995).

4. *Punitive damages.* In most cases, the extracontractual compensatory damages likely to be caused by the insurer's bad faith will be modest. The treasure trove for the plaintiff-insured will be the punitive damage claim. To the extent punitive damage liability, as a general matter, is constricted in the future, the importance of bad faith claims will be diminished. (For more information on trends in punitive damage liability, see the materials in § 5.03[1], *supra.*) Pending retrenchment in the availability of punitive damages generally, are you confident about the ability of judges to discriminate between insurer conduct that deserves to be punished and insurer denials of coverage that has sound justification? Alan Sykes offers the following assessment:

> [S]ome theoretical justification exists for punitive damages when the insurer's refusal to pay a claim is utterly baseless and strategic — cases defined here as "intentional breach." Perhaps the strongest argument for stiff extracontractual penalties in these cases is that insurers might otherwise exploit the prospect of delay in litigation to extract favorable settlements from insureds with high implicit discount rates But the importance of this possibility should not be exaggerated. Impatient insureds may have some viable counterstrategies against an opportunistic insurer, such as assignment and borrowing. Moreover, additional damage remedies for the wrongful denial of meritorious claims could be provided by contract, and it is important to consider what inference should be drawn from their failure to emerge in competitive insurance markets. Perhaps the proper inference is that error costs in the administration of such measures would swamp any benefits. And even if the absence of contractual remedies reflects market failure, it is possible that measures to reduce delay in litigation, such as mandatory arbitration, would better serve the parties joint interests than measures to increase the damages award.

Alan O. Sykes, *"Bad Faith" Breach of Contract by First-Party Insurers,* 25 J. Leg. Studies 405, 407 (1996). If the insurer's breach is not intentional, do you think, as Professor Sykes frames the question, that "it may be impossible as a practical matter for courts to distinguish opportunistic behavior by an insurer in the face of uncertainty about the merits of a claim [which may deserve a penalty for claim denial given that the only consequence is perhaps having to pay the claim later] from behavior that has sound justification"? See *id.*

5. *The fall of insurer bad faith?* By the 1990s, much of the bad faith turmoil had ebbed. One of the most important reasons for the relative calm was the Supreme Court's 1987 decision in *Pilot Life Insurance Co. v. Dedeaux,* 481 U.S. 41 (1987). In that case, the Court held that the Employee Retirement Income Security Act of 1974 (ERISA), 88 Stat. 829, as amended, 29 U.S.C. § 1001 *et seq.,* preempts state common law tort and contract actions asserting improper processing of a claim for benefits under an insured employee benefit plan. This affects claimants who are insured through group contracts provided by their employers and which cover medical, surgical, or hospital care, or benefits in the event of sickness, accident, disability or death. Under the holding in *Pilot Life,* the civil enforcement remedies set forth in ERISA are exclusive.

Pilot Life has been subject to strong criticism; further, subsequent Supreme Court ERISA preemption cases have hardly been a model of consistency. See Robert H. Jerry, II, Understanding Insurance Law § 21[e] (2d ed. 1996). Nevertheless, it appears, under the authority of *Pilot Life* and its progeny, that ERISA preempts all state remedies, including those under statutes like the Model Unfair Trade Practices Act. Because the vast preponderance of private health and disability and most life insurance is provided through employer-sponsored group plans, the tort of bad faith is preempted in these large segments of the market. What is left are property and liability insurance policies, which are hardly ever marketed on a group basis, and life, disability, and health insurance purchased by individuals. Does it make sense that insureds under individual policies have more rights under state law than insureds under group policies? Does it make sense that ERISA, which was designed to increase employees' rights, has the effect of constricting employees' rights with respect to employer-provided insurance policies?

At 2000, the controversy over ERISA preemption is particularly intense with respect to health insurance and health care services. Because most health insurance and managed care plans are employer-provided welfare benefit plans, the only remedies for contract-related denials of care are those provided by the ERISA remedial scheme, and these remedies do not include tort damages. A public consensus seems to be emerging that the full measure of ERISA preemption is unwise, although exactly what should take its place remains the subject of intensely partisan disagreement in Washington, D.C.

·[2] Third-Party Insurance

When an insurer breaches the duty to defend, the insurer is liable for damages calculated in accordance with familiar contract formulas. This subject was explored in § 8.02[6]. Should the insurer's liability increase if the refusal to defend is in "bad faith?" If insurers are liable in tort for bad faith denials of coverage and bad faith claims processing in first-party insurance, why not have the same outcome in third-party insurance? The "third-party" question was broached in § 8.02[5], where the insurer's liability for breach of settlement obligations was explored. Where this liability is grounded in tort, as it is in most jurisdictions, the questions are answered in the affirmative.

As it turns out, the tort of bad faith in first-party insurance has its roots in third-party cases. Actually, it was a series of decisions in California involving liability insurance that ignited the evolution of the bad faith tort. A 1957 California appeals court decision used "good faith" as the standard to describe the circumstances in which the insurer incurs a liability in excess of the policy limits for failing to accept a settlement offer. *See Brown v. Guarantee Insurance Co.,* 155 Cal. App. 2d 679, 319 P.2d 69 (1957). One year later, the California Supreme Court in *Comunale v. Traders & General Insurance Co.,* 50 Cal. 2d 654, 328 P.2d 198 (1958), held that an insurer which refused without justification to undertake the defense of a claim against the insured and which refused to accept a reasonable settlement offer within the policy limits violated "its duty to consider in good faith the interest of the insured in the settlement," that this duty sounded either in contract or in tort, and that the insurer was liable for the entire judgment against the insured, including the amount in excess of the policy limits.

After *Brown* and *Comunale,* it could not be said with certainty that anything more had been decided than that an insurer which fails to accept a reasonable settlement offer to dispose of a claim against its insured (which includes, necessarily, an insurer which fails to respond to a settlement offer because it has not undertaken the defense) is liable for the resulting excess judgment. Because such an outcome was well within the reach of contract law, the evolution through *Comunale* could hardly have been considered revolutionary.

All of this changed in *Crisci v. Security Insurance Co.,* 66 Cal. 2d 425, 426 P.2d 173, 58 Cal. Rptr. 13 (1967), which appears in § 8.02[5], when the California Supreme Court reaffirmed *Comunale's* observation that the cause of action for breach of the duty to settle lies in both contract and tort and then upheld an award to the insured for mental suffering. This aspect of *Crisci* made clear that the broader remedies of tort law — a broader range of consequential damages; damages for mental anguish; and the possibility of punitive damages — were available for the insurer's bad faith performance of its duties in the third-party setting.

Capitalizing on the third-party cases, the courts then began to recognize the tort of bad faith in first-party cases. *See, e.g., Gruenberg v. Aetna Insurance Co.,* 9 Cal. 3d 566, 510 P.2d 1032, 108 Cal. Rptr. 480 (1973). The cases in the prior subsection illustrate how the courts have fleshed out that area of law, recognizing damages both for breach of contract and tort.

From any vantage point one might have occupied in the late 1970s and early 1980s, one could reasonably have predicted that the tort of bad faith would grow and prosper as much in the third-party setting as it would prosper (and has prospered, notwithstanding the substantial constraint of ERISA) in the first-party setting. Such a prediction has been vindicated to some extent; the law of bad faith breach of the duty to settle has matured and ripened, and the insurer's liability in tort for this breach is well-settled in most jurisdictions. But carrying out a settlement obligation is much different from determining a coverage obligation. With respect to bad faith determinations of coverage, the law is considerably less robust in the third-party setting than the first-party setting. Before taking up the question why this might be so, consider the situation where an insurer is alleged to have committed the tort of bad faith in refusing to undertake the defense of the insured.

SMITH v. AMERICAN FAMILY MUTUAL INSURANCE CO.

294 N.W.2d 751 (N.D. 1980), 20 A.L.R.4th 1 (1983)

VANDE WALLE, JUSTICE.

American Family Mutual Insurance Company ("American Family") appeals from a judgment entered against it upon a jury verdict in favor of Kenneth A. Smith. It also appeals from the trial court's order denying its motions for judgment notwithstanding the verdict or, in the alternative, a new trial. We affirm.

In February 1976, American Family, through James Erickson as agent, sold an automobile insurance policy to Smith providing liability and collision coverage for Smith's 1970 automobile. At that time Smith was working as a contract deputy sheriff in Wildrose, North Dakota. There is some dispute in the testimony as to whether or not Erickson was informed that Smith used his automobile in his police work although Smith's automobile was specially equipped for police work. Subsequently, Smith accepted employment as chief of police at Pembina, North Dakota. On June 10, 1976, Smith, while off duty and driving his own automobile, answered an assistance call from a deputy sheriff in Cavalier County. The deputy was pursuing a van and, according to Smith's testimony, he asked the deputy if he (Smith) should set up a roadblock. Smith testified that the officer replied in the affirmative and Smith did drive his car crosswise on the two-laned highway, blocking the northbound lane. Smith placed a revolving red light on the top of his car and waited on the side of the road. The driver of the van which was being pursued did not stop and ran into Smith's car, demolishing it. Smith reported the loss to Erickson but Erickson told Smith the loss was not covered.[1] American Family apparently had taken the position that Smith's actions in equipping the insured vehicle with a revolving red light, a special police radio and firearms, and using his car as a roadblock brought into play this exclusion. The interpretation of the policy terms as applied to the facts is not one of the issues before us.

Smith and his wife, Joyce, lived in Langdon; Joyce worked in Cavalier and Smith also needed a car to drive to work in Pembina. Because they both

---

[1] The insurance policy provided:

> The company shall pay on behalf of the insured all sums which the insured shall become legally obligated to pay as damages because of bodily injury or property damage arising out of the ownership, maintenance or use of an owned automobile or the use of a nonowned automobile, and the company shall defend with counsel of its choice any suit alleging such bodily injury or property damage and seeking damages which are payable under the terms of this policy, even if any of the allegations of the suit are groundless, false or fraudulent; but the company may make such investigation and settlement of any claim or suit as it deems expedient.

> The policy contained a further provision that coverage did not apply "to liability assumed by the insured under any contract or agreement."

needed automobiles to drive to work, Smith was anxious to have his claim settled. Smith asked Erickson on several occasions when an insurance adjuster would come to investigate the claim. Erickson told Smith the adjusters were busy. On June 24, an independent adjuster did investigate the accident. He agreed on the amount of the loss but requested that Smith sign a nonwaiver agreement, which the adjuster also executed on behalf of American Family, wherein Smith and American Family agreed that any action taken by American Family in investigating the accident would not operate to invalidate any of the provisions of the policy and that if a suit were filed as a result of the accident and American Family elected to defend the suit, such action would not be construed as a waiver of any of the conditions of the policy. The agreement further provided:

> It is the intention of this agreement to preserve all the rights of the parties hereto and provide for an investigation of the said accident without in any way affecting, impairing or adding to the liability of the Company under said policy or under any statutes or the common law, and no act of the Company hereunder shall be construed as an admission of its liability or coverage.

Although Smith was asked to execute and did execute the agreement, he testified the agent told him that in his opinion the collision was covered and Smith should get a check in a week or two. When Smith contacted Erickson inquiring why the check was not forthcoming, Erickson told him the reason could be that the loss was not covered. Smith had another car he owned, which had motor problems, repaired for $770 in order that he and his wife would have cars to drive to their places of employment. American Family paid the claim for the loss of Smith's car some two months later. Prior to the time the check arrived, Erickson, when asked about the delay, gave various excuses including the response that there was no coverage under the policy. When the check did arrive, Erickson told Smith the only reason American Family paid the loss was that the adjusters had determined that a badly hurt passenger (Herzog) in the van which collided with Smith's automobile had decided not to sue Smith.

Herzog did sue Smith later. Smith immediately delivered the papers to Erickson. Erickson told Smith that American Family was not named in the lawsuit and therefore the company did not have to defend Smith, and that Smith must secure his own attorney to defend the suit because American Family was not liable. Smith became very upset and contacted an attorney (Sillers) who agreed to represent Smith for $50 per hour.

Sillers contacted Harrington, American Family's claim counsel, by telephone on September 29, 1976, inquiring as to what American Family was going to do on the defense of the Herzog lawsuit. Harrington informed Sillers he had called Herzog's attorney and asked for an extension to file an answer. He also told Sillers the matter was being forwarded to the Letnes & Marshall law firm in Grand Forks to commence a declaratory-judgment action to determine American Family's liability under the insurance contract. Harrington told Sillers it was American Family's position that when Smith agreed with the deputy sheriff of Pembina County to use Smith's car as a roadblock it came within the provision of the policy excluding liability assumed by the insured under any contract or agreement.

In October 1976, Sillers called American Family and asked for an immediate decision by American Family on the matter of defending Smith in the action brought against him by Herzog. Sillers spoke with Harrington, who told Sillers he would deny the claim. Harrington then wrote a letter on October 11, 1976, to Sillers denying coverage on the part of American Family. Sillers commenced this lawsuit against American Family on Smith's behalf on October 18, 1976. Subsequently, Sillers received a copy of a letter from American Family's claim counsel, Harrington, addressed to the Letnes & Marshall law firm of Grand Forks, requesting that firm to defend American Family and Erickson in the lawsuit filed by Smith against them. In that letter Harrington suggested filing a counterclaim against Sillers for abuse of process in the amount of $1,000,000. Because of that letter Sillers advised Smith there might be a conflict of interest if he were sued by American Family and continued to represent Smith in the lawsuit against American Family. Smith requested Sillers to continue the lawsuit but, at Sillers's suggestion, another attorney was retained to work with Sillers in the matter.

In January 1977, Sillers told Smith that American Family had reversed its position and would take over Smith's defense in the action brought by the passenger in the van, but the company refused to pay Sillers the full $50 per hour. Sillers advised Smith that if he accepted American Family's offer, Smith would still owe him the difference between the $50 per hour agreed upon as his fee and the amount American Family agreed to pay. Smith told Sillers to use his best judgment. American Family did take over defense of the lawsuit against Smith but made no direct contact with Smith prior to the trial of this action. At the time this action was tried the action against Smith was still pending. The evidence at trial indicated that Smith was upset and worried over the pending action against him, whether or not American Family would defend the action, and whether or not, if a verdict was rendered against Smith, American Family would pay the judgment to the limits of the insurance policy.

In his action against American Family, Smith alleged breach of contract of his automobile liability insurance policy, tortious breach of the implied covenant of good faith and fair dealing, malice, oppression, and fraud, and intentional infliction of severe emotional distress on the part of American Family. After trial to a jury, the jury found that Smith failed to prove he suffered severe emotional distress caused by the conduct of American Family; the jury dismissed any claim against American Family's agent, James Erickson; but found against American Family in the sum of $4,120 for breach of contract, $3,000 for breach of an implied covenant of good faith and fair dealing, and $50,000 for exemplary damages. American Family moved for judgment notwithstanding the verdict or, in the alternative, a new trial. The motion was denied by the district court and American Family took this appeal. In its appeal American Family raises several issues, some of which we will consider separately and others together.

I

In its first issue American Family argues that the trial court erred in refusing to dismiss Smith's action in tort because it failed to state a claim upon which relief could be granted. American Family's position is that a failure to defend an insured as required by the insurance policy is a breach of contract on the part of the insurer and does not constitute a tort on the part of the insurer. In support of its position American Family cites *Prince v. Universal Underwriters Insurance Co.*, 143 N.W.2d 708 (N.D. 1966), in which this court held that a failure to defend was a breach of the insurer's obligation under the policy which renders the insurer liable to the insured to the extent of the insured's costs and expenses incurred in defending the action. The decision in *Prince* is not applicable to the issue raised by American Family. . . . In *Prince* the insured did not bring action against the insurer in tort nor did the court consider whether or not that action was permitted. Furthermore, since the decision in *Prince*, this court decided *Corwin Chrysler-Plymouth v. Westchester Fire Insurance Company*, 279 N.W.2d 638 (N.D. 1979), wherein we quoted with approval the following statement of the Oklahoma Supreme Court in *Christian v. American Home Assurance Company*, 577 P.2d 899, 904–905 (Okl. 1978):

> "We approve and adopt the rule that an insurer has an implied duty to deal fairly and act in good faith with its insured and that the violation of this duty gives rise to an action in tort for which consequential and, in a proper case, punitive, damages may be sought. We do not hold that an insurer who resists and litigates a claim made by its insured does so at its peril that if it loses the suit or suffers a judgment against it for a larger amount than it had offered in payment, it will be held to have breached its duty to act fairly and in good faith and thus will be liable in tort."

279 N.W.2d at 645.

In *Corwin Chrysler-Plymouth*,[2] we also cited and relied upon *Gruenberg v. Aetna Insurance Company*, 9 Cal. 3d 566, 108 Cal. Rptr. 480, 510 P.2d 1032 (1973), and *Mustachio v. Ohio Farmers Insurance Company*, 44 Cal. App. 3d 358, 118 Cal. Rptr. 581 (1975), in affirming a decision of the district court that an insurer, which initially refused to pay a portion of an embezzlement claim representing funds taken subsequent to the expiration of its policy but which continued to refuse to pay after being informed that the embezzler had admitted the funds had been taken prior to the expiration of the policy, did, under the facts of that case, breach its obligation to deal with its insured in good faith.

American Family attempts to distinguish this holding on the basis that *Corwin Chrysler-Plymouth* and the California decisions upon which it relies give rise to tort liability only where the insurer fails to accept a reasonable settlement and not where, as here, there is only a wrongful refusal by an insurer to defend an insured. It points to *Comunale v. Traders & General Insurance Co.*, 50 Cal. 2d 654, 328 P.2d 198 (1958), and *Hogan v. Midland*

---

[2] Our decision in *Corwin Chrysler-Plymouth* was not announced until May 22, 1979. Judge Heen's memorandum decision denying American Family's motions for judgment notwithstanding the verdict or, in the alternative, a motion for a new trial was issued on March 3, 1979. Judge Heen cited *Gruenberg v. Aetna Insurance Company*, 9 Cal. 3d 566, 108 Cal. Rptr. 480, 510 P.2d 1032 (1973), as illustrative of the development of the law holding the insurer liable to the insured in tort for a breach of the implied duty of good faith and fair dealing.

National Insurance Company, 3 Cal. 3d 553, 91 Cal. Rptr. 153, 476 P.2d 825 (1970), as supporting its position. *Comunale* involved an action against an insurer to recover the portion of a judgment which was in excess of policy limits. The California Supreme Court held that where the insurer wrongfully refused to defend the insured and refused a reasonable settlement within limits of the policy, the insurer's breach of its express obligation to defend did not release it from its implied duty to consider the insured's interest in settlement. The court held the insurer liable for the entire judgment rendered against the insured even though the judgment exceeded policy limits. . . . As dictum the California court noted that where there is no opportunity to compromise the claim and the only wrongful act of the insurer is the refusal to defend, the liability of the insurer is ordinarily limited to the amount of the policy plus attorney fees and costs; . . .

Hogan cited *Comunale* for the proposition that the insurer is liable for amounts over the policy limit because of its wrongful refusal to settle the underlying action and noted the *Comunale* opinion distinguished the consequences of a wrongful refusal to settle and a wrongful refusal to defend, pointing out that as to a wrongful refusal to defend the liability of the insurer is ordinarily limited to the amount of the policy plus attorney fees and costs.

Although we believe the statements of the California Supreme Court in *Comunale* and *Hogan* to be dicta as used in those opinions, we note both opinions were issued prior to the 1973 decision in *Gruenberg v. Aetna Insurance Company, supra.* . . .

Significantly, the court in *Gruenberg,* relying upon its decision in *Crisci, supra,* upheld recovery for mental suffering and emotional distress because an action against an insurer for breach of its implied duty of good faith sounds in tort as well as contract. We cannot differentiate between a failure to pay, as in *Gruenberg,* and, here, a failure to defend, if the insurer breaches its covenant to act fairly and in good faith in discharging its contractual responsibilities. Insofar as claims for emotional distress and mental suffering are made, the failure of the insurer to defend the insured against a multithousand-dollar action filed by a third party against the insured may be significantly greater than the failure to pay a claim to the insured under a fire policy such as in *Gruenberg.* To limit the recovery by the insured and the liability of the insurer to the amount of the policy plus attorney fees and costs in instances in which the insured has breached its duty to act fairly and in good faith by failing to defend the insured would, in many instances, preclude recovery by the insured for damages for emotional distress.

In *Farris v. U.S. Fidelity and Guaranty Co.,* 284 Or. 453, 587 P.2d 1015 (1978), the Oregon Supreme Court considered the issue of whether or not the failure of the insurer to defend the insured under a liability policy could give rise to a tort action. The majority of the Oregon court concluded that, in view of its previous decision in *Santilli v. State Farm Life Ins. Co.,* 278 Or. 53, 562 P.2d 965 (1977), an insurer's failure to undertake representation of the insured could only have been a breach of contract for which no recovery for mental distress because of threat of pecuniary loss was available. In reaching its decision, the majority in *Farris* relied in part upon the unfair-trade-practices provisions of that State's Insurance Code (Or. Rev. Stat. Chapter

746) and the civil penalties provided for the violation of the Insurance Code (Or. Rev. Stat. Section 731.988). Similar provisions are found in our statutes. Secs. 26-30-04 and 26-30-11, N.D.C.C. The Oregon court also recognized a distinction between failure of the insurer to settle within the policy limits and failure to defend, concluding that in the case of failure to settle the insurer was acting in a fiduciary capacity which imposed a higher duty of good faith and fair dealing upon the insurer, but that failure to defend was merely a breach of contract for which no recovery for mental distress because of threat of pecuniary loss is recoverable.

Significantly, however, the Oregon court recognized that *Gruenberg* and related decisions would permit an action in tort for failure to defend but refused to adopt the rationale of those decisions, stating:

> The California courts have not, however, made the distinction pointed out here or in *Santilli* but have, without recognition that it was the fiduciary position of the insurer which arises when it represents the insured in litigation which gives rise to the good faith language, transposed the language into cases in which insurance companies have not undertaken representation of the insured at all. As a result, they have held an action in tort can lie for the breach of contract.
>
> . . . .
>
> Contrary to the California holdings, for the reasons given in *Santilli*, we believe defendant's failure to undertake representation of plaintiffs which required them to represent themselves could only have been a breach of contract, and, in cases of breach, the law is clear that no recovery for mental distress because of threat of pecuniary loss is recoverable.

284 Or. at 464–465, 587 P.2d at 1021.

The minority opinion in *Farris* would have permitted the tort action for failure to defend, stating:

> In fact, the basis of liability insurance is not just the assumption of actual cost and losses that result from a lawsuit but also the assumption of the risk of being sued, of the selection of an attorney, of the responsibility and control of the litigation, and even of the risk of losing. It is because of this special responsibility and relationship arising from the contract, rather than any implied covenant of good faith in the insurance contract, that the law imposes a duty of good faith on the insurer and thus the bad faith breach of a liability insurance contract is a tort.
>
> . . . .
>
> In fact, under the majority opinion in *this* case of bad faith refusal to perform the liability insurance contract, all the insurer has to lose is the costs and losses it would have borne anyway if it had accepted the case. If anything, a liability insurer intending to breach its contract in bad faith is encouraged to do so at the outset rather than risk the tort liability applicable to bad faith breaches *in performance*.

284 Or. at 477–478, 587 P.2d at 1028.

We adopted the rationale of *Gruenberg* in *Corwin Chrysler-Plymouth*. The Oregon Supreme Court has rejected that rationale but its decision in *Farris* reveals that it also finds *Gruenberg* and related decisions applicable to failure to defend as well as failure to settle within the policy limits.

An insurer's obligation to defend and an insurer's obligation to indemnify are separate and distinct contractual elements. We agree with the trial court that the defense and vindication of an insured by his insurance carrier against third-party claims is one of the chief benefits of the insurance contract.

Smith's cause of action in this instance alleged tortious breach of the implied covenant of good faith and fair dealing, malice, oppression, and fraud against American Family. That allegation was predicated on American Family's failure to defend as required by its policy with Smith. To adopt a rationale that distinguishes between the insurer's failure to defend and the failure to accept a settlement would, as the trial court noted in its memorandum opinion denying American Family's post-trial motions, "encourage insurance companies to exert whatever coercion in whatever manner and under whatever circumstances as would serve their financial interest, and under the circumstances here present would leave the plaintiff without a remedy for damages for the failure to defend beyond attorney's fees and legal costs."

American Family also argues that even if there is an implied tort remedy for failure by the insurer to defend the insured, Smith's complaint should have been dismissed because it was brought prior to the resolution of the Herzog suit against him. In support of its argument, American Family refers us to the decision in *Critz v. Farmers Insurance Group*, 230 Cal. App. 2d 788, 41 Cal. Rptr. 401 (1965), wherein the California Court of Appeals, in deciding whether or not an insured could assign to another party his right to maintain a bad-faith action against his insurer prior to the time he suffered adverse judgment in a personal-injury action, held the insured could make the assignment because the breach of the duty of good faith was complete when it occurred. That court also held, however, that the breach of the duty would not result in an immediately enforceable chose in action against the insurer because of the uncertainty as to the damages — which would be determined only when the insured incurred a binding judgment in excess of the policy limit.

In this instance Smith claimed damages of $4,900 for loss of employment as a result of American Family's failure to defend the action filed against him by Herzog; $300 in costs for repairing an automobile; traveling expenses in the amount of $125; medical expenses in the amount of $115 for treatment and evaluation of mental injury and depression resulting from American Family's failure to defend him; $50,000 for mental distress and emotional injury; and $3,861.89 for legal expenses incurred in defending the lawsuit brought against him by Herzog. In addition, Smith made a claim for future costs of defending the Herzog suit in an unspecified amount. Smith also asked that American Family be required to pay on Smith's behalf all sums for which Smith might be adjudged liable in the suit brought by Herzog and he requested $1,000,000 in exemplary damages. The jury awarded Smith $4,120 for breach of contract; $3,000 for American Family's breach of its obligation to deal fairly and in good faith with Smith; and $50,000 in punitive (exemplary) damages. It is apparent from an examination of the special jury verdict that the jury did not award Smith any speculative damages for a judgment which might be entered against him in the Herzog action. The actual damages which were awarded Smith were for injury he had already suffered. It is best explained by the trial court's memorandum opinion denying American Family's motions:

> Smith's cause of action is not grounded upon the carrier's refusal to settle, but rather upon the company's refusal to defend, a cause of action complete under the facts of this case at the time of trial. Future refusal to defend is unlikely and should not be presumed. If the plaintiff wishes to chance a splitting of a cause of action then he takes the election made in this instance.

Because the limit of liability of American Family under the insurance policy was $50,000 and because the jury returned a verdict of $50,000 in exemplary damages, American Family argues that the jury did speculate as to the outcome of the Herzog lawsuit inasmuch as the $50,000 exemplary damages awarded equals the liability limit of Smith's insurance policy. This is conjecture on the part of American Family and a theory we refuse to adopt.

. . . .

American Family also attacks the instruction given by the trial court on emotional distress.[3] American Family took exception to the instruction because it did not require "severe" emotional distress as a requisite to a damage award. Although recognizing that *Gruenberg, supra,* upon which we relied in *Corwin Chrysler-Plymouth, supra,* abolished the "severity" requirement, American Family notes that applies only in cases where the claim is actionable and has resulted in substantial damage due to emotional distress. It argues that the only other damage Smith was able to prove was that flowing from breach of contract, i.e., attorney fees. There was, however, testimony introduced as to damage other than attorney fees, such as the loss of his job with the City of Pembina because of his job performance and lost employment opportunities in North Dakota, Montana, and Alaska because of prospective employers' learning of his action against his own insurance company. These are not "contractual" damages which would have been paid under the insurance contract. Although there was conflicting evidence introduced as to these damages, they are not unlike the type of damages which the court in *Gruenberg* found sufficient as an award for emotional distress. The jury did not award an excessive amount in damages for breach of the covenant of good faith and fair dealing. The award was $3,000. Moreover, in *Corwin Chrysler-Plymouth, supra,* we quoted with approval *Mustachio v. Ohio Farmers Insurance Company, supra,* which in turn quoted from *Fletcher v. Western National Life Insurance Co.,* 10 Cal. App. 3d 376, 401–402, 89 Cal. Rptr. 78, 93–94 (1970), as follows:

> We further hold that, independent of the tort of intentional infliction of emotional distress, such conduct on the part of a disability insurer

---

[3] The trial court's instruction on damages permitted reasonable compensation "for any pain, discomfort, fears, anxiety and other emotional distress suffered by the plaintiff and for similar suffering reasonably certain to be experienced in the future from the same cause."

constitutes a tortious interference with a protected property interest of its insured for which damages may be recovered to compensate for *all detriment proximately resulting therefrom,* including economic loss *as well as emotional distress* resulting from the conduct or from the economic losses caused by the conduct, and, in a proper case, punitive damages. [Emphasis supplied.]

In the alternative, American Family urges that because of our decision in *Whetham v. Bismarck Hospital,* 197 N.W.2d 678 (N.D. 1972), the instruction was erroneous in that North Dakota does not recognize recovery for emotional distress without some accompanying physical harm unless the plaintiff was in personal danger of physical impact. We agree with Smith that the *Whetham* decision, which involved the witnessing of a tortious act by the plaintiff and involved the impact rule, is not applicable to a tortious breach of an insurer's duty of good faith and fair dealing. Our decision in *Corwin Chrysler-Plymouth* clearly requires us to reject American Family's contention in matters involving an insurer's tortious breach of the duty of good faith and fair dealing.

. . . .

VII

Finally, American Family urges us to conclude that the damages awarded are excessive. Looking first to the $3,000 in compensatory damages awarded for breach of the implied obligation of good faith and fair dealing, American Family again points to the evidence concerning Smith's emotional condition and argues it does not support a conclusion that Smith suffered severe emotional distress. The jury did not award damages for severe emotional distress. As we have already noted, the jury found in its special verdict that Smith did not suffer severe emotional distress. Our review is limited to the consideration of whether or not there is substantial evidence to sustain the verdict. If there is such evidence we are bound by the verdict. The evidence we have referred to heretofore is sufficient to support the award of compensatory damages of $3,000 for breach of the obligation of American Family to deal fairly and in good faith with Smith and to support the $4,120 awarded by the jury for breach of contract.

Insofar as the award of $50,000 in punitive damages is concerned, American Family again argues that it is more than coincidence that such damages are exactly equal to Smith's automobile liability insurance policy limits. We have already indicated we do not intend to conjecture as to the basis for the jury's verdict. It is not the function of this court to make computations to show how the jury arrived at its verdict.

In this case the comments of the trial judge, made in a memorandum opinion denying a motion for a new trial, are pertinent:

> In the case at hand, American Family's denial of coverage coupled with its letter (P's Ex. 30) which directed legal assertion of a $1,000,000 claim against their own assured's privately retained lawyer for filing the declaratory judgment action and a claim of exemplary damages scarcely can be termed conscionable conduct. Substantial evidence supported the jury finding that Ex. 30 was inconsistent with the company's duty to give the interest of the insured as much concern

by exercise of good faith and fair dealing as that of the carrier. The purpose of Ex. 30, according to Harrington, admittedly was coercive and would justify the jury in finding that the letter expressly conveyed an intended message of intimidation coloring the denial of policy coverage by the company with a lack of good faith and fair dealing.

Although we believe the award of $50,000 in punitive damages is ample, it is not, under the facts of this case, excessive.

The order denying American Family's motions for judgment notwithstanding the verdict or, in the alternative, a new trial and the judgment are affirmed.

ERICKSTAD, C.J., and PEDERSON, PAULSON and SAND, J.J., concur.

NOTES

1. *Bad faith and the emotional distress torts.* Does the court in *Smith,* in effect, recognize a cause of action in tort for negligent infliction of emotional distress? How does the tort of bad faith compare with that for intentional infliction of emotional distress? If the court is not saying that negligent or intentional conduct is the basis of culpability for compensatory damages, what is the basis? What is the basis of culpability for punitive damages? What connections do you see between this case and *Rawlings v. Apodaca, supra?*

2. *Settlement compared.* In § 8.02[5], the materials considered the question of the insurer's liability for failure to fulfill the insurer's settlement obligations. In § 8.02[6], the insured's remedies for breach of the insurer's duty to defend were considered. What makes *Smith* different from the cases discussed in those subsections?

In addition to breaching a settlement obligation or refusing to defend a covered claim, what other kinds of insurer conduct in the third-party setting might constitute the tort of bad faith? *See Commercial Union Insurance Co. v. Liberty Mutual Insurance Co.,* 393 N.W.2d 161 (Mich. 1986).

3. *The paucity of bad-faith refusal-to-defend cases.* Few reported cases have applied the tort of bad faith to remedy an insurer's refusal to provide a defense in the third-party situation. Other rare examples include *Lunsford v. American Guaranty & Liability Insurance Co.,* 18 F.3d 653 (9th Cir. 1994), and *North Iowa State Bank v. Allied Mutual Insurance Co.,* 471 N.W.2d 824 (Iowa 1991). Why is this so? Has the threat of extracontractual liability deterred insurers from breaching their obligations? If so, why has the same thing not happened in first-party insurance, where extracontractual liability is much more common? Have the law's requirements for when a duty to defend exists and the defense-under-reservation-of-rights option affected the frequency of bad faith liability in third-party insurance for denial of coverage?

4. *Third-party's rights.* Should the third-party claimant be allowed to sue the insurer directly for breach of the insurer's duty of good faith? Where the insurer's duty is *statutorily* based, the overwhelming weight of authority holds that the third party does not have a cause of action directly against the

insurer. *See Herrig v. Herrig,* 844 P.2d 487 (Wyo. 1992); *Hart-Anderson v. Hauck,* 230 Mont. 63, 748 P.2d 937 (1988); *Tank v. State Farm Fire & Casualty Co.,* 105 Wash. 2d 381, 715 P.2d 1133 (1986). The most notable case to the contrary, *Royal Globe Insurance Co. v. Superior Court,* 23 Cal. 3d 880, 153 Cal. Rptr. 842, 592 P.2d 329 (1979), was subsequently overruled in *Moradi-Shalal v. Fireman's Fund Insurance Cos.,* 46 Cal. App. 3d 287, 250 Cal. Rptr. 116, 758 P.2d 58 (1988). Although the California legislature revived the rule, a voter referendum re-buried it. See note 6 following the *White* case in § 8.03[1], *supra.* Should the same result be reached when the third party asserts the insurer's breach of the common law duty of good faith? *See Coleman v. Gulf Insurance Group,* 41 Cal. 3d 782, 718 P.2d 77, 226 Cal. Rptr. 90 (1986).

Is the idea of a third-party claim for the tort of bad faith against the liability carrier a tempest in a teapot given that in many jurisdictions the insured can assign his or her cause of action against the liability carrier to the third-party? Would the insured want to assign her cause of action for consequential damages as compared to the cause of action for the policy proceeds?

If a third-party action against the liability insurer is recognized for the tort of bad faith, should the third-party be entitled to recover consequential damages arising from the liability insurer's wrongful conduct?

5. *"Reverse" or "comparative" bad faith?* If the insurer can be held liable to the insured for the tort of bad faith, what about the insured's reciprocal obligations to the insurer? In other words, is "bad faith" a one-way or two-way street? Is a two-way street more attractive if good faith is deemed a contract duty and not a tort duty? Independent of the question of whether the insurer should have a bad faith cause of action against the insured, should the insured's bad faith offset the insurer's bad faith under comparative or contributory fault principles?

Notwithstanding a kind of "symmetric appeal" of the two-way street position, the clear weight of authority, notwithstanding some isolated indications to the contrary, is that the tort of bad faith is a one-way street. *See Kransco v. American Empire Surplus Lines Insurance Co.,* 97 Cal. Rptr. 2d 151, 2 P.3d 1 (Cal. 2000); *Stephens v. Safeco Insurance Co. of Am.,* 852 P.2d 565 (Mont. 1993) (disapproving doctrine); *Tokles & Son, Inc. v. Midwestern Indemnity Co.,* 605 N.E.2d 936 (Ohio 1992) (disapproving doctrine). For more discussion, see Ellen Smith Pryor, *Comparative Fault and Insurance Bad Faith,* 72 Tex. L. Rev. 1505 (1994); Douglas R. Richmond, *Insured's Bad Faith as Shield or Sword: Litigation Relief for Insurers?,* 77 Marq. L. Rev. 41 (1993). Insurers might like to have a bad faith remedy against insureds, but do they need it?

APPENDICES·

APPENDIX A

FIRST PAGE OF STANDARD FIRE POLICY

No. . . . .

[Space for insertion of name of company or companies issuing the policy and other matter permitted to be stated at the head of the policy.]

[Space for listing amounts of insurance, rates and premiums for the basic coverages insured under the standard form of policy and for additional coverages or perils insured under endorsements attached.]

In Consideration of the Provisions and Stipulations herein or added hereto

and of . . . . .Dollars Premium

this Company, for the term | from the . . . . day of . . . ., 19. . . . | at noon, Standard Time, at
of . . . . | to the . . . . day of . . . ., 19. . . . | location of property involved,

to an amount not exceeding . . . . Dollars,

does insure . . . .:

and legal representatives, to the extent of the actual cash value of the property at the time of loss, but not exceeding the amount which it would cost to repair or replace the property with material of like kind and quality within a reasonable time after such loss, without allowance for any increased cost of repair or reconstruction by reason of any ordinance or law regulating construction or repair, and without compensation for loss resulting from interruption of business or manufacture, nor in any event for more than the interest of the insured, against all DIRECT LOSS BY FIRE, LIGHTNING AND BY REMOVAL FROM PREMISES ENDANGERED BY THE PERILS INSURED AGAINST IN THIS POLICY. EXCEPT AS HEREINAFTER PROVIDED, to the property described hereinafter while located or contained as described in this policy, or pro rata for five days at each proper place to which any of the property shall necessarily be removed for preservation from the perils insured against in this policy, but not elsewhere.

Assignment of this policy shall not be valid except with the written consent of this Company.

This policy is made and accepted subject to the foregoing provisions and stipulations and those hereinafter stated, which are hereby made a part of this policy, together with such other provisions, stipulations and agreements as may be added hereto, as provided in this policy.

𝕴𝖓 𝖂𝖎𝖙𝖓𝖊𝖘𝖘 𝖂𝖍𝖊𝖗𝖊𝖔𝖋, this Company has executed and attested these presents; but this policy shall not be valid unless countersigned by the duly authorized Agent of this Company at . . . .

. . . .

Secretary.   *President.*

Countersigned this . . . . day of . . . ., 19. . . .   .
                                                                                                               AGENT.

SECOND PAGE OF STANDARD FIRE POLICY

1 **Concealment,** This entire policy shall be void if, whether
2 **fraud.** before or after a loss, the insured has wil-
3 fully concealed or misrepresented any ma-
4 terial fact or circumstance concerning this insurance or the
5 subject thereof, or the interest of the insured therein, or in case
6 of any fraud or false swearing by the insured relating thereto.
7 **Uninsurable** This policy shall not cover accounts, bills,
8 **and** currency, deeds, evidences of debt, money or
9 **excepted property.** securities; nor, unless specifically named
10 hereon in writing, bullion or manuscripts.
11 **Perils not** This Company shall not be liable for loss by
12 **included.** fire or other perils insured against in this
13 policy caused, directly or indirectly, by: (a)
14 enemy attack by armed forces, including action taken by mili-
15 tary, naval or air forces in resisting an actual or an immediately
16 impending enemy attack; (b) invasion; (c) insurrection; (d)
17 rebellion; (e) revolution; (f) civil war; (g) usurped power; (h)
18 order of any civil authority except acts of destruction at the time
19 of and for the purpose of preventing the spread of fire, provided
20 that such fire did not originate from any of the perils excluded
21 by this policy; (i) neglect of the insured to use all reasonable
22 means to save and preserve the property at and after a loss, or
23 when the property is endangered by fire in neighboring prem-
24 ises; (j) nor shall this Company be liable for loss by theft.
25 **Other insurance.** Other insurance may be prohibited or the
26 amount of insurance may be limited by en-
27 dorsement attached hereto.
28 **Conditions suspending or restricting insurance.** Unless other-
29 wise provided in writing added hereto this Company shall not
30 be liable for loss occurring
31 (a) while the hazard is increased by any means within the con-
32 trol or knowledge of the insured; or
33 (b) while a described building, whether intended for occupancy
34 by owner or tenant, is vacant or unoccupied beyond a period of
35 sixty consecutive days; or
36 (c) as a result of explosion or riot, unless fire ensue, and in
37 that event for loss by fire only.
38 **Other perils** Any other peril to be insured against or sub-
39 **or subjects.** ject of insurance to be covered in this policy
40 shall be by endorsement in writing hereon or
41 added hereto.
42 **Added provisions.** The extent of the application of insurance
43 under this policy and of the contribution to
44 be made by this Company in case of loss, and any other pro-
45 vision or agreement not inconsistent with the provisions of this
46 policy, may be provided for in writing added hereto, but no pro-
47 vision may be waived except such as by the terms of this policy
48 is subject to change.
49 **Waiver** No permission affecting this insurance shall
50 **provisions.** exist, or waiver of any provision be valid,
51 unless granted herein or expressed in writing
52 added hereto. No provision, stipulation or forfeiture shall be
53 held to be waived by any requirement or proceeding on the part
54 of this Company relating to appraisal or to any examination
55 provided for herein.
56 **Cancellation** This policy shall be cancelled at any time
57 **of policy.** at the request of the insured, in which case
58 this Company shall, upon demand and sur-
59 render of this policy, refund the excess of paid premium above
60 the customary short rates for the expired time. This pol-
61 icy may be cancelled at any time by this Company by giving
62 to the insured a five days' written notice of cancellation with
63 or without tender of the excess of paid premium above the pro
64 rata premium for the expired time, which excess, if not ten-
65 dered, shall be refunded on demand. Notice of cancellation shall
66 state that said excess premium (if not tendered) will be re-
67 funded on demand.
68 **Mortgagee** If loss hereunder is made payable, in whole
69 **interests and** or in part, to a designated mortgagee not
70 **obligations.** named herein as the insured, such interest in
71 this policy may be cancelled by giving to such
72 mortgagee a ten days' written notice of can-
73 cellation.
74 If the insured fails to render proof of loss such mortgagee, upon
75 notice, shall render proof of loss in the form herein specified
76 within sixty (60) days thereafter and shall be subject to the pro-
77 visions hereof relating to appraisal and time of payment and of
78 bringing suit. If this Company shall claim that no liability ex-
79 isted as to the mortgagor or owner, it shall, to the extent of pay-
80 ment of loss to the mortgagee, be subrogated to all the mort-
81 gagee's rights of recovery, but without impairing mortgagee's
82 right to sue; or it may pay off the mortgage debt and require
83 an assignment thereof and of the mortgage. Other provisions

84 relating to the interests and obligations of such mortgagee may
85 be added hereto by agreement in writing.
86 **Pro rata liability.** This Company shall not be liable for a greater
87 proportion of any loss than the amount
88 hereby insured shall bear to the whole insurance covering the
89 property against the peril involved, whether collectible or not.
90 **Requirements in** The insured shall give immediate written
91 **case loss occurs.** notice to this Company of any loss, protect
92 the property from further damage, forthwith
93 separate the damaged and undamaged personal property, put
94 it in the best possible order, furnish a complete inventory of
95 the destroyed, damaged and undamaged property, showing in
96 detail quantities, costs, actual cash value and amount of loss
97 claimed; and within sixty days after the loss, unless such time
98 is extended in writing by this Company, the insured shall render
99 to this Company a proof of loss, signed and sworn to by the
100 insured, stating the knowledge and belief of the insured as to
101 the following: the time and origin of the loss, the interest of the
102 insured and of all others in the property, the actual cash value of
103 each item thereof and the amount of loss thereto, all encum-
104 brances thereon, all other contracts of insurance, whether valid
105 or not, covering any of said property, any changes in the title,
106 use, occupation, location, possession or exposures of said prop-
107 erty since the issuing of this policy, by whom and for what
108 purpose any building herein described and the several parts
109 thereof were occupied at the time of loss and whether or not it
110 then stood on leased ground, and shall furnish a copy of all the
111 descriptions and schedules in all policies and, if required, verified
112 plans and specifications of any building, fixtures or machinery
113 destroyed or damaged. The insured, as often as may be reason-
114 ably required, shall exhibit to any person designated by this
115 Company all that remains of any property herein described, and
116 submit to examinations under oath by any person named by this
117 Company, and subscribe the same; and, as often as may be
118 reasonably required, shall produce for examination all books of
119 account, bills, invoices and other vouchers, or certified copies
120 thereof if originals be lost, at such reasonable time and place as
121 may be designated by this Company or its representative, and
122 shall permit extracts and copies thereof to be made.
123 **Appraisal.** In case the insured and this Company shall
124 fail to agree as to the actual cash value or
125 the amount of loss, then, on the written demand of either, each
126 shall select a competent and disinterested appraiser and notify
127 the other of the appraiser selected within twenty days of such
128 demand. The appraisers shall first select a competent and dis-
129 interested umpire; and failing for fifteen days to agree upon
130 such umpire, then, on request of the insured or this Company,
131 such umpire shall be selected by a judge of a court of record in
132 the state in which the property covered is located. The ap-
133 praisers shall then appraise the loss, stating separately actual
134 cash value and loss of each item; and, failing to agree, shall
135 submit their differences, only, to the umpire. An award in writ-
136 ing, so itemized, of any two when filed with this Company shall
137 determine the amount of actual cash value and loss. Each
138 appraiser shall be paid by the party selecting him and the ex-
139 penses of appraisal and umpire shall be paid by the parties
140 equally.
141 **Company's** It shall be optional with this Company to
142 **options.** take all, or any part, of the property at the
143 agreed or appraised value, and also to re-
144 pair, rebuild or replace the property destroyed or damaged with
145 other of like kind and quality within a reasonable time, on giv-
146 ing notice of its intention so to do within thirty days after the
147 receipt of the proof of loss herein required.
148 **Abandonment.** There can be no abandonment to this Com-
149 pany of any property.
150 **When loss** The amount of loss for which this Company
151 **payable.** may be liable shall be payable sixty days
152 after proof of loss, as herein provided, is
153 received by this Company and ascertainment of the loss is made
154 either by agreement between the insured and this Company ex-
155 pressed in writing or by the filing with this Company of an
156 award as herein provided.
157 **Suit.** No suit or action on this policy for the recov-
158 ery of any claim shall be sustainable in any
159 court of law or equity unless all the requirements of this policy
160 shall have been complied with, and unless commenced within
161 twelve months next after inception of the loss.
162 **Subrogation.** This Company may require from the insured
163 an assignment of all right of recovery against
164 any party for loss to the extent that payment therefor is made
165 by this Company.

APPENDIX B(1)

COMMERCIAL GENERAL LIABILITY
CG 00 01 07 98

COMMERCIAL GENERAL LIABILITY COVERAGE FORM

Various provisions in this policy restrict coverage. Read the entire policy carefully to determine rights, duties and what is and is not covered.

Throughout this policy the words "you" and "your" refer to the Named Insured shown in the Declarations, and any other person or organization qualifying as a Named Insured under this policy. The words "we", "us" and "our" refer to the company providing this insurance.

The word "insured" means any person or organization qualifying as such under Section II – Who Is An Insured.

Other words and phrases that appear in quotation marks have special meaning. Refer to Section V – Definitions.

SECTION I – COVERAGES

COVERAGE A BODILY INJURY AND PROPERTY DAMAGE LIABILITY

1. Insuring Agreement

a. We will pay those sums that the insured becomes legally obligated to pay as damages because of "bodily injury" or "property damage" to which this insurance applies. We will have the right and duty to defend the insured against any "suit" seeking those damages. However, we will have no duty to defend the insured against any "suit" seeking damages for "bodily injury" or "property damage" to which this insurance does not apply. We may, at our discretion, investigate any "occurrence" and settle any claim or "suit" that may result. But:

(1) The amount we will pay for damages is limited as described in Section III – Limits Of Insurance; and

(2) Our right and duty to defend end when we have used up the applicable limit of insurance in the payment of judgments or settlements under Coverages **A** or **B** or medical expenses under Coverage **C**.

No other obligation or liability to pay sums or perform acts or services is covered unless explicitly provided for under Supplementary Payments – Coverages **A** and **B**.

b. This insurance applies to "bodily injury" and "property damage" only if:

(1) The "bodily injury" or "property damage" is caused by an "occurrence" that takes place in the "coverage territory"; and

(2) The "bodily injury" or "property damage" occurs during the policy period.

c. Damages because of "bodily injury" include damages claimed by any person or organization for care, loss of services or death resulting at any time from the "bodily injury".

2. Exclusions

This insurance does not apply to:

a. **Expected Or Intended Injury**

"Bodily injury" or "property damage" expected or intended from the standpoint of the insured. This exclusion does not apply to "bodily injury" resulting from the use of reasonable force to protect persons or property.

b. **Contractual Liability**

"Bodily injury" or "property damage" for which the insured is obligated to pay damages by reason of the assumption of liability in a contract or agreement. This exclusion does not apply to liability for damages:

(1) That the insured would have in the absence of the contract or agreement; or

(2) Assumed in a contract or agreement that is an "insured contract", provided the "bodily injury" or "property damage" occurs subsequent to the execution of the contract or agreement. Solely for the purposes of liability assumed in an "insured contract", reasonable attorney fees and necessary litigation expenses incurred by or for a party other than an insured are deemed to be damages because of "bodily injury" or "property damage", provided:

(a) Liability to such party for, or for the cost of, that party's defense has also been assumed in the same "insured contract"; and

(b) Such attorney fees and litigation expenses are for defense of that party against a civil or alternative dispute resolution proceeding in which damages to which this insurance applies are alleged.

c. Liquor Liability

"Bodily injury" or "property damage" for which any insured may be held liable by reason of:

(1) Causing or contributing to the intoxication of any person;

(2) The furnishing of alcoholic beverages to a person under the legal drinking age or under the influence of alcohol; or

(3) Any statute, ordinance or regulation relating to the sale, gift, distribution or use of alcoholic beverages.

This exclusion applies only if you are in the business of manufacturing, distributing, selling, serving or furnishing alcoholic beverages.

d. Workers' Compensation And Similar Laws

Any obligation of the insured under a workers' compensation, disability benefits or unemployment compensation law or any similar law.

e. Employer's Liability

"Bodily injury" to:

(1) An "employee" of the insured arising out of and in the course of:

    (a) Employment by the insured; or

    (b) Performing duties related to the conduct of the insured's business; or

(2) The spouse, child, parent, brother or sister of that "employee" as a consequence of Paragraph **(1)** above.

This exclusion applies:

(1) Whether the insured may be liable as an employer or in any other capacity; and

(2) To any obligation to share damages with or repay someone else who must pay damages because of the injury.

This exclusion does not apply to liability assumed by the insured under an "insured contract".

f. Pollution

(1) "Bodily injury" or "property damage" arising out of the actual, alleged or threatened discharge, dispersal, seepage, migration, release or escape of "pollutants":

    (a) At or from any premises, site or location which is or was at any time owned or occupied by, or rented or loaned to, any insured. However, this subparagraph does not apply to:

        (i) "Bodily injury" if sustained within a building and caused by smoke, fumes, vapor or soot from equipment used to heat that building;

        (ii) "Bodily injury" or "property damage" for which you may be held liable, if you are a contractor and the owner or lessee of such premises, site or location has been added to your policy as an additional insured with respect to your ongoing operations performed for that additional insured at that premises, site or location and such premises, site or location is not and never was owned or occupied by, or rented or loaned to, any insured, other than that additional insured; or

        (iii) "Bodily injury" or "property damage" arising out of heat, smoke or fumes from a "hostile fire";

    (b) At or from any premises, site or location which is or was at any time used by or for any insured or others for the handling, storage, disposal, processing or treatment of waste;

    (c) Which are or were at any time transported, handled, stored, treated, disposed of, or processed as waste by or for any insured or any person or organization for whom you may be legally responsible; or

(d) At or from any premises, site or location on which any insured or any contractors or subcontractors working directly or indirectly on any insured's behalf are performing operations if the "pollutants" are brought on or to the premises, site or location in connection with such operations by such insured, contractor or subcontractor. However, this subparagraph does not apply to:

  (i) "Bodily injury" or "property damage" arising out of the escape of fuels, lubricants or other operating fluids which are needed to perform the normal electrical, hydraulic or mechanical functions necessary for the operation of "mobile equipment" or its parts, if such fuels, lubricants or other operating fluids escape from a vehicle part designed to hold, store or receive them. This exception does not apply if the "bodily injury" or "property damage" arises out of the intentional discharge, dispersal or release of the fuels, lubricants or other operating fluids, or if such fuels, lubricants or other operating fluids are brought on or to the premises, site or location with the intent that they be discharged, dispersed or released as part of the operations being performed by such insured, contractor or subcontractor;

  (ii) "Bodily injury" or "property damage" sustained within a building and caused by the release of gases, fumes or vapors from materials brought into that building in connection with operations being performed by you or on your behalf by a contractor or subcontractor; or

  (iii) "Bodily injury" or "property damage" arising out of heat, smoke or fumes from a "hostile fire".

(e) At or from any premises, site or location on which any insured or any contractors or subcontractors working directly or indirectly on any insured's behalf are performing operations if the operations are to test for, monitor, clean up, remove, contain, treat, detoxify or neutralize, or in any way respond to, or assess the effects of, "pollutants".

(2) Any loss, cost or expense arising out of any:

  (a) Request, demand, order or statutory or regulatory requirement that any insured or others test for, monitor, clean up, remove, contain, treat, detoxify or neutralize, or in any way respond to, or assess the effects of, "pollutants"; or

  (b) Claim or suit by or on behalf of a governmental authority for damages because of testing for, monitoring, cleaning up, removing, containing, treating, detoxifying or neutralizing, or in any way responding to, or assessing the effects of, "pollutants".

However, this paragraph does not apply to liability for damages because of "property damage" that the insured would have in the absence of such request, demand, order or statutory or regulatory requirement, or such claim or "suit" by or on behalf of a governmental authority.

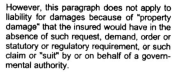

g. **Aircraft, Auto Or Watercraft**

"Bodily injury" or "property damage" arising out of the ownership, maintenance, use or entrustment to others of any aircraft, "auto" or watercraft owned or operated by or rented or loaned to any insured. Use includes operation and "loading or unloading".

This exclusion does not apply to:

(1) A watercraft while ashore on premises you own or rent;

(2) A watercraft you do not own that is:

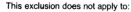

  (a) Less than 26 feet long, and

  (b) Not being used to carry persons or property for a charge;

(3) Parking an "auto" on, or on the ways next to, premises you own or rent, provided the "auto" is not owned by or rented or loaned to you or the insured;

(4) Liability assumed under any "insured contract" for the ownership, maintenance or use of aircraft or watercraft; or

(5) "Bodily injury" or "property damage" arising out of the operation of any of the equipment listed in Paragraph f.(2) or f.(3) of the definition of "mobile equipment".

h. Mobile Equipment

"Bodily Injury" or "property damage" arising out of:

(1) The transportation of "mobile equipment" by an "auto" owned or operated by or rented or loaned to any insured; or

(2) The use of "mobile equipment" in, or while in practice for, or while being prepared for, any prearranged racing, speed, demolition, or stunting activity.

i. War

"Bodily injury" or "property damage" due to war, whether or not declared, or any act or condition incident to war. War includes civil war, insurrection, rebellion or revolution. This exclusion applies only to liability assumed under a contract or agreement.

j. Damage To Property

"Property damage" to:

(1) Property you own, rent, or occupy;

(2) Premises you sell, give away or abandon, if the "property damage" arises out of any part of those premises;

(3) Property loaned to you;

(4) Personal property in the care, custody or control of the insured;

(5) That particular part of real property on which you or any contractors or subcontractors working directly or indirectly on your behalf are performing operations, if the "property damage" arises out of those operations; or

(6) That particular part of any property that must be restored, repaired or replaced because "your work" was incorrectly performed on it.

Paragraphs **(1)**, **(3)** and **(4)** of this exclusion do not apply to "property damage" (other than damage by fire) to premises, including the contents of such premises, rented to you for a period of 7 or fewer consecutive days. A separate limit of insurance applies to Damage To Premises Rented To You as described in Section III – Limits Of Insurance.

Paragraph **(2)** of this exclusion does not apply if the premises are "your work" and were never occupied, rented or held for rental by you.

Paragraphs **(3)**, **(4)**, **(5)** and **(6)** of this exclusion do not apply to liability assumed under a sidetrack agreement.

Paragraph **(6)** of this exclusion does not apply to "property damage" included in the "products-completed operations hazard".

k. Damage To Your Product

"Property damage" to "your product" arising out of it or any part of it.

l. Damage To Your Work

"Property damage" to "your work" arising out of it or any part of it and included in the "products-completed operations hazard".

This exclusion does not apply if the damaged work or the work out of which the damage arises was performed on your behalf by a subcontractor.

m. Damage To Impaired Property Or Property Not Physically Injured

"Property damage" to "impaired property" or property that has not been physically injured, arising out of:

(1) A defect, deficiency, inadequacy or dangerous condition in "your product" or "your work"; or

(2) A delay or failure by you or anyone acting on your behalf to perform a contract or agreement in accordance with its terms.

This exclusion does not apply to the loss of use of other property arising out of sudden and accidental physical injury to "your product" or "your work" after it has been put to its intended use.

n. Recall Of Products, Work Or Impaired Property

Damages claimed for any loss, cost or expense incurred by you or others for the loss of use, withdrawal, recall, inspection, repair, replacement, adjustment, removal or disposal of:

(1) "Your product";

(2) "Your work"; or

(3) "Impaired property";

if such product, work, or property is withdrawn or recalled from the market or from use by any person or organization because of a known or suspected defect, deficiency, inadequacy or dangerous condition in it.

o. Personal And Advertising Injury

"Bodily injury" arising out of "personal and advertising injury".

Exclusions **c.** through **n.** do not apply to damage by fire to premises while rented to you or temporarily occupied by you with permission of the owner. A separate limit of insurance applies to this coverage as described in Section III – Limits Of Insurance.

 CG 00 01 07 98 □

COVERAGE B PERSONAL AND ADVERTISING INJURY LIABILITY

1. Insuring Agreement

a. We will pay those sums that the insured becomes legally obligated to pay as damages because of "personal and advertising injury" to which this insurance applies. We will have the right and duty to defend the insured against any "suit" seeking those damages. However, we will have no duty to defend the insured against any "suit" seeking damages for "personal and advertising injury" to which this insurance does not apply. We may, at our discretion, investigate any offense and settle any claim or "suit" that may result. But:

(1) The amount we will pay for damages is limited as described in Section III – Limits Of Insurance ; and

(2) Our right and duty to defend end when we have used up the applicable limit of insurance in the payment of judgments or settlements under Coverages **A** or **B** or medical expenses under Coverage **C**.

No other obligation or liability to pay sums or perform acts or services is covered unless explicitly provided for under Supplementary Payments – Coverages **A** and **B**.

b. This insurance applies to "personal and advertising injury" caused by an offense arising out of your business but only if the offense was committed in the "coverage territory" during the policy period.

2. Exclusions

This insurance does not apply to:

a. "Personal and advertising injury":

(1) Caused by or at the direction of the insured with the knowledge that the act would violate the rights of another and would inflict "personal and advertising injury";

(2) Arising out of oral or written publication of material, if done by or at the direction of the insured with knowledge of its falsity;

(3) Arising out of oral or written publication of material whose first publication took place before the beginning of the policy period;

(4) Arising out of a criminal act committed by or at the direction of any insured;

(5) For which the insured has assumed liability in a contract or agreement. This exclusion does not apply to liability for damages that the insured would have in the absence of the contract or agreement;

(6) Arising out of a breach of contract, except an implied contract to use another's advertising idea in your "advertisement";

(7) Arising out of the failure of goods, products or services to conform with any statement of quality or performance made in your "advertisement";

(8) Arising out of the wrong description of the price of goods, products or services stated in your "advertisement";

(9) Committed by an insured whose business is advertising, broadcasting, publishing or telecasting. However, this exclusion does not apply to Paragraphs **14.a.**, **b.** and **c.** of "personal and advertising injury" under the Definitions Section; or

(10) Arising out of the actual, alleged or threatened discharge, dispersal, seepage, migration, release or escape of "pollutants" at any time.

b. Any loss, cost or expense arising out of any:

(1) Request, demand or order that any insured or others test for, monitor, clean up, remove, contain, treat, detoxify or neutralize, or in any way respond to, or assess the effects of, "pollutants"; or

(2) Claim or suit by or on behalf of a governmental authority for damages because of testing for, monitoring, cleaning up, removing, containing, treating, detoxifying or neutralizing, or in any way responding to, or assessing the effects of, "pollutants".

COVERAGE C MEDICAL PAYMENTS

1. Insuring Agreement

a. We will pay medical expenses as described below for "bodily injury" caused by an accident:

(1) On premises you own or rent;

(2) On ways next to premises you own or rent; or

(3) Because of your operations;

provided that:

(1) The accident takes place in the "coverage territory" and during the policy period;

(2) The expenses are incurred and reported to us within one year of the date of the accident; and

(3) The injured person submits to examination, at our expense, by physicians of our choice as often as we reasonably require.

b. We will make these payments regardless of fault. These payments will not exceed the applicable limit of insurance. We will pay reasonable expenses for:

(1) First aid administered at the time of an accident;

(2) Necessary medical, surgical, x-ray and dental services, including prosthetic devices; and

(3) Necessary ambulance, hospital, professional nursing and funeral services.

2. **Exclusions**

We will not pay expenses for "bodily injury":

a. To any insured.

b. To a person hired to do work for or on behalf of any insured or a tenant of any insured.

c. To a person injured on that part of premises you own or rent that the person normally occupies.

d. To a person, whether or not an "employee" of any insured, if benefits for the "bodily injury" are payable or must be provided under a workers' compensation or disability benefits law or a similar law.

e. To a person injured while taking part in athletics.

f. Included within the "products-completed operations hazard".

g. Excluded under Coverage A.

h. Due to war, whether or not declared, or any act or condition incident to war. War includes civil war, insurrection, rebellion or revolution.

SUPPLEMENTARY PAYMENTS – COVERAGES A AND B

1. We will pay, with respect to any claim we investigate or settle, or any "suit" against an insured we defend:

a. All expenses we incur.

b. Up to $250 for cost of bail bonds required because of accidents or traffic law violations arising out of the use of any vehicle to which the Bodily Injury Liability Coverage applies. We do not have to furnish these bonds.

c. The cost of bonds to release attachments, but only for bond amounts within the applicable limit of insurance. We do not have to furnish these bonds.

d. All reasonable expenses incurred by the insured at our request to assist us in the investigation or defense of the claim or "suit", including actual loss of earnings up to $250 a day because of time off from work.

e. All costs taxed against the insured in the "suit".

f. Prejudgment interest awarded against the insured on that part of the judgment we pay. If we make an offer to pay the applicable limit of insurance, we will not pay any prejudgment interest based on that period of time after the offer.

g. All interest on the full amount of any judgment that accrues after entry of the judgment and before we have paid, offered to pay, or deposited in court the part of the judgment that is within the applicable limit of insurance.

These payments will not reduce the limits of insurance.

2. If we defend an insured against a "suit" and an indemnitee of the insured is also named as a party to the "suit", we will defend that indemnitee if all of the following conditions are met:

a. The "suit" against the indemnitee seeks damages for which the insured has assumed the liability of the indemnitee in a contract or agreement that is an "insured contract";

b. This insurance applies to such liability assumed by the insured;

c. The obligation to defend, or the cost of the defense of, that indemnitee, has also been assumed by the insured in the same "insured contract";

d. The allegations in the "suit" and the information we know about the "occurrence" are such that no conflict appears to exist between the interests of the insured and the interests of the indemnitee;

e. The indemnitee and the insured ask us to conduct and control the defense of that indemnitee against such "suit" and agree that we can assign the same counsel to defend the insured and the indemnitee; and

f. The indemnitee:

(1) Agrees in writing to:

(a) Cooperate with us in the investigation, settlement or defense of the "suit";

(b) Immediately send us copies of any demands, notices, summonses or legal papers received in connection with the "suit";

(c) Notify any other insurer whose coverage is available to the indemnitee; and

(d) Cooperate with us with respect to coordinating other applicable insurance available to the indemnitee; and

CG 00 01 07 98   □

(2) Provides us with written authorization to:

    (a) Obtain records and other information related to the "suit"; and

    (b) Conduct and control the defense of the indemnitee in such "suit".

So long as the above conditions are met, attorneys' fees incurred by us in the defense of that indemnitee, necessary litigation expenses incurred by us and necessary litigation expenses incurred by the indemnitee at our request will be paid as Supplementary Payments. Notwithstanding the provisions of Paragraph **2.b.(2)** of Section **I** – Coverage A – Bodily Injury And Property Damage Liability, such payments will not be deemed to be damages for "bodily injury" and "property damage" and will not reduce the limits of insurance.

Our obligation to defend an insured's indemnitee and to pay for attorneys' fees and necessary litigation expenses as Supplementary Payments ends when:

a. We have used up the applicable limit of insurance in the payment of judgments or settlements; or

b. The conditions set forth above, or the terms of the agreement described in Paragraph f. above, are no longer met.

SECTION II – WHO IS AN INSURED

1. If you are designated in the Declarations as:

a. An individual, you and your spouse are insureds, but only with respect to the conduct of a business of which you are the sole owner.

b. A partnership or joint venture, you are an insured. Your members, your partners, and their spouses are also insureds, but only with respect to the conduct of your business.

c. A limited liability company, you are an insured. Your members are also insureds, but only with respect to the conduct of your business. Your managers are insureds, but only with respect to their duties as your managers.

d. An organization other than a partnership, joint venture or limited liability company, you are an insured. Your "executive officers" and directors are insureds, but only with respect to their duties as your officers or directors. Your stockholders are also insureds, but only with respect to their liability as stockholders.

2. Each of the following is also an insured:

a. Your "employees", other than either your "executive officers" (if you are an organization other than a partnership, joint venture or limited liability company) or your managers (if you are a limited liability company), but only for acts within the scope of their employment by you or while performing duties related to the conduct of your business. However, none of these "employees" is an insured for:

    (1) "Bodily injury" or "personal and advertising injury":

        (a) To you, to your partners or members (if you are a partnership or joint venture), to your members (if you are a limited liability company), or to a co-"employee" while that co-"employee" is either in the course of his or her employment or performing duties related to the conduct of your business;

        (b) To the spouse, child, parent, brother or sister of that co-"employee" as a consequence of Paragraph (1)(a) above;

        (c) For which there is any obligation to share damages with or repay someone else who must pay damages because of the injury described in Paragraphs (1)(a) or (b) above; or

        (d) Arising out of his or her providing or failing to provide professional health care services.

    (2) "Property damage" to property:

        (a) Owned, occupied or used by,

        (b) Rented to, in the care, custody or control of, or over which physical control is being exercised for any purpose by

    you, any of your "employees", any partner or member (if you are a partnership or joint venture), or any member (if you are a limited liability company).

b. Any person (other than your "employee"), or any organization while acting as your real estate manager.

c. Any person or organization having proper temporary custody of your property if you die, but only:

    (1) With respect to liability arising out of the maintenance or use of that property; and

    (2) Until your legal representative has been appointed.

d. Your legal representative if you die, but only with respect to duties as such. That representative will have all your rights and duties under this Coverage Part.

3. With respect to "mobile equipment" registered in your name under any motor vehicle registration law, any person is an insured while driving such equipment along a public highway with your permission. Any other person or organization responsible for the conduct of such person is also an insured, but only with respect to liability arising out of the operation of the equipment, and only if no other insurance of any kind is available to that person or organization for this liability. However, no person or organization is an insured with respect to:

a. "Bodily injury" to a co-"employee" of the person driving the equipment; or

b. "Property damage" to property owned by, rented to, in the charge of or occupied by you or the employer of any person who is an insured under this provision.

4. Any organization you newly acquire or form, other than a partnership, joint venture or limited liability company, and over which you maintain ownership or majority interest, will qualify as a Named Insured if there is no other similar insurance available to that organization. However:

a. Coverage under this provision is afforded only until the 90th day after you acquire or form the organization or the end of the policy period, whichever is earlier;

b. Coverage A does not apply to "bodily injury" or "property damage" that occurred before you acquired or formed the organization; and

c. Coverage B does not apply to "personal and advertising injury" arising out of an offense committed before you acquired or formed the organization.

No person or organization is an insured with respect to the conduct of any current or past partnership, joint venture or limited liability company that is not shown as a Named Insured in the Declarations.

SECTION III – LIMITS OF INSURANCE

1. The Limits of Insurance shown in the Declarations and the rules below fix the most we will pay regardless of the number of:

a. Insureds;

b. Claims made or "suits" brought; or

c. Persons or organizations making claims or bringing "suits".

2. The General Aggregate Limit is the most we will pay for the sum of:

a. Medical expenses under Coverage C;

b. Damages under Coverage A, except damages because of "bodily injury" or "property damage" included in the "products-completed operations hazard"; and

c. Damages under Coverage B.

3. The Products-Completed Operations Aggregate Limit is the most we will pay under Coverage A for damages because of "bodily injury" and "property damage" included in the "products-completed operations hazard".

4. Subject to 2. above, the Personal and Advertising Injury Limit is the most we will pay under Coverage B for the sum of all damages because of all "personal and advertising injury" sustained by any one person or organization.

5. Subject to 2. or 3. above, whichever applies, the Each Occurrence Limit is the most we will pay for the sum of:

a. Damages under Coverage A; and

b. Medical expenses under Coverage C

because of all "bodily injury" and "property damage" arising out of any one "occurrence".

6. Subject to 5. above, the Damage To Premises Rented To You Limit is the most we will pay under Coverage A for damages because of "property damage" to any one premises, while rented to you, or in the case of damage by fire, while rented to you or temporarily occupied by you with permission of the owner.

7. Subject to 5. above, the Medical Expense Limit is the most we will pay under Coverage C for all medical expenses because of "bodily injury" sustained by any one person.

The Limits of Insurance of this Coverage Part apply separately to each consecutive annual period and to any remaining period of less than 12 months, starting with the beginning of the policy period shown in the Declarations, unless the policy period is extended after issuance for an additional period of less than 12 months. In that case, the additional period will be deemed part of the last preceding period for purposes of determining the Limits of Insurance.

CG 00 01 07 98 □

SECTION IV – COMMERCIAL GENERAL LIABILITY CONDITIONS

1. Bankruptcy

Bankruptcy or insolvency of the Insured or of the insured's estate will not relieve us of our obligations under this Coverage Part.

2. Duties In The Event Of Occurrence, Offense, Claim Or Suit

a. You must see to it that we are notified as soon as practicable of an "occurrence" or an offense which may result in a claim. To the extent possible, notice should include:

   (1) How, when and where the "occurrence" or offense took place;

   (2) The names and addresses of any injured persons and witnesses; and

   (3) The nature and location of any injury or damage arising out of the "occurrence" or offense.

b. If a claim is made or "suit" is brought against any insured, you must:

   (1) Immediately record the specifics of the claim or "suit" and the date received; and

   (2) Notify us as soon as practicable.

You must see to it that we receive written notice of the claim or "suit" as soon as practicable.

c. You and any other involved insured must:

   (1) Immediately send us copies of any demands, notices, summonses or legal papers received in connection with the claim or "suit";

   (2) Authorize us to obtain records and other information;

   (3) Cooperate with us in the investigation or settlement of the claim or defense against the "suit"; and

   (4) Assist us, upon our request, in the enforcement of any right against any person or organization which may be liable to the insured because of injury or damage to which this insurance may also apply.

d. No insured will, except at that insured's own cost, voluntarily make a payment, assume any obligation, or incur any expense, other than for first aid, without our consent.

3. Legal Action Against Us

No person or organization has a right under this Coverage Part:

a. To join us as a party or otherwise bring us into a "suit" asking for damages from an insured; or

b. To sue us on this Coverage Part unless all of its terms have been fully complied with.

A person or organization may sue us to recover on an agreed settlement or on a final judgment against an insured obtained after an actual trial; but we will not be liable for damages that are not payable under the terms of this Coverage Part or that are in excess of the applicable limit of insurance. An agreed settlement means a settlement and release of liability signed by us, the insured and the claimant or the claimant's legal representative.

4. Other Insurance

If other valid and collectible insurance is available to the insured for a loss we cover under Coverages A or B of this Coverage Part, our obligations are limited as follows:

a. **Primary Insurance**

This insurance is primary except when b. below applies. If this insurance is primary, our obligations are not affected unless any of the other insurance is also primary. Then, we will share with all that other insurance by the method described in c. below.

b. **Excess Insurance**

This insurance is excess over:

   (1) Any of the other insurance, whether primary, excess, contingent or on any other basis:

     (a) That is Fire, Extended Coverage, Builder's Risk, Installation Risk or similar coverage for "your work";

     (b) That is Fire insurance for premises rented to you or temporarily occupied by you with permission of the owner;

     (c) That is insurance purchased by you to cover your liability as a tenant for "property damage" to premises rented to you or temporarily occupied by you with permission of the owner; or

     (d) If the loss arises out of the maintenance or use of aircraft, "autos" or watercraft to the extent not subject to Exclusion g. of Section I – Coverage A – Bodily Injury And Property Damage Liability.

   (2) Any other primary insurance available to you covering liability for damages arising out of the premises or operations for which you have been added as an additional insured by attachment of an endorsement.

When this insurance is excess, we will have no duty under Coverages **A** or **B** to defend the insured against any "suit" if any other insurer has a duty to defend the insured against that "suit". If no other insurer defends, we will undertake to do so, but we will be entitled to the insured's rights against all those other insurers.

When this insurance is excess over other insurance, we will pay only our share of the amount of the loss, if any, that exceeds the sum of:

(1) The total amount that all such other insurance would pay for the loss in the absence of this insurance; and

(2) The total of all deductible and self-insured amounts under all that other insurance.

We will share the remaining loss, if any, with any other insurance that is not described in this Excess Insurance provision and was not bought specifically to apply in excess of the Limits of Insurance shown in the Declarations of this Coverage Part.

c. Method Of Sharing

If all of the other insurance permits contribution by equal shares, we will follow this method also. Under this approach each insurer contributes equal amounts until it has paid its applicable limit of insurance or none of the loss remains, whichever comes first.

If any of the other insurance does not permit contribution by equal shares, we will contribute by limits. Under this method, each insurer's share is based on the ratio of its applicable limit of insurance to the total applicable limits of insurance of all insurers.

5. Premium Audit

a. We will compute all premiums for this Coverage Part in accordance with our rules and rates.

b. Premium shown in this Coverage Part as advance premium is a deposit premium only. At the close of each audit period we will compute the earned premium for that period. Audit premiums are due and payable on notice to the first Named Insured. If the sum of the advance and audit premiums paid for the policy period is greater than the earned premium, we will return the excess to the first Named Insured.

c. The first Named Insured must keep records of the information we need for premium computation, and send us copies at such times as we may request.

6. Representations

By accepting this policy, you agree:

a. The statements in the Declarations are accurate and complete;

b. Those statements are based upon representations you made to us; and

c. We have issued this policy in reliance upon your representations.

7. Separation Of Insureds

Except with respect to the Limits of Insurance, and any rights or duties specifically assigned in this Coverage Part to the first Named Insured, this insurance applies:

a. As if each Named Insured were the only Named Insured; and

b. Separately to each insured against whom claim is made or "suit" is brought.

8. Transfer Of Rights Of Recovery Against Others To Us

If the insured has rights to recover all or part of any payment we have made under this Coverage Part, those rights are transferred to us. The insured must do nothing after loss to impair them. At our request, the insured will bring "suit" or transfer those rights to us and help us enforce them.

9. When We Do Not Renew

If we decide not to renew this Coverage Part, we will mail or deliver to the first Named Insured shown in the Declarations written notice of the nonrenewal not less than 30 days before the expiration date.

If notice is mailed, proof of mailing will be sufficient proof of notice.

SECTION V – DEFINITIONS

1. "Advertisement" means a notice that is broadcast or published to the general public or specific market segments about your goods, products or services for the purpose of attracting customers or supporters.

2. "Auto" means a land motor vehicle, trailer or semitrailer designed for travel on public roads, including any attached machinery or equipment. But "auto" does not include "mobile equipment".

3. "Bodily injury" means bodily injury, sickness or disease sustained by a person, including death resulting from any of these at any time.

4. "Coverage territory" means:

a. The United States of America (including its territories and possessions), Puerto Rico and Canada;

 CG 00 01 07 98 □

b. International waters or airspace, provided the injury or damage does not occur in the course of travel or transportation to or from any place not included in a. above; or

c. All parts of the world if:

  (1) The injury or damage arises out of:

    (a) Goods or products made or sold by you in the territory described in a. above; or

    (b) The activities of a person whose home is in the territory described in a. above, but is away for a short time on your business; and

  (2) The insured's responsibility to pay damages is determined in a "suit" on the merits, in the territory described in a. above or in a settlement we agree to.

5. "Employee" includes a "leased worker". "Employee" does not include a "temporary worker".

6. "Executive officer" means a person holding any of the officer positions created by your charter, constitution, by-laws or any other similar governing document.

7. "Hostile fire" means one which becomes uncontrollable or breaks out from where it was intended to be.

8. "Impaired property" means tangible property other than "your product" or "your work", that cannot be used or is less useful because:

a. It incorporates "your product" or "your work" that is known or thought to be defective, deficient, inadequate or dangerous; or

b. You have failed to fulfill the terms of a contract or agreement;

if such property can be restored to use by:

a. The repair, replacement, adjustment or removal of "your product" or "your work"; or

b. Your fulfilling the terms of the contract or agreement.

9. "Insured contract" means:

a. A contract for a lease of premises. However, that portion of the contract for a lease of premises that indemnifies any person or organization for damage by fire to premises while rented to you or temporarily occupied by you with permission of the owner is not an "insured contract";

b. A sidetrack agreement;

c. Any easement or license agreement, except in connection with construction or demolition operations on or within 50 feet of a railroad;

d. An obligation, as required by ordinance, to indemnify a municipality, except in connection with work for a municipality;

e. An elevator maintenance agreement;

f. That part of any other contract or agreement pertaining to your business (including an indemnification of a municipality in connection with work performed for a municipality) under which you assume the tort liability of another party to pay for "bodily injury" or "property damage" to a third person or organization. Tort liability means a liability that would be imposed by law in the absence of any contract or agreement.

Paragraph f. does not include that part of any contract or agreement:

  (1) That indemnifies a railroad for "bodily injury" or "property damage" arising out of construction or demolition operations, within 50 feet of any railroad property and affecting any railroad bridge or trestle, tracks, road-beds, tunnel, underpass or crossing;

  (2) That indemnifies an architect, engineer or surveyor for injury or damage arising out of:

    (a) Preparing, approving, or failing to prepare or approve, maps, shop drawings, opinions, reports, surveys, field orders, change orders or drawings and specifications; or

    (b) Giving directions or instructions, or failing to give them, if that is the primary cause of the injury or damage; or

  (3) Under which the insured, if an architect, engineer or surveyor, assumes liability for an injury or damage arising out of the insured's rendering or failure to render professional services, including those listed in (2) above and supervisory, inspection, architectural or engineering activities.

10. "Leased worker" means a person leased to you by a labor leasing firm under an agreement between you and the labor leasing firm, to perform duties related to the conduct of your business. "Leased worker" does not include a "temporary worker".

11. "Loading or unloading" means the handling of property:

a. After it is moved from the place where it is accepted for movement into or onto an aircraft, watercraft or "auto";

b. While it is in or on an aircraft, watercraft or "auto"; or

c. While it is being moved from an aircraft, watercraft or "auto" to the place where it is finally delivered;

but "loading or unloading" does not include the movement of property by means of a mechanical device, other than a hand truck, that is not attached to the aircraft, watercraft or "auto".

12. "Mobile equipment" means any of the following types of land vehicles, including any attached machinery or equipment:

a. Bulldozers, farm machinery, forklifts and other vehicles designed for use principally off public roads;

b. Vehicles maintained for use solely on or next to premises you own or rent;

c. Vehicles that travel on crawler treads;

d. Vehicles, whether self-propelled or not, maintained primarily to provide mobility to permanently mounted:

   (1) Power cranes, shovels, loaders, diggers or drills; or

   (2) Road construction or resurfacing equipment such as graders, scrapers or rollers;

e. Vehicles not described in a., b., c. or d. above that are not self-propelled and are maintained primarily to provide mobility to permanently attached equipment of the following types:

   (1) Air compressors, pumps and generators, including spraying, welding, building cleaning, geophysical exploration, lighting and well servicing equipment; or

   (2) Cherry pickers and similar devices used to raise or lower workers;

f. Vehicles not described in a., b., c. or d. above maintained primarily for purposes other than the transportation of persons or cargo.

However, self-propelled vehicles with the following types of permanently attached equipment are not "mobile equipment" but will be considered "autos":

   (1) Equipment designed primarily for:

      (a) Snow removal;

      (b) Road maintenance, but not construction or resurfacing; or

      (c) Street cleaning;

   (2) Cherry pickers and similar devices mounted on automobile or truck chassis and used to raise or lower workers; and

   (3) Air compressors, pumps and generators, including spraying, welding, building cleaning, geophysical exploration, lighting and well servicing equipment.

13. "Occurrence" means an accident, including continuous or repeated exposure to substantially the same general harmful conditions.

14. "Personal and advertising injury" means injury, including consequential "bodily injury", arising out of one or more of the following offenses:

a. False arrest, detention or imprisonment;

b. Malicious prosecution;

c. The wrongful eviction from, wrongful entry into, or invasion of the right of private occupancy of a room, dwelling or premises that a person occupies, committed by or on behalf of its owner, landlord or lessor;

d. Oral or written publication of material that slanders or libels a person or organization or disparages a person's or organization's goods, products or services;

e. Oral or written publication of material that violates a person's right of privacy;

f. The use of another's advertising idea in your "advertisement"; or

g. Infringing upon another's copyright, trade dress or slogan in your "advertisement".

15. "Pollutants" mean any solid, liquid, gaseous or thermal irritant or contaminant, including smoke, vapor, soot, fumes, acids, alkalis, chemicals and waste. Waste includes materials to be recycled, reconditioned or reclaimed.

16. "Products-completed operations hazard":

a. Includes all "bodily injury" and "property damage" occurring away from premises you own or rent and arising out of "your product" or "your work" except:

   (1) Products that are still in your physical possession; or

   (2) Work that has not yet been completed or abandoned. However, "your work" will be deemed completed at the earliest of the following times:

      (a) When all of the work called for in your contract has been completed.

      (b) When all of the work to be done at the job site has been completed if your contract calls for work at more than one job site.

      (c) When that part of the work done at a job site has been put to its intended use by any person or organization other than another contractor or subcontractor working on the same project.

   Work that may need service, maintenance, correction, repair or replacement, but which is otherwise complete, will be treated as completed.

 CG 00 01 07 98

b. Does not include "bodily injury" or "property damage" arising out of:

(1) The transportation of property, unless the injury or damage arises out of a condition in or on a vehicle not owned or operated by you, and that condition was created by the "loading or unloading" of that vehicle by any insured;

(2) The existence of tools, uninstalled equipment or abandoned or unused materials; or

(3) Products or operations for which the classification, listed in the Declarations or in a policy schedule, states that products-completed operations are subject to the General Aggregate Limit.

17. "Property damage" means:

a. Physical injury to tangible property, including all resulting loss of use of that property. All such loss of use shall be deemed to occur at the time of the physical injury that caused it; or

b. Loss of use of tangible property that is not physically injured. All such loss of use shall be deemed to occur at the time of the "occurrence" that caused it.

18. "Suit" means a civil proceeding in which damages because of "bodily injury", "property damage" or "personal and advertising injury" to which this insurance applies are alleged. "Suit" includes:

a. An arbitration proceeding in which such damages are claimed and to which the insured must submit or does submit with our consent; or

b. Any other alternative dispute resolution proceeding in which such damages are claimed and to which the insured submits with our consent.

19. "Temporary worker" means a person who is furnished to you to substitute for a permanent "employee" on leave or to meet seasonal or short-term workload conditions.

20. "Your product" means:

a. Any goods or products, other than real property, manufactured, sold, handled, distributed or disposed of by:

(1) You;

(2) Others trading under your name; or

(3) A person or organization whose business or assets you have acquired; and

b. Containers (other than vehicles), materials, parts or equipment furnished in connection with such goods or products.

"Your product" includes:

a. Warranties or representations made at any time with respect to the fitness, quality, durability, performance or use of "your product"; and

b. The providing of or failure to provide warnings or instructions.

"Your product" does not include vending machines or other property rented to or located for the use of others but not sold.

21. "Your work" means:

a. Work or operations performed by you or on your behalf; and

b. Materials, parts or equipment furnished in connection with such work or operations.

"Your work" includes:

a. Warranties or representations made at any time with respect to the fitness, quality, durability, performance or use of "your work"; and

b. The providing of or failure to provide warnings or instructions.

APPENDIX B(2)

COMMERCIAL GENERAL LIABILITY
CG 00 02 07 98

COMMERCIAL GENERAL LIABILITY COVERAGE FORM

COVERAGES A AND B PROVIDE
CLAIMS-MADE COVERAGE
PLEASE READ THE ENTIRE FORM CAREFULLY

Various provisions in this policy restrict coverage. Read the entire policy carefully to determine rights, duties and what is and is not covered.

Throughout this policy the words "you" and "your" refer to the Named Insured shown in the Declarations, and any other person or organization qualifying as a Named Insured under this policy. The words "we", "us" and "our" refer to the Company providing this insurance.

The word "insured" means any person or organization qualifying as such under Section II – Who Is An Insured.

Other words and phrases that appear in quotation marks have special meaning. Refer to Section VI – Definitions.

SECTION I – COVERAGES

COVERAGE A BODILY INJURY AND PROPERTY DAMAGE LIABILITY

1. Insuring Agreement

  a. We will pay those sums that the insured becomes legally obligated to pay as damages because of "bodily injury" or "property damage" to which this insurance applies. We will have the right and duty to defend the insured against any "suit" seeking those damages. However, we will have no duty to defend the insured against any "suit" seeking damages for "bodily injury" or "property damage" to which this insurance does not apply. We may, at our discretion, investigate any "occurrence" and settle any claim or "suit" that may result. But:

    (1) The amount we will pay for damages is limited as described in Section III – Limits Of Insurance; and

    (2) Our right and duty to defend end when we have used up the applicable limit of insurance in the payment of judgments or settlements under Coverages A or B or medical expenses under Coverage C.

  No other obligation or liability to pay sums or perform acts or services is covered unless explicitly provided for under Supplementary Payments – Coverages A and B.

  b. This insurance applies to "bodily injury" and "property damage" only if:

    (1) The "bodily injury" or "property damage" is caused by an "occurrence" that takes place in the "coverage territory";

    (2) The "bodily injury" or "property damage" did not occur before the Retroactive Date, if any, shown in the Declarations or after the end of the policy period; and

    (3) A claim for damages because of the "bodily injury" or "property damage" is first made against any insured, in accordance with Paragraph c. below, during the policy period or any Extended Reporting Period we provide under Section V – Extended Reporting Periods.

  c. A claim by a person or organization seeking damages will be deemed to have been made at the earlier of the following times:

    (1) When notice of such claim is received and recorded by any insured or by us, whichever comes first; or

    (2) When we make settlement in accordance with Paragraph 1.a. above.

  All claims for damages because of "bodily injury" to the same person, including damages claimed by any person or organization for care, loss of services, or death resulting at any time from the "bodily injury", will be deemed to have been made at the time the first of those claims is made against any insured.

  All claims for damages because of "property damage" causing loss to the same person or organization will be deemed to have been made at the time the first of those claims is made against any insured.

2. Exclusions

This insurance does not apply to:

  a. Expected Or Intended Injury

  "Bodily injury" or "property damage" expected or intended from the standpoint of the insured. This exclusion does not apply to "bodily injury" resulting from the use of reasonable force to protect persons or property.

b. **Contractual Liability**

"Bodily injury" or "property damage" for which the insured is obligated to pay damages by reason of the assumption of liability in a contract or agreement. This exclusion does not apply to liability for damages:

(1) That the insured would have in the absence of the contract or agreement; or

(2) Assumed in a contract or agreement that is an "insured contract", provided the "bodily injury" or "property damage" occurs subsequent to the execution of the contract or agreement. Solely for the purposes of liability assumed in an "insured contract", reasonable attorney fees and necessary litigation expenses incurred by or for a party other than an insured are deemed to be damages because of "bodily injury" or "property damage", provided:

　(a) Liability to such party for, or for the cost of, that party's defense has also been assumed in the same "insured contract"; and

　(b) Such attorney fees and litigation expenses are for defense of that party against a civil or alternative dispute resolution proceeding in which damages to which this insurance applies are alleged.

c. **Liquor Liability**

"Bodily injury" or "property damage" for which any insured may be held liable by reason of:

(1) Causing or contributing to the intoxication of any person;

(2) The furnishing of alcoholic beverages to a person under the legal drinking age or under the influence of alcohol; or

(3) Any statute, ordinance or regulation relating to the sale, gift, distribution or use of alcoholic beverages.

This exclusion applies only if you are in the business of manufacturing, distributing, selling, serving or furnishing alcoholic beverages.

d. **Workers' Compensation And Similar Laws**

Any obligation of the insured under a workers' compensation, disability benefits or unemployment compensation law or any similar law.

e. **Employer's Liability**

"Bodily injury" to:

(1) An "employee" of the insured arising out of and in the course of:

　(a) Employment by the insured; or

　(b) Performing duties related to the conduct of the insured's business; or

(2) The spouse, child, parent, brother or sister of that "employee" as a consequence of Paragraph (1) above.

This exclusion applies:

(1) Whether the insured may be liable as an employer or in any other capacity; and

(2) To any obligation to share damages with or repay someone else who must pay damages because of the injury.

This exclusion does not apply to liability assumed by the insured under an "insured contract".

f. **Pollution**

(1) "Bodily injury" or "property damage" arising out of the actual, alleged or threatened discharge, dispersal, seepage, migration, release or escape of "pollutants":

　(a) At or from any premises, site or location which is or was at any time owned or occupied by, or rented or loaned to, any insured. However, this subparagraph does not apply to:

　　(i) "Bodily injury" if sustained within a building and caused by smoke, fumes, vapor or soot from equipment used to heat that building;

　　(ii) "Bodily injury" or "property damage" for which you may be held liable, if you are a contractor and the owner or lessee of such premises, site or location has been added to your policy as an additional insured with respect to your ongoing operations performed for that additional insured at that premises, site or location and such premises, site or location is not or never was owned or occupied by, or rented or loaned to, any insured, other than that additional insured; or

　　(iii) "Bodily injury" or "property damage" arising out of heat, smoke or fumes from a "hostile fire";

　(b) At or from any premises, site or location which is or was at any time used by or for any insured or others for the handling, storage, disposal, processing or treatment of waste;

　(c) Which are or were at any time transported, handled, stored, treated, disposed of, or processed as waste by or for any insured or any person or organization for whom you may be legally responsible; or

(d) At or from any premises, site or location on which any insured or any contractors or subcontractors working directly or indirectly on any insured's behalf are performing operations if the "pollutants" are brought on or to the premises, site or location in connection with such operations by such insured, contractor or subcontractor. However, this subparagraph does not apply to:

(i) "Bodily injury" or "property damage" arising out of the escape of fuels, lubricants or other operating fluids which are needed to perform the normal electrical, hydraulic or mechanical functions necessary for the operation of "mobile equipment" or its parts, if such fuels, lubricants or other operating fluids escape from a vehicle part designed to hold, store or receive them. This exception does not apply if the "bodily injury" or "property damage" arises out of the intentional discharge, dispersal or release of the fuels, lubricants or other operating fluids, or if such fuels, lubricants or other operating fluids are brought on or to the premises, site or location with the intent that they be discharged, dispersed or released as part of the operations being performed by such insured, contractor or subcontractor;

(ii) "Bodily injury" or "property damage" sustained within a building and caused by the release of gases, fumes or vapors from materials brought into that building in connection with operations being performed by you or on your behalf by a contractor or subcontractor; or

(iii) "Bodily injury" or "property damage" arising out of heat, smoke or fumes from a "hostile fire".

(e) At or from any premises, site or location on which any insured or any contractors or subcontractors working directly or indirectly on any insured's behalf are performing operations if the operations are to test for, monitor, clean up, remove, contain, treat, detoxify or neutralize, or in any way respond to, or assess the effects of, "pollutants".

(2) Any loss, cost or expense arising out of any:

(a) Request, demand, order or statutory or regulatory requirement that any insured or others test for, monitor, clean up, remove, contain, treat, detoxify or neutralize, or in any way respond to, or assess the effects of, "pollutants"; or

(b) Claim or suit by or on behalf of a governmental authority for damages because of testing for, monitoring, cleaning up, removing, containing, treating, detoxifying or neutralizing, or in any way responding to, or assessing the effects of, "pollutants".

However, this paragraph does not apply to liability for damages because of "property damage" that the insured would have in the absence of such request, demand, order or statutory or regulatory requirement, or such claim or "suit" by or on behalf of a governmental authority.

g. Aircraft, Auto Or Watercraft

"Bodily injury" or "property damage" arising out of the ownership, maintenance, use or entrustment to others of any aircraft, "auto" or watercraft owned or operated by or rented or loaned to any insured. Use includes operation and "loading or unloading".

This exclusion does not apply to:

(1) A watercraft while ashore on premises you own or rent;

(2) A watercraft you do not own that is:

(a) Less than 26 feet long; and

(b) Not being used to carry persons or property for a charge;

(3) Parking an "auto" on, or on the ways next to, premises you own or rent, provided the "auto" is not owned by or rented or loaned to you or the insured;

(4) Liability assumed under any "insured contract" for the ownership, maintenance or use of aircraft or watercraft; or

(5) "Bodily injury" or "property damage" arising out of the operation of any of the equipment listed in Paragraph f.(2) or f.(3) of the definition of "mobile equipment".

h. **Mobile Equipment**

"Bodily injury" or "property damage" arising out of:

(1) The transportation of "mobile equipment" by an "auto" owned or operated by or rented or loaned to any insured; or

(2) The use of "mobile equipment" in, or while in practice for, or while being prepared for, any prearranged racing, speed, demolition, or stunting activity.

i. **War**

"Bodily injury" or "property damage" due to war, whether or not declared, or any act or condition incident to war. War includes civil war, insurrection, rebellion or revolution. This exclusion applies only to liability assumed under a contract or agreement.

j. **Damage To Property**

"Property damage" to:

(1) Property you own, rent, or occupy;

(2) Premises you sell, give away or abandon, if the "property damage" arises out of any part of those premises;

(3) Property loaned to you;

(4) Personal property in the care, custody or control of the insured;

(5) That particular part of real property on which you or any contractors or subcontractors working directly or indirectly on your behalf are performing operations, if the "property damage" arises out of those operations; or

(6) That particular part of any property that must be restored, repaired or replaced because "your work" was incorrectly performed on it.

Paragraphs (1), (3) and (4) of this exclusion do not apply to "property damage" (other than damage by fire) to premises, including the contents of such premises, rented to you for a period of 7 or fewer consecutive days. A separate limit of insurance applies to Damage To Premises Rented To You as described in Section III – Limits Of Insurance.

Paragraph (2) of this exclusion does not apply if the premises are "your work" and were never occupied, rented or held for rental by you.

Paragraphs (3), (4), (5) and (6) of this exclusion do not apply to liability assumed under a sidetrack agreement.

Paragraph (6) of this exclusion does not apply to "property damage" included in the "products-completed operations hazard".

k. **Damage To Your Product**

"Property damage" to "your product" arising out of it or any part of it.

l. **Damage To Your Work**

"Property damage" to "your work" arising out of it or any part of it and included in the "products-completed operations hazard".

This exclusion does not apply if the damaged work or the work out of which the damage arises was performed on your behalf by a subcontractor.

m. **Damage To Impaired Property Or Property Not Physically Injured**

"Property damage" to "impaired property" or property that has not been physically injured, arising out of:

(1) A defect, deficiency, inadequacy or dangerous condition in "your product" or "your work"; or

(2) A delay or failure by you or anyone acting on your behalf to perform a contract or agreement in accordance with its terms.

This exclusion does not apply to the loss of use of other property arising out of sudden and accidental physical injury to "your product" or "your work" after it has been put to its intended use.

n. **Recall Of Products, Work Or Impaired Property**

Damages claimed for any loss, cost or expense incurred by you or others for the loss of use, withdrawal, recall, inspection, repair, replacement, adjustment, removal or disposal of:

(1) "Your product";

(2) "Your work"; or

(3) "Impaired property";

if such product, work, or property is withdrawn or recalled from the market or from use by any person or organization because of a known or suspected defect, deficiency, inadequacy or dangerous condition in it.

o. **Personal And Advertising Injury**

"Bodily injury" arising out of "personal and advertising injury".

Exclusions c. through n. do not apply to damage by fire to premises while rented to you or temporarily occupied by you with permission of the owner. A separate limit of insurance applies to this coverage as described in Section III – Limits Of Insurance.

 CG 00 02 07 98 ☐

COVERAGE B PERSONAL AND ADVERTISING INJURY LIABILITY

1. Insuring Agreement

a. We will pay those sums that the insured becomes legally obligated to pay as damages because of "personal and advertising injury" to which this insurance applies. We will have the right and duty to defend the insured against any "suit" seeking those damages. However, we will have no duty to defend the insured against any "suit" seeking damages for "personal and advertising injury" to which this insurance does not apply. We may, at our discretion, investigate any offense and settle any claim or "suit" that may result. But:

(1) The amount we will pay for damages is limited as described in Section **III** – Limits Of Insurance; and

(2) Our right and duty to defend end when we have used up the applicable limit of insurance in the payment of judgments or settlements under Coverages **A** or **B** or medical expenses under Coverage **C**.

No other obligation or liability to pay sums or perform acts or services is covered unless explicitly provided for under Supplementary Payments – Coverages **A** and **B**.

b. This insurance applies to "personal and advertising injury" caused by an offense arising out of your business, but only if:

(1) The offense was committed in the "coverage territory";

(2) The offense was not committed before the Retroactive Date, if any, shown in the Declarations or after the end of the policy period; and

(3) A claim for damages because of the "personal and advertising injury" is first made against any insured, in accordance with Paragraph c. below, during the policy period or any Extended Reporting Period we provide under Section **V** – Extended Reporting Periods.

c. A claim made by a person or organization seeking damages will be deemed to have been made at the earlier of the following times:

(1) When notice of such claim is received and recorded by any insured or by us, whichever comes first; or

(2) When we make settlement in accordance with Paragraph **1.a.** above.

All claims for damages because of "personal injury and advertising injury" to the same person or organization as a result of an offense will be deemed to have been made at the time the first of those claims is made against any insured.

2. Exclusions

This insurance does not apply to:

a. "Personal and advertising injury":

(1) Caused by or at the direction of the insured with the knowledge that the act would violate the rights of another and would inflict "personal and advertising injury";

(2) Arising out of oral or written publication of material, if done by or at the direction of the insured with knowledge of its falsity;

(3) Arising out of oral or written publication of material whose first publication took place before the Retroactive Date, if any, shown in the Declarations;

(4) Arising out of a criminal act committed by or at the direction of any insured;

(5) For which the insured has assumed liability in a contract or agreement. This exclusion does not apply to liability for damages that the insured would have in the absence of the contract or agreement;

(6) Arising out of a breach of contract, except an implied contract to use another's advertising idea in your "advertisement";

(7) Arising out of the failure of goods, products or services to conform with any statement of quality or performance made in your "advertisement";

(8) Arising out of the wrong description of the price of goods, products or services stated in your "advertisement";

(9) Committed by an insured whose business is advertising, broadcasting, publishing or telecasting. However, this exclusion does not apply to Paragraphs **14.a., b.** and **c.** of "personal and advertising injury" under the Definitions Section; or

(10) Arising out of the actual, alleged or threatened discharge, dispersal, seepage, migration, release or escape of pollutants at any time.

b. Any loss, cost or expense arising out of any:

(1) Request, demand or order that any insured or others test for, monitor, clean up, remove, contain, treat, detoxify or neutralize, or in any way respond to, or assess the effects of, "pollutants"; or

(2) Claim or suit by or on behalf of a governmental authority for damages because of testing for, monitoring, cleaning up, removing, containing, treating, detoxifying or neutralizing, or in any way responding to, or assessing the effects of, "pollutants".

COVERAGE C MEDICAL PAYMENTS

1. Insuring Agreement

a. We will pay medical expenses as described below for "bodily injury" caused by an accident:

(1) On premises you own or rent;

(2) On ways next to premises you own or rent; or

(3) Because of your operations;

provided that:

(1) The accident takes place in the "coverage territory" and during the policy period;

(2) The expenses are incurred and reported to us within one year of the date of the accident; and

(3) The injured person submits to examination, at our expense, by physicians of our choice as often as we reasonably require.

b. We will make these payments regardless of fault. These payments will not exceed the applicable limit of insurance. We will pay reasonable expenses for:

(1) First aid administered at the time of an accident;

(2) Necessary medical, surgical, x-ray and dental services, including prosthetic devices; and

(3) Necessary ambulance, hospital, professional nursing and funeral services.

2. Exclusions

We will not pay expenses for "bodily injury":

a. To any insured.

b. To a person hired to do work for or on behalf of any insured or a tenant of any insured.

c. To a person injured on that part of premises you own or rent that the person normally occupies.

d. To a person, whether or not an "employee" of any insured, if benefits for the "bodily injury" are payable or must be provided under a workers' compensation or disability benefits law or a similar law.

e. To a person injured while taking part in athletics.

f. Included within the "products-completed operations hazard".

g. Excluded under Coverage **A**.

h. Due to war, whether or not declared, or any act or condition incident to war. War includes civil war, insurrection, rebellion or revolution.

SUPPLEMENTARY PAYMENTS – COVERAGES A AND B

1. We will pay, with respect to any claim we investigate or settle or any "suit" against an insured we defend:

a. All expenses we incur.

b. Up to $250 for cost of bail bonds required because of accidents or traffic law violations arising out of the use of any vehicle to which the Bodily Injury Liability Coverage applies. We do not have to furnish these bonds.

c. The cost of bonds to release attachments, but only for bond amounts within the applicable limit of insurance. We do not have to furnish these bonds.

d. All reasonable expenses incurred by the insured at our request to assist us in the investigation or defense of the claim or "suit", including actual loss of earnings up to $250 a day because of time off from work.

e. All costs taxed against the insured in the "suit".

f. Prejudgment interest awarded against the insured on that part of the judgment we pay. If we make an offer to pay the applicable limit of insurance, we will not pay any prejudgment interest based on that period of time after the offer.

g. All interest on the full amount of any judgment that accrues after entry of the judgment and before we have paid, offered to pay, or deposited in court the part of the judgment that is within the applicable limit of insurance.

These payments will not reduce the limits of insurance.

 CG 00 02 07 98 □

2. If we defend an insured against a "suit" and an indemnitee of the insured is also named as a party to the "suit", we will defend that indemnitee if all of the following conditions are met:

a. The "suit" against the indemnitee seeks damages for which the insured has assumed the liability of the indemnitee in a contract or agreement that is an "insured contract";

b. This insurance applies to such liability assumed by the insured;

c. The obligation to defend, or the cost of the defense of, that indemnitee, has also been assumed by the insured in the same "insured contract";

d. The allegations in the "suit" and the information we know about the "occurrence" are such that no conflict appears to exist between the interests of the insured and the interests of the indemnitee;

e. The indemnitee and the insured ask us to conduct and control the defense of that indemnitee against such "suit" and agree that we can assign the same counsel to defend the insured and the indemnitee; and

f. The indemnitee:

(1) Agrees in writing to:

(a) Cooperate with us in the investigation, settlement or defense of the "suit";

(b) Immediately send us copies of any demands, notices, summonses or legal papers received in connection with the "suit";

(c) Notify any other insurer whose coverage is available to the indemnitee; and

(d) Cooperate with us with respect to coordinating other applicable insurance available to the indemnitee; and

(2) Provides us with written authorization to:

(a) Obtain records and other information related to the "suit"; and

(b) Conduct and control the defense of the indemnitee in such "suit".

So long as the above conditions are met, attorneys' fees incurred by us in the defense of that indemnitee, necessary litigation expenses incurred by us and necessary litigation expenses incurred by the indemnitee at our request will be paid as Supplementary Payments. Notwithstanding the provisions of Paragraph 2.b.(2) of Section I – Coverage A – Bodily Injury And Property Damage Liability, such payments will not be deemed to be damages for "bodily injury" and "property damage" and will not reduce the limits of insurance.

Our obligation to defend an insured's indemnitee and to pay for attorneys' fees and necessary litigation expenses as Supplementary Payments ends when:

a. We have used up the applicable limit of insurance in the payment of judgments or settlements; or

b. The conditions set forth above, or the terms of the agreement described in Paragraph f. above, are no longer met.

SECTION II – WHO IS AN INSURED

1. If you are designated in the Declarations as:

a. An individual, you and your spouse are insureds, but only with respect to the conduct of a business of which you are the sole owner.

b. A partnership or joint venture, you are an insured. Your members, your partners, and their spouses are also insureds, but only with respect to the conduct of your business.

c. A limited liability company, you are an insured. Your members are also insureds, but only with respect to the conduct of your business. Your managers are insureds, but only with respect to their duties as your managers.

d. An organization other than a partnership, joint venture or limited liability company, you are an insured. Your "executive officers" and directors are insureds, but only with respect to their duties as your officers or directors. Your stockholders are also insureds, but only with respect to their liability as stockholders.

2. Each of the following is also an insured:

a. Your "employees", other than either your "executive officers" (if you are an organization other than a partnership, joint venture or limited liability company) or your managers (if you are a limited liability company), but only for acts within the scope of their employment by you or while performing duties related to the conduct of your business. However, none of these "employees" is an insured for:

(1) "Bodily injury" or "personal and advertising injury":

(a) To you, to your partners or members (if you are a partnership or joint venture), to your members (if you are a limited liability company), or to a co-"employee" while that co-"employee" is either in the course of his or her employment or while performing duties related to the conduct of your business;

(b) To the spouse, child, parent, brother or sister of that co-"employee" as a consequence of Paragraph (1)(a) above;

(c) For which there is any obligation to share damages with or repay someone else who must pay damages because of the injury described in Paragraphs **(1)(a)** or **(b)** above; or

(d) Arising out of his or her providing or failing to provide professional health care services.

(2) "Property damage" to property:

(a) Owned, occupied or used by,

(b) Rented to, in the care, custody or control of, or over which physical control is being exercised for any purpose by

you, any of your "employees", any partner or member (if you are a partnership or joint venture), or any member (if you are a limited liability company).

b. Any person (other than your "employee") or any organization while acting as your real estate manager.

c. Any person or organization having proper temporary custody of your property if you die, but only:

(1) With respect to liability arising out of the maintenance or use of that property; and

(2) Until your legal representative has been appointed.

d. Your legal representative if you die, but only with respect to duties as such. That representative will have all your rights and duties under this Coverage Part.

3. With respect to "mobile equipment" registered in your name under any motor vehicle registration law, any person is an insured while driving such equipment along a public highway with your permission. Any other person or organization responsible for the conduct of such person is also an insured, but only with respect to liability arising out of the operation of the equipment, and only if no other insurance of any kind is available to that person or organization for this liability. However, no person or organization is an insured with respect to:

a. "Bodily injury" to a co-"employee" of the person driving the equipment; or

b. "Property damage" to property owned by, rented to, in the charge of or occupied by you or the employer of any person who is an insured under this provision.

4. Any organization you newly acquire or form, other than a partnership, joint venture or limited liability company, and over which you maintain ownership or majority interest, will qualify as a Named Insured if there is no other similar insurance available to that organization. However:

a. Coverage under this provision is afforded only until the 90th day after you acquire or form the organization or the end of the policy period, whichever is earlier;

b. Coverage A does not apply to "bodily injury" or "property damage" that occurred before you acquired or formed the organization; and

c. Coverage B does not apply to "personal and advertising injury" arising out of an offense committed before you acquired or formed the organization.

No person or organization is an insured with respect to the conduct of any current or past partnership, joint venture or limited liability company that is not shown as a Named Insured in the Declarations.

SECTION III – LIMITS OF INSURANCE

1. The Limits of Insurance shown in the Declarations and the rules below fix the most we will pay regardless of the number of:

a. Insureds;

b. Claims made or "suits" brought; or

c. Persons or organizations making claims or bringing "suits".

2. The General Aggregate Limit is the most we will pay for the sum of:

a. Medical expenses under Coverage C;

b. Damages under Coverage A, except damages because of "bodily injury" or "property damage" included in the "products-completed operations hazard"; and

c. Damages under Coverage B.

3. The Products-Completed Operations Aggregate Limit is the most we will pay under Coverage A for damages because of "bodily injury" and "property damage" included in the "products-completed operations hazard".

4. Subject to **2.** above, the Personal and Advertising Injury Limit is the most we will pay under Coverage B for the sum of all damages because of all "personal and advertising injury" sustained by any one person or organization.

 CG 00 02 07 98 ☐

5. Subject to **2.** or **3.** above, whichever applies, the Each Occurrence Limit is the most we will pay for the sum of:

   a. Damages under Coverage **A**; and

   b. Medical expenses under Coverage **C**

   because of all "bodily injury" and "property damage" arising out of any one "occurrence".

6. Subject to **5.** above, the Damage To Premises Rented To You Limit is the most we will pay under Coverage **A** for damages because of "property damage" to any one premises, while rented to you, or in the case of damage by fire, while rented to you or temporarily occupied by you with permission of the owner.

7. Subject to **5.** above, the Medical Expense Limit is the most we will pay under Coverage **C** for all medical expenses because of "bodily injury" sustained by any one person.

The Limits of Insurance of this Coverage Part apply separately to each consecutive annual period and to any remaining period of less than 12 months, starting with the beginning of the policy period shown in the Declarations, unless the policy period is extended after issuance for an additional period of less than 12 months. In that case, the additional period will be deemed part of the last preceding period for purposes of determining the Limits of Insurance.

SECTION IV – COMMERCIAL GENERAL LIABILITY CONDITIONS

1. **Bankruptcy**

   Bankruptcy or insolvency of the insured or of the insured's estate will not relieve us of our obligations under this Coverage Part.

2. **Duties In The Event Of Occurrence, Offense, Claim Or Suit**

   a. You must see to it that we are notified as soon as practicable of an "occurrence" or offense which may result in a claim. To the extent possible, notice should include:

      (1) How, when and where the "occurrence" or offense took place;

      (2) The names and addresses of any injured persons and witnesses; and

      (3) The nature and location of any injury or damage arising out of the "occurrence" or offense.

      Notice of an "occurrence" or offense is not notice of a claim.

   b. If a claim is received by any insured, you must:

      (1) Immediately record the specifics of the claim and the date received; and

      (2) Notify us as soon as practicable.

      You must see to it that we receive written notice of the claim as soon as practicable.

   c. You and any other involved insured must:

      (1) Immediately send us copies of any demands, notices, summonses or legal papers received in connection with the claim or a "suit";

      (2) Authorize us to obtain records and other information;

      (3) Cooperate with us in the investigation or settlement of the claim or defense against the "suit"; and

      (4) Assist us, upon our request, in the enforcement of any right against any person or organization which may be liable to the insured because of injury or damage to which this insurance may also apply.

   d. No insured will, except at that insured's own cost, voluntarily make a payment, assume any obligation, or incur any expense, other than for first aid, without our consent.

3. **Legal Action Against Us**

   No person or organization has a right under this Coverage Part:

   a. To join us as a party or otherwise bring us into a "suit" asking for damages from an insured; or

   b. To sue us on this Coverage Part unless all of its terms have been fully complied with.

   A person or organization may sue us to recover on an agreed settlement or on a final judgment against an insured obtained after an actual trial; but we will not be liable for damages that are not payable under the terms of this Coverage Part or that are in excess of the applicable limit of insurance. An agreed settlement means a settlement and release of liability signed by us, the insured and the claimant or the claimant's legal representative.

4. **Other Insurance**

   If other valid and collectible insurance is available to the insured for a loss we cover under Coverages **A** or **B** of this Coverage Part, our obligations are limited as follows:

   a. **Primary Insurance**

      This insurance is primary except when **b.** below applies. If this insurance is primary, our obligations are not affected unless any of the other insurance is also primary. Then, we will share with all that other insurance by the method described in **c.** below.

b. Excess Insurance

This insurance is excess over:

(1) Any of the other insurance, whether primary, excess, contingent or on any other basis:

(a) That is effective prior to the beginning of the policy period shown in the Declarations of this insurance and applies to "bodily injury" or "property damage" on other than a claims-made basis, if:

(i) No Retroactive Date is shown in the Declarations of this insurance; or

(ii) The other insurance has a policy period which continues after the Retroactive Date shown in the Declarations of this insurance;

(b) That is Fire, Extended Coverage, Builders' Risk, Installation Risk or similar coverage for "your work";

(c) That is Fire insurance for premises rented to you or temporarily occupied by you with permission of the owner;

(d) That is insurance purchased by you to cover your liability as a tenant for "property damage" to premises rented to you or temporarily occupied by you with permission of the owner; or

(e) If the loss arises out of the maintenance or use of aircraft, "autos" or watercraft to the extent not subject to Exclusion **g.** of Section I – Coverage **A** – Bodily Injury And Property Damage Liability.

(2) Any other primary insurance available to you covering liability for damages arising out of the premises or operations for which you have been added as an additional insured by attachment of an endorsement.

When this insurance is excess, we will have no duty under Coverages A or B to defend the insured against any "suit" if any other insurer has a duty to defend the insured against that "suit". If no other insurer defends, we will undertake to do so, but we will be entitled to the insured's rights against all those other insurers.

When this insurance is excess over other insurance, we will pay only our share of the amount of the loss, if any, that exceeds the sum of:

(1) The total amount that all such other insurance would pay for the loss in the absence of this insurance; and

(2) The total of all deductible and self-insured amounts under all that other insurance.

We will share the remaining loss, if any, with any other insurance that is not described in this Excess Insurance provision and was not bought specifically to apply in excess of the Limits of Insurance shown in the Declarations of this Coverage Part.

c. Method Of Sharing

If all of the other insurance permits contribution by equal shares, we will follow this method also. Under this approach each insurer contributes equal amounts until it has paid its applicable limit of insurance or none of the loss remains, whichever comes first.

If any of the other insurance does not permit contribution by equal shares, we will contribute by limits. Under this method, each insurer's share is based on the ratio of its applicable limit of insurance to the total applicable limits of insurance of all insurers.

5. Premium Audit

a. We will compute all premiums for this Coverage Part in accordance with our rules and rates.

b. Premium shown in this Coverage Part as advance premium is a deposit premium only. At the close of each audit period we will compute the earned premium for that period.

Audit premiums are due and payable on notice to the first Named Insured. If the sum of the advance and audit premiums paid for the policy period is greater than the earned premium, we will return the excess to the first Named Insured.

c. The first Named Insured must keep records of the information we need for premium computation, and send us copies at such times as we may request.

6. Representations

By accepting this policy, you agree:

a. The statements in the Declarations are accurate and complete;

b. Those statements are based upon representations you made to us; and

c. We have issued this policy in reliance upon your representations.

7. Separation Of Insureds

Except with respect to the Limits of Insurance, and any rights or duties specifically assigned in this Coverage Part to the first Named Insured, this insurance applies:

a. As if each Named Insured were the only Named Insured; and

b. Separately to each insured against whom claim is made or "suit" is brought.

Copyright, Insurance Services Office, Inc., 1997   CG 00 02 07 98

8. Transfer Of Rights Of Recovery Against Others To Us

If the insured has rights to recover all or part of any payment we have made under this Coverage Part, those rights are transferred to us. The insured must do nothing after loss to impair them. At our request, the insured will bring "suit" or transfer those rights to us and help us enforce them.

9. When We Do Not Renew

If we decide not to renew this Coverage Part, we will mail or deliver to the first Named Insured shown in the Declarations written notice of the nonrenewal not less than 30 days before the expiration date.

If notice is mailed, proof of mailing will be sufficient proof of notice.

10. Your Right To Claim And "Occurrence" Information

We will provide the first Named Insured shown in the Declarations the following information relating to this and any preceding general liability claims-made Coverage Part we have issued to you during the previous three years:

a. A list or other record of each "occurrence", not previously reported to any other insurer, of which we were notified in accordance with Paragraph 2.a. of the Section IV – Duties In The Event Of Occurrence, Offense, Claim Or Suit Condition. We will include the date and brief description of the "occurrence" if that information was in the notice we received.

b. A summary by policy year, of payments made and amounts reserved, stated separately, under any applicable General Aggregate Limit and Products-Completed Operations Aggregate Limit.

Amounts reserved are based on our judgment. They are subject to change and should not be regarded as ultimate settlement values.

You must not disclose this information to any claimant or any claimant's representative without our consent.

If we cancel or elect not to renew this Coverage Part, we will provide such information no later than 30 days before the date of policy termination. In other circumstances, we will provide this information only if we receive a written request from the first Named Insured within 60 days after the end of the policy period. In this case, we will provide this information within 45 days of receipt of the request.

We compile claim and "occurrence" information for our own business purposes and exercise reasonable care in doing so. In providing this information to the first Named Insured, we make no representations or warranties to insureds, insurers, or others to whom this information is furnished by or on behalf of any insured. Cancellation or non-renewal will be effective even if we inadvertently provide inaccurate information.

SECTION V – EXTENDED REPORTING PERIODS

1. We will provide one or more Extended Reporting Periods, as described below, if:

a. This Coverage Part is canceled or not renewed; or

b. We renew or replace this Coverage Part with insurance that:

(1) Has a Retroactive Date later than the date shown in the Declarations of this Coverage Part; or

(2) Does not apply to "bodily injury", "property damage" or "personal and advertising injury" on a claims-made basis.

2. Extended Reporting Periods do not extend the policy period or change the scope of coverage provided. They apply only to claims for:

a. "Bodily injury" or "property damage" that occurs before the end of the policy period but not before the Retroactive Date, if any, shown in the Declarations; or

b. "Personal injury and advertising injury" caused by an offense committed before the end of the policy period but not before the Retroactive Date, if any, shown in the Declarations.

Once in effect, Extended Reporting Periods may not be canceled.

3. A Basic Extended Reporting Period is automatically provided without additional charge. This period starts with the end of the policy period and lasts for:

a. Five years with respect to claims because of "bodily injury" and "property damage" arising out of an "occurrence" reported to us, not later than 60 days after the end of the policy period, in accordance with Paragraph 2.a. of the Section IV – Duties In The Event Of Occurrence, Offense, Claim Or Suit Condition;

b. Five years with respect to claims because of "personal and advertising injury" arising out of an offense reported to us, not later than 60 days after the end of the policy period, in accordance with Paragraph 2.a. of the Section IV – Duties In The Event Of Occurrence, Offense, Claim Or Suit Condition; and

c. Sixty days with respect to claims arising from "occurrences" or offenses not previously reported to us.

The Basic Extended Reporting Period does not apply to claims that are covered under any subsequent insurance you purchase, or that would be covered but for exhaustion of the amount of insurance applicable to such claims.

4. The Basic Extended Reporting Period does not reinstate or increase the Limits of Insurance.

5. A Supplemental Extended Reporting Period of unlimited duration is available, but only by an endorsement and for an extra charge. This supplemental period starts when the Basic Extended Reporting Period, set forth in Paragraph 3. above, ends.

You must give us a written request for the endorsement within 60 days after the end of the policy period. The Supplemental Extended Reporting Period will not go into effect unless you pay the additional premium promptly when due.

We will determine the additional premium in accordance with our rules and rates. In doing so, we may take into account the following:

a. The exposures insured;

b. Previous types and amounts of insurance;

c. Limits of Insurance available under this Coverage Part for future payment of damages; and

d. Other related factors.

The additional premium will not exceed 200% of the annual premium for this Coverage Part.

This endorsement shall set forth the terms, not inconsistent with this Section, applicable to the Supplemental Extended Reporting Period, including a provision to the effect that the insurance afforded for claims first received during such period is excess over any other valid and collectible insurance available under policies in force after the Supplemental Extended Reporting Period starts.

6. If the Supplemental Extended Reporting Period is in effect, we will provide the supplemental aggregate limits of insurance described below, but only for claims first received and recorded during the Supplemental Extended Reporting Period.

The supplemental aggregate limits of insurance will be equal to the dollar amount shown in the Declarations in effect at the end of the policy period for such of the following limits of insurance for which a dollar amount has been entered:

General Aggregate Limit
Products-Completed Operations Aggregate Limit

Paragraphs 2. and 3. of Section III – Limits Of Insurance will be amended accordingly. The Personal and Advertising Injury Limit, the Each Occurrence Limit and the Fire Damage Limit shown in the Declarations will then continue to apply, as set forth in Paragraphs 4., 5. and 6. of that Section.

SECTION VI – DEFINITIONS

1. "Advertisement" means a notice that is broadcast or published to the general public or specific market segments about your goods, products or services for the purpose of attracting customers or supporters.

2. "Auto" means a land motor vehicle, trailer or semitrailer designed for travel on public roads, including any attached machinery or equipment. But "auto" does not include "mobile equipment".

3. "Bodily injury" means bodily injury, sickness or disease sustained by a person, including death resulting from any of these at any time.

4. "Coverage territory" means:

   a. The United States of America (including its territories and possessions), Puerto Rico and Canada;

   b. International waters or airspace, provided the injury or damage does not occur in the course of travel or transportation to or from any place not included in a. above; or

   c. All parts of the world if:

      (1) The injury or damage arises out of:

         (a) Goods or products made or sold by you in the territory described in a. above; or

         (b) The activities of a person whose home is in the territory described in a. above, but is away for a short time on your business; and

      (2) The insured's responsibility to pay damages is determined in a "suit" on the merits, in the territory described in a. above or in a settlement we agree to.

5. "Employee" includes a "leased worker". "Employee" does not include a "temporary worker".

6. "Executive officer" means a person holding any of the officer positions created by your charter, constitution, by-laws or any other similar governing document.

7. "Hostile fire" means one which becomes uncontrollable or breaks out from where it was intended to be.

 CG 00 02 07 98 ☐

8. "Impaired property" means tangible property, other than "your product" or "your work", that cannot be used or is less useful because:

   a. It incorporates "your product" or "your work" that is known or thought to be defective, deficient, inadequate or dangerous; or

   b. You have failed to fulfill the terms of a contract or agreement;

   if such property can be restored to use by:

   a. The repair, replacement, adjustment or removal of "your product" or "your work"; or

   b. Your fulfilling the terms of the contract or agreement.

9. "Insured contract" means:

   a. A contract for a lease of premises. However, that portion of the contract for a lease of premises that indemnifies any person or organization for damage by fire to premises while rented to you or temporarily occupied by you with permission of the owner is not an "insured contract";

   b. A sidetrack agreement;

   c. Any easement or license agreement, except in connection with construction or demolition operations on or within 50 feet of a railroad;

   d. An obligation, as required by ordinance, to indemnify a municipality, except in connection with work for a municipality;

   e. An elevator maintenance agreement;

   f. That part of any other contract or agreement pertaining to your business (including an indemnification of a municipality in connection with work performed for a municipality) under which you assume the tort liability of another party to pay for "bodily injury" or "property damage" to a third person or organization. Tort liability means a liability that would be imposed by law in the absence of any contract or agreement.

   Paragraph f. does not include that part of any contract or agreement:

   (1) That indemnifies a railroad for "bodily injury" or "property damage" arising out of construction or demolition operations, within 50 feet of any railroad property and affecting any railroad bridge or trestle, tracks, road-beds, tunnel, underpass or crossing;

   (2) That indemnifies an architect, engineer or surveyor for injury or damage arising out of:

   (a) Preparing, approving, or failing to prepare or approve, maps, shop drawings, opinions, reports, surveys, field orders, change orders or drawings and specifications; or

   (b) Giving directions or instructions, or failing to give them, if that is the primary cause of the injury or damage; or

   (3) Under which the insured, if an architect, engineer or surveyor, assumes liability for an injury or damage arising out of the insured's rendering or failure to render professional services, including those listed in (2) above and supervisory, inspection, architectural or engineering activities.

10. "Leased worker" means a person leased to you by a labor leasing firm under an agreement between you and the labor leasing firm, to perform duties related to the conduct of your business. "Leased worker" does not include a "temporary worker".

11. "Loading or unloading" means the handling of property:

    a. After it is moved from the place where it is accepted for movement into or onto an aircraft, watercraft or "auto";

    b. While it is in or on an aircraft, watercraft or "auto"; or

    c. While it is being moved from an aircraft, watercraft or "auto" to the place where it is finally delivered;

    but "loading or unloading" does not include the movement of property by means of a mechanical device, other than a hand truck, that is not attached to the aircraft, watercraft or "auto".

12. "Mobile equipment" means any of the following types of land vehicles, including any attached machinery or equipment:

    a. Bulldozers, farm machinery, forklifts and other vehicles designed for use principally off public roads;

    b. Vehicles maintained for use solely on or next to premises you own or rent;

    c. Vehicles that travel on crawler treads;

    d. Vehicles, whether self-propelled or not, maintained primarily to provide mobility to permanently mounted:

    (1) Power cranes, shovels, loaders, diggers or drills; or

    (2) Road construction or resurfacing equipment such as graders, scrapers or rollers;

    e. Vehicles not described in a., b., c. or d. above that are not self-propelled and are maintained primarily to provide mobility to permanently attached equipment of the following types:

    (1) Air compressors, pumps and generators, including spraying, welding, building cleaning, geophysical exploration, lighting and well servicing equipment; or

    (2) Cherry pickers and similar devices used to raise or lower workers;

f. Vehicles not described in **a.**, **b.**, **c.** or **d.** above maintained primarily for purposes other than the transportation of persons or cargo.

However, self-propelled vehicles with the following types of permanently attached equipment are not "mobile equipment" but will be considered "autos":

(1) Equipment designed primarily for:

    (a) Snow removal;

    (b) Road maintenance, but not construction or resurfacing; or

    (c) Street cleaning;

(2) Cherry pickers and similar devices mounted on automobile or truck chassis and used to raise or lower workers; and

(3) Air compressors, pumps and generators, including spraying, welding, building cleaning, geophysical exploration, lighting and well servicing equipment.

13. "Occurrence" means an accident, including continuous or repeated exposure to substantially the same general harmful conditions.

14. "Personal and advertising injury" means injury, including consequential "bodily injury", arising out of one or more of the following offenses:

a. False arrest, detention or imprisonment;

b. Malicious prosecution;

c. The wrongful eviction from, wrongful entry into, or invasion of the right of private occupancy of a room, dwelling or premises that a person occupies, committed by or on behalf of its owner, landlord or lessor;

d. Oral or written publication of material that slanders or libels a person or organization or disparages a person's or organization's goods, products or services;

e. Oral or written publication of material that violates a person's right of privacy;

f. The use of another's advertising idea in your "advertisement"; or

g. Infringing upon another's copyright, trade dress or slogan in your "advertisement".

15. "Pollutants" mean any solid, liquid, gaseous or thermal irritant or contaminant, including smoke, vapor, soot, fumes, acids, alkalis, chemicals and waste. Waste includes materials to be recycled, reconditioned or reclaimed.

16. "Products-completed operations hazard":

a. Includes all "bodily injury" and "property damage" occurring away from premises you own or rent and arising out of "your product" or "your work" except:

    (1) Products that are still in your physical possession; or

(2) Work that has not yet been completed or abandoned. However, "your work" will be deemed completed at the earliest of the following times:

    (a) When all of the work called for in your contract has been completed.

    (b) When all of the work to be done at the job site has been completed if your contract calls for work at more than one job site.

    (c) When that part of the work done at a job site has been put to its intended use by any person or organization other than another contractor or subcontractor working on the same project.

Work that may need service, maintenance, correction, repair or replacement, but which is otherwise complete, will be treated as completed.

b. Does not include "bodily injury" or "property damage" arising out of:

(1) The transportation of property, unless the injury or damage arises out of a condition in or on a vehicle not owned or operated by you, and that condition was created by the "loading or unloading" of that vehicle by any insured;

(2) The existence of tools, uninstalled equipment or abandoned or unused materials; or

(3) Products or operations for which the classification, listed in the Declarations or in a policy schedule, states that products-completed operations are subject to the General Aggregate Limit.

17. "Property damage" means:

a. Physical injury to tangible property, including all resulting loss of use of that property. All such loss of use shall be deemed to occur at the time of the physical injury that caused it; or

b. Loss of use of tangible property that is not physically injured. All such loss of use shall be deemed to occur at the time of the "occurrence" that caused it.

18. "Suit" means a civil proceeding in which damages because of "bodily injury", "property damage" or "personal and advertising injury" to which this insurance applies are alleged. "Suit" includes:

a. An arbitration proceeding in which such damages are claimed and to which the insured must submit or does submit with our consent; or

b. Any other alternative dispute resolution proceeding in which such damages are claimed and to which the insured submits with our consent.

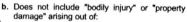

19. "Temporary worker" means a person who is furnished to you to substitute for a permanent "employee" on leave or to meet seasonal or short-term workload conditions.

20. "Your product" means:

a. Any goods or products, other than real property, manufactured, sold, handled, distributed or disposed of by:

　(1) You;

　(2) Others trading under your name; or

　(3) A person or organization whose business or assets you have acquired; and

b. Containers (other than vehicles), materials, parts or equipment furnished in connection with such goods or products.

"Your product" includes:

a. Warranties or representations made at any time with respect to the fitness, quality, durability, performance or use of "your product"; and

b. The providing of or failure to provide warnings or instructions.

"Your product" does not include vending machines or other property rented to or located for the use of others but not sold.

21. "Your work" means:

a. Work or operations performed by you or on your behalf; and

b. Materials, parts or equipment furnished in connection with such work or operations.

"Your work" includes:

a. Warranties or representations made at any time with respect to the fitness, quality, durability, performance or use of "your work"; and

b. The providing of or failure to provide warnings or instructions.

APPENDIX C

HOMEOWNERS
HO 00 02 04 91

HOMEOWNERS 2
BROAD FORM

AGREEMENT

We will provide the insurance described in this policy in return for the premium and compliance with all applicable provisions of this policy.

DEFINITIONS

In this policy, "you" and "your" refer to the "named insured" shown in the Declarations and the spouse if a resident of the same household. "We," "us" and "our" refer to the Company providing this insurance. In addition, certain words and phrases are defined as follows:

1. "Bodily injury" means bodily harm, sickness or disease, including required care, loss of services and death that results.

2. "Business" includes trade, profession or occupation.

3. "Insured" means you and residents of your household who are:

   a. Your relatives; or

   b. Other persons under the age of 21 and in the care of any person named above.

   Under Section II, "insured" also means:

   c. With respect to animals or watercraft to which this policy applies, any person or organization legally responsible for these animals or watercraft which are owned by you or any person included in 3.a. or 3.b. above. A person or organization using or having custody of these animals or watercraft in the course of any "business" or without consent of the owner is not an "insured";

   d. With respect to any vehicle to which this policy applies:

      (1) Persons while engaged in your employ or that of any person included in 3.a. or 3.b. above; or

      (2) Other persons using the vehicle on an "insured location" with your consent.

4. "Insured location" means:

   a. The "residence premises";

   b. The part of other premises, other structures and grounds used by you as a residence and:

      (1) Which is shown in the Declarations; or

      (2) Which is acquired by you during the policy period for your use as a residence;

   c. Any premises used by you in connection with a premises in 4.a. and 4.b. above;

   d. Any part of a premises:

      (1) Not owned by an "insured"; and

      (2) Where an "insured" is temporarily residing;

   e. Vacant land, other than farm land, owned by or rented to an "insured";

   f. Land owned by or rented to an "insured" on which a one or two family dwelling is being built as a residence for an "insured";

   g. Individual or family cemetery plots or burial vaults of an "insured"; or

   h. Any part of a premises occasionally rented to an "insured" for other than "business" use.

5. "Occurrence" means an accident, including continuous or repeated exposure to substantially the same general harmful conditions, which results, during the policy period, in:

   a. "Bodily injury"; or

   b. "Property damage."

6. "Property damage" means physical injury to, destruction of, or loss of use of tangible property.

7. "Residence employee" means:

   a. An employee of an "insured" whose duties are related to the maintenance or use of the "residence premises," including household or domestic services; or

   b. One who performs similar duties elsewhere not related to the "business" of an "insured."

8. "Residence premises" means:

   a. The one family dwelling, other structures, and grounds; or

   b. That part of any other building;

   where you reside and which is shown as the "residence premises" in the Declarations.

   "Residence premises" also means a two family dwelling where you reside in at least one of the family units and which is shown as the "residence premises" in the Declarations.

SECTION I – PROPERTY COVERAGES

COVERAGE A – Dwelling

We cover:

1. The dwelling on the "residence premises" shown in the Declarations, including structures attached to the dwelling; and

2. Materials and supplies located on or next to the "residence premises" used to construct, alter or repair the dwelling or other structures on the "residence premises."

This coverage does not apply to land, including land on which the dwelling is located.

COVERAGE B – Other Structures

We cover other structures on the "residence premises" set apart from the dwelling by clear space. This includes structures connected to the dwelling by only a fence, utility line, or similar connection.

This coverage does not apply to land, including land on which the other structures are located.

We do not cover other structures:

1. Used in whole or in part for "business"; or

2. Rented or held for rental to any person not a tenant of the dwelling, unless used solely as a private garage.

The limit of liability for this coverage will not be more than 10% of the limit of liability that applies to Coverage A. Use of this coverage does not reduce the Coverage A limit of liability.

COVERAGE C – Personal Property

We cover personal property owned or used by an "insured" while it is anywhere in the world. At your request, we will cover personal property owned by:

1. Others while the property is on the part of the "residence premises" occupied by an "insured";

2. A guest or a "residence employee," while the property is in any residence occupied by an "insured."

Our limit of liability for personal property usually located at an "insured's" residence, other than the "residence premises," is 10% of the limit of liability for Coverage C, or $1000, whichever is greater. Personal property in a newly acquired principal residence is not subject to this limitation for the 30 days from the time you begin to move the property there.

Special Limits of Liability. These limits do not increase the Coverage C limit of liability. The special limit for each numbered category below is the total limit for each loss for all property in that category.

1. $200 on money, bank notes, bullion, gold other than goldware, silver other than silverware, platinum, coins and medals.

2. $1000 on securities, accounts, deeds, evidences of debt, letters of credit, notes other than bank notes, manuscripts, personal records, passports, tickets and stamps. This dollar limit applies to these categories regardless of the medium (such as paper or computer software) on which the material exists.

   This limit includes the cost to research, replace or restore the information from the lost or damaged material.

3. $1000 on watercraft, including their trailers, furnishings, equipment and outboard engines or motors.

4. $1000 on trailers not used with watercraft.

5. $1000 for loss by theft of jewelry, watches, furs, precious and semi-precious stones.

6. $2000 for loss by theft of firearms.

7. $2500 for loss by theft of silverware, silver-plated ware, goldware, gold-plated ware and pewterware. This includes flatware, hollowware, tea sets, trays and trophies made of or including silver, gold or pewter.

8. $2500 on property, on the "residence premises," used at any time or in any manner for any "business" purpose.

9. $250 on property, away from the "residence premises," used at any time or in any manner for any "business" purpose. However, this limit does not apply to loss to adaptable electronic apparatus as described in Special Limits 10. and 11. below.

10. $1000 for loss to electronic apparatus, while in or upon a motor vehicle or other motorized land conveyance, if the electronic apparatus is equipped to be operated by power from the electrical system of the vehicle or conveyance while retaining its capability of being operated by other sources of power. Electronic apparatus includes:

    a. Accessories and antennas; or

    b. Tapes, wires, records, discs or other media;

    for use with any electronic apparatus.

11. $1000 for loss to electronic apparatus, while not in or upon a motor vehicle or other motorized land conveyance, if the electronic apparatus:

    a. Is equipped to be operated by power from the electrical system of the vehicle or conveyance while retaining its capability of being operated by other sources of power;

    b. Is away from the "residence premises"; and

               HO 00 02 04 91

   c. Is used at any time or in any manner for any "business" purpose.

Electronic apparatus includes:

   a. Accessories and antennas; or

   b. Tapes, wires, records, discs or other media;

for use with any electronic apparatus.

Property Not Covered. We do not cover:

1. Articles separately described and specifically insured in this or other insurance;

2. Animals, birds or fish;

3. Motor vehicles or all other motorized land conveyances. This includes:

   a. Their equipment and accessories; or

   b. Electronic apparatus that is designed to be operated solely by use of the power from the electrical system of motor vehicles or all other motorized land conveyances. Electronic apparatus includes:

     (1) Accessories or antennas; or

     (2) Tapes, wires, records, discs or other media; for use with any electronic apparatus.

   The exclusion of property described in **3.a.** and **3.b.** above applies only while the property is in or upon the vehicle or conveyance.

We do cover vehicles or conveyances not subject to motor vehicle registration which are:

   a. Used to service an "insured's" residence; or

   b. Designed for assisting the handicapped;

4. Aircraft and parts. Aircraft means any contrivance used or designed for flight, except model or hobby aircraft not used or designed to carry people or cargo;

5. Property of roomers, boarders and other tenants, except property of roomers and boarders related to an "insured";

6. Property in an apartment regularly rented or held for rental to others by an "insured," except as provided in Additional Coverages 10.;

7. Property rented or held for rental to others off the "residence premises";

8. "Business" data, including such data stored in:

   a. Books of account, drawings or other paper records; or

   b. Electronic data processing tapes, wires, records, discs or other software media.

   However, we do cover the cost of blank recording or storage media, and of pre-recorded computer programs available on the retail market; or

9. Credit cards or fund transfer cards except as provided in Additional Coverages 6.

COVERAGE D – Loss Of Use

The limit of liability for Coverage D is the total limit for all the coverages that follow.

1. If a loss covered under this Section makes that part of the "residence premises" where you reside not fit to live in, we cover, at your choice, either of the following. However, if the "residence premises" is not your principal place of residence, we will not provide the option under paragraph **b.** below.

   a. **Additional Living Expense,** meaning any necessary increase in living expenses incurred by you so that your household can maintain its normal standard of living; or

   b. **Fair Rental Value,** meaning the fair rental value of that part of the "residence premises" where you reside less any expenses that do not continue while the premises is not fit to live in.

Payment under **a.** or **b.** will be for the shortest time required to repair or replace the damage or, if you permanently relocate, the shortest time required for your household to settle elsewhere.

2. If a loss covered under this Section makes that part of the "residence premises" rented to others or held for rental by you not fit to live in, we cover the:

   Fair Rental Value, meaning the fair rental value of that part of the "residence premises" rented to others or held for rental by you less any expenses that do not continue while the premises is not fit to live in.

Payment will be for the shortest time required to repair or replace that part of the premises rented or held for rental.

3. If a civil authority prohibits you from use of the "residence premises" as a result of direct damage to neighboring premises by a Peril Insured Against in this policy, we cover the Additional Living Expense and Fair Rental Value loss as provided under **1.** and **2.** above for no more than two weeks.

The periods of time under **1., 2.** and **3.** above are not limited by expiration of this policy.

We do not cover loss or expense due to cancellation of a lease or agreement.

ADDITIONAL COVERAGES

1. **Debris Removal.** We will pay your reasonable expense for the removal of:

   a. Debris of covered property if a Peril Insured Against that applies to the damaged property causes the loss; or

   b. Ash, dust or particles from a volcanic eruption that has caused direct loss to a building or property contained in a building.

This expense is included in the limit of liability that applies to the damaged property. If the amount to be paid for the actual damage to the property plus the debris removal expense is more than the limit of liability for the damaged property, an additional 5% of that limit of liability is available for debris removal expense.

We will also pay your reasonable expense, up to $500, for the removal from the "residence premises" of:

a. Your tree(s) felled by the peril of Windstorm or Hail;

b. Your tree(s) felled by the peril of Weight of Ice, Snow or Sleet; or

c. A neighbor's tree(s) felled by a Peril Insured Against under Coverage C;

provided the tree(s) damages a covered structure. The $500 limit is the most we will pay in any one loss regardless of the number of fallen trees.

2. **Reasonable Repairs.** In the event that covered property is damaged by an applicable Peril Insured Against, we will pay the reasonable cost incurred by you for necessary measures taken solely to protect against further damage. If the measures taken involve repair to other damaged property, we will pay for those measures only if that property is covered under this policy and the damage to that property is caused by an applicable Peril Insured Against.

This coverage:

a. Does not increase the limit of liability that applies to the covered property;

b. Does not relieve you of your duties, in case of a loss to covered property, as set forth in SECTION I – CONDITION **2.d.**

3. **Trees, Shrubs and Other Plants.** We cover trees, shrubs, plants or lawns, on the "residence premises," for loss caused by the following Perils Insured Against: Fire or lightning, Explosion, Riot or civil commotion, Aircraft, Vehicles not owned or operated by a resident of the "residence premises," Vandalism or malicious mischief or Theft.

We will pay up to 5% of the limit of liability that applies to the dwelling, for all trees, shrubs, plants or lawns. No more than $500 of this limit will be available for any one tree, shrub or plant. We do not cover property grown for "business" purposes.

This coverage is additional insurance.

4. **Fire Department Service Charge.** We will pay up to $500 for your liability assumed by contract or agreement for fire department charges incurred when the fire department is called to save or protect covered property from a Peril Insured Against. We do not cover fire department service charges if the property is located within the limits of the city, municipality or protection district furnishing the fire department response.

This coverage is additional insurance. No deductible applies to this coverage.

5. **Property Removed.** We insure covered property against direct loss from any cause while being removed from a premises endangered by a Peril Insured Against and for no more than 30 days while removed. This coverage does not change the limit of liability that applies to the property being removed.

6. **Credit Card, Fund Transfer Card, Forgery and Counterfeit Money.**

We will pay up to $500 for:

a. The legal obligation of an "insured" to pay because of the theft or unauthorized use of credit cards issued to or registered in an "insured's" name;

b. Loss resulting from theft or unauthorized use of a fund transfer card used for deposit, withdrawal or transfer of funds, issued to or registered in an "insured's" name;

c. Loss to an "insured" caused by forgery or alteration of any check or negotiable instrument; and

d. Loss to an "insured" through acceptance in good faith of counterfeit United States or Canadian paper currency.

We do not cover use of a credit card or fund transfer card:

a. By a resident of your household;

b. By a person who has been entrusted with either type of card; or

c. If an "insured" has not complied with all terms and conditions under which the cards are issued.

All loss resulting from a series of acts committed by any one person or in which any one person is concerned or implicated is considered to be one loss.

We do not cover loss arising out of "business" use or dishonesty of an "insured."

This coverage is additional insurance. No deductible applies to this coverage.

Defense:

a. We may investigate and settle any claim or suit that we decide is appropriate. Our duty to defend a claim or suit ends when the amount we pay for the loss equals our limit of liability.

b. If a suit is brought against an "insured" for liability under the Credit Card or Fund Transfer Card coverage, we will provide a defense at our expense by counsel of our choice.

c. We have the option to defend at our expense an "insured" or an "insured's" bank against any suit for the enforcement of payment under the Forgery coverage.

7. **Loss Assessment.** We will pay up to $1000 for your share of loss assessment charged during the policy period against you by a corporation or association of property owners, when the assessment is made as a result of direct loss to the property, owned by all members collectively, caused by a Peril Insured Against under COVERAGE A – DWELLING, other than earthquake or land shock waves or tremors before, during or after a volcanic eruption.

This coverage applies only to loss assessments charged against you as owner or tenant of the "residence premises."

We do not cover loss assessments charged against you or a corporation or association of property owners by any governmental body.

The limit of $1000 is the most we will pay with respect to any one loss, regardless of the number of assessments.

Condition 1. Policy Period, under SECTIONS I AND II CONDITIONS, does not apply to this coverage.

8. **Collapse.** We insure for direct physical loss to covered property involving collapse of a building or any part of a building caused only by one or more of the following:

a. Perils Insured Against in COVERAGE C – PERSONAL PROPERTY. These perils apply to covered buildings and personal property for loss insured by this additional coverage;

b. Hidden decay;

c. Hidden insect or vermin damage;

d. Weight of contents, equipment, animals or people;

e. Weight of rain which collects on a roof; or

f. Use of defective material or methods in construction, remodeling or renovation if the collapse occurs during the course of the construction, remodeling or renovation.

Loss to an awning, fence, patio, pavement, swimming pool, underground pipe, flue, drain, cesspool, septic tank, foundation, retaining wall, bulkhead, pier, wharf or dock is not included under items b., c., d., e., and f. unless the loss is a direct result of the collapse of a building.

Collapse does not include settling, cracking, shrinking, bulging or expansion.

This coverage does not increase the limit of liability applying to the damaged covered property.

9. **Glass or Safety Glazing Material.**

We cover:

a. The breakage of glass or safety glazing material which is part of a covered building, storm door or storm window; and

b. Damage to covered property by glass or safety glazing material which is part of a building, storm door or storm window.

This coverage does not include loss on the "residence premises" if the dwelling has been vacant for more than 30 consecutive days immediately before the loss. A dwelling being constructed is not considered vacant.

Loss for damage to glass will be settled on the basis of replacement with safety glazing materials when required by ordinance or law.

This coverage does not increase the limit of liability that applies to the damaged property.

10. **Landlord's Furnishings.** We will pay up to $2500 for your appliances, carpeting and other household furnishings, in an apartment on the "residence premises" regularly rented or held for rental to others by an "insured," for loss caused by all Perils Insured Against other than the peril of Theft.

The $2500 limit is the most we will pay in any one loss regardless of the number of appliances, carpeting or other household furnishings involved in the loss.

SECTION I – PERILS INSURED AGAINST

We insure for direct physical loss to the property described in Coverages A, B and C caused by a peril listed below unless the loss is excluded in SECTION I – EXCLUSIONS.

1. **Fire or lightning.**

2. **Windstorm or hail.**

   This peril does not include loss to the inside of a building or the property contained in a building caused by rain, snow, sleet, sand or dust unless the direct force of wind or hail damages the building causing an opening in a roof or wall and the rain, snow, sleet, sand or dust enters through this opening.

   This peril includes loss to watercraft and their trailers, furnishings, equipment, and outboard engines or motors, only while inside a fully enclosed building.

3. **Explosion.**

4. **Riot or civil commotion.**

5. **Aircraft,** including self-propelled missiles and spacecraft.

6. **Vehicles.**

   This peril does not include loss to a fence, driveway or walk caused by a vehicle owned or operated by a resident of the "residence premises."

7. **Smoke,** meaning sudden and accidental damage from smoke.

   This peril does not include loss caused by smoke from agricultural smudging or industrial operations.

8. **Vandalism or malicious mischief.**

   This peril does not include loss to property on the "residence premises" if the dwelling has been vacant for more than 30 consecutive days immediately before the loss. A dwelling being constructed is not considered vacant.

9. **Theft,** including attempted theft and loss of property from a known place when it is likely that the property has been stolen.

   This peril does not include loss caused by theft:

   a. Committed by an "insured";

   b. In or to a dwelling under construction, or of materials and supplies for use in the construction until the dwelling is finished and occupied; or

   c. From that part of a "residence premises" rented by an "insured" to other than an "insured."

This peril does not include loss caused by theft that occurs off the "residence premises" of:

   a. Property while at any other residence owned by, rented to, or occupied by an "insured," except while an "insured" is temporarily living there. Property of a student who is an "insured" is covered while at a residence away from home if the student has been there at any time during the 45 days immediately before the loss;

   b. Watercraft, and their furnishings, equipment and outboard engines or motors; or

   c. Trailers and campers.

10. **Falling objects.**

    This peril does not include loss to the inside of a building or property contained in the building unless the roof or an outside wall of the building is first damaged by a falling object. Damage to the falling object itself is not included.

11. **Weight of ice, snow or sleet** which causes damage to a building or property contained in the building.

    This peril does not include loss to an awning, fence, patio, pavement, swimming pool, foundation, retaining wall, bulkhead, pier, wharf, or dock.

12. **Accidental discharge or overflow of water or steam** from within a plumbing, heating, air conditioning or automatic fire protective sprinkler system or from within a household appliance. We also pay for tearing out and replacing any part of the building on the "residence premises" necessary to repair the system or appliance from which the water or steam escaped.

    This peril does not include loss:

    a. On the "residence premises," if the dwelling has been vacant for more than 30 consecutive days immediately before the loss. A dwelling being constructed is not considered vacant.

    b. To the system or appliance from which the water or steam escaped;

    c. Caused by or resulting from freezing except as provided in the peril of freezing below; or

    d. On the "residence premises" caused by accidental discharge or overflow which occurs off the "residence premises."

    In this peril, a plumbing system does not include a sump, sump pump or related equipment.

HO 00 02 04 91

13. **Sudden and accidental tearing apart, cracking, burning or bulging** of a steam or hot water heating system, an air conditioning or automatic fire protective sprinkler system, or an appliance for heating water.

This peril does not include loss caused by or resulting from freezing except as provided in the peril of freezing below.

14. **Freezing** of a plumbing, heating, air conditioning or automatic fire protective sprinkler system or of a household appliance.

This peril does not include loss on the "residence premises" while the dwelling is vacant, unoccupied or being constructed, unless you have used reasonable care to:

a. Maintain heat in the building; or

b. Shut off the water supply and drain the system and appliances of water.

15. **Sudden and accidental damage from artificially generated electrical current.**

This peril does not include loss to a tube, transistor or similar electronic component.

16. **Volcanic eruption** other than loss caused by earthquake, land shock waves or tremors.

SECTION I—EXCLUSIONS

We do not insure for loss caused directly or indirectly by any of the following. Such loss is excluded regardless of any other cause or event contributing concurrently or in any sequence to the loss.

1. **Ordinance or Law,** meaning enforcement of any ordinance or law regulating the construction, repair, or demolition of a building or other structure, unless specifically provided under this policy.

2. **Earth Movement,** meaning earthquake including land shock waves or tremors before, during or after a volcanic eruption; landslide; mine subsidence; mudflow; earth sinking, rising or shifting unless direct loss by:

a. Fire;

b. Explosion; or

c. Breakage of glass or safety glazing material which is part of a building, storm door or storm window;

ensues and then we will pay only for the ensuing loss.

This exclusion does not apply to loss by theft.

3. **Water Damage,** meaning:

a. Flood, surface water, waves, tidal water, overflow of a body of water, or spray from any of these, whether or not driven by wind;

b. Water which backs up through sewers or drains or which overflows from a sump; or

c. Water below the surface of the ground, including water which exerts pressure on or seeps or leaks through a building, sidewalk, driveway, foundation, swimming pool or other structure.

Direct loss by fire, explosion or theft resulting from water damage is covered.

4. **Power Failure,** meaning the failure of power or other utility service if the failure takes place off the "residence premises." But, if a Peril Insured Against ensues on the "residence premises," we will pay only for that ensuing loss.

5. **Neglect,** meaning neglect of the "insured" to use all reasonable means to save and preserve property at and after the time of a loss.

6. **War,** including the following and any consequence of any of the following:

a. Undeclared war, civil war, insurrection, rebellion or revolution;

b. Warlike act by a military force or military personnel; or

c. Destruction, seizure or use for a military purpose.

Discharge of a nuclear weapon will be deemed a warlike act even if accidental.

7. **Nuclear Hazard,** to the extent set forth in the Nuclear Hazard Clause of SECTION I — CONDITIONS.

8. **Intentional Loss,** meaning any loss arising out of any act committed:

a. By or at the direction of an "insured"; and

b. With the intent to cause a loss.

SECTION I – CONDITIONS

1. Insurable Interest and Limit of Liability. Even if more than one person has an insurable interest in the property covered, we will not be liable in any one loss:

a. To the "insured" for more than the amount of the "insured's" interest at the time of loss; or

b. For more than the applicable limit of liability.

2. Your Duties After Loss. In case of a loss to covered property, you must see that the following are done:

a. Give prompt notice to us or our agent;

b. Notify the police in case of loss by theft;

c. Notify the credit card or fund transfer card company in case of loss under Credit Card or Fund Transfer Card coverage;

d. Protect the property from further damage. If repairs to the property are required, you must:

(1) Make reasonable and necessary repairs to protect the property; and

(2) Keep an accurate record of repair expenses;

e. Prepare an inventory of damaged personal property showing the quantity, description, actual cash value and amount of loss. Attach all bills, receipts and related documents that justify the figures in the inventory;

f. As often as we reasonably require:

(1) Show the damaged property;

(2) Provide us with records and documents we request and permit us to make copies; and

(3) Submit to examination under oath, while not in the presence of any other "insured," and sign the same;

g. Send to us, within 60 days after our request, your signed, sworn proof of loss which sets forth, to the best of your knowledge and belief:

(1) The time and cause of loss;

(2) The interest of the "insured" and all others in the property involved and all liens on the property;

(3) Other insurance which may cover the loss;

(4) Changes in title or occupancy of the property during the term of the policy;

(5) Specifications of damaged buildings and detailed repair estimates;

(6) The inventory of damaged personal property described in **2.e.** above;

(7) Receipts for additional living expenses incurred and records that support the fair rental value loss; and

(8) Evidence or affidavit that supports a claim under the Credit Card, Fund Transfer Card, Forgery and Counterfeit Money coverage, stating the amount and cause of loss.

3. Loss Settlement. Covered property losses are settled as follows:

a. Property of the following type:

(1) Personal property;

(2) Awnings, carpeting, household appliances, outdoor antennas and outdoor equipment, whether or not attached to buildings; and

(3) Structures that are not buildings;

at actual cash value at the time of loss but not more than the amount required to repair or replace.

b. Buildings under Coverage A or B at replacement cost without deduction for depreciation, subject to the following:

(1) If, at the time of loss, the amount of insurance in this policy on the damaged building is 80% or more of the full replacement cost of the building immediately before the loss, we will pay the cost to repair or replace, after application of deductible and without deduction for depreciation, but not more than the least of the following amounts:

(a) The limit of liability under this policy that applies to the building;

(b) The replacement cost of that part of the building damaged for like construction and use on the same premises; or

(c) The necessary amount actually spent to repair or replace the damaged building.

(2) If, at the time of loss, the amount of insurance in this policy on the damaged building is less than 80% of the full replacement cost of the building immediately before the loss, we will pay the greater of the following amounts, but not more than the limit of liability under this policy that applies to the building:

    (a) The actual cash value of that part of the building damaged; or

    (b) That proportion of the cost to repair or replace, after application of deductible and without deduction for depreciation, that part of the building damaged, which the total amount of insurance in this policy on the damaged building bears to 80% of the replacement cost of the building.

  (3) To determine the amount of insurance required to equal 80% of the full replacement cost of the building immediately before the loss, do not include the value of:

    (a) Excavations, foundations, piers or any supports which are below the undersurface of the lowest basement floor;

    (b) Those supports in **(a)** above which are below the surface of the ground inside the foundation walls, if there is no basement; and

    (c) Underground flues, pipes, wiring and drains.

  (4) We will pay no more than the actual cash value of the damage until actual repair or replacement is complete. Once actual repair or replacement is complete, we will settle the loss according to the provisions of **b.(1)** and **b.(2)** above.

    However, if the cost to repair or replace the damage is both:

    (a) Less than 5% of the amount of insurance in this policy on the building; and

    (b) Less than $2500;

    we will settle the loss according to the provisions of **b.(1)** and **b.(2)** above whether or not actual repair or replacement is complete.

  (5) You may disregard the replacement cost loss settlement provisions and make claim under this policy for loss or damage to buildings on an actual cash value basis. You may then make claim within 180 days after loss for any additional liability according to the provisions of this Condition 3. Loss Settlement.

4. Loss to a Pair or Set. In case of loss to a pair or set we may elect to:

  a. Repair or replace any part to restore the pair or set to its value before the loss; or

  b. Pay the difference between actual cash value of the property before and after the loss.

5. Glass Replacement. Loss for damage to glass caused by a Peril Insured Against will be settled on the basis of replacement with safety glazing materials when required by ordinance or law.

6. Appraisal. If you and we fail to agree on the amount of loss, either may demand an appraisal of the loss. In this event, each party will choose a competent appraiser within 20 days after receiving a written request from the other. The two appraisers will choose an umpire. If they cannot agree upon an umpire within 15 days, you or we may request that the choice be made by a judge of a court of record in the state where the "residence premises" is located. The appraisers will separately set the amount of loss. If the appraisers submit a written report of an agreement to us, the amount agreed upon will be the amount of loss. If they fail to agree, they will submit their differences to the umpire. A decision agreed to by any two will set the amount of loss.

Each party will:

  a. Pay its own appraiser; and

  b. Bear the other expenses of the appraisal and umpire equally.

7. Other Insurance. If a loss covered by this policy is also covered by other insurance, we will pay only the proportion of the loss that the limit of liability that applies under this policy bears to the total amount of insurance covering the loss.

8. Suit Against Us. No action can be brought unless the policy provisions have been complied with and the action is started within one year after the date of loss.

9. Our Option. If we give you written notice within 30 days after we receive your signed, sworn proof of loss, we may repair or replace any part of the damaged property with like property.

10. Loss Payment. We will adjust all losses with you. We will pay you unless some other person is named in the policy or is legally entitled to receive payment. Loss will be payable 60 days after we receive your proof of loss and:

  a. Reach an agreement with you;

  b. There is an entry of a final judgment; or

  c. There is a filing of an appraisal award with us.

11. Abandonment of Property. We need not accept any property abandoned by an "insured."

12. Mortgage Clause.

  The word "mortgagee" includes trustee.

If a mortgagee is named in this policy, any loss payable under Coverage A or B will be paid to the mortgagee and you, as interests appear. If more than one mortgagee is named, the order of payment will be the same as the order of precedence of the mortgages. If we deny your claim, that denial will not apply to a valid claim of the mortgagee, if the mortgagee:

a. Notifies us of any change in ownership, occupancy or substantial change in risk of which the mortgagee is aware;

b. Pays any premium due under this policy on demand if you have neglected to pay the premium; and

c. Submits a signed, sworn statement of loss within 60 days after receiving notice from us of your failure to do so. Policy conditions relating to Appraisal, Suit Against Us and Loss Payment apply to the mortgagee.

If we decide to cancel or not to renew this policy, the mortgagee will be notified at least 10 days before the date cancellation or nonrenewal takes effect.

If we pay the mortgagee for any loss and deny payment to you:

a. We are subrogated to all the rights of the mortgagee granted under the mortgage on the property; or

b. At our option, we may pay to the mortgagee the whole principal on the mortgage plus any accrued interest. In this event, we will receive a full assignment and transfer of the mortgage and all securities held as collateral to the mortgage debt.

Subrogation will not impair the right of the mortgagee to recover the full amount of the mortgagee's claim.

13. **No Benefit to Bailee.** We will not recognize any assignment or grant any coverage that benefits a person or organization holding, storing or moving property for a fee regardless of any other provision of this policy.

14. **Nuclear Hazard Clause.**

a. "Nuclear Hazard" means any nuclear reaction, radiation, or radioactive contamination, all whether controlled or uncontrolled or however caused, or any consequence of any of these.

b. Loss caused by the nuclear hazard will not be considered loss caused by fire, explosion, or smoke, whether these perils are specifically named in or otherwise included within the Perils Insured Against in Section I.

c. This policy does not apply under Section I to loss caused directly or indirectly by nuclear hazard, except that direct loss by fire resulting from the nuclear hazard is covered.

15. **Recovered Property.** If you or we recover any property for which we have made payment under this policy, you or we will notify the other of the recovery. At your option, the property will be returned to or retained by you or it will become our property. If the recovered property is returned to or retained by you, the loss payment will be adjusted based on the amount you received for the recovered property.

16. **Volcanic Eruption Period.** One or more volcanic eruptions that occur within a 72-hour period will be considered as one volcanic eruption.

SECTION II – LIABILITY COVERAGES

COVERAGE E – Personal Liability

If a claim is made or a suit is brought against an "insured" for damages because of "bodily injury" or "property damage" caused by an "occurrence" to which this coverage applies, we will:

1. Pay up to our limit of liability for the damages for which the "insured" is legally liable. Damages include prejudgment interest awarded against the "insured"; and

2. Provide a defense at our expense by counsel of our choice, even if the suit is groundless, false or fraudulent. We may investigate and settle any claim or suit that we decide is appropriate. Our duty to settle or defend ends when the amount we pay for damages resulting from the "occurrence" equals our limit of liability.

COVERAGE F – Medical Payments To Others

We will pay the necessary medical expenses that are incurred or medically ascertained within three years from the date of an accident causing "bodily injury." Medical expenses means reasonable charges for medical, surgical, x-ray, dental, ambulance, hospital, professional nursing, prosthetic devices and funeral services. This coverage does not apply to you or regular residents of your household except "residence employees." As to others, this coverage applies only:

1. To a person on the "insured location" with the permission of an "insured"; or

2. To a person off the "insured location," if the "bodily injury":

a. Arises out of a condition on the "insured location" or the ways immediately adjoining;

b. Is caused by the activities of an "insured";

c. Is caused by a "residence employee" in the course of the "residence employee's" employment by an "insured"; or

d. Is caused by an animal owned by or in the care of an "insured."

SECTION II – EXCLUSIONS

1. Coverage E – Personal Liability and **Coverage F – Medical Payments to Others** do not apply to "bodily injury" or "property damage":

a. Which is expected or intended by the "insured";

b. Arising out of or in connection with a "business" engaged in by an "insured." This exclusion applies but is not limited to an act or omission, regardless of its nature or circumstance, involving a service or duty rendered, promised, owed, or implied to be provided because of the nature of the "business";

c. Arising out of the rental or holding for rental of any part of any premises by an "insured." This exclusion does not apply to the rental or holding for rental of an "insured location":

  (1) On an occasional basis if used only as a residence;

  (2) In part for use only as a residence, unless a single family unit is intended for use by the occupying family to lodge more than two roomers or boarders; or

  (3) In part, as an office, school, studio or private garage;

d. Arising out of the rendering of or failure to render professional services;

e. Arising out of a premises:

  (1) Owned by an "insured";

  (2) Rented to an "insured"; or

  (3) Rented to others by an "insured";

  that is not an "insured location";

f. Arising out of:

  (1) The ownership, maintenance, use, loading or unloading of motor vehicles or all other motorized land conveyances, including trailers, owned or operated by or rented or loaned to an "insured";

  (2) The entrustment by an "insured" of a motor vehicle or any other motorized land conveyance to any person; or

  (3) Vicarious liability, whether or not statutorily imposed, for the actions of a child or minor using a conveyance excluded in paragraph **(1)** or **(2)** above.

This exclusion does not apply to:

(1) A trailer not towed by or carried on a motorized land conveyance;

(2) A motorized land conveyance designed for recreational use off public roads, not subject to motor vehicle registration and:

  (a) Not owned by an "insured"; or

  (b) Owned by an "insured" and on an "insured location";

(3) A motorized golf cart when used to play golf on a golf course;

(4) A vehicle or conveyance not subject to motor vehicle registration which is:

  (a) Used to service an "insured's" residence;

  (b) Designed for assisting the handicapped; or

  (c) In dead storage on an "insured location";

g. Arising out of:

  (1) The ownership, maintenance, use, loading or unloading of an excluded watercraft described below;

  (2) The entrustment by an "insured" of an excluded watercraft described below to any person; or

  (3) Vicarious liability, whether or not statutorily imposed, for the actions of a child or minor using an excluded watercraft described below.

Excluded watercraft are those that are principally designed to be propelled by engine power or electric motor, or are sailing vessels, whether owned by or rented to an "insured." This exclusion does not apply to watercraft:

(1) That are not sailing vessels and are powered by:

  (a) Inboard or inboard-outdrive engine or motor power of 50 horsepower or less not owned by an "insured";

  (b) Inboard or inboard-outdrive engine or motor power of more than 50 horsepower not owned by or rented to an "insured";

(c) One or more outboard engines or motors with 25 total horsepower or less;

(d) One or more outboard engines or motors with more than 25 total horsepower if the outboard engine or motor is not owned by an "insured";

(e) Outboard engines or motors of more than 25 total horsepower owned by an "insured" if:

(i) You acquire them prior to the policy period; and

(a) You declare them at policy inception; or

(b) Your intention to insure is reported to us in writing within 45 days after you acquire the outboard engines or motors.

(ii) You acquire them during the policy period.

This coverage applies for the policy period.

(2) That are sailing vessels, with or without auxiliary power:

(a) Less than 26 feet in overall length;

(b) 26 feet or more in overall length, not owned by or rented to an "insured."

(3) That are stored;

h. Arising out of:

(1) The ownership, maintenance, use, loading or unloading of an aircraft;

(2) The entrustment by an "insured" of an aircraft to any person; or

(3) Vicarious liability, whether or not statutorily imposed, for the actions of a child or minor using an aircraft.

An aircraft means any contrivance used or designed for flight, except model or hobby aircraft not used or designed to carry people or cargo;

i. Caused directly or indirectly by war, including the following and any consequence of any of the following:

(1) Undeclared war, civil war, insurrection, rebellion or revolution;

(2) Warlike act by a military force or military personnel; or

(3) Destruction, seizure or use for a military purpose.

Discharge of a nuclear weapon will be deemed a warlike act even if accidental;

j. Which arises out of the transmission of a communicable disease by an "insured";

k. Arising out of sexual molestation, corporal punishment or physical or mental abuse; or

l. Arising out of the use, sale, manufacture, delivery, transfer or possession by any person of a Controlled Substance(s) as defined by the Federal Food and Drug Law at 21 U.S.C.A. Sections 811 and 812. Controlled Substances include but are not limited to cocaine, LSD, marijuana and all narcotic drugs. However, this exclusion does not apply to the legitimate use of prescription drugs by a person following the orders of a licensed physician.

Exclusions **e.**, **f.**, **g.**, and **h.** do not apply to "bodily injury" to a "residence employee" arising out of and in the course of the "residence employee's" employment by an "insured."

2. **Coverage E – Personal Liability**, does not apply to:

a. Liability:

(1) For any loss assessment charged against you as a member of an association, corporation or community of property owners;

(2) Under any contract or agreement. However, this exclusion does not apply to written contracts:

(a) That directly relate to the ownership, maintenance or use of an "insured location"; or

(b) Where the liability of others is assumed by the "insured" prior to an "occurrence";

unless excluded in (1) above or elsewhere in this policy;

b. "Property damage" to property owned by the "insured";

c. "Property damage" to property rented to, occupied or used by or in the care of the "insured." This exclusion does not apply to "property damage" caused by fire, smoke or explosion;

d. "Bodily injury" to any person eligible to receive any benefits:

(1) Voluntarily provided; or

(2) Required to be provided;

by the "insured" under any:

(1) Workers' compensation law;

(2) Non-occupational disability law; or

(3) Occupational disease law;

e. "Bodily injury" or "property damage" for which an "insured" under this policy:

 HO 00 02 04 91

(1) Is also an insured under a nuclear energy liability policy; or

(2) Would be an insured under that policy but for the exhaustion of its limit of liability.

A nuclear energy liability policy is one issued by:

(1) American Nuclear Insurers;

(2) Mutual Atomic Energy Liability Underwriters;

(3) Nuclear Insurance Association of Canada;

or any of their successors; or

f. "Bodily injury" to you or an "insured" within the meaning of part **a.** or **b.** of "insured" as defined.

3. Coverage F – Medical Payments to Others, does not apply to "bodily injury":

a. To a "residence employee" if the "bodily injury":

(1) Occurs off the "insured location"; and

(2) Does not arise out of or in the course of the "residence employee's" employment by an "insured";

b. To any person eligible to receive benefits:

(1) Voluntarily provided; or

(2) Required to be provided;

under any:

(1) Workers' compensation law;

(2) Non-occupational disability law; or

(3) Occupational disease law;

c. From any:

(1) Nuclear reaction;

(2) Nuclear radiation; or

(3) Radioactive contamination;

all whether controlled or uncontrolled or however caused; or

(4) Any consequence of any of these; or

d. To any person, other than a "residence employee" of an "insured," regularly residing on any part of the "insured location."

SECTION II – ADDITIONAL COVERAGES

We cover the following in addition to the limits of liability:

1. Claim Expenses. We pay:

a. Expenses we incur and costs taxed against an "insured" in any suit we defend;

b. Premiums on bonds required in a suit we defend, but not for bond amounts more than the limit of liability for Coverage E. We need not apply for or furnish any bond;

c. Reasonable expenses incurred by an "insured" at our request, including actual loss of earnings (but not loss of other income) up to $50 per day, for assisting us in the investigation or defense of a claim or suit; and

d. Interest on the entire judgment which accrues after entry of the judgment and before we pay or tender, or deposit in court that part of the judgment which does not exceed the limit of liability that applies.

2. First Aid Expenses. We will pay expenses for first aid to others incurred by an "insured" for "bodily injury" covered under this policy. We will not pay for first aid to you or any other "insured."

3. Damage to Property of Others. We will pay, at replacement cost, up to $500 per "occurrence" for "property damage" to property of others caused by an "insured."

We will not pay for "property damage":

a. To the extent of any amount recoverable under Section I of this policy;

b. Caused intentionally by an "insured" who is 13 years of age or older;

c. To property owned by an "insured";

d. To property owned by or rented to a tenant of an "insured" or a resident in your household; or

e. Arising out of:

(1) A "business" engaged in by an "insured";

(2) Any act or omission in connection with a premises owned, rented or controlled by an "insured," other than the "insured location"; or

(3) The ownership, maintenance, or use of aircraft, watercraft or motor vehicles or all other motorized land conveyances.

This exclusion does not apply to a motorized land conveyance designed for recreational use off public roads, not subject to motor vehicle registration and not owned by an "insured."

4. Loss Assessment. We will pay up to $1000 for your share of loss assessment charged during the policy period against you by a corporation or association of property owners, when the assessment is made as a result of:

a. "Bodily injury" or "property damage" not excluded under Section II of this policy; or

b. Liability for an act of a director, officer or trustee in the capacity as a director, officer or trustee, provided:

(1) The director, officer or trustee is elected by the members of a corporation or association of property owners; and

(2) The director, officer or trustee serves without deriving any income from the exercise of duties which are solely on behalf of a corporation or association of property owners.

This coverage applies only to loss assessments charged against you as owner or tenant of the "residence premises."

We do not cover loss assessments charged against you or a corporation or association of property owners by any governmental body.

Regardless of the number of assessments, the limit of $1000 is the most we will pay for loss arising out of:

a. One accident, including continuous or repeated exposure to substantially the same general harmful condition; or

b. A covered act of a director, officer or trustee. An act involving more than one director, officer or trustee is considered to be a single act.

The following do not apply to this coverage:

1. Section II – Coverage E – Personal Liability Exclusion 2.a.(1);

2. Condition 1. Policy Period, under SECTIONS I AND II CONDITIONS.

SECTION II – CONDITIONS

1. Limit of Liability. Our total liability under Coverage E for all damages resulting from any one "occurrence" will not be more than the limit of liability for Coverage E as shown in the Declarations. This limit is the same regardless of the number of "insureds," claims made or persons injured. All "bodily injury" and "property damage" resulting from any one accident or from continuous or repeated exposure to substantially the same general harmful conditions shall be considered to be the result of one "occurrence."

Our total liability under Coverage F for all medical expense payable for "bodily injury" to one person as the result of one accident will not be more than the limit of liability for Coverage F as shown in the Declarations.

2. Severability of Insurance. This insurance applies separately to each "insured." This condition will not increase our limit of liability for any one "occurrence."

3. Duties After Loss. In case of an accident or "occurrence," the "insured" will perform the following duties that apply. You will help us by seeing that these duties are performed:

a. Give written notice to us or our agent as soon as is practical, which sets forth:

(1) The identity of the policy and "insured";

(2) Reasonably available information on the time, place and circumstances of the accident or "occurrence"; and

(3) Names and addresses of any claimants and witnesses;

b. Promptly forward to us every notice, demand, summons or other process relating to the accident or "occurrence";

c. At our request, help us:

(1) To make settlement;

(2) To enforce any right of contribution or indemnity against any person or organization who may be liable to an "insured";

(3) With the conduct of suits and attend hearings and trials; and

(4) To secure and give evidence and obtain the attendance of witnesses;

d. Under the coverage – Damage to Property of Others – submit to us within 60 days after the loss, a sworn statement of loss and show the damaged property, if in the "insured's" control;

e. The "insured" will not, except at the "insured's" own cost, voluntarily make payment, assume obligation or incur expense other than for first aid to others at the time of the "bodily injury."

4. Duties of an Injured Person – Coverage F – Medical Payments to Others.

The injured person or someone acting for the injured person will:

   a. Give us written proof of claim, under oath if required, as soon as is practical; and

   b. Authorize us to obtain copies of medical reports and records.

The injured person will submit to a physical exam by a doctor of our choice when and as often as we reasonably require.

5. **Payment of Claim – Coverage F – Medical Payments to Others.** Payment under this coverage is not an admission of liability by an "insured" or us.

6. **Suit Against Us.** No action can be brought against us unless there has been compliance with the policy provisions.

No one will have the right to join us as a party to any action against an "insured." Also, no action with respect to Coverage E can be brought against us until the obligation of the "insured" has been determined by final judgment or agreement signed by us.

7. **Bankruptcy of an Insured.** Bankruptcy or insolvency of an "insured" will not relieve us of our obligations under this policy.

8. **Other Insurance – Coverage E – Personal Liability.** This insurance is excess over other valid and collectible insurance except insurance written specifically to cover as excess over the limits of liability that apply in this policy.

SECTIONS I AND II – CONDITIONS

1. **Policy Period.** This policy applies only to loss in Section I or "bodily injury" or "property damage" in Section II, which occurs during the policy period.

2. **Concealment or Fraud.** The entire policy will be void if, whether before or after a loss, an "insured" has:

   a. Intentionally concealed or misrepresented any material fact or circumstance;

   b. Engaged in fraudulent conduct; or

   c. Made false statements;

relating to this insurance.

3. **Liberalization Clause.** If we make a change which broadens coverage under this edition of our policy without additional premium charge, that change will automatically apply to your insurance as of the date we implement the change in your state, provided that this implementation date falls within 60 days prior to or during the policy period stated in the Declarations.

This Liberalization Clause does not apply to changes implemented through introduction of a subsequent edition of our policy.

4. **Waiver or Change of Policy Provisions.**

A waiver or change of a provision of this policy must be in writing by us to be valid. Our request for an appraisal or examination will not waive any of our rights.

5. **Cancellation.**

   a. You may cancel this policy at any time by returning it to us or by letting us know in writing of the date cancellation is to take effect.

   b. We may cancel this policy only for the reasons stated below by letting you know in writing of the date cancellation takes effect. This cancellation notice may be delivered to you, or mailed to you at your mailing address shown in the Declarations.

   Proof of mailing will be sufficient proof of notice.

   (1) When you have not paid the premium, we may cancel at any time by letting you know at least 10 days before the date cancellation takes effect.

   (2) When this policy has been in effect for less than 60 days and is not a renewal with us, we may cancel for any reason by letting you know at least 10 days before the date cancellation takes effect.

   (3) When this policy has been in effect for 60 days or more, or at any time if it is a renewal with us, we may cancel:

     (a) If there has been a material misrepresentation of fact which if known to us would have caused us not to issue the policy; or

     (b) If the risk has changed substantially since the policy was issued.

     This can be done by letting you know at least 30 days before the date cancellation takes effect.

   (4) When this policy is written for a period of more than one year, we may cancel for any reason at anniversary by letting you know at least 30 days before the date cancellation takes effect.

c. When this policy is cancelled, the premium for the period from the date of cancellation to the expiration date will be refunded pro rata.

d. If the return premium is not refunded with the notice of cancellation or when this policy is returned to us, we will refund it within a reasonable time after the date cancellation takes effect.

6. **Nonrenewal.** We may elect not to renew this policy. We may do so by delivering to you, or mailing to you at your mailing address shown in the Declarations, written notice at least 30 days before the expiration date of this policy. Proof of mailing will be sufficient proof of notice.

7. **Assignment.** Assignment of this policy will not be valid unless we give our written consent.

8. **Subrogation.** An "insured" may waive in writing before a loss all rights of recovery against any person. If not waived, we may require an assignment of rights of recovery for a loss to the extent that payment is made by us.

If an assignment is sought, an "insured" must sign and deliver all related papers and cooperate with us.

Subrogation does not apply under Section II to Medical Payments to Others or Damage to Property of Others.

9. **Death.** If any person named in the Declarations or the spouse, if a resident of the same household, dies:

a. We insure the legal representative of the deceased but only with respect to the premises and property of the deceased covered under the policy at the time of death;

b. "Insured" includes:

(1) Any member of your household who is an "insured" at the time of your death, but only while a resident of the "residence premises"; and

(2) With respect to your property, the person having proper temporary custody of the property until appointment and qualification of a legal representative.

APPENDIX D

PORTIONS OMITTED

SECTION I – PERILS INSURED AGAINST

COVERAGE A – DWELLING and COVERAGE B – OTHER STRUCTURES

We insure against risk of direct loss to property described in Coverages A and B only if that loss is a physical loss to property. We do not insure, however, for loss:

1. Involving collapse, other than as provided in Additional Coverage **8.**;

2. Caused by:

     HO 00 03 04 91

a. Freezing of a plumbing, heating, air conditioning or automatic fire protective sprinkler system or of a household appliance, or by discharge, leakage or overflow from within the system or appliance caused by freezing. This exclusion applies only while the dwelling is vacant, unoccupied or being constructed, unless you have used reasonable care to:

(1) Maintain heat in the building; or

(2) Shut off the water supply and drain the system and appliances of water;

b. Freezing, thawing, pressure or weight of water or ice, whether driven by wind or not, to a:

(1) Fence, pavement, patio or swimming pool;

(2) Foundation, retaining wall, or bulkhead; or

(3) Pier, wharf or dock;

c. Theft in or to a dwelling under construction, or of materials and supplies for use in the construction until the dwelling is finished and occupied;

d. Vandalism and malicious mischief if the dwelling has been vacant for more than 30 consecutive days immediately before the loss. A dwelling being constructed is not considered vacant;

e. Any of the following:

(1) Wear and tear, marring, deterioration;

(2) Inherent vice, latent defect, mechanical breakdown;

(3) Smog, rust or other corrosion, mold, wet or dry rot;

(4) Smoke from agricultural smudging or industrial operations;

(5) Discharge, dispersal, seepage, migration, release or escape of pollutants unless the discharge, dispersal, seepage, migration, release or escape is itself caused by a Peril Insured Against under Coverage C of this policy.

Pollutants means any solid, liquid, gaseous or thermal irritant or contaminant, including smoke, vapor, soot, fumes, acids, alkalis, chemicals and waste. Waste includes materials to be recycled, reconditioned or reclaimed;

(6) Settling, shrinking, bulging or expansion, including resultant cracking, of pavements, patios, foundations, walls, floors, roofs or ceilings;

(7) Birds, vermin, rodents, or insects; or

(8) Animals owned or kept by an "insured."

If any of these cause water damage not otherwise excluded, from a plumbing, heating, air conditioning or automatic fire protective sprinkler system or household appliance, we cover loss caused by the water including the cost of tearing out and replacing any part of a building necessary to repair the system or appliance. We do not cover loss to the system or appliance from which this water escaped.

3. Excluded under Section I – Exclusions.

Under items 1. and 2., any ensuing loss to property described in Coverages A and B not excluded or excepted in this policy is covered.

COVERAGE C – PERSONAL PROPERTY

We insure for direct physical loss to the property described in Coverage C caused by a peril listed below unless the loss is excluded in SECTION I – EXCLUSIONS.

1. **Fire or lightning.**

2. **Windstorm or hail.**

This peril does not include loss to the property contained in a building caused by rain, snow, sleet, sand or dust unless the direct force of wind or hail damages the building causing an opening in a roof or wall and the rain, snow, sleet, sand or dust enters through this opening.

This peril includes loss to watercraft and their trailers, furnishings, equipment, and outboard engines or motors, only while inside a fully enclosed building.

3. **Explosion.**

4. **Riot or civil commotion.**

5. **Aircraft,** including self-propelled missiles and spacecraft.

6. **Vehicles.**

7. **Smoke,** meaning sudden and accidental damage from smoke.

This peril does not include loss caused by smoke from agricultural smudging or industrial operations.

8. **Vandalism or malicious mischief.**

9. **Theft,** including attempted theft and loss of property from a known place when it is likely that the property has been stolen.

This peril does not include loss caused by theft:

a. Committed by an "insured";

b. In or to a dwelling under construction, or of materials and supplies for use in the construction until the dwelling is finished and occupied; or

c. From that part of a "residence premises" rented by an "insured" to other than an "insured."

This peril does not include loss caused by theft that occurs off the "residence premises" of:

a. Property while at any other residence owned by, rented to, or occupied by an "insured," except while an "insured" is temporarily living there. Property of a student who is an "insured" is covered while at a residence away from home if the student has been there at any time during the 45 days immediately before the loss;

b. Watercraft, and their furnishings, equipment and outboard engines or motors; or

c. Trailers and campers.

10. **Falling objects.**

This peril does not include loss to property contained in a building unless the roof or an outside wall of the building is first damaged by a falling object. Damage to the falling object itself is not included.

11. **Weight of ice, snow or sleet** which causes damage to property contained in a building.

12. **Accidental discharge or overflow of water or steam** from within a plumbing, heating, air conditioning or automatic fire protective sprinkler system or from within a household appliance.

This peril does not include loss:

a. To the system or appliance from which the water or steam escaped;

b. Caused by or resulting from freezing except as provided in the peril of freezing below; or

c. On the "residence premises" caused by accidental discharge or overflow which occurs off the "residence premises."

In this peril, a plumbing system does not include a sump, sump pump or related equipment.

13. **Sudden and accidental tearing apart, cracking, burning or bulging** of a steam or hot water heating system, an air conditioning or automatic fire protective sprinkler system, or an appliance for heating water.

We do not cover loss caused by or resulting from freezing under this peril.

14. **Freezing** of a plumbing, heating, air conditioning or automatic fire protective sprinkler system or of a household appliance.

This peril does not include loss on the "residence premises" while the dwelling is unoccupied, unless you have used reasonable care to:

a. Maintain heat in the building; or

b. Shut off the water supply and drain the system and appliances of water.

15. **Sudden and accidental damage from artificially generated electrical current.**

This peril does not include loss to a tube, transistor or similar electronic component.

16. **Volcanic eruption** other than loss caused by earthquake, land shock waves or tremors.

SECTION I – EXCLUSIONS

1. We do not insure for loss caused directly or indirectly by any of the following. Such loss is excluded regardless of any other cause or event contributing concurrently or in any sequence to the loss.

   a. **Ordinance or Law,** meaning enforcement of any ordinance or law regulating the construction, repair, or demolition of a building or other structure, unless specifically provided under this policy.

   b. **Earth Movement,** meaning earthquake including land shock waves or tremors before, during or after a volcanic eruption; landslide; mine subsidence; mudflow; earth sinking, rising or shifting; unless direct loss by:

      (1) Fire;

      (2) Explosion; or

   (3) Breakage of glass or safety glazing material which is part of a building, storm door or storm window;

   ensues and then we will pay only for the ensuing loss.

   This exclusion does not apply to loss by theft.

   c. **Water Damage,** meaning:

      (1) Flood, surface water, waves, tidal water, overflow of a body of water, or spray from any of these, whether or not driven by wind;

      (2) Water which backs up through sewers or drains or which overflows from a sump; or

Copyright, Insurance Services Office, Inc., 1990   HO 00 03 04 91

(3) Water below the surface of the ground, including water which exerts pressure on or seeps or leaks through a building, sidewalk, driveway, foundation, swimming pool or other structure.

Direct loss by fire, explosion or theft resulting from water damage is covered.

d. Power Failure, meaning the failure of power or other utility service if the failure takes place off the "residence premises." But, if a Peril Insured Against ensues on the "residence premises," we will pay only for that ensuing loss.

e. Neglect, meaning neglect of the "insured" to use all reasonable means to save and preserve property at and after the time of a loss.

f. War, including the following and any consequence of any of the following:

(1) Undeclared war, civil war, insurrection, rebellion or revolution;

(2) Warlike act by a military force or military personnel; or

(3) Destruction, seizure or use for a military purpose.

Discharge of a nuclear weapon will be deemed a warlike act even if accidental.

g. Nuclear Hazard, to the extent set forth in the Nuclear Hazard Clause of SECTION I – CONDITIONS.

h. Intentional Loss, meaning any loss arising out of any act committed:

(1) By or at the direction of an "insured"; and

(2) With the intent to cause a loss.

2. We do not insure for loss to property described in Coverages A and B caused by any of the following. However, any ensuing loss to property described in Coverages A and B not excluded or excepted in this policy is covered.

a. Weather conditions. However, this exclusion only applies if weather conditions contribute in any way with a cause or event excluded in paragraph **1.** above to produce the loss;

b. Acts or decisions, including the failure to act or decide, of any person, group, organization or governmental body;

c. Faulty, inadequate or defective:

(1) Planning, zoning, development, surveying, siting;

(2) Design, specifications, workmanship, repair, construction, renovation, remodeling, grading, compaction;

(3) Materials used in repair, construction, renovation or remodeling; or

(4) Maintenance;

of part or all of any property whether on or off the "residence premises."

APPENDIX E

PERSONAL AUTO
PP 00 01 06 98

PERSONAL AUTO POLICY

AGREEMENT

In return for payment of the premium and subject to all the terms of this policy, we agree with you as follows:

DEFINITIONS

A. Throughout this policy, "you" and "your" refer to:

1. The "named insured" shown in the Declarations; and

2. The spouse if a resident of the same household.

If the spouse ceases to be a resident of the same household during the policy period or prior to the inception of this policy, the spouse will be considered "you" and "your" under this policy but only until the earlier of:

1. The end of 90 days following the spouse's change of residency;

2. The effective date of another policy listing the spouse as a named insured; or

3. The end of the policy period.

B. "We", "us" and "our" refer to the Company providing this insurance.

C. For purposes of this policy, a private passenger type auto, pickup or van shall be deemed to be owned by a person if leased:

1. Under a written agreement to that person; and

2. For a continuous period of at least 6 months.

Other words and phrases are defined. They are in quotation marks when used.

D. "Bodily injury" means bodily harm, sickness or disease, including death that results.

E. "Business" includes trade, profession or occupation

F. "Family member" means a person related to you by blood, marriage or adoption who is a resident of your household. This includes a ward or foster child.

G. "Occupying" means in, upon, getting in, on, out or off.

H. "Property damage" means physical injury to, destruction of or loss of use of tangible property.

I. "Trailer" means a vehicle designed to be pulled by a:

1. Private passenger auto; or

2. Pickup or van.

It also means a farm wagon or farm implement while towed by a vehicle listed in **1.** or **2.** above.

J. "Your covered auto" means:

1. Any vehicle shown in the Declarations.

2. A "newly acquired auto".

3. Any "trailer" you own.

4. Any auto or "trailer" you do not own while used as a temporary substitute for any other vehicle described in this definition which is out of normal use because of its:

   a. Breakdown;

   b. Repair;

   c. Servicing;

   d. Loss; or

   e. Destruction.

   This Provision (**J.4.**) does not apply to Coverage For Damage To Your Auto.

K. "Newly acquired auto":

1. "Newly acquired auto" means any of the following types of vehicles you become the owner of during the policy period:

   a. A private passenger auto; or

   b. A pickup or van, for which no other insurance policy provides coverage, that:

      (1) Has a Gross Vehicle Weight of less than 10,000 lbs.; and

      (2) Is not used for the delivery or transportation of goods and materials unless such use is:

         (a) Incidental to your "business" of installing, maintaining or repairing furnishings or equipment; or

         (b) For farming or ranching.

2. Coverage for a "newly acquired auto" is provided as described below. If you ask us to insure a "newly acquired auto" after a specified time period described below has elapsed, any coverage we provide for a "newly acquired auto" will begin at the time you request the coverage.

   a. For any coverage provided in this policy except Coverage For Damage To Your Auto, a "newly acquired auto" will have the broadest coverage we now provide for any vehicle shown in the Declarations. Coverage begins on the date you become the owner. However, for this coverage to apply to a "newly acquired auto" which is in addition to any vehicle shown in the Declarations, you must ask us to insure it within 14 days after you become the owner.

If a "newly acquired auto" replaces a vehicle shown in the Declarations, coverage is provided for this vehicle without your having to ask us to insure it.

b. Collision Coverage for a "newly acquired auto" begins on the date you become the owner. However, for this coverage to apply, you must ask us to insure it within:

(1) 14 days after you become the owner if the Declarations indicate that Collision Coverage applies to at least one auto. In this case, the "newly acquired auto" will have the broadest coverage we now provide for any auto shown in the Declarations.

(2) Four days after you become the owner if the Declarations do not indicate that Collision Coverage applies to at least one auto. If you comply with the 4 day requirement and a loss occurred before you asked us to insure the "newly acquired auto", a Collision deductible of $500 will apply.

c. Other Than Collision Coverage for a "newly acquired auto" begins on the date you become the owner. However, for this coverage to apply, you must ask us to insure it within:

(1) 14 days after you become the owner if the Declarations indicate that Other Than Collision Coverage applies to at least one auto. In this case, the "newly acquired auto" will have the broadest coverage we now provide for any auto shown in the Declarations.

(2) Four days after you become the owner if the Declarations do not indicate that Other Than Collision Coverage applies to at least one auto. If you comply with the 4 day requirement and a loss occurred before you asked us to insure the "newly acquired auto", an Other Than Collision deductible of $500 will apply.

PART A – LIABILITY COVERAGE

INSURING AGREEMENT

A. We will pay damages for "bodily injury" or "property damage" for which any "insured" becomes legally responsible because of an auto accident. Damages include prejudgment interest awarded against the "insured". We will settle or defend, as we consider appropriate, any claim or suit asking for these damages. In addition to our limit of liability, we will pay all defense costs we incur. Our duty to settle or defend ends when our limit of liability for this coverage has been exhausted by payment of judgments or settlements. We have no duty to defend any suit or settle any claim for "bodily injury" or "property damage" not covered under this policy.

B. "Insured" as used in this Part means:

1. You or any "family member" for the ownership, maintenance or use of any auto or "trailer".

2. Any person using "your covered auto".

3. For "your covered auto", any person or organization but only with respect to legal responsibility for acts or omissions of a person for whom coverage is afforded under this Part.

4. For any auto or "trailer", other than "your covered auto", any other person or organization but only with respect to legal responsibility for acts or omissions of you or any "family member" for whom coverage is afforded under this Part. This Provision (B.4.) applies only if the person or organization does not own or hire the auto or "trailer".

SUPPLEMENTARY PAYMENTS

In addition to our limit of liability, we will pay on behalf of an "insured":

1. Up to $250 for the cost of bail bonds required because of an accident, including related traffic law violations. The accident must result in "bodily injury" or "property damage" covered under this policy.

2. Premiums on appeal bonds and bonds to release attachments in any suit we defend.

3. Interest accruing after a judgment is entered in any suit we defend. Our duty to pay interest ends when we offer to pay that part of the judgment which does not exceed our limit of liability for this coverage.

4. Up to $200 a day for loss of earnings, but not other income, because of attendance at hearings or trials at our request.

5. Other reasonable expenses incurred at our request.

EXCLUSIONS

A. We do not provide Liability Coverage for any "insured":

1. Who intentionally causes "bodily injury" or "property damage".

2. For "property damage" to property owned or being transported by that "insured".

 PP 00 01 06 98

3. For "property damage" to property:

   a. Rented to;

   b. Used by; or

   c. In the care of;

that "insured".

This Exclusion **(A.3.)** does not apply to "property damage" to a residence or private garage.

4. For "bodily injury" to an employee of that "insured" during the course of employment. This Exclusion **(A.4.)** does not apply to "bodily injury" to a domestic employee unless workers' compensation benefits are required or available for that domestic employee.

5. For that "insured's" liability arising out of the ownership or operation of a vehicle while it is being used as a public or livery conveyance. This Exclusion **(A.5.)** does not apply to a share-the-expense car pool.

6. While employed or otherwise engaged in the "business" of:

   a. Selling;

   b. Repairing;

   c. Servicing;

   d. Storing; or

   e. Parking;

vehicles designed for use mainly on public highways. This includes road testing and delivery. This Exclusion **(A.6.)** does not apply to the ownership, maintenance or use of "your covered auto" by:

   a. You;

   b. Any "family member"; or

   c. Any partner, agent or employee of you or any "family member".

7. Maintaining or using any vehicle while that "insured" is employed or otherwise engaged in any "business" (other than farming or ranching) not described in Exclusion A.6.

This Exclusion **(A.7.)** does not apply to the maintenance or use of a:

   a. Private passenger auto;

   b. Pickup or van; or

   c. "Trailer" used with a vehicle described in **a.** or **b.** above.

8. Using a vehicle without a reasonable belief that that "insured" is entitled to do so. This Exclusion **(A.8.)** does not apply to a "family member" using "your covered auto" which is owned by you.

9. For "bodily injury" or "property damage" for which that "insured":

   a. Is an insured under a nuclear energy liability policy; or

   b. Would be an insured under a nuclear energy liability policy but for its termination upon exhaustion of its limit of liability.

A nuclear energy liability policy is a policy issued by any of the following or their successors:

   a. Nuclear Energy Liability Insurance Association;

   b. Mutual Atomic Energy Liability Underwriters; or

   c. Nuclear Insurance Association of Canada.

B. We do not provide Liability Coverage for the ownership, maintenance or use of:

1. Any vehicle which:

   a. Has fewer than four wheels; or

   b. Is designed mainly for use off public roads.

This Exclusion **(B.1.)** does not apply:

   a. While such vehicle is being used by an "insured" in a medical emergency;

   b. To any "trailer"; or

   c. To any non-owned golf cart.

2. Any vehicle, other than "your covered auto", which is:

   a. Owned by you; or

   b. Furnished or available for your regular use.

3. Any vehicle, other than "your covered auto", which is:

   a. Owned by any "family member"; or

   b. Furnished or available for the regular use of any "family member".

However, this Exclusion **(B.3.)** does not apply to you while you are maintaining or "occupying" any vehicle which is:

   a. Owned by a "family member"; or

   b. Furnished or available for the regular use of a "family member".

4. Any vehicle, located inside a facility designed for racing, for the purpose of:

   a. Competing in; or

   b. Practicing or preparing for;

any prearranged or organized racing or speed contest.

LIMIT OF LIABILITY

A. The limit of liability shown in the Declarations for each person for Bodily Injury Liability is our maximum limit of liability for all damages, including damages for care, loss of services or death, arising out of "bodily injury" sustained by any one person in any one auto accident. Subject to this limit for each person, the limit of liability shown in the Declarations for each accident for Bodily Injury Liability is our maximum limit of liability for all damages for "bodily injury" resulting from any one auto accident.

The limit of liability shown in the Declarations for each accident for Property Damage Liability is our maximum limit of liability for all "property damage" resulting from any one auto accident.

This is the most we will pay regardless of the number of:

1. "Insureds";

2. Claims made;

3. Vehicles or premiums shown in the Declarations; or

4. Vehicles involved in the auto accident.

B. No one will be entitled to receive duplicate payments for the same elements of loss under this coverage and:

1. Part B or Part C of this policy; or

2. Any Underinsured Motorists Coverage provided by this policy.

OUT OF STATE COVERAGE

If an auto accident to which this policy applies occurs in any state or province other than the one in which "your covered auto" is principally garaged, we will interpret your policy for that accident as follows:

A. If the state or province has:

1. A financial responsibility or similar law specifying limits of liability for "bodily injury" or "property damage" higher than the limit shown in the Declarations, your policy will provide the higher specified limit.

2. A compulsory insurance or similar law requiring a nonresident to maintain insurance whenever the nonresident uses a vehicle in that state or province, your policy will provide at least the required minimum amounts and types of coverage.

B. No one will be entitled to duplicate payments for the same elements of loss.

FINANCIAL RESPONSIBILITY

When this policy is certified as future proof of financial responsibility, this policy shall comply with the law to the extent required.

OTHER INSURANCE

If there is other applicable liability insurance we will pay only our share of the loss. Our share is the proportion that our limit of liability bears to the total of all applicable limits. However, any insurance we provide for a vehicle you do not own shall be excess over any other collectible insurance.

PART B – MEDICAL PAYMENTS COVERAGE

INSURING AGREEMENT

A. We will pay reasonable expenses incurred for necessary medical and funeral services because of "bodily injury":

1. Caused by accident; and

2. Sustained by an "insured".

We will pay only those expenses incurred for services rendered within 3 years from the date of the accident.

B. "Insured" as used in this Part means:

1. You or any "family member":

   a. While "occupying"; or

   b. As a pedestrian when struck by;

   a motor vehicle designed for use mainly on public roads or a trailer of any type.

2. Any other person while "occupying" "your covered auto".

EXCLUSIONS

We do not provide Medical Payments Coverage for any "insured" for "bodily injury":

1. Sustained while "occupying" any motorized vehicle having fewer than four wheels.

2. Sustained while "occupying" "your covered auto" when it is being used as a public or livery conveyance. This Exclusion (2.) does not apply to a share-the-expense car pool.

3. Sustained while "occupying" any vehicle located for use as a residence or premises.

4. Occurring during the course of employment if workers' compensation benefits are required or available for the "bodily injury".

5. Sustained while "occupying", or when struck by, any vehicle (other than "your covered auto") which is:

   a. Owned by you; or

   b. Furnished or available for your regular use.

6. Sustained while "occupying", or when struck by, any vehicle (other than "your covered auto") which is:

   a. Owned by any "family member"; or

   b. Furnished or available for the regular use of any "family member".

   However, this Exclusion (6.) does not apply to you.

Copyright, Insurance Services Office, Inc., 1997   **PP 00 01 06 98**

7. Sustained while "occupying" a vehicle without a reasonable belief that that "insured" is entitled to do so. This Exclusion (7.) does not apply to a "family member" using "your covered auto" which is owned by you.

8. Sustained while "occupying" a vehicle when it is being used in the "business" of an "insured". This Exclusion (8.) does not apply to "bodily injury" sustained while "occupying" a:

   a. Private passenger auto;

   b. Pickup or van that you own; or

   c. "Trailer" used with a vehicle described in a. or b. above.

9. Caused by or as a consequence of:

   a. Discharge of a nuclear weapon (even if accidental);

   b. War (declared or undeclared);

   c. Civil war;

   d. Insurrection; or

   e. Rebellion or revolution.

10. From or as a consequence of the following, whether controlled or uncontrolled or however caused:

   a. Nuclear reaction;

   b. Radiation; or

   c. Radioactive contamination.

11. Sustained while "occupying" any vehicle located inside a facility designed for racing, for the purpose of:

   a. Competing in; or

b. Practicing or preparing for;

any prearranged or organized racing or speed contest.

LIMIT OF LIABILITY

A. The limit of liability shown in the Declarations for this coverage is our maximum limit of liability for each person injured in any one accident. This is the most we will pay regardless of the number of:

   1. "Insureds";

   2. Claims made;

   3. Vehicles or premiums shown in the Declarations; or

   4. Vehicles involved in the accident.

B. No one will be entitled to receive duplicate payments for the same elements of loss under this coverage and:

   1. Part A or Part C of this policy; or

   2. Any Underinsured Motorists Coverage provided by this policy.

OTHER INSURANCE

If there is other applicable auto medical payments insurance we will pay only our share of the loss. Our share is the proportion that our limit of liability bears to the total of all applicable limits. However, any insurance we provide with respect to a vehicle you do not own shall be excess over any other collectible auto insurance providing payments for medical or funeral expenses.

PART C – UNINSURED MOTORISTS COVERAGE

INSURING AGREEMENT

A. We will pay compensatory damages which an "insured" is legally entitled to recover from the owner or operator of an "uninsured motor vehicle" because of "bodily injury":

   1. Sustained by an "insured"; and

   2. Caused by an accident.

The owner's or operator's liability for these damages must arise out of the ownership, maintenance or use of the "uninsured motor vehicle".

Any judgment for damages arising out of a suit brought without our written consent is not binding on us.

B. "Insured" as used in this Part means:

   1. You or any "family member".

   2. Any other person "occupying" "your covered auto".

   3. Any person for damages that person is entitled to recover because of "bodily injury" to which this coverage applies sustained by a person described in 1. or 2. above.

C. "Uninsured motor vehicle" means a land motor vehicle or trailer of any type:

   1. To which no bodily injury liability bond or policy applies at the time of the accident.

   2. To which a bodily injury liability bond or policy applies at the time of the accident. In this case its limit for bodily injury liability must be less than the minimum limit for bodily injury liability specified by the financial responsibility law of the state in which "your covered auto" is principally garaged.

3. Which is a hit-and-run vehicle whose operator or owner cannot be identified and which hits:

   a. You or any "family member";

   b. A vehicle which you or any "family member" are "occupying"; or

   c. "Your covered auto".

4. To which a bodily injury liability bond or policy applies at the time of the accident but the bonding or insuring company:

   a. Denies coverage; or

   b. Is or becomes insolvent.

However, "uninsured motor vehicle" does not include any vehicle or equipment:

1. Owned by or furnished or available for the regular use of you or any "family member".

2. Owned or operated by a self-insurer under any applicable motor vehicle law, except a self-insurer which is or becomes insolvent.

3. Owned by any governmental unit or agency.

4. Operated on rails or crawler treads.

5. Designed mainly for use off public roads while not on public roads.

6. While located for use as a residence or premises.

EXCLUSIONS

A. We do not provide Uninsured Motorists Coverage for "bodily injury" sustained:

1. By an "insured" while "occupying", or when struck by, any motor vehicle owned by that "insured" which is not insured for this coverage under this policy. This includes a trailer of any type used with that vehicle.

2. By any "family member" while "occupying", or when struck by, any motor vehicle you own which is insured for this coverage on a primary basis under any other policy.

B. We do not provide Uninsured Motorists Coverage for "bodily injury" sustained by any "insured":

1. If that "insured" or the legal representative settles the "bodily injury" claim without our consent.

2. While "occupying" "your covered auto" when it is being used as a public or livery conveyance. This Exclusion (**B.2.**) does not apply to a share-the-expense car pool.

3. Using a vehicle without a reasonable belief that that "insured" is entitled to do so. This Exclusion (**B.3.**) does not apply to a "family member" using "your covered auto" which is owned by you.

C. This coverage shall not apply directly or indirectly to benefit any insurer or self-insurer under any of the following or similar law:

1. Workers' compensation law; or

2. Disability benefits law.

D. We do not provide Uninsured Motorists Coverage for punitive or exemplary damages.

LIMIT OF LIABILITY

A. The limit of liability shown in the Declarations for each person for Uninsured Motorists Coverage is our maximum limit of liability for all damages, including damages for care, loss of services or death, arising out of "bodily injury" sustained by any one person in any one accident. Subject to this limit for each person, the limit of liability shown in the Declarations for each accident for Uninsured Motorists Coverage is our maximum limit of liability for all damages for "bodily injury" resulting from any one accident.

This is the most we will pay regardless of the number of:

1. "Insureds";

2. Claims made;

3. Vehicles or premiums shown in the Declarations; or

4. Vehicles involved in the accident.

B. No one will be entitled to receive duplicate payments for the same elements of loss under this coverage and:

1. Part **A.** or Part **B.** of this policy; or

2. Any Underinsured Motorists Coverage provided by this policy.

C. We will not make a duplicate payment under this coverage for any element of loss for which payment has been made by or on behalf of persons or organizations who may be legally responsible.

D. We will not pay for any element of loss if a person is entitled to receive payment for the same element of loss under any of the following or similar law:

1. Workers' compensation law; or

2. Disability benefits law.

OTHER INSURANCE

If there is other applicable insurance available under one or more policies or provisions of coverage that is similar to the insurance provided under this Part of the policy:

1. Any recovery for damages under all such policies or provisions of coverage may equal but not exceed the highest applicable limit for any one vehicle under any insurance providing coverage on either a primary or excess basis.

2. Any insurance we provide with respect to a vehicle you do not own shall be excess over any collectible insurance providing such coverage on a primary basis.

       PP 00 01 06 98

3. If the coverage under this policy is provided:

   a. On a primary basis, we will pay only our share of the loss that must be paid under insurance providing coverage on a primary basis. Our share is the proportion that our limit of liability bears to the total of all applicable limits of liability for coverage provided on a primary basis.

   b. On an excess basis, we will pay only our share of the loss that must be paid under insurance providing coverage on an excess basis. Our share is the proportion that our limit of liability bears to the total of all applicable limits of liability for coverage provided on an excess basis.

ARBITRATION

A. If we and an "insured" do not agree:

   1. Whether that "insured" is legally entitled to recover damages; or

   2. As to the amount of damages which are recoverable by that "insured";

from the owner or operator of an "uninsured motor vehicle", then the matter may be arbitrated. However, disputes concerning coverage under this Part may not be arbitrated.

Both parties must agree to arbitration. If so agreed, each party will select an arbitrator. The two arbitrators will select a third. If they cannot agree within 30 days, either may request that selection be made by a judge of a court having jurisdiction.

B. Each party will:

   1. Pay the expenses it incurs; and

   2. Bear the expenses of the third arbitrator equally.

C. Unless both parties agree otherwise, arbitration will take place in the county in which the "insured" lives. Local rules of law as to procedure and evidence will apply. A decision agreed to by two of the arbitrators will be binding as to:

   1. Whether the "insured" is legally entitled to recover damages; and

   2. The amount of damages. This applies only if the amount does not exceed the minimum limit for bodily injury liability specified by the financial responsibility law of the state in which "your covered auto" is principally garaged. If the amount exceeds that limit, either party may demand the right to a trial. This demand must be made within 60 days of the arbitrators' decision. If this demand is not made, the amount of damages agreed to by the arbitrators will be binding.

PART D – COVERAGE FOR DAMAGE TO YOUR AUTO

INSURING AGREEMENT

A. We will pay for direct and accidental loss to "your covered auto" or any "non-owned auto", including their equipment, minus any applicable deductible shown in the Declarations. If loss to more than one "your covered auto" or "non-owned auto" results from the same "collision", only the highest applicable deductible will apply. We will pay for loss to "your covered auto" caused by:

   1. Other than "collision" only if the Declarations indicate that Other Than Collision Coverage is provided for that auto.

   2. "Collision" only if the Declarations indicate that Collision Coverage is provided for that auto.

If there is a loss to a "non-owned auto", we will provide the broadest coverage applicable to any "your covered auto" shown in the Declarations.

B. "Collision" means the upset of "your covered auto" or a "non-owned auto" or their impact with another vehicle or object.

Loss caused by the following is considered other than "collision":

   1. Missiles or falling objects;

   2. Fire;

   3. Theft or larceny;

   4. Explosion or earthquake;

   5. Windstorm;

   6. Hail, water or flood;

   7. Malicious mischief or vandalism;

   8. Riot or civil commotion;

   9. Contact with bird or animal; or

  10. Breakage of glass.

If breakage of glass is caused by a "collision", you may elect to have it considered a loss caused by "collision".

C. "Non-owned auto" means:

   1. Any private passenger auto, pickup, van or "trailer" not owned by or furnished or available for the regular use of you or any "family member" while in the custody of or being operated by you or any "family member"; or

   2. Any auto or "trailer" you do not own while used as a temporary substitute for "your covered auto" which is out of normal use because of its:

     a. Breakdown;

     b. Repair;

     c. Servicing;

     d. Loss; or

     e. Destruction.

TRANSPORTATION EXPENSES

A. In addition, we will pay, without application of a deductible, up to a maximum of $600 for:

1. Temporary transportation expenses not exceeding $20 per day incurred by you in the event of a loss to "your covered auto". We will pay for such expenses if the loss is caused by:

a. Other than "collision" only if the Declarations indicate that Other Than Collision Coverage is provided for that auto.

b. "Collision" only if the Declarations indicate that Collision Coverage is provided for that auto.

2. Expenses for which you become legally responsible in the event of loss to a "non-owned auto". We will pay for such expenses if the loss is caused by:

a. Other than "collision" only if the Declarations indicate that Other Than Collision Coverage is provided for any "your covered auto".

b. "Collision" only if the Declarations indicate that Collision Coverage is provided for any "your covered auto".

However, the most we will pay for any expenses for loss of use is $20 per day.

B. If the loss is caused by:

1. A total theft of "your covered auto" or a "non-owned auto", we will pay only expenses incurred during the period:

a. Beginning 48 hours after the theft; and

b. Ending when "your covered auto" or the "non-owned auto" is returned to use or we pay for its loss.

2. Other than theft of a "your covered auto" or a "non-owned auto", we will pay only expenses beginning when the auto is withdrawn from use for more than 24 hours.

C. Our payment will be limited to that period of time reasonably required to repair or replace the "your covered auto" or the "non-owned auto".

EXCLUSIONS

We will not pay for:

1. Loss to "your covered auto" or any "non-owned auto" which occurs while it is being used as a public or livery conveyance. This Exclusion (1.) does not apply to a share-the-expense car pool.

2. Damage due and confined to:

a. Wear and tear;

b. Freezing;

c. Mechanical or electrical breakdown or failure; or

d. Road damage to tires.

This Exclusion (2.) does not apply if the damage results from the total theft of "your covered auto" or any "non-owned auto".

3. Loss due to or as a consequence of:

a. Radioactive contamination;

b. Discharge of any nuclear weapon (even if accidental);

c. War (declared or undeclared);

d. Civil war;

e. Insurrection; or

f. Rebellion or revolution.

4. Loss to any electronic equipment designed for the reproduction of sound and any accessories used with such equipment. This includes but is not limited to:

a. Radios and stereos;

b. Tape decks; or

c. Compact disc players.

This Exclusion (4.) does not apply to equipment designed solely for the reproduction of sound and accessories used with such equipment, provided:

a. The equipment is permanently installed in "your covered auto" or any "non-owned auto"; or

b. The equipment is:

(1) Removable from a housing unit which is permanently installed in the auto;

(2) Designed to be solely operated by use of the power from the auto's electrical system; and

(3) In or upon "your covered auto" or any "non-owned auto" at the time of loss.

5. Loss to any electronic equipment that receives or transmits audio, visual or data signals and any accessories used with such equipment. This includes but is not limited to:

a. Citizens band radios;

b. Telephones;

c. Two-way mobile radios;

d. Scanning monitor receivers;

e. Television monitor receivers;

f. Video cassette recorders;

g. Audio cassette recorders; or

h. Personal computers.

This Exclusion (5.) does not apply to:

a. Any electronic equipment that is necessary for the normal operation of the auto or the monitoring of the auto's operating systems; or

b. A permanently installed telephone designed to be operated by use of the power from the auto's electrical system and any accessories used with the telephone.

6. Loss to tapes, records, discs or other media used with equipment described in Exclusions 4. and 5.

7. A total loss to "your covered auto" or any "non-owned auto" due to destruction or confiscation by governmental or civil authorities.

This Exclusion (7.) does not apply to the interests of Loss Payees in "your covered auto".

8. Loss to:

a. A "trailer", camper body, or motor home, which is not shown in the Declarations; or

b. Facilities or equipment used with such "trailer", camper body or motor home. Facilities or equipment include but are not limited to:

(1) Cooking, dining, plumbing or refrigeration facilities;

(2) Awnings or cabanas; or

(3) Any other facilities or equipment used with a "trailer", camper body, or motor home.

This Exclusion (8.) does not apply to a:

a. "Trailer", and its facilities or equipment which you do not own; or

b. "Trailer", camper body, or the facilities or equipment in or attached to the "trailer" or camper body, which you:

(1) Acquire during the policy period; and

(2) Ask us to insure within 14 days after you become the owner.

9. Loss to any "non-owned auto" when used by you or any "family member" without a reasonable belief that you or that "family member" are entitled to do so.

10. Loss to equipment designed or used for the detection or location of radar or laser.

11. Loss to any custom furnishings or equipment in or upon any pickup or van. Custom furnishings or equipment include but are not limited to:

a. Special carpeting or insulation;

b. Furniture or bars;

c. Height-extending roofs; or

d. Custom murals, paintings or other decals or graphics.

This Exclusion (11.) does not apply to a cap, cover or bedliner in or upon any "your covered auto" which is a pickup.

12. Loss to any "non-owned auto" being maintained or used by any person while employed or otherwise engaged in the "business" of:

a. Selling;

b. Repairing;

c. Servicing;

d. Storing; or

e. Parking;

vehicles designed for use on public highways. This includes road testing and delivery.

13. Loss to "your covered auto" or any "non-owned auto", located inside a facility designed for racing, for the purpose of:

a. Competing in; or

b. Practicing or preparing for;

any prearranged or organized racing or speed contest.

14. Loss to, or loss of use of, a "non-owned auto" rented by:

a. You; or

b. Any "family member";

if a rental vehicle company is precluded from recovering such loss or loss of use, from you or that "family member", pursuant to the provisions of any applicable rental agreement or state law.

LIMIT OF LIABILITY

A. Our limit of liability for loss will be the lesser of the:

1. Actual cash value of the stolen or damaged property; or

2. Amount necessary to repair or replace the property with other property of like kind and quality.

However, the most we will pay for loss to:

1. Any "non-owned auto" which is a trailer is $500.

2. Equipment designed solely for the reproduction of sound, including any accessories used with such equipment, which is installed in locations not used by the auto manufacturer for installation of such equipment or accessories, is $1,000.

B. An adjustment for depreciation and physical condition will be made in determining actual cash value in the event of a total loss.

C. If a repair or replacement results in better than like kind or quality, we will not pay for the amount of the betterment.

PAYMENT OF LOSS

We may pay for loss in money or repair or replace the damaged or stolen property. We may, at our expense, return any stolen property to:

1. You; or

2. The address shown in this policy.

If we return stolen property we will pay for any damage resulting from the theft. We may keep all or part of the property at an agreed or appraised value.

If we pay for loss in money, our payment will include the applicable sales tax for the damaged or stolen property.

NO BENEFIT TO BAILEE

This insurance shall not directly or indirectly benefit any carrier or other bailee for hire.

OTHER SOURCES OF RECOVERY

If other sources of recovery also cover the loss, we will pay only our share of the loss. Our share is the proportion that our limit of liability bears to the total of all applicable limits. However, any insurance we provide with respect to a "non-owned auto" shall be excess over any other collectible source of recovery including, but not limited to:

1. Any coverage provided by the owner of the "non-owned auto";

2. Any other applicable physical damage insurance;

3. Any other source of recovery applicable to the loss.

APPRAISAL

A. If we and you do not agree on the amount of loss, either may demand an appraisal of the loss. In this event, each party will select a competent appraiser. The two appraisers will select an umpire. The appraisers will state separately the actual cash value and the amount of loss. If they fail to agree, they will submit their differences to the umpire. A decision agreed to by any two will be binding. Each party will:

1. Pay its chosen appraiser; and

2. Bear the expenses of the appraisal and umpire equally.

B. We do not waive any of our rights under this policy by agreeing to an appraisal.

PART E – DUTIES AFTER AN ACCIDENT OR LOSS

We have no duty to provide coverage under this policy unless there has been full compliance with the following duties:

A. We must be notified promptly of how, when and where the accident or loss happened. Notice should also include the names and addresses of any injured persons and of any witnesses.

B. A person seeking any coverage must:

1. Cooperate with us in the investigation, settlement or defense of any claim or suit.

2. Promptly send us copies of any notices or legal papers received in connection with the accident or loss.

3. Submit, as often as we reasonably require:

   a. To physical exams by physicians we select. We will pay for these exams.

   b. To examination under oath and subscribe the same.

4. Authorize us to obtain:

   a. Medical reports; and

b. Other pertinent records.

5. Submit a proof of loss when required by us.

C. A person seeking Uninsured Motorists Coverage must also:

1. Promptly notify the police if a hit-and-run driver is involved.

2. Promptly send us copies of the legal papers if a suit is brought.

D. A person seeking Coverage For Damage To Your Auto must also:

1. Take reasonable steps after loss to protect "your covered auto" or any "non-owned auto" and their equipment from further loss. We will pay reasonable expenses incurred to do this.

2. Promptly notify the police if "your covered auto" or any "non-owned auto" is stolen.

3. Permit us to inspect and appraise the damaged property before its repair or disposal.

PART F – GENERAL PROVISIONS

BANKRUPTCY

Bankruptcy or insolvency of the "insured" shall not relieve us of any obligations under this policy.

CHANGES

A. This policy contains all the agreements between you and us. Its terms may not be changed or waived except by endorsement issued by us.

B. If there is a change to the information used to develop the policy premium, we may adjust your premium. Changes during the policy term that may result in a premium increase or decrease include, but are not limited to, changes in:

1. The number, type or use classification of insured vehicles;

2. Operators using insured vehicles;

3. The place of principal garaging of insured vehicles;

4. Coverage, deductible or limits.

If a change resulting from A. or B. requires a premium adjustment, we will make the premium adjustment in accordance with our manual rules.

C. If we make a change which broadens coverage under this edition of your policy without additional premium charge, that change will automatically apply to your policy as of the date we implement the change in your state. This Paragraph (C.) does not apply to changes implemented with a general program revision that includes both broadenings and restrictions in coverage, whether that general program revision is implemented through introduction of:

1. A subsequent edition of your policy; or

2. An Amendatory Endorsement.

FRAUD

We do not provide coverage for any "insured" who has made fraudulent statements or engaged in fraudulent conduct in connection with any accident or loss for which coverage is sought under this policy.

LEGAL ACTION AGAINST US

A. No legal action may be brought against us until there has been full compliance with all the terms of this policy. In addition, under Part A, no legal action may be brought against us until:

1. We agree in writing that the "insured" has an obligation to pay; or

2. The amount of that obligation has been finally determined by judgment after trial.

B. No person or organization has any right under this policy to bring us into any action to determine the liability of an "insured".

OUR RIGHT TO RECOVER PAYMENT

A. If we make a payment under this policy and the person to or for whom payment was made has a right to recover damages from another we shall be subrogated to that right. That person shall do:

1. Whatever is necessary to enable us to exercise our rights; and

2. Nothing after loss to prejudice them.

However, our rights in this Paragraph (A.) do not apply under Part D, against any person using "your covered auto" with a reasonable belief that that person is entitled to do so.

B. If we make a payment under this policy and the person to or for whom payment is made recovers damages from another, that person shall:

1. Hold in trust for us the proceeds of the recovery; and

2. Reimburse us to the extent of our payment.

POLICY PERIOD AND TERRITORY

A. This policy applies only to accidents and losses which occur:

1. During the policy period as shown in the Declarations; and

2. Within the policy territory.

B. The policy territory is:

1. The United States of America, its territories or possessions;

2. Puerto Rico; or

3. Canada.

This policy also applies to loss to, or accidents involving, "your covered auto" while being transported between their ports.

TERMINATION

A. Cancellation

This policy may be cancelled during the policy period as follows:

1. The named insured shown in the Declarations may cancel by:

a. Returning this policy to us; or

b. Giving us advance written notice of the date cancellation is to take effect.

2. We may cancel by mailing to the named insured shown in the Declarations at the address shown in this policy:

a. At least 10 days notice:

(1) If cancellation is for nonpayment of premium; or

(2) If notice is mailed during the first 60 days this policy is in effect and this is not a renewal or continuation policy; or

b. At least 20 days notice in all other cases.

3. After this policy is in effect for 60 days, or if this is a renewal or continuation policy, we will cancel only:

a. For nonpayment of premium; or

b. If your driver's license or that of:

(1) Any driver who lives with you; or

(2) Any driver who customarily uses "your covered auto";

has been suspended or revoked. This must have occurred:

(1) During the policy period; or

(2) Since the last anniversary of the original effective date if the policy period is other than 1 year; or

c. If the policy was obtained through material misrepresentation.

B. Nonrenewal

If we decide not to renew or continue this policy, we will mail notice to the named insured shown in the Declarations at the address shown in this policy. Notice will be mailed at least 20 days before the end of the policy period. Subject to this notice requirement, if the policy period is:

1. Less than 6 months, we will have the right not to renew or continue this policy every 6 months, beginning 6 months after its original effective date.

2. 6 months or longer, but less than one year, we will have the right not to renew or continue this policy at the end of the policy period.

3. 1 year or longer, we will have the right not to renew or continue this policy at each anniversary of its original effective date.

C. Automatic Termination

If we offer to renew or continue and you or your representative do not accept, this policy will automatically terminate at the end of the current policy period. Failure to pay the required renewal or continuation premium when due shall mean that you have not accepted our offer.

If you obtain other insurance on "your covered auto", any similar insurance provided by this policy will terminate as to that auto on the effective date of the other insurance.

D. Other Termination Provisions

1. We may deliver any notice instead of mailing it. Proof of mailing of any notice shall be sufficient proof of notice.

2. If this policy is cancelled, you may be entitled to a premium refund. If so, we will send you the refund. The premium refund, if any, will be computed according to our manuals. However, making or offering to make the refund is not a condition of cancellation.

3. The effective date of cancellation stated in the notice shall become the end of the policy period.

TRANSFER OF YOUR INTEREST IN THIS POLICY

A. Your rights and duties under this policy may not be assigned without our written consent. However, if a named insured shown in the Declarations dies, coverage will be provided for:

1. The surviving spouse if resident in the same household at the time of death. Coverage applies to the spouse as if a named insured shown in the Declarations; and

2. The legal representative of the deceased person as if a named insured shown in the Declarations. This applies only with respect to the representative's legal responsibility to maintain or use "your covered auto".

B. Coverage will only be provided until the end of the policy period.

TWO OR MORE AUTO POLICIES

If this policy and any other auto insurance policy issued to you by us apply to the same accident, the maximum limit of our liability under all the policies shall not exceed the highest applicable limit of liability under any one policy.

Copyright, Insurance Services Office, Inc., 1997 **PP 00 01 06 98**

POLICY NUMBER: **PERSONAL AUTO**
                                                        PP 03 11 06 98

THIS ENDORSEMENT CHANGES THE POLICY. PLEASE READ IT CAREFULLY.

UNDERINSURED MOTORISTS COVERAGE

SCHEDULE

Limit Of Liability	Premium		
	Auto 1	Auto 2	Auto 3
$ _____ each person	$ _____	$ _____	$ _____
$ _____ each accident			

With respect to the coverage provided by this endorsement, the provisions of the policy apply unless modified by the endorsement.

INSURING AGREEMENT

A. We will pay compensatory damages which an "insured" is legally entitled to recover from the owner or operator of an "underinsured motor vehicle" because of "bodily injury":

1. Sustained by an "insured"; and

2. Caused by an accident.

The owner's or operator's liability for these damages must arise out of the ownership, maintenance or use of the "underinsured motor vehicle".

We will pay under this coverage only if 1. or 2. below applies:

1. The limits of liability under any bodily injury liability bonds or policies applicable to the "underinsured motor vehicle" have been exhausted by payment of judgments or settlements; or

2. A tentative settlement has been made between an "insured" and the insurer of the "underinsured motor vehicle" and we:

   a. Have been given prompt written notice of such tentative settlement; and

   b. Advance payment to the "insured" in an amount equal to the tentative settlement within 30 days after receipt of notification.

B. "Insured" as used in this endorsement means:

1. You or any "family member".

2. Any other person "occupying" "your covered auto".

3. Any person for damages that person is entitled to recover because of "bodily injury" to which this coverage applies sustained by a person described in 1. or 2. above.

C. "Underinsured motor vehicle" means a land motor vehicle or trailer of any type to which a bodily injury liability bond or policy applies at the time of the accident but its limit for bodily injury liability is less than the limit of liability for this coverage.

However, "underinsured motor vehicle" does not include any vehicle or equipment:

1. To which a bodily injury liability bond or policy applies at the time of the accident but its limit for bodily injury liability is less than the minimum limit for bodily injury liability specified by the financial responsibility law of the state in which "your covered auto" is principally garaged.

2. Owned by or furnished or available for the regular use of you or any "family member".

3. Owned by any governmental unit or agency.

4. Operated on rails or crawler treads.

5. Designed mainly for use off public roads while not upon public roads.

6. While located for use as a residence or premises.

7. Owned or operated by a person qualifying as a self-insurer under any applicable motor vehicle law.

8. To which a bodily injury liability bond or policy applies at the time of the accident but the bonding or insuring company:

   a. Denies coverage; or

   b. Is or becomes insolvent.

EXCLUSIONS

A. We do not provide Underinsured Motorists Coverage for "bodily injury" sustained:

1. By an "insured" while "occupying", or when struck by, any motor vehicle owned by that "insured" which is not insured for this coverage under this policy. This includes a trailer of any type used with that vehicle.

2. By any "family member" while "occupying", or when struck by, any motor vehicle you own which is insured for this coverage on a primary basis under any other policy.

B. We do not provide Underinsured Motorists Coverage for "bodily injury" sustained by any "insured":

1. While "occupying" "your covered auto" when it is being used as a public or livery conveyance. This Exclusion (**B.1.**) does not apply to a share-the-expense car pool.

2. Using a vehicle without a reasonable belief that that "insured" is entitled to do so. This Exclusion (**B.2.**) does not apply to a "family member" using "your covered auto" which is owned by you.

C. This coverage shall not apply directly or indirectly to benefit any insurer or self-insurer under any of the following or similar law:

1. Workers' compensation law; or

2. Disability benefits law.

D. We do not provide Underinsured Motorists Coverage for punitive or exemplary damages.

LIMIT OF LIABILITY

A. The limit of liability shown in the Schedule or in the Declarations for each person for Underinsured Motorists Coverage is our maximum limit of liability for all damages, including damages for care, loss of services or death, arising out of "bodily injury" sustained by any one person in any one accident. Subject to this limit for each person, the limit of liability shown in the Schedule or in the Declarations for each accident for Underinsured Motorists Coverage is our maximum limit of liability for all damages for "bodily injury" resulting from any one accident.

This is the most we will pay regardless of the number of:

1. "Insureds";

2. Claims made;

3. Vehicles or premiums shown in the Schedule or in the Declarations; or

4. Vehicles involved in the accident.

B. The limit of liability shall be reduced by all sums paid because of the "bodily injury" by or on behalf of persons or organizations who may be legally responsible. This includes all sums paid under Part **A** of this policy.

C. No one will be entitled to receive duplicate payments for the same elements of loss under this coverage and Part **A**, Part **B** or Part **C** of this policy.

D. We will not make a duplicate payment under this coverage for any element of loss for which payment has been made by or on behalf of persons or organizations who may be legally responsible.

E. We will not pay for any element of loss if a person is entitled to receive payment for the same element of loss under any of the following or similar law;

1. Workers' compensation law; or

2. Disability benefits law.

OTHER INSURANCE

If there is other applicable insurance available under one or more policies or provisions of coverage that is similar to the insurance provided by this endorsement:

1. Any recovery for damages under all such policies or provisions of coverage may equal but not exceed the highest applicable limit for any one vehicle under any insurance providing coverage on either a primary or excess basis.

2. Any insurance we provide with respect to a vehicle you do not own shall be excess over any collectible insurance providing such coverage on a primary basis.

3. If the coverage under this policy is provided:

   a. On a primary basis, we will pay only our share of the loss that must be paid under insurance providing coverage on a primary basis. Our share is the proportion that our limit of liability bears to the total of all applicable limits of liability for coverage provided on a primary basis.

   b. On an excess basis, we will pay only our share of the loss that must be paid under insurance providing coverage on an excess basis. Our share is the proportion that our limit of liability bears to the total of all applicable limits of liability for coverage provided on an excess basis.

 PP 03 11 06 98

ARBITRATION

A. If we and an "insured" do not agree:

1. Whether that "insured" is legally entitled to recover damages; or

2. As to the amount of damages which are recoverable by that "insured";

from the owner or operator of an "underinsured motor vehicle", then the matter may be arbitrated. However, disputes concerning coverage under this endorsement may not be arbitrated.

Both parties must agree to arbitration. If so agreed, each party will select an arbitrator. The two arbitrators will select a third. If they cannot agree within 30 days, either may request that selection be made by a judge of a court having jurisdiction.

B. Each party will:

1. Pay the expenses it incurs; and

2. Bear the expenses of the third arbitrator equally.

C. Unless both parties agree otherwise, arbitration will take place in the county in which the "insured" lives. Local rules of law as to procedure and evidence will apply. A decision agreed to by two of the arbitrators will be binding as to:

1. Whether the "insured" is legally entitled to recover damages; and

2. The amount of damages. This applies only if the amount does not exceed the minimum limit for bodily injury liability specified by the financial responsibility law of the state in which "your covered auto" is principally garaged. If the amount exceeds that limit, either party may demand the right to a trial. This demand must be made within 60 days of the arbitrators' decision. If this demand is not made, the amount of damages agreed to by the arbitrators will be binding.

ADDITIONAL DUTIES

A person seeking coverage under this endorsement must also promptly:

1. Send us copies of the legal papers if a suit is brought; and

2. Notify us in writing of a tentative settlement between the "insured" and the insurer of the "underinsured motor vehicle" and allow us 30 days to advance payment to that "insured" in an amount equal to the tentative settlement to preserve our rights against the insurer, owner or operator of such "underinsured motor vehicle".

GENERAL PROVISIONS

The following is added to the **Our Right To Recover Payment** Provision in Part F:

OUR RIGHT TO RECOVER PAYMENT

Our rights do not apply under Paragraph **A.** with respect to Underinsured Motorists Coverage if we:

1. Have been given prompt written notice of a tentative settlement between an "insured" and the insurer of an "underinsured motor vehicle", and

2. Fail to advance payment to the "insured" in an amount equal to the tentative settlement within 30 days after receipt of notification.

If we advance payment to the "insured" in an amount equal to the tentative settlement within 30 days after receipt of notification:

1. That payment will be separate from any amount the "insured" is entitled to recover under the provisions of Underinsured Motorists Coverage; and

2. We also have a right to recover the advanced payment.

This endorsement must be attached to the Change Endorsement when issued after the policy is written.

APPENDIX F

THE BAR PLAN

MUTUAL INSURANCE COMPANY
1717 Hidden Creek Court
St. Louis, MO 63131
(314) 965-3333 or (800) 843-2277
Fax: (314) 821-0534

Lawyers Professional
Liability Insurance Policy

SPECIMEN

IMPORTANT NOTICE: Automatic coverage for attorneys who first become associated with the Policyholder during the Policy Period is restricted to the first 60 days of association and does not automatically include coverage for prior acts. (Refer to Section I., Definitions, Paragraph B.3. for the definition of Insured.) Coverage for such attorneys is all conditioned upon the Policyholder notifying the Company WITHIN SIXTY (60) DAYS of the date of association, completion of an application and underwriting approval.

In order to avoid a lapse in coverage or to secure a quotation for Optional Extended Reporting Coverage, termination of coverage for any attorney must be reported to your agent or The Company NO LATER THAN THIRTY (30) DAYS from the date of termination. (Refer to Section II. Coverage, Paragraphs D., E. and F. for Extended Reporting Coverage Options.)

All changes affecting this Policy must be reported immediately to the Company in order to avoid a lapse in coverage.

Form TBP-2 (1-2000)

1

THE BAR PLAN
MUTUAL INSURANCE COMPANY

PROFESSIONAL LIABILITY INSURANCE FOR LAWYERS

SPECIMEN

IMPORTANT NOTICES

This is a Claims-Made and Reported Policy. Only those Claims first made against an Insured and reported to the Company during the Policy Period are covered, subject to the terms and conditions of this Policy.

Defense Expenses are within the Limits of Liability; meaning that payment of Defense Expenses will reduce the Limits of Liability available to pay Damages.

The Bar Plan Mutual Insurance Company is organized in accordance with the provisions of Chapter 379, R.S.Mo.

PLEASE READ CAREFULLY

In consideration of the undertaking of the Named Insured to pay, when due, all premiums, and the deductible described herein, in the amounts stated in the Declarations, and in reliance upon the statements in the application attached hereto and made a part hereof, subject to the Limits of Liability shown in the Declarations and all of the terms and conditions of this Policy, and in accordance with the provisions of the Company's Articles and Bylaws, the Company agrees with the Named Insured as follows:

Form TBP-2 (1-2000)

2

INDEX

PAGE

I. DEFINITIONS. Whenever used in this Policy:

A. **"NAMED INSURED"** means each lawyer and each Partnership, Professional Legal Corporation or Association, Limited Liability Company, Limited Liability Partnership or Charter named in the DECLARATIONS of this Policy.

B. **"INSURED"** means:

 1. Any Named Insured;

SPECIMEN

 2. Any lawyer who is a former partner, member, officer, director, stockholder, associate, or employee of the Policyholder named in the Declarations of this Policy or the Policyholder's Predecessor Firm(s), but solely for acts or omissions while acting within a professional capacity providing Legal Services on behalf of the Policyholder or its Predecessor Firm(s) for acts or omissions prior to leaving or retiring from such firm;

 3. Any lawyer who, during the Policy Period, first becomes associated with the Policyholder either as a partner, member, officer, director, stockholder, associate, or employee, but only for a period of not longer than sixty (60) days from the date the association begins and solely for acts or omissions while acting in a professional capacity on behalf of the Policyholder, all on condition that the Policyholder notify the Company within sixty (60) days of the date of association. Upon receipt of an application, the Company may, at its discretion, provide prior acts coverage for the new lawyer;

 4. The heirs, executors, administrators, beneficiaries, assigns, appointed legal representatives, guardians and conservators of an Insured who is dead, disabled or incapacitated, and the trustee or estate of an Insured in bankruptcy, but solely with respect to the liability of the Insured as is otherwise covered by this Policy; and

 5. Any non-lawyer who was, is now, or hereinafter becomes an employee of the Named Insured or Predecessor Firm(s), but solely for acts or omissions while acting within the scope of such person's duties as an employee of the Policyholder.

C. **"ASSOCIATE"** means: Any lawyer who is not a partner, member, officer, director, or stockholder of the Policyholder for whom the Policyholder is legally responsible.

D. **"CLAIM"** means: Receipt by an Insured of a demand for money or services (including the service of suit or the institution of arbitration proceedings) against the Insured from one other than that Insured.

E. **"THE COMPANY"** means: **The Bar Plan Mutual Insurance Company.**

F. **"DAMAGES"** means: A monetary judgment, final arbitration award or settlement, but specifically excludes:

 1. Fines, penalties, sanctions, costs, expenses or fees imposed under state or federal laws, regulations, statutes or rules of procedure, punitive or exemplary damages and damages which are a multiple of compensatory damages, including, but not limited to double and treble damages; provided, however, that **DAMAGES** do include an award arising under 15 U.S.C. Section 1640;

Form TBP-2 (1-2000)

2.   Restitution, reduction or set off of any monies or other consideration paid to an Insured as fees or expenses, which are to be reimbursed or discharged as part of the judgment, settlement or final arbitration award;

3.   Fees charged for an Insured's own work; or costs, fees or expenses incurred by an Insured in the course of the provision of Legal Services, including, but not limited to, expert witness fees, court costs, and costs and expenses associated with depositions or transcripts; and

4.   Matters deemed uninsurable by law.

G.   "DEFENSE EXPENSE" means:

1.   Fees charged by a lawyer designated by the Company to defend a Claim;

2.   All other fees, costs and expenses resulting from the investigation, adjustment, defense and appeal of a Claim, if incurred by the Company after receiving proper notice of the Claim;

3.   Fees charged by a lawyer designated by an Insured to defend a Claim with the written consent of the Company.

Defense Expense does not include salary charges of regular employees or officials of the Company or any supervisory counsel retained by the Company. The determination of the Company as to the reasonableness of Defense Expense shall be conclusive as to an Insured.

H.   "LEGAL SERVICES" means: Services performed by an Insured in an Insured's professional capacity as:

1.   A lawyer or notary public;

2.   A mediator or arbitrator; or

3.   An administrator, conservator, executor, guardian, trustee, receiver, or any similar fiduciary capacity.

I.   "PERSONAL INJURY" means: False arrest, humiliation, detention or imprisonment, wrongful entry or eviction or other invasion of private occupancy, publication of libel, utterance of slander, or other defamatory or disparaging material, or a publication or utterance in violation of an individual's right of privacy.

J.   "POLICY PERIOD" means: The one-year period from the effective date of this Policy to the expiration date as set forth in the Declarations or its earlier cancellation or termination date, plus any Extension Period Coverage.

K.   "POLICYHOLDER" means: The lawyer, Partnership, Professional Legal Corporation or Association, Limited Liability Company, Limited Liability Partnership or Charter named as such in the Declarations of this Policy.

L.   "PREDECESSOR FIRM" means: Any lawyer, Partnership, Professional Legal Corporation or Association, Limited Liability Company, Limited Liability Partnership or Charter engaged in the practice of law in whose assets and liabilities the entity named as Policyholder in the Declarations of this Policy is the majority successor in interest and which is designated as a Predecessor firm in the application for coverage.

Form TBP-2 (1-2000)

II. COVERAGE

A. PROFESSIONAL LIABILITY AND CLAIMS MADE AND REPORTED CLAUSE:

The Company will pay on behalf of an Insured all sums, subject to the Limit(s) of Liability, Exclusions and terms and conditions contained in this Policy, which an Insured shall become legally obligated to pay as Damages and/or Defense Expenses as a result of CLAIMS (INCLUDING CLAIMS FOR PERSONAL INJURY) FIRST MADE AGAINST AN INSURED DURING THE POLICY PERIOD AND REPORTED TO THE COMPANY DURING THE POLICY PERIOD by reason of any act or omission by an Insured acting in a professional capacity providing Legal Services.

PROVIDED ALWAYS THAT such act or omission happens:

1.   During the Policy Period; or

2.   Prior to the Policy Period, provided that prior to the effective date of this Policy:

    (A)   An Insured did not give notice to any insurer of any such act or omission; and

    (B)   No Claim based on such act or omission has been made against an Insured.

Note: It is a condition precedent to coverage under this Policy that all Claims be reported in compliance with Section VII. CLAIMS, Paragraph A.

B. DEFENSE AND CONSENT TO SETTLE:

1.   **DUTY TO DEFEND.** Subject to Paragraph B. 3., below, the Company has the right and duty to defend any Claim seeking Damages to which this insurance applies.

2.   **INVESTIGATION, SETTLEMENT AND DEFENSE EXPENSE PAYMENTS.** When the Company has the duty to defend:

    (A)   The Company may investigate any Claim at its discretion;

    (B)   The Company will pay for all Defense Expenses incurred after its duty to defend begins, until its duty to defend ends; and

    (C)   If by mutual agreement or court order, a Named Insured assumes control of the defense before the applicable amount available as provided under the Limits of Liability is exhausted, the Company will reimburse that Insured for reasonable Defense Expenses, until the Company's duty to defend ends.

3.   **END OF DUTY TO DEFEND.** The Company's duty to defend any new or existing Claim(s) ends once the applicable LIMITS OF LIABILITY (Each Claim and/or Aggregate Limit(s)) is (are) exhausted.

4.   **TRANSFER OF DEFENSE AT END OF DUTY TO DEFEND.**

    (A)   As soon as practicable after the Company becomes aware that the Each Claim Limit and/or Aggregate Limit of Liability is exhausted:

        (1)   The Company will notify the Named Insured of any outstanding Claim(s) which is (are) affected by the exhausted limit(s); and

Form TBP-2 (1-2000)

(2)   The Named Insured will promptly arrange for defense of such Claim(s) against the Named Insured or any other Insured under this policy when the Company's right and duty to defend them ends.

(B)   The Company will assist the Named Insured in the transfer of control of the defense of Claims under Paragraph (A), above. Until such arrangements are completed, the Company will take on behalf of any Insured those steps that the Company, at its sole discretion, determines are appropriate:

(1)   To avoid a default in a Claim; or

(2)   To the continued defense of Cla**SPECIMEN**

5.   **CONSENT TO SETTLE.** The Company shall not settle any Claim without the consent of the Named Insured. In the event the Company shall recommend settlement and the Named Insured shall refuse to consent to any settlement proposal to which the claimant and the Company would agree, and the Named Insured thereby elects to contest or continue any legal proceeding in connection therewith, then the Company, at its sole discretion, may choose to limit its Each Claim Limit of Liability for the Claim under this Policy to the amount for which the Claim could have been settled, less Deductible, plus Defense Expenses incurred with the consent of the Company up to the date of the refusal. Should the Company elect to so limit its liability to the amount of the recommended settlement, the Company shall notify the Named Insured by fifteen (15) days written notice of its election. Thereafter, the Each Claim Limit for the Policy for this particular Claim shall be deemed amended to the amount disclosed in the notice.

C.   **DISCOVERY CLAUSE:**

If during the Policy Period, or any Extension Period elected hereunder, an Insured first becomes aware of a specific incident, act or omission while acting in a professional capacity providing Legal Services, which may give rise to a Claim for which coverage is provided under this Policy, and during the Policy Period, or any Extension Period Coverage, the Insured gives written notice to the Company of:

1.   The specific incident, act or omission;

2.   The injury or damage which has or may result from such incident, act or omission; and

3.   The circumstance(s) by which the Insured first became aware of such incident, act or omission;

then any Claim that may subsequently be made against the Insured arising out of such incident, act or omission shall be deemed for the purposes of this insurance to have been made during the Policy Period, or any Extension Period elected hereunder. The Insured shall cooperate fully with the Company as provided in Section VII. CLAIMS, Paragraphs A. and B., and any investigation conducted by the Company or its representatives shall be subject to the terms set forth in this Policy.

D.   **OPTION TO PURCHASE EXTENSION PERIOD COVERAGE:**

If, prior to receiving a notice of cancellation or termination from the Company, an Insured terminates the Policy, either during the Policy Period or at the expiration date, and such

Form TBP-2 (1-2000)

Insured has complied with all the terms and conditions thereof including the payment of all premiums and deductibles when due, then that Insured, upon payment of an additional premium as set forth herein, shall have the option to extend the insurance afforded by this Policy subject otherwise to its terms (including Limits of Liability, EXCLUSIONS and CONDITIONS), to apply to CLAIMS FIRST MADE AGAINST THE INSURED AND REPORTED TO THE COMPANY DURING THE OPTIONAL EXTENSION PERIOD immediately following the effective date of such termination, but only for Claims made by reason of any act or omission in a professional capacity providing Legal Services rendered before such effective termination date and otherwise covered by this insurance. The Optional Extension Period of Coverage for Claims made subsequent to termination or cancellation of the Policy can be extended for intervals of: (a) 12 MONTHS; (b) 24 MONTHS; or (C) 36 MONTHS shall be endorsed hereto, if purchased, and shall hereinafter be referred to as the "OPTIONAL EXTENSION PERIOD COVERAGE."

The premium for the OPTIONAL EXTENSION PERIOD COVERAGE elected by an Insured if an Insured terminates this Policy shall be a percentage of the current full annual premium for this Policy, as follow: (a) 85% for 12 MONTHS; (b) 125% for 24 MONTHS and (c) 160% for 36 MONTHS.

If an Insured exercises the OPTION TO PURCHASE EXTENSION PERIOD COVERAGE, the Policy Period is enlarged accordingly, but the Limits of Liability remain the same for the period which begins at the policy Inception date and ends at the end of the extension period. Consequently:

1. The liability of the Company for ~~EACH CLAIM FIRST MADE AGAINST~~ THE INSURED AND REPORTED TO THE ~~COMPANY DURING THE POLICY~~ PERIOD INCLUDING THE OPTIONAL EXTENSION PERIOD shall be the Each Claim Limit as shown in the Declarations; and

2. The liability of the Company for ALL CLAIMS FIRST MADE AGAINST THE INSURED AND REPORTED TO THE COMPANY DURING THE POLICY PERIOD INCLUDING THE OPTIONAL EXTENSION PERIOD shall not exceed the Aggregate Limit as shown in the Declarations.

E. **OPTION TO PURCHASE NON-PRACTICING EXTENSION PERIOD COVERAGE:**

If, prior to receiving a notice of cancellation or termination from the Company, an Insured ceases the private practice of law during the Policy Period other than as the result of disbarment, revocation, surrender or suspension of a license to practice law, then upon payment of an additional premium as set forth herein, such Insured shall have the option to extend the insurance afforded by this Policy to apply to CLAIMS FIRST MADE AGAINST THE INSURED AND REPORTED TO THE COMPANY DURING THE NON-PRACTICING EXTENSION PERIOD, but only for Claims made by reason of any act or omission in a professional capacity providing Legal Services rendered before the date of the Insured's cessation of private practice and otherwise covered by this insurance. The coverage can be extended for an UNLIMITED PERIOD, or for an interval of: (a) 12 MONTHS; (b) 24 MONTHS; or (c) 36 MONTHS (all periods commencing immediately following the expiration date of this Policy as stated in the Declarations).

The extension of coverage purchased by an Insured for Claims made subsequent to the Insured's cessation of private practice shall be endorsed hereto, and shall hereinafter be referred to as "NON-PRACTICING EXTENSION PERIOD COVERAGE."

The premium for the NON-PRACTICING EXTENSION PERIOD COVERAGE elected by an Insured shall be a percentage of the current full annual premium for the Insured under

Form TBP-2 (1-2000)

this Policy, as follows: (a) 85% for 12 MONTHS; (b) 125% for 24 MONTHS; (c) 160% for 36 MONTHS; or (d) 200% for an UNLIMITED PERIOD.

In the event of death or permanent total disability of an Insured preventing further conduct of that Insured's profession as a lawyer, such Insured shall be entitled, at no additional premium, to NON-PRACTICING EXTENSION PERIOD COVERAGE for an unlimited period, PROVIDED that such Insured has been an Insured of the Company for at least five (5) consecutive years prior to the date of permanent total disability or death.

If an Insured purchases or is given the NON-PRACTICING EXTENSION PERIOD COVERAGE, the Policy Period is enlarged accordingly, but the Limits of Liability remain the same for the period which begins at the policy Inception date and ends at the end of the extension period. Consequently:

1.   The liability of the Company for EACH CLAIM FIRST MADE AGAINST THE INSURED AND REPORTED TO THE COMPANY DURING THE POLICY PERIOD INCLUDING THE NON-PRACTICING EXTENSION PERIOD shall be the Each Claim Limit as shown in the Declarations; and

2.   The liability of the Company for ALL CLAIMS FIRST MADE AGAINST THE INSURED AND REPORTED TO THE COMPANY DURING THE POLICY PERIOD INCLUDING THE NON-PRACTICING EXTENSION PERIOD elected by the Insured shall not exceed the Aggregate Limit as shown in the Declarations.

F.   **CONDITIONS:**

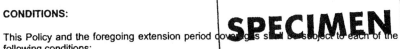

This Policy and the foregoing extension period coverages shall be subject to each of the following conditions:

1.   ALL PREMIUMS, INCLUDING THE PREMIUM, IF ANY, FOR SUCH EXTENSION PERIOD, as well as all Deductibles due the Company, must be paid within thirty (30) days of the quotation.

2.   An Insured's right to EXTENSION PERIOD COVERAGE described in Section II., COVERAGE, Paragraphs D. and E., is conditioned upon notice in writing to the Company not later than thirty (30) days after the cancellation or termination date of coverage for such Insured, specifying the total extension period desired.

3.   In the event of death or permanent total disability of an Insured, written proof of death or permanent total disability must be provided to the Company on behalf of Insureds who are eligible for the NON-PRACTICING EXTENSION PERIOD COVERAGE at no additional premium.

4.   At the commencement of any NON-PRACTICING EXTENSION PERIOD COVERAGE or OPTIONAL EXTENSION PERIOD COVERAGE, the entire premium therefor shall be deemed earned and in the event the Insured terminates the NON-PRACTICING EXTENSION PERIOD COVERAGE or OPTIONAL EXTENSION PERIOD COVERAGE before its contractual termination, the Company shall not be liable for the return to the Insured any portion of the premium for the NON-PRACTICING EXTENSION PERIOD COVERAGE or OPTIONAL EXTENSION PERIOD COVERAGE.

Form TBP-2 (1-2000)

III. EXCLUSIONS

THIS POLICY DOES NOT PROVIDE COVERAGE FOR ANY CLAIM BASED UPON OR ARISING OUT OF:

A. Any dishonest, deliberately fraudulent, criminal, malicious or deliberately wrongful acts or omissions by an Insured; however, the Company will provide a defense for any Claim alleging such acts or omissions by an Insured acting in a professional capacity providing legal services, but the Company will not pay any sums the Insured shall become legally obligated to pay as Damages for any such Claim. This exclusion is waived with respect to each Insured who did not know of, or participate or acquiesce in, the act or omission.

B. An Insured's capacity as:

   1. A public official or employee of a governmental body, subdivision or agency, provided however that if, independent of that capacity, the Insured is regularly engaged in the provision of Legal Services in return for financial remuneration, this exclusion shall not apply, but in that event, the insurance afforded by this policy shall be excess over any other applicable valid and collectible insurance or statutory indemnity, notwithstanding any other language in this policy;

   2. A fiduciary under the Employee Retirement Income Security Act of 1974 and its amendments or any regulation or order issued pursuant thereto, except if an Insured under this Policy is deemed to be a fiduciary solely by reason of rendering Legal Services in a professional capacity with respect to an employee benefit plan;

   3. An investment advisor, securities broker or dealer, insurance agent or broker, real estate agent or broker, or accountant; and

   4. A legal representative of investors in regard to and resulting in investment in an enterprise in which an Insured owns an equity interest or for which the Insured receives a fee or commission from an entity other than the investor;

C. Any business or charitable enterprise not named in the Declarations, which is or was owned by an Insured, or of which an Insured is a general partner, officer, director or employee, or which is directly or indirectly controlled, operated or managed by an Insured, either individually or in a fiduciary capacity;

D. The Insured's notarization of a signature, the signing of which was not seen by the Insured and not acknowledged to the Insured by the signer;

E. An Insured being the beneficiary or distributee of any trust or estate;

F. Bodily injury, sickness, disease or death of any person, or injury to or destruction of any tangible property, including loss of use resulting therefrom, except that this exclusion does not apply to mental illness, emotional distress or humiliation arising from rendering or failing to render Legal Services in a professional capacity;

G. Enforcement of any indemnity agreement entered into by an Insured without obtaining prior written approval from the Company;

H. Employment practices by an Insured;

I. Any expense incurred by an Insured in defense of a grievance or complaint filed with a bar regulatory agency;

Form TBP-2 (1-2000)

J.   Fines, penalties, restitution, sanctions, costs, expenses or fees imposed under state or federal statutes or rules of procedure, punitive or exemplary damages or multiple damages, except a Claim for damages arising under Section 15 U.S.C. 1640(a)(2)(a);

K.   Matters deemed uninsurable by law; and

THIS POLICY DOES NOT PROVIDE COVERAGE FOR ANY CLAIM MADE BY OR ON BEHALF OF:

L.   A present or former partner, officer, director, stockholder, associate or employee of the Named Insured, unless such Claim arises out of an Insured providing Legal Services to that claimant as a client.

IV.   INNOCENT INSURED PROVISION

Although this Policy does not provide coverage for a Claim against an Insured made but not reported to the Company as required by Section VII. CLAIMS, Paragraph A., this policy does provide coverage for that Claim with respect to all other Insureds who, within twenty (20) days after obtaining knowledge of the Claim during the Policy Period, give written notice of that Claim to the Company and forward any documentation or papers obtained and related thereto.

V.   TERRITORY

The insurance afforded applies worldwide provided that the Claim is made or suit is brought within the United States of America, its territories, or Canada.

VI.   LIMITS OF LIABILITY

SPECIMEN

A.   **LIMITS OF LIABILITY:**

The Limits of Liability shown in the Declarations and the provisions of this Policy fix the maximum amount the Company will pay for Damages and Defense Expense regardless of the number of:

1.   Insureds;

2.   Claims; or

3.   Persons or entities making Claims.

Defense Expenses are included within the Limits of Liability. As a result, Defense Expenses will be paid first and such payment will reduce the amount available to pay Damages.

B.   **EACH CLAIM LIMIT:**

The liability of the Company for each Claim first made against an Insured during the Policy Period, including any extension period, shall not exceed the amount stated in the Declarations for each Claim for the sum of Damages and Defense Expense.

Form TBP-2 (1-2000)

11

C. **MULTIPLE INSUREDS, CLAIMS AND CLAIMANTS:**

SPECIMEN

The demand for money or services by more than one person or entity shall not operate to increase the Company's liability. Two or more demands arising out of a single act or omission or a series of related acts or omissions shall be treated as a single Claim. Any such Claim, whenever made, shall be considered for the purposes of this insurance to have been first made and reported during the Policy Period, OPTIONAL EXTENSION PERIOD, or NON-PRACTICING EXTENSION PERIOD in which the earliest demand arising out of such act or omission was first made, provided that such demand is, in fact, asserted against an Insured and reported to the Company during a period in which the Company provided coverage. All such demands for money or services shall be considered a single Claim subject to a single Limit of Liability, regardless of the number of Insureds against which the demands are made.

The following is a *non-exhaustive* list of a series of related acts or omissions that constitute *a single Claim* under the Policy where a single Limit of Liability will apply:

1. All activities pertaining to handling a probate estate from its inception to its conclusion, including, but not limited to, the advice and preparation of tax returns for the decedent or the estate;

2. All activities, including but not limited to, settlement negotiations, discovery, trial and appeal, conducted on behalf of an injured client pertaining to all possible Claims and theories of recovery against all possible parties arising out of injury or loss to that client;

3. All activities pertaining to the defense of a client in a civil case, including but not limited to settlement negotiations, discovery, trial and appeal;

4. All activities pertaining to the defense of a criminal case including but not limited to plea-bargaining, discovery, trial, sentencing, and appeal;

5. All activities pertaining to a real estate transaction including but not limited to negotiating and/or drafting listing contract, contract for sale, related loan documents and deeds; performing title search, examining title and conducting closing(s), etc;

6. All activities pertaining to a sale of a business including but not limited to negotiations, preparation of documents, due diligence and investigation, obtaining licenses, attending closing, etc; and

In the event the Insured is covered for the same Claim by more than one Policy issued by the Company, the Other Insurance provision (Section VIII. B.), shall not apply as to that, and this section shall apply to determine the applicable LIMIT(S) OF LIABILITY for this Policy as follows:

1. If all of the acts or omissions were committed by the Insured while the Insured was with the firm or entity covered by this policy as a Named Insured, then this policy will cover that Claim to the extent of its available LIMIT(S) OF LIABILITY.

2. If all of the acts or omissions were committed by the Insured while the Insured was not with the firm or entity covered by this policy as a Named Insured, then this policy will not provide any coverage for that Claim, meaning that as to that Claim the Each Claim Limit on this policy will be zero, except that if the available LIMIT(S) OF LIABILITY on this policy is higher than on the other Company policy, then this policy

Form TBP-2 (1-2000)

will provide coverage for that Claim, but only in excess of the other Company policy, and only for an amount equal to the numerical difference in Limits of Liability between the other Company policy and this one.

3. If the Insured committed some of the acts or omissions pertaining to the same Claim while the Insured was with the Named Insured for this policy and also committed some of the acts or omission at another entity also insured by a Company policy, then the LIMITS OF LIABILITY for that particular Claim will be reduced proportionately to a percentage of the limit which would have applied if there were no other Company policy insuring that Claim, said percentage to be computed by: the ratio of the limit of this policy (if there were no other Company policy insuring that Claim) divided by the total of the limits of the two Company policies (if there were no other Company policies insuring that Claim).

D. **AGGREGATE LIMIT:**

The Aggregate Limit of Insurance shall not exceed the amount stated in the Declarations. The Aggregate is the sum of:

1. All Damages for all Claims first made against an Insured during the Policy Period including any Extension Period Coverage; and

2. All Defense Expenses for all Claims seeking Damages payable under paragraph 1., above.

SPECIMEN

E. **DEDUCTIBLE:**

The Deductible amount stated in the Declarations shall be paid by the Named Insured and shall be applicable to all Damages paid for each Claim first made and reported during the Policy Period. If the OPTIONAL EXTENSION PERIOD COVERAGE is purchased OR NON-PRACTICING EXTENSION PERIOD COVERAGE is purchased (or provided without cost, if the Insured will qualifies) the Deductible will be reinstated to the full amount shown in the Declarations and shall be applicable to all Damages paid for each Claim first made under the OPTIONAL EXTENSION PERIOD COVERAGE OR NON-PRACTICING EXTENSION PERIOD COVERAGE. Such amounts shall, upon written demand by the Company, be paid by the Named Insured within thirty (30) days.

F. **REIMBURSEMENT TO THE COMPANY:**

An Insured shall be liable to the Company upon demand for:

1. The amount of the Deductible stated in the Declaration; and

2. The amounts paid by the Company in excess of the Each Claim Limit or Aggregate Limit.

G. **VOLUNTARY RESOLUTION REFUND:**

1. For a Claim that is voluntarily resolved within twelve (12) months after the date the Claim is properly reported to the Company in compliance with Paragraph A. of Section VII. CLAIMS, fifty percent (50%) of the deductible, but not to exceed a maximum of $12,500 for each Claim, shall be reimbursed within thirty (30) days of payment of the full deductible; or

Form TBP-2 (1-2000)

2. For a Claim that is voluntarily resolved between twelve (12) months and twenty-four (24) months, after the date the Claim is properly reported to the Company, in compliance with Paragraph A. of Section VII. CLAIMS, twenty-five percent (25%) of the deductible, but not to exceed a maximum $6,250 for each Claim, shall be reimbursed within thirty (30) days of payment of the full deductible.

Voluntary Resolution (or settlement) means that parties to a Claim voluntarily enter into an agreement, with written consent of the Company, whereby the parties ascertain and delineate precisely what is coming from one to the other and vice versa, other than by reason of a verdict or judgement. A Claim is deemed **resolved** when all documents necessary to effectuate settlement of all Claims and all aspects thereof are properly executed and filed. A Claim resolved through the use of formal arbitration or mediation shall also be deemed a voluntary resolution, provided that the parties to the Claim obtain the written consent of the Company to the use of such means of resolution and to the choice of arbitrator or mediator.

VII. CLAIMS

A. NOTICE OF A CLAIM:

SPECIMEN

As a condition precedent to the coverage provided by this Policy, an Insured shall, within twenty (20) days of the date any Claim is first made against that Insured, give written notice of that Claim to the Company.

In the event suit is brought against an Insured, the Insured shall immediately forward to the Company every demand, notice, summons or other process received directly or by the Insured's representatives.

B. ASSISTANCE AND COOPERATION OF INSUREDS:

Each Insured shall cooperate with the Company and upon the Company's request shall meet with Company representatives and defense counsel, give written statements to and submit to examination and interrogation by representatives of the Company and defense counsel, under oath if required, and shall attend hearings, depositions and trials and shall assist in effectuating settlement, securing and giving evidence, obtaining the attendance of witnesses and in the conduct of suits, all without charge to the Company. The Insured shall exercise the Insured's rights to reject or demand the arbitration of any Claim made against the Insured in accordance with the written instructions of the Company. The Insured shall not, except at the Insured's own cost, make any payment, admit any liability, settle any Claims, assume any obligation or incur any expense without the written consent of the Company.

C. SUBROGATION:

In the event of any payment under this Policy, the Company shall be subrogated to all the Insured's rights of recovery against any person or entity and the Insured shall execute and deliver instruments and papers and do whatever else is necessary to secure such rights. The Insured shall do nothing to prejudice such rights.

Any amount so recovered shall be apportioned as follows:

1. First, to the repayment of expenses of recovery; and

2. Second, to Damages and Defense Expense paid by the Company on behalf of the

Form TBP-2 (1-2000)

14

Named Insured and Damages and Defense Expense paid by the Named Insured in the proportion each paid to the total of all such damages.

The Company shall not exercise any such rights against any Insured as defined in this Policy (See Definitions, Section I.). Except that the Company reserves the right to exercise any rights of subrogation against an Insured in respect to any Claim brought about or contributed to by the dishonest, deliberately fraudulent, criminal, maliciously or deliberately wrongful act or omission of such Insured.

D. **ACTION AGAINST THE COMPANY:**

No action shall lie against the Company until the Insured shall have fully complied with all the terms of this Policy and the amount of the Insured's obligation to pay shall have been finally determined either by judgement against the Insured after actual trial or by written agreement of the Company.

Any person or entity or legal representative thereof who has secured such judgement or written agreement shall thereafter be entitled to recover under this Policy to the extent of the insurance afforded by this Policy. No person or entity shall have any rights under this Policy to join the Company as a party to any action against an Insured or any legal representative of the Insured.

Bankruptcy or insolvency of an Insured or of an Insured's estate shall not relieve the Company of any of its obligations hereunder.

E. **FALSE OR FRAUDULENT CLAIMS:**

If an Insured shall commit fraud in proffering any Claim, this insurance shall become void as to such Insured from the date such fraudulent Claim is proffered.

VIII. OTHER CONDITIONS

SPECIMEN

A. **APPLICATION:**

By acceptance of this Policy, all Insureds agree that the representations made in the Declaration Letter and Application (including all supplements) attached hereto and hereby made part of this Policy are true and complete to the best of the knowledge of all Insureds. This Policy is issued in reliance upon the truth of such representations and all Insureds warrant that no facts have been suppressed or misstated. This Policy embodies all agreements existing between the Insureds and the Company and any agents of the Company relating to this Policy of insurance.

B. **OTHER INSURANCE:**

If any Insured has insurance provided by other companies covering a Claim covered by this Policy, the Company shall not be liable under this Policy for a greater proportion of such Damages and Defense Expenses than the applicable Limit of Liability stated in the Declarations or as determined by LIMITS OF LIABILITY (Section VI., Paragraphs A. - D.), bears to the total applicable Limits of Liability of all valid and collectible insurance covering such Claim; provided, however, with respect to acts or omissions which occur prior to the inception date of this Policy, but for which this Policy provides prior acts coverage, the insurance hereunder shall apply only as excess insurance over any other valid and collectible insurance and shall then apply only in the amount by which the applicable Limits of Liability of this Policy exceed the sum of the applicable Limits of Liability of all such other insurance.

Form TBP-2 (1-2000)

15

C. CHANGES:

The terms of this Policy shall not be changed, except by endorsement to this Policy. Notice to and knowledge of an agent of the Company shall be considered notice to and knowledge of the Company. Any breach of this Policy known to an agent prior to a Claim shall not void this Policy or prevent coverage of such Claim. Defense counsel are not agents of the Company.

D. ASSIGNMENT:

Assignment of any interest under this Policy shall not bind the Company unless its consent is endorsed hereon.

SPECIMEN

E. CANCELLATION OR TERMINATION:

This Policy may be cancelled by the Named Insured by surrender hereof to the Company or by mailing the Company written notice stating when thereafter such cancellation shall be effective. If cancelled by the Named Insured, the Company shall retain the customary short-rate proportion of the premium.

In the event of the failure of the Named Insured to pay any premium when due, or any default in payment of a premium financing installment or part thereof, this Policy may be cancelled by the Company by mailing to the Named Insured written notice stating when, not less than ten (10) days thereafter, such cancellation shall be effective.

This Policy may be cancelled by the Company, other than for non-payment of premium or premium financing installment, by mailing to the Named Insured written notice stating when, not less than sixty (60) days thereafter, such cancellation shall be effective.

If the Company declines to issue an annual Policy to the Named Insured, the Company shall mail to the Named Insured, not less than sixty (60) days prior to the expiration of this Policy, written notice of such election.

The mailing of notice of cancellation or termination shall be sufficient notice and the effective date of cancellation stated in any notice shall become the end of the Policy Period. Delivery of such written notice to the Named Insured by the Company shall be equivalent to mailing. If cancelled by the Company other than for non-payment of premium, earned premium shall be computed pro-rata. Premium adjustment may be made at the time cancellation is effective or as soon as practicable thereafter.

F. ARTICLES AND BYLAWS:

The Articles and Bylaws of the Company as amended from time to time are expressly incorporated into and made a part of this Policy.

G. NON-ASSESSABLE POLICY:

This Policy is not assessable. The liability of Policyholders and members of The Bar Plan Mutual Insurance Company under this Policy is limited to payment of premium. This provision does not alter rights or obligations under any previous assessable Policy issued by the Company or any predecessor Company.

Form TBP-2 (1-2000)

IN WITNESS THEREOF, the Company has caused this Policy to be signed by the Chairman of its Board and Secretary, but this Policy shall not be valid unless countersigned on the Declarations by a duly authorized representative of the Company.

David E. Larson

CHAIRMAN OF THE BOARD

Ann P. Hagan

SECRETARY

SPECIMEN

Form TBP-2 (1-2000)

17

Staple Application Here

Form TBP-2 (1-2000)

APPENDIX G

SAMPLE POLICY

Sample Whole Life Insurance Policy

TO THE READER:

There are no "standard" life insurance policies, and the contracts vary in wording and appearance from company to company. Sometimes there are also significant differences in policy provisions. This policy is generally representative of contracts issued in the United States.

Source: LIFE AND HEALTH INSURANCE: A TEACHING MANUAL
Washington, DC: American Council of Life Insurance/Health Insurance Association of America

SAMPLE

INSURED	THOMAS A. BENSON	$50,000	AMOUNT
DATE OF ISSUE	NOVEMBER 1, 1985		
PLAN	WHOLE LIFE PAID UP AT 90	000/000	POLICY NUMBER
POLICY DATE	NOVEMBER 1, 1985	37, MALE	AGE AND SEX

WHOLE LIFE INSURANCE POLICY

OUR INSURING AGREEMENT

The Council Life Insurance Company agrees to pay the benefits provided in this policy, subject to its terms and conditions. Executed at New York, New York on the Date of Issue.

YOUR RIGHT TO RETURN YOUR POLICY

Please read this policy carefully. The Owner may return the policy for any reason within ten days after receiving it. If returned, the policy will be considered void from the beginning and any premium paid will be refunded. The policy may be returned to your agent or to the Home Office of the Council Life Insurance Company.

Secretary

President

POLICY HIGHLIGHTS

- WHOLE LIFE POLICY—PARTICIPATING
- AMOUNT PAYABLE AT DEATH OF INSURED $50,000.
- PREMIUMS PAYABLE TO AGE 90.
- SCHEDULE OF BENEFITS AND PREMIUMS PAGE 2.

This policy is a legal contract between the Owner and The Council Life Insurance Company. Read your policy carefully.

A GUIDE TO POLICY PROVISIONS

Accidental Death Benefit	15	Dividends	5
Beneficiaries	8	Loans	7
Cash Value, Extended Term	5	Ownership	3
and Paid-Up Insurance		Payment of Policy Benefit	9
Change of Policy	7	Premiums and Reinstatement	4
Contract	3	Specification	2
		Waiver of Premium Right	14

Endorsements Made At Issue Appear After "General Provisions." Additional Benefits, If Any, Are Provided By Rider.

1

Source: LIFE AND HEALTH INSURANCE: A TEACHING MANUAL. Washington, DC: American Council of Life Insurance/Health Insurance Association of America.

POLICY SPECIFICATIONS

INSURED—	THOMAS A. BENSON	$50,000	—AMOUNT
POLICY DATE—	NOVEMBER 1, 1985	000/00	—POLICY NUMBER
DATE OF ISSUE—	NOVEMBER 1, 1985	37 MALE	—AGE AND SEX
PLAN—	WHOLE LIFE PAID UP AT 90		

PLAN AND ADDITIONAL BENEFITS	AMOUNT	PREMIUM	YEARS PAYABLE
WHOLE LIFE (PREMIUMS PAYABLE TO AGE 90)	$50,000	$927.00	53
WAIVER OF PREMIUM (TO AGE 65)		22.50	28
ACCIDENTAL DEATH (TO AGE 70)	$50,000	39.00	33

A PREMIUM IS PAYABLE ON THE POLICY DATE AND EVERY 12 POLICY MONTHS THEREAFTER.
THE FIRST PREMIUM IS $988.50.

TABLE OF GUARANTEED VALUES

END OF POLICY YEAR	CASH OR LOAN VALUE	PAID-UP INSURANCE	EXTENDED TERM INSURANCE YEARS	DAYS
1	$ 0	$ 0	0	0
2	515	1,650	2	149
3	1,253	3,900	5	47
4	2,011	6,100	7	94
5	2,786	8,200	8	339
6	3,579	10,200	10	118
7	4,390	12,150	11	250
8	5,220	14,000	12	280
9	6,068	15,800	13	228
10	6,932	17,500	14	109
11	7,783	19,100	14	282
12	8,648	20,600	15	48
13	9,526	22,050	15	142
14	10,417	23,450	15	205
15	11,319	24,750	15	240
16	12,233	26,000	15	251
17	13,156	27,250	15	241
18	14,089	28,400	15	213
19	15,031	29,500	15	169
20	15,979	30,600	15	113
AGE 60	18,853	33,500		
AGE 65	23,647	37,550		

PAID-UP ADDITIONS AND DIVIDEND ACCUMULATIONS INCREASE THE CASH VALUES;
INDEBTEDNESS DECREASES THEM.
THE PERCENTAGE REFERRED TO IN SECTION 5.6 IS 83.000%.

DIRECT BENEFICIARY   HELEN M. BENSON, WIFE OF THE INSURED
OWNER   THOMAS A. BENSON, THE INSURED

2

Source: LIFE AND HEALTH INSURANCE: A TEACHING MANUAL. Washington, DC: American Council of Life Insurance/Health Insurance Association of America

SECTION 1. THE CONTRACT

1.1 LIFE INSURANCE BENEFIT

The Council Life Insurance Company agrees, subject to the terms and conditions of this policy, to pay the Amount shown on page 2 to the beneficiary upon receipt at its Home Office of proof of the death of the Insured.

1.2 INCONTESTABILITY

This policy shall be incontestable after it has been in force during the lifetime of the Insured for two years from the Date of Issue.

1.3 SUICIDE

If within two years from the Date of Issue the Insured dies by suicide, the amount payable by the Company shall be limited to the premiums paid.

1.4 DATES

The contestable and suicide periods commence with the Date of Issue. Policy months, years and anniversaries are computed from the Policy Date. Both dates are shown on page 2 of this policy.

1.5 MISSTATEMENT OF AGE

If the age of the Insured has been misstated, the amount payable shall be the amount which the premiums paid would have purchased at the correct age.

1.6 GENERAL

This policy and the application, a copy of which is attached when the policy is issued, constitute the entire contract. All statements in the application are representations and not warranties. No statement shall void this policy or be used in defense of a claim under it unless contained in the application.

Only an officer of the Company is authorized to alter this policy or to waive any of the Company's rights or requirements.

All payments by the Company under this policy are payable at its Home Office.

SECTION 2. OWNERSHIP

2.1 THE OWNER

The Owner is as shown on page 2, or his successor or transferee. All policy rights and privileges may be exercised by the Owner without the consent of any beneficiary. Such rights and privileges may be exercised only during the lifetime of the Insured and thereafter to the extent permitted by Sections 8 and 9.

2.2 TRANSFER OF OWNERSHIP

The Owner may transfer the ownership of this policy by filing written evidence of transfer satisfactory to the Company at its Home Office and, unless waived by the Company, submitting the policy for endorsement to show the transfer.

2.3 COLLATERAL ASSIGNMENT

The Owner may assign this policy as collateral security. The Company assumes no responsibility for the validity or effect of any collateral assignment of this policy. The Company shall not be charged with notice of any assignment unless the assignment is in writing and filed at its Home Office before payment is made.

The interest of any beneficiary shall be subordinate to any collateral assignment made either before or after the beneficiary designation.

A collateral assignee is not an Owner and a collateral assignment is not a transfer of ownership.

3

SECTION 3. PREMIUMS AND REINSTATEMENT

3.1 PREMIUMS

(a) **Payment.** All premiums after the first are payable at the Home Office or to an authorized agent. A receipt signed by an officer of the Company will be provided upon request.

(b) **Frequency.** Premiums may be paid annually, semiannually, or quarterly at the published rates for this policy. A change to any such frequency shall be effective upon acceptance by the Company of the premium for the changed frequency. Premiums may be paid on any other frequency approved by the Company.

(c) **Default.** If a premium is not paid on or before its due date, this policy shall terminate on the due date except as provided in Sections 3.1(d), 5.3 and 5.4.

(d) **Grace Period.** A grace period of 31 days shall be allowed for payment of a premium not paid on its due date. The policy shall continue in full force during this period. If the Insured dies during the grace period, the overdue premium shall be paid from the proceeds of the policy.

(e) **Premium Refund at Death.** The portion of any premium paid which applies to a period beyond the policy month in which the Insured died shall be refunded as part of the proceeds of this policy.

3.2 REINSTATEMENT

If the policy has not been surrendered for its cash value, it may be reinstated within five years after the due date of the unpaid premium provided the following conditions are satisfied:

(a) Within 31 days following expiration of the grace period, reinstatement may be made without evidence of insurability during the lifetime of the Insured by payment of the overdue premium.

(b) After 31 days following expiration of the grace period, reinstatement is subject to:

(i) receipt of evidence of insurability of the Insured satisfactory to the Company;
(ii) payment of all overdue premiums with interest from the due date of each at the rate of 6% compounded annually; or any lower rate established by the Company.

Any policy indebtedness existing on the due date of the unpaid premium, together with interest from that date, must be repaid or reinstated.

Source: LIFE AND HEALTH INSURANCE: A TEACHING MANUAL. Washington, DC: American Council of Life Insurance/Health Insurance Association of America

4

SECTION 4. DIVIDENDS

4.1 ANNUAL DIVIDENDS

This policy shall share in the divisible surplus, if any, of the Company. This policy's share shall be determined annually and credited as a dividend. Payment of the first dividend is contingent upon payment of the premium or premiums for the second policy year and shall be credited proportionately as each premium is paid. Thereafter, each dividend shall be payable on the policy anniversary.

4.2 USE OF DIVIDENDS

As directed by the Owner, dividends may be paid in cash or applied under one of the following:

(a) **Paid-Up Additions.** Dividends may be applied to purchase fully paid-up additional insurance. Paid-up additions will also share in the divisible surplus.

(b) **Dividend Accumulations.** Dividends may be left to accumulate at interest. Interest is credited at a rate of 3½% compounded annually, or any higher rate established by the Company.

(c) **Premium Payment.** Dividends may be applied toward payment of any premium due within one year, if the balance of the premium is paid. If the balance is not paid, or if this policy is in force as paid-up insurance, the dividend will be applied to purchase paid-up additions.

If no direction is given by the Owner, dividends will be applied to purchase paid-up additions.

4.3 USE OF ADDITIONS AND ACCUMULATIONS

Paid-up additions and dividend accumulations increase the policy's cash value and loan value and are payable as part of the policy proceeds. Additions may be surrendered and accumulations withdrawn unless required under the Loan, Extended Term Insurance, or Paid-up Insurance provisions.

4.4 DIVIDEND AT DEATH

A dividend for the period from the beginning of the policy year to the end of the policy month in which the Insured dies shall be paid as part of the policy proceeds.

SECTION 5. CASH VALUE, EXTENDED TERM AND PAID-UP INSURANCE

5.1 CASH VALUE

The cash value, when all premiums due have been paid, shall be the reserve on this policy less the deduction described in Section 5.5, plus the reserve for any paid-up additions and the amount of any dividend accumulations.

The cash value within three months after the due date of any unpaid premium shall be the cash value on the due date reduced by any subsequent surrender of paid-up additions or withdrawl of dividend accumulations. The cash value at any time after such three months shall be the reserve on the form of insurance then in force, plus the reserve for any paid-up additions and the amount of any dividend accumulations.

If this policy is surrendered within 31 days after a policy anniversary, the cash value shall be not less than the cash value on that anniversary.

5.2 CASH SURRENDER

The Owner may surrender this policy for its cash value less any indebtedness. The policy shall terminate upon receipt at the Home Office of this policy and a written surrender of all claims. Receipt of the policy may be waived by the Company.

The Company may defer paying the cash value for a period not exceeding six months from the date of surrender. If payment is deferred 30 days or more, interest shall be paid on the cash value

5

Source: LIFE AND HEALTH INSURANCE. A TEACHING MANUAL. Washington DC. American Council of Life Insurance—Health Insurance Association of America.

less any indebtedness at the rate of 4% compounded annually from the date of surrender to the date of payment.

5.3 EXTENDED TERM INSURANCE

If any premium remains unpaid at the end of the grace period, this policy shall continue in force as nonparticipating extended term insurance. The amount of insurance shall be the amount of this policy, plus any paid up additions and dividend accumulations, less any indebtedness. The term insurance shall begin as of the due date of the unpaid premium and its duration shall be determined by applying the cash value less any indebtedness as a net single premium at the attained age of the Insured. If the term insurance would extend to or beyond attained age 100, paid-up insurance under Section 5.4 below will be provided instead.

5.4 PAID-UP INSURANCE

In lieu of extended term insurance this policy may be continued in force as participating paid-up life insurance.

Paid-up insurance may be requested by written notice filed at the Home Office before, or within three months after, the due date of the unpaid premium. The insurance will be for the amount that the cash value will purchase as a net single premium at the attained age of the Insured. Any indebtedness shall remain outstanding.

5.5 TABLE OF GUARANTEED VALUES

The cash values, paid-up insurance, and extended term insurance shown on page 2 are for the end of the policy year indicated. These values are based on the assumption that premiums have been paid for the number of years stated and are exclusive of any paid-up additions, dividend accumulations, or indebtedness. During the policy year allowance shall be made for any portion of a year's premium paid and for the time elapsed in that year. Values for policy years not shown are calculated on the same basis as this table and will be furnished on request. All values are equal to or greater than those required by the State in which this policy is delivered.

In determining cash values a deduction is made from the reserve. During the first five policy years, the deduction for each $1,000 of Amount is $9 plus $.15 for each year of the Insured's issue age. After the fifth policy year, the deduction decreases yearly by one-fifth of the initial deduction until there is no deduction in the tenth and subsequent policy years. If the premium paying period is less than ten years, there is no deduction in the last two policy years of the premium paying period or thereafter.

5.6 RESERVES AND NET PREMIUMS

Reserves, net premiums and present values are determined in accordance with the Commissioners 1958 Standard Ordinary Mortality Table and 4% interest, except that for the first five years of any extended term insurance, the Commissioners 1958 Extended Term Insurance Table is used. All reserves are based on continuous payment of premiums and immediate payment of claims. Net annual premiums are the same in each policy year, except that if premiums are payable for more than 20 years, the net annual premium in the 21st and subsequent policy years is determined by applying the percentage shown on page 2 to the net annual premium for the 20th policy year. On the Policy Date, the present value of all future guaranteed benefits equals the present value of all future net annual premiums. The reserve at the end of any policy year is the excess of the present value of all future guaranteed benefits over the present value of all future net annual premiums. The reserve is exclusive of any additional benefits.

6

SECTION 6. LOANS

6.1 POLICY LOAN

The Owner may obtain a policy loan by assignment of this policy to the Company. The amount of the loan, plus any existing indebtedness, shall not exceed the loan value. No loan shall be granted if the policy is in force as extended term insurance. The Company may defer making a loan for six months unless the loan is to be used to pay premiums on policies issued by the Company.

6.2 PREMIUM LOAN

A premium loan shall be granted to pay an overdue premium if the premium loan option is in effect. If the loan value, less any indebtedness, is insufficient to pay the overdue premium, a premium will be paid for any other frequency permitted by this policy for which the loan value less any indebtedness is sufficient. The premium loan option may be elected or revoked by written notice filed at the Home Office.

6.3 LOAN VALUE

The loan value is the largest amount which, with accrued interest, does not exceed the cash value either on the next premium due date or at the end of one year from the date of the loan.

6.4 LOAN INTEREST

Interest is payable at the rate of 8% compounded annually, or at any lower rate established by the Company for any period during which the loan is outstanding.

The Company shall provide at least 30 days written notice to the Owner (or any other party designated by the Owner to receive notice under this policy) and any assignee recorded at the Home Office of any increase in interest rate on loans outstanding 40 or more days prior to the effective date of the increase.

Interest accrues on a daily basis from the date of the loan on policy loans and from the premium due date on premium loans, and is compounded annually. Interest unpaid on a loan anniversary is added to and becomes part of the loan principal and bears interest on the same terms.

6.5 INDEBTEDNESS

Indebtedness consists of unpaid policy and premium loans on the policy including accrued interest. Indebtedness may be repaid at any time. Any unpaid indebtedness will be deducted from the policy proceeds.

If indebtedness equals or exceeds the cash value, this policy shall terminate. Termination shall occur 31 days after a notice has been mailed to the address of record of the Owner and of any assignee recorded at the Home Office.

SECTION 7. CHANGE OF POLICY

7. CHANGE OF PLAN

The Owner may change this policy to any permanent life or endowment plan offered by the Company on the Date of Issue of this policy. The change may be made upon payment of any cost and subject to the conditions determined by the Company. For a change made after the first year to a plan having a higher reserve, the cost shall not exceed the difference in cash values or the difference in reserves, whichever is greater, plus 3½% of such difference.

Source: LIFE AND HEALTH INSURANCE: A TEACHING MANUAL. Washington, DC. American Council of Life Insurance/Health Insurance Association of America.

7

SECTION 8. BENEFICIARIES

8.1 DESIGNATION AND CHANGE OF BENEFICIARIES

(a) By Owner. The Owner may designate and change direct and contingent beneficiaries and further payees of death proceeds:

    (1) during the lifetime of the Insured.

    (2) during the 60 days following the date of death of the Insured, if the Insured immediately before his death was not the Owner. Any such designation of direct beneficiary may not be changed. If the Owner is the direct beneficiary and elects a payment plan, any such designation of contingent beneficiaries and further payees may be changed.

(b) By Direct Beneficiary. The direct beneficiary may designate and change contingent beneficiaries and further payees if:

    (1) the direct beneficiary is the Owner.

    (2) at any time after the death of the Insured, no contingent beneficiary or further payee is living, and no designation is made by the Owner under Section 8.1 (a) (2).

    (3) the direct beneficiary elects a payment plan after the death of the Insured, in which case the interest in the share of such direct beneficiary or any other payee designated by the Owner shall terminate.

(c) By Spouse (Marital Deduction Provision). Notwithstanding any provision of Section 8 or 9 of this policy to the contrary, if the Insured immediately before death was the Owner and if the direct beneficiary is the spouse of the Insured and survives the Insured, such direct beneficiary shall have the power to appoint all amounts payable under the policy either to the executors or administrators of the direct beneficiary's estate or to such other contingent beneficiaries and further payees as he may designate. The exercise of that power shall revoke any then existing designation of contingent beneficiaries and further payees and any election of a payment plan applying to them.

(d) Effective Date. Any designation or change of beneficiary shall be made by the filing and recording at the Home Office of a written request satisfactory to the Company. Unless waived by the Company, the request must be endorsed on the policy. Upon the recording, the request will take effect as of the date it was signed. The Company will not be held responsible for any payment or other action taken by it before the recording of the request.

8.2 SUCCESSION IN INTEREST OF BENEFICIARIES

(a) Direct Beneficiaries. The proceeds of this policy shall be payable in equal shares to the direct beneficiaries who survive to receive payment. The unpaid share of any direct beneficiary who dies while receiving payment shall be payable in equal shares to the direct beneficiaries who survive to receive payment.

(b) Contingent Beneficiaries. At the death of the last surviving direct beneficiary, payments due or to become due shall be payable in equal shares to the contingent beneficiaries who survive to receive payment. The unpaid share of any contingent beneficiary who dies while receiving payment shall be payable in equal shares to the contingent beneficiaries who survive to receive payment.

(c) Further Payees. At the death of the last to survive of the direct and contingent beneficiaries, the proceeds, or the withdrawal value of any payments due or to become due if a payment plan is in effect, shall be paid in one sum:

8

(1) in equal shares to the further payees who survive to receive payment; or

(2) if no further payees survive to receive payment, to the executors or administrators of the last to survive of the direct and contingent beneficiaries.

(d) **Estate of Owner.** If no direct or contingent beneficiaries or further payees survive the Insured, the proceeds shall be paid to the Owner or the executors or administrators of the Owner.

8.3 GENERAL

(a) **Transfer of Ownership.** A transfer of ownership will not change the interest of any beneficiary.

(b) **Claims of Creditors.** So far as permitted by law, no amount payable under this policy shall be subject to the claims of creditors of the payee.

(c) **Succession under Payment Plans.** A direct or contingent beneficiary succeeding to an interest in a payment plan shall continue under such plan subject to its terms, with the rights of transfer between plans and of withdrawal under plans as provided in this policy.

SECTION 9. PAYMENT OF POLICY BENEFITS

9.1 PAYMENT

Payment of policy benefits upon surrender or maturity will be made in cash or under one of the payment plans described in Section 9.2, if elected.

If policy benefits become payable by reason of the Insured's death, payment will be made under any payment plan then in effect. If no election of a payment plan is in effect, the proceeds will be held under the Interest Income Plan (Option A) with interest accumulating from the date of death until an election or cash withdrawal is made.

9.2 PAYMENT PLANS

(a) **Interest Income Plan (Option A).** The proceeds will earn interest which may be received in monthly payments or accumulated. The first interest payment is due one month after the plan becomes effective. Withdrawal of accumulated interest as well as full or partial proceeds may be made at any time.

(b) **Installment Income Plans.** Monthly installment income payments will be made as provided by the plan elected. The first payment is due on the date the plan becomes effective.

(1) **Specified Period (Option B).** Monthly installment income payments will be made providing for payment of the proceeds with interest over a specified period of one to 30 years. Withdrawal of the present value of any unpaid installments may be made at any time.

(2) **Specified Amount (Option D).** Monthly installment income payments will be made for a specified amount of not less than $10 per $1,000 of proceeds. Payments will continue until the entire proceeds with interest are paid, with the final payment not exceeding the unpaid balance. Withdrawal of the unpaid balance may be made at any time.

(c) **Life Income Plans.** Monthly life income payments will be made as provided by the plan elected. The first payment is due on the date the plan becomes effective. Proof of date of birth satisfactory to the Company must be furnished for any individual upon whose life income payments depend.

9

(1) Single Life Income (Option C). Monthly payments will be made for the selected certain period, if any, and thereafter during the remaining lifetime of the individual upon whose life income payments depend. The selections available are:

  (i) no certain period,

  (ii) a certain period of 10 or 20 years, or

  (iii) a refund certain period such that the sum of the income payments during the certain period will be equal to the proceeds applied under the plan, with the final payment not exceeding the unpaid balance.

(2) Joint and Survivor Life Income (Option E). Monthly payments will be made for a 10 year certain period and thereafter during the joint lifetime of the two individuals upon whose lives income payments depend and continuing during the remaining lifetime of the survivor.

(3) Withdrawal. Withdrawal of the present value of any unpaid income payments which were to be made during a certain period may be made at any time after the death of all individuals upon whose lives income payments depend.

(d) Payment Frequency. In lieu of monthly payments a quarterly, semiannual or annual frequency may be selected.

9.3 PAYMENT PLAN RATES

(a) Interest Income and Installment Income Plans. Proceeds under the Interest Income and Installment Income plans will earn interest at rates declared annually by the Company, but not less than a rate of 3½% compounded annually. Interest in excess of 3½% will increase payments, except that for the Installment Income Specified Amount Plan (Option D), excess interest will be applied to lengthen the period during which payments are made.

The present value for withdrawal purposes will be based on a rate of 3½% compounded annually.

The Company may from time to time also make available higher guaranteed interest rates under the Interest Income and Installment Income plans, with certain conditions on withdrawal as then published by the Company for those plans.

(b) Life Income Plans. Life Income Plan payments will be based on rates declared by the Company. These rates will provide not less than 104% of the income provided by the Company's Immediate Annuities being offered on the date the plan becomes effective. The rates are based on the sex and age nearest birthday of any individual upon whose life income payments depend, and adjusted for any certain period and the immediate payment of the first income payment. In no event will payments of the first income payment. In no event will payments under these rates be less than the minimums described in Section 9.3(c).

(c) Minimum Income Payments. Minimum monthly income payments for the Installment Income Plans (Options B and D) and the Life Income Plans (Options C and E) are shown in the Minimum Income Table. The minimum Life Income payments are determined as of the date the payment plan becomes effective and depend on the age nearest birthday adjusted for policy duration.

The Life Income Plan payment rates in that table depend on the sex and on the adjusted age of each person on whose life the payments are based. The adjusted age is:

10

Source: LIFE AND HEALTH INSURANCE: A TEACHING MANUAL - Washington DC: American Council of Life Insurance/Health Insurance Association of America

■ the age on the birthday that is nearest to the date on which the payment plan takes effect; plus

■ the age adjustment shown below for the number of policy years that have elapsed from the Policy Date to the date that the payment plan takes effect. A part of a policy year is counted as a full year.

POLICY YEARS ELAPSED	AGE ADJUSTMENT	POLICY YEARS ELAPSED	AGE ADJUSTMENT
1 to 10	+ 8	31 to 35	− 1
11 to 15	+ 6	36 to 40	− 2
16 to 20	+ 4	41 to 45	− 3
21 to 25	+ 2	46 to 50	− 4
26 to 30	0	51 or more	− 5

9.4 ELECTION OF PAYMENT PLANS

(a) **Effective Date.** Election of payment plans for death proceeds made by the Owner and filed at the Home Office during the Insured's lifetime will be effective on the date of death of the Insured. All other elections of payment plans will be effective when filed at the Home Office, or later if specified.

(b) **Death Proceeds.** Payment plans for death proceeds may be elected:

(1) by the Owner during the lifetime of the Insured.

(2) by the Owner during the 60 days following the date of death of the Insured, if the Insured immediately before his death was not the Owner. Any such election may not be changed by the Owner.

(3) by a direct or contingent beneficiary to whom such proceeds become payable, if no election is then in effect and no election is made by the Owner under Section 9.4(b) (2).

(c) **Surrender or Maturity Proceeds.** Payment plans for surrender or maturity proceeds may be elected by the Owner for himself as direct beneficiary.

(d) **Transfers Between Payment Plans.** A direct or contingent beneficiary receiving payment under a payment plan with the right to withdraw may elect to transfer the withdrawal value to any other payment plan then available.

(e) **Life Income Plan Limitations.** An individual beneficiary may receive payments under a Life Income Plan only if the payments depend upon his life. A corporation may receive payments under a Life Income Plan only if the payments depend upon the life of the Insured, or a surviving spouse or dependent of the Insured.

(f) **Minimum Amounts.** Proceeds of less than $5,000 may not be applied without the Company's approval under any payment plan except the Interest Income Plan (Option A) with interest accumulated. The Company retains the right to change the payment frequency or pay the withdrawal value if payments under a payment plan are or become less than $25.

9.5 INCREASE OF MONTHLY INCOME

The direct beneficiary who is to receive the proceeds of this policy under a payment plan may increase the total monthly income by payment of an annuity premium to the Company. The premium, after deduction of charges not exceeding 2% and any applicable premium tax, shall be applied under the payment plan at the same rates as the policy proceeds. The net amount so applied may not exceed twice the proceeds payable under this policy.

Source: LIFE AND HEALTH INSURANCE A TEACHING MANUAL. Washington DC: American Council of Life Insurance: Health Insurance Association of America

11

MINIMUM INCOME TABLE

Minimum Monthly Income Payments Per $1,000 Proceeds

INSTALLMENT INCOME PLANS (Options B and D)

PERIOD (YEARS)	MONTHLY PAYMENT	PERIOD (YEARS)	MONTHLY PAYMENT	PERIOD (YEARS)	MONTHLY PAYMENT
1	$84.65	11	$9.09	21	$5.56
2	43.05	12	8.46	22	5.39
3	29.19	13	7.90	23	5.24
4	22.27	14	7.49	24	5.09
5	18.12	15	7.10	25	4.96
6	15.35	16	6.76	26	4.84
7	13.38	17	6.47	27	4.73
8	11.90	18	6.20	28	4.63
9	10.75	19	5.97	29	4.53
10	9.83	20	5.25	30	4.45

12

MINIMUM INCOME TABLE

Minimum Monthly Income Payments Per $1,000 Proceeds

LIFE INCOME PLANS (Options C and E)

SINGLE LIFE MONTHLY PAYMENTS (Option C)

MALE ADJUSTED AGE*	CERTAIN PERIOD (YEARS)				FEMALE ADJUSTED AGE*	CERTAIN PERIOD (YEARS)			
	NONE	10	20	REFUND		NONE	10	20	REFUND
55	$ 5.39	$ 5.24	$ 4.85	$ 5.00	55	$ 4.75	$4.70	$ 4.53	$4.57
56	5.51	5.34	4.91	5.09	56	4.85	4.78	4.59	4.64
57	5.63	5.45	4.97	5.19	57	4.94	4.87	4.66	4.72
58	5.77	5.56	5.03	5.29	58	4.05	4.97	4.73	4.81
59	5.91	5.68	5.10	5.39	59	5.16	5.07	4.80	4.90
60	6.06	5.80	5.16	5.50	60	5.27	5.17	4.87	4.99
61	6.22	5.93	5.21	5.62	61	5.40	5.28	4.94	5.09
62	6.39	6.07	5.27	5.74	62	5.53	5.40	5.01	5.20
63	6.58	6.21	5.33	5.87	63	5.67	5.52	5.08	5.31
64	6.77	6.35	5.38	6.01	64	5.82	5.66	5.15	5.43
65	6.99	6.50	5.43	6.16	65	5.97	5.80	5.22	5.55
66	7.21	6.66	5.48	6.31	66	6.14	5.95	5.28	5.69
67	7.46	6.83	5.52	6.47	67	6.31	6.10	5.35	5.83
68	7.72	7.00	5.56	6.65	68	6.50	6.27	5.40	5.99
69	7.97	7.17	5.60	6.83	69	6.70	6.45	5.46	6.15
70	8.23	7.35	5.63	7.03	70	6.90	6.63	5.51	6.32
71	8.49	7.53	5.66	7.23	71	7.11	6.82	5.55	6.51
72	8.76	7.71	5.68	7.45	72	7.33	7.02	5.59	6.71
73	9.03	7.89	5.70	7.69	73	7.55	7.22	5.62	6.92
74	9.30	8.07	5.72	7.94	74	7.79	7.43	5.65	7.15
75	9.57	8.25	5.73	8.21	75	8.02	7.64	5.68	7.39
76	9.85	8.43	5.74	8.49	76	8.26	7.85	5.69	7.65
77	10.11	8.60	5.74	8.80	77	8.48	8.05	5.71	7.92
78	10.38	8.77	5.75	9.13	78	8.72	8.26	5.72	8.21
79	10.64	8.93	5.75	9.48	79	8.94	8.45	5.73	8.52
80	10.90	9.08	5.75	9.85	80	9.16	8.64	5.74	8.85
81	11.13	9.21	5.75	10.26	81	9.36	8.81	5.74	9.21
82	11.36	9.34	5.75	10.70	82	9.53	8.96	5.75	9.57
83	11.55	9.44	5.75	11.17	83	9.70	9.10	5.75	9.97
84	11.75	9.54	5.75	11.70	84	9.85	9.22	5.75	10.39
85 and over	11.92	9.61	5.75	12.26	85 and over	9.98	9.33	5.75	10.81

JOINT AND SURVIVOR MONTHLY PAYMENTS (Option E)

MALE ADJUSTED AGE*	FEMALE ADJUSTED AGE*						
	55	60	65	70	75	80	85 and over
55	$4.33	$4.55	$4.76	$4.94	$5.08	$5.17	$5.22
60	4.45	4.73	5.03	5.30	5.53	5.68	5.76
65	4.54	4.89	5.28	5.68	6.04	6.29	6.43
70	4.61	5.01	5.49	6.04	6.57	6.97	7.20
75	4.66	5.09	5.65	6.32	7.04	7.65	8.02
80	4.68	5.14	5.74	6.51	7.39	8.20	8.72
85 and over	4.69	5.16	5.78	6.60	7.57	8.52	9.15

*See Section 9.3.

13

WAIVER OF PREMIUM BENEFIT

1. THE BENEFIT

If total disability of the Insured commences before the policy anniversary nearest his 60th birthday, the Company will waive the payment of premium becoming due during total disability of the Insured.

If total disability of the Insured commences on or after the policy anniversary nearest his 60th birthday but before the policy anniversary nearest his 65th birthday, the Company will waive the payment of premiums becoming due during total disability of the Insured and before the policy anniversary nearest his 65th birthday.

The Company will refund that portion of any premium paid which applies to a period of total disability beyond the policy month in which the disability began.

The premium for this benefit is shown on page 2.

2. DEFINITION OF TOTAL DISABILITY

Total disability means disability which:

(a) resulted from bodily injury or disease;

(b) began after the Date of Issue of this policy and before the policy anniversary nearest the Insured's 65th birthday;

(c) has existed continuously for at least six months; and

(d) prevents the Insured from engaging in an occupation. During the first 24 months of disability, occupation means the occupation of the Insured at the time such disability began; thereafter it means any occupation for which he is reasonably fitted by education, training or experience, with due regard to his vocation and earnings prior to disability.

The total and irrecoverable loss of the sight of both eyes, or of speech or hearing, or of the use of both hands, or of both feet, or of one hand and one foot, shall be considered total disability, even if the Insured shall engage in an occupation.

3. PROOF OF DISABILITY

Before any premium is waived, proof of total disability must be received by the Company at its Home Office:

(a) during the lifetime of the Insured;

(b) during the continuance of total disability; and

(c) not later than one year after the policy anniversary nearest the Insured's 65th birthday.

Premiums will be waived although proof of total disability was not given within the time specified, if it is shown that it was given as soon as reasonably possible, but not later than one year after recovery.

4. PROOF OF CONTINUANCE OF DISABILITY

Proof of the continuance of total disability may be required once a year. If such proof is not furnished, no further premiums shall be waived. Further proof of continuance of disability will no longer be required if, on the policy anniversary nearest the Insured's 65th birthday, the Insured is then and has been totally and continuously disabled for five or more years.

5. PREMIUMS

Any premium becoming due during disability and before receipt of proof of total disability is payable and should be paid. Any such premiums paid shall be refunded by the Company upon acceptance of proof of total disability. If such premiums are not paid, this benefit shall be allowed if total disability is shown to have begun before the end of the grace period of the first unpaid premium.

14

If on any policy anniversary following the date of disablement the Insured continues to be disabled and this benefit has not terminated, an annual premium will be waived.

6. TERMINATION

This benefit shall be in effect while this policy is in force, but shall terminate on the policy anniversary nearest the Insured's 65th birthday unless the Insured is then totally disabled and such disability occurred prior to the policy anniversary nearest the Insured's 60th birthday. It may also be terminated within 31 days of a premium due date upon receipt at the Home Office of the Owner's written request.

ACCIDENTAL DEATH BENEFIT

1. THE BENEFIT

The Company agrees to pay an Accidental Death Benefit upon receipt at its Home Office of proof that the death of the Insured resulted, directly and independently of all other causes, from accidental bodily injury, provided that death occurred while this benefit was in effect.

2. PREMIUM AND AMOUNT OF BENEFIT

The premium for and the amount of this benefit are shown on page 2. This benefit shall be payable as part of the policy proceeds.

3. RISKS NOT ASSUMED

This benefit shall not be payable for death of the Insured resulting from suicide, for death resulting from or contributed to by bodily or mental infirmity or disease, or for any other death which did not result, directly and independently of all other causes, from accidental bodily injury.

Even though death resulted directly and independently of all other causes from accidental bodily injury, this benefit shall not be payable if the death of the Insured resulted from:

(a) Any act or incident of war. The word "war" includes any war, declared or undeclared, and armed aggression resisted by the armed forces of any country or combination of countries.

(b) Riding in any kind of aircraft, unless the Insured was riding solely as a passenger in an aircraft not operated by or for the Armed Forces, or descent from any kind of aircraft while in flight. An Insured who had any duties whatsoever at any time on the flight or any leg of the flight with respect to any purpose of the flight or to the aircraft or who was participating in training shall not be considered a passenger.

4. TERMINATION

This benefit shall be in effect while this policy is in force other than under the Extended Term Insurance or Paid-up Insurance provisions, but shall terminate on the policy anniversary nearest the Insured's 70th birthday. It may also be terminated within 31 days of a premium due date upon receipt at the Home Office of the Owner's written request.

David Olson

Secretary
THE COUNCIL LIFE INSURANCE COMPANY

15

RECEIPT FOR PAYMENT AND CONDITIONAL LIFE INSURANCE AGREEMENT

Thomas A. Benson $50,000 LIFE POLICY PARTICIPATING

Name of Proposed Insured   Face Amount   Plan

Received of *Thomas A. Benson*

the sum of $ *241.60* for the policy applied for in the application to THE COUNCIL INSURANCE COMPANY (CL) with the same date and number as this receipt. Checks, drafts, and money orders are accepted subject to collection.

New York, N.Y., Nov 1 19 *85* *J R Washington* Agent.

Place and Date

When premium is paid at the time of application, complete this Agreement and give to the Applicant. No other Agreement will be recognized by the Company. If premium is not paid—do not detach.

CONDITIONAL LIFE INSURANCE AGREEMENT

I. **No Insurance Ever in Force.** No insurance shall be in force at any time if the proposed insured is not an acceptable risk on the Underwriting Date for the policy applied for according to CL's rules and standards. No insurance shall be in force under an Additional Benefit for which the proposed insured is not an acceptable risk.

II. **Conditional Life Insurance.** If the proposed insured is an acceptable risk on the Underwriting Date, the insurance shall be in force subject to the following maximum amounts if the proposed insured dies before the policy is issued:

Life Insurance		Accidental Death Benefit	
Age at Issue	Policies Issued at Standard Premiums	Policies Issued at Higher Premiums	Age at Issue	Maximum Amount
0–24	$ 500,000	$250,000	0–14	$ 25,000
25–45	1,000,000	500,000	15–19	50,000
46–55	800,000	400,000	20–24	75,000
56–65	400,000	200,000	25–60	150,000
66–70	200,000	100,000	Over 60	-0-
Over 70	-0-	-0-		

Reduction in Maximum Amounts. The maximum amounts set forth in the preceding table shall be reduced by any existing CL insurance on the life of the proposed insured with an Issue Date within 90 days of the date of this Agreement or by any pending prepaid applications for CL insurance on the life of the proposed insured with an Underwriting Date within 90 days of the date of this Agreement.

Termination of Conditional Life Insurance. If the proposed insured is an acceptable risk for the policy applied for according to CL's rules and standards only at a premium higher than the premium paid, any insurance under this Agreement shall terminate on the date stated in a notice mailed by CL to the applicant unless by such date the applicant accepts delivery of the policy and pays the additional premium required.

Underwriting Date. The Underwriting Date is the date of page 2 (90-2) of the application or the date of the medical examination (if required, otherwise the date of the nonmedical, page 4 (90-4)), whichever is the later.

III. **Premium Adjustment.** If the proposed insured is an acceptable risk for the policy applied for only at a premium higher than the premium paid and dies before paying the additional premium required, that additional premium shall be subtracted from the insurance benefit payable to the beneficiary.

IV. **Premium Refund.** Any premium paid for any insurance or Additional Benefit not issued or issued at a higher premium but not accepted by the applicant shall be returned to the applicant.

NOT A "BINDER"—NO INSURANCE WHERE SECTION I APPLIES—NO AGENT MAY MODIFY

Source: LIFE AND HEALTH INSURANCE A TEACHING MANUAL, Washington, DC: American Council of Life Insurance/Health Insurance Association of America

16

PART I   Life Insurance Application to *The COUNCIL Life Insurance Company*

IMPORTANT NOTICE—This application is subject to approval by the Company's Home Office. Be sure all questions in all parts of the application are answered completely and accurately, since the application is the basis of the insurance contract and will become part of any policy issued.

1. Insured's Full Name (Please Print-Give title as Mr. Dr. Rev., etc.)

MR. THOMAS A. BENSON

	Mo., Day, Yr. of Birth	Ins. Age	Sex	Place of Birth	Social Security No.
Single ☐ Married ☑ Widowed ☐ Divorced ☐ Separated ☐	APRIL 6, 1948	37	M	BOSTON, MASS	000-00-0000

2. Addresses last 5 yrs.

		Number	Street	City	State	Zip Code	County	Yrs.
Mail to ☐ Home:	Present	217 E 62 STREET, NEW YORK, N.Y.				10017	NEW YORK	6
	Former							
☑ Business:	Present	PEPPER, GRIMSTEAD, & CROUCH 552 49th ST				10017	NEW YORK	7
	Former							

3. Occupation

	Title	Describe Exact Duties	Yrs.
Present	ATTORNEY REPRESENTS CLIENTS IN LEGAL MATTERS		7
Former			

4. a) Employer

b)

Any change contemplated? Yes ☐ (Explain in Remarks)   No ☑

5. Have you ever   Yes   No

a) been rejected, deferred or discharged by the Armed Forces for medical reasons or applied for a government disability rating?   ☐ ☑

b) applied for insurance or for reinstatement which was declined, postponed, modified or rated?   ☐ ☑

c) used LSD, heroin, cocaine or methadone?   ☐ ☑

6. a) In the past 3 years have you

(i) had your driver's license suspended or revoked or been convicted of more than one speeding violation?   ☐ ☑

(ii) operated, been a crew member of, or had any duties aboard any kind of aircraft?   ☐ ☑

(iii) engaged in underwater diving below 40 feet, parachuting, or motor vehicle racing?   ☐ ☑

b) In the future, do you intend to engage in any activities mentioned in (ii) and (iii) of a) above?   ☐ ☑
(If "Yes" to 5a or any of 6, complete Supplemental Form 3375)

7. Have you smoked one or more cigarettes within the past 12 months?   ☑ ☐

8. Are other insurance applications pending or contemplated?   ☐ ☑

9. Do you intend to go to any foreign country?   ☑ ☐

10. Will coverage applied for replace or change any life insurance or annuities? (If "Yes", submit Replacement form)   ☐ ☑

11. Total Life Insurance in force $ 35,000   None ☐

12. Face Amount $ 50,000   Plan WL

Accidental Death ☐   Waiver of Premium ☐

Purchase Option—Regular ☐   Preferred ☐   PEP ☐   GOR ☐

_____ units of Wife's Term—name: _____

$ _____ initial amount Decreasing Term, _____ Years

(Joint ☐)   (Mot. Pro. ☐)   (Straight Line ☐)

Children's Term ☐   Other: _____

13. Auto. Prem. Loan provision operative if available?   Yes ☐ No ☑

14. Dividend Option

Additions (for other than term policies)   Deposits ☐
Reduce premium, if applicable, otherwise cash
Supplemental Protection (term only) ☐
1 Year Term—any balance to ☐
Deposits ☐ Additions ☐ Reduce prem. (cash if mo.) ☐

15. Beneficiary—for children's, wife's or joint insurance as provided in contract; for other insurance as follows, subject to policy's beneficiary provisions:

	(Name)	(Relationship to insured)	
1st	HELEN M. BENSON	WIFE	if living, if not
2nd	DAVID A. BENSON	SON	if living, if not
3rd			if living, if not

the executors or administrators of: Insured ☐   Other (see Remarks) ☐
(Joint beneficiaries will receive equally or survivor, unless otherwise specified.)

16. Flexible Plan settlement (personal beneficiary only)   ☐

17. Rights—During Insured's lifetime all rights belong to
Insured ☐   Other:
Trustee ☐
(attach Trust)
(After Insured's death as provided in contract on wife's insurance.)

18. Premium—Frequency ANNUAL Amt. Paid $ 241.60   None ☐
Have you received a Conditional Receipt?   Yes ☑   No ☐

REMARKS (Include details (company, date, amt., etc.) for all "yes" answers to questions 4b, 5b, 5c, 8, 9 and 10)

Q9: PLANS VACATION IN SWITZERLAND

I agree that: (1) No one but the Company's President, a Vice-President or Secretary has authority to accept information not contained in the application, to modify or enlarge any contract, or to waive any requirement. (2) Except as otherwise provided in any conditional receipt issued, any policy issued shall take effect upon its delivery and payment of the first premium during the lifetime of each person to be insured. Due dates of later premiums shall be as specified in the policy.

Date at NEW YORK, N.Y. on NOVEMBER 1 19 85   Signature of Insured   *Thomas A Benson*

Signature of Applicant (if other than Insured) who agrees to be bound by the representations and agreements in this and any other part of this

application _____
(Name)   (Relationship)   (Complete address of Applicant)

Countersigned by *Ed Hatey* _____
Field Underwriter (Licensed Resident Agent)

17

| PART 1A | Statements Forming Part Of Application To *The COUNCIL Life Insurance Company* [Complete this Part if any Non-Medical or Family Insurance is Applied For] | | | | | | | |

1. Name of Insured **THOMAS A. BENSON**   Ins. Age **37**   Height **6** ft. **1** in.   Weight **185** lbs.

2. If Family, Children's Wife's or Joint Insurance desired, other family members proposed for insurance:

Wife (include maiden name)		Ins. Age	Mo., Day, Yr. of Birth	Height ft. in.	Weight lbs.	Life in Force $	Place of Birth

Children	Sex	Ins. Age	Mo., Day, Yr. of Birth	Children	Sex	Ins. Age	Mo., Day, Yr. of Birth

3. Has any eligible dependent (a) been omitted from 2? Yes ☐ No ☐   (b) applied for insurance or for reinstatement which was declined, postponed, modified or rated or had a policy cancelled or renewal refused? Yes ☐ No ☐ (Give name, date, company in 8)

4. Have you or anyone else proposed for insurance, so far as you know, ever been treated for or had indication of (underline applicable item)

	Yes	No
a) high blood pressure? (If "Yes", list drugs prescribed and dates taken.)	☐	☑
b) chest pain, heart attack, rheumatic fever, heart murmur, irregular pulse or other disorder of the heart or blood vessels?	☐	☑
c) cancer, tumor, cyst, or any disorder of the thyroid, skin, or lymph glands?	☐	☑
d) diabetes or anemia or other blood disorder?	☐	☑
e) sugar, albumin, blood or pus in the urine, or veneral disease?	☐	☑
f) any disorder of the kidney, bladder, prostate, breast or reproductive organs?	☐	☑
g) ulcer, intestinal bleeding, hepatitis, colitis, or other disorder of the stomach, intestine, spleen, pancreas, liver or gall bladder?	☐	☑
h) asthma, tuberculosis, bronchitis, emphysema or other disorder of the lungs?	☐	☑
i) fainting, convulsions, migraine headache, paralysis, epilepsy or any mental or nervous disorder?	☐	☑
j) arthritis, gout, amputation, sciatica, back pain or other disorder of the muscles, bones or joints?	☐	☑
k) disorder of the eyes, ears, nose, throat or sinuses?	☐	☑
l) varicose veins, hemorrhoids, hernia or rectal disorder?	☐	☑
m) alcoholism or drug habit?	☐	☑

5. Have you or anyone else proposed for insurance, so far as you know, (underline applicable item)

	Yes	No
a) consulted or been underline examined or treated by any physician or practitioner in the past 5 years?	☑	☐
b) had, or been advised to have, an x-ray, cardiogram, blood or other diagnostic test in the past 5 years?	☑	☐
c) been a patient in a hospital, clinic, or other medical facility in the past 5 years?	☐	☑
d) ever had a surgical operation performed or advised?	☑	☐
e) ever made claim for disability or applied for compensation or retirement based on accident or sickness?	☐	☑

6. Are you or any other person proposed for insurance, so far as you know, in impaired physical or mental health, or under any kind of medication? ☐ ☑

7. Weight change in last 6 months of adults proposed for insurance: **N. A.**

Name	Gain	Loss	Cause

8. Details of all "Yes" answers. For any checkup or routine examination, indicate what symptoms, if any, prompted it and include results of the examination and any special tests. Include clinic number if applicable.

Question No.	Name of Person	Illness & Treatment	No. of Attacks	Dates: Onset–Recovery	Doctor, Clinic or Hospital and Complete Address
5a.	THOMAS A. BENSON	ANNUAL CHECK UP	—	—	LIFE EXAMINATION INSTITUTE
5b	THOMAS A. BENSON	ROUTINE OF ANNUAL CHECKUP	—	—	
5d	THOMAS A. BENSON	TONSILLECTOMY – AGE 5	1	JUNE 1949	BOSTON HOSPITAL 2 PITTS STREET, BOSTON MASS

So far as may be lawful, I waive for myself and all persons claiming an interest in any insurance issued on this application, all provisions of law forbidding any physician or other person who has attended or examined, or who may attend or examine, me or any other person covered by such insurance, from disclosing any knowledge or information which he thereby acquired.

I represent the statements and answers in this and in any other part of this application to be true and complete to the best of my knowledge and belief, and offer them to the Company for the purpose of inducing it to issue the policy or policies and to accept the payment of premiums thereunder. I also agree that payment of the first premium (if after this date) shall be a representation by me that such statements and answers would be the same if made at the time of such payment.

Date at **NEW YORK, N.Y.** on **NOV 1** 19 **85**   Signature of Insured **Thomas A. Benson**

Witnessed by **Ed Hatey**   Signature of Wife (if insured) _____
Field Underwriter (Licensed Resident Agent)

AUTHORIZATION

For purposes of determining my eligibility for insurance, I hereby authorize any physician, practitioner, hospital, clinic, institution, insurance company, Medical Information Bureau, or other organization or person that has records or knowledge of me or my health to give any such information to the Council Life Insurance Company.
If application is made to The Council Life Insurance Company for insurance on any member of my family, this authorization also applies to such member. A photostatic copy of this authorization shall be as valid as the original.

Signed on **NOVEMBER 1** 19 **85**   **Thomas A. Benson**
Signature of Insured

18

TABLE OF CASES

[Principal cases appear in all capital letters; references are to pages.]

[Principal cases appear in all capital letters; references are to pages.]

[Principal cases appear in all capital letters; references are to pages.]

[Principal cases appear in all capital letters; references are to pages.]

[Principal cases appear in all capital letters; references are to pages.]

[Principal cases appear in all capital letters; references are to pages.]

[Principal cases appear in all capital letters; references are to pages.]

E

[Principal cases appear in all capital letters; references are to pages.]

[Principal cases appear in all capital letters; references are to pages.]

[Principal cases appear in all capital letters; references are to pages.]

[Principal cases appear in all capital letters; references are to pages.]

H

[Principal cases appear in all capital letters; references are to pages.]

[Principal cases appear in all capital letters; references are to pages.]

[Principal cases appear in all capital letters; references are to pages.]

[Principal cases appear in all capital letters; references are to pages.]

[Principal cases appear in all capital letters; references are to pages.]

M

[Principal cases appear in all capital letters; references are to pages.]

[Principal cases appear in all capital letters; references are to pages.]

[Principal cases appear in all capital letters; references are to pages.]

[Principal cases appear in all capital letters; references are to pages.]

[Principal cases appear in all capital letters; references are to pages.]

[Principal cases appear in all capital letters; references are to pages.]

[Principal cases appear in all capital letters; references are to pages.]

[Principal cases appear in all capital letters; references are to pages.]

[Principal cases appear in all capital letters; references are to pages.]

[Principal cases appear in all capital letters; references are to pages.]

[Principal cases appear in all capital letters; references are to pages.]

U

[Principal cases appear in all capital letters; references are to pages.]

[Principal cases appear in all capital letters; references are to pages.]

INDEX

[References are to pages.]

[References are to pages.]

[References are to pages.]

[References are to pages.]

[References are to pages.]

[References are to pages.]

[References are to pages.]